John A. Macdonald

The Young Politician

* * *

The Old Chieftain

John A. Macdonald

The Young Politician

* * *

The Old Chieftain

DONALD CREIGHTON

With a new introduction by P. B. Waite

UNIVERSITY OF TORONTO PRESS
Toronto Buffalo London

Toronto Buffalo London

Printed in Canada

ISBN 0-8020-7164-3 (paper)

Printed on acid-free paper

Canadian Cataloguing in Publication Data

Creighton, Donald, 1902–1979
John A. Macdonald : the young politician, the old chieftain

(Reprints in Canadian history)
ISBN 0-8020-7164-3

1. Macdonald, John A. (John Alexander), 1815–1891.   2. Canada – Politics and
government – 1867–1896.   3. Prime ministers – Canada – Biography.   I. Title.
II. Series.

FC521.M3C74 1998   971.05'092   C97-932482-3
F1033.M13C74 1998

University of Toronto Press acknowledges the financial assistance to its publishing
program of the Canada Council for the Arts and the Ontario Arts Council.

We also thank the Estate of Donald Creighton and the Sir John A. Macdonald
Historical Society, whose contributions made the republication of
this work possible.

FOREWORD

John A. Macdonald and his colleagues intended that Canada would derive its strength from its diverse provinces and territories and would, as a federation, be stronger than any of its parts. John A. contributed his time and effort to building his vision of Canada into a strong reality. He set a standard of service to country that all readers of this new one-volume edition of his biography by Professor Creighton might follow.

In the months leading up to the celebration of Canada's Centennial Year, 1967, many Canadians became involved in planning various Centennial projects. One group of British Columbians, inspired by the leadership of Sir John in the founding of Canada, decided to commemorate him by founding the Sir John A. Macdonald Historical Society.

Since then, the Society has tried to stimulate the pride of Canadians in their identity. It has sponsored various speakers and sent its own energetic members across the country to communicate Sir John's concept of the equality and partnership of Canada.

With the help of generous donors, the Society bestowed a statue of Sir John on the City of Victoria. For a number of years, the Society has also sponsored the award-winning Sir John A. Macdonald Society Pipe Band. Now, through a special distribution of this book, the Society hopes to acquaint every high school student in British Columbia with the fascinating story of the early years of this country from the perspective of its first Prime Minister.

SIR JOHN A. MACDONALD HISTORICAL SOCIETY

Introduction

Donald Creighton and His Macdonald

P.B. WAITE

Half a century ago the History Department at the University of Toronto inhabited a spacious old house at the corner of St. George and College streets that once belonged to Robert Baldwin, the Reform politician from the 1840s and 1850s. Hence it was called Baldwin House. In 1950–51, in a large west room on the ground floor, for two hours Donald Creighton held his weekly graduate seminar in Canadian history, 1840 to 1900. There were a dozen graduate students there that year, some of them war veterans, from several universities—Dalhousie, U.N.B., Queen's, Manitoba, U.B.C., as well as Toronto. The topic for discussion one January afternoon in 1951 was the Pacific Scandal, with a paper given by an M.A. student from western Canada. The paper was not all that good, a slapdash affair grubbed up from secondary sources, mostly from Sir Joseph Pope's biography of Macdonald published in 1894. There was little use of primary sources, nothing from the Royal Commission Report on the scandal, nothing from the newspapers. Creighton, long, lean and pensive, presided at the head of the table.

In our experience he had always been fair. That he had opinions we knew, but he rarely obtruded them. He seemed to be after what had really happened; he neither wanted nor expected conformity with his own views. So he did not ride roughshod over student papers, bullying as Chester Martin, head of the department from 1928 to 1952, was wont to do. Creighton respected evidence and taught us to do so also. You could tell him anything if you could prove it from the documents. He wanted you to reach for the truth, whatever that might be. But he did expect you to make the effort of reaching. Now, however, after fifteen minutes it was all too patent that this Pacific Scandal paper was thin and the effort put into it negligible. Creighton raised his hand. "I think," he said coolly and politely, "that we shall have to tidy this up a little." Creighton had never done this before; we sat silent, a little abashed that one of our number had, so to speak, let the side down.

We soon forgot our discomfort, however, and Creighton made no further mention of the matter. We soon forgot even the winter afternoon closing in outside. Creighton began to weave—there is no better word for it—the story of the Pacific Scandal, the railway negotiations, the struggle between Montreal and Toronto over C.P.R. control, the blackmail once the Americans got themselves in, how the Liberals bribed the clerk in J.J.C. Abbott's Montreal office, how he stole in and got at the files, pulled out the incriminating letters and telegrams and sidled out into the Montreal night, how they were published in the newspapers in July, 1873, and how Macdonald handled the whole messy affair—not all that well. We were on the edge of our seats; Creighton was like a sorcerer around a campfire telling the story of a great adventure. He was enjoying himself. Finally, at 6:10 p.m., Macdonald having resigned with his government in ruins, Creighton stopped. "That, gentlemen," said he, "is the Pacific Scandal."

We burst into applause. Most of us had never heard anything like it before; some of us have heard nothing like it since. It was a bravura performance. We knew it and he knew it. He was moved by our demonstration, though he tried not to let that show. We stood around talking admiringly after he left, then slowly dispersed to our several lodgings across the big Toronto campus through the gathering winter night.[1]

Donald Creighton came from a literary family, the son of Laura Harvie and William Black Creighton, editor of the Methodist *Christian Guardian*. Born in Toronto on July 15, 1902, he was brought up in a modest home on Hewitt Avenue, just east of High Park, and went to Humberside Collegiate. He then took Honour English and History at Victoria College, where he graduated in 1925. He went on to Balliol College, Oxford, in the autumn of

1925 on a scholarship, feeling very much the colonial in accent, style, clothing, manners and money. He was a product of the Methodist Toronto of the 1920s—a narrow and earnest society, though in its decidedly bourgeois way it tried to be civilized. In some ways it was. Its high-school education was still solid; at Humberside Collegiate Creighton had learned by heart a good deal of English poetry: Browning's "Home-Thoughts, from the Sea"—"Nobly, nobly, Cape St. Vincent to the North-West died away"—and more radically for that time, Matthew Arnold's "Dover Beach." In some ways that poem sums up Creighton's early alternations of love and despair:

> ... for the world, which seems
> To lie before us like a land of dreams,
> So various, so beautiful, so new,
> Hath really neither joy, nor love, nor light,
> Nor certitude, nor peace, nor help for pain;
> And we are here as on a darkling plain
> Swept with confused alarms of struggle and flight
> Where ignorant armies clash by night.

He had an extraordinary knowledge of, and memory for, poetry. He was well-read in English literature and in French; he believed scholars should be. He was difficult to beat in that game played over drinks and friendship when one added, if one could, to the first line of a poem the next, or even the rest of the stanza.

At Oxford, Creighton read little in the constitutional history of the British Empire, often the heartland for Canadian students as the only historical ground that touched on Canada. Instead he read mainly European and British history, and slowly gathered around him, like a cloak, the great traditions of European civilization. But a Canadian he was born and it showed. Indeed, he soon came to resent not having been born and brought up English; that Humberside schooling was not Marlborough or Winchester. He would resent even more the airs and contempt reserved by the English for colonials, however talented, who might occasionally affront well-established manners and traditions.

One of those traditions was certainly that Oxford undergraduates did not marry. In London on June 23, 1926, after his first

year, Creighton married Luella Bruce, a sprightly Canadian girl
from Stouffville, Ontario. They eventually came to a decision to
live for a time separately, Luella in Paris and her young husband at
Balliol. Creighton wanted to do graduate work at the University
of Paris when he finished his Oxford B.A. in 1927. His spoken
French was not as good as his wife's; like many English Canadians
he had grown up without hearing French, coming to it via French
grammar. Though he was well-versed in the language and spoke it
accurately, his French was heavy with English accents, his French
"u" and his French "r" both sounding like west Toronto, which
they were.

What determined Creighton's fate, however, was not his French
but his lack of money. When in the autumn of 1927 he accepted a
lectureship in history at the University of Toronto he did not give
up ambitions of research in French history, and teaching a course
in the French Revolution whettted his appetite. But on a lecturer's
salary a summer's research in Paris was desperately draining, and
the young couple came home from the first summer's work in
1928 in parlous financial circumstances. There was no money for a
bright Canadian student who wanted to study the French Revolution in Paris and write a Ph.D. thesis on the Girondins, and who
hoped to end up teaching in Britain. Creighton would have liked
to live in an ample and aged English country house, surrounded by
lawns, gardens, history and civilization, with Luella as Lady
Creighton, and himself as Sir Donald Creighton. Instead, in his
research, in his mode of living, he got Canada—primitive, grubby,
thinly civilized and preoccupied with the bourgeois savagery of
making money.[2] Thus to Toronto he returned and in Toronto
would he remain to the end of his life, save for the odd research
trip abroad. He was made assistant professor in 1932, associate in
1939, and the top rank in 1945.

His early years in Canadian research produced *The Commercial
Empire of the St. Lawrence, 1760–1850*, published in 1937. The
Laurentian interpretation of Canadian history at the core of this
book was derived from Harold Adams Innis. It rested on Canadian
geographic reality and an economic view of Canadian history that
came out of the fur trade, with its vast western and northern
reaches. It was Canadian experience with a perspective out of central Canada, in which Confederation would later become the

centrepiece. Further, the work that Creighton did for the Rowell Sirois Commission, *British North America at Confederation* (1939), reinforced his conviction that the strong powers given to the Dominion government in 1867 had been systematically weakened by decisions of the Judicial Committee of the Privy Council in London. Through all this, Creighton's nationalism came gradually into being: Canadian geography made vibrant, Canadian history made articulate, and Canadian constitutional law revealed as a constant betrayal by distant British courts unknowing of Canadian ways.

So he came naturally to work on the development of Canadian nationality after 1867. After a Guggenheim fellowship in 1940–41 and a Rockefeller in 1944–45, he settled on Sir John A. Macdonald as the focus of his research. When he applied for a Nuffield grant to enable him to go to England for the winter of 1951–52, the research for the Macdonald biography was two-thirds complete and a good deal of Volume 1 had already been written, much of it in the ancient Canadian Archives building on Sussex Drive that now houses the War Museum. Luella wrote from Port Carling, Muskoka, on July 5, 1951: "I hope you are roaring through chapter nine, and looking forward with happy anticipation to chapter ten and that all your [Ottawa] friends are rallying round."[3] That was all very well out in cool Muskoka, but in summer that old Archives building in Ottawa reeked of heat, and humanity in shirt sleeves.

Creighton wrote *Macdonald* from the documents, from Macdonald's letters and others', aiming continually to reveal Macdonald through his own words and his actions. C.M. MacInnes, a Canadian and historian then at the University of Bristol, thought that Creighton, as a result of this approach, came to be a bit hard on Joseph Howe. Creighton conceded the point:

Perhaps I was a bit hard on Joseph Howe, or perhaps, in justice to myself, I ought to say that I had not enough space to be really fair to him. I have always felt attracted to him rather than the reverse. In a biography, one must concentrate upon the central character to such an extent that the rest of the cast has to be given rather summary treatment.

There was more to it than that. Creighton was not just concentrating on the central character, he was trying to *be* the central character, to see the world through Macdonald's eyes, to measure it with Macdonald's thinking. Perhaps, as H.V. Nelles has suggested, this was the result of Creighton's intense communion with the past. He liked pictures, photographs, old textures, fabrics, furniture, things that allowed him, literally in some cases, to get the feel of the past. It was as if his senses were antennae set out to bring that lost world into his mind. He would ask his students to look intently at any old photographs of their subject in order to submerge themselves in that distant *ambiance*. As he told Margaret Aitken of the *Toronto Telegram*, "one pours oneself into it." Perhaps a little too much so. Norman Ward remarked in the *Saskatoon Star-Phoenix* that Creighton not only liked and disliked the same people as Macdonald but that he sometimes disliked Macdonald's opponents more than Macdonald did himself.

Macdonald was also more malleable than Creighton; R.C. Brown noted that Macdonald "had the master politician's sense that a conciliatory word or gesture could turn yesterday's enemy into today's ally." Would Creighton have done that? In cabinet Macdonald lived for nine years with J.A. Chapleau's unrestrained love of intrigue; when in 1885 Chapleau's death was falsely reported, Macdonald praised mainly Chapleau's good qualities even to his private secretary, Joseph Pope, though he knew well what Chapleau was capable of. Creighton described Francis Hincks (vol. 1, p. 217) as "bleakly clever, drably efficient," as if he enjoyed a certain vein of malice against Macdonald's opponents. Unlike Macdonald, who claimed a public man could have no resentments, Creighton seemed to have a number of them. The Hincks reference, and others to George Brown, Edward Blake, Oliver Mowat, prompted F.H. Underhill to comment in 1958 that he would have had more confidence in *Macdonald* as history were it not that Macdonald's political opponents "were not only intellectually deficient and morally delinquent but also physically repulsive."

Creighton delighted in resonant adjectives, rotund adverbs, piling them up: the countryside west of Kingston broadening out "comfortably in pleasant and fertile amplitudes" (vol. 1, p. 9); the bedroom of Isabella in 1852 "full of equivocal silences and nervous apprehensions" (vol. 1, p. 174). Such phrases call up Arthur

Lower's comment in the *United Church Observer* in 1952 that "the adjective kills the noun." Still, "equivocal silences" has its own special resonance, and doubtless Creighton so intended it.

Norman Ward loved Creighton's marvellous way with the research materials of history, the way Creighton had made a glowing canvas from the primitive colours research provided. Ward quoted with delight a long passage from page 224, where Macdonald has brought his wife, Isabella, to Toronto for the legislative session. She became ill; it is January, 1856, in a boardinghouse west on Wellington Street:

At night, when he walked homeward along King Street, the brief, sullen winter sunset had already faded in the west ... A dozen times he really expected to find her dead when he arrived ... Yet, with her feeble but persistent resolution, she lived on. She waited for him in the dim sickroom; and there, night after night, he stayed with her. The town was busy with dances, dinners, and parties ... He was inundated with invitations; but he refused them all. Night after night, while the frost struck the desolate little street into icy stillness, he sat up with Isabella; and night after night the candle burned itself slowly downward to the socket.

That's good writing. It is also sustainable history, as close to Ranke's *wie es eigentlich gewesen ist* ('as it really was') as one could have any reason to expect. Yet the documentary authority for it is probably thin—weather reports in the newspapers, a letter or two about Macdonald's wife's health and his life in Toronto. It illustrates Creighton's belief that history was literature, of a special kind, indeed, but grounded in the same canon, with form, plot, structure, that details would come into afterwards, the shafts of light and life that Creighton, imbued with the *Zeitgeist*, could evoke almost at a touch. Indeed, once the research was finished and a skeletal structure assembled, the actual writing would go quickly, page after page in Creighton's small, neat hand, with hardly an emendation.[4]

From the start of his work on Macdonald, Creighton was encouraged by Harold Innis, a considerable historian himself, whom Creighton much admired. The feeling was mutual. When Creighton dedicated the first volume of *Macdonald* to Innis, Innis was visibly moved. George Ferguson of the *Montreal Star*, visiting Innis, who was in hospital with cancer, wrote Creighton that the dedication was the finest thing Creighton had ever done. "If you had heard his [Innis's] voice and seen the charming smile and the look in his eyes ... I nearly wept." When Creighton asked Innis if he could dedicate *Macdonald* to him, probably neither knew that Innis was mortally ill. Discharged from hospital after treatment, Innis went home to Dunvegan Road and settled in to read the proofs of Volume I. He was highly approving. "I am of course confirmed in my earlier view that this marks a new epoch in historical writing in Canada ... and will compel a rewriting and a drastic revision of the content of Canadian history. What a contrast with Mackenzie King!" Innis told Ferguson that "it would set a mark so high that it might scare MacGregor Dawson off the task he had undertaken [the biography of King]!" His only complaint to Creighton was that each chapter read all too quickly. As for Creighton's dedication of *Macdonald* to him, Innis said it was "the highest honour, academic or otherwise which I will ever achieve ..."[5]

If the highest, it was also the last. Innis hoped "to get back to normal in the not too distant future but it is exasperatingly slow. I still write letters only to the Creightons ..." That was in August, 1952. Innis died on November 8. As the news of Innis's cancer circulated among his friends, Gerald Graham, Rhodes Professor of Imperial History, wrote to Creighton: "I can hardly bear the thought of getting along without him ... I shall never have another friend like him, and it's going to be a bloody lonely world."[6] Like Graham, Creighton loved Innis. Innis was his intellectual mentor, and Creighton was Innis's interpreter. One had difficulty with Innis's gnarled and abstruse prose; Creighton made its themes manifest in *The Commercial Empire of the St. Lawrence* (1937), *Dominion of the North* (1944) and *Macdonald*. Creighton remembered Innis in a biography published in 1957. He also felt that this biography, like some of his other books, had never had its proper due.

That was Creighton's besetting sin. Envy unnerved his spirit, clouded his thought, made a Dover Beach of his joy. Ultimately Creighton would receive all the accolades Canada and friends could offer, including the Order of Canada; but in the important world of Britain, who knew or cared much about Canada, dead Canadian politicians, or even live Canadian historians? Or about the fact that Max Beloff in the *Spectator* declared in 1953 that in "Donald Creighton the University of Toronto has one of the half dozen best historians now writing anywhere in the English-speaking world"? When Creighton went to England he was warmly greeted by his friends, but otherwise the great society of London paid little attention to one of the six best historians writing in the English-speaking world. Macmillan of London took only 250 copies of his *Macdonald*. It was gall and wormwood.

That may have been one reason why by the 1960s Creighton had come to dislike the English, their ways, their sublime indifference to things Canadian. He believed in the Crown and the Commonwealth, but now he often found the English intolerable. Of anglophile Canadians like Vincent Massey he was contemptuous. What created this change was a combination of things, not least his Canadian nationalism, but also the difference between the young impressionable Creighton of the mid-1920s and the mature historian of the mid-1960s, made bitter by accomplishment insufficiently recognized.

Cyril James, Principal of McGill University from 1939 to 1962, asked by the Rockefeller Foundation to supervise the work going forward on the Mackenzie King biography, asked Creighton about his mode of operation. There was resentment in Creighton's reply. While he had had some grants—in 1944–45 a Rockefeller, in 1951–52 a Nuffield, and a few short summer grants from the University of Toronto—"no other body and no other person has supported my project either directly or indirectly. I have done all the work myself, and have never had any secretarial assistance. I must confess that I have often envied the lavish fashion in which Mr. King's biography has been supported."

Creighton's other deadly sin was anger. He had a short temper that could be aroused by ignorance and by offences against history or his vanity. He was a member of the Historic Sites and Monuments Board of Canada from 1957 to 1971; once at Niagara-on-the-Lake in the late 1960s he was accidentally left behind at the hotel, while his colleagues went off surveying Fort George. Someone remembered him and went back. There he was, all 6 foot, 2 inches of him, pacing up and down the sidewalk outside the Oban Inn. He was in a smoking fury. As he got in the car he gave one contemptuous snort, "You sons of bitches!" In half an hour it had all passed.

Creighton's reputed insensitivity was apt to be his own astringent mixture of those two sins, envy and anger. He was not a boor, even if occasionally he could behave like one. He could be extraordinarily perceptive. In a conversation with Historic Sites colleagues once, the talk had come around to the tenderness and delicacy of women. Someone said, "It's not exactly like that, is it? Women are creatures of blood and earth. In many ways they are tougher than men. Delicacy is a cover for their elemental nature." Creighton looked up, his eyes wide and shining. "A wonderful remark," he said.

He was sympathetic and generous to his graduate students and that usually comprehended wives, children and income. When one graduate student and his wife both had to set to and teach Basic English at night school to make ends meet, Creighton was horrified. "Oh, God, so it's come to this!" He sought out Vincent Bladen and between them they found $1,200 to establish the student as an Innis Memorial Scholar. "There," he said, "now you can find your way more comfortably in the wake of a great Canadian scholar."[7]

John A. Macdonald: The Young Politician was published by Macmillan of Canada in mid-October, 1952. John Gray, the company president from 1946 to 1978, took an active interest from the start. Macmillan printed five thousand copies, a big printing. It was exhausted in six months, and at least two further printings were needed. Macmillan was probably made bold by the current success of Bruce Hutchison's book on Mackenzie King, which sold fifteen thousand copies in its first year. *The Incredible Canadian* was part reminiscence, part history—in some ways a terrible book, but vivid it was. The vividness found in Lytton Strachey and others prompted Grattan O'Leary to note that new techniques in biography "added a new terror to death." Creighton could quote chunks from Lytton Strachey and would chuckle "like a schoolboy at Strachey's subtlety and wickedness."[8]

Creighton's book was received with tremendous acclaim. It was the first substantial Canadian biography published in many years, really since O.D. Skelton's *Laurier* of 1921. Gratton O'Leary in the *Ottawa Journal* said it was the best since Willison's *Laurier* of 1905. There were a few caveats from Arthur Ford of the *London Free Press*, and the *Peterborough Examiner* did not like the opening sentence; but really there was an explosion of enthusiasm. Macdonald's granddaughter, Isabella Macdonald Gainsford, whom Sir John used to call "Puss," liked it. Arthur Meighen was delighted, although he could not agree with Creighton's implied criticism of the Double Shuffle of 1858. (The Cartier-Macdonald government, said Meighen, "complied strictly with the law" and with its spirit.) C.M. MacInnes wrote Creighton the minute he finished the last page with his "very great admiration ... The function of the historian is to tell a story ... there are still some left who believe that history should also be literature."[9]

Creighton was in Ottawa in October, 1952, for the launching of Volume 1, and, fresh from the accolades above, returned to England for the research and writing of Volume 2, this time on a Rockefeller grant. The Canadian research was already in hand, but he needed to work in English collections. While in England he was solicited to stand for the presidency of the University of New Brunswick. That was almost certainly Beaverbrook's doing. Creighton was annoyed with the University of Toronto for the lack of recognition for his three substantial works already published, and his *Macdonald* just launched. One of the last things Innis did, in the summer of 1952, was to tell Claude Bissell, the new vice-president of Toronto, that they could very well lose Creighton, and that Creighton's complaints to Sidney Smith were justified. Bissell acted, Smith accepted, and by mid-September, 1952, Creighton was appointed chairman of Division I of Graduate Studies for three years, in recognition of his "outstanding contribution to the University." He would be paid an extra $500 a year, bringing his salary to $8,100. That did not prevent him from being interested in the presidency of U.N.B. In the event, Colin B. McKay was appointed and Creighton's aspirations as university president seem to have gone no further.[10]

He stayed in England writing until the last minute, arriving in

Toronto just before the start of lectures, in late September 1953. He was on the second-last chapter, but he was now plunged into academic responsibilities. He was hoping to finish by the summer of 1954. Macmillan did not push him. We'll welcome your manuscript when it comes, John Gray said, and added, "I expect to print 15,000 (count 'em)."[11]

Gray was reading chapters as Creighton sent them, and by December, 1954, he had read the first eleven and had a few comments. The Red River Rebellion of 1869–70 was unclear, especially its outcome. That was not surprising, for it was a difficult story to make clear. Moreover, though Gray professed this a minor point,

the impression that comes through of your own complete lack of sympathy toward the half-breeds. This may be entirely designed, but if not you should be aware of it. The feeling is conveyed in your choice of adjectives (at the time of the 1870 rebellion and again in '84) intractable, improvident, restless, unpredictable—and the very fact that they are almost always referred to as half-breeds instead of metis. The adjectives are, of course, accurate but I feel sure you have more sympathy for them than the reader would think. As it stands this impression would give much offence in the West.

Gray knew the West. All through the 1930s he had canvassed it by train two or three times a year from Winnipeg to Vancouver, weeks at a time, selling Macmillan's books to provincial Departments of Education. It is difficult to know what changes Gray's comments effected. It was Creighton's business, and Gray thoroughly admired the manuscript. "I am congratulating us," he said; "We are going to be very proud of this book." Nevertheless, Creighton was Ontario-born just seventeen years after the Saskatchewan rebellion, and did not really know the West. The point is not irrelevant. It's a long way by train (or any other way) from Toronto to Winnipeg. Macdonald wrote Cartier, November 27, 1869, sympathizing with the position of the Métis. Creighton quoted the letter (vol. 2, pp. 46–47): "All these poor people know is that Canada has bought the country from the Hudson's Bay Company, and that they are handed over like a flock of sheep to

us ..." But Creighton omitted what some might have considered
the most important part of that letter. It goes on: "and they are
told that they may lose their lands and everything they value.
Under these circumstances it is not to be wondered at that they
should be dissatisfied, and show their discontent." It is impossible
to say whether Creighton deliberately suppressed this second section. The quotation was already sufficiently long, and Creighton
did not like long quotations. They cluttered narrative. Gray could
not have known what this omission was, but Creighton's suppression of it, if that is what it was, may have been an illustration of
what was nagging at the back of Gray's mind.[12]

If Volume 1 created delight, Volume 2 created sensation.
Creighton opened up a good deal; invigorated, emboldened by
the success of Volume 1, he shook himself free of any lingering
academic hesitations and launched himself into the Macdonald of
the post-1867 years. His boldness was in effect sanctified by the
tremendous increase in the range and quality of the Macdonald
Papers from 1867 to 1891 and by his access to Lady Macdonald's
diary. That made up for the woeful lack of domestic correspondence between Macdonald and Agnes, for the disappearance of
which she had been mainly responsible. Agnes outlived her husband by thirty years (she died in 1921) and she had ample time to
destroy correspondence, both her letters in her husband's papers,
and his letters in hers.

Volume 2 brought out the superlatives, in Arthur Meighen not
least: "This is the finest biography any Canadian has produced. We
must never forget the years of toil, the dauntless perseverance
which these volumes have cost you. I comfort myself in the
thought that my children and my children's children will feel the
same inspiration that I have felt." George Stanley in the *Queen's
Quarterly* agreed. It was the combination of scholarship and literary
skill, "too rarely found in historians, that gives Mr. Creighton's
work the quality of greatness." Stanley disagreed with Creighton's
interpretation of Louis Riel and with Creighton's views of Macdonald's French-Canadian colleagues, but all that was forgiven in a
book that "blazes with spirit ... It fulfils the hardest task of the historian, that of breathing life into the past. Macdonald stands before
us warm, humorous, clever, lovable."

Hilda Neatby entered, however, a discerning critique on the CBC's "Critically Speaking." We don't get into Macdonald's mind, she said,

> and for a curious reason. Professor Creighton is constantly opening the door, but having done so he stands in the way and blocks the view. And we hear a voice, but we are not quite sure whether it is Macdonald or Creighton who speaks. Is it, for example, Macdonald or his biographer who defends the gerrymander of 1885 as essential for the winning of the election? This method, used throughout the book, of blending his voice with the voice of his subject, prevents Mr. Creighton from offering the mature and informed judgments on Macdonald that he is so abundantly qualified to make.[13]

The first volume of *Macdonald* took the Governor General's gold medal for literature in 1952, and Volume 2 took it in 1955. *Macdonald* came out in paperback. But within twenty years much had changed. Political history, and political biography, had become less fashionable; the younger spirits of the historical academy had shifted their interest to social history. Fashion is apt to be heedless as well as ruthless. By the 1960s Creighton's personal glory had come to be clouded by new ideas and movements that buffeted his sensibilities. He had never held back from expressing his opinions on public questions; he could put his marvellous turn for language to polemical uses, and that had begun very early. Public affairs, public policy, mattered; the anguish of his last ten years came from his profound knowledge of Canadian history, especially of Confederation, and from its juxtaposition with Canada's present, of the Quiet Revolution and the indignity of the FLQ crisis in 1970.

Creighton had always had an appreciation of French-Canadian scholarship. He admired Georges-Henri Lévesque, Dean of Social Sciences at Laval, and he had rewarding relations with Michel Brunet of the Université de Montréal. He helped to bring Brunet to Toronto as the Gray Lecturer in 1958. In 1959 he had to decline chairing a Canadian Historical Association meeting at which Brunet would speak, not because of Brunet, but because he, Creighton, was not sufficiently bilingual.

What eventually alienated Creighton was French-Canadian

nationalism. It made him angry. In May of 1971 he told Eugene
Forsey that French-Canadian nationalism had "succeeded in
weakening my nation." Donald Wright, in a comprehensive and
able analysis of Creighton's attitudes to French Canada, makes the
point that Creighton's anger too often was taken for intolerance.
Creighton was rather, Wright argues,

defending the truth as he understood it ... While he could tolerate differences of interpretation, he could not abide what he saw as outright fabri-
cation ... Two nations, associate state, special status: these were all notions
Creighton found big-hearted, soft-headed, rooted in bad history and
ultimately dangerous to his country. On this point he was not alone.

But by the mid-1970s he was largely beyond those positions,
which at least had historical justification. At times he could be
venomous, even paranoid about French Canadians, their hands "in
the till" as he put it. It warped his judgment, inflamed his mind;
Mirabel airport sent him down "deep ... in the caverns of his
rage."[14]
   Creighton's alienation by French-Canadian attitudes came also
because he viewed Quebec nationalism from premises that were
old and even then not always at one with French-Canadian realities. Had he understood the ambiguity in Louis Fréchette's poem
of the 1880s, "Le Drapeau Anglais"? A young boy and his father
are in Montreal and the boy notices the Union Jack flying at the
top of a building. His father explains that it's a fine flag, it has
made his country prosperous and has given him political freedom.
Then the boy asks,

   —Mais, père, pardonnez si j'ose ...
   N'en est-il pas un autre, à nous?
   —Ah, celui-là, c'est autre chose,
   Il faut le baiser à genoux!

That other flag represented French Canada's attachment to France
and to French. The British flag also represented the conquest,
however generous British rule had, mostly, been. Brunet reminded
Creighton in August, 1956, "Survivre n'est pas vivre."[15] Creighton

seemed not to understand, either, the French-Canadian sense of being continually threatened, surrounded as it really was now, by a tide of English growing incrementally. The new television programs of the 1960s, so many of them in English from both Canada and the United States, made the threat to the French language all the more palpable.

Towards the end of the 1970s, when Creighton was already ill with cancer, some friends took him to a performance of Richard Strauss's *Der Rosenkavalier*, an opera that Creighton knew only distantly. Towards the end of the first act the Marschallin, the Princess von Werdenberg, in her mid-thirties, embraces her seventeen-year-old lover Octavian, first with love, then with philosophy. You will love and marry someone else, she says, someone younger and prettier than me. Time runs off with us all. You can't hold it.

> Time flows on, silently, like sand in an hour-glass.
> Oh, Quinquin! Very often I hear it running—inexorably.

It was not the first time such reflections had come to Creighton. He himself used to say, "all, all is ashes." It is evoked magically in the splendid third act of *Rosenkavalier* when the Marschallin, with Viennese elegance and restraint, ushers Octavian out of her life and gives him to a younger woman. Creighton was in tears.[16]

Cancer caught him finally, on December 19, 1979.

A few months later, in the September, 1980, issue of the *Canadian Forum*, H.V. Nelles published "Creighton's Seminar," a vivid portrait of Creighton the professor. "He taught us first and foremost to respect our evidence. We were expected to plunge into the documents at an early stage and face the bewildering past directly ... to exhaust all of the readily available primary sources for our papers." It is a measure of Creighton's integrity as professor and scholar that what had been true in 1950–51 was still true two decades later.[17]

Creighton had a scholar's passion for accuracy and a dramatist's urge to tell a good story. There may have been other historians who took their page proofs to the archives to check the quotations; I don't know of any but Creighton who did. He might well have resented one's saying that *Macdonald* was his greatest work, but in the perspective of his whole career, it is. Of course there are things wrong with it. Not a few of the critics were at least partly correct: Underhill's spite had some reason in it; Hilda Neatby came as close as anyone to being right, but even she was an admirer, even with her reservations. Sometimes one has to reckon with touches of apparent verisimilitude that are Creighton's sense of drama grounded on a careful reading of the sources and of newspaper weather reports. Anyone who has tried knows how difficult it is to do what Creighton did with Macdonald. The men and women he described, all, all, are dead; their parties, their talk, have disappeared almost, but not quite, without a trace. The traces they left in the archives and in the old newspapers were enough to allow Creighton to make a vivid history of Macdonald's life.

Creighton's work is inimitable: for its grace, its sheer power of evocation, driven by Creighton's passion for making the past alive and breathing. History happened; Creighton never forgot that elementary lesson. Whatever he touched in those two volumes seemed to want to shake off accumulated dust, stand to its feet, and move. Though dead, Macdonald speaks; his jokes and stories are still with us. Creighton died in 1979; his *Macdonald* lives on.

NOTES

1 This recollection is obviously personal, but it has been read, along with the rest of this introduction, by Alan Wilson, a fellow Ph.D. student in the seminar, recently retired as Professor of History, Trent University. He was a graduate student of Creighton's in the 1950s, and his recollections and comments have added much to this account. Viv Nelles of York University raised fascinating (and profound) questions, some that came from his encounter with Cynthia Creighton Flood's story cited immediately below. (Viv Nelles to P.B.W., 13 June, 23 October, 1997.) Michael Cross, a younger colleague of Creighton's at Toronto, now at Dalhousie, offered perceptive comments on this introduction and on the later Creighton. To all three my gratitude; I hope I have translated their suggestions not too imperfectly.

2 Derived from what is perhaps the most challenging work on Creighton, by his daughter, Cynthia Creighton Flood, "My Father Took a Cake to France," in *Malahat Review,* 87 (Summer, 1989), especially pp. 114–15, 118–19, 123.

3 National Archives of Canada (NA), D.G. Creighton Papers, MG31 D77, vol. 2, Luella to D.G. Creighton (hereafter DGC), 5 July, 1951. I am grateful for the discernment and kindness of Robert Fisher of the Manuscript Division of the Archives for making available to me during half a week's visit to Ottawa a selected group of the Creighton Papers.

4 Ibid., C.M. MacInnes to DGC, 1 September, 1953; ibid., vol. 16, DGC to MacInnes, 23 October, 1953; Toronto Telegram, 23 February, 1956, reported by Margaret Aitken; R.C. Brown, "The Historian as Biographer," Canadian Forum, vol. LX, no. 702 (September, 1980), p. 10; Norman Ward in the Saskatoon Star-Phoenix, November, 1952, in DGC Papers, vol. 17; the Underhill remark is quoted by Carl Berger, The Writing of Canadian History: Aspects of English-Canadian Historical Writing, 1900–1970 (Toronto, 1976), p. 225.

Ramsay Derry comments on Creighton's methods and style of writing in the introduction to Donald Creighton, The Passionate Observer: Selected Writings (Toronto, 1980), p. ix. Viv Nelles notes Creighton's view of history as literature, Nelles to PBW, 23 October, 1997.

5 DGC Papers, vol. 2, G.V. Ferguson to DGC, 14 May, 1952; Innis to DGC, 15 July, 1952, from 92 Dunvegan Road; vol. 28, Innis to DGC, 2 August, 1952, addressed to 18 Rawlinson Road, Oxford, where Creighton and his wife were staying while Creighton was writing Volume 2.

6 DGC Papers, vol. 2, Graham to DGC, 29 April, 1952, from Princeton.

7 The Spectator (London), 6 March, 1953; DGC Papers, vol. 2, DGC to Cyril James, 9 January, 1953.

The Historical Sites and Monuments Board recollections of Creighton are mine. The graduate student and his wife whom Creighton helped were Alan and Budge Wilson. (Alan Wilson to PBW, 26 June, 1997.)

8 Cited by Grattan O'Leary in his review of Macdonald, Ottawa Journal, 25 October, 1952; Alan Wilson to PBW, 26 June, 1997.

9 For a history of Canadian biography, see Carl Berger, The Writing of Canadian History, especially chapter 9, "Donald Creighton and the Artistry of History," pp. 208–37. Arthur Ford's review is in London Free Press, 25 October, 1952, the Peterborough Examiner's, 12 November, 1952. For Mrs. Isabella Macdonald Gainsford's letter, see DGC Papers, vol. 6, 15 February, 1953; Arthur Meighen's is in ibid., 1 December, 1952; for C.M. MacInnes, see ibid., vol. 2, 1 September, 1953.

10 Ibid., vol. 2, DGC to B.F. Macaulay, 27 June, 1953, from Oxford; Macaulay to DGC, 18 September, 1953, personal and confidential, from Fredericton.

Creighton's annoyances with University of Toronto were various, some of them with the chief accountant. Harold Innis intervened about what he considered the university's shabby treatment of Creighton; see ibid., vol. 28, Innis to DGC, 2 August, 1952; ibid., Sidney Smith to DGC, 17 September, 1952. Creighton after his stint as chairman of Division I, Graduate Studies, was appointed Acting Chairman of the Department of History as of 1 January,

1955 (replacing Ralph Flenley) and chairman as of 1 July, 1955, which post he held until 1959.

11 *Ibid.*, vol. 2, DGC to W.L. Morton, 18 November, 1953; Gray to DGC, 3 September, 1953.

12 *Ibid.*, vol. 16, Gray to DGC, 17 December, 1954. For John Gray's life, see his *Fun Tomorrow: Learning to Be a Publisher and Much Else* (Toronto, 1978), pp. 179, 182–83. It is sad to record that this marvellous man died four months after writing the preface to his book.

Macdonald's letter to Cartier is in vol. 516 of the Macdonald Papers, in the letterbooks, which are quite complete for this period. The original letter Cartier sent on to Hector Langevin; thus it was not destroyed with Cartier's papers, and is in ANQ, Langevin Papers, boîte 18.

13 DGC Papers, vol. 6, Arthur Meighen to DGC, 7 October, 1955; G.F.G. Stanley's review in *Queen's Quarterly* (1955), pp. 592–94, also in DGC Papers, vol. 16; Hilda Neatby, "Critically Speaking," 9 October, 1955, typescript in *ibid.*

14 *Ibid.*, vol. 26, DGC to Eugene Forsey, 9 May, 1971, quoted in Donald A. Wright, "Donald Creighton and the French Fact, 1920s–1970s," in *Journal of the Canadian Historical Association*, vol. 6 (1955), p. 259; *ibid.*, p. 266.

Creighton's paranoia in his late years is noted by Michael Cross, a former colleague, Cross to PBW, 16 July, 1997, and especially by Creighton's daughter. See Cynthia Flood, "My Father Took a Cake to France," p. 121.

15 DGC Papers, vol. 3, Brunet to DGC, 11 August, 1956, cited in Wright, "Donald Creighton," p. 254.

16 For Creighton's remark, "All, all is ashes," see Cynthia Flood, "My Father Took a Cake to France," p. 115. The recollection of Creighton at *Der Rosenkavalier* is Ramsay Derry's. See his introduction to Creighton's *The Passionate Observer*, pp. vii–viii.

17 H.V. Nelles, "Creighton's Seminar," *Canadian Forum*, vol. LX, no. 702 (September, 1980), p. 6.

BIBLIOGRAPHICAL NOTE

There is no book about Donald Creighton but there are many articles and other shorter works. The most important is by his daughter, Cynthia Creighton Flood, "My Father Took a Cake to France," in the *Malahat Review*, vol. 87 (Summer, 1989), pp. 119–24. The *Canadian Forum* (September, 1980) has a Creighton symposium with five articles, the most perceptive of which is Viv Nelles's "Creighton's Seminar," pp. 5–6. Also valuable is R.C. Brown's "The Historian as Biographer," pp. 9–10. A recent, comprehensive and well-made academic piece is Donald A. Wright, "Donald Creighton and the French Fact, 1920s–1970s," in

Journal of the Canadian Historical Association, New Series, vol. 6 (1995), pp. 243–72. Readers will find in Wright's footnotes a cornucopia of articles on Creighton's career. Carl Berger has a fine chapter on Creighton in his *The Writing of Canadian History: Aspects of English-Canadian Historical Writing, 1900 to 1970* (Toronto, 1976), "Donald Creighton and the Artistry of History," pp. 208–37. A *Festschrift* for Creighton was published by Macmillan in 1970: John S. Moir, ed., *Character and Circumstance: Essays in Honour of Donald Grant Creighton*. This book includes Moir, "Donald Grant Creighton," pp. 1–8, and J.M.S. Careless, "Donald Creighton and Canadian History: Some Reflections," pp. 8–22. Ramsay Derry provides a handsome introduction about Creighton in the collection *The Passionate Observer: Selected Writings by Donald Creighton* (Toronto, 1980). My obituary of Creighton is published in the Royal Society of Canada, *Proceedings*, vol. XVIII (1980), pp. 73–77, some bits of which have surfaced in this introduction.

John A. Macdonald

* * *

The Young Politician

TO

HAROLD ADAMS INNIS

PREFACE

It is now nearly sixty years since Sir Joseph Pope published, in two volumes, his *Memoirs of the Right Honourable Sir John Alexander Macdonald, G.C.B., First Prime Minister of The Dominion of Canada.* Sir Joseph was Macdonald's literary executor; to him was entrusted the vast mass of the Macdonald correspondence; and his biography, solidly based upon these private papers, has long remained the standard work on the subject. Other biographies of Macdonald have been published, of course, since the *Memoirs* first appeared in 1894; but they were shorter and slighter works, and without independent authority. This was inevitable as long as the correspondence remained in the custody of Macdonald's literary executor; but in 1917 Sir Joseph Pope transferred the entire collection to the Public Archives of Canada. Since that time—thirty-five years ago now—the Macdonald Papers have certainly not been left unused. Historians have searched them—or, at least, parts of them—in pursuit of evidence on a variety of special topics. But, somewhat curiously, the principal subject of the collection, Macdonald himself, has never been made the main theme of an extended study. In view of the richness of the Papers, this neglect is surprising; and it is all the more surprising when one realizes how many other collections of original materials, relating in whole or in part to Canadian affairs during the long period of Macdonald's career, have been opened to students, in both Canada and Great Britain, during the past twenty-five years. It would seem, therefore, that the time has perhaps arrived for a re-examination of Macdonald's career in the light of all the evidence now available. That, at least is the excuse for the present study. The volume which is here presented covers the first of the two great periods into which Macdonald's career naturally falls. A second and concluding volume will deal with the years from 1867 to Macdonald's death in 1891.

I have to acknowledge Her Majesty's gracious permission to make use of material in the Royal Archives, Windsor Castle. I am indebted, for much kind assistance, to Dr. W. Kaye Lamb, Dominion Archivist, and his assistants in the Public Archives of Canada, especially Miss Norah Story and Mr. W. G. Ormsby of the Manuscript Division; to Dr. G. W. Spragge, Department of Public Records and Archives, Ontario; and to Mr. H. P. Gundy, Librarian, Queen's University, Kingston. For help in finding material in England, I am under obligation to Sir Campbell Stuart, Mr. R. L. Atkinson, of the Historical Manuscripts Commission, Colonel G. E. G. Malet, of the National Register of Archives, and Miss D. E. Eldred, representative of the Public Archives of Canada at the Public Record Office, London. I have also to thank the officials of the National Trust for permission to consult the Beaconsfield Papers at Hughenden Manor. Professor J. M. S. Careless, my colleague in the Department of History, University of Toronto, has verified a number of my references; and I should like to record my appreciation of his assistance.

Finally, I gratefully acknowledge my indebtedness to the University of Toronto, the Rockefeller Corporation, and the Nuffield Foundation for the grants which have enabled me to give my undivided attention to this work over considerable periods of time.

D. G. CREIGHTON

OXFORD, DOMINION DAY, 1952.

CONTENTS

Chapter One

The Immigrant Macdonalds

I

In those days they came usually by boat. A few immigrants may have made the long journey from Montreal by land, taking several weeks and stopping at a score of friendly farm-houses as they pushed their way through the green forest. But most people travelled westward by the river—either in *bateaux*, camping out at night on the shore under the stars, or by schooner, or by one of the new steamers which in the last few years had begun to chug noisily up and down the long stretches between the rapids. In its upper reaches, the St. Lawrence widened promisingly; but here the rocky formation of the Laurentian Plateau thrust a huge knotted fist southward, across the river into New York State; and the St. Lawrence was crowded with islands, big and little, long and low, or towering and crested with pine trees, which parted the vast expanse of water into innumerable channels and masked the approach to Lake Ontario. As the boats slipped at length past Howe Island, out of the river's last channel and into the lake itself, their destination was still hidden by a bulging promontory of mainland, dented with deep inlets, which jutted south into Lake Ontario. They passed Deadman Bay, and then Navy Bay—where Sir James Yeo had urged his shipwrights forward in the frantic struggle for the mastery of Lake Ontario during the War of 1812—and finally rounded Point Frederick. Here was another wide body of water, the estuary of the Cataraqui River, which drained into Lake Ontario from the rocky highland to the north.

And beyond that, on low land rising gently towards the west, was the town of Kingston.

From the site of Frontenac's old fort, the town's shore-line curved southward in a slow arc to Mississauga Point, with its battery and the blockhouse beyond. A paddle-wheel steamer, a half-dozen schooners were moored at Cartwright's and Forsyth's and the newer docks to the south; and behind them, the town lay like an outspread fan, its east-west streets, like ribs, converging on Store Street, less than a mile inland. In 1820 it was thirty-six years since Captain Michael Grass and his small company of United Empire Loyalists had drawn lots for their properties in the new town-site. Kingston had not done badly in the race for prominence and prestige which the little Loyalist villages had begun back in 1784. York had become the seat of government; York was already threatening to acquire the financial and commercial leadership of the province. But Kingston, with its three to four thousand inhabitants equalled, if it did not exceed, the population of the capital, and had far outstripped the other river and lake towns. Kingston, in fact, had been the real, though not the titular, capital of the early province of Upper Canada, the province of the Loyalists, with its concentration on the upper St. Lawrence. And the solid advantages which had given it this early pre-eminence lasted stubbornly on, long after settlement had begun to spill into the rich peninsula between Lakes Erie and Huron, and the whole centre of gravity of the province was shifted slowly westward.

The town stood at the head of the St. Lawrence, at the foot of the vast, interconnecting system of the Great Lakes; and this commanding position was important for all sorts of reasons, military and naval, as well as commercial and political. Like York, Kingston was one of the principal garrison towns in the upper province; but, in addition—and this was an unique advantage—it had since 1789 been the British naval base on Lake Ontario. It was true that the Peace of Ghent had silenced the busy activity of the dockyard at Point Henry. It was true, and more important, that the Rush-Bagot Treaty, limiting future naval construction on the Great Lakes, had seemed to drop the curtain on Kingston's briefly dramatic career as a naval base.

Those two giants, H.M.S. *Wolfe* and H.M.S. *Canada* lay un-finished on the stocks, just where they had been abruptly abandoned in 1815; and the *St. Lawrence* and the little flotilla of ships that had gained command of the lake in the last weeks of the war rode at anchor, in decaying splendour, in Navy Bay. Formally, peace had come; but it was a doubtful and uneasy period of tranquillity, during which the province waited, seized by recurring fits of apprehension; and Kingston, and other stra-tegic centres, remained watchfully upon the defensive. East of the Cataraqui River, at the naval base, the decaying little fleet was not finally destroyed, and the "stone frigate", the largest structure yet built at Point Frederick, was erected in 1820. West of the river, in the town itself, the commandant still kept up his fine house, and the garrison occupied the site of Frontenac's old fort, just below where the scow ferry plied from one side to the other of the river. The town was full of soldiers. They were as familiar as the citizens; and some were becoming citizens themselves. Veterans of the Napoleonic and American Wars, they were settling down in the lands which they had fought to keep British; and along with them, or after them, there often came their sweethearts, wives, children, relations or friends. It was a characteristic episode of the period when, on a July day in 1820, a little group of Scottish immigrants arrived at the house of their kinsman, Lieutenant-Colonel Donald Mac-pherson, a retired British Army officer living in Kingston.

There were six of them—Hugh Macdonald, his wife Helen, and their four children, Margaret, John Alexander, James, and Louisa.[1] It was Helen Macdonald who provided the link with the Macpherson family and the claim upon the Colonel's benevolence. She was a big woman, sturdily built, with a firm, prominent nose, and wide-set, dark, intelligent eyes. She and Anna Macpherson, the Colonel's wife, were half-sisters. They were both members of a stout, intricate family connection of Macphersons, Clarks, Grants and Shaws, who inhabited a half-dozen tiny villages in Badenoch and Speyside, Inverness-shire. Their mother, Margaret Grant, had been twice married, first to William Shaw, of Dalnavert, and then to James Shaw, a clansman, but not a relation of her first husband, who came

from Kinrara, a tiny neighbouring village in the same parish of
Alvie. Anna and Margaret were daughters of the first marriage,[2]
Helen of the second; and Helen's father, James Shaw, was a
soldier who had fought for the Pretender at Culloden and who,
like so many other more famous heads of Jacobite families, had
taken service in the Hanoverian armies after the ruin of the
Stuart cause.

Helen grew up in Dalnavert, in the house which her much
older half-sisters had once occupied, in that professional military
atmosphere which was common to so many Highland families
in the two generations after Culloden. Her father had been a
soldier; her elder half-sister, Anna Shaw, had married young
Lieutenant Donald Macpherson; her younger half-sister, Margaret, had married another Highland officer, Alexander Clark.
It might have been confidently expected that Helen, in her turn,
would follow the example of her sisters and choose one of these
men of high pride; and small means, and splendid courage, who
had been fighting the battles of the British Empire in Europe
and America since 1757. But she did nothing of the kind. Somewhere about 1811, she met and married Hugh Macdonald;
and with him, as a sober merchant's wife, she settled down in
Glasgow.

Hugh Macdonald introduced a distinct and novel strain into
the Badenoch connection of Grants, Macphersons, Clarks, and
Shaws. He came not from Inverness-shire but from Sutherland,
and his family background lay not in military service with
Stuart and Hanoverian armies, but in small farming and trade.[3]
His father, John Macdonald, a tall, spare man, with abundant,
black, curly hair, had been born in 1736 in Rogart; and Rogart
was one of the few inland parishes, in the south-eastern part of
the country, which had been carved out by occupation from the
immense, sombre, treeless expanse of moorland which was
Sutherland. Here, in little villages in the Strathfleet valley, he
lived and worked; here in 1778 he married a clanswoman, Jean
Macdonald; and here several of his children, including his
second son, Hugh, were born. It was not until comparatively
late in life that he made the great move of his career—a move
that carried him only a few miles in space, but a considerable

distance in opportunity—to the county town, Dornoch. In Dornoch, close to the edge of the North Sea, at the entrance to the long arm of Dornoch Firth, he slowly prospered. For a time he may have leased and farmed a part of the property known locally as "Fourpenny" in the vicinity of the borough; but he also kept a shop in town, apparently near the cathedral; and it was for these mercantile pursuits that he was evidently best known. For long afterward the old people of Dornoch used to remember him by his Gaelic title "the merchant Macdonald".[4]

John Macdonald's virtues were simple and solid ones; but his son, Hugh, was a much more complicated and unstable character. He had been born in 1782, and the new century was probably not very far advanced before he began to fret inside the grey walls of his father's shop. Amiable, a little indolent, he was fond of talk and company and the bottle; but he responded quickly to young faces, new landscapes, and fresh opportunities. He was at once ambitious and good-natured, restless yet fundamentally easy-going, enterprising and at the same time curiously lacking in persistence. He always seemed to believe that he was made for success, and he was in fact invariably susceptible to failure. Dornoch, a little northern county town, had proved ample enough for his father's ambition, and had generously repaid his father's hard work. But, once Hugh had attained his majority, nothing but the big city of Glasgow would satisfy him. In Glasgow, he set up in business with a partner as a manufacturer of cottons in a small way, and failed. He then tried a new and similar enterprise on his own account and succeeded no better. It was true that the times were scarcely propitious. The conclusion of the Napoleonic Wars was followed, after only a few years, by a depression which threw Glasgow, all Scotland, and the whole of the United Kingdom into a state of profound discouragement and unrest. Failure was epidemic; and so was the counter-contagion, emigration. After a long interval, the western movement of the British peoples was resumed once more; and, for the first time in their history, the northern provinces which had survived the American Revolution began to attract the interested attention of prospective migrants in the Motherland. It was only natural that the mercurial, avid, restless Hugh should think of emigration. It was inevitable, once the decision to leave Scotland was made, that he should get in touch with his wife's relatives, the Donald Macphersons, the one branch of the connection that had settled in British North America.

The Macphersons had been living in the Canadas for over twelve years, and the Colonel had spent an even longer portion of his agitated career in North America, defending British authority and British territory against bellicose republicans.[5] In 1775, when he was just a young man, he had joined the muster of Fraser's Highlanders, the 71st Regiment; and he had fought all through the American Revolutionary War until the surrender of Cornwallis's army at Yorktown. When, in 1783, Fraser's Highlanders were disbanded at Perth, and young Macpherson, a lieutenant on half-pay, returned to Inverness-shire, and settled down at Dalnavert, he may very well have assumed that his connection with North America was ended for ever. It was true that he did not remain very long in the Highlands, for when the war with Revolutionary France broke out in 1793, he at once resumed his old profession of soldiering; and if he had been a slightly younger man, he might have ended his long military career with his new regiment, the Gordon Highlanders, in the triumphs and endurances of the Peninsular and Waterloo campaigns. But one lifetime was too short to support active service in three wars which together covered a space of nearly forty years. In 1806—a major now—Macpherson was transferred to one of the veterans' units;[6] a year later he crossed the Atlantic for the third time to take up garrison duty in the distant yet supposedly far less hazardous theatre of action, British North America; and, on September 10, 1807, he landed at Quebec, with the Tenth Royal Veteran Battalion, commanded by Lieutenant-General Lowther Pennington.[7] When the War of 1812 broke out, five years later, he was stationed at Kingston; and the old man resumed the familiar exercise of fighting Americans. In 1813, as a reward of long service, he was promoted Lieutenant-Colonel. For a brief while he was apparently commandant of the garrison; and then, in 1815, the war came to an end.[8]

He did not return to Scotland. He retired on full pay, received an ample grant of land, and settled down in Kingston with a comfortable air of finality. His children were growing up. John Alexander, the eldest son, and his younger brother, Lowther Pennington, named in honour of the Colonel's old commander, were now lads in their teens; and there was a third boy, Evan, and four girls as well.[9] They were the children of Macpherson's mature years who, in effect, had known no home but Kingston and no country but Canada; and in Canada their circumstances were easy and their prospects promising. Kingston, in fact, had ceased to be a temporary advanced post from which soldiers of fortune inevitably returned. It had become a new home base round which a part, at least, of the vast Macpherson connection might be happily reunited. Back from this Upper Canadian household, solidly established in a promising wilderness, there flowed the encouragement, advice and assistance that were to lure the Macpherson clan from the old world to the new. Hugh Macdonald accepted it all eagerly. He was a born migrant whom failure and misfortune had made ready for travel again. In the early summer of 1820 he set sail for Canada; and on July 17, he and his wife, Helen, and their four children "entered Colonel Macpherson's house at Kingston".[10]

II

It could hardly have been a more pleasant introduction to Canada. The Macphersons lived in relative ease and dignity. The house was full of children, and the younger Macpherson boys and girls were much of an age with the Macdonald children. Anna Macpherson had a wealth of practical information to give to Helen Macdonald; and the Colonel, than whom nobody in Kingston was better known or more respected, had acquired a copious store of knowledge about the little town and its ways which was of immediate value to Hugh. For Hugh had determined to settle in Kingston. He had no intention whatever of submitting himself and his family to the terrible fatigues and privations of real pioneer life. The frontier homestead, won with incredible difficulty out of the bush in the remote north or west, the "improved farm" somewhere "out front" in the first row of townships—these hard destinies, which were the common lot of thousands of the first two generations of immigrants after Waterloo, were to form no part of the history of the Macdonald family. Hugh Macdonald knew village and town life. Commerce—petty trade and small-scale manufacturing—had formed the chief economic thread in the fortunes of his family for two decades. He had experience. He had some capital, not a great deal perhaps, but more, certainly, than the majority of his fellow-emigrants. And in the prosperous and benevolent Colonel Macpherson he possessed a commercial asset of high importance through which he could anticipate good will, make connections, and acquire credit.

Finally, he was fortunate in coming to the town of Kingston. Without any question, the commercial advantages of Kingston were superior to those of any other town in the eastern part of Upper Canada. The military barracks, the naval establishment at Point Frederick, the huge, if spasmodic, expenditures for defence, were all official endorsations of the basic importance of its position. Kingston was the capital of the Midland District; and, although the Midland District comprised only the four counties, Frontenac, Lennox and Addington, Prince Edward, and Hastings, these were very populous and prosperous counties. And, indeed, the prominence of the Midland District was such that people in other parts of Upper Canada often spoke and wrote of it, in a loose, inaccurate, but highly flattering fashion, as if it occupied the whole of the east-central part of the province. Even within its official boundaries, it extended over a vast and varied domain. To the north-east lay the plateau of the Precambrian shield, the gnarled and shaggy country of rock and forest and intricately connected waterways, from which the Cataraqui River brought the great red and white pine timbers down to the Kingston mills. It was true that the infertile rock-land crowded Kingston closely, a little oppressively, to the north-east, in somewhat the same way as the great moors of central Sutherland had crowded Rogart and Lairg and Dornoch, the little parishes of Hugh Macdonald's youth. But south-west ol

Kingston, along the Bath and Napanee roads, the country broadened out comfortably in pleasant and fertile amplitudes; and across the narrow strait from Adolphustown lay the peninsula of Prince Edward county, nearly encircled by the warm, shallow waters of the Bay of Quinte, and rich with farms and barns and orchards. A score of villages and little towns—Bath, Ameliasburgh, Adolphustown, Hallowell, Napanee, and Belleville—looked up respectfully to Kingston as their local capital; and Kingston's economic hinterland extended far beyond the limits of its administrative authority. It had become the little commercial metropolis for all the eastern part of the province; and it was a major point of transhipment on the northern trade route which extended from England and the ports of Europe across the Atlantic, up the St. Lawrence and the Great Lakes system and far into the interior of the continent.

To Hugh Macdonald the town itself must have seemed not only novel and exciting, but also, in an odd way, vaguely familiar. There was a grey, sober, earnest, downright, yet not ungracious air about it which might have reminded him of the villages and towns of his youth. Many of the shops and houses of Kingston were built of limestone, which was obtained with ease in the ample quarries nearby; and the flat, grey shop fronts, with their rows of pleasantly spaced sashed windows, climbed in slowly ascending levels up Store Street from the harbour. Despite its smallness, the town had an eighteenth-century urban appearance, an old-fashioned inclination towards regularity and symmetry and perspectives, which was to yield only slowly and partially to the violent idiosyncrasies of Victorian stone- and brick-work. In the homely austerity of Lower Town, on the pavements of Store, Grass, Church and Grave Streets—grey thoroughfares which only later were to be given less hard-bitten names—Hugh might, at times, have thought himself back among the stone walls of Dornoch. And on autumn nights, when the wind blew chill from the west, and the waters of the huge, troubled lake roared outside the harbour he could have fancied himself looking out towards Dornoch Firth and the North Sea. He was done with big cities. His father had won his decent reputation and his sober success in a small town;

and, town for town, Kingston was infinitely more promising than Dornoch. Hugh was not yet thirty-eight years old. He had been unfortunate; but, in this new world, everything could be, and would be, repaired. He arranged his credits, obtained his stock, engaged a highly dubious assistant—an old soldier named Kennedy, who drank in secret even more than his easy-going master would have considered desirable—and, on October 16, 1820, almost exactly three months after his arrival, he opened his first shop in Kingston.[11]

He and his wife and children lived above the shop, as did the families of most merchants and professional men, even the most affluent, in Kingston at the time. It was a relatively small family, judged by the standards of that age, smaller certainly than the Macpherson brood, and death, through disease and accident, had been busy already with its members. Life was uncertain enough for the adult population of the early nineteenth century. It was doubly precarious for children; and, of the five sons and daughters born to Hugh and Helen, only three survived the tragic disasters of childhood. William, apparently the eldest son, died in infancy long before they left Scotland; and they had not been two years in Canada when their second surviving boy, James, was killed in a frightful accident. A little thing—he was not yet six years old when the tragedy took place—he was left one spring evening in the care of the old soldier, Kennedy, who, apparently, could be brutal as well as bibulous; and Kennedy, either in impatience or anger, struck him with such force that he fell, injuring himself fatally.[12] Of the three children who remained, two were girls. Margaret —"Moll"—was the elder, a gentle little girl, with a round, sweet, serious countenance, and regular diminutive features. The baby, Louisa—"Lou" she was called—was a sturdy, rather plain child, not more than two years old when they arrived in Canada; and, as she grew up, she came to resemble her brother very closely.

Her brother, Hugh's only surviving son, was called John Alexander. The third child, a year and a half younger than his sister Margaret, he had been born on January 11, 1815, in Glasgow. He remembered something of his native city, in the

queer disconnected flashes of childish recollection; and his accent
and mode of speech were formed in a family and among relatives where broad Scots was continually spoken. But he was
only five and a half years old when he was brought to Canada;
and he grew up a typical Midland District boy, with the expressions and turns of phrase which were characteristic of the
region.[13] Tall for his age, slight and yet sturdy, with an increasingly lanky and almost angular frame, he had his mother's
prominent nose, her generous mouth, her wide-set dark eyes.
These rugged lines, apparent already in the smooth countenance
of early boyhood, were set off by another characteristic feature,
a copious crop of dark, curly, almost frizzy hair—a legacy, apparently, of his paternal grandfather, old "merchant Macdonald"
of Dornoch. In 1820, when his parents arrived in Canada, he
had almost reached the end of the first free, happily unfettered
phase of childhood. A rather quiet, thoughtful small boy—and
yet, at times, full of exuberant fun and inventive mischief—, he
must have learnt to read early, for he quickly became passionately interested in books. Now he was almost ready for school.

In the meantime, while Helen bore her domestic tragedy and
coped with the thousand novelties of her new situation, things
had not been going at all well with Hugh. The shop did not
prosper—at least to his satisfaction. Its fortunes began to have
a distressingly close resemblance to those of his abandoned
enterprises in Glasgow. The fault, of course, must be a quite
simple one, easily remedied. It was probably that his location
was unfortunate—his shop inconvenient and remote from the
main business of the town. He changed his location; but,
strangely enough, he could not change his luck. And some time
early in 1824, less than four years after he had arrived from
Scotland, he came restlessly to the conclusion that he was
through with the capital of the Midland District. There may
have been talk, as he discussed the matter with his wife Helen,
and with Donald and Anna Macpherson, of a move to one of
the newer settlements, farther west along the shore of Lake
Ontario, and an attempt at farming; but, in the end, Hugh made
a much more modest and sensible choice, which had at least
a definite relation with his training and previous experience.

He moved westward, indeed, but only a little westward, as the long ungainly province measured its distances; and on Hay Bay, one of the deep inlets of the Bay of Quinte, and in a small, clap-boarded building painted red, he opened his third shop.[14] Here, in the third concession of Adolphustown, the "Fourth Town" west of the capital of the Midland District, he was still in Kingston's economic hinterland, in long-settled country which had been occupied since the first coming of the Loyalists. In these pleasant surroundings, and in fairly short order, the third shop failed.

Even yet, Hugh was far from daunted. With his easy-going, well established migratory habits, he determined to abandon Lennox and Addington County as he had already abandoned Frontenac. A little to the south-west, across a narrow reach of water, lay the irregular peninsula of Prince Edward County, with a little settlement, later called Glenora, at its very edge. Immediately beyond Glenora, the land soared abruptly upward, in steep, wooded heights, to form a wide tableland, hundreds of feet above the level of Lake Ontario. High on this dominating plateau, set in thick woods, mysteriously suspended above the great stretch of water below, was a little lake, the "Lake on the Mountain". All around, to the north-east and north-west, lay spread out the immense, tranquil landscape of the Bay of Quinte and its counties, in an intricate pattern of deep bays and coves and reaches, of long projecting headlands, capes, and points, which, as they stretched away towards the horizon, became a succession of narrow, contrasting strokes of colour, blue water, dark woods, and yellowing farmlands. A small channel had been cut from the Lake on the Mountain to the cliff's edge, and from there a roaring stream of water tumbled down a wooden race-way to turn the machinery of a large stone mill, several storeys in height, which stood by the shore of Adolphus Reach.[15] This property, the "Stone Mills", as the place was known at the time, was Hugh Macdonald's last major investment. It was a grist-mill, where Hugh also carried on the carding of wool, and the fulling, dyeing and dressing of cloth.[16] An ill-fated but indomitable enterpriser, he had been both manufacturer and shop-keeper. Now he was to become a miller.

The stock of prudence and pertinacity which had been so laboriously accumulated during generations of hard living in Rogart and Dornoch parishes was apparently being frittered away during a single lifetime. It was true that Hugh Macdonald, unlike some of the gentlemen immigrants who lost everything, including the last shreds of their dignity, in the Canadian bush, never completely succumbed to his reverses. In his hopeful, amiable, ineffectual way, he managed, if but barely, to keep some kind of shaky foundation for his family's life. The mill was never more than a mediocre success; but at least, for a number of years, it avoided failure. And the countryside about the Stone Mills—the waters of Adolphus Reach, the wooded heights, the mountain, and its diminutive lake—all this formed an agreeable landscape through which John Alexander and his sisters rambled happily down the long, golden road of summer. Yet Hugh, though he always provided a house, and though, perhaps, he could teach his family some of the simplest arts of living, was never quite able to remove the uneasy sense of uncertainty and precariousness from his children's lives. It was Helen who succeeded in maintaining the family in effective being during those years of reverses and abandonments.[17] In her strong, solid frame there was an immense vitality and an immense power of endurance. Hugh grew rapidly older; for him the great hopes of immigration had failed. But Helen kept alive a family sense of purpose and direction. It was she who was always remembering the past. It was she who was planning for the future—for her children, for her only surviving son.

III

As far back, probably, as the winter of 1822, John Alexander had started to school in Kingston.[18] He was only nine years old when the family moved to Hay Bay, and probably for the first year he stayed at home, and tramped down the country roads to John Hughes's school at Adolphustown.[19] Then—and the change may have coincided with the move to the Stone Mills

—a different and more ambitious educational programme was adopted; and he was sent back, for the winter months at least, to continue his schooling at Kingston. It was a characteristic Scottish decision. It meant long separations, and additional expense, which Hugh could ill afford; but both he and Helen —and perhaps particularly Helen—believed in their stubborn way that it was essential; and, somehow or other, they managed to meet the fees and the charges for board and lodging. John Hughes had a decent reputation as a teacher; but there was probably no school within many miles of the Stone Mills; and, in general, even in such old-established counties as Frontenac, Lennox and Addington and Prince Edward, the common schools were few, badly equipped and even more badly taught. The District Grammar Schools, usually established at the capital of each administrative district, were the one great exception to the general rule of poor and inadequate teaching. It was a standing Radical grievance, repeatedly ventilated in the Legislative Assembly, that the provincial school system favoured the rich of the towns at the expense of the poor of the countryside. But the fact was that, at that time, Upper Canada could simply not afford a substantial number of competent schools; and another twenty-five years elapsed before Egerton Ryerson began to lay down the broad solid foundations of a truly provincial educational system. In the meantime, the District Grammar Schools, together with a few private academies, provided the best education that the province could afford; and it was only by unusual arrangements and some sacrifices that a country boy like John Alexander could attend a good school.

He was, on the whole, lucky in the Midland District Grammar School. It was a small stone building, standing on the north side of School Street, a little below Church, and kept by two masters—the Reverend John Wilson, who was headmaster from 1817 to the close of 1824, and his assistant George Baxter.[20] Wilson was an old Oxonian, a member of Queen's College, and a clergyman of the Established Church, whose reputation as a scholar was not forgotten when he buried himself in the little frontier Upper Canadian town; and the standard of teaching at the Midland District Grammar School was probably pretty high. John Alexander was well grounded in Latin; he was almost certainly taught some French, though what is likely to have been his first French grammar, still surviving, has a suspiciously unused appearance. And by 1827, when he was just twelve years old, he had worked his way through numbers and their properties, decimals, ratios and geometrical proportions, and was deep in square and cube root.[21] He wrote a round, clear, careful hand, which soon became easy and flowing. His books were neatly kept, with careful spacing, indentations, and headings; and it was only on the covers that he allowed himself to indulge in supplementary and unacademic expression—in repeated, grotesque representations of the human profile, in a few imaginary and euphonious appellations such as "Timothy Mudlark Toenail", and in the inspiring reflection, "God Save the King, and the Devil Take the Preacher".

He lodged and boarded in town, probably with several different landladies. But the Macpherson household was a second home, and he must have been in and out of it constantly. His uncle, the old Colonel, who had begun his fighting career over fifty years before, died at length in 1828. The citizens of Kingston shut their shops in honour of his memory, and the battery guns boomed out in a last salute. The two older Macpherson boys, John Alexander and Lowther Pennington, who by this time had reached their twenties, may already have left their home; and in 1826 one of the elder girls had married an able, pushing Scot named Francis Harper, who seemed to acquire capital and important friends with ease, and who was soon to become one of the financial standbys of the connection. The family circle shrank and altered; but Aunt Anna Macpherson kept the old household going, and the younger children, Helen and Catharine and Evan, were much of John Alexander's age and remained good friends with him. He used to slip into the Macpherson house after school, and Helen would supply him with slices of pudding and other delicacies not too frequently present on the table at his lodgings. Already he was a voracious reader, and he would sit for hours deep in a book, almost oblivious to what was going on, while the friendly tumult of the Macpherson household raged around him.[22] Then, when the summer came, he was away again to the Stone Mills for the long vacation.

He had profited from John Wilson's training in the first years of his schooling, before the family had left for Hay Bay. But, by the time he returned to Kingston, Wilson had resigned his headmastership and had returned to England to take up a post in his old university. The trustees of the Midland District Grammar School—the Archdeacon, George Okill Stuart, those two Loyalist worthies, John Macaulay and Thomas Markland, and the laconic Dr. Sampson, Kingston's principal physician for many years—pondered, at somewhat lengthy intervals, the question of Wilson's successor. Baxter was, of course, available. Baxter wanted the job; and Baxter, though it was regrettably true that he had once been a Presbyterian, was now definitely a member of the Church of England in good standing. Yet, the trustees, with the memory of Wilson's headmastership to inspire them, aimed at better talent. They wanted a man with an English university degree—a priest of the Church of England. This second requirement was included partly for reasons of religious conviction and considerations of prestige; but also partly on grounds of economy. The trustees could offer an annual salary of £350; but they believed that a clergyman could be more easily induced to accept it, since a clergyman would have the opportunity of increasing his income by doing a variety of odd jobs for the Archdeacon. In the end, however, these complicated and ambitious plans fell through. Baxter was made temporary headmaster, and then, in 1826, he was given the permanent appointment.[23] There may have been dissatisfaction with his principalship, or dissatisfaction with the grammar-school system in general, which some people, in places like Kingston, believed was certain to be injured by the large sums which Lieutenant-Governor Colborne seemed likely to divert to his pet project, Upper Canada College, at York. At any rate, the Kingston Scots began to be concerned about the education of their children.

The Protestant Scots community in Kingston had been growing fairly rapidly during these years. Scots had formed no important part of the original Loyalist settlement; but after the conclusion of the War of 1812 they began to come in increasing numbers. Up to 1820, they had lacked a church of their own; but in that year, the year in which the Macdonalds arrived in town, St. Andrews, in connection with the Church of Scotland, was built at the corner of Clergy and Store Streets. Its first minister, John Barclay, died in 1826, after only five years in Kingston; but again the Scottish community approached the Presbytery of Edinburgh, and the Presbytery of Edinburgh appointed John Machar, a young man from Forfarshire, a graduate of King's College, Aberdeen, and of Edinburgh University.[24] When he arrived in Kingston in the autumn of 1827, Machar was not yet thirty-one. He was a slight, rather frail man, with fine, fastidious features and thoughtful eyes, who combined a disciplined, intellectual faith with a gentle, non-combative tolerance. His congregation, he found on his arrival, was the "most numerous Protestant one in the place"; and aided by substantial elders like John Mowat and George Mackenzie, he took up its needs and interests with quiet but purposeful enthusiasm. One of these needs was education. St. Andrews was plainly dissatisfied with the management of the Midland District Grammar School. And it was not the last time that the sober Presbyterians were to show themselves ready to criticize and reject the leadership of the Anglican Loyalists who up to that time had run the province and the town.

The founding of the new school was the last important event in John Alexander's boyhood. Late in the autumn of 1828 another young Scotsman arrived in Kingston. He came with the encouragement, and probably at the invitation, of the Kingston Presbyterians; and everybody at St. Andrews was impressed with his credentials and recommendations. He was the Reverend John Cruickshank, a product, like Machar, of the Scottish universities, but younger than Machar by half-a-dozen years, a tall, handsome man, with curly hair, well-shaped nose and mouth, and clear intense eyes.[25] In January, 1829, he opened his school "for classical and general education" at Owen Macdougall's shop on Store Street.[26] Unlike the Midland District Grammar, it was a co-educational school, one of the first of such in the province. The Scots residents of Kingston hastened

to give it their support; and among others John Alexander Mac
donald was transferred to Cruickshank's care.

He sat in a small room, crowded with desks and forms, and
twenty or twenty-five children, of all ages from six to sixteen.
Some of them he would never see again; some would remain
mere acquaintances whose names he would make a point of
trying to remember in later years. But, by a curious chance,
he was to know two of them very well. Two of them were
to have careers as public and almost as prominent as his own,
and were to cross and re-cross his path repeatedly in future.
One was young Oliver Mowat, John Mowat's elder son, a
short, stocky boy, not yet ten years old, with a round cherubic
countenance. The other was John Hillyard Cameron. It was
almost by accident that John Hillyard attended Cruickshank's
school, for his father, Angus Cameron, quartermaster of the
79th Regiment, was soon to be posted to York, and young
Cameron was to become one of the earliest and most distinguished graduates of Upper Canada College. He was a tall
youth, with a broad, heavy, rather unprepossessing face which
was redeemed from unattractiveness by the friendly charm of
his smile and manner. Already there was an air about him of
precocious brilliance and easy accomplishment. His memory
and inventive powers were remarkable; and, with affable condescension he used to whisper jokes to the smaller boys, or tell
them long, fabulous stories to which Oliver Mowat listened with
round-eyed attention.[27]

The year 1829 drew to its close. John Alexander was nearly
fifteen, a "big boy" now, as the school population of Upper
Canada reckoned its ages; a promising boy too, fondly regarded,
no doubt, by Cruickshank, who long after kept a little sheaf of
his pupil's compositions. But, promising or not, John was
finished with formal education for ever when he walked for
the last time out of the classroom in Owen Macdougall's shop.
His was not an exceptionally unfortunate fate, for only a
favoured few of his contemporaries were permitted to continue
their studies much further. Richard Cartwright, legislative
councillor, chairman of the Quarter Sessions, and one of the
richest of Kingston's first generation of merchants, could afford

to send his twin sons to England for their education—Robert David to Oxford, and John Solomon to Lincoln's Inn.²⁸ But the Cartwrights lived an existence of inimitable splendour. Most boys, even the sons of fathers in comparatively comfortable circumstances, had to be content with the training which the Province of Upper Canada afforded; and, at that time, there were not even rough provincial substitutes for the venerable institutions of England. In 1830, it was a decade and more before King's College and Queen's College would open their doors to students; and, although the Law Society of Upper Canada examined pupils at the beginning and end of their legal training, there was no formal instruction in law in the province. Students were articled for both practical and theoretical training; and the old-established legal firms, together with the abler and more energetic of the younger lawyers, offered, in effect, the best professional education which could be had in the province. Many ambitious youths began in this way. They started early; even John Solomon Cartwright, long before he departed for Lincoln's Inn, had, as a boy of sixteen, begun his legal studies in John Beverley Robinson's office at York. The law was a broad, well-trodden path to comfort, influence, even to power; and back at the Stone Mills, after long and anxious conclaves, no doubt, it was decided that John Alexander should follow it. Hugh Macdonald had been a mediocre, ineffectual enterpriser; but the men of the Macpherson-Shaw-Clark connection had been successful professional soldiers. The professions were a part of the family tradition; the law was the obvious choice for a boy who seemed as attracted to study as he was uninterested in trade.

It was all settled in 1830. John was articled to a young Scottish lawyer, George Mackenzie, late of Ernesttown, and now of Kingston; and possibly in April of that year, when the assizes were on and the spring term in progress, he journeyed up by steamboat to York, the capital of the province, to confront the Benchers of the Law Society. He found lodgings at Osgoode Hall, or at one of the hotels or boarding-houses in its vicinity; dutifully he presented his petition and paid his fee of £10 to the secretary of the Society; and in a day or so, when a quorum of the Benchers could be got together for the purpose, he appeared formally to sit the examination required of a student at law.[29] There was, inevitably, a passage of Latin to translate; a little Latin parsing to do; some mathematical propositions to expound and a few questions in history to answer; and then the ordeal was over. In a few days John was given his certificate and formally admitted to the society as a student at law. In a few days more, which he spent attending the courts and watching the law officers of the Crown and the barristers of the capital perform, the assizes came to an end and he had "kept" the first of his four terms. He boarded the steamboat back to Kingston and plunged at once into the work of his new employer's office.

Chapter Two

The Lawyer's Apprentice

I

It was a highly respectable establishment, and also, in a sober, provincial fashion, distinguished. George Mackenzie, who reached the age of thirty-five in the year John began his apprenticeship, was still a comparatively young man, in the early stages of his career;[1] but already he occupied a place of special importance in the eyes of Kingston townsfolk in general and of his Scottish fellow-citizens in particular. John Machar of St. Andrews admired and respected him.[2] The long-headed merchants and lawyers of Store Street held his professional ability and integrity in the highest estimation. And throughout Kingston and its neighbourhood there was a growing opinion, which soon became a confident belief, that if Mackenzie wanted a parliamentary career, his knowledge, his interest in his own town, and his concern for the affairs of the whole province would easily win him a seat in the provincial legislature.[3] He was almost a model of virtue, certainly a pattern of professional rectitude. Yet, at the same time, he was a robust, genial, warm-hearted man, who, though he did not hesitate to correct and admonish those who served him, was quick to recognize ability and never niggardly in his praise.

In 1830 John took his inconspicuous place in George Mac-kenzie's office. It was a tumultuous year, with revolution in France, strikes and riots in England, and, even on the small stage of Upper Canadian affairs, a general election. But inside Mackenzie's busy establishment, the far-off dramatic clamour of international affairs, and even the more intimate homely argument of provincial politics must have sunk to a low, barely audible rumour. For John the demands of his own situation and his own future were loud and peremptory. He lodged and boarded with the Mackenzies; and, despite his professional articles, he was still very much the schoolboy, dependent upon authority and direction, hard to waken in the mornings, and watched over by Mrs. Mackenzie with kindly solicitude.[4] All day he was at work, running errands, establishing titles, transcribing letters and documents, and making pressed copies of Mackenzie's correspondence on the wetted tissue leaves of the letter books. At night, under his master's benevolent direction, he began to read law. It was, no doubt, a tight routine of study, of small tasks and responsibilities, beyond which, as yet, he did not think to venture very far. His mother and father, his sisters, Margaret and Louisa, were a long journey away at the Stone Mills. The dispersal of the Macpherson family continued; and in 1830—the year in which he began his apprenticeship—Anna Macpherson married young Thomas Wilson, the Deputy Assistant Commissary-General of the garrison.[5] But the old household which had served him as a second home all through his school-days was maintained for a few years longer, and he must often have visited it. Some of his earliest friendships—that with Charles Stuart, the grandson of Archdeacon George Okill Stuart, for example—probably date from this period. His reading broadened, and sometimes, of an evening, he would visit the precentor of St. Andrews—in secret a deplorable freethinker—and argue with him about religion.[6]

His place was small and inconspicuous. Yet—though this was perhaps apparent only to his elders at the moment—it was a position of considerable strategic importance. For Mackenzie was in touch with most affairs of any consequence in Kingston. His friends, associates, clients, and acquaintances formed a large and staunch company. His practice was already great and rapidly growing. Its main staple was, of course, the little contentions and affairs of farmers and small tradesmen scattered about in Kingston and its vicinity; but, in addition, there were a few of the luxuries of the profession—large accounts of merchants, and landowners, and forwarding companies, which Mackenzie already possessed, and still larger accounts which would come to him, if only the town prospered. Everybody believed it would prosper. The region of the lower lakes was being rapidly settled; and a struggle between the St. Lawrence and the New York routes for the prize of the western trade was now at hand. Already men were planning seriously for the first St. Lawrence canals; and far away, in the dense forests to the north-east, Lieutenant-Colonel John By was superintending the construction of the Rideau Canal, which was to link Kingston with the Ottawa, via the Rideau and the Cataraqui Rivers. The canal, which was designed as a military work to provide a route more northerly and safer than that of the exposed St. Lawrence, was certainly a fresh testimony to Kingston's strategic importance. But it was also a valuable addition to its commercial strength. It brought men, and money, and business to the town. And Kingston, busy and comfortably prosperous, began to desire the financial institutions appropriate to its new affluence. In January, 1830, the townsfolk assembled to petition the legislature for a new bank, their own bank, the future Commercial Bank of the Midland District.[7] For John and his employer, and the Macpherson-Macdonald clan, this project was charged with the greatest significance. Francis Harper, who had married John's cousin, was to be for many years the bank's cashier, or general manager; and George Mackenzie was its first solicitor.

During the next two years, while John sat soberly in his employer's office, performing his small tasks and learning something of the vast mysteries of the law, the Kingstonians, with Mackenzie in assiduous professional attendance, struggled earnestly for their bank. The first need, of course, was for an act of incorporation, which could be obtained only from the provincial legislature. But in 1830 the Kingstonians had the best of reasons for believing that the political way lay open and unobstructed before them. The bank's promoters were respectable Conservatives; George Mackenzie was a prominent Conservative; the general election of 1830 had returned a comfortable Conservative majority to the provincial Assembly; and—best of all—the newly elected member for Kingston, the tall, thickset, burly, overbearing Loyalist, Christopher Alexander Hagerman, had been appointed, one year earlier, to the post of Solicitor-General of the province. Yet for two years Kingston's hopes and expectations were denied by its old rival, York. For two years the supporters of York, entrenched in the Legislative Council, defended the monopoly of the Bank of Upper Canada, hitherto the one chartered bank in the province, which had its headquarters in the capital. In the end, however, the Conservatives grew tired of this unseemly and unprofitable controversy. The Assembly generously increased the capital stock of the Bank of Upper Canada; the Council handsomely accepted the charter of the Commercial Bank of the Midland District.⁸ And Mackenzie received the most important company account in Kingston.

The years 1832 and 1833 were successful years for Mackenzie, for his firm, and for Kingston. Mackenzie's repute grew; and Kingston flourished. When young John and his fellow-Kingstonians read the newspapers or walked about the town and its environs with curious interest, they seemed to see on every hand the plain evidence of government favour and commercial prosperity. The completion of the Rideau Canal, the commencement of the great fortress on Point Henry, the government's decision to build the provincial penitentiary at Portsmouth, a little west of Kingston—all this appeared to show that the town was just at the beginning of a great new stage in its development. Kingston, with its busy new bank, its splendid public works, its obviously influential leaders in politics and finance, was re-asserting its old importance in the life of Upper Canada. Business flowed into it from the Midland District, from the whole eastern part of the province. Mackenzie's practice expanded, and he began to think seriously of setting up a small branch establishment, in the fashion of the time, a little to the west, in the Bay of Quinte region. Some time in 1832 he decided that Napanee was to be the new outpost and John Alexander was to be its manager.

In the late summer or early autumn of 1832 John set out. Napanee was nothing more than a little inland village which had had its first beginnings in the early years of Loyalist settlement. A sawmill, a grist-mill, a carding-and-fulling mill, and a tannery had been built on the banks of the Napanee River, which, a few miles farther south, drained into the eastern end of the Bay of Quinte; and around these prosaic little establishments—the inevitable first requirements of any pioneer community—there clustered a small group of shops and houses.[9] Napanee was fewer than thirty miles away from Kingston, and John was within reach—though not too readily within reach—of his employer's advice and assistance. George Mackenzie promised to ride over that autumn to give his pupil's quarters and activities a paternal inspection;[10] and a certain Dier, who was, apparently, Napanee's solitary physician and who occasionally travelled to Kingston "a horseback", used sometimes to bring back letters, parcels and instructions. A fundamental change in John's circumstances had taken place. Napanee meant much more independence and much more responsibility. For the first time he was nearly on his own.

One of the three or four shops at Napanee was kept by Thomas Ramsay, a young man about John's age, and with all John's bookish interests and love of literary conversations; and it was here that young Macdonald established himself. He may at times have helped Tom Ramsay behind the counter, weighing out the tea and sugar; and his first independent "office" was probably nothing more than his own bedroom, or a corner of the small shop, crowded with stoves and hardware, barrels of pork, bolts of cloth, and kegs of beer and spirits. He was seventeen now, at the perilous middle point of the journey between boyhood and manhood, when the vagaries, the complications and the contradictions of adolescence were at their most painful and baffling stage. The landscape of his character, if it had passed through the first primitive period of upheaval and subsidence, was still a new, unknown land, with hazy and uncertain outlines. But to Mackenzie, peering with kindly interest through the obscurity, there were a few solid, rocky contours which were at once quite certain and entirely satisfactory. Mackenzie, as in duty bound, used occasionally to write John orthodox injunctions: "be industrious", "be assiduous"; but in reality these platitudinous exhortations were unnecessary, and probably nobody was better aware of the fact than George Mackenzie himself. John was certainly quick and efficient and reliable. Only once, apparently, during that first perplexing autumn at Napanee, did he make a serious mistake. In casual and regrettably unprofessional conversation, he talked incautiously to a prospective client, "old Moore", about his pending suit, only to discover a little later, to his consternation, that "old Moore's" opponent had formally asked George Mackenzie to act for him. Mackenzie was annoyed to discover that he was likely to lose a paying client through the gift of free advice; but, with his stiff code of professional ethics, he saw no way out of the difficulty. He stood by his junior colleague's indiscreet commitments and informed Moore's opponent that he could not act for him "with propriety". In private he unburdened himself to John in what was less a reprimand than a little lecture on the economics of the legal profession. "This shows," he wrote, "the necessity you have to say nothing to anyone on business without receiving a fee in advance."[11]

Meanwhile John was getting ahead with the studies which formed the other important part of his job. He must have taken a few law books with him to Napanee; and when he applied to Mackenzie to forward a book, as he did at least once in the winter of 1833, it can hardly have been anything but a legal treatise. Yet these professional studies were evidently only a small part of his reading at this time. In the Macpherson household he had always been known as a bookworm; and now, when he was just turning eighteen, and with the literary Tom Ramsay to guide and inspire him, he plunged into a wide variety of reading—novels, history and biography, a sampling of the new books on economics and politics, and quantities of poetry. He wrote some verses; he may have tried his hand at other forms of literary composition. There was a touch of reserve about him, an evident relish in solitude, an occasional air of preoccupation in things very different from his immediate surroundings. His manner was often quiet; he could be laconic and a little stand-offish. His cousin, Helen Macpherson, noticed this, and it was, apparently, one of the few things about his pupil that bothered

Mackenzie. A genial, open-hearted, downright person himself, Mackenzie must have pondered over the mysterious complications of his pupil's character. John was a good boy—almost an exemplary boy, or he would never have been chosen for the important commission at Napanee. But was he, perhaps, a little too good—a little too quiet, reserved and bookish for his own welfare? "I do not think," he wrote in his abrupt, kindly fashion, "that you are so free and lively with the people as a young man eager for their good will should be. A dead-and-alive way with them never does." [12]

George Mackenzie knew best the boy who had lived respectfully with him at Kingston. But at Napanee, John became a young man, with all a young man's desired freedom, and at least some of his opportunities. His two best friends in the village—Tom Ramsay and the Highlander, Donald Stuart—were lively young men. The rest of the settlers—Andrew Quackenbush, the tavern-keeper, William Templeton who owned the tannery, and James Henry and Archie McNeil—were, no doubt, many of them young people, bachelors or newly married, the inevitable youthful and energetic enterprisers of a tiny pioneer community. Allan Macpherson, the "Laird of Napanee" who owned the saw- and grist-mill, and who watched over the little village with a kind of benevolent despotism, was Colonel Macpherson's eldest son by his first wife, and thus a connection of John's. He was very hospitable; and his large house, with its prim, pleasant Georgian lines, must have been opened freely and frequently to the young law student and his companions. There were parties and dances; there were long evenings of talk and jollification at Ramsay's and Quackenbush's. And on occasional Sundays, when Mr. Givens, the itinerant Anglican clergyman, visited the settlement and read service in the school-house—for there was no church—John used to sing in the choir. [13] Once out of his reserve, and in congenial company, he showed a lively and inventive gaiety. He was getting to be known for his store of anecdotes, for his burlesques and his absurdly comic improvisations. It began to seem probable that this tall, saturnine, rather ugly young man, with his reserved, studious manner, and off-hand, non-committal ways, might have a special talent for friendship, an almost creative ability for companionship and conviviality.

II

Some time in the spring or summer of 1833 John returned to Kingston. He found the town in an uproar, for during the winter the Colonial Office had made one of its sudden, well-intentioned but highly disconcerting interventions into Canadian politics. For some time past the imperial authorities had been gravely perturbed by certain actions of the legislature and government of Upper Canada. The new bank acts—the statutes which had enlarged the capital of the Bank of Upper Canada and established the Commercial Bank of the Midland District —were couched in terms which seemed inexcusably lax; and William Lyon Mackenzie, the new leader of the radical section of the Reform party, had been repeatedly expelled from the Assembly by its Conservative majority, in utter disregard of all the inconvenient precedents established by the case of John Wilkes. The Assembly, when mildly reproached about these and other matters, remained obstinately unrepentant; and the law officers of the Crown, who ought to have been anxious to support the wishes of the home government, blustered openly and defiantly against them. The Colonial Office, wearied by this insubordination and legislative incompetence, decided to act. Boulton and Hagerman, the Attorney-General and Solicitor-General, were dismissed; and it was announced that the bank acts, unless they were substantially amended, would be disallowed.

During the summer, when John had returned to Kingston, the excitement was still at its height. The town was aghast at the dismissal of its favourite son, its repeatedly elected member in the Legislative Assembly; while Francis Harper and George Mackenzie and their associates were seriously perturbed by the threatened disallowance of the charter of the Commercial Bank. Part of Kingston's resentment was almost immediately allayed, for the Colonial Office, with one of those important second

thoughts which made its name a byword for arbitrary inconsistency, reappointed Hagerman to his old post;[14] but the
danger of imperial cancellation still hung over the bank acts.
The Macpherson connection as well as Mackenzie's office was
deeply concerned in the outcome, and John must have shared
in the general perturbation. He was higher than ever in his
employer's esteem and confidence, and when, early in August,
after the assizes of the Midland District were over, Mackenzie
set out on a business trip down the river to Montreal and Quebec,
he left John in complete charge of the office. It was the most
important charge which the pupil had yet been given, and he
must have stuck closely to his task, performing the duties of
the practice with exactitude, and writing his employer a long
reassuring report which reached him at Brockville. "I am
sensible of your attention to the duties of the office," Mackenzie
replied, "and I trust that I may have it in my power to mark
my sense of your zeal and fidelity." [15]

Mackenzie's sincerity was not long to go untested. For in
that autumn of 1833 there came another small turn of John
Alexander's wheel of fortune. It was not so much an offer as
a request which he received, and it came out of the misfortunes
of the Macpherson family, the family who had given the
Macdonalds so much help, hospitality, and clannish friendliness
in the past. Lowther Pennington Macpherson, who had established himself as a lawyer in Hallowell, Prince Edward County,
became seriously ill. His malady was not one of those dreadful
and so often fatal diseases, such as cholera and tuberculosis,
which killed so many hundreds of Canadians during the migration period, but a supposedly far less dangerous illness, bronchitis.[16] But the provincial medical men proved mysteriously
unable to cure or even to relieve him. His cough grew chronic
and exhausting; his strength drained ominously away. There
was still assurance of recovery, if only he could obtain a period
of complete rest, if only he could find an able assistant who
would free him from the everlasting routine of the office. It was
inevitable that he should think of John. John was his cousin,
the pride of George Mackenzie's office, the successful founder
of the branch establishment at Napanee.

Mackenzie may well have hesitated. It was no time to be losing able assistants. The dreadful fate of undeserved extinction hovered over the Commercial Bank of the Midland District; and there was work and worry for all. Yet Mackenzie, as he himself had acknowledged, had a debt to pay to his pupil; and his pupil was evidently anxious to go, partly, perhaps, for financial reasons, partly for the zest of the job itself, but largely, it may be assumed, out of loyalty to his kinsmen, the Macphersons. George Mackenzie gave his consent and the way was open. Tom Ramsay wrote from Napanee, congratulating John on the "high compliment" paid to him, on "so positive a step to preferment", declaring that he didn't know which to praise more, Mackenzie's disinterestedness or Macpherson's generosity, and ending up with the rather pious hope that John would amply reward his new employer by "a vigorous employment of those talents in his service which you so fully possess".[17] The assignment was, in fact, a formidable one; Hallowell meant a good deal more responsibility than Napanee had done. For now John had a general practice, not a small branch office, to manage; and this for an employer who was ill, who needed rest, and who was soon to seek the milder air and more expert medical advice of England.

John could feel instantly and easily at home in Hallowell. The village, which stood at the end of the long narrow arm of Picton Bay, had by this time become the real centre of the Macpherson-Macdonald-Clark connection. John Alexander, the eldest Macpherson boy, who married Maria Clark in the following year,[18] lived at Hillier, a little way to the west. Hugh and Helen Macdonald were still established at the Stone Mills, which was even closer to Hallowell on the other side. And when, at about this time, old Mrs. Macpherson finally gave up the house at Kingston and took refuge in Hallowell with her married son, the family circle was virtually complete. It was pleasantly easy for the clan to gather at Hallowell under the presidency of the aged Mrs. Macpherson; easy, too, for John Alexander to slip down to the Stone Mills to visit his parents and his sisters, Moll and Lou. And the warm, intimate routine of family visits, and conferences, and occasions must have continued in much the same way as it used to do at Kingston, when the old Colonel was alive.

But, for John, Hallowell was interesting for other reasons than this. Though it was a smaller place than Kingston, it was definitely more important than the tiny pioneer village at Napanee. It was, in fact, composed of two fair-sized settlements, Hallowell and Picton, divided only by a small stream which flowed into the head of Picton Bay. Between these two sections of the same community there reigned the fiercest and most unremitting rivalry.[19] They competed for place and prominence in everything; and when, in due course, Prince Edward was made a separate judicial district, and it became necessary to build a court-house and a gaol, the two villages struggled valiantly and jealously for the possession of these important public works. In the end, through the unparalleled exertions of the Reverend William Macaulay, Picton's founder and principal squire, the smaller village won. The gaol and court-house were built in Picton and completed just about the time when John arrived to take over Lowther Pennington's practice;[20] and, despite all the wrangles they had occasioned, the new buildings were complacently regarded by the villagers as an appropriate sign of their community's coming-of-age. Hallowell was a growing place, full of bustle, and debate, and organized activity; and for these reasons all the more interesting to a young man with a zest for company and a developing interest in public affairs. At Hallowell—he turned nineteen there—his early uncertainty and diffidence began to wear off; at Hallowell, in a modest fashion, his career as an executive began. He became the first secretary of the Hallowell Young Men's Society. The Prince Edward District School Board appointed him secretary—it was his first municipal office—and he signed the board's advertisement inviting applications from prospective teachers. He even took part in an abortive effort to amalgamate the old rivals Picton and Hallowell and to christen the united village Port William, in honour of the Sailor King.[21]

Yet, despite the temporary attractions of Hallowell, the problem of his professional future became gradually more insistent. By the summer of 1834, Lowther Pennington Macpherson was back from England, still uncured of his malady and increasingly despairing about the future. "I am almost discouraged about my health," he wrote gloomily from Hillier, where he was visiting his brother. "Nothing now remains on my stomach and my cough is if anything worse. God only knows how it is to terminate."[22] John must have begun to suspect that his career as a *locum tenens* might be indefinitely prolonged. If he wished to, he might even establish himself permanently in Hallowell. But did he really want to stay? There was Kingston, as well as Hallowell—Kingston, the larger town, in which he had begun his apprenticeship, with which he was intimately associated; and at Kingston, during the summer of 1834 there occurred a tragic series of events which struck at his old employer and utterly changed his own professional prospects. The blow came at the very height of Mackenzie's career. The perplexities of 1833 were over. The Colonial Office, intimidated by the vast hubbub it had roused in Upper Canada, withdrew its threat of disallowance against the Commercial Bank. Mackenzie, victorious and successful, had achieved most of his ambitions. Was it not time now to fulfil those political expectations which his friends had held so long on his behalf? A general election—the first since 1830—was approaching, and Mackenzie was nominated as one of the Conservative candidates for Frontenac.[23] He never lived to contest the seat. In the last days of July, at the still middle point of the long hot summer, the Asiatic cholera returned to Canada, raging widely through the province, and killing with its appalling suddenness and terrible frequency. At Kingston the slaughter was at its height. There were eight burials in the Scots cemetery on the second day of the epidemic; John Machar stood waiting in the churchyard nearly the whole day for the dreary procession of coffins.[24] And a month later, when at last the violence of the plague was declining, the total dead in Kingston amounted to 265.[25] One of the long list of victims was George Mackenzie. On Sunday, August 3, a day of still, intense heat, he had sat as usual in his pew in St. Andrews Church. Before the day was out he was attacked with all the dread familiar symptoms, and by Monday morning he was dead.[26]

The tragedy helped in various ways to decide John Alexander's professional future. It must certainly have settled his immediate problem. There was no point now in an early return to Kingston, for his old master was gone and he could not recommence his apprenticeship. The only sensible thing was to stay on in Hallowell—as, indeed, his clannish loyalty prompted him to do—and round out his apprenticeship with what perfunctory supervision he could get from the ailing Lowther Pennington. For another year he stuck by his cousin's practice; he even tried to extend it, returning for a while to Napanee to recover some of the business which two years before he had tried to drum up for his old employer. And it was at Napanee, in the congenial company of Tom Ramsay and Donald Stuart, that he concocted the most elaborate of his serio-comic burlesques. The "Société de la Vache Rouge" had a political origin. In 1834 the Conservatives had lost the general elections in both Upper and Lower Canada; and in Lower Canada the victorious *Patriotes* were indulging in vaguely revolutionary gestures. The "Constitutionalists", as they called themselves, rallied pugnaciously in both provinces; and the "Société de la Vache Rouge", with its mock Gallic title and its curious mixture of medieval chivalry and Highland Scottish fervour, was, in its own absurd way, young John's riposte to the approaching revolution in the Canadas. Tom Ramsay, who was deeply read in heraldry, supplied the knightly organization with its necessary information. Donald Stuart, the young man with the royal name, was created "Lord Lyon, King of Arms"; and Helen Macpherson—"The Lady Helen o' that Ilk"—worked a banner "Sans Peur et Sans Reproche", which was presented with appropriate ceremonies at Allan Macpherson's house. That Christmas, the Christmas of 1834, John brought the whole company down with him to the Stone Mills for Christmas; and one night his mother, "Queen Helen", was enthroned with a long cardboard sword in her hand and the "Lady Helen" standing in attendance at her side, while the knights came forward one by one to do their obeisance and to make their vows.[27] Then, when it was all over and the knights were singing wassail songs, Helen Macdonald, who knew and loved Scots stories and legends, laughed until the tears ran down. It was the last Christmas but one that they were to spend at the Stone Mills. The fires burned brightly; and outside the dark trees rose behind them, tier on tier, to the crest of the mountain, and in front the waters of Adolphus Reach lay spread out still and white with ice.

By the summer of 1835 John Alexander was getting close to his majority—the solemn age at which he could be admitted to the bar. He made his decision to return to Kingston. It was true that at Hallowell he might soon be called upon—all too soon, it appeared—to succeed his cousin Lowther Pennington. But this was not the destiny he wanted. Hallowell, for all its bustle and pretensions, was only a large village. Kingston was the rival of York, the acknowledged capital of the eastern part of the province; and above all, at Kingston, there lay waiting the yet unclaimed inheritance of George Mackenzie. John, of course, was not the heir apparent. Mackenzie, dying in the brief agony of the cholera, could have made no provision for the future. But Mackenzie had liked him, valued his abilities, and given him responsible tasks; and, in the absence of any heirs of direct descent, the facts of his old employer's trust and approval were not bad credentials. And the inheritance was a prize worthy of real struggle! For Mackenzie had left not merely the obvious assets of his large practice and wide connections, but also the more intangible though no less real legacy of his genial distinction, his acknowledged prestige and the unrealized possibilities of his public career. Some time during the summer of 1835, John returned to Kingston, and on August 24 he wrote out and dated his first professional advertisement, which was printed two days later in the Kingston *Chronicle and Gazette*. "John A. Macdonald, attorney, &c," he announced, "has opened his office in the brick building belonging to Mr. Collar, opposite the shop of D. Prentiss, Esq., Quarry Street, where he will attend to all the duties of the profession."[28]

III

Store Street, which was Kingston's main avenue of commerce,

and which in due course changed itself into the through high-way to Toronto and the West, was crossed, on its way up from the harbour, by other streets, some of them nearly as long and important as itself. Quarry Street was the third of these. It was a lengthy thoroughfare which stretched from Brock Street up to the northern suburbs, and, under the different name of Grass Street—given in honour of Kingston's old Loyalist founder—prolonged itself to the town limit on the south. The shops and offices of Quarry Street were thickest towards the centre of town; and it was here, on the east side of the short section between Brock and Store Streets, and nearly midway between the two, that the building belonging to Mr. Collar stood. Unlike so many of the town's shops and houses, it was built not of limestone, but of small neat bricks. It had the flat, straight, severe front, the high-pitched roof, and the small dormer windows which were characteristic of so much of Kingston's architecture. On the ground floor there were two small shops, with a common entrance between, and twin doors set at angles to each other.[29] And in one of these little low-ceilinged rooms, with a window looking out on Quarry Street, young Macdonald established his first office.

It was well situated. The coach from Toronto rattled past him down Store Street to the post office; the market was held a little to the south-west, on ground where the splendid municipal buildings were to be erected in the future; and the steamers and schooners from Prescott, Port Hope, Toronto, and Hamilton lay moored at the foot of Brock and Clarence and Store Streets. John had been away from Kingston—though not, of course, continuously—for nearly three years; and, as he walked about the streets, surveying his new office and the town he had come back to conquer, he must have found a curious mixture of hopeful and depressing portents. The great cholera epidemic of 1834 had left Kingston in a state of numbed prostration. The dreadful fire of November 1833[30] had been followed by others almost equally destructive, and John did not have to travel far from his Quarry Street office before he encountered long stretches of desolate waste. Yet the town pulled itself slowly together. The first year of the Quarry Street office was a year of returning confidence and reviving hope.[81] And, from young Macdonald's point of view, the professional prospects were surely as promising as they had ever been. It was true that there were numerous lawyers, all of them senior to himself and better known. But nobody had yet incontestably occupied the proud place once held by George Mackenzie. It was a free field, full of uncertainties, but full of chances as well.

The young man who was to become so pleasantly familiar to Kingstonians in the next decade had now emerged from the awkward indecisions of adolescence. He was tall, as he had given promise of being, a lanky, loose-limbed young man, with alert, humorous eyes, a big, prominent nose, and a wide mouth that curved easily in an amused and disarming smile. He was at home, physically, in the fashions and conventions of the period. The close-cropped hair styles, so modish in the first decades of the century, with their affectation of republican simplicity, had given place to the more copious, flowing coiffures of the 1830's; but, on the other hand, whiskers and moustaches were still so rare that, to the country boys of the Midland District, they appeared almost as outlandish monstrosities. John's long, spare, oval face, with its wide cheek-bones and firm chin, was always shaven. His thick, black, curly hair rose to a crested wave on the top of his head and fell away in bushy amplitudes over his ears. He was far from being handsome; but, at the same time, he had his own odd air of distinction. He wore his best clothes—tall hat, black neckcloth, full-skirted, high-waisted coat, and checked or pale grey trousers—in a discreetly foppish manner. In his office, seated before his new desk, he fell easily into negligent, lounging postures; and outside, on Quarry Street, he carried himself in a confident, jaunty fashion.

In his first advertisement, he had called himself by the non-committal, ambiguously professional name of "attorney", added a vaguely generous "etcetera" for good measure, and announced that he was prepared to "attend to all the duties of the profession". The description was an aspiring one, but hardly accurate, for he had not yet been admitted to the bar. During that first autumn at Kingston, while he was waiting for the coming of his majority, he must have been busy with his books in preparation for the final ordeal; and he had scarcely passed his twenty-first birthday, on January 11, 1836, when the little office on Quarry Street achieved its proper status and took on a new air of professional consequence. Late in January or early in February he journeyed up to Toronto to confront the Benchers of the Law Society of Upper Canada; and shortly afterwards the official *Upper Canada Gazette* announced that on February 6, in the Hilary Term, 1836, John Alexander Macdonald had been admitted to the degree of Barrister at Law.[32] Less than a fortnight before, on January 27, the new barrister had acquired his first articled pupil. It was Oliver Mowat, John Mowat's eldest son.[33] The chubby boy, who had listened so attentively to John Hillyard Cameron's stories, had now become a slight, short youth of nearly sixteen, with a disarming smile and a cherubic countenance, whose expression of guileless and confiding innocence was accentuated by a pair of small circular spectacles. Small, neat, and quick, all intelligence, purpose, and assurance, Oliver Mowat was likely to be an asset in any office. But he brought much more than energy and ability to his new employer. His mere presence—the mere fact of a Mowat in the small room in Quarry Street—was, for Macdonald, a matter of incalculable importance. For John Mowat, though he would never attain to Mackenzie's eminence, was a man of some consequence in the Scottish community at Kingston. He inspired confidence and guaranteed respectability. And if he consented to send his son to Macdonald's office, did it not surely imply that Mowat and the Kingston Scots in general were coming to regard the new Quarry Street lawyer as their own professional man, the man to whom their bright boys and their business would be sent, just as they had been sent a few years before to the great George Mackenzie himself?

Moreover, Macdonald was not only a recognized professional man, but also a virtual householder. Only a year or two before, the Macpherson-Macdonald-Clark connection had seemed securely established in Prince Edward County; but now it began to shift its base back to Kingston, as a new strong centre of family unity made its appearance and as the old began noticeably to lose its cohesive power. Old Mrs. Macpherson, the Colonel's widow, had died in April, 1835, before Macdonald had left Hallowell.[34] Thomas Wilson, the Deputy Assistant Commissary-General, with his wife Anna, had set out on a series of missions which took him as far away as the West Indies, Central America and North Africa.[35] And it was while Wilson was in Jamaica, in November, 1835, that Lowther Pennington determined to visit his brother-in-law, in a last effort to seek a climate in which he could cure himself of his affliction. He never returned to Upper Canada.[36] His death and the break-up of his house and practice at Hallowell were signs that one phase of the family's history had ended; and an even more significant indication was the return of Hugh and his wife and daughters to Kingston. Hugh was only fifty-four; but his long, hopeful, erratic, and unsuccessful career had ended in the qualified failure of the Stone Mills. Francis Harper, the financial head of the connection, got him a small clerkship in the Commercial Bank; and the Macdonald family circle, which had been broken for so long by John's repeated and prolonged absences, was now again complete.[37] Yet its inner organization, if not its outward form, had been profoundly altered. Hugh was titular leader. But John was the family's real head. John was becoming an important member of the Macpherson-Macdonald-Clark connection, which, in exemplary Scottish fashion, was a tight, consciously united group organized for the protection, security, and advancement of its members.

The family was the first important association in young Macdonald's life; the second was the Scottish community at Kingston. Upper Canada was made up of such small, fairly distinct communities, for the settled homogeneous mixture of a new provincial society had not yet emerged out of the angry agitations of the migration period; and the new settlers, English, Scots, Irish, and Americans, who were almost as strange to each other as they were to their new physical environment, had yet to make their final peace with either. The Kingston Scots formed a group which was fairly typical of the others in the province, though perhaps better organized and more purposeful than most; and its Protestant members, who were in the majority, had their spiritual and intellectual centre in St. Andrews

Church. St. Andrews, which had been founded carefully "in connection with the Church of Scotland", regarded itself proudly as part of one of the two established churches of the Empire, with rights and privileges, guaranteed by the Act of Union of 1707, which were exactly coequal with those of the Church of England itself. Macdonald was made to feel that he was a member not of a dissenting sect, but of an ancient and venerable establishment, which emphasized the authority of law and history, and assumed the unity of the Empire as the basis of its claims. A son of the nineteenth, not of the eighteenth, century, he grew up in a Christian community which was mature in its organization, sober in temper, and proudly conscious of its historical traditions. If the sceptical detachment and rationalist absolutes of the Age of Reason formed no part of his experience, neither did the pious fervour and puritanical eccentricities of early nineteenth-century evangelism. He became a friend of the gentle and fastidious John Machar, who loaned him books and watched with interest over his welfare. And he was to take a modest part in promoting the interest and fighting the battles of the Kingston Presbyterians.

St. Andrews was not the only bond of union among the Kingston Scots. In the first years after Macdonald's return to the capital of the Midland District, they were founding secular organizations as well, of which the Celtic Society was the first. To a large extent these associations cut across religious divisions, and old Alexander Macdonell, the beloved Roman Catholic Bishop of Regiopolis, took an active part in their formation. Like the St. George's Societies and the Orange Order, the Scottish organizations were products of the increasingly disturbed political condition of the Canadas. The English, Scots, and Ulster settlers, worried by the growing truculence of the French Canadians and the republican demonstrations of the Upper Canadian Radicals, began to draw together for defence. At a later time, when a new "native" generation had made its appearance, their patriotism would have taken a different, more "nationalist" form; but in the 1830's, when the groups of new British immigrants, still strange to each other, were united mainly by their determination to defend British institutions against French and

American republicanism, it was natural, it was inevitable, that the old historic names should be used. The Celtic Society, like the Orange Order, which was much more powerful politically, was stoutly Conservative in politics; and when it met, in February, 1836, under president Bishop Macdonell, for its semi-annual celebration of the capture of Quebec, it toasted the Earl of Gosford, the new Governor of Lower Canada, and expressed the fervent hope that the British constitution would be "the sheet anchor of his administration".[38] Soon after Macdonald's return to Kingston, he became the Society's recording secretary; and it was he who signed its advertisement offering a gold medal for the best essay on Upper Canada as a guide for intending immigrants.[39]

Beyond the Macpherson-Macdonald connection, and St. Andrews and the Celtic Society, was Kingston as a whole and the wider world of Upper Canada. Macdonald was a young man with a lusty appetite for people, talk, debate, literary conversation, and conviviality; so it was as much his inclination as it was to his interest to increase his friendships and take a becoming part in public affairs. He had to begin modestly—even more modestly than he had at Hallowell. There were no small secretarial jobs that wanted doing; but he joined the Young Men's Society of Kingston, and debated the somewhat solemn subjects which its executive devised. And although he was too young and too little known to take a more prominent part, these small activities were making him pleasantly familiar to an increasing number of people in Kingston. The province, up to that time, had probably been a rather dim background in his life—a background only occasionally brought into sharp focus by the coming of a general election. But now, as a real political storm roared up over the horizon, Upper Canada and its affairs seemed all of a sudden to stand out with vivid clarity, lit by flashes of lightning. The political crisis in the province coincided almost exactly with his own coming-of-age, with the first beginnings of his professional life. In midwinter of 1836, when he had travelled up to Toronto to face the Benchers of the Law Society, the capital had been fluttering with excitement over the arrival of a new governor, a dapper little man with curly hair and a precise, opinionated mouth, called Sir Francis Bond Head. Within a few short months, Sir Francis had quarrelled with his Executive Council, quarrelled with the Reform Assembly, dissolved the House, and appealed, with grandiloquent gestures, to the whole province to join him in the defence of British institutions against ultra-democracy and republicanism.

The crisis was a real one, as the approaching rebellion proved; and it confirmed, beyond all doubt, the fundamental assumptions of Macdonald's political career. He had grown up in an environment in which there could be no trifling on these basic issues. Kingston, since it had been granted a separate seat in the Assembly, had invariably returned Conservative members. Old Colonel Macpherson had fought to preserve a united Empire, and there was no doubt about the political allegiance of the Macdonalds and Macphersons. George Mackenzie had been a Conservative; and St. Andrews Church and the Celtic Society, when it came to a plain question of the survival of the Canadas as British provinces, flung the full weight of their support in favour of the "Constitutional" cause. In the general election of June, 1836, the entire Midland District—Kingston itself, Frontenac, Lennox and Addington, Hastings, and Prince Edward—went solidly Conservative.[40] And on Thursday night, June 30, when it finally became certain that the Reform candidates in Lennox and Addington had gone down to defeat, the citizens of Kingston assembled on the commons to light triumphal bonfires and to cheer for their "glorious emancipation from the fangs of a ruthless and revolutionary party".[41]

And yet, though Kingston and the Kingston Scots stood squarely in support of constitutional rule and the British connection, they were not entirely comfortable inside the old Tory party, nor entirely submissive to its old leadership. And these reservations and qualifications—just as much as the basic loyalties which they modified—were an important part of the political tradition which Macdonald inherited. Kingston had never relished the political leadership of Toronto; the Kingston Scots had always been sensitively resentful of the ecclesiastical claims of the Church of England; and, to both town and kirk, the rule of the so-called "Family Compact", most of whose members were both Torontonians and Anglicans, could, on occasion, be violently objectionable. There came a day, in February, 1837, when even Christopher Alexander Hagerman, Kingston's own member in the Assembly, and Kingston's representative in the provincial government, turned savagely upon his old allies, the Presbyterian Scots. Some of the Presbyterians had just presented a new petition in which they had vindicated once more the status of the Church of Scotland as one of the established churches of the Empire, and reasserted its claim, along with that of the Church of England, to a portion of the revenues of the Clergy Reserves—the lands set apart by the Constitutional Act of 1791 for the support of a Protestant Clergy.[42] Hagerman, with a pugnacious and pontifical manner reminiscent at once of the pulpit, the schoolroom, and the parade ground, fell upon this petition, overwhelmed it with invective, abuse, and ferocious banter, and contemptuously reduced the Presbyterians to the humiliating level of mere tolerated sectaries.[43] The Kingston Scots were aghast. In March, St. Andrews met, in the greatest agitation, to record its disapproval and restate its position.[44] In April a general meeting of the Presbyterian churches—to which Francis Harper was sent as the Kingston delegate—assembled at Cobourg to take action; and William Morris was sent over to England to plead the cause of the Church of Scotland at the Colonial Office. Even the Quarry Street office took an unobtrusive part in this affair, for Oliver Mowat seconded one of the resolutions passed at the meeting at St. Andrews; and, although Macdonald did not participate in this fashion, it was not, as subsequent events clearly proved, because of any lukewarmness in his support of the Presbyterian cause. He must have shared the angry disappointment at Hagerman's betrayal of his old friends. He had come of age in a community which was British and Conservative yet sharply critical of Toronto Toryism.

IV

During the summer of 1837, while the political situation in the province went from bad to worse, and while the banking crisis and the commercial depression heightened the general feeling of miserable uncertainty, Macdonald approached the second anniversary of the opening of his office. For him, as for any young ambitious lawyer at the time, it was essential to make a name in the courts. But he had gone on for two years now, relatively unnoticed, without the prestige or notoriety of an exciting case; and to his cronies in the Young Men's Society he was probably better known for his love of books and fondness for conversation and debate than for the depth of his legal knowledge or for the expertness of his court-room strategy. Then, in the autumn of 1837, came a significant change. The assizes of the Midland District opened; and in a long, rather dull docket, the one really exciting item was a horrible case of the rape of a child. William Henry Draper, the new Solicitor-General—Hagerman had been promoted to the attorney-general-ship—prosecuted for the Crown; and the defence of the accused man, William Brass, fell to Henry Cassady and young Macdonald. In the circumstances, the outcome of the trial was almost a certainty; and the accomplished Draper, sure of his verdict, approached the prosecution with that air of restraint, of dignified moderation, and judicious impartiality which was so characteristic of him. Macdonald could not save William Brass from the death sentence; but he evidently made a prolonged and adroit effort on his behalf. One of the local newspapers, in a flattering paragraph, described the defence as "ingenious, reflecting credit upon a young member of the bar".[45] And for the first time, apparently, it began to be noticed that this tall, ugly, genial young man seemed to possess a curiously winning way with juries and a casual but cunning expertness in the management of a case.

People still had time to be interested in this modest professional triumph, despite the rising clamour of political agitation in the province as a whole. Kingston itself seemed completely at peace. Early in August, in the presence of a great crowd of officials and citizens, Richard Bullock, the sheriff of the Midland District, proclaimed the accession of the young Queen Victoria. The whole district—the entire eastern part of the province—appeared settled in its loyalty, relatively unperturbed by the ominously rising excitement about Toronto, and concerned only at the prospect of serious trouble in the sister province of Lower Canada. On October 31, eight days after the French Canadians had held their vast assemblies at Montreal and St. Charles, over 250 grave and determined heads of households in Kingston, among them Hugh Macdonald, signed a petition requesting Richard Bullock to call a public meeting in order that they might "take into consideration the peculiar situation of affairs in Lower Canada".[46] Three days later the meeting was held; and the assembled Kingstonians resolved that "We cannot any longer defer the declaration of our determination to support with our lives and fortunes the supremacy of the British Constitution and the just dependence of the Canadas upon the British Crown".[47] It was Thursday, November 2; and on the very next night the Kingston Young Men's Society, with a fine independence of contemporary agitations, assembled for its opening "soirée" of the autumn, elected Macdonald its president and Oliver Mowat its recording secretary, and announced that the first subject of debate in the winter programme would be: "Are the works of Nature sufficient in themselves to prove the existence of a Supreme Being?"[48]

On Monday, November 6, before the Society ever got down to its serious debate, the long-awaited clash between the *Patriotes* and the Constitutionalists occurred in Montreal. All during November, while the news of rebel concentrations and troop movements drifted slowly in, the eyes of everybody in Kingston were fixed on Lower Canada, and all the regular troops in the province had been sent there. The militia had not yet been called up, and although the Frontenac Light Dragoons, a voluntary troop of horsemen, trotted with ostentatious loyalty through the streets of Kingston, everybody expected that, if the Dragoons were used at all, they would be used against the French Canadians. One editor reflected proudly that "if called into active service under their gallant commander they will soon bring the affairs of Jean Baptiste into a pretty narrow focus".[49] Even this possibility seemed more and more unlikely as the troubled month drew to its close. The news of the battles of St. Charles and St. Denis, fought on November 23 and November 25, came into town in confused but increasingly reassuring batches. By the beginning of December it seemed perfectly clear that the rebels had been routed and that their leaders had fled headlong into exile.

On Wednesday morning, December 6, in the midst of this satisfied calm, the regular stage coach from the west, which had left Toronto on Sunday, arrived in Kingston. It bore alarming news—all the more alarming since it was now three days old.[50] The Radicals—so the report ran—had been seen drilling, in large numbers, to the north of Toronto. An attack on the city had been feared on the previous Saturday and it was expected that on Monday the Lieutenant-Governor would issue a proclamation calling up the militia for duty. All day the news spread; all day the town waited anxiously; and the early December dark was already falling when another stage—an express direct from Toronto—clattered down Store Street to the post office.[51] This time the news was both definite and stupendous. The rebels to the number of about 400 had assembled with arms within a few miles of Toronto and an attack on the capital was hourly expected. Now, in peaceful Upper Canada, the revolt had broken out.

Chapter Three

First Public Appearances

I

That night, only an hour or so after the stage had brought the tidings of the rebellion, the magistrates called a meeting of the citizens at the court-house. The regular troops had left for Lower Canada. Apart from a few small detachments of Royal Artillery and Royal Engineers, there were no imperial soldiers in Kingston; and there, as elsewhere in the province, it was the plain citizens who rushed together, in a great spontaneous movement, to improvise their own defence. On the first night, in a strange atmosphere of ignorance, and worry and excitement, only the sketchiest arrangements could be made. The town was divided into wards for protective purposes; the townsmen were hurriedly enrolled and armed; and all night long, stout patrols, each headed by a magistrate, tramped through the echoing streets.[1] The next morning, Thursday, the steamboat *Traveller* arrived from Toronto, bringing the welcome news that the Gore Militia had landed at the capital the day before, and that the rapidly growing citizen army would probably soon take the offensive against the rebels. Arms, ammunition, and a couple of field pieces—all watched over by a strong, volunteer guard—were despatched back to Toronto by the *Traveller*.[2] But the first duty of Kingston, Frontenac County, and the Midland District generally was to defend Fort Henry and the naval base, and to secure the eastern part of the province. Actually, there was no danger east of Toronto; and at Toronto itself—on the day before the *Traveller* returned with its consignment of arms—the little amateur army of farmers, mechanics, and professional men which had gathered at the capital marched north up Yonge Street and easily scattered Mackenzie's dwindling forces. But in those first excited, bewildered days, precise news came slowly and vague rumours spread with incredible rapidity. And rebellion, which had not been seriously feared even at Toronto, was now expected almost anywhere and everywhere in the province.

Macdonald was, of course, a member of the Sedentary Militia. Every able-bodied male in the province, between the ages of eighteen and sixty, was, by law at least, a member of the Sedentary Militia. It was a vast, cumbrous, and, in many ways, a comically inefficient organization, which existed not so much to give the population an adequate military training—there was neither time nor money for that—as to acquaint the inhabitants with their responsibilities for the defence of the province and to muster them swiftly in times of actual danger. Once every year, on "training day"—June 4, George III's birthday—the awkward files of farmers and mechanics went through a few cheerfully simple manoeuvres in response to the uncertain orders of their amateur officers; and then everybody gratefully adjourned, in the pleasant June sunshine, for sports, picnics, robustious drinking, and general jollification.[8] Nothing could have been more chaotically unprofessional; but, at the same time, nothing could have been closer to the people of the small, half-organized province, or more suitable as a vehicle for their own angry determination, and the rough simple task they had in hand. In the ten days that followed the coming of the news of the rebellion, the two Frontenac regiments mustered companies; a company of Lennox and Addington Militia tramped into Kingston; and other eager citizens, not included in the regular militia formations, were joining independent companies, and volunteering as marines and artillerymen and civic guards. There were detachments at Fort Henry, at Point Frederick, at the Tête du Pont barracks, and at the blockhouses about the town; and in Kingston itself, the Frontenac Dragoons, careering about valiantly on horseback, were regarded complacently as "indefatigable".[4] Kingston was proud of its hastily collected, amateur army of over 500 men; and the "loyal ladies" of the town, meeting at Mrs. Harper's, at the Commercial Bank, quickly raised £44 to buy a set of colours for their husbands and sons in the Frontenac Militia.

Macdonald shouldered his musket with the rest. His professional friends, his cronies in the Young Men's Society, his relations, and his fellow-members of St. Andrews Church were prominent in Kingston's citizen army, some of them as officers.[5] Macdonald himself was considered for promotion when a new regiment, the Third or East Frontenac Regiment was formed in the following month, January, 1838. His name, with that of one of his best friends, Charles Stuart, immediately below, headed the list of those who were recommended as ensigns in the new regiment.[6] In the end, his appointment did not take place, for reasons which are unknown;[7] but it is possible that Macdonald—a virtual householder, with a family largely dependent upon him—may have pleaded his responsibilities as an excuse from the additional duty. In any event, he and fellow-privates and officers had comparatively little to do. There was, no doubt, some drill and target-practice, some marching and counter-marching; and long afterward Macdonald remembered vividly one gruelling march in which, though weary with the weight of his heavy musket, he had managed to keep up with his companion, "a grim old soldier who seemed impervious to fatigue".[8] But there was no fighting whatever, for the whole eastern part of the province was tranquilly loyal. West of Toronto, the disturbances continued for a little while longer, and there was some rather officious rebel-hunting; but, in effect, the rebellion collapsed on December 7, in the little skirmish on Yonge Street. Within a week the people of Upper Canada, by their own efforts and without the slightest professional military assistance, had overwhelmed a small internal revolt.

Yet, despite the conclusive defeat of the rebellion, the turmoil into which it had plunged the province lasted fully twelve months more. The tiny battle on Yonge Street, and the flight of Mackenzie and a few other fugitives across the border sufficed to rouse, in the northern United States, a mass of uninformed, credulous, and violently anti-British opinion, which for a year kept the international boundary in a state of actual or threatened violence. Inspired by the impulse to liberate the "oppressed" Canadians, to assist a republican movement which had scarcely ever had any real existence, large bodies of American citizens periodically assembled and armed themselves with little or no concealment, for the invasion of Canada. And on half a dozen occasions, while the military authorities of the northern states looked on with benevolent detachment, and while a few zealous American federal officers and a handful of federal troops struggled vainly to preserve their country's neutrality, these American "sympathizers"—these "pirates" or "bandits" as the Canadians called them—actually succeeded in carrying out raids on Canadian territory. The "rebellion", as a native uprising, had lasted only a matter of days; now it threatened to continue indefinitely as an undeclared guerilla war with the citizens of the northern United States. "It may be also safely affirmed," wrote the editor of one Kingston newspaper, "that had not some of the Americans taken by the hand a few discomfited leaders of the late rebellion, the inhabitants of Upper Canada would, within the short period of a week, without military aid, and almost without bloodshed, have extirpated this miserable faction, and have again returned to their peaceful and happy homes."[9]

The citizens of Kingston were not at first directly affected by these excitements on the frontier, for the first of the "pirate" bases was established, during December, 1837 and January, 1838, on Navy Island, in the Niagara River. But in February the danger began to spread eastward, towards the St. Lawrence River, directly threatening Kingston. During the third week of February, startling reports of the pillage of the Watertown arsenal, of "bandit" assemblies and drilling, began to filter into town;[10] and on February 22—what more appropriate day for the enterprise could have been chosen than Washington's birthday?—the "sympathizers" began to gather at the mouth of French Creek, a stream flowing into the St. Lawrence from the American side, nearly opposite to Gananoque. The Kingston garrison of British regulars had not yet returned, and once again the town was dependent upon its own citizen army. The whole Midland District rallied for the defence. The Frontenac Militia was called out, and militia regiments and volunteer companies from Hastings, and from Lennox and Addington moved into town to their support. Macdonald and his friends and relatives were almost certainly among the 1500 militiamen and armed civilians who assembled in Kingston on that February day; and, in the late afternoon, part of the little force marched out to occupy advanced positions along the shore and in some of the neighbouring Canadian islands.[11] In the gathering darkness the amateur soldiers waited in vain. The tiny "army" of American "sympathizers", watched by an enthusiastic crowd of spectators from New York State, did not finally get under way until the day was far advanced. It moved—only 300 to 500 strong—from Grindstone Island, safe in American jurisdiction, to Hickory Island, on the Canadian side. It was dark by now. The island was shelterless and it was February. The invaders fell back to the American side with such expedition that they left a good part of their supplies and accoutrements behind.[12]

For Macdonald and his generation, this was the first affair, since the troubles in the Canadas had begun, which had brought with it any real prospect of fighting. The danger had come not from their own discontented fellow-subjects, but from some bellicose citizens of northern New York State; and from then on, the "American sympathizer" became the chief object of the baffled indignation of the Kingstonians. In March, when the first round of raids was over, and when a great crowd assembled one evening in the Kingston market place to hang and burn their enemies in effigy, the symbolic figure of the United States was singled out for special treatment. At seven o'clock, eight stuffed figures were strung up on a tall gallows before an amused and satisfied crowd of thousands. It was a curious collection of criminals. The English Philosophical Radicals—Hume, Grote, Molesworth, Leader, and Roebuck—hung dangling beside the Canadian rebels Mackenzie and Papineau. A special place, outside the main gallows, was given to Uncle Sam or "Brother Jonathan the Sympathizer". He was "a tall, gaunt figure—real Connecticut phiz—green spectacles—white hat, with a streamer

of black crape—a dapper cloak—in short, what our readers may
readily consider a real republican of the old school, full of the
recollections of the rebellion of '76, modernized into the in-
famous sympathizer, ready for pelf and plunder".[18] Dangling
by himself, holding the placards "sham neutrality" and "authorized sympathy" in his limp hands, he was not even judged a fit
participant of "honour among thieves" and even in this simple
fact, as the editor carefully explained to his readers, there was
exhibited that deep-seated sense of injury at the "vile conduct
of our detestable neighbours".

II

In March and April, Macdonald, like the other young men
of Kingston, could begin to think once more of his own affairs.
The rebellion was over, and the border seemed quiet again.
The night watches in Kingston were given up, and the zealous,
inexpert militiamen returned to their homes. Sir Francis Bond
Head, the Governor of the rebellion period, passed through
Kingston on his way back to England; and everybody knew
now that John George Lambton, Lord Durham, had been appointed Governor-in-Chief and High Commissioner to inquire
into the affairs of British North America. Things were settling
down to something like their old courses, amid a flurry of talk
and speculation about the political future. Nobody knew, of
course, what was going to happen to Upper Canada, though
some of the Kingston Conservatives were already disturbed by
slight misgivings; but Kingston, at any rate, was given a new
and more appropriate status in the spring of 1838. In the
opinion of the townsmen, it was high time. Other towns, far
less important than Kingston, had recently been created municipalities, and it was four years now since the old rival York had
been made a city and rechristened Toronto. Now, at length,
Kingston was granted self-government, and on March 24, the
first civic elections took place.[14] Macdonald was not a candidate
—that would come later—but he was important enough to be
associated, in a minor way, with this first stage in the history of

the new municipality. He was appointed returning officer for Ward Three, and duly declared Edward Noble and Walter McCuniffe elected.[15]

As spring went on, the premature sense of returning peace and security grew stronger. Actually, it was during May that the Hunters' Lodges, the most formidable of all the secret associations formed for the forcible republicanization of Canada, began to spread outward from Vermont through the northern American states.[16] But the Canadians were, as yet, blissfully unaware of these developments, and in Kingston people went about their ways with confidence. Early in May, the 83rd Regiment, with Colonel the Honourable Henry Dundas in command, arrived in town to occupy Fort Henry; and when it turned out for its first church parade, the Kingstonians, listening to the splendid band and watching the long, reassuring lines of red-coats, felt agreeably confirmed in their new sense of security.[17] On May 17—it was one of the last sessions under Macdonald's presidency—the Young Men's Society met to debate the practical professional question: "How far is circumstantial evidence to be admitted as constituting satisfactory evidence, and what objections bear against the admission of circumstantial evidence generally?"[18]

Ten days later, on May 27, the *Hastings* dropped anchor off Quebec; and on May 29, Lord Durham, mounted on his fine white horse, rode up to the old Castle of St. Louis. The post rebellion settlement of the Canadas was obviously about to commence; and the Kingston Conservatives were impressed but not entirely reassured by the reputation of the nobleman who had been appointed to direct it. Lord Durham's record as a Radical Whig was certainly disquieting. The highly dubious morals of some of the members of his staff—Edward Gibbon Wakefield's elopements and Thomas Turton's infidelities—must have shocked the sober Christians of St. Andrews Church. And it was perturbing, as well as annoying, to see the jaunty confidence with which the Canadian Radicals tried to appropriate Lord Durham.[19] The doubts and misgivings grew; and, with Durham's first important public actions, they were turned into positive apprehensions. On June 28, which was observed throughout the province as Queen Victoria's coronation day, the citizens of Kingston assembled at block-house No. 3 to watch the "loyal ladies"—represented by Mrs. Smith, Mrs. Harper, and Mrs. Kirby—present the colours they had procured from England to the First Frontenac Regiment of Militia.[20] On the same day, at Quebec, Durham issued the famous Royal Proclamation which granted an amnesty to the great mass of the political prisoners in Lower Canada, and sentenced the small remainder to exile in Bermuda. The Conservatives were shocked by this prodigal clemency; a few newspapers ventured a mild protest. But in general the Upper Canadians choked back their alarms. They were waiting for Durham. It was most strange that he had not yet visited the province. It was July now and he had been in the Canadas two months.

In all this process of settlement, a young lawyer like Macdonald, with a small provincial practice, could expect to take only a very modest part. There was, of course, plenty of professional work—conspicuous, if not profitable, professional work—to be done. The gaols, particularly the Toronto gaols, were crowded—so crowded that the authorities despatched to Fort Henry at Kingston a small batch of political prisoners, including John Montgomery, the innkeeper at whose Yonge Street tavern Mackenzie's rebels had congregated. But the great political trials were Toronto trials, monopolized by the lawyers of the capital; and the Midland District, which had been relatively so unaffected by the rebellion, produced only one important treason case during the busy judicial summer of 1838. Macdonald took it, and took it this time alone. Eight men—residents apparently of Hastings, and Lennox and Addington Counties—were arraigned before Mr. Justice McLean in the first week in July.[21] The case against them looked dark enough. Some of them had been caught with arms in their hands; some had been persuaded or coerced by a vigorous, officious magistrate to sign affidavits in which they had sworn to their guilt. And the Kingston townsfolk clearly expected a verdict of guilty. But there was a new spirit of clemency abroad, affecting both courts and juries. John S. Cartwright, who prosecuted for the Crown, allowed the prisoners a good deal of indulgence; and Macdonald's defence was skilful. The compromising affidavits were summarily rejected as an outrage upon the administration of justice; the witnesses for the Crown, under close cross-examination, broke down and began to contradict each other; and the prosecution failed to establish any deliberate continuity of purpose on the part of the accused. To the very last, the outcome was uncertain. On the four most important of the cases, the jury was out from Saturday afternoon until Monday evening. But at last it brought in a verdict of not guilty, and in the end all the prisoners were acquitted. One young man sitting in the court and watching the trial's climax with absorbed interest remembered Macdonald's "marked triumph" long afterward;[22] and a Kingston newspaper informed its readers that "the prisoners were defended with much ingenuity and ability by Mr. J. A. Macdonald, who, though one of the youngest barristers in the Province, is rapidly rising in his profession".[23]

Macdonald could afford to feel pleasantly satisfied. For him, the post-rebellion settlement had not been very rich in professional chances. But he had been given one; he had taken it; and the result had perceptibly raised his prestige. The only trouble was that the period for such opportunities seemed now to be over; and, indeed, the whole grand investigation of Upper Canada, to which everybody had looked forward eagerly and anxiously, appeared to be coming to a sudden and unexpected end. For weeks the Upper Canadians had waited for Lord Durham; for weeks—for months—he had remained fixed in Quebec. And then, with almost unceremonious precipitation, he began to move west. On July 10, he left Montreal. On July 11, at about midnight, nearly twenty-four hours before he was expected, he arrived in Kingston by the steamer *Brockville* to find most of the town in darkness and a somewhat hastily improvised guard of honour drawn up on the dock to receive him. The next day it was rather better. At about the middle of the morning two barges, tastefully protected by awnings from the July sun, carried the Governor-General and his suite out from the Clarence Street dock for a tour of the harbour and its military and naval establishments. Lord Durham visited the dock-yard, inspected Fort Henry, cantered back across the penny bridge on his white horse, ate an expeditious lunch at the British American Hotel, and then, in the early afternoon, boarded the *Cobourg* and was off up the lake to Niagara.[24] What followed was even more disconcerting. The Kingstonians had barely time to learn that Her Majesty's High Commissioner had stayed a few days at Niagara, like any other tourist, and that he had cut short his visit to Toronto to twenty-four hours, when the vice-regal steamer, with Lord Durham on board, was back again in Kingston harbour! This time—it was Friday, July 20—Lady Durham did not trouble to go ashore, as a brief visit only was intended. A respectable guard of honour attended the Governor-General, and John S. Cartwright, Chairman of the Quarter Sessions, presented an address of welcome.[25] Then, after only a few hours delay, the *Cobourg* steamed off down the river for Prescott. The grand tour of Upper Canada was over, and Kingston sank back again into its midsummer repose.

It did not remain there long. Fewer than ten days later an astounding event occurred, which instantly revived all the old political excitement, and presented Macdonald with a curious, and slightly dangerous professional opportunity.

III

The night of Sunday, July 29, was violent with a prolonged summer thunderstorm. And when, after hours of blinding rain and crashing thunder, the summer day broke clear, wet and fresh, it was discovered that the fifteen political prisoners, newly incarcerated at Fort Henry, had broken out and had apparently got clear away. Their tortuous route out through the fortifications was easily traced. They had cleverly taken advantage of every characteristic feature of a building which was designed, not to keep people in, but to keep them out. It was a completely successful gaol-break. Yet it was obvious that it could not possibly have succeeded without somebody's assistance and advice.[26] The rough tools which the prisoners had used—a flat bar of iron, a long, poker-like spike, a makeshift lantern, and a primitive ladder constructed by cutting toeholds in a plank or "banquette"—could hardly have been secured without help; and when a rough plan of the fort and its underground passages was discovered in the prisoners' casemate, that put the matter beyond any possible doubt. There had been an accomplice, or accomplices, inside the fort. Somebody had helped the prisoners to escape.

This was the sub-plot inside the main drama of the gaol-break; and it was the sub-plot which involved Macdonald. Things happened fast on that Monday morning, July 23. Colonel Dundas, rushing to the fort in angry agitation, surveyed the evidence with mounting suspicion and quickly decided that the prisoners must have been aided and abetted in their escape. Almost as quickly—too quickly—he came to the conclusion that John Ashley, the gaoler whom the sheriff had appointed to look after these civilian prisoners, must be the guilty man. Ashley was arrested as soon as he appeared at the fort that morning. He spent almost eight hours in the guardhouse before a warrant was finally secured for his arrest; and very shortly after his detention was finally legalized, he was released by the magistrates on the ground that there was no case against him whatever.[27] Here the matter might have been dropped—an unfortunate accident, the consequence of legitimate, if excessive, zeal. But Ashley was not prepared to let it drop. He was a sober citizen, a respectable church-goer, who valued his reputation and had not enjoyed his eight hours' detention in the guardhouse. He promptly brought suit against Colonel Dundas for illegal arrest, and he engaged Henry Smith, Jr. and John Macdonald as his legal advisers.

The case came up at the autumn assizes of the Midland District before Mr. Justice McLean.[28] It was a major sensation in Kingston; and as he watched the crowded court-room on the evening of September 18, Macdonald may very well have wondered not merely whether success was possible, but also whether it was even desirable, in either Ashley's interest or his own. Arrayed against them were the two sacred symbolic figures of law and order. Dundas was the town's protector, the Commandant of the garrison; and for his counsel he had secured no less a person than Christopher Alexander Hagerman, the member for Kingston, the Attorney-General of the province, with all his prestige, his eloquence, and the pugnacious, masterful confidence of his manner. It was a formidable combination. Hagerman, the town's most distinguished legal authority, had a case in which he sincerely believed, both personally and professionally; and Dundas, Colonel of the 83rd, the regiment which had been welcomed with such relief and gratitude a few months before, was the indispensable military leader upon whom the whole of Kingston relied. Perhaps he had acted a little hastily —but out of excess of zeal, not malice. Perhaps he had failed for too long to secure the necessary warrant—but there were unfortunate circumstances which would amply account for the delay. He was a plain soldier, trying to do his duty in a sudden crisis, in the midst of a troubled period of rebellion and raids.

Yet, at the same time, Ashley undeniably had a case. His arrest had been ordered summarily, after what must have been a very cursory examination; and so solid was his reputation in Kingston that the three highly respectable magistrates—John S. Cartwright, John Mowat, and Alexander Pringle—who had accompanied him out to the fort, were astonished when he was suddenly torn from their midst and clapped in gaol. Their astonishment, moreover, was very quickly confirmed, when once they began an investigation into the escape. They discovered, beyond any possibility of doubt, that the guilty accessories to the gaol-break were two men employed in the engineering department at the fort, Organ, a master carpenter, and a casual labourer named Davis.[29] There never had been any basis for the Colonel's suspicions; there was no excuse—not even the need of organizing the pursuit of the escaped prisoners—which could justify his failure to seek a warrant, once the fatal order had been given. All day Ashley's lawyers sought to drive these points home. Macdonald, who acted in support of Smith, apparently pursued the military in general and Colonel Dundas in particular with a disrespectfully incisive vigour which was long remembered by at least one of the listeners in the court-room;[30] and a Kingston newspaper remarked, with almost unwilling admiration, that the young barrister "displayed much ingenuity and legal knowledge during the trial".[31] This, however, did not greatly impress the court. Mr. Justice McLean, in his summing up, tried to direct the attention of the jury to the "true matter at issue" which, according to him, was "whether the arrest was made by Colonel Dundas under a conviction that he was faithfully discharging his duty, or whether he was actuated by malicious or vindictive feelings". After that, every unprejudiced person could hardly fail to reach the conclusion that a verdict should be returned for the defendant. But the jury—the jury of plain people whom Macdonald was learning to influence and convince—decided otherwise. The original arrest, they found, was justifiable. But the long, unwarranted detention in the guardhouse was an excess for which Dundas was ultimately responsible. And they awarded Ashley damages of £200.

The trial was an important episode in Macdonald's career. He was now a fairly conspicuous young man—noticed, and yet not marked, for nothing could be said against him. He had simply done his professional duty; he had acted a legitimate, a necessary, part, in the venerable processes of British justice. The officers at Fort Henry and Tête du Pont barracks might grind their teeth at his irreverent treatment of soldiers; the sober, conservative citizens of Kingston might shake their heads in bewilderment, if not disapproval, at the decision in *Ashley* vs. *Dundas*. But the finger of public scorn and indignation could not be levelled at Macdonald. His professional reputation had not been undermined; it had probably grown stronger and more secure. Yet, at the same time, it had been slightly, subtly, but unmistakably changed. He had been associated, if he had not been identified, with the liberties of the subject, with the defence of the plain people against the encroachments of military power. The solid blue of his inherited conservatism was varied now, in a pleasantly interesting fashion, with a few threads of a different and livelier colour.

IV

It was at this point, when the political trials were over and when the first phase of the post-Rebellion reconstruction seemed at an end, that the troubles of the Canadas recommenced. In the very week in which the trial of *Ashley* vs. *Dundas* took place, two highly significant events occurred. On September 19, the day after Smith and Macdonald had won their verdict, Lord Durham received at Quebec the shattering news that his ordinance, exiling the state prisoners to Bermuda, had been disallowed by the Melbourne government in England; and on Sunday, September 16, two days before the Ashley affair, the Hunters' Society held the first session of its Cleveland convention, at which plans were adopted for concerted raids upon the Canadas.[32] The news of Lord Durham's imminent return to England, which very soon became public property, was bewailed by almost everybody in the Canadas without distinction of race or class or political affiliation; but the sense of resentment and indignation at the Governor's betrayal, which even the Conservatives shared, was very quickly followed by other and graver feelings of apprehension for the political future. Barely a week had elapsed since the pro-Durham meeting at Kingston, before the familiar, the too familiar, reports from the south began to spread once more.[33] The whole border was in an ominous ferment; and by October 10 the Kingston and Prescott newspapers were warning their readers that some of the most active preparations for invasion were apparently going on along the shore of Lake Ontario and the upper St. Lawrence River, in the region between Syracuse and Ogdensburg. The Midland District pulled itself together once again for defence. It was a familiar exercise, which up to that time had been rather frustrating. But apparently it had not lost its zest.

The Sedentary Militia was not called out—even in part— until October 23; but, in the meantime, there were various ways in which young men like Macdonald could satisfy their need for training and practice. During the troubled year 1838 a number of the militia regiments, particularly those in the exposed border counties, organized so-called "flank companies", which were kept as far as possible in a state of readiness for instant action. And in addition, independent, volunteer companies, which served without pay and allowances, were formed fairly frequently, some of them with official approval—such as the Kingston company which the new Governor, Sir George Arthur, sanctioned on October 15—and some, perhaps, without. The little, highly irregular unit, the "Société de la Vache Rouge", was the first of these extra-official organizations to which Macdonald belonged; the second, similar to the first in its Scottish character, but far more resplendent, was organized at Kingston in the autumn of 1838. It went by the resounding name of the "Loyal Scotch Volunteer Independent Light Infantry Company", and its uniform was Highland feather bonnets, blue jackets, and Royal Stuart trews. Alexander McNabb, a member in good standing of St. Andrews and an officer in the Frontenac Militia, was the unofficial captain; and Macdonald stood side by side in the ranks with Oliver Mowat and William Gunn.[34]

By the last week in October, when the long, mild, rainy autumn turned sharply to frost and snow, the reports of assemblies and drilling on the American side became more frequent and detailed. On November 1—the very day that Durham boarded the *Inconstant* for England—the Kingstonians assembled in public meeting, divided the town into five wards for protective purposes and re-established the night watch which had been formed first nearly a year before.[35] Four days later, Sir George Arthur issued his proclamation warning the people of the possibility of invasion, and attempting at the same time to appeal to their patriotism and allay their fears.[36] The second regiment of the Frontenac Militia was called out; the volunteer company of artillery was stationed at Fort Henry; over 500 citizens were armed; and at night the civic guard perambulated the town and cavalry patrols trotted through the silent streets.[37] Still the days went by and nothing happened. Periods of the wildest excitement alternated with periods of complete scepticism. And, as late as Monday, November 12, a Kingston newspaper could still predict that there would be no invasion from the United States until the New Year. Actually it was on Sunday, the previous day, that the steamer *United States*, crowded with a suspiciously large number of male travellers and heavily freighted with bulky pieces of luggage, was moving down the river on her adventurous journey from Oswego to Ogdensburg, taking on passengers at every stop.[38] Kingston might have learnt the truth earlier. But the Americans detained the Wolfe Island Ferry at Cape Vincent, in order to prevent the news from reaching the Canadian side. And it was late on Monday before the Kingstonians began to realize the tremendous fact that the invasion was under way, and that the invaders had probably landed already, sixty miles down the river, at Prescott.

Late that night, Captain Sandom, R.N., set out for Prescott with his little armed flotilla, the steamer *Victoria* and the schooner *Cobourg*; and early next morning, Tuesday, the *Brockville* and *Kingston*, with Colonel Dundas and four companies of 83rd on board, moved off down the river from Kingston harbour.[39] Once more the Midland District was left to defend its own capital. Late on Tuesday, the clear, still weather broke, and snow came swirling out of the north-west in the wake of a stiff wind. But all day the Frontenac Militia was mustering; and on Wednesday, with snow and freezing rain still falling, companies of four Lennox and Addington regiments tramped into town.[40] By this time people knew that the Pirates, repulsed at Prescott town, had made a landing about a mile and a half farther down the river at Windmill Point, and that on Tuesday morning, before the arrival of Dundas and his reinforcements, the Johnstown Militia had marched out to meet them. Late Wednesday night, when Colonel Dundas and the companies of the 83rd returned unexpectedly to Kingston, the town learnt, in official detail, of the bloody little battle at the windmill and its outcome. The militia, with the assistance of a few regulars, had captured the outbuildings from the Pirates; but they had spent themselves in vain in futile charges against the ponderous stone walls of the windmill. About sixty of all ranks had been wounded, and sixteen killed; and one of the corpses, that of a Lieutenant Johnston, was subsequently discovered to have been mutilated, supposedly by the invaders. Dundas had determined not to risk any more lives; he had come back to Kingston to await the arrival of heavy artillery from Toronto. In the meantime—the Kingstonians learnt to their satisfaction—the Bandits were cooped up in the mill and its stone outbuildings, closely surrounded by the militia, without hope of release and without prospect of reinforcement. At the appropriate moment they could be destroyed.

Late Thursday afternoon—nearly twenty-four hours later— the *Brockville* and *Kingston* churned their way out from the docks once again, with Dundas, and the 83rd, and two eighteen-pounders and a howitzer on board.[41] The town, crowded with militia and tense with excitement, settled down to wait as best it could. Friday passed by. The hours on Saturday crawled along with heavy slowness; but by this time rumours of a victory and the capture of the Bandits had begun to filter in from the east and, long after night had fallen, the town stayed up, waiting and expectant. It was nearly midnight when across the dark harbour the citizens could see at last the twinkling lights of the approaching steamers. The houses were illuminated; the crowd rushed down Brock Street to Scobel's wharf. And then, between guarding rows of red-coats, a long, double file of prisoners began to wind its way down the dock to the street.[42] A tall, well-formed, darkly handsome man strode at its head. His clothes hung in ribbons around him; his shirt had been nearly torn off his back. A great rope was knotted around his chest, and behind him plodded his followers, in two long silent rows, each with his right or left hand tied to the rope.[43] They marched through streets which were lurid with lights and torches and excited faces, and clamorous with exultant cheers. They marched past the town and over the bridge, and out through the friendly darkness to Fort Henry.

V

It was the trial of the captured American prisoners which gave Macdonald his last important case of the year. The trial was, of course, to be by court martial. A special statute, "An Act to Protect the Inhabitants of this Province against Lawless Aggressions from the Subjects of Foreign Countries at Peace with Her Majesty", prescribed this summary form of trial for invading American "sympathizers" found in arms. In a court martial, civilian counsel had no status whatever and could not plead: they could do nothing more than advise and assist prisoners who quite literally had to conduct their own defence themselves. It was a poor, second-best kind of legal assistance; but one man in Kingston, who happened to be the brother-in-law of Daniel George, the paymaster of the Pirates, determined to secure it for his imprisoned relative. In the brief ten days which intervened before the opening of the trial, he tried at least twice to get help; and twice he was turned down. By now time was running short. And it may have been very shortly before the trial, and probably on the day of its opening, that the frantic brother-in-law knocked one morning early on the Macdonald door before John was even out of bed.[44]

Macdonald may very well have hesitated to take the case. It was a difficult, unprofessional, unpopular, and possibly danger-ous task. In a court martial, bereft of his usual status and pre-rogatives, he would be a nobody in an alien and perhaps hostile world. It would be almost impossible for him to secure an acquittal, or even to mitigate the death sentence, for the statute was clear and comprehensive enough, and the prisoners had been caught red-handed. Yet even an ineffectual defence might arouse the whole community against him. The prisoners were hated, as only foreigners who interfere by force in the affairs of others can be hated. The town was mad with grief and rage and horror. The futile enormity of the invasion itself, the long, needless list of dead and wounded at the Battle of the Wind-mill, the revolting mutilation of Lieutenant Johnston's body, and the heap of carved, double-edged bowie knives which had been taken from the Bandits and exhibited to the astounded Kingstonians—all worked like madness in the minds of the townspeople. Every circumstance seemed unfavourable. It was surely wisdom to have nothing to do with the whole affair. And yet, he took the case. Even he might have found it difficult to say why. A curious interest in people, a relish for cases which were odd and difficult, a jaunty recognition of the fact that professional prestige involved publicity, and, perhaps, a certain stubborn, independent conviction that these helpless and de-luded men deserved at least the bare minimum of assistance—

all these may have helped to move him to his decision. It was a solitary part that he had to play. Henry Smith, member for Frontenac, had shared with him the honours and the obloquy of the Dundas suit. But Macdonald went out to Fort Henry alone.

On Wednesday, November 28, when he arrived hurriedly at the fort, the court martial had already commenced its sombre business. John B. Marks, Colonel of the Third Frontenac Regiment, presided. The long, low casemate, with its bare, white-washed walls, was crowded with officers of the Midland District Militia, stiff in their scarlet and silver uniforms; and William Henry Draper, Solicitor-General of the province, who had been appointed Judge-Advocate for the occasion, had just concluded his first address to the court in the prosecution of Daniel George.[45] Urbane, learned, resourceful in the management of a case, yet not ungenerous to the prisoners, Draper had begun by setting out the terms of the governing statute, 1st Victoria, c. 3. The simple facts of the invasion were completely beyond dispute; but, by the statute, Draper was required to prove that the prisoners were citizens of a foreign country at peace with the United Kingdom, that they had associated themselves with traitorous and rebellious British subjects, and that they had made war against the Queen, and slain and wounded divers of her subjects. The second point was covered, but only barely covered; for not a solitary subject of the Queen had joined the American force after it landed at the windmill, and only three or four ex-Canadians had come with it from the United States. These people—Levi Chipman and two tearful French-Canadian lads—promptly turned Queen's evidence; and it was upon their testimony, and that of a little group of officers and men from the navy, the marines and the 83rd Regiment, that the Judge-Advocate chiefly relied. The first witness, Lieutenant Leary, R.N., had already begun his evidence, when Daniel George requested a brief delay, in order to obtain counsel. Macdonald arrived and the two held a hurried consultation. And then the trial went on.[46]

George was scarcely an heroic republican crusader. Actually he had attempted to "desert" the Pirate army immediately after the Battle of the Windmill, leaving his companions to fight it out on Canadian soil as best they could; and he had been picked up in a small boat just off Windmill Point. The whole plan of his hastily improvised defence was to dissociate himself as completely as possible from the enterprise; and he concentrated on the testimony by which the Judge-Advocate tried to identify him as an American citizen, and on the evidence of his actually levying war against the Queen. Prompted, no doubt, by Macdonald, he asked Lieutenant Leary a number of searching questions; and he sought not unskilfully to break down the credibility of the dishonourable Levi Chipman. "Has the witness ever stated that he would swear to anything to save himself?" he inquired. His trial lasted the whole of Wednesday; and it was well into Thursday, November 29, when Draper finished the case for the prosecution. George immediately requested a delay in which to prepare his defence, as he had not had sufficient time to consult with his counsel.[47] The court granted him until Saturday; and it then passed on at once to the second case, the case of "General" Nils Szoltevcky Von Schoultz.

Macdonald may have seen the dark, exotic Von Schoultz as he strode proudly through the streets of Kingston on that wild Saturday night ten days before, at the head of the long sullen line of prisoners. Von Schoultz and the other "officer" of the Pirate army, "Colonel" Dorethus Abbey, probably shared a casemate with Daniel George; and Macdonald almost certainly met the "General" on Wednesday night as he talked over the case of his first client. George and Abbey were colourless, if not spiritless, characters, broken by the disasters which had overtaken them; but the Pole, Von Schoultz, was purer and harder metal, tempered in really revolutionary fires.[48] His family, Swedish in origin, cultivated, and distinguished in government service, had for some time been established in Poland. His father, who owned salt mines in the neighbourhood of Cracow, was a major in a Polish regiment; and Nils Von Schoultz, brought up in an atmosphere of ease and dignity, had been trained as a chemist in the universities of northern Europe. In 1830, when the Poles revolted to save their dwindling freedoms from the grasp of Russia, this pleasant family existence was ended; and Nils, who had been elected to succeed his father as major in the defence of Warsaw, escaped, apparently alone among all the members of his family, and for half a dozen years wandered aimlessly over the face of Europe. He served in the French Foreign Legion, taught music in Florence, contracted a romantic but unfortunate marriage with an English girl; and then, in 1836, cutting himself clear from the past, he fled to the United States. His training as a chemist, his experience in salt manufacture, his experimental interest in the improvement of the refining process took him first to Virginia, and then to Salina, the salt-making town in northern New York State. Here, under the emphatic but dubious instruction of the Hunters, he reached the romantic conclusion that the Canadians were serfs groaning under an oppression indistinguishable from that of the Poles. He boarded the steamer *United States* on the fateful Sunday, November 11, without any very clear idea of what was going to happen; and the next day, to his consternation, he found himself the virtual leader of the little abandoned army of men who had been dumped down by their bragging compatriots at Windmill Point. Neither of the acknowledged "commanders" was with him. Bill Johnston, the river pirate, the self-styled "Commodore of the Navy of the Canadian Republic", with his picturesque belt of bowie knives and pistols, evidently decided that his duty lay with the "fleet"; and John W. Birge, the "General" of the land forces, resplendent with flashing sword and glittering gold braid, was suddenly afflicted with a stomachic disorder, which caused him unostentatiously to seek the seclusion of his cabin on the steamboat, and, as fast as possible, the safety of the United States. Von Schoultz bore himself well, with a vain, stoical bravery, in this last, grotesquely tragic episode of his career. A tall man, handsome and gentle-spoken, with fine manners, and an aristocratic reserve, he had about him a romantic air of strange tongues, and far countries, and lost causes. He consulted with Macdonald, he told the long, agitated story of his life. But Macdonald could do nothing for him. For the Pole had determined upon his course and nothing could swerve him from it.

He pleaded guilty. The answer to the fatal question was made with complete composure. While George and Abbey, the Canadian newspapers noted, were terrified men, Von Schoultz was "as unmoved as a rock".[49] Draper cautioned him against such a plea, pointing out its probable consequences; but the Pole tranquilly rejected the last slight opportunity offered him.[50] He had, he said, been terribly deceived; the whole enterprise had been conceived and carried out in ignorance and misrepresentation. But it was useless to deny that he had led the little army at Windmill Point. He persisted in his plea of guilty. The court, after a brief pause to consider the position, continued to take evidence. Von Schoultz listened to it with stoical impassivity. He asked the French-Canadian boys a perfunctory question or two; he inquired of the despicable Levi Chipman if he did not know that "General" Birge was the real leader of the expedition. But the witness who really shook him was Dr. Gardner, the surgeon of the 83rd, who told the court how he had examined the dead body of Lieutenant Johnston and had discovered its mutilation. Von Schoultz said nothing at the time, but he evidently brooded over this shameful revelation, to the exclusion of almost everything else. And when the trial was over, and he rose to address the court for the last time, it was the one subject on which he dwelt at any length. He spoke not, like George and Abbey, to save his life, but to clear his honour. He denied that he had treated the dead and wounded with inhumanity. He had done all he could to protect them; and he, and those about him, had spoken highly of Johnston as a brave man who deserved every honour.

On Friday, as soon as the court opened, Von Schoultz was condemned to death by hanging; and the next day, after George had read the written defence which Macdonald had prepared for him, he and Abbey were sentenced to the same fate. They were the first three of the principals who suffered the death penalty; and thereafter the trials became increasingly perfunctory and, in great batches, the rank-and-file were released. Macdonald apparently took no part in all these later proceedings. The court martial, despite its inevitable professional defeats, had been an important event in his career; and long afterwards it remained in his memory, though in an imperfect, uneven fashion, with vivid patches of clear recollection in the ambiguous shadow of forgetfulness, like a deep wood under strong summer sunlight. George and Abbey, the two rather nondescript Americans, made little permanent impression upon him, and in after years he could not even remember George's name. But Von Schoultz was an unforgettable person. Macdonald must have spent long and absorbed hours in his company. He drew the Pole's will; and Von Schoultz was evidently so grateful to the young lawyer, and so appreciative of his friendly counsel that he tried to leave him a small legacy, which Macdonald, of course, had to refuse. To the very last years of his life Macdonald remembered all the material details of the Pole's story with unfaded clarity.[51] Von Schoultz was one memory—a tragic memory—of the rebellion period. The Ashley affair was a comedy-drama which, in recollection, must have given him a certain acid amusement. The rebellion had made him as a lawyer; it had given him the reputation of a conservative who was not afraid to battle for liberal principles; and it had left him with one clear and uneffaceable general impression. For him, and for Kingston and the whole Midland District, the "rebellion" had been not so much a native uprising as a succession of American raids; and from then on he never quite lost a certain lingering anxiety for the problem of British North American defence.

Chapter Four

The New Conservative Candidate

I

In January, 1839, he passed his twenty-fourth birthday. Less than a month later, *The Times* printed a large first instalment of Lord Durham's *Report;* and, within another month, Kingstonians, as well as Canadians everywhere, were reading the famous document with varying degrees of interest, enthusiasm, apprehension, disgust, and anger. The peaceful reorganization of the Canadas, for which the *Report* appeared to be the official programme, could hardly have come at a more appropriate period of Macdonald's career. If he had been older, even, perhaps, only a few years older, he would have belonged to the pre-Rebellion generation of Canadian public men; and it is a curious fact that the members of that generation, whether they were comparatively young, or middle-aged, or old, failed, with astonishing uniformity, to survive very long in the new political atmosphere. For them, the adjustment was too difficult; but in Macdonald's case, it was made with ease. The commencement of the new era in Canadian politics coincided almost exactly with the beginnings of his public career. He had almost nothing to unlearn from the vanishing past. He could adapt himself with facility to the requirements, and the opportunities, of the present and the future.

Moreover, the shape of things to come, which Lord Durham had revealed with such reckless effrontery, must have seemed a good deal less dismaying to him, and to Kingston, and to Scots Presbyterians in general, than it did to the Anglican Tories of

Toronto. It was true, of course, that most Upper Canadian Conservatives, whether they were young or old, moderate or ultra, could hardly help being scandalized by the *Report*. The brief but notorious section on Upper Canada, with its grotesque inaccuracies, its perverse misinterpretations, its unashamed Radical prejudices and assumptions, appeared to them like a vulgar, journalistic lampoon on the affairs of their province.[1] They felt certain that responsible government, which was one of the two principal recommendations of the *Report,* was utterly inconsistent with what they called "the just dependence of the colonies upon the parent state"; and they looked upon the second main proposal, the legislative union of Upper and Lower Canada, with doubts and misgivings. They were still worried about the future and sore with the humiliation of disparagement and misrepresentation when the new Governor, Charles Poulett Thomson, arrived in September. The Conservatives eyed him doubtfully. A Baltic timber merchant, an ex-President of the Board of Trade, a brisk, opinionated, engagingly cocksure man, ready with snap judgments and eager for quick returns, he seemed, even more than Durham, to have all the dread appearance of a bright, irreverent, impatient Radical Whig. This was the first uneasy view; but it rapidly altered. Within a few months, Thomson had become the accepted leader of the great central mass of moderate Conservatives, and the inspiration and exemplar of the young men of Macdonald's generation.

Thomson, in fact, was one of the great founders of the Liberal-Conservative party. With his drive, his enthusiasm, his easy competence, and his none too scrupulous dexterity, he invested the programme of the moderates with an air of modernity and adventurous purpose. If he kept himself somewhat impatiently aloof from the old official set, he was far from becoming the obsequious familiar of the Radicals; and while he continued restlessly urging a giant programme of provincial reforms, there were evidently certain untouchable absolutes with which he had no intention of tampering. In a few crisp sentences, he and the Colonial Secretary, Lord John Russell, dismissed the extreme Reform interpretation of the doctrine of responsible government. Coolly, almost contemptuously, he exposed the waste and inefficiency of party rule; and with the engaging, peremptory address of a company promoter, he appealed to all sensible men to drop their meaningless debate over theoretical points of government and to unite in a great joint campaign for the improvement and prosperity of their province. The moderate Conservatives gasped with both relief and enthusiasm. The imperial connection was to remain undisturbed: the governor—no longer the tool of a clique, but the real leader of a province—was still to rule. Reassured, if not entirely satisfied, the moderates faced the future with more confidence, and prepared to accept the legislative union of Upper and Lower Canada, the basic political reform upon which Thomson had obviously set his heart. When in December, 1839, the Governor submitted the measure for the acceptance of the Upper Canadian legislature, the representatives of the old Toryism, Boulton and Sherwood of Toronto, and even Hagerman and Cartwright from the Midland District were opposed, or doubtful, or lukewarm; but it was significant that William Morris, the moderate Conservative who had been appointed to plead the cause of the Church of Scotland at the Colonial Office, declared his willingness to accept the union frankly and without conditions.[2] The Presbyterians throughout the province were prepared to follow him; and the Conservative papers in Kingston gave the union their support. During the early summer of 1840, the bill uniting the two provinces was pushed through the imperial Parliament; and in a special supplement of August 22, the *Chronicle and Gazette* printed the full text of the statute for the enlightenment of its Kingston readers. The union had come when Macdonald was only twenty-five; and it rigged the stage on which his political career was to be acted out for the next quarter-century and more.

He was almost, but not quite, ready to take his place. He had come a long way in a little while. In those days a young and ambitious man could legitimately expect to have accomplished a good deal by the time he was twenty-five; and, judged by those standards, Macdonald had not done at all badly. It was not yet five years since he had first opened the office in Quarry Street, and not yet six years since George Mackenzie's death. But could it not be said already that he had nearly won George Mackenzie's place? Without any question he was the preferred legal adviser of the Scots community; it might even be argued now that he was one of the most popular lawyers in the town as a whole. He was getting to be known professionally as an ingenious young man, persuasive with juries, adroitly clever in the management of cases—"a dangerous man to encounter in the courts", as one of his contemporaries phrased it long afterwards.[3] In his youthful readiness to take on cases which were difficult, or doubtful, or unpopular, there were pleasant signs of a professional adventurousness, a generous tolerance of attitude, a jaunty independence of mind. Yet nothing could be even hinted against the respectability of his associations or the soundness of his Conservative principles. He was gay, genial, even, perhaps, a little lightheartedly adventurous; but eminently safe. In 1839, the Commercial Bank of the Midland District affixed its broad impressive seal to the titles of his professional merit. In June—just six months after the Von Schoultz trial—he was elected a member of the Board of Directors;[4] and in the autumn, following the death of Henry Cassady, Kingston's second mayor, he became the bank's solicitor. Could anything prove more conclusively that George Mackenzie's old pupil had stepped firmly and decisively into his master's shoes?

With this increase in business and professional consequence, there came an augmentation of staff. Oliver Mowat had been Macdonald's first pupil; in the autumn of 1839, there came a second, Alexander Campbell, who had been articled to Henry Cassady.[5] A Scotsman by origin—though the Campbell family had lived for at least one generation in Yorkshire—young Alexander was a youth of seventeen when he joined Macdonald's office. He was slight in build, shorter than his youthful employer, with a reserved, serious face whose solemnity was accentuated by a slightly pendulous underlip. A sensitive and thoughtful young man, emotional yet scrupulous and cautious, Campbell was in many ways a more complex character than either his employer or his fellow-pupil. He brooded. He philosophized. His standards were obstinately high; he was rather dourly conscientious; he developed stubborn loyalties. And although Oliver Mowat was soon to abandon Kingston and to seek an independent career for himself in Toronto, the association between Macdonald and Campbell was never so summarily or so completely broken. With young Alexander's coming, the Macdonald establishment took on a size and grandeur which, except in the capital, were distinctly unusual at the time. Two articled pupils, when even the great George Mackenzie had had only one! Early that winter, in December, Macdonald gave up the tiny Quarry Street office, and moved to larger quarters, immediately adjoining the dry-goods shop of Douglas Prentiss, in the town's principal thoroughfare, Store Street.[6]

Things were going swimmingly. He was well on the way to becoming—what Alexander Campbell later claimed him to be—*facile princeps* of the Kingston bar. He was clever, and courageous, and friendly, and cheerfully resourceful. But he had had luck as well—luck, and good connections, and strong support. Back of him was the Macdonald clan, and back of that was the vigorous and cohesive Scots community of Kingston. His father, the agreeable and hopeful Hugh, his mother with her sturdy tranquillity and robust good humour, his sisters, Margaret and Louisa, the Macpherson boys and their wives, the Macpherson girls and their husbands and sweethearts were linked together, not only by the conventions, and affections, and small accepted antagonisms of family life, but also by the closest and most practical of material interests. The Commercial Bank was the main source of their welfare and the chief focus of their economic connections. The family had, indeed, moved into the bank solidly, bag and baggage, with a familiar, proprietorial air. Francis Archibald Harper continued to be its general manager. Appropriately enough, he lived on the premises in Kingston—though, it was true, he also owned a large and pleasant country residence, west of the town, along the lake front and close to Kingston's largest mansion, Alwington House. Hugh still kept his small clerkship in the institution. Thomas Wilson, the Deputy Assistant Commissary-General who had returned from his travels abroad and was soon to retire from the service with an injured arm, was appointed the Commercial Bank's representative in Montreal. And finally John Macdonald had

also become a director and the bank's solicitor. John S. Cartwright, the son of one of the town's founding fathers, the typical
representative of the Anglican Loyalist group, was still president
of the bank; but the firm hold which the Macpherson-Macdonald
group had secured upon it revealed only too clearly how the
new British immigrants who had come in since Waterloo were
effectively transferring the direction of affairs from the old
Loyalist leaders to themselves.

The Scottish community of Kingston was one of the strongest
of these immigrant groups. Macdonald was one of its chosen
younger representatives, clearly one of its favourite sons. And
Kingston, even, perhaps, more than Toronto, was becoming
recognized as the main citadel of Presbyterianism in Upper
Canada. St. Andrews Church had always been among the first
to urge the rights, and state the needs, and plan the future of
the Scottish community in the province. Kingston was frequently the meeting place of the synod; and it was soon to
become the permanent seat of the new Presbyterian university,
Queen's College. Macdonald, like Harper and other members
of the family, was closely identified with these causes and
enterprises. Back in the troubled autumn of 1838, when the
members of St. Andrews had met once more to take into consideration "the present state of the Presbyterian Church in
Canada", Macdonald, seconded by Harper, moved the first and
basic resolution which asserted that "the Church of Scotland,
in virtue of the Articles of Union between the two Kingdoms,
is as much an Established Church of the Empire as the Church
of England; and her Members, in every Colony acquired since
the Union, are entitled to the same religious liberty, and to an
equal participation in all rights and privileges with those of
the sister establishment".[7] Over a year later, in December, 1839,
just after Macdonald had moved to his new Store Street office,
the congregation met again to organize support for the new
Presbyterian college, which it was planned to establish in
Kingston. John Machar acted as chairman. Great "good feeling" prevailed; and before the meeting was over £1100 had been
subscribed. It was John Macdonald who seconded the first
resolution, proposed by Major Logie, which read "that this

meeting deeply regret the limited means afforded the youth of this country, of acquiring a liberal education, founded on Christian principles, and, more especially, the total want of an institution for educating and preparing young men for the Ministry in connection with the Church of Scotland".[8]

These public appearances were growing steadily more numerous. Up until the summer of 1840, they had been largely for Presbyterian causes; but, after the Union Bill had finally passed the imperial Parliament, Macdonald moved openly into the general politics of his town. That summer everybody expected that a general election—the first general election in the united Province of Canada—would immediately take place; and in Kingston it was clear that the growing influence of the Scottish community, and of its representatives such as Macdonald, could no longer be ignored or disregarded. In all probability the Scots Conservatives would never again have willingly accepted Hagerman—Hagerman who had disgraced himself by his terrible outburst of February, 1837, against the Presbyterian Church; but, by a fortunate accident, they were spared the embarrassment of open opposition to his candidature. Hagerman could not run. His long professional career had been crowned by an appointment to the bench. He was now definitely out of politics and a successor to the Kingston constituency would have to be found. Who was it to be? It was not really a controversy between Radicals and Tories, for no admitted Reform candidate dared to present himself. It was really a question—a delicate and fascinating question—of what kind of Conservative the capital of the Midland District would send to the new, united Assembly. The curious and significant fact was that there was no generally acceptable representative of the Tory and Anglican Loyalist group, which up to that time had so largely controlled both the province and the town. Anthony Manahan, a man in his forties, with some political experience, who had been elected for Hastings county in 1836 along with Edmund Murney, was put forward by one group in Kingston as a possible candidate. But the Scots Presbyterians were plainly no more satisfied with Manahan than they would have been with a second edition of Hagerman. Manahan, it was true, was a Conservative, a sensible moderate Conservative, who was turning into a good follower of Thomson. But he was also an Irishman and a Roman Catholic; and, from the point of view of the Kingston Scots, these were fatal defects. And, along with others of the same stubborn opinion, they set about obtaining a rival candidate.

Macdonald—it was a significant indication of his growing influence in politics—played a major part in these negotiations. He was one of a committee of two which interviewed Thomas Kirkpatrick, Kingston's first mayor, and begged him to run. And when Kirkpatrick finally declined, and the problem of a substitute was put before a general meeting of the Kingston electors early in August, 1840, Macdonald's competent generalship was in evidence at every stage of the meeting.[9] The candidate whom he and Thomas Kirkpatrick proposed to the little assembly was John Richardson Forsyth, a member of one of Kingston's oldest founding families, and related also, as his second name indicated, to the venerable commercial house of Richardson, in Montreal. The hereditary titles of Forsyth's conservatism were certainly good—so good that Radicals, and even moderates, might be disposed to look at them a little askance. But, on the other hand, Forsyth was a young man, a Presbyterian, who, like Macdonald, had done his share of fighting for the rights of the Church of Scotland, and who therefore could hardly be regarded as too closely connected with the old Anglican governing set. The election address which he published, shortly after the meeting had accepted his candidature, seemed to bear out this satisfactory impression. Forsyth spoke with fitting impressiveness of the importance of the British connection; but he also showed himself a moderate, a follower of the popular Thomson, and he declared that he would give all the aid he could in the task of "leading the people of these colonies from fruitless and idle disputes upon theoretical points of government to the consideration of their real and practical interests".[10]

Yet the general election did not take place that summer, for Thomson—he had become Baron Sydenham now—had not yet issued the proclamation which would bring the union into effect and the new constitution into operation. All that autumn and winter of 1840-41, while the Canadians of the two old provinces waited expectantly for the official beginning of their new political existence, there was one topic, of inexhaustible fascination, upon which everybody's attention was focused. Where was the capital of this new, enormous, empire province to be? The imperial Act of Union, maintaining a discreet silence on this controversial subject, merely empowered the governor to select; and Sydenham had pressed to be permitted to exercise his leisurely discretion in the matter, on the plea that the selection was a very difficult problem, requiring prolonged and serious study.[11] In reality, he made up his mind quickly; but he did not choose to reveal it. And for long, dragging months, the province waited restlessly, in a state of agonized conjecture. The old capital cities, Quebec and Toronto, as well as the commercial metropolis, Montreal, and an odd little place on the Ottawa River called Bytown, all had their fervent partisans and their elaborate supporting arguments. But from the very beginning there was a strong, persistent, and confident rumour that Kingston would be the inevitable choice. As early as mid-August, 1840, the editor of one Kingston newspaper claimed that this decision was a certainty;[12] and when, a few days later, Sydenham visited the town for the second time, he received a rapturous greeting which differed markedly from the cool, reserved reception he had been accorded in the previous autumn. And young Macdonald, along with the other members of a select committee, presented him with a highly laudatory address.[13]

For another six months the matter of the capital slumbered. And then, one famous day in late January, it was suddenly discovered that Hamilton Killaly, the Chairman of the Board of Works, was in town, making a severely quiet inspection of all the available public buildings.[14] Hopes were raised at once to fever pitch; they were as quickly dashed by the doleful rumours that Kingston's accommodation had been found unsufficient; and they were raised once more when these rumours were indignantly and authoritatively denied. On Saturday, February 6, 1841, the Kingstonians were definitely informed that their town had been chosen as the seat of government;[15] and four days later the union, by Sydenham's proclamation, went into effect. A little town, of less than five thousand population, and fewer than five hundred houses, had suddenly become the capital of an enormous province, vastly larger than any which had existed in the nineteenth century in British North America; and Macdonald, a young man just turned twenty-six, discovered that provincial politics had been deposited on his own front door-step.

II

During these first years of Kingston's sudden greatness, Macdonald went through a period of illness more serious than he had experienced before. He had been ill during the winter of 1840;[16] there was, apparently, a return of the same trouble some time late in 1841. But these attacks came at intervals; and he was far too interested, and far too prominent, to sit back and watch others monopolize the arrangements for Kingston's reception of the new Canadian government. The town was busy with preparations and nearly frantic with excitement. Killaly, with the impressive authority of the Board of Works, hurried back and forward between Kingston and the temporary seat of government in Montreal. George Browne, the architect in charge of the reconstruction of the public buildings, was busy with plans and specifications. Down by the lake front, on the Penitentiary Road, about a mile from the centre of town, scores of labourers were remodelling the recently completed municipal hospital in preparation for its reception of the two Houses of Parliament and the government offices; and further west, another contingent of workmen was hurriedly constructing two additional and spacious wings for the handsome Grant mansion, Alwington House, which was to serve as the Governor's residence.[17] Accommodation—weeks before the parliamentarians and the civil servants could possibly arrive to occupy it—was suddenly found to be at a premium; rents went dramatically up. And, as early as February 17, barely ten days after the wonderful announcement had been made public, a Kingston editor found it necessary to rebuke his fellow-citizens for taking undue advantage of their town's new-found glory.[18]

In the meantime, while Kingston waited for the Governor's coming and the opening of the legislature, Macdonald had lots to do. The Kingston election, for which all the preparations had been made during the previous summer, was scheduled to begin on Monday, March 22; and he acted as young Forsyth's counsel and probably as his principal assistant in the campaign. The election address—in which both young men no doubt had a hand—seemed to strike exactly the right note of discreet modernity and forward-looking conservatism. Forsyth reminded the electors of how long he had believed in the union, how loyally he was prepared to follow Sydenham, and how anxious was his determination to assist the parent government in carrying out its beneficent intentions for Canada's welfare.[19] The Kingston newspapers, the *British Whig* and the *Chronicle and Gazette,* faced with two such equally acceptable Conservative candidates, seemed almost inclined to praise young Forsyth as much as they did his senior, Manahan. And yet, from the beginning, there were a few peevish criticisms, a few captious references to Forsyth's family and its past. "If he has a drawback," declared the *British Whig* of the Scottish candidate, "it is perhaps a too intimate connection with the oligarchy of Upper Canada, who have, by a long-continued series of successes, been led to consider the representation of certain towns and counties as their own private property".[20] This was bad enough; but there was worse to follow. For Forsyth, despite a well-meaning, rather obvious effort to conciliate the Irish by pleasant references to the hospitality he had received on a recent visit to Ireland, turned out to be a lamentably poor speaker. On the fatal Monday, March 22, while his stiff speech was received coolly, Manahan, with his rich and tactful blarney, was repeatedly cheered. Forsyth lost; but he lost by only twenty votes.[21] And Macdonald, contemplating the defeated young candidate, may very well have wondered whether, if their roles had been reversed, the decision would not have been altered also.

During late April and early May, when the workmen had

nearly finished their hasty alterations of the public buildings, a steady persistent avalanche of public officials, civil servants, records, papers, books and furniture began to descend upon Kingston. Down in the converted hospital building, in a situation which everybody agreed was "delightful and salubrious" in the extreme, the government offices were fitted out; and the Assembly room—a little exiguous, the newspapermen thought, for its full complement of legislators—was furnished with eighty-four handsome stuffed armchairs, of black walnut, covered in dark green moreen, with a small projection on the side to write upon.[22] Everything was now ready for the entrance of the principal; and, on a day in May, a little group of Kingstonians assembled in the town hall to make preparations for the final and crowning event—the arrival of the Governor—which would complete and validate everything that had gone before. Macdonald was there in his capacity as vice-president of the St. Andrews Society. On the previous November 30, in the absence of the president, he had taken the chair at the Society's great annual banquet. And now—the president being again out of town—he sat down with Dr. Sampson, Henry Smith, Jr., Thomas Kirkpatrick, and his friend Charles Stuart, to plan an imposing reception for Governor Sydenham.[23]

Friday, May 28, was a delightful day, clear and bright, with a gentle breeze, and a few white, comfortable clouds travelling with easy rapidity across a blue sky. It was nearly one o'clock, when the Traveller, commanded by Captain Sandom, the hero of the naval operations off Prescott nearly three years before, rounded Point Frederick into the harbour; and the guns of Fort Henry and the gaily decorated ships roared into the long official salute. The town was crammed with citizens and visitors, for all the shops were shut and people for miles around had come in to celebrate the general holiday. The crowd was packed thick by the Commercial Wharf, at the foot of Store Street, where Sydenham landed, attended by his guard of honour. And all the way up Store Street to the King Street intersection, along an avenue which was decorated and arched with evergreens, and gay with flags and defiant Britannic mottoes, there stood the Mayor and corporation, the local members of parliament and lawyers, the members of the national societies, of the Mechanics Institute and the Volunteer Fire Brigade, drawn up in two continuous ranks and cheering like mad. As Sydenham's carriage rolled slowly up Store Street, and under the festooned arch of evergreens, the citizens formed up behind him, with Macdonald and his St. Andrews Society among the first. A piper, Donald McKay, strode at their head. Macdonald and many of the members were in kilts; and a huge banner, with the red lion of Scotland, floated over their heads. In the brilliant spring sunshine, they marched along King Street and the lake front to Alwington House, to conduct their Governor home. Sydenham stood on the steps of the main entrance; and Macdonald and his Highlanders and the long cavalcade of citizens drew up in a great semicircle on the lawn before the Governor, with their banners to the front, and the pale green of the spring leaves and the dark blue of the lake behind them. The sheriff of the Midland District read the official address of welcome, to which Sydenham graciously replied. Then the procession paraded round the circular drive before the Governor, and down the road, and home.[24]

From that moment Macdonald drew back, an interested but relatively unimportant onlooker, while the stage was occupied by other and more commanding figures. Parliament, the first which Kingston had ever known, met early in June with impressive ceremonies. The opposition, under Baldwin and Lafontaine, massed themselves for a concerted attack on the government; but Sydenham, with his bland confidence and dexterity, divided and scattered his enemies. Kingston, the town, buzzed with interest in these national affairs; and Kingston the constituency—it seemed symbolic of the new capital's altered status —was swept out of the control of its local politicians and into the sphere of executive affairs. Shortly after the legislature met, Anthony Manahan, who had obligingly accepted an office of profit, was required to resign his seat; and Samuel Bealey Harrison, the Provincial Secretary in Sydenham's Cabinet, who up to that time had failed to win a constituency, intimated that he would be prepared to run. Obviously he would run without opposition. The Kingston newspapers, in a rather perfunctory effort to placate the surviving remnant of local independence, tried to convert Harrison into a Kingstonian by pointing out that he had purchased a lot on the outskirts of the town; but these efforts were clearly unnecessary, for pride and gratification in the possession of a cabinet minister as a member would certainly triumph over every other consideration.[25] Forsyth prudently declined to run again; and if the vague, pleasant thought had ever crossed Macdonald's mind that another rather more popular young man might succeed where Forsyth had unfortunately failed, he must now have tucked that thought away in the bottom drawer of his ambitions. In any case, he had enough to do during those spring and summer months. Oliver Mowat had left finally for Toronto, and the two remaining members of the firm were no doubt busy transferring masses of property to Kingston's new householders and arranging loans for Kingston's ambitious merchants. There was even a small amount of parliamentary business to be done; and in July Macdonald acted as counsel for Henry Smith, Jr., in the Frontenac contested election case.

In September, as the short summer slipped into autumn, there came a double tragedy, which flung a shadow over the radiance of Kingston's new political existence, and brought one phase of Macdonald's personal life to its close. On Saturday, September 4, while Sydenham was out riding unaccompanied he was thrown from his horse. And on Sunday, September 19, he died as a result of his injuries. His death must have come almost as a personal loss to Macdonald and the moderates; and it was only four days after he had been laid away in the earth of "Regiopolis", as he had once banteringly called Kingston, that the second, more intimate tragedy occurred, and the quiet, rather nondescript Scotsman, Hugh Macdonald, went off on the last long migration of his troubled career.[26] He was only fifty-nine. His life, which had ended in a mean little clerkship, seemed all too obviously a failure. But the small family which he had brought all the way from Glasgow had started promisingly in the New World. He had left an able son; and from him the son drew qualities important though not easily definable—

a love of people, and their company and talk, a ready and courageous adaptability, an easy, generous tolerance for men and the infinite variety of their views and ways.

It was, apparently, shortly after his father's death that the most serious illness of Macdonald's young manhood occurred.[27] By the end of November he was so far recovered that he was able to take up police court work again and to appear at his place as vice-president at the annual St. Andrews dinner. In mid-December, when the town decided patriotically to plan a monster celebration of the birth of the Prince of Wales, Macdonald was, as usual, a member of the committee in charge. On December 22, while a sleigh dragged a huge roasted ox through the snow to the market place, and the whole of Kingston's poor sat down to a vast dinner of roast beef, mutton, ham, venison, coffee and beer, he and the other members of the "Committee of Bachelors" were coping with a cheerfully refractory mass of Kingston's children who were given a competitive banquet in the town hall.[28] He enjoyed these affairs, as his father would have, and was good at them. But from then on his public appearances grew fewer; and when, early in January, 1842, the new Governor, Sir Charles Bagot, was drawn across the ice from Cape Vincent in a racing "gig", Macdonald was not among the rather small informal company which gathered to meet Sydenham's successor. His illness had apparently trailed off in a long convalescence, which left him easily tired, without much appetite, and restless. He determined to go "home". Kingston, capital of Canada as well as of the Midland District, was satisfactory enough; but beyond Kingston, and Canada, and British North America, lay another world, imperial and international in scope, remote, and splendid, and vastly more exciting than anything he had yet known. From a practical point of view, there were probably family affairs to be settled in Scotland, following his father's death. In any case, he wanted the change and the rest, and the practice, which had certainly been booming during the last few years, could supply him with all the funds he needed for his travels.

John Machar recommended Butler's *Analogy of Natural and*

Revealed Religion and suggested that there was nothing so good as a sea voyage for serious and prolonged reflection.[29] For three nights—about the only three nights in his life when he tried cards for money—he played loo with John S. Cartwright, George W. Yarker of the Commercial Bank and two other fellow-spirits, and won with miraculous and unbroken consistency.[30] With his heavy winnings tucked in his pocket, along with John Machar's letter commending him to the protection of a gracious Providence, he set out from Kingston, some time late in January, 1842. He was accompanied by Tom Wilson, who was going back to England to interview the officials of the War Office in an effort to persuade them to take a serious view of the compensation which should be granted him for his injured arm. It was the depth of winter when they sailed from Boston. The ocean was white with tempest; and London, in February and March, was only doubtfully clement. But almost at once his health began miraculously to improve. He discovered, to his own astonishment, and to that of Tom Wilson and his well-to-do brother-in-law Edward Wanklyn, that he was eating plenteous breakfasts and even more bountiful dinners; and along with this suddenly voracious appetite, there went a surprised and delighted sensation of vitality, of conscious well-being, of easy and effortless strength. He went everywhere. Streets, shops, public buildings, theatres, exhibitions, dinners, parties, and balls were all crowded into an enormous programme which took his sleep, and tired his legs, and taxed his pocketbook. With intense interest, but without being moved to any very profound political or legal reflections, he watched the jury trials at the Guildhall, listened to a debate in the Lords, and heard Peel, Russell, Stanley, Goulburn and Sir James Graham in the Commons. And one bland, delightful day in late February, which was like a sweet breath of the coming spring, he visited Windsor, peeped, by special permission, into the Queen's private apartments while the pretty Margaret Wanklyn hung upon his arm, compared impressions of royal domesticity with his companion, and discovered, to his intense satisfaction, that they were in happily sympathetic agreement upon all the main points.[81] He lived in a state of continual high spirits. Amused, conscious of his amusement, conscious of things to be enjoyed and of his almost limitless capacity for quizzical enjoyment, he was realizing and perfecting his own style, his characteristic way with things and people, the easy, jaunty fashion in which he was to saunter through life.

There was some, but not much, evidence of practical purpose in his itinerary. London was pure fun. The projected tour of the Lake Country, and the visits to Oxford and Cambridge were all parts of a general programme of diversion and recuperation. Only occasionally was there some slight tangible sign of concern for the life which must soon be resumed in the far-off house and office in Kingston. In Chancery Lane, he bought a substantial law library which cost him a little over £160.[82] He wrote his mother that at Manchester he proposed to purchase a quantity of house furnishings—wall-paper, damask, ornaments, iron railings, and a kitchen stove—all intended for the house in Kingston, of which he had now become the proprietor. For the rest, there must certainly be visits with his British relatives. Evan Macpherson, a soldier like his father, the old Colonel, was now stationed at Chester; and at Arbroath were Major and Mrs. Bruce Gardyne—she had been Catharine Macpherson. In Scotland, other members of the family surrounded and claimed him. He met them all, and, among the rest, his first cousin, Isabella Clark, the second daughter of his Aunt Margaret Shaw, and the sister of that Maria Clark who back in 1834 had married John Alexander Macpherson in Hallowell.[83] Her gentle, tranquil features, her hair brushed smoothly away from its centre part in the demure fashion of the 1840's, have survived only in a faded picture whose blurred outlines seem to frustrate the enquirer with gently mocking modesty. When Macdonald left for Scotland, he was, and perhaps expected to remain for some time, a bachelor. Perhaps he carried with him back to Canada only the pleasant memory of her face. Perhaps, when he left, he had already secured from her at least one promise, that next year she might herself cross the ocean to visit her long-absent sister Maria in Kingston.

III

When Macdonald arrived home, some time in the summer of 1842, he was probably in much better health than he had been for years. Kingston also was prospering. Since the moment, in the summer of 1840, when the first intimations of its new grandeur had begun to circulate, the town had nearly doubled in population. The sense of well-being and vitality, which Macdonald had recovered so vividly in London, had been shared now for nearly two years by the moderate Liberal-Conservatives and by the new capital of the new province. For nearly two years the glittering but unsubstantial fabric reared by the magician Sydenham had lasted; and then in the autumn of 1842, almost without warning, it began to collapse. In September, the first parliament of the united Province of Canada met for its second session; and it had barely been sitting a week when the new Governor, Sir Charles Bagot, was obliged to reconstitute his Cabinet and to admit Robert Baldwin and his French-Canadian friends to office. The Tories were out; Draper, the principal hope of the moderate Conservatives, had gone. And yet, though some of the Kingston newspapers began to refer contemptuously to "Granny Bagot" and to print abusive burlesques on the subject of "Bagot, Hincks and Company, General Office Brokers and Cabinet Makers", public opinion in the town was inclined to be discreetly cautious in its attitude to the new government.[34] After all, Samuel Bealey Harrison, Secretary for Canada West and Kingston's own member in the provincial parliament, remained, with a few others, to provide a tenuous connection with the past. Surely Harrison would defend Kingston's interests? And surely it was common prudence for Kingston to give a decent welcome to the administration which governed in its midst?

Macdonald, who had no reason to qualify his known and definite Conservative position, was of course opposed to the political change which had just taken place. He must have been aware of the vague feeling of unease in the town, and must have watched with interest for the first sign of any policy which might render the new ministers objectionable to his fellow-townsmen. He had not long to wait. The new government had not been in office a week when a sinister rumour began to spread rapidly through Kingston that, at the determined instance of Lafontaine and the French Canadians, the seat of government was to be moved, probably to Montreal. The town waited in nervous apprehension. Late in September, Harrison read in the Assembly a despatch from the Colonial Office on the subject, a despatch in which Stanley, the Colonial Secretary, had poured a deluge of very cold water on the proposed removal, declaring that it could be done only under the "clearest necessity" and with "the general sense of the Province unequivocally expressed in its favour".[35] The government newspapers in Kingston drew a breath of relief. That settled the matter. Yet the ominous rumours persisted. "Our firm belief is," wrote one editor, "that in the arrangements lately effected, the interests of Kingston were actually and virtually sold."[36] As if to give point to this blunt assertion, the Assembly, a few days later, took up the embarrassing subject once again and, for some hours, expatiated offensively on Kingston's limitations as a capital. Even government supporters in the town now took alarm. The French Canadians were given downright warning not to abuse their power. "We do not know anything," wrote one government newspaper, "calculated to enter more deeply into the minds of the inhabitants of the Upper Province, than the removal of our Parliament to Lower Canada".[37]

All this was both alarming and encouraging. The transfer to Montreal would provide excellent political capital for the Conservative party; but, on the other hand, it would mean the certain ruin of the new-found prosperity of Kingston. Macdonald's feelings must have been mixed, for his political hopes grew bright as his professional prospects darkened. But the Kingston city fathers, who were responsible for the town's well-being, could naturally take only one view of the situation. They had realized for some time that their rapidly growing capital was badly in need of a new town hall and new market buildings; and they were aware also—and the thought hovered always at the back of their speculations—that the provincial legislature, completely ignoring the need of permanent provision, still occupied its avowedly temporary quarters, the four-storey limestone building which had been erected as a hospital. Contemplating these two necessities, the town council reached an audacious and grandiose decision. It would build an elegant, spacious, and splendid town hall, a town hall amply sufficient to accommodate not merely the offices and council rooms which a rising town like Kingston was certain to require, but also still larger chambers, fit, perhaps, for the deliberations of still greater and more august assemblies.[38] John Counter, thick-set, square-jawed, black-haired—Kingston's energetic and repeatedly elected Mayor—departed for England to raise the necessary funds, armed with £20,000 in corporation securities. The mission was a complete success and on his return in March John Counter was given a hero's reception. Ground was broken and the council's grand design marched steadily forward.[39] George Browne, who had supervised the alteration of the government buildings in Kingston, was the architect; and Browne had made an interesting and significant use of his space. The ground floor of the new building was to contain a variety of smaller rooms and offices; but upstairs, in the second storey, there were to be, not one, but two large and lofty chambers, larger certainly than any common council would presumably require, but not, on the other hand, too large for a provincial Legislative Council and a Legislative Assembly.

It was at this point, when the civic affairs of Kingston were taking on a new pomp and circumstance, that Macdonald decided to run as alderman. A municipal career, in and for itself, would be vastly more interesting than it would have been even a few years before. Also, though the fate of the Kingston constituency seemed settled for years to come, municipal office was in general a most suitable beginning for public life. He was certainly well known and popular. He had participated in the most intimate councils of the Conservative party and had taken part in every important civic affair for years. Moreover, during the previous autumn—it was a crowning honour for a member of the Scottish community—he had been

elected president of the St. Andrews Society, with Harper and
J. R. Forsyth as first and second vice-presidents.⁴⁰ Early in
February, when he modestly announced that he proposed to
run for the vacant seat in the Fourth Ward, the Kingston newspapers, of all political opinions, welcomed and supported his
candidature with flattering unanimity. "We are not aware,"
said the editor of the *Chronicle and Gazette*, "that a more
eligible person could offer. His experience in public business,
his well-known talents and high character, render him peculiarly fit for the office, and we sincerely hope, for the sake of
the Town, that he will be elected."⁴¹ The *British Whig* assured
the electors that they would never have cause to regret choosing Macdonald and his team-mate, Robert Anglen, who was
running for the post of common councilman. The *Loyalist*
wound up the chorus of praise with a soaring finale, when it
confidently predicted that Macdonald would be returned with
a triumphant majority. It proved to be exactly right. When,
on March 28, the election finally took place, Macdonald and
Anglen were returned with ease and were chaired in triumph
through the town.⁴²

Macdonald barely won his seat in council in time. For, on
the very next day, March 29, one of the most important civic
affairs of the year occurred. A new governor—the third since
Kingston had been declared the seat of government—arrived in
the capital. Sir Charles Bagot had fallen a victim to that
curiously implacable fatality which seemed to hover over the
lives of all the first representatives of the Crown who had tried
to rule the united Province of Canada from Alwington House.
Since December, 1842, he had been ill; and he still lingered,
slipping daily closer to death, when his successor, Sir Charles
Metcalfe, arrived to take over the governorship. Macdonald,
as before, had met with others to plan a proper reception for
their new ruler;⁴³ but the gloom at Alwington House made too
great enthusiasm inappropriate, and with the arrival of the
third governor in two years, it was a little hard to maintain the
first thrill of novelty. The winter had been a terrible one; and
the thousands of people who crowded into Kingston on that

late March day stood about uncomfortably in piles of deep snow and slush. The ice was still feet thick in the river when Sir Charles crossed from Cape Vincent in a carriage, changing, just as he reached Kingston, into an open sleigh, with four fine grey horses, which drew him through the capital.[44] The town corporation—with the new alderman for Ward Four among them—went over to the American side to greet the Governor; and there Macdonald caught his first glimpse of the man who was to have such a decisive effect upon the fortunes of the Conservative party. He may not have been very impressed. Metcalfe, a veteran colonial administrator with long and successful experience in the West Indies and India, was a stout, dumpy, aging man, with iron-grey hair, and fat, rather pendulous cheeks, upon one of which, already noticeable, was a frightening and venomous sore.

What was going on behind the grey and unrevealing exterior of Government House when Metcalfe met his Reform ministers? Macdonald, like most other people in Kingston, probably had very little idea. But not even a fortnight had elapsed since the new Governor's arrival, when the old horrible rumours about the transfer of the seat of government were revived once more, and this time with the most circumstantial particulars. It was said in Montreal that Lafontaine, the Attorney-General for Canada East, was decidedly in favour of a move to Montreal;[45] it was rumoured from Quebec that the French-Canadian members of the government had, in a body, threatened the Governor with resignation, if their demands were not complied with.[46] In the midst of these depressing and unnerving rumours, and in the vilest possible weather, the Kingstonians stubbornly continued to build their town hall. All that April and May it rained and snowed, thawed and froze, with wearisome consistency; and on Monday, June 5—"Training Day"—when Governor Metcalfe came down in state to the waterfront to lay the cornerstone of the new municipal buildings, "the day was cold and showery, which threw a damp upon the proceedings".[47] That evening Macdonald, the other members of the corporation, and a long list of guests were entertained at dinner by the

Governor at the British American Hotel. A grey uneasiness, which matched the gloomy night outside, with its east wind and gusts of rain, may very well have fallen upon the company; and it must have been with a certain forced bravado that speaker after speaker arose to extol the glories of Kingston and to predict its prosperity in the future.

Yet, if the affairs of the province and the destiny of Kingston remained veiled in ominous ambiguity, Macdonald continued, unaffected, on his own cheerful way. Last year, in England, he had gained what seemed a long, strong, unshakable lease on life. He was a lawyer with a large practice, an alderman with a good deal of popularity, and a genial young man with quantities of friends. He was enjoying existence to the full; and that summer, which opened warmly and agreeably after the terrible prolonged winter, Isabella Clark arrived in Kingston. Her sister Maria, and her sister's husband, John Alexander Macpherson, who had lived in Hillier, in Prince Edward County, during the 1830's, had now migrated back to Kingston, like so many others of the Macpherson-Macdonald clan; and one of their children, a very small boy named James Pennington in memory of his uncle and in honour of his grandfather's old commander, remembered long afterwards how this strange, delightful aunt from overseas had captivated him with her sweetness, and gentleness, and tender sympathy.[48] "Cousin John" had always been a frequent visitor at the Macpherson household; now his visits became even more assiduous. And he and Isabella fell in love. This was first love, spontaneous, unpremeditated and impulsive; and within a few months, perhaps even a few weeks, it had brought the lovers to that quick, sure decision upon which happy marriages are based. On September 1, 1843, Macdonald did two things, accepted two contracts, the delicious incongruity of which may have amused his half-practical and half-romantic nature. He agreed to form a legal partnership with his old pupil Alexander Campbell, who had just recently been called to the bar;[49] and in St. Andrews Church, with John Machar as officiating clergyman and his two friends Tom Wilson and Charles Stuart as witnesses, he married his cousin, Isabella Clark.[50]

IV

The young man was twenty-eight. He was married, an alderman, the senior partner in a young but flourishing firm, an able practitioner who could work with ease and efficiency and who now, after years of effort, had reached a comfortable level of prosperity. On September 2, the day after the wedding had been performed and the partnership sealed, Macdonald and Campbell announced the opening of their office on what had long been Store Street, but was now renamed Princess Street, in honour of the Princess Royal.[51] A little later, when the bridegroom and his bride had returned from their honeymoon, they settled down in a house in Brock Street, spacious and comfortable, replete with all the modern conveniences of a wonderful mechanical age.[52] There was a library, for Macdonald had always bought and read books; there was a carriage and a pair of horses, "Mohawk" and "Charlie". Sometimes the young James Pennington Macpherson would be permitted the enormous honour of sitting beside the coachman on his box. Sometimes, coming home from school, he might meet his uncle in the street, and his uncle, indulging the pleasant fiction that he owed James vast sums of money, would proceed to liquidate the debt with all the coppers in his pocket; and James Pennington would go on his happy ways, confirmed in the unshakable conviction that his uncle was the richest and most generous man in the world.

The Macdonalds were barely established in the handsome house on Brock Street, when the crisis in the affairs of Kingston and the province, which had been gathering slowly for a period of months, finally broke. The legislature was scheduled to meet on September 28. A few days before, the town was thrown into a state of angry excitement by a new and positive rumour that Secretary Harrison and possibly one or two other members of the Cabinet were about to resign in protest against a definite official decision to transfer the seat of government from Kingston to Montreal.[53] It was only too true. On September 30, Harrison's resignation was formally announced. Six days later, the government introduced its proposal of removal;

and on November 3, after a long and acrimonious debate in which a growing opposition exhausted every device of obstruction, the transfer to Montreal was finally voted in principle. "And so, at the will of a few, and without any petitions or agitations . . . the hopes and means of many in Kingston are destroyed . . . the 600 houses erected here are to be left tenantless to moulder into ruin. The Market Building, than which nothing more noble has been erected in North America, is to be left a curse to the place."[54] Summarily, and—as it turned out—for ever, the political destiny of Kingston had been determined. And a profound sense of depression—of disappointment, injury, resentment and frustration—settled down upon the town.

Macdonald was affected as a Kingstonian, for his prospects were altered and injured, like those of every other townsman. He was affected also as a Conservative, for the Tory leaders, local and provincial—Sir Allan MacNab, John S. Cartwright, and Henry Smith, Jr.—at once leaped forward to direct the storm of protest to their profit. But what hope was there of upsetting the government, of ending—what now seemed to be a proved reality—the sinister, pervasive, and irresistible influence of Lafontaine and his French Canadians? It was true that the Seat of Government Bill was arousing a mass of opposition in Canada West. Undoubtedly, also, Baldwin's plan for a great, non-sectarian, provincial university was certain to alienate those who supported the small church colleges, Queen's, King's and Victoria, and who believed in the indissoluble union of "science and religion". And, finally, there could be no question that the Secret Societies Bill, a frank and undisguised effort—"unexampled in British legislation", Metcalfe called it—to destroy the Orange Order, had goaded the Grand Master, Ogle Robert Gowan, and his followers into a crusade more determined and furious than any which the Order had inspired since the election of 1836. But, though Harrison had resigned and a few other Reformers were now opposed or doubtful, the government still seemed to hold a commanding majority. The session went solidly forward. Then, suddenly, when nobody but a few initiates expected it, there came another sharp turn of Fortune's wheel. The year 1843, which had been an important one for Macdonald, full of new ventures and significant decisions, had one last, and more general, surprise in store. On Sunday, November 26, alleging a dispute over appointments and patronage, which they declared involved the principle of responsible government, nine out of the ten members of the provincial administration tendered their resignations to the Governor-General.

The crisis gave Macdonald his first great political chance. He rushed into the struggle—and in Kingston it was a popular struggle—for the defence of the legitimate prerogative of the Crown against the evils of extreme party government. On November 30, four days after the resignation of the ministers, when he presided once more at the annual dinner of the St. Andrews Society, the occasion took on an even more defiantly Conservative aspect than usual; and the guests and members sang "Charlie is my Darling" when they toasted the Governor-General.[55] The following Monday Macdonald and his Conservative friends were present and prominent at the public meeting which the Mayor called to take into consideration the question of an address to Metcalfe in the existing crisis. It was a rowdy meeting, in a packed hall, with a large preponderance of Metcalfe supporters; and for the first time Macdonald and the new generation of Kingston Conservatives appeared as popular leaders before a large crowd of their fellow-citizens. Charles Stuart moved the first resolution; Macdonald followed with a resolution which declared "that the firm, manly, and vigorous manner in which His Excellency has maintained the Prerogative of the Crown and at the same time upheld the just rights of all classes of the people, entitles him to our confidence". It was a fighting political speech which followed. With enthusiasm, and with a certain colloquial familiarity of address, he began his defence of the imperial connection, of the Governor who was its prime symbol, and of the Governor's just authority, outside the limits of responsible government as sanctioned by Sydenham in 1841, to protect the rights of both races and all classes of the population against the extremes of party rule.[56]

He started on a note which must have sounded real and

authentic, as nothing else could have done, to an audience which, only six years before, had lived through the perils of the rebellion and the American raids. The basic issue of the controversy, he insisted, was the question of British supremacy. He reminded his listeners of the benefits of the imperial connection, of the protection it could be counted upon to provide, of the vitally necessary defence it had given in 1837 and 1838. Most men in the crowd before him could remember well what militant republicanism had meant. He told them roundly that those who did not rally round the Governor were, in effect, supporting republican principles. From these large generalities in political theory, he pressed on, shrewdly, rapidly, to the more intimate matters of local concern. The people, he declared, had the right to expect a constructive programme from government; but all the ministry had done was to effect the ruin of Kingston. The plea of the ministers, that they had resigned in defence of the principle of responsible government, was so much claptrap; it was no important political issue, but merely the question of the party management of patronage, which had caused them to resign. How could they be trusted now to fill the offices in the Midland District appropriately, when, once the legislature had been moved to Montreal, every place in the government would be stuffed with the friends of Lafontaine?

The speech, and the meeting as a whole, which, to the annoyance of the Reformers, had been a triumphant success, thrust Macdonald publicly and openly into the front rank of Kingston Conservatives. From that moment he was certain to be one of the leading figures, if not the central figure, in the popular defence of Metcalfe in Kingston; and he and his fellow-moderates must have looked with deepening anxiety to Government House for the first signs of the policy which could betray them just as easily as it could invigorate their defence. On December 7, parliament was suddenly prorogued. A few days later, the Governor announced the first appointments to his new Council. It was a curious collection of individuals—William Henry Draper, the moderate Liberal-Conservative Englishman; Denis Benjamin Viger, the repentant French-Canadian revolutionary; and Dominick Daly, the veteran, unpolitical Irish

bureaucrat, who had sat in Sydenham's government, and in
Bagot's government, who saw no reason why he should ever
surrender his job, and who must have regarded the whole disturbing business of responsible government with uncomprehend-
ing distaste. Incomplete, ill-assorted, incongruous—the new
ministry was all of these; but it proved to Macdonald and the
moderates that Metcalfe, in his sharp recoil from the Reformers,
had not fallen automatically into the waiting arms of the old
Tory Compact. The portly, commonplace-looking, stiffly formal
man who had accepted the tragedy of his life with stoical resignation, and who knew now that he could never be cured of the
hideous cancer that had eaten its way through his cheek, was
determined never to yield to the extremes of either party. He
embodied the spirit, not of Sir Francis Bond Head, but of Lord
Sydenham. His aim from the first was a composite, moderate
administration, representing both races and all groups. The
moderates were mystified and embarrassed by the long delays
in the completion of the Council. They could not know the
details of those long months of unavailing negotiations, during
which Metcalfe, still sticking obstinately to his plan, hawked
the offices of government around with a frequency which was
scarcely calculated to increase their prestige. But the few
appointments which were made were highly satisfactory; and it
became increasingly clear that the Toronto Tories, confident
that the Governor must fall back upon them in the end, and
furious that he had not done so already, were holding back
their support with callous indifference.[57] Badgered from both
sides, attacked by their enemies and betrayed by their friends,
the moderates closed their ranks in the defence of Sir Charles.

During March, 1844, though the Governor's Council was still
incomplete, and though parliament had not been dissolved,
the Kingston Conservatives decided that it was time to begin
preparations for the general election. Whom were they to
choose as their candidate? Forsyth had failed, though not too
badly, in 1841. Harrison, though he had resigned on the seat-
of-government question, was suspected of having refused a
place in Metcalfe's new Cabinet. The Kingstonians turned their
backs on both these possibilities, and selected Macdonald; and

a little later their invitation, signed by 225 people, together with Macdonald's reply, was printed in the *Kingston Herald*.[58] The young lawyer's first political declaration was about as brief and as laconically non-committal as Forsyth's had been. But, amid vague benevolent professions of devotion to the interests of Kingston, and of loyalty to "sound and liberal" principles of public policy, there was one long and significant sentence. "In a young country like Canada," declared Macdonald, "I am of opinion that it is of more consequence to endeavour to develop its resources and improve its physical advantages, than to waste the time of the legislature and the money of the people in fruitless discussions on abstract and theoretical questions of government." Perhaps it was, in part, a real profession of faith. Certainly, in the politics of the time, it was an instantly recognizable party label. It identified Macdonald as a moderate, as a Sydenhamite, as a man who would support the Governor, but who was not necessarily associated with the old Tory party. Ten days later, on May 2, he and his friends met at the Court House, to organize the United Empire Association, the electoral organization by which they intended to fight the campaign.[59]

A long halt followed. For weeks, for months, the harassed Governor made no significant move. And during the long summer, while the newspapers fired acrimonious editorials at each other and while R. B. Sullivan and Egerton Ryerson, the heavy guns of the Conservative and Reform parties, kept up their long artillery duel over the meaning of responsible government, Kingston was a dull and depressed place. By the middle of June, most of the public officers, with their records and their furniture, had left town for Montreal. On June 20, Metcalfe, standing on the promenade deck of the steamer *Caledonia*, waved a last farewell to the citizens of what had been, all too briefly, the capital of united Canada.[60] Early in July, Macdonald and his wife left for the United States to visit one of Isabella's sisters, Mrs. Greene; and they had probably been back only a short time when, early in September, Metcalfe ended the long political suspense with a decisive move. The names of the new ministers were made public, and although some of these qualified as moderates simply because they had been political nonentities in the past, others, such as William Morris, had already proved the zeal and the quality of their moderate Conservatism. Obviously a dissolution of the Assembly was now imminent. It was time for Macdonald to act.

Towards the end of September, he called a meeting of his supporters at Metcalfe's Inn.[61] He explained his own position with ingratiating candour. The requisition of the previous spring was months old and he would hold no man bound to it. He would run if they wished; and if they wished, he would cheerfully retire. It was a polite and adroit move. But the minds of the Kingston Conservatives were made up now. When John Richardson Forsyth, the defeated principal of 1841, proposed Macdonald's name, it was voted by acclamation. On October 5, Macdonald published his first election manifesto, and four days later, at a crowded meeting in the court-house, he and Anthony Manahan were nominated as rival candidates.[62] Macdonald was far from underrating the generous, affable Manahan, with his solid Irish Roman Catholic support. He expected, as he said, to be "hard run by the Papishes".[63] He knew, too, that the Scots Presbyterians, upon whose united support he might have counted, had been divided by the "Great Disruption" between "Old Kirk" and "Free Kirk", with the Free Kirkers following the Reformist lead of George Brown and the Toronto *Globe*. It was all true. It was true also that Manahan, for all his good humour and his good stories, was a highly embarrassed man. He tried vainly to explain that he had resigned his seat in 1841 at Sydenham's own request; but he could never quite live down the imputation that he had sold the constituency for a job.

At nine o'clock on Monday, October 14, the voting began. These were the days of the open poll, when each vote was a blow which was known and cheered, and when the electors on both sides marched to the hustings like the men-at-arms of two medieval private armies. By noon of the first day, Manahan, overwhelmed with reverses, had retired under protest, and his discomforted and leaderless followers were scattered. But all that afternoon and all the next day, the Macdonald men continued to press forward, as if the contest were still on, and the issue yet in doubt.[64] At the close of the second day's poll, the vote stood 275 for Macdonald and 42 for Manahan. The election "terminated in a most peaceable and orderly manner, without the slightest attempt at disturbance".[65] It was true that Manahan's supporters, in a formal petition to the Returning Officer, protested the entire election, giving nine separate reasons why it should be declared invalid. But this was normal and rather routine procedure. The vote stood. Macdonald was member for Kingston.

Chapter Five

Minister of the Crown

I

Macdonald stayed in town long enough to attend the dinner in honour of the completion of the new municipal building, which was held on Thursday, November 21, in the town hall itself, in one of the spacious assembly halls which Kingston had vainly hoped would house the two branches of the provincial legislature.[1] Then, early in the next week, it was time to leave for the first session of the newly elected parliament in Montreal. The first great moment in his political career had come; and yet it is probable that he did not depart for Montreal in a mood of carefree triumph. His constituency, despite the drunken hilarity of the great civic dinner, was still sunk in depression and sullen resentment; and he was well aware of the fact that the new government could not possibly restore the town's artificial prosperity, for it did not dare to reverse the decision concerning the seat of government. The state of Kingston, and—intimately associated with it—the state of his own popularity, were problems which he carried away with him. And these worries were matched by other, more intimate, and more serious apprehensions concerning his own and his family affairs. It was true that he was leaving the practice in a most satisfactory state. The arrangement with Campbell, by which the junior partner was to have one-third of the profits of the practice, exclusive of the proceeds of Macdonald's retainer by the Commercial Bank of the Midland District, was an excellent arrangement which, from Macdonald's point of view, could hardly have been made more opportunely. Campbell, young, sober, conscientious, doggedly loyal, could be counted upon, as few men could have been, to maintain the practice which was Macdonald's one source of income and the necessary basis of his political career. The office was all right. If his family had been in as flourishing a condition, Macdonald would have been happy. But old Mrs. Macdonald, despite her iron will and her enormous vitality, was frailer now; and what was worse, infinitely worse, was that Isabella, "Isa", the healthy, happy bride of only a little over a year before, was suffering from occasional and debilitating attacks of illness.

Some time in the last week of November, Macdonald strolled down the streets of Montreal to take his first view of the new provincial parliament buildings. Kingston had built an extravagantly splendid town hall for the benefit of an ungrateful provincial legislature. But Montreal, well looked after by Providence, in the shape of Lafontaine and his impressive phalanx of French-Canadian votes, had not the slightest need to extend itself in this fashion; and all it did was to lease a market building to the Canadian government, which the Canadian government —with the advice, once again, of the inevitable architect, George Browne—proceeded to rearrange and redecorate at its own expense. The new parliament house—it had been called St. Ann's Market—stood just east of McGill Street in the wide irregular square since known as Place Youville. It was a long, low, narrow, two-storey building, with a pillared portico at each end, and a slight elevation in the centre which broke the roof-line without rising to the stature of a proper tower.[2] The ground floor, with its spacious hall in the centre of the building, and its long corridors running from end to end, was crowded with the offices of government. The first floor was occupied by the two assembly halls, the Council chamber in the east wing, the Legislative Assembly room in the west wing towards McGill Street, and each with its appropriate complement of robing-room, lounge, and bar. On the afternoon of Thursday, November 28, Macdonald took his seat for the first time in the Legislative Assembly, and shortly after, he and thirty-eight Conservatives elected Sir Allan Napier MacNab as their Speaker.[3]

As Macdonald sat, a relatively inconspicuous back-bencher, in his place in the St. Ann's Market building, two obvious things about the Conservative majority in the House must have struck him immediately. In the first place, the majority was very small; and in the second, it was almost exclusively English-speaking. The Conservatives elected MacNab to the Speaker's chair by thirty-nine to thirty-six votes; and though their majorities improved slightly during the next week or so, this first division was to remain an unhappily accurate revelation of the precarious margin of Tory power. The party drew almost no support from French Canada. Only a very few odd, unrepresentative French Canadians, who promptly forfeited the support of their old followers, and who were popularly despised by their compatriots as renegades and *vendus*, were to be found voting with the government in the first crucial divisions of the session. The towns—the "rotten boroughs" as the Reformers called them—had gone solidly Tory, with the exception of Quebec. In the far east, in the English-speaking districts of the Eastern Townships, the Conservatives had carried every seat; and in the far west, in the great peninsula between Lake Erie and Lake Huron, where American influences were regrettably strong and Reformist delusions notoriously influential, they had succeeded in taking Kent, Oxford, Middlesex, Huron, Simcoe, South Lincoln, and the two Haltons, East and West. In the main, however, the strength of the Conservative party lay, where it had always lain before, in the long narrow strip of farming country, homeland of the first Loyalist settlements, which stretched from Toronto eastward to the old interprovincial boundary. In fact, what the Conservatives had really done in the election of 1844 was to maximize their ancient strength.

The limitations of that strength were painfully apparent to Macdonald, as to others. He realized that the Conservative party, as then constituted, was a weak party. As time passed and he gradually acclimatized himself to the legislature and got to know his fellow party members, he became aware of another, and perhaps even more serious, defect in the structure of provincial Conservatism. The party was not only weak; it was also divided. It was struggling with difficulty through the first, perilous period of a great metamorphosis, and it hovered ambiguously, painfully, between its old and new selves, between the Toryism of the past and the Liberal Conservatism of the future. On the one hand were the Liberal Tories, distinctly the larger group in the party, but composed, for the most part, of men who were either young or relatively unknown. On the other hand were the surviving members of the Family Compact and the Chateau Clique—men like Badgeley, Hale, and Moffatt from Canada East, like MacNab, Boulton, Robinson, and the Sherwood brothers from Canada West. Despite everything that the moderates and the Governor could do, these relics of the past—surprisingly young, some of them, and surprisingly alive —had forced their way back into the centre of affairs. In the administration which Metcalfe had formed, back in September, 1844, not a single one of the old Conservative names had been included; but after the election, and after the upsurge of primitive Tory strength which it witnessed, the representatives of the old oligarchies could no longer be disregarded with impunity. Sir Allan MacNab, stout, hearty, emptily genial, was made Speaker; W. B. Robinson, brother of the old Chief Justice, Sir John Beverley Robinson, was given the portfolio of Inspector-General; and Henry Sherwood, one of the Toronto members, a young man, younger than Macdonald, with straight features, and curly hair, and an expression of arrogant assertiveness, was appointed to the solicitor-generalship, though without a seat at the Council board.

From the beginning, Macdonald must have regarded these men as doubtful and difficult friends. His background and all his early associations had made him a moderate, a Sydenhamite; and, once inside the Assembly, he gravitated immediately to the Liberal Conservative wing. Some of its members he knew already. William Morris, the defender of the Scottish Church and the patron of Queen's University, who held a seat in the Legislative Council, was probably an old acquaintance; and Ogle Robert Gowan, the Grand Master of the Orange Lodge, a man who combined the airs of a demagogue with the practices of a cool realist, was one of the key members of the Assembly with whom Macdonald quickly struck up a firm and lasting association. But the man who, above all others in the party, became Macdonald's leader and inspiration during the early part of his career was William Henry Draper, the prophet of Liberal Conservatism on Canadian earth, if Sydenham and Metcalfe were its presiding deities in the imperial heaven. Draper was an interesting and complex person who, despite the unimpeachable respectability of his origins, views, and habits, had had an adventurous career.[4] The son of a Church of England clergyman, brought up in a remote rural parish in Devon, he had run away to sea when he was a mere boy, had served, for some years, in an East India merchantman, and had turned up in Canada in 1820, when he was nineteen years old. At first his activities in the New World seemed unremarkable and were certainly unnoticed. He taught school in Port Hope. He studied law. And then, one fortunate day, shortly after he had been admitted to the bar, he was noticed favourably at the Cobourg assizes by no less a person than the great John Beverley Robinson himself, then Attorney-General of the province. Robinson—a man not given to facile enthusiasms—was impressed; he determined to persuade the clever young man to enter his Toronto office. And from then on, Draper's career was made. He became a Member of Parliament, the colonel of a York militia regiment, Solicitor-General and then Attorney-General in succession to Hagerman. And now, under Governor Metcalfe, he was back at his old post of the attorney-generalship once more.

Macdonald had met Draper for the first time professionally at the autumn assizes of the Midland District in 1837. Draper had acted also as Judge-Advocate in the trial of Von Schoultz and the other "pirate" prisoners caught in the battle at Windmill Point in the autumn of 1838; and his physical presence and public manner must have been perfectly familiar to Macdonald long before the opening of the first session of the new parliament in 1844. Draper was a big man, with a rugged, resilient frame, a capacity for brisk, long walks, and a considerable prowess at cricket which he played with zest until he was quite old. To his followers, if not to all his contemporaries, he must have seemed a genuinely distinguished man. Cultivated, urbane, learned in the law, skilled in languages both ancient and modern, with a talent for lucid, if elaborate, exposition and a persuasive eloquence which earned him the title of "Sweet William", he might have seemed designed by Providence to lead the Tory party out of the old ways of routine and into the rewarding paths of experiment. Macdonald and the young moderates certainly accepted his leadership eagerly. Moreover, Draper's poise, his learning, his devout Anglicanism, and the irreproachable respectability of his professional connections in Toronto—all ought to have endeared him to the members of the Old Guard. Yet they obviously did not. The Toronto Tories may have been jealous of this successful young interloper from overseas. They certainly disliked him. They intrigued against him. And Macdonald had not been a member of the Legislative Assembly for more than a few weeks when it must have become perfectly clear to him that there could be no genuine negotiated peace between Draper and the Old Guard, and that the war between them—a war both of personalities and of principles—was certain to continue as a struggle for extermination. Macdonald became a devoted follower of Draper. He and the other moderates viewed their distinguished leader with a respect, a hope, and a confidence in which there was only one small flaw of doubt. Draper would infallibly succeed —if only he fought the struggle out to a conclusion. But could he be persuaded to continue? It was known that he had accepted office under Metcalfe reluctantly and as a matter of public duty. He was inclined to view the indecorous hurly-burly of democratic politics with an old-fashioned and fastidious aversion. He grew tired of the open quarrelling and the incessant subterranean intrigue. His eye wandered wistfully towards the seclusion of the bench and the legal library—towards the calm and unhurried composition of those elaborate judicial opinions, full of exact definitions, refined distinctions and learned allusions, which he did so well and enjoyed so much.

II

Macdonald had to familiarize himself with the large strategy of these conflicts between principles and personalities as well as with the detailed tactics of party manoeuvre inside the House. Newly elected, a humble back-bencher, inexperienced yet not intimidated, and never disposed to take himself or anybody else too seriously, he made his way slowly and cautiously through new and difficult situations. From the start he was a fairly good parliamentarian, sensibly obedient to party whips, present unfailingly at every important division. But during his first two sessions, he spoke only at rare intervals and with modest brevity. Yet he was by no means afraid to catch the Speaker's eye; and it was characteristic of him that he seemed even readier to enter the hurly-burly of debate, to take part, as few novices did, in the frightening business of exchange and parry, than to deliver a set prepared oration before a nodding House. The session was barely three weeks old when, on November 19, he made his first intervention.[5] The debate concerned a controverted election, an important election in the urban constituency of Montreal, and one by one the leaders on both sides had risen to attack or defend the petition which had been presented against it. The ample Baldwin, Reform leader for Canada West, with his solemn, slightly Pecksniffian air of conscious rectitude, had just sat down when the young member for Kingston arose to make his maiden speech. Macdonald knew the election law; he was well equipped with the precedents. Calmly, logically, in a brief speech of a few paragraphs, he proceeded to demolish the validity of the petition against the Montreal election. He was the only new member who had ventured to take part in a debate which had been almost monopolized by the great names on both sides; but curiously enough, he was not crowded back into obscurity and forgotten. "Mr. Macdonald, who moved the adjournment," wrote the reporter in the great *Montreal Gazette*, "is evidently not used to parliamentary debate, but he as evidently has the stuff in him. He gathered up the scattered strands of argument with great dexterity, and knitted them up like a man used to the work of reply."⁶

This was one Macdonald—the skilful practitioner of the Midland District courts, the adroit parliamentary tactician of the future. Yet there was another Macdonald, the student, the reader of learned reviews and books, the reasoning, theoretical conservative who had grounded his beliefs on history and philosophy; and this Macdonald, who, to Tom Ramsay, and Alex Campbell and Charles Stuart, must have seemed the real man, had at least one chance to show himself in the session of 1844-45. Late in January, when the House had nearly finished its debate on Roblin's bill for the equal distribution of intestate estates in Canada West, Macdonald rose to speak. To him, as to Burke, any serious change in the established law of private property implied, without any question, the utter subversion of the existing social and political order. His speech was an elaborate one, full of echoes of Burke, and references to *Blackwood's* and the learned reviews, and appeals to the great names of English history. "The great majority of the people," he declared, "were against this measure as anti-British and anti-Monarchical; it ought not to be introduced here, for the very reason that it had been introduced into the United States; and it was folly to raise a monarchical structure upon a republican foundation. The law of primogeniture was the great bulwark between the people and the Crown and the Crown and the people."⁷ Primogeniture was an essential basis of the constitution; it was a vital principle of political economy. The measure before the House, like all other such measures, was calculated to make "that which was a comfortable farmhouse in one generation, a cottage in the second, and a hovel in the third; and, under it, agriculture, instead of becoming a science, would be degraded, as it was in Ireland and France, to a mere means of life." The best economic authorities were opposed to such a division of lands; and the experience of the United States had amply demonstrated the evils of the partition law. "The greatness of England," Macdonald went on, rounding into his peroration, "was owing to its younger sons; it was they who had spread the name, the fame, and the glory of England all over the world—they formed its colonies, led its armies and navies—they were its statesmen and its scholars . . . What would have been the younger Pitt or Fox, if, instead of being sent forth to seek their fortunes, the estate of their father had been divided? They would have been mere country squires, instead of becoming, as they did, the lights of the world. What would the Duke of Wellington have been, if the paternal estate had been divided? It was fortunate for him, for his country, and the world, that he was left with his sword in his hand, and that sword all he had."[8]

This was a special effort, not repeated in the first session. He would never be famous for his oratory alone. Yet the gift for an occasional good speech was one item in the extended list of assets which was gradually making him known as a good parliamentarian. Rapidly he came to possess a cool and disconcertingly exact knowledge of the rules; and sometimes, when the Assembly became a turbulent verbal milling ground, he could intervene with devastating effect. On a day in mid-February, when Moffatt, goaded by Aylwin's repeated interruptions, had finally protested and when the House became at once a babel of excited controversy, it was Macdonald who gave generalship to the Tories and who gradually pushed Aylwin back from one humiliation to another.[9] He was at his best—cool and resourceful—in these encounters. He was efficient also in the more humdrum work of committee. The House—its rules, its ways, its members, and their varied interests and contrasted backgrounds—were all becoming an intimate part of his consciousness. Easily, almost effortlessly, he was compiling the first important pages of that vast catalogue of names, faces, personalities, constituencies, institutions, associations and churches, which he came to know so intimately, and which served him so well until the end.

He was an important acquisition for the party. As one of Draper's young men, he was an important addition to the ranks of the moderates. But Liberal Conservatism was still ringed round with enemies, Tories as well as Reformers; and as the session wore on it became lamentably clear how far the modernists were from dominating their party and how weak and distracted it still remained. Draper was determined to settle the university question—the problem of King's College, with its enormous endowment, and of the newer sectarian colleges, Queen's, Victoria, and Regiopolis. This question of higher education in the province, which involved the basic issues of the relation of church and state and the connection between science and religion, was the one thing, above all others, which was almost certain to drive the Anglican Tories, the supporters of King's and its vast exclusive endowment, into furious opposition against their moderate leaders. Yet the question was an important one, long and violently agitated in the province, clamouring for settlement; and Draper did not see how he could possibly avoid it. In his urbane gentlemanly way, he tried to compromise. The Reformers, under Baldwin, had hoped to establish a single, great, non-sectarian university, completely controlled by the state and its appointees; a university in which the colleges were to be reduced to the level of divinity halls. The Conservatives, who got their educational ideals from England rather than from Scotland and the Continent, believed in colleges as well as in a university, in tutorials as much as lectures, in academic management more than in external control, and in church influence rather than in irreligious secular authority. Draper tried to steer a tactful course between these two extremes. To placate the High Tories, he re-introduced a moderate religious test, gave the colleges a larger place in the life of the university, and strengthened its academic control. To please his own moderate followers—and possibly also to gain a few Reform votes—he kept all the main features of the Baldwin measure, the unification and centralization of higher learning, and the division of the university endowment, hitherto enjoyed solely by King's.[10]

Macdonald had all Draper's interest in the university question. Like Draper, he believed that the Conservative party should tackle and settle the problem; and the debate which followed the introduction of Draper's bill must, for him, have been a dismaying revelation of the difficulties in the way. Robinson, the Inspector-General, resigned his portfolio in protest against the government's policy. W. H. Boulton and George Sherwood of Brockville felt perfectly free, despite their recognized political affiliations, to oppose the measure on the floor of the House, and even dared, with insolent discourtesy, to move the six months' hoist for the second reading.[11] Draper was furious. Despite his mellifluous voice and his suave, urbane manner, there was a strain of quick, combative emotionalism in the man who long ago had run away to sea. " . . . To allow the bill to be stopped before its second reading," he cried, "and to permit the whole proceedings of the House to be stultified—never, Sir, will I hold office on such terms."[12] Outwardly, it was a bold defiance; and yet, in reality, Draper had been forced to yield. The possibility—indeed, the probability—that a premature and violent breach with the Toronto Tories might involve the complete break-up of the party and the utter ruin of all his hopes, hovered alarmingly before him. It was not yet time to force the controversy to its climax. He drew back cautiously. The University Bills were postponed. It was clear to Macdonald and the moderates that the crisis had been an abortive one, that the problem of leadership and direction was still unsolved, and that the whole future of the Conservative party rested in suspense.

III

Parliament was prorogued before the end of March and Macdonald was soon back in Kingston. The session, in many ways, had been a disappointing one; but these small concerns for the future of the party must have been quickly crowded from his mind by a host of personal troubles which rushed in upon him in the spring and early summer of 1845. His mother was gravely ill. Late that spring she suffered one of the first of a series of small apoplectic seizures which at intervals over a long period of time wracked her strong and enduring frame. "Oh, God," wrote Isabella, "it was dreadful to see her face so twisted."[13] Yet the twisted face recovered its serene composure, and the iron constitution survived; and it was not the indomitable old woman but the young wife who had caused

Macdonald's worries to grow so horribly out of nothing during the past few months. Isa was not well—far from well. She had been very ill indeed. And already, less than two years after her marriage, less than a year after her happy visit to her sister Margaret Greene in the summer of 1844, the pattern of this dreadful recurring illness had become established and known in all its details. Her attacks came at intervals, rising in spasms to terrible climaxes, which left her exhausted, sunk in complete prostration, incapable almost of moving, or of bearing the company of anybody but those she loved the most.

Yet, in the spring and early summer of 1845, she was, apparently, much better; and Macdonald planned to carry her off again to visit her sister, Margaret, who was living now in New Haven, and to whom she was very devoted. Old Mrs. Macdonald's seizure postponed the visit for some time, and then Macdonald had to go to Toronto on professional business. But it was all arranged that they would set out as soon as he returned; and on June 11, just at the beginning of summer, Isa was writing happily to her sister, giving her all the family news, chattering about lavender bonnets and yellow stockings, and promising that she and John would leave Kingston for the United States shortly after the 21st of the month.[14] She never finished and sealed the letter. The crisis came, and seemed to pass; and with its passing there followed the inevitable debility, which this time did not improve but deepened into an appalling exhaustion. On July 12, Macdonald faced the medical man, old Dr. Sampson, who had dealt with the troubles of so many Kingstonians; and Sampson told him that he could do no more. "God bless and protect both of you, my beloved sisters," Macdonald wrote to Margaret, "and enable you to meet the impending anguish with fortitude and resignation."[15] That day he expected her to die. And even if she did live, live at least for a little time, what chance did they really have of winning this race against time, this race for the warm air and the long sunlight of the south, which now, he had come to believe, held out the one real hope for her recovery? "It may be days—nay, weeks—before she has rallied sufficiently to attempt any journey. What to say or do, I know not. The summer is wearing away and may have nearly terminated before the invalid can be moved."[16]

The warm, pleasant edifice of his domestic happiness was crumbling towards utter ruin. He waited, planning and hoping, drawing on the cool, deep reserves of his fortitude. There was —or seemed to be—one last chance; and suddenly he took it, though the risks involved were frightful. Less than a week after the crisis, at the first fluttering, barely perceptible sign of Isabella's returning health, they set out by steamboat for Oswego, to New Haven and the south. Moll and Lou were with them, and there was work for all to do as they carried the exhausted Isabella down to the dock. At the last moment they almost turned back. They had risked everything. It was a chance, a wild, dangerous chance; but Macdonald was convinced that it was the one hope of survival which remained to Isa. The boat put out. That day the lake was violently stormy. Macdonald was sick, they were all sick, Isabella dreadfully so. "We thought she would die on the deck."[17] And it was not until the dead of night, an hour after midnight, that they finally reached the Welland House in Oswego.

And yet, as she lay on the couch that morning, she seemed— faintly, miraculously—to be improved. Her pulse, her whole appearance were better than they had been just before leaving Kingston. Now, with no thought of turning back, they pushed ahead slowly but hopefully. All the summer and early autumn were spent with Annie and Margaret at New Haven, in prolonged recuperation; but the doctor, as Macdonald had anticipated, ordered Isabella south for the winter, and they were determined to reach Savannah, which was their ultimate goal, before the real coming of the cold. Some time late in October, Macdonald and Isabella set out again. The journey was incredibly long and involved, but Isabella bore its tortuous difficulties with a tranquil and patient resignation which became habitual with her. Shifted from railway to steamboat and back again to railway, borne over cobbled streets in jolting hacks, carried in chairs up the steep, twisting steps of a long succession of hotels, and sleeping, often drugged with opium to dull her pain, through long exhausted days in order to prepare herself for the next stage of the journey, she passed, with Macdonald always at her side, in a dim, long confusion of movement, distress and torpor, through Jersey City, Philadelphia, Baltimore, Wilmington, Charleston, and finally, after over two weeks of broken travel, to "this city of sandy streets and circular squares"—Savannah.

It was a terrible journey. But Macdonald was always helpful, almost always hopeful, almost always light-heartedly ready to find something—even if it were only his own awkward attentions to his wife—which awoke his ready humour or prompted amused, ironic comment. ". . . Annie and I do our d——dest (as the Methodists say) to make her comfortable," he wrote.[18] At Philadelphia, seduced temporarily "from my allegiance to my petticoat government", and carried off by a Mr. Robinson to a highly intellectual conversazione, he found that the champagne and the terrapin supper lingered even more pleasantly in his memory than the scientific and literary discussion.[19] Penned up in dull little hotel parlours and bedrooms, he galloped through a strange variety of books—*Tom Burke*, *The Bible in Spain*, *Rookwood*, Carlyle's *Life of Schiller*, Bishop Moore's *Sermons*, and Lord Mahon's *History of England*, which he found "impartial and amusing".[20] He was charmed and delighted, he told his sister-in-law Margaret cheerfully, by the prettiness of the women friends to whom she had written, and who called occasionally on Isabella on their journey south. "By the way, sister," he wrote, "there is a Latin proverb 'Noscitur a sociis' which may be translated for the benefit of the Country Members 'birds of a feather flock together'. I always considered you a *charming woman*, but I did not calculate on all your friends being so. From those I have seen, I have only to say, that you will confer a great favour on me by sitting down and writing me Letters of Credence to *every one* of your Yankee lady friends, and it will go hard but I deliver most of them."[21]

At Savannah, he established Isabella in rooms and set about getting a more comfortable permanent boarding-house. Within a few nights of his arrival, he was taken off to a Whig political meeting; but his views of the two-hour oration delivered by

one of the local judges were a trifle mixed. "He is evidently
an able man, with great fluency and force of expression," he
wrote, "but he has the great fault of American speakers (with,
I believe, the single exception of Webster) of being too
theatrical in manner, and turgid in style."[22] He continued to
prefer English to Yankee oratory; but he found, that night,
that the Americans could, at any rate, concoct a most acceptable
kind of peach brandy. It was pleasant enough in Savannah,
and, if only there had been sufficient money, he would have
liked to stay and to have at least one "warm winter" in his life.
But that was quite impossible, and now he was impatient to be
away. Isabella was, of course, to remain with the southern sunlight which might cure her; and he comforted himself with the
thought that the faithful Margaret would soon come down
from New Haven to take his place beside the invalid. When
he first reached Savannah, late in November, he hoped and
expected to be able to leave by the beginning of the next month.
But Isabella's slow recovery from the terrible fatigues of the
journey must have delayed his departure. He was still in the
south on New Year's Day, and probably for some weeks thereafter. But some time early in February, back once more "among
the frosts and snows of Canada, sucking my paws like any other
bear", he was waiting for Isabella's letters, and reading with
pleasure Margaret's good news of the continued improvement
of her charge.[23]

IV

His absence had lasted six months. Altogether, counting his
long attendance at the first session of the provincial parliament,
he had been away from Kingston for by far the greater part
of 1845. The practice was undeniably suffering; and Campbell,
overburdened with work, was harried and inclined to be resentful. But though Macdonald's difficulties were accumulating,
and his expenses mounting in a frightening fashion, he showed
no sign of abandoning his parliamentary career; and when the
legislature met for the second time, late in March, he was in

his place as usual.[24] Outwardly his position and importance in
the House did not seem to have altered greatly; his speeches
were not more numerous nor very different in character. He
was, once again, the thoughtful young theorist, quoting freely
from Bentham and Sir James Mackintosh, when he defended
free trade in money against the old usury laws;[25] and his pro-
British nationalism reappeared in a new, economic dress when
he vigorously supported differential duties against imports from
the United States, claiming that it was American—not British—
manufacturers that the Canadians had to fear.[26] These infrequent public appearances were satisfactory enough; but they
were no index of the important place which he was gradually
and unostentatiously winning in the councils of the party. He
was one of Draper's most promising young men. Draper began
to realize it. And he looked upon the young member for Kingston with a fatherly benevolence.

It was at this point that Draper, weary, baffled, but indomitable, decided to make one more effort to strengthen the
government and to popularize the Conservative party. During
the previous summer he had attempted to gain the support of
the French Canadians by giving them a certain number of
places in the government. The attempt had finally failed. The
correspondence, betrayed to Lafontaine, was read triumphantly
to the House in April; and the whole affair had exploded in
the most lamentable and damaging publicity. Yet Draper was
not quite ready to give in. Even if the sullen, reluctant French
Canadians still remained unapproachable, he could at least
reorganize the existing government, secure the support of some
of the able young moderates, and openly dismiss the Tory in-
triguers who had successfully paralysed almost everything he
had tried to do. On June 10, 1846, the day after the Conservative government had finally pulled through its second,
lame parliamentary session, he wrote a long, confidential
memorandum to Lord Cathcart, the undistinguished nobleman
who had succeeded temporarily to the governor-generalship,
when Metcalfe, utterly overwhelmed by his terrible affliction,
had gone home to die.[27]

Only a "due infusion" of French Canadians, Draper insisted,

could make the government really strong; but, at any rate, it might be made less weak by the elimination of its inefficient and obstructive members, the incompetent Viger and the notoriously intriguing Sherwood. For the places thus left vacant, Draper made two definite recommendations: one was "a gentleman of great legal eminence, considerable talent, and irreproachable character"—later identified as John Hillyard Cameron, Macdonald's old fellow-pupil at John Cruickshank's school in Store Street. The other was John A. Macdonald himself. The Commissionership of Crown Lands—the office for which Draper recommended the member for Kingston—imperatively required "a man of activity of mind and familiar with business details". Macdonald's brisk efficiency, the easy swiftness with which, when it suited his purpose, he could get through masses of work must have impressed the harassed leader of the government; and if Draper had come to learn indirectly that, on an evening in the previous April, his prospective young lieutenant had spoken so disrespectfully of a member of the Boulton family that he had risked a duel with young William Henry Boulton, the Tory Toronto member,[28] he might have appeared outwardly shocked, but secretly he could hardly have helped being delighted. Macdonald was a good man—and sound on the Toronto "gang". But there was something else as well—something far more attractive and promising—the unmistakable first signs of charm and popularity, of political wisdom, and insight and tact—the accumulating, promising evidence, not only of open debate, of sober work in committee and caucus, but also of casual talks and convivial occasions, of little arrangements, and negotiations, and manoeuvres.

At the age of thirty-one, when he had had only two years' experience in parliament, Macdonald had been recommended for office under the Crown. Cathcart sanctioned the recommendation, writing to Draper that "the Governor-General has a very high opinion of Mr. J. A. Macdonald and his appointment to office in the administration would afford him much satisfaction".[29] But, for one reason or another, the appointment was not made at this time. Draper, still vainly pursuing his hoped-for alliance with the French, may have preferred to reserve the portfolio of the Crown Lands, pending a general reconstruction of his Cabinet; and it is just as likely that Macdonald himself was, at the moment, in no position to accept public office. He had overspent his income, overworked Campbell, and endangered the practice. The embarrassment of his position was plainly evident in September, 1846, when, after three years, the partnership arrangement came up for renewal.[30] Macdonald had to agree to pay his junior partner £500, in three annual instalments, as compensation for his own prolonged absences during the first period of the partnership. For the future, Campbell was to have one-third of the proceeds as before, but this time the third was to include the profits of the Commercial Bank business, hitherto reserved; and also—and this was a still more significant indication of Macdonald's vulnerable position—the head of the firm had to agree not to take more than £600 annually from the business during the next four years. Yet even these concessions were not all. For if, at the moment, Macdonald was obliged to forgo office, he was obviously thinking of it for the future—for a future not very far away. He agreed—and the concession was written formally into the new agreement—that if he accepted office, Campbell was to be allowed an additional annual payment of £250, beginning in June, 1847. Macdonald was in no position to drive a good bargain. He had piled a staggering burden of personal responsibilities and political ambitions on his neglected practice and long-suffering partner; and during the summer and autumn, he must have stuck closely to Kingston, slaving away at his desk. Isabella was still in the United States. During the greater part of 1846, she probably remained in Savannah, at Mrs. Hardie's boarding-house, improving slowly and with frequent setbacks; and then, possibly some time in the autumn, she was moved north to New York, with the object, no doubt, of obtaining more expert medical attention and more systematic treatment. There Macdonald visited her for the Christmas holiday season of 1846. They had been separated for very nearly a year.

On December 19, while he was away in New York, he was appointed Queen's Counsel, along with Thomas Kirkpatrick, one-time Mayor of Kingston, and Henry Smith, the member for Frontenac, who had acted with him in the famous Ashley-Dundas case. He treated his new honour with characteristic lightness of touch, informing Margaret Greene that it gave him "the *mighty* right of wearing a silk gown instead of a stuff one".[31] He was, however, pleased enough with the appointment, which came unsolicited and unexpected; and he must have read with interest the press comments on it, which, in their vituperative detail, were a sure indication of his growing consequence. "Mr. John A. Macdonald," declared the *Globe*, in its best vein of ferocious denigration, "stands some degrees below Mr. Kirkpatrick. Overlooking his short but discreditable political career, he is a man of perfect respectability—industrious, and successful in his profession—but far from possessing such talent as would warrant his being made a Queen's Counsel. He is, however, a Presbyterian Tory; of that species of respectable 'loose-fish' who denounce High Churchism and Family Compactism, and prate about opening King's College; who are guided more by *personal feeling* than by *principle,* and are prepared to *take office* under any administration, at the shortest notice".[32] Macdonald must have smiled with sardonic amusement. Overlooking (as the *Globe* would have said) the pert imputations and consistent depreciation, he had to admit that the picture of him which the Reform newspaper was industriously circulating, was both accurate and politically advantageous. Gradually, to both friends and foes alike, he was getting to be known as a moderate, as a "Presbyterian Tory", as a follower of William Henry Draper.

It was thus that Draper saw him. And Draper, approaching the final crisis of his political career, began to rely more and more upon his young subordinate, and to give him a larger and larger measure of his confidence. The position of the head of the government was becoming almost intolerable. Sherwood had been ejected from office; for the moment, the High Tories were held at bay; but the French Canadians, appealed to once more to join the government, had once more refused. Draper was sick of office. And then, before his longing eyes, he saw, slowly opening, the door of his escape. Judge Christopher

Alexander Hagerman, once Kingston's member and Attorney-General, was clearly at the point of death; and Draper, after all his services, could justly claim the right of succession. Yet he hesitated. "My thirst for relief from the responsibility of office . . . ," he wrote to Egerton Ryerson, "gets stronger and stronger. I should gladly avail myself of the first *just cause* to slake it, but I have not nerve enough to subject myself to the charge of weakening and perhaps breaking up the party Lord Metcalfe brought together by an act of personal desertion."[33] No! He would not leave yet. A new Governor, Lord Elgin, had arrived; and, under him, he would make one last effort to reorganize the government, to get the support of the French Canadians, and to strengthen the position of the moderates in the party. Macdonald would be useful to him—useful on his own account, useful also for his friendly association with Ogle Gowan, the Grand Master of the Orange Lodge, and one of the most popular and obstreperous opponents of the Family Compact in the party. He offered Macdonald the solicitor-generalship, which was refused. He begged Macdonald to pay a "flying visit" to Montreal, to persuade Gowan to accompany him, and to join with the Orangeman in the important work of convincing Lord Elgin that Conservatism did not necessarily mean ultra-Toryism.[34]

For Macdonald, all these political agitations—the arrival of Elgin, the threat of Draper's retirement, the approaching struggle within the party for the inheritance of leadership—coincided, with painful exactitude, with a crisis in his domestic affairs. He heard regularly from New York, for his own sister, Margaret, had gone down to look after Isabella; and early in January Isabella herself wrote him a note of congratulation, in her "trembling handwriting", for his birthday on the 11th. Then, just when she seemed to be improving, though slowly and with difficulty, a fresh complication was revealed. She had become pregnant. Late in March Margaret became so frightened at the state of her patient that she appealed for help. Macdonald rushed down to New York, taking with him Maria Macpherson, Isabella's sister, who, as the mother of a fine family, regarded herself as an expert in these matters, and who cheerfully volun-

teered to take Margaret's place. They found Isabella in a doubtful state. Her new medical adviser, Dr. Washington, reported
frankly that she was in a critical condition as a result of
repeated attacks of "uterine neuralgia". "These attacks . . . ,"
Macdonald wrote to Margaret Greene, "may bring on a premature confinement, and if so, God alone knows what may be
the consequence".³⁵ Isabella herself, lying all day in utter quiet,
was calm and resolute. Macdonald could not be always with
her, for the doctor would permit only one visitor at a time.
There was little he could do, besides. And, within a week, he
was on his way back to Kingston, carrying his consuming
anxiety with him.

When he arrived home, he found the Cabinet in the throes
of reconstruction and the opposition newspapers jubilantly
celebrating the embarrassments of the government and the
rivalries of the "Gowanites" and the "MacNabmen". Draper's
final effort to obtain the support of the French Canadians had
failed, like the others. But, inside the Cabinet, he and the
moderates were trying desperately to strengthen their position,
and, on May 6, William Morris wrote to Macdonald, offering
him the portfolio of Receiver-General, appealing for his assistance, and reminding him that "if you will not put your
shoulder to the wheel, you assist those who, it may be, desire to
regain power which you and I helped to deprive them of; I
mean the 'family'."³⁶ It was a cunningly worded appeal. And
Macdonald replied three days later, on the 9th. He accepted
office, on condition that Morris himself would remain in the
ministry, and with the hope that Draper might continue at least
until the end of the approaching session, and that his acquaintance, Gowan, might receive some political reward.³⁷ On May 11,
the perennial, unpolitical secretary, Dominick Daly, wrote, informing him that his commission had been issued on the same
day, and less than a fortnight later his appointment was
officially announced. The announcement created no great
uproar, either of delight or disapproval. The opposition papers
treated it with tolerant contempt. Macdonald was, the *Globe*
assured its readers, a "*harmless* man", a "third-class lawyer" who
had sat two sessions in parliament and "scarcely opened his

mouth during the whole time".[38] Yet Elgin, a fairly astute observer, was rather more flattering. "Since my last letter to you was despatched," he wrote to Grey, "the prospects of the administration are brighter—a certain Mr. Macdonald, a person of consideration among the *moderate Conservative, anti-Compact* Party has consented to accept the office of Receiver-General . . . ."[39]

He accepted it at a moment when the government was in the final agonies of reconstruction. During the last half of May, the fortnight which preceded the long-delayed opening of the legislature, the fortunes of the ultras and the moderates wavered backwards and forwards across the trampled battleground of the Conservative administration. Hagerman had died, Draper was determined to resign. And for his post, the attorney-generalship, the key post in the Cabinet, a successor would have to be found. Who was it to be? John Hillyard Cameron, the first invited, refused the office; and there was—or seemed to be—nobody else but Sherwood.[40] Less than a year before, Sherwood had been virtually dismissed from the office of solicitor-general. Now, on the heels of Draper's retirement, he entered the ministry again to occupy the post of leadership which his old rival had just vacated. It looked like a complete victory for the ultras. It looked as if the Tory party had openly and officially disavowed Draper's Liberal-Conservatism. But nothing in that period of Canadian Conservatism was ever conclusive or final. Draper might have abdicated, but he had appointed his successor. And Macdonald, as well as Morris, was there to carry on the fight for his tradition.

On June 2, when parliament opened, Macdonald took his seat on the treasury benches for the first time. He was badly worried during the first ten days at Montreal, for Isabella was drawing closer to her time, and he had no news from New York, except a scrap which had been forwarded from Kingston.[41] He was bothered too by the problems of his job, by the difficulties of an embarrassing session; and it must have given him a certain wry amusement to reflect that, just when he expected to become a father, he was to appear in parliament as the principal author of an important piece of government legislation. Back in May,

when he had written to Morris accepting office, he had insisted
that the university question was the great stumbling-block in
the path of the Conservatives, a stumbling-block which must
in some way be removed. "Many questions of more real importance may arise," he pointed out, "but none which operates
more strongly on the principles or prejudices of the public, and
if the Conservatives hope to retain power, they must settle it
before the general election." It was the first unmistakable sign
of his purposeful sense of direction, of his sensitive alertness
to popular demand. And for some reason, which can only be
guessed at with difficulty, for the purposes of that erratic and
distracted ministry are never easily explicable, he was given
the chance of settling the matter once and for all.

On Friday, July 9, he was on his feet to sponsor the first
government bills of his career.[42] His speech—brief, factual,
straightforward—was in utter contrast to the elaborate eloquence
of Draper.[43] Yet the terse, laconic exposition disclosed a policy
which was a better compromise, a compromise potentially far
more popular, than any that Draper had thought of. Daringly,
Macdonald rejected the plans of his old chief, and of his old
chief's great opponent, Baldwin. The idea of a unified, non-
sectarian, provincial university was abandoned. The principle
of collegiate organization and sectarian control, beloved of the
High Tories, became the main basis of Macdonald's plan.
King's College, which had been partly secularized by the amending statute of 1837, was to have its old charter restored to it
almost unchanged, and was to become once more a strictly
Church of England institution. All the colleges—King's, Queen's,
Victoria, and Regiopolis—would thus conform roughly to the
same pattern of clerical organization and management; and all
—this was the great popular feature of Macdonald's bill—were to
share in the splendid endowment. "Yet, in the division," Macdonald explained, "particular attention was to be paid to the
Church of England, for they have just and equitable claims".
Out of the annual revenue of the endowment, King's College,
which had once had the whole, was to be given £3000, and
the other colleges £1500 each. The plan was shrewd. More
than shrewd, it was wise. It was based on the idea—the idea

which commanded widespread support for this and another generation—that the union of science and religion was indissoluble. The claims of a wide variety of communions for government support in their educational work were generously recognized; and yet a fair preference had been given to the historic rights of the Church of England.

For the moment, the success of the bills looked comfortably certain. Macdonald appeared to have achieved the impossible: he had united both sections of the Conservative party in the support of his measure. John Hillyard Cameron, though he gave a regretful glance backward to King's College as it once had been, declared that the plan was just and that he was prepared to accede to it.[44] Sherwood, who had opposed Draper's bills so bitterly two years before, promised his support. Boulton, the second of the Toronto Tories, amiably asserted that the bills would satisfy all parties. And, on the other side, Ogle Gowan, the anti-Compact moderate, had a flattering word of praise for his friend, the man who "should feel proud at having solved the problem that baffled so many others".[45] Yet had he solved it, had he really settled it? "Settling the question, indeed," cried Baldwin, with sombre indignation, "by sweeping the University from the face of the earth, and giving the Country, in its stead, a few paltry Institutions, in none of which could there be any pretensions to those attributes which it was the highest behest to a University to possess."[46] This kind of stuff might be expected from the secular-minded Reformers, though Macdonald hoped to detach a few Methodists from their number. But, when two supposedly faithful Conservatives unaccountably arose to make the same secular criticisms, then the young member on the treasury bench began to feel uneasy.

Oddly enough, yet not so oddly in view of the violent passions which the issue aroused, the debate had taken place on the first reading of the bills. They were postponed for a while; but they were due to come up again for consideration on July 26. And in the meantime, Macdonald, worried by the news which kept arriving from New York, tried anxiously to consider the position. It was the old, endless problem of the feeble Conservative majority, of the perilous insecurity of the government. He wrote gloomily to the Principal of Victoria College that two Methodist Reformers, whose support he had hoped for, would vote against the bill; the Roman Catholic Reformers were also in opposition; and, what was even worse, the two Conservatives, Dickson and Wilson, refused obstinately to be won round.[47] Regretfully he decided that the bills would have to be postponed, and that he must wait for the organization of popular support in their favour. He had failed—almost as badly as Draper, and for much the same reasons.

On Wednesday, July 28, two days after the second reading of the University Bills had been perfunctorily discharged without debate, the legislature was prorogued. Immediately, with few or no explanations to his political colleagues, he hastened back to Kingston; and along with Mrs. Harper he set out for New York. The frantic travellers arrived on Saturday to find Isabella reasonably well, and Maria elated at their coming. But they were only just in time. For the next day Isabella became obviously distressed, and Dr. Washington, hastily summoned in the evening, declared that she was in labour. For some hours she continued to suffer. And then, in desperation, they called in another physician, a Dr. Rodgers, "celebrated for the use and application of the *Lethean* or somnific gas". But Isabella's weak and nervously disordered state intimidated him, and he did not dare to give her enough of the gas to put her comfortably asleep. All night, and far into the morning of August 2, the long agony went on. At length it became only too clear that Isabella was unable to deliver herself. The doctors determined to use forceps, and, at a little after 8 o'clock in the morning, her child, a boy, apparently strong and healthy, was born. "The first word the poor thing said," Macdonald wrote to his mother, "after being informed that the child was alive and not deformed, was to tell me to write you and to ask you to give it a name—which in her name and my own I now do."[48]

Chapter Six

The Twilight of the Tory Party

I

The boy was thin. As Maria said to Dr. Washington, that was scarcely to be wondered at, since he had been living on pills so long. But he was tall, and seemed strong and healthy.[1] His eyes, dark blue in colour, were very large, and his nose— his father's nose—was generous also. They had not much chance to admire him, for he was whisked off almost immediately to Kingston by Maria; and Macdonald settled down in New York to watch anxiously over his wife's convalescence. It was very slow. The neuralgic pains in her side and leg kept recurring; and Macdonald, impatiently sceptical of the leeching and blistering which had been prescribed for her, called in another physician who varied the treatment. She seemed slowly to improve. Yet her condition was so vulnerable, and the improvement so uncertain and precarious that when the doctor finally suggested that she might try to walk across the room, this little convalescent's adventure ended in a violent return of pain, and a recourse, once more, to the old anodyne, opium.[2]

The long, aching apprehensions, the sudden, recurring seizures of fear, like spurts of pain, seemed never to end or to subside. He scarcely knew what to do. Campbell and the practice would have to get along as best they could; but he was a minister of the Crown now, at a critical moment in the history of the government, and he could not stay away indefinitely. Cayley, the new Inspector-General, wrote him considerately from Montreal, assuring him "from our colleagues and myself that we will cheerfully submit to a longer deprivation of your services and assistance here should the continued illness of Mrs. Macdonald claim your care, rather than add to your anxiety by pressing your return".[3] These assurances were kind, but they could not be presumed upon. Obviously he would have to return, and obviously also—however much they might wish it—Isabella could not accompany him. How was he to leave her? The Macpherson-Clark women, who had come loyally to his assistance so often in the past, were now, for one reason or another, in no position to lend him aid. His sister Louisa was ill; his mother, attacked once again by an apoplectic seizure, and still weak and prostrate, required her daughter Margaret's constant attention. Maria Macpherson had enough to do to cope with her own children and to look after the infant John Alexander Macdonald, so called after his father. And Isabella's other sisters, including the faithful Margaret Greene, were far away and unable to come. He would have to leave his wife, for a time at least, with strangers. He said good-bye to her—ill, lonely, frightened at the thought of his departure—and tore himself away.

Back in Montreal, living in lodgings, "quite solitary and miserable" and comforted mainly by the news of young John Alexander's flourishing progress, he picked up departmental routine and political strategy once more. The arrears were cleared up with his usual expedition; and he found administrative work acceptable enough, for there was enough of it to keep him from boredom without absorbing all his attention. The really perplexing problem, which occupied the ministry at intervals during the greater part of the autumn, was the lamentable condition of the Conservative government. On the one hand, though the existing parliament still had some time to run, it would be difficult and very humiliating politically to stagger through yet another session with such a shaky majority. On the other hand, though Lord Elgin's consent to an early dissolution could probably be secured, the government would certainly run a very good chance of defeat at a general election. There was no doubt that the ministers were caught, partly by their own failures—the University Bills being the most notorious example—and partly by the general commercial depression, which neither they, nor anybody else in Canada, could conceivably have avoided. Already, during the whole of 1846, the timber trade had been seriously depressed. The first season which followed the repeal of the British Corn Laws was, to be sure, a good one for Canadian agriculture, for the terrible scarcity in the British Isles which had, indeed, dictated Peel's measure, created, for a time, an apparently bottomless demand for food-stuffs from North America. Prices kept up fairly well during the first few months of 1847; and then, with the dead weight of a stone, they dropped. By the autumn of the year, the whole province, and the whole of British North America, was becalmed in a windless commercial stagnation.

All autumn, Macdonald and his colleagues looked doubtfully at the problem, backed away from it, and returned to continue their morbid scrutiny. In the end they decided in favour of a dissolution. It was a choice between two evils, almost a choice between lingering and sudden death; but the ministry preferred the quick way, even though some of its members may have felt sure that their action amounted to political suicide. As early as October 30, Macdonald wrote H. D. Jessup of Grenville, informing him that a dissolution had already been under serious consideration;[4] and a few days later the first rumour of a general election began to appear in the Kingston newspapers. Parliament was not finally dissolved and the new writs issued until early in December; but at least a week before that Macdonald was back in Kingston, organizing his campaign. It was good to escape from his gloomy bachelor quarters and to be back with the family once again; and although Isabella still lingered in New York—for now it had been determined that she must spend another winter there—he could at least solace himself with the pleasant sight of young John Alexander, a sturdy little thing, nearly four months old. But he was very busy in Kingston. Now, it seemed, he might have a real fight on his hands.

Though the Reformers put up a candidate, a relatively unknown young man named Kenneth Mackenzie, this familiar type of opposition probably did not cause Macdonald a great deal of concern. What really gave him pause was the proposed candidature of Thomas Kirkpatrick—a disconcerting and preposterous candidature which threatened to divide the Conservative vote.[5] The trouble with Kirkpatrick was that he was —or would have been in other circumstances—such an unexceptionable candidate. A Conservative like Macdonald, quite as well known and apparently as popular—for at the time he was Kingston's Mayor—Kirkpatrick had, in addition, a special claim upon the Irish vote; and the Irish vote, as Manahan had demonstrated in 1841 in his contest with Forsyth, was important enough to cause the Conservative newspapers grave concern. The *Chronicle and News* reminded its readers that union was strength, deplored the possibility of an unnatural blow aimed "at the vitality of our existence as a Conservative Constituency", and roundly asserted that "no Conservative, who understands his duty, as such, will for a moment countenance a division as Mr. Kirkpatrick threatens".[6] Mr. Kirkpatrick began to realize that he had no press, but a good deal of opprobrium, in Kingston. He thought twice about the matter and retired.

Macdonald, as might have been expected, built most of his campaign around the University Bill. It was his bill, it was one of the government's most popular measures, and, above all, it had an intimate and direct connection with his constituency, for—by a special dispensation of Providence—two of the institutions, Queen's and Regiopolis, which were to be granted support under the new scheme, were actually situated in Kingston. The Radicals, uncomfortably aware of these circumstances, labelled Macdonald as a designing Tory "of the Draper, or crafty school", denounced his bill as a bill of "proscription, of injustice, and delusion", and tried to explain how it had deceived the Roman Catholics, Methodists, and Scots Presbyterians, and utterly proscribed the Baptists, Free Kirkers, and Episcopal Methodists.[7] These blows, watched by Kingstonians without much interest or alarm, did not drive Macdonald back upon the defensive. On December 20, when he addressed a large crowd of his supporters at one of the final meetings of the campaign, he was still dwelling proudly on the positive advantages which the lucky Kingston would derive from his measure.[8] He gave a brief, sidelong glance of disapproval at Baldwin's "great godless university, in which it was proposed to teach men everything but that which it most concerned them to know". Religion, the bond of social union, the preparation for the life hereafter, was the essential basis of all education. It was the basis of his plan; and his plan had secured the support of all religious authorities, Anglican, Presbyterian, Methodist, and Roman Catholic. No Christian communion was excluded from its benefits, as the Reformers had unjustly claimed; if other colleges, under other religious authorities, were established and obtained charters, they might participate, along with the original beneficiaries, in the proceeds of the endowment. His plan, which embraced all communions and all classes, was aimed at bringing education within the reach of the mass of the people. Earlier university bills had designed "one great institution at Toronto, inaccessible to the great body of the people"; but he, believing that parents would prefer to have their sons educated under their own supervision rather than to send them to Toronto from all parts of the province, had tried to place the advantages of an education within easy reach of all.

On December 22, at the nomination meeting, which was invaded by a large crowd of enthusiasts, many of them without votes, the show of hands seemed to be in favour of Mackenzie. "Mr. Macdonald is truly chop-fallen", exulted the *Kingston Herald*.[9] But Macdonald had suffered exactly the same small tactical defeat in his contest with Manahan; and as he said on the hustings, after the poll had been demanded, "he was quite content to take the voters, and to give his opponent all the advantage he could possess by enjoying the confidence of the remainder".[10] The voters in fact rolled up in impressive numbers in Macdonald's favour when the poll opened at 9 o'clock on December 28. And when, on the following day, it finally closed, the vote stood 386 for Macdonald to 84 for Mackenzie.[11] It was nearly, though not quite, as bad a defeat as Manahan's had been.

Yet, unfortunately, Macdonald's success was completely untypical of the fortunes of the Conservative party as a whole. Nearly two months later, on February 28, when the new parliament met in Montreal for its first session, the wastage of Conservatism was apparent all too literally in the flesh. Many of the leaders—MacNab, Cayley, Cameron, Robinson, Boulton, the Sherwoods, as well as Macdonald himself—had all been safely returned; but the truth was—there could be no denying it—that the party had actually been cut to about half its strength in the previous House. There were no French Canadians and virtually no westerners who voted on the Conservative side in the opening divisions. The party, now wholly English-speaking, had been reduced to its primitive Loyalist nucleus; and for the government there was no escape from defeat. In a few days, it came. On February 25, MacNab failed of re-election as Speaker by a vote of 54 to 19; and on March 3, Baldwin's amendment to the address in reply to the speech from the throne was carried by 54 to 20.[12] The next day the entire ministry resigned. Macdonald was a free man, and within a month—for the rest of the brief, uninteresting session was over before the end of March—he was back in Kingston again.

II

The first spring days had come by then, and the great event of the early summer was the long-awaited return of Isabella. It was in June, 1848, nearly three years after the terrible day in July when they had set out for Oswego by the steamer, that she finally arrived back in Kingston. Her longing for her husband and for young John Alexander, her desperate, continually thwarted desire to begin the only life that mattered to her once more, had sustained her to the end; and, as Macdonald reported, "she bore the journey wonderfully well". But the reaction was swift and disconcertingly severe. For days she lay in her half-darkened room, sunk in lassitude and discomfort, overcome by the excitements and fatigues of the journey, capable only of the exertion of sitting up for about ten minutes each day, and occasionally drugging her pain with opium. At first the boy was shy with her. Weak as she was, "she could not dandle him, or toss him about—a ceremony which the young gentleman insists upon from all who approach him".[13] This strangeness must have hurt her a little, even in her torpor. But soon, as she grew slightly better, Macdonald reported that they had become great friends, and the baby used to sit "most contentedly in the bed with her, surrounded by his toys, which he throws about, much to her inconvenience, I am sure, though she will not allow it". She watched him with all the starved, fierce intensity of her emotional nature, watched him while he played with happy aimlessness beside her, bent over his small face when he fell so suddenly asleep. "Oh! darling, darling sister," she confessed, "my very soul is bound up in him. God pardon me if I sin in this. But did I not purchase him dearly?"[14] Now he was nearly a year old—a fine little boy "in high spirits and in capital condition". "Certainly," Macdonald reported proudly, "there never was a child who has got through his first year with less trouble or illness of any kind. God grant it may continue so."[15]

These were happy days of reunion. And yet as he watched Isabella and talked with her in the dim room, Macdonald grew more and more profoundly uneasy. The recurring neuralgia, the sudden violent attacks of pain, the opium, and the drear lassitude of recovery—all these, though dreadful, were known, familiar, even tolerable, for they had been borne so often before. But now there was something new—a small matter, perhaps, small at any rate in comparison with her accustomed miseries, but terrible in its sinister significance. Even before she had left New York she had been troubled by an occasional pain in her chest and a slight cough; and on her way up to Kingston, in the middle of June, she had unaccountably caught cold. For the first week after her arrival, the cough, though still not hacking or exhausting, was almost incessant; and although a new prescription which Dr. Hayward of Kingston supplied seemed for a while to give her some relief, the cough never completely disappeared. Once or twice, on the journey up from New York, she had discovered blood upon her handkerchief; and now at intervals, the small stains reappeared. The doctors conducted long examinations, failed to discover any signs of serious, permanent affection, and, for a while, talked soothingly about the fatigues and excitements of the journey. Her pulse was not feverish; there was no hectic flush on her cheek. But obviously, as the medical men admitted in the end, there must be some tenderness which time, and nature, and local remedies, it was hoped, would cure. Macdonald remained disquieted. "I fear," he wrote his sister-in-law, "I fear."[16]

If rest, and peace, and fresh air would help to cure her, he was determined that they should be hers. Some little distance from town, half-way down the long hill which sloped towards Lake Ontario, there stood a large, absurdly ornate "villa", with two long wings at right angles to each other, and, at the centre, a square, incongruous tower, which seemed almost to have a separate and disconnected existence of its own. The rent would certainly be heavy; and already—for there were servants and a nurse for the child—he was probably spending up to the limit of his income. But whatever financial worries he may have had were concealed under an easy flow of raillery at the expense of the architectural horror, "the most fantastic concern imaginable", which he proposed to rent. It had been built, he explained, by a retired grocer, who had dreamed romantically of an "Eyetalian Willar"; and in Kingston it was variously known—from the "laudable tho' rather prosaic pursuits of the worthy landlord"— as Tea Caddy Castle, Molasses Hall, and Muscovado Cottage.[17] Macdonald called it "Pekoe Pagoda" to his intimates and named it "Bellevue" for public consumption. They moved out towards the end of August. It was very quiet there, and the trees grew thick about the place, and a sweet fresh breeze blew in from Lake Ontario. The short journey—it was less than a mile from home—had exhausted Isabella and brought on a return of her neuralgia. But Macdonald was still sanguine that she would improve rapidly in the new surroundings. The boy was fine. "He sits by the hour now with his mother, as contentedly as possible," he wrote, "and smiles and crows away from one end of the day to the other."[18]

They had nearly a month of quiet happiness in Pekoe Pagoda. And then, on September 21, 1848, young John Alexander died. "Convulsions", a sudden, terrible fall—the accounts of the tragedy differ; and the newspaper notices simply announced the

death of "the infant son of the Hon. John A. Macdonald".[19]
He had lost his child; he never expected now to have another;
and the hope which still mitigated the enormous concern he
felt for his wife was sustained as much by his stubborn will as
by the warm, strong current of his sanguine temperament. That
dark autumn he and Isabella drew even closer together in their
loneliness. In October—far too soon after the tragedy—he was
obliged to go to Toronto for a fortnight on professional business.
But Isabella, childishly eager to surprise and please him with
her improvement, practised sitting up a while each day during
his absence, and, the night he returned, a little table was brought
into her bedroom, and they dined in state together.[20] Gradually
the household began to approximate what still, after all their
misfortunes, must have seemed a delicious novelty—the ordinary
routine of family life. Macdonald became a typical, overworked
professional man, away to the office by nine o'clock in the
morning and absent until six at night; and Isabella, though she
was always confined to her room, and often—ill with pain—to
her bed, managed somehow, in her frail but persistent fashion,
to play the welcome role of housekeeper. And the house, under
her remote but methodical Scottish management, fell gracefully
into neat routines of order, regularity, and cleanliness. The
great event, the domestic climax of the day, was Macdonald's
dinner, "about which poor Isa takes the greatest pains". Sometimes he would draw her in on a chair to the table in the dining-
room; but often he sat there alone, eating a far too solitary meal.
Then, in the evening, he would read to her, while she lay with
a piece of sewing or knitting in her hand, and then it would
be tea-time and the day would be over.

The autumn passed with imperceptible and dismaying swiftness. It was December before they knew it, and parliament was
scheduled to meet in the following month. The very thought
of his absence, coming so swiftly after the death of their child,
distressed her pitiably. He almost decided not to go; but then
his stubborn loyalty to the party, in its period of trouble, reasserted itself, and he was not yet willing to abandon his own
political career. It was, he told his sister-in-law, "a matter of
necessity".[21] He would go; but not for long. And he set out

from Kingston, carrying the new waistcoat Isabella had made him, "which I am to sport as a winter vest".

III

He found his fellow-Conservatives in a black mood. In the Assembly, they were a pitiable minority, capable of mustering, at best, about twenty-five votes; and all over the province their old and stoutest supporters seemed crushed to earth by an accumulation of misfortunes. The depression, sullenly continuing, made the present almost unendurable; and the repeal of the British Corn Laws and Timber Duties, which at one stroke had ended Canada's old preferences in imperial markets, seemed to have cut short the hope of any real revival along traditional lines for the future. The Old Colonial System, to which the Tories had clung tenaciously in the past and which seemed at once the basis of their material success and the foundation of their old political supremacy, appeared to be tottering to its fall. The Canadian Conservatives acted like men who had been cheated of their inheritance and robbed of their faith. In the towns, and particularly in Montreal, where the depression was at its blackest, people began shamelessly to air strange, heterodox opinions and to bow down before outlandish pagan gods. There was discussion of protection to native industry, and a growing agitation for a wide reciprocal trade agreement with the United States, and even—this was the final apostasy—talk of annexation to the American republic. The Conservatives had reached these dangerous extremes, even before the meeting of parliament, even though they might have expected that there was more and worse to come. The ministry, now solidly Reform and backed by a solid Reform majority in the House, had been working out a great programme of new legislation ever since the brief perfunctory session of 1848. And one of the first measures to be introduced was Lafontaine's proposal to use public funds to compensate those persons in Lower Canada who had suffered property losses during the troubles of 1837 and 1838.

It was the Rebellion Losses Bill which completed the ruin of the old Tory philosophy and drove the Conservatives to the excesses of desperation. The bill, introduced first in the shape of seven resolutions, was a highly provocative measure, and, in all probability, intended as such by Lafontaine and his French-Canadian friends. The proposed benefits were apparently thrown open to everybody, without any defined exceptions whatever. Conceivably rebels who had sustained losses as a result of the action of the civil and military authorities might secure compensation just as easily as loyal citizens who had suffered at the hands of the rebels. To many people in Canada West, Reformers as well as Conservatives, the proposed bill meant, in effect, the formal annulment of the political decision of 1837 and the legitimization of the Lower Canadian revolts. The Tories were scandalized. This huge and shameless affront to their principles drove from their heads all prudent calculations of compromise with the French Canadians; and, without any reserves or qualifications or hesitations, they leaped upon what was for them the crucial point of the whole question. Did the government actually intend to compensate those who had taken part in the revolts? Did it—to take an embarrassing but pointed example—intend to pay over money to Dr. Wolfred Nelson, member for Richelieu, who had certainly, though ineffectually, tried to lead the rebels in 1837, and who afterwards, in 1845, had shyly presented a modest bill for £12,000 against the government he had defied by force of arms? All these interrogations and rhetorical questions were in vain. The government, either in embarrassment, or stubbornness, or complacency, remained silent. Even Dr. Nelson, who was occasionally goaded to reply by his tormentors, was scarcely more illuminating in his answers. Had not Nelson, inquired Sir Allan MacNab bluntly, been a "rank rebel" in 1837? "Not to my God," replied Dr. Nelson affectingly.[22] This removal of the whole question to the elevated plane of theology was scarcely calculated to advance its solution. Did Dr. Nelson's innocence before the Almighty entitle him to £12,000 from the government of the Province of Canada?

During two long sessions in committee while the debate centred, with ever mounting violence, upon the scandalous ambiguity of the measure, Macdonald maintained his accustomed silence. A fairly strict parliamentarian, not very much inclined to verbal heroics, he took no part in these emotional recriminations, these excited charges and counter-charges. But his temper was quick and occasionally it escaped from the cool control which he habitually imposed upon it; and his intervention in the debate of February 1849, when it finally came, was sudden and characteristic. It was William Hume Blake who goaded him to action. Blake, who came of a good family and who had been educated at Trinity College, Dublin, was a member of that cultivated and prosperous group of Anglo-Irish Reformers, led by the Baldwins, who repaid the supercilious disdain of the Family Compact with an equally cold and arrogant dislike. Elected for one of the York constituencies in the general election of 1847, he speedily came to be recognized as an acquisition of immense value to the Reform party; and on February 15, after MacNab, Sherwood, Gugy, and the other principal Tory speakers had had their prolonged say, he rose to attack the problem of Rebellion Losses. His speech, delivered in an assertive, dogmatic, passionate fashion, and with a prodigally copious flow of offensive Irish oratory, had lasted between two and three hours when it was suddenly interrupted. Blake, carried away by his invective, dared to call MacNab and his friends the real "rebels" of 1837! MacNab rose passionately to his feet. It was a falsehood, he shouted. The Speaker called him to order. MacNab insisted on repeating his statement, unless Blake would withdraw his. "Never!" cried Blake. A pandemonium of recriminations followed. The galleries erupted in fist fights; and the onlooking ladies, tumbling in charming disarray over the low barrier, were conducted by a gallant parliamentarian to the little island of safety behind the Speaker's chair.[28]

In this first skirmish, Macdonald took no part. But the events of February 15 were only a preliminary, for Blake had several thousand more words that he wanted to say; and next day, refreshed, and eager, and declamatory, he returned to the charge. Macdonald must have listened to him with rising impatience. Most parliamentary speeches left him tolerably unconcerned, if not cheerfully amused. But this was different. Blake's speech, which purported to be a long historical and legal review of the background of the rebellion, was so shamelessly vitiated by its evasions and omissions, and so grotesquely Irish in its rasping belligerency, that Macdonald grew white with Highland Scots fury. For long minutes he must have fidgeted and hesitated. And then, while Blake continued his interminable reading from old dispatches—garbling their contents, so the *Montreal Gazette* assured its readers, to "justify rebellion"— he could bear it no longer. He rose suddenly, to a point of order.[24]

"I should feel obliged," he remarked tensely, "by the honourable member reading all the words."

"What does the honourable member mean?" Blake inquired.

"I want the honourable member to read the whole of it," Macdonald explained. "I shall do it for him myself, if he wishes. Is it parliamentary, in reading documents, to leave out whole sentences and parts of sentences?"

MacNab jumped to his feet to support his lieutenant. Such a partial reading of documents, he declared, would certainly be considered irregular at Westminster.

Blake regarded them both with contemptuous defiance.

"I shall read any part I like," he declared.

The Speaker quieted the resulting uproar. Blake swept on his way, unchecked and unrepentant, and finished shortly after in a fierce peroration. The debate continued on a more humdrum and less provocative note. But, in the meantime, Macdonald had been busy. Duels, which had been a reality twenty-five years before, were still a diminishing possibility in the 1840's; and challenges, by which an explanation or an apology could frequently be extorted, were regarded with enormous seriousness. While the debate proceeded, Macdonald sent his challenge, his "threatening communication", and, shortly after, both he and Blake quietly left the Assembly hall. The Speaker was informed; the galleries were cleared of reporters and spectators; and the sergeant-at-arms, bearing the mace, went off solemnly to seek the culprits and to require their immediate attendance in the House. Macdonald was found, returned, and made his submission. But Blake, curiously enough, was not at home. Presumably, if the sergeant-at-arms was unable to find him, Macdonald's seconds would have been in a similar difficulty. It all ended happily on Monday, February 18, when the sergeant reported that he had also taken Mr. Blake into custody, and both repentant culprits bound themselves to keep the peace.[25]

The incident was over. And, as it turned out, the troubled passage of the Rebellion Losses Bill was nearly over as well. On February 22, Henry John Boulton, once a Conservative and now an independent Reformer eager for political preferment, introduced an important amendment to the resolutions— an amendment which he had actually persuaded Wolfred Nelson to second, and which had had the previous concurrence of the principal chiefs of the Reform party.[26] By the amendment, all those people in Lower Canada who had been convicted by the courts in 1837-38 or had been banished to Bermuda in accordance with Lord Durham's Ordinance, were excluded from the financial benefits of the proposed bill.[27] If the Conservatives had thought of this amendment, which was, in reality, the minimum amendment capable of satisfying Canada West, they might very well have overthrown the government. But Boulton, the busy, obsequious friend of the ministry, had forestalled them, and, once his device had been publicly accepted by the Reform leaders, the rank and file of the party, which up to that time had been dubious and reluctant, swung gratefully into line.

The passage of the Rebellion Losses Bill was now certain. Even so, the final debate on the subject lasted all through the night of Thursday, February 22, and on until nearly noon of Friday morning. Macdonald spoke late, when the long, all-night session was nearly over. This—his sole contribution of any length on the subject of Rebellion Losses—was a typical Macdonald speech, just as characteristic of his usual political strategy, as his brush with Blake had been typical of his hot Highland temperament. "They had been hurried into the consideration of the Resolutions," he declared, "without any notice, or without any explanation being given of the measure

. . .".[28] The ministers were now anxious to push the bill through in a hurry, because, if they waited, their supporters might be influenced by the rising popular clamour against it. The opposition, sure ultimately of popular support, would make no compromise; "they would speak when they liked, as long as they liked, and as often as they liked". Here the appeal was to popular opinion rather than to principle; and, indeed, Macdonald was one of the few leading Conservatives who did not take advantage of the Rebellion Losses Bill to fight the whole issue of the Rebellion all over again verbally.

He did not even witness—let alone participate in—the violent crisis which followed Lord Elgin's acceptance of the bill. Early in April, he secured leave of absence from the House. His ostensible reason was "urgent private business";[29] but it was probably Isabella as much as his practice that called him back. Although his leave, which was originally for fifteen days, does not seem to have been officially renewed, his name does not reappear in the proceedings until early in May. In the meantime Lord Elgin had signed the Rebellion Losses Bill, and the Conservatives were left in a mood of furious and self-destructive bewilderment. In their blind rage, they could not see that Lord Elgin had been wise and right to confirm responsible government by playing the constitutional role which it required of him; they only knew that they had relied upon a British governor to veto or reserve the bill, and that a British governor had failed them. Their unquestioned assumptions, their traditional beliefs, their hereditary loyalties, lay strewn about in the broken confusion of a rout; and grief and fury had planted their angry banners on the wreckage. For the Tories, "Elginism" had finished the dreadful work that "Cobdenism" had begun. The Rebellion Losses Bill was the political counterpart of the repeal of the Corn Laws; and the downfall of the Old Colonial System had been crowned and completed by the defeat of the Loyalists who had forfeited everything in its defence. After the passage of the Rebellion Losses Bill, Canada could no longer regard itself as a British province; and with the repeal of the Corn Laws, the reality of its membership in the British Empire had come to an end. It had become a foreign country, governed by an alien race. So the Conservatives felt rather than reasoned. And when, on April 25, Lord Elgin came in from Monklands to give his official acceptance to a number of measures, including the Rebellion Losses Bill, the Tory, anti-French mob of Montreal plunged into an orgy of violence and incendiarism which lasted for over a week. Macdonald did not, apparently, witness the blazing spectacle of the burning parliament buildings. He was absent on April 26, the morning after the fire, when the chastened Assembly met in the Bonsecours Market Place. Once again—though this time in an accidental fashion—he had been dissociated from the maddened extremism of his party.

IV

Yet he was far from being unaware of the baffled fury of the Conservatives, or indifferent to its serious implications. On May 1, when he was still at home on leave of absence, the Kingston Conservatives held a protest meeting in the city hall, with the Mayor in the chair. One by one Macdonald's friends and supporters—sober Tories such as J. R. Forsyth, John Counter, Major Logie, Joseph Bruce and his own partner, Alexander Campbell—arose to move strangely novel resolutions in strangely excited language.[30] It was true that they deplored the explosion of violence and the destruction of property at Montreal, and that they insisted that redress of grievances must be sought by legal and constitutional means only; but at the same time they resolved that the Governor-General had betrayed his trust and set at nought the wishes of the loyal inhabitants, that his recall was necessary, and that the only course now remaining was to petition the Queen to disallow the Rebellion Losses Act. All over the province such meetings were being held, such resolutions were being passed. All over the province, Conservatives, shaken in their old faith and absolved from their old loyalties, were groping, in angry perplexity, towards new policies and perhaps towards new principles. Already—and this was a significant indication of the general sense of political crisis—a new association, the British American League, had been formed, largely by Conservatives;[31] and from the beginning it was planned that the League should hold a great convention of delegates in order to determine its programme. A struggle began for the control of policy. On the one hand were the Conservatives apostates, the disillusioned extremists, with their terribly simple solution—annexation to the United States; on the other hand were the moderates, angry, confused, and anxious. What was their programme to be?

At the end of May, when the provincial parliament was prorogued and when the time for the convention of the British American League was rapidly approaching, Macdonald returned to Kingston. His own personal affairs, which during these years were almost never free from worries, had become tangled in a new knot of embarrassment and anxiety. It was true that Isabella had apparently thrown off the distressing symptoms of the previous year, and that all during the spring and early summer she had gained most promisingly. But, as he had come to realize, her improvement was always unstable, and this was proved true once again that summer when her brother John came to see them on a three weeks' visit. Although John was invariably careful not to overtire his sister himself, his presence naturally attracted Maria and a concourse of other relatives and friends, whom Isabella, with her hospitable instincts, felt she ought to see. The fatigue and the agitation were all too much for her, and when John had gone, she fell seriously ill with dysentery. "The whole gain of the spring is gone," wrote Macdonald morosely.[32] He was utterly despondent about his wife; and he was worried also about Campbell and the practice, for now at length the consequences of his heavy expenditures and enforced absences were coming back upon him. He had scarcely returned to Kingston, early in June, when Campbell began to broach the ominous question of a dissolution of their partnership. "The more I reflect on our conversations on the subject of a dissolution of our partnership," he wrote on June 8, "the more I am persuaded that it is desirable on very many grounds that it should take place".[33]

Yet, despite all these anxieties, Macdonald could not fail

to be deeply interested in the approaching convention of the British American League and in the unsolved problem of Conservative policy. From the beginning of his political career, he had been fighting extremists—first, the ultras of Toronto, who had tried to impose Anglican, Tory institutions upon the province, and now the ultras of Montreal, who were attempting to submerge it in the United States. This new extremism, which like that of the rebel Reformers of 1837 was directed towards continental union, was obviously by far the more crucial of the two, since it involved the total disappearance of a separate British North America. The first task of 1849, as Macdonald and the moderates saw it, was to defeat the desperate annexationist proposals. The convention was to be held at Kingston, symbolically the appropriate place. For if Montreal represented trade and Toronto government, Kingston, from the beginning, had stood for defence, and defence particularly against the United States. The convention "will, I think," wrote Macdonald hopefully, "put its foot on the idea of annexation".[34] It was his principal hope. But obviously the moderates would have to have some programme to substitute for the violent expedient they were determined to reject. During July, while Macdonald was busy trying to round up his moderate friends and associates and to persuade them to take part in the convention, he was already formulating alternative proposals. The programme which he sent to D. B. Stevenson, of Prince Edward County, was already fairly complete and specific: "Protection to native industry and home manufactures—connection with Great Britain—Reciprocity with the United States in agricultural products—and Repeal of the Municipal and Tariff monstrosities of last session. No French domination, but equal rights to all. *These* are the ruling principles of the League."[35]

On Wednesday, July 25, when the convention began its first session in one of the spacious upper chambers of Kingston's ambitious and slighted town hall, Macdonald joined the large but somewhat undistinguished crowd in attendance.[36] There was a small sprinkling of Conservative politicians, men like Edward Ermatinger, Rolland Macdonnell, Edmund Murney, back-benchers, most of them, who had sat in the parliament of 1844-47 and who had not been re-elected. George Moffatt, the ex-member for Montreal, and Ogle Gowan who had nearly attained office in 1847, might be regarded as rather more important politically. But, of the leading members of the Conservative opposition—MacNab, Cayley, Boulton, Cameron and the Sherwoods—not one had been tempted to put in an appearance. Macdonald was the only ex-minister of the Crown present. It was a meeting of the interested rank and file, entirely English-speaking, largely Conservative in its political leanings, but with a few independents and worried Reformers, who helped to give it a non-partisan character which was more apparent than real. Macdonald, perhaps out of prudent regard for his party, spoke little, even less than he might have been expected to do; but from the start he was busy organizing the conference and ensuring that it would run with smoothness. Perhaps, in their very different ways, the unobtrusive Macdonald and the talkative and theatrical Gowan were the two most important people at the conference. It was one of the first illustrations of a political partnership which was to last for years.

The next day the convention got down to a regular routine of morning, afternoon, and evening sessions. In the main, it followed the currently fashionable Conservative line. It spoke with the outraged voice of English-speaking Canada, of Canada West in particular, shouting its convictions in belligerent disregard of the susceptibilities of the French Canadians and of the respect due to the representative of the Crown. The recall of Lord Elgin was frankly demanded; the Rebellion Losses Bill was vigorously denounced. The convention insisted at length, and with gloomy particularity, upon the economic paralysis, the feverish popular excitement, the social and moral instability, and the decline and degradation of established authority, which constituted, in its opinion, the chief distinguishing features of the existing state of provincial affairs. But lamentations and denunciations were not the only, nor the chief, part of its work. With open talk of annexation and vague discussion of an elected Legislative Council in the air, with Conservatives everywhere subjected to the imputation of disloyalty, and the convention itself regarded as a "Yankee League", it was vitally necessary for the delegates to take their stand with decision on the major issues of the day. Annexation was not even debated in the Kingston town hall during those last days of July. The motion for an elected Legislative Council was rejected. The convention affirmed its loyalty to the Crown, to the British connection, to monarchical institutions, and the "mixed forms of government" of the parliamentary system.[37] Macdonald might well have been satisfied. The convention had, indeed, "put its foot on the idea of annexation" with decisive firmness.

He must have been equally pleased with the main motion on economic policy. Here the convention was compelled, by force of circumstances, to take an even more positive stand. The Old Colonial System, with its tariff preferences and shipping monopolies, to which Conservatives in Canada had clung tenaciously for generations, had now been shattered by the introduction of British free trade. The Canadians, for really the first time in their collective history, were obliged to face the basic economic problem of their existence as a separate community in North America. In his letter to Stevenson, Macdonald had spoken of protection to native industry and home manufactures as well as of reciprocal free trade with the United States in natural products. Both projects had been discussed with rising interest during the black days of the depression, as the Canadians sought worriedly for some escape from the economic troubles which surrounded them. But, of the two, protection was the more patently nationalist, the more defiantly anti-American policy; and it was possibly for these reasons that the convention accepted it and neglected to consider the idea of reciprocity. Gowan introduced the motion in favour of protection; but Macdonald, as far back as 1846, when he had been discussing Cayley's tariff, had sounded the note of alarm at the dangers of American industrial competition. The two of them were to argue strenuously in support of a protective tariff in future; and the resolution in its favour is perhaps one of the best illustrations of their co-operation in the convention of the British American League.

In one respect, however,—and this in a matter of crucial importance—the convention evidently went beyond anything that Macdonald had intended or expected. On Saturday, July 28, John Duggan and Rolland Macdonnell moved a resolution in favour of the federal union of all the British North American colonies.[38] It was true that, after the first wild enthusiasm had expended itself, the conference drew back a little in prudent hesitation; and all that it resolved in the end was that a scheme of such immense magnitude must receive the most careful study, and that a committee of ten should be appointed to discuss it with representatives from the Maritime Provinces. Macdonald was not made a member of the committee. In one of his very few appearances before the convention, he suggested mildly that the scheme was premature and impractical for the moment; and his friend Gowan opposed and criticized Duggan's motion with much greater fervour. Yet the debate may have accomplished an important stage in their political education. Duggan's motion was evidently a popular one, for speaker after speaker arose to discuss it, and to support it with arguments which anticipated those of a later date with curious exactitude.[39] From the moment of this declaration by the British American League, the Conservatives never lost a certain persistent, if tenuous, interest in the federal union of British North America.

On Monday and Tuesday, July 30 and 31, when the convention met for the last times, Macdonald was at hand, nominating officers, providing for publicity, arranging for the reassembling of the convention, giving the final smooth, efficient touches to the proceedings. He had been a member of the committee which drafted the convention's address to the people of Canada; but he was not elected an officer of the League nor a member of the permanent executive committee. It was probably his own wish, for, at the moment, he did not dare to take on any other commitments, even in the interests of the Conservative party. Isabella, thank God, was mending again. But Campbell, with his all too legitimate feeling of resentment for the injustices of the past, was obstinately bent on a separation, and if the partnership were to survive, it would require all the diplomacy of which Macdonald was capable. He was working hard, no doubt, with his usual easy, tireless speed, in order to make amends for the past, to propitiate Campbell, and to meet his own mounting obligations; but although, at the moment, he felt that he could give no more time to the British American League, he must have felt reasonably satisfied with what he had helped it to do at Kingston. It was true that the annexationist cry was still rising shrilly; and nobody, of course, could predict what the excited, irresponsible merchants of Montreal might yet do. But he had tried to ensure—and he must have thought successfully—that his own section of the province, Canada West, would stick to the idea of a separate, British future in North America.

Chapter Seven

Years of Recovery

I

Once the conference had ended, he could give himself without distraction to the task of pacifying Campbell. It was a formidable business. For Campbell, sensitive, warm-hearted, dourly cautious yet not unambitious in his shrewd way, was troubled not only by his own personal grievances, but also by his worries for the business as a whole. He certainly had a good deal to complain of. For years he had done by far the greater part of the work and had received only a third of the profits; and of the bonus which was supposed to have compensated him for his additional labours, £420 had not yet been paid. "So I feel," he wrote bluntly, "that I have been doing too much and getting too little."[1] It was the principal point of difference, for Campbell was stubborn in the defence of his own interests. But there were other, more general, and perhaps more fundamental differences, as well. The mere size of Macdonald's operations must have slightly intimidated his prudent colleague. Yet it was not size alone, for Campbell himself was keen enough where money was concerned; it was rather the complexity of the business, the embarrassments in which it was involved, and the almost cheerfully casual fashion in which Macdonald managed it, which created, in the junior partner, a dull, unappeasable sense of unease. Their bank account, Campbell pointed out accusingly, was overdrawn: the firm owed £1800, a debt which was a bad blot on their business escutcheon. And these painful embarrassments had been continued and ag-

gravated by Macdonald's long absences, by his political preoccupations, and by his easy-going habit of drawing upon the
firm's revenues to meet his own immediate financial needs.
"Your absence from home and your necessities," Campbell
wound up his case, "have been I think the *main* although not
by any means the only cause of the annoyances that have
arisen."[2]

As August passed rapidly along, as September, the anniversary
of the commencement of the partnership, drew closer and closer,
Macdonald struggled to overcome Campbell's timidities and
to appease his sense of injustice. For years now, the junior
partner had served him like a stout, serviceable, extremely
comfortable pair of boots, which had only occasionally squeaked
a little. He did not see how he could get along without Campbell. The practice—a big affair now, despite the depression
and his debts—was supremely useful, perhaps even vital, to
the continuance of his parliamentary career. He used every
argument and every form of persuasion: he even pleaded with
Campbell not to desert him at this crucial moment; and Campbell, who, despite all his slow resentments and nagging worries,
never wavered in his belief in his friend's political future, was
particularly susceptible to such an appeal. "I am willing, indeed anxious," he wrote, "that your political career should not
be cut short at this moment . . .".[3] And, apparently at his own
suggestion, they succeeded, towards the end of August, in
working out a new agreement whereby the partnership was to
be continued, on the basis of a half share for each, for a further
experimental period of two years.[4] On August 30, the draft
agreement was ready. Then, at the last moment, Campbell
drew back. The new arrangement, he admitted generously, was
"fair and everything he could desire"; but, after dismal worries
and sleepless nights, he decided to reject it. He acknowledged
that he was probably sacrificing as much as £2000. "I do it
with a sore heart," he wrote, ". . . but after giving the matter
every consideration I have *finally* determined (with your permission) to abandon all the advantages it offered for the *comfort*
of a smaller business."[5] Comfort, security—he had diplomatically
identified these with a small practice; but he must have been

well aware of the fact that they were far from alien to a large
and lucrative practice, so long as it was under his own control.
He stuck to his decision. Macdonald agreed to buy him out
for £1250; and after September 1, when the partnership came
to an end, they commenced the painful and haggling business
of settling their complicated accounts.

Macdonald abandoned the Princess Street establishment
which he had shared with Campbell and moved into a new
and probably less expensive set of offices at 343 King Street.[6]
The loss of a partner, who had complemented and corrected
his own qualities so exactly and who had stood by him through
all their early difficulties with his own special kind of dogged,
complaining devotion, must have seemed an irremediable disaster. There was nobody, at the moment, whom he wanted, or
could persuade, to take Campbell's place; and all that autumn,
he must have stuck to his desk, working away at a mass of
humdrum, prosaic matters, to which he had grown unaccustomed during the easy years of the partnership and which probably irked him profoundly. He had little time for politics. And
yet, all the while, the state of politics grew steadily gloomier,
as the current of Tory extremism continued in its fatal, self-
destructive way. Early in October, the Montreal merchants,
utterly forgetting their city's long historic struggle to establish
a separate British commercial empire in North America, issued
their long-awaited, notorious manifesto, advocating the political
union of Canada with the United States.[7] The desperate action
had been finally taken, despite all that the moderates had tried
to do; and if the effect of the manifesto was to be counteracted,
and the feverish contagion of continentalism checked, it was
highly desirable that the British American League should carry
out its intention of holding a second meeting of the adjourned
convention. On November 1, when the agitation following the
publication of the manifesto was at its height, the League met
again, this time at Toronto. John Richardson Forsyth, the
defeated Conservative candidate of 1841, was Kingston's delegate. Macdonald, who in the autumn of 1849 had no time
for conventions, however much he might have wished to attend
this one, was forced to stay at home. He must have found the

news from Toronto puzzling—at once reassuring and disquieting. It was true that the convention disavowed annexation
once more, and with unqualified decisiveness: it was true also
that the project of an elected Legislative Council, raised a
second time, was again rejected, after a protracted wrangle.
But although these desperate courses, these republican innovations, were pushed firmly aside, there was a good deal of evidence
that, even in this assembly of self-declared moderates, the current of extremism, restless, impatient, and exasperated, was still
running very strong. The original recommendations of the
League—retrenchment, protection to native industry, maintenance of the British connection—were, the delegates seemed to
say, all well enough, but inadequate in the existing crisis. Other
changes, more drastic and fundamental, were necessary for
colonies which had reached the extreme point of their endurance, which could not "continue in their present political or
commercial state". The Kingston meeting, to Macdonald's surprise and probably against his will, had advocated British North
American union; and it was upon this project, and the project
of constitutional change generally, that the delegates at Toronto
spent by far the greater part of their time. The League's committee, which had discussed federal union at Montreal with
a few representatives from New Brunswick, presented its report
to the convention. A torrent of vague, grandiose, irresponsible
constitution-making was immediately unloosed; and there were
repeated demands for a general convention of the people of
the whole of British North America to discuss the proposed
union.[8]

To Macdonald—busy, detached, and coolly sceptical—all this,
which went so far beyond his own modest, concrete proposals
of July, must have seemed mere theorizing, premature, nebulous,
and dangerous. The Conservatives had not closed their ranks
on a sensible and modest programme. They had continued to
fly apart, as if determined on dispersal and self-annihilation,
along various contrasted paths of hazardous eccentricity. And,
as the autumn wore on, and he continued his desultory bickering
with Campbell over the winding up of their joint affairs, there
was only one feature of the political situation to give him much

satisfaction. This was the fact—dimly apparent early in October and increasingly manifest as the autumn continued—that political division was not peculiar to the Conservatives alone, and that the unity of the huge and varied Reform party was threatened, much as Baldwin had earlier feared it would be,[9] by the revolt of its radical members. The first sign of trouble was the sudden political reappearance of Peter Perry, an "old Reformer", a gnarled veteran of the pre-Rebellion period in Upper Canadian politics, who, after a decade of oblivion, now came forward as a candidate for the third riding of York, in a by-election made necessary by the appointment of William Hume Blake to the chancellorship.[10] Perry was known to be dissatisfied with the "stale moderation" of the Reform government; he was suspected of favouring annexation to the United States; and to the Reform leaders, who wished on grounds of principle and political expediency to stamp annexationism as a purely Tory heresy, his candidature appeared particularly displeasing. Baldwin tried to discipline Perry publicly, but the attempt was a dismal failure. The "old Reformer" remained defiantly mutinous; he was elected to the vacant constituency without the slightest opposition. Before the autumn was out he had acquired a small but obstreperous following, a heterogeneous group of young Radicals and old Reformers, who drew their inspiration both from the tradition of the Rebellion of 1837 and from the new political philosophies of the 1840's, including Chartism. A new Radical movement, the "Clear Grit" movement, so called at first in derision by its opponents and then with complacent self-satisfaction by its own members, had arisen to trouble the comfortable well-being of the Reform party.

It was pleasant for Macdonald to observe these ructions going on in the large, ostentatiously affectionate family of the Reformers. It was gratifying to see a little of the annexationist mud sticking tenaciously to the respectable black broadcloth of Mr. Baldwin's trousers. These were the small consolations of an autumn which seemed full of nothing but work, of bickering over the past, and worry for the future. It was true that the settlement with Campbell, which had threatened on more than one occasion to become acrimonious, had reached a peaceful and satisfactory conclusion in the end. At one of their last conferences over a small contentious account, Campbell had characteristically pleaded for "a little forbearance on both sides". "It will never do," he wrote, "for us to disagree about the fag end of the affair, after escaping through so much."[11] They had indeed escaped through much—much which was ultimately Macdonald's responsibility; and in the end, after all the tangled, vexatious complexities of the partnership, they emerged good friends. It was something to have saved out of the wreck. But Macdonald was, as Campbell had shrewdly suspected, badly in debt. His political chances were jeopardized, for a time at least, and the practice, which had certainly declined in value since the beginning of the depression, now depended entirely upon his own exertions and tied him for long hours to his desk. But these were not his only worries. For a new crisis in his domestic affairs was looming up. Isabella had become pregnant once again.

When young John Alexander had died, a year ago in September, Macdonald had never expected to have another child. But the stoical, taciturn resignation, which was the last, invulnerable citadel of his spirit, offered no real refuge for Isabella from the tragedy of the nursery. The whole meaning of her painful existence lay centred in her own family, in her own household, in her husband and her child. Apart from the one brief setback, which had followed hard on her brother's visit in July, she had, on the whole, been better, a great deal better, during the spring and summer of 1849; and she must have realized her condition with a thrill of anxious, excited joy. From then on, despite her previous improvement, she became more than ever vulnerable to the slightest over-exertion, and to every crisis of her own febrile, emotional nature. When, early in December, the news arrived of the death of her sister Jane, who had been living with Margaret Greene in Athens, Georgia, she attempted desperately though vainly, for the sake of the child she carried, to control her overwhelming grief. But sleep, despite her feeble resolution, would not come to quiet her anguish, and the utter exhaustion into which she finally fell brought on a new and terrible attack of neuralgia, and the familiar ominous bleeding at the mouth.[12] These were the old familiar crises of her disease; and, as the old year ended and her pregnancy drew toward its conclusion, a new and painful set of symptoms, which she remembered dimly from the first experience in New York, seemed to herald her approaching confinement.[13] She bore the discomfort and the recurring pain with less apprehension than on the first occasion and with equal tranquillity and fortitude. All day long she lay in bed, burdened with her body, often drugged with opiates, yet sensitively aware of every incident in the routine of her household, and intent, with feeble but tenacious persistence, in imposing her sense of order and decorum upon its operations. Macdonald, as he watched and marvelled, compared her comically with the "invisible lady" of the circuses of the day, who was "exhibited" but did not "show" herself. "The invisible lady's voice, orders, and behests," he wrote to Margaret Greene, "are heard and obeyed all over the house, and are carried out as to cupboards which she never sees, and pots and pans that have no acquaintance with her. Not a glass is broken, or a set of dishes diminished, but she knows of, and calls the criminal to account for. In fact she carries on the whole machinery as well, to appearance, as if she were bustling from *but* to *ben* in person."[14]

Early in January of 1850, on the advice of the doctors, Macdonald began to expect that the baby would be born within a week or two. Everything was in readiness. One physician was in constant attendance: another, a specialist in "midwifery", was to be called in at the crucial moment; and a nurse was already installed in the room adjoining Isabella's own.[15] "Isa is in God's hands," wrote Macdonald, "and there we must leave her." They waited miserably, while the weeks of January and February went by, marked only by the increasing frequency and increasing severity of Isabella's pain. At home, the agony of suspense was almost unbearable for Macdonald; and, at the office, the piled papers before him never seemed to diminish. "Isa says I work too hard," he confessed, "and in truth I begin to feel that I do, but like a thief on the treadmill, I *must* step on, or be dragged."[16] So far as politics were concerned there was some satisfaction in the now evident fact that the annexa-

tion cry had met with "very little encouragement". Also, it
must have been agreeable to notice that Peter Perry's insurgent
group was still receiving recruits, that a new Radical newspaper,
the *North American,* had joined the *Examiner* in its crusade
against the ministry, and that Caleb Hopkins, another unre-
generate survival of the Radical past, had turned Clear Grit
and was busily contesting East Halton against Wetenhall, the
government candidate. But all these brief interests disappeared
quickly in the dark, bottomless well of his concern for Isabella.
He feared; and yet, in his characteristic fashion, and despite
all the ominous recent tragedies in the family circle, he continued to hope. "The rod cannot be always smiting," he told
himself. To cling to these hopes, to accept, at their face value,
the repeated assurances of the doctors that all would be well in
the end was a task almost beyond his capacity. For days and
weeks, Isabella lay prostrate in a condition apparently unchanged; "she still lingers on, and suffers, and submits".[17]
February passed, as January had slowly passed before it. He
was still waiting, watching his wife's struggles and sufferings,
still hoping for the best. And at last, on March 13, when it
seemed as if Isabella could endure no longer, the child was
born.[18]

II

"We have got Johnnie back again—almost his image," wrote
Macdonald to his sister. "I don't think he is so pretty, but he
is not so delicate."[19] The male parent, from the slight detachment of his position, could afford to make these realistic com-
parisons; but Isabella, who, in her state of emotional ecstasy,
had almost brought herself to believe that her dead baby,
purchased by her own suffering, had been restored to life by
Providence, was anxious that the boy should be called John
Alexander. Old Mrs. Macdonald, Maria Macpherson, and
Margaret Greene—an impressive array of authoritative female
opinion—looked doubtfully, with pursed apprehensive lips, at
the ominous practice of giving a new baby his dead brother's

name. In the end the child was christened Hugh John, after both his father and grandfather, and Hugh became the name by which he was usually called. It was comforting to realize that these simple, homely, family debates had mercifully succeeded to the agonizing worries of the winter; but the crisis which had passed had brought no real resolution of his troubles, and they continued, like a sombre formless story which had no meaning and could only have one end. Old Mrs. Macdonald, who had trudged stoutly through the snow to visit Isabella during the winter, had been attacked again with one of her seizures. Tom Wilson, his friend and relation in Montreal, the companion of his happy trip to England in 1843, had just lost his youngest child. And what was even harder to bear—for it touched his own youth and his earliest associations so closely—was the consumption which threatened at any moment now to end the life of his friend, Charles Stuart.[20] The friendship with Stuart went back to the time of his schooldays and apprenticeship, to the old days at Napanee and Hallowell; and it was Stuart who, in the first great meeting of his political career, had stood up beside him on that December day of 1843, to defend Sir Charles Metcalfe before the thrilling, cheering crowd of Kingstonians. All that was ended now. He knew it as he tried with joking, peremptory affection to play the doctor for a man who, with fatalistic obstinacy, refused all medicine and all advice. It was strange that so many of his earliest friends were gone or going. He could speak of this; but he would not admit the central tragedy of his life—the wreck of his marriage—which everybody about him knew and lamented. Isabella, he was writing, nearly a month after the birth of Hugh John, "still lingers very much in her recovery". Her recovery! He still believed in it with the same invincible gaiety of spirit with which he looked forward to the rebuilding of his practice and the success of his political career. But the troubles of the last year had taught him at least some sense of limitations, some realization that, with all his powers, there were choices which must be made. His wife, his small son, and the work which kept them all in existence—this was the real concern of the moment. Politics, and the future of the distracted Conservative party would have to wait.

Montreal had been punished for its incendiary violence by the removal of the government. It had been decided—and the decision had revealed clearly what a price in efficiency had to be paid by the Province of Canada for the blessings of its dual culture—that legislation and administration were to alternate, every few years, between Toronto and Quebec. Toronto had been selected as temporary capital for the fag end of the existing parliament; and when the legislature commenced its sittings there, on May 14, 1850, Macdonald was not in his place. For the first time in his political career he had missed an opening. He gave no excuses, sought and obtained no formal leave of absence; but it was not until early in June, nearly a month after the commencement of the session, that he finally took his seat.[21] The old parliament buildings of Upper Canada—three unpretentious, red-brick Georgian structures, with somewhat unsightly wooden passages connecting them, which stood, with their backs to Wellington Street, in a wide open space fronting on Toronto bay—were, of course, entirely new to him. The grounds around, which had been almost completely denuded of trees and shrubs, seemed incongruously bare and depressing in the early summer sunshine; but the setting, with its wide view of the bay, had real natural beauty. Inside the central building, the Council and Assembly chambers had been most sumptuously redecorated, with crimson carpets and crimson hangings, glittering chandeliers and desks with royal-blue covered tops, and black walnut armchairs with crimson morocco cushions.[22] For about ten days, worried and uneasy, Macdonald kept his place. He was present on June 18, when the resolutions proposed by J. H. Price precipitated a great debate on the Clergy Reserves, in which the hesitations and uncertainties of the moderate Reformers were revealed with painful clarity by the intransigent demands of the Clear Grits. It was the conviction of the Clear Grits that no support should be given by the state to any religious communion; and they now demanded that the revenues from the Clergy Reserves—the portion of the Crown lands reserved for the support of "a Protestant Clergy"

—should be appropriated to secular uses, and employed for education or any other of the general purposes of the state. Macdonald did not take any part in the debate; and it was John Hillyard Cameron, his old fellow pupil at Cruickshank's school, and his old rival for the affectionate approval of Draper, who made, apparently, the most eloquent defence of the Tory position, that the existing division of the Reserves among the different Protestant communions should be left undisturbed.[23] Macdonald sat the debate out; but a few days later the letters from Kingston must have brought the dread familiar story of a new crisis. He left at once; and on June 28, when a call of the House was made, he was found absent and declared "excused on account of sickness in his family".[24]

It was not until after the end of the first week in July that he was able to return. From then on he was a regular attendant; but he had almost nothing to say on general issues—even those issues in which he had been particularly active in the past. For the moment, in the tight, difficult position in which he found himself, it suited his purpose to become a typical, parochial back-bencher, interested mainly in the concerns of his own constituency. The case of the Trust and Loan Company of Upper Canada revealed clearly how close the connection could be between the interests of Kingston and the interests of John A. Macdonald's law practice. Macdonald was determined, if possible, to revive the fortunes of the loan company. Ever since it had been founded, back in 1844, he had been its solicitor; and along with the Commercial Bank of the Midland District, it had been one of the two most important company accounts of the Macdonald and Campbell firm. The depression, which had hit agricultural prices and farm properties so hard, had brought about a grievous decline in the Trust and Loan Company's business; and in one of those lugubriously pessimistic reviews of the prospects of the firm which Campbell had made on the eve of the dissolution of the partnership, he had declared, with terse finality, that the loan company account had been "knocked on the head". In 1850, however, the directors of the company, led by Oliver Mowat, attempted to revive it from unconsciousness; and Macdonald sponsored a private bill which was framed to amend the original terms of the incorporating statutes.[25] The bill, which was pushed briskly through parliament with the significant assistance of Francis Hincks, the Inspector-General, contained one small, inconspicuous, but immensely important change: it raised the limits on the rates which the company was permitted to charge for interest. As Elgin explained later, with much satisfaction, to Grey, the act had given "a thrust at our usury laws through its side".[26] The inevitable annual bill for the repeal of the usury laws, presented this time by Sherwood of Toronto, was, as usual, rejected by an overwhelming majority of French Canadians, with the addition of a few Clear Grits and Tories.[27] But the Trust Company Bill, with its tiny, significant amendment, had got clear through; and now, with better times and more attractive rates, there was a good prospect of acquiring a real supply of British capital.

There was one other local matter with which Macdonald busied himself in the closing days of the session of 1850. Outwardly it seemed to be of no direct interest to him whatever, for it merely concerned the provincial penitentiary at Portsmouth; but the sequel of his intervention in the affairs of the provincial penitentiary was of immense importance, for it brought him the personal enmity of George Brown. Until a little over a year before, Brown, in Macdonald's eyes, had simply been the too vigorous editor, the too successful publisher, of the Toronto *Globe*, a newspaper which, ever since its establishment in March, 1844, had been one of the most pugnaciously effective of the official journals on the Reform side. As a buzzing, waspish—though somewhat remote—journalistic nuisance, Brown could have been endured. But he was not destined to remain solely a journalist; and ever since the day, in the spring of 1843, when he had entered Samuel Thompson's office in Toronto with such healthy assurance and had begun his acquaintance with Canadian newspapermen and Canadian publishing,[28] he had been pushing himself steadily into a position from which he could exercise real influence and cause real trouble. He was an awkward, red-haired, extremely tall, extremely serious young Scotsman of firm views, great ambitions, and superabundant physical energy. In temperament, character, and convictions, he was almost the exact antithesis of Macdonald. A Reformer, a stiff Free Kirker, an ardent voluntarist who abominated any connection between church and state, a passionately serious dogmatist to whom all compromise and accommodation were alien and difficult, Brown contradicted Macdonald's instinctive habit of thought with the whole force of his downright, positive nature. The two men were almost certain to clash; and as Brown's popularity and prestige grew, as he became more discontented with the journalistic task of "puffing" the work of others and more determined to play a great political role himself,[29] the chances of such an encounter rapidly increased. It was fated to come; but it might have come without the bitterness of a savage personal enmity, if it had not been for Brown's first political appointment in the spring of 1848. The new Reform government, anxious to give some polite recognition to the editor of the *Globe*, and busy with the congenial task of sacking officials, investigating old abuses and planning new reforms, had decided to appoint a prison commission, and to make George Brown one of its members and its secretary. In the autumn of 1848, the commission had moved in upon the provincial penitentiary at Portsmouth with all the horrid purposefulness of an armoured regiment. It had carried out a minute, particular, uncompromising and exhaustive inquiry into the affairs of the penitentiary. The Warden, Henry Smith, Senior, had been suspended from office; and a huge indictment, consisting of eleven separate charges, divided into 121 distinct counts, and occupying 300 folio pages of manuscript, was finally preferred against him.

Macdonald had been immediately made aware of these scandalous happenings. He knew the Smiths well, for the Smiths were an old Kingston Conservative family. And since it was obviously impossible for Henry Smith, Junior, the Tory member for Frontenac, to intervene directly on his father's behalf in parliament, the main burden of the defence had fallen inevitably upon Macdonald. In the winter of 1849, immediately after the opening of the legislature, he had received a cascading series of letters from the senior Smith—one by almost every post—in which the injured Warden, vigorously denouncing his tormentors as "arrant scoundrels" and "unblushing liars", had attacked the malice, prejudice, and vindictive partiality which he discerned everywhere in the conduct of the investigation.[30] He had followed this up—once Brown had finished his voluminous report—with a lengthy, though not nearly so voluminous, refutation of its charges.[31] All these outraged effusions had been read by Macdonald with sympathetic attention. The penitentiary was in his bailiwick, the Smiths were his acquaintances and associates, and the investigation, with its secrecy and unprofessional informality, had revolted his lawyer's sense of the proprieties. Whatever the doubtful merits of the case may have been, he at least came to the definite conclusion that much of the evidence against Smith was of questionable origin, that a good deal of it had been scandalously manipulated and distorted, that Smith had never been given a reasonable chance to answer the charges against him, and that, in sum, a substantial injustice had been done. His complaint was, of course, against the commission as a whole. But, in his mind, the chief culprit was Brown, who, as the secretary of the commission and the chief author of the report, had systematically juggled the evidence. Once these conclusions had been formed, he clung to them with a peculiarly stubborn tenacity. He had brought one phase of the matter up before parliament early in the session of 1849.[32] And now, on August 5, as one of his last acts of the session, he presented Smith's petition—Smith in the meantime had been finally dismissed from office—and asked that it should be referred to a special committee of inquiry.[33] The request, of course, was voted down. Nothing resulted to the advantage of Smith. But Brown, sensitive and irascible, began to notice Macdonald's pertinacious attacks on his newspaper. The feud had begun.

At the moment, neither of the two contestants paid very much attention to it. Macdonald, anxious to exploit the new Trust and Loan Company's bill, was planning to leave for England as soon as the session ended. The recovery of his practice was evidently still his major preoccupation; and the prison controversy and political issues in general had declined

in interest, perhaps because the Tory party still seemed so immovably stuck in futility. The annexationist cry, it was true,
was dead; the extravagant excesses of 1849 were mercifully over;
but the party, though chastened, had not found in its humiliation a new unity or a new sense of direction. If the Reformers
had grown weaker through internal division, the Conservatives
had not apparently increased in strength; and while the Clear
Grits, at what was somewhat pompously described as the
"Markham Convention", had drawn up a fashionably formidable
list of Radical principles, the Tories had seemingly not even
bothered to search the somewhat muddled proceedings of the
British American League for a few new ideas. They did not
press for protection to home industry, or urge the federal union
of British North America, or even succeed in making the
somewhat banal idea of "retrenchment" peculiarly their own.
When they did take up a modish notion, it was likely to be
some such highly questionable proposal as an elective Legislative Council, which the British American League had twice
discussed, and twice rejected, and which the Clear Grits had
appropriated as part of their general campaign for elective
institutions. In the Conservative defence of the Clergy Reserves as a legitimate source of support for all recognized
Protestant communions, there had been an appropriate appeal
to British precedents and to old loyalties and affections; but it
was apparently just as easy for some of the Tories to reject
tradition completely, without any sense of incongruity, and
with a commonplace North American contempt indistinguishable from that of the Clear Grits. There was a comic occasion
on which William Henry Boulton, supposedly one of the old
Family Compact Conservatives, brought two hammers and
two adzes into the Assembly, one set British and one set American, and blandly proceeded, by an unflattering comparison,
to prove the superiority of American enterprise, resourcefulness,
and practical efficiency, and the consequent and inevitable
superiority of American political institutions.[34] This attempt
to substitute shirt-sleeves and galluses for neckcloths and sober
Tory broadcloth, this effort to smarten up a roomful of Chip-
pendale furniture by the introduction of an efficient American

box-stove, was all slightly depressing; and the Conservative front-benchers—the bragging Sherwood, the timid Cayley, Mac-Nab with his tiresome geniality and tiresome rages, Boulton with his stage properties and conjuring tricks—were an uninspiring lot. They could not even stick together in public. And the session was still in mid-career when Boulton and Sherwood, the two Toronto members, began an unedifying controversy in the press.[35] Perhaps the best hope for the future was not in these men at all, but in their avowed enemies—in the prospect, now growing rapidly more certain, of a real break-up in the Reform party.

III

Late in the summer Macdonald sailed for England. It was eight years since he had last crossed the ocean; and now—for nearly a decade of disillusioning trouble had intervened—his plans were far more definite and practical than they had been before. He travelled as the accredited representative of the Trust and Loan Company of Upper Canada, and his main purpose was to secure new British capital for the concern and to carry out the enlargement and reorganization of its activities. It was highly desirable that he should gain admittance to British financial circles through the *porte cochère* of the governing class, and, despite his not altogether happy relations with Lord Elgin in the past, he had no hesitation in asking the Governor for a letter of introduction to the Colonial Secretary, Earl Grey. Elgin obligingly complied, describing his ex-minister somewhat patronizingly as "a respectable man and tolerably moderate in his views", and ending up with the comment—in itself an odd gloss upon his own vaunted political detachment—that Macdonald belonged to "the section of the Conservatives who are becoming reasonable".[36] Macdonald reached England some time in September, but Grey did not become aware of his presence until later, and November came before the Colonial Secretary invited the young solicitor of the Trust and Loan Company to dinner. It was quite a distinguished gathering, with Lord Lansdowne, the President of the Council, Sir Charles Wood, the Chancellor of the Exchequer, and another visiting Canadian, the Reverend Egerton Ryerson, Superintendent of Schools for Canada West, as guests. Ryerson, with his ready tongue, his copious store of knowledge, and his air of easy self-assurance, evidently outshone his fellow-colonial at dinner. Grey described the portly clergyman as "a very superior man", and had nothing at all to say about Macdonald.[37] But for all that he did not neglect the agent of the Trust and Loan Company, and the introductions and advice which he gave Macdonald probably helped him considerably in his task.[38] The mission was a triumphant success. The Trust and Loan Company, which Campbell had morosely regarded as defunct, rose again in splendid vitality with a capital of £500,000, an impressive set of British directors, and Thomas Baring and George Carr Glyn as trustees.

In the midst of these successes, Macdonald probably gave little thought to the subject of Canadian politics. But while he was still in England, busy with financial negotiations, there occurred a curious episode in British affairs which was to have violent repercussions in Canada, and which was to affect his new enemy, George Brown, and the Reform party, and even, indirectly, the Canadian Conservatives as well. On October 7, a few weeks before the dinner at Lord Grey's London house, Cardinal Wiseman, newly appointed Roman Catholic Archbishop of Westminster, had made public in a famous pastoral "From out the Flaminian Gate of Rome" a recent brief of the Papacy affecting Great Britain. The brief established the Roman Catholic hierarchy in England with, for the first time, English territorial titles, of which "Westminster" itself was obviously one of the most presumptuous and notorious. Englishmen, who for centuries had been unaccustomed to the sweeping rhetoric of papal pronouncements, learnt to their indignant astonishment that, as a result of this beneficent Roman brief, Catholic England, at length "restored to its orbit in the ecclesiastical firmament" was now to begin "its course of regularly adjusted action round the centre of unity", and that Cardinal Wiseman, the appointed emissary from this centre of unity, was to "govern the counties of Middlesex, Hertford, Essex, Surrey, Sussex, Kent, Berkshire, and Hampshire".[39] This parcelling off of English counties into Roman dioceses "with all the authority and minuteness of an Act of Parliament" aroused a storm of Protestant protest in England. The bishops and the press spluttered with indignation; and, on November 4, the Prime Minister, Lord John Russell, in a public letter to the Bishop of Durham, denounced the Pope's action as "insolent and insidious".[40] In Canada, as Macdonald knew very well, the first point in the dispute—the establishment of Roman Catholic dioceses with British territorial names—had really no meaning, since such titles had existed in British North America for a long time without any noticeable enslavement of the Protestant population. But Canada West was a cultural province of the United Kingdom, influenced by every important religious disturbance in the Mother Country, as the recent disruption of the Church of Scotland had proved once again. And the presence of the large, compact body of French-Canadian Roman Catholics helped to make the Upper Canadian Protestants peculiarly responsive to the charge of "papal usurpation". Somebody was almost bound to raise the "Protestant Cry", and fate had appointed the appropriate man and the appropriate megaphone through which it was to be sounded. On December 10 and December 19, 1850—fateful days for the Reform party and for George Brown—the *Globe* published two long and outspoken articles on the religious controversy in England.[41]

When Macdonald returned to Kingston, some time in the winter of 1851, the feverish symptoms of infection in the robust body of the Reform party were becoming more alarmingly conspicuous than they had ever been before. The Clear Grits, waxing stronger with every by-election, had recently published a revised and expanded edition of their reform programme in the *North American*;[42] but even their rising popularity, important as it was, could hardly have seemed more promising to Macdonald than the obviously growing estrangement between the leaders of the Reform party and their terrible newspaper ally, George Brown. To the dismay of the government, which now began to fear for its French-Canadian and Irish Roman

Catholic support, Brown had waged his anti-Catholic campaign all winter, with passionate conviction and complete disregard for all probable political consequences. Yet there were important consequences, as he was soon to discover. In April, 1851, in a by-election in Haldimand, he made his first attempt to enter parliament; and he was badly defeated by no less a person than William Lyon Mackenzie, the returned exile, the most notorious of all the "Old Reformers", who had attached himself loosely to the Clear Grits.⁴³ Brown was furious with Mackenzie and his associates; he blamed the interfering priesthood for his defeat. But his irritation with the Clear Grits and the Roman Catholics was little more than a weak reflection of his righteous anger with the official Reform leaders and the "party". The party, which owed him support both because of his principles and the services he had given in the past, had in fact let him down shamelessly out of a timorous and time-serving concern for the Roman Catholic vote.⁴⁴ He brooded sullenly over his accumulating wrongs. He had reached an ominous stage of rankling disappointment and angry determination.

It was in these rather more hopeful political circumstances that parliament met, late in May, for the last time before the approaching general election. Macdonald was present from the beginning. Since the terrible winter of 1849-50 his affairs had improved in almost every way. Isabella was better, despite her slow recovery after the birth of Hugh John. The return of good times and the beginnings of the railway boom had re-animated the law practice; and the Trust and Loan Company, firmly re-established in Canada with himself as solicitor and Francis Archibald Harper as one of the two Canadian commissioners, was preparing to enter the investment field once again in a vigorous fashion.⁴⁵ It was true that the Clear Grits, led by William Lyon Mackenzie, made a savage attack on the company's special privileges in the session of 1851; but both the Tory opposition and the government Reformers joined in defence of the now highly respectable financial institution, and Macdonald was not even required to say a word in its behalf.⁴⁶ His position was more secure than it had been; it seemed to be growing almost easy. There were no lengthy absences from parliament, authorized or unauthorized, during the session of 1851. He had fewer preoccupations than before, and more time and zest for politics. And as his experience grew and his confidence came back with a rush, he began to develop, with more freedom, his own characteristic parliamentary style, his easy, conversational, half-bantering manner, his terse, occasionally flippant, and dangerously adroit method of attack. He could put the virtuous Baldwin into a state of mild embarrassment by supporting a transference of controverted elections to the courts; and, when he sponsored a bill for the incorporation of the medical profession, he made the House giggle with a tale of his own amateur efforts to cope with a case of lumbago, as a horrible example of the evils attending the activities of unauthorized practitioners.[47]

Yet the main task of the session was to encourage the divisions in the Reform party, to promote by every possible means the ill-concealed estrangement between George Brown and the government leaders. Here Macdonald found that he could make excellent use of the everlasting question of the report of the Penitentiary Commission. On June 24 he rose to make his annual demand for a parliamentary inquiry. He drew, of course, an affecting picture of the senior Smith, a virtuous man, "accused of the meanest peculation and the greatest cruelty", condemned on the basis of garbled evidence which had been originally supplied by "every unhanged scoundrel about the penitentiary", and thrust forth, with vindictive unceremoniousness, from his office without a decent chance of reply. The injustice was patent and unquestionable, but Macdonald concentrated more upon the question of responsibility for Smith's dismissal than upon the enormity of Smith's misfortunes. He explained tolerantly that he did not believe the ministers had nursed any real enmity against the luckless warden in the beginning; and although in the end they had certainly inflicted a grinding injustice, they had done so largely "from their cowardly fear of George Brown, who had so completely bullied them".[48] In the circumstance, this was a neat, calculated jab at the sensitive quick of Brown's relations with the ministry, and its results were highly satisfactory. Baldwin, opposing the inquiry, spoke

very temperately in reply. Lafontaine, defending the commissioners against the charge of falsifying the evidence, made,
oddly enough, no reference at all to the secretary, thus "giving
poor Brown the go-by, though a like charge had been made
against him".⁴⁹ It was all a little tepid and unenthusiastic. Brown
had sustained a fresh injury and had been given a new reason
for resentment; and two days later, in the *Globe*, he printed an
enormous editorial, three columns in length, in which he fell
upon both his false friends and his open enemies, in a scandalized tone of shocked betrayal.⁵⁰ Macdonald must have been
satisfied with the protean uses to which he had put the report
of the Penitentiary Commission. The Reform leaders and the
editor of the *Globe* had now one further reason for their open
recriminations.

IV

Yet nobody—not even the hungry Tories—could really have
expected that a disgruntled publisher and a handful of Clear
Grits had much immediate chance of upsetting the "Great
Ministry" of Baldwin and Lafontaine. And, in fact, the Cabinet would probably have continued calmly on its way for some
months to come at least, if it had not been for Baldwin's weariness of office and the hypersensitivity of his temperament. On
June 26, William Lyon Mackenzie proposed the abolition of
the Court of Chancery, a court which Baldwin had reorganized
two years before and which he regarded affectionately as one
of his greatest achievements. A majority of the whole House
rejected this intransigent proposal, but a majority of the members
from Upper Canada supported it. Baldwin was wounded by
the defection of his own followers in a matter where he thought
he could count upon their loyalty. He at once resigned. Lafontaine followed with the announcement that he also would
retire at the close of the present session; and in the fluid circumstances of Canadian politics, the imminent retirement of
the two great leaders seemed almost certain to bring about a
reshuffling of groups, and even a realignment of parties. The

crisis—for which Macdonald and the Tories had hoped but which they had scarcely expected so soon—was now at hand. What profit could they possibly derive from it?

The essential basis of political power was an alliance with the main body of the French-Canadian members. Macdonald had inherited the idea of such a union from Draper, the father of Liberal Conservatism, who had tried three times in vain to carry it out. And despite Draper's repeated failures, the project still haunted the imaginations of the Conservatives with its tantalizing possibilities. They fortified their hopes by arguing that the existing coalition of the essentially Conservative French Canadians and the Radicals of Canada West was an unnatural coalition, an accident of history rather than a logical consequence of political realities.[51] Even Lord Elgin, though he dreaded the break-up of the existing Reform alliance, was convinced that it was only a recollection of their snubbing by the "old official set, and the fear that the union had been designed to swamp them" which kept the French Canadians away from their natural allies, the Conservatives of Canada West.[52] It was true that these old French-Canadian fears and grievances, slumbering peacefully away in the decade after the Rebellion, had been suddenly and violently reawakened by the excesses of the Conservatives during the controversy over the Rebellion Losses Bill. But if recent happenings in Canada had tended to revive the old fear and dislike of Conservative professions, the course of events on the continent of Europe was now bringing with it a rapid decline and discredit of the Liberal creed, both political and religious. Canada East, a French and Roman Catholic province, was bound to be influenced by the remarkable change which had come over European politics since the Revolutions of 1848, by the decline of the Second French Republic, the rise of Louis Napoleon, and the altered policies of the disillusioned Pius IX. Rome and Paris, which had so often contradicted each other in the past to the bewilderment of French Canadians, might now unite to proclaim a persuasive and authoritative anti-Liberal gospel. And if the Clear Grits grew too obstreperous, or if a radical, anti-clerical movement—similar to that of the Clear Grits—arose to embarrass the Reform party in Canada East, then the main body of French Canadians might be persuaded or frightened into an abandonment of their old alliance. They were already a little concerned over the intemperate politics of the western Radicals. Their concern might be judiciously heightened. And if, as seemed probable in the days that followed Baldwin's resignation, the Reformers could be kept in power only by a reunion of all their groups, however radical, and including the Clear Grits, the desertion of the French Canadians might come immediately.

Macdonald and the Conservatives, as they planned their campaign during the exciting summer of 1851, tried to take advantage of these vaguely discerned contours of the political landscape. They pointed to the ominous violence of George Brown's anti-Catholic campaign. They expatiated on the Clear Grits' dislike of clerical influence and unconcealed hatred of religious endowments. They repeated the solemn warning, made over a year ago by John Hillyard Cameron, that if the Roman Catholics of Canada East continued to act with the would-be spoliators of Protestant Church property, they would be endangering the principle by which their own ecclesiastical endowments were secured and that they might sow the wind and reap the whirlwind.[53] For a brief moment, these Tory manoeuvres may have had a chance of success; and through the thick murk, pierced feebly by flashes of rumour and conjecture, which still envelops the crisis of July, 1851, there are brief glimpses of the Conservatives, with Macdonald prominent in the foreground, making and receiving overtures for a *rapprochement* with the moderate Reformers, French and English. It was reported that Macdonald, with other Conservatives, had been sounded by the Ministerialists on the possibility of a coalition.[54] And McDougall, the editor of the *North American*, who was manoeuvring on behalf of the Clear Grits, declared that "the Tories have been making all sorts of humiliating overtures" to the French. "They thought they had the cherry in their mouths," he added, "but with the blessing of God we will disappoint them."[55]

And, at the last moment, the Conservatives were disappointed. The old feeling for unity among the Reformers, the urge towards the reconciliation of their recent unnatural feuds, was still too strong to be circumvented. By the end of July it was generally known that a new basis for the existing government had been laid in an alliance of the main body of Reformers with the Clear Grits; and in October the new Cabinet, headed by Francis Hincks and A. N. Morin, was formally constituted. Once again the Conservatives had failed to obtain power; once again they had failed to exploit successfully the admitted divisions of their opponents; and in the autumn of 1851 almost their sole consolation lay in the obvious fact that the new Reform coalition had been achieved with difficulty, that it was not really complete, and that its future career was uncertain. How would the Clear Grits enjoy the large concessions and compromises which their leaders now admitted must be made? How high a price would have to be paid by everybody in future embarrassments, frustrations, and perplexities? And what, above all, were the probable consequences of the sinister isolation of George Brown? For Brown—and herein lay the largest measure of consolation for the Conservatives—stood apart from the whole arrangement. Moody, resentful, jealous of Hincks, disappointed of an expected place in the new Cabinet, and determined to continue his struggle against the dark forces of the Roman Catholic hierarchy, he now broke openly and defiantly with the new government. And with his defection, the split in the Reform party, first noticed in the autumn of 1849, was continued in a different but possibly more dangerous fashion.

These cheerful circumstances, and the improvement of his own personal affairs, gave Macdonald fresh energy that autumn, despite the failure of the grand plan for a union with the French. The old zest in provincial politics had come back: and, as the general election steadily approached, he took the whole Midland District under his superintendence with easy and exuberant efficiency. In mid-September, though the formal reorganization of the government was still to come and the election months away, he was writing to his friend, D. B. Stevenson of Prince Edward County, warning him that "the Rads are working like blazes" and urging him "to take the stump manfully" and at once.[56] It was not until late in November, to the accompaniment of mountainous snowfalls which unfortunately blocked up the door of one of the Reform newspapers and prevented its appearance for a day, that the electoral campaign in Kingston began to get under way. Then the Conservatives discovered, to their shocked astonishment, that the Radicals, despairing of finding a genuine candidate of their own, had cunningly decided to requisition Kingston's popular ex-Mayor, John Counter, in a last diabolical effort to "throw John A. Macdonald overboard".[57] On December 6, at the hustings outside the city hall, Counter was actually nominated, although he was not present at the meeting; but after the crowd had pushed its way inside the hall to hear Macdonald's speech, the ex-Mayor suddenly appeared. It was utterly impossible for him to accept the nomination, he explained, and he must therefore decline it.[58] Despite this blunt disavowal, his dubious friends persisted in their nomination and demanded a poll on his behalf; but the opposition had now become so obviously frivolous and fraudulent that Macdonald could afford to treat it with benign contempt. Counter, he explained blandly in his nomination speech, was not really a Reformer and had been put up solely on the grounds that he, Macdonald, had not paid sufficient attention to the local interests of Kingston in parliament. For the first two-thirds of his speech he continued in a severely parochial strain, dwelling upon his devotion and his services to his own city; and it was only towards the end of the usual lengthy nomination speech that he approached really provincial affairs. There was an echo of the old programme of the British American League, in his demand for protection to native industry; and he clung closely to Tory policy in respect of religious endowments when he declared that "the Clergy Reserves he would hold sacred to religious purposes . . .".[59] He desired, he said, to see no inequality in the rights of the different denominations of Christians, but he hoped to establish equality, not by levelling down, but by raising up those which were now in an inferior position to the enjoyment of the privileges held by others.

On Monday, December 15, the poll opened. The vote was

light, partly because of the spurious nature of Counter's un-willing candidacy, and partly because of another terrific snow-storm, which began on Monday and continued in blinding downfalls all the next day.[60] On Wednesday, at noon, when the final totals were announced, Macdonald had received 291 votes and Counter 15. The entire Midland District, Kingston, Frontenac, Hastings, and Lennox and Addington—everything but Prince Edward County—had now been secured for the Conservatives; and when he thanked his supporters briefly from the steps of the city hall, Macdonald explained that there was still work to be done for the party and that he was leaving immediately for Picton to cast his vote for the Tory candidate, Stevenson. Back in September, when he had written Steven-son, he had promised that he would bring over all the Kingston Conservative voters who held property in Prince Edward; and that afternoon he, and Alexander Campbell, John Richardson Forsyth and Henry Smith, Jr., piled into a sleigh and were driven off up the snow-choked road to the south-west.[61] They stopped for the night at an inn at Adolphustown. The day before, a far-seeing Reformer of the district had thoughtfully collected all the small skiffs on the other side of Adolphus Reach, by Macdonald's old home, the Stone Mills. The ruse was simple, ingenious, but unnecessary; for a severe frost, which followed the snowstorm, had frozen the Reach, and immobilized everything, including the ferry, at Glenora. The ice was too thin in places to bear a sleigh or horses; but the cheerful and undaunted members of the voting party each secured two planks and, pushing these tentatively ahead, crawled slowly on their stomachs over the weakest parts of the Reach towards the Stone Mills. There a sleigh whisked them quickly over the snowy road to Picton, and they cast their votes in time.

Stevenson was elected. The entire Midland District had now been won for the Conservatives, and the drive back to the Stone Mills, in the dark December evening, was a triumphal progress. Down by Adolphus Reach, the inevitable crowd of faithful Conservatives had assembled; and Macdonald, cheer-ful, irreverent, elated with whisky and triumph, mounted the platform of Teddy McGuire's saloon to address the crowd. He was back in his old district, joking with his old neighbours, talking to old friends and acquaintances who already rolled his stories, and escapades, and burlesques about their palates like a well-loved spirit. For five minutes or so they shouted with laughter while he imitated the ridiculous sing-song manner in which a poor worthy Quaker clergyman, well known in the district, used to intone his interminable sermons. A young man, Canniff Haight, who had driven the sleigh back from Picton, stood watching the platform, and the flaring lights of the hotel, and the laughing faces of the spectators. Long afterwards he remembered: and it was out of episodes such as these —at ferries and by roadsides, in hotels and village inns, in city halls and on rural hustings—that the incredible Macdonald legend began to grow.

Chapter Eight

The Liberal-Conservative Coalition

I

In the new parliament—it was the third of which he had been a member—Macdonald stepped easily into a new prominence. He turned thirty-seven in January, 1852. His powers had matured; he had grown increasingly expert in their use; and he had kept his political good fortune in the midst of catastrophes which had eliminated, at least temporarily, so many of his rivals. The financial worries and emotional disturbances of the winter of 1849 were apparently a thing of the past. He stood on some admitted limitations and some abandoned hopes; but the ground, if less pleasant than it might have been, was still solid. He would never be a very great, or, perhaps, a very wealthy, lawyer; but money, or legal fame, was not his real ambition. With the Commercial Bank and the Trust Company accounts, he had enough to permit him to continue in politics and to keep his small family in reasonable ease and comfort. Hugh John, who would be two years old next March, had come through the first, anxious stage of babyhood. Isabella had crept slowly and painfully out of the never-to-be-repeated agonies of motherhood and into that feeble, uneasy state of convalescence which had come to be her best substitute for health. She could never be a normal wife, a normal mother, a normal mistress of a married establishment; and the house, which might have been crowded with company and talk and laughter, kept at its very centre a dim, hushed room, full of equivocal silences and nervous apprehensions. Isabella could match Macdonald's silent, dogged fortitude; she could rival the warmth of his emotional intensity; but it was beyond the strength of her broken body and injured spirit to respond to his gaiety, his buoyant vitality, his irrepressible genial interest in a multitude of people and things. At the very heart of his existence there was, not a denial—for Isabella never had the opportunity to give or refuse her part—but the utter impossibility of any real response. The long, hopeless years, with the familiar crises, and recoveries, and relapses of the sick-room, never apparently calloused the tenderness of his anxious affection with the hard skin of impatient familiarity. But there was a strong, warm current of his nature which could find only a part of its scope and encouragement in his own home and his own office. He liked and understood people; he enjoyed the pace and bustle of affairs; he had convictions; and he wanted power. Politics could not absorb him completely. Politics was not yet a vocation in Canada; and, even if it had been, he was probably not yet ready to accept the tyranny which such a vocation would certainly impose. He was a gifted amateur who had not yet decided to become a professional. There was a new confidence, as well as the old zest, in the way he played his part.

The fortunes of politics favoured his sudden advance. He had always been regarded as Draper's protégé and heir—as the best of the possible moderates, as the potential leader of the Liberal-Conservatives. And now a film of discredit, the discredit of defeat or of temporary political disfavour, had apparently dulled the prestige of his old rivals, the High Tories, the survivors of the Family Compact group. He had kept his tight, unshakable hold on Kingston and the Midland District, while several among his more important colleagues had failed to meet the basic political requirement of holding their ridings. The party as a whole had done just as badly in the general election of 1851 as it had in the general election of 1847; and its few reinforcements—men like John Gamble from York South and T. C. Street from Welland—were not enough to fill the wide gaps where the veterans had fallen. William Cayley, John Hillyard Cameron, George and Henry Sherwood, had all been defeated. It was a wholesale clearance of the general staff. Henry Sherwood had been Attorney-General, titular leader of Canada West in the Conservative government in 1847; Cayley and Cameron had both held office; and all of them could have been regarded as potential successors to Sir Allan MacNab. They were all out of parliament now, and they were out at a time when the question of the succession to Sir Allan—a question propounded with hopeful frequency by the moderates in the party—was being raised once more. For nearly six years, ever since the retirement of Draper and the discredit of Sherwood in the election of 1847, MacNab had been the tacitly accepted Conservative leader. The son of a United Empire Loyalist, a soldier like his father, he had fought through the War of 1812 while still a boy in his teens, and had gained his knighthood for services in the Rebellion of 1837; and in his red-faced, jovial, downright fashion, he gave the philosophy of the Family Compact what was perhaps its most primitive military expression. He had long been odious to the "Gowan-ites"; he was becoming objectionably tiresome to larger sections of the party; and recently a new political disturbance had deposited a small cloud of disapproval about his ruddy, genial countenance.

The fact was that he appeared far too intimately connected with the government's ambitious railway policy.[1] A hearty, simple-minded soul who enjoyed every minute of his robust existence, and who alternated with genial ease between a rather ostentatious wealth and an unabashed impecuniosity, MacNab had always been a somewhat needy, greedy, not too scrupulous speculator. Now, in his older, more expansive years, he took to railways like a cheerful child to jam. He became president of the Great Western Railway. He was made chairman—though his party was in opposition—of the parliamentary committee on railways; and he was alleged to have said—and the newspapers frequently repeated the aphorism—"my politics now are railroads". As the summer of 1852 passed on, and the time for the opening of the first session of parliament drew closer and closer, it began to be hinted, with unpleasant openness, that the "gallant knight" was no longer free to oppose the government on any vital issue. From these insinuations some Conservative newspapers in both Toronto and Montreal went on to make the most damaging general assessments of Sir Allan's fitness for the post of leader.[2] Then, having pronounced judgment against him, they took the final step of advocating the claims of John A. Macdonald.

The chorus of approval was impressive and sustained. The *Montreal Gazette* referred regularly to the Conservatives of Canada West "led by Macdonald of Kingston".[3] "We believe it is now settled, with the unanimous consent of the party," wrote the editor of the Toronto *Patriot*, "that the Hon. John A. Macdonald, member for the city of Kingston, is to be the future parliamentary leader".[4] These calm assumptions and confident prophecies naturally aroused protests among some of the older Tories; and a long, unseemly dispute, in which a number of Conservative newspapers joined, went on for some weeks over the question of the leadership of the party. The *Globe*, which, though opposed to the government, still took the keenest relish in Tory squabbles, assured its readers, in a stern biblical metaphor, that "the Conservatives remind us just now of the inhabitants of Jerusalem when Titus was besieging their city".[5] Macdonald would probably have agreed that these demoralizing quarrels in the party simply emphasized its divisions and invited its defeat. The argument over the leadership had no doubt done him some good, but it was certainly doing the party harm. He had no wish to oust the still indispensable MacNab, and he was apparently one of a number of Conservative members of parliament who tried to put a stop to the controversy by signing a formal resolution in which they expressed confidence once more in their old leader.[6]

He was not yet head of the party, but it was significant that no other heir apparent had even been mentioned during the debate. These great expectations had apparently bred in him a greater sense of responsibility, a more becoming gravity. But even yet there was a certain light-hearted, amateurish inconsistency in his devotion to the party. In the first session of the new parliament, which began in Quebec in August, 1852, adjourned in November and reopened in the following February, he was certainly more prominent than ever before, but still not uniformly faithful in his attendance. At times, when the pressure of affairs was running strong at Quebec, he found he could not even spare the time for such important family occasions as the marriage of his sister Margaret to James Williamson, the Professor of Mathematics and Natural Philosophy at Queen's University.[7] "I wish that Moll should have a good kit," he wrote characteristically to his sister Louisa, "and I wish you to expend £25 for her on such things as you like. Don't say anything to her about it, but when I go up I will settle the bills. Get the things."[8] He added that he would "strain every nerve to be up on the 19th", which was the day in October fixed for the wedding. But on October 18 an important election petition came up for debate—he was a member of the election committee—and at the last moment it was impossible for him to get away.[9] Yet, despite these proofs of self-sacrificing zeal, his devotion was not consistent. He was nearly three weeks late when parliament met in the winter of 1853, after the long adjournment; and he left in the spring when the lengthy session had still a month to run.[10] His professional interests in Kingston, a certain cheerful casualness of attitude which some of the sterner members of the party were perhaps beginning to find a little exasperating, and a disinclination to commit himself too far to either the Conservative party or Canadian politics in general, all helped to keep him in a position of slight detachment. But when he was at Quebec—and for long months he stuck faithfully to his post—he was certainly busier than ever before, intervening more frequently in debate, making longer speeches, cultivating the French Canadians, drinking and dining with his fellow-members, and making plans and concocting plots and surprises for the day-by-day battle in the House.

As he grew better known to the Assembly and the country, the popular picture of his character as a politician, of his distinctive style as a public man, became filled out in detail and warmer in colour. Nobody, not even his most enthusiastic supporters, ever thought of complimenting him upon what were known in mid-nineteenth-century North America as the "higher graces of oratory". But he had never liked and never tried to imitate the fashionable rhetoric of the period, with its ornate vocabulary and inflated periods. These turgid pomposities he had long regarded as characteristically American and highly undesirable. The easy, informal, rather conversational manner, rising occasionally and naturally to bursts of eloquence, which he had always regarded as the great traditional style of the British House of Commons, was his own instinctive preference. He was a debater by intention; and it was as a debater, as "an exceedingly close reasoner", laconic, cogent, persuasive, and entertaining, that he was getting to be known.[11] There was a touch of the old eighteenth-century manner in his occasional Latin tags, in his not infrequent quotations from satiric or comic literary classics such as *Hudibras,* in his appeals to the great traditions of Chatham, Pitt, Burke, Fox, and Wellington. He dealt frequently and easily in irony, in comic exaggeration; and the note of light-hearted humour which crept disconcertingly in and out of his speeches delighted his own followers and drove his opponents into a baffled state of half-amused exasperation. Drummond, Attorney-General for Canada East, who, on one occasion, had to admit to making an absurd error in the government's railway legislation, was pursued by Macdonald with such genial dexterity, that, in his blind rage, he scarcely knew where to turn. He began by accusing his tormentor of "flippancy"; then, with a brief effort to put the best face on the matter, went on to insist that Macdonald's "pleasant lecture" had really afforded him intense amusement; and ended up, in a badgered, truculent fashion, by demanding proof of the errors of omission and commission with which he had been charged. Macdonald blandly admitted that he always tried to be good-humoured in debate, noted how excessively disagreeable Drummond had found his pleasantries, wondered why a government whose politics were admittedly "railway politics" should be so ignorant of its own basic legislation, and finally advised Francis Hincks—the "Emperor Francis I" as the Conservative newspapers called him—never to be out of the House in view of the "awful messes" into which his colleagues got themselves during his absence.[12]

The manner was distinctive, characteristic and becoming increasingly well known. The matter—the sum total of his views on the constitutional and politico-religious questions of the day—was equally a typical expression of his character. Although, on occasion, he could quote authorities and appeal to abstract ideas, these references back to a fundamental political and social philosophy were usually implied rather than explicit. Unlike the formidable Brown, who appeared in parliament for the first time in the session of 1852-53, he was not a crusader with a mission. Equally he was not a rationalist who believed that government was a series of general objectives which could be attained by the application of timeless and universal rules. He thumped no tubs and banged no pulpits. He was far too concerned with the intricate details of concrete problems, far too interested in the curious and manifold complexities of human situations, to follow an ideal faithfully or to settle everything by scrupulous reference to a given set of rules. For him government was neither a quest for political justice nor an exercise in political arithmetic. Government was a craft, which one learnt chiefly by doing and by watching others do—a craft which consisted essentially in managing a small group of men which a far larger group of men had selected to govern them. There were no text-books and no divine revelations. The craft had its traditions, its conventions, its techniques, its stock of forms and variations—all of which were historical products. It found its raw material in the problems of a particular landscape and a particular people. It was the task of a politician to work within the tradition, and to respect the limitations and exploit the possibilities of the medium. He might remain a competent craftsman; he might become a great, creative artist. But he should never aspire to the alien roles of prophet, philosopher, or engineer.

In Macdonald's eyes, one of the main points of the tradition of his craft was the British parliamentary system of government. For him, the parliamentary system was, in fact, the grand style in which all his operations must be carried out. There was a slight, instinctive bias in his mind against any change in the system, even when change was clearly of native inspiration, and when it amounted to little more than a modification of the style. The bias grew appreciably stronger when it became a question of alien borrowings, and particularly of imports from the exotic theory or practice of the congressional system in the United States. The old campaign for "elective institutions" which the Clear Grits had revived in 1851 had now dwindled away into a demand, fairly regularly repeated, for an elective Legislative Council. A number of Conservatives were, rather surprisingly, in favour of the change, for they believed that, if the upper chamber were elected on a stiff property franchise, they would have a good chance of wresting its control away from the Reformers. Macdonald had to treat these mild aberrations of his colleagues seriously; but he showed little interest, and took no part, in the campaign to smarten up the parliamentary system with a few day-before-yesterday republican improvements.[13] For him, responsible government, and the institutions out of which it had naturally developed, were amply sufficient. And when George Brown, who was in other respects a stout defender of the parliamentary system, proposed a fixed date for the annual meeting of the legislature, Macdonald objected that this would limit the use of the ancient royal prerogative to summon and prorogue parliament.[14] He looked with detachment on proposals to broaden the already fairly generous Canadian franchise; and even such an outwardly innocuous measure as the Representation Bill of 1853, which increased the representation of each section of the province to sixty-five members, found him dubious and critical. He had a number of debating points to make against the bill; he considered it unnecessary and uncalled for. "If there is one thing to be avoided," he declared, "it is meddling with the constitution of the country, which should not be altered till it is evident that the people are suffering from the effects of that constitution as it actually exists."[15]

If in politics he stressed the value of the constitutional inheritance, so in cultural matters he was prepared to recognize the strength and importance of the Christian tradition. His upbringing, his political experience, and the instinctive, easygoing tolerance of his nature all helped to make it easy for him to realize how vital, and how endlessly varied, was the religious life of early Victorian Canada. Confronted with this uniform passion for religion, and these passionate religious differences, both the secular-minded anticlerical and the deeply religious "voluntarist" were accustomed to preach the doctrine of the separation of church and state. But this simple and decisive solution was not Macdonald's first choice. He was quite prepared to accept the old Conservative view that the state should recognize and assist the religious and cultural activities of the churches. He made, in fact, only one change—but a change of enormous importance—in this venerable programme. From the start he had tried to convince his Conservative associates that they must liberalize and democratize the principles of recognition and assistance by extending their scope to all Christian communions without distinction. The Constitutional Act of 1791 provided that one-seventh of all the public lands granted by the Crown should be reserved for the support of a Protestant Clergy. The endless difficulties in the definition of the term "a Protestant Clergy" had convinced many Christians that it would be best to "secularize" the Clergy Reserves—to appropriate their revenues to the general purposes of government. But Macdonald would have preferred to maintain the revised settlement, established by the imperial statute of 1840, which divided the proceeds of the Reserves among the principal Protestant churches. There were difficulties, of course, in the equitable division of state support—difficulties which were augmented by the utter refusal of certain communions to accept any share whatever: and these problems, which had led to the abandonment of the University Bills in 1847, might in the end force the acceptance of the secularization of the Clergy Reserves. He was better prepared than some of his associates to accept secularization, for his interest in the Reserves was not special privilege but fair division. In his view, the Conservatives must learn to recognize and respect not only the multiple religious divisions of Canada West, but also the single basic cultural division between English-speaking and French-speaking Canada.

It was this idea which governed his policy during the excited politico-religious dispute of the early 1850's. He was prepared to accept the cultural duality of Canadian life, to recognize that what was in form a unitary province was in fact a half-acknowledged federal state. The union could only be preserved by a series of compromises and conventions which sanctioned this cultural duality; and one of the most important of these compromises was the equal representation of the two sections of the province in the Assembly. Up until the session of 1852-53, the sectional political equality had not been very sharply questioned; but in March, 1853, George Brown first began his frontal attack on it by moving, in an amendment to the Representation Bill, that "the Representation of the people in Parliament should be based upon Population . . . and without regard to any separating line between Upper and Lower Canada".[16] This was the first emphatic and unambiguous expression of the principle of "Rep. by Pop."—the principle which, if adopted, was certain to upset the quasi-federal structure of the province, and to give Canada West, now rapidly surpassing the eastern section of the province in population, a dominant place in the union. Macdonald—a deplorably late arrival at Quebec that winter—was not in his place when Brown's amendment was debated:[17] but there can be little doubt that he eyed it very doubtfully from the start. For him, "Rep. by Pop." was an abstract idea, whose value could never be judged apart from the existing circumstances of time and place; and if, as the French Canadians insisted, the abandonment of sectional equality was tantamount to the dissolution of the union, then obviously the abstract idea was politically impossible. For the union of 1841 must be maintained. Macdonald did not, as yet, believe in the practicability of a general British North American federation; but at Kingston he had grown up into the conviction that the British lands bordering on the great river were indissolubly one. It was only through their union with each other and their connection with Great Britain that the St. Lawrence communities could hope to maintain their separate existence in North America. And for these reasons, the union, with all its necessary compromises, must be preserved.

II

This was the assortment of goods which Macdonald, now MacNab's principal assistant, could arrange inside the somewhat small and grimy panes of the Conservative shop window. To drum up trade among conservative Liberals and liberal Conservatives, to win the custom of the French Canadians—this was the old objective. And now that the Clear Grits were in the ministry, and the religious, cultural controversy in full swing, it was possible for the Conservatives to give a new and persuasive twist to the old propaganda by which they had tried to convince the French Canadians that they were taking their patronage to the wrong shop. In the speech which Macdonald delivered, early in September, 1852, on the address in reply to the speech from the throne, this new direction was at least vaguely indicated.[18] Already, he informed his listeners, the Radicals were jubilantly predicting that great and "progressive" reforms were bound to come, now that the "drag" of Baldwin and Lafontaine had been removed from the government. What could this possibly portend? Baldwin and Lafontaine, he informed Hincks reproachfully, "were the most upright men with whom the Inspector-General was ever allied". They had dignified the past of the Reform party. But now, with the Clear Grits in the government, who could safeguard its future? Macdonald glanced briefly, apprehensively, at that future. Possibly the Clergy Reserves question, now slumbering peacefully, would be revived. Possibly some equally fundamental attack on the established order would be begun. The future was dark with menace. The new alliance on the treasury bench was a preposterous and horrible partnership, a conspiracy merely to retain office, which could survive only through inconsistency, hypocrisy and deceit, and which promised to end in the treachery of the Clear Grits and the betrayal of the French Canadians.

On September 17, when, for the first time in his political career, Macdonald spoke at length on the subject of the Clergy Reserves, he took advantage of the occasion to picture the probable results of the alliance with the Clear Grits in still more horrifying detail. This, the third great debate on the

Reserves, marked another stage in the stumbling, erratic, and somewhat equivocal progress of the question. Lord John Russell's government, on receipt of the Canadian resolutions of 1850, had decided that it would repeal the imperial act of 1840 and permit the provincial parliament to legislate as it pleased on the subject. But the Russell government fell before it could carry out its expressed intention, and the Conservatives under Lord Derby succeeded to power. The Conservatives in England looked just as disapprovingly as the Conservatives in Canada upon any disturbance of the existing settlement of the Reserves; and the new Colonial Secretary, Sir John Pakington, informed Lord Elgin that his government was not disposed to touch the question. It was easy, fairly popular, and politically cheap for the Reformers to enter a valiant protest against this imperial veto.[19] It was equally easy for the Conservatives to take cover behind the Colonial Office, to justify the wisdom of its stand, and to deprecate the "collision" with the imperial authorities which the Canadian government seemed to threaten. Macdonald found Hincks's resolutions meaningless, insolent, and revolutionary. The imperial act of 1840 was, he insisted, a moderate, reasonable settlement of the problem. The deliberate resuscitation of the question of the Reserves, with a transparently fraudulent affectation of strong feeling, was a "solemn and discreditable mockery". Its one aim—for the ministers did not dare to pledge their followers to a policy of secularization— was simply to keep the country in an uproar. The interests of peace and equity required that this agitation should be stopped, and French Canadians had a special obligation to quiet a senseless and mischievous controversy which was full of peril for themselves. "They had it in their power," Macdonald declared deliberately, "to put a stop to the turmoil and the agitation and hypocrisy upon this question: and they should do it, as well to protect the constitutional rights of others, as to prevent the same violent hands being laid upon their own property and institutions in turn".[20] If they joined the spoliators of religious endowments in Canada West, they would inevitably endanger their own cultural institutions; and every French-Canadian member who voted for Hincks's resolutions "lent his influence and support to a party who were seeking to destroy all ecclesiastical institutions, who would never rest until they tore down every church establishment in British America".

Macdonald's dire predictions remained unsubstantiated during the first part of the session. But when the House met again, in the middle of a snowy February, after a long adjournment, it was at once evident that the question of the Clergy Reserves had entered a new and still more exciting phase. In the interval, the Derby ministry in England had been succeeded by a coalition of Whigs and Peelites under Lord Aberdeen; and the new Colonial Secretary, the Duke of Newcastle, promptly informed Lord Elgin that the new government was ready to honour the pledge made by the previous Liberal administration. This despatch, read on February 15, the second evening after the opening, was listened to with "breathless attention".[21] Would the Conservatives, now that the support of the Colonial Office had been removed, continue their efforts to quiet the angry agitation over the Reserves? Would the work of secularization and spoliation now proceed unhindered to the satisfaction of those covetous anticlericals, the Clear Grits? These were natural questions, but they remained unanswered. Time went on, and nothing seemed to happen. On the one hand, the government maintained a mysterious silence on the subject of the Reserves; on the other, it seemed disposed to give every legislative assistance to a great variety of religious groups and societies in French Canada, who were covering the eastern section of the province with a network of monasteries, nunneries, schools, colleges, hospitals, and charities, all under ecclesiastical control. Was it true that the favoured institutions of French Canada, far from being menaced, were actually multiplying themselves with impunity? Could it be that the Clear Grits, and not the French Canadians, were the real dupes of the coalition of 1851? And, if so, how were Macdonald and the Conservatives to revise the strategy by which they hoped to detach the French Canadians from their "unnatural alliance", and thus attain political power themselves?

One obvious device was at hand. Macdonald and his friends could intensify their campaign to prove that these concessions

on the part of the Clear Grits were utterly insincere and calculating; they could redouble their efforts to reveal the Radicals
as a group which was infinitely contemptible and yet infinitely
dangerous. For months the Conservative newspapers made this
form of caricature their favourite pastime. The Clear Grits
were represented, in the first place, as an unsavoury and illiterate
crew of yokels. "Coon" Cameron's hair resembled "a disarranged
brush heap".[22] His followers occupied their leisure time in the
Assembly in the "elegant operation" of picking their teeth and
scratching their heads.[23] On formal occasions, they wore coats
"evidently made when the broad-bottomed Dutch style was
in vogue"; they acknowledged gracious salutations "with a
picturesque chop of their heads and hoist of their heels"; and
they found the parties at Government House a sad disappointment because the refreshments unfortunately contained no
pork and beans, sauerkraut, or pumpkin pie.[24] Uncouth, ill-bred,
bad-mannered, with nothing but a low animal cunning to serve
them in the place of intelligence, they were just as morally
reprehensible as they were physically dirty. Usually their convenient "sliding-scale" of principles permitted them to sit in
the House and vote for anything the government demanded.
But sometimes even their coarse radical stomachs were revolted
by a strong and unchanging diet of ecclesiastical corporation
bills. They sought refuge from humiliation in precipitate retreat; and Dr. Rolph, their second representative in the ministry,
became known as "Old Dissolving Views" from the frantic haste
with which he left the chamber, his coat-tails flying out, when
a particularly embarrassing division was at hand.[25] All this
transparent evasion and dissimulation was simply a device to
permit the Clear Grits to enjoy the benefits of office. Their
real views had not changed: their real views were indistinguishable from those of George Brown, the editor of the *Globe*, the
newly elected member for Kent, who had carried into the Assembly his great campaign against the sinister forces of the
Papacy, and who was now denouncing French and Roman
Catholic domination in religious and cultural matters with
terrific energy and passionate emotional conviction. "The spirit
which the member for Kent has openly avowed through the

columns of the *Globe* rankles in all their breasts and is only hidden now from motives of policy".[26]

Macdonald accepted these useful propagandist devices, but he must have realized that they had certain limitations. However much the Conservatives might denounce the unreality of the coalition of 1851, however much they might prophesy the eventual betrayal of the French Canadians, the fact remained that at the moment the government was pursuing a moderate policy in cultural and religious matters, a policy which could hardly have been anything but satisfactory to the French Canadians, and which was not very different from that which the Conservatives themselves would have followed. Yet if the Conservatives accepted the government programme too meekly they would forfeit their right to be regarded as a serious opposition, just as they would wreck the whole plan of a union with the moderates and French Canadians if they followed the intransigent opposition of Brown. It was a tight situation, and its difficulties were never better illustrated than by the so-called Ecclesiastical Corporations Bill of 1853. The government, wearied and perhaps embarrassed by the frequently repeated necessity of chartering individual Roman Catholic institutions, decided to introduce a general measure for the incorporation of such religious, charitable and educational bodies.[27] It was certain that George Brown would oppose the bill. But what of the Clear Grits, those restless, unhappy, conscience-stricken creatures, who listened dully, with one unwilling ear, to the orders of their government whips, and, with the other, hearkened yearningly to Brown's irrefutable logic? Obviously their vote was very uncertain; and after March 8, when Brown delivered his enormous, vituperative oration against the bill,[28] the rumours of dissatisfaction and impending revolt among the Clear Grits, the Baldwin Reformers, and even among the French Canadians began to grow and circulate rapidly.[29] Could it be that the government would be defeated on the measure? And in such a crisis, what policy should the Conservative party adopt?

Macdonald obviously enjoyed surprise, shock tactics—"plots" he called them to Captain Strachan; and it is not too difficult to see his guiding hand in the dispositions of the Conservatives on this occasion. The party waited developments in ambush. Not a single Conservative arose to debate Brown's amendment; and on March 10, when the debate was resumed, MacNab's entire following still remained fixed in mysterious and sinister silence. That night the galleries were crowded; rows of priests and Roman Catholic dignitaries sat watching anxiously for the result. And as Drummond, the Attorney-General for Canada East, ramblingly continued his protracted—perhaps deliberately protracted—speech, the desperate struggle for votes went on. Dr. Rolph, and Messrs. Richards and Cameron were observed "flying about the house, now soft-sawdering a refractory Grit, and again pulling the traces on the right side of the legs of a kicking French Canadian".[30] There was, a Tory correspondent noted with malicious satisfaction, a peculiar "goneness" in the stricken countenance of the Clear Grit David Christie as he contemplated the horrifying vision of his angry Free Kirk constituents back in Wentworth; and "as for poor Amos Wright, of East York, he was so flattered and fondled by great men in high offices, that he looked as bewildered with unexpected honours as an interesting young widow giving herself away in matrimony for the fourth time".[31] Then at last, when Drummond's long speech grew to its close, the vote came. The entire body of Conservatives, together with Brown and his few followers, and Cauchon, Sicotte, and a handful of French Canadians, voted for the amendment and against the bill. They mustered thirty-four votes. No, only thirty-three! For the once vigilant and terrible William Lyon Mackenzie, awakening in bewilderment out of a deep and stupefying sleep, voted for the amendment, then announced that he had made a mistake and voted the other way, while the House amused itself at the fretful old man's expense. Thirty-three votes! But the government had obtained thirty-nine. It had won; but only with the support and the humiliation of the Clear Grits.

Macdonald had now to talk his way out of the position in which the vote had placed the Conservative party. The opposition had done better than in any previous division in the new House. But the Conservative ruse had failed of its daring objective—the overthrow of the ministry. The party had voted as a body with Brown, and its course, to say the least, required some defence and explanation. Hincks rose, immediately after the vote, to taunt the "great Conservative party" with voting factiously for an amendment which it had not dared to support in debate. MacNab's defence was brief and rather feeble, and a good deal depended on Macdonald's reply. He did what probably nobody in the House beside himself would have thought of doing, or dared to do. He gave only the briefest of explanations, assuring the French Canadians, at the very end of his speech, that the Conservatives did not, of course, object to ecclesiastical corporations as such, but only to the generality and laxity of the present bill. He hardly bothered with a defence at all. Instead, he burlesqued the whole episode of the vote which the House had just recorded, covered the unhappy Grits with ridicule, and kept the whole House laughing over the preposterous divisions in the government.[82] Never before, he declared, had there been "such a whipping in" in Canadian parliamentary history. During the whole evening, ministers had been looking anxiously out into the corridors for skulkers; the President of the Council had been flitting restlessly about the room in search of recalcitrants. And yet, when, after all their efforts, they had got their last man in, they could muster a majority of only six votes—of only five "before the honourable member for Haldimand saw which way the wind was blowing and changed his mind". Poor Mackenzie, chattering with rage, got indignantly to his feet to refute this insinuation and to tell the humiliating story of his slumbers. But Brown retorted incisively that only the day before, Mackenzie had informed him that he would oppose the bill; and the resulting altercation between the member for Kent and the member for Haldimand continued for a moment or two, while the House rocked with laughter. Everybody was in a good humour when Macdonald resumed his description of the monstrous, hydra-headed government, whose agonized convulsions were so fascinating to behold that the Conservatives preferred to watch them in attentive silence. Office was the one thing that kept the government together; and office—and the well-filled purse of a developing young country— had brought the Clear Grits submissively to heel once again.

"These honourable gentlemen of more than common political virtue, these purists who would sweep everything away for their principles, these Clear Grits, the pure silica of Upper Canada, voted for the government against their principles".[33] Never again could they face their constituencies with impunity: "the member for Kent had ungritted them".

Macdonald's defence was ingenious, but it could not get the party out of the fundamental difficulty of its position. The fact was that the quarrel over cultural and religious institutions, over the relation of church and state, had aroused strong and conflicting opinions, which were inhibited and muffled by the existing divisions of the Canadian party system. Until recent times it had been chiefly the Conservatives who, for obvious reasons, had attacked the existing divisions; but now it was the turn of the Radicals to grow angry over the deceptions and frustrations of Canadian party politics. The secularization of the Clergy Reserves had been repeatedly and mysteriously postponed; the ecclesiastical institutions of Canada East had been steadily strengthened; the common school system of Canada West had been progressively modified to admit separate Roman Catholic schools. And all this had happened under a Reform government, of which the radical Clear Grits were a constituent party! William McDougall, the architect of the coalition of 1851, was now alarmed by the results of his handiwork.[34] The Radical leaders, Rolph and Cameron, steadily declined in prestige, and George Brown loomed larger and larger as the real leader of western Canadian discontent. He had become, in one short parliamentary session, a commanding figure in the House and the country. Humourless, blunt in diction, awkward in gesture—the stiff arm, jerking monotonously up and down like a dull saw on an obstinate log of hardwood, was the characteristic accompaniment of his speeches—he seemed, in the downright, purposeful simplicity of his thought and manner, to be the authentic, vital voice of Protestant Upper Canada. For him the existing party system was simply a sham. He had no doubt whatever that the Radicals, in accepting office with French-Canadian support, had debased their Liberalism and abandoned their entire programme of reform. The French Canadians, he insisted over and over again, were not real reformers at all: and "to think that the Liberals of Upper Canada can long continue in close alliance with the Lower Canadian party, as at present constituted, is absurd".[35] Once the unnatural union were broken, the western Liberals would be released from their thraldom, and the Ultramontanes of Canada East could make an appropriate alliance with the Tories of Canada West. "The two parties were in fact made for each other," he wrote bluntly, "and should embrace as soon as possible. Everybody is in a false position just now".[36]

Macdonald would have emphatically agreed that everybody was in a false position. It was natural that these two men, the coming Conservative and Reform leaders, the great political rivals of the future, should concur so nearly in their analysis of Canadian parties. Both men wished to break up the existing party system. Both hoped to establish great middle parties from which only a few extremists would be excluded. They were of one mind up to this point; but at this point their agreement ended. Macdonald believed that his Liberal-Conservative party could absorb the great body of the Reformers with the exception of a few radical Clear Grits from Canada West and a few *Rouges* from Canada East. Brown aspired to take over the majority of the Conservatives minus only an impotent handful of ultras and reactionaries. "It is the real Tory High-Churchmen of Upper Canada and the thorough ultramontanists of Lower Canada who must join," the *Globe* argued persuasively.[37] The two plans conflicted; the success of one meant inevitably the complete failure of the other. And from 1853 on, as the coalition of 1851 grew more insecure and the Hincks government more vulnerable, the two schemes began to stand out against each other with greater and greater clarity.

III

Early in May, when Macdonald left Quebec and returned to Kingston, the long, meandering session had still a month to run. It was probably the practice that drew him back; but a weary discouragement with the results of the session may have made it easier for him to leave. Back in Kingston, as he talked over the probable future of the party with a friendly observer like Alexander Campbell, he sometimes showed a cheerfully cynical despair.[38] The fact was that the session, with its heavy concentration on cultural and religious matters, had not advanced the fortunes of Conservatism nearly as much as he had perhaps expected. In one way, the battles over schools, and Clergy Reserves, and religious corporations had been useful to the Conservatives, for they gave the party a chance of demonstrating its basic sympathy with French-Canadian needs. But, in another and equally important way, the cultural struggle was dangerous to the Conservatives, and to any other political group which was, in fact or by intention, a truly provincial party. Disputes over schools and churches brought out into the open the fundamental antagonism between the two divisions of the province. Cultural disputes emphasized the sectional rather than the provincial interest. They led to mutual recriminations, to charges and counter-charges that one section of the province was imposing a cultural domination on the other. They supplied a cogent justification for George Brown's plan of representation by population, and a plausible excuse for George Brown's scheme of a great sectional crusade against conservative French Canada. In such dangerous circumstances it was difficult for Canadians to combine, as Canadians; and it was altogether too easy for the Conservatives themselves to hark back to their old anti-French prejudices of the past. The party might not only fail to win the alliance of the French of Canada East; it might also lose its following among the Protestant English of Canada West. The danger was real, and it would almost certainly grow greater, if the cultural conflict became more acrimonious. And the trouble was that in the spring and early summer of 1853 religious and sectional antagonism reached a new and almost unexampled pitch of violence.

Partly it was the actions and inactions of the provincial legislature—the new public school law and the failure to do anything about the Clergy Reserves—which aggravated the voluntarist and anti-Catholic grievances of Canada West. But, to a very large extent, the emotional explosion of June and July was the result of the sudden appearance of a strange and exotic figure from abroad who, as not infrequently happens in provincial societies, touched off the charge of anger with an ease which no native could have approached. Towards the end of May, Father Alessandro Gavazzi, a veteran of the Italian Revolutions of 1848 and an ex-friar of the Roman Catholic Church, arrived in Toronto to begin a Canadian lecture tour. Gavazzi was a Liberal in politics who had become an evangelical Protestant in religion;[39] and after the collapse of the Roman Republic had driven him into exile in 1849, he had travelled about the English-speaking world, lecturing to large, responsive audiences on such currently exciting topics as the authority of the Bible, the doctrine of transubstantiation, and the evils of the Inquisition, ancient and modern.[40] His mission, he announced with grandiloquent comprehensiveness, was nothing less than the total destruction of the Pope and Popery. He was a tall, stout man, with a powerful voice, at once insinuating and commanding, and a strongly marked, extremely expressive countenance, radiating magnetic force and vehement conviction.[41] When he appeared before an audience, he wore a long, full, black robe, ornamented with a purple cross on the breast and left shoulder. His appearance was sufficiently startling; his platform manner was more than a little theatrical; and it seemed at first as if his Canadian tour was certain to be a triumphant success. On the last day of May and the first of June, 1853, he delivered two highly successful lectures to huge audiences in Toronto. From Toronto he travelled quickly eastward to Quebec, where the legislature was still sitting; and at Quebec, a riot occurred when he attempted to lecture in the Free Wesleyan Chapel in St. Ursula Street.[42] Almost immediately he left the capital; but instead of abandoning the province, as prudence might have suggested, he simply sailed up the river to Montreal. There, on the evening of June 8, at Zion Church in Haymarket Square, the tragedy occurred. A large crowd hostile to Gavazzi collected; a riot threatened, and the military were called out. The soldiers, acting in response to a fatal order, whose origin was hotly disputed afterwards, fired upon a section of the crowd, composed, as it happened, chiefly of the members of Gavazzi's audience, killing several people and fatally wounding others.[43]

This dreadful event put Macdonald, and the Conservatives, and indeed all the moderates, into a most embarrassing position. The tragedy was a terrible one, and its perpetrators seemed to have escaped with impunity from all consequences. No successful prosecutions were ever carried out in Montreal. Not even the thought of possible prosecution seemed to intimidate the rioters. For some time after June 8, so the newspapers alleged, crowds of Montrealers, completely contemptuous of the law, roamed the streets at will, breaking the windows of Protestant chapels and molesting and abusing evangelical Protestant clergymen.[44] And all the while, the governments, both municipal and provincial, seemed strangely unconcerned in the whole affair. No other series of events could have so effectively proved, in the excited popular mind, the justice of George Brown's crusade against the Roman Catholic domination of Canada East. Brown was a sectional leader—the defender of Upper Canadian sectional interests; but the tragedy of June 8—and this, for the Conservatives, was perhaps its most serious consequence—had invested his anti-Catholic crusade with a truly provincial significance and popularity. Down in Montreal, people began to argue hysterically that Protestants must combine to protect themselves with arms against the "thuggism" and "barbarism" which were "patronized by the legal authorities".[45] There was an ominous drift back towards the violence of 1849; there was an equally ominous tendency away from the compromises and accommodations which the dual culture seemed to require, and which Macdonald and some of the Conservatives had been trying to prove they were ready to accept. In these new and difficult circumstances, could the party hold to its chosen course, or would it slip back into the old anti-French direction, and so into the waiting arms of George Brown? In the weeks that followed the Gavazzi riots, the future seemed uncertain. Towards the end of June the Orange Order split. A minority of lodges, led by George Benjamin, withdrew in protest against the moderation of Ogle Gowan's pro-Catholic and pro-French policies: and it was significant that, in the political field, the "Benjaminites" preached a union with the Clear Grits to defeat Popery. In August, there came a dreadful day when even the *Montreal Gazette* admitted that the Conservative party, as then constituted, was moribund and incapable of resuscitation. A new party, the *Gazette* predicted, would arise—a new party which would labour to undo the iniquities of the past four years; and "this party," the prophetic editorial continued, "will demand equality for all sects and classes, gradual fusion of U.C. and L.C., free schools for the whole people, and Rep. by Pop.".[46] Was this not really the programme of the *Globe*? What was there to distinguish this "new party" from the party which George Brown was actually trying to create?

Macdonald's whole conception of the future of Conservatism was in danger. Some of his followers were ready to bolt; his policies had apparently been made meaningless by the horrors of the Gavazzi riots. He did not reappear in parliament for the last month of the session. He said and did little. He simply waited, hoping, no doubt, that the furious cultural and sectional antagonisms would wear themselves out through the very excess of their own violence. And, as the summer of 1853 passed slowly along, it began to seem possible that he had not waited entirely in vain. August was not ended before a new and very different political scandal began slowly and tantalizingly to be revealed to the fascinated gaze of the Canadians. It concerned no less a person than Francis Hincks himself, the Inspector-General, and the somewhat mysterious good fortune which had come to him in the last two years. For some weeks, the newspapers merely busied themselves with vague but interested inquiries into the source of Hincks's "sudden and inexplicable acquisition of great wealth";[47] and it was not until September, when the City of Toronto brought suit in chancery against its Mayor, John G. Bowes, that definite evidence of some of Hincks's financial operations at length became available. Then a tangled and curious story was revealed.[48] It appeared that the City of Toronto, wishing to aid the Toronto, Simcoe, and Huron Railway which was then in financial difficulties, had agreed to grant £50,000 in Toronto municipal debentures to the railway company. Sub-

sequently it was discovered that the authority by which the
city had made the grant was defective; and the debentures,
which had been paid out by the railway to its contractors, depreciated in value. The City of Toronto, moved by its Mayor,
John G. Bowes, now decided to consolidate the entire municipal debt with a refunding operation which would redeem all
its old or defective debentures at par; and the government of
Canada, with Francis Hincks as its finance minister, accommodatingly sponsored the consolidation act by which this operation was carried out. So far the case—a not unusual case of
Canadian municipal generosity and inefficiency—had not been
very remarkable. But there was more to come. It was now
revealed that Bowes and Hincks, the principals in the refunding operation, were also the purchasers of the old and depreciated debentures. They had bought the old bonds for £40,000;
they exchanged them for new bonds worth £50,000. They had
cleared £10,000 upon the deal.

This—the so-called "£10,000 job"—was a major sensation of
the autumn and winter of 1853-54. In September the chancery
suit began; in February three whole days were occupied in
receiving the testimony of Francis Hincks.[49] His evidence,
printed in long, close columns in the newspapers, almost competed in interest with the exciting despatches from England
which recounted the diplomatic prologue to the Crimean War.
A host of speculations and rumours, each clamouring for certainty, now gathered about the Inspector-General. Mr. Hincks,
the *Montreal Gazette* assured its readers, had been "financing
to a tune . . . of which the first notes are only now falling on
the public ear".[50] All that autumn and winter the public ear
was attentively cocked. What were the other high notes in
Mr. Hincks's soaring financial melody? Who had paid for the
1008 shares of stock with which he was credited in the books
of his own creation, the Grand Trunk Railway? Had he known,
when he speculated in the stock of the St. Lawrence and Atlantic Railway, that it was certain to be absorbed, on advantageous terms, by the Grand Trunk? By what means had he
possessed himself of a piece of government property which
happened to lie so conveniently close to the destined junction

of the railway at Point Levis? A clever little man—a typical sharp-eyed child of that unpleasantly prolific marriage between railways and responsible government, Hincks had gone about the business of furthering his own personal interests with the direct, uncomplicated ingenuity of a precocious infant. He had presented the public with a scandal so simple, so instantly comprehensible, so wholly malodorous that it brought unmitigated damage to the government and no embarrassment to the opposition. From the winter of 1854, it was almost certain that Hincks's political career was at an end; it was almost certain that the government which he had led would have to be reconstituted, and the only question, as William McDougall put it, was how were men to combine anew?[51]

Macdonald's objective remained exactly the same. He still hoped to build a party which would be liberal in its Conservatism and truly provincial in its scope. He still hoped to attract the bulk of the French Canadians and a large number of their associates, the Baldwin Reformers. For him the great political advantage of the Hincks scandals lay in the fact that they tended to direct attention away from the religious grievances and sectional resentments which for a year now had prejudiced this old Conservative programme. It was true that these resentments and grievances still rankled angrily in the minds of some Conservatives; and it was true too that George Brown, more openly than ever in the past, was seeking to seduce those waverers with his own special kind of blunt, argumentative wooing. "Between the great mass of the Reformers of Upper Canada and this largest or liberal section of the Conservatives," he argued, "there is little difference of opinion. Not one great principle divides them. Nothing but old recollections of antagonism, and a reluctance to yield up the Reserves, for which many of them have so long contended—prevents them working cordially together. When they do unite—when they unite on clearly defined, progressive principles—*French Canadian supremacy will be at an end*, and the political prospects of our country very different from now."[52] "French-Canadian supremacy will be at an end"—it was the old catch-cry, seductive and illusory, which the Conservatives had hearkened to long before. Macdonald had no desire to follow that mocking voice once more into the political wilderness. "I believe also," he wrote to Captain Strachan in February, 1854, "that there must be a change of ministry after the election, and from my friendly relations with the French, I am inclined to believe my assistance will be sought."[53] The French-Canadian alliance was still a main objective: so also was the liberalization of the old Conservative programme in Canada West. And although the Conservatives must never be led away into the fatal error of identifying their profession of faith with that of George Brown, yet they must struggle to convince moderate Reformers that there was a real prospect of progressive Reform in Liberal-Conservatism. "Our aim," Macdonald wrote to Captain Strachan, "should be to enlarge the bounds of our party so as to embrace every person desirous of being counted as a progressive Conservative, and who will join in a series of measures to put an end to the corruption which has ruined the present government and debauched all its followers."[54]

The theme of government corruption became the main theme of Macdonald's attack when parliament met again in June, 1854. In the meantime, the government of Canada, which, for nearly fifteen years, had been flitting unhappily about, like a distracted, migratory family of tenants, from one set of makeshift lodgings to another, had sustained a double tragedy in rapid succession. In the early morning of February 1, the old parliament buildings of Lower Canada, which had housed the government and legislature of the united provinces since their move from Toronto, were totally destroyed by fire;[55] and early in May, barely three months later, a second and equally spectacular conflagration wiped out the convent on the edge of the town which had been altered and redecorated at great expense for parliament's temporary accommodation.[56] It was the third time in five years that the lodgings of the luckless Canadian government had been burnt up by accident or arson; and, in this all too familiar emergency, the dwindling piles of books and records were packed up once more, the Legislative Council was transferred to the Quebec court-house, and the public Music Hall was hurriedly prepared for the reception of the

Assembly. The Assembly had barely met in these ironically incongruous surroundings when it became quite clear that even Macdonald had underestimated the amount of impatient disapproval which Hincks had aroused since the prorogation of the previous summer. Yet the Inspector-General apparently viewed this climbing wave of criticism with contemptuous unconcern. Badgered by many problems, and restrained by Elgin's cautionary advice, he presented only a very brief, perfunctory programme of legislation, which touched none of the controversial issues of the day; and he now surprisingly argued— echoing the arguments which the Governor-General had used to him—that, since the new representation bill was now upon the statute books, it would be better to seek the sense of the people again before beginning any radical changes. The House felt frustrated and irritated; the debate on the address in reply to the speech from the throne was prolonged and stormy; and when, on the night of Monday, June 19, Macdonald rose to speak, he may have believed that at last there was a real chance of doing something decisive. He began by attacking Hincks for the transparent self-interest which had dictated his change of attitude to a dissolution. Last year, when criticized for introducing a representation bill into the first session of a new parliament, the government had argued that the House, in passing such a measure, would not thereby confess itself to be an unrepresentative assembly which was incompetent to deal with serious matters. Last session, every government spokesman had insisted on the omnicompetence of the existing legislature; this session, with equal unanimity, they had proclaimed parliament's lack of moral authority to make law. It was an absurdly obvious contradiction, Macdonald argued, which arose solely from the government's desire to evade a parliamentary inquiry into its own misdeeds. Those corrupt misdeeds had been repudiated by everybody, including Reformers, including even the Inspector-General's own colleagues, for Malcolm Cameron, the Postmaster-General, had declared, at a public dinner in Perth, that he did not approve of the Point Levis purchase. The first, primitive duty of a member of any administration was not to speculate in public funds and public property. Pitt—

and here came one of Macdonald's characteristic appeals to the conduct of his favourite statesman—had for years remained completely unmoved by all the attacks made upon him; but, when once it was charged that he had speculated in public funds, then immediately he had filed suit in slander. Had the members of the present Canadian government been equally sensitive? They had not—and for a simple reason. They were terrified of the consequences which such a prosecution would entail.[57]

It was a particularly savage attack: and even the Toronto *Leader*, a government newspaper which the Conservative journals delighted to refer to as "Tsar Francis I's Court Circular", admitted rather wryly that Macdonald had "displayed more talent in the assault than the world usually gives him credit for possessing".[58] Hincks, pushed unceremoniously into an awkward corner, arose to give a somewhat laboured account of his purchase of the Point Levis property; Cameron got up to explain away his statement at the Perth dinner and to denounce Macdonald for repeating the falsehoods which foul-mouthed slanderers had been spreading for months against the government. Charges, recriminations and counter-charges were bandied about for a couple of hours between the alleged Reform railway plunderers of the present and the alleged Conservative land-grabbers of the past. The next day the debate was resumed with a new vigour and purposefulness. Cauchon, an ex-Reformer who had acted with Macdonald in the previous session, had already moved an amendment to the address, censuring the government for its failure to produce a bill for the "immediate settlement of the seigniorial question". Hartman, a Clear Grit, now produced a sub-amendment, which gave expression to the principal Upper Canadian grievance, and lamented the absence of a measure for "secularization of the Clergy Reserves". The horrid, definite word "secularization" was too much for the House: the Clear Grit sub-amendment was voted down. But where Hartman and Sicotte, the Clear Grit and the *Rouge*, had failed, it was possible for Sicotte and Cauchon, the Conservative, to succeed. Together they introduced a second sub-amendment which merely deplored the absence of a bill for the "immediate settlement of the Clergy Reserves". All the various, discontented sections of the House swung in behind this new, vaguely critical sub-amendment. It was passed by forty-two to twenty-nine votes; and Cauchon's main amendment, so altered, was accepted by the same majority.[59] The Hincks government had suddenly been defeated, and on two issues of major importance.

That night, when the long debate ended, Macdonald probably expected an immediate invitation to office. It was rumoured that next day, June 21, he and MacNab stayed patiently in their hotel rooms, waiting for a messenger from the Governor-General.[60] The House stood adjourned all day; all day the government debated its future course of action; but night fell and there was still no indication that Hincks had resigned and that a new government was about to be formed. It was not, apparently, until the morning of June 22 that the members began uneasily to suspect that Hincks had decided upon a very different course. Then, as the House assembled in the early afternoon, these suspicions were quickly converted into shocking certainties. Outside, the booming guns heralded the approach of the Governor-General to the nearby court-house; and inside the Music Hall, Hincks, in reply to a question from Sir Allan MacNab, calmly informed the House that the government had decided upon an immediate prorogation. At first the members seemed shocked into speechlessness. MacNab's brief protest was heard "amid a silence deep as death". Then William Lyon Mackenzie rose, somewhat more excitedly, to support the plea of the leader of the opposition that the Franchise Bill be passed immediately. But it was not until Black Rod had been admitted and the notice of prorogation given, that the House really seemed to realize what was happening, and then all order and decorum were suddenly blown into tatters as a furious storm of rage and disappointment swept through the Assembly. The hall was clamorous with cries and murmurs; a dozen members were struggling to voice their bitter protests; and the excitable Mackenzie, pointing a passionate finger at the ministers, screamed "shame on them, shame on them", over and over again. Yet it was Macdonald who seemed to ride over the whole enormous tumult as its principal avenging fury. For the first time in his career he had become a fighter in a parliamentary milling ground. He had always disliked Elgin. And now Elgin and Hincks, by a too successful trick, had defrauded him of office and robbed him of his revenge. He was a political principal who was almost required to make a protest. But he was also a furious Highlander who was ready and willing for a fight. And for nearly a quarter of an hour he stood in his place, his face contorted with excitement, gesticulating violently and shouting his denunciations at the top of his voice.[61] Other angry voices succeeded to his. Drummond, Robinson, Brown, and Langton took up the vehement argument. But these were briefer utterances, briefer exchanges, which trailed away into ineffectuality, as the Speaker, and the government members, and the whole body of the Reformers began to move out of the room.

Within a fortnight the province was plunged into the excitement of an election. The Crimean War in which Great Britain was now engaged had become stalled in its first phase of laborious inactivity; and, for a moment at least, Canada could give a nearly undivided attention to provincial politics. It was the first general election since Macdonald had been publicly accepted as MacNab's principal lieutenant; and although, in those days, a party could exercise only a feeble control over its wayward and eccentric members, there were more than a few signs of Macdonald's guiding hand in the disposition of Conservative strategy. The ground for manoeuvre was difficult in the highest degree. The great main object of the campaign—the overthrow of the Hincks government—was an object shared by a variety of political groups; and there was inevitably some degree of association—desirable but dangerous association—among the different sections of the opposition. George Brown continued to make the most forthright and indiscreet advances. He did not trouble to conceal his preference for certain Conservative candidates, even in his home bailiwick, Toronto:[62] he announced publicly that the *Globe* would have supported John A. Macdonald, if he had run against Francis Hincks. The ministerial Reformers professed themselves bewildered and scandalized by this preposterous behaviour.

"Either the Tory party are the only true Reformers," wrote
the Toronto *Leader*, "or Mr. George Brown is no true Reformer
but a Tory."[63] But Brown remained cheerfully unrepentant in
the face of these rebukes. "Moreover," the *Globe* concluded a
long editorial in explanation of its conduct during the general
election, "we are free to admit that we have never failed to
keep in view the small differences which now divide the Reformers and Conservatives of Upper Canada and the exceeding probability that ere long they will be found in the same
harness working against the common enemy."[64] Macdonald
believed also in the probability of a union—but on his own, not
George Brown's, terms. And although the demonstrative expressions of Brown's rough wooing could not be rejected contemptuously, the Conservative party must set itself to prove that
it had not compromised its independence by any too intimate
political engagement.

Macdonald had tried to make the question of personal
honesty in government the first issue in the campaign; and
in the main the Conservative press followed him obediently.
"Let us rid the country of its corrupt rulers," said the *Montreal
Gazette*, "and ascertain how much damage they may have
inflicted; and then, having repaired the leaks in the strong box,
proceed to other reforms".[65] The nature of these "other reforms"
was indicated vaguely with those moderate reforming gestures
which Macdonald had been teaching his associates to employ.
The Conservatives were not disposed to change their basic
views on the relation of church and state; and they realized
that the adoption of Brown's extreme voluntarist and anti-
Catholic position would wreck their chances in Canada East.
But, at the same time, they knew also that, if they wished to
win moderate Reform support in Canada West, they must now
show their willingness to compromise on the subject of the
Clergy Reserves. They felt, and revealed, little enthusiasm for
secularization; they announced simply that they were ready to
face facts. The unpopularity of the Reserves must be conceded;
and the vast hubbub, which, despite Conservative warnings,
had been deliberately aroused over the settlement of 1840,
could not be permitted to disturb society indefinitely. "Men

have become wearied of the perpetual jangle," observed the *Montreal Gazette* temperately, "and are content to have the thing got rid of in some way—in any way so far as the bulk of the population were concerned . . .".[66] Badgley and Sherwood, it was reported, were prepared for new legislation on the subject;[67] and even MacNab, though his opinions remained unchanged, was alleged to have declared that he "knew when to bow to the voice of the country". It was rumoured, from Quebec, that at their last caucus of the session, the Conservatives had determined upon a fundamental change of policy with respect to the Reserves.[68] Evidently the party as a whole was preparing "to bow to the voice of the country".

So far as Macdonald's own election was concerned, the contest was a comparatively easy one. On July 17, at noon, outside the Kingston town hall, while a broiling sun beat down on the hustings and the perspiring crowd, Macdonald and John Counter were nominated as the two candidates for the riding.[69] Counter was, of course, the popular ex-mayor who had been nominated back in 1851, but who had refused to run on that occasion. With his hearty jokes and his bad grammar, he was the same cheerful, loquacious partisan of Kingston that he had always been. If he had any general politics they did not differ materially from Macdonald's. But the main public concern of his life had been Kingston; his principal interest in provincial politics was Kingston; and he was prolific in criticisms of what Macdonald had failed to do for the "good old town"—and voluble with promises of what he himself would certainly accomplish if he were elected. A new post office, a new customs house, the transfer of the "outer station" to the city, and even the return of the seat of government to Kingston—these were the spacious inducements in which Counter and his supporters dealt. "We are told by these immaculate persons," said a Conservative newspaper severely, "that Mr. Counter's politics are expressed in the simple word 'Kingston'; that he knows nothing but 'Kingston'; and that he will do anything and everything (if he *can* do anything) for 'Kingston'. If this has any meaning at all, it means that, be the government radical, whig, or tory . . . Kingston will be placed at its disposal, under any and all circumstances, *for a consideration*."⁷⁰ This effort to disparage poor Counter's politics as selfish and time-serving was apparently all that was needed; and Macdonald won his seat again by 437 to 265 votes.⁷¹

It was a severely local contest, peculiar in its almost exclusive concern with parochial issues, and unusual also as an easy Conservative success. The party, of course, won more seats than it had possessed in the previous House, for, now that the Representation Bill had gone into effect, there were many more seats to win. But, in general, success fell far short of Macdonald's hopeful expectations. The old, unreconciled disputes between the "progressive" Conservatives and the Tories still continued; the split between the "Gowanites" and the "Benjaminites" in the Orange Order was a serious weakness in several constituencies; and Macdonald faced a long and disappointing string of defeats. The ministerial papers joyfully announced that, after eight fruitless years of struggle, the Conservatives were now ready to "throw up the whole affair in disgust". It was even rumoured that "one of their leaders has made up his mind to resign his seat in Parliament, and leave the deluded country to its fate".⁷² Whether the gossip-monger had the member for Kingston in mind or not, the rumour was apparently an all too accurate description of Macdonald's feelings during the dark weeks of July and August. He was sick of the apparently profitless and hopeless struggle. "The party is nowhere—damned everlastingly," he told Alexander Campbell in his blunt, realistic way. "I will go down and get the bank bill passed and retire. I am resolved upon it."⁷³

It was an odd declaration, in the light of what happened in the first ten days of September. During the late summer Hincks had tried in vain to strengthen the support of his government;⁷⁴ and on September 5, when he met the House, a large House now of 130 members—"such immense shoals of loose fish were never before witnessed"—it became immediately evident that anything might happen, and happen quickly. On the first day the government candidate for the speakership was defeated; and on September 7, before the House ever really got down to the debate on the speech from the throne, Hincks sustained two tactical reverses in the case of the disputed Bagot election. On the morning of Friday, September 8, he and his colleagues resigned; and Lord Elgin sent at once for Sir Allan MacNab. Even then, and even among the Conservatives, the contradictory hopes and fears which had been bred of the bewildering confusion of Canadian party politics still continued to divide men; and the *Montreal Gazette* assured its readers that Sir Allan would probably fail in his task, and that then J. A. Macdonald and the "advanced Conservatives" would unite with the *Rouges* and the Brownites to form a government.[75] These confident calculations, so obviously copied from George Brown's exercise book in political arithmetic, could hardly have led to a more inaccurate conclusion. The next day MacNab saw Morin and Hincks; and Egerton Ryerson, who met him as he was coming out from his interview with the late Inspector-General, reported that Sir Allan was laughing heartily.[76] It was all arranged. The Conservatives were to unite with the moderates of the Reform party. The Lower Canadian section of the ministry was to continue unaltered; there were to be two Hincksite Reformers in the Upper Canadian section, and three Conservatives, MacNab, Cayley, and Macdonald. Macdonald was Attorney-General of Canada West, the office which both Draper and Baldwin had occupied. He was heir to the policies of both. He had won office with the support of a coalition which was provincial and moderate, rather than sectional and intransigent, in character. He, and not George Brown, had succeeded.

Chapter Nine

The Victory of the Progressive-Conservatives

I

Yet, in the autumn of 1854, the victory must have appeared doubtful and impermanent. Who could be certain that the coalition of 1854 was not simply one more of the many political arrangements and rearrangements of a troubled decade? And, in any case, had it not raised almost as many problems as it had solved? Even on the personal, the domestic, side, this sudden rise to office had certainly disturbed the rather genial, easy-going course of Macdonald's affairs. The new and welcome salary— it was £1250 a year[1]—had transformed him from a casual amateur into a responsible professional who, however hard or efficiently he worked at his duties, would have to spend at least a large part of the year away from Kingston, at the Canadian capital. The practice could be left with safety to his new, recently acquired partner, A. J. Macdonnell; but Isabella and the four-year-old Hugh John could not be disposed of so easily. Isabella was a woman who lived for her family, and who yet could not play her appropriate and desired role in family life. If she accompanied Macdonald to the capital, what could she bring but the burden of her invalidism; and if she stopped in Kingston with her female relatives, how could she support her husband's interminable absences? It was not easy to see a way through this new phase of an old anxiety, just as it was not easy to devise methods of consolidating the rather cramped position of political strength in which luck and astute management had suddenly landed him. How was he to strengthen and preserve the Liberal-Conservative coalition, without either affronting the old Tories or alienating the impatient Reformers, and thus destroying the great, middle, constitutional party which had always been his hope?

The first weeks of autumn were agitatedly busy. The by-election in Kingston, made necessary by his acceptance of office, came off late in September.[2] It was an easy formality, rather than a contest; and early in October he was back in Quebec once more.[3] The House had adjourned for a week, to meet again on October 10; and, during the brief interval, the ministers feverishly planned their programme of legislation and doubtfully considered the political future. In the Assembly, where a big majority stood for the moment at their bidding, the position seemed solid enough; but in the country as a whole it almost appeared for a while as if the new coalition was being regarded, not as a pleasant surprise, but as a painful shock. The outraged comment of the *Globe*—"Never did politicians make a 'grab' for office with less apparent regard for past professions than these gentlemen"[4]—could, of course, be ascribed simply to the fury of envious disappointment. But the cynical enjoyment of George Brown's discomfiture, which the *Leader* and other moderate newspapers exhibited, was not necessarily accompanied by any great enthusiasm for Macdonald's success.[5] A number of journals continued to regard the coalition with a frigid, stand-offish curiosity, as if it were something artificial, faintly discreditable, and inevitably temporary. It would take time to win popular support, to create a respectable following in the press; and there was a lamentable weakness even in those journals which were ready to give the new government immediate and enthusiastic aid. Macdonald had not arrived back in Quebec before importunate appeals began to arrive from Gowan of the *Patriot* and Samuel Thompson of the *Colonist*.[6] They had, it appeared, huge debts and almost no money. The task of maintaining journalistic competition in Toronto with George Brown's *Globe* was evidently going to be a formidable business.

But the first and main task faced the Conservatives at Quebec. They had to prove to the Assembly that the coalition of 1854 was not a factious combination of office-hungry politicians,

but a real union, based on a substantial identity of views, and
fortified with a constructive programme for the future. Inevitably their sincerity was called in question. In consenting to
enter the ministry, the Conservatives had accepted the elected
Legislative Council, the secularization of the Clergy Reserves,
and the abolition of the Seigniorial Tenure—policies which in the
past they had opposed or sharply criticized, and which had
formed the three main points in the late government's programme, as laid down in the speech from the throne. Charges
of political opportunism and political inconsistency were certain
to be hurled from both sides of the House—from outraged old
Tories as well as jeering Radicals; and the session had barely
recommenced after the adjournment, when Edmund Murney,
the Loyalist member for Hastings, arose to deride his old friends
for sacrificing their principles for power—for holding office "at
the mere whim of those to whom they had been opposed all
their lives".[7] Murney indignantly denied that the Conservative
party had ever authorized its leaders to change their policy
with respect to the Reserves: and Macdonald was obliged to
tell in public the story of the caucus of the previous June—
the caucus at which it had been decided that if the election
registered a conclusive popular verdict in favour of secularization, the Conservatives would not oppose it any longer.[8] It
was important for him, on purely personal grounds, to clear
the party's record respecting the Reserves. Drummond, Attorney-General East, would sponsor the Seigniorial Tenure
Bill; Morin would take up his old hobby of the elected Legislative Council; and MacNab, whose ancient martial valour
had been reawakened by the opening of the war with Russia
and by the allied landing in the Crimea, had already moved
for a commission of four to report on the Canadian militia
system. The Reserves—the most important item for Upper
Canada in this first instalment of the new government's programme—were left for Macdonald.

Tuesday, October 17, 1854, was, for more than one reason,
an exciting day. On the previous evening, vague garbled reports
of a great action in the Crimea had reached Canadian cities
by telegraph; and the men who sat down to listen to the

Attorney-General West on the afternoon of the seventeenth had just finished reading the newspaper accounts of the Battle of the Alma. In such a tense atmosphere, it was well to be brief; and with such subject matter, at once highly technical and highly controversial, Macdonald evidently judged it best to return to the straightforward, matter-of-fact manner, and the serious tone which he had used long before in introducing his University Bills.[9] He reminded his listeners that the Canadian parliament had been permitted to legislate on the Reserves only on the express condition that the stipends or allowances actually being paid to the clergy of the different denominations should be continued until the death of these incumbents. The bill provided that these stipends were either to be continued annually, as a first charge upon the fund, or that, alternatively, they might be commuted or capitalized, with the consent of the ecclesiastical body to which the incumbent belonged. After these first charges and the expenses of collection had been met, the entire proceeds of the Reserves, divided into two funds, one for Canada East and one for Canada West, were to be apportioned yearly among the different municipalities of both sections of the province in accordance with population as determined by the last census. The bill was astonishingly brief: the introduction was equally laconic. Macdonald explained a few technical difficulties, countered the argument that the money ought to be transferred to consolidated revenue and used for education, and ended by appealing to all members to co-operate in making the bill as final and definitive as possible. Then MacNab moved "that in consideration of the news arrived this day from the theatre of war in the Crimea of a series of brilliant victories gained by the combined fleets and armies of France and England, it is the duty of this House to testify its high gratification at the event . . .".[10] The members poured tumultuously out of the House to celebrate.

The debates on the Clergy Reserves Bill, as they dragged on from second reading into committee, revealed only too clearly the nature of the double attack—from the right as well as from the left—which the Liberal-Conservative coalition would have to face. On November 2, John Hillyard Cameron, supporting himself with an elaborate, closely-reasoned legal argument, moved an amendment which would have saved a large portion of the Reserves for the churches. Other Conservatives—Powell, Bowes, Robinson, Gamble, and Murney—were expected to support this last diehard attempt to salvage something of the old rights of the Church of England.[11] But the members of this brave little band, including the obstreperous Murney, did not really need to be taken very seriously. "Is Murney as foolish as ever," Gowan inquired with heavy sarcasm, "or has he given up drinking?"[12] Murney, though he had been rather tiresomely talkative of late, was scarcely a dreaded opponent; but John Hillyard Cameron's opposition, as Macdonald knew very well, was a different and much more dangerous matter. Cameron was back in parliament once again, after an absence of three years. His political career, as brilliant as it was erratic and enigmatic, had been suddenly renewed. Macdonald's other contemporaries and rivals, Toronto Tories such as Henry Sherwood and William Henry Boulton, were dying or fading out of political life. But, at the last election, Cameron had been returned for Toronto at the head of the poll. A cultivated, prosperous, highly successful lawyer, who, as Samuel Thompson said, "ruled the Bench by force of argument and the jury by power of persuasion", Cameron was now nearly at the apex of his popularity, authority and influence.[13] It was no longer so easy to make fun, as the *Globe* had tried to do back in 1847, of his fluent rhetoric and elegant manner—to deride his "flute-like" voice, his "demnition-foin" vocabulary, and his affected, "dancing-master" attitude.[14] It was not good enough to write his abilities down—as Macdonald himself had done only six months before—to "a good memory and a vicious fluency of speech". Had Macdonald, in fact, not been betrayed, either by resentment or jealousy, into a serious undervaluation of his old rival's abilities? "Cameron was useful in legal matters when in the House," he had conceded rather patronizingly, "but he lacks general intelligence and is altogether devoid of political reading. . . . If he came in for Niagara, or fought some doubtful county, it would be all very well and he could be kept in his place."[15] Grotesquely vain assumptions! Cameron had not "come in for Niagara or fought some doubtful county". He had headed the poll in Toronto! Could he be "kept in his place"? He was a power in the Church of England, a growing force in the Orange association; and his professional income, magnified now by daring and successful speculations in real estate and foreign exchange transactions, was amply sufficient for him to play the patron to Samuel Thompson's *Colonist*. He had a press and a following. And he was dangerous to Liberal-Conservatism and the French alliance because he represented the old tradition of concern for Upper Canadian Protestantism and Upper Canadian sectional interests, which the old Tories had cherished in the past and which they had never yet distinctly repudiated.

On the other side of the House—and, if possible, still more dangerous politically—was the tall, ungainly and vehement figure of George Brown. On October 31, two days before John Hillyard Cameron spoke, Brown had led the Reform attack on the Clergy Reserves Bill. His criticisms, despite the pugnacity and portentous seriousness of his manner, were largely debating points; but there was nothing picayune in the formidable ascendancy which Brown seemed so rapidly to be establishing in the new Assembly. Two years ago he had been a loud but almost solitary and unapplauded voice in the Assembly, a would-be but unaccepted leader, a huge engine, with steam up, frantic to be going, and attached only to a pathetic string of carriages. Six months ago, in his desperate search for power and place, he had openly coquetted with the Conservative party. Another had won the game he tried to play, and Brown himself had been crushed beneath a load of humiliation and ridicule. For the moment it looked as if his—and all—opposition was in ruins. But no such assumption could have been more unreal. The new Liberal-Conservative coalition, despite the crowded regiment of its followers, had not, of course, ended opposition: it had merely ended, for the time at least, the frustrating ambiguities and unrealities which had bedevilled Canadian party politics for the last few years. Brown's own few faithful followers, the remnant of the Clear Grit party, and the few disgruntled Hincksites who had refused to join the coalition—the elements of a new Reform party were there, waiting to be welded together, and linked in some effective fashion with the *Rouges* of Canada East. Who could perform the task? Baldwin had long retired. Hincks was supporting the new coalition, and Malcolm Cameron and John Rolph, the two Clear Grit leaders of yesteryear, had been thoroughly discredited in Radical eyes by their compromising association with the defeated Inspector-General. There remained John Sandfield Macdonald, an ex-Speaker, an ex-minister in Baldwin's Cabinet, a veteran Reformer with obviously a good deal more experience than Brown could boast. But, apart from this diminutive pawky Scotsman, with his little "tail" of followers from the eastern counties of Canada West, who was there but Brown? More and more conspicuously, Brown's huge figure stood out from the ruck of his followers. And his rivalry with Macdonald, glimpsed for a long time only dimly through the confusing fog of Canadian party politics, now began to emerge as the central fact of the new parliament.

Macdonald took Brown's and Cameron's opposition seriously —at least in part. The easy levity which he used when countering attacks on the alleged opportunism and inconsistency of the Conservatives was dropped when he came to defend his principal measure, the Clergy Reserves Bill. His answer to Brown was a matter-of-fact, point-by-point rebuttal of specific criticisms;[16] his reply to Cameron was a deliberate, serious, almost emotional appeal from the new Conservatives to the old.[17] "I view this subject," he told the House frankly, "from the same point of view as the honourable gentleman . . . I have never disguised my opinion on that subject." At bottom, he insisted, he had always believed that in a country where the majority of people were of one religion, and that religion Christian, the state ought to acknowledge itself to be a Christian state, and to make provision accordingly for its church. The connection between church and state had been beneficial in England; but it had been most injurious in Ireland. He had been driven to the conclusion that the multiplicity of sects in Canada, and the uncertain division of the population among them, would make the connection equally injurious in Canada. He had reached this decision reluctantly, sorrowfully. But Cameron and his mistaken friends had refused to accept the irrefutable lesson of experience. They had prejudiced their own position and aroused a hideous public clamour by their protracted and stubborn resistance. "I believe it is a great mistake in politics and private life to resist when resistance is hopeless . . . ," Macdonald told the House. "There is no maxim which experience teaches more clearly than this, that you must yield to the times. Resistance may be protracted until it produces revolution. Resistance was protracted in this country until it produced rebellion." The immovability of the Family Compact could be copied, in this day and age, only at the risk of real peril: but the decision of the Duke of Wellington and Sir Robert Peel to accept Catholic Emancipation was an example, Macdonald declared, which had guided himself, and might very well guide the other members of his party.

The Clergy Reserves measure and the Seigniorial Tenure Bill marched nearly abreast through the legislature during November. On November 23, they were both read for the third time and passed by large majorities, the Clergy Reserves Bill receiving 62 to 39 votes.[18] For the government, the most important work of the first part of the session was ended; and a little over three weeks later, on December 18, the House was adjourned for the Christmas recess. Lord Elgin made his last public appearance at the adjournment. The next day, to the secret but probably immense delight of Macdonald and the Conservatives, he handed over the governorship of the Province of Canada to Sir Edmund Walker Head.[19]

II

Late in January, 1855, when Macdonald returned to Quebec, the general feeling that the province was settling down to a new phase of its political existence had perceptibly strengthened. A new Governor, a Governor very different from the last, was now in formal command of affairs. Head, who had been a Fellow of Merton College, and a Poor Law Commissioner in England

before he accepted the lieutenant-governorship of New Brunswick, obviously did not belong to the exalted social and political
circles which the eighth Earl of Elgin had entered freely by
right of birth and marriage. The new Governor was a reserved
and thoughtful man, a scholar with literary and artistic interests,
who wrote verses and translated art histories from the German.
There was a touch of the common-room in his manner, an echo
of the lecture hall in his tentative yet architectonic speculations,
an air of boards and committee rooms in his dry, unsentimental,
bureaucratic precision. His life as a don and as a rather humdrum administrator had strengthened his native caution and
sharpened his native efficiency for office work. It was these
administrative powers which Macdonald naturally got to know
first, and which, with his own nimble efficiency in administration, he was quick to appreciate. "I like Sir Edmund very
much," he wrote laconically to his sister Louisa. "He is a
thorough man of business and attends to the public interests
con amore."[20]

The coming of the new Governor was followed quickly by
a partial reorganization of the new government. Morin and
two undistinguished mediocrities disappeared from the Canada
East section of the Cabinet. They were replaced by two equally
undistinguished and, as it turned out, equally temporary mediocrities, and by a third French Canadian, a squat, solid, square-
faced man, with immense physical powers, and an explosive,
rapid, rather bullying manner in debate, called George Étienne
Cartier. Macdonald remained blandly unaware of the fact
that in Cartier he had found his most effective French-Canadian
team-mate. He was temperately, almost tepidly, enthusiastic
about the new Provincial Secretary. The district of Montreal,
he explained carefully, required another representative in the
Cabinet; and Cartier, "a Montrealer body and soul", was the
obvious choice. The secretaryship required only "industry and
method", both of which the new minister possessed in a remarkable degree.[21] "He is active—too active," Macdonald wrote
a little patronizingly, "and will do his work."[22] Cartier, obviously,
was still regarded as a diligent, slightly officious bureaucrat who
could quite easily be kept in his place.

The triumvirate of the future—Head, Macdonald and Cartier—had arrived on the stage which they were to occupy as principals. But the stage was still bewilderingly crowded with personages, and the eminence of the three could not yet be taken for granted. It was still possible to misjudge Cartier's future position; and what Macdonald's place was to be, his associates and even his closest political friends would perhaps have found it difficult to say. His odd, ugly, memorable head, with its pile of dark, curly hair, its big nose, its gay friendly eyes and genially sardonic smile, did not inevitably suggest the great political idealist or the great practical politician of the future. In his speech, his easy-going manner, his whole youthful appearance, he did not seem to conform exactly to any of the plates in the political fashion book of the period. Certainly his garments had not been cut from the sober, heavy black broadcloth in which Canadian party leaders had usually appeared in the past. Draper had been a serious man, Baldwin a very solemn man; and Hincks, though on occasion he had displayed an acid wit, like that of a precociously knowledgeable street-gamin, had been a bleakly clever, drably efficient administrator. Macdonald differed from all these predecessors in a fashion at once puzzling and disarming. He obviously enjoyed politics, just as he apparently enjoyed every other part of life. His conviviality, his exuberant gaiety, his perpetual flow of robust animal good spirits had by now become famous. "I dare say," his old partner Alexander Campbell wrote, "you are very busy from night until morning, and again from noon 'til night. The drinking the refractory members is in your department, I take for granted. Another glass of champagne and a *story of doubtful moral tendency* with a little of the Hon. John Macdonald's peculiar 'sawder' are elements in the political strength of a Canadian ministry not to be despised, as I have no doubt all parties in the House are fully aware."[23] Undoubtedly, his smiling capacity for liquor, and his bawdy stories, and his "soft sawder" were all elements of strength; but he was occasionally a hard drinker, who took too much and kept on taking too much; and the knowledge of these habits strengthened the impression of easy-going conviviality, and possibly helped to lead the undiscerning into a serious under-estimate of his basic abilities. Yet there were some good qualities which even the sceptics and the puritans were willing to concede him. "He can get through more work in a given time than anybody I ever saw, and do it well," recorded John Langton, the member for Peterborough whom Macdonald had just made the new Auditor-General.[24] And it was the same caustic and critical John Langton who generously insisted that Macdonald's "talent was undoubted" and that "his character for integrity stood very high". Almost everybody—opponents as well as friends—agreed that Macdonald's conservative inheritance was qualified by a genuine liberalism. Even William Lyon Mackenzie rather grudgingly admitted that Macdonald had "something of the liberal spirit" in him;[25] and Langton recalled that his "instincts and associations were all with the Liberals, and people thought that he had been thrown by circumstances on to the wrong side of the house". These, for a man who wanted to modernize and liberalize his party, were assets of a very high order. But were they not, even so, outbalanced by those liabilities which seemed so lamentable in the eyes of the provincial society of early Victorian Canada? "He is fond of pleasure," Langton wrote with grave severity, "and has an almost boyish exuberance of animal spirits, and a poco-curantism, and want of earnestness in any pursuit which will always prevent him from being a successful leader." What was to be done with such a scandalously flippant creature? Could a man who did not even bother to pretend to seriousness be taken very seriously? Langton did not believe so. In his judicious, tolerant but disapproving manner, he wrote Macdonald down. "His instincts are all good," he summed up, "but he takes the world too easily to be much depended on."

Macdonald was certainly taking the world of Canadian politics very easily in this winter of 1855. "I am, thank God, in good health and spirits," he wrote his sister Louisa in February, "and quite ready for the parliamentary campaign."[26] The campaign that winter was an easy walkover, with the new coalition, and its swollen army of followers, marching irresistibly forward. The achievements of the session—the secularization of the Reserves, the commutation of Seigniorial Tenure, the elective Legislative Council, the reform of the Canadian militia system, and the new Reciprocity Treaty with the United States —formed an impressive total which seemed to prove, beyond all doubt, that the new coalition was a genuinely liberal-minded government which could settle old grievances and open up new opportunities as no previous administration had been able to do. For the moment, John Hillyard Cameron and the old Tories were silenced; the Hincksite Reformers of Canada West seemed genuinely satisfied; and Macdonald, confident that the coalition was making its way, was zestfully eager to bury every attack upon its sincerity and good faith with shovelfuls of raillery and ridicule. Sometimes he could not resist a joke for the joke's own sake. "Did not the honourable gentleman drill *his* men more than ten days?" he inquired urbanely of William Lyon Mackenzie,[27] when that forlorn leader of the rebels at Montgomery's Tavern objected to the amount of training imposed on the new volunteers by the Militia Bill. Sometimes, when George Brown and John Sandfield Macdonald kept reminding him of his attacks on the corruption of the Hincks government and his criticisms of an elected Legislative Council, he countered by jovially recalling how vigorously the *Globe* had supported his own and MacNab's candidature in the election of 1854. More and more frequently and lovingly he dwelt on Brown himself—on his outstanding abilities, his increasingly dominant position in the Reform party, and the monopolizing authority of his newspaper. Poor feeble John Sandfield Macdonald had almost believed himself to be the real leader of the opposition during the first days of the session; but once the mighty member for Lambton had arrived, he had humbly abdicated this absurdly fancied eminence. Poor William McDougall had once been the proprietor of a popular and aggressive Reform newspaper the *North American*: but now, "like some languishing lady falling into the arms of her admirer", the fainting *North American* was "clinging to the strong and robust form of his honourable friend opposite for support".[28] The continental *North American* had, in fact, become absorbed into the universality of the *Globe*. The Reform press was Brown's:

the Reform party was Brown's. It was scarcely to be wondered at that next day the *Globe* took occasion to rebuke the petty way in which Macdonald had tried to sow personal jealousies among the members of the opposition. "The harmony of the Liberal party," it announced majestically, "is not to be disturbed by the shabby manoeuvres of Mr. John Alexander Macdonald."[29]

Harmony had never been, and was not to be, a distinguishing feature of the party which Brown was even then licking into shape in his rough, imperious, but not unskilful, way. The session rolled on, the coalition appeared impregnably popular, and it was not until nearly the end of the year's proceedings that the opposition found itself suddenly in possession of most acceptable grounds for attack. On May 12, when the long session had less than three weeks to run, Dr. E. P. Taché introduced, in the Legislative Council, a bill which clarified, confirmed and, to some degree, extended the privileges of the Separate Schools of Canada West.[30] The subject matter of the bill— the educational privileges of Roman Catholics—was dangerously delicate; the circumstances of its introduction seemed sinister and suspicious in the highest degree. It had been introduced in the fag-end of the session, in the Legislative Council and not in the Assembly, by a French-Canadian minister from Canada East and without the concurrence, or even the knowledge, of Egerton Ryerson, the superintendent of the school system in the western part of the province. J. W. Gamble, one of the Tories who had followed John Hillyard Cameron in his defence of the Reserves, wired Ryerson, warning him of the bill;[31] Brown, the old critic of Separate Schools, prepared himself again for his favourite battle; and by May 22, when Macdonald got up to introduce the bill in the Assembly, it was clear that the great majority of the Upper Canadian contingent, whether they were Tory, Conservative, moderate Reform, or Clear Grit, regarded the bill with miserable uncertainty or downright disapproval.

Macdonald did his best. He might have pointed out how far short the bill fell of the demands which Charbonnel and the other Roman Catholic bishops had been pressing upon the government during the previous winter; but obviously this was a suicidally dangerous course. Instead he tried to persuade his audience how faithfully the measure ran along established lines. He tried to prove that the clauses which facilitated the establishment of Roman Catholic Separate Schools and governed the calculation of their government grant were clauses which either made merely minor and formal changes in existing procedures, or embodied sensible principles which had been approved by Ryerson himself.[32] When attacks were made upon Separate Schools in principle—and Brown, of course, launched such attacks repeatedly and at enormous length—Macdonald simply took refuge behind the utter impossibility of destroying an establishment to which the province had already pledged its faith by repeated legislation. "If they could make the world all of one way of thinking it might work more harmoniously," he conceded with genially tolerant scepticism, "but yet he doubted very much if things would go on one bit better on that account. The severance of opinion, the right of private judgment tended to the elevation of man, and he should be sorry if a legislature, the majority of whose members were Protestants professing to recognize the great Protestant principle of the right of private judgment, should yet seek to deprive Roman Catholics of the power to educate their children according to their own principles. . . . "[33] The defence was not bad: and, although any, even the most innocuous, measure on such a subject would have been vulnerable, the bill was a defensible one. But the tactics of the government had been stupidly maladroit. The bill had been introduced in an equivocal, furtive, almost conspiratorial fashion. Had Macdonald been merely careless, or had his importunate Roman Catholic associates tried to be too clever by half? Now the Attorney-General West was acutely embarrassed. Gamble told the story of his telegram to Ryerson and of the Superintendent of Education's complete ignorance of the government's legislation. Langton, Hartman, Brown—the independent Conservative, the Clear Grit, and the Liberal Reformer—all pressed the case against the good faith of the administration. The remnant of the Upper Canadian members—for many of them had gone home believing the session over—looked on doubtfully or mutinously. The bill passed, but it passed by virtue of French-Canadian, Roman Catholic votes. A measure to amend the Separate School system of Canada West had been opposed by a majority of Western Canadian members. For the first time, on an issue of major importance, the government had given its enemies an excuse to argue that Canada West was still governed by the pressure and at the will of Canada East. Within a year of its establishment, the prestige and popularity of the coalition had received a profound shock in Protestant Upper Canada.

III

That autumn the unhappy peripatetic government moved again, back to Toronto. On Monday, October 8, the Governor-General, accompanied by his Western Canadian ministers, MacNab, Spence and Macdonald, bade farewell to Quebec and started out for his new capital. The vice-regal progress continued placidly, in a deliberate and dignified fashion, with loyal addresses, triumphal arches, and public dinners; there was an inspection of the provincial agricultural exhibition at Cobourg, a visit to Niagara Falls, and a triumphant reception at Hamilton, organized by MacNab, and unfortunately accompanied by a persistent drizzle of icy rain.[34] In the third week in October, the gubernatorial party swept westward still, in a leisurely tour of the peninsula between Lake Huron and Lake Erie. But Macdonald, leaving the superintending honours of these vice-regal perambulations to the eager and officious MacNab, remained behind in Toronto and began the task of settling in. There was a good deal to do. It was a question not only of organizing his department in new offices, but also of finding suitable quarters for an invalid wife and a small boy. He viewed the whole business of the family move from Kingston doubtfully. As late as a month before he had still been undecided as to whether Isabella and Hugh John should accompany him to Toronto.[35] There had, of course, been really no question of Isabella's going to Quebec. At Quebec, where the government's days were already numbered, she would have been in an unfamiliar world, with little opportunity to acquire a fresh set of friends. But Toronto was different for various and obvious reasons. And at Toronto, the government, and her husband with it, would be established for four clear years. Almost certainly she wanted to go to Toronto. And Macdonald agreed.

At Toronto, the little empire of provincial government and legislation was mainly centred in a long parallelogram of territory, bounded by Wellington Street on the south, King Street on the north, Simcoe Street on the east, and which, on the west, stretched out past isolated houses and summer villas into the open fields and orchards of the countryside. The heart of this administrative world—Government House and the parliament buildings—stood physically at its eastern frontier by Simcoe Street. The Attorney-General's office—the Crown Law Department, as it was called—was housed in an old building, once the town's general hospital, which stood on the north side of King Street, between John and Peter. King Street was mainly commercial and administrative in character, though there were a few, and some very splendid, private houses on it. Wellington Street was largely residential, and out west, at the town's outskirts, between Portland and Brock Streets, where the street changed its name to Wellington Place, Macdonald found the quarters he desired.[36] There could be no question of buying or leasing a private house, for Isabella was quite incapable of housekeeping. But one of the scattered buildings in Wellington Place was a boarding-house. And here the reunited Macdonald family was established.[37]

The place had its advantages. It was quiet for Isabella, for westward the town petered out rapidly, and all the noise and bustle and confusion of the city lay down Wellington Street to the east. The friendly houses of Macdonald's colleagues and acquaintances—John Hillyard Cameron, David Macpherson, and Philip Vankoughnet—at all of which were young children, were near enough for Hugh to visit frequently and with relative ease. Macdonald himself, once he had left his office, had but to walk a little way west on King Street, and down a block on Portland Street, to find himself at his lodgings. In its cramped, makeshift, unsatisfactory way, it was the nearest thing to a

home together that they had had for years; and they had
ventured much—more than they had dared to do since Isabella's
return from the United States—to make it a success. It ought
to have succeeded. But they had not been more than a month
or so in Toronto before Macdonald knew in his heart that the
enterprise was a tragic failure. For, in January of 1856, Isabella
became terribly ill.[38] Janet, the nurse and companion who,
Macdonald had no doubt expected, would help to look after
five-year-old Hugh, had to give up the boy to slave over her
spent and weary mistress; and Hugh was packed off almost
unceremoniously in the mornings to spend the day under the
kindly care of Rose Cameron at The Meadows, John Hillyard
Cameron's pleasant house on Queen Street West. Macdonald
hated to leave Wellington Place in the mornings. Once, fear-
ing the very worst, the doctor had sent for him at the Crown Law
Office; and afterwards he could hardly bear the sight of unfamiliar messengers. At night, when he walked homeward
along King Street, the brief, sullen winter sunset had already
faded in the west. A harsh wind roared along the road out of
a blue-black sky; and such a grinding sense of foreboding and
desolation overwhelmed him that he could hardly force his
steps along the homeward way. A dozen times he really expected to find her dead when he arrived. A dozen times, in
fact, she hovered upon the point of death. Yet, with her feeble
but persistent resolution, she lived on. She waited for him in
the dim sickroom; and there, night after night, he stayed with
her. The town was busy with dances, dinners, and parties,
with all the first events of the season, and all the preliminaries
of the approaching parliamentary session. He was inundated
with invitations; but he refused them all. Night after night,
while the frost struck the desolate little street into icy stillness,
he sat up with Isabella; and night after night the candle burned
itself slowly downward to the socket.

There was something decidedly ominous also in the aspect
of public affairs. The coalition had run through its first great
programme of legislation and had used up its first supply of
generous and uncritical support. The difficult passage of the
Separate School Bill seemed to mark a turn by which the decline

of government confidence and the rise of opposition hopes could be equally well dated. Ever since the prorogation of the summer, Brown had undeniably waxed in importance, as a journalist, as a party leader, as an accepted spokesman for injured Canada West. In February, 1855, the *Globe* had bought up William McDougall's *North American*; and this had been followed, in September of the same year, by the amalgamation of the *Globe* and the *Examiner*, the other principal Clear Grit newspaper in Toronto. McDougall joined the *Globe* staff; the erstwhile Clear Grit leaders admitted their own past political miscalculations and publicly admired the rugged consistency of George Brown. And all that summer and autumn, using the detested Separate School Bill of 1855 as a hideous example of French-Canadian tyranny, Brown was preaching a united Reform party for the defence of Upper Canadian sectional interests through the principle of representation by population in parliament. Macdonald at first affected a cheerful indifference to "Rep. by Pop.". It was, he had told Brown Chamberlin of the *Montreal Gazette*, back in August, "too abstract a question to be enthusiastic about".[39] Airily brave words! They were quite untrue. The "abstract principle" was an effective cure for real, substantial and sensitively felt grievances. For Upper Canadians, Conservatives as well as Reformers, it held a dangerously strong appeal. It not only meant the release of Canada West from the domination and exploitation of Roman Catholic Canada East; it also implied—what, indeed, George Brown made no pretence whatever to conceal— the "assimilation of the laws" of the two sections of the province, and therefore ultimately the extinction of the peculiar culture of French Canada, just as Lord Durham had foretold.

Macdonald was instinctively opposed to all this, as well because of temperament and personal conviction as because of party commitments. Once at least during that dreadful January of 1856, as he sat up beside his troubled wife, he tried to set out his own views in some detail. Isabella lay back exhausted, half glimpsed in the obscurity of the room: the "single dip" flamed feebly. He was writing to Brown Chamberlin, of the *Montreal Gazette*, one of the journalists whom he was now beginning to cultivate, writing a long letter, full of his jokes, his flippant pleasantries, his cunningly worded appeals, and his fundamental tolerant sound sense.[40] The letter was not addressed to George Brown, and it dealt only with Canada East and its English-speaking minority; but it might have served as a reply and a rebuke to the newly rebuilt Reform party and its campaign for the "liberation" of Canada West through "Rep. by Pop.". "The truth is," Macdonald argued, "that you British Lower Canadians never can forget that you were once supreme—that Jean Baptiste was your hewer of wood and drawer of water. You struggle, like the Protestant Irish in Ireland, like the Norman invaders in England, not for equality, but *ascendancy*—the difference between you and those interesting and amiable people being that you have not the honesty to admit it. You can't and won't admit the principle that the majority must govern. The Gallicans may fairly be reckoned as two thirds against one third of all the other races who are lumped together as Anglo-Saxons—Heaven save the mark! . . . The only remedies are immigration and copulation and these will work wonders. The laws are equally administered to the British as the French, at least if we may judge by the names of your judges it ought to be so. Lumping your judges of the Queen's Bench, Supreme and Circuit courts, you have full one half British. More than one half of the Revenue officers, indeed of all offices of emolument, are held by men not of French origin. It would surprise you to go over the names of officials in a Lower Canada almanac and reckon the *ascendancy* you yet hold of official positions. Take care the French don't find it out and make a counter-cry. True, you suffer occasionally from a Gavazzi riot or so, but in the first place you Anglo-Saxons are not bad hands at a riot yourselves, and, in the second place, the rioters are not Franco-Canadians, nor Canadians of any kind. A proper jury law, if the present one does not suit, is all you can want. But you must be represented in the cabinet . . ."

His pen flowed on smoothly. The immediate and practical note must now be sounded. The British of Canada East, split into several contemptible fragments, must be convinced that a united support of one party (and, of course, it could only be the Liberal-Conservative party) would alone win them representation in the provincial government. He made the appeal in his brief, rather off-hand, apparently disinterested fashion; but the practical politics of government support and cabinet-making did not detain him long; and he returned to the basic cultural problem of Canada in a vein which, if he had been noted for solemn speculation, might almost have been regarded as prophetic. "No man in his senses," he wrote, "can suppose that this country can for a century to come be governed by a totally unfrenchified government. If a Lower Canadian British desires to conquer he must 'stoop to conquer'. He must make friends with the French, without sacrificing the status of his race or language, he must respect their nationality. Treat them as a nation and they will act as a free people generally do—generously. Call them a faction and they become factious. Supposing the numerical preponderance of British in Canada becomes much greater than it is, I think the French would give more trouble than they are said now to do. At present they divide as we do, they are split up into several sections, and are governed by more or less defined principles of action. As they become smaller and feebler, so they will be more united; from a sense of self-preservation, they will act as one man and hold the balance of power. Look how in a house of 600 Pitt was supported through Dundas by the whole Scotch vote, and remember that O'Connell with his tail absolutely governed England after the Lichfield House bargain. So long as the French have twenty votes they will be a power, and must be conciliated. I doubt much however if the French will lose their numerical majority in L. C. in a hurry. What with the cessation of emigration from Europe, their own spread in the Townships, the opening up of the Ottawa and St. Maurice, and the certainty that they will ere long be the labourers in our factories that are fast coming, I am inclined to think they will hold their own for many a day yet."

He could discuss the future with Brown Chamberlin in this jocular, laconic and curiously discerning fashion. But the present, and the existing position of the Liberal-Conservative government were very different matters, requiring different arguments and different solutions. The long, unhappy Toronto winter dragged on, and February 15, the day of the opening of parliament, drew closer. It was bitterly cold, and he was overwhelmed with work in preparation for the session; but this was the kind of labour he dispatched with cheerful ease, and, as he told his sister Louisa rather boastingly, "I thrive wonderfully under it".[41] His real trouble was totally different. The fact was that the coalition had lost ground, and was still steadily losing ground, in Canada West. The ministry and the party, Liberal-Conservative by name, were also in reality an imperfect combination of two rival elements, each of which was still struggling for mastery. The scarcely concealed animosities inside the Cabinet—between John Ross, the leader of the Hincksite Liberals, and the genial, greedy, impecunious Sir Allan MacNab, the titular chieftain of the Conservatives—were repeated in the jarring ranks of the coalition as a whole. A group of Conservatives, ranging themselves behind John Hillyard Cameron, were reported to be sullenly opposed to the continuance of Macdonald's influence in the party; and embarrassed Hincksite Liberals, smarting under Brown's charge that the ministry had accepted the dictation of Canada East, were drifting back into the swelling ranks of the reorganized Reform party. Macdonald's political handiwork—the Liberal-Conservative coalition—was falling apart in less than two years. And back in Wellington Place, in a few rented rooms in a boarding-house, all that remained of his domestic happiness continued in hopeless jeopardy. His spirit was rasped raw by worry and foreboding. Beneath his almost limitless good nature, which was not a carefully cultivated pose but a cheerful instinct, there lurked, far below, an uncertain temper—a temper which, that winter, must often have struggled to be free. An outburst was probably inevitable. And it came.

It came on Tuesday, February 26, when the debate on the address in reply to the speech from the throne had droned on for nearly a week. That night they were threshing over a lot of singularly dry and brittle straw—the divisions in the Conservative government, the animosities in the Reform opposition, the Conservative betrayal of their principles for the sake of office, and Brown's support of the Conservatives in the previous election for the sake of political power. Brown had already spoken in the debate at enormous length on the previous Thursday; but he was on his feet again on the fatal Tuesday evening, as provocative and belligerent as ever. When, towards midnight, Macdonald got up to speak, it soon became plain that he had been goaded too far. Yet he began quietly enough. His manner tense, his voice trembling a little, he started by exposing a few of what he said were the characteristic contradictions and inconsistencies of Brown's speech. Brown's assertions—and here the words began to come faster with excitement—were contradictory and inconsistent for the very simple reason that they were untrue. They always had been untrue. And how could people be expected to keep their tempers when they were assailed by the habitual untruths of a man who, years ago, at the very beginning of his public career, had abused his position on the Penitentiary Commission by perverting the testimony and falsifying the evidence! The words poured out in a furious torrent. The last restraints were gone now, the last inhibitions had been washed away. Macdonald was white with passion. All the old charges—the brutal intimidation of the aged Warden Smith, the suborning of convicted criminals as witnesses, the elaborate falsification of evidence, the calculated secrecy of the commission's proceedings, and Brown's resolute determination to prevent a parliamentary investigation of its work—all the accusations which dated back as far as the sessions of 1849 and 1850 were hurled again at Brown's head.[42] The House sat silent with shocked amazement. When Brown rose to reply, he was white with anger and excitement. But he was curiously brief as well. This was not to be one of his lusty, hard-hitting, long-winded attacks. He merely announced, in a low voice, that he would ask for a committee of inquiry into Macdonald's charges. There was a pause. The House got the ominous impression that something irremediable had happened, that the unforgettable and unforgivable had been said.

It was an unfortunate beginning. The session, which, unlike its predecessor, had no great programme of important practical reforms, seemed bereft of purpose and direction. It was the easy prey of bad temper and fortuitous accident; and the chief preoccupation of the House appeared to be its own chaotic condition—the disintegration of the coalition, the rivalries of Liberals and Conservatives, and the confused state of parties in the Assembly as a whole. Behind this confusion lay, as always, the central cultural division of the province; and, in the circumstances, a crisis could be precipitated by almost any revival of the old politico-religious disputes. The House had not long to wait. During the winter there occurred the trial of several Roman Catholics, Kelly and others, for the murder of an Irish Protestant, Edward Corrigan; and at the conclusion of the trial, the judge, Judge Duval, a French-Canadian Roman Catholic justice, delivered the accustomed final charge to the Roman Catholic French-Canadian jury. It was, as it was reported in the newspapers, a curious charge; and it was followed by what was, in the eyes of the Protestant Canada West, an inexplicable event—the acquittal of Kelly and the other Roman Catholic prisoners. Somebody in the Assembly was almost certain to raise the question of Judge Duval's charge. It ought, perhaps, to have been George Brown. But it was not George Brown. On Friday, March 7, John Hillyard Cameron moved, seconded by his faithful lieutenant Gamble, for an address to the Governor-General requesting a copy of the charge delivered to the jury by Judge Duval in the trial of Kelly and others for the murder of Edward Corrigan.[48]

IV

Macdonald, in all probability, had confidently expected some such move. In his mind, it was probably a question merely as to which of the two quarrelling divisions of the Liberal-Conservative coalition—the Progressive Conservatives or the Tories —would first begin the attack. He was well aware of the fact that Ross and Spence, the two Hincksite Liberals in the Cabinet, had become increasingly weary of Sir Allan MacNab, and his gout, and his absences, and the "infernal lot of hangers on" that he had to provide with jobs and militia commissions.[44] He may even have known that the Hincksites were now determined upon the gallant knight's removal. But, in a letter which he wrote to Brown Chamberlin late in January, he had still felt justified in deriding "the absurd grounds of suspicion that we want to get rid of MacNab";[45] and in the end it had been the Tories, and not the Progressive Conservatives, who had taken the initiative in the struggle. MacNab, racked with gout, had been absent from the House almost from the beginning of the session. But, from his sickbed, had he helped to inspire this movement of the ultras against a Francophile government of which he was the titular head? Was this supposedly bluff, hearty, downright old man secretly jealous of Macdonald and anxious to push John Hillyard Cameron forward as his own designated heir? For some time, Cameron's conduct itself had been curiously equivocal. Early in the session, he had called a meeting of his fellow-Tories, Murney, Powell, Gamble, Robinson and others, to discuss the government's educational policy; and from this meeting had sprung the rumour that the ultras were about to form a new party with Cameron as leader.[46] Equally curious speculations were provoked by the resolution of March 7. By putting himself forward so ostentatiously at the head of the insurgent group, Cameron seemed openly to be flirting with the invitation to accept its leadership. By moving the resolution in the Corrigan affair, he had opened an indirect but very real onslaught on the general policy of the Liberal-Conservative government; and, by choosing his ground for attack in the highly provocative field of race and religion, he had appeared frankly to invite the support of George Brown and the outraged Protestant radicals of Canada West. Cameron, "with his usual versatility," wrote one newspaper editor, "has served the double purpose of state physician to Sir Allan Mac-Nab and temporary leader of the anti-ministerial opposition in the House".[47] It looked as if Cameron had finally decided to precipitate a quarrel for the leadership of the coalition and the control of its policies, and that he had accepted the questionable alliance of the Reform opposition for the purpose.

Macdonald was determined to smother the quick flames of

this fire before Brown could fan it into another huge conflagration. The continuance of the Hincksite Liberals' support, the very existence of the coalition, depended upon the rapid extinction of the insurgent blaze. On March 7, the opening date of the debate, he argued long and learnedly with Hillyard Cameron over the limits of the Crown's power to require reports and information from the judges.[48] Even if the request for the charge were not unconstitutional, he insisted, it was still extremely inexpedient. It could not alter the course of justice in the slightest degree, for the accused in the trial for the murder of Edward Corrigan had already been irrevocably acquitted: it could only deal a serious blow at the independence of the bench. The House, listening with delight to Cameron's elegantly expressed learning and Brown's Protestant moral indignation, remained unimpressed by Macdonald's reasoned, moderate appeal; and, on March 10, with virtually the entire body of the members for Canada West voting in its favour, the motion requiring the production of the charge to the jury was passed by a vote of forty-eight to forty-four. This was extremely serious. On March 11, the House was adjourned for two days; and on March 13, when it met again, Drummond, on behalf of the government, demanded that the resolution requiring the production of Judge Duval's charge be formally rescinded. J. S. Macdonald and A. A. Dorion promptly moved the previous question, which was treated as a motion of want of confidence and soundly defeated by seventy-five to forty-two votes. Macdonald must have drawn a long breath of relief. The government made no further difficulty about the resolution to which, of course, it now advised the Governor-General to refuse compliance. Head's reply denied that Duval's charge could be "presumed to exist as a distinct document"; and it insisted that to call a judge to account for his words, at the request of one branch of the legislature only, might serve as a precedent for interference by the Crown with the independence of the judiciary.[49] The request for the production of Duval's charge was politely refused. The House accepted the refusal passively; and although, a little later, Dorion made a final attempt to defeat the government on the issue, he was again unsuccessful. It looked as if Macdonald had won. The first effort of the Tories, backed by the questionable support of the Reformers, to upset the administration and break up the coalition had been a failure.

The Tories had begun the struggle. Who would finish it? The Hincksites, the few remaining Liberal supporters of the coalition in Canada West, grew more open in their opposition to MacNab and "fossilism", and more outspoken in their support of Macdonald. They were justified, so the editor of the *Leader* argued, by Cameron's provocative attempt to foist himself upon the party as its leader.[50] They may even have been justified by a shameless intrigue between the Tories and the Grits, for long afterwards Samuel Thompson, the editor of the *Colonist*, recollected how he had encountered George Brown in Sir Allan's house in Ritchie's Terrace, Adelaide Street, and how John Hillyard Cameron had burst in upon the conference with the announcement that the Liberal-Conservatives had elected Macdonald as their leader.[51] Certainly, towards the end of March, a circumstantial rumour began to run about town that the Liberal-Conservatives had assembled lately and had given their support to the Attorney-General West; and a few days later, the *Globe,* with a curiously affectionate interest in the fate of the doughty, stout-hearted old knight, began to refer openly to the campaign for the removal of Sir Allan and the substitution of a man who, it declared, was "scarcely known out of Kingston, save as a barrister of good standing, and what is called a jolly good fellow".[52] The whole matter had become public property, and questions had begun to be asked in the House. Macdonald finally decided to make a statement. "No such leadership was ever offered me," he declared, "and no such leadership was ever accepted by me." A deputation of three Liberal-Conservatives had, he admitted, come to him from a meeting of their fellows, held because of the growing rumours of a change of government. They did not, they said, desire a change: "but they wanted to state to me that if any change or reconstruction should take place under any exigency whatever, they had confidence in me, and they would support any reconstruction which I should advise. My answer was that there was no truth in the rumours and that there was no chance of any reconstruction at present."⁵³ Macdonald probably believed the matter would stop there. As he said himself, he was prepared to follow as long as Sir Allan could lead. But it was becoming increasingly difficult for the gallant knight to lead at all, and impossible for him to lead the members of Canada West. The western division of the party held another meeting and determined that MacNab should be invited to retire. Macdonald intervened with decision and at once. The protest movement was temporarily dropped. But it was renewed once more; and finally the representatives of the remaining western Reformers in the coalition announced that, if MacNab continued in the government, circumstances might compel them to vote against it.⁵⁴ As soon as this notice was given, early in April, John Ross, the senior Hincksite in the Cabinet, at once resigned.

Obviously the climax of the whole confused affair was rapidly approaching. It had been a terrible winter. And almost nothing had occurred, either at his rooms or at the Crown Law Office, to release Macdonald's real good nature from the prison of its chronic, irritating anxiety. "Hugh is, thank God, in prime health," he wrote his mother towards the end of March.⁵⁵ And here, at least, was one source of unalloyed satisfaction. It was pleasant to realize that Hugh had grown from a baby to a healthy small boy of six, to watch him preside over a lively assembly of his playmates at his birthday party on March 13, and to note proudly that "he is quite tall now and is putting on almost a manly appearance".⁵⁶ But Isabella was ill again in March, this time with erysipelas. He was never really free of the dull ache of his anxiety for her, and he was rasped and irritated by the endless proceedings of the House committee appointed to investigate his charges against George Brown. "I am carrying on a war against that scoundrel George Brown," he told his mother, "and I will teach him a lesson he never learnt before. I shall prove him a most dishonest, dishonourable fellow and in so doing I will only pay him a debt I owe him for abusing me for months together in his newspaper."⁵⁷ He was eager to pay off old scores, apt to take new offence quickly, and ready to use his own bantering humour to drive others into fury. Early in the session George Brown had made him lose his temper; but, in the debate of April 16, it was he who provoked Colonel Arthur Rankin to outbursts of violent unparliamentary language.[58] Parliament was an almost continual verbal milling ground. As John Langton said, "the whole of this session has been a state of chronic crisis for the ministry".[59] The unresolved conflict in the Liberal-Conservative party continued; and the opposition, knowing this fact, pressed forward with their votes of want of confidence. It was almost too much for him. "John A. Macdonald is now the recognized leader," wrote Langton with cheerful harshness, "but he is anything but strong in reality."[60]

The long ordeal drew towards its close, as spring blossomed into summer. It was the question of the seat of government which brought the crisis to a head. Obviously the selection of a permanent capital for the united province was a question of deep cultural and sectional prestige to both English and French, to both Canada West and Canada East. It was only after the most protracted debate that the Assembly finally decided, on April 16, that Quebec was the most eligible place, that parliament be permanently established there after 1859, and that suitable buildings be commenced at once for the legislature and the government departments. Macdonald had expected the result. "The French will, I think, be too strong for us," he wrote his mother, "and we must submit to going to Lower Canada. . . . I am afraid that we have no chance for Kingston. We shall, however, make a fight for it."[61] He did, indeed, make a fight for it. He voted for Kingston, and for other towns in Canada West against Quebec: he even voted against the main motion declaring Quebec the most eligible town.[62] The issue was, in fact, not regarded as a "ministerial question", and members voted freely upon it; and it was this apparent exhibition of governmental irresponsibility which provided the opposition with its last great chance for a want-of-confidence debate. On Wednesday, May 14, just as the House was about to go into supply, Papin moved in amendment "that the position which His Excellency's administration have assumed up to the present day, on the question of the seat of government, does not inspire this House with the confidence necessary to entrust that administration with the moneys required for the construction of the necessary buildings at the seat of government".[63] The very next day, in further refinement of Papin's verbal attack, Holton moved in amendment that "the course of the administration with reference to the question of the seat of government and other important public questions has disappointed the just expectations of the great majority of the people of this province".[64]

In the great debate which followed, a debate which lasted almost exactly a week, Macdonald was most prominent. As he himself proudly said afterward, "I fought the ship to the last". Even after John Ross's resignation he had succeeded in patching up the government once again: he and Spence, the Postmaster-General, had between them persuaded J. C. Morrison, another old Baldwin Reformer, to enter the Cabinet under MacNab's leadership. But both Spence and Morrison had insisted they would resign if ever the remaining Hincksite Reformers carried out their implied threat and brought the verdict of Canada West against the government. On Friday evening, when the debate was adjourned for the week-end, it looked as if the defection of the western Reformers was a certainty. Even so, the ministers resumed the battle on Monday, May 19. The debate continued, before crowded, excited galleries, without interruption, day and night, for over thirty hours; and it was not until midnight on Tuesday that the final vote was taken. Holton's sub-amendment was defeated, seventy to forty-seven; Papin's amendment was voted down seventy-three to forty-three.[65] The government had been sustained; but in Canada West it stood in a minority of six. Immediately the long-awaited train of events began. The next day, when the House assembled, the ministers were conspicuously absent. Spence, Morrison and Macdonald, later joined by Cayley, had decided to resign. They did not believe, they insisted, in the double or sectional majority as an abstract principle; but Morrison and Spence, who felt themselves to represent the Reform side in the coalition, were dismayed by the defection of their old followers; and Macdonald, who knew that if his colleagues resigned they would take the last western Reform votes with them, realized that the government and the coalition would then be broken up.[66] MacNab, faced by the mass resignation of the entire western division of his government, could do nothing but place his own portfolio at the disposition of the Governor-General; and Head found himself in the embarrassing position of reorganizing a government which had not been defeated, but which would have no peace with itself until it had ejected Sir Allan.[67] On Saturday evening, May 24, the new administration was constituted, with E. P. Taché, President of the Legislative Council, as first minister, and Macdonald as Attorney-General West and leader of the government in the Assembly. The new Cabinet, little changed otherwise, met the House the following Monday, and four days later it pulled through its first want-of-confidence debate with the narrow majority of four.[68] The gallant old Sir Allan, crippled with gout, swathed in flannel bandages, appearing heroically like another Pitt to confront his successful enemies, was a pathetic spectacle which the Grit opposition loved to exhibit.[69] But many contemporaries, who knew some of the facts and suspected others, were not greatly impressed, and Macdonald, when he was sufficiently provoked, grew openly defiant. "Heap as many epithets and reproaches on me as you like," he declared, "but this I contend, that having performed my portion of the contract, having stuck to my leader, having tried every means to keep the cabinet together, that I had a right as a gentleman and a man of honour to go into a new government, with the speaker of the Legislative Council, or anyone else."[70]

One great episode in his career was finished. The struggle between the ultras and moderates in the Conservative party, which had begun years before with the beginning of the union, had ended at last. The moderates had triumphed, and Macdonald was the accepted leader of the Conservatives of Canada West.

Chapter Ten

Double Shuffle

I

Draper—it had been a characteristic sign of the two equally authentic elements in his Liberal-Conservatism—had thought of both John Hillyard Cameron and John Alexander Macdonald as his possible successors. The decade which had elapsed since Draper's retirement in 1847, when regarded from the point of view of the Conservative party, had been, in effect, a long struggle between the principles represented by these two men. Indeed their rivalry itself was only the last phase of a conflict, which had begun before the Rebellion, between the High Toryism of the past and the Liberal-Conservatism of the future. The coalition of 1854 had marked the first great victory of Liberal-Conservatism. The extrusion of MacNab, and the rejection of his lieutenant, Cameron, had clinched it. Macdonald, and the philosophy he represented, had won. He had not, of course, finished with Toryism, for Toryism was to remain a strong constituent element in the party, without which Liberal-Conservatism would have lost its essential character. He had not even finished with John Hillyard Cameron, for Cameron was to appear again, with all his old prestige and following, though never—such was the tragedy of chance—with quite the same striking power. There would be insurgent groups and party divisions in the future; but they were never to be quite the same as those of the past. The Rebellion, and all the rancorous disputes which had preceded and accompanied it, was at last ended; and the secularization of the Clergy Reserves had been the last chapter in an old book of troubles. Macdonald was done with all that. He and the province were growing up. From then on, Canada was to become more continuously aware than it ever had been of its difficult position and uncertain future in North America; and Macdonald, at forty-one, was called upon to grapple with a new and inter-related set of problems, the problems of approaching maturity.

One of these problems had already appeared, in a brief, but sharply acute, fashion. The Crimean War, the first great war which the British Empire had fought since the Napoleonic conflict nearly forty years before, had compelled the province to think seriously about its defences; and the Conservative government, with Sir Allan MacNab taking the principal initiative, had overhauled the venerable militia system and established a small but fairly efficient volunteer force. A certain amount of military enthusiasm and reforming zeal was thus an early product of the war; but by the time it ended it had brought on something not very far removed from a panic, at least in the innermost circles of government. Once again, as had happened during the Napoleonic wars, a major military struggle in the Old World was accompanied by a crisis with the United States of America—a crisis in which Canada would inevitably be involved, though she had no responsibility whatever for its creation. It had been brought on by Great Britain, which, in the desperate need for men, had passed the Foreign Enlistment Act, and by the British minister to Washington, J. F. T. Crampton, and the Nova Scotian politician Joseph Howe, who, with imprudent patriotism, set out to apply the act in the United States, despite all the stringent American neutrality laws.[1] Howe, who was moving about the United States like a somewhat theatrical conspirator in his search for men, appealed to the Canadian government to accept recruits. But MacNab and his Cabinet, advised by the cautious Head, would have nothing to do with the whole affair; and a year later, when the United States exacted its delayed revenge, and dismissed Crampton and three British consuls, they could at least congratulate themselves on their caution. Yet inevitably the province became the innocent victim of the storm of anti-

British and annexationist rage which swept through the United States. Palmerston and the Secretary for War, Panmure, realizing the danger of an explosion, and freed now from the demands of the Crimean War, despatched five regiments to Canada and a vast quantity of military stores.² For a while the peril seemed real. "If I am carried off to Boston or New York," wrote Head cheerfully to a correspondent, "I will apprise you of the change in my address but I think we should have a fight for it first".³ The fight never came, as it had never really come back in 1838; but the crisis brought back a sudden recollection of the old anxiety, which must have struck Macdonald like a blow. Within two years of accepting an important office in government, he had been compelled to take up the most basic of all Canadian problems, the problem of survival against the imperialist designs of the United States; and for the next fifteen years this was a problem which left him undisturbed for only the briefest of intervals.

Quickly he discovered that it lowered over most other problems like a huge, vague, sinister presence. It forced him, as it forced other people, to think in terms of a far-flung and daring strategy. Obviously the security of Canada was inseparable from the security of British North America as a whole. Canada could not be defended, it could not grow prosperous in isolation, but only as a part of a wider whole; and its relations with the other colonies and with the vast uncolonized west were certainly of prime importance for both opulence and defence. A whole host of absorbing and difficult questions had been raised by the Crimean War and the crisis with the United States. Was this the moment to revive the old idea of a general union of British North America, or was it wiser, for a while yet, to plan for a series of preliminary, regional unions? In the east, had the strategic necessity of the Intercolonial Railway been proved beyond a doubt by the threat of war with the United States? And, in the west, what was to be done with the Hudson's Bay Company, whose licence of exclusive trade in the North West Territories was soon to expire, and whose loose and uncertain hold over its enormous dominions might seem to justify some different and more effective provision against the encroaching Americans? These questions were asked, not only in Canada, which was nearly ready to expand its interests, but also in Great Britain, which had already begun to contract its obligations, so far as British North America was concerned. In the late summer of 1856 Head was visited in Toronto by Robert Lowe, the Vice-President of the Board of Trade in Palmerston's Cabinet, a quick-tempered intellectual, impatient of colonial commitments, and anxious that Canada should become Great Britain's residuary legatee on the North American continent. He and Head talked over a wide range of British North American affairs;[4] and, as a result of these discussions, Macdonald became aware that the imperial government was seriously considering several problems, including that of the Hudson's Bay Company, which deeply affected Canada. There was probably no very great surprise when, towards the end of the year, the expected dispatch arrived from Labouchere, the Colonial Secretary, informing the Canadian administration that the imperial government had decided to set up, at the next session of parliament, a committee of the House of Commons to explore the whole subject of the Hudson's Bay Company.[5] The question of the renewal of the exclusive licence to trade in the North West Territories would be the particular point at issue; but the inquiry was expected to range freely over the present and future position of the company as a whole. Inevitably the interests of the Province of Canada would be involved. Labouchere ended the dispatch by politely requesting the Canadian government to send witnesses and make representations to the proposed committee. There was no escaping the question. What policy was the Canadian government to adopt?

This was one of the principal questions which faced Macdonald as he and his small family settled down again in Wellington Place for the winter session of 1857. There were many confident voices, in the press as a whole and among the Reform newspapers in particular, which urged that Canada should adopt a vigorous policy of expansion. The Hudson's Bay Company charter was dismissed contemptuously as invalid. Canada's title to the entire territory was asserted with unabashed conviction, and the Canadian legislature was clamorously required to take instant, practical steps to acquire what was properly its own. Early in January, 1857, as a part of George Brown's comprehensive drive for the reorganization of the Grit party, a great convention of western Reformers was held at Toronto. Among the half dozen basic planks in its new platform, the convention adopted a resolution calling for the incorporation of Hudson's Bay Company's territory in Canada.[6] The opposition, with the spacious irresponsibility which is the prerogative of all oppositions, had pronounced in favour of western expansion; and, without any doubt, there was a good deal to be said for the course which the Reformers had so hastily adopted. It was popular in Canada at the moment, and it would very likely be the course which Canada would adopt in the end. But how could the province dare to undertake such a heavy responsibility at present or in the immediate future? Macdonald and the Cabinet drew back cautiously. The newspapers, even the *Globe*'s brassy voice of command, were all very well; but there were other more intimate and more prudent councils which were having their effect upon the willing Macdonald.

In the first place there was the influence of Head himself. Head had made no secret of the fact that he preferred his new government to the old one which MacNab had led. It was true that Taché was the titular head of the new administration, but Macdonald was now its principal Upper Canadian member. In Toronto, he lived conveniently close to Government House. He and the Governor saw a great deal of each other; they exchanged ideas and confidences; and their habits of mind, which were not dissimilar, led them unerringly towards the same general conclusions. Head distrusted popular clamour. He was impatient with the idle "dreams and speculations" about the west which he found "floating in the public mind here, even among sober and good men".[7] He told people, a little acidly, that Canada could not govern properly the dominions which she already possessed; and he was convinced that the Hudson's Bay Company's territories, even as a free gift, would be far too great a responsibility for Canada to accept at the present. The real point about territory was, not how to acquire

it, but how to administer it. Could Canada possibly cope with
an empire which occupied a quarter of a continent?

This kind of advice was coming to Macdonald also from
another and very different source, from a young Scotsman
living in Montreal, named John Rose. Rose was half a dozen
years younger than Macdonald, and he had arrived in Canada
much more recently; but some time in the late 1840's or early
1850's they met and became close friends. They were light-
hearted and still fairly irresponsible young men who enjoyed
life to the full without taking it very seriously; and once,
when Macdonald at least was old enough to know better,
they went off on an absurd adventure in the United States,
and wandered around as travelling showmen, with Rose caper-
ing about as a dancing bear, and Macdonald playing some
"rude instrument" in accompaniment.[8] In the meantime, back
in the sedate professional circles of Montreal, Rose was building up a very large and flourishing law practice. There was
little likelihood that he would ever be Macdonald's rival. Ambitious enough in his own way, and tranquilly assuming that
the good things of life would come to him, Rose had no very
great interest in public office or recognized political power.
He preferred to do things unostentatiously and by indirection;
he was born to conduct negotiations, to carry out delicate missions, to make adroit and rewarding arrangements. He was
an instinctive diplomatist who was by nature an urbane and
charming man; and already, although he was still comparatively
young, his sources of information were many and his influence
wide. Rose knew Head and Macdonald and the other members
of the Canadian government, and was well acquainted with the
business and professional people in Montreal. He even seemed
to possess a fairly large number of confidential correspondents
in financial and governmental circles in England. One of
them was Edward Ellice, old "Bear" Ellice, the veteran British
fur trader, who had helped to bring about the union of the
North West Company and the Hudson's Bay Company in
1821, and who ever since had been a potent influence in the
amalgamated concern. Rose had become Ellice's legal adviser
in Canada, and his agent for the Ellice seigniory at Beau-

harnois; and the old man, in a series of vigorous, cynically realistic letters, expounded to his Canadian subordinate the real position of the Hudson's Bay Company, as he saw it. It might have been—it obviously was—Hudson's Bay Company propaganda. But it also looked remarkably like good sense.

Ellice began by conceding—what Macdonald, Rose and other prudent Canadians were already prepared to admit—that in the end the Hudson's Bay Company would probably lose its chartered as well as its licensed territories. The lands would either become part of Canada, or they would be formed by Great Britain into new colonies, having, perhaps, some connection with Canada. Sooner or later they would probably gravitate to the St. Lawrence colony, for the sufficient reason that they could never be permitted to become a part of the United States. All this could be granted. It was not a question of principle, but a question of timing. When should the proposed change in administration take place? "It is neither the monopoly, nor the proprietary right of the Company, which is of much importance," old Edward Ellice argued shrewdly. "The great point is, how govern the territory. . . . Let anybody refer to the history and experience of the past, and they will be satisfied that these extensive and remote regions can only be governed by monopoly, and that the monopoly must be profitable to pay them who will undertake it. It is now profitable—it has never been more so—but if the Province of Canada, not having sufficient work on hand to govern themselves, covet this extension of their Dominion, its trade and its administration, nothing is as easy as to acquire it. For a million sterling, they may buy the fee simple of the whole territory north of forty-nine and between Canada and the Rocky Mountains, the whole trade and establishment of the Hudson's Bay Company, but they must saddle themselves at the same time with the expense, and what is of infinitely more importance, the responsibility of a territory extending some 6000 miles."[9] It was an intimidating prospect. Rose, who found it frankly terrifying, no doubt communicated the contents of Ellice's letter to Macdonald; and when the Governor next visited Montreal, he read a part of it to him. Head, Rose reported, was deeply impressed with the wisdom of Ellice's views. "I am sure he will exercise extreme caution," Rose wrote back to Ellice, "before he involves us in the heavy responsibility of protecting such an extent of territory, even were it given up to us for nothing."[10] Purchase or gift—it really made very little difference. If Canada were induced to accept major responsibility for the Hudson's Bay territories, would not Great Britain gladly and swiftly accelerate her withdrawal, certainly from the west, and perhaps even from British North America as a whole?

Yet, as Macdonald fully realized, some answer would have to be made to Labouchere's invitation. It would have to be a confident and perhaps assertive response, for public opinion in Canada obviously expected some clear declaration with respect to the Hudson's Bay Company's territories; but it need not be either very explicit or very compromising. And about the middle of January, Council got down to the business of concocting a suitable reply.[11] It began by asserting that the Canadian government "rejoiced" that the Hudson's Bay Company was about to be investigated. Then there was a reference to the unhappy uncertainty of the boundary between Canada and the United States, and another reference to the danger of encroaching American settlement. Canada, the order-in-council continued, had a natural interest in the affairs of every part of British North America; and, so far as her own claims were concerned, "the general feeling here is strongly that the western boundary of Canada extends to the Pacific Ocean". From all these rather vague and grandiose premises, Council drew the conclusion that Canada ought to be properly represented before the proposed parliamentary committee; and a few weeks later it decided that the proper representative could be none other than William Henry Draper, the first architect of the Liberal-Conservative party, and now the Chief Justice of Canada West. The instructions which Draper received were scarcely a great deal more definite than the language of the minute which had justified his appointment.[12] He was bidden to watch over the interests of Canada in the investigation and to assert her "legal and equitable claims"—whatever they might. be. The provision of tracts of land fit for settlement ought to be ensured in any settlement with the Hudson's Bay Company. Above all else, the international boundary must be defined and protected "against sudden and unauthorized immigration from the United States". But Draper was not to feel free to require, or conclude, any plan of settlement without reference back to the Canadian government. The Canadian government, in fact, had no very definite "plan of settlement" to press. It wished to protect Canadian interests for the future, but without serious obligations at the present.

II

By the time these decisions were taken, the Macdonalds John Alexander, Isabella, and Hugh John, were established once again in the rented apartments in the house on Wellington Place. It was a constricted, unhappy family existence. The narrow rooms were crowded with the paraphernalia of the sick-room and hushed by the presence of invalidism; it was almost like carrying on domestic life in all the depressing discomforts of a field-hospital tent. Isabella, it was true, had no recurrence of the terrible crisis of the previous winter. Sometimes Macdonald, in his letters back to Kingston, merely announced briefly that his wife was "as usual"; and once, towards the end of the winter, he was even able to report that she had been "in very unusual health and strength". But this, as everybody knew now, was only a brief interval of well-being in an incurable disease; and even so, the joy at Isabella's temporary improvement was darkened by concern for Hugh. The boy—he was seven years old in March—was ill most of the winter.[18] Afflicted with recurring but diminishing attacks of pain, treated with special diets and frequent hot baths, he was kept sternly in the house for weeks on end and permitted virtually no exercise. His education, which was obviously suffering, was already a concern to his parents. They worried over the fact that the seven-year-old was not able to attend a Toronto school; and a tutor was secured who, during the difficult period of the winter, appeared daily for a token lesson of an hour.[14] In March, when the sun climbed higher and the air grew warmer, Hugh emerged to play in the open air. Now the tutor's visits lengthened: Hugh "takes a two hours lesson every day and is a wonderful arithmetician", Macdonald reported proudly to his sister Louisa.[15] It was pleasant to record the small boy's steady improvement; it was a hopeful episode in a family history which sometimes looked like an unbroken chronicle of illness. Even Macdonald himself, who was usually so robustly healthy, was ill that winter. The session began late, towards the end of February; and a little after the opening, he gave his arm a severe sprain—a sprain which shook him far more than might have been expected. He kept the arm wrapped up in flannel for some time; but he continued to feel weak and depressed in spirit. It was a bad state in which to meet parliament for what was destined to be the last session before a general election.

It was an important session in other ways as well. The problems of Canada's approaching maturity emerged gradually out of the haze of distance like the harsh, forbidding features of some newly discovered and formidable landscape. The question of defence against the United States, the problems of Canadian westward expansion, of communications with the eastern seaboard, and of British North American union, were all important matters which had jolted Macdonald and his colleagues out of the rutted tracks of normal provincial speculation. They were pushed further, protestingly, along the paths of invention and experiment, by the very condition of their province itself, by the incessantly recurring difficulties of a country which was in form a unitary state, and in fact a half-acknowledged federal system. The choice of a capital, the selection of the province's spiritual centre symbolized, as perhaps nothing else could have done, the irreconcilable conflict between unity and duality. The debate on the "seat-of-government" question had been going on almost without interruption from the moment that Sydenham had first selected Kingston back in 1841. For years it had not been considered a "ministerial question". No recent government had dared to take up a decided stand on the issue; and in the previous session, the MacNab administration had, ostensibly at least, permitted the debate on the subject to develop in complete freedom. The debate had resulted in the choice of Quebec. Macdonald and his colleagues, dutifully accepting the decision of the legislature, had included in the budget an appropriation for the construction of appropriate permanent buildings at the province's new capital. It looked as if the whole business was ended, when there came another odd turn in the erratic course of the provincial legislature. The Legislative Council threw out the appropriation for buildings. The whole affair had been deposited back again at the starting point.

The government was not quite nonplussed. The new session approached, and Macdonald was one of the originators of a completely new plan. He had probably not been very well pleased with the choice of Quebec, against which he had voted consistently in the last session. On the other hand, he disliked the ambulatory system even more, for the ambulatory system implied division, and he liked to believe in the continued existence of the united province, either by itself, or as part of a possible wider unity. Why not refer the whole perplexing issue to the Queen, and respectfully invite Her Majesty to make a decision which the Canadian legislature seemed incapable of making by itself? Surely this was an ingenious suggestion with a good deal to recommend it. In the first place, it would ensure delay, while Her Majesty deliberately made up her mind; and delay, which was always good anyway, could in this case be prolonged until after the next general election. In the second place, it was a patriotically unexceptionable course, which could only be criticized with difficulty, and which would probably end in a selection less easily disturbed than any which the Canadian legislature could make itself. The argument seemed sound and Macdonald launched the resolutions inviting the Queen's arbitrament early in the session. There was some criticism. John Hillyard Cameron attacked the government for its abandonment of responsibility. The request for the Queen's decision, he declared, was a retrograde step constitutionally, which would, of course, not prevent the Canadian ministers from offering surreptitious advice. "They will secretly exercise an influence," Cameron declared in his smoothest fashion, "the responsibility of which they are afraid openly to assume."[16] Macdonald jovially twitted the High Tory Cameron with being a late and doubtful convert to responsible government, insisted that the present administration, in proposing the reference to the Queen, had in fact assumed more responsibility than any previous government, and defended the course he proposed as the only remaining method of settling the contentious question. The baffled and weary House was inclined to agree with him. One last concession, it was true, had to be made to the Conservative supporters in Canada East. Macdonald, pressed by Alleyn and Lemieux, was forced to agree that the seat of government should be transferred for a last term to the city of Quebec before the final and permanent removal to the new capital, wherever it might be.[17] But this was a cheap price to pay for what might possibly be a lasting settlement, and what would certainly result in a welcome period of peace. Before March was out, Head had sent to the Colonial Office the reference to the Queen.[18] "It will not be expedient," he told Herman Merivale, the Permanent Under-Secretary, in a private letter dispatched the same day, "that any answer should be given for 8 or 10 months, *except the acceptance of the reference*. The sooner that comes the better." The Colonial Office acted with commendable promptitude. The Queen graciously accepted the reference. And Macdonald gratefully pushed the matter out of his mind as something which could be conveniently forgotten for nearly a twelvemonth.

He was not permitted to indulge his feeling of relief too long. The crisis with the United States in the spring of 1856 and the dispatch of the imperial reinforcements to Canada had raised the whole general question of British North American communications. In Canada a phase of the same problem was brought up again by the perennial difficulties of the Grand Trunk Railway. The Conservative government had not, of course, begun the Grand Trunk—that had been the work of Hincks; but from the beginning Liberal-Conservatives, as individuals, had played a conspicuous part in the financial melodrama of the railway age. MacNab, the first leader of the administration, was president of the Great Western Railway; Ross, the ex-President of the Council, was the president of the Grand Trunk Railway; and Cartier, the Attorney-General for Canada East and the effective leader of the French-Canadian bloc in the Assembly, was the Grand Trunk's principal solicitor. It was an intimate, all too vulnerable, personal connection; and it grew all the more easily open to attack as the Grand Trunk became an established fact, as its benefits tended to be taken for granted, and as its requirements and necessities rapidly became the subject of acrid public debate. A huge, though still incomplete, system, which stretched from Quebec and Portland in the east towards Sarnia and London in the west, the railway had in fact become the most important enterprise in Canada— an enterprise which was at once an economic and social asset to the province and a financial and political liability to the provincial government.[19] Repeatedly, the new Liberal-Conservative administration had had to rush to the assistance of the railway. Financial help had been given in 1855, and again in 1856; and with the opening of the session of 1857, it became perfectly clear that a new Grand Trunk aid bill would inevitably be an embarrassing item in the government's programme of legislation. The support of the government entailed the attack of the opposition; and resistance to the Grand Trunk and its financial exactions became an integral part of the new Liberalism which Brown and his associates were building up in Canada West. The railway was represented to the edified populace of Upper Canada as a malign creation of Montreal finance, which robbed the public treasury, debauched the country with the bribery of jobs and contracts, and impoverished the poor patient farmers of Canada West with exorbitant freight rates. The influence of the Grand Trunk, like the influence of the Roman Catholic priesthood, rested ultimately, the *Globe* explained to its readers, upon the votes of the French-Canadian bloc in parliament; and Rep. by Pop. would defeat both the despotism of the popish hierarchy and the financial tyranny of Montreal.

Macdonald, though he had never taken much interest in the detail of finance, found that he was being pushed more and more deeply into Grand Trunk affairs. It was, of course,

Cayley's job, as Inspector-General, to introduce the bill. But Cayley, with his diffident, gentlemanly manner, and weak voice, was ineffective in the House; and a good deal of the defence fell to Macdonald. Macdonald tried, as he always did, to avoid technical detail, and to confine himself to the broad basic considerations which would really determine the matter. The aid which the government proposed, he told the House, was not intended to relieve the shareholders, or to put money into anybody's pocket; it was designed simply to restore public confidence in the property, to facilitate the raising of fresh capital, and, above all else, to complete the road.[20] When, a few minutes later in the speech, Brown laughed cynically at the request that the bill be passed with as little delay as possible, Macdonald, in a moment of sheer exasperation, informed his tormentor savagely that he might very well laugh on the other side of his face, if, six months from then, he found himself at the head of a Reform administration, with the work on the Victoria Bridge suspended, the G.T.R. rolling stock handed over to the railway's creditors and the railway itself in bankruptcy. Nobody, Brown included, really believed that the railway could be abandoned. But, before this danger-point was even approached, criticism could be pushed a very long way indeed, for the financial history of the Grand Trunk was a tangled and somewhat questionable story. Brown exploited his advantage with his usual intemperate righteousness. He attacked the relief bill in violent diatribes; he secured a parliamentary committee for the investigation of the entire financial record of the Grand Trunk Railway Company; he flung accusations, insinuations, and reproaches in all directions. And at a certain point, which Macdonald saw approaching with delight, and which Brown himself seemed utterly incapable of anticipating, he went too far. His wholesale condemnations began to include the eastern members of his own party; the violent Upper Canadianism of his crusade began to awaken an indignant response even in Liberal Canada East. Alexander Tilloch Galt, the *Rouge* member for Sherbrooke, a railway promoter and contractor who had had a good deal to do with the Grand Trunk Railway, was subjected to a prolonged and merciless inquisition in Brown's special committee of investigation. When Galt had the temerity to interrupt Brown in the full flow of one of his speeches and question him on a point of fact, Brown turned furiously upon the member for Sherbrooke and screamed out his accusations of bad faith and bribery to the whole House. When Luther Holton, another *Rouge* who was also a railway contractor, attempted to deny Brown's pet thesis and to argue that the Grand Trunk was really of more benefit to Canada West than to Canada East, Brown instantly attributed this infatuated delusion to the basest of pecuniary motives. "There was a time," he told the House furiously, "when the honourable gentleman opposed the Grand Trunk as strongly as I did; but that opposition ceased when he got a Grand Trunk directorship and a Grand Trunk contract. There was a time when he professed to act with the opposition, but his conduct on this question has done more injury to the Liberal party than has been done by all the efforts of the gentlemen opposite."[21] The situation was comically grotesque. Brown, in one of his hysterias of arrogant righteousness, seemed actually to be trying to read Dorion, Galt, and Holton out of the party! But the *Rouges* owed him no allegiance, and Dorion and the others were far from being his submissive lieutenants. They protested indignantly, and the unseemly public row went on. It was a good illustration of how difficult it was going to be to build a provincial Reform party on the basis of militant sectionalism.

Macdonald amiably watched the opposition leaders indulging in the traditional Reform game of fighting with each other in public. He tucked the idea away in his mind that this might be a suitable moment to begin detaching Dorion, Holton, and Galt from their censorious and dictatorial western colleague. But this delicate operation would have to be postponed until autumn, for he had other and still more urgent affairs on hand for the summer. Early in the session he had reached the conclusion that railways in general and the Grand Trunk in particular would require him to go off to England as soon as parliament rose. As the exacting session dragged on, his resolution wavered; he had become ill shortly after the opening and his illness continued for most of the following three months.

He began to dream longingly of a real holiday at the seashore for Isabella and Hugh and himself—a holiday such as they had never had before. "On the rising of Parliament," he told his sister Louisa towards the end of April, "I intend to go to the seashore and not to England. I hope to have six weeks of sea bathing which will put me all right again."[22] That was in early spring; but by the middle of June, when the session had at length ended, the earlier decision prevailed. The condition of the Grand Trunk—three times in succession rescued by government—was desperate in the extreme; and both on financial and political grounds the embarrassed government was bound to make another effort to obtain imperial support. Besides, the summer of 1857 was in many ways a suitable moment for the mission. In London he would enjoy strong Canadian support. Draper was already there on the business of the Hudson's Bay investigation. Head, the Governor-General, had sought and obtained leave to return home, partly on the ground that his presence on the spot might be useful in the Hudson's Bay matter and in the seat-of-government question.[23] And Head and Macdonald were a formidable team in Canadian affairs.

In mid-July, council authorized Macdonald's mission to England;[24] and Eyre, the General Officer Commanding, who acted as administrator in Head's absence, wrote a letter introducing the Attorney-General West to Labouchere at the Colonial Office.[25] In its order of July 18, Council declared that Macdonald was to "have authority to call to his aid the services of any gentleman whom he may deem necessary to the success of the negotiations". At that late date the identity of the "gentleman" was still apparently unknown; but, in reality, Macdonald had made his choice some time before. It was John Rose—the pleasant fellow, the good companion, with his affable manner and his wide circle of influential London friends. Rose wrote off to Edward Ellice that Macdonald had been begging him to go. "I don't quite see my way to leave," he explained, "nor do I quite relish the mission, but he, as well as others, are so urgent that I may go."[26] He went indeed; and before a fortnight had passed he and Macdonald were aboard the

Anglo-Saxon and bound for Liverpool. After the long grind of the session, Macdonald enjoyed the sea voyage. He admitted, in a letter to his mother, that he had felt a "little squeamish" at intervals for three days and had been decidedly sick one morning; but, he concluded proudly, "I never lost my dinner —a great and wonderful change for me".[27] It was a pleasant but uneventful voyage—"a couple of icebergs and a few whales being all our wonders"—and before the month was out he and Rose had docked at Liverpool, travelled down to London and were installed in the York Hotel, Albemarle Street. That first evening they went off together to the opera; but the next morning early he was "up to his eyes in business".[28]

It was, for him, a new kind of entrance to the capital of the Empire. He had come before as a young man on his travels or as the agent of a commercial company; now he appeared as the accredited representative of the senior colony in British North America. He appeared, moreover, with what could be defended as a practical scheme, which, far from laying all the burdens on Great Britain, would certainly place real and substantial obligations on the Province of Canada. They would be heavy obligations; but, according to the new plan, they would be somewhat differently distributed, and hence possibly more bearable. Canada had in fact determined to revive the old project of the Intercolonial Railway and to transfer some of its financial responsibilities from the provincial Grand Trunk to the interprovincial road. Macdonald and Rose proposed to the Colonial Office that if Great Britain should relieve Canada of the repayment of the £1,500,000 loan of 1841 and of the sinking fund established in connection with it, the province would agree to pay the entire cost of its share of the line from Rivière du Loup to Halifax.[29] During the first weeks of August, they were busy memorializing the British government and interviewing its various members. They saw Labouchere, the Colonial Secretary, Sir George Cornewall Lewis, the Chancellor of the Exchequer and Lord Panmure, the Secretary for War.[30] Head gave them his weighty assistance. Even Edward Ellice, "somewhat against my conscience", wrote to Lord Panmure to give what help he could towards "your military road".[31]

Everybody was very polite. Yet they seemed to make curiously little progress, as, indeed, Edward Ellice had anticipated. "You will be received with great civility," the old man had told Rose, "matters will be discussed with you, as if there was a disposition to assist you—'fair words butter no parsnips'—but when the real point of engagement comes on the tapis they will do nothing for you".[32] It soon began to look ominously as if Ellice's prophecy were only too correct; and, indeed, the circumstances of the summer of 1857 were unhappily unpropitious for Macdonald's proposal. The crisis with the United States of the summer of 1856 was a thing of the past; the Indian Mutiny had already broken out, and the whole focus of imperial concern had shifted from west to east. The Canadian mission, as a mission, was pretty obviously a failure; but as a diverting holiday for Macdonald, it had been a pronounced success. He found Rose, as he had anticipated, a pleasant companion, and they got on very well together. "I am, thank God," he wrote his mother, "in good health and spirits and enjoying myself amazingly."[33] He paid a series of visits to the members of the Macdonald-Macpherson connection, went off to Paris for an extra-official three-day visit, and bought a few things to take back to Canada, including a highland kilt for Hugh. "I have no doubt," he told his mother, "he will bare his bottom with due Celtic dignity."[34] Then it was September and time to return home. The problem of British North American transportation had not been solved in the brief summer of 1857.

III

That autumn he took up the delicate business of Cabinet reorganization. It was high time to be mending political fences. Parliament expired by the effluxion of time in the summer of 1858; and, as Head had anticipated, the government decided that it would be better to hold the election a little earlier, before the end of the current year. It was certainly not a particularly good moment to appeal to the constituencies, for

the Crimean War boom broke in the autumn of 1857 and the
province, like the rest of the western world, was soon deep
in the pit of an economic depression. But there was not much
point in delaying the election a few months, in the vain hope
that things would improve. In any case, the reorganization
of the Cabinet must take place immediately, for Colonel Taché,
the titular head of the administration, was anxious to resign,
and there were two other places to fill as well. Before he sailed
for England Macdonald had been aware of the fact that an
extensive shake-up in the Canada East section of the Cabinet
was necessary; and in the autumn, after he had returned to
the province, Head asked him to accept the major responsibility
for making the new appointments.[35] At the age of forty-
two, he was first minister of the government of the Province
of Canada. Cartier, who had pushed his way rapidly to the
front of the rather feeble and fluctuating group of French-
Canadian politicians, was to be his principal assistant, almost
his political equal; and Cartier's prodigious authority and influence in all that concerned Canada East could not be gain-
said. Together they sat down to recruit the eastern section of
the Cabinet.

Macdonald knew the complicated rules well. And Cartier
was always willing to expound them in his vigorous staccato
style. Apart from the Solicitor-General, who was not formally
a member of the Cabinet, there had to be in every self-
respecting administration two members from the District of
Quebec and three from the District of Montreal. One of
these—it did not matter much from which district he came—
had to be a "Britisher", not a French Canadian. There might
even, at a pinch, be two Britishers, though Cartier looked very
doubtfully at this augmentation of the English-speaking side.
One of the Britishers was required to be a Protestant; the
second—in case there unfortunately had to be a second—might
very usefully be an Irish Roman Catholic. Macdonald left
most of the details to Cartier, who every once in a while, like
a minor prophet bursting into revelation, would be "delivered"
of a fresh set of names.[36] Macdonald's principal purpose was
to use the reorganization in such a way as to steal a little

opposition support. He had divined the angry discontent of the
Rouges with astonishing accuracy. The rift in the unhappy
Liberal family was, in fact, very serious. "Have you and I any
particular inducement," Holton inquired sourly of Galt, "to
assist in playing the Opposition's game after the treatment we
received last session?"[37] Macdonald pressed his sympathetic
inducements in his most persuasive manner. Dorion was offered
a Cabinet post; and when Dorion at length and somewhat
hesitatingly declined, Galt was approached for his support in
a jocularly friendly fashion. "You call yourself a *Rouge,*"
wrote Macdonald affably. "There may have been at one time
a reddish tinge about you, but I could observe it becoming by
degrees fainter. In fact you are like Byron's Dying Dolphin,
exhibiting a series of colours—'the last still loveliest'—and that
last is 'true blue', being the colour I affect. Seriously, you
would make a decent Conservative, if you gave your own
judgment a fair chance and cut loose from Holton and Dorion
and those other beggars. So pray do become true blue at once:
it is a good standing colour and bears washing."[38]

Galt did not become "true blue" at once. But it was significant that he had disapproved of Dorion's decision not to
accept a Cabinet post; and in a little while he was to announce
himself an Independent and to begin a vigorous attack upon
his former colleagues in the opposition. The hope of obtaining
the support of some of the prominent *Rouge* leaders had to be
given up, at least temporarily; but Sicotte brought with him
a Liberal flavour to the eastern division of the Cabinet and
John Rose certainly raised the level of its intellectual ability.
Rose was not very acceptable, as a second English-speaking
member, to Cartier; but he was, if anything, even more objectionable to the ministers from Canada West, who looked
on the Montreal lawyer as a very imperfectly disguised agent
of the Hudson's Bay Company. "I will do almost anything to
serve you," Philip Vankoughnet wrote to Macdonald, "but
giving up to Lower Canada the Commissioner of Crown Lands
and taking in John Rose also is too much. Rose will and must
be regarded as the agent of Ellice . . . and as I have no doubt
we will run the ship ashore with him it is as well to give it

up now with credit."³⁹ Macdonald blandly disregarded this
outspoken warning. Sicotte was made Commissioner of Crown
Lands, and John Rose became the Solicitor-General, Canada
East.

It remained to be seen whether they would run the ship
upon the rocks, as Vankoughnet had so gloomily prophesied.
After the reconstruction of the Cabinet was complete, Macdonald enjoyed a very brief holiday in Kingston; but on November 29 he left again for Toronto and by half-past nine that night
he was comfortably installed in the new Rossin House.⁴⁰ There
was no thought, at the moment, of Isabella and Hugh accompanying him or of a resumption of their life together in Toronto
lodgings. Isabella was seriously ill again; and next day, the
last day of November, he waited impatiently for the agreed-
upon telegram which would tell him that all was well at home.
The election was less than a fortnight away. The Reform
alliance, the new Reform organization which had been fashioned
at the convention in the previous January, was sweeping the
whole west in a boisterous campaign which extolled Rep. by
Pop. as the single sovereign remedy for all the cultural and
economic ills under which Canada West suffered and groaned.
The counter-campaign which Macdonald tried to organize from
Toronto was essentially defensive. He was unremittingly busy
—so busy that he could hardly spare a moment for the minor
engagement of his own election in Kingston. On December
9, he rushed down at the last moment and appeared the following day at the hustings before the city hall for the nomination
meeting. A local man, John Shaw, had been put up to oppose
him; but, as the local Conservative newspaper announced contemptuously, Shaw's candidature was so trivial that it was
generally believed to have been originated by wags for sport.⁴¹
And Macdonald, addressing the crowd in "his usual friendly
happy manner", hardly bothered to talk politics, either local or
general, in his election speech, and reminisced instead about
the old days in "the good old town".⁴² That very night he
returned to Toronto, announcing confidently that he "entrusted
his return to Parliament to the people of Kingston". The
confiding appeal could not be resisted. "Electors of Kingston,"

exhorted the editor of the *News*, "stand by your Political Child, and trample under foot the factious opposition that seeks to bring discredit upon our good old city".[43] On December 16, a mild day of dull, cloudy skies and muddy streets, the poll opened. Before the day was out John Shaw formally withdrew from the unequal contest; but his withdrawal did not prevent him from being burnt in effigy that night in the market place. And next evening, when the poll finally closed, Macdonald's total had mounted to 1189 votes, whilst poor Shaw had secured only nine.[44]

It was a walkover. But unfortunately it bore no resemblance to the results in the majority of the constituencies of Canada West. Three Conservative cabinet ministers—Cayley, Spence, and Morrison—were defeated; while George Brown was successful, not only in North Oxford, but actually in Toronto as well. Three years ago, when the Liberal-Conservative coalition had first faced parliament, John Hillyard Cameron, the Tory, had seemed almost as formidable an antagonist as the Reformer, George Brown; but now, in so short a time, their relative importance had completely altered. Cameron, who had not even sought re-election, had become one of the first and most tragic victims of the depression. The New York house through which he had carried on his ambitious exchange business had failed suddenly and its drafts on London were dishonoured. The securities which he had placed in the hands of his English bankers were sold at a loss of over £100,-000.[45] He was terribly, almost hopelessly, in debt. But he refused all financial compromises and swore he would pay twenty shillings on the pound. The great house on Queen Street was given up; the patronage of Samuel Thompson's *British Colonist* was abandoned; and he became the grimly willing slave of his profession. Never again would he be able to afford the time for a really active political career. He had fallen—fallen at almost exactly the same moment as Brown's most sudden and dramatic rise. Brown now towered above all his Radical rivals; he seemed to loom portentously over the whole Canadian political scene. For him the election had been a personal as well as a party triumph; it had demonstrated the justice of his convictions and the wisdom of his strategy. It was true that in Canada East the demoralized *Rouges* lost almost as heavily as the Grits gained in Canada West; but this, though it might save the Liberal-Conservative government, could not lessen Brown's feeling of triumph nor remove Macdonald's sense of personal defeat. Canada West was his own particular baili-wick; and in Canada West his party had now been put unquestionably in a minority.

The election had not yet finished when the holiday came. He had not intended to go home for Christmas; and he was still in Toronto, carrying on the battle for the last constituencies, when the message arrived from Kingston. There had been such messages before, and he had obeyed them instantly, hurrying home in a terror of apprehension as he had done from the Crown Law Office on that winter day almost a year before. In one sense his whole married life, ever since the terrible summer of 1845, had been one long frightened expectation of the tragic message which, in the end, must infallibly come. By Christmas night he was in Kingston, by Isabella's bedside, watching hope-fully as he had watched so often before. This time, as he must have seen immediately, there were no alternatives ahead. For three days more she dragged her broken existence along; and then on December 28, in the last exhaustion from which there was no recovery, she died.[46] It was the expected, inevitable end for what had been for almost a dozen years a grey, un-relieved tragedy. Life had cheated him terribly; he had given everything where, in the very nature of the case, there could never be a full and satisfying response. By the two supreme efforts of her life, Isabella had borne children, one of whom had lived; but for years she had been a bedridden invalid, who was physically incapable of giving him the love, the sup-port, and the companionship which he had craved. It was all over now—the agony of worry, the aching feeling of incom-pleteness, the patched habit of cheerful resignation. But for twelve years it had twisted his whole life. He had become a family man whose home was a hotel or a lodging-house; a bachelor husband who had to go for companionship to bars and lounges and smoking-rooms; a frustrated host who drank too much on occasion, partly because it was the only way he could entertain, and because it passed the empty time, and because it was an easy way to forget.

IV

He had spent the autumn reconstructing the Canada East section of the Cabinet. The first task of the dreary New Year was to recruit its broken contingent from Canada West. Two months before, he had cautiously felt out the discontented and half-rebellious forces of the enemy's eastern wing; and now, in the same kind of delicate manoeuvre, he sought tentatively for the weak spot on the western flank. John Sandfield Macdonald, the independent Reformer from the upper St. Lawrence valley, who had never accepted Brown's dictatorship, seemed to respond a little to these approaches; and late in January he was actually offered a choice of offices in the Cabinet. John Alexander Macdonald hoped for the telegraphic reply "All right" to his hastily written letters; what he received from his clansman was the equally laconic but unfortunately negative rejoinder "No go".[47] In the end John Ross returned to the Cabinet, and Sidney Smith, an authentic Reformer whose election the *Globe* had celebrated, was also persuaded to join. In some way the ranks were reformed. But it had been a difficult and disheartening task; and he was a depressed and lonely man during the winter of 1858 in Toronto. His wife was dead; his small son was a long day's journey away in Kingston; and now that the family apartments in Wellington Place had been given up for ever, he was living with a Mr. Salt, in bachelor quarters on Bay Street.

In the Assembly, George Brown led a clamorous and exultant opposition. Politically Macdonald lived from day to day, in a state of constant and irritating uncertainty. The House was a tossing ship in which, at almost any moment, he expected to lose his balance and fall headlong. During the first month of the long session he became ill, as he had done in the previous March; and for days of convalescence he dragged himself around with painful difficulty. It was pleasant to escape for week-ends to John Ross's house five miles out in the country on the Davenport Road, to have two good nights' rest, and to spend Sunday lounging in peaceful ease on the sofa. But this respite was very brief, and on Monday he found himself facing George Brown and his confident, truculent supporters once more. "We are having a hard fight in the House," he told his sister Margaret, "and shall beat them in the votes, but it will, I think, end in my retiring as soon as I can with honour. I find the work and annoyance too much for me."[48] He was depressed by weariness, by the continued drear sense of personal loss, by the unhappy realization of political defeat in his own old province of Upper Canada, and finally, perhaps, by a vague feeling that his own political mission was finished. He had formed the Liberal-Conservative party; and in the Clergy Reserves and Seigniorial Tenure measures he had helped to settle the outstanding issues of the past. But it was not the past that counted; it was the present and future. And here he could still not see a bold and easy course ahead.

For two years now the new and wider problems of approaching political maturity had been crowding about his government. For two years now his government had done little more than fumble with them cautiously and indecisively. It was true that he had thought of a new method, sensible as well as merely ingenious, for the solution of the seat-of-government question; and Sir Edmund Head's recommendation of Ottawa may very well have been his own private suggestion, though for many obvious reasons, he could hardly claim the credit for it. There were other quite different choices, from other advisers, civil and military, in the papers which were presented to the Queen.[49] But the Colonial Office, following Head, had decided for Ottawa; and General Grey, the Queen's secretary, drew the same conclusion from the evidence. "An attentive perusal of the papers relative to the seat of government in Canada," he wrote, "leads to the conviction that the choice of Ottawa will be the right and politic one."[50] It was all settled. The Queen had selected Ottawa, and the only remaining question was when the benevolent royal choice should be communicated to the devoted Canadians. "Sir Edmund Head is of opinion," wrote Labouchere to the Queen, "that the decision had better arrive in Canada about Christmas."[51] It was the Queen's Christmas present to the Province of Canada; and the dispatch announcing it arrived early in January, a little late for the holiday, but just after the elections, and comfortably before the first session of the new parliament.[52]

As far as could be seen, Macdonald had cleared one problem out of the way with a dexterous flourish. But in other matters, the government had either not been very adventurously constructive, or, when it had tried to take a bold course, it had not been very successful. The effort to persuade the imperial government to give assistance in the construction of the Intercolonial Railway had turned out to be completely unsuccessful. And the grand investigation of the Hudson's Bay Company, about which there had been so much vainglorious talk in the Canadian newspapers, had ended, not in the dramatic recognition of Canadian rights or the acquisition of new Canadian territory, but in the virtual humdrum continuation of the existing regime in the west. Worst of all, the Conservatives seemed to have no solution whatever for the endless problems created by the cultural division of the province. Almost every other party, or fragment of a party, had a solution. They represented all degrees of political decisiveness, from the completely catastrophic to the mildly reformist. Any one of them could be made to look plausible; and all of them were given lengthy hearing in the session of 1858, when the new parliament, weary with union yet frightened of separation, wore down many doorsteps in its frantic search for a new and comfortable shelter. Mackenzie, as of old the greatest extremist, advocated a simple dissolution of the union. Brown, proudly conscious that he was the chosen mouthpiece for the outraged and powerful voice of Canada West, presented Rep. by Pop. once again, the official policy of the Reform Alliance. John Sandfield Macdonald, the invariable Liberal individualist, spoke up for the so-called Double Majority, a scheme far more advocated than practised, which required any truly legitimate government to have a parliamentary majority in both sections of the province. And finally Alexander Tilloch Galt, the one-time *Rouge* who had now broken with his old associates, revived the old idea—advocated years before by the British American League and by such Tories as Henry Sherwood—that the peculiar problems of the Canadian union could best be solved in a federation of British North America. At the moment Macdonald was willing to support none of these proposals. On the subject of Galt's scheme, which was the only broadly constructive one of the lot, he simply kept his opinions in reserve; but all the others he opposed, for, in his opinion, all the others were wholly negative and destructive. Mackenzie would dissolve the union. Brown would break it up equally effectively by destroying its peculiar character. And Sandfield Macdonald would make it impossible to govern by responsible government according to the parliamentary model. Macdonald could do nothing more than stick by the union.[53] It was a cautious, sensible, defensive policy—like so many other of the government's policies; and, in the wild exasperation of the moment, it could hardly be very popular.

Yet Macdonald somehow kept the weak, embarrassed, and vulnerable government going. The winter and spring passed slowly. Summer came, and still the interminable session prolonged itself. It was almost unthinkable that Brown would fail to grasp what seemed to be his greatest opportunity. A huge, earnest, clumsily vital man, he was now at the height of his physical and mental powers; and his confident belief in his own future and in the political destiny of Canada West had become a fanatical conviction. Yet it was not until nearly the end of the session that he and his followers were able to precipitate the overthrow of the government, and even then their sudden and almost unexpected success was achieved by a method, which, if they had been less eager and over-confident, they might have regarded as dubious if not dangerous. Clearly the government's tenure of office was based upon its large majority of members from Canada East; and clearly the government's defeat could be encompassed by the method of detaching, if only temporarily, a considerable bloc of its Canada East supporters. The simple—far too simple—way of accomplishing this was obvious; it was by reviving the ancient seat-of-government question once more. Quebec and Montreal—and particularly Quebec which had had high hopes of becoming Canada's future capital—were resentfully disappointed at the Queen's choice of Ottawa. On this matter, if on no other, the members of Canada East might be moved by an irrepressible burst of local feeling to desert the government. This was the manoeuvre which the opposition finally decided to adopt. On Wednesday, July 28, an address to the Queen on the subject of the capital was mooted; amendments and still more ingenious amendments were suggested; and finally Piché moved that "in the opinion of this House the City of Ottawa ought not to be the permanent seat of government of this Province".[54] Macdonald intervened late in the debate. He reminded the House of the long acrimonious dispute which had moved the legislature itself to seek the royal intervention; he insisted that the Queen's choice had been made freely without the slightest advice from the Canadian government; and he condemned the resolution before the House as "a brusque and uncourteous insult to Her Majesty".[55] A few minutes later the vote came; and, as the Brownites had gleefully anticipated, the necessary bloc of French-Canadian votes changed sides. The government had been defeated sixty-four to fifty.

Flushed and excited Brown jumped to his feet at once. The vote which had just been carried, he explained triumphantly to the House, was in reality an express disapproval of the entire policy of the government; but, in order to put this interpretation of the event to the test, he would move the adjournment. Macdonald accepted the motion to adjourn as a deliberate challenge to his government; and the House, as most people, except the over-confident Grits, might have expected, immediately reversed itself.[56] The whole incident could have been dismissed as unimportant, but Macdonald decided at once that he would take it seriously. The appeal to the Queen, if it had not been his invention, had at least received his emphatic support. He may have intended merely to repudiate the vote as a reversal of his government's declared policy. He may have hoped to escape from a difficult position, to teach the irrespons-

ible Assembly the consequences of its folly, to force a sobered
House to take him back again on his own terms. And finally,
was he not clearly aware from the beginning that the resignation of the Liberal-Conservative government would place before
the blindly over-confident Brown the greatest temptation of
his career—the temptation to accept office on the basis of a
majority which, in the nature of the case, could only be
ephemeral, the temptation to wreck his own future and the
prospects of the Grit party by a premature grasp of power?
That night, when a new and this time insignificant motion
to adjourn had been passed, Macdonald called a late informal
meeting of his colleagues in the Assembly. Before they went
to bed, a majority of the ministers had decided to resign; and
their decision, communicated next morning to their colleagues
in the Legislative Council, was quickly made unanimous. Early
in the forenoon of Thursday, July 29, the Macdonald-Cartier
ministry tendered its collective resignation to Governor Head.
A quarter of an hour later, when the Assembly opened at the
unusual hour of 10 o'clock in the morning, Macdonald gave
a lengthy explanation of the course he and his colleagues had
taken.[57] After the adjournment, at his last brief conversation
with Head, he learnt that the Governor had sent for Brown
and that Brown had asked for time to consult his friends. "After
that," Macdonald later concluded his account of the affair,
"I had no conversation, direct or indirect, with His Excellency,
of any kind, or by means of any agency."[58]

The next day, July 30, during a scene of odd and somewhat
equivocal hilarity, the ex-ministers gave up their places on the
treasury benches; and Macdonald seated himself comfortably
on the opposition side to watch with interest what would
happen. He had not long to wait for the denouement. The
gods finished their sport with George Brown very quickly;
and indeed they had little need to manipulate circumstances,
for Brown's infatuated presumption had brought about his
own swift undoing. He had, as he no doubt realized from the
beginning, no chance whatever in the existing House. The
members of his new Cabinet, in accepting office, would automatically forfeit their seats and be obliged to seek re-election;

and this would temporarily remove eight or ten stout Reformers
from the Assembly. In a fairly evenly balanced House, where
small numbers counted seriously, this temporary loss would
be important; but far more important was the undoubted fact
that the original majority on the seat-of-government question
had been purely accidental, the result of special circumstances,
unlikely to be repeated. Everything, then, depended upon
Brown securing a dissolution; but here he came up against
Governor Head, and the Crown's prerogative of the dissolution
of parliament, and the Crown's necessary concern for the
welfare of the country as a whole, irrespective of party. The
present House had been elected only seven months previously;
part of the supplies were still unvoted and several important
measures awaited completion; and August, the harvest season,
was the worst possible time for an appeal to the people.[59]
For all these reasons Head hesitated to exercise the royal prerogative. Was he as impartial as he thought himself, or as his
role required him to be? Was he influenced by distrusts and
preferences which were inarticulate but compelling? The ground
he stood on, at any rate, was solid; and his position was explained with complete candour. He warned Brown verbally,
at their first meetings, that he could give no promise respecting
a dissolution; he carefully repeated his warning in writing.
But Brown swept on. "Some fish require to be toyed with,"
Macdonald explained amiably, a little later, to the House. "A
prudent fish will play around with the bait some time before
he takes it, but in this instance the fish scarcely waited till
the bait was let down. He jumped out of the water to catch
it."[60] Perhaps Brown expected that, in the end, the Governor
would feel obliged to give way. In the lobbies and corridors
of the legislature, the Grits were jubilantly predicting a dissolution; and Macdonald and his followers, in grave uncertainty,
waited unhappily for the outcome. It came quickly. At noon
on Monday, August 2, the Brown-Dorion government was
sworn in; and a little after the House met for its afternoon
session, one of the writs of election made necessary by the
new appointments to office was proposed, and the motion
immediately amended by a want-of-confidence resolution.

Before the House adjourned, at midnight, the amendment had been carried by the large majority of forty.[61] The next day, both verbally and in writing, the new ministers advised the Governor to dissolve the House and appeal to the people. Head refused; and on Wednesday, August 4, after having lasted almost exactly two days, the Brown-Dorion government ceased to exist.[62]

Macdonald waited a while longer. The Liberal-Conservatives had been defeated on a chance vote; the Reformers had been rejected far more decisively on a straight want-of-confidence amendment. To whom would the Governor turn? Head first invited Galt, a prominent independent, unconnected with either party, to form a government; but in short order Galt abandoned the task. The Governor then summoned Cartier, who immediately enlisted the help of Macdonald; and with little difficulty, the Macdonald-Cartier government was reconstituted, this time under the leadership of Cartier as first minister, and with only two changes of personnel, of which one, the substitution of Galt for Cayley as Inspector-General, was alone of real importance. The old government was back again; but when, on Friday, August 6, the ex-ministers were sworn in once more, each was appointed to an office different from that which he had held before. Somebody—it was more than probably Macdonald, the old master of manoeuvre in the courts—had conveniently recollected the seventh clause of the Independence of Parliament Act, passed the previous year, in 1857; and the seventh clause provided that if any one of the principal officers of government should resign his office and within one month accept another one, he should not be obliged thereby to vacate his seat in parliament.[63] It was not one month, it was only eight days, since Macdonald and his colleagues had tendered their resignations on July 29; and although clause seven had been pretty obviously designed to permit individual changes of portfolio without the expense of an election, there seemed no reason to believe that it would not validate a general shift of an entire ministry.

It was a clever device; in one way a little too clever, and in another not quite clever enough. It was not neat and finished;

in fact, it landed the ministers in a further difficulty. Did the words of the statute, "any other of the said offices", necessarily mean an office different from that previously occupied? There was some doubt on the subject; but the Cabinet decided that in a matter of this kind, it was far better to be on the safe side. On August 6, Macdonald was sworn in as Postmaster-General, and most, though not all, of his colleagues were similarly assigned to offices which they had no intention of occupying permanently. They occupied them, in fact, only one day; and on August 7 they all changed back to their proper portfolios once more.[64] By this time the device had become laboured and obvious and more than a little cheap. But it was none the less effective. The double shift—or, as it soon became popularly known, the "double shuffle"—permitted all the old members of the Macdonald-Cartier government to keep their seats in the Assembly at the very moment when the ex-ministers of the Brown-Dorion Cabinet had lost their parliamentary places as well as their political power. For the baffled and furious Grits, this was the last insufferable affront. They denounced it as a fraudulent evasion of the Independence of Parliament Act—an evasion made possible by an act of mass perjury on the part of the ministers, who had sworn to perform the duties of offices which they had no intention of occupying. It was an outrageous swindle—the last piece of knavery in a long and complicated plot, which had begun with the resignation of the Macdonald-Cartier government, which had involved the Governor and Macdonald in collusion, and which had been devised to defeat the innocent Reformers and defraud the long-suffering people of Canada.

Macdonald rejected this melodramatic invention with a sweeping denial. "It is a charge that I am a dishonourable man," he told the House, "a charge that the representative of our sovereign, myself, and all my colleagues, if they have any concern in the matter, are alike dishonourable conspirators, and here in my place in parliament, I say it is *false as Hell*."[65] It was fairly easy to dispose of the romantic horrors of Brown's excited imagination; but it was rather more difficult to brush off the dust which clung to him from the political mêlée of the summer. He had not been particularly anxious to retain power. For some time he had been considering hopefully the idea of resignation—of release from the "irritation" and "annoyance" of parliamentary life. But once the crisis was upon him, once he was engaged in the heat of the political battle, he had put forth all the resources of his cunning and experience. He had fought to win. On one occasion at least he had been guilty of sharp practice. He had paid his way back into power with some good money, and a few counterfeit coins. And his Governor, who had rejected the legitimate usage of the dissolution in such dignified terms, was obliged in the end to accept the contrivance of the "double shuffle". It was all a little unfortunate, and the trouble was that Macdonald could not tell at the moment just how unfortunate its consequences were likely to be.

But if Macdonald had been compromised, so also had George Brown. Macdonald had purchased success with a little cheap trickery; Brown had bought failure, humiliating and ridiculous, at the expense of his reputation for sincerity and consistency. There was no need for Macdonald to remain long upon the defensive. The comically pathetic performance of the two-day Brown-Dorion government—of "His Excellency's most ephemeral administration"—gave him an inexhaustible supply of material for raillery. What a curious spectacle that government had presented to the reflecting! Brown, the embodiment of militant Protestantism, had actually included six Roman Catholics in his Cabinet! Brown, the personification of the indignant sectionalism of Canada West, had apparently compromised all his main principles for the sake of office with a handful of Lower Canadian *Rouges*. It was true that he had not had time to frame and announce a programme; but, almost immediately after the resignation of his government, his ex-ministers and their friends and acquaintances began to make the most damaging revelations about the concessions he had apparently been prepared to make. Macdonald told the House jovially that it reminded him of a candidate in an election contest in Kingston, who had prudently equipped himself with a green handkerchief and an orange handkerchief which he flourished alternately before the beaming faces of the Irish Roman Catholics and the Protestant Orangemen.[66] Brown was never permitted to forget the "short administration". It had apparently existed for two days. But it did not really die on August 4, 1858. It lived on as a legend, at once sinister and ludicrous, which dragged a long, coiling tail of consequences for the Reform party.

There were to be consequences for both parties. And one of the first and most important of these was a dramatic change in the policy of the Liberal-Conservatives. Up to that time the party had devised no solution for the cultural problem of United Canada which it could oppose to the variety of other cures—Rep. by Pop., Double Majority, and Dissolution of the Union—currently being flaunted before the public. But now, in the last days of the troubled session, the ministers announced that they would attempt to initiate discussions for the federal union of British North America. Head had for some time been privately considering, in his speculative, academic fashion, the rival possibilities of a legislative union of the Maritime Provinces and a federal union of the whole of British North America. And Galt, the new Inspector-General, had advocated federal union during the great debates on the state of the province which had preceded the ministerial crisis at the end of July. Galt was a volatile and romantic character who took up new ideas with great ease, urged them with great persuasiveness, and altered them with great rapidity; and his inclusion in the Cabinet marked the adoption of the new policy and had probably helped to precipitate it. But the governing factor was different. What mattered most was the fact that Macdonald and Cartier, the two sectional leaders of the party, had been converted to the idea of a federal union. There can be little doubt that the crisis of July, with its peremptory warning of the growing difficulties of governing a divided and distracted Canada, had hastened their conversion. "I found him [Galt] and several of the gentlemen about to assume office," Head reported to the Colonial Secretary, "deeply impressed with the idea that in some such union alone could be found the ultimate solution of the great question which had been made a ground of agitation by Mr. Brown at the general election, viz.—the existing equality of representation of Upper and Lower Canada, and the alleged injustice inflicted on the former by such equality."[67] All the other solutions—Rep. by Pop. and the rest—Macdonald had openly and strongly opposed; but he had never opposed federation—at least in principle. He may, in 1849, have considered it impractical for the moment; in the years that followed he had simply not mentioned the subject at all. Whilst almost everybody had rushed impatiently forward with his solution, Macdonald had waited; and now he was free to commit himself and his party to the most ambitious and splendid solution of all.

In the explanations which he gave to the House on August 7, Cartier briefly alluded to the new policy; and on August 16, when he finally prorogued parliament, Head gave an even more formal announcement of the course which the new government proposed to follow. "I propose in the course of the recess," he told the House, "to communicate with Her Majesty's Government, and with the Governments of the sister Colonies, on another matter of very great importance. I am desirous of inviting them to discuss with us the principles on which a bond of a federal character, uniting the Provinces of British North America, may perhaps hereafter be practicable."[68] Less than three weeks later, on September 4, Council submitted a minute, which Head subsequently approved, outlining in some detail the steps which should be taken to start the discussions "with as little delay as possible".[69] On September 9, Head sent off this order-in-council, together with a covering letter, to the Colonial Secretary and to each of the British American Governors. A start, and a fairly quick one, had been made—so far as it could be made with letters and dispatches. But the government was not willing to rely solely on paper, and it decided to send a strong delegation to press the federation proposal upon the authorities in England. Macdonald was not to be a member of it. He was no longer the leader of the government, and the burden of the Canadian mission to England in the previous summer had been chiefly his. Cartier, the new first minister, John Ross, and Alexander Tilloch Galt were chosen as delegates; and early in October they set sail for England.

Chapter Eleven

The Humiliation of George Brown

I

The affairs with which Macdonald had been dealing for the past two years—communications, defence, and political reorganization—were by no means exclusively Canadian. They were imperial. They involved the other British North American colonies; they involved Great Britain itself: and their solution could only be reached through a complicated process of correspondence and discussions. The long series of pilgrimages to the Colonial Office, of conferences in British North America, had already commenced. During the previous summer Macdonald and Rose had joined forces with the Nova Scotians in an attempt to persuade the imperial government to support the Intercolonial Railway; and now, in the autumn of 1858, Canada had sent its federal proposal to all the capitals of British North America and had dispatched a strong contingent to press the plan upon the Colonial Office. Five different, highly individualistic, and largely unpredictable governments were concerned. What would Nova Scotia, New Brunswick, Prince Edward Island and Newfoundland think of the plan? How would they—and their Governors—enjoy being jerked out of the comfortable routine of provincial politics and required to consider an ambitious scheme proposed by their pushing and turbulent neighbour, Canada? Above all, and this was a crucial element in the general uncertainty, what impression would the plan make upon the Colonial Office and the British government?

In the short time which had elapsed since Macdonald's visit

in 1857, the political scene at Westminster had completely altered. Lord Palmerston's government had fallen; the Conservatives, under Derby and Disraeli, were in power once more; and the novelist, Sir Edward Bulwer Lytton, facile, versatile, charming, yet occasionally quick tempered, was installed at the Colonial Office. Lytton was genuinely interested in the colonies. He believed firmly in the continuation of the imperial tie; and, in his capricious, rather temperamental fashion, he realized, better than some of his contemporaries, the fact that the colonies were growing up and had become acutely sensitive to criticism and dictation. "To lecture any free Colony is dangerous," he told Disraeli bluntly, "to accuse the grand Province of Canada of corruption as the natural consequence of Democracy (which by the way is wrong in fact), would be madness."[1] Lytton had the novelist's gift of sympathetic understanding, and he was plentifully endowed with natural charm. But, at the same time, he was himself a sensitive, rather self-conscious person, who was by no means at ease in his new position. It was his first tenure of political office; and, although he had apparently been promised the colonial secretaryship some time before the Conservatives came into power, he got it only by reversion after Lord Stanley, the first Tory holder of the office, had been transferred to another department.[2] Lytton was justifiably annoyed. It was only natural that he should view his predecessor's policies with some distaste. It was equally natural that, as a novice, he should slightly resent the free and easy practices of the veterans in the colonial service. All the old hands knew that a good deal of the most important correspondence was by private letter and that a great governor like Head was sometimes a little late with the official dispatches. Lytton, who was not noticeably systematic in other things, desired more formality. He wanted to know. He wanted to control things. And he was uneasily conscious of the fact that about many matters he was still in the dark.

Thus, during that critical summer, while Macdonald had been coping with the ministerial crisis and devising the programme of his new government, an unmistakable grievance against Sir Edmund Head and the Canadian government had been slowly building itself up in the sensitive mind of Sir Edward Bulwer Lytton. He convinced himself in the first place that Head's communications had, in general, been singularly "meagre" and "defective".[3] There was, for example, the Hudson's Bay Company question. On that matter Head had left the Colonial Office "wholly unenlightened" where he ought to have given "explicit information". There was also the whole business of the ministerial crisis—the "conditions" imposed on Brown and the "contrivance" by which the members of the Cartier-Macdonald ministry had managed to avoid the necessity of re-election; and although Carnarvon, the Under-Secretary, believed that Head had acted rightly in refusing to dissolve,[4] Lytton continued to have grave doubts about Head's "conduct throughout the recent transactions". These doubts were quickly magnified when the English newspapers, gaining their information from the somewhat dubious source of George Brown's *Globe*, began to criticize the course which the Governor had followed. Lytton foresaw questions in the House—perhaps a short debate—the very kind of thing in which he, with his set speeches, was poorest.[5] And he had nothing to fall back upon! There were private letters, but not a single public dispatch of explanation or justification—nothing which could be produced to satisfy a noisy and captious Commons.

It was at this point that the news of the Canadian federation proposal arrived in England. To the Colonial Office officials and to Sir Edward Bulwer Lytton, both the matter of the Canadian proposal and the manner of its introduction were alike astounding in the highest degree. The Canadian legislature had been notified of the new plan, not only by Cartier, but also by the Governor himself, who had referred to it in the last paragraph of the speech with which he closed the legislature on August 16. A matter of the utmost magnitude— a truly imperial matter which involved the other colonies and Great Britain—had been brought forward publicly by the Governor "already more than half impressed with the mark of his concurrence";[6] and before he could possibly have received any intimation of approval from the centre of Empire, his Executive Council had calmly proceeded to make arrangements for the discussion of their daring proposal "just as if the consent of the Queen and Her Government had been formally and previously secured". The Colonial Office viewed this casual conduct with the lifted eyebrows and pursed lips of disapproval. "The last paragraph of the Governor's speech is, to me, very startling," wrote Arthur Blackwood, one of the senior clerks;[7] and Lytton, in his impulsive, theatrical fashion, was, of course, far more outspoken. "It is absolutely necessary," he raged, "to administer a reproof to Sir E. Head for his paragraph on Confederation. It has caused the greatest displeasure and I have been even urged to recall him on account of it."[8] Heroic action of this kind was clearly not in the tradition of the Colonial Office; and even if it had been, there were reasons why such a savage penalty could not possibly be applied to Head. Herman Merivale, the Permanent Under-Secretary, recalled that Labouchere had "particularly" requested the Governor to take the matter of union in hand:[9] and Carnarvon subsequently discovered that Lord Stanley's private letters also gave undeniable support to the policy which Head had tried to pursue.[10] Moreover, there was the undoubted fact that the question of federal union had already been raised in the Canadian legislature by Galt. Lord Carnarvon concluded that Head's proposal to discuss the matter with the British government and the other Colonies was not "entirely gratuitous". Still, the Governor had been unwise. He had taken far too much for granted. He had assumed that Lytton would concur in the policies of his predecessors—an assumption which, in the circumstances, Lytton found peculiarly irritating. Yet the Colonial Secretary's first spasm of annoyance had spent itself. He admitted that his views had been "modified".[11] He administered a rather avuncular lecture to Head on the subject of private correspondence and official dispatches. He reminded the Governor that the question of federation involved all the British North American governments and that it therefore properly belonged "to the executive authority of the Empire, and not that of any separate province, to initiate".[12] And there, for the moment, the matter rested.

Macdonald, of course, saw all public dispatches from the

Colonial Office. He was probably made aware of the gist of the private letters of each Colonial Secretary as well. And he and Head tried to divine what lay behind the carefully guarded sentences of these communications. The Colonial Office had criticized Canadian procedure; it had not touched principle. But the two were not entirely separable, and even before the delegation sailed for England in the early part of October, Macdonald may have begun to suspect that the federation proposal would not receive any very enthusiastic support from the London officials. Cartier, Ross, and Galt soon proved the truth of this surmise. Outwardly their reception was a flatteringly attentive one. They had an audience of the Queen. Lytton entertained them at Knebworth, and Carnarvon at Highclere Castle; but this agreeable procession of dinners and week-ends could not disguise the continuance of delay, nor quell the suspicion that delay was at least partly caused by uncertainty and doubt. In fact, the Colonial Office officials were in no position to be very enthusiastic about the Canadian proposal. They did not dare to commit the British government without some indication of a favourable response from all, or most, of the other British North American provinces; and the replies from the other British North American provinces, tepid and non-committal in character, did not begin to come in until the New Year. The only really prompt response came from New Brunswick. A highly negative and inconclusive document, it intimated that New Brunswick would like to consider a legislative, as well as a federative, union;[13] and it was followed, after only a brief interval, by a long argumentative dispatch in which Manners Sutton, New Brunswick's Lieutenant-Governor, attacked the Canadian proposal with great vigour and expatiated upon the advantages of yet a third type of union—a legislative union of the Maritime Provinces alone.[14]

In the most natural fashion, therefore, the Colonial Office was confirmed in its original suspicion that the federation scheme had been conceived in parochial selfishness, with the sole purpose of solving the peculiar difficulties of the Province of Canada, and in complete disregard of the interests and requirements of all the rest of British North America. From the beginning the London officials had been rather sharply critical of federal union. "In Canada, I suspect," wrote Herman Merivale, "it is chiefly popular with politicians, not with the community, and rather as a mode of getting out of the inextricable scrape in which they seem involved by the present union."[15] By the time T. F. Elliot drew up his lengthy memorandum on the subject for the consideration of the Cabinet, the Canadian scheme had come to be regarded unsympathetically as a gratuitous and barefaced attempt to drag the other colonies into the inextricable mess of Canadian politics.[16] Federal union had not been asked for by any other British North American government: it was not an answer to any really British North American problem. It was a purely Canadian remedy for a purely Canadian difficulty. Yet not even the Canadians appeared to agree upon its virtues: and certainly the Reformers had not hastened to embrace the new scheme in preference to that of Rep. by Pop. "At this moment," Lytton summed up, "Federation is really a question raised for the convenience of the present Canadian administration, and upon which the formidable Opposition, headed by Mr. Brown, have not decidedly committed their policy. An imperial interest of the utmost magnitude is, in short, in the crude state of a party question, embittered and obscured by fierce party passions. If the British Government were to take a pronounced course either way, it would thus appear to side with one party, be exposed to the assault of the other, and by participating in the contests of rival politicians, it would lose the character of a calm and impartial arbiter . . . "[17] At all costs, England must keep the "character of a calm and impartial arbiter"—an arbiter not only between Canadian parties, but also among the governments of the British North American provinces. "We think we should be wanting in proper consideration for those governments," Lytton wrote in a final rejection of the Canadian proposal, "if we were to authorize without any previous knowledge of their views, a meeting of delegates from the Executive Councils, and thus to commit them to a preliminary step towards the settlement of a momentous question, of which they have not yet signified their assent to the principle."[18] This dispatch, dated November 26, was given to Galt, who had waited in London to receive it;[19] and by the middle of December Macdonald and his colleagues had been made aware of the fate of their scheme. A meeting to discuss federal union could not be held without imperial authorization; and imperial authorization would not be given unless the colonies involved in the project had at least signified their willingness to discuss it. The Canadian proposal had not in the least been rejected by the imperial authorities; it had been temporarily postponed out of consideration for the other provinces. It could be taken up again. But the omens, so far, were not very favourable.

II

Yet, in the autumn and winter of 1858-59, Macdonald still confidently carried the ball which he had caught so unexpectedly in the political scrum of the previous summer. His audacity and cleverness seemed to have been rewarded rather than punished. It was true his government had received a check; but the check might be no more than temporary, and, in other and equally important respects, he had emerged triumphantly from the difficulties which had threatened him at first. Lytton and some of the Colonial Office officials had originally questioned the "contrivance" of the "double shuffle": George Brown and the *Globe* had denounced its flagrant illegality and hideous moral turpitude. The Reformers apparently believed that Providence would not permit such villainy to go unpunished. The courts, if appealed to, would surely deal in an exemplary fashion with this perjured and profligate government! Accordingly, three test legal actions were begun that autumn against Macdonald, Vankoughnet and Sidney Smith. The *Globe* invariably referred to them with awful solemnity as the "State Trials"; and the first, which concerned Macdonald, opened at Toronto on November 19, before Chief Justice Draper and Justice Richards.[20] John Hillyard Cameron headed the battery of lawyers who acted for Macdonald: and Cameron, in a speech which the *Globe* denounced as all too speciously fluent, approached the

question from a severely legal point of view. "They had not
to discuss here, as if the question was being debated in either
branch of the legislature," he pointed out, "what would be the
constitutional effect of the proceedings complained of. . . .
Whatever they might desire as politicians, they could not as
lawyers take any other view than the statute pointed out."[21]
And the statute—the seventh clause of the Independence of
Parliament Act (20 Vic. cap. 22)—pointed unmistakably and
emphatically in Macdonald's direction.

Macdonald waited a month, not very uneasily in all likelihood, for his vindication. On December 18, when the judges'
decision was read, Draper seemed to have very little difficulty
in giving judgment for the defendant. The state of the facts,
he thought, came expressly within the words of the seventh
clause; and the only question in his mind was whether the
section permitted more than one resignation and more than
one appointment to a different office. If the court were at
liberty to assume that the power to change offices frequently
was a beneficial power tending to the good of the public
service, then there would be no difficulty in construing the
section so as to give the necessary permission. "I do not feel
warranted in making that assumption," Draper continued
smoothly, "but I am just as little warranted in making a contrary one; so that, after all, the construction must be made on
the words used . . . and so taken, they are, in my humble
judgment, so large as not to be confined to one change only,
and therefore I feel bound to hold that the legislature meant
to authorize more than one change, and, as a consequence, I
am of opinion that the defendant should have the judgment. . . ."[22] On Monday, December 20, when this decision
was made public, the *Globe* excelled even itself in vituperation.
Up to that point Brown had maintained at least some slight
check upon the violence of his newspaper. He may have in-
dulged real hopes in the "State Trials": he knew at least that
he must pretend to reserve judgment until they were finished.
But now the last need for reserve had been swept away. All
the accumulating, fermenting feelings of humiliation, disgust,
anger and disillusionment suddenly vented themselves upon the

"double shuffle" and its perpetrators. The deed itself was "the most shameful example of executive licentiousness ever perpetrated in Canada". It was a fraud to which the criminal ministers and the Governor-General were both parties: and it had been judicially condoned by a judge who had been "the pliant tool of Lord Metcalfe" and the "political father" of John A. Macdonald! "Mr. Draper," the *Globe* concluded savagely, "has mistaken the place and the age. He would have made a very fair Jeffreys, and might have served even for the Bloody Assize, but neither the governor who plays the part of James, nor his servile judge, are fit to breathe the free atmosphere of Canada in the middle of the nineteenth century."[23]

Macdonald may have noticed something else—something much more significant than these wild vituperative exaggerations. Brown was no longer content to criticize the "double shuffle" itself and its authors; he had begun to attack the constitution, the system of parliamentary government which apparently permitted such acts of ministerial knavery. "The unwritten constitution may do in England where rulers are scrupulous and careful," the *Globe* conceded, "but it is different here; and the decision in these cases will materially strengthen the hands of those who demand a written constitution, after the American model. With his unwarrantable exercise of the prerogative, and his tampering with the usages of the constitution, Sir Edmund has done more to Americanize our institutions than all other influences combined, although they have been both numerous and powerful. His reckless rule has weakened the confidence of even the most devoted advocates of the British model."[24] Brown himself, the old critic of the early "Yankee Grits", the old opponent of American "elective institutions", had certainly been one of the most sincere supporters of the British parliamentary system. And was not his strange mood of disillusionment in responsible government a most revealing sign of the state of moral collapse to which his party had been brought? The Reformers had tasted the extreme humiliation of defeat; and now, confirmed in their incapacity to win the game, they sought in desperation to change the

rules. The ministerial crisis of 1858 was certainly having consequences—consequences perhaps more serious for the van-
quished than for the victors. The Reformers had come perilously
close to apostasy. Were they about to repeat, in another form,
the Annexation Manifesto of 1849?

Macdonald could feel heartened. There had been a most
laughable miscarriage of that frightful retribution which the
Grits had been promising ever since the ministerial crisis. He
was far from being out of the woods, but he kept to his chosen
path with the serene stubbornness which was characteristic of
him. In the summer his government had been overthrown and
his party rocked to its foundations; and, in the months that
followed, Liberal-Conservatism seemed for a while to meet
nothing but obstacles and receive nothing but blows. But
Macdonald was not much inclined to alter his direction. Others
were ready for changes—were indeed anxious to alter the party's
policy with respect to such notoriously dangerous matters as
the seat-of-government question. "Oh that her Majesty had
refused the reference," lamented John Rose to Edward Ellice,
"or been advised to choose some other spot than the Romantic
Hill we looked on!"[25] Rose himself was prepared to "modify"
his opinions; and Sicotte, the Reformer who next to Cartier
was the most important French Canadian in the Cabinet,
insisted that the government should give up all attempts to
defend the Queen's choice. The Attorney-General West opposed
an urbane but flat refusal. " . . . Macdonald and those who
had brought about the reference could not with honour recede,"
John Rose explained, "and the alternative offered was between
breaking up the Government at *once* and without meeting the
House, or taking the course we have."[26] Macdonald, who in
any case was ready enough to escape from the tiresome burden
of parliamentary life, was evidently quite prepared to resign
upon the issue; but in the end it was Sicotte, the Commissioner
of Public Works, and not the Attorney-General West who left
the government.[27] The government pushed on sturdily. The
address in reply to the speech from the throne, defiantly recognizing the Queen's choice and thus reversing the vote of the
previous summer, was passed unaltered. "Cartier deserves great

credit," Head explained to Herman Merivale; "he has parried
abuse and odium from his civil supporters most manfully."[28]
The Macdonald-Cartier combination was an efficient machine
which was now reaching the apex of its smooth perfection.

Yet, if the Cabinet had at least held its ground on the seat-
of-government issue, it had made no spectacular gains with
the projects which had been taken up in the previous autumn.
Cartier, Ross, and Galt had gone to London empowered to
discuss two major schemes with the Colonial Office: one was
the federation proposal and the other was a revised version of
that favourite British North American plan—the plan of securing imperial support for the Intercolonial Railway. Lytton
himself was ready to give some imperial aid to the railway.
"I am of opinion," he told Disraeli, "that if we can do something we ought. . . ."[29] But a Conservative Chancellor of the
Exchequer was just as little inclined as a Liberal Chancellor
of the Exchequer to divert imperial funds to a public work
which would always be physically remote and which would
only occasionally become politically important. Lytton talked
the matter over sympathetically with Galt, "who begged me
for the sake of the imperial interest generally not to shut the
door for ever in their faces";[30] and when the final negative reply
came to be written, he composed it carefully "with a desire
to soften as much as possible our refusal". The dispatch did
handsomely admit the imperial interests and advantages of
the Intercolonial Railway. "But still," it concluded, "the national
expenditure must be regulated by the national resources."[31]
There was no money for the Intercolonial Railway; and that
was that. Cartier, Ross, and Galt had failed just as badly in
1858 as Macdonald and Rose had failed in 1857.

But, on the whole, the Confederation scheme was an even
greater embarrassment to Macdonald. The Intercolonial Railway was a veteran, an almost tiresomely familiar, project, in
which failure, by becoming habitual, had ceased to have much
political significance. But Confederation was a brand new
solution for an old and anguishing Canadian difficulty—a
difficulty for which rival and much advertised remedies were
constantly being pushed upon the market. The new remedy

had certainly not been greeted with wild enthusiasm. But its virtues had not been very fully explained to its intended consumers either at home or in the Maritime Provinces; and obviously the first task of the Canadian government, which at this time had no thought of giving up its federal scheme, was to explain and justify the proposal to the phlegmatic and unresponsive Maritimers. In January, 1859, when the Canadian Council took the matter up in earnest, it was decided to acquaint the governments of the Lower Provinces fully with all the steps which had been taken in the matter, and, in particular, to send them copies of the elaborate letters which Cartier, Ross, and Galt had given to Lytton in the previous October.[32] The Maritime Provinces might respond in the end. But it would take time. Meanwhile, the Canadian opposition, sniffing eagerly for anything that might be used to disparage the government's new proposal, must be answered and silenced in some fashion. Dorion asked flatly whether the negotiations for federal union had been broken off. Macdonald denied this. The co-operation of the other colonies had been invited by Canada: but they were apparently not yet ready to take a decided course in the matter, and until all, or most, of them had accepted the invitation, further real progress must be delayed. The imperial government had certainly not rejected the proposal or stopped the negotiations. "But as the interests of all the British North American Provinces," Macdonald concluded, "as well as those of Canada and the mother country were involved, the answer of the Imperial Government was simply that until they were approached on the subject by the other colonies, they could give no answer in the matter."[38]

In the matter of federal union, Macdonald was compelled by circumstances to mark time: in the affair of the Hudson's Bay Company's territories he moved forward slowly by deliberate preference. Here, once again, he felt under no compulsion to change the policy of his government: it was exactly the same policy as before, cautious, realistic if not unambitious in character and completely unspectacular in results. It might, of course, have been very different if the project of federal union had made rapid progress, for federation could have provided the strength necessary for a more rapid westward expansion. Head had pointed out in one of his efforts to gain support for his union scheme that the new western colony or colonies might be "aggregated" to the federation: " . . . and it is, perhaps," he went on, "one great recommendation of this scheme at the present moment that it will thus admit of extending westward the body of our North American colonies."[84] New colonies could be "aggregated" to a federal union more easily and with less danger to Canada East than new territory could be "aggregated" to the existing Province of Canada. Cartier, as well as Macdonald, had no doubt appreciated this point; but it was useless to urge it, for the union scheme had come to a dead stop, and the Cabinet must think of some other way to still the vast hubbub over the Hudson's Bay Company. The Canadian newspapers were crowded with speculations about a vast array of romantic Western enterprises—settlements, colonies, staple trades, roads, telegraphs, and railways. But it was not merely the acquisitive clamour of the Reform press which embarrassed the Canadian government; it was also the somewhat irritated persistence of the Colonial Office. Time was getting on. The House of Commons committee on the Hudson's Bay Company had long ago finished its labours: the Company's licence for exclusive trade came to an end in 1859, and some legislation respecting the matter would have to be presented in the approaching session of the imperial Parliament. Yet Canada delayed, equivocated and remained unaccountably silent. It was the source of one of Lytton's chief irritations with Head. What did the province really want? She had seen fit vaguely to question the validity of the charter and had voiced certain equally vague claims to the territory over which it ran. Was she ready to test the charter by a reference to a judicial tribunal? Would she be prepared to acquire—which meant, of course, to govern and colonize—two new provinces on the Red and Saskatchewan Rivers?[85]

These, as Macdonald knew very well, were highly inconvenient questions. They had to be answered; and they could not be answered by aggressive yet academic claims for territory and grandiose yet unsubstantial projects for railways. The fact was, as Head explained to Lytton, there was a general belief that "the reversion of the fee of the colony ought to be vested in Canada". Ultimately the property must be hers. But not now. Now the inheritance would be too dangerous and too costly to be borne. It was not only, and certainly not mainly, a question of the expense of civil government. It was the inescapable consideration of defence—of protection against both Americans and Indians—which intimidated the Canadian government, not so much because of its cost as because of its dangers for a small and dependent power. "Canada," Head explained, "will not readily undertake the government of the Red River settlement as a charge on her own revenues. She will assert her claims and rights in the abstract, but she will object either to compensate the company, or pay continuously for the maintenance of military protection or civil government."[36] She objected to all these things, which were admittedly costly and might be very dangerous: she even hesitated to accept the rather inconsiderable undertaking of testing the Hudson's Bay Company's charter. Lytton had pressed this procedure upon the colony as an indispensable first step in assessing the value of the Hudson's Bay Company's titles. Canada agreed that, on the whole, the step was a sensible one, and ought to be made —by the imperial government. If the charter were proved invalid, then the lands which it covered would simply revert to the imperial Crown: if the validity of the charter were confirmed then the liquidation of the Hudson's Bay Company's rights was a task which only the imperial government could undertake.[37] From any and every point of view, the whole business was clearly an imperial affair, and even if the lands came to Canada gratis, Macdonald insisted that at the moment she would accept them at her peril. "If we obtained that territory," he told the House during the debate in April, "we would have no proper means of supervision over it—people would rush into it who from want of restraint would grow up into anything but a creditable population."[38]

All these obstacles and inhibitions had put the Conservative government in an inconclusive and uninspiring position. Macdonald knew it: but he had already begun to suspect that the state of the Reform party was even more miserable—that it had been dealt a far more shattering blow by the ministerial crisis of the previous summer. Macdonald had found a narrow, devious path through the blind thickets in which his party had been trapped. He had led his followers into the open. And was it not time now, and legitimately possible, for him to retire, as he had so often hoped to do during the previous twelve months? Surely the moment was appropriate? Isabella's death had altered things domestic in much the same drastic way as the ministerial crisis had changed affairs political. He was living in lodgings in Toronto and his nine-year-old son, Hugh, remained of course in Kingston with his grandmother and his aunts, Margaret and Louisa. Hugh had lost his mother and, as things stood, he might almost have lost his father as well. The three women relatives were all very well and all very necessary; but they could hardly take a male parent's place, even if they had been free, which they were not, from other preoccupations. Margaret, Mrs. Williamson, had of course her own separate domestic establishment. Old Mrs. Macdonald, who had now survived her husband Hugh for nearly twenty years, was shattered occasionally by apoplectic strokes;[39] and Louisa, tall, raw-boned and devoted, was obliged to look after her for lengthy periods. Obviously Hugh needed a father. And obviously also the father needed more leisure, and less annoyance, and more income. In September 1859 he would have completed five years of political power; and, at about the same time, the legislature and government were to move back to Quebec for a last period before the final transfer to Ottawa. Did he want to go to Quebec and start the whole business over again? Could he even contemplate settling down permanently with the government in Ottawa? In Kingston he was still the head of a prosperous and respected legal firm (Macdonald, Macdonnell, Draper and Wilkinson) which occupied a handsome apartment, lit by eight windows, in a pleasant little Renaissance-style building, which looked across Clarence Street to the post office.[40] Why not move back to Kingston, to his son, to his family and his practice, and lead the easy, comfortable life to which he had always meant to return?

And yet—could he really go? In the end all moments seemed inappropriate for a break so conclusive and so final. There was the province, and the Liberal-Conservative party, and his own small special band of Conservative followers who, since Cayley's departure, looked up to him as their only remaining leader, and who begged him not to desert them at this stage.[41] There was, despite all the sudden irritations and nagging annoyances, his own unquenchable interest in the game itself, in its puzzles and problems and solutions, in its devices and traps and surprises. And even if retirement in a session or two were certain, there was always the feeling, natural in a born and victorious commander, that only one more campaign was necessary to convert the defeat of the enemy into a complete annihilation. The truth was that in the session of 1859 the Reformers were a divided, confused, and irritable lot. Their brief two days' association in office seemed to have bred more animosities among them than a lifetime's partnership could possibly have done. It was their tragedy that in two days of power they had been able to sketch, but not to complete, a programme; and from this abortive reconciliation of their ideas came serious trouble. If they remained studiously vague about what they had intended to do in such vital matters as Separate Schools and electoral reform, they invited Conservative ridicule; and if, on the other hand, they made the fatal mistake of trying to be precise, they instantly revealed differences of opinion among themselves which quickly led to charges of deception and bad faith. Wiser heads such as Dorion and John Sandfield Macdonald might have steered safely clear of trouble; but between Brown and his late Lower Canadian colleagues there soon developed the most appalling disputes. Thibaudeau, who had been President of the Council in the Reform administration, announced, early in the session of 1859, that he would never have consented to accept office if he had not been perfectly assured that the Brown-Dorion government was prepared to do full justice to the Roman Catholics of Canada West.[42] Laberge, the two-day Solicitor-General East, informed the House that, according to his understanding, the Reform administration had intended to liquidate the remaining seigniorial obligations in

Canada East with moneys from the consolidated revenue of the province, and that therefore Brown's claim that his government would have relieved the *censitaires* "without taking money out of the pockets of the people of Upper Canada" was quite simply false.[43] All these arguments, contradictions and denials, all these miserable disputes over the dead body of a failure, were a pure gift to Macdonald. Almost every speech at the beginning of the session included a satirical passage at the expense of "His Excellency's most ephemeral administration". "They had intended to 'grapple' or rather to grope—and that in the dark too—" for a policy, he told the House, paraphrasing one of Brown's rather laboured explanations.[44] "There never was such an exhibition of political profligacy as in the formation of the Brown-Dorion Government."

No, he would stay as the leader of the Liberal-Conservatives for a while longer. He would stay for at least a session and complete the ruin of the great Liberal party which Brown had been labouring to create ever since the autumn of 1857. Already it was becoming apparent that the terrible fiasco of the two-day government had not been an ordinary unfortunate episode in the life of Brown or in the history of Grittism. It was much more: it was that kind of demoralizing crisis which can change a man's political philosophy or alter the whole direction of a party. Brown had been put into an abject position, and his deep personal humiliation had come at a time when he was physically and mentally least capable of sustaining it. For almost the first time in his life, the clumsy, impetuous giant was ill: and for the first time certainly in a career of unbroken commercial success in Canada, the robust publisher and promoter had become the prey of real financial worries. His prodigal energy had led him to take on too much. He had not been content to remain the proprietor of what was probably the most influential, and certainly the most popular, newspaper in Canada West: he had hoped to become an experimental land owner, a commercial farmer on the grand scale; and at Bothwell, in Kent county,[45] he had purchased very extensive holdings of land. For a few years, the "Laird of Bothwell" became a territorial magnate of some importance.

Then came the depression and the terrible fall in the prices of raw materials. The commercial collapse did not affect Brown so quickly and dramatically as it had John Hillyard Cameron; but, as 1858 dragged itself to an end, and a new and dismally unprosperous year began, he began to feel acutely embarrassed. The depression of 1857-58 had already virtually removed one rival from Macdonald's path. Was it about to remove his other rival and his greatest opponent?

Macdonald watched Brown's increasingly erratic course with curious interest. Surely the unhappy, frustrated publisher was being driven into ways of the most preposterous extremism! The reckless criticisms with which the *Globe* had greeted Draper's decisions in the "State Trials" were evidently not the products of a temporary outburst of temper; they were, it seemed, merely the first signs of a profound and permanent disillusionment with the existing political system. Beaten, humiliated, quarrelling with his friends and supporters, yet no doubt bitterly accusing himself, Brown must have felt disgust with Canadian parliamentarism rise in him like nausea. And he was at once too physically ill, too intellectually confused, too haunted by nervous worries, to direct his sense of deception into a critical and constructive assessment of the Canadian political system. He left that to others. He left it in particular to George Sheppard, a radical journalist from England, who now began to assume a sinister importance in the *Globe's* editorial staff and who was the principal author of a long series of editorials advocating "organic changes" in the system of responsible government and parliamentary institutions.[46] Rep. by Pop., the *Globe's* astonished readers were now told, was not enough! There must be a written constitution, a clear separation of executive and legislative functions, and definite checks upon the power of the provincial administration. There must even be, the *Globe* finally announced, a dissolution of the Canadian union! The Conservatives gasped with delight and surprise as they beheld Brown, like a huge, bewildered, wayward child, stumbling down the path which led past the dubious structure of "elective institutions" to the congressional system at Washington. "He has made the grand mistake," Spence wrote to Macdonald, "of assailing the system as well as the men working it out—charging as it were the hands with ineptitude and treachery and at the same time declaring that the ship's bottom was so rotten she must founder. . . . In no quarter, to any extent worth speaking of, will annexation leanings have any support—and changes of any kind will be looked upon with great distrust inasmuch as failure in constitutional tinkering might ultimately bring about such a result."[47]

Such a moment, when Brown seemed to be rushing precipitately towards political extinction and when all the signs pointed towards a commercial recovery, was no time to think about resigning. "Everything, my dear Macdonald," Spence wrote beseechingly, "looks well, and now, my old fellow, after five years' service, don't give up the ship when you and your colleagues are just nearing Port." No, he would stay a while longer, if only to see what would happen and to extract all possible advantage from it. Parliament came to the end of its session on a fine day early in May. The last prorogation that Toronto was to witness in a long time passed off to the accompaniment of royal salutes, crashing band music, and a flutter of gay spring dresses; and down in the Crown Law Office on King Street they began soberly to pack up in preparation for the move to Quebec. It could hardly be said that the summer was uneventful, for early in July Macdonald nearly lost his life when the *Ploughboy*, a steamer carrying him and a large party on an excursion to Sault Ste. Marie, drifted helplessly before a gale and was nearly lost upon the rocks.[48] In August, he got what he had wanted for some years now, a little sea-bathing off the coast of Maine; but he was called back to Toronto in the middle of the holiday and the imminent move to Quebec prevented him from returning and accompanying Hugh and his sister, Louisa, on their return journey to Kingston.[49] All that spring and summer, he—like every other Conservative—had been watching the columns of the *Globe* with unwearied attention. For a while everything seemed to go well. For a while the constitutional indiscretions of the newspaper reached and maintained a climax of awful impropriety.

And then something seemed to happen. It was as if Brown

had been suddenly awakened out of his mournful and be-wildered apathy to realize with astonishment the commitments that had already been made for him and for his party. From somewhere, quietly but forcefully, the brakes were applied. The *Globe*'s headlong career towards constitutional reform perceptibly slackened. The articles in favour of "organic changes" were fewer and more closely hedged by conditions and ambiguities. Brown, a sobered and repentant Brown, was plainly in control of his journal once again; and plainly also he was determined to make another great effort to reorganize the party which had been so morally shattered by the ministerial crisis of 1858, and which—in part because of his own weariness and preoccupation—had fallen into the control of Radicals and Republicans. The great Reform convention of January, 1857, had been the prelude to the triumphant Grit success in the general election of the following December; and now another great Reform convention would repair the ravages of the past twelve months and prepare the way for the even greater electoral triumph of the future. That autumn, on November 9, nearly six hundred Reformers, coming from all parts of Canada West —except, significantly, its eastern portion, where John Sandfield Macdonald kept control—descended upon Toronto for a three-day convention.⁵⁰ Macdonald, seizing upon what seemed to him to be the essential point, tried to discover whether there had been any incipient revolt against Brown. But Lindsey, of the Toronto *Leader*, to whom he appealed for information, had to confess that, so far as he could discover, the leadership had never been mentioned, even in secret session. "Whatever was thought," he wrote, "nothing appears to have been said."⁵¹ It was the same all the way through the convention. The reawakened Brown and his powerful directorate of Toronto Reform politicians steered the convention smoothly and dexterously back towards a moderate liberalism.⁵² The Radicals and extremists—bred of the crisis of 1858-59—were silenced or defeated. "Organic Changes" were tacitly dismissed, and although Rep. by Pop., the sovereign remedy of 1857, was admitted now to be in-sufficient, its virtual successor, dissolution of union, was re-pudiated even more firmly. The convention decided upon a federal union of Canada East and Canada West, with "some joint authority" connecting them, yet leaving each free for most purposes to go its own way. Alongside the Conservative plan—federation of British North America—there had now been competitively placed the Reform scheme for the federal union of Canada East and Canada West. Was the federal union of the Canadas a policy upon which the shattered forces of the Grit party could effectively reunite and by which they could win the next general election?

III

As the testing time—the session of 1860—rapidly approached, Macdonald may very well have had some apprehension. Once again he had comparatively little to offer parliament—at least in respect of the major problem of the constitution of the Canadas. Time had gone on. The Conservatives seemed to be making very little progress with their federal scheme. And, in the meantime, the project of the legislative union of the Maritime Provinces—a scheme which might be regarded either as the complement or the rival of the federal union of British North America—was being vigorously advocated once more. Manners Sutton, the Lieutenant-Governor of New Brunswick, had for some time been pressing it upon the attention of the Colonial Office; and even Head, who had, of course, supported both schemes, giving first one and then the other a slight emphasis of preference, now indicated that he thought the time was favourable for the undertaking of the smaller union.[53] With all these small regional plans—the federal union of the Canadas, the legislative union of the Maritime Provinces—in the air about them, the Canadian Conservatives may have felt somewhat intimidated about their own ambitious project. But they persevered for a while longer. Galt, the Minister of Finance (the old title of Inspector-General had been abandoned) had been perhaps the most ardent supporter of federation in the Cabinet; and since, in the autumn of 1859, he planned to visit the United Kingdom on the financial affairs of the province, the ministry passed an order-in-council authorizing him to put himself in communication with the Colonial Secretary "with the view of ascertaining what action has been taken by the Imperial Government thereon, and what communications, if any, have passed between them and the other Provinces on the subject. . . . "⁵⁴ The Canadians were anxious, in the first place, to clear up a serious misconception which, they suspected, had probably been created by Lytton's dispatch of November 26, 1858, and which was no doubt having a most unfortunate effect on the governments of the Maritime Provinces. Lytton's dispatch, Galt suggested, in a letter to the Duke of Newcastle, the new Liberal Colonial Secretary, "has been somewhat misunderstood as indicating a disinclination to entertain the question while it was, we believe, only intended to express the unwillingness of the imperial authorities to initiate discussion of the subject which it was conceived more properly should proceed from the Colonies themselves."⁵⁵ This, Galt intimated pleasantly, was a very acceptable attitude; it was a gratifying further proof of the imperial government's firm adherence to the well-tried colonial policy of self-government. Nevertheless, it had had somewhat unfortunate results. ". . . There is no doubt that the dispatch has been misunderstood and an objection to the mode of action has been construed into a condemnation of the policy." Would the Colonial Secretary be good enough to remove all doubt about Lytton's dispatch, and, if the other provinces agreed to the proposal, would he authorize a meeting of delegates to discuss British North American union?

Faced with repeated and importunate demands to clarify the imperial views and to support this or that scheme, the Duke of Newcastle responded in a brief but classic explanation of colonial policy. He had his own private ideas about the stages through which British North American reorganization ought to proceed; but he knew also—and it was the first principle of his policy—that the imperial government must never be betrayed into the premature expression of a preference for any particular kind of union. "Her Majesty's Government," he informed all the colonial governors in a circular dispatch, "see no reason to depart from the general line of policy which they have hitherto pronounced it their intention to adopt if the occasion should arise. They do not think it their duty to initiate any movement towards such union, but they have no wish to impede any well considered scheme which may have the concurrence of the people of the provinces through their legislatures, assuming of course that it does not interfere with imperial interests."[56] It was a free field for all kinds of advocates and all types of union; and the only condition was that the governors, before authorizing delegates to a conference, must beforehand communicate with the Colonial Secretary. As late as the middle of February, 1860, the Canadian government was still interested in its scheme and disposed to press it.[57] But after that it was quietly laid on one side. Galt, in London, had probably been given the gist of the lukewarm replies of the other British North American provinces; and if the Canadian government had at first been eager to compete with their general federation scheme against the regional plan of the Grits, they soon began to see the dangers of such obvious competition. The two plans, and the reasons which justified each, could all too easily be confused and confounded in the public mind; and at the moment the strategy of the Conservatives was to isolate the Reformers' proposal as something scandalous, and to damn it as a device for breaking up the existing union. "It was true," Macdonald declared during the session of 1860, "that the government had proposed a Confederation of the British North American provinces—that they would like to take into it the Red River on the one side, and the Lower Provinces on the other, so as to make a great empire, stronger by wealth, position, and general standing than the parts could be while divided. But they were not prepared to admit that there were any internal grievances which could not be constitutionally remedied—cured without any alteration in the constitution whatever."[58]

Meanwhile, and some time before these words were uttered, Macdonald had begun to realize that it was probably not going to be very difficult to discredit and defeat the new Reform scheme. The Toronto convention had adopted it by a resounding majority; but it now began to appear that the Toronto convention and the Reform caucus at Quebec were two quite different things, with two quite different ideas of the wisdom of a federal union of the Canadas. Back in the autumn there had been most delicious rumours of the grumbling resentment in Grit ranks at the dictatorial fashion in which Brown and the Toronto gang had managed the Reform convention; and the session had barely started when it began to be noised abroad that the Reformers were quarrelling furiously—and over the federal union of the Canadas, the very policy which was supposed to have reunited their divided ranks! Foley's no-confidence motion, which was intended to censure the government for its persistent minority rule in Canada West, gave Macdonald an opportunity to exploit these rumours, to isolate Brown as a brilliant but hated ruler, and to taunt his followers with their abject submission to his rule. "No one knew better than he (Mr. Brown) himself," he told the House, "that his party was at the present moment breaking up. No one knew better than he that the honourable members around and beside him, while they feared him, did not love him. No one knew better than he that they would like to remove him but dare not face him. . . . By his superior will, by his superior ability, he wielded them as he wished; he held the lash over them. . . . The honourable gentleman was the Louis Napoleon of his party, but he had an Austrian army. . . . There was the Italian portion of it, and there was the Hungarian portion of it . . . and horse, foot and artillery would find a common Solferino in the next election."[59]

Macdonald could be embarrassingly contemporary in his topical allusions, and the "Austrian army" speech was a delight to his followers. ". . . you seem to have been in full force," wrote John Ross delightedly from London, "hitting out right and left in splendid style."[60] Macdonald was enjoying himself immensely. "We are having great fun just now with the opposition," he wrote to Charles Lindsey of the Toronto *Leader*. "They are quarrelling like fury and do not affect concealment. I pat Brown on the back occasionally by calling him the only man in the party worth *tuppence* and then I please his recalcitrant followers by pitching into him as a dishonest and inconsistent politician. In other words, I call him a 'knave' and them 'fools', an expression of which you will recognize the justice."[61] It was good fun and it was excellent value politically, for the Grits, whose private wrangles in caucus had now become notorious, were perilously close to the point of an open row in the House. On Monday, April 23, the explosion finally came.[62] For weeks Brown had been vainly attempting to speak to his constitutional resolutions—his version of the programme of the Toronto convention; and repeatedly, or so it seemed to him, his notice of motion had been postponed. On April 23, Cartier moved its postponement once again; and to Brown's amazement and indignation, Foley, the Grit member for Waterloo, arose to support the Conservative leader! It was the one thing needed to provoke Brown to another tirade of his scandalous accusations. Foley was no true Reformer. He had not given his leader proper support. He had a secret understanding with the members of the government! Foley replied hotly. There were excited replies and still more excited rejoinders; and it ended by Foley declaring furiously that he had been a Reformer long before Brown had even had a seat in the House, and that he did not doubt he would continue to be a Reformer long after Brown had ceased to vex and distress the party. At this felicitous point, Macdonald rose to intervene. The Reform party, he announced pleasantly, was in fragments: it "amounted to nothing more than a number of atoms accidentally placed together but without any principle of adhesion and indeed without any principle at all".

"You will see," Rose wrote to Edward Ellice, "that there is an open rupture between Brown and his followers—indeed the opposition is now a mere congeries of discordant opinions."[63] The divisions and the quarrelling were bad enough even while the main subject of Reform disagreement was still being postponed; but once Brown's constitutional resolutions began to be debated, the chances of a really serious rupture became much greater. McGee and John Sandfield Macdonald—the first principal Reform leaders to debate the resolutions after Brown had introduced them—showed themselves either unenthusiastic or opposed. But there was worse to come. On May 7, after the debate had been going on with intervals for a week, Foley got up to speak. He began by announcing bluntly that he had been charged with infidelity to his party and with inconsistency in his attitude to the constitutional resolutions. And he then proceeded to tell a curious story.[64] The whole Reform convention, he charged, had been run by the Toronto Grits; the Toronto Grits had packed the all-important resolutions committee and dominated its proceedings. McDougall, a Toronto man, had proposed the compromise federal scheme with "some joint authority" connecting the two sections of the province; and Brown, the head of this small domineering cabal, had insisted, before he had properly consulted the Reform caucus, on placing his own version of the convention's resolutions upon the order paper. Caucus had protested indignantly in a series of meetings; and finally the public storm had burst. "From that day to this," Foley concluded sombrely, "the members of the opposition had never been called together to consult upon any subject."

No more was needed. By the time the session ended the phrase "joint authority" had degenerated into a rather painful joke and the Reform party had become a body of men united chiefly by the emotional warmth of their antagonisms. Macdonald, for all his weariness with politics, must have felt elated. It was very nearly two years now since the great ministerial crisis of the summer of 1858; and, to all appearances, the Liberal-Conservative party was stronger than ever. The long months of the depression and the short week of political crisis between July 29 and August 6, 1858, had between them ruined his principal political rivals and enemies. The desperate efforts of the Grits to recreate their organization and their programme had apparently failed. The Reform party was broken in fragments; the depression had ended, and, best of all, the gangling, growing, ambitious Province of Canada was to be honoured that very summer by something entirely new in the history of colonies, by the first of all the royal overseas tours, the visit of Edward, Prince of Wales, to British North America. A year before, in the summer of 1859, Henry Smith—son of the ex-Warden of Kingston penitentiary and Speaker of the Legislative Assembly—had carried an invitation to Queen Victoria to visit

Canada with her husband, the Prince Consort, and such other members of the Royal Family as might be selected to come. This novel and almost breath-taking request had produced scarcely less remarkable results. It was impossible, the Queen announced, for her to go herself; but she promised that within another year the Prince of Wales would pay Canada a visit. And on July 9, 1860, the Prince, accompanied by the Duke of Newcastle and a little contingent of minor functionaries, boarded the *Hero* at Southampton and set sail for British North America.[65] It was a thrilling but rather frightening thought that in about a month's time he would be actually sailing up the St. Lawrence River!

The excited members of the Canadian government redoubled their efforts; and poor John Rose discovered that there was a multiplicity of unusual tasks attached to the Commissionership of Public Works. "I am again the packhorse in this business," he told Ellice dolefully, "—all the work and arrangements falling to my department. . . ."[66] The drab legislative buildings at Quebec were converted into what the newspapers described rather grandly as a palace, with apartments for the Prince and his suite, a dining-room and a magnificent reception room with a yellow and purple flowered velvet carpet.[67] The Canadian ministers donned the British civil uniform appointed for the principal officers in Colonial governments. It was a handsome costume of dark blue cloth with gold braid, gold facings, a cocked hat and a sword. "A great deal of time," the *Globe* announced ironically, "has been wasted by John A. Macdonald in learning to walk, for the sword suspended to his waist has an awkward knack of getting between his legs, especially after dinner. . . . Galt is the best-looking footman of the whole lot. He advocated knee breeches, it is said, that he might show his fine calves; but John A. opposed the idea with great ferocity."[68] There was no doubt that they were all immensely excited, immensely proud, and more than a little nervous. The royal tour was to be the final authoritative rebuke to the constitutional tinkering of the Grits. It was to be a wreath of honour placed with truly imperial dignity upon the loyal achievements of the Conservative party.

At first all went superbly well. On Friday, August 10, Macdonald along with the Governor and the other members of the
Cabinet arrived at Gaspé harbour on board the Canadian
government steamer, *Queen Victoria*. Head had determined
to greet the Prince like some medieval sheriff, the moment he
entered the territorial limits of the Province of Canada; and he
waited for two days, in a frenzy of apprehension lest the royal
convoy should unhappily get past him and up the St. Lawrence.[69] At length, at 7 o'clock on the evening of Sunday,
just at the climax of a spectacular Canadian sunset, the *Hero*
and her little escort of ships sailed majestically into Gaspé
harbour. The next day, Macdonald and the other Canadian
ministers went on board and were presented. They lunched
and talked with the Prince;[70] and meanwhile the royal fleet
resumed its extremely deliberate way up the River of Canada.
It was Saturday, August 18—a dull, murky day, appallingly hot,
with not a breath of air stirring—when the Prince landed at
Quebec. On the platform were the Canadian ministers, perspiring profusely in their new uniforms, and looking, so the
Globe assured its readers, "as uncomfortable as so many pigs
in armour". Macdonald, no doubt, was nervously agitated as
the crucial moment approached; but he wore his clothes with
something of an air, as even his critics tacitly acknowledged.
"The thin, spare frame of John A. Macdonald was in ceaseless
motion," the *Globe* reported. "He put on a devil-may-care air,
managed to get his cocked hat stuck on one side and elevated
at the front in a most ridiculous fashion."[71] Then came the
procession through the hot streets, and presentations and addresses; and on Tuesday, August, 21—the climax of the royal
visit to Quebec—the Prince held a formal levee in the parliament buildings and knighted Narcisse Belleau, Speaker of
the Legislative Council, and the portly Henry Smith, Speaker
of the Commons. Then the royal party moved westward, in a
stately fashion, to Montreal, Sherbrooke and Ottawa; and, as
the Prince and his suite passed along, the Canadian rivers and
railway lines became avenues of almost uninterrupted jubilation. "Here is the universal programme," declared one newspaper correspondent sourly, "—spruce arches, cannon, procession,

levee, lunch, ball, departure; cheers, crowds, men, women, enthusiasm, militia, Sunday school children, illuminations, fire works, etcetera, etcetera, *ad infinitum*." The imposing Victoria Bridge, spanning the St. Lawrence at Montreal, was officially declared open; the cornerstone of the new parliament buildings at Ottawa was solemnly laid. On Monday, September 3, the royal party, accompanied by Macdonald and a number of the Canadian ministers, proceeded up the Ottawa River by steamer and canoe to Arnprior, drove inland to the village of Almonte and at Almonte boarded a special south-bound train on the Brockville and Ottawa Railway. It was dark by the time they reached Brockville. The loyal addresses had to be read with the aid of lamps, and they then drove at a foot's pace through dense crowds down to the St. Lawrence, where the steamer *Kingston* was waiting to receive them. "Our carriages," the Prince reported to his father, "were accompanied by firemen who carried lighted torches, and all the houses were illuminated, and the throng of people following cheering and hallooing gave it a very pretty effect."[78]

It was superb. The Upper Canadian part of the tour could hardly have opened more auspiciously. Macdonald ought to have been completely satisfied. But he was not. As the train drove through the gathering darkness to Brockville, his worries and fears steadily deepened. All day he had known that at Brockville he would be given a last slim chance of averting what threatened to be a hideous contretemps. For days—ever since their visit to Montreal—he had seen it ominously approaching. He knew that he could not escape being involved. It concerned Kingston, which had been his faithful constituency since he had entered politics. It concerned the Orangemen, who under Gowan's leadership had gradually and largely become the zealous followers of the Conservative party. In Canada, the parades, banners, and insignia of the Orange Order were all perfectly legal; but in the United Kingdom they were not. The Duke of Newcastle, who accepted full responsibility for the actions of his royal charge, decided that the Prince could not be permitted to compromise himself by acknowledging an illegal organization; and he therefore wrote a formal letter

to the Governor, which Head forwarded to the mayors of
Kingston and Toronto, warning all concerned that there must
be no Orange banners or insignia along any route on which
the Prince would pass. Most of the Orangemen, wisely advised
by the new Grand Master, John Hillyard Cameron, grumblingly
accepted this incredible veto. But some did not. And among
these latter—to the discomfiture of Macdonald—were the Kingston Orangemen. A large and important body, nearly all stout
Conservatives, they clamoured so long and so loudly to be
permitted to parade under their Orange arch and in their
Orange costumes that in the end the corporation of Kingston
appointed a special delegation, which was to see the Duke and
beg him to modify his decision. The delegation—the Mayor,
Colonel Strange, Macdonald's old partner, Alexander Campbell,
and two other Kingston worthies—reached Brockville some time
before the Prince and his suite arrived.[74]

It was eleven o'clock at night before the Duke was free to
see the Kingstonians. They boarded the steamer apprehensively;
Macdonald made the necessary introductions, and for two and
a half hours the fruitless discussion lasted. The Mayor reminded
the Duke that the Orange Order was entirely legal in Canada
and that its members could not be prevented from parading
as they pleased; and Macdonald argued that, since the favours
extended to Roman Catholics during the Prince's tour in
Canada East had been widely publicized, the Protestants of
Canada West would be correspondingly quick to resent a slight
offered to any part of their body.[75] It was all quite useless. The
Duke remained adamant. And so, as it turned out, did the
Orangemen. On the afternoon of Tuesday, September 4, as
the steamer drew close to Kingston harbour, the horrified members of the Prince's suite could plainly perceive an Orange arch,
Orange banners, and a "large concourse" of defiant Orangemen,
"occupying the street in great force so that the Prince could
not enter the Town without passing through the demonstration
they had prepared".[76] The Mayor was hurriedly sent for and
informed that the Orangemen would be given until the following morning to reconsider their scandalous conduct. The
Kingston, with offended dignity, remained all night in the

harbour, in the hope that a new day would bring repentance. But the new day had barely dawned when the incorrigible Orangemen began to reassemble. Once again, clad in their full regalia, they took up a position in the immediate neighbourhood of the landing-place, from which neither threats, remonstrances, nor supplications could move them. The Duke was affable but firm. In such circumstances the Prince could not be permitted to land and pay the town the expected visit. The *Kingston*, which had remained in the harbour for twenty-two embarrassing hours, now steamed away up the lake.

Macdonald was not on board. He had decided to stay with his injured constituents. He had actually abandoned the royal tour in mid-career! The opposition newspapers made the most of this conspicuous and astounding absence. "Where is John A.?" a *Globe* editorial began gaily. And from Toronto, whither the Prince had proceeded, Macdonald's colleagues and friends dispatched puzzled and importunate letters. "Your absence is very much remarked," John Ross wrote, "and I wish you would either come up or write and let us know what you propose to do."[77] The Governor-General, Philip Vankoughnet reported, felt very keenly about Macdonald's mortification. He had insisted that the decision was not his but the Duke's, and that the Duke would publicly accept full responsibility for it. "I think," he added, "that till the visit is over you should be here."[78] But it was no use. Macdonald, unmoved and unrepentant, continued to remain in Kingston for a few days more. No doubt he was worried by the political implications of the "Orange affair", but he was also genuinely annoyed that the Prince had been made publicly to disregard the laws of one of his own future dominions. It was not until later, towards the close of the Prince's tour, that he reappeared at a Hamilton celebration in "full fig", the newspapers noted, but "looking very hard".[79] He had much to think about. The royal tour had been expected to complete and crown the Liberal-Conservative recovery. But had it seriously miscarried? Were the Orangemen alienated? Had Protestant Upper Canada been given one more proof of its belief in the prevalence and power of Roman Catholic influence in Canada? These were serious questions: for within another year a new general election would have to be held.

IV

The more Macdonald and his colleagues considered the matter, the more likely it seemed that the consequences of the "Orange affair" would be deplorable. How rosy political prospects had appeared in the spring of 1860! How seriously they had been altered now! It was irritating to remember that all this had come about as the result of a stupid, meaningless contretemps. It was provoking for Macdonald to realize that his two old rivals, George Brown and John Hillyard Cameron, who, a few months ago, had seemed buried under an avalanche of misfortunes and humiliations, were now up and doing, and, in their different ways, exploiting the Orange affair to his disadvantage. Cameron, as leader of the Order, journeyed to England to present a monster petition, signed supposedly by 100,000 Orangemen, complaining of the Duke of Newcastle's decision and protesting their loyalty to the Crown. Acclaimed once more, brought suddenly back to something like his old prominence, Cameron was virtually leading an anti-ministerial wing of Conservative Orangemen; and George Brown, who had never ceased up to that moment to abuse the Order, now shyly revealed himself and the Grit party as the Orangemen's devoted champions! The part which Macdonald had played in the affair, and the extent to which his government was responsible for its outcome, were misunderstood by his friends and, of course, deliberately misrepresented by his opponents. Alexander Campbell, in one of his characteristically gloomy letters, begged his friend not to entertain the idea of an early dissolution of parliament. "To my mind," he wrote, "there is no room whatever to anticipate a result favourable to the existing government from that step."[80]

Macdonald agreed. Parliament could not be dissolved until much closer to the date of its legal expiration. But there was over a year, if need be, in which to make reparation and preparation: and the first task was obviously to explain his own course and the position of the government in the Orange affair. He decided to undertake something which was new in both his career and Canadian politics generally—a speaking tour. It began at Brantford on Friday, November 9, a few days after a famous and portentous electoral contest had resulted in the return of Abraham Lincoln to the presidency of the United States. November 9 was a dull, inauspicious, autumn day, gloomy with boisterous gales and heavy falls of rain; but at the Kirby House in Brantford nearly three hundred sat down to dinner, prepared to eat their way with pleasant deliberation through half a dozen courses, to drink eight or ten florid toasts, and to listen to nearly as many heavily political speeches.[81] Macdonald began with a long and careful account of the royal visit, of the constitutional conventions governing it, and of the responsibility accepted and exercised by the Duke of Newcastle. It was the most important part of his address; but during the time—literally hours—in which his admiring audience was prepared to listen to him, there was opportunity for a good many other topics. He reviewed the accomplishments of his six-year tenure of power, exposed the laughable absurdity of the very idea of "French Domination", lingered jocosely over the humours of the two-day Brown-Dorion ministry, and ended up with a stirring appeal for the preservation of the union against the machinations of the anti-unionist Grits. It was long after midnight that he got to bed, and next day, as had been promised during the dinner, he stayed at the Brantford hotel to meet a large company of the "intelligent yeomanry" of the country.

It was only the beginning. The success of the Brantford dinner inspired St. Thomas, London and Hamilton to send invitations; then, in a long procession, came Toronto, Guelph, Kingston, Belleville, Caledonia, St. Catharines, Simcoe, and Millbrook. Usually Macdonald was accompanied by some other member, or members, of the Liberal-Conservative government—by J. C. Morrison, Sidney Smith and Philip Vankoughnet; but invariably he was the chief speaker and the principal attraction. Hotel dining-rooms, town halls, mechanics institutes and athenaeums were hung with flags and streamers welcoming "John A." and honouring "the pilot that weathered the storm"; and over the gallery at the St. Lawrence Hall in Toronto, his name shone out in flaming gas jets. Invariably the crowd was stupendous. Such enthusiastic gatherings, according to Conservative newspapers, had never been seen in the history of the town or the county; they overflowed the available rooms and overtaxed the resources of the caterers. "The leading gentlemen of the district, the bone and sinew of the country", were present, 150, 300, 500, 800 strong; and the ladies, lending "a grace and brilliancy to the scene", watched the proceedings demurely from the gallery, or joined the company after the first toast had been given, while the diners, cheering enthusiastically, rose *en masse*, and the band played "Here's a health for all good lasses." Almost always there was a band—and sometimes two, for good measure of fellowship; and when Macdonald entered the room, or when the great moment arrived for him to respond to the toast "to the provincial administration", the big brass throats blared out into "For he's a right good fellow" and "See the conquering hero comes". At Simcoe they sang a song composed specially in his honour—a highly laudatory concoction, nine verses long and each verse ending "Nine cheers for Macdonald, hurra!", while at Guelph a Mr. Douglas, sticking firmly to the popular nautical motif, sang an original composition called, "The Pilot that stands by the Helm" in a good bass voice. Then came the speech, which might last for anything up to two hours; and then, when the toasts were all drunk, and the supplementary speeches finished, and the chairman duly thanked for "his able conduct in the chair", the long meeting at length broke up in a happy babel of greetings, introductions, recognitions, jokes and stories. Usually there was a "levee" the following day, if one had not already been held before the dinner, at which Macdonald met "the intelligent gentlemen and yeomen" of the county; and sometimes for hours the long file continued—lawyers, merchants, farmers, young men who were just learning to be fanatical Macdonald followers, and old men who had fought in a dozen political battles and bore the medals of the War of 1812 upon their chests.[82]

The series ended at length with the dinner at Millbrook on December 7. It had been a long affair—twelve meetings and twelve lengthy speeches—but surely it had been worth while.

The opposition newspapers tried to make fun of the "lean and hungry" Attorney-General travelling about the country "looking for dinners", but the complete absence of any notices of these dinners in the columns of the opposition newspapers at least suggested a fear that they had been a success. It began to look as if the effort to accumulate a large amount of political capital out of the Orange affair was likely to be a dismal failure; and by the time the legislature assembled again, in March 1861, it had become clear that the Reform party was relapsing back again into its old state of division and weakness. When Mc-Dougall offered an amendment to the address, censuring the Cabinet for its conduct in the Orange affair and for the abdication of its functions as a responsible ministry, he could muster only a large handful of votes in support.[83] The "joint authority" federal scheme, the masterpiece of the great convention of 1859, had been hurriedly removed from sight as if it were something disreputable if not positively obscene. The western Grits returned for solace and inspiration to the old battle-cry of Rep. by Pop., and the unrepentant John Sandfield Macdonald was busy once again "trotting out his hobby", the Double Majority.[84] The old lamentable divisions were still there; but the old imperious master, who had at once provoked and dominated them, was not.

For the first time since 1852 George Brown was absent from his place in the legislature. For eight years he had led and captained the Reform party. He had even seemed to personify and represent Grittism, like a medieval champion riding out to do battle in single combat before his watching army. But now, when the legislature met in that uneasy March, a month after the southern states had founded the Confederacy, Brown was not in his accustomed place. He was ill, and worried, and sick at heart. For most of the session he was absent. And Michael Foley, who had been his principal critic in the previous session, and who had publicly exposed the shameful divisions of the Grit party, was destined to succeed him as leader in the House.

The Reformers had tacitly given up their federal scheme. And this abandonment was naturally followed by an imme-

diate revival of the old agitation for Rep. by Pop. After a
period in which they had pessimistically believed that Rep. by
Pop. was impossible of achievement, the Upper Canadian Reformers returned to it with greater determination than ever
before, and for a new and conclusive reason. The new decennial
census, published recently, had suddenly supplied a statistical
proof for all the old arguments based on alleged preponderance
of Upper Canada's population. It was revealed, beyond any
possibility of doubt or argument, that the citizens of Canada
West outnumbered those of Canada East by approximately
285,000.[85] This revelation profoundly startled Canada West,
whether Grit or Tory; it impelled a growing number of Conservatives to announce publicly that they wished to see "justice
done to Upper Canada". Sidney Smith in the Cabinet, Sir
Henry Smith, J. B. Robinson, and George Benjamin in the
Assembly, were plainly all in favour of electoral reform, and
Macdonald and Cartier, faced by the growing opposition, were
driven to agree that differences of opinion must be respected
and that the matter could not be regarded as a "ministerial
question". Superficially this decision seemed impartial, but
actually it was not, for, as Cartier announced candidly to the
House, the government had no intention of introducing a bill
which would disturb the electoral equality of the two sections.
Cartier, roused as he seldom was by any issue, spoke for nearly
five hours against any change in the existing system,[86] and
two weeks later, on April 19, Macdonald followed with a
speech which, if shorter than his chief's, was an equally lively
denunciation of the Grit resolution.

The date was significant. Exactly a week before, on April
12, the Confederate guns had opened fire upon Fort Sumter
in Charleston harbour; and the beginning of the American
Civil War was to mark an important stage in the development
of Macdonald's views on federalism. Cartier, in his speech,
had not even mentioned the Conservative plan for the federal
union of British North America; but Macdonald had returned
to it at least once during his speaking tour in the previous
autumn and now, as he faced the House on the night of April
19, he returned to it again—and with a new argument which

the troubles in the United States were already beginning to impress upon him. In his view, federation was still the only really acceptable solution for the difficulties of the Canadian union. Yet the future federation of British North America must not be a federation in the decentralized American sense. The failure of the American system, Macdonald told the House, had been proved by the present lamentable conflict in the United States. The Americans had committed the fatal error of making each state a distinct sovereignty and giving to each a distinct sovereign power. The Canadians, warned by the tragic consequences of this mistake, must realize that the true principle of Confederation lay in giving to the general government all the functions and powers of sovereignty. With such a powerful central government, Macdonald argued, British North America would be an important nation in its own right. Already Canada was fast ceasing to be a dependency, and was assuming the position of an ally of Great Britain. Great Britain, the centre of a vast interdependent organization, would be sustained by alliances with Australasia and British North America; and there would thus be formed "an immense confederation of free men, the greatest confederacy of civilized and intelligent men that had ever had an existence on the face of the globe."[87]

He had begun his speech late. Sidney Smith and others had already spoken and it was nearly eleven o'clock before he had got to his feet. "There was a general rush for places throughout the House," the correspondent of the *Leader* reported. "The Reporters' Gallery, lately empty, was overflowing in a moment, and everyone eagerly bent over to hear something good. It was without exception the best speech Mr. Macdonald ever delivered. Those who are acquainted with his style of delivery need not be told that he is not what is called a 'flowery orator'. There is no prepared introduction—no tragical allusions—no straining after effect."[88] It was a good, hard-hitting speech, a speech which was at once typical of him and exceptionally good of its kind, a speech which inspired his followers to rounds of uproarious applause. He sat down tense and excited. As the House gradually subsided, as he began to relax in the pleasant consciousness of his triumph, he was still in no state to endure the waspish note of a critic. And yet it was precisely at this unfortunate moment that a determined critic presented himself. It was Oliver Mowat, his old legal pupil, stocky, rotund, short-sighted, but completely self-assured, who rose to confront him. And Mowat had a grievance to air. During the course of his speech Macdonald had jovially twitted his old junior with inconsistency—inconsistency in now supporting Rep. by Pop. when he had abandoned it so conclusively at the Reform convention at Toronto. Mowat interrupted his tormentor briefly at the time to say that he had been misrepresented; but as soon as Macdonald had sat down he rose and read in full the actual words he had spoken at the convention. There must have been some provocation in his remarks —some charge that Macdonald had wilfully falsified his views. Macdonald gasped. These impertinences were actually coming from the fat boy who had been his inky junior at school and his respectful apprentice at law! Suddenly, as the plump, bespectacled, rather self-important little man finished his statement, Macdonald's brittle temper was shattered into splinters as at a blow. In a minute—as soon as the Speaker had left the chair—he walked quickly across the gangway. Blind rage in his heart, he confronted Mowat.[89]

"You damned pup," he roared, "I'll slap your chops!"

John Sandfield Macdonald quickly stepped between the antagonists. Others helped to pull them apart. It was over in a minute—an abortive encounter, which had ended without violence. But, nevertheless, it had what was almost certainly a deliberate and intended sequel. Mowat had publicly suffered an indignity, if not a humiliation. A short, round, physically negligible man, who had a lively sense of his own importance and a lusty urge towards domination, he was not likely to be above thoughts of revenge; and within a few weeks chance gave him what he must have thought was a gorgeous opportunity. The session was a short one, as Macdonald had hoped. It ended on May 18, and three days later Macdonald was writing to Samuel Amsden the warning which he had probably dispatched to all his principal followers that day: "Get ready for War!" "Get your voters' lists ready as soon as possible," he continued three days later, "and begin your canvass. Act as if the polling was to come on next week. . . . Keep all this dark."⁹⁰ It could only, of course, be kept dark long enough to give the Conservatives a good head start, and within another week the province knew that parliament had been dissolved and that writs had been issued for the new general election. It was then that Mowat decided to spring the trap of his own private surprise. He had a good safe seat in South Ontario, and Macdonald's constituency in Kingston was so solid that nobody of any political consequence had ever ventured to run against him. But towards the end of the first week of June a requisition requesting Mowat to offer himself as a candidate against Macdonald was busily circulating through Kingston.⁹¹ By the end of the week, the stupendous news arrived that Mowat would reach town on Monday, June 10, to see his friends and investigate the situation.

Macdonald arrived at Kingston by the express on Sunday morning. He was only twenty-four hours ahead of Mowat: and from the very start Mowat or Mowat's men seemed always ready to meet and check and embarrass his every movement. He had, he thought, scored an initial advantage by reserving the town hall for his first big public meeting on Monday night, but Mowat countered this with a surprise manoeuvre of the greatest cunning. The Reform candidate, preceded significantly by a large and proudly blaring Orange band, was escorted directly to the town hall as soon as he arrived at Kingston Monday morning;⁹² and at the town hall a large crowd, composed principally of Grits, who had assembled quietly according to plans, gave him a thunderous reception. When night came and the hour of Macdonald's meeting arrived, the Mowat supporters were free to marshal themselves *en masse* again at the municipal buildings. The town hall was full of hecklers; and when Macdonald began by saying, "Gentlemen, I am on my trial—I feel that I am on my trial," the literal as well as the metaphorical truth of his words was quickly proved.⁹³ There were groans, hisses, cheers, counter-cheers and constant interruptions. When question time came, a particularly pugnacious heckler provoked Macdonald to an open altercation;

and the meeting was barely finished when the platform was invaded and a free fight began. The next day it was almost as bad. Mowat's large and successful meeting in the City Park was concluded before night fell and when Macdonald had finished only one of the series of ward meetings which he had planned for that evening. The second meeting, at the Grammar School House, where the voters of Sydenham and Victoria Wards were assembled, had barely begun when a sudden violent uproar outside announced the arrival of the Mowat men, fresh from the meeting at the Park where Mowat had announced his candidature; and for nearly an hour the little body of Conservative voters, penned in an upper room of the school-house, endured a kind of siege, rearing forms and desks against the windows to protect themselves against the fusillades of stones, and again and again hurling the charging Mowat men back down the staircase.[94] All this was new—surprisingly and intimidatingly new—in the usual placid and perfunctory history of Macdonald electoral contests. Now, for the first time, there was force and cunning on the other side. There was more. There was purpose and confidence.

Macdonald was uneasily conscious that his position had changed and that some of his strongest supporters were publicly admitting the fact. "While we feel confident," the News remarked editorially, "that his place in the affections of a majority of the electors is still unimpaired, we cannot conceal the fact that a good deal of the support which he has hitherto received is about to be withdrawn from him."[95] There was little uncertainty about the danger of this withdrawal and there could be no doubt at all that it was caused by Macdonald's recently expressed opposition to Rep. by Pop. Other Conservatives had bent themselves accommodatingly and adroitly before the weighty revelations of the new census. But he stood awkwardly apart. He had been committed once again by his speech of April 19, and in Kingston, during the campaign, he did nothing to modify his position. He defended the union—the union, apparently, as it was, with its conventional inequalities. As at Quebec, the only kind of political reorganization which he was prepared to support was a federal union of the British

North American provinces. Federation was one of the policies announced in the electoral manifesto which he addressed to the electors of Kingston;[96] and he advocated it again in his first great speech of the campaign, in the turbulent city hall. "It is the policy of the government," he told the noisy and quarrelling audience, "to try to secure the union of the Lower Provinces of New Brunswick and Nova Scotia and perhaps Newfoundland, but when unhappily we see the fratricidal strife which rages across the line, we must take advantage of the faults and defects in their constitution. We must take care that we will not, like them, have a weak central government. We must have local governments for local purposes only, and not run the risk in this country, which we see on the other side of the frontier, of one part of the country destroying the other part."[97] Union and strength—certainly for Canada, and, if possible, for British North America—these were theories which he had made peculiarly his own. But they were not very popular theories. Everybody was talking about the sectional grievances of Canada West.

Yet Macdonald continued resolutely on his way, and as the contest approached its climax, the outcome seemed to grow more and more doubtful. When, on Saturday, June 22, nomination day finally arrived, each side struggled desperately to provide its candidate with the larger escort to the hustings. Macdonald's procession, headed by two bands and by a long string of decorated waggons and carriages, was apparently the more numerous. But both sides were strong; there were continual interruptions and noisy exchanges; and Mowat, who gave the longer of the two speeches, seemed exhausted when he sat down after his great effort in the hot June sunlight.[98] Macdonald, using this most public occasion of the entire campaign, openly attacked Rep. by Pop. once more, insisting that the interests of Kingston were inseparably bound up with the St. Lawrence and the central Canadian region, and that it would be outrageous folly for such a constituency to assist in giving the West a numerical preponderance in parliament. For a while, after this daringly outspoken speech, Conservative support seemed to falter. The men of the Mowat party contemptuously resumed their rowdyism once more, and even the chief Conservative newspaper in the town rebuked Macdonald in a long and sorrowful editorial. The issue was still apparently uncertain when at length the poll opened on Monday, July 1. During the first day, which was clear and beautiful, the voters came forward in large numbers; but on Tuesday, a raw, chilly, rainy day, the totals mounted much more slowly. Yet, from the beginning, there was never really any doubt. Macdonald was ahead on the first day's polling; and by Tuesday night, when the poll closed, the vote stood 785 for Macdonald and 474 for Mowat.[99] He had won, by a majority of 311, over a man who had deliberately invaded his territory, looking for revenge.

This time, moreover, his success was no longer so exceptional. The Reform party, weakened by its unconcealed divisions, its frequent changes of programme, and its quarrelling and maladroit leadership, had received a sudden setback in Canada West. For the first time in five years the parties were almost exactly balanced: the Conservatives might even have a majority of one in the sixty-five Upper Canadian seats. Macdonald had apparently been rescued from his political dependence upon Canada East. He had recovered his pre-eminence in his own territory; and on Friday when the return of the Kingston election was formally declared at the court-house, a special effort was made to mark the joint victory of the candidate and his party. When he had given his thanks to the great crowd assembled at the hustings, Macdonald, along with a few of his principal supporters, got into a "beautifully decorated triumphal carriage, drawn by six horses". Followed by a long line of other carriages, it moved proudly through the city streets and out along the road to Portsmouth, where old Mrs. Macdonald and Hugh and Louisa lived. It was the last electoral triumph of her son which Helen Macdonald would ever see. She stood waiting for him in the summer sunlight, and beside her "a bountiful collation was spread on tables beneath the pleasant shade of the trees".

Chapter Twelve

Impasse

I

The famous victory had been adequately celebrated. It had been accompanied by so many blessings—including as a crowning mercy the defeat of George Brown in Toronto—that it might have seemed to have ended the very possibility of political worries and annoyances. But, in a curious and inexplicable fashion, they persisted. There were, of course, certain huge preoccupations, such as the problem of Anglo-American relations and the enigma of the political future of the North American continent, which had been raised by the American Civil War and which were beyond the healing power of even a Canadian general election. These large and sinister uncertainties might be expected to continue. The really disturbing fact was that the little annoyances, the petty irritations, of Canadian party politics should continue as well. But they did. In the complicated state to which politics had been reduced in the united Province of Canada almost no election could have a conclusive outcome. In accordance with what had now come to be regarded as a natural law of Canadian affairs, a party's gains in one section of the province were certain, or nearly certain, to be balanced by its losses in the other. The Conservatives had done badly in Canada East for the same reasons that they had done well in Canada West. The advocacy of Rep. by Pop., which had gained them constituencies in the west, had awakened a slight shudder of apprehension among their French-Canadian supporters. The party, as a whole, had not improved its position. Numerically it was about as large as it had been; and it was now split down the middle on a really important issue. A number of western Conservative members had definitely pledged themselves to their constituents to uphold electoral reform. But the government could not possibly bring in a measure which would really establish representation by population throughout the province. A section of its Upper Canadian supporters still opposed the idea; and the entire body of its followers in Lower Canada utterly abominated it. Yet, if humanly possible, the Radicals in the party must be conciliated, for otherwise they would certainly join George Brown. How could this fatality be avoided?

This was the problem which Macdonald faced in the autumn and winter of 1861. His problems had an unfortunate habit of finding appropriate personifications, and this particular problem was no exception. It was embodied, so he discovered to his rather bored annoyance, in the dignified person of John Hillyard Cameron. This was not the kind of political resurrection which was likely to bring him to his knees in gratitude. Everybody knew that Cameron was politically dead. A pathetic victim of the depression of 1857, he had been buried under an avalanche of debts and obligations; and if he were ever again to revisit, in a fleeting fashion, his old political haunts, it must surely be as a ghost, a spectral slave of his profession, burdened with a long chain of briefs and law books. Yet here he was once more miraculously restored to life, a very solid political personality, and bowing gracefully to the plaudits of an unexpectant but delighted audience. As Grand Master of the Orange Lodge, he had made the most of the deplorable affair at Kingston. He had returned, virtually a popular hero, from his mission of dignified protest to the Queen. And when he had decided to re-enter politics in the general election of 1861, he had scored an easy victory over his Grit antagonist in Peel County. Back in the troubles of 1856, he had represented the Tory element in the Liberal-Conservative party— the element which had always stood stoutly by the Protestant religion and the sectional interests of Canada West. Now, by publicly espousing electoral reform he had put himself once more at the head of the little group of discontented Conservatives who were threatening to desert the ministry.

Macdonald hardly knew what to do. From all quarters news of incipient revolts and impending desertions kept coming in; and almost invariably at the centre of these disconcerting rumours was the name of Cameron. "What is in the wind?" George Allen enquired from Toronto. "William F. Powell has been in Toronto abusing the ministry and holding conferences with J. H. Cameron. Dr. Clarke has also been down and has been talking of 'independence'. . . . I am afraid there is a party growing up amongst those for whom you have done most, desirous of supplanting you. I therefore warn you."[1] It was a warning that was repeated by others, including one gentleman who had just enjoyed the fearful pleasure of an interview with George Brown; and to him Brown had prophesied confidently that Hillyard Cameron would detach a considerable part of Macdonald's support.[2] How was he to cope with this threat? Would it be best to attempt to pacify Cameron and his Tories? Or should he try, as he had done in 1854 and 1856, to recoup his losses from the Reform side? After all, if the Conservatives were divided, the Grits were also divided and more seriously still. Rep. by Pop. was a solvent which had left politics in a highly fluid state. And by a dexterous movement he might scoop up quite as much as he spilled.

He had at hand an easy method of clinching the support of possible new friends. There were places in the Cabinet which would soon need to be filled; there were almost always places in the Cabinet which were vacant or soon would be vacant. Macdonald had never been able to build up a trained and experienced team; he played most of his matches with what amounted to a long procession of dubious substitutes. Ministers were always resigning or thinking about resigning. They were lusting irrepressibly to go back to their professions, or on to the bench, or into business. Cayley, Spence, Drummond, John Rose and a long line of French Canadians had already vanished, like the faces glimpsed momentarily in a crowd. And now it was only too clear that Ross, who was tired of politics, and Morrison, who never seemed able to get a seat, and Vankoughnet, who had an eye cocked in the direction of the vacant chancellorship, were all eagerly considering the question of resignation. Three places would probably be open soon. How should he fill them? If, on the one hand, he tried to make still another coalition with the moderate Reformers, then, as one of his correspondents pointed out, it would be only too natural for Cameron "to ally himself with the remainder and more numerous body of the Grits". If, on the other hand, he attempted to make his peace with Cameron and the Conservative supporters of Rep. by Pop., then what changes of policy would have to be accepted to gain their support, and whom should he select to represent their views in the Cabinet? There was T. C. Street, or John Carling of London, or J. B. Robinson of Toronto, or Alexander Campbell of Kingston. There was even the great John Hillyard Cameron himself. But was Cameron in a position to accept office? George Brown had assured one of Macdonald's correspondents that Cameron was looking forward to power;[3] J. C. Morrison, another correspondent, informed Macdonald that Cameron had given up all hope of any real release from the tyranny of his debts and his profession.[4] This sounded conclusive. But was it really? Was Cameron simply trying to enhance his own value? And what price would have to be paid for the support of his followers? Cameron informed Morrison that he would be content with the smallest instalment of increase in the representation of Canada West. But some increase there would certainly have to be. Macdonald turned the matter over and over in his mind. Could he invent some scheme that Cartier could be induced to accept and which would yet enable the Conservative supporters of electoral reform to fulfil their election pledge?

No, the election had not ended the weaknesses and divisions of the Liberal-Conservative party, for it had not settled the basic politico-cultural problem of the Canadian union. It had left provincial politics in a state of uncertain equilibrium; and this at the very moment when the whole continent seemed rocked by the shocks of the American Civil War. From the

moment he had assumed power, back in 1857, Macdonald
had been only intermittently able to consider the Canadian
question by itself and in isolation. All too frequently the
problem of governing a united yet divided province had been
inextricably yet distractingly connected with other puzzles—with
the questions of western expansion, interprovincial union,
and external defence. In the past these complications had
been intermittent; but now, as a result of the American Civil
War, they threatened to become continuous. The peaceful
relations between England and Canada on the one hand and
the United States on the other might be endangered now at
any moment and for years to come. The war might end in a
division of the original republic and the independence of the
Confederacy. It might end in a political turmoil throughout
the entire continent, which would render meaningless all the old
divisions and boundaries. These obvious threats to the independence and separateness, to the very existence, of British
North America were a main consideration in the minds of
Macdonald and his contemporaries; but there were other and
more subtle ways in which the war influenced their speculations.
It brought up for re-examination the whole question of political
unions in general, and federal unions in particular. It raised
the still more fundamental problem of the validity of the
democratic and republican form of government.

Macdonald approached these matters with little prejudice
against the United States and with a good deal of respect for
the American character and American political experience.
Although Conservative opinion in Canada, as in the United
Kingdom, tended to sympathize with the Southern Confederacy, he gave little sign of a marked preference one way or the
other; and although, in the days which followed Great Britain's
recognition of the South as a belligerent power, the insulting
and provocative threats of a section of the American press
caused the deepest resentment in Canada, he was not very
apt to be disturbed by this kind of journalistic imperialism.[5]
In his great speech in April, at the beginning of the American
conflict, he had told the House that he regarded the apparent
break-up of the union, not with any sense of vindictive satis-

faction, but with feelings of sincere regret.[6] His belief in the
vigour of the Anglo-Saxon character, in the worth of Anglo-
Saxon institutions, whether in their British or American dress,
made it easy for him to sympathize with the misfortunes of
the republic. But, on the other hand, this sympathy did not
weaken his conviction that the war had its lessons which must
be heeded, and the American constitution its faults which must
be avoided at all costs. He dwelt on the fatal defect of state
sovereignty with growing emphasis in his speeches. But he
also shared the widely spread belief that the Civil War was,
in some sense, the inevitable bloody outcome of mob rule and
presidential despotism. To many English-speaking Canadians
of his generation, the American Civil War marked the final
stage in the discredit, not merely of federation, but also of
democracy and republicanism.[7] Since 1848, in both Europe
and North America, republican institutions had been in retreat.
The collapse of English Chartism, the defeat of the European
revolutions, marked the successive stages in their decline; and
now, in the United States, they were about to disappear in a
welter of blood and corruption.

Macdonald held a modified and highly particularized version
of this view. He had always believed in monarchical as
opposed to republican institutions and in responsible parliamentary government as opposed to divided powers and constitutional checks. In the 1850's, when "elective institutions" were
still popular with his own Conservative colleagues and followers, as well as with French-Canadian Reformers and Western Clear Grits, he had had to give way, at least to some
extent. But the introduction of the elected Legislative Council
in 1856 had been, in effect, the last victory of the supporters
of the "congressional system"; and thereafter the winds shifted
and began to blow with increasing strength the other way. The
Grit campaign for "organic changes"—a written constitution
and executive checks—had been disavowed by the Toronto
convention and disavowed even by those who later criticized
the work of the Toronto convention. It was possible now, as
it had not been before, for Macdonald to take the offensive on
behalf of British parliamentary institutions, and to blacken sug-

gested changes with the stigma of their alleged American parentage. When the Grit, McDougall, describing with a rhetorical flourish the desperate courses into which Canada West might be forced by its accumulated wrongs, happened incautiously to picture the Upper Canadians "looking for help to Washington",[8] Macdonald and his followers pounced on this fatal remark as a particularly delectable piece of prey. They exhibited it with telling effect to various shocked audiences during the election of 1861; and, indeed, Macdonald in a private letter to Egerton Ryerson declared that the election might "determine the future of Canada, and whether it will be a limited Constitutional Monarchy or a Yankee democracy".[9] "Let these people not look to Washington," he told one audience, "but let them go thither. The loyal population will stay here, happier that the others are away, and if they try to return, with an army at their back, why, in the name of the militiamen of Canada, let them come."[10] These heroics, which did heavy duty in the election of 1861, were politically safer and more effective than they had been. Morin, the original leader of the French-Canadian division in the coalition of 1854, had sponsored the first bill for making the Legislative Council elective; but Cartier, who sometimes seemed to imply that the American lack of responsible government was the sole cause of the Civil War, was, if anything, an even more outspoken critic of the "congressional system" than Macdonald. The Civil War in the United States gave support both for those who believed in British institutions and for those who desired a strong federal union. If Canada survived, it would work for Conservative principles. If Canada survived . . . . It was a condition at the end of which the war itself had written a large mark of interrogation.

II

It was the autumn of 1861, nearly four years after Isabella's death. Time may have dulled what even in the beginning must have been an old ache rather than a fresh wound of grief; but his feelings for the dead, as for the living, Isabella, were kept securely within the firm wall of his reserve. People sometimes dimly suspected that he must have his unhappy moments—that there were thoughts which, with all his prodigal cameraderie, he had no intention of sharing with others. "I am of opinion," Spence wrote with rather ponderous kindness, "that with all your appearance of almost continual mirthfulness you are not without your seasons of serious reflection."[11] But these seasons he kept to himself. Then he was either a solitary or his one companion was a bottle. And to the little political world of Quebec he presented the appearance of a jocund widower, who was enjoying life to the full, who rose above the irritations of Canadian politics with careless ease, and who only occasionally astounded his friends by a sudden and unaccountable outburst of temper. He had apparently yielded, with smiling good humour, to the importunate appeals of his political friends. While everybody else wandered off in search of lucrative jobs or secure places, he remained at Quebec, an imperturbable fixture, a pleasant and approachable permanency, with whom one could always joke and on whom one could always rely. Little by little, Kingston and most of its affairs receded into the background of his mind; but Hughey, Lou, Moll and "the Parson" and his mother maintained their prominence in the light of his affection. Somehow, despite the long distances and the distracting preoccupations, he managed to hold them tenaciously close. He was a good son, who worried over the successive shocks which prostrated his mother, and a good father—interested, proud, generous and yet not over-indulgent. Hugh was to have the Shetland pony he desired; but he must ride it every day. "When it rains, let him wear the waterproof I sent him," he wrote to Louisa, "but he must ride daily."[12] He must also if possible do well at school; but equally his progress must be appreciated, and a good report from his master handsomely praised. ". . . in the first place," he wrote his sister, "tell Hugh that I am extremely pleased at the report of Mr. May. Tell him that I am quite proud of it and that I have shewn it to all my friends. Let him go on and prosper and he will make his mark in the country yet."[18]

November, which was to usher in such an exciting period for Canada, began with an appropriately important change. Sir Edmund Walker Head relinquished the office of Governor-General, and Viscount Monck, an Irish peer who had been a Member of Parliament for Portsmouth, arrived to take his place. Head had first assumed his duties nearly seven years before, when the Liberal-Conservative government was only a few months old; and except for the famous two days when Brown and his colleagues briefly supplanted the Conservatives, Macdonald had held office under him for the entire period. He had come to know and respect the Governor deeply. It was the kind of friendly acquaintanceship which could not easily be re-established with another person, and perhaps might never be established with Lord Monck. For Monck differed markedly from Sir Edmund. A large, comfortably built, heavily bearded man, less original, more sluggish, but perhaps more tenacious in his mental processes than his predecessor, he had little of Head's imaginative grasp or creative power in British North American affairs. Still, as Macdonald quickly discovered, he was a workmanlike efficient administrator; and, as the first events of his governorship soon proved, he was a man of wise prudence, of deep if somewhat narrow wisdom. No governor had ever had more need of these qualities. Monck had arrived and had taken the oaths of office in the last days of October. He had not been two weeks in his new position, when there occurred the "incident"—the incident almost doomed to happen by the ominous state of Anglo-American relations. On November 8, Captain Wilkes of the U.S.S. *San Jacinto* stopped the British mail packet *Trent,* and took from her by force two Confederate diplomatic agents, James Murray Mason and John Slidell. About a week later, this astounding piece of news became public property in the United States, where it was apparently greeted by the exultation of the people, and the complacent approval of the government. It became known in Canada about the same time, and, two weeks later, in England.

In both countries it aroused intense excitement. A British

note, modified by the faltering hand of the dying Prince Albert, demanded an apology and the instant return of the captured envoys. And Canadians, recollecting the awkward fact that their country was the inevitable battlefield of any Anglo-American struggle, wondered whether the jubilation of the American people would permit their government to give way. In those early days of December, 1861, Macdonald and his colleagues found that their private advices, as well as the public prints, were equally dismaying. On December 4, at the height of the crisis, Galt, who happened to be in Washington on business connected with the Reciprocity Treaty, had a private interview with President Lincoln.[14] He liked the President's sombre, strongly marked features, his simple, straightforward manner, and his remarkable fund of anecdotes. And yet the interview perturbed him. It was true that Lincoln suggested, in a reassuring off-hand fashion, that the Mason-Slidell affair would be "gotten along with" some way or other. But when Galt reproached him mildly for the rather formidable defensive measures that the government of the United States had already taken, the President replied significantly, "We must say something to satisfy the people."[15] It was not the first time that Canadians and British had heard the most provocative actions defended on the straight commercial grounds that there was a big demand for them in the home market of the United States; and Galt brought a doubtful report back to Macdonald and the Cabinet. All that December, Canadians and British worked feverishly to repair the defective defences of the province. Transports, bearing a total of nearly 14,000 imperial troops, raced for the St. Lawrence; and when the frost sealed the river and foiled them of their destination, they turned back to the Maritime ports, and the regiments they carried travelled laboriously over the snow-choked Temiscouata passage from northern New Brunswick to Canada East.[16] In the meantime, while a patriotic wave of enthusiasm swept through the entire province, the Conservative government decided to increase the volunteers, prepared to call up nearly 40,000 of the Sedentary Militia, and placed orders for 100,000 uniforms in the United Kingdom.[17] Finally—a last convincing

proof that defence had suddenly become big government business—a new portfolio of Militia Affairs was created; and Macdonald, the Attorney-General West, was appointed the first
minister.[18]

For a little while the new Minister of Militia Affairs expected to become very literally a Minister of War. But the
United States decided to restore the captured diplomatists; Great
Britain countermanded the dispatch of further troops to Canada;
and Macdonald, a little breathless with excitement, was able
to set down the biggest pack of his anxieties. The particular
danger was apparently over. But the general problem of provincial defence in a highly troubled period remained; and the
new Minister of Militia Affairs was not prepared to push it
back into the lumber room of neglect, where it had been pushed
so often before. If the first Conservative improvement of the
militia had been justified by the necessities of the Crimean
War, then the present crisis, so much closer and more dangerous,
called imperatively for a still more thorough reorganization.
Towards the end of January, 1862, the Governor appointed a
militia commission, whose membership, significantly enough,
included not only the expected imperial and colonial officers,
but also such political figures as Cartier, the leader of the
government, Galt, the Minister of Finance, and Macdonald
himself, the new Minister of Militia Affairs.[19] The personnel
of the new commission suggested an important change in policy:
and so did the terms of reference which guided its labours.
Its main assignment was to recommend a scheme for the reorganization of the militia and the building up of an efficient
and economical system of defence. Finally, to bring all these
investigations to a practical issue, it was commanded to prepare
a bill on the subject for submission to the colonial legislature.

In the meantime, while these vast rumbling international
disturbances kept the Canadian government in a state of continual agitation, Macdonald slowly pursued the business of the
reorganization of his Cabinet. A tedious, provoking, yet immensely important affair, for on it depended the recruitment
of political strength and the continuance of political power, its
complications seemed never to be ended. The uncertainties,

hesitations, conditions, scruples, and convictions of his retiring ministers and their possible successors—all had to be taken into consideration. He mystified and annoyed people with his changes and procrastinations. Gowan, protesting that this was "probably the last letter I shall ever address to you," stalked off in a tremendous sulk;[20] and Alexander Campbell, who had told Macdonald several times that he would not accept office unless the assistance of Street and Cameron were also secured, now bluntly informed his old partner that unless the originally suggested changes were made, "then with many thanks to you for the honour you have done me, I retire altogether from the field".[21] The problem seemed insoluble. The opening of parliament on March 20 steadily approached. The old ministers resigned; and still their places were unfilled. "One day more!" the Globe announced cheerily, "And no government yet. We advance. Van is gone. Joe is gone. Ross is gone. There is nobody left but John A., Sidney Smith, and George Sherwood. And parliament meets tomorrow."[22] It met tomorrow, and three days later, on March 23, Macdonald was still negotiating, through Hillyard Cameron, with Street, and Street was still "standing out on the representation question".[23]

Four days later, on March 27, when the appointments had at last been made, Macdonald rose to make the necessary explanations in the House. The new ministers—John Carling of London, and James Patton and John Beverley Robinson of Toronto—were all open and avowed supporters of Rep. by Pop.; but yet, as Macdonald announced firmly, the government was not prepared to introduce any measure which would disturb the existing sectional equality of representation. The question was not a ministerial question at all. "Every member of the Government," Macdonald told the House, "in his capacity as a member of Parliament could vote as his conscientious convictions induced him to do on that question."[24] It remained to be seen whether this promise was to be taken literally, and whether, even if it were taken literally, it would satisfy the large number of Conservative supporters of Rep. by Pop. The test came almost immediately, in the debate on the address, and therefore in its most difficult and politically embarrassing form; both McDougall, the Grit, and John Hillyard Cameron, the Tory, submitted amendments advocating a change in the system of parliamentary representation.²⁵ Faced with these two amendments—one of them introduced by a Tory of high standing and great influence—the Conservative supporters of electoral reform discovered that they had no choice at all. They would have to vote for the amendments. They were bound by their engagements to do so. Yet Macdonald was equally certain to look on their defection in the most serious light. Rep. by Pop. had not been placed before the House as a substantive motion, on which his followers could vote with the freedom he had promised them. It had been introduced as an amendment to the address, in effect a motion of want of confidence, which all Conservatives were bound to unite to resist. But they were not going to do so. And he was suddenly angry. Fretted and weary with a burden which everybody seemed to take for granted that he should carry indefinitely, he looked upon the inconveniently righteous convictions of his followers with cold annoyance. He may have intimated his displeasure. He may even, as the newspapers hinted, have threatened to resign.²⁶

He must have been astounded at the result. True, the McDougall and Cameron amendments were defeated, for the bulk of the votes from Canada East were, of course, cast against them; but this outcome had already been expected and discounted as obvious. The really significant part of the vote— the part which would reveal the extent of the defection of Macdonald's English-speaking supporters—was the sectional vote of Canada West. On that night of April 1, forty-three Upper Canadian members voted for the two amendments and, in both cases, only sixteen voted against.²⁷ It was a sectional majority of twenty-seven in favour of Rep. by Pop.—a sectional majority of twenty-seven against the avowed policy of the government. The bulk of the western Conservatives had completely disregarded their leader's well-known preferences. They had voted exactly as they wanted to do with utter indifference for the interests of the party. He was furious; and that night everybody was aware of his fury. "The general talk on the ministerial side," the *Globe* reported complacently, "is of an

immediate break-up." John Campbell, one of the Upper Canadian Conservatives who had voted for the amendments, hastened
to write Macdonald a little letter of explanation and regret that
very night.[28]

Next morning, a general assembly of the Upper Canadian
supporters, a sobered and perhaps slightly frightened group of
men, headed by John Hillyard Cameron, met to state their
position and to appease the sudden wrath of their genial leader.
"I have been directed by the unanimous voice of the meeting,"
George Benjamin wrote, "to state to you, that on the votes
which were given on Mr. Cameron's motion on the question
of representation, as well as on the motion of Mr. McDougall
on the same question, it was not their intention to vote a want
of confidence."[29] They believed, Benjamin went on to explain,
that the government was quite safe. They felt that they must
honour the solemn pledges made to their constituents. And
they hoped—here the letter became a little pathetic—that Macdonald would sympathize with them. "I can only say," Benjamin concluded, "I never attended a more cordial meeting
of friends, nor one where the feeling was more united in favour
of yourself as their leader, and in confidence in your ability
to conduct the affairs of the country." This was very handsome.
And anyway Macdonald's anger had probably gone. It was
a sparkling wine that left no sediment of resentment. Yet,
when the whole episode was over, a certain sense of disillusionment and discouragement remained. Was it really possible to
win at all in Canadian politics? Not a year had passed since
the last general election, since his recovery of the majority in
Canada West, and his great personal triumph over Mowat.
Not a year had passed; and yet his support in Canada East
had been sharply reduced and his followers in Canada West
were divided. Could the problem of the Canadian union ever
be solved? Would they ever escape from this apparently inevitable tendency towards a balance of parties, and from its
inevitable consequences—political stalemate and governmental
impotence?

He went ahead; but with, perhaps, a slightly more cynical
recklessness than before. There was no attempt to renew the

negotiations for Confederation; but, on the other hand, he had evidently determined upon something that was even more immediately hazardous—the radical reform of the Canadian militia system. On March 15, two weeks before the crisis over the McDougall and Cameron amendments, the commission on Canadian defence had presented its report;[30] and even in the circumstances of the moment—a crisis, barely over, in Anglo-American relations, and a mounting wave of patriotic fervour in the Province of Canada—this was a very formidable document indeed. The commissioners, after having briefly and somewhat pessimistically reviewed the primary factors which governed Canadian defence, went rapidly on to make their principal recommendations. "In order to provide an efficient force for the defence of the province," they declared, "we are of opinion that a far greater number of trained men will be required than have hitherto been sanctioned, and recommend the organization of an active force of 50,000 men of all arms, with a reserve of the same number." These were startling totals; and the means by which they were to be achieved were highly unusual as well. Yet the province was not given a very long time to accustom itself to these drastic recommendations. On Friday, May 2, Macdonald introduced the government Militia Bill—a bill which was frankly based upon the report.

It was a rather equivocal episode. The tone of the Minister of Militia Affairs was defensive, conciliatory, almost apologetic. His speech was an accomplished effort at extenuation, a masterly exercise in the difficult art of explaining away.[31] It was true that he began bravely enough by pointing out the dangerous position in which the province stood, and the wisdom and moderation of the recommendations of the report—"any honourable gentleman who looks at the map will admit the calculation to be a moderate one". He was frank enough also in the description of the composition of the new force, and of the methods by which it was to be recruited. In the cities and towns, the volunteer corps would simply be enlarged; but in the country districts active battalions of regular militia were to be raised from the old sedentary force, by voluntary enlistment, as far as possible, and if necessary by ballot or

conscription. Drill would be carried on regularly in the evenings
or the week-ends in the cities, where it was possible for the
militiamen to assemble fairly regularly; but in the country,
where such short, frequent drills were impracticable, a fairly
long training period each year was proposed for the active
militia battalions. All this looked definite enough. The reserved
powers of conscription and the weeks of training were shockingly
unusual; but there was no doubt what was meant. Still, the
structure of the new system depended upon its details; and
these, on investigation, turned out to be extremely hazy. Macdonald described the bill, a little too persuasively, as an "enabling
bill". The Mutiny Act, it seemed, was an analogous measure.
How many men would be called out under the new statute?
That was for parliament to decide subsequently. How much
would the first year's operations cost? That also was for parliament to decide. The whole bill was clearly "permissive";
and the new system could be expanded or contracted as the
House thought best. These rather evasive explanations did
not satisfy the critics. They pressed for concrete details and
estimates, and Drummond complained that it was like drawing
teeth to get governmental explanations. Macdonald relented a
little; but it was not until four days later, when Galt announced
that the government proposed, for the first year, to call out
30,000 men for fourteen days' training at an estimated cost
of about $480,000, that the House really learnt the full truth.[32]
It was a staggering revelation. "It is plainly and obviously our
duty," Macdonald had argued in his peroration, "to provide a
large and efficient force for the purpose of fighting upon our
own soil, for our own possessions, our own privileges, and our
own liberties." All very true, no doubt. But who had expected
that a colony would be suddenly asked to do so much for
defence?

The opposition to the bill began to mount. The French-
Canadian supporters of government may have felt a lingering
resentment at the ease with which their friends from Canada
West had abandoned the principle of sectional equality in
parliament. They may have been ready enough to desert their
Upper Canadian colleagues and thus to get a little revenge for

the votes on the McDougall and Cameron amendments. And in any case they firmly believed that the Militia Bill imposed too large burdens and sacrifices upon a small colonial community. This conviction that the scheme was too absurdly heroic was the main, but not the only, source of opposition to the bill. The government, which had been in power continuously since 1854, had become old but not venerable. It seemed almost a provincial oligarchy, determined to prolong its rickety existence by the most dubious methods. It had become distinctly unsavoury through what the *Globe* called the "Ottawa jobberies" and other scandals; and its Finance Minister, Galt, had just been obliged to disclose in his budget speech a most unsatisfactory state of the finances. Monck actually believed that parliament and the people in general were reluctant to trust the large amounts of money required by the Militia Bill to such a suspect government;[33] and John Rose, who had significantly resigned the Commissionership of Public Works some time before, was only a little less censorious in a long letter of explanation which he wrote to Edward Ellice immediately after the crisis was over. The government, he explained—he was often a little sanctimoniously proper in his letters to Ellice—"lived too long, resorted to too many shifts to prolong existence, and people had begun to complain of the political oligarchy that ruled the country. They were anxious to reform but *couldn't*—they were surrounded by place hunters, jobbers, and had all manner of entangling antecedents. Galt's budget disclosed an alarming state of the finances; and all of us who had neither political regrets nor aspirations felt that we must set the house in order."[34]

But even this was not all. Another event, at once comic and awful, occurred. Macdonald suddenly ceased to be the captain of the ship and became an irresponsible stowaway. He was drinking heavily;[35] and he went on drinking heavily in complete and cheerful disregard for the Militia Bill, the Canadian government, the Conservative party, and the military necessities of the British Empire. The bout may have been accompanied or preceded by the depressing troubles of a real illness; but there were other than physical reasons for this prolonged relapse into irresponsibility. All that winter he had been troubled by the realization that the government was weak and the party divided. All that winter he had been growing increasingly irritated by the bland assumption that he would invariably continue at his post with patient fidelity, while everybody else was happily free to vote, accept or reject office, indulge all eccentric scruples and whimsical convictions exactly as it pleased him. He was bored and sick and tired with the whole business—with the endless deceptions and frustrations of Canadian politics. He kept to his room; and on Tuesday, May 13, nearly a week after the first debate on the Militia Bill, the *Globe* reported that he was unwell. "He has one of his old attacks," the correspondent continued jocosely. "It must be confessed that Mr. Macdonald's 'illnesses' occur at very inconvenient times."[36] On Thursday, May 15, he was reported still unwell. On Friday he was better; on Saturday he was still unable to leave his bed; and on Monday, May 19, he was said at last to be recovering. All during this deplorable absence the opposition to the Militia Bill was steadily increasing. "Rumours are getting thick again . . . ," one correspondent reported. "It is well known that the supporters of Government are very much dissatisfied with the militia bill. Nobody makes any secret of that."[37] Yet Macdonald was still not at his post. "The Attorney General West, I am told," the *Globe* correspondent admitted, "has really been very ill—ill in earnest, though at first the 'illness' was rather peculiar. Doubtless the one illness was the consequence of the other."

He was back at length on May 20. In the meantime, "a conviction is settling down in the minds of everybody that a break-up is imminent".[38] Yet Macdonald apparently did little to avoid it. He may even have welcomed it as the only way out of an impossible situation. "There seems little reason to doubt," one correspondent argued, "that Mr. Cartier and his colleagues have known for some time that they could not get through the session and that they elected to fall on the militia bill."[39] It was—like the seat-of-government question—a highly respectable, highly patriotic issue, an issue on which a slightly disreputable government could make a most dignified exit.

It was, in fact, such a lordly form of withdrawal that the Conservative malcontents and the regular opposition hoped to compel departure by a more ignominious route. But Macdonald was too much for them. Within half an hour of the opening of the House on May 20, the second reading of the Militia Bill took place. A little group of French-Canadian votes changed sides; the measure was defeated by sixty-one to fifty-four votes; and the next day he and Cartier and the entire ministry resigned. Macdonald's first feeling was an overwhelming sense of relief; and the letter which he wrote a few days later to the family in Kingston glows with the joyous consciousness of freedom. "You complain of my not having written," he told his sister. "It is true, but I had the excuse of overwork. I have that no longer. You will have seen that I am out of office. I am at last free, thank God! and can now feel as a free man. I have longed for this hour and only a sense of honour has kept me chained to my post . . . I have now fulfilled my duty to my party and can begin to think of myself."⁴⁶

III

Yet he did not begin to think of himself in what, for political men at that time, were the most obvious ways. Tradition, firmly established by a number of honourable examples, gave a retiring attorney-general the choice of all the vacant legal positions at the time; and retiring attorney-generals, even after only a brief term in office, were not infrequently in a hurry to press their claims. He had held the position—with the exception of a few days only—for nearly eight years. Two important offices had been open that winter, the chief justiceship and the chancellorship of Canada West; the one left vacant by the retirement of Sir John Beverley Robinson, and the other by the resignation of William H. Blake. Macdonald could have had either, and he refused them both. It was clear, at any rate, that he was not going to break dramatically and completely with politics, that he was not going to accept a position which would make it impossible to return. He finished out the session;

he did not resign his seat; he did not inform his followers that he would not take up the leadership of the opposition once more. His followers, of course, wanted one last great effort from him. They were out. They wanted to be in. Well, he would help them. He could hardly, if only for the sake of his own self-respect, leave the party at such an unfortunate moment. Privately he decided that he would not again accept office. That at least was settled. But the overthrow of the new government—there, surely, was an easier thing. Surely, in the light of all the savage divisions among the Reformers, it ought to be really easy?

In fact, the stage was rigged in such a fashion that the new government seemed destined for a tragic role. The terrible George Brown was still out of parliament; and his successor— the temporary leader at least of the Western Grits—was Brown's old critic, Michael Foley. But the portly and bibulous Foley did not stand out nearly so conspicuously as Brown had done from among his unfriendly associates, the other Reform leaders. It was possible to ignore him; and Monck, probably advised by Cartier, did ignore him, inviting John Sandfield Mac-donald instead to form a government. John Sandfield Mac-donald's cure for the political troubles of Canada was the so-called Double Majority; and L. V. Sicotte, who acted as the leader of the French-Canadian division in the new govern-ment, had supported the same principle. For the Conservatives, therefore, the elevation of Sicotte and John Sandfield Mac-donald to power was an excellent form of political insurance. It ensured, in the first place, that no immediate effort would be made to introduce Rep. by Pop., and, in the second place, that the new government would be attacked with the greatest possible venom by George Brown and his die-hard followers. Sandfield Macdonald and Sicotte had set out on what seemed to be a most difficult and unpopular course. In Canada they were heartily disliked by an influential section of the Reform party, and in England they were regarded with outraged dis-approval as unpatriotic colonials who had risen to political power on the wreck of that entirely necessary measure, the Militia Bill. "I have had two long interviews with the Duke of Newcastle," Edward Watkin of the Grand Trunk Railway wrote to John Sandfield Macdonald, "and found him at first very angry and full of doubts as to the new ministry. He said that he feared in the event of another danger the English government dared not make the effort of last December over again."[41] This was a very sad beginning in external relations. But there was worse to come. Before the year ended, the Macdonald-Sicotte government was to be dismally out of favour with the colonial governments of Nova Scotia and New Brunswick as well as with Great Britain.

Macdonald did not believe that the new government would last more than a twelvemonth. He told one of his correspondents, Samuel Amsden, that the policy of the party was "to keep together and prepare for an election next year". Probably not much effort would be necessary. The opposition could forgo heroics and content itself with the most guilelessly modest behaviour. "When Cartier and I crossed the floor," Macdonald told Amsden blandly, "we resolved to show the country what a gentlemanlike and patriotic opposition was. We resolved to give the new-comers fair play and offer no factious opposition. Some hot-headed friends of ours were dissatisfied with this, but I think they see now that we were correct. We have shown that we did not wish to cling to office for its own sake and we wish to show that we prefer the good of the country to mere party triumph. . . . When the House meets I will endeavour to prevent any vote of want of confidence. Let the Ministry have every chance to propose their measures. If they are for the good of the country, pass them. If not, oppose them. My opinion is that they are incapable of satisfying the wishes of the country and that they must fall from their own weakness and want of administrative ability. Their absurd programme or platform with 'Double Majority', etc., etc., must turn the country against them. Brown will fight them on Rep. by Pop. and split them in two. If the Government are defeated, it will be their own fault, and my own opinion is that defeated they will be, but not by our opposition. They will crumble to pieces before the end of the session from their own weakness."[42]

In one way, there was nothing very daring about these prophecies. They were based, not on any little-known, special weaknesses of the Reform party, but on the general and notorious defects of all Canadian parties in the third decade of the union. John Sandfield Macdonald's administration might, indeed, fall within a year. But if John Alexander Macdonald's government succeeded, what guarantee was there, in the existing state of things, that it could last any longer? "I will play the party game if allowed to do so . . . ," he had told Samuel Amsden. But would he be allowed to do so? Had the time not arrived when he, and everybody else, must stop playing the party game for a while—when all parties, or, at least, the bigger, more responsible parties, must unite to bring about a radical change in the constitution? That summer he had several long and significant conversations with a curious, apparently self-appointed intermediary named David Shaw, who, in a strictly private fashion, was trying to promote a union of parties to carry constitutional reform. Shaw saw George Brown and then Macdonald. He reported to Brown that Macdonald was prepared to support Rep. by Pop. as a less serious evil than the Double Majority; he told Macdonald that Brown would be prepared to join with him in a union government pledged to carry that great measure.[43] But like a good many intermediaries, before and since, Shaw found himself quickly disavowed by his principals. He probably misrepresented Macdonald; he certainly misrepresented Brown; and Brown wrote in some heat to say that his remarks had been entirely misconceived, that he had never suggested such a demoralizing thing as a coalition of parties, and that he did not contemplate for a moment renewing friendly personal intercourse with Macdonald, who had made charges against him of such a character "that until entirely withdrawn must debar any other than Parliamentary intercourse between us".[44] After this, Shaw's negotiations rather languished; but their life, however brief, had had a certain cloudy significance. Macdonald may merely have been trying to trap Brown into giving open assistance in the attack on the Macdonald-Sicotte administration; but, on the other hand, he may have been genuinely prepared to sink party differences for the sake of radical but necessary reform. He could look at the matter disinterestedly, at any rate, for his own ambitions were not involved. And Shaw grasped this fact clearly. ". . . My intention," Macdonald wrote privately to another correspondent at this time, "is *entre nous* to keep out of the government myself. I have had enough of it and must set to work to make a little money."[45]

This feeling, that the year 1862 would mark a firm period in his career, must have been greatly strengthened by another event which took place that autumn. On October 24, his mother died. It was almost exactly forty-two years since she and her husband had opened the first of their shops in Kingston, and slightly over twenty-one years since Hugh himself had died. Despite the shocks which, for years now, had racked and prostrated her body, she had lived sturdily on. She had clung tenaciously to her independence, to her own separate establishment—the house at Portsmouth—where she and Louisa and Hugh lived, and where a room was always kept in readiness for the return of her famous son. She was gone now, and with her went a good deal of the past—the old stories of Scotland, the clearest recollections of his father, of his own childhood, of the shops in Kingston, and the long summers at the Stone Mills. His wife was dead. His mother was dead. He had lost political power, and all these conclusions, big and little, seemed to combine to mark the end of a definite period of his existence. He was still only forty-seven. With a good third of his life still to come, he could resume his lucrative practice and pick up all the other interests that he had had to drop so largely during the last eight years. That autumn, shortly after his mother's death, he sailed for England. There may have been matters connected with the maternal estate in Scotland which had to be attended to. But now he was free to investigate the prospects of the future as well as to wind up the affairs of the past. He could discuss the business of the Trust and Loan Company in a leisurely fashion with Frederick Fearon. He could talk over possible speculations with Edward Watkin—and at a fortunate moment, too, for Watkin and his pushing friends were already negotiating for the purchase of the Hudson's Bay Company.

It was over twelve years since he had last visited England in an unofficial capacity. His reception this time was very different. He was, of course, far better known than he had been; and he could hardly have been more favourably known than he was at that very moment. To official London, he appeared as the patriotic sponsor of the Militia Bill, while his opponents, two of whom happened to be in London at the same time, were naturally distrusted as the authors of its defeat. Sicotte and Howland, together with representatives from Nova Scotia and New Brunswick, had come over to complete the financial arrangements for the Intercolonial Railway. At last, after years of vain negotiations, this project seemed actually to be under way. Great Britain, alarmed by the transport difficulties at the time of the *Trent* crisis, had offered to guarantee a provincial loan to be used for the purpose of the railway; and, in September, the three provinces concerned had finally agreed on a division of the costs. Everything appeared to be settled when the delegates assembled in London. But the Canadians, refusing to accept the sinking fund which the British government had insisted upon as the indispensable condition of its financial guarantee, suddenly and completely broke off the negotiations. They were now in bad odour with everybody; and they flung angrily away almost at the moment that Macdonald arrived. His appearance could hardly have been better timed. His reception, though unofficial, could hardly have been more pleasant. He was given a temporary membership at the Athenaeum. Various people competed for his company at week-ends; and the Duke of Newcastle himself was graciously pleased to grant him an interview. "I shall be very glad," wrote C. B. Adderley, one of the sternest of the "anti-colonials" in Parliament, "to let you see in me the lamentable ignorance prevailing here of Canada and to get you to cure it as far as possible in my case."[46]

He reached Quebec again on February 18, only a few days after the session opened. Outwardly his role was very much what it had been before. "I find our friends in the House—

indeed in both Houses—in very good health and spirits and eager for the fray," he told Samuel Amsden.[47] Apparently he was still "playing the party game", making the usual small moves on the battered political chessboard, guarding with jealous fondness every piece that could possibly be pressed into service in the attack against Macdonald and Sicotte. Even the old animosities—the venerable rivalry with John Hillyard Cameron and the irreconcilable quarrel with George Brown— were now discovered to be luxuries too costly to keep up during the rigorous poverty of opposition. At a dinner, which was given to Macdonald at Russell's Hotel the day after he arrived in Quebec, Cameron told the delighted company that the hatchet—if it had ever been lifted between Macdonald and himself—was now solemnly buried.[48] And when George Brown at last sought to re-enter parliament by contesting the vacant seat in North Oxford, the local Conservatives decided to repay his slashing attacks on the Macdonald-Sicotte government by giving him their enthusiastic support.[49] Secretly Macdonald was going a good deal further. At his instigation, no doubt, Malcolm Cameron, the old leader of the Clear Grits, renewed the delicate conversations with George Brown, which David Shaw had taken it upon himself to begin the previous summer. "I saw Brown," he reported to Macdonald, "and nothing is nearer to his heart than to upset the ship, but it is to him impossible unless Rep. by Pop. is in some way got over, and he says he understands the Cartier party was prepared to give two or three members to the West."[50] This was a big affair, very unlike the small change of party manoeuvres. He still could not see his way through it; and, in the meantime, the Conservative rank and file grew more impatient for a final, frontal assault. "We can put the ministry out whenever we like," Macdonald wrote to Amsden, "but the pear is not yet ripe." What was he to do? Where would a new and stable government get its support? Who was to lead it and what were its policies to be? The great difficulty, Rose wrote to Ellice, was to know what to put in the place of the Macdonald-Sicotte administration. "Your old friend Cartier is unbecomingly eager to get back to power, but there are very great objections to him, and yet there is hardly a Frenchmen to take his place. If he would but show himself superior to office, and agree to support some friendly government for a time, he would do himself lasting credit and the country a service. Macdonald—the late Attorney-General—is all for taking this course and anxious that Cartier should."[51]

Macdonald held his hand for a while yet. He had told Amsden that he fully expected the Macdonald-Sicotte government to ruin itself; and it suited his purpose to wait while the ministry reeled onward on its career of prodigal ineptitude. Already, within a year of taking office, it had chalked up a fairly consistent record of disavowed engagements and abandoned principles. It had, as John Rose put it, "shuffled out" of its responsibilities for defence and its railway engagements. And what was perhaps even worse, several of its members from Canada West, the old followers of Brown, had most obviously "shuffled out" of their Grit principles. From the very beginning it had been clear, from their mere acceptance of office in a government whose avowed policy was the Double Majority, that they had abandoned Rep. by Pop.; and during the session of 1863 it became equally apparent, as a result of the debates on R. W. Scott's Separate School Bill, that they had given up their old beliefs in non-sectarian schools. The whole history of the Scott bill was, in itself, a faltering, unhappy confession of weakness. The ministry as a whole, fearful of losing its strong support in Canada West, had not dared to introduce the bill as a government measure; but the ministers individually, worried by the prospect of arraying the whole of Canada East against them, had decided that they must give it their support. McDougall, the first leader of the Clear Grits, the author of the revolutionary Grit programme of 1851, actually voted in favour of Separate Schools; and for an amusing quarter of an hour Macdonald read maddeningly from the official journals of the Assembly to prove how frequently and consistently the poor Commissioner of Crown Lands had voted, while in opposition, against their extension, and in favour of their total abolition.[52] Yet even ignominious reversals such as this were not the end of the government's humiliations. The Scott

Separate School Bill passed, but in a fashion characteristic of such measures. A majority of the whole House voted in its favour; a majority of the members from Canada West voted against it. It was, in other words, a sectional, a "single", majority. Yet Double Majority was professedly the fundamental guiding principle of the government. What would it do? What explanation could it possibly give? It did nothing. It said nothing. It gave no explanations, yet it continued in office.

Macdonald decided that it would not remain in office much longer. As early as March 3, Rose had prophesied that the ministry would be turned out by a direct vote of want of confidence shortly after the Easter recess. The Easter recess came and went. The House reassembled and the Conservatives grew hourly more impatient. James Patton wrote from Toronto to ask how long Macdonald intended to keep McDougall, Foley and Co. in suspense. "Have they not had enough rope yet?" he enquired.[53] It was Friday, May 1, before Macdonald finally rose to address the House on his want-of-confidence motion.[54] He spoke for two hours—a long attack on the government's failure to live up to its professions. Almost exactly a week later—at 1.25 a.m. on the morning of Friday, May 8 —the vote finally came. The government was defeated by sixty-four to fifty-nine votes. John Sandfield Macdonald asked for a dissolution; and unlike Brown, he got it. A short while after, the seventh parliament of the Province of Canada ceased to exist.

IV

On Tuesday, May 19, Macdonald arrived in Kingston by the late night train, and the next day he appeared in the streets, talking with friends and acquaintances and "looking in most excellent health and evidently in the best of spirits".[55] He viewed the election—as he viewed all elections—with a cynically jocular smile. For him they had only some of the excitement, and all of the uncertainty, of a horse race; and he had to admit that in the last few hours of the old parliament the odds against him had perceptibly lengthened. Sandfield Macdonald had abandoned the now obviously untenable principle of Double Majority and had made his peace with George Brown. In the Cabinet, Oliver Mowat, a zealous follower of Brown, had been substituted for Michael Foley, his fat and frequently inebriated critic; and the places which Sicotte and the moderates from Canada East had once occupied were now filled by Dorion and his more radical followers. It was as clear as it could be that Sandfield Macdonald, now strengthened by George Brown's vehement support, was bent, at all costs, upon the recovery of Canada West. Electoral reform, which, of course, had been proscribed before, was now to be treated as an open question; and the Separate School Bill, which was law in any case, was in some sense redeemed by the grace of George Brown's forgiveness. The angry floodwaters seemed to be returning to their original channels. There was no longer any opportunity, for John A. Macdonald, of new alliances and new and radical policies. It was a straight party fight of the old kind. And he was far less fitted to win a straight party fight in Canada West in 1863 than he had been in 1861. Then the Conservatives had campaigned freely with Rep. by Pop. as an open question. Now they were committed by their stand on Scott's Separate School Bill. Most of the Conservatives had followed Macdonald and voted for the bill, while the Reformers had rejected the leadership of McDougall and others and voted against it. The rank and file of Grits were free from stigma, and their party was united as it had not been for years.

Macdonald once again accepted the inescapable burden of leadership. There was no way out of it. He knew everybody and everybody looked to him. Weeks before the election commenced he was busily writing his innumerable little letters to his political correspondents in each riding, recommending candidates, advising about strategy and tactics, pleading for reconciliations and unity—"let there be no splits". Everybody wrote to him in return. Everybody confided in him, appealed to him, demanded his presence, and drew upon his campaign money. "I can get them to do absolutely nothing," John

Duggan wrote from Toronto, ". . . they say, 'we'll wait till John A. comes up . . . .'"[56] He was so bothered and driven by these ceaseless importunities—by these repeated and rather peremptory requests to raise drooping spirits and to unravel angry political tangles—that he must have been relieved at the prospect of a comparatively easy contest in Kingston. This time it was not an important secondary politician such as Oliver Mowat, but another one of those worthy, respectable, unknown Kingstonians, O. S. Gildersleeve, who was put up to oppose him. When nomination day came on June 12, poor Gildersleeve's single flag and tiny troop of followers contrasted comically with Macdonald's three bands, gaily decorated waggons and carriages, and hundreds of defiantly marching Conservatives.[57] "As for Kingston," Patton wrote from Toronto, "everyone laughs at Gildersleeve's vanity in supposing that he could rob you of your old and tried friends. . . ."[58] Gildersleeve was, of course, infinitely ridiculous. Gildersleeve, unlike Oliver Mowat, was not to be taken seriously. Yet, when the votes were counted, it was discovered that Gildersleeve had received only one vote less than Mowat and that Macdonald had barely bettered his majority. It was a shock; and other and worse shocks were to follow it. The defeats began to accumulate. Sometimes, of course, failure was expected and discounted in advance—as it was, for example, in the case of poor Ephraim Cook, who campaigned valiantly against George Brown in South Oxford. "It is impossible to meet such a man in a back country as this," Cook told Macdonald lugubriously, "—500 devils could not begin to tell the yarns he does—and not one word of truth."[59] Yet in other ridings, untroubled by Brown's furious presence, where the Conservatives imagined they had a real chance, the toll of casualties grew longer and longer. The Conservatives went down. But they went down battling. "We had a fight," T. M. Daly reported from Stratford, "and twenty of the Grits are under medical treatment yet, only two of my men got hurt and they were up next day."[60]

It was impossible to escape the plain facts. The Conservatives had done badly in Canada West. The scant victory of 1861 had been converted into a defeat as serious as that of

1857. It was bad; but it was, quite literally, only half bad. For in Canadian elections there was always another, and a very different, side of the story. The thesis of Canada West invariably provoked the antithesis of Canada East; the Upper Canadian action was followed automatically by the Lower Canadian reaction. In exactly the same fashion as the Conservatives in 1861, the Reformers had won in the west and lost in the east. The Lower Canadian Conservatives were almost jubilant. "Things have not gone so well as you expected in U. Canada," Cauchon wrote to Macdonald. "Nevertheless there is no cause for despair and your only duty now is to gather your scattered soldiers and to bring them in good spirits with our Lower Canadian troops on the field of battle."[61] With good management, Cauchon thought, and a little judicious yielding on Cartier's part, they could muster fifty votes from Canada East; and Macdonald's reduced contingent from Canada West would number another twenty at least. "That would make seventy in all," Cauchon concluded hopefully, "and more than necessary to upset the fellows." The old game was about to begin again, and on almost exactly the same terms. The old and rather ignominious search for allies had already recommenced. Cartier was sounding out Sicotte. Patton—so he wrote Macdonald—was listening with sympathetic attentiveness while Foley unburdened his mind on the "damned treachery" of Sandfield Macdonald.

"I leave here for Quebec on Friday," Macdonald wrote a friend from Kingston on August 5, "so as to be early on the ground."[62] An autumn meeting of the new parliament was necessary because the sudden dissolution had prevented the completion of a good deal of business; and later in August the Assembly met with the two parties in an exquisitely dangerous state of near balance. "We are going to upset these fellows, I think, this week," Macdonald wrote in September.[63] But at the last moment the government collected sufficient votes to defeat a want-of-confidence motion; and when the session closed on October 15, Sandfield Macdonald was still precariously in power. This kind of thing could apparently go on for ever. It was not exactly stalemate. There were always

a few small moves that could be made. There were always a
few votes that might be won. John A. Macdonald had gained
the increasingly popular McGee, and, as the autumn wore on,
it looked also as if he were going to capture Foley. The
ousted Reform leader had already begun to write plaintively ingratiating letters to him; and now he redoubled the fervour
of his professions. He would turn over an absolutely new leaf![64]
He had already joined the Sons of Temperance! He would
soon declare himself unreservedly a supporter of the Conservative party. One vote more! It would almost do it. Two—
and the thing would be a certainty! And, as everybody had
known all autumn, the second vote would soon be open for
competition. The government had not yet appointed a Solicitor-
General for Canada West; and the appointment, which would
require the new official to seek re-election, would instantly
open a solitary seat for contest. "If they lose this election in
U.C.," wrote Macdonald, appealing for funds to Brown Chamberlin of Montreal, "it will be Sandfield's coup de grace. Herein
fail not an thou lovest me!"[65] Everybody was on the alert. Who
would get the appointment? What seat would be thrown open?
There were repeated rumours. And towards the last of December, 1863, the government finally made its move. A. N.
Richards was appointed Solicitor-General; and the open constituency was South Leeds.

It might have been a general election. "If you decide on
war to the knife," wrote Alleyn, "draw on me at seven days'
sight for five hundred dollars. I regret it is not five thousand."[66]
It was to be, Macdonald decided, "war to the knife", and the
whole party began to roll into action. D. F. Jones, the Conservative candidate opposing Richards, wrote from Gananoque,
modestly suggesting that if Macdonald, McGee, Campbell,
and one or two others would range through the riding following his opponent, a great deal would be gained. "Chrysler
says," he wrote, "they want to see John A.—and I think if
he shewed himself in the county, and at the nomination, etc.,
it would have a good effect—but the great thing will be the
needful."[67] The "needful" poured in in fairly copious quantities. It was true that at first there was a dreadful rumour

that the Bank of Montreal was secretly aiding Richards; but John Rose went quickly to interview the president and the general manager, and the rumour turned out happily to be false. Railwaymen such as Brydges of the Grand Trunk, and contractors such as David Macpherson, who wished to get ahead with the Intercolonial Railway, contributed readily enough in support of the Conservative cause. "As long as the present men remain in power," Brydges wrote, "we can do nothing and the Lower Provinces will be driven to connect with Portland instead of Quebec."[68] Armed with these resources, Macdonald and his new ally, Thomas D'Arcy McGee, plunged into the riding on an extended speaking tour. These two "outsiders", as the *Globe* called them contemptuously—the "pretended" Orangeman and the "pretended" Roman Catholic—together accomplished the defeat of poor Mr. Richards, and in the last days of January the letters and telegrams of congratulation began to flow in.

"We have no difficulty in acknowledging," the *Globe* declared editorially with a somewhat odd, detached realism, "that the defeat of Mr. Richards is a serious blow to the administration. After the defection of Mr. Foley, parties being so nearly balanced last session, they could ill afford to lose the vote of the Solicitor-General."[69] The Conservatives were, of course, triumphant. Everybody was suddenly talking about preparing for a new general election, and building a new political organization, and taking "the Grits in the hour of their prostration". It was all very well, and Macdonald himself had been talking about the need of organization as recently as December; but as the prospect of the defeat of the government grew clearer and clearer, the old questions—which he had been asking himself for years now—came back with renewed force. Upon what basis could a really stable government be formed? And who was to assume the leadership that he had grown so tired of? Back in the previous spring, Rose had suggested that Campbell, who had had no part in the history of the old Conservative government, might suitably take over; and others, of only less importance, agreed that the Grits might be robbed of half their powers of attack if the Conservatives could only present themselves to the public under a different name. Campbell would certainly make a respectable titular head: but would the Conservatives ever accept him as the actual leader? Macpherson thought not. He told Macdonald that he did not believe it would be possible for him to transfer his command to another:[70] and James Patton of Toronto—another correspondent to whom Macdonald had confided his plan of retirement—rejected the idea even more conclusively. "I believe," he wrote, "that a Ministry formed on our side, without you and Cartier as the master minds, *would not hold together*." Macdonald must not even suggest the possibility of resigning. He could not effectively play Brown's role; and if he abandoned the leadership in the Assembly, the party would simply break up piecemeal. "No!" Patton concluded forcibly. "Your position is such, by common consent, that proper deference would always be paid to your advice, for it is felt that your generalship can carry the Party through when another man—no matter how able—would fail. *You* bring to bear the experience of a quarter century in Parliamentary warfare and *no man* on our side *can take your place*."[71]

Well, he would see. But obviously the moment in which a decision would have to be made was coming closer and closer. And the question of leadership was inextricably bound up with the question of policy—policy for the Province of Canada, and perhaps for British North America as a whole. For months, almost for years now, he and his opponents had gone on making these small adjustments, fighting these mimic battles, rejoicing over these insignificant victories; but the time was surely coming when some government—a government in which he might exercise an influence if he did not play a leading part—would have to grapple at last with the really big issues. During the American Civil War, these problems had grown more serious; and ever since the summer of 1863, when the loss of the battle of Gettysburg had put the southern Confederacy upon the defensive, they had become more urgent still. What was to be done about this knotted tangle of problems—defence, the West, British North American communications and British North American political reorganization? The

Americans, irritated with both Great Britain and her colonies, were threatening to abrogate the Reciprocity Treaty and to repeal the bonding laws which made possible the free transit of Canadian goods through the republic. Great Britain, which had already sent one group of military experts to investigate and report upon Canadian defences, might be expected soon to raise the military problem in a more acute form. The newly reorganized Hudson's Bay Company was making great plans for the development of the West. The Grand Trunk authorities, worried at the prospect of a connection between the Maritime and American railways, were anxiously promoting the old Intercolonial once more. Nothing whatever had been done about the central difficulty of the Canadian union. It had left everybody baffled and exhausted. The plan for a federal union of the Canadas, and the rival plan for a federal union of British North America, were both apparently dead. And in the meantime, down in Halifax and Fredericton, they were beginning to talk seriously of a legislative union of the Maritime Provinces.

Could anything be done without a coalition of major parties? It was over eighteen months now since the officious Shaw had first begun the very tentative overtures to Brown. Was it possible that the time had arrived to renew them, even more hopefully? Later in December he noted with interest that the *Globe* had been "pitching into" McDougall for his abandonment of Rep. by Pop. Was the reconciliation between Brown and the members of the Sandfield Macdonald government already wearing a little thin? These were questions which he must have pondered deeply during the long three-day journey from Kingston to Quebec through the snow-piled landscape of winter. C. J. Brydges, who, as a promoter of the Intercolonial, had his own reasons for being interested in Brown and the *Globe*, agreed to see the western Grit leader when he was in Quebec on railway business and to report back to Macdonald. Brydges, who suspected that the post office, under the pure administration of Sandfield Macdonald, was systematically tampering with his correspondence, was careful to send his reports through an intermediary. He had a curiously interesting but inconclusive story to tell. Brown, he reported, was certainly angry with the Sandfield Macdonald government and fully expected its immediate fall. The great editor was prepared to talk future politics, and even to consider Brydges' offers in a gingerly fashion; but, as Brydges admitted sadly, "it did not go as far as could be wished", for Brown would not give him the opening. "I offered him the chair of the Canada Board of Hudson's Bay," the manager of the Grand Trunk wrote Macdonald, "at which I think he was a good deal impressed, but would not say positively. . . . I showed him that nothing could be done about Northwest without the Intercolonial. On the latter point he is much mollified—thinks that the action of the Yankees about reciprocity and bonding has put an entirely new phase on the question, and that it ought now to be seriously taken into consideration. . . . He does not object I think to the marrying of Northwest and Intercolonial but wants the number of items enlarged. He wishes an omnibus arrangement to include Northwest, Intercolonial, Representation, and change of tariff by lowering duties."[72] Brown, Brydges reported, would support such a programme and believed that it could be carried; but that was as far as the editor of the Globe was prepared to go. "He could not be secured at the moment," Brydges admitted, "but you can now judge if it is best to press him further now."[73]

No, it would not be best, Macdonald decided, to press him any further at the moment. It would be useless, as well as undignified, to follow that faint but tantalizing trail any longer. As the session opened, he settled down in Quebec without any clear plan for the future. His new quarters, which were much nearer the legislature than the old, were comfortable enough; and, as he told his sister, Louisa, "I am pretty well just now, barring an occasional colic, which sticks to me with wonderful pertinacity."[74] His health was all right, he was in the best of spirits; and, amid the general fog of uncertainty, there were at least some desired objectives that he could see clearly. A broad coalition government, in which the old Liberal-Conservatives would be fittingly represented, must be formed, capable of dealing at last with the really big issues. He himself, having assisted in its formation and given it his blessing, would gracefully retire. All this—and his retirement in particular—was quite clear. It was like a far hill lit by a single shaft of sunlight. But all around was dark with shadow. And, like everybody else, he was frightened of losing his way, frightened of bumping into difficulties, frightened of taking positive steps in any direction. He had always stood for the unity of the British lands bordering on the St. Lawrence River system. He had always held that, if the legislative union of Upper and Lower Canada were to be given up, it must be surrendered only for a really strong union of the whole of British North America; and, from the very beginning of the American Civil War, he had repeatedly warned his fellow-countrymen that in their proposed general union, they must at all costs avoid the manifest weaknesses of American federalism. With this important change of emphasis, he had still stuck to the Conservative plan of 1858. But in the meantime his unhappy doubts had been growing stronger. Was it possible to frame a plan of federal union which would be immune from the dangers which American experience had revealed?

He could no longer be certain. His first objective was the strength of real unity; and if federation could not ensure that strength, then another and safer form of union might have to be substituted for federation. He must have realized that these vigorous conclusions would embarrass the unity of the party; but that did not prevent him from speaking his mind when, on March 14, Brown moved for a select committee of nineteen on the problem of the constitution. Galt, who spoke early in the debate, insisted that the plan of the Liberal-Conservative government had been, and remained, Confederation, and that the proposed legislative union of the Maritime Provinces was an important preliminary step towards it. Scoble, who followed Galt, declared roundly that he did not believe in federal union, and did not wish to see repeated in Canada a plan which had so manifestly failed in the United States. Macdonald called out, "hear, hear", and later, when he himself was on his feet, he told the House that British North American union, if it ever came, must be a complete union.

"The sad experience on the other side," he continued, "proved it must not be merely a federal one; that instead of having a federal one, we should have a Legislative Union in fact, in principle and in practice."[75] This, in view of the past, was an oddly independent pronouncement; and Brown inquired satirically whether that was the policy which the Liberal-Conservative government had previously announced. "That is not my policy," Cartier said grimly, and the House laughed. It was a tempting opportunity for the Reformers; and Brown promptly denounced Macdonald as a man who had proved his want of fixed principles by a total abandonment of the Conservative Confederation scheme of 1858. Macdonald, who had already attacked Brown in much the same fashion for his apparently waning interest in Rep. by Pop., might have retorted that his old antagonist relied far too much on principles, programmes, and resolutions, and far too little on the humdrum but necessary machinery of cabinet government. Macdonald realized at any rate that a broad coalition government could alone tackle the enigma of the Canadian constitution. But what was the solution to be? Once he had thought he knew. And he still believed that above all else a strong union was necessary. That was the most important principle and he clung to it.

In the meantime, the desired and dreaded event which he had anticipated so long drew rapidly closer. The Conservatives massed their full strength for the defeat of the government; and on March 21, without even waiting for the vote on the want-of-confidence motion, John Sandfield Macdonald and his Cabinet resigned. Now was the moment for which he had hoped. Years ago he had told his sister, Margaret, that he intended to give up politics as soon as he could "with honour". Surely now he could honourably retire! Surely this was the moment to form that broad administration composed of the veteran moderates of both parties! For obvious reasons, the Governor shared these views and was prepared to act on them. The old leaders of both old parties had failed him. He could legitimately look elsewhere. And the search for new men began. Monck turned first to Fergusson Blair, who had been a member of the Sandfield Macdonald government. When Fergusson

Blair reported his failure, he then invited Alexander Campbell to undertake the task. For months the Conservatives had been grooming Macdonald's old partner for this very role; and now that his moment had arrived Campbell struggled long and desperately to gain the necessary support. Yet he failed as well. There was still no government. The days went by; and, as time passed fruitlessly, the pressure upon Macdonald steadily increased. It came from all directions, from both circumstances and persons, from ex-cabinet ministers, Members of Parliament, and from obscure followers of the Liberal-Conservative party who wrote or spoke to him, begging him not to desert them. "If you take the helm all is well," one of them wrote, "if not, disaster is certain to follow . . . Surely all our conquests, our fights, our triumphs are not to end in this way. John A. not the U.C. leader!—bosh, the Government won't stand."[76] It was this very argument, couched, no doubt, in more literary terms, that old Dr. Etienne Taché was now pressing upon him; and to Taché, as a last resort, the now nearly frantic Governor had turned. Macdonald gave in, as he had given in so often before. He would make one last effort. On March 30, after nine days of interregnum, the Taché government was formed; and the next day the weary House adjourned.

A stiff north-west wind had filled the St. Lawrence opposite Quebec with drifting ice. The steamer which carried passengers across the river to the Grand Trunk station at Levis—there was no North Shore Railway then—was stopped; and Macdonald and Campbell, who dared, like a few others, to cross in a canoe, were driven through drifting ice to a point far below their destination.[77] There was need for haste. So much had to be done in the brief interval of the adjournment. So much; and yet what, after all, would it possibly avail? The old government had, in effect, come back again. Dr. Taché had admittedly been out of politics for a few years; but everybody remembered that he had been first minister of the Liberal-Conservative government as recently as 1857. Campbell, who had accepted the post of Commissioner of Crown Lands, was known as a respected semi-independent, and Foley and McGee, who had also joined the new government, had been Reformers of some prominence in the past; but, whatever their previous affiliations, they could not bring with them sufficient support to change the character of the Taché government in any essential. It would stand as a Liberal-Conservative government; and—what was even more important—it would probably fall as a Liberal-Conservative government, and in short order. When parliament met again on May 3 after the adjournment, Macdonald doubtless had very little hope. The poor, unfortunate Foley had already been defeated in his by-election, and in the House the two sides were almost in perfect balance. The government stuck it out for nearly a month; but at last, on June 14, it was defeated by a majority of two.[78] Macdonald told the House next day that, as a result of the vote, he and his colleagues had decided that it was their duty to communicate with the Governor. What would happen he had, as yet, almost no idea. But he knew at least that the last card in the old game had been played.

Chapter Thirteen

British North America in Conference

I

Yet, even on Wednesday, June 15, there were a few slight signs that this "ministerial crisis" would not end as all ministerial crises had done before. When Macdonald had finished his announcement, John Sandfield Macdonald got up immediately to demand further information. It was the usual opposition request. But George Brown did not give it exactly the usual support that might have been expected of him. He agreed, of course, that the House had a right to information; but he felt "that in the position of great gravity in which the honourable gentlemen opposite were now placed, they should be allowed every fair opportunity to consider what course they should pursue".[1] A new attitude of concern and conciliation was faintly suggested even in this public pronouncement. In private Brown had already gone much further. On Tuesday evening and Wednesday morning he had spoken to several Conservatives, urging strongly that the present crisis should be used to settle the Canadian constitutional problem for ever, and stating that he was prepared to co-operate with the existing, or any other, government that would deal with that problem promptly and firmly. These words were, by permission, communicated to John A. Macdonald and Galt; and Macdonald immediately changed the direction which his baffled government had already taken. The ministers, in despair of achieving a stable government in the existing House, had advised a dissolution and an appeal to the people. But there was no guarantee that a new general election would give either party a solid majority, and no hope whatever that it could end the sectional difficulty. Brown's words implied something quite different and infinitely more promising. It was what Macdonald had been hoping and working for, through tentative, indirect approaches, ever since the summer of 1862. He had made advances himself in the past. Now he was ready to respond to the advances of others. On Thursday, just before three o'clock in the afternoon, when the galleries were rapidly filling up with eager spectators, and the members were chatting idly in the Assembly room, waiting for the Speaker to take the chair, he approached the member for South Oxford. Would Brown have any objection to meeting Galt and himself to talk the matter over? And Brown replied, "Certainly not."[2]

On Friday, at about one o'clock, Macdonald and Galt called on Brown at the St. Louis Hotel. Only three days before, Macdonald had still felt at liberty to record his theoretical preference for legislative union. On June 14, the very day of the defeat of his government, Brown's constitutional committee had reported that "a strong feeling was found to exist among the members of the committee in favour of changes in the direction of a federative system, applied either to Canada alone, or to the whole British North American Provinces. . . ."[3] And Macdonald had publicly dissented. He had stuck to his own private convictions, in their extremest form, as long as the issue remained an academic question. But now it had been transferred from the debating society of a committee to the practical politics of government; and as he and Galt walked that day into the lobby of the St. Louis Hotel, he realized that he must give way. When Brown inquired courteously what remedy the government proposed for the constitutional difficulty, Macdonald and Galt replied that their remedy was a federal union of British North America. And when Brown, in his turn, was asked what solution he preferred, he answered that he advocated parliamentary reform based on population. Each side rejected the other's initial proposal with equal firmness; and the preliminary exchange of diplomatic courtesies was over. Then the two Conservatives made the obvious suggestion that the recommendations of Brown's constitutional committee offered the best basis for an agreement; and "after much discussion on both sides, it was found that a compromise might probably be had in the adoption either of the federal principle for all British North American Provinces, as the larger question, or for Canada alone. . . ."⁴ The two policies, Conservatives and Reform, were to be combined as alternatives in a single programme. But which was to come first? For obviously no government could pursue both policies together. It was the crucial question. They were still discussing it, and Brown was still insisting "that the Canadian Federation should be constituted first", when they all realized that their time was almost up. It was nearly three o'clock. They would have to meet the House. But they could confidently ask it for a further and longer adjournment, now that there was a real hope of an agreement.

The galleries were crowded once again when Macdonald rose to make his announcement. He told the House that the Governor had, that very morning, given the Cabinet permission to dissolve. He informed the eagerly listening members that the ministry, reserving the newly granted authority, had already begun discussions with the member for Oxford in the hope of finding a basis for a stronger government in the existing House.⁵ Dorion complained that the government was using the power of dissolution to coerce the Assembly. John Sandfield Macdonald supported his objections. It was clear that the little group of *Rouges* from Canada East, and the still smaller "tail" of Sandfield Macdonald Reformers from the Ottawa valley, would certainly oppose any agreement that might be made in the next few days. But that hardly mattered. For Brown was now on his feet, making the most dramatic announcement of his political career. He was sure, he said, that the members would acquit him of any desire to aid the government in coercing the House. Only the pressure of most extreme circumstances could have justified the government in making its approaches to him; and only the force of the same extreme circumstances could have justified him in meeting men to whom he had been so long and strongly opposed. He paid tribute to the spirit in which the members of the government had made their advances; and he promised that there would be no secrecy. Then he sat down. In another minute the Speaker rose. There was a great roar of applause from either side; and Dufresne, one of the members for Montreal, walked quickly across the floor of the House to shake Brown's hand. Then they were all shaking hands. And, in spirit at least, the new coalition was made.

After this, the principals could hardly fail. Next day, Saturday, June 18, they got down to it in earnest. There were repeated conferences between Brown on the one hand, and Macdonald, Galt, and Cartier on the other. Brown had an interview with the Governor-General, and saw a number of his own followers. Macdonald called a ministerial caucus, and sought, and obtained, approval for the course which he and Cartier were pursuing. At night, when the third of the conferences ended, they had at least agreed upon the main point of policy. Brown had made a vain last attempt to insist upon the immediate federation of the Canadas, with a provision for the future admission of the Maritime Provinces and the North West Territories. But Macdonald and his colleagues had declared that they would not consent to waive the larger issue; and in the verbal formula which was finally adopted as an alleged compromise, there was no doubt that the coalition would be committed to an immediate attempt to seek a general federation.[6] On this matter, Brown had had to give way; and, when the conference closed on Saturday night, Macdonald and Cartier were contending that he must also abandon his extreme demand that the Reformers should be given one-half the places in the coalition Cabinet. On Monday, when the discussions were resumed, with Sir E. P. Taché in attendance, this question of Grit representation in the coalition ministry had become the principal subject. Macdonald said that he was ready and willing to resign if his resignation would help matters. But he made it clear that if he remained in the Cabinet, he would not be content with any serious alteration in his position; and he refused to concede more than three places—exactly half the Upper Canadian division in the ministry—to the Reformers.

This was the arrangement which, after a good deal of further debate, was finally accepted on Tuesday. And this was the result which Macdonald communicated to the House in his "ministerial explanations" on Wednesday, June 22. A week later, on June 30, the House was finally prorogued. On the same day, George Brown, Oliver Mowat, and William Mc-Dougall were sworn into the Executive Council of the Province of Canada.

It had happened. The hopes held stubbornly for years had been realized. The union with George Brown was a fact; the broad coalition government had been brought into actual being; and its declared policy, though admittedly a compromise, was the compromise which Macdonald had proposed from the first. He had committed the new administration not to a division, but to an enlargement, of Canada, in a general federal union of British North America. It was his task now—the task for which he had clung to a place in the Cabinet—to see that the proposed federation was as strong as it could possibly be made. At the moment, circumstances seemed propitious—more propitious certainly than they had been back in 1858. On at least two occasions in the last few years, Newcastle, the recent Colonial Secretary, had declared that he was ready to consider sympathetically any scheme of union, regional or general, which had the consent of the parties concerned. The American Civil War had strengthened a mental attitude favourable to Macdonald's scheme; and the approaching conference of the Maritime Provinces supplied an occasion on which to launch it. This conference, which the Canadians had, of course, known about since the winter, could hardly help but be an important element in all their calculations. It was true that the Maritimers were scheduled to discuss only a union of their own legislatures. But, from the reports of the debates and from other more confidential sources of information, Macdonald may have begun to suspect that Maritime union, by itself, was a somewhat academic subject, which had aroused very little public enthusiasm, and which was favoured more by Maritime governors than it was by Maritime politicians. In any case, the delegates at the conference would probably be willing to interrupt their official discussions to listen while the Canadians presented unofficially the advantages of a different type of union.

It was in this sense that Monck wrote, on June 30, to the Governors of Nova Scotia, New Brunswick and Prince Edward Island. Would a delegation from the new coalition government of Canada be permitted to attend the proposed Maritime Conference to present a plan for a general federal union of British North America? This polite but unexpected request revealed an odd state of unpreparedness in the Maritime governments, which scarcely suggested any great zeal for legislative union. The three provincial legislatures had authorized their governments to appoint delegates to the approaching conference; but no delegates had in fact been appointed by any colony, and the very date and place of the conference were still unsettled.[7] The Maritime governments, jarred somewhat from their curious lethargy, answered courteously that of course the Canadians would be welcome. But two of the replies stressed the fact that Canadian participation must be entirely unofficial; and one Governor, Sir Richard Graves MacDonnell of Nova Scotia, was so uncertain about the matter, and so troubled about his own power to appoint any delegates without previous authorization from the imperial government, that he wrote back for reassurance to the Colonial Office.[8] By the end of July, the dilatory Maritime governments had at last decided on the time and place of their proposed meeting. It was to be at Charlottetown, Prince Edward Island, on September 1. At least there was to be a conference for the Canadians to attend.

Obviously the Maritime attitude to the general question of union was very different from what it had been back in 1858. That, as Macdonald knew very well from experience, was one very important point gained. But what of the Colonial Office? Had the rather cold neutrality that was so evident in Lytton's day altered for the better? There were several good reasons for believing that it had. In the first place, the very readiness of the Maritime governments to welcome a visit from the Canadians was sufficient in itself to remove one of Lytton's chief objections. It was true, although Macdonald had probably no means of knowing this, that the Duke of Newcastle had always privately believed that Maritime union ought to precede Confederation, and that the Intercolonial Railway ought to precede both.[9] It was also true that the permanent officials of the Colonial Office, converted by the persuasive dispatches of a succession of Maritime governors, had come to believe devoutly in the wisdom and expediency of a legislative union of the three Lower Provinces. But Newcastle had never for a moment imagined that the imperial government should take the initiative in the matter, or that the private preferences of imperial officers should be permitted to disturb that attitude of benevolent neutrality which the Mother Country should maintain until the colonists had made up their minds. Moreover—a point of some importance—Newcastle was no longer at the Colonial Office. He had been succeeded by Edward Cardwell. There was no particular reason to assume in advance that Cardwell's private preferences on the subject of British North American unions would be the same as Newcastle's. There was, in short order, a good deal of reason to be certain that they were quite different.

During that July of 1864 the new Colonial Secretary was particularly preoccupied with Canadian affairs. There was Monck's laconic dispatch announcing the formation of the coalition government; there was Sir Richard MacDonnell's puzzled communication, with its news of the Canadian request to attend the Maritime Conference. Above all, there were the protracted discussions in the imperial Cabinet on the question of British North American, and particularly Canadian, defence —a question raised once more by the report of the military expert, Lieutenant-Colonel Jervois, who had made a tour of Canada and the Maritime Provinces in the autumn of 1863. There were members in the Cabinet—Gladstone by his own confession was the most prominent among them—who wished to make serious changes, "to shift the centre of responsibility", in the matter of British North American defence.[10] But these members, though they voiced the currently fashionable dogmas on the subject, did not yet form the most numerous or influential body in the Cabinet. "I cannot admit," Palmerston wrote in a lengthy minute on a suggested change in Cardwell's proposed dispatch to Monck, "that it is a question for consideration or division whether our North American Provinces are to be fought for or abandoned. There may be much to be said for the theory put forward by some, that our Colonies are an encumbrance and an expense, and that we should be better without them, but that is not the opinion of England, and it is not mine."[11] It was not, indeed. And Palmerston's opinions, in a somewhat less robust form, were shared by other members of the Cabinet. Even Gladstone acknowledged that "the Cabinet as a whole is not prepared at the present time, and perhaps never may be prepared, to proceed upon such a basis" as he had laid down. The dispatch which Cardwell sent to Monck on August 6 assumed the continuance of imperial military help; but it also asserted the principle that the security of Canada must depend largely on the efforts and courage of its own people; and it invited the Canadian government to make definite proposals for the improvement of its defences in the light of the Jervois report.[12] A little later, towards the end of August, the British government also decided to send Colonel Jervois, the author of this disturbing document, back to Canada to assist the colonial authorities in making their decisions.

At the end of July, when these discussions of Canadian defence were going on, Cardwell was already well aware of the new Canadian coalition government and its project of a general British North American federation. In the minutes and letters which the ministers exchanged on the military question, there was no connection drawn between federation and defence, and no suggestion made that the former would promote the effectiveness of the latter. Yet the Colonial Office was obviously interested, in a speculative, academic way, in the Canadian proposal; and Gordon, the Lieutenant-Governor of New Brunswick, who was in London on leave during July, later recalled a conversation he had had on the subject with Cardwell and T. F. Elliot.[13] As might have been expected, the Colonial Office officials were a little bit jealous for the success of their pet project, Maritime union. The copious comments which they made on MacDonnell's dispatch, announcing the Canadian request, showed quite clearly that even Frederic

Rogers, the Permanent Under-Secretary, and Fortescue, the Parliamentary Under-Secretary, were very insistent that "the smaller union may not be imperilled or delayed by the discussion of a larger union. . . ."[14] But Cardwell obviously did not share these apprehensions. There was no sign of them in the minute which he himself wrote on Sir Richard's communication or in the reassuring dispatch which was sent back to him on August 9.[15] There was equally little sign of displeasure at the presumption of the Canadians in the dispatch which was written, after a few more leisurely days, to Monck, asking for further information about Canada's request to attend the Maritime Conference. It was not until September 10, when the delegates had actually left Charlottetown, that Monck's explanatory reply reached the Colonial Office. The clerks were plainly dissatisfied. Monck ought to have done this. He most certainly should have done that. It was all most regrettably informal. But Cardwell was evidently not much impressed with their strictures. "Put by," he wrote briefly on the dispatch.[16]

II

On Monday, August 29, Macdonald boarded the Canadian government steamer, *Queen Victoria,* at Quebec.[17] With him was a large company of people. There were the seniors in the Cabinet, Cartier, Brown and Galt, and their junior colleagues, McDougall, McGee, Campbell and Langevin; and —what was distinctly unusual in British North American conferences—a secretarial staff of three. It was, for the times, a large, determined, and well-equipped delegation that set out from Quebec. But it had only the vaguest notion of what its reception was likely to be at Charlottetown. The letters from the Maritime government had been polite—but very formally polite. The Maritimers might be simply annoyed by this uninvited Canadian intrusion. The whole affair might have a most deplorable ending. And yet, at the same time, it was impossible not to regard the meeting at Charlottetown

as a divinely granted opportunity. The Canadians might succeed, though their mission was strictly unofficial; and if at
the end of the conference there it seemed a reasonable prospect
that a general federal union could be formed, then it would
be easy to call a formal conference on the subject.[18] The great
thing was to convince the Maritimers; and, as the *Queen
Victoria* travelled slowly down the Gulf of the St. Lawrence
towards Prince Edward Island, the Canadians must have been
frantically busy, putting the last touches to their federal plan
and deciding who had best speak on this or that phase of it.
It was late Wednesday night, the last day of August, when
the steamer began slowly to approach Charlottetown. The
somewhat incurious citizens of the capital city of Prince
Edward Island casually noticed a strange vessel just off the
harbour that night; and next morning the strange vessel, which
was without benefit of pilot, came timidly up the harbour,
casting the lead for safety at every few feet.[19] The exciting
news spread that the Canadians had arrived; and W. H. Pope,
a member of the Prince Edward Island government, procured
a small boat and rowed manfully out to the steamer to greet
them. The *Queen Victoria* hoisted its flag. The breathless
Pope presented the greetings of Charlottetown and Prince
Edward Island. And shortly after, while it was still morning,
the formidable Canadian delegation came ashore.

Charlottetown was crowded with a sudden influx of visitors.
The *Heather Belle* had brought the Nova Scotian delegation
on the afternoon of August 31; the New Brunswickers had
arrived on the *Prince of Wales* a little before midnight on the
same day. But the conference on Maritime union was not the
only, nor, indeed, the main, attraction which drew people towards the somnolent little town of Charlottetown on the last
day of August, 1864. There was also a circus, the first circus
to visit the Island, it was said, in twenty-one years, and people
were travelling eagerly from sixty miles away to behold it.
"What is the cause of this 'wonderful migration'?" the correspondent of the Saint John *Morning Telegraph* enquired
satirically. "The circus, Sir, the circus," came the answer from
a dozen throats as the "surging throng" swept past him.[20] The

circus not only attracted people from all over the Island; it also
apparently attracted a good many members of the Prince Edward
Island government. At any rate they were not on the dock to
greet the delegates. Not a soul was on hand to give an official
welcome to the Nova Scotians. There was not even a carriage
or a waggon, so it was said, to take them or their belongings
to hotels.[21] Pope, the indefatigable Provincial Secretary, hurried
out alone to welcome the New Brunswickers, and the Canadians. And after this rather meagre reception, it was discovered
that there was difficulty about lodging. The New Brunswickers
could be put up at the Mansion House; but there was not
enough room for the Canadians at the Franklin. The embarrassed Islanders subsequently tried to excuse themselves for
this unfortunate lack of accommodation by pointing out that
Monck had indicated a Canadian delegation of only four.[22] In
the end, some of the Canadians stayed in town at the Franklin
House; but most of them remained in the *Queen Victoria,*
and among these, with his secretaries, was Macdonald.

It was an awkward beginning. Was it an unhappy symbol
of the Canadians' real position? Physically their delegation was
half in town and half out in the harbour; morally, they were
a part, yet not a real part, of the conference. Was the whole
enterprise to end in embarrassment, irritation, and defeat? The
first hour or so after the landing at Charlottetown must have
been full of painful uncertainties. And yet, though the Canadians were, of course, unaware of it, their problem was already
solved in a fashion which could hardly have been more favourable. On Thursday morning, September 1, as the *Queen Victoria* was moving deliberately up the harbour towards Charlottetown, the Maritime Conference had held its first meeting. The
delegates had scarcely assembled when the news of the imminent arrival of the Canadians was announced. And then an
odd but revealing event occurred. With a unanimity and
alacrity which almost suggested a general sense of mental
relief, the conference decided that it would postpone the discussion of Maritime union until the unofficial visitors, the
Canadians, had had a chance to present their very different
plan.[23] This was the wonderful news that greeted the ad-

venturers from the *Queen Victoria*. They may have heard it first at about twelve o'clock when all the delegates went out to Government House, on the outskirts of the town, to pay an official visit to Lieutenant-Governor Dundas. They were to be heard at once! The conference had cleared its agenda for them! Everybody was ready to give immediate attention to what they had to say. It could hardly have been a more courteous reception. And that evening, when the Canadians went out again to Government House for the opening dinner of the conference, they must have been in a pleased and excited frame of mind.

Next day, Friday, at a little past ten o'clock in the morning, Cartier began the presentation of their case for federal union. He spoke for some time—a fairly carefully prepared address— and then, for the rest of the session, a general discussion followed, with the Maritimers asking questions, and the Canadians attempting to supply satisfactory answers.[24] It was the pattern which the meetings were to follow for the next few days. Cartier had given a general survey of the advantages which union might be expected to bring. Macdonald, in all probability, had planned to analyse the general character of the proposed federation; and next morning he got up to face the conference.[25] He was, in appearance, though not in age, nearly the youngest of the delegates. His pearl-grey trousers contrasted almost frivolously with the funereal expanse of black broadcloth around him. He was clean-shaven in the midst of a grizzled and rather forbidding forest of beards, side-whiskers, and moustaches. And the spare lines of his long, oval face, his high forehead, and the graceful mass of his dark curly hair gave him a sensitive, thoughtful, even vaguely poetic expression. He could be earnest and persuasive; but his frequent smile, which was charming, belied any suggestion of undue gravity. He was full of his subject. British history and constitutional practice, the precedents in the other colonies of the Empire, the tragic experience of the United States, and the brief experiments of the Southern Confederacy—he knew them all. His speech—probably the longest given at the conference, and certainly one of the most serious efforts he had ever made—lasted most of that day's session. He was a good advocate. But, as the Canadians knew very well, he was also a convivial host; and it was only appropriate that his speech should be followed by a lavish exhibition of Canadian hospitality. At three o'clock in the afternoon, all the delegates—thirty-three in number—adjourned to the *Queen Victoria* for an elaborate luncheon. They were still there, talking and drinking toasts, until late in the evening.

On Monday, after Brown and Galt had spoken at length on the economic and financial aspects of the proposed federation, a definite impression began to form rapidly in the minds of the delegates. The conference had almost ceased to be a meeting for the consideration of a Maritime legislative union; it was becoming a conference for the promotion of British North American federation. Everything that subsequently occurred seemed to confirm this tacitly accepted view. On Tuesday —before the Maritime delegates had devoted so much as a single session to their own separate project—the conference decided that it would adjourn two days later and proceed to Halifax. On Wednesday—when at long last the Maritimers got down to the subject for which the conference had ostensibly been called—a complete impasse was quickly reached as a result of Prince Edward Island's impossible demand that the capital of the united province should be established at Charlottetown. It was not that Macdonald and the Canadians were hostile to Maritime union—so long, of course, as it did not get in the way of federation. According to a rumour which the correspondent of the Halifax *Morning Chronicle* retailed to his readers, the Canadians were reported to be quite indifferent as to whether the Maritime Provinces should enter their proposed federation as one government or three.[26] But the Maritimers simply could not agree. And now the best chance of reaching an agreement had gone by. The conference was on the move. On Thursday, September 8, the delegates went off on an excursion to the northern part of the Island; and that night, when they returned, came the final ball.

The Province Building, where the conference had held its sittings, had been hurriedly prepared for the festivities during the brief absence of the delegates. The Legislative Council chamber had been fitted up as a reception room. In the legislative library—now a refreshment room of a rather different character—tea, coffee, sherry, claret, and champagne were available in copious quantities; and the Assembly, where the dancing was to take place, had been decorated with flags, flowers, and evergreens, with tall and cunningly placed mirrors, and with the most brilliant lighting effects which the superintendent of the local gas works could produce.[27] Macdonald was paired off with Mrs. Dundas, the wife of the Island's Lieutenant-Governor, for the first quadrille. And at one o'clock, when supper-time came, he took his seat to the right of the chairman, Colonel John Hamilton Gray of Prince Edward Island. In the eyes of everybody he had come to represent the visitors, and he responded first to the toast in their honour. He was beginning to win the Maritimers, as he had already won the Canadians and, from his point of view, the conference could hardly have been a more complete success. But now he was anxious for the next move, and ready to be gone. It was after three o'clock in the morning. The Canadians had agreed to carry the entire conference across the straits to the Nova Scotia mainland in their steamer; and the delegates, having torn themselves away from the ball, packed their bags frantically and hurried down to the harbour in the early hours of the morning. By Saturday they were supposed to be in Halifax.

The *Queen Victoria*—the "Confederate Cruiser" as the Islanders jocularly called her—was lying in the harbour, with steam up. But for some hours yet she could not stir. A dense fog—the like of which, the Maritimers assured their visitors, had not been seen in a matter of ten years—settled down over the Island and Northumberland Strait, obscuring everything. It was eight o'clock in the morning, and the delegates, who had had little, if any, rest in the previous twenty-four hours, were just about to sit down to a substantial breakfast, when at last the mist cleared sufficiently to permit the *Queen Victoria* to get away. Now it promised to be a fine day. The sea was smooth, the sky clear. A little after midday they reached

Pictou where most of the party disembarked, and started off
on a long overland excursion, by carriage and railway train,
which would show them something of the sights of Nova
Scotia. But Macdonald, along with McGee, Langevin, and
the secretaries, remained on board the steamer.[28] He enjoyed
a welcome rest and a good night's sleep as the *Queen Victoria*
ploughed her deliberate way along the North Shore and around
Cape Canso. It was noon on Saturday, September 10, before
they reached Halifax; but even so they were half an hour
earlier than the overland party.[29] That afternoon, at four
o'clock, the conference reconvened. As they discussed plans
and problems fully, with "visitors" and official delegates taking
an equal part in the debate, it began to look as if the ultimate
purpose which had brought the Canadians down to Charlottetown was about to be achieved. On Monday these hopes
were at last confirmed. At ten o'clock on the morning of that
day, the Maritime delegates held another meeting by themselves, in a final effort to come to some conclusion about Maritime union. The attempt failed; and within another hour, the
doors were opened and the Canadians admitted once more.
By the time the session adjourned at half-past one it had
reached the stupendous decision that a new conference, to
discuss a federal union for the whole of British North America,
was to be held at Quebec, beginning October 10. Macdonald
and his secretaries immediately began their hurried preparations.
A telegram was sent off to the premier of Newfoundland inviting that island to send representatives to the Quebec Conference. Another telegram was dispatched to Sir E. P. Taché
informing him of the decision that had been taken and promising that the *Queen Victoria* would be back in Quebec by
Sunday, September 18.[30] Now the matter was clinched.

That night, September 12, a dinner in honour of the
"Colonial Delegates" was given at the Halifax Hotel. Tupper
was in the chair. Macdonald sat next to the Lieutenant-
Governor of Nova Scotia; and it was he who responded to
the toast given by Tupper to "Colonial Union". His theme—
the theme which he had made peculiarly his own for the last
three years—was the need of a strong federation. He began

with the constitution of the United States. He praised its wisdom; he admitted its defects; "and it is for us," he told the great audience of Haligonians, "to take advantage by experience, and endeavour to see if we cannot arrive by careful study at such a plan as will avoid the mistakes of our neighbours." The British North American provinces could avoid the mistakes of their neighbours if only they could agree upon forming a strong federal union which would have all the rights of sovereignty except those that were specifically reserved to the local governments. "If we can only attain that object—a vigorous general government—we shall not be New Brunswickers, nor Nova Scotians, nor Canadians, but British Americans, under the sway of the British sovereign."[31] It was true, of course, he hastened to add, that they would have to consider what was practicable as well as what was desirable, that they must consult local ambitions, and that they should try to preserve the identity of the separate provinces. But this was not the note on which he ended. He told his audience that they could make British North America a great nation capable of defending itself. He reminded his listeners of "the gallant defence that is being made by the Southern Republic —at this moment they have not much more than four millions of men—not much exceeding our own numbers—yet what a brave fight they have made. . . ." The purpose of the British North American federalists was a noble one. Theirs was the object of "founding a great British Monarchy, in connection with the British Empire, and under the British Queen".[32]

The conference was over. The Canadians had achieved their original purpose; and, in their anxiety to prepare for Quebec, the last of their Maritime travels may have seemed a little superfluous. But they had visited both Prince Edward Island and Nova Scotia. It was extremely important, even from the point of view of the federation they were trying to create, to pay New Brunswick the courtesy of a visit as well; and on Wednesday, September 14, after a complete day of welcome rest, they set out on their travels once more. Most of the party went by rail to Windsor, and across the Bay of Fundy by the steamer *Emperor* to Saint John;[33] but once again

Macdonald adroitly dodged the public excursion for the peaceful quiet of the half-empty steamer *Queen Victoria*.[34] It was
foggy when they set out for the North Shore—a less unusual
circumstance at Halifax than it was at Charlottetown. The
ship was late in arriving at Shediac. He missed the train,
missed the big public dinner at Saint John, and only caught
up with the perambulating conference at Fredericton. By the
late afternoon of Friday the whole party was back once more
in Saint John, and there at last the delegations separated. The
Canadians left town for Shediac on a special train, and late
that night they finally boarded the *Queen Victoria* and were
off up the St. Lawrence.[35]

Once back in Quebec there was time only for the briefest
of rests. By the middle of the week the Cabinet was reunited
and hard at work again; and on September 22 Macdonald
wired Charles Tupper, the premier of Nova Scotia, that the
formal invitations to the Quebec Conference had been sanctioned and would go out the following day.[36] There was no
doubt about the answers. That had been decided at Halifax.
All the Maritime Provinces would certainly send delegations.
Their authority—as the Canadian ministry was careful to
point out in the order-in-council of September 23—was that
invaluable document, the dispatch of July 6, 1862, from the
Duke of Newcastle to the Lieutenant-Governor of Nova Scotia.[37]

The Canadians thought they could assume the permission
of the Colonial Secretary; and if, as seems probable, Macdonald
knew something of the private correspondence between Monck
and Cardwell, he doubtless realized that he could assume something a good deal more cordial than permission. For Cardwell
was being converted to the Canadian plan; and, as the promising Quebec Conference drew nearer, he was not in a mood
to be interested in the points of procedure raised by the officials
in the Colonial Office, or in the doubts and criticisms of the
Governors of Nova Scotia or New Brunswick. MacDonnell, of
Nova Scotia, who had doubted his own authority to appoint
delegates to the Charlottetown Conference, was similarly uncertain about his power to send representatives to Quebec, and
wrote in to the Colonial Office asking for permission. Cardwell,

in the comments which he made on this request, noted that
time was important, and added, "I have no hesitation in giving
the required permission."[38] Three days later, in a private letter
to Gordon of New Brunswick, he revealed much more clearly
how far he had already been won over to the Canadian scheme.
Gordon had written as quickly as possible, giving his criticisms
of the proposed union. Cardwell, in his reply, defended federation against this stout partisan of Maritime legislative union.
"Monck assures me," he wrote, "that there is no idea of that
feeble legislature which you so justly object to; that they wish
a strong central legislature with subordinate municipal Institutions."[39]

III

By Saturday, October 8, Macdonald was ready. The Canadian ministers, with the exception of McDougall and Cockburn,
were all at their posts at Quebec; and it was hoped that the
preparations for the guests were complete. Russell, the proprietor of one of the biggest hotels in Quebec, had been persuaded to keep his establishment open much later in the
season than was usual, with the idea of avoiding the shortage
of accommodation experienced at Charlottetown; and the Canadian Cabinet had planned a long series of dinners, *déjeuners*
and balls. Before midnight on Saturday a number of the
visitors had arrived.[40] The Newfoundland and Prince Edward
Island delegations, and Tilley and a few of the New Brunswickers, were already there. On Sunday the *Queen Victoria*,
which the Canadians had hospitably sent down east for the
transport of their guests, reached Quebec, with Sir Richard
MacDonnell and the remainder of the Maritime delegates on
board.[41] The conference was now complete. It was a large
company, considerably larger than that which had assembled
at Charlottetown, for the entire Canadian Executive Council
attended; and Newfoundland had, for the first time, sent a
delegation of two, and both Prince Edward Island and New
Brunswick were represented by two additional delegates. They

were all greeted with attentive and flattering welcomes, and were barely installed in their lodgings, when the parade of entertainments began. There was a dinner at the St. Louis Hotel on Saturday night, and on Sunday night both Monck and his Executive Council were entertaining again.

On Monday morning, October 10, the Quebec Conference assembled for its first official session. Its quarters were adequate, though hardly splendid. The original parliament buildings at Quebec had been burnt down over ten years before; and since then the government of Canada had had to be content with makeshift accommodation. The building which they then occupied had been constructed originally as a general post office.[42] It was an unpretentious, yet not undignified structure, three storeys in height, built of grey stone and in a simplified Renaissance style. Its situation was magnificent. Perched near the edge of the high cliff of the Upper Town, it commanded an immense perspective; and from the tall round-arched windows of the room on the second storey where the conference met, the delegates could see the wide river and its lofty banks recede slowly in tones of diminishing blue towards the remote horizon. It was a noble prospect. If only it had not rained so much! The weather, on the whole, had been fine for the Charlottetown Conference. But it broke at Quebec. The rain drummed relentlessly on the tall windows; it drowned the curves of the river and the long line of the Laurentians in pale washes of indigo.

From the start Macdonald exercised a directing control over affairs. He had had twenty years of parliamentary experience. Hewitt Bernard, the chief clerk in the office of the Attorney-General, Canada West, was appointed executive secretary to the conference on its second day; and the master and his confidential servant were an efficient, smoothly working machine. Other members of the Canadian delegation apparently took little active part in the proceedings; and even Cartier, who was often so voluble, remained relatively silent. But the easy pressure of Macdonald's guidance can be felt in a long list of motions, in a thick bundle of slips of paper on which the principal resolutions of the conference are set out in his clear, flowing hand. It was true that the plan was a Canadian one, the submission of the Canadian Cabinet as a whole; but he alone, of all the ministers, seemed to have a truly architectonic view of the entire structure. During the first two days he worked his hardest to get things going smoothly. They were critical days—days of formalities, of rather stiff beginnings, when it was essential to create an atmosphere of ease and friendly concord, and when an awkward motion or an unfortunate wrangle might prove absolutely fatal. Once, on the very first day, he barely avoided serious trouble. As soon as the conference was properly constituted, Edward Palmer of Prince Edward Island and Robert Dickey of Nova Scotia moved that in all questions but those of order each delegation should have one vote.[43] It was a clever manoeuvre on the part of these two men, who were so soon to become known as outspoken champions of provincial rights. The Canadians were at once put into a distinctly awkward position, for they could not possibly accept an arrangement which would give Canada only one vote as against the four possessed by the Atlantic provinces. At the very start, they were forced to argue—to insist upon the exceptional importance of their province. The debate was unfortunate, and it went on. It threatened—on the first day of the conference—to become a serious altercation. But Macdonald intervened. It was essential to divert the attention of the delegates—to awaken their enthusiasm, if possible. He moved, with Tilley seconding the motion, "that the best interests and present and future prosperity of British North America will be promoted by a Federal Union under the Crown of Great Britain, provided such union can be effected on principles just to the several provinces."[44]

Next morning, when the second session was well advanced, he got up to speak to this key resolution. Already, on that second day, he had been busy enough. He had sponsored a successful amendment to Palmer's motion, providing that Canada should have two votes, in virtue of its two historic divisions, Canada East and Canada West.[45] And, with Tilley seconding as on the previous day, he moved a series of six sensible resolutions for the order of proceedings.[46] The tension relaxed. The conference was warming up like a social function which people were now ready to make go. And yet, as he got to his feet to begin what was undoubtedly one of the greatest efforts of his career, he could have no certainty whatever as to the outcome. This was not the Canadian legislature. The men facing him were not his faithful and devoted Conservatives, willing to do almost anything at his bidding. They were virtually strangers, at best mere acquaintances, some of whom he had met for the first time as late as the previous Saturday, and only a very few of whom he had known before the Charlottetown Conference. As he looked at the rows of heavily bearded faces, the serious, non-committal faces of men who had come to hear and to judge, he could probably detect only a few which he knew already to be sympathetic. There was Charles Tupper, the premier of Nova Scotia, with his round youthful face encircled in a glossy frame of black hair and beard; there was Samuel Leonard Tilley, premier of New Brunswick, a short, neat man, with small, sharp features and bright eyes. These, and some of their followers, were already half converted; but in the eyes of others he could read the unmistakable signs of watchful hostility. Dickey, with his grey head set at an opinionated angle, might be the only determined sceptic in the approving Nova Scotia delegation; but the prevailing attitude of the group from Prince Edward Island was distinctly more unsympathetic. George Coles and Edward Palmer—a tall man with huge features and a bushy, ragged beard—had already been making embarrassing motions and awkward criticisms. They —and how many others?—might prove troublesome. Yet somehow a majority of delegates in a majority of delegations must be won. Among them the Atlantic provinces had four votes. If they wanted to, they could out-vote Canada two to one.

He began to talk. It was the speech for which he had been consciously preparing for the last five years, for which, indeed, his entire career had been an unconscious preparation.[47] All the material was ready in his mind. He could state the leading themes with precision and emphasis; he could develop them with the rich variations of detail and example. And two *motifs* which kept coming back and back, and sounding emphatically as if with the authority of the horns and percussion, were the need of a strong central government, and the desirability of maintaining British institutions and British parliamentary government. Their constitution, he told the delegates, must, in the words of Governor Simcoe, be an image and transcript of the British constitution; and their federal system must avoid those fatal errors which had wrecked the American experiment. By the existing practice of responsible government under the Crown, the British North American provinces had already escaped most of the defects of the American constitution; and the elected Legislative Council—the only feature of the congressional system which had been adopted, and that by two colonies only—might now be abandoned as a well-meaning but mistaken departure from British parliamentary rule. So far as basic institutions were concerned, only a few minor corrections and modifications were needed. They had but to return to the original purity of a well-known and well-loved system. But, for the federal aspects of their future constitution, a more sustained and comprehensive attempt must be made, Macdonald insisted, to create a central government strong enough to withstand the shocks that had divided the United States. The provinces, as parts of the British Empire, could not, of course, regard themselves as separate and distinct sovereignties; and, in the new constitution which was to unite them, nothing should be done to encourage these absurd pretensions. There should be regional, not provincial, equality, in the federal Upper House, or Legislative Council; and in the division of legislative authority, all powers—except the few granted to the local governments for local purposes only—should be reserved to strengthen the central government.

Macdonald finished his speech at a little after one o'clock; and before the day's session was over, his general motion, in favour of a British North American federation, had been carried unanimously and with a burst of applause that could be heard outside the hall.[48] It would be some time before such a united enthusiasm would be voiced again. The expositions and the generalities were over. It was time to come to particulars and debate. Macdonald brought up the subject of the composition of the Legislative Council; and at once the little provinces by the sea began a determined and protracted resistance. For them the importance of the federal Upper House was very great. They knew very well—from what had been said at Charlottetown—that the Canadians would propose a federal Assembly based on representation by population; and they were sadly aware of the fact that in such an Assembly the Maritime members would be heavily outnumbered. Their one hope of redressing the political balance lay in the Legislative Council. Why should they not demand provincial equality there, as the small American states had at Philadelphia? But it was precisely this unfortunate American precedent which Macdonald was determined to avoid if he possibly could; and his resolution divided British North America into three divisions or sections—Canada West, Canada East, and the four Atlantic provinces together—and gave each section an equal number of representatives in the federal Upper House.[49] This arrangement left the Maritime delegates deeply dissatisfied. In their view such representation was pitiably inadequate. They hungrily wanted more members in the Legislative Council. And yet—in somewhat the same fashion as the Canadians—they did not think in terms of the Philadelphia precedent, and did not dream of asserting their demand for larger representation as a right based on provincial sovereignty. A. A. Macdonald of Prince Edward Island hinted at the principle; but even he did not draw the logical conclusions from his premises.[50] The delegates from the east exhausted their ingenuity in producing a great variety of resolutions, all aimed at giving the Maritime Provinces a larger membership in the Council, and all unfortunately failing to win the united support of the Maritime delegations. Yet the debate continued—through Thursday, Friday, Saturday, and on into Monday, October 17. The Canadians tried to maintain an atmosphere of hearty conviviality by frequent dinners and balls; but the rain never seemed to stop falling, and, by the weekend, everybody was depressed by the weather and irritated by the standstill to which the conference seemed to have been brought.[51] Yet the Canadians stuck to their plan of sectional equality. And finally, on Monday, they won their point—though only by dint of a concession which certainly modified the rigour of the original scheme. Newfoundland was removed from the list of provinces making up the third, or Maritime, division and given four additional members in the Council in her own right.[52]

Macdonald had saved his principle. This compromise was nothing like provincial equality. But the victory had been purchased at the cost of a concession, and even the concession had not satisfied all the delegates. Several of the Prince Edward Islanders—Coles, Palmer and A. A. Macdonald—remained resentfully unconvinced; and the entire delegation may, as A. A. Macdonald claimed, have voted against the compromise. Regional equality in the Legislative Council—with four seats for Prince Edward Island—was bad enough; and the next Canadian resolution, which provided that the legislative councillors were to be appointed for life by the Crown under the great seal of the general government, was almost as objectionable.[53] Appointment by the federal power would surely make meaningless any remaining belief that the Legislative Council could act as the defender of regional, let alone provincial, rights; and Coles and A. A. Macdonald apparently opposed Macdonald's resolution, demanding instead appointment by the provincial legislatures.[54] The anger, and the number, of the Prince Edward Island malcontents was growing; but they still could not invariably swing their delegation. Macdonald's resolution was unanimously accepted; and, by the close of the Wednesday morning session, the remaining problems of the Legislative Council were satisfactorily settled. It was not until the evening of Wednesday, October 19, when the conference had already been in session for nearly nine days, that it finally reached the question of the composition of the federal Assembly. Then, at a stroke, the disgust of the Prince Edward Island delegation became general and complete. George Brown, appropriately enough, introduced a series of resolutions providing for representation by population in the new Lower House. Canada East was to have sixty-five seats, its existing strength in the legislature of United Canada, and the other provinces in proportion. This would give Canada West, the most populous province, a total of eighty-nine seats, and Prince Edward Island, the smallest numerically, a total of five. The entire Island delegation revolted against this contemptible number. The delegates—Reformers and Conservatives—were obviously quarrelling among themselves; but this did not prevent them from uniting in their outraged demand for more representation. They begged—basing their appeal on nothing much better than the difficulty of dividing the Island's three counties into five constituencies—for one more seat. But even this electoral morsel was denied them. And with this denial Prince Edward Island settled down into a state of sullen, permanent opposition.

The conference was nearing the end of its second week, and already the chances of making a comprehensive British North American union had grown slight indeed. Newfoundland, a little-known colony which so far had taken almost no part in the union movement, could certainly not be counted upon to join; and Prince Edward Island, whose delegation had now relapsed into a state of chronic negativism, would probably remain aloof. But, after all, the scheme would not fail from the absence of one or both of the two island colonies. The mainland provinces were the important provinces; and both Nova Scotia and New Brunswick had accepted the compromise over the Legislative Council, and had supported Canada consistently in the battle for representation by population in the Lower House. The first part of the new structure—the federal institutions of government—was almost finished, and finished, in the main, as Macdonald wanted it.

Yet the division of legislative powers—the most important part of the whole work, from his point of view—was still to come. For years he had been arguing that, above all else, British North America must reject the theory of the United States, and grant residuary power to the central government; and on Friday, October 21, when he got up to move a series of resolutions on the powers of the federal legislature, this major principle of his scheme came up for acceptance or rejection.[55] No crucial objections appeared in Friday's debate; and on Monday, October 24, Mowat, for the Canadians, introduced a complementary set of resolutions on the powers of the local legislatures. At this point trouble broke out. George Coles moved that "the local legislatures shall have power to make all laws not given by this conference to the General Legislature expressly".[56] It was the exact opposite of Macdonald's principle.

Prince Edward Island had done it again. Though most of the members of its delegation were morally outside the conference, they were still physically a part of it. They could still perplex its proceedings. They could fight for the sheer pleasure of fighting, though victory would scarcely have mollified them; and Coles, once again, had been successful in putting the issue in its sharpest form. Yet if Coles and the Prince Edward Island malcontents had been alone, it would not have mattered so much, for their attitude was now notorious. But Coles was not alone. He was joined by E. B. Chandler, a member of the New Brunswick delegation, who argued strongly that the subjects given to the provincial legislatures were so insignificant that the union would, in effect, be a legislative union. Tupper, of Nova Scotia, got up to answer him. Macdonald must have been pleased by Tupper's support. It was better that, if possible, Maritimers should reply to Maritimers, and Tupper argued in his best downright style, asserting stoutly that the closer the approximation to legislative union, the better pleased he would be.[57] Yet the debate dragged on with angry inconclusiveness. Chandler complained that his argument was being answered, not on its merits, but on the basis of what was alleged to have been decided at Charlottetown. Macdonald saw that the case for his sacred principle had not really been made and, late in the long evening of discussion, he got up to reply. He was desperately serious. There was a strange note of extreme vehemence in his phrases. He drove Coles's resolution back to its origin in the American constitution. He told the conference that to grant residuary powers to the local legislatures would be to adopt the worst error of the American constitution, the error upon which all writers had expatiated, the error whose awful consequences de Tocqueville had foretold. "A source of radical weakness" would be introduced into the new constitution of British North America. "It would ruin us," Macdonald declared emphatically, "in the eyes of the civilized world."[58]

The appeal succeeded. In the end, no provincial delegation, not even that of Prince Edward Island, voted against Macdonald's principle. It was his last great triumph in the conference. Galt carried the main burden of presenting and defending the Canadian government's financial proposals; and although Macdonald was deeply preoccupied with the delicate problems of uniting the common-law provinces with Canada East and its very different legal tradition, these were settled fairly easily, without any serious disagreement in public. By Wednesday, the delegates, although still considering fresh items, were already engaged in the task of reviewing and rounding out their work; and on the late afternoon of Thursday, October 27, the conference drew to a hurried close. The room, with its tall windows and its magnificent view, now darkening rapidly in the late October twilight, was full of lassitude, of scarcely concealed impatience, of a sense of impending departure. Yet also present, and perhaps even dominant, was a surprised, excited realization of accomplishment. Less than two months before, Macdonald had set out, a self-invited guest, for Charlottetown. Now all the provinces, with the doubtful exception of Prince Edward Island, had apparently agreed to the Canadian scheme for federation. The union was to embrace not only the existing provinces but, in the end, the whole of British North America; in the ambitious plans of the delegates, it was to become a transcontinental federation. During the last hours of the last session, the conference declared that the communications with the North West Territories, and the improvements required for the development of its trade with the seaboard, were subjects of the highest importance which should be attacked as soon as the finances of the new federation would permit; and it was provided that British Columbia and Vancouver Island, as well as the North West, should be admitted into the union upon terms agreeable to all parties. Then, amid a flurry of last moment revisions and formalities, the conference came to an end. Already, at four o'clock, a large party, chiefly Maritimers, had left in a special train provided by Brydges. A second group, including about half the members of the Canadian Cabinet, departed by the regular Grand Trunk Railway night express at nine o'clock.[59] Among them was Macdonald. In the mass of papers which weighted his luggage were all but three of the seventy-two resolutions which subsequently came to be known as the "Quebec Plan". The conference was over.

IV

Yet it was obvious, of course, that the real work of making Confederation had barely begun. The provincial legislatures would have to accept the plan; the Colonial Office would have to approve it; and the elaborate bill necessary for carrying out the decisions of the conference would have to be drafted and pushed through the imperial Parliament. As Macdonald faced the future, a long, grim line of dispatches, interviews, speeches, debates, elections and conferences seemed to stretch forward interminably until it disappeared at length over the edge of his mental horizon. Yet one small but pressing need stood out in the immediate foreground. The Quebec Conference, like the Charlottetown Conference before it, had met behind closed doors; and unless something were done fairly quickly to enlighten and conciliate public opinion, it would be all too easy to disparage the federal plan as the work of a gang of guilty conspirators. The Canadians had already been presented to Maritime audiences in the tour which followed the Charlottetown Conference. Now a similarly modest triumphal progress was to introduce the Maritime delegates to the Canadian public, and to disclose, in discreet generalities, the main provisions of the Quebec plan. Brown hurried back to Toronto to make preparations for the reception there; Macdonald was selected to preside over the proceedings at the new capital, Ottawa; and Cartier was the obvious choice as master of ceremonies at Montreal. At Montreal, which was the first port of call, the delegates found time to hold a final official session of the conference, and to pass the three supplementary Montreal resolutions, in one of which the Queen was requested "to determine the rank and name of the Federated Provinces". This, appropriately enough, was almost the last official action of the conference, and the rest of the proceedings were purely social. Macdonald, clad in his dark-blue civil uniform, attended the ball on Friday night. But he was apparently not present at the long-drawn-out *déjeuner* on Saturday afternoon, and Cartier gave the formal reply to the toast to the Canadian ministry.[60]

Macdonald was worn out. For two months he had been almost continuously under pressure; and during the last three weeks, his work had been incessant. By far the biggest part of the burden at the conference had fallen upon his straining shoulders; and the inevitable reaction had already set in when the steamer carrying the touring delegates started up the Ottawa River early in the morning of Monday, October 31. The day was crisply cool. There were only a few hours of fitful sunshine, and the chill autumn night had fallen long before the steamer reached Ottawa, where a shouting, welcoming crowd of citizens had carried the delegates off in triumph to Russell's Hotel. Macdonald had not visited the broad promontory, which was soon to be known as Parliament Hill, for some time at least, and possibly not since the Prince of Wales had laid the cornerstone of the central building back in the late summer of 1860. Now the lines of the three great structures were beginning to emerge clearly from the chaos of scaffoldings and building material. But the roof of the Legislative Council chamber was only half finished, the roof of the Assembly room was as yet untouched; and next day, when the delegates sat down to a luncheon given by the contractors, they had to be accommodated in the future "picture gallery", which at least had a covering, and which was decorated bravely, for all the cool, autumnal weather, with wreaths of flowers.

Yet the buildings were—as Brown had declared them to be during the summer—"surpassingly fine". The site was magnificent. From the edge of Parliament Hill, Macdonald was able to show his visitors another enormous perspective. Below, down an almost sheer drop, lay the Ottawa River. A little distance to the west, it plunged into the vast agitations of the Chaudière Falls, recovered itself, and swept serenely past Parliament Hill and away to the north-east. On the other side, the green lush river meadows ended abruptly in dense masses of pine trees, which climbed up, in tier after tier of darkening green, to the long, low, blue line of the Laurentian Plateau. Here geography confronted politics. Here the men who had made a federal union on paper came face to face with the ancient geological system which covered nearly half of British North America, and which in some way must be conquered before a transcontinental federation could be achieved in fact. Macdonald was to spend the rest of his life in these tasks; but now he could not finish the first speech he ever tried to make in the Canadian parliament. He was supposed to have been sickening with the illness that kept him away from the rest of the triumphal tour. Perhaps he had been drinking. He managed to get out a few of his casual, friendly phrases. And then, without warning, he stopped. He could not continue, and, after an awkward pause, Galt got up to reply in his place to the toast to the Canadian ministry.[61]

At the conference, he had carried almost everything. Now he was wearied of it all. Next day, Wednesday, November 2, while the special train carrying the delegates continued westward towards Toronto, he got off gratefully at Kingston. The sight-seeing and the speech-making went on without him. He stayed where he was, needing the relaxation; and the only trouble was that he had such a few days in which to lounge about and recruit his strength. By Sunday the last of the Maritime delegates were on their way back east; and on Tuesday, November 8, the Canadian Cabinet began to reassemble at Quebec. There was a great deal still to be done. And the first task, which must be completed before the union scheme was submitted to the provincial legislatures, was to secure the approval of the Colonial Office. Monck had already sent the Seventy-two Resolutions over to the imperial government, and had written a long, confidential dispatch in their support.[62] But from the first it had been planned to send a confidential envoy to consult with the imperial authorities on the question of union, and, as far back as the coalition negotiations in June, Brown had been selected for the mission. Brown's departure had been several times postponed while the Charlottetown and Quebec Conferences dragged on; and it was postponed a last time to permit the Cabinet to assemble once again and to come to some conclusions on the problems of Rupert's Land and of defence—two problems which were intimately related to each other and to Confederation, and which were certain to come up in the discussions at the Colonial Office. Answers must be sent back to Cardwell. Brown must be briefed for his mission. On the night of November 9, the special train bearing Macdonald pulled in at the railway station at Levis.[63]

The near prospect of a general federal union of British North America certainly had its influence on the Cabinet's decisions. It was true that in the matter of the Hudson's Bay Company the ministers still kept on coolly insisting that all the cost of extinguishing the monopoly must be borne by the imperial government; but, on the other hand, they showed a livelier enthusiasm for westward expansion, and a new readiness to co-operate with the British government in opening up communications with the Territories, and in promoting their settlement and providing for their local government.[64] These western gestures were still rather vaguely hearty; but in the matter of defence, the Canadians evidently felt obliged to be a good deal more definite. Cardwell's dispatch of August 6, which had asked the government of Canada to set out its military proposals, had lain for months unanswered; and Colonel Jervois, the author of the report which had prompted Cardwell's inquiries, had travelled across the ocean again expressly to help the Canadian ministers make up their minds. On October 12, when the Quebec Conference had barely begun, he had had a long interview with them. He had gone away to work out answers to a series of practical questions put to him by the Cabinet. But before he had finished this supplementary report, an event occurred which suddenly sharpened everybody's interest in defence. Early on the morning of Thursday, October

20, when the delegates were just about to begin their last attempt to persuade the offended Prince Edward Islanders to accept five seats in the federal Assembly, Monck received a highly excited telegram from Gregory Smith, the Governor of the State of Vermont, which seemed to suggest that a small-sized army of desperadoes from Canada had been committing wholesale murder in the town of St. Albans.⁶⁵ Subsequently, when this intelligence had been somewhat deflated, it turned out that on October 19 a small party of about twenty-five ununiformed Confederate soldiers had indeed descended from Canadian territory upon the town of St. Albans in Vermont. There they destroyed a little property, robbed the banks, wounded two people, one of them fatally, and escaped over the border again into Canada.

Macdonald must have been reminded of the American invasions of his young manhood. In one alone of these invasions —the American descent on the stone windmill near Prescott— the Canadians had suffered as many casualties as they had in the Battle of Queenston Heights; and to regard the trifling incidents of the St. Albans "raid" in the same light as this wholesale and gratuitous slaughter must have seemed, to the men of Macdonald's generation, to be a monstrous impertinence. Yet the St. Albans raid, whatever its real significance, was certain to be politically important. For one thing it came at a time when American dislike of British, and British American, behaviour during the Civil War had already reached alarming proportions; and, for another, it unfortunately happened to occur when the American presidential election was only three weeks away. "We must be prepared," Lyons wrote from Washington to Earl Russell, "for demonstrations of a *'spirited foreign policy'* by Mr. Seward during the next fortnight, for electioneering purposes."⁶⁶ And, indeed, for the next few days there was a tremendous hubbub in the United States. General Dix, the American Commander on the north-eastern frontier, ordered his men to pursue the St. Albans raiders, if necessary, into Canadian territory. And, a little later, Seward instructed Adams, the American minister in London, to give the six-months' notice required for the abrogation of the Convention of 1817, limiting naval forces on the Great Lakes. "In conversation both with Mr. Burnley and me," Lyons reported to Russell, "he [Seward] said it would be impossible to resist the pressure which would be put upon the Government to abrogate the Reciprocity Treaty also, if these invasions from Canada continued."[67] All this—and most of it was known unofficially in Quebec at an early date—must certainly have seemed serious to Macdonald. Yet, on the other hand, the signals were not all for danger. In short order the Canadian police captured thirteen of the raiders; and Monck was thanked by Seward for the zeal and efficiency which his government had shown. In a very few days the commotion in the United States died down.

The Canadian ministry, therefore, took up the subject of defence in circumstances which were certainly pressing—they had been that for years—but which had not yet become unusually urgent. On November 10, the day after Macdonald had arrived at Quebec, Jervois presented his supplementary report.[68] This formidable document called for an armed force of 110,000 men, and the construction of large fortifications at Quebec, Montreal, and Kingston, at an estimated cost of £1,754,000. As they contemplated these monstrous figures, Macdonald and the other members of the Cabinet must have experienced a sudden access of colonial feeling. Wars, they insisted in a long minute of Council, were the result of imperial policy.[69] Defence, they argued, was properly an imperial concern. Canada was totally incapable of providing the enormous forces and footing the huge bills which Jervois thought necessary; and federal union, which promised in the end to strengthen British North American defences, was at the moment largely an embarrassment, for it would be dangerous to prejudice the Quebec scheme with heavy military commitments. Much of this argument was in the traditional Canadian manner. Yet the whole minute of Council was far from being an exercise in colonial irresponsibility and procrastination. The Cabinet agreed to construct the works at Montreal, the cost of which Jervois had estimated at £443,000, provided Great Britain would undertake the Quebec fortifications and supply the armament for both. In addition, the ministers promised to propose a vote of a million dollars for the militia in the next session of parliament.

The programme was complete. Brown was well armed, surely very acceptably armed, for his encounter with the Colonial Office; and on Wednesday, November 16, he sailed from New York for England. There was nothing that could be done now but wait and hope for the best from the Colonial Office. In the meantime, Macdonald kept himself occupied in clearing off the arrears of his departmental work and in preparing for the next session of the provincial parliament. The main business of the session would certainly be the consideration of the Quebec Resolutions. At the conference the delegates had generally agreed that it would be best to follow British practice and to submit the resolutions to the provincial legislature rather than to the people. And Macdonald was only occasionally called upon to reassure some of his followers who had perhaps expected a plebiscite. "It would be unconstitutional and anti-British to have a plebiscite," he told Samuel Amsden. "If by petitions and public meetings Parliament is satisfied that the Country do not want the measure, they will refuse to adopt it. If on the other hand Parliament sees that the country is in favour of the Federation, there is no use in an appeal to it. Submission of the complicated details to the Country is an obvious absurdity."[70] No, parliament would have to settle the matter; and they decided to call it, a little earlier than usual, for January 19, 1865. He noted that Dorion had rushed into print with a manifesto against the Quebec scheme, and that the *Rouges* and John Sandfield Macdonald were "beating up for recruits everywhere".[71] But he had very little doubt about the easy passage of the resolutions through the Canadian legislature. Yet what was done at Quebec was now only a beginning. He was already learning to think of the other provinces; and the news from the other provinces was far from reassuring. Not a word had come from Prince Edward Island. Shea, of Newfoundland, had written optimistically but somewhat vaguely, about the prospects in the other island colony. Tupper, who was usually so sanguine, admitted frankly that he and his colleagues had met "a strong opposition" in Nova Scotia.[72] But the very worst news of all came from New Brunswick. Tilley wrote briefly to say that the feeling in his province against the Quebec plan was so strong that he had been obliged to promise that the government would not press the resolutions in the existing House.[73] The New Brunswick Assembly was due to expire shortly in any case; now it was decided to dissolve it within a few months. Almost at once the Quebec plan would have to stand the rough passage of a provincial election.

"Will you let me know what you hear from the British government?" Tupper inquired anxiously of Macdonald. As their difficulties grew, the provincial leaders naturally looked to London for encouragement and support. What would the Colonial Office think of their federal scheme? The Maritime premiers may have been quite uncertain; but Macdonald very probably knew, for Cardwell, in his private letters, had been at no pains to conceal his views. The Colonial Secretary had, in fact, made up his mind fairly quickly, and yet independently of the pressure of unusual circumstances. The real crisis in the affair of the St. Albans raid did not begin until the middle of December. The first news of the raid itself did not reach the Colonial Office until November 10, and long before that time Cardwell's declared preferences were quite definite. He had reached them, indeed, at a time when, in his own view, Anglo-American relations were in a much better state than had been previously expected. "If McClellan had carried the Presidency," he wrote to Gladstone on October 27, "and peace had been made on Southern and pro-slavery conditions: which was a sufficiently possible contingency not to be excluded from our view—the immediate danger to our small force in Canada might have been considerable. That hazard does not seem to be great now."[74] It continued to seem only a small hazard for a few weeks longer. On November 23, Adams gave notice of the abrogation of the Rush-Bagot Convention; but this, by itself, was not sufficient to cause any great alarm, and in any case it came too late to have any appreciable effect on the Cabinet's decision on British American union. The Quebec Resolutions arrived at the Colonial Office on November 22, and four days later, in a private letter to Gordon of New Brunswick, Cardwell was predicting the government's unanimous and enthusiastic approval.[75]

Earl Russell, the Foreign Secretary, had expressed his preference for a federal union of British America over two years before, while Newcastle was still at the Colonial Office.[76] And Cardwell seems never to have believed in any other solution but the strong federation which Macdonald and Monck desired. "My principal fear," he wrote to Gladstone on October 27, "is that the selfish interests of the men in the smaller Provinces should lead them to insist on *federation* as against *union*:— on the policy of Jefferson as against that of Washington and Hamilton;—on a policy which would run B.N. America upon the rock on which the Union has gone to pieces." He was ready to admit in advance all the criticisms which could be brought against federations in general. But, like Macdonald and Monck, he had come to believe that a federation might be made sufficiently strong and centralized so as to approximate to a legislative union. "Of course," he wrote realistically to Gordon, "it signifies very little what name is employed. What we wish is a central and strong government as distinguished from a number of small states united by a feeble bond."[77] Monck had convinced him that this was what the Canadians intended. He was prepared to accept their plan in advance; and in a private letter of November 14—over a week before the Quebec Resolutions reached the Colonial Office—Monck thanked him for the consistent support that the Colonial Secretary had afforded.[78] Cardwell was not only giving the Canadians direct encouragement at every stage; he was also defending them indirectly by rebuking their critics. Usually he was polite enough with Gordon, the fervent advocate of Maritime union; but once he ventured a sardonic reference to the "selfish interests" of the Maritimers. "The bold, ambitious leaders of public opinion in Canada," he wrote on October 14, "are more likely to wish for a complete fusion, which would extend their powers, than are the ministry and parliament men of New Brunswick, whose occupation would in that case be ended."[79]

His conclusions had already been reached. There was no hesitation or delay. On December 3, the Colonial Secretary sent off the public dispatch which, in almost enthusiastic terms, announced Great Britain's warm acceptance of the Quebec Resolutions.

Chapter Fourteen

Checkmate

I

Yet before Cardwell's inspiring dispatch arrived, real trouble had broken out for Canada. It had been coming closer, despite the false appearances of calm, ever since the St. Albans raid on October 19. The American people had, it was true, temporarily dismissed the thoughts of the raid from their minds and had returned to the gorgeous excitement of the presidential election; but they had done so on the evident assumption that a savage retribution would be meted out to the raiders. "There can be no doubt," Burnley wrote to Russell from Washington, "that considerable irritation exists in the minds of the American people on the general subject of these repeated raids from Canada, and I am afraid that if the Canadian Law Courts should look upon the men concerned in the St. Albans affair as regular commissioned Belligerents rather than as criminals to be given up under the Extradition Treaty that we may expect a very serious outburst of feeling against Her Majesty's Government."[1] Seward had, of course, peremptorily demanded that the "criminals" be given up to his government; and Monck had temperately replied that as soon as the proofs required by the extradition treaty had been furnished, the prisoners would be handed over to the American authorities.[2] Yet, on December 13, when the question of the extradition of the raiders at last came up for a preliminary hearing before Magistrate Coursol of Montreal, a most unexpected and astounding event occurred. Coursol never got to the crucial point of whether the raiders were extraditable criminals or regularly commissioned officers of a country whose belligerent rights Great Britain had recognized. He simply asserted want of jurisdiction on the ground of technical defects in the British and Canadian statutes implementing the Ashburton Treaty.[3] And he dismissed the raiders, who promptly walked out of the court free men.

Both as a lawyer and as a politician, Macdonald was seriously annoyed with this judgment. "The unhappy and mistaken decision of Coursol at Montreal," he wrote, "has had a most unfortunate tendency. From the fact of his being called 'Judge' Coursol, his decision is considered a judicial one in the United States. He was however merely acting in his capacity as police magistrate, and altogether mistook his duty, when he presumed to judge as to his right to discharge those prisoners. It was his duty to assume that he had the authority under the statute, and the question of jurisdiction should only have been brought up to be solemnly decided by the Superior Courts."[4] It was all very regrettable, and, as Macdonald realized, its consequences were likely to be extremely unfortunate. But even he may possibly not have been prepared for the violence of the reaction in the United States. The American press returned at once to that continental military imperialism which was one of its best loved themes. The conquest of Canada was earnestly advocated as a suitable small exercise for the victorious union army after the conclusion of the American Civil War. The American executive and the American Congress, which had just reassembled, revealed the national displeasure in actions which were almost as pugnacious as the words of the newspapers. On December 17, for the first time in the relations of British North America and the United States, the American executive issued an order requiring passports from all persons entering the republic from the provinces. In his message to Congress at the opening of the session, Lincoln had already revealed the fact that the United States had given the required notice for the abrogation of the Rush-Bagot Convention; and almost at once both the Senate and the House of Representatives took up the question of the

Reciprocity Treaty.⁵ There was, unfortunately, not the slightest doubt that the treaty would be abrogated just as soon as it was legally possible for the United States to terminate it. The sky was by now nearly opaque with threatening gloom. And the one pale gleam of hope lay in the fact that General Dix's order had been disavowed at Washington—a disavowal which certainly came belatedly, but at a fortunate moment, in the end.

Macdonald watched all these developments with his accustomed calm. He was not inclined to get excited. He refused to be hustled by circumstances into heroics of one kind or another. "We must perform our duty, however, irrespective of the smiles or frowns of any foreign body," he told one correspondent, "and will never be hurried into extra exertions by proclamations like those of General Dix, or prevented by any feeling of indignation from carrying our laws into full force."⁶ In a few rapid and energetic moves, the government tried to cope with the new situation. The released St. Albans raiders were pursued once more and most of them were recaptured in New Brunswick. To prevent a recurrence of the raids, nearly 2,000 volunteers were called up and stationed at appropriate points along the border. In addition—and this was the most novel of Macdonald's measures—it was decided "to organize a detective and preventive police force, for the purpose of watching and patrolling the whole frontier from Toronto to Sarnia. . . ." This force which was soon in its modest fashion to become a most efficient instrument of counter-espionage and prevention, was put under the control of a newly appointed stipendiary magistrate, Gilbert McMicken. "He is a shrewd, cool, and determined man," Macdonald wrote, "who won't easily lose his head, and who will fearlessly perform his duty."⁷ McMicken was to deserve every word of the encomium which Macdonald wrote for him.

"I think," wrote Burnley to Russell, "we have got safely out of the Canadian troubles thanks to Lord Monck's extremely energetic and conciliatory policy towards this country, which has been duly appreciated by Mr. Seward and the cabinet. . . ."⁸ There was no doubt whatever about Canadian effort. But as Burnley observed, it was equally true that "with all this there

is a general latent feeling of dislike to the English which it
would be useless to disguise. . . ." Macdonald was well aware
of this old animosity. He realized that the new passport regulations and the threatened abrogation of the Rush-Bagot Convention and the Reciprocity Treaty had all been prompted
largely by the desire for political retaliation. It was useless to
hope that commercial considerations, or any kind of reasoned
argument, would have the slightest effect. At the moment,
the republic was like an aged and irritable female relative, who
had been deeply offended by behaviour lacking in deference,
and whom it was quite impossible to propitiate. Thomas Swinyard, of the Great Western Railway, and Brydges, of the Grand
Trunk, were in despair at the effect of the passports on their
traffic; and Swinyard wanted an immediate effort made at
Washington to have the restriction removed. Macdonald thought
such a proposal quite unwise. He believed that, so far as
immediate steps were concerned, it would be best to appoint
agents on the Canadian side who would make it their business
to establish friendly relations with the American passport officers.
As for the future, the right policy would be to put up with the
annoyance, and try to bring private influences to bear at
Washington.[9] "I think," he wrote to Swinyard, "it would be
extremely impolitic and, indeed, defeat our object, if the
Canadian Government went on its knees to the United States
Government for the purpose of procuring a revocation of the
late order. It would give Mr. Seward an exaggerated idea of
the inconvenience and the loss sustained by Canada and would
be kept up as a means of punishment or for purposes of coercion. The true way to succeed is for the Canadian Government to assume an indifferent tone in the matter, leaving it
to the Western States and private solicitation to effect the
purpose."[10]

In the meantime, while relations with the United States
still remained in this state of worrying uncertainty, the Confederation scheme had run into several large snags. Tilley's
unhappy admission that he had agreed not to submit the Quebec Resolutions to the existing House in New Brunswick was
the most disturbing piece of news. But the advices, public and

private, which now began to reach Macdonald from Nova Scotia, were almost as bad. At Quebec, the cheerful Tupper had been fairly confident of the success of the scheme in his native province. He felt that he could count not only upon the united support of his government and his party, but also upon the favourable influence of A. G. Archibald and Jonathan McCully, two prominent members of the Reform party, who had been delegates to the Quebec Conference and who were enthusiastic supporters of the Seventy-two Resolutions. The fact that McCully was the editor of the Halifax *Morning Chronicle* served to ensure that this most important of the Reform newspapers would be on the side of Confederation. And as for Joseph Howe, the leader of the Reform party and prime minister of the previous government, Tupper assumed, with some justification at least, that the old tribune's appointment as imperial Fisheries Commissioner would neutralize him fairly effectively, particularly if the imperial government could be persuaded to give vigorous support to the Quebec scheme.[11] These confident expectations lasted for a little while after Tupper's return from Quebec to Halifax. He was still fairly complacently optimistic at the end of the second week in December. He admitted the existence of "a strong opposition"; but he was frankly delighted with the success of its first public meeting for Confederation, and full of hope for the future. By the beginning of January this note of lusty confidence had changed. "We have had hard work here," he confessed to Macdonald. "A great body of the leading men comprising the most wealthy merchants in the city are exerting themselves to the utmost to defeat the scheme. Archibald and McCully have stood by me like trumps and I hope we will carry the day."[12] Hope—a little battered—was still surviving. Archibald and McCully were a stout support. But their old leader, Joseph Howe, had tossed away his neutrality as a civil servant and had flung himself into the struggle against the Quebec scheme. As Tupper confessed ruefully, his old opponent had become overnight the chief centre of the opposition to Confederation in Nova Scotia.

As the circle of Macdonald's influence widened the number

and variety of his enemies increased. He probably knew something about Howe's career, for he made it his business to inform himself generally about British North American politics. He may even have met Howe briefly in London on one of his expeditions to the Colonial Office. But in 1864 the two men can hardly have been more than mere acquaintances at best. And then, almost overnight, a virtual stranger, a blurred recollection, a name in the papers, became one of the most important figures in Macdonald's career. The two men belonged almost to two different political generations, though in age they were separated by only a little over ten years. That winter, on December 13, Howe turned sixty. It was not a great age, though he had always used and abused his strength with careless prodigality. But it was an age at which, in the life of any man, a settled and inescapable sense of dissatisfaction might at length become an agonizing conviction of failure. His consciousness of his own powers, his relish for important people and great affairs, his everlasting and grinding need for money, had kept him fluttering around the bright flame of office and position like a moth, at once attracted, wounded and repelled. Three years before, he had attained the premiership—the highest executive office in the province then open to a colonial—but without exhilaration, and without much conviction of great work still to be done. For a long time now he had manoeuvred and struggled and humiliated himself for the sake of an imperial appointment which would be commensurate with his talents; and at long last he had been awarded the Commissionership of Fisheries, a post not indeed completely insignificant, but of an appalling mediocrity, a mediocrity made all the more emphatic by a salary which was just big enough to compel him to accept it. Cooped up in H.M.S. *Greyhound* or H.M.S. *Lily* for two or three months of every year, with nothing but the company of the captain and his own drunken secretary, fishing, shooting ducks and curlew, writing unimportant reports which nobody of any political importance would ever consider for a moment—this was the mean way in which he was dragging out the last years of his life.[13] This was the almost sordid duty which had kept him from accepting the invitation to

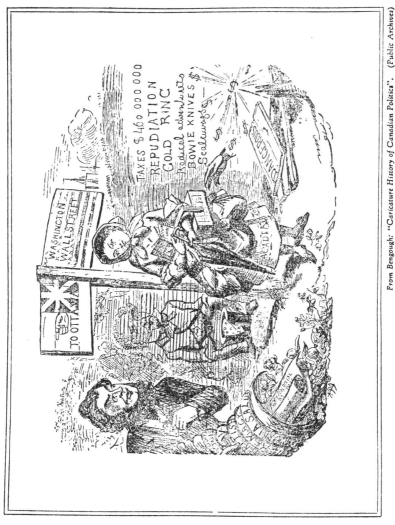

From Bengough: *"Caricature History of Canadian Politics".* (Public Archives)

CROSS ROADS

SHALL WE GO TO WASHINGTON FIRST, OR HOW(E)?

attend the conference on Maritime union. It had been Charles Tupper, and not Joseph Howe, who had gone to Charlottetown and Quebec, who had argued, debated and resolved, who had spoken for Nova Scotia and accepted the honours due to her. Others had always occupied the commanding positions at the crucial moments; others had known how to bring the dream and the reality together. He brooded, his big face, with its rather coarse features, once ennobled by vitality and conviction, now dulled and heavy with care and disillusionment and fatigue. In his absence, without his help, without his knowledge, others had dared to rearrange British North America to their liking. Well, they could not. They could not, for he, Joseph Howe, would prevent them.

He did not believe in Confederation. It was true that in his facile—too facile—way, he had spoken rhetorically of a British North American dominion stretching from the Atlantic to the Pacific Ocean. But he was so much a Nova Scotian, so spiritually a part of the old British maritime world of "ships, colonies, and commerce", that these visions of transcontinental empires could be only transitory and artificial. The federation which was closest to his heart was a federation of the whole British Empire, with a great federal imperial parliament at Westminster.[14] It was this old belief, sharpened now by his haunting sense of neglect and failure and, perhaps, by the tormented urge to undo the work of others more successful than himself, that drove him into the last unhappy crusade of his career. Once his decision was taken, events followed rapidly. McCully was deposed from the editorship of the *Morning Chronicle*. Annand, a stout anti-Confederationist, reigned in his place; and early in January the first of a series of articles by Howe called *The Botheration Scheme*, attacking Confederation, appeared in Annand's newspaper. Rallied and emboldened by Howe's leadership, the anti-Confederation forces drew together in an imposing array, and Tupper suddenly found himself upon the defensive. Howe demanded that an appeal should be made to the people on the Quebec scheme. It was, in the circumstances, an extremely adroit move, which took advantage of the weakness of Tupper's position—a weakness which had been caused by Tilley's reluctant consent to dissolve the New Brunswick Assembly and go to the country.

If only Tilley could be persuaded not to give the anti-Confederationists everywhere the benefit of this fatal example! "I hope you will assist me," Tupper wrote to Macdonald, "in pressing Tilley to put it through without going first to the people."[15] Macdonald was thoroughly convinced of the unwisdom of Tilley's decision. He always maintained that Tilley should have held a final session of the legislature, and had the Quebec scheme discussed, so that the subject would at least have been understood by the people. "It would have been much better, as you say," he wrote later to a correspondent in New Brunswick, "to have called the House together, and to have had the subject thoroughly ventilated, and then to have tried the vote. If the vote had been carried, all well, if not, you still had recourse to the people."[16] There was, in short, almost everything to gain and nothing to lose in submitting the Quebec Resolutions to the House in a final session. Macdonald certainly considered Tilley's plan of campaign timorous and inept. But, at the same time, he characteristically assumed that Tilley must make his own decisions, for Tilley alone was in full possession of all the relevant facts. And, indeed, the premier of New Brunswick was already hard pressed: by his own colleagues and followers; by an opposition which was already exploiting the growing dislike of the Quebec scheme; and, last but not least, by the Governor himself, Arthur Hamilton Gordon.

Gordon was another one of the personalities from the Maritime Provinces who played an important part in the troubled passage of the Quebec scheme. Macdonald had met him first at Charlottetown, where Gordon had appeared for the early part of the conference. In 1864, he was still a comparatively young man, thirty-five years old, with a long, lugubrious, bearded face and sad, heavily-lidded eyes. The son of the Earl of Aberdeen, Prime Minister of Great Britain from 1852 to 1855, young Gordon had been private secretary, first to his father, and then to that increasingly important architect of the new Liberalism, William Ewart Gladstone; and Gladstone, who kept up an intermittent correspondence with his protégé, always saluted him affectionately as "Arthur". New Brunswick was Arthur's first colonial appointment. He cannot be said to have liked it. He was not long in Fredericton before he conceived a marked distaste for colonial politicians in general, whom he regarded as uncouth, illiterate, corrupt, and curiously obstinate in holding opinions different from his own. When Cardwell, hoping to mollify him, reported the flattering tribute that George Brown had paid to the Lieutenant-Governor of New Brunswick during his visit to the Colonial Office, Gordon was not greatly impressed by Brown's compliments. "They at least shew," he conceded tartly, "that I succeeded in carefully concealing from him my true opinion—viz., that he is the most dangerous and most unscrupulous demagogue in British North America."[17] On the whole, however, he held a relatively high opinion of the Canadians. Cartier, at all events, was a "thorough gentleman", Galt "a remarkably clever fellow", and "Macdonald (when not drunk) is a really powerful man".[18] But as for the provincial politicians of New Brunswick, they were, with the exception of Tilley, almost contemptible. And to Gordon it was insufferably galling that creatures like this should actually rule in fact whilst he merely governed in form. When Cardwell mildly reminded him that government in one of the democratic colonies was very much like government in the constitutional monarchy of Great Britain, Gordon indignantly rejected this respectable analogy. "I hold," he wrote, "that . . . the position of the Governor is less like that of the Queen than that of Louis XVI during the Constitution of 1791."[19] He wanted to be free from this degrading servitude. He wanted more power, or, as he rather quaintly put it, more "opportunity for usefulness". He dreamed longingly of an appointment to a submissive Crown Colony, with a nice climate, and a nice salary, and, above all, no Assembly and no "parliamentary eloquences".

Gordon had been an ardent believer in Maritime union. At every stage in the proceedings of the Charlottetown and Quebec Conferences, he had attacked the federal scheme, and impugned the motives of its authors, the Canadians. Cardwell's dispatch of December 3 announcing the British government's hearty support for the Seventy-two Resolutions must have come to him as a profound disappointment, a personally mortifying disappointment. In his complaining, argumentative fashion, he kept on reiterating his criticisms of federations in general and the Quebec plan in particular; but he at least indicated that he would "act in conformity with Her Majesty's gracious commands".[20] He did more. All of a sudden, almost without warning, he was eager for immediate action. Could it be that those veiled sardonic eyes had already discerned an appropriate revenge for the shameful neglect with which he and his opinions had been treated by both British and colonials? Had he realized that he could embarrass Confederation even more by clumsy and inept support than he possibly could by outright opposition? Or was he merely trying once again to assert himself, to show that he was not under Tilley's thumb, to demonstrate that he was not a contemptible cipher in the government of New Brunswick? At all events, he was all haste and all confidence, where Tilley, who ought to have been the best judge of the situation, was plainly hesitant and doubtful. Tilley had promised not to submit the Quebec scheme to the expiring House; but he was anxious, nevertheless, to hold a final session of the legislature, to postpone the general election until June, when the legal term of the parliament was up. He wanted time—time to complete the speaking tour on which he was then engaged—time to explain the merits of the Quebec scheme and to weaken the prejudice against it. But time was the very thing that the Governor was unwilling to concede. He wanted an immediate dissolution and a winter election. He saw, apparently, no reason for Tilley's programme of education; he gauged public opinion with a strangely optimistic eye. It was not until January 16 that he admitted in a dispatch to Cardwell that the apathetic attitude of New Brunswick to the Quebec scheme had of late been somewhat altered and that it had been replaced "by a sentiment more decidedly hostile to the proposed arrangement".[21] But even then—even later—he showed no alarm for the safety of Confederation at the polls. While Tilley hesitated, he pressed him vigorously with arguments; and in the end the Governor got his way. On January 19, 1865, the Executive Council decided in favour of an immediate dissolution. Tilley acquiesced. But he permitted himself one last reproachful remark. "I cannot refrain, however, from stating," he wrote, "that our chances of success would have been increased by adhering to our original design."[22]

II

The disturbing news of the imminent New Brunswick election reached Macdonald only a little after the Canadian legislature had assembled for its winter session. He arrived in Quebec on January 22, three days late for the opening.[23] He had been ill; and when, on the cold evening of Monday, February 6, he rose in the Assembly to move the adoption of the Quebec Resolutions, his voice was still a little weak from the effects of ill health. It was not a new speech. He had given much of it before, in various forms, at Charlottetown, at Halifax, and, above all, at Quebec. But the rank and file of the Canadian legislature had not heard it yet; and never before had it been given in such a full and finished form, and with such a wealth of illustrative detail. Yet the main themes —the need of a strong central government, and the importance of maintaining British institutions, and British principles of government—stood out as clearly as before. The imperial Parliament, he told the House, would have to decide the title which the federal Legislative Assembly would bear. But the Canadians hoped it would be "House of Commons", with all that that historic name implied; and as for the Upper House, with its councillors appointed by the central government on a regional basis, it had been designed "in accordance with the British system as nearly as circumstances would allow". Executive authority was vested, as it always had been, in the Crown, and administered "according to the well understood principles of the British Constitution". Responsible government under the Crown had served the colonies well in the past; and, in their new federal state, they could still avoid the despotic powers and party label of the American presidency by sticking firmly to the monarchical principle. "I believe," Macdonald went on, "that it is of the utmost importance to have that principle recognized, so that we shall have a sovereign who is placed above the region of party—to whom all parties look up —who is not elevated by the action of one party nor depressed by the action of another, who is the common head and sovereign of all."[24]

Yet the lessons of the British constitution, Macdonald implied, were not confined to the sphere of political institutions and principles of government. The British constitution was an almost equally valuable guide in the purely federal parts of the projected union. For the Empire, with its sovereign imperial Parliament and dependent colonial legislatures, was itself an informal federal system; and the rules which had governed the old imperial connection could be easily transferred to regulate the relationships of the central and local governments in British North America. "As this is to be one united province," Macdonald explained, "with the local governments and legislatures subordinate to the General Government and Legislature, it is obvious that the chief executive officer in each of the provinces must be subordinate as well."[25] In the Old Colonial System, the governors and lieutenant-governors had been appointed by the imperial authorities; in the new federation, the lieutenant-governors of the subordinate provinces were to be nominated by the central government. "The General Government," said Macdonald, appealing directly to the imperial analogy, "assumes towards the local governments precisely the same position as the Imperial Government holds with respect to each of the colonies now."[26] The main origins of the Quebec scheme, in short, were British origins. The federation had been planned to achieve that close unity which was symbolized by the imperial Crown; it had been designed to avoid the fatally divided sovereignties of the United States. "We have strengthened the General Government," Macdonald declared. "We have given the General Legislature all the great subjects of legislation." Above all, they had given it—and not the local legislatures—the residuary power. "We thereby strengthen the Central Parliament," Macdonald went on, "and make the Confederation one people and one government, instead of five peoples and five governments, with merely a point of authority connecting us to a limited and insufficient extent."[27]

Cartier followed the next night, Tuesday, February 7; and on Wednesday Brown held a crowded House for over four hours. The debate, which promised to last until virtually every member of the legislature had said his say on the subject of the Quebec Resolutions, was now well under way; and, unfortunately for the success of both, it coincided almost exactly with the New Brunswick election campaign. Macdonald was worried by the possible influence that each might have upon the other. He had far more doubts about the result of the election than he had about the outcome of the debate; but he realized that Tilley and the New Brunswickers would be watching with interest the reports in the Canadian newspapers, drawing ammunition and confidence from the course of the argument. Yet even with his awareness of the growing interdependence of British North American politics, he was betrayed into a fairly serious mistake. The *Rouges* and John Sandfield Macdonald, who together constituted the only opposition in the House, were loftily contemptuous of number sixty-eight of the Quebec Resolutions, which declared that the general government of the new federation would complete the Intercolonial Railway without delay. Macdonald, in reply to a question from Holton, admitted that the guarantee of the Intercolonial could hardly form a part of the new federal constitution proper. In a few days this statement was public property in New Brunswick. It created the greatest consternation in government circles. From Tilley's point of view, the Intercolonial was one of the few immediate and practical benefits which he could claim that Confederation would bring to his province. Why, asked his anti-Confederate opponents, was a doubt now cast upon the formality of the guarantee? Were the Canadians getting ready to betray the New Brunswickers once again, as they had betrayed them back in 1862? Tilley, bombarded with questions and jibes, wrote immediately to Macdonald. "Now

I can assure you," he declared emphatically, "that no Delegate from this Province will consent to Union unless we have this guarantee. And we will certainly fail in all our elections unless I have word by you, and to be in time must be by telegraph, saying that this security will be given us. All will be lost without this. . . ."[28] This nearly frantic appeal drew an immediate reply from Macdonald. "My remark," he telegraphed back, "was that an agreement to build a Railroad could not be a portion of a Constitution. In our case it was one of the conditions on which Constitution was adopted. Such condition will of course be inserted in the Imperial Act."[29]

In the meantime, the diplomatic bag had brought another, and an only slightly less disturbing, communication. It was a dispatch from Cardwell, in which the Colonial Secretary reported the reply of his government to the long Canadian Council minute of the previous November on the subject of defence. On January 19 and 20—at the very moment when the Canadian parliament was assembling again—the British Cabinet had been considering the fortifications of Quebec. Gladstone, still eager to "shift the centre of responsibility" in colonial defences and still confronting his impatient colleagues with long, involved paragraphs of argument, had been, in Lord Palmerston's words, particularly "troublesome and wrong-headed".[30] With equal prolixity and tenacity he had objected to the fortification of Quebec and urged a reduction of 500 men in the navy. He had been overborne, of course; and the decision of the majority of the Cabinet was "that the best security against a conflict with the United States will be found in an adequate defensive force". Yet the conclusions drawn from this general principle were curiously meagre. Jervois had estimated the total cost of the Quebec fortifications at £200,000. The Cabinet merely decided to put an item of £50,000 in the army estimates for the current year, towards the construction of the works. As for the general problem of the organization of Canadian defences, Cardwell agreed, almost too readily, to postpone the whole business until after Confederation.[31] At this leisurely rate of progress it would be years before anything solid was done. There was remarkably little evidence of a sense of acute peril, of desperate urgency, in Great Britain; but in Canada there was certainly a greater feeling of apprehension than there had been back in the previous November. The fate of the St. Albans prisoners was not yet determined. The passport nuisance still continued. Worst of all, the Americans were evidently in dead earnest about the abrogation of the Reciprocity Treaty.

There was a good deal to worry about. Macdonald was ill, also, with a severe cold; and for the last week in February he obeyed doctor's orders and stayed away from the House.[82] The New Brunswick election drew closer and closer; and his convalescence was not yet over when on Saturday, March 4, the news began to come in over the telegraph wires. The halls of the legislature in Quebec were crowded. The little knot of *Rouges* and Sandfield Macdonald Grits were excited and triumphant.[83] Tilley and Watters, the two Confederate candidates in Saint John, were both defeated; and, before Saturday was out, the downfall of the union government was conceded. The Quebec scheme was not only stopped; it was derailed. On Monday Dorion's followers were predicting a crisis for the Canadian ministers. The Cabinet met early that morning. Macdonald was back at his post again; and when the House met for the afternoon session, he rose to make the expected statement of government policy.

He began by admitting frankly that the New Brunswick election had been "a declaration against the policy of Confederation".[84] But, he went on—and the argument was far from being merely specious—, Confederation was by no means the only issue involved in the contest. What was at stake in this, as in all other elections under the British system, was the total record of the government. To a very large extent, the contest was simply the usual battle between the ins and the outs. It was also a battle between the rival railway policies competing for the favour of the New Brunswick electorate. Macdonald was well aware—though he took no time to deal with this in his brief explanation—of the basic division of interest between the North Shore of New Brunswick, which identified itself with the St. Lawrence and British North

America, and the Saint John and Bay of Fundy region, which often sought its prosperity in trade with the United States. The Intercolonial Railway was an essentially Laurentian, British North American enterprise. "Western Extension", which meant the extension of the existing New Brunswick railway—the European and North American—south-westward, so as to connect with the railway lines of the United States, was an equally good expression of the urge towards the American market. Tilley's opponents, led by a group of Saint John merchants, had, of course, taken up "Western Extension". But back of the Saint John merchants was a still more powerful group, the railway capitalists of the north-eastern United States, who had for years been competing with Watkin and Brydges for the control of the Maritime Provinces, and who were ready to put a good deal of money into the election for the sake of defeating the Intercolonial Railway. "It was a fair stand-up fight," D'Arcy McGee said bluntly, "of Yankee interests on the one side and British interests on the other."[35] Macdonald was rather less outspoken. He merely hinted at the widespread suspicion that American money had helped materially to decide the New Brunswick election.

His main task was to explain government policy for the future. The ministers, he told the House, wished it to be "most distinctly understood" that they regarded the New Brunswick election not as a reason for changing direction, but as an additional cause for perseverance in their original course. Since the previous June, when the coalition government was formed, a scheme of union had been worked out, had been sanctioned by all the governments of British North America, and approved by the Colonial Office. The project, on the whole, had been a success, rather than a failure. The Canadian government had no intention of abandoning it. The ministers proposed, Macdonald announced crisply, to put the Quebec Resolutions to a vote as soon as possible, to prorogue the House as soon as possible, and then to send a mission to England to discuss Confederation and related questions with the British government.[36] One of these questions was the unsatisfactory state of trade relations with the United States, and the other was defence. Last autumn it had been hoped that a new federal government would soon be able to deal with the question of British North American defence in general. But now, since the New Brunswick election, there was no immediate prospect of united action; and the Canadian military problem could be postponed no longer. This was Macdonald's defiantly energetic announcement to Dorion, Sandfield Macdonald, and their followers; and, having made it, he sat down.

III

On Tuesday and Wednesday, March 21 and 22, the Canadian Cabinet held two long sessions which lasted on until after six o'clock at night.[37] Everybody knew that the personnel and programme of the delegation to England was up for discussion. Macdonald did not want to go. He had accepted office in the previous June as an emergency task. But now the temporary emergency seemed to be aging into a permanent ordeal. He had been ill again, for the third time since the New Year, and he would have been perfectly content to stay at home and let his colleagues have the excitement and the honour of the negotiations in England. Yet this was perhaps the most important mission that Canada had ever sent to the imperial government. The other members of the Cabinet pressed him to go; and, once a rumour of his reluctance got abroad, others added their appeals to the pressure of the ministers. "I pray you go to England," wrote Brown Chamberlin of the *Montreal Gazette*. "There are many true hearts will not rest satisfied unless you do. If the wit of men can help it, there must be no failure to come to an agreement with the Mother Country. . . . The greatest interests, the very birthright of Britons in Canada are in your keeping. . . . Five years hence we shall be more truly British or altogether Yankee. Whose will be the fault if the latter should be our fate?"[38]

No, it was impossible for him to stay at home. He would have to go to England. He would have to try to give direction and encouragement to the union movement everywhere, to watch

over the different provinces of British North America as he
had watched over the constituencies of Canada West for the
last fifteen years. Everywhere things seemed to have gone
wrong. There was still no word from Newfoundland. The
legislature of Prince Edward had rejected Confederation and
Maritime union with equal decisiveness and announced firmly
that it wished to be left alone. From the defeated unionists
in New Brunswick—Tilley, Charles Fisher, and Colonel J. H.
Gray—there came a series of unhappy letters, bewailing the
catastrophe of the election, and trying miserably to account
for it. Even Nova Scotia was involved in the general retreat. The
magic of Howe's name and the evil spell of the New Brunswick
defeat had between them confounded Charles Tupper. He told
Macdonald that, if Tilley had only succeeded, he might have
got the Quebec Resolutions through the Nova Scotian Assembly
with a bare majority; "but the moment he failed," he went on
dismally, "I found that all my ingenuity would be required
to avert the passage of a hostile Resolution."[39] Since the anti-
unionists were professing an unreal love for Maritime union,
Tupper was forced to adopt the defensive manoeuvre of taking
up that defunct project himself. On April 10, he moved that
"whereas under existing circumstances an immediate Union of
the British North American Colonies has become impracticable",
the negotiations for a legislative union of the three Maritime
Provinces should be renewed.[40] In every province but Canada
Confederation had been brought to a dead stop. From every
province the gloomy news kept coming in during March and
April as Macdonald made his preparations for the mission to
England. He tried to keep his correspondents in good heart.
The tactics in New Brunswick had been wrong, he said frankly;
but it was "easy to be wise after the event", and for the future
he promised assistance. "I do not at all despair," he wrote to
one of the faithful delegates in Prince Edward Island, "of
carrying out our great project sooner or later."[41]

The prospect abroad was almost as bad as the outlook at
home. It was true that early in March—just after the New
Brunswick election—there had come a slight relaxation in the
portentous displeasure of the American Secretary of State. On

March 10, the Canadian papers reported that the hated pass-ports were no longer being required at the American border;[42] and two days earlier Seward had instructed Adams, the American minister in London, to notify Earl Russell that the United States was willing to let the Rush-Bagot Convention remain "practically in force".[43] The irritating annoyances, the direct threats seemed to be disappearing; but now a huge though vague peril was taking their place. Spring had come, and early in April Grant was pursuing Lee down the last twisting turns of that desperate flight that ended at Appomattox Court House. In a few weeks the Civil War would be over. In a few weeks the victorious north would be able to give its undivided attention to its grievances against Great Britain and British America, and the Grand Army of the Republic would be free to win any military objective that was set for it in the continent of North America. Macdonald was fearful of a revival of American military imperialism; but he was even more worried by the state of Canadian defences and Canadian morale, and by the half-hearted response that the British government and the British Parliament seemed to be making to the Canadian danger. "The indiscreet publication of Colonel Jervois' report in England," he wrote to J. H. Gray of New Brunswick, "has at the present caused a panic in Western Canada, as it shows the defencelessness of most of our Province, unless protected by permanent works, and the wretched debate in the House of Lords has not diminished the dread of forced annexation and abandonment by Great Britain. Fancy the British Empire for the purpose of defending Canada and the British Flag from an impending war voting £200,000 in all, to be expended at £50,000 a year! . . . In order to shame them we carried the vote for a million of dollars, and we go home with that sum in our hands."[44] This was frank enough; but to Watkin, of the Grand Trunk Railway and the Hudson's Bay Company, he was even more reproachfully downright. "But if England," he wrote, "can do nothing better for us than to vote £50,000 a year for four years to fortify Quebec, we may give up the idea of resistance as hopeless. . . ."[45]

In any case, it was time to be away. On April 20, five days after Galt and Cartier had departed, he sailed with Brown on the *China* for England.[46] Only eight years before, they had had their fearful row in the House—a row which had made Brown swear a deep and passionate oath that never again would there be anything but purely "parliamentary intercourse" between them. Yet here they were sailing in the same ship and bound on the same mission! It was certainly a delicate, precious relationship, which Macdonald treated in a gingerly, almost deferential, fashion. He even appeared to regard Brown as his senior. Although the proprietor of the *Globe* was, in fact, five years younger than himself, he referred to him blandly as "the old fellow", and "the covenanting old chap". There was, indeed, a strain of intense, brooding seriousness in Brown which made his companion's high spirits seem almost frivolously youthful. The Reform leader was a difficult colleague: reserved, sensitive, moody, and impulsive; touchy about everything that concerned seniority and precedence, and already quite obviously jealous of Galt. But the coalition had lasted now for nearly a year without any serious trouble; and the long voyage across the Atlantic to England was one of its most pleasant incidents. The wind blew steadily from the east, and there was scarcely ever any point in hoisting their auxiliary sails; but the *China* ploughed steadily ahead, making a regular twelve miles an hour all the way.[47] It was a gay company on board. They played round games, fenced for exercise, and got up balls and parties and concerts. There was only a brief stop in the Mersey for quarantine, and then they were off by the night mail for London. Next morning—the morning of May 3—they walked into the Westminster Palace Hotel. Macdonald was to become almost wearisomely familiar with the Westminster Palace Hotel in the next two years.

Its doorway must have seemed, in the days that followed, like a triumphal arch into the heart of imperial London. The London press had given a good welcome to Confederation;[48] and now its chief authors, the four principal members of the Canadian Cabinet, were honoured with a fatherly greeting from *The Times*. On May 16, they were presented to the

Queen (with Galt confessing a slight doubt as to the tenacity of the trousers of his new uniform).[49] In the days that followed, the members of the royal family, cabinet ministers, titled personages, railway magnates and London livery companies all seemed to be competing with a flattering enthusiasm for even a few hours of the delegates' time; and for over a month they travelled round the circuit of the West End houses through a pleasant succession of balls, dinner parties and receptions. Macdonald enjoyed it all—less naïvely than Cartier, who frankly delighted in big and splendid affairs, but more wholeheartedly than his two introspective Scots colleagues, Brown and Galt. Brown, the most recently married of the lot, a most passionately devoted family man, was always fretting to be back to his wife and little daughters in Toronto. Galt, who, in his own way, was just as temperamental as Brown, was very much the self-conscious colonial, doubtfully analysing his sensations in London society, and occasionally reminding himself of the obvious fact that if he had not been Finance Minister of Canada, not one of these pleasant hosts and hostesses would have paid the slightest attention to him.

The political reception of the delegates was quite as impressive as the social accolade with which they were received. They began with informal talks with Cardwell, the Colonial Secretary, and went on to more official discussions with a committee of the Cabinet, which included Gladstone—still arguing interminably over "this most formidable Canadian question"— as one of its principal members. The committee had decided, as Gladstone later explained privately to Gordon of New Brunswick, to treat with Canada "as morally in the attitude of an independent Power".[50] Galt, who regarded himself very gravely as a virtual "independent"—and who would have been far more furious if the delegation had received a condescending reception—brooded darkly, with suspicious colonial misgivings, over this ceremonious treatment. The British, on their part, were puzzled by the new note of desperate urgency which the Canadians sounded, and by the unprecedented scope of Galt's first defence proposals. What had happened to the Canadians? Were they in deadly earnest? Or were they simply presenting views which they imagined would be highly acceptable in London? Gladstone, who continued to wrestle heroically with his enormous doubts, suspected that some of the Canadian views were "derivative and factitious". He wanted to make quite sure that the Canadian proposals were "spontaneous and not mere reflections of imaginary wishes here".[51]

By the time Macdonald and Brown arrived, Cardwell and his colleagues had already given their promise to use all the influence they possessed to forward the Quebec scheme, and Galt's first gigantic programme of defence measures had been tacitly dropped. The Canadians abandoned their rather melo-dramatic manner; and, basing their representations on the Jervois reports and on a new report which was furnished by the im-perial defence committee, they returned pretty much to their suggestions of the previous November. They offered to build the fortifications west of Quebec, to improve the provincial canals, and to spend up to $1,000,000 annually on the training of the militia—provided the imperial government would guar-antee the loans necessary to finance these works, and would also supply a naval force for the defence of the Great Lakes.[52] The guarantee, they demanded with reiterated insistence, must be granted at once. It must be authorized in the current session of the imperial Parliament. Without it the fortifications west of Quebec would have to be postponed a year, to a time when heavy military commitments would merely embarrass the project of Confederation. The demand was a rather peremptory one, awkward for the British to concede, for the army estimates for the year were already passed; and, as May drew to its close, they and the Canadians were still arguing about the matter.

The last day of May was Derby Day. Business was sus-pended. Everybody was out of town. The Canadians made up a party of eleven, with Russell of *The Times,* Grant and Brydges of the Grand Trunk, and D'Arcy McGee, the Canadian Minister of Agriculture, who had also arrived in London. They set out for Epsom at nine o'clock, in two stout carriages with postillions, and with a huge basket of food and wines from Fort-num and Mason's tucked away inside.[53] The road was jammed with an unending stream of vehicles. They took hours to

414 THE YOUNG POLITICIAN [1865

cover the sixteen miles to the Downs; and it was twelve o'clock
before they had established their carriage in a good position
and were washing away the dust of the journey with sherry
and seltzer water. The crowd thickened every minute. Macdonald and Galt walked about for a bit, with Russell as their
guide, and when they turned back could scarcely discover
their own carriages in the dense mass of vehicles. Somebody
suggested a pool at a guinea a draw. Galt—he was always a
person to whom things happened—drew the favourite, the
French horse, Gladiateur. Macdonald drew the field.

"You are a lucky fellow," said Macdonald.

Galt gazed at his ticket doubtfully. He would have gazed
doubtfully at any ticket he could possibly have drawn. "I do not
know about that," he said slowly. "There are fourteen horses
running, and it is a great chance if one of them does not come
in ahead."

"Well," said Macdonald, "I will swop and give you a guinea
to boot."[54]

They swopped and then it was time for Macdonald and
Galt to go. Russell, who knew everybody, had got the pair an
invitation to the pavilion and stand, just opposite the royal
party, which was provided by Todd Heatly, the wine merchant,
for his race-going patrons and friends. Inside the pavilion
there was turtle soup, "and all the delicacies and substantials
of the season", and a brimming fountain of champagne. Outside, on the stand, was an uninterrupted and magnificent view
of the entire course. There were a dozen false breaks, and then,
just at two minutes to four, the horses were off at last and
streaming up the hill. Wild Charley, Christmas Carol, Eltham,
Broomielaw, and Oppressor were out in front; and somewhere
in the ruck, almost unnoticed at first, were the blue and red
sleeves of the "Frenchman", with Harry Grimshaw up, carrying
Macdonald's guineas as a part of his enormous baggage of
metal. It was the crowd, rather than the race, that fascinated
Macdonald. As the horses pounded round Tattenham Corner,
the enormous black mass of spectators turned as one man;
and—it was like a flash of lightning—a multitude of white
staring faces rushed in a second into view. Now the horses

were into the straight. Broomielaw was still going very fast; but soon "those light back ribs could do no more". The two "magpie jackets", Eltham and Christmas Carol, shot out together; but deep on the inside was a stealing blur of blue and red that swept into a lead, "and nothing else was in it".[55] Macdonald could have dropped his handkerchief on Gladiateur's head, as the horse passed the post, a winner by two lengths. Then it was all over; and the crowd, shouting, pushing, gesticulating, and fighting, poured out onto the course.

"The Road", the creeping cavalcade back from Epsom to London, was a licensed saturnalia of horse-play and broad good humour. The Canadians buttoned up their greatcoats tightly, crammed their hats down on their heads, and armed themselves with peas, pea-shooters, pincushions of bran and little bags of flour. Macdonald, greatly daring, even bought a bag of peas for the "old chap", George Brown; and Brown, for a few wild, uncovenanting hours, developed an unexpected zeal for the pea-shooter. Galt thought himself lucky to be in the same carriage with Macdonald and Russell, who were "past masters at the art of chaffing". Macdonald kept up a constant raillery with the strangers on every side; and once, when they were blocked for an hour at a railway bridge, Russell got up on his seat and addressed the crowd in an eloquent extempore election speech. Assaulted in turn with cheers, jeers, peas, flour, and uproarious abuse, their carriage maintained its reputation for originality and high spirits all the way to London. It took them five hours to reach the capital. They were tired out when they walked into the Westminster Palace Hotel, and white as millers with dust and pelted flour.

The next day, June 1, they were back in conference once more. It was clear by now that the prospect of a comprehensive military settlement had faded. Macdonald and his colleagues wanted to start the defence construction programme during the current season. The British ministers could not understand the frantic haste of the Canadians and did not believe it was justified by the state of relations with the United States. "I frankly own my entire inability," Gladstone wrote to Cardwell, "to comprehend the feverish impatience of the Deputation, and their repeated declarations that the spring of 1866 is the crisis of their danger."⁵⁶ It was difficult for the British to grant the financial guarantee immediately, and equally hard, now that the Rush-Bagot Convention had just been restored, to start planning for a force of small ships in the Great Lakes. Yet the Canadians attached an enormous importance to their conditions; and Macdonald argued that if they could not be met, then the whole plan, including the expenditure of the $1,000,-000 already voted for the militia, would become politically difficult and embarrassing, and would have to be delayed beyond a year.⁵⁷ The British ministers, taking these arguments very literally indeed, proposed, in their turn, that the entire question of Canadian defences should be postponed once more until after Confederation. In the end, after all the investigations, reports, and proposals of the past eighteen months, this was what was decided. It was not quite all that was decided, however, for Great Britain and Canada exchanged pledges to assist each other with all their resources, in the event of war; and this British promise, though in fact it pledged nothing new, cleared at a stroke the unhappy uncertainty of the past few months. Yet the big Canadian armament programme had come to nothing. Defence, like Confederation, had ended in delay and postponement. And once again there was that depressing feeling of unfulfilment, of spiritual deflation.

The conference was over, and on June 17 Galt and Brown sailed for Canada. Macdonald waited another week. He had, he told his sister Louisa, a good deal of private business to attend to; besides, Oxford University had invited him to accept the honorary degree of D.C.L. "This is the greatest honour they can confer," he told his sister, "and is much sought after by the first men, so that I of course was only too happy to wait for it."⁵⁸ He stayed the last week-end at Strawberry Hill, Horace Walpole's old house, as a guest of the Countess Waldegrave; and on Tuesday, June 20, he travelled up to Oxford. That evening the Vice-Chancellor gave a dinner party, to which he was invited; and early next day—a morning of cloudless skies and brilliant sun—the "saturnalia of undergraduate Oxford", "the well-known melodrama of grave ceremony and uproarious fun was once more enacted" at the Sheldonian Theatre.[59] The undergraduates, who had taken their seats first, enlivened the wait by giving alternate cheers and groans for a long list of public figures and members of the audience. This had just begun to pall, and a loud voice had suggested that a policeman be sent to fetch the Vice-Chancellor in, when the organ struck up the national anthem, and the academic procession entered. Macdonald was in distinguished, though hardly splendid, company: Lord Lyons, the Minister to the United States, who had just returned from Washington, Sir Hugh Rose, late Commander-in-Chief in India, Henry Maine, Regius Professor of Law at Cambridge, and three more British and foreign scholars were the other recipients of degrees. Lord Lyons and Sir Hugh Rose were most loudly cheered, "the next in popularity being Mr. Macdonald".[60] He sat in his gorgeous robes and listened to the public orator trying to complete a Latin oration which one undergraduate invited him "to finish off tonight over a bottle of port". The prize essayists read their English and Latin compositions amid a hubbub of genial undergraduate comment, and the Newdigate poet fumbled feebly through his verses on "Mexico". Then the young gentlemen of the University gave a final cheer "to ourselves for being so good" and *Encaenia* was over. Macdonald carried away pleasant memories of Oxford in the June sunshine; and three days later, on June 24, he sailed for Boston on the *China*.

IV

He arrived in Montreal on July 7. Monck wrote him a friendly note of greeting, congratulating him on his reception in England. "I hope," he added, "you were as well pleased with H.M. Ministers as they—from all I hear—were with you."[61] It was amusing to be announced as "Dr. Macdonald" by Monck's butler, Lambkin, as he went in for his first interview with the Governor-General on reaching Quebec. But Monck was anxious for a variety of reasons, public and private, to reassemble the legislature as quickly as possible, and Macdonald found himself plunged at once into public affairs. The Cabinet met on July 12; and the next day a proclamation was issued calling parliament for August 8. Then the ministers separated and, at long last, Macdonald went back for a brief holiday to Kingston.

He was not permitted to enjoy as much rest as he had hoped or expected. On July 30, old Sir Etienne Taché, the titular head of the Canadian ministry, died at his home at Montmagny. It was a shock, in more ways than one. Taché was a link with the past—a necessary link in the present, also, for he helped to bind the disparate elements of the coalition government together. Back in 1856 he had succeeded Sir Allan MacNab as the second head of the Liberal-Conservative government; and he had presided over the deliberations of the Quebec Conference, a benevolent old chairman, with his round friendly countenance and his nimbus of white hair. He had been very fond of Macdonald. Two days after the ministers had separated, when he already knew that his end was close, he had written a last little note on public business to the Attorney-General West, begging Macdonald to let him know as soon as he returned to Quebec. "J'aimerais à vous voir encore une fois," he wrote, "avant le long voyage que je vais bientôt entreprendre."[62] Now that last meeting could never take place. Taché was gone. And his going produced a political crisis of the first importance. A magnanimous old neutral who had no political ambitions and of whom nobody could be jealous, he had held the coalition together. Who was to succeed him?

Early in the morning of Thursday, August 3—the day after he had gone out to Montmagny for Taché's funeral—Macdonald received a note from the Governor-General. Could he come out that very morning to Spencer Wood for breakfast?[63] There could be only one meaning in such an invitation and within an hour it was made plain. At Spencer Wood, Monck invited him to take Taché's place as first minister and to form a new administration. Ever since June, 1864, he had been, in reality, the effective head of the government. Now he was asked to become its formal leader. He probably wanted the leadership. He knew that, in fact, nobody deserved it more than he. But, as he accepted the Governor-General's commission, he realized that nothing could be more conditional than his acceptance. He would have to confront Brown. And Brown was almost certain to make difficulties. Nobody could be more generous in his enthusiasms, more willing in his sacrifices, than Brown; but nobody also was more acutely sensitive, more prone to irritations, jealousies, and resentments, more apt to take offence, to stand upon his dignity, or to stick upon some absurd point of punctilio as if it were a major question of principle. In Brown's view, the Cabinet had been a triumvirate of equals—Macdonald, Cartier, and Brown—with Taché as merely nominal head. But, as time went on, it seemed to him that his own position was being threatened by a long and calculated succession of slights and indignities. He became convinced that Macdonald was ambitious to rise above this senior committee of three, and that Galt was intent upon thrusting his way into it from below. He had given up much. He knew it; and behind those sunken, smouldering eyes there now lay a sullen determination to yield no more. When Macdonald met him on the morning of August 3, with the Governor-General's commission, he would have nothing to do with it.[64] He refused to accept Macdonald as titular leader.

The crisis lasted for three indecisive days. Yet its outcome, as Macdonald must have realized, was inevitable from the beginning. He wanted the leadership—yes. But he was content to wait; then, and always, he was content to wait—for, in all the larger strategy of his career, he was gifted with a limitless patience. At that moment, nothing must be done which would permanently alienate Brown. With the movement for federal union stopped in apparent frustration, with Canada's whole future in a state of dangerous uncertainty, the coalition government could not possibly be permitted to dissolve. At first he suggested Cartier as Taché's successor; and then, since Brown still hesitated and demurred, he proposed that Sir Narcisse Belleau, a much less important member of the Legislative Council than old Taché had been, should be elevated to the empty honour of leadership, leaving the equality of the triumvirate, Macdonald, Cartier, and Brown, undisturbed.[65] Sir

Narcisse was not anxious for political office of any kind; but he yielded to the solicitations of Macdonald and Cartier. Brown accepted the arrangement. And on Tuesday, August 8, one day after Belleau had been sworn in, parliament met. It had been done in the nick of time.

Back in March, when it had been first announced, the summer meeting of parliament had seemed almost like an emergency session. But by now ministers might have been willing to dispense with it altogether, if only they had been able to do so. They had little to communicate and even less to propose. Though the British had promised to do all they could to forward Confederation, it would take time for their influence, and all other influences, to have any effect whatever; and although the fundamental pledges of military assistance given at London had profoundly reassured the Canadians, the big defence programme had been postponed once more. The seven-point statement of government policy which Cartier read to the House on August 15 was singularly negative and indecisive.[66] The government proposed no further action on the plan of federal union, no immediate construction of works for the defence of the province, no votes of money for the Intercolonial Railway, and no revisions of the tariff. The whole problem of the militia would have to wait for a further government investigation. The question of the Reciprocity Treaty and of foreign trade in general would have to be postponed until after the meeting of the interprovincial conference, which was scheduled for the autumn. Very evidently, and rather wearily, the government was marking time. It was a lame session. And, for a good part of it, Macdonald was absent. He was ill and for a while under doctor's orders.[67]

A sense of bafflement and suspense, a feeling of uncertainty and frustration seemed to infect the Canadians like a low fever. What could, or should, be done about defence, about their external relations with the United States? On the one hand, that enormous and dreaded fighting force, the Union army, was now being rapidly demobilized; but, on the other, the undiminished American resentment at Great Britain and her colonies seemed to promise, at least, a long period of diplomatic fights and economic retaliations. The Americans had never been satisfied with the dragging inconclusiveness of the St. Albans trials. They now proceeded to vie with each other in suggesting outrageous totals for the damages which the United States must demand of Great Britain for the havoc wrought by the *Alabama,* the cruiser which had been built in a British shipyard and acquired by the Confederate States. It was true that most of the retaliatory moves which had been so far prompted by these grievances had not lasted very long. But the notice of the abrogation of the Reciprocity Treaty had never been cancelled; and Galt and Howland, who had gone down to Washington in July to discuss with Sir Frederick Bruce the prospects of renewal, returned with a very pessimistic report. It looked now as if, in less than a year, the international border would be closed to the free passage of Canadian raw materials.

All this was bad enough. Now there was one thing more. The Union army was, indeed, being demobilized; but a fairly large number of its Irish veterans were promptly re-enlisting in the unofficial forces of a new militant organization, the Fenian Brotherhood. The Brotherhood dated back to 1858. Its original objective had been the liberation of Ireland from English "tyranny" and its establishment as a free and independent republic. It was perhaps too much to expect that an Irish revolutionary society should remain very long united on a single objective. At any rate its members in the United States soon began to quarrel bitterly over high policy. One lot, led by John O'Mahony, the original "Head Centre" of the movement, continued to preach the pure, original evangel of revolution in Ireland. Another group, captained by W. R. Roberts and R. W. Sweeny, now began to advocate the invasion and occupation of British North America, as a base for future heroic but unspecified operations against Great Britain.[63] Macdonald, on the death of Taché, had taken over the Department of Militia Affairs once again; and by the autumn he was receiving a good deal of information about the Fenians and their activities through the espionage organization which Gilbert McMicken had built up. "I am watching them very closely with his assistance," Macdonald wrote to Monck, "and think that the movement must not be despised, either in America or Ireland. I am so strongly of that opinion that I shall spare no expense in watching them on both sides of the line."[69]

There were all sorts of reasons for Macdonald's anxiety and uncertainty, for the delays and embarrassments of the Canadian government's policy. But, without any doubt, the most important of them all was the impasse into which Confederation had blundered. So much was bound up with Confederation— was dependent upon Confederation; and its abrupt stoppage not merely held up the entire programme, but also filled everyone with a discouraged, paralysing feeling of futility and exasperation. Nothing whatever could be done until the decision in New Brunswick was reversed. But what chance was there yet of upsetting the apparently powerful new government, led by A. J. Smith and R. D. Wilmot, which had come into office only six months before as a result of a triumphant victory at the polls? The British government had done its part nobly. Cardwell and his colleagues, who believed that union was desirable on general imperial grounds, British as well as British North American, were quite ready, without any prompting from Canada, to push Confederation with all their power. "I wish to avoid all appearance of *undue* pressure or of dictation," Cardwell wrote to Gordon during his conversations with the Canadians in May, "but at the same time to let it be thoroughly understood that this question of Confederation is one in which the Home Government is quite in earnest; and considers that its wishes ought to have and will have great weight in the Provinces."[70] On June 24, when he wrote again to the Lieutenant-Governor of New Brunswick, transmitting the results of the conference with the Canadian ministers, the Colonial Secretary stated these wishes once more without ambiguity and in a tone of earnest admonition.[71] Later in the summer, Smith and Allen, the New Brunswick delegates, arrived in England in an attempt to counteract the evil influence of the Canadians. But they were received at the Colonial Office by men whose minds were firmly made up and who politely refused to be budged an inch. As for the opposition in Nova Scotia, Cardwell wrote a private letter to Earl Russell, at the Foreign Office, suggesting that "anything you could do to bring round Mr. Howe might help exceedingly".[72]

Surely all that could be done had been done. What further action was possible, unless the British government resorted frankly to coercion? There were some at least who were willing to consider even this. Russell, in the gloomy days in early September, when everything in British North America seemed to have reached a standstill, wrote Cardwell that he thought the colonies must be united for their own preservation, and that "some coercion" would be necessary. "The question will be," he went on, "whether the Maritime Provinces should be coerced in order to form a Federal Union, or whether the Province of Lower Canada should be forced to consent to a Legislative Union, with their separate privileges and laws being secured to them in the Act of Union. I incline to the latter plan."[73] It could scarcely be called a "plan", for drastic deeds of this kind still lay in the realm of speculation. And so long as they remained in the realm of speculation, the British government had clearly reached the end of its influence. The "earnestness and just authority" of Her Majesty's imperial ministers had not availed very much. "My present information about the prospect of Confederation is not very favourable," Cardwell wrote to Russell late in the summer. Everything possible had been done to win over A. J. Smith. "Yet I fear," Cardwell went on sadly, "he is unshaken in his determination to oppose to the uttermost."[74]

The gloom appeared unbroken. Yet back in British North America, where everything effective would have to originate in any case, there seemed suddenly to be a small gap in the curtain. In August Charles Fisher wrote quite optimistically to Macdonald from Fredericton.[75] Early in September Tilley came up to Quebec and spent two days talking over the situation in his native province with Monck and Macdonald and the other members of the Canadian ministry.[76] The fact was, as Tilley and Fisher had already begun to appreciate, that the Smith government, despite its appearance of strength, was already pretty seriously weakened and divided. A common dislike of the Quebec scheme was the one thing that had drawn this odd collection of Liberals and Conservatives together; and they found it almost impossible to discover an alternative policy which was at all practicable, and upon which they could agree. Maritime union, despite Prince Edward Island's obstinate refusal to consider the matter further, was a faint possibility; but the members of the Smith government had not really the slightest interest in Maritime union. The one positive plank in their programme was the promotion of railway and commercial relations with the United States. But the province was too poor to build "Western Extension" itself; and it could not offer sufficiently attractive terms to persuade private capitalists to undertake the project. Finally—and this in itself was a fatal blow—the approaching end of the Reciprocity Treaty would certainly make meaningless the whole pro-American commercial policy for which Smith and his friends stood. The government began to lose confidence and direction. It was becoming vulnerable. "We will watch the moment," Tilley wrote to Macdonald, "and be ready to strike a blow if there appears to be a chance of success."[77] Now the chance appeared. A by-election in York county was necessary. Fisher himself believed he could win. "I am quite certain," Tilley wrote to Macdonald, "Fisher can be returned under any circumstances, with an expenditure of eight or ten thousand dollars. If this should be considered necessary, is there any chance of the friends in Canada providing half the expenditure, not to exceed five thousand dollars, for their share?"

Macdonald promised Canadian aid. He told Fisher that if he went into the York election, he must go in to win at any cost. Now there was something to hope for. But the New Brunswick contest was nearly two months away; and meanwhile there was nothing to do but mark time. Monck left on the morning of September 26 for a brief holiday in England; and the Canadian government was already on the move to its new home in Ottawa.[78] As soon as he had said good-bye to Monck, Macdonald hurried off to seek quarters in the new capital. At Ottawa he found Parliament Hill still littered with unsightly masses of building materials. The steam-heating system, one of the wonders of the new buildings, was in good working order. There was a plentiful supply of water; but oil lamps flared in the rooms in the late afternoon, for Parliament Hill had not yet been connected with the municipal gas-works. In the streets—streets which seemed so curiously wide and empty after the crowded thoroughfares of Quebec—the civil servants tramped about, looking for flats and houses. Macdonald himself found a house, one of a terrace at the south-west corner of Daly and Cumberland Streets. A day later, as the steamer carried him down the river again to Montreal, he was writing to Louisa, inquiring about bed and table linen.[79] Yet for some time the house on Daly Street—the "Quadrilateral" as it came to be called—was only a somewhat temporary resting place. Ottawa itself was like a handsome new residence which its owner had formally purchased, but which was still un-finished and unfit for tranquil occupation. Ottawa, in fact, was very much like Confederation.

V

On November 6, Charles Fisher defeated John Pickard in the York by-election. Macdonald learnt the news the same day; and, a few days later, he received a long jubilant letter from Fisher recounting his victory.[80] The precise value of that victory to Confederation was more than a little obscure. For Fisher, in his election campaign, had said as little as he could on the subject of federal union, and at one point had been driven publicly to declare that Confederation could not be proceeded with until the people of New Brunswick had had another chance to pronounce their will on the subject at the polls.[81] But, despite all these tactical reservations, the mean-ing of Fisher's election was clear and very heartening. He had been a delegate to the Quebec Conference and was a known admirer of the Quebec scheme. He had cleverly tried to identify Smith and his pro-American policies with the growing menace of Fenianism, and he had aroused the Loyalists and the Orangemen of the province by an appeal to the British connection. Monck, to whom Macdonald wrote as soon as he had received the news from York, was suddenly all confidence again. "I think," he wrote back from England, "this is the most important thing that has happened since the Quebec Conference and if followed up judicially affords a good omen of success in our spring campaign."[82]

Of course, it could be, and would be, followed up by other judicious Canadian moves. Yet by themselves these Canadian efforts would have been ineffectual. What gave them their value was the persistent deterioration of the Smith government. The defeat of Pickard in York was merely the outward sign of serious inward decay. Two weeks later, T. W. Anglin, one of the staunchest supporters of "Western Extension" in the administration, resigned as a result of the failure to proceed with his favourite scheme. The policies which gave the Smith-Wilmot government its only meaning and justification were breaking against immovable obstacles; and as Smith and his colleagues grew more muddled and divided, the Canadian government rushed in to take up the position of an unofficial opposition. "We look to you to help us out of the scrape," Fisher wrote to Macdonald, presenting his bill of expenses in York, "for if every dollar is not paid it will kill us at the general election. . . . Do not allow us to want now or we are all gone together." The Canadian ministers prepared to honour Macdonald's pledge; and in November, when George Brown visited Fredericton on business connected with the Reciprocity Treaty, he and the now confident Gordon laid plans for the triumph of Confederation in New Brunswick. "We confidentially settled the whole course of operations to be pursued here," Gordon confided to Cardwell, "and found ourselves almost perfectly agreed. I am convinced I can make (or buy) a union majority in the Legislature. . . ."[83]

The feeling of anxiety and frustration which had got on everybody's nerves during the summer had magically vanished. The York by-election—an equivocal victory by itself—had, in some strange fashion, changed everything. The Canadian government was stronger morally than it had been at any time

since the news of Tilley's defeat in the previous March. It was
strong enough even to survive George Brown's resignation,
which, if it had come five months earlier at the time of Taché's
death, would in all probability have wrecked the coalition.
Brown had disagreed with the policy which Galt and the rest
of the Cabinet wished to pursue in a last effort to persuade the
United States to continue the Reciprocity Treaty; but this disagreement, while it was not simply an occasion or an excuse
for his resignation, was at the same time not its only cause.
There were incompatibilities of temperament in the coalition
which had been endured only by a supreme effort of patience
and good will on all sides; and when Brown finally left, everybody, including Brown himself, must have felt a profound
sense of relief. Yet the original political agreements of the
coalition had remained unbroken. The rather strained cordiality of its members had lasted to the end; and when the
break finally came, Brown's last letters, addressed to Cartier,
not Macdonald, were friendly and even generous.[84] He promised that if the government stuck to the policies already agreed
upon, he would give it his "best aid". He offered $500 towards
the New Brunswick fund and pledged himself to give more
if further help was required. The continued support of the
Grits was assured. Macdonald accepted it gratefully, making
the necessary promises to Howland, now the senior Reformer
in the Cabinet. And the coalition went on. Yet the time in
which it could achieve its first objective was now running out.
In August, when Belleau had been appointed, it had been
agreed that if a general British North American union should
be still impracticable by the time the Canadian parliament
met for its next session, then the government must proceed
immediately with the federal union of Canada East and Canada
West alone. The meeting of the Canadian legislature could
not be delayed beyond the summer of 1866. Macdonald had
about six months left.

Yet by now he was beginning to believe that scarcely half
that time would be necessary. "Mr. Cardwell showed me his
private communications from Mr. Gordon," Monck wrote confidently from London, "and from them I have come to the

conclusion that the success of the Union next spring in New Brunswick may be looked upon as *certain*."⁸⁵ All the news from Fredericton seemed to confirm Macdonald's impression that the disintegration of the Smith government was proceeding apace; and early in January the rickety administration received the worst blow it had yet sustained. R. D. Wilmot sent in his resignation. From the start Wilmot and Smith had been regarded as the joint leaders of the anti-Confederate Cabinet. Even by itself, Wilmot's resignation would have been serious enough; but its significance was magnified by the reasons which had caused it. For Wilmot, the anti-Confederate, had been converted to Confederation. A delegate to the inter-provincial conference on trade, held at Quebec in September, 1865, he had come to believe in the prospects of a united British North American commerce; and, at the same time, he had come to recognize the hopelessness of all attempts to renew the Reciprocity Treaty.⁸⁶ His resignation was, in essence, a public admission of the fact that the policies of the Wilmot-Smith government had now been invalidated by circumstances. Within a few weeks, his interpretation of the facts was proved correct. Galt and Howland of Canada, Henry of Nova Scotia, and Smith of New Brunswick journeyed down to Washington in January, 1866, to make a last attempt to continue the Reciprocity Treaty. But the one offer which they finally received from the members of the Ways and Means Committee of the House of Representatives could hardly have been more derisory if it had been intended as a deliberate insult. The Reciprocity Treaty had gone. And with it went the main policy, and one of the two leaders, of the Smith-Wilmot government.

What would Gordon do with his wonderful opportunity? Macdonald knew, from what Brown and Monck had told him, that the Lieutenant-Governor had counted much on Wilmot's support in his plans for gaining a union majority in the legislature. But could he not derive even more advantage from Wilmot's retirement from the ministry than from his presence in it? Could he not use it to break up the existing government completely and to replace it by a new administration really favourable to Confederation? At first, from the news that Macdonald received from Tilley, it seemed that this was precisely the course that Gordon intended to follow. "I have had one or two interviews of late with our Governor," Tilley wrote, describing the approaching crisis, "and find that he is determined to put matters through without delay. He has declined to accept Wilmot's resignation and it is probable that one or two members of the Government beside Wilmot will take ground in favour of Confederation and that a break up will be the result."[87] Obviously this final, happy denouement could not take place until Smith had returned from the Reciprocity Treaty negotiations in Washington. On February 15, 1866, the day after he reached Fredericton, the Governor tackled him firmly. And then occurred the most astounding episode in the whole ambiguous and tortuous history of the Smith-Wilmot government. Smith, though still intensely disliking the Quebec Resolutions, professed himself not opposed in principle to British North American union. He consented to a paragraph on the subject being inserted in the speech from the throne. He even promised that in due course, and in a somewhat indirect, face-saving fashion, his government would carry out the union policy which the imperial authorities had so strongly recommended.[88] In the end the Lieutenant-Governor closed with this curious offer. The crisis passed. And Smith and most of his colleagues remained in power.

What had happened? Were both the principals in this strange compact acting in good faith? Or, if not, who was deceiving whom? Fisher, who had always suspected that the Governor was determined to injure Confederation in every possible way, naturally doubted Gordon's sincerity. Tilley, who was a good deal closer to the centre of affairs than Fisher, never believed that Smith and his colleagues really intended to carry out their promises. To Macdonald, far away in Canada, the whole course of the affair must have seemed tangled and equivocal to the last degree. On March 8, the New Brunswick legislature met. The paragraph on Confederation in the speech from the throne seemed non-committal and innocuous; but, on the other hand, it certainly had the effect of indicating to Smith's diehard anti-Confederate followers that a change in policy was imminent.[89] The debate on the address began in both Houses, while the Governor waited impatiently for the new policy to be declared. In the Assembly, days and weeks dragged by in an inconclusive argument prompted by Fisher's want-of-confidence amendment; but in the Legislative Council, where a strong pro-Confederation majority had existed from the start, the outcome was quick and decisive. Early in April the telegrams from Fredericton began to warn Macdonald that a crisis was at hand. "Address to Queen for Confederation on basis of Quebec Conference carried in Legislative Council thirteen to five," Peter Mitchell wired on April 7. "Government opposed but powerless. They cannot stand long."[90] Macdonald may have wondered how the passage of an address in the Legislative Council could cause the downfall of a government; but he was soon enlightened. For Gordon had determined to answer the address of the Council at once; and he had determined also, despite the delays and evasions of the past few weeks, to answer it in the favourable sense which he thought was justified as a result of his agreement with Smith. He prepared an answer expressing satisfaction. Smith and his colleagues objected to it. They refused to accept responsibility. But the Governor had decided to "brusquer les choses". He read his prepared reply to the legislative councillors; and three days later he briefly announced its consequences to the Canadians. "My answer to Legislative Council address," he wired Monck, "proved too strong for my government who have resigned today."[91]

Chapter Fifteen

Triumph

I

Macdonald's first feeling was one of enormous relief. "The *Telegraph* of yesterday informed me," he wrote to Peter Mitchell on the morning of April 10, before Gordon's telegram had arrived, "that you have not yet got through your vote of want of confidence in the Lower House, but that you are in the midst of a ministerial crisis, in consequence of Mr. Gordon's reply to the address from your branch of the Legislature. I hope this is correct, and that you will be able to form an administration that will at once carry Confederation."[1] These hopes were strong—stronger now than they had been for months; but even so, they were still mixed with apprehensions and doubts. For months the handling of affairs in New Brunswick had seemed to him curiously clumsy and inept. What he thought of Gordon's conduct he kept carefully to himself. But he had criticized Tilley for promising not to submit the Quebec scheme to the legislature in a final session; and he was very suspicious of Fisher's want-of-confidence amendment to the address, which the Assembly had still been debating when the ministerial crisis occurred. He suspected that Fisher was "playing Mr. Smith's game". He was certain, at any rate, that everybody down in New Brunswick had been playing party politics a great deal too much. If Smith were, indeed, half converted to federal union, why was it not possible to form a coalition of both parties and to carry Confederation through the present House without a general election? What was needed in New

Brunswick, after all these devious meanderings, was a little straightforward action. "Can Mr. Gordon not be moved," he wired Monck on April 11, "to form coalition ministry so as to secure passage of address without waiting for re-election of ministers?"[2]

These early impressions vanished quickly. Tilley's letters—cool, realistic, yet resolute—supplied a full analysis of the "ministerial crisis" and of the awkward position in which it had left all the New Brunswick unionists. There was no doubt whatever—Gordon had put his foot into it most decisively. The long-faced, sad-eyed young man, with his unsubdued preference for Maritime union, his cold contempt for colonial politicians, and his secret longings for a nice biddable Crown colony, had chosen to "forward" Confederation by the brusque action of a benevolent despot. Even if all the worst suspicions of him had been true, even if he had been really trying to injure Confederation by his maladroit championship, he could hardly have acted with more tragic ineptitude. "In the particular case of your reply to the Legislative Council," Cardwell wrote privately a little later, "you made, as I thought and as you said yourself, a great mistake in acting alone and giving occasion for complaint which might easily have been avoided."[3] The indignant clamour raised immediately by Smith and his colleagues against the "arbitrary" action of the Lieutenant-Governor introduced a new and difficult element into the contest, and utterly changed the campaign which Tilley and the unionists would have to fight. "It is unfortunate for the cause of Confederation," Tilley explained to Macdonald, "that the break up was brought about in the manner in which it has been. . . . The Governor was indiscreet in dealing with his advisers on one point, though I think we can make a fair defence of him. Smith and the Antis now desire to make the issue one of a violation of the principles of Responsible Government, not a test of Confederation. Had the case not come up in this shape, we could have beaten them with great ease, but this new issue arising, it complicates matters."[4]

It did indeed. And Macdonald, up in Canada, hardly knew how to cope with the complications. What they had all hoped

and longed for had come, but it had come in such a questionable shape as to be hardly recognizable. Yet out of this disappointing and dangerous opportunity, an advantage must be
plucked, and at once. Time was rapidly running out. In
another three months at most, the Canadian parliament would
have to be called. And if, at the time it reassembled, there
was not an absolutely clear course for Confederation, then he
would have to do what he had repeatedly promised Brown
that he would do—he would have to deal with the constitutional problem of the Province of Canada alone. "If we fail
this year in New Brunswick," Monck wrote to him ominously
at the height of the crisis in Fredericton, "would it be possible
to pass Representation by Population for Canada on the basis
proposed at Quebec, with effective guarantees to Lower Canada
for her peculiar institutions and laws?"[5] The time was coming
fast when he would have to consider these desperate alternatives seriously. But not yet. The game was not quite played
out yet. Down in the Maritime Provinces there was now a
chance, as well as a hazard. And if Tilley and his new ministry
could only get the existing New Brunswick House to sanction
renewed negotiations for union, then they would be through in
safety. In Nova Scotia, where the legislature was also sitting,
Tupper had introduced a non-committal resolution, which,
while it said nothing whatever about the Quebec scheme,
did authorize the provincial government to continue the
negotiations for a federal union of British North America.
If Tupper could get his resolution passed, there would be a
clear way for Confederation. And Tupper, with his skill and
robust confidence, would probably succeed, if only his doubtful and restless Assembly were not panicked by the news of
an impending general election in New Brunswick. Tilley, if
he could possibly avoid it, must not risk another dissolution.
Macdonald telegraphed to him, begging him to get a union
resolution passed without going again to the country.

But this was precisely what Tilley could not do. If the
break-up of the late government had come over the issue of
Confederation, it might perhaps have been fairly easy for him
to have picked up a good deal of support from among Smith's

divided and bewildered followers. But Smith and his colleagues had resigned in protest against what they termed a "gross violation" of the principles of responsible government; and before adjournment of the House, which took place only a few days after the formation of the new government, the leader of the "Antis" had succeeded in reuniting his followers in an attack on the Governor for his arbitrary conduct. After this, Tilley could scarcely meet the same House again. If he did, the same majority would commence its constitutional tirade all over again; and the unionists would be prevented from getting at the question of Confederation.[6] No, it was obvious—there was no way of avoiding another general election in New Brunswick. It would be a difficult contest—just how difficult Macdonald began to realize as the long letters from Tilley kept coming in. It was rumoured that Howe would come over from Nova Scotia to aid the New Brunswick anti-Confederates; and there was no doubt, Tilley reported, that the American imperialists would supply Smith with money as generously as they had in the election of 1865. "The opposition are raising Heaven and Earth . . ." he told Macdonald gloomily. "Smith and his friends now attempt to keep Confederation out of sight and make it a constitutional test, and you know how the masses of the people view any supposed infringement of their constitutional rights."[7]

Macdonald realized that the Canadians must now make their supreme effort. In September, 1865, when Tilley had visited Quebec, they had discussed the possibility of Canadian assistance in the event of another New Brunswick election. Already the Canadians had paid over a good bit on account. The bills for Fisher's contest in York had come in; and early in January, Brydges had reported that he had "sent the needful to Tilley and kept all our names here off the document".[8] Now—from the estimates which kept coming in from Fredericton—it was clear that a much bigger effort was required. "I think we can with good management and with means," Tilley reported realistically, "carry a majority in the province. . . . If you can give us funds, we can send a responsible man (such as Mr. Wright of Saint John, one of our wealthiest merchants) to

Portland where he might meet Brydges or some other person to arrange finances. It will require some $40,000 or $50,000 to do the work in all our counties. . . ."[9] The sum was not unusually large for a provincial general election in mid-Victorian times; but the Canadians had to find it largely among themselves and their closest friends, for the rank and file of party contributors could not be expected to have a very lively interest in New Brunswick politics. Everybody—including the Governor-General—was agreed that aid should be sent and at once. "Cartier and Galt both think that someone in the confidence of the Canadian ministry should have an interview with Mr. Tilley," Monck reported to Macdonald. "I think if Galt were to go to Portland and get Tilley to meet him there it would be the best plan."[10]

When the money had been scraped together and Galt, or someone else, had gone down to Portland to give it to the New Brunswickers, the Canadians would have done all they could. The rest was up to Tilley and his followers. The election had been fixed for the last days of May and the first of June; and Macdonald was ready to delay the meeting of the Canadian parliament until the verdict in New Brunswick had been given. There was still time; and he was prepared to wait a little longer for certainty. But he had not reckoned with the unexpected, the unprecedented zeal of the Governor-General, Lord Monck. Monck may not have been a very profound or a very original political philosopher—"though the Prince of good fellows," said Gordon caustically, "he never appears to me to see anything with his own eyes or to look below the surface."[11] But, up to that moment at any rate, he had been —in his comfortable, rather sluggish fashion—a very sensible and cautious guide. Now the news that came up from the Maritime Provinces seemed to electrify him with a frantic zeal for instant action. On April 17 the union resolution had successfully passed the Nova Scotian Assembly; and, at about the same time, letters arrived from the Lieutenant-Governors of both Newfoundland and Prince Edward Island, speaking in optimistic terms of the prospects of Confederation in these provinces.[12] "I think the time has come," Monck wrote to

Macdonald, "when we ought to call our Parliament together."[18] It must meet, he thought, almost immediately, in the first week in May. The local constitutions for Canada East and Canada West—the last part of the Confederation settlement which still remained to be completed—must be framed and passed as quickly as possible, without even waiting for the longed-for action in Fredericton. Then, whether the results of the New Brunswick elections were good or bad, they must hurry over to London in time to get the required legislation passed in the present session of the imperial Parliament. Legislation by the imperial Parliament was, of course, absolutely essential. In no other way could the British North American Provinces be constitutionally joined together in a federal union. The northern provinces were not independent states; they had never renounced their allegiance to the Crown; and as Colonel Gray had pointed out, "they still recognized a paramount and sovereign authority, without whose consent and legislative sanction the Union could not be framed". Obviously the independent making of such a union required the exercise of two essential sovereign powers which the provinces had not acquired, and never even thought of claiming; they could not formally amend their own constitutions, and they could not negotiate formal agreements among themselves or with foreign powers. Legislation by the imperial Parliament was necessary—particularly necessary in the case of the Province of Canada, for there a long series of imperial statutes, of which the Quebec Act, the Constitutional Act, and the Act of Union were the most important, had established the constitution; and what had been done by the imperial Parliament only the imperial Parliament itself could alter. Everybody took for granted that the Quebec Resolutions, and their possible amendments, were simply the basis of a bill which would have to be drafted in Whitehall, sponsored by the British government, and passed by Lords and Commons at Westminster. This, in fact, was the final goal of the whole union movement. And now Monck was all impatience to reach it. "To use a phrase of your own," he wrote persuasively to Macdonald, "the thing should be completed *per saltum*. . . . If we are ready and present ourselves

at the Colonial Office in time I am very much inclined to think
that New Brunswick—particularly divided as she now is—would
not be allowed to stop the way."[14]

It was a question of tactics. It was a delicate problem in
timing. And Macdonald did not want to be hustled into
precipitate action. There were half a dozen different parliaments
—including the imperial Parliament—to be considered. Newfoundland and Prince Edward Island, where the prospects of
success were still very vague, could be dismissed without
much attention; but the others counted seriously, and each
was a problem in itself. The Nova Scotian parliament would
expire by law in the spring of 1867; and unless Confederation
were completed before that date, it would run the grave risk
of another defeat in another provincial general election. In
Great Britain, the government was obviously in serious difficulties with its Reform Bill; and if the legislation uniting British
North America were not presented at once, there might be
a change of government, or a dissolution and an appeal to the
people, which would delay the whole business for months.
Both these considerations were important. They both suggested
speed. But there was a third factor in the problem—the New
Brunswick general election; and, for an equally important
reason, it invited delay. The Canadian parliament had formally
accepted the Quebec Resolutions without amendment. But in
Nova Scotia and New Brunswick it was hardly possible to
talk in public about the Quebec Resolutions without a storm.
The most that could be hoped for in these provinces was a
general resolution authorizing the continuation of the negotiations for union; but the passage of these resolutions would
certainly be imperilled if the Canadian legislature met at once.
If parliament met for its first session in Ottawa before the
New Brunswick general election, Dorion and John Sandfield
Macdonald would hardly neglect the delightful opportunity
of asking the coalition government whether it still adhered
to the Quebec scheme. "Had we answered in the affirmative,"
Macdonald later explained to Tilley, "you would have been
defeated, as you were never in a position to go to the polls on
those resolutions. Had we replied in the negative, and stated

that it was an open question, and that the resolutions were liable to alteration, Lower Canada would have risen as one man, and good-bye to Federation."15 No, it would be fatal to run such a risk before the New Brunswick election had taken place. But the Canadians could meet as soon after as possible, if only to quiet Monck's feverish impatience. And it was decided to call parliament for June.

In the meantime, another matter, which was to reach a crisis before the Canadian parliament assembled and which was to have a profound effect upon the general election in New Brunswick, had already begun to take up a very large amount of Macdonald's time. This was the Fenian Brotherhood which, in the spring of 1866, seemed to be working itself into a paroxysm of crazy activity. As far back as the late autumn of 1865, the two provinces with long land frontiers had become so alarmed by the threats of Fenian raids that Canada had called out nine companies of volunteers for service and New Brunswick had set about enrolling a home guard. During the winter the Fenian advocates of the plan of invading British North America had been stirred into even more frenzied demonstrations by the controversy over high policy which was still convulsing the Brotherhood. A Fenian convention, called in January, vindicated O'Mahony and the old gospel of revolution in Ireland. A second Fenian convention, called in February, upheld Sweeny and Roberts and their new revelation of "on to Canada". Sweeny and Roberts were, by their own confession, the more intrepid crusaders. Theirs was the more immediate objective. It was obviously up to them to do something spectacular. And, as March 17 drew closer and closer, reports began to come in from all along the border that the Brotherhood had chosen the symbolic occasion of St. Patrick's Day for the great adventure of their attack on Canada. "Be at all times on the lookout," "Oliver", the spy, wrote to Mc-Micken at Windsor. "A desperate advance and attack will be made along the whole of the frontier on or about the 17th instant. You may depend that a struggle is at hand. . . ."16

As Attorney-General West and Minister of Militia Affairs, Macdonald had to accept the main responsibility of preparing

for the Fenians. He accumulated masses of material about
them. The Fenians themselves always advertised their proceedings in public with vainglorious garrulity. Moreover, news
of their plans and doings poured in from the British minister
at Washington, from British consuls in the various cities of
the republic, and above all from Gilbert McMicken, the stipendiary magistrate at Windsor, who had organized an excellent detective force along the frontier, and who had a wide
acquaintance of spies and informers. Macdonald usually knew
more about the plans of the Fenians than the Fenians did
themselves. This, to be sure, did not mean a great deal. But
it may have meant too much. For Macdonald was usually
inclined, in a laudable spirit of prudence, to give the Fenians
credit for more sanity than they possessed, and to invest the
kaleidoscopic chaos of their plans with a degree of order and
coherence never remotely approached. On March 7, ten days
before the dreaded attack was expected to take place, he insisted, despite the doubts of several members of the Canadian
ministry, on calling out 10,000 of the Canadian militia.[17] When
the famous day came, the volunteers were strung out along
the frontier, waiting for raids; and the police of Toronto—
where a riot of St. Patrick's Day demonstrators was expected—
were watching the streets with apprehension. Yet nothing
happened. March 17 had passed in complete and baffling
peace. It began to look as if the only real result of all the
machinations of the Fenians would be a remarkable outburst
of British North American patriotism, a remarkable demonstration of the new British North American national feeling.

There was, however, another result—a result of still more
immediate and practical value. New Brunswick, as well as
Canada, was embraced in the comic grand strategy of the
Fenians. "At the moment I am writing this letter," Macdonald
observed in his brief note to Mitchell of April 10, "you are,
I fancy, in great excitement about the Fenians. I really would
not be surprised if these rascals gave you some trouble."[18] In
fact, the "ministerial crisis" in New Brunswick coincided almost
exactly with the threat of a great Fenian invasion—a threat
which ended in a few characteristically dirty deeds of incen-

diarism—and the coincidence was highly unfortunate for Smith. Smith and his followers were already upon the defensive. As Tilley had foretold, the leader of the anti-unionists had tried to shift the main issue of the election away from Confederation and back to the sacred principles of "responsible government". The attempt was not much of a success. The Governor, defending himself with a good deal of force and plausibility, publicly revealed his agreement with Smith; and Smith was obliged to admit, in his own elegant phraseology, that he had told the Governor that he "would go for a union provided one could be obtained upon fair and equitable terms".[19] Convicted at the worst of double dealing and at the best of wavering procrastination, Smith was a highly damaged man. His policies —"Western Extension" and increased trade with the United States—had proved impossible to carry out. Worst of all, the whole pro-American attitude of his government had now become doubly suspect and unpopular as a result of the Fenian raids.

Both sides, of course, tried to draw political capital out of the raids. But the Confederates were by far the more successful. "The Fenian excitement continues on our borders," Tilley reported to Macdonald on April 21, "and you will laugh when you see that the Antis are endeavouring to make the people believe that you Canadians have sent them here to aid Confederation."[20] There was, indeed, something of the quality of bad amateur theatricals about the Fenian movement, but there ran through it also a very real strain of vicious gangsterism; and the attempt to explain away the Irish-American menace as a clumsy Canadian imposture had the natural effect of increasing the public suspicion of Smith and his colleagues. Timothy Anglin, an original member of the Smith government who had fled from Ireland after the Rebellion of 1848, was declared to be in daily communication with the Fenians; and it was reported that Smith himself had become an enthusiastic convert to the movement during his visit to Washington on the business of the Reciprocity Treaty. The unionists, in their campaign, used the bogey of external danger to the limit. The

Fenian threat aroused doubts of their opponents' loyalty. It gave a new meaning to the grave warning of the British government that Confederation was necessary for effective defence.

Up in Ottawa, where everybody was now getting ready for the approaching session of the Canadian parliament, Macdonald waited with growing confidence for the outcome of the New Brunswick elections. Towards the end of May, the news began to come in over the telegraph wires. As was usual at that time, the elections were spread out over about a fortnight; and it was not until June 12 that the returns from the last constituencies came in. But there was no doubt, from the beginning, that the decision of the previous year had been completely reversed and that Tilley and the unionists were victorious. Only two of the ex-ministers of the Smith government survived the general defeat; only six of the twenty-two members of the old House who had signed the protest against the "unconstitutional" action of Gordon had been re-elected to the new parliament. This time, everything, including even the Fenian menace, had worked together to produce a smashing success. The Fenians almost deserved Macdonald's and Tilley's gratitude. The nuisance had a value. But it was an interminable nuisance, nevertheless; and just at the very moment when the news of Tilley's triumph was reaching Ottawa, the rumours of Fenian movements along the Canadian frontier were beginning to pour in once more, growing more precise and ominous with every passing minute. On May 31, the government called out 14,000 volunteers. These youthful, half-trained companies might have encountered nothing but the peaceful calm which had reigned on March 17; but chance decided differently. In the cowardly incompetence of Fenianism there was still the Irish element of the unpredictable; and among all the vainglorious "head centres", "generals" and "grand organizers" who had shouted for the capture of Canada, there was one man— John O'Neill—who was not afraid to fight. On the night of May 31, he led a body of Fenians across the Niagara River into Canada; and two days later he drove back a detached column of Canadian volunteers at Ridgeway. By the night of June 2, the invaders had hurriedly retreated to the United States; but they left behind them nine dead and thirty wounded Canadian militiamen.

II

It had all happened before, as Macdonald knew very well. There had been the large American invasions of his young manhood, and, much more recently, the tiny Confederate raid on St. Albans in Vermont. But this gratuitous act of mass murder had not even the justification of the feeblest of rebellions, of the smallest of internal disturbances. The St. Albans raiders had been native Americans, the commissioned officers of a power whose belligerent rights had been recognized, and which was engaged in fighting a great war. But there was no civil war going on in Canada and the Fenians were not Canadians; they were Irish Americans who had crossed an international border to bring death and havoc to a completely peaceful land. The incredible wantonness of their attack, which seemed to imply that a large section of the American people regarded the mere separate existence of British North America as a permanent offence, provoked, in response, an angry outburst of genuine national feeling. The entire body of the volunteers—over 20,000 strong—turned out eagerly to guard the frontiers; the Canadian parliament, meeting in the exciting atmosphere of an emergency, proceeded to suspend habeas corpus, vote lavish credits for defence, and re-enact the old law by which Von Schoultz and the other officers of the invading American force had been executed back in 1838. "The autonomy of British America," declared the *Globe*, "its independence of all control save that to which its people willingly submit, is cemented by the blood shed in battle on the 2nd June."[21] Macdonald's profoundest purpose in political life was to preserve that autonomy, in co-operation with Great Britain, and against the United States. Confederation, his most ambitious political project, was in essence a design for the defence of that separateness. And the Fenian raids had given a new significance and meaning to the federal scheme. They clothed the bare bones of the Quebec Resolutions with the living tissue of popular enthusiasm and popular will.

But this was not all. The raids, which in one way were a positive inspiration to the new nationality, were in another a mere added complication in the already difficult time-table of Confederation. How, while the Fenian crisis continued, could the necessary delegation leave Canada for England to help prepare the legislation which would unite British North America? Yet the whole constitutional process must be completed within a year or infinite trouble would certainly result. The New Brunswick anti-Confederates had been thoroughly silenced by the overwhelming defeat of June. But in Nova Scotia, Howe was still vigorously at work, gaining converts at every stage of his passionate anti-unionist crusade, and threatening almost certain defeat for Tupper, if the old constitution should last long enough to permit another general election. Archibald and Tupper were becoming almost frantic. "We *must* obtain action during the present session of the Imperial Parliament," Tupper wrote in great excitement, "or all may be lost. Our House expires by law in May next when a general election must be held and for reasons which it is not necessary to enter into here the result would be most disastrous to Confederation and probably defeat it altogether. I am sure I need not add a word more to convince you of the necessity of prompt and immediate action."[22] Further words might have been quite unnecessary but within three days Tupper added them.[23] And his importunate appeals for haste were reinforced by Lord Monck who, although the session of the Canadian parliament had not lasted more than a fortnight, was already fretting with impatience for the completion of the local constitutions of Canada East and Canada West.[24] Badgered by importunities and scarcely veiled threats, Macdonald kept his temper fairly well. He had always intended to have the local constitutions passed at the summer session, and he knew very well that the Nova Scotian legislature expired in the following May. It was a question now, not of strategy, but of tactics, he told Lord Monck; and he politely reminded the Governor-General that "somewhat" should be left to the Canadian parliamentary experience of his principal minister.²⁵ Yet on the main point he yielded to combined pressure. Tupper and Archibald came up to Ottawa towards the end of June to press their case; and it was decided that an effort should be made to get legislation through the present session of the imperial Parliament. The Maritime delegates were to leave for England on July 19. The Canadians—Fenians or no Fenians—would sail two days later.

Everything now depended on the continuation of the present session of the imperial Parliament, and on the survival of the Whig government under whose benevolent supervision the whole union scheme had been worked out. Yet it was at this highly unfortunate moment that the long-awaited crisis in British politics occurred. Lord Russell's government, defeated on its Reform Bill, resigned; and on July 7 Cardwell wrote regretfully to Monck announcing that he had left office the day before, and that he could no longer look forward to moving the British North America Bill in the House of Commons.²⁶ Only a week later, on July 14, the first news of the English crisis reached Canada. Its effects were shattering. What was to be done? With the prospect of the session in England being wound up almost immediately, whatever party was in power, was there any point in trying to carry out the plan that had been agreed upon with Tupper at the end of June? Monck and Macdonald decided that it would be useless at the moment to send delegates to London. They reached agreement easily. But it soon became clear that the Maritimers took a completely different view. They were determined to sail for England so long as there remained the shadow of a hope of legislation in the current session of Parliament; and Tupper gave a peremptory answer to Monck's first telegram, politely intimating the Canadian desire for delay. "Nova Scotia and New Brunswick delegates," he announced very firmly, "will leave on nineteenth as agreed with you. Any delay on the part of Canada for reasons personally explained will undoubtedly be fatal to Confederation."²⁷ Monck wired back the same day to Sir Fenwick Williams, the Lieutenant-Governor of Nova Scotia, arguing that it would be "simply absurd to send delegates home until we have some communication with the new Secretary of State", and begging Williams to "keep your people quiet if you can".[28] But it was difficult to keep the strong-minded and voluble Tupper quiet, and impossible to persuade him and Tilley to alter their decision. "New Brunswick and Nova Scotia delegates go by steamer tonight," they telegraphed Macdonald peremptorily on the fatal July 19, "and rely upon Canadian delegates meeting them promptly in London as agreed on."[29] But the Canadians had no intention of meeting their fellow British Americans in London promptly. Monck refused to stir himself and refused to authorize the appointment of a delegation.[30] The Canadians and the Maritimers were already out of step. They were also extremely annoyed with one another.

Meanwhile, the new Conservative government in England, underestimating the effect of an imperial political crisis on colonial plans, was going ahead on the assumption that all the British North American delegates would be arriving in England early in August. Lord Carnarvon, the new Colonial Secretary—he had been Under-Secretary during the Bulwer Lytton regime eight years before—was just as eager as Cardwell had been to complete the Quebec scheme in the current year. The session was very far advanced; but he believed it would just be possible, if he could count on the hearty support of the opposition, to get the required legislation through before the House prorogued. It would have to be a very odd, rudimentary bill, a mere legislative framework, which would leave most things—even the division of powers itself—to be settled by order-in-council, after they had been thrashed out with the delegates. He appealed to Cardwell.[31] Would the Liberals consent to help? Cardwell, of course, was sympathetic, and he reported that Earl Russell was most eager to have the Confederation Bill "ratified" that year by parliament.[32] It was true that the ex-ministers were very anxious that nothing should be done until the arrival of the delegates, and that they were a little perturbed at the amount of important matter that was to be left for order-in-council.[33] But an agreement was quite within the range of probability. On July 21, Cardwell had a long interview with Carnarvon; and on July 27 he pledged the support of the Liberals for the bill, on two conditions which could have easily been met. It was all useless. The very next day the news arrived that the North American steamer was in with the Maritimers, but not the Canadians, on board. There was, moreover, not the slightest indication of when they might be expected.

Carnarvon instantly gave up the idea of legislation in the current session;[34] and the Maritime delegates reached London breathlessly to discover that the cup of political security had been quite literally dashed from their lips. They had felt vexed and injured before. Now they were almost seething with exasperation. If the Canadians had only kept to the agreement and sailed on July 21 as they had promised to do, the union of British North America might have been made irrevocable by the end of the first week in August. Now everything must be postponed again—how long? In a long, complaining, and foreboding letter to Galt, Tilley mingled his angry reproaches with the darkest prophecies for the future.[35] The imperial Parliament, he informed the Canadians, was expected to be prorogued on August 10; and even when it reassembled, there was no certainty of the passage of the British North America Bill. A want-of-confidence motion might be carried against the unsteady Conservative government. There would be a dissolution and a general election. Months would be lost in these interminable delays. And all the time the fatal hour of the demise of the Nova Scotia parliament would be drawing closer and closer.

Macdonald remained unconvinced by these arguments and unimpressed by this show of moral indignation. "As the English Parliament has risen by this time," he wrote briefly to Oliver Mowat, "there is no use in my going home just now, and probably I shall not leave until the end of October or beginning of November."[36] He reminded Tilley that the Maritime delegates had sailed in the full knowledge that the Canadians had no intention of following them; and he could never be convinced that, even if the Canadians had yielded and followed in the next boat, the British North America Bill could have been pushed through in the fag end of the session of 1866. "The settlement of the terms of the Bill is not the work of a day," he reminded Tilley a little tartly, "—it must take weeks of anxious and constant labour."[37] The British Parliament could not meet again until January or February of the New Year; and if the British North American delegates assembled in London in the autumn, there would be ample time to prepare the bill. Tilley protested in outraged astonishment at this suggestion, and threatened that the Maritime delegates would come home. But the Canadians stayed in Ottawa. They had found, in the meantime, another and an excellent reason for delay. Once again the rumours of a Fenian raid began to multiply; and a wave of panic excitement swept over the entire province.

Macdonald, who had considered early in July that "the Fenians are thoroughly disheartened," refused to be over-excited by these threats.[38] "The *Globe*'s idea about calling out all the volunteers is all nonsense," he wrote to Gilbert McMicken on August 25, "and no one knows better than Brown that it is so, but he desires to make a fuss and cause discontent."[39] Without much doubt, the opposition newspapers were exploiting the public fear. But, during the next few days, the rumours became more circumstantial and alarming hour by hour. On August 27, Monck and Sir John Michel, the General Officer Commanding the imperial forces in Canada, suddenly sent off an appeal to the British government for reinforcements. Only a very little while before, the appeal would have gone by diplomatic bag in the next Atlantic mail; but this message sped over to England through the newly laid cable; and the very next day Carnarvon was himself telegraphing Disraeli at Hughenden Manor, trying to arrange for an immediate meeting of the Cabinet on the Canadian crisis.[40] There was no doubt about what the imperial government would do in such an emergency. Carnarvon acted with speed and efficiency;[41] and in the last days of the month he was seeking ocean transports for the troops, while Macdonald was writing to Michel about the barracks in which they were to be accommodated when they reached Canada.[42] In the next few weeks there was a vast amount of work for a Canadian Minister of Militia to do. It began to seem almost providential that the Canadians had decided to stay in Ottawa. And in Ottawa they would certainly have to remain, until the approach of winter made Fenian military "operations" impossible. Monck, in the midst of the crisis, reported that he had received a dispatch from Carnarvon, inviting the Canadians to be in England by the end of September. "The present Fenian excitement has given me the opportunity of telling him," Monck confided to Macdonald, "that it is impossible for the leading members of the Government to leave until the season is so far advanced as to render an attack impossible."[43]

It was all very sensible, but its immediate consequences were unfortunate. The Maritime delegates, despite their threats, were still in London, kicking their heels resentfully; and what was still worse, Joseph Howe, who had followed them over to England, was busily employing the interval of their enforced inactivity in presenting the case of the anti-Confederates of Nova Scotia in long and persuasively rhetorical papers. He and his fellow-delegate, Annand, were writing something else as well—some more intimate, more decidedly personal communications—to the new Colonial Secretary. Macdonald was the principal subject of these effusions; and they were prompted by a shower of mingled eulogy and abuse which had fallen on the Attorney-General West in Canada during the last weeks of the summer of 1866. Late in August the *Globe* began an open attack against what it claimed was Macdonald's disgraceful intemperance. Macdonald, it assured its readers in scandalized tones, had been drunk at the time of the Fenian raid in June, and repeatedly intoxicated during the final fortnight of the summer session. The Attorney-General, his "utterance so thick as to be almost incomprehensible", had had to cling to his desk in the House to prevent himself from falling; and what was even more deplorable, he had been utterly incapable of performing his duty as Minister of Militia at the perilous moment when the enemy was on Canadian soil. On September 6, after several weeks of this abusive campaign, and as if in answer to it, the city of Kingston gave a dinner in Macdonald's honour; and, on that occasion, D'Arcy McGee paid tribute to his leader as the principal author of the Quebec Resolutions, and as the resolute defender of Canada during the Fenian raid. On the very day before the dinner, and with the apparent intention of discounting in advance all possible eulogies that might be made at it, the *Globe* amplified and summed up its lofty indictment of Macdonald's "weakness".[44] These charges were widely reprinted and commented on in Canada West; and in due course the Canadian newspapers reached England. Howe was deeply impressed. How better could he employ his time than in communicating this sad intelligence about Macdonald to the Colonial Secretary? He felt it his duty, he told Carnarvon gravely, to call his attention to the "impropriety and peril" of entrusting the defence of the Maritime Provinces to a man who could not govern himself. This gentleman, "whose habits and gross neglect of important public duties have been thus rendered notorious by the Canadian and English Press", was—so D'Arcy McGee asserted—the author of fifty of the seventy-two Quebec Resolutions. "Assuming the statement to be accurate," Howe went on jocularly, "the undersigned, while charitably attributing to the inveterate habits referred to the incoherent and defective character of the whole scheme, would respectfully submit to Her Majesty's Government whether the knowledge of its paternity is likely to make it more acceptable to the Imperial Parliament, or to the people of the Maritime Provinces whose institutions it is proposed to disturb."[45]

Macdonald and the Canadians were hardly enjoying a good press in London. Carnarvon wrote very sorrowfully to Monck, enclosing Howe's charges. Howe himself continued his indefatigable lobbying against Confederation, and the Maritime delegates had nothing to do but watch his activities apprehensively and nurse their grievances against the Canadian government. Brydges, who had received an extremely gloomy letter from London about the Maritimers, reported that they were completely disgusted with the long delay and on the point of abandoning the enterprise and returning home.[46] Macdonald did not believe it. Tilley and Tupper had committed themselves too far. They would have to wait. And, despite all these minor irritations and misunderstandings, Confederation was safe now —provided, of course, that there was no major political upheaval in England during the next six months. Yet it was bad politics to alienate Tilley and Tupper, with whom he had already made a defensive and offensive compact for the future. He wrote a long, frank, but conciliatory letter of explanation to Tilley, and Monck wired to Carnarvon that the Canadians would positively sail on November 7. "I think," the Governor-General wrote jocularly to Macdonald, "it is of very great importance that this arrangement should now be carried into effect and that the *feelings* of these gentlemen should not be further 'trifled with'!!"[47] Macdonald, who had carried the main burden both of Confederation and the Fenian crisis, was hurriedly preparing for the departure in the last weeks of October. "I have been working night and day to get ready for England," he told Thomas White, "and scarcely know how I shall be through in time. The Fenian prisoners and their fate may perhaps keep me for a while, but this is strictly *entre nous* for I am supposed to sail on the 7th without fail."[48] Actually, he was still frantically writing to Gilbert McMicken about the Fenians on November 8, and it was not until November 14 that he finally sailed from New York. There was still ample time, he was convinced; and a little before his departure, he and Monck carefully worked out a time-table for the next few months.[49] The three or four weeks between the time of Macdonald's arrival in London and the Christmas holidays could be spent in the last crucial discussions with the Nova Scotians and New Brunswickers. Before the Christmas break-up the delegates would be able to present their plan, in its final form, to Carnarvon. The conferences with Carnarvon and the Colonial Office officials could be begun with the New Year; and by the time the imperial Parliament opened, at the end of January or the beginning of February, the British North America Bill would be ready for presentation.

III

All the delegates were staying at the Westminster Palace Hotel. It stood at the junction of Victoria and Tothill Streets, a long, narrow, wedge-shaped building, which overlooked Westminster Abbey, and St. Margaret's, and the Houses of Parliament beyond. The entrance was on Victoria Street; and beyond the reception desk a short passage led to a long, handsome room—rather ornately decorated in the Corinthian style—which was then used as a lecture hall or concert room. Here, on the morning of Tuesday, December 4, 1866, the "London Conference" opened its sessions. It was a much smaller company than that which had assembled at either Charlottetown or Quebec. Neither Prince Edward Island nor Newfoundland had sent delegates, for neither island was as yet prepared to enter Confederation. Five Nova Scotians, five New Brunswickers, and six Canadians made up the group that settled down on December 4 to decide the last details of the federal union of their governments.

On the very first day, Tupper and Tilley proposed that Macdonald should be chairman of the conference.[50] Sir Narcisse Belleau, the amiable figurehead of the Canadian administration, had stayed at home; and there was no George Brown to deny to Macdonald the pre-eminence that everybody else was so willing to concede him. The chairmanship at the Westminster Palace Hotel was delicate and exacting, but not a really dangerous task. The men facing him were already convinced and had already committed themselves; and everybody knew that whatever their differences of opinion might be, a final set of resolutions would certainly be sent off to Lord Carnarvon in a few weeks. But the Quebec scheme, which had been accepted without amendment by the Canadian parliament, had never even been presented to the legislatures of the Maritime Provinces. The Canadians were bound, in theory at least, to stick to the letter of the Seventy-two Resolutions; the Maritimers felt themselves equally obliged to stress the changes which, they hoped, would make the plan more popular back in Nova Scotia and New Brunswick. They did not, of course, want any very serious alterations. The Quebec scheme, which was partly their own creation, was still fundamentally their own preference. But they were convinced that, at the very least, something must be done to make the scheme financially more acceptable—a "better bargain"—for the small provinces. On the very first day they announced bluntly that their authority to act was contingent upon a guarantee of the construction of the Intercolonial Railway; and a fortnight later Galt complained rather sadly that "our friends from the Maritime Provinces are excessively fond of talking, and very naturally wish to have some changes made in their interest."[51] Macdonald dealt in an easy off-hand fashion with the theoretically conflicting authorities of the different delegations. "We are quite free to discuss points as if they were open," he announced with bland inconsistency, "although we may be bound to adhere to the Quebec scheme."[52] On December 4, the conference began a rapid preliminary survey of the Seventy-two Resolutions as a whole, leaving difficult and contentious items for further consideration; and by the end of the first day they had got down as far as resolution twenty-nine.

While the discussions were going on inside the Westminster Palace Hotel, Macdonald was getting to know Carnarvon and renewing his acquaintance with the Colonial Office officials. The new Secretary, Henry Howard Molyneux Herbert, fourth Earl of Carnarvon, was still, at thirty-six, a comparatively young man. A gracious and cultivated person, at once urbane in manner and chivalrous in spirit, Carnarvon nevertheless clung strongly to his basic convictions. One of those convictions was a well-grounded belief in the wisdom of the Quebec scheme. Like Cardwell before him, he had an emphatic theoretical preference for a federal union with a strong central government. In July, when, for a brief while, he had hoped to push the British North America Bill through parliament in the last days of the session, he had confessed to Cardwell that his "foremost object would be to strengthen, as far as practicable, the central Government against the excessive power or the encroachments of the local administrations".[53] The new Colonial Secretary, just like the old, had been con-

verted in advance to Macdonald's plan. Macdonald was fortunate in this; but he was lucky in having Carnarvon for a
more general, and perhaps more important reason. Unlike
the coldly intellectual Cardwell—who had looked upon the
colonies with a little of Gladstone's calculating detachment—
Carnarvon believed in the continuance of the Empire, and
the future greatness of its principal colonies, with a warm
emotional conviction. Macdonald always remembered this
generous enthusiasm; and long afterwards he still believed that
Carnarvon, almost alone of the men of his generation, had
had a real and splendid vision of the great nation he was
helping to create.

Highclere Castle, with its lovely setting of gently rolling
parkland and noble beech trees, became, in its own pleasantly
informal fashion, a drafting-room for the British North America
Bill. On Tuesday, December 11, when Macdonald, Cartier,
and Galt travelled down to Newbury as guests of the Colonial
Secretary, the conference had already, after a week's work,
completed its preliminary survey of the Quebec Resolutions
and was deep in the consideration of the reserved contentious
points. They stayed overnight at Highclere, had a long talk
with Carnarvon on the problems of Confederation, and enjoyed their day's relaxation in the country.

It was late on Wednesday night before they got back to the
Westminster Palace Hotel. Macdonald was already tired out
and sleepy by the time he got into bed, gathered the newspapers about him, and began that final reading of the day's
political news which was his invariable custom before he blew
out the light. In a few minutes he was asleep with the candle
still burning beside him: and—how long later he knew not—
he was suddenly awakened by a sensation of intense heat, and
started up to discover that the bed, bed-clothes, and curtains
were blazing about him. He pulled the curtains down, emptied
the water jug upon them, yanked the burning bed-clothes on
to the floor, and, ripping open bolster and pillows, "poured
an avalanche of feathers on the blazing mass". The flames
were very nearly under control by this time; but he hurried
into Cartier's room and then into Galt's—the three had ad-

joining bedrooms and a common sitting-room—and waked his companions. Together, collecting all the water available, they put out the fire.[54]

It was only then, after the excitement was all over, that he discovered that he himself had been scorched about the head and hands, and that his right shoulder-blade was badly burnt. "So I got it dressed," he told his sister Louisa, "and thought no more of it." On the very next day—Thursday, December 13—the old problem of the Legislative Council, which had caused so much trouble at Quebec, came up once more. What was to be done with the twenty-four seats in the Maritime division, now divided equally between Nova Scotia and New Brunswick, if and when Prince Edward Island came in? And, even more important, should not some method be devised of increasing the membership of this body of immovable oligarchs, if it should get into a serious deadlock with the House of Commons? The conference debated a long time.[55] Provision was made for the entrance of Prince Edward Island; but otherwise the clauses on the Legislative Council were not disturbed. Indeed, there were relatively few changes in the whole plan, and none at all that affected its fundamental character. The conference emphatically bound the general government to build the Intercolonial Railway, substantially increased the subsidies which were to be paid to the local governments, and amplified the educational clauses in the interests of religious minorities. By December 19—two weeks after the conference had begun—the delegates had pretty well finished their work. It was just in time, for Macdonald at the moment could no longer act as chairman. The burn on his right shoulder, which he had characteristically made light of, was not healing at all. It had suddenly taken on an ugly look, and he had to submit himself to a doctor. For three days he stayed in bed, stubbornly reading. For eight days—while Christmas came and went—he was kept firmly inside the Westminster Palace Hotel. "I had a merry Xmas alone in my own room," he told Louisa, "and my dinner of tea and toast. I drank all your healths in Bohea though you didn't deserve it."

On the day before Christmas, he reported to Carnarvon that

the delegates had finished their preliminary discussions and on Christmas Day he dispatched the London Resolutions to the Colonial Office.[56] Almost at once, Carnarvon replied from Highclere Castle, saying that he had sent the resolutions off to London to be printed for the benefit of the Cabinet and the officials in the Colonial Office. Everything looked to be well in train, and Macdonald, who was tired with his work at the conference and bored with ten days of enforced seclusion in the Westminster Palace Hotel, badly wanted a holiday before the difficult business of drafting the bill began. But, at the back of his mind, he was always conscious of the inevitable approach of spring and the equally inevitable expiration of the Nova Scotian legislature. The bill, if possible, must be completely ready by the opening of the imperial Parliament. Was there time enough, he wondered unhappily, and wrote off to Monck, confiding some of his apprehensions. Monck, who had already followed him across the ocean and had reached his house, Charleville, at Enniskerry, replied comfortably that the imperial Parliament would not meet until February 5, and that there would be ample time before that date. He himself, he told Macdonald, expected to reach London on January 7. Carnarvon would probably return to town on the same day, and nothing much could happen until his arrival.[57] The coast was obviously clear, and Macdonald decided to take advantage of the respite. He hurried off to France for a few days' holiday.

It was his last holiday alone. His wife had died a little over nine years before; and now he was about to marry again. At fifty-two, he was very far from being the young barrister who had made his vows at St. Andrews Church, Kingston, back in 1843, and Susan Agnes Bernard belonged to a world very different from that which the simple and devoted Isabella had inhabited. Her father had been a member of the Privy Council for Jamaica; her brother, Lieutenant-Colonel Hewitt Bernard became a senior official in the office of the Attorney-General, Canada West, shortly after the family migrated to Canada in the middle 1850's. Macdonald came to rely a great deal upon the tall, handsome colonel, and for a time they shared bachelors' quarters together in the "Quadrilateral" in Ottawa. But, despite this close acquaintanceship, he saw very little of Susan Agnes; and it was not until late in the autumn of 1866 that the rapid courtship began. Mrs. Bernard and her daughter had returned to England to live, over a year before; and Macdonald met them, quite by accident, in Bond Street, during the early days of the London Conference. Though she was, of course, considerably younger than Macdonald, Agnes Bernard was a mature woman, tall and handsome like her brother, with a good deal of natural poise and dignity and a fair amount of social experience. She would make a charming companion, a distinguished chatelaine; and now that Hugh had nearly reached seventeen and was far less dependent upon him, his sense of loneliness may have increased. Before the end of the year he had proposed to Susan Agnes and had been accepted. They decided that they would be married very shortly, after only a brief engagement, while the delegates were still in London awaiting the passage of the British North America Bill.[58]

It began to look as if the marriage ceremony might coincide with the most important debate on the bill. By the beginning of the second week in January, Carnarvon had come back to town and Monck was installing himself in his house in Hill Street, Berkeley Square. There was a series of discussions and conferences with the Colonial Office officials and, in the meantime, F. S. Reilly, the professional legal expert, worked on the first draft of the measure. Carnarvon had hoped to be able to send Macdonald a copy of the first draft by January 20;[59] but there were the usual delays in drafting and printing, and Carnarvon himself was ill with influenza and preoccupied with his stand in the matter of the projected Conservative Reform Bill. It was Thursday, January 24, before Macdonald and his colleagues had received their copies of the draft; and another two days passed before they sat down, at Carnarvon's house in Grosvenor Street, with the Colonial Secretary, Adderley, Rogers, and Reilly, to go through its provisions systematically.[60] Carnarvon was in the chair, and he and his subordinates had only one really important criticism to make of the draft that lay before them. They did not object to the appointment of the senators by the central government, nor even, in principle, to their tenure of office for life. What worried them was the fact that this body of immovable life members was fixed at a total of seventy-two. They argued, as some of the delegates had already argued in the discussions at the Westminster Palace Hotel, that there was at least the possibility of a serious deadlock between the Senate and the House of Commons; and the draft on the table provided no method of escape from it.[61] In Great Britain, the Crown could always increase the number of peers and thus overcome the obstinate resistance of the House of Lords. But, in the proposed constitution of Canada, there was no comparable means of ensuring the ultimate triumph of the popular branch of the legislature.

Macdonald must have groaned inwardly as he saw this venerable difficulty coming up once again. The problem of the Upper House had very nearly wrecked the Quebec Conference and had preoccupied the London Conference with further long hours of argument. The plan, for which he had fought so hard and so long, must now be altered in a small but important particular; and to carry out even the tiniest of changes in the clauses relating to the Senate was an operation almost as delicate as the removal of a thorn from the injured paw of a lion. He took up the task once more, while the delegates and the Colonial Office officials watched him with a jealous or an anxious scrutiny. "Macdonald was the ruling genius and spokesman," Sir Frederic Rogers wrote later, "and I was very greatly struck by his power of management and adroitness. The French delegates were keenly on the watch for anything which weakened their securities; on the contrary, the Nova Scotia and New Brunswick delegates were very jealous of concession to the *arriérée* province. . . . Macdonald had to argue the question with the Home Government on a point on which the slightest divergence from the narrow line already agreed on in Canada was watched for—here by the French, and there by the English—as eager dogs watch a rat hole; a snap on one side might have provoked a snap on the other, and put an end to the concord. He stated and argued the case with cool, ready fluency, while at the same time you saw that every word was measured, and that while he was making for a point ahead, he was never for a moment unconscious of any of the rocks among which he had to steer."⁶² There were indeed, a good many rocks ahead; but in the end the very variety of the conflicting interests involved became a help rather than a hindrance. The different objections cancelled each other out; and what might have been a complicated compromise ended by becoming a fairly simple one. They had not quite finished with the difficulty by the end of the month, but on February 2 Macdonald wrote to Carnarvon enclosing a final draft of the clause.⁶³ On the recommendation of the Governor-General, the Queen might direct the appointment of three or six additional senators, representing equally the three divisions of Canada. And there, at last, the matter rested.

Macdonald, on his part, had another and a quite different criticism to make of the first draft of the bill. Reilly had throughout described the product of the proposed union as the "United Province". He was thinking, naturally enough, in the old provincial terms; but Macdonald believed in the national stature of the country he was creating. He had spoken more than once of founding "a great Kingdom, in connection with the British monarchy and under the British flag": and the title "Kingdom of Canada", which was undoubtedly his own preference, was written into the delegates' revision of the first draft of the bill.⁶⁴ It might very probably have been accepted by Carnarvon, for nobody believed more sincerely than he in the dignity of the country he was helping to create. But Carnarvon was not the only member of the Cabinet. There were others more important; and one of them was Lord Stanley, the son of the Prime Minister, who was Foreign Secretary. Derby, whom Disraeli later unkindly described as living "in a region of perpetual funk", was frightened of the possible international consequences of this defiant monarchical title.⁶⁵ Would it wound the republican sensibilities of the United States? Derby decided that it would; and the accuracy of his assumption was soon borne out by the facts. On February 27, H. J. Raymond of New York tried to introduce a resolution requesting the president to inform the House of Representatives "whether any remonstrance has been made by this Government against the proposed consolidation of all the British North American Provinces into a single confederation under the imperial rule of an English prince. . . ."[66] The Raymond resolution did not provoke much discussion in the House; even its sublime arrogance was apparently regarded as quite unremarkable. But Sir Frederick Bruce, the British Minister at Washington, sent a copy of Raymond's enquiry to the Foreign Office. The title "Kingdom of Canada" had, he informed Lord Derby, aroused "much remark of an unfriendly character in the United States".[67]

Although the preferred title had been rejected and Canadian hopes had been sacrificed once more to the fear of a dangerous outburst of American dislike, the delegates and the Colonial Office officials quickly found an alternative designation upon which they were all agreed. The name "Canada" proposed by one of the representatives of the Maritime Provinces, had already been unanimously accepted by all the delegates;[68] and they now proceeded to link it with the designation "Dominion" to complete the title. "The North American delegates are anxious," Carnarvon explained to the Queen, "that the United Provinces should be designated as the 'Dominion of Canada'. It is a new title: but intended on their part as a tribute to the monarchical principle which they earnestly desire to uphold. . . . It will give greater dignity to the commencement of this great scheme and consequently greater self-respect to those who take part in the administration of affairs there."[69] The Queen graciously accepted the proposal. She had been invited, by the second last of the Quebec Resolutions to "determine the rank and name" of the new nation; and when she had confirmed the title *Dominion of Canada*, the British North America Bill was at last complete. It was only just in time. Parliament had opened on February 5; but the next day, Rogers was still begging Macdonald for some important details for a few of the sections of the bill; and the Queen's final answer to Lord Carnarvon on the subject of the title probably did not come in until Friday or Saturday of that week. The last clauses were completed over the week-end;

and on Tuesday, February 12, the bill was read for the first time in the House of Lords.

Macdonald's last-minute delays with the material for the educational clauses and the powers of the local legislatures may very well have had their explanation in his frantic preparations for matrimony. On Saturday, February 16, four days after the first reading of the British North America Bill, the marriage ceremony was performed at St. George's Church, Hanover Square.[70] The Bishop of Montreal, Metropolitan of Canada, read the service; and four of the daughters of the delegates, the Misses McDougall, McGee, Tupper and Archibald, attended the bride. Seventy people sat down to the wedding breakfast at the Westminster Palace Hotel; and Francis Hincks, Governor of British Guiana, Macdonald's great opponent in times past, proposed the toast to the bride. It was mid-afternoon before the newly married couple left for what could only be called with some courtesy their honeymoon. It could not be longer than two or three days at most; for the second and crucial reading of the bill was scheduled to come up in the House of Lords on the following Tuesday, and Macdonald knew that he could not possibly miss it. Before the short February day had ended they were in Oxford. The university city was scarcely at its best in the middle of the dull Hilary term. But Macdonald could now regard Oxford as his Alma Mater; and the memories that he had carried away from it on the previous June were very pleasant ones.

He was back in London on Tuesday in time for Carnarvon's great effort. Surely the whole business was as good as finished now. There could be hardly any doubt as to the outcome; and yet, as he watched the operations of a Parliament in which he had no part or influence whatever, he could hardly quiet his nervous apprehensions. All this time Howe and Annand had been continuing their lobbying and propaganda against the British North America Bill. It was known that they were about to present a monster petition, signed supposedly by thirty thousand people, begging the imperial Parliament to delay the consideration of the bill until after the approaching general election in Nova Scotia. In the present state of affairs at

Westminster, with a ministry holding office precariously and a House almost distracted by the question of electoral reform, it was still possible for a sudden catastrophe to overwhelm the bill. Yet the debate on Tuesday night was unquestionably reassuring. Carnarvon, who was at the height of his form, gave the best speech that anybody was to give on the measure in the imperial Parliament. Normanby, Monck and Lyveden supported him; and Russell, though he again gave expression to his old preference for a legislative as opposed to a federal union, practically committed the opposition to an acceptance of the bill. It was comforting to hear how effectively Carnarvon dealt in advance with the case which Howe had been building up against the measure. And it must have been a moving experience to listen while the Colonial Secretary pictured the future which Macdonald himself had dreamed for his country. "We are laying the foundation of a great State," Carnarvon declared in the last eloquent sentences of his speech, "—perhaps one which at a future day may even overshadow this country. But, come what may, we shall rejoice that we have shown neither indifference to their wishes nor jealousy of their aspirations, but that we honestly and sincerely, to the utmost of our power and knowledge, fostered their growth, recognizing in it the conditions of our own greatness."[71]

From his uneasy position on the side-lines, Macdonald watched the rapid passage of the measure through the House of Lords. On Friday, February 22, the bill slipped easily through the committee stage, with only a brief reference to the petition which was expected from the dissentients in Nova Scotia. The third reading was to come up on the following Tuesday: but already Macdonald was worried about a different and even more exacting test—the decision in the House of Commons—that lay ahead. Could an appeal be made to Gladstone and Cardwell for their support, he asked Carnarvon unhappily? Carnarvon tried to soothe him as best he could;[72] but Carnarvon himself was now struggling, in agonies of indecision, to determine his own course in a political crisis which threatened to divide, and possibly to upset, the government. On Saturday, the day after the British North America Bill had got safely through committee in the House of Lords, Disraeli proposed to the Cabinet a new and more radical scheme of electoral reform in place of the moderate measure which had been so coldly received at the beginning of the session. Over the week-end, Lord Cranborne, the future Marquess of Salisbury, Carnarvon and General Peel decided that they could not accept the revised plan; and, early on Monday morning, they demanded another Cabinet for reconsideration.[73] "The enclosed, just received, is utter ruin," Derby wrote in a hastily scribbled note to Disraeli. "What on earth are we to do?"[74] Another Cabinet was called. In frantic haste, a new moderate compromise—the "Ten Minutes Bill"—was put together. Disraeli went down to the House of Commons with it, and Carnarvon and the others stood by their posts. But the compromise was received with noisy dissatisfaction; the Cabinet was obviously divided; and the mind of the whole Parliament was centred on nothing but electoral reform. What could be more sensible than to decide that the British North America Bill should be delayed? "A more unhappy moment could not be selected for sending the Bill to the other House of Parliament," Lord Campbell declared weightily at the third reading in the House of Lords, "unless the avowed object is to bar deliberation and make a chorus to repeat the statement of a Minister, or tribunal to register the edicts of his office. Distracted by a prospect which affects its own existence, the House of Commons cannot give its mind to British North America."[75]

Yet Carnarvon was determined that it must give its mind to British North America. With only a few days or a few hours of office left, he was fighting hard to get his bill through in time. On Tuesday, February 26, the bill finally passed the House of Lords, despite Lord Campbell's plea for delay; and immediately it was transferred to the House of Commons. It had its first reading on Wednesday; the second, crucial, reading was scheduled for Thursday. Wednesday, with a fine though unwitting sense of dramatic appropriateness, was the day selected for the presentation of Macdonald and the four other principal delegates to the Queen. It was, as he carefully pointed out to his sister, a special court, at which only those specially summoned appeared; and before it took place, at half-past twelve in the afternoon, the colonial ministers had, in succession, a private audience of the Queen. Macdonald, as chairman of the conference, went in first. There was nobody in the big room but Princess Louise, and Lord Carnarvon, and the small figure with the grave face and the sombre garments. He knelt and kissed the Queen's hand. She told him that she was glad to see him on this mission, that she realized the importance of the bill he was sponsoring, and that she was aware of the loyalty that the British Americans had shown. "We have desired in this measure," he replied, "to declare in the most solemn and emphatic manner our resolve to be under the Sovereignty of Your Majesty and your family for ever."[76] It was only a sentence; but if he had been asked to state the political purpose of his life in a single sentence he could hardly have done better. Then the audience was over, and he bowed his way out.

The next day, with Agnes at his side, he watched while Adderley moved the second reading of the British North America Bill. Already there were small signs of restiveness in the Commons. On the preceding day Hadfield had demanded an explanation of the curious haste with which the bill was being rushed through the House. It was known that Howe had received some kind of assurance from John Bright; and there was good reason to fear that the proposed imperial guarantee for the Intercolonial Railway loan—a guarantee fairly clearly foreshadowed in the bill itself—would provoke some caustic criticism from the inveterate anti-colonials. Adderley's speech, which had nothing of the eloquence of Carnarvon's, was practically designed to meet these criticisms and to stave off the demand for delay in the interests of the anti-Confederate minority in Nova Scotia. It looked for a while as if he had succeeded. Cardwell, who followed immediately afterwards and who spoke strongly in favour of the bill, committed the Liberal rank-and-file to its support in the same way as Russell had already done in the House of Lords. But the Radical voice of Birmingham was not governed by these commitments; and, in a few moments,

Bright rose to make his expected attack. He told the familiar story of the opposition in Nova Scotia. He made the familiar charge of indecent haste, and the familiar demand for delay. But it soon became apparent that his main concern was not for Nova Scotia or British North America, but for the financial and military assistance which Great Britain had so far granted them. "But if," he told the House, with that unctuous mixture of pecuniary considerations and moral values which was so characteristic of his school, "they are to be constantly applying to us for guarantees for railways and for fortresses and for works of defence . . . then I think it would be better for them and for us—cheaper for us and less demoralizing for them—that they should become an independent State—and maintain their own fortresses, fight their own cause, and build up their own future without relying on us."[77]

Yet, as Macdonald and the watching delegates were quick to notice, Bright ended on a somewhat lame and indecisive note. Nobody of any importance supported him in his attack; and after only a relatively brief debate, in which most of the participants spoke strongly in favour of the bill, it passed the second reading with triumphant ease. The detailed consideration in committee was expected to come up at the beginning of the next week; and Monck reported that on Friday night, in an attempt to ease the way for the committee stage, he had had a long discussion with Cardwell and Robert Lowe.[78] Lowe, another notorious anti-colonial who had not yet spoken on the subject, was expected to oppose the bill out of dislike for the Intercolonial Railway loan; and on Monday, March 4, when the House went into committee, he and Roebuck repeated their familiar arguments. Yet the bill went through with only trifling amendments, and Macdonald could draw a long breath of relief. They had taken almost all the fences. Now they were nearly out into the clear. Carnarvon had done his work and done it well. And it had been finished just in time. For on Friday Disraeli had again presented his radical scheme of reform to the Cabinet, and it had been accepted. Cranborne, Carnarvon and Peel had at once resigned; and on Monday, the very day that the British North America Bill passed through committee in the House of Commons, Carnarvon revealed his resignation in the Lords. The next day Macdonald sat down to write to him. He lamented Carnarvon's resignation, hoped that he would be soon back again at his old post at the Colonial Office, and ended by thanking him "as a Canadian for the sincere and great heartiness with which you addressed yourself to the object of our mission and for the able manner in which you ensured its success."[79]

Carnarvon had gone; but Macdonald knew now that "their" measure was safe. Adderley was worried that when the amended bill came up for consideration, Hadfield would move for delay until after the forthcoming general election in Nova Scotia. But, in the end, no protest was made, and the bill passed third reading on Friday, March 8, without a word of debate. The work that Macdonald had begun nearly three years before was finished. After all the fears and frustrations of the past months, he had completed it on time; and nothing remained now but the final problem of the guaranteed loan. "Pray tell Mr. Watkin," Adderley wrote to Macdonald, "that I shall be much obliged to him if he will speak in defence of the proposed guarantee which I hear is to be attacked strongly."[80] It was attacked strongly, by Lowe and others, with their accustomed arguments. But Gladstone, though he echoed some of these anti-colonial banalities in a long and characteristically involved speech, came down heavily in the end in favour of the guarantee, and its success was assured. The imperial Parliament had finished its work for the new Dominion of Canada. It had done, and done generously, all that had been asked of it by the British North Americans; and its members might, in Carnarvon's own words, "rejoice that we have shown neither indifference to their wishes nor jealousy of their aspirations, but that we honestly and sincerely, to the utmost of our power and knowledge, fostered their growth, recognizing in it the conditions of our own greatness."

Epilogue

The First of July, 1867

I

The day was his, if it was anybody's. He, above all others, had ensured its coming, and he had prescribed the order of its celebration. But the actual day—July 1—was not his first choice. For simple and practical reasons—he did not believe the preparations could be completed earlier—he would have preferred a date a fortnight later. But he was far away from London when the matter was finally settled; and on May 22 a royal proclamation announced that the union of British North America was to come into effect two weeks before his chosen date. "So you see," he wrote off to Fisher of New Brunswick, "we are to be united in Holy Matrimony on 1st July—just a fortnight too soon."[1] There was certainly not a great deal of time to make the necessary arrangements. "Much has to be done before then—," he told Tilley, "the members of the cabinet to be determined, the offices distributed, the policy considered, and the whole machinery set in motion."[2] But even with the weight of all these practical, political matters, he found time to give some attention to the day itself. Others would expatiate eloquently upon its significance—after he had done the work of bringing it about. He was neither an orator nor a prophet. And it was characteristic of him to speak of what was so largely his own creation with jocular understatement rather than with rhetorical hyperbole. "By the exercise of common sense and a limited amount of that patriotism which goes by the name of self-interest," he wrote frankly to Shea of Newfoundland, "I have no doubt that the Union will be for the common weal."³ He would never exaggerate any occasion or glorify any future; but he had the conservative's feeling for historical continuity, for the stages in the process of national growth; and from the first he had determined that the day of the Dominion's beginning should have its appropriate celebration. "On the 1st July, as you know," he wrote Denis Godley, Monck's secretary, "Confederation will be a fixed fact and we think it well that some ceremony should be used in inaugurating the new system."⁴ It was decided to make the day a general holiday. The volunteers were to turn out; and Sir John Michel, the Commander of the Forces, was requested to make sure that, in the various garrisons throughout the country, "Royal salutes should be fired, and the Royal standard hoisted, with such other military show as is usual on festive occasions."

He could prescribe the order of the day; but he could not determine the weather. Yet it did not disappoint him. Officially the northern hemisphere was ten days away from the summer solstice; but in the Maritime Provinces and along the St. Lawrence River valley there were as yet almost no signs that this long six-months' period, in which the sun's power had daily and majestically increased, had ended at last in its appointed fashion. The first of July belonged, by natural right, to the little group of the richest days of the year; and in 1867 no accident occurred to rob it of its birthright. On the previous night certain Canadians, watching the sky anxiously, had been disturbed by the appearance of a few ominous clouds; but by the morning these threats had vanished completely. All through the federation, the day dawned fair and warm, with a clear, cobalt-blue sky, and a little breeze that took the hottest edge off the bright sun. Everybody noticed the beauty of the day; everybody observed how auspicious was its splendour. "On aimera à se rappeler," declared the editor of the *Journal des Trois Rivières*, "quand la Confédération aura subi l'épreuve du temps, combien a été beau le jour de son inauguration."⁵

The day began long before Macdonald was up; in Ottawa it probably began even before he had gone to bed. Just after midnight struck, a long salute of 101 guns was fired, while all the church bells pealed, and a huge bonfire was kindled.⁶ Then, presumably, the people of Ottawa went to bed; but neither they nor Her Majesty's loyal subjects in other parts of the new Dominion were permitted to enjoy too long a rest on that short summer night. Early in the morning, when the sky was hardly yet paling with the approach of sunrise, the royal salutes began. At Saint John, New Brunswick, the twenty-one guns in "honour of this greatest of all modern marriages" were fired off at four o'clock.⁷ At six, they sounded out from Fort Henry, just across the river from Kingston. And at eight, when it was now full day, the Volunteer Artillery of Halifax discharged a long salvo from the Grand Parade, which came back, as if in booming echoes, from the guns of the naval brigade on the Dartmouth side of the harbour.⁸ The bells were ringing also, in town halls, and clock towers, and church steeples. High Mass was sung in the cathedral at Three Rivers at seven o'clock in the morning; and all over the country, people dressed in their Sunday best were walking soberly along the streets to pray, in early church services, for the welfare of the Dominion.

By nine o'clock, the sun was already high. The air was warm; the sky's benignant promise was unqualified. People thronged the streets of their own cities and towns, or crowded into excursion trains and steamers to join in the celebrations of their neighbours. The steamer *America* brought nearly 300 visitors across the lake from St. Catharines to swell the crowds in Toronto. And down in the Eastern Townships, the little villages of Missisquoi—Philipsburg, Bedford, Dunham, and Frelighsburg—arranged a common celebration to which people flocked from all over the county. All the shops were shut; the streets were bright with flags and bunting. "Bientôt," wrote one correspondent of a French-Canadian town, "St. Jean disparut dans les drapeaux et les pavillons."⁹ Down in the Maritime Provinces, where the anti-Confederates watched the bright day with sullen disapproval, a few shops stayed ostentatiously open; a few doors were hung with bunches of funereal black crepe; and in Saint John, New Brunswick, a certain doctor

defiantly flew his flag at half-mast until a party of volunteers
happened to come along, offered politely to assist him in raising it, and, on receiving a furious refusal, raised it anyway
and went on their way rejoicing. But there were few enough
such incidents; and everywhere it was a good-humoured crowd
that pressed along, on foot and in carriages, under the banners,
and triumphal arches and the great inscriptions and transparencies which, in English and French, offered "success to
the Confederacy" and "Bienvenue à la nouvelle puissance".

It was mid-morning—nearly eleven o'clock. The crowds were
thicker now, and they pushed their way along more purposefully, as if towards an important objective. The day marked
the greatest state occasion in the history of British North
America, and now its solemn, official climax was at hand. The
Grand Parade at Halifax, Barrack Square at Saint John, Queen's
Park at Toronto, and Victoria Square and the Place d'Armes
in Montreal were rapidly filling up with waiting citizens. And
all over the country, in scores of market squares, parks, and
parade grounds, the little officials of Canada, the mayors, and
town clerks, and reeves, and wardens, were about to read the
Queen's proclamation, bringing the new federation into official
existence. In Kingston, the mayor and committee stood on a
great scaffolding which workmen had been busily erecting in
the market square since early morning.[10] The town clerk of
Sarnia carried the proclamation honourably in a carriage, while
the Sarnia band and the volunteers paraded proudly in front,
and behind came another carriage and four, with four young
girls, all in white, representing the four provinces of the new
Dominion.[11] At the parade ground in Montreal, the troops,
regulars and militia, formed the three sides of a great square.
Sir John Michel, the Commander of the Forces, waited with
his officers in its centre; and then the Mayor and the Recorder,
bearing the proclamation, arrived resplendently in a fine carriage drawn by six white horses. The proclamation was read;
the bands crashed into "God Save the Queen"; there were
cheers for the Queen and the new Dominion. Then the Volunteer Field Battery began another royal salute; down on the

river the guns of the *Wolverine* boomed their response. And, at every seventh explosion, the *feu de joie* "cracked deafeningly along, up and down the lines, from the new breach-loaders".[12]

II

In Ottawa also, it had just turned eleven o'clock when the Mayor appeared at the entrance of the City Hall on Elgin Street to read the proclamation. There was a little crowd of listeners to applaud him; but most of the citizens of the capital were making their way along Rideau and Wellington Streets, and up Metcalfe and O'Connor, towards Parliament Hill. Macdonald, an early traveller along Rideau Street, had reached the parliament buildings in good time; and long before eleven o'clock approached he was ready and waiting in his office in the Eastern Departmental Building. The official inauguration was about to take place. He hoped everything was in order. It had taken him nearly three years to get the British North America Act passed, and over a month to prepare for the day when it was to go into effect. The work had been barely finished in time and his had been the major responsibility for its completion. The old thoughts of retirement had vanished now. He was to be the first Prime Minister of the new Canada. As far back as March 21, he had confided to his sister Louisa that Lord Monck had charged him "with the formation of the first Government as Premier". He was the obvious choice. There was no method of discovering what individual possessed the confidence of a parliament which did not yet exist; and Monck had fallen back upon the fact that the delegates of all the British North American provinces, assembled in conference at London, had unanimously chosen Macdonald as their chairman. "In authorizing you to undertake the duty of forming an administration for the Dominion of Canada," Monck wrote to him formally on May 24, "I desire to express my strong opinion that, in future, it shall be distinctly understood that the position of First Minister shall be held by *one* person, who shall be responsible to the Governor-General for the appointment of the other ministers, and that the system of dual First Ministers, which has hitherto prevailed, shall be put an end to."[13] The Provinces of Ontario and Quebec had replaced the old united Province of Canada; and with its passing had gone all those dual offices and dual departments which were the mark of its half-acknowledged federal system. Now, for really the first time, he was Prime Minister in form as well as in fact.

From the end of May, when Monck's commission and the news of the royal proclamation had reached him from London, he had been struggling to complete the arrangements for his Cabinet. It was the old task—a little larger and more complicated than it had been, but essentially the same. A few more jagged and intractable pieces had simply been added to the original heap of the Canadian puzzle. There were, as there always had been, racial interests, religious interests, and territorial interests to be considered; and there was the additional and vastly complicating fact that the new government could only be a government of Confederates, a government which drew its support and its leadership from the unionists of both parties in every province of the Dominion. It was true that in Nova Scotia there was a certain unreality about this assumption of concord. And in Ontario, the great coalition, which had been an inspiring fact three years before, was now rapidly degenerating into a rather dubious fiction. George Brown, who had left the government eighteen months earlier, was now busily reorganizing the Grits for the coming struggle against the coalition; and at the great Reform convention, held in Toronto early in June, Howland and McDougall—the two ministers who were supposed to represent the Grits in the coalition government—were excommunicated and overwhelmed with anathemas, in the lavish manner of an early Christian council. To his colleagues, Macdonald tried to put the best face on these depressing developments. "McDougall and Howland have returned from Toronto in good spirits," he wrote to one correspondent. "It is believed that they have made a great impression upon the members of the convention by their manly conduct there. The split in the Reform ranks seems to be permanent. . . ."[14] A split was all he could hope for now, whereas Brown had brought a united party with him in June, 1864; and it must often have seemed that to regard Howland and McDougall as effective Grit leaders was simply to alienate good Liberal-Conservatives without even the hope of gaining much Reform support. Yet McDougall and Howland had fought for him as best they could. He was pledged to them —and to everyone, Grit or Tory, who had supported Confederation. And the coalition must go on.

At first it had seemed relatively easy to maintain its impartial spirit so far as the Maritime appointments to the Cabinet were concerned. Tupper was a Conservative; and Archibald, who had come to be recognized as his principal lieutenant, was a Reformer. "You will of course come on with Tupper," Macdonald wrote to Archibald, urging both of them to be at hand in Ottawa for the first meeting of the future Cabinet on June 15.[15] Tilley, another Reformer, was also a certainty; and there was only a small hesitation about the other New Brunswick representative. "I note your suggestion to bring an associate with me," Tilley answered Macdonald's letter of invitation. "At this moment I am a little puzzled who to ask."[16] It was a choice between two people only—Fisher and Mitchell; and Mitchell, who, to do him justice, probably had no very great desire for office, settled the matter by reminding Macdonald and Tilley that his section of the province, the northeastern section, which had always given its support to Confederation and the Intercolonial Railway, must have some representation in the Cabinet. Where was the Intercolonial Railway to run—by the St. John River valley or by the North Shore? Macdonald could easily appreciate Mitchell's argument that his constituents would expect an advocate for their interests in the government. "It would certainly appear to me, on the first impression, as the lawyers say," Macdonald wrote back to Mitchell, "that it would be politic to select a St. John's river man and a northern route man for the Cabinet."[17] Tilley agreed. The Maritime contingent was complete; and towards the end of June, Tupper, Tilley, Mitchell and Archibald had arrived in Ottawa.

To their surprise, they found the whole matter of the Cabinet chaotically unsettled and Macdonald almost in despair of effecting a settlement. As far back as May 30, he had told Tilley that he had already made preliminary arrangements for Ontario and Quebec; but possibly even he did not expect the variety and the truculent strength of the demands that were made of him. Though McDougall could always fall back upon the need of maintaining the principle of the coalition, his bargaining power, as a Reform leader, was obviously in decline. Yet he demanded no fewer than three places for himself and his associates in the Cabinet. "You admitted," he reminded Macdonald, "that if Ontario should be represented by five members in the Cabinet, the Liberal party should have three, your position as Premier equalizing the preponderance of Liberals in that Province."[18] This would leave Macdonald only two places for his faithful Liberal-Conservatives. He was anxious to have Alexander Campbell, his old partner, in the Cabinet. But Campbell had always been regarded as a moderate "Rep.-by-Pop." Conservative; and his inclusion would leave no room for a representative of the old Tories, the followers of MacNab and Hillyard Cameron, who up to a few years before had been such an important factor in the party. Still, as McDougall said, he would himself be Prime Minister. He had forced the poor Tories to accept a good many unpleasant things in the past two decades. Perhaps they would follow him grumblingly still.

The real difficulty was not in Ontario at all, but in Quebec. McDougall and Howland had insisted not only that Ontario must have five seats, and that three of the five should be given to Reformers, but also that Quebec would have to be content with one seat fewer than her sister province. This somewhat perverted application of Rep. by Pop. to the business of cabinet-making instantly created the most awful difficulties. Cartier was ready to agree that Quebec could have only four cabinet ministers; but he would not consider for even a minute the suggestion that the French-Canadian membership should be reduced by one. Whatever happened, he and Hector Langevin and Jean Charles Chapais must be ministers. That would leave only one seat. But there were still two important interests in the province which were unrepresented—the English-speaking, Protestant minority, which had long looked up to Galt of Sherbrooke as its leader, and the Irish Roman Catholics, who had grown greatly in numbers in the past few decades, and who had fixed their affections upon Thomas D'Arcy McGee. Galt, however wayward and temperamental he might be, was undeniably one of the ablest men in Canadian politics. But McGee had been the chief public prophet of Confederation; and he was quite conscious of his enormous popularity. "I certainly have no desire to embarrass future arrangements which will naturally be under your direction," he had written Macdonald as early as April 9, "but in a Confederation Government, founded on principles which I have always zealously advocated, I will, if in Parliament, give way neither to Galt, nor to a third Frenchman, 'nor to any other man'."[19]

There were demands, stubborn and unyielding demands, on all sides. How could he satisfy them? He was almost ready to throw the whole business up in disgust, when at nearly the last moment—it was one week away from July 1—a way out was found. Charles Tupper, with his robust optimism and friendly good nature, was a man more generous in spirit than many of those who had gathered at Ottawa. He offered to give up his own strong claim to office, and suggested a method by which his withdrawal could be used to settle the difficulty. In his place there might be appointed another Nova Scotian who was also a Roman Catholic, a Nova Scotian who might thus satisfy both the claims of his own province and the aspirations of his co-religionists in Canada as a whole. Tupper's resignation was essential to the success of this plan; but so also was McGee's; and McGee, despite his pugnacious protestations of a few weeks ago, yielded his personal claims. On June 24 Macdonald wired offering a seat in the new Cabinet to Edward Kenny, who happened to be both a Nova Scotian and a Roman Catholic. He had few other claims to distinction or to office; but in the circumstances, he was apparently worth both the veterans, Tupper and McGee. The first Confederate government was complete.

III

As eleven o'clock drew close, they were all waiting—all
except Edward Kenny, of course, who had hardly had time
to collect his senses and his luggage, let alone make the long
journey between Nova Scotia and Ottawa. A crowd of Ottawa
citizens had gathered outside the Eastern Departmental Building,
and people had even pushed their way along the corridors to the
doors of the Privy Council chamber. Monck was expected at
almost any minute. The Governor-General, in his characteristic
easy-going fashion, had not sailed from England until the last
possible moment, and had reached Quebec on June 25. "I
bring out with me," he wrote reassuringly to Macdonald, "my
new commission and the Great Seal of Canada, Ontario, and
Quebec, so that everything is ready to start the new coach
on Monday next."[20] The new coach was indeed ready; but
Monck was apparently unaware that he should contribute
anything special to the pomp and circumstance of its send-off.
"I hope the people of Ottawa," he wrote anxiously to Macdonald, "will be satisfied to postpone any *demonstration* until
I come to remain at Rideau Hall as I should like that my
present visit should be considered one for business only." To
be told that the inauguration of Confederation was "business
only" was a little depressing to the spirit. Yet Monck had
some justification for looking rather coolly upon the visit to
Ottawa that he was about to undertake. It was nearly three
years ago that George Brown had described Rideau Hall as
a "miserable little house". "To patch up that building," he had
insisted to Macdonald, "will cost more than a new one. . . ."[21]
But, despite this advice, the government had decided to "patch
up" instead of building anew, and even after three years the
"patching up" process was not complete. Monck could camp
out for a night or two at Rideau Hall; but permanent residence would certainly have to be deferred till later. He may
have been slightly annoyed. He would hardly have been
human if he had not been. But there was more than a little
temporary irritation back of his casual attitude to July first.
He had believed firmly in Confederation, and had done all in

his power to strengthen it and forward its progress. But Carnarvon's visions would have been quickly dissipated in his practical, workaday mind. A "good man", Macdonald described him later, but quite unable, from the constitution of his mind, "to rise to the occasion".

Along with a large crowd of people, Macdonald had waited on the dock for the steamer *Queen Victoria*, which had borne Monck up to Ottawa on Friday, June 28. He would have liked to see Lord Monck, as head now of the new state, in a role more imposing than his former one. In April, after the British North America Act had been passed, he had suggested that it would be gratifying to the people of Canada if the Governor-General could be styled Viceroy as in India.[22] But such touches of purple had not been applied; if Canada could not be a kingdom, presumably she could not have a viceroy. And it was simply a very typical mid-Victorian gentleman, in civilian clothes, and with only his private secretary, Godley, as attendant, who had landed at Ottawa and driven away in a carriage to Rideau Hall.[23] There had been no reception on Friday night, and no ceremony; and now, as he waited anxiously for the Governor on the morning of July 1, Macdonald knew very well that he could expect a repetition of the same kind of gentlemanly informality. He was not disappointed. Monck drove up to the East Block in plain clothes and with Godley as his only companion.[24] The crowd of waiting people was hardly aware of his arrival, and there was no demonstration. He walked along the corridors to the Privy Council chamber. The prospective councillors, the judges, and a few officers in uniform were waiting for him there; and after he had entered the room, the doors were thrown open to the public.

The brief, business-like ceremony began. Godley read Monck's new commission; and the judges—Chief Justice Draper, Chief Justice Richards, and Justices Mondelet, Hagarty, and Wilson—administered the oaths.[25] The Governor, his hand resting on the Bible, spoke the solemn words in a clear, firm voice; and then, having shaken hands with the judges, he seated himself in the chair of state. Up to this point the proceedings had been unremarkable, and could easily have been anticipated; but now came an announcement which Macdonald could have foretold in only the most general fashion. Monck had determined that the coming of Confederation should be marked by the distribution of honours; and, in conformity with a custom which up to that time had been invariable, he and the Colonial Office officials had among them decided what the honours were to be. Cartier, Galt, Tupper, Tilley, McDougall, and Howland were to be made Companions of the Bath—there was no doubt about that. There was equally no doubt that Macdonald should be given a superior honour, for in Monck's opinion he had unquestionably been the principal architect of federal union. But what form should this special royal favour take? At first Monck thought of a Baronetcy; but in the end he agreed with the new Colonial Secretary, the Duke of Buckingham and Chandos, that Macdonald should be made a Knight Commander of the Bath.[26] It was a sharp distinction between the new Prime Minister and his colleagues; and, as Macdonald heard Monck make the announcement that morning, he must have realized instantly that it would be regarded as an invidious distinction as well. In one minute a grave political mistake had been made. But the public session was over; the onlookers withdrew from the Privy Council chamber—the newspaper correspondents among them; and in a few minutes the news of the awards would be speeding over the telegraph wires. The thing had been done; and a little while later Monck and his new councillors, including his new Knight, adjourned their meeting to review the troops on Parliament Hill.

It was high noon now, and for the last hour and a half, all through the four provinces, the military parades and reviews had been going on. At an early hour in the morning the citizens of Kingston had been streaming across the Cataraqui Bridge and up to the Barriefield Common to secure the choicest positions for the spectacle; and before half-past ten, when the review began in Toronto, the Torontonians had gathered in an "immense circle" round the reviewing grounds to the north-west of the city.[27] In little places like Cayuga, where the 37th Battalion of Haldimand Rifles paraded—"the 37th cannot be surpassed by any Battalion in Canada"—it was the volunteers, of course, who made up the review.[28] But in the larger towns of Halifax, Quebec, and Montreal, where there were imperial garrisons, the regular soldiers gave a smart professional air to the exercises; and at Toronto the most romantic feature of the whole day's entertainment was the presence of the 13th Hussars, the "Noble Six Hundred" of Balaclava, who had newly arrived in town. For a couple of hours, while the bright day grew rapidly warmer, and the vendors of soda water, ice cream and confectionery did a roaring trade, the troops marched, and drilled and fought mimic battles. Cavalry crashed against hollow squares and "thin red lines"; the Hussars went by at the gallop in a blur of blue and silver; and everybody admired the wonders of the new Snider-Enfield breech-loading rifles. Then came the grand march past, and the general salute, and the review was over.

IV

In Ottawa, the last of the troops marched down Parliament Hill and away, and the crowd, in search of its midday meal, began slowly to disperse. The square, with the fountain playing in the middle, was nearly empty. But Monck, Macdonald, and the other ministers, after only a brief interval, returned to the Privy Council chamber to complete the list of essential actions, without which government in Canada and its provinces could not have functioned at all. It was early afternoon —the climax of the long summer's day. In the height of the sky, the sun seemed scarcely to have moved; and the whole earth sunned itself luxuriously in the careless assurance of the long hours of warmth that lay ahead. From the windows of the Privy Council chamber, one could watch the river, all splashed with sunshine, flowing smoothly away past the high cliffs of Major Hill Park towards the north-east. Beyond the far bank stretched the pale green river flats, and beyond them, rising abruptly in wave after long, low wave of pine trees, were the Laurentian hills. In that far country where all the colours seemed to darken so swiftly into sombre blues, there was, on most days and in most lights, the harsh suggestion of something vast and gnarled and forbiddingly inhospitable. But on this day of brilliant sunshine, the colours of the whole ragged landscape had mysteriously lightened and freshened; the dull blue had narrowed to a thin line at the horizon, and it was possible to distinguish clearings, and perhaps a village or a winding road—the signs of indomitable human life. It was warmer now—the heat of an unruffled summer's day. And they must have felt it in the Privy Council office as they worked away, swearing in the ministers to their respective offices, appointing the Lieutenant-Governors of the different provinces, setting the coach in motion, in Monck's own phrase.

In the meantime, most of the population of Canada had gone on holiday. The parades were over; the proclamation had been read; everything official—civil or military—was finished. And the people had packed up, left their houses, and gone off to sports, games and picnics. At Three Rivers, a large crowd of spectators watched the Union Club and the Canadian Club play "une partie de cricket". There were games in the cricket grounds at Kingston, while the band of the Royal Canadian Rifles played faithfully on during the long afternoon; and out on the waters of the bay the competing sailboats moved gracefully along the course round Garden Island and back. The citizens of Barrie turned out to Kempenfelt Bay to watch the sailing and sculling races, and to amuse themselves at the comic efforts of successive competitors to "walk the greasy pole" which extended thirty feet beyond the railway wharf, with a small flag fluttering at its end.[29] At Dunnville, down in the Niagara peninsula, a new race-course had just been laid out. People came from all around "to witness the birthday of the course as well as that of the nation"; and while "the Dunnville and Wellandport brass bands discoursed sweet music to the multitude", the spectators watched the exciting harness race between Black Bess and Jenny Lind.

In dozens of small villages, where there were no bands or race-courses, and where there could be no water sports, the farmers and their wives and children thronged out early in

the afternoon to the local fair grounds or picnic place. Sometimes this common occupied a piece of high ground just outside the village, where a great grove of maple trees gave a
pleasant shelter from the heat; and sometimes it lay a mile
or two away—a broad, flat stretch of meadowland, through
which a shallow river ran. The waggons and buggies stood
together in a row; the unharnessed horses were tethered in the
shade of a group of tall elm trees; and out in the sunshine the
young people and the children played their games and ran off
their sports. For an hour or two the small boys who were
later to drive the Canadian Pacific Railway across their country
and who were to found the first homesteads in the remote
prairies, jumped across bars and ran races. The long shadows
were creeping rapidly across the turf when they all sat down
to a substantial supper at the trestle tables underneath the
trees. Afterwards they gossiped and chattered idly in the still
calm evening. Then it grew slowly darker, and the children
became sleepy; and they drove home over the dusty summer
roads.

By nine o'clock, the public buildings and many large houses
were illuminated all across Canada. And in Toronto the
Queen's Park and the grounds of the private houses surrounding it were transformed by hundreds of Chinese lanterns hung
through the trees. When the true darkness had at last fallen,
the firework displays began; and simultaneously throughout
the four provinces, the night was assaulted by minute explosions
of coloured light, as the roman candles popped away, and the
rockets raced up into the sky. In the cities and large towns,
the spectacle always concluded with elaborate set pieces. The
Montrealers arranged an intricate design with emblems representing the three uniting provinces—a beaver for Canada, a
mayflower for Nova Scotia, and a pine for New Brunswick.
At Toronto the words "God Save the Queen" were surrounded
by a twined wreath of roses, thistles, shamrocks, and *fleur-de-lys*;
and at Hamilton, while the last set pieces were blazing, four
huge bonfires were kindled on the crest of the mountain. In
Ottawa, long before this, Monck and Macdonald and the other
ministers had quitted the Privy Council chamber; and Par-

liament Hill was crowded once again with people who had
come to watch the last spectacle of the day. The parliament
buildings were illuminated. They stood out boldly against the
sky; and far behind them, hidden in darkness, were the ridges
of the Laurentians, stretching away, mile after mile, towards
the north-west.

A NOTE ON AUTHORITIES

This book is based on materials contemporary with the events described in the text. The principal sources are collections of manuscripts, which are to be found in a number of different archives and libraries in Canada and Great Britain.

Of these repositories, the richest in material relating to Macdonald is undoubtedly the Public Archives of Canada, at Ottawa. At the Public Archives are the Macdonald Papers, a magnificent collection of letters and documents, bound in 545 portfolios. The Macdonald Papers are more voluminous for the latter part of Macdonald's career than for the period covered by this volume; but the correspondence up to 1867 is considerable in quantity and high in quality. Obviously this collection has been of unique importance in the making of this book.

A number of other manuscript collections at the Public Archives of Canada have proved useful. The state papers of the different provinces of British North America are indispensable for an understanding of the period. The G series, which contains the dispatches from the Secretary of State for the Colonies to the Governor-General of Canada, is of obvious importance for a study which centres in Canadian politics; and the similar collections of the official correspondence of the Maritime Provinces, the Nova Scotia and New Brunswick Dispatches, are necessary sources for the history of British North American federation. The Minutes of the Executive Council of the Province of Canada are an essential record of government policy during the periods of Macdonald's tenure of office. Other collections of Canadian state papers—the C series, the J series, and the Upper Canada Sundries—have also provided occasional pieces of valuable material. In addition there are also at the Public Archives of Canada numerous collections of private papers, of which the Baring Papers, the Brown Chamberlin Papers, and the John Sandfield Macdonald Papers have been the most useful.

The other principal Canadian libraries and archives, from which material was obtained, are at Toronto. The John Langton Papers, at the University of Toronto Library, and the Baldwin Papers, at the Toronto Public Reference Library, yielded a few items of interest. At the Public Records and Archives of Ontario, there are several relatively small collections of private papers which have proved useful. Of these the most important are the Hodgins Papers, the Clarke Papers, the Buell Papers, the Stevenson Papers, and the Alexander Campbell Papers.

For the student of Canadian affairs during the pre-Confederation period, the Public Record Office is the most important repository of material in Great Britain. Here is to be found the other side of the official correspondence between the colonial governments and the imperial authorities—the dispatches from Canada and the other North American provinces to the Secretary of State for the Colonies. These state papers—series C.O. 42 for Canada, C.O. 188 for New Brunswick, and C.O. 217 for Nova Scotia—have been extensively used; and the dispatches from the British Minister at Washington to the Foreign Secretary, contained in series F.O. 5, have also been consulted for particular periods. In addition, the Public Record Office has acquired a number of collections of private papers, of which several—the Russell Papers, Carnarvon Papers, and Cardwell Papers—have been significant sources of material for this book. In particular these collections are essential to an understanding of British policy on Canadian federation.

In addition to the Public Record Office, several other British archives and libraries contain material important for this study. At the Royal Archives, Windsor Castle, a number of interesting letters were found. The Beaconsfield Collection, at Hughenden Manor, High Wycombe, and the Gladstone Papers, at the British Museum, illustrate British colonial policy as it was developed under both Conservative and Liberal governments. Finally, the Ellice Papers, at the National Library of Scotland, contributed some valuable information.

Contemporary printed material, of which there is a great quantity, has also been extensively used. The *Journals* of the Legislative Assembly and the Legislative Council provide essential information on parliamentary proceedings and government activities. The newspapers of the period are an indispensable source. Since there was no official *Hansard* at that time, they supply the only record of the debates in the Canadian legislature; and they also contain a good deal of useful information on electoral campaigns and public affairs in general. Valuable files of newspapers were found at the Public Archives of Canada and the Parliamentary Library, Ottawa; Queen's University Library, Kingston; the Legislative Library, Toronto; and the Toronto Public Reference Library.

NOTES

CHAPTER ONE: *The Immigrant Macdonalds*
(Pages 1 to 20)

[1] Public Archives of Canada, Macdonald Papers, vol. 540, Hugh Macdonald's Memorandum Book.

[2] *Ibid.*, vol. 538, Louisa Macdonald to Macdonald, 28 March, 1879.

[3] Joseph Pope, *Memoirs of the Right Honourable Sir John Alexander Macdonald, G.C.B., First Prime Minister of the Dominion of Canada* (London, 1894), vol. 1, pp. 1-2.

[4] Gilbert Gunn, "Sir John Alexander Macdonald of Canada and his Sutherland Forbears", *Northern Times* (Sutherland, Scotland), 27 September, 1923.

[5] J. P. Macpherson, *Life of the Right Hon. Sir John A. Macdonald* (Saint John, 1891), vol. 1, pp. 78-80.

[6] *A List of All the Officers of the Army and Royal Marines* (London, 1807), p. 369.

[7] *Quebec Gazette*, 17 September, 1807.

[8] Macpherson, *Macdonald*, vol. 1, pp. 79-80.

[9] Macdonald Papers, vol. 540, Hugh Macdonald's Memorandum Book.

[10] *Ibid.*

[11] *Ibid.*

[12] *Chronicle* (Kingston), 3 May, 1822.

[13] Public Records and Archives of Ontario, Alexander Campbell Papers. Undated Memorandum on Campbell's early association with Macdonald.

[14] *Chronicle*, 30 July, 1824. H. Macdonald is listed as the agent of *The Chronicle* at Hay Bay; Canniff Haight, *Country Life in Canada Fifty Years Ago: Personal Recollections and Reminiscences of a Sexagenarian* (Toronto, 1885), p. 296.

[15] *Chronicle and Gazette* (Kingston), 16 August, 1834, contains a contemporary description of the Stone Mills.

[16] *Hallowell Free Press*, 4 June, 1833.

[17] Macpherson, *Macdonald*, vol. 1, pp. 80-81.

[18] T. S. Webster, John A. Macdonald and Kingston (M.A. Thesis, Queen's University, 1944), pp. 1-5.

[19] W. S. Herrington, *History of the County of Lennox and Addington* (Toronto, 1913), pp. 98-99. The inscription on the fly-leaf of Macdonald's French grammar is dated Kingston, 23 May, 1825, which suggests that he did not attend school at Adolphustown for more than a year at most. The French grammar is in the possession of Percy Ghent, Esq., of Toronto, who kindly supplied the author with information concerning it.

[20] D. A. Lapp, The Schools of Kingston, their First Hundred and Fifty Years (M.A. Thesis, Queen's University, 1937), pp. 69-79.

[21] Macdonald Papers, vol. 540, John Alexander Macdonald's Exercise Book.

[22] Macpherson, *Macdonald*, vol. 1, pp. 80-81.

[23] Lapp, The Schools of Kingston, pp. 69-79.
[24] *Memorials of the Life and Ministry of the Rev. John Machar, D.D., Late Minister of St. Andrew's Church, Kingston,* ed. by Members of his Family (Toronto, 1873), pp. 11-37.
[25] J. Carnochan, *Centennial, St. Andrews, Niagara, 1794-1894* (Toronto, 1895), pp. 47-48. This volume contains Sir Oliver Mowat's reminiscences of his school days. There is a photograph of Cruickshank.
[26] *Chronicle,* 17 January, 1829.
[27] Carnochan, *Centennial, St. Andrews,* pp. 48-49.
[28] A Shortt, "Founders of Canadian Banking: John Solomon Cartwright, Banker, Legislator, and Judge", *Journal of the Canadian Bankers Association,* vol. 30 (July, 1923), pp. 475-487.
[29] No record of Macdonald's appearance before the Benchers of the Law Society exists; but the procedure described in the text was evidently required of all legal students at the time, and is described in some detail in the diary of Patrick MacGregor, M.A. (Edin.), 1815-1882, who was a candidate at the spring examination of 1834. A typescript copy of the original diary is in the possession of Professor D. C. MacGregor, University of Toronto, who kindly brought it to the author's attention. As the diary makes clear, Patrick MacGregor was accompanied to Toronto by Macdonald, who, in the spring of 1834, was evidently keeping another of the four terms required of students at law.

CHAPTER TWO: *The Lawyer's Apprentice*

(Pages 21 to 45)

[1] Notice of his marriage was given in the *Chronicle,* 23 May, 1829.
[2] *Memorials of the Life and Ministry of John Machar,* p. 56.
[3] Carnochan, *Centennial, St. Andrews,* p. 48.
[4] Macpherson, *Macdonald,* vol. 1, p. 81.
[5] *Chronicle,* 4 December, 1830.
[6] Macpherson, *Macdonald,* vol. 1, p. 81.
[7] Shortt, "Founders of Canadian Banking: John Solomon Cartwright", *Journal of the Canadian Bankers Association,* vol. 30, pp. 475-487.
[8] D. G. Creighton, *The Commercial Empire of the St. Lawrence, 1760-1850* (New Haven and Toronto, 1937), p. 280.
[9] Herrington, *History of the County of Lennox and Addington,* pp. 208-233.
[10] Macdonald Papers, vol. 336, Mackenzie to Macdonald, 29 September, 1832.
[11] *Ibid.,* Mackenzie to Macdonald, 17 December, 1832.
[12] *Ibid.*
[13] Herrington, *History of the County of Lennox and Addington,* pp. 214-215.
[14] *Chronicle and Gazette,* 3 August, 1833.
[15] Macdonald Papers, vol. 336, Mackenzie to Macdonald, 19 August, 1833.
[16] Macpherson, *Macdonald,* vol. 1, p. 82.
[17] Macdonald Papers, vol. 336, Ramsay to Macdonald, 3 December, 1833.

[18] *Chronicle and Gazette*, 25 October, 1834.

[19] *Illustrated Historical Atlas of the Counties of Hastings and Prince Edward, Ont.* (Toronto, 1878), pp. xiv-xv.

[20] *Hallowell Free Press*, 30 July, 1833.

[21] *Picton Gazette*, 11 March, 1931, contains an article on Macdonald's activities in Hallowell, based on the early files of the *Hallowell Free Press*.

[22] Macdonald Papers, vol. 336, Macpherson to Macdonald, 1 August, 1834.

[23] *Chronicle and Gazette*, 12 July, 1834.

[24] *Memorials of the Life and Ministry of John Machar*, pp. 55-56.

[25] *Chronicle and Gazette*, 6 September, 1834.

[26] *Ibid.*, 9 August, 1834.

[27] Macpherson, *Macdonald*, vol. 1, pp. 82-83.

[28] *Chronicle and Gazette*, 26 August, 1835.

[29] E. E. Horsey, Sir John Alexander Macdonald, His School Days and Law Offices (Typescript pamphlet, Queen's University Library, 1942), p. 3.

[30] *Hallowell Free Press*, 11 November, 1833.

[31] *Chronicle and Gazette*, 20 April, 1836.

[32] *Ibid.*, 9 March, 1836.

[33] C. R. W. Biggar, *Sir Oliver Mowat: a Biographical Study* (Toronto, 1905), vol. 1, pp. 6-18.

[34] *Chronicle and Gazette*, 30 May, 1835.

[35] Public Archives of Canada, C, vol. 148, pp. 355-356.

[36] *Chronicle and Gazette*, 27 April, 1836.

[37] Macpherson, *Macdonald*, vol. 1, p. 78.

[38] *Chronicle and Gazette*, 17 February, 1836.

[39] *Ibid.*, 6 February, 1836.

[40] *Quebec Gazette*, 15 July, 1836.

[41] *Ibid.*, 8 July, 1836.

[42] *Journals of the House of Assembly of Upper Canada* (1836-1837), p. 157.

[43] *Chronicle and Gazette*, 22, 25 February, 1837.

[44] *Ibid.*, 29 March, 1837.

[45] *Ibid.*, 11 October, 1837.

[46] *Ibid.*, 1 November, 1837.

[47] *Ibid.*, 4 November, 1837.

[48] *Ibid.*, 11 November, 1837.

[49] *Ibid.*, 22 November, 1837.

[50] *Ibid.*, 6 December, 1837.

[51] *Ibid.*, 9 December, 1837.

CHAPTER THREE: *First Public Appearances*

(Pages 46 to 68)

[1] *Chronicle and Gazette*, 9 December, 1837.

[2] *Ibid.*

[3] A. Jameson, *Winter Studies and Summer Rambles in Canada* (London, 1838), vol. 1, pp. 300-303.

[4] *Chronicle and Gazette*, 18 December, 1837.

[5] C, vol. 1968A, pp. 18-19; *ibid.*, vol. 1968C, pp. 25-27.

[6] *Upper Canada Gazette,* 15 February, 1838.

[7] *Ibid.,* 22 February, 1838.

[8] Pope, *Memoirs,* vol. 1, p. 9.

[9] *Chronicle and Gazette,* 10 January, 1838.

[10] *Ibid.,* 21 February, 1838.

[11] *Ibid.,* 24 February, 1838.

[12] A. B. Corey, *The Crisis of 1830-1842 in Canadian-American Relations* (New Haven and Toronto, 1941), p. 41.

[13] *Chronicle and Gazette,* 21 March, 1838.

[14] E. E. Horsey, *Kingston a Century Ago* (Kingston, 1938), pp. 16-19.

[15] *Chronicle and Gazette,* 28 March, 1838.

[16] Corey, *The Crisis of 1830-1842,* pp. 75-76.

[17] *Chronicle and Gazette,* 16 May, 1838.

[18] *Ibid.,* 19 May, 1838.

[19] For example see the *Mirror* (Toronto), 16 June, 1838.

[20] *Chronicle and Gazette,* 30 June, 1838.

[21] *Ibid.,* 11 July, 1838.

[22] Alexander Campbell Papers, Undated Memorandum on Campbell's early association with Macdonald.

[23] *Chronicle and Gazette,* 11 July, 1838.

[24] *Ibid.,* 14 July, 1838.

[25] *Ibid.,* 21 July, 1838.

[26] C, vol. 611, pp. 24-30, Bonnycastle to Wright, 30 July, 1838.

[27] Public Archives of Canada, Upper Canada Sundries, Cartwright to Macaulay, 8 August, 1838. This is the complete report of the Kingston magistrates on the escape of the state prisoners. It contains depositions by eleven persons, including John Ashley.

[28] *Chronicle and Gazette,* 19 September, 1838.

[29] Upper Canada Sundries, Cartwright to Macaulay, 8 August, 1838.

[30] Macpherson, *Macdonald,* vol. 1, p. 88.

[31] *Chronicle and Gazette,* 19 September, 1838.

[32] Corey, *The Crisis of 1830-1842,* pp. 77-78.

[33] *Chronicle and Gazette,* 10 October, 1838.

[34] Macdonald Papers, vol. 538, William Gunn to Joseph Pope, 11 July, 1891.

[35] *Quebec Gazette,* 12 November, 1838.

[36] *Upper Canada Gazette,* 6 November, 1838.

[37] *Quebec Gazette,* 18 November, 1838.

[38] C. Carmer, *Dark Trees to the Wind, a Cycle of York State Years* (New York, 1949), pp. 225-226.

[39] *Chronicle and Gazette,* 14 November, 1838.

[40] *Ibid.*

[41] *Ibid.,* 17 November, 1838.

[42] *Ibid.*

[43] Macpherson, *Macdonald,* vol. 1, p. 88.

[44] Macdonald Papers, vol. 538, Memorandum by Pope of a Conversation with Macdonald about Von Schoultz, 17 May, 1890.

[45] Public Archives of Canada, R.G. 5, B. 41. Copy of proceedings of the Militia General Court Martial, Fort Henry, 1838.

[46] *Ibid.;* Cobourg Star, 12 December, 1838.

[47] R.G. 5, B. 41, Court Martial of Daniel George.

[48] Carmer, *Dark Trees to the Wind*, pp. 218-225.

[49] *Cobourg Star*, 12 December, 1838.

[50] R.G. 5, B. 41, Copy of The Proceedings of a Militia General Court Martial, holden at Fort Henry, at Kingston, for the trial of Nils Szoltevcky Von Schoultz.

[51] Macdonald Papers, vol. 538, Macdonald to Overlander, 8 December, 1890.

CHAPTER FOUR: *The New Conservative Candidate*

(Pages 69 to 99)

[1] *Journals of the House of Assembly of Upper Canada* (1839), Appendix, Report on the State of the Province, 30 April, 1839.

[2] *Cobourg Star*, 25 December, 1839, 1 January, 1840.

[3] Alexander Campbell Papers, Undated Memorandum on Campbell's early association with Macdonald.

[4] *Chronicle and Gazette*, 12 June, 1839.

[5] Webster, Macdonald and Kingston, p. 14.

[6] *Chronicle and Gazette*, 18 December, 1839.

[7] *Quebec Gazette*, 22 October, 1838.

[8] *Chronicle and Gazette*, 18 December, 1839.

[9] *Ibid.*, 8 August, 1840.

[10] *Ibid.*

[11] D. J. Pierce and J. P. Pritchett, "The Choice of Kingston as the Capital of Canada", *Canadian Historical Association Report* (1929), pp. 57-63.

[12] *Chronicle and Gazette*, 15 August, 1840.

[13] *Ibid.*, 22 August, 1840.

[14] *Ibid.*, 3 February, 1841.

[15] *Ibid.*, 6 February, 1841.

[16] Macdonald Papers, vol. 336, Wilson to Macdonald, 23 March, 1840.

[17] *Chronicle and Gazette*, 27 February, 3 March, 1841.

[18] *Ibid.*, 17 February, 1841.

[19] *Ibid.*, 27 February, 1841.

[20] *Ibid.*, 8 August, 1840.

[21] *Ibid.*, 24 March, 1841.

[22] *Montreal Gazette*, 21 May, 1841.

[23] *Chronicle and Gazette*, 8 May, 1841.

[24] *Montreal Gazette*, 31 May, 1841.

[25] *Chronicle and Gazette*, 19 June, 1841.

[26] *Ibid.*, 29 September, 1841.

[27] Macpherson, *Macdonald*, vol. 1, p. 85.

[28] *Chronicle and Gazette*, 24 December, 1841.

[29] Macdonald Papers, vol. 336, Machar to Macdonald, n.d.

[30] Pope, *Memoirs*, vol. 2, p. 270.

[31] Macdonald Papers, vol. 539, Macdonald to his Mother, 3 March, 1842.

[32] *Ibid.*, vol. 336, Account of H. Sweet, Chancery Lane, 27 April, 1842.

[33] Macpherson, *Macdonald*, vol. 1, pp. 85-86.

[34] *British Whig* (Kingston), 17 September, 1842.

[35] *Chronicle and Gazette*, 28 September, 1842.

[36] *British Whig*, 20 September, 1842.

[37] *Chronicle and Gazette*, 8 October, 1842.

[38] Horsey, *Kingston a Century Ago*, p. 23.

[39] *Ibid.*, pp. 23-24.

[40] *British Whig*, 21 November, 1842.

[41] *Chronicle and Gazette*, 4 February, 1843.

[42] *Ibid.*, 29 March, 1843.

[43] *Quebec Gazette*, 24 March, 1843.

[44] *Ibid.*, 3 April, 1843.

[45] *Chronicle and Gazette*, 8 April, 1843.

[46] *Quebec Gazette*, 12 April, 1843.

[47] *Ibid.*, 9 June, 1843.

[48] Macpherson, *Macdonald*, vol. 1, p. v.

[49] Macdonald Papers, vol. 194, Memorandum of the Terms of Co-partnership between Macdonald and Campbell, n.d.

[50] Macdonald Papers, vol. 545, Macdonald's Marriage Certificate, 1 September, 1843.

[51] *Chronicle and Gazette*, 2 September, 1843.

[52] Macpherson, *Macdonald*, vol. 1, pp. v-vi.

[53] *Chronicle and Gazette*, 27 September, 1843.

[54] *Ibid.*, 11 October, 1843.

[55] *Ibid.*, 6 November, 1843.

[56] *Ibid.*, 6 December, 1843.

[57] C. B. Sissons, "Letters of 1844 and 1846 from Scobie to Ryerson", *Canadian Historical Review*, vol. 29 (Dec. 1948), pp. 393-411.

[58] *Herald* (Kingston), 23 April, 1844.

[59] *British Whig*, 3 May, 1844.

[60] *Chronicle and Gazette*, 22 June, 1844.

[61] *News* (Kingston), 3 October, 1844, quoted in Macpherson, *Macdonald*, vol. 1, pp. 92-93.

[62] *British Whig*, 11 October, 1844.

[63] Macdonald Papers, Macdonald to Thirkell, 10 October, 1844.

[64] *British Whig*, 15 October, 1844.

[65] *Chronicle and Gazette*, 16 October, 1844.

Chapter Five: *Minister of the Crown*

(Pages 100 to 124)

[1] *Chronicle and Gazette*, 23 November, 1844.

[2] N. Bosworth, *Hochelaga Depicta* (Montreal, 1839), pp. 149-150.

[3] *Journals of the Legislative Assembly of the Province of Canada* (1844-1845), p. 1.

[4] D. B. Read, *The Lives of the Judges of Upper Canada and Ontario* (Toronto, 1888) pp. 222-236.

[5] *Montreal Gazette*, 21 December, 1844.

[6] *Ibid.*

[7] *Ibid.*, 1 February, 1845.

[8] *Ibid.*

[9] *Ibid.*, 20 February, 1845.

[10] J. G. Hodgins, *Documentary History of Education in Upper Canada from the Passing of the Constitutional Act in 1791, to the Close of the Reverend Doctor Ryerson's Administration of the Education Department in 1876* (Toronto), vol. 5, pp. 159-164.

[11] *Christian Guardian* (Toronto), 26 March, 1845; *Journals of the Assembly* (1844-1845), p. 374.

[12] Hodgins, *Documentary History*, vol. 5, pp. 191-192.

[13] Macdonald Papers, vol. 545, Isabella Macdonald to Margaret Greene, 11 June, 1845.

[14] *Ibid.*

[15] *Ibid.*, Macdonald to Margaret Greene, 12 July, 1845.

[16] *Ibid.*, Macdonald to Margaret Greene, 11 July, 1845.

[17] *Ibid.*, Macdonald to Margaret Greene, 18 July, 1845.

[18] *Ibid.*, Macdonald to Margaret Greene, 31 October, 1845.

[19] *Ibid.*, Macdonald to Margaret Greene, 3 November, 1845.

[20] *Ibid.*, Macdonald to Margaret Greene, 15 November, 1845. Macdonald was fairly up-to-date in his reading. George Borrow's *The Bible in Spain* appeared in 1843, Charles Lever's *Tom Burke of Ours* in 1844, and Harrison Ainsworth's *Rookwood* in 1834. A new edition of Carlyle's *Life of Schiller* was published in 1845. *The History of England from the Peace of Utrecht to the Peace of Versailles, 1713-1783*, was a work in seven volumes which appeared at intervals in the years 1836-1853. Its author, Philip Henry Stanhope, Viscount Mahon, later fifth Earl of Stanhope, was an historian whom Macdonald much admired; Stanhope's *Life of William Pitt* (1861) later became one of Macdonald's favourite biographies. The *Sermons* were probably those of John Moore, Bishop of Ely; they were published early in the eighteenth century.

[21] *Ibid.*, Macdonald to Margaret Greene, 3 November, 1845.

[22] *Ibid.*, Macdonald to Margaret Greene, 20 November, 1845.

[23] *Ibid.*, Macdonald to Margaret Greene, 27 February, 1846.

[24] *Journals of the Legislative Assembly of the Province of Canada* (1846), p. 6.

[25] *Mirror of Parliament of the Province of Canada* (Montreal, 1846), pp. 104-105.

[26] *Ibid.*, pp. 109-110.

[27] Macdonald Papers, vol. 209, Draper to Cathcart, 10 June, 1846, quoted in Pope, *Memoirs*, vol. 1, pp. 43-44.

[28] *Ibid.*, vol. 336, W. H. Boulton to R. Maitland, 10 May, 1846.

[29] *Ibid.*, vol. 209, Draper to Cathcart, 10 June, 1846.

[30] *Ibid.*, vol. 194, Memorandum of the Terms of Co-partnership between Macdonald and Campbell.

[31] *Ibid.*, vol. 539, Macdonald to Margaret Greene, 20 January, 1847.

[32] *Globe* (Toronto), 9 January, 1847.

[33] Public Records and Archives of Ontario, Hodgins Papers, Draper to Ryerson, 22 February, 1847.

[34] Macdonald Papers, vol. 209, Draper to Macdonald, 4 March, 1847.

[35] *Ibid.*, vol. 545, Macdonald to Margaret Greene, 5 April, 1847.

[36] *Ibid.*, vol. 336, Morris to Macdonald, 6 May, 1847.

[37] *Ibid.*, Macdonald to Morris, 9 May, 1847.

[38] *Globe*, 22 May, 1847.

[39] Sir A. G. Doughty, (ed.) *The Elgin-Grey Papers, 1846-1852* (Ottawa, 1937), vol. 1, pp. 39-40, Elgin to Grey, 18 May, 1847.

[40] Macdonald Papers, vol. 336, Cayley to Macdonald, 22 May, 1847.

[41] *Ibid.*, vol. 539, Macdonald to his Mother, 10 June, 1847.

[42] Hodgins, *Documentary History*, vol. 7, pp. 4-6.

[43] *Ibid.*, pp. 6-7.

[44] *Christian Guardian*, 21 July, 1847.

[45] *Ibid.*

[46] Hodgins, *Documentary History*, vol. 7, p. 8.

[47] *Ibid.*, p. 52.

[48] Macdonald Papers, vol. 539, Macdonald to his Mother, 2 August, 1847.

CHAPTER SIX: *The Twilight of the Tory Party*
(Pages 125 to 146)

[1] Macdonald Papers, vol. 545, Macdonald to Margaret Greene, 31 August, 1847.

[2] *Ibid.*, Macdonald to Margaret Greene, 28 September, 1847.

[3] *Ibid.*, vol. 336, Cayley to Macdonald, 4 September, 1847.

[4] *Ibid.*, additional, vol. 1, Macdonald to Jessup, 30 October, 1847.

[5] *Herald*, 3 November, 1847.

[6] *Chronicle and Gazette*, 27 November, 1 December, 1847.

[7] *Herald*, 8 December, 1847.

[8] *Chronicle and Gazette*, 22 December, 1847.

[9] *Herald*, 22 December, 1847.

[10] *Chronicle and Gazette*, 24 December, 1847.

[11] *Ibid.*, 29 December, 1847, 1 January, 1848.

[12] *Journals of the Legislative Assembly of the Province of Canada* (1848), p. 17.

[13] Macdonald Papers, vol. 545, Macdonald to Margaret Greene, 9 July, 1848.

[14] *Ibid.*, Isabella Macdonald to Margaret Greene, n.d.

[15] *Ibid.*, Macdonald to Margaret Greene, 1 August, 1848.

[16] *Ibid.*

[17] *Ibid.*, Macdonald to Margaret Greene, 15 August, 1848.

[18] *Ibid.*, Macdonald to Margaret Greene, 29 August, 1848.

[19] *Chronicle and Gazette*, 23 September, 1848.

[20] Macdonald Papers, vol. 545, Macdonald to Margaret Greene, 3 December, 1848.

[21] *Ibid.*, Macdonald to Margaret Greene, 17 December, 1848.

[22] *Montreal Gazette*, 16 February, 1849.

[23] *Examiner* (Toronto) 21, 28 February, 1849.

[24] *Montreal Gazette*, 19 February, 1849.

[25] *Journals of the Legislative Assembly of the Province of Canada* (1849), p. 88.

[26] Toronto Public Libraries, Baldwin Papers, H. J. Boulton to Baldwin, 2 January, 1850.

[27] *Montreal Gazette*, 26 February, 1849.

[28] *Ibid.*

29 *Journals of the Legislative Assembly of the Province of Canada* (1849), p. 219.

30 Macpherson, *Macdonald*, vol. 1, pp. 148-149.

31 C. D. Allin and G. M. Jones, *Annexation, Preferential Trade and Reciprocity, an Outline of the Canadian Annexation Movement of 1849-50, with Special Reference to the Questions of Preferential Trade and Reciprocity* (Toronto, n.d.), pp. 49-60.

32 Macdonald Papers, vol. 545, Macdonald to Margaret Greene, 24 July, 1849.

33 *Ibid.*, vol. 194, Campbell to Macdonald, 8 June, 1849.

34 *Ibid.*, vol. 545, Macdonald to Margaret Greene, 24 July, 1849.

35 Public Records and Archives of Ontario, Miscellaneous Papers, 1849, Macdonald to Stevenson, 5 July, 1849.

36 *Montreal Gazette*, 28 July, 1849.

37 *Minutes of the Proceedings of a Convention of Delegates of the British American League held at Kingston (Canada West) on the 25th, and by Adjournment on the 26th, 27th, 28th, and 31st Days of July, 1849* (Kingston, 1849), pp. 7-8.

38 *Ibid.*, pp. 11-12.

39 *Montreal Gazette*, 31 July, 1849.

CHAPTER SEVEN: *Years of Recovery*

(Pages 147 to 173)

1 Macdonald Papers, vol. 194, Campbell to Macdonald, 8 June, 1849.

2 *Ibid.*

3 *Ibid.*, Campbell to Macdonald, n.d.

4 *Ibid.*, New Terms of Agreement, 30 August, 1849.

5 *Ibid.*, Campbell to Macdonald, n.d.

6 Horsey, *Macdonald, His School Days and Law Offices*, p. 4.

7 G. N. Tucker, *The Canadian Commercial Revolution, 1845-1851* (New Haven, 1936), pp. 178-201, 227-233.

8 *Minutes of the Proceedings of the Second Convention of Delegates of the British American League held at Toronto, C.W., on Thursday, November 1, and by Adjournment on the 2nd, 3rd, 5th, 6th and 7th of November, 1849* (Toronto, 1849).

9 Public Archives of Canada, John Sandfield Macdonald Papers, Baldwin to Macdonald, 1 February, 1848.

10 G. M. Jones, "The Peter Perry Election and the Rise of the Clear Grit Party", *Ontario Historical Society Papers and Records*, vol. 12 (1914), pp. 164-175.

11 Macdonald Papers, vol. 194, Campbell to Macdonald, n.d.

12 *Ibid.*, vol. 545, Macdonald to Margaret Greene, 9 December, 1849.

13 *Ibid.*, Macdonald to Margaret Greene, 6 January, 1850.

14 *Ibid.*, Macdonald to Margaret Greene, 20 January, 1850.

15 *Ibid.*, Macdonald to Margaret Greene, 27 January, 1850.

16 *Ibid.*, Macdonald to Margaret Greene, 20 January, 1850.

17 *Ibid.*, Macdonald to Margaret Greene, 2 February, 1850.

18 *Ibid.*, vol. 540, Hugh Macdonald's Memorandum Book.

[19] *Ibid.*, vol. 539, Macdonald to Margaret Macdonald, 2 April, 1850.

[20] *Ibid.*

[21] *Journals of the Legislative Assembly of the Province of Canada* (1850), p. 63.

[22] *Montreal Gazette*, 18, 21 May, 1850.

[23] *Globe*, 22 June, 1850.

[24] *Journals of the Legislative Assembly of the Province of Canada* (1850), p. 106.

[25] *Ibid.*, pp. 158, 165.

[26] Doughty, *Elgin-Grey Papers*, vol. 2, p. 715, Elgin to Grey, 27 September, 1850.

[27] *Globe*, 29 June, 1850.

[28] Samuel Thompson, *Reminiscences of a Canadian Pioneer, for the Last Fifty Years, an Autobiography* (Toronto, 1884), pp. 215-216.

[29] Baldwin Papers, Brown to Baldwin, 9 October, 1848.

[30] Macdonald Papers, vol. 297, Smith to Macdonald, 23, 26, 28, 29 January, 1 February, 1849.

[31] *Ibid.*, Statement of Charges preferred by the Penitentiary Commission against the Warden, with his Comments, 15 February, 1849.

[32] *Montreal Gazette*, 26 January, 1849.

[33] Macdonald Papers, vol. 297, Humble Petition of Henry Smith, late Warden of the Provincial Penitentiary; *North American* (Toronto), 9 August, 1850.

[34] *Globe*, 27 June, 1850.

[35] *British Colonist* (Toronto), 5 July, 1850.

[36] Doughty, *Elgin-Grey Papers*, vol. 2, p. 715, Elgin to Grey, 27 September, 1850.

[37] *Ibid.*, p. 736, Grey to Elgin, 15 November, 1850.

[38] *Ibid.*, p. 748, Grey to Elgin, 13 December, 1850.

[39] W. Ward, *The Life and Times of Cardinal Wiseman* (London, 1912), vol. 1, pp. 542-543.

[40] *Ibid.*, pp. 547-548.

[41] *Globe*, 10, 19 December, 1850.

[42] Charles Clarke, *Sixty Years in Upper Canada, with Autobiographical Recollections* (Toronto, 1908), p. 65.

[43] *Globe*, 8, 17 April, 1851.

[44] *Ibid.*, 19 April, 1851.

[45] *News* (Kingston), 2 January, 1852.

[46] *Globe*, 27 May, 1851; *Montreal Gazette*, 30 May, 1851.

[47] *Montreal Gazette*, 25 July, 1851.

[48] *Globe*, 26 June, 1851.

[49] *Montreal Gazette*, 30 June, 1851.

[50] *Globe*, 26 June, 1851.

[51] *Montreal Gazette*, 1 August, 1851.

[52] Doughty, *Elgin-Grey Papers*, vol. 2, pp. 745-747, Elgin to Grey, 22 November, 1850.

[53] *Globe*, 22 June, 1850.

[54] *Montreal Gazette*, 11 August, 1851.

[55] Public Records and Archives of Ontario, Clarke Papers, McDougall to Clarke, 26 July, 1851.

56 Public Records and Archives of Ontario, Stevenson Papers, Macdonald to Stevenson, 14 September, 1851.

57 *News*, 26, 27 November, 1851.

58 *Ibid.*, 8 December, 1851.

59 *Ibid.*, 10 December, 1851.

60 *Ibid.*, 16, 18 December, 1851.

61 Macdonald Papers, vol. 538, Harcourt Vernon to Pope, 19 May, 1892.

62 Haight, *Country Life in Canada Fifty Years Ago*, pp. 297-298.

CHAPTER EIGHT: *The Liberal-Conservative Coalition*

(Pages 174 to 207)

1 *Leader* (Toronto), 25 August, 1852.

2 *Patriot* (Toronto), 25 August, 1852; *Montreal Gazette*, 29 October, 1852.

3 *Montreal Gazette*, 18 August, 1852.

4 *Patriot*, 15 September, 1852.

5 *Globe*, 12 October, 1852.

6 *Montreal Gazette*, 29 October, 1852.

7 *News*, 20 October, 1852.

8 Macdonald Papers, vol. 539, Macdonald to Louisa Macdonald, 13 October, 1852.

9 *Journals of the Legislative Assembly of the Province of Canada* (1852-1853), p. 313.

10 His name appears on the division lists for the first time on 8 March, and for the last time on 4 May, 1853. See *Journals of the Legislative Assembly of the Province of Canada* (1852-1853).

11 *Patriot*, 24 September, 1852.

12 *Globe*, 14 October, 1852.

13 *Ibid.*, 21 October, 1852.

14 *Ibid.*, 14 April, 1853.

15 *Ibid.*, 12 April, 1853.

16 *Journals of the Legislative Assembly of the Province of Canada* (1852-1853), p. 539.

17 *Globe*, 15 March, 1853; *Leader*, 23 March, 1853.

18 *Patriot*, 4 September, 1852.

19 *Journals of the Legislative Assembly of the Province of Canada* (1852-1853), p. 143.

20 *Patriot*, 24 September, 1852.

21 Clarke Papers, Thomson to Clarke, February, 1853.

22 *Patriot*, 25 August, 1852.

23 *Patriot*, 21 February, 1853.

24 *Ibid.*, 8 September, 1852.

25 *Montreal Gazette*, 13 September, 1852; *Patriot*, 23 February, 1853.

26 *Montreal Gazette*, 20 August, 1852.

27 *Patriot*, 17 March, 1853.

28 *Globe*, 22 March, 1853.

[29] *Montreal Gazette,* 16 March, 1853.

[30] *Patriot,* 18 March, 1853.

[31] *Ibid.*

[32] *Globe,* 24 March, 1853.

[33] *Ibid.*

[34] Clarke Papers, McDougall to Clarke, 2 February, 1853.

[35] *Globe,* 2 April, 1853.

[36] *Ibid.,* 14 May, 1853.

[37] *Ibid.*

[38] Macdonald Papers, vol. 194, Campbell to Macdonald, 8 March, 1855.

[39] G. M. Trevelyan, *Garibaldi's Defence of the Roman Republic, 1848-9* (London, 1928), Chapter V.

[40] Alessandro Gavazzi, *Six Lectures delivered in the Round Room of the Rotunda, Dublin, with a Biographical Sketch of the Author* (Toronto), 1853.

[41] *Globe,* 2, 4 June, 1853.

[42] *Ibid.,* 9 June, 1853.

[43] *Ibid.,* 14 June, 1853.

[44] *Ibid.,* 18 June, 1853.

[45] *Montreal Gazette,* 15 July, 1853.

[46] *Ibid.,* 18 August, 1853.

[47] *Ibid.,* 19 August, 1853.

[48] R. S. Longley, *Sir Francis Hincks, a Study of Canadian Politics, Railways, and Finance in the Nineteenth Century* (Toronto, 1943), pp. 238-239.

[49] *Leader,* 28 February, 1854.

[50] *Montreal Gazette,* 20 September, 1853.

[51] Clarke Papers, McDougall to Clarke, 17 September, 1853.

[52] *Globe,* 27 February, 1854.

[53] Macdonald Papers, vol. 336, Macdonald to Strachan, 9 February, 1854.

[54] *Ibid.*

[55] *Globe,* 2 February, 1854.

[56] *Leader,* 5 May, 1854.

[57] *Globe,* 24 June, 1854; Public Records and Archives of Ontario, Buell Papers, Cameron to Buell, 21 June, 1854.

[58] *Leader,* 27 June, 1854.

[59] *Journals of the Legislative Assembly of the Province of Canada* (1854), pp. 29-30.

[60] *Leader,* 30 June, 1854.

[61] *Globe,* 24 June, 1854.

[62] *Ibid.,* 14 July, 1854.

[63] *Leader,* 8 August, 1854.

[64] *Globe,* 7 August, 1854.

[65] *Montreal Gazette,* 19 July, 1854.

[66] *Ibid.,* 11 August, 1854.

[67] *Leader,* 14 July, 1854.

[68] *Globe,* 3 July, 1854.

[69] *News,* 18 July, 1854.

[70] *Ibid.,* 20 July, 1854.

[71] *Ibid.,* 28 July, 1854.

[72] *Leader,* 11 August, 1854.

[73] Macdonald Papers, vol. 194, Campbell to Macdonald, 8 March, 1855.

[74] O. D. Skelton, *The Life and Times of Alexander Tilloch Galt* (Toronto, 1920), pp. 187-192.

[75] *Montreal Gazette*, 9 September, 1854.

[76] C. B. Sissons, *Egerton Ryerson, his Life and Letters* (Toronto, 1947), vol. 2, p. 281.

CHAPTER NINE: *The Victory of the Progressive-Conservatives*

(Pages 208 to 237)

[1] *Journals of the Legislative Assembly of the Province of Canada* (1856), Appendix 30.

[2] *Ibid.* (1854-1855), p. 144.

[3] *Globe*, 16 October, 1854.

[4] *Ibid.*, 13 September, 1854.

[5] *Leader*, 15 September, 1854.

[6] Macdonald Papers, vol. 336, Thompson to Macdonald, 22 September, 1854, Gowan to Macdonald, 25 September, 1854.

[7] *Globe*, 19 October, 1854.

[8] *Leader*, 19 October, 1854.

[9] *Globe*, 23 October, 1854.

[10] *Journals of the Legislative Assembly of the Province of Canada* (1854-1855), p. 194.

[11] *Leader*, 25 October, 1854.

[12] Macdonald Papers, vol. 336, Gowan to Macdonald, 13 December, 1854.

[13] Thompson, *Reminiscences of a Canadian Pioneer*, pp. 336-338.

[14] *Globe*, 2 October, 1847.

[15] Macdonald Papers, vol. 336, Macdonald to Strachan, 9 February, 1854.

[16] *Globe*, 9 November, 1854.

[17] *Ibid.*, 10 November, 1854.

[18] *Journals of the Legislative Assembly of the Province of Canada* (1854-1855), p. 385.

[19] *Quebec Gazette*, 21 December, 1854.

[20] Macdonald Papers, vol. 539, Macdonald to Louisa Macdonald, 21 February, 1855.

[21] Public Archives of Canada, Brown Chamberlin Papers, vol. 2, Macdonald to Chamberlin, 2 February, 1855.

[22] W. A. Langton (ed.), *Early Days in Upper Canada, Letters of John Langton* (Toronto, 1926), p. 216.

[23] Macdonald Papers, vol. 194, Campbell to Macdonald, 8 March, 1855.

[24] University of Toronto Library, John Langton Papers, Langton's Estimate of Macdonald, 1855.

[25] *Globe*, 12 March, 1855.

[26] Macdonald Papers, vol. 539, Macdonald to Louisa Macdonald, 21 February, 1855.

[27] *Globe*, 23 April, 1855.

[28] *Ibid.*, 12 March, 1855.

[29] *Ibid.*

[30] Sissons, *Egerton Ryerson*, vol. 2, pp. 328-331.

[31] J. G. Hodgins, *The Legislation and History of Separate Schools in Upper Canada: From 1841 until the Close of the Reverend Doctor Ryerson's Administration of the Education Department of Ontario in 1876* (Toronto, 1897), p. 93.

[32] *Globe*, 6 June, 1855.

[33] *Ibid.*, 11 June, 1855.

[34] *Leader*, 9, 13, 18 October, 1855.

[35] Macdonald Papers, vol. 539, Macdonald to Louisa Macdonald, 21 September, 1855.

[36] *Brown's Toronto General Directory, 1856* (Toronto, 1856), p. 323.

[37] Macdonald Papers, vol. 539, Williamson to Pope, 10 October, 1892.

[38] *Ibid.*, Macdonald to his Mother, 26 January, 1856.

[39] Brown Chamberlin Papers, vol. 2, Macdonald to Chamberlin, 7 August, 1855.

[40] *Ibid.*, Macdonald to Chamberlin, 21 January, 1856.

[41] Macdonald Papers, vol. 539, Macdonald to his Mother, 4 February, 1856.

[42] *Leader*, 28 February, 1856; *Globe*, 27 February, 1856.

[43] *Journals of the Legislative Assembly of the Province of Canada* (1856), p. 116.

[44] Macdonald Papers, vol. 336, John Ross to Macdonald, 23 August, 1855.

[45] Brown Chamberlin Papers, vol. 2, Macdonald to Chamberlin, 21 January, 1856.

[46] *Leader*, 20 February, 1856.

[47] *Ibid.*, 8 April, 1856.

[48] *Globe*, 11 March, 1856.

[49] *Journals of the Legislative Assembly of the Province of Canada* (1856), p. 144.

[50] *Leader*, 25 March, 1856.

[51] Thompson, *Reminiscences of a Canadian Pioneer*, p. 294.

[52] *Globe*, 27 March, 1856.

[53] *Leader*, 8 April, 1856.

[54] *Globe*, 30 May, 1856.

[55] Macdonald Papers, vol. 539, Macdonald to his Mother, 17 March, 1856.

[56] *Ibid.*, Macdonald to his Mother, 21 April, 1856.

[57] *Ibid.*, Macdonald to his Mother, 17 March, 1856.

[58] *Leader*, 17 April, 1856.

[59] Langton, *Early Days in Upper Canada*, p. 257.

[60] *Ibid.*

[61] Macdonald Papers, vol. 539, Macdonald to his Mother, 17 March, 1856.

[62] *Journals of the Legislative Assembly of the Province of Canada* (1856), pp. 322-330.

[63] *Ibid.*, p. 514.

[64] *Ibid.*, p. 522.

[65] *Ibid.*, pp. 538-539.

[66] *Globe*, 27 May, 1856.

[67] Public Archives of Canada, G10, vol. 2, Head to Labouchere, 23 May, 1856; G12, vol. 66, Head to Labouchere, 24 May, 1856.

[68] *Journals of the Legislative Assembly of the Province of Canada* (1856), pp. 554-555.

[69] *Globe*, 24 May, 1856.
[70] *Ibid.*, 30 May, 1856.

CHAPTER TEN: *Double Shuffle*
(Pages 238 to 272)

[1] J. B. Brebner, "Joseph Howe and the Crimean War Enlistment Controversy between Great Britain and the United States", *Canadian Historical Review*, vol. 11 (Dec. 1930), pp. 300-327.
[2] C. P. Stacey, *Canada and the British Army, 1846-1871, a Study in the Practice of Responsible Government* (London, 1936), pp. 98-99.
[3] D. G. G. Kerr, "Edmund Head, Robert Lowe, and Confederation", *Canadian Historical Review*, vol. 20 (Dec. 1939), pp. 409-420.
[4] *Ibid.*
[5] *Journals of the Legislative Assembly of the Province of Canada* (1857), Appendix 17, Labouchere to Head, 4 December, 1856.
[6] *Globe*, 9 January, 1851.
[7] Public Archives of Canada, G9, vol. 32, Head to Labouchere, 3 September, 1856.
[8] Sir Arthur Hardinge, *The Life of Henry Howard Molyneux Herbert, Fourth Earl of Carnarvon, 1831-1890* (Oxford, 1925), vol. 3, pp. 92-93.
[9] National Library of Scotland, Ellice Papers, first instalment, bundle 29a, Ellice to Rose, 6 October, 1856.
[10] *Ibid.*, Rose to Ellice, 15 December, 1856.
[11] *Journals of the Legislative Assembly of the Province of Canada* (1857), Appendix 17, Order-in-Council, 17 January, 1857.
[12] *Ibid.*, Order-in-Council, 16 February, 1857.
[13] Macdonald Papers, vol. 539, Macdonald to his Mother, 27 January, 1857.
[14] *Ibid.*, Macdonald to his Mother, 4 February, 1857.
[15] *Ibid.*, Macdonald to Louisa Macdonald, 17 March, 1857.
[16] *Globe*, 20 March, 1857.
[17] *Ibid.*, 26 March, 1857.
[18] Public Record Office, London, C.O.42, vol. 609, Head to Labouchere, 28 March, 1857, minute by Merivale, 13 April, 1857.
[19] G. P. de T. Glazebrook, *A History of Transportation in Canada* (Toronto and New Haven, 1938), pp. 179-180.
[20] *Globe*, 30 April, 1857.
[21] *Ibid.*, 13 May, 1857.
[22] Macdonald Papers, vol. 539, Macdonald to Louisa Macdonald, 27 April, 1857.
[23] C.O.42, vol. 609, Head to Labouchere, 23 March, 1857.
[24] Public Archives of Canada, Canada, Executive Council Minutes, State Book R, Order-in-Council, 18 July, 1857.
[25] C.O.42, vol. 610, Eyre to Labouchere, 12 July, 1857.
[26] Ellice Papers, first instalment, bundle 29a, Rose to Ellice, 3 July, 1857.
[27] Macdonald Papers, vol. 539, Macdonald to his Mother, 28 July, 1857.
[28] *Ibid.*, Macdonald to his Mother, 31 July, 1857.

[29] *Ibid.*, vol. 120, Memorandum on the Intercolonial Railway, August, 1857.

[30] *Ibid.*, Macdonald to Provincial Secretary, 1 February, 1858.

[31] Ellice Papers, first instalment, bundle 29a, Ellice to Rose, 9 August, 1857.

[32] *Ibid.*, Ellice to Rose, 1 August, 1857.

[33] Macdonald Papers, vol. 539, Macdonald to his Mother, 11 August, 1857.

[34] *Ibid.*, Macdonald to his Mother, 21 August, 1857.

[35] C.O.42, vol. 610, Head to Labouchere, 26 November, 1857.

[36] Macdonald Papers, vol. 336, Cayley to Macdonald, 11 November [1857].

[37] Skelton, *Galt*, p. 229.

[38] *Ibid.*, pp. 229-230.

[39] Macdonald Papers, vol. 293, Vankoughnet to Macdonald, n.d.

[40] *Ibid.*, vol. 539, Macdonald to his Mother, 30 November, 1857.

[41] *News*, 9 December, 1857.

[42] *News*, 11 December, 1857.

[43] *Ibid.*, 17 December, 1857.

[44] *Ibid.*, 18 December, 1857.

[45] Thompson, *Reminiscences of a Canadian Pioneer*, pp. 338-339.

[46] *News*, 29 December, 1857.

[47] Pope, *Memoirs*, vol. 1, p. 180.

[48] Macdonald Papers, vol. 539, Macdonald to Margaret Williamson, 20 March, 1858.

[49] Public Record Office, London, P.R.O. 30/6 (Carnarvon Papers), vol. 69, *Papers Relative to the Seat of Government of Canada*, October, 1857.

[50] Royal Archives, Windsor, P22, Draft Memorandum by General Grey, October, 1857.

[51] *Ibid.*, Labouchere to the Queen, 16 October, 1857.

[52] G1, vol. 143, Labouchere to Head, 31 December, 1857.

[53] *Leader*, 20 July, 1858.

[54] *Journals of the Legislative Assembly of the Province of Canada* (1858), p. 931.

[55] *Leader*, 29 July, 1858.

[56] *Assembly Journals* (1858), pp. 931-932.

[57] *Globe*, 30 July, 1858.

[58] *Atlas* (Toronto), 6 August, 1858.

[59] Pope, *Memoirs*, vol. 1, Appendix 3, pp. 339-341; E. A. Forsey, *The Royal Power of Dissolution of Parliament in the British Commonwealth* (Toronto, 1943), pp. 50-52.

[60] *Atlas*, 6 August, 1858.

[61] *Assembly Journals* (1858), pp. 935-936.

[62] C.O. 42, vol. 614, Head to Lytton, 9 August, 1858.

[63] Pope, *Memoirs*, vol. 1, p. 200.

[64] C.O. 42, vol. 614, Head to Lytton, 18 August, 1858.

[65] *Atlas*, 6 August, 1858.

[66] *Ibid.*

[67] C.O. 42, vol. 615, Head to Lytton, 22 October, 1858.

[68] *Assembly Journals* (1858), p. 1043.

[69] Canada, Executive Council Minutes, State Book T, Order-in-Council, 9 September, 1858.

CHAPTER ELEVEN: *The Humiliation of George Brown*

(Pages 273 to 314)

¹ Hughenden Manor, Beaconsfield Papers, bundle 13, Lytton to Disraeli, 14 December, 1858.

² Hardinge, *Carnarvon*, vol. 1, p. 119.

³ C.O. 42, vol. 614, Head to Lytton, 16 August, 1858, minute by Lytton.

⁴ *Ibid.*, Head to Lytton, 9 August, 1858, minute by Carnarvon.

⁵ P.R.O. 30/6, vol. 69, Lytton to Head, 24 September, 1858, printed in *Question of the Federation of the British Provinces in America* (Colonial Office, Nov. 1858).

⁶ C.O. 42, vol. 614, Head to Lytton, 16 August, 1858, minute by Carnarvon, 1 September, 1858.

⁷ *Ibid.*, minute by Blackwood, 30 August, 1858.

⁸ *Ibid.*, minute by Lytton.

⁹ *Ibid.*, minute by Merivale, 31 August, 1858.

¹⁰ *Ibid.*, vol. 615, Head to Lytton, 22 October, 1858, minute by Carnarvon, 8 November, 1858.

¹¹ *Ibid.*, vol. 614, Head to Lytton, 31 July, 1858, minute by Lytton.

¹² G1, vol. 146, Lytton to Head, 10 September, 1858.

¹³ P.R.O. 30/6, vol. 69, Sutton to Lytton, 29 September, 1858, printed in *Question of Federation of the British Provinces in America.*

¹⁴ *Ibid.*, Sutton to Lytton, 2 October, 1858.

¹⁵ C.O. 42, vol. 614, Head to Lytton, 16 August, 1858, minute by Merivale, 31 August, 1858.

¹⁶ P.R.O. 30/6, vol. 69, T. F. Elliot, *Memorandum on the Question of the Federation of the British Provinces in North America*; R. G. Trotter, "The British Government and the Proposal of Federation in 1858", *Canadian Historical Review*, vol. 14 (September, 1933), pp. 287-292.

¹⁷ P.R.O. 30/6, vol. 69, *Memorandum for the Cabinet*, 10 November, 1858.

¹⁸ G1, vol. 146, Lytton to Head, 26 November, 1858.

¹⁹ Beaconsfield Papers, bundle 13, Lytton to Disraeli, n.d.

²⁰ *Globe*, 20 November, 1858.

²¹ *Ibid.*, 23 November, 1858.

²² *Ibid.*, 20 December, 1858.

²³ *Ibid.*

²⁴ *Ibid.*

²⁵ Ellice Papers, first instalment, bundle 29a, Rose to Ellice, 3 January, 1859.

²⁶ *Ibid.*

²⁷ C.O. 42, vol. 617, Head to Lytton, 8 January, 1859.

²⁸ *Ibid.*, Head to Merivale, 12 February, 1859.

²⁹ Beaconsfield Papers, Lytton to Disraeli, n.d.

³⁰ *Ibid.*, Lytton to Disraeli, 19 December, 1858.

³¹ G1, vol. 146, Lytton to Head, 24 December, 1858.

³² Canada, Executive Council Minutes, State Book T, Order-in-Council, 6 January, 1859.

³³ *Leader*, 2 February, 1859.

³⁴ C.O. 42, vol. 615, Head to Lytton, 9 September, 1858.

[35] G1, vol. 145, Lytton to Head, 20 August, 1858.

[36] C.O. 42, vol. 615, Head to Lytton, 9 September, 1858.

[37] C.O. 42, vol. 618, Head to Lytton, 7 May, 1859.

[38] *Leader*, 30 April, 1859.

[39] Macdonald Papers, vol. 539, Macdonald to his Mother, 2 October, 1858.

[40] Horsey, *Macdonald, His School Days and Law Offices*, p. 5.

[41] Pope, *Memoirs*, vol. 1, p. 206.

[42] *Leader*, 10 February, 1859.

[43] *Ibid.*, 16 April, 1859.

[44] *Ibid.*, 12 February, 1859.

[45] J. M. S. Careless, "Who was George Brown?", *Ontario History*, vol. 52 (April, 1950), pp. 57-66.

[46] G. W. Brown, "The Grit Party and the Great Reform Convention of 1859", *Canadian Historical Review*, vol. 16, (September, 1935), pp. 245-256.

[47] Macdonald Papers, vol. 336, Spence to Macdonald, 14 October, 1859.

[48] Pope, *Memoirs*, vol. 1, pp. 215-216.

[49] Macdonald Papers, vol. 539, Macdonald to Louisa Macdonald, 1 September, 1859.

[50] Brown, "The Grit Party and the Great Reform Convention".

[51] Macdonald Papers, vol. 336, Lindsey to Macdonald, 24 November, 1859.

[52] J. M. S. Careless, "The Toronto Globe and Agrarian Radicalism", *Canadian Historical Review*, vol. 29 (March, 1948), pp. 14-39.

[53] G10, vol. 2, Head to Newcastle, 1 December, 1859.

[54] Canada, Executive Council Minutes, State Book U, Order-in-Council on federation, 22 November, 1859.

[55] *Ibid.*, Galt to Colonial Secretary, 18 January, 1860.

[56] G1, vol. 150, Newcastle to Head, 27 January, 1860.

[57] Canada, Executive Council Minutes, State Book U, Order-in-Council on federation, 13 February, 1860.

[58] *Leader*, 30 April, 1860.

[59] *Thompson's Mirror of Parliament, being a Report of the Debates in both Houses of the Canadian Legislature* (Quebec, n.d.), no. 19, pp. 6-7.

[60] Macdonald Papers, vol. 260, Ross to Macdonald, 14 April, 1860.

[61] *Ibid.*, vol. 188, Macdonald to Lindsey, 19 April, 1860.

[62] *Thompson's Mirror of Parliament*, no. 31, pp. 6-8, no. 32, pp. 1-4.

[63] Ellice Papers, first instalment, bundle 29a, Rose to Ellice, 26 April, 1860.

[64] *Thompson's Mirror of Parliament*, no. 4, pp. 1-7.

[65] Sir Sidney Lee, *King Edward VII, a Biography* (London, 1925), vol. 1, p. 88.

[66] Ellice Papers, first instalment, bundle 29a, Rose to Ellice, 26 April, 1860.

[67] *Globe*, 18 August, 1860.

[68] *Ibid.*, 21 August, 1860.

[69] Robert Cellem, *Visit of His Royal Highness, the Prince of Wales, to the British North American Provinces and the United States in the Year 1860* (Toronto, 1861), p. 113.

[70] Royal Archives, Z466, Bruce to the Prince Consort, 14 August, 1860.

[71] *Globe*, 22 August, 1860.

[72] *Ibid.*, 3 September, 1860.

[73] Royal Archives, Z461, Prince of Wales to Prince Consort, 6 September, 1860.

[74] Macdonald Papers, vol. 297, Kirkpatrick's Memorandum on the Brockville Interview, September, 1860.

[75] *Ibid.*, Campbell's Memorandum on the Brockville Interview, September, 1860.

[76] Royal Archives, Z467, Newcastle to the Queen, 6 September, 1860.

[77] Macdonald Papers, vol. 260, Ross to Macdonald, 10 September, 1860.

[78] Pope, *Memoirs*, vol. 1, pp. 226-227.

[79] *Globe,* 20 September, 1860.

[80] Macdonald Papers, vol. 297, Campbell to Macdonald, 30 September, 1860.

[81] *Leader,* 12 November, 1860.

[82] *Ibid.,* 16, 17, 21, 22, 26, 30 November, and 1, 3, 8, 11, 12 December, 1860.

[83] *Journals of the Legislative Assembly of the Province of Canada* (1861), pp. 19-20.

[84] *Leader,* 21 March, 1861.

[85] *Census of the Canadas, 1860-61* (Quebec, 1863), vol. 1, pp. 42-43, 78-79.

[86] *Globe,* 11 April, 1861.

[87] *Montreal Gazette,* 24 April, 1861.

[88] *Leader,* 25 April, 1861.

[89] *News,* 24 April, 1861; *Globe,* 22 April, 1861.

[90] Macdonald Papers, additional, vol. 1, Macdonald to Amsden, 31 May, 1861.

[91] *News,* 8 June, 1861.

[92] *Ibid.,* 11 June, 1861.

[93] *Ibid.,* 12 June, 1861.

[94] *Ibid.,* 13 June, 1861.

[95] *Ibid.,* 11 June, 1861.

[96] *Address of the Hon. John A. Macdonald to the Electors of the City of Kingston with Extracts from Mr. Macdonald's Speeches delivered on various occasions in the Years 1860 and 1861,* p. viii.

[97] *News,* 12 June, 1861.

[98] *Ibid.,* 24 June, 1861.

[99] *Ibid.,* 3 July, 1861.

CHAPTER TWELVE: *Impasse*

(Pages 315 to 353)

[1] Macdonald Papers, vol. 337, Allen to Macdonald, 5 September, 1861.

[2] *Ibid.,* Feebar to Macdonald, 29 July, 1861.

[3] *Ibid.*

[4] *Ibid.,* vol. 253, Morrison to Macdonald, 1 December, 1861.

[5] L. B. Shippee, *Canadian-American Relations, 1849-1874* (New Haven and Toronto, 1939), pp. 114-116; Skelton, *Galt,* pp. 307-311.

[6] *Montreal Gazette,* 24 April, 1861.

[7] *News,* 14 May, 1861.

8 *Leader,* 18 April, 1861.

9 Sissons, *Egerton Ryerson,* vol. 2, p. 426.

10 *Leader,* 15 June, 1861.

11 Macdonald Papers, vol. 336, Spence to Macdonald, 14 October, 1859.

12 *Ibid.,* vol. 539, Macdonald to Louisa Macdonald, 18 October, 1860.

13 *Ibid.,* Macdonald to Louisa Macdonald, 11 April, 1861.

14 Skelton, *Galt,* pp. 314-316.

15 Lord Newton, *Lord Lyons, a Record of British Diplomacy* (London, n.d.), p. 48.

16 Stacey, *Canada and the British Army,* pp. 120-121.

17 C.O. 42, vol. 628, Monck to Newcastle, 19, 27 December, 1861.

18 Canada, Executive Council Minutes, State Book W, Order-in-Council, 28 December, 1861.

19 Macdonald Papers, vol. 99, Provincial Secretary to Macdonald, 28 January, 1862.

20 *Ibid.,* vol. 337, Gowan to Macdonald, 4 February, 1862.

21 *Ibid.,* vol. 194, Campbell to Macdonald, 13 December, 1861.

22 *Globe,* 19 March, 1862.

23 Macdonald Papers, vol. 337, Cameron to Macdonald [23 March, 1862].

24 *Globe,* 31 March, 1862.

25 *Ibid.,* 3 April, 1862.

26 *Ibid.,* 2 April, 1862.

27 *Journals of the Legislative Assembly of the Province of Canada* (1862), pp. 33-36.

28 Macdonald Papers, vol. 337, Campbell to Macdonald, 1 April, 1862.

29 Pope, *Memoirs,* vol. 1, pp. 234-235.

30 Macdonald Papers, vol. 99, *Report of the Commissioners Appointed to Prepare a Plan for the better Organization of the Department of Adjutant General of Militia, and the Best Means of Reorganizing the Militia of this Province and to Prepare a Bill Thereon* (Quebec, 15 March, 1862).

31 *Globe,* 9 May, 1862.

32 *Ibid.,* 7 May, 1862.

33 John Martineau, *The Life of Henry Pelham, Fifth Duke of Newcastle, 1811-1864* (London, 1908), p. 310.

34 Ellice Papers, first instalment, bundle 29a, Rose to Ellice, 23 May, 1862.

35 Martineau, *Newcastle,* p. 310.

36 *Globe,* 14 May, 1862.

37 *Ibid.,* 20 May, 1862.

38 *Ibid.*

39 *Ibid.,* 21 May, 1862.

40 Macdonald Papers, vol. 539, Macdonald to Margaret Williamson, 23 May, 1862.

41 John Sandfield Macdonald Papers, Watkin to Macdonald, 28 June, 1862.

42 Macdonald Papers, additional, vol. 1, Macdonald to Amsden, 30 July, 1862.

43 *Ibid.,* vol. 188, Shaw to Brown, 28 July, 1862.

44 *Ibid.,* Brown to Shaw, 3 September, 1862.

45 *Ibid.,* additional, vol. 1, Macdonald to Amsden, 30 July, 1862.

46 *Ibid.,* vol. 161, Adderley to Macdonald, 26 December, 1862.

47 *Ibid.,* additional, vol. 1, Macdonald to Amsden, 23 February, 1863.

⁴⁸ *Globe*, 20 February, 1863.
⁴⁹ Macdonald Papers, vol. 188, McWhinnie to Macdonald, 27 February, 1863.
⁵⁰ *Ibid.*, vol. 188, Cameron to Macdonald [16 March, 1863].
⁵¹ Ellice Papers, first instalment, bundle 29a, Rose to Ellice, 3 March, 1863.
⁵² *Globe*, 20 March, 1863.
⁵³ Macdonald Papers, vol. 338, Patton to Macdonald, 20 April, 1863.
⁵⁴ *Globe*, 6 May, 1863.
⁵⁵ *News*, 21 May, 1863.
⁵⁶ Macdonald Papers, vol. 338, Duggan to Macdonald, 26 May, 1863.
⁵⁷ *News*, 13 June, 1863.
⁵⁸ Macdonald Papers, vol. 338, Patton to Macdonald, 10 June, 1863.
⁵⁹ *Ibid.*, Cook to Macdonald, 14 June, 1863.
⁶⁰ *Ibid.*, Daly to Macdonald, 1 July, 1863.
⁶¹ *Ibid.*, Cauchon to Macdonald, 27 June, 1863.
⁶² *Ibid.*, additional, vol. 1, Macdonald to Amsden, 5 August, 1863.
⁶³ *Ibid.*, Macdonald to Amsden, 14 September, 1863.
⁶⁴ *Ibid.*, vol. 215, Foley to Macdonald, 24 November, 1863.
⁶⁵ Chamberlin Papers, vol. 2, Macdonald to Chamberlin, 20 November, 1863.
⁶⁶ Macdonald Papers, vol. 338, Alleyn to Macdonald, 29 December, 1863.
⁶⁷ *Ibid.*, Jones to Macdonald, 1 January, 1864.
⁶⁸ *Ibid.*, vol. 191, Brydges to Macdonald, 16 January, 1864.
⁶⁹ *Globe*, 30 January, 1864.
⁷⁰ Macdonald Papers, vol. 247, Macpherson to Macdonald, 27 February, 1864.
⁷¹ *Ibid.*, vol. 338, Patton to Macdonald, 19 November, 1863.
⁷² *Ibid.*, vol. 191, Brydges to Macdonald, 24 February, 1864.
⁷³ *Ibid.*, Brydges to Macdonald, 22 February, 1864.
⁷⁴ *Ibid.*, vol. 539, Macdonald to Louisa Macdonald, 24 February, 1864.
⁷⁵ *Globe*, 15 March, 1864.
⁷⁶ Macdonald Papers, vol. 338, O'Reilly to Macdonald, 25 March, 1864.
⁷⁷ *Globe*, 1 April, 1864.
⁷⁸ *Journals of the Legislative Assembly of the Province of Canada* (1864), pp. 387-390.

CHAPTER THIRTEEN: *British North America in Conference*
(Pages 354 to 390)

1 *Globe*, 16 June, 1864.
2 Pope, *Memoirs*, vol. 1, appendix 5, pp. 344-350.
3 *Journals of the Legislative Assembly of the Province of Canada* (1864), pp. 383-384.
4 Pope, *Memoirs*, vol. 1, appendix 5.
5 *Globe*, 18 June, 1864.
6 Pope, *Memoirs*, vol. 1, appendix 5.

[7] W. M. Whitelaw, *The Maritimes and Canada before Confederation* (Toronto, 1934), pp. 211-217.

[8] Public Record Office, C.O. 217, vol. 234, MacDonnell to Cardwell, 18 July, 1864.

[9] *Ibid.*, vol. 230, Mulgrave to Newcastle, 21 May, 1864, minute by Newcastle.

[10] British Museum, Additional MSS. 44118 (Gladstone Papers), Gladstone to Cardwell, 25 July, 1864.

[11] Public Record Office, P.R.O. 30/22 (Russell Papers), vol. 27, minute by Palmerston on Cardwell's draft dispatch to Monck, 29 July, 1864.

[12] Stacey, *Canada and the British Army*, pp. 160-161.

[13] Public Record Office, P.R.O. 30/48 (Cardwell Papers), vol. 39, Gordon to Cardwell, 10 April, 1865.

[14] C.O. 217, vol. 234, MacDonnell to Cardwell, 18 July, 1864, minute by Fortescue, 4 August, 1864.

[15] Public Archives of Canada, Nova Scotia Dispatches, vol. 108, pt. 2, Cardwell to MacDonnell, 9 August, 1864.

[16] C.O. 42, vol, 642, Monck to Cardwell, 26 August, 1864, minute by Cardwell, 1 October, 1864.

[17] *Montreal Gazette*, 1 September, 1864.

[18] Canada, Executive Council Minutes, State Book AA, Order-in-Council, 29 August, 1864.

[19] *Islander* (Charlottetown), 9 September, 1864.

[20] *Morning Telegraph* (Saint John), 5 September, 1864, quoted in *Islander*, 9 September, 1864.

[21] *Examiner* (Charlottetown), quoted in *Globe*, 20 September, 1864.

[22] *Islander*, 9 September, 1864.

[23] J. H. Gray, *Confederation; or the Political and Parliamentary History of Canada, from the Conference at Quebec in October, 1864, to the Admission of British Columbia, in July, 1871* (Toronto, 1872), vol. 1, p. 30.

[24] *Globe*, 21 September, 1864.

[25] *Ibid.*

[26] *Morning Chronicle* (Halifax), 10 September, 1864.

[27] *Islander*, 16 September, 1864.

[28] *Ibid.*, 23 September, 1864.

[29] *Morning Chronicle*, 12 September, 1864.

[30] Macdonald Papers, vol. 51, Macdonald to Taché (draft), 12 September, 1864.

[31] *Globe*, 21 September, 1864.

[32] *Ibid.*

[33] *Evening Express* (Halifax), 14 September, 1864.

[34] *Montreal Gazette*, 19 September, 1864.

[35] *Morning News* (Saint John), 19 September, 1864.

[36] Macdonald Papers, vol. 51, Macdonald to Tupper (draft), 22 September, 1864.

[37] Canada, Executive Council Minutes, State Book AA, Order-in-Council, 23 September, 1864.

[38] Whitelaw, *The Maritimes and Canada*, p. 230.

[39] P.R.O. 30/48, vol. 39, Cardwell to Gordon, 1 October, 1864.

[40] *Globe*, 10 October, 1864.

[41] *Ibid.*, 11 October, 1864.

[42] W. M. Whitelaw, "Reconstructing the Quebec Conference", *Canadian Historical Review*, vol. 19 (June, 1938), pp. 123-137.

[43] Macdonald Papers, vol. 46, p. 13.

[44] *Ibid.*, p. 14.

[45] *Ibid.*, p. 27.

[46] *Ibid.*, pp. 21, 24-25.

[47] *Ibid.*, pp. 29-38.

[48] *Globe*, 12 October, 1864.

[49] Macdonald Papers, vol. 46, pp. 51-57.

[50] A. G. Doughty (ed.), "Notes on the Quebec Conference, 1864", *Canadian Historical Review*, vol. 1 (March, 1920), pp. 26-47.

[51] *Globe*, 15 October, 1864.

[52] Macdonald Papers, vol. 46, pp. 64-70.

[53] *Ibid.*, pp. 65-72.

[54] Doughty, "Notes on the Quebec Conference", pp. 36-37.

[55] Macdonald Papers, vol. 46, pp. 142-149.

[56] *Ibid.*, p. 161.

[57] Joseph Pope, *Confederation, being a Series of hitherto unpublished Documents bearing on the British North America Act* (Toronto, 1895), pp. 84-85.

[58] Macdonald Papers, vol. 46, pp. 167-168.

[59] *Globe*, 28 October, 1864.

[60] *Ibid.*, 29, 31 October, 1864.

[61] *Ibid.*, 2 November, 1864.

[62] C.O. 42, vol. 643, Monck to Cardwell (confidential), 7 November, 1864.

[63] *Globe*, 9 November, 1864.

[64] Canada, Executive Council Minutes, State Book AA, Order-in-Council, 16 November, 1864.

[65] C.O. 42, vol. 643, Monck to Cardwell, 27 October, 1864.

[66] P.R.O. 30/22, vol. 38, Lyons to Russell, 24 October, 1864.

[67] *Ibid.*, Lyons to Russell, 28 October, 1864.

[68] Stacey, *Canada and the British Army*, pp. 165-166.

[69] Canada, Executive Council Minutes, State Book AA, Order-in-Council, 16 November, 1864.

[70] Macdonald Papers, additional, vol. 1, Macdonald to Amsden, 1 December, 1864.

[71] Sir Joseph Pope, *Correspondence of Sir John Macdonald* (Toronto n.d.), pp. 13-15, Macdonald to Tupper, 14 November, 1864.

[72] *Ibid.*, pp. 17-18, Tupper to Macdonald, 13 December, 1864.

[73] Macdonald Papers, vol. 51, Tilley to Macdonald, 23 November, 1864.

[74] British Museum, Additional MSS. 44118, Cardwell to Gladstone, 27 October, 1864.

[75] P.R.O. 30/48, vol. 39, Cardwell to Gordon, 26 November, 1864.

[76] P.R.O. 30/22, vol. 31, Russell to Newcastle, 12 June, 1862.

[77] P.R.O. 30/48, vol. 39, Cardwell to Gordon, 12 November, 1864.

[78] Royal Archives, P 22, Monck to Cardwell, 14 November, 1864.

[79] P.R.O. 30/48, vol. 39, Cardwell to Gordon, 14 October, 1864.

CHAPTER FOURTEEN: *Checkmate*

(Pages 391 to 430)

[1] F.O. 5, vol. 963, Burnley to Russell, 21 November, 1864.

[2] C.O. 42, vol. 643, Monck to Lyons, 12 November, 1864, enclosed in Monck to Cardwell, 12 November, 1864.

[3] Shippee, *Canadian-American Relations*, p. 148.

[4] Pope, *Correspondence*, p. 19, Macdonald to Swinyard, 19 December, 1864.

[5] Shippee, *Canadian-American Relations*, pp. 177-179.

[6] Pope, *Correspondence*, pp. 19-20, Macdonald to Swinyard, 19 December, 1864.

[7] *Ibid.*, p. 18.

[8] P.R.O. 30/22, vol. 38, Burnley to Russell, 27 December, 1864.

[9] Macdonald Papers, vol. 510, Macdonald to Brydges, 1 January, 1865.

[10] *Ibid.*, Macdonald to Swinyard, 1 January, 1865.

[11] Pope, *Correspondence*, pp. 24-26, Tupper to Macdonald, 9 April, 1865.

[12] Macdonald Papers, vol. 51, Tupper to Macdonald, 4 January, 1865.

[13] J. A. Roy, *Joseph Howe, a Study in Achievement and Frustration* (Toronto, 1925), p. 259.

[14] J. A. Chisholm, *The Speeches and Public Letters of Joseph Howe* (Halifax, 1909), vol. 2, pp. 268-295.

[15] Macdonald Papers, vol. 51, Tupper to Macdonald, 4 January, 1865.

[16] *Ibid.*, vol. 510, Macdonald to Fisher, 24 March, 1865.

[17] P.R.O. 30/48, vol. 39, Gordon to Cardwell, 15 January, 1865.

[18] *Ibid.*, Gordon to Cardwell, 10 April, 1865.

[19] *Ibid.*, Gordon to Cardwell, 24 October, 1864.

[20] Public Archives of Canada, New Brunswick, C.O. 189, vol. 2, Gordon to Cardwell, 2 January, 1865.

[21] Public Record Office, C.O. 188, vol. 143, Gordon to Cardwell, 16 January, 1865.

[22] *Ibid.*, Tilley to Gordon, 30 January, 1865, enclosed in Gordon to Cardwell, 30 January, 1865.

[23] *Globe*, 21 January, 1865.

[24] *Parliamentary Debates on the Subject of the Confederation of the British North American Provinces* (Quebec, 1865), p. 33.

[25] *Ibid.*, p. 42.

[26] *Ibid.*

[27] *Ibid.*, p. 41.

[28] Macdonald Papers, vol. 51, Tilley to Macdonald, 13 February, 1865.

[29] *Ibid.*, Macdonald to Tilley, 20 February, 1865.

[30] G. E. Buckle (ed.), *Letters of Queen Victoria* (London, 1926), Series 2, vol. 1, pp. 248-249, Palmerston to the Queen, 20 January, 1865.

[31] G1, vol. 161, Cardwell to Monck, 21 January, 1865.

[32] *Globe*, 6 March, 1865.

[33] *Ibid.*, 7 March, 1865.

[34] *Confederation Debates*, p. 648.

[35] *Ibid.*, p. 669.

[36] *Ibid.*, pp. 649-650.

[37] *Globe*, 22 March, 1865.

[38] Macdonald Papers, vol. 339, Chamberlin to Macdonald, 22 March, 1865.

[39] Pope, *Correspondence*, p. 25, Tupper to Macdonald, 9 April, 1865.

[40] *Debates and Proceedings of the House of Assembly of Nova Scotia* (1865), p. 203.

[41] Pope, *Correspondence*, p. 24, Macdonald to Gray, 24 March, 1865.

[42] *Globe*, 10 March, 1865.

[43] Shippee, *Canadian-American Relations*, p. 134.

[44] Macdonald Papers, vol. 511, Macdonald to Gray, 27 March, 1865.

[45] *Ibid.*, Macdonald to Watkin, 27 March, 1865.

[46] A. Mackenzie, *The Life and Speeches of George Brown* (Toronto, 1882), p. 233.

[47] *Ibid.*, pp. 233-234.

[48] *The Times* (London), 28 April, 1865.

[49] Skelton, *Galt*, pp. 379-380; *Times*, 17 May, 1865.

[50] British Museum, Additional MSS. 44320 (Gladstone Papers), Gladstone to Gordon, 11 July, 1865.

[51] *Ibid.*

[52] Stacey, *Canada and the British Army*, pp. 185-186.

[53] Skelton, *Galt*, pp. 383-386.

[54] Pope, *Memoirs*, vol. 1, pp. 283-284.

[55] *Illustrated London News*, 3 June, 1865, pp. 526-527.

[56] British Museum, Additional MSS. 44118, Gladstone to Cardwell, 23 May, 1865.

[57] Macdonald Papers, vol. 161, Observations on the Answer to our Memo. of Yesterday, 2 June [1865].

[58] *Ibid.*, vol. 539, Macdonald to Louisa Macdonald, 17 June, 1865.

[59] *The Times*, 22 June, 1865.

[60] *Jackson's Oxford Journal*, 24 June, 1865.

[61] Macdonald Papers, vol. 74, Monck to Macdonald, 7 July, 1865.

[62] Pope, *Memoirs*, vol. 1, p. 285.

[63] Macdonald Papers, vol. 74, Monck to Macdonald, 3 August, 1865.

[64] Pope, *Memoirs*, vol. 1, Appendix 9, pp. 362-364.

[65] *Ibid.*, pp. 365-366, Macdonald to Brown, 5 August, 1865.

[66] *Globe*, 16 August, 1865.

[67] Macdonald Papers, vol. 539, Macdonald to Louisa Macdonald, 23 August, 1865.

[68] C. P. Stacey, "Fenianism and the Rise of National Feeling in Canada at the Time of Confederation", *Canadian Historical Review*, vol. 12 (September, 1931), pp. 238-261.

[69] Macdonald Papers, vol. 511, Macdonald to Monck, 18 September, 1865.

[70] P.R.O. 30/48, vol. 39, Cardwell to Gordon, 13 May, 1865.

[71] Public Archives of Canada, New Brunswick, Dispatches Received, vol. 45, Cardwell to Gordon, 24 June, 1865.

[72] P.R.O. 30/22, vol. 26, Cardwell to Russell, 22 July, 1865.

[73] *Ibid.*, vol. 31, Russell to Cardwell, 4 September, 1865.

[74] *Ibid.*, vol. 26, Cardwell to Russell, 15 August, 1865.

[75] Macdonald Papers, vol. 51, Fisher to Macdonald, 13 August, 1865.

[76] *Globe*, 4 September, 1865.

[77] Macdonald Papers, vol. 51, Tilley to Macdonald, 13 September, 1865.

[78] *Globe*, 27, 29 September, 1865.

79 Pope, *Memoirs,* vol. 1, p. 291, Macdonald to Louisa Macdonald, 28 September [1865].

80 Macdonald Papers, vol. 51, Fisher to Macdonald, 11 November, 1865.

81 New Brunswick, C.O. 189, vol. 2, Gordon to Cardwell, 20 November, 1865.

82 Macdonald Papers, vol. 51, Monck to Macdonald, 22 November, 1865.

83 P.R.O. 30/48, vol. 39, Gordon to Cardwell, 20 November, 1865.

84 Pope, *Memoirs,* vol. 1, appendix 11, pp. 370-371.

85 Pope, *Correspondence,* p. 30, Monck to Macdonald, 20 December, 1865.

86 *Reports of the Debates of the House of Assembly of the Province of New Brunswick During the Session of 1866, First Session,* p. 34.

87 Macdonald Papers, vol. 51, Tilley to Macdonald, 13 February, 1866.

88 New Brunswick C.O. 189, vol. 2, Gordon to Cardwell, 21 February, 1866.

89 *Journal of the House of Assembly of the Province of New Brunswick* (1866—First Session), pp. 12-13; *New Brunswick Assembly Debates,* 1866, pp. 23, 34, 62-64.

90 Macdonald Papers, vol. 51, Mitchell to Macdonald, 7 April, 1866.

91 Public Archives of Canada, G13, vol. 2, Gordon to Monck, 10 April, 1866.

CHAPTER FIFTEEN: *Triumph*

(Pages 431 to 465)

1 Pope, *Correspondence,* p. 32, Macdonald to Mitchell, 10 April, 1866.

2 Public Archives of Canada, G13, vol. 12, Macdonald to Monck, 11 April, 1866.

3 P.R.O. 30/48, vol. 39, Cardwell to Gordon, 1 July, 1866.

4 Macdonald Papers, vol. 51, Tilley to Macdonald, 17 April, 1866.

5 *Ibid.,* Monck to Macdonald, 23 April, 1866.

6 *Ibid.,* Tilley to Macdonald, 21 April, 1866.

7 *Ibid.,* Tilley to Macdonald, 20 April, 1866.

8 *Ibid.,* vol. 191, Brydges to Macdonald, 17 January, 1866.

9 *Ibid.,* vol. 51, Tilley to Macdonald, 17, 20 April, 1866.

10 *Ibid.,* Monck to Macdonald, 23 April, 1866.

11 P.R.O. 30/48, vol. 39, Gordon to Cardwell, 14 January, 1866.

12 Macdonald Papers, vol. 51, Monck to Macdonald, 18 April, 1866.

13 *Ibid.,* Monck to Macdonald, 17 April, 1866.

14 *Ibid.*

15 Pope, *Memoirs,* vol. 1, p. 306, Macdonald to Tilley, 8 October, 1866.

16 Macdonald Papers, vol. 237, McMicken to Macdonald, 12 March, 1866.

17 Stacey, "Fenianism and the Rise of National Feeling in Canada", p. 244.

18 Pope, *Correspondence,* p. 33, Macdonald to Mitchell, 10 April, 1866.

19 *Journal of the House of Assembly of the Province of New Brunswick* (1866—First Session), p. 217.

20 Macdonald Papers, vol. 51, Tilley to Macdonald, 21 April, 1866.

21 Stacey, "Fenianism and the Rise of National Feeling in Canada", p. 252.

22 Macdonald Papers, vol. 51, Tupper to Macdonald, 17 June, 1866.

23 *Ibid.,* Tupper to Macdonald, 19 June, 1866.

24 *Ibid.,* Monck to Macdonald, 21 June, 1866.

[25] Pope, *Memoirs*, vol. 1, pp. 300-302, Macdonald to Monck, 22 June, 1866.

[26] P.R.O. 30/48, vol. 40, Cardwell to Monck, 7 July, 1866.

[27] Macdonald Papers, vol. 51, Tupper to Macdonald, 14 July, 1866.

[28] Pope, *Memoirs*, vol. 1, p. 304, Monck to Williams, 14 July, 1866.

[29] Macdonald Papers, vol. 51, Tilley and Tupper to Macdonald, 19 July, 1866.

[30] *Ibid.*, Macdonald to Tupper, 19 July, 1866.

[31] P.R.O. 30/48, vol. 40, Carnarvon to Cardwell, 14, 19, 20 July, 1866.

[32] *Ibid.*, Cardwell to Carnarvon, 19 July, 1866.

[33] *Ibid.*, Cardwell to Carnarvon, 27 July, 1866.

[34] *Ibid.*, Carnarvon to Cardwell, 28 July, 1866.

[35] Macdonald Papers, vol. 51, Tilley to Galt, 9 August, 1866.

[36] *Ibid.*, vol. 512, Macdonald to Mowat, 13 August, 1866.

[37] Pope, *Memoirs*, vol. 1, p. 307, Macdonald to Tilley, 8 October, 1866.

[38] Macdonald Papers, vol. 512, Macdonald to Mayor of Cornwall, 2 July, 1866.

[39] *Ibid.*, vol. 513, Macdonald to McMicken, 25 August, 1866.

[40] Beaconsfield Papers, bundle 12, Carnarvon to Disraeli, 27 August, 1866.

[41] *Ibid.*, Carnarvon to Disraeli, 30 August, 1 September, 1866.

[42] Pope, *Correspondence*, pp. 34-35, Macdonald to Michel, 28 August, 1866.

[43] Macdonald Papers, vol. 74, Monck to Macdonald, 29 August, 1866.

[44] *Globe*, 17, 22 August, 5 September, 1866.

[45] G10, vol. 1, Howe and Annand to Carnarvon, 3 October, 1866.

[46] Macdonald Papers, vol. 51, Brydges to Macdonald, 8 October, 1866.

[47] *Ibid.*, Monck to Macdonald, 11 October, 1866.

[48] *Ibid.*, vol. 513, Macdonald to White, 20 October, 1866.

[49] *Ibid.*, vol. 51, Monck to Macdonald, 12 October, 1866.

[50] *Ibid.*, vol. 47, pp. 3-4.

[51] Skelton, *Galt*, p. 408.

[52] Pope, *Confederation Documents*, p. 122.

[53] P.R.O. 30/48, vol. 40, Carnarvon to Cardwell, 19 July, 1866.

[54] Pope, *Memoirs*, vol. 1, pp. 316-317, Macdonald to Louisa Macdonald, 27 December, 1866.

[55] Macdonald Papers, vol. 47, pp. 46-52.

[56] *Ibid.*, vol. 51, Macdonald to Carnarvon, 24 December, 1866.

[57] *Ibid.*, Monck to Macdonald, 31 December, 1866.

[58] Pope, *Memoirs*, vol. 1, pp. 314-315.

[59] Macdonald Papers, vol. 51, Carnarvon to Macdonald, 23 January, 1867.

[60] Hardinge, *Carnarvon*, vol. 1, p. 303-304.

[61] Macdonald Papers, vol. 51, Macdonald to Carnarvon, 30 January, 1867.

[62] G. E. Marinden (ed.), *Letters of Frederic, Lord Blachford, Under-Secretary of State for the Colonies, 1860-1871* (London, 1896), pp. 301-302.

[63] Macdonald Papers, vol. 51, Macdonald to Carnarvon, 2 February, 1867.

[64] Pope, *Confederation Documents*, pp. 158-176.

[65] Pope, *Correspondence*, p. 451, Macdonald to Knutsford, 18 July, 1889.

[66] *The Congressional Globe: Containing the Debates and Proceedings of the Second Session of the Thirty-Ninth Congress* (Washington, 1867), p. 1617.

[67] Shippee, *Canadian-American Relations, 1849-1874*, p. 196.

[68] Royal Archives, B23, Carnarvon to the Queen, 4 February, 1867, Carnarvon to Grey, 6 February, 1867.

[69] *Ibid.*, Carnarvon to Grey, 7 February, 1867.

[70] *The Times*, 21 February, 1867.

[71] *Hansard's Parliamentary Debates* (London, 1867), third series, vol. 185, p. 576-b.

[72] Macdonald Papers, vol. 51, Carnarvon to Macdonald, 21 February, 1867.

[73] Hardinge, *Carnarvon*, vol. 1, pp. 346-347.

[74] G. E. Buckle, *The Life of Benjamin Disraeli, Earl of Beaconsfield* (London, 1916), vol. 4, p. 498.

[75] *Hansard*, third series, vol. 185, pp. 1016-1017.

[76] Pope, *Memoirs*, vol. 1, p. 338, Macdonald to Louisa Macdonald, 21 March, 1867.

[77] *Hansard*, third series, vol. 185, p. 1184.

[78] Macdonald Papers, vol. 75, Monck to Macdonald, 2 March, 1867.

[79] *Ibid.*, vol. 51, Macdonald to Carnarvon [5 March, 1867].

[80] *Ibid.*, Adderley to Macdonald, n.d.

EPILOGUE—*The First of July, 1867*

(Pages 466 to 484)

[1] Macdonald Papers, vol. 51, Macdonald to Fisher, 30 May, 1867.

[2] *Ibid.*, Macdonald to Tilley, 30 May, 1867.

[3] *Ibid.*, vol. 513, Macdonald to Shea, 3 June, 1867.

[4] *Ibid.*, Macdonald to Godley, 1 June, 1867.

[5] *Journal des Trois Rivières*, quoted in *La Minerve* (Montreal), 6 July, 1867.

[6] *Ottawa Times*, 3 July, 1867.

[7] *Morning News* (Saint John), 3 July, 1867.

[8] *British Colonist* (Halifax), 2 July, 1867.

[9] *La Minerve*, 8 July, 1867.

[10] *News* (Kingston), 2 July, 1867.

[11] *Observer* (Sarnia), 5 July, 1867.

[12] *Montreal Gazette*, 3 July, 1867.

[13] Pope, *Correspondence*, p. 46, Monck to Macdonald, 24 May, 1867.

[14] Macdonald Papers, vol. 513, Macdonald to Morris, 1 July, 1867.

[15] *Ibid.*, vol. 51, Macdonald to Archibald, 30 May, 1867.

[16] *Ibid.*, Tilley to Macdonald, 5 June, 1867.

[17] *Ibid.*, vol. 513, Macdonald to Mitchell, 1 June, 1867.

[18] *Ibid.*, vol. 230, McDougall to Macdonald, 5 June, 1867.

[19] Pope, *Correspondence*, p. 43, McGee to Macdonald, 9 April, 1867.

[20] Macdonald Papers, vol. 51, Monck to Macdonald, 26 June, 1867.

[21] *Ibid.*, vol. 188, Brown to Macdonald, 15 August, 1864.

[22] *Ibid.*, vol. 51, Macdonald to Monck, 5 April, 1867.

[23] *Ottawa Times*, 29 June, 1867.

[24] *Ibid.*, 3 July, 1867.

[25] Canada, Privy Council Minutes, 1 July, 1867.

[26] Royal Archives, B23, Buckingham and Chandos to Pakington, 22 June, 1867.

[27] *Leader* (Toronto), 2 July, 1867.

[28] *Grand River Sachem*, 10 July, 1867.

[29] *Northern Advance* (Barrie), 4 July, 1867

INDEX

Abbey, Dorethus, 65, 67-8
Aberdeen, George Hamilton Gordon, 4th Earl of, 186
Act to Protect the Inhabitants of this Province against Lawless Aggressions from the Subjects of Foreign Countries at Peace with Her Majesty, An, 62
Act of Union, 436
Adams, Charles Francis, 385, 388, 410
Adderley, Sir Charles Bowyer, 338, 456, 465
Adolphus Reach, 12
Adolphustown, 9, 12; John Hughes's school at, 13
Alabama, cruiser, 421
Albert, Prince, 299, 324
Allen, George, 317
Allen, John Campbell, 422
Alleyn, Charles, 249, 345
Alwington House, Kingston, 73, 78, 81
Ameliasburgh, 9
American Civil War, 318, 358
American "sympathizers", 49, 50
Anglin, Timothy W., 426, 440
Annand, William, 448, 460
Appomattox Court House, 410
Archibald, Adams George, 395, 472
Arthur, Sir George, Bart., 60; issued proclamation, 60
Ashburton Treaty, 392
Ashley, John, 56, 57, 58
Ashley vs. *Dundas*, 58
Aylwin, Thomas Cushing, 108

Badgeley, William, 103
Bagot, Sir Charles, Bart., 83, 86, 89
Baldwin, Robert, 81, 86, 106, 109, 123, 129, 130, 151, 166, 167; planned non-sectarian provincial university, 93
Bank acts, the, 28; Colonial Office threatens to disallow, 28
Bank of Montreal, 346
Bank of Upper Canada, 24, 28; capital stock increased, 24
Barclay, John, 17
Baring, Thomas, 163
Bath, 9

Battle of the Alma, 211
Battle of Gettysburg, 347
Baxter, George, 14, 16
Bay of Quinte, 9, 12, 25
Beaconsfield, Benjamin Disraeli, 1st Earl of, 274, 462, 464
Belleau, Sir Narcisse Fortunat, 300, 419
Belleville, 9, 305
Bellevue, 132
Benjamin, George, 195, 308, 328
Bernard, Hewitt, 372
Bernard, Susan Agnes, 455, 456
Birge, John W., 66
Blackwood, Arthur, 276
Blair, Fergusson, 351
Blake, William Hume, 136, 137, 151
Bonsecours Market, 140
Bothwell, George Brown's farm at, 289
Boulton, Henry John, 28, 71, 103, 123, 130, 138
Boulton, William Henry, 109, 116, 161, 162
Bowes, John G., 196, 212
Brantford, 305
Brass, William, 43
Bright, John, 463, 464
British American League, 141, 149; Kingston convention of, 142-146; Toronto convention of, 149-150
British Colonist, 209, 213, 259
British Columbia on union, 380
British Corn Laws, repeal of, 127, 134, 139
British North America federation, carried, 375; delegates, 445; Bill, 459, 460
British Whig, Kingston, 79, 89
Brockville, steamer, 61, 62
Brown, George, 158, 159, 167, 170, 181, 183, 187, 189, 190, 191, 195, 198, 203, 213, 221, 229, 259, 261, 263, 271, 280, 281, 289, 304, 307, 336, 339, 343, 349, 350, 354, 355-8, 366, 377, 381, 382, 384, 400, 404, 411, 415, 416, 419, 427; Free Kirkers led by, 98; and Grand Trunk Railway, 251-3; constitutional resolutions of, 297-8
Brown-Dorion government, 267, 289

PROPOSED WINDOW FOR THE
PARLIAMENT BUILDING

*(From Bengough: "Caricature History of Canadian
Politics." Public Archives)*

John A. Macdonald

* * *

The Old Chieftain

PREFACE

I have to acknowledge Her Majesty the Queen's gracious permission to make use of material in the Royal Archives, Windsor Castle. I am grateful to the Duke of Argyll, the Marquess of Lansdowne, the Earl of Kimberley, the Earl of Iddesleigh, and the Earl St. Aldwyn for generously giving me access to their family papers relating to Canada. I have been fortunate in the number of diaries and letters that have been placed at my disposal; and I am particularly indebted, for the privilege of using such material, to Mrs. D. F. Pepler, Mr. C. P. Meredith, Mr. Oscar Orr, and Mr. W. F. Nickle. I should like to thank Sir Archibald Nye, High Commissioner for the United Kingdom in Canada, for enabling me to become better acquainted with Earnscliffe, Sir John Macdonald's old residence; and I am under obligation to Professor W. L. Morton of the University of Manitoba and Miss Heather Donald for permitting me to read in manuscript their studies on this period in Canadian history. Mr. Norman A. Robertson, High Commissioner for Canada in the United Kingdom, Mr. E. H. Coleman, Brigadier J. M. S. Wardell, Dr. T. P. Morley, Mr. J. S. Moir and Mr. G. D. Scroggie have all kindly assisted me in my search for material, or have furnished me with valuable information; and I should like to record my appreciation of their help. I am again indebted, for generous assistance, to Dr. W. Kaye Lamb, Dominion Archivist, and his assistants in the Public Archives of Canada, especially Miss Norah Story and Mr. W. G. Ormsby of the Manuscript Division; to Miss W. D. Coates and the staff of the National Register of Archives, London; and to Colonel C. P. Stacey, of the Historical Section, General Staff, Ottawa.

For help in finding illustrations and for permission to republish cartoons, my thanks are due to the Public Archives of Canada and to Rapid Grip and Batten, Limited, of Toronto.

Finally I should like again to acknowledge my indebtedness to the University of Toronto, the Rockefeller Corporation, and the Nuffield Foundation for the grants which have enabled me to carry this work forward to its completion.

TORONTO, DOMINION DAY, 1955   D. G. CREIGHTON

CONTENTS

Chapter One

The Pacification of Nova Scotia

I

On Thursday afternoon, November 7, 1867, Macdonald, along with the other members of the Commons, stood waiting expectantly and somewhat nervously in the Senate chamber of the Parliament Buildings at Ottawa. The Governor-General, Lord Monck, was reading the speech from the throne to the first federal Parliament of Canada. The legislative history of the new Dominion was about to commence. Outside, though the season was far advanced in autumn, the day was fine. Most of the shops in town were shut. A great crowd had pressed behind the rows of regulars and militia which lined the carriage drive up to the great central door of the building; and inside, in the Senate chamber, the galleries were crowded with people.[1] Behind the rows of Senators, nearly a hundred ladies, the wives and daughters of the members, gay in crinoline toilettes, watched the ceremony: and out in front, close to the Governor-General's chair, a little group of seats had been specially reserved for Lady Monck and the wives of the Cabinet ministers. Susan Agnes was prominent among them. For the first time in Macdonald's career, his wife was taking her appointed place in the ceremonial of Canadian politics. He noted appreciatively how much she seemed to enjoy such affairs and how instinctively expert she was at them. She was a tall woman, dark, with rather large but regular features, and fine, serious eyes. Her grave, almost statuesque appearance, her poised, easy manner made her an appropriate part of the formal scene.

Macdonald wore his court costume. He was fifty-two now —getting on for fifty-three; but it was difficult to see his age in his tall, slight, erect figure, in the easy nonchalance of his pose. The crested wave of his black hair had subsided only a little. The skin of his long oval face was still boyishly unlined; and his sardonic smile was as quick and genial as ever. He tired more quickly than he had done. Now, when he read, he liked to lie extended on a sofa, and, after luncheon, he would often seek a quick midday rest. Sometimes there was a weary pallor in his face that brought Agnes a sudden pang of fear. But he had remarkable powers of recovery. His spirits seemed as resilient and mercurial as ever. "He can throw off a weight of business in a wonderfully short time," his wife confided to her diary. "Oftentimes he comes in with a very moody brow, tired and oppressed, his voice weak, his step slow; and ten minutes after he is making clever jokes, and laughing like any school boy, with his hands in his pockets, and his head thrown back."[2] His high spirits were just as refreshing as they had been before. His good nature seemed to have lost none of its old easy-going tolerance. "I tell him," his wife wrote admiringly, "his good heart and amiable temper are the great secrets of his success."[3]

He had need of his secret recipe still. In a very few minutes he would have to confront the faithful Commons of the first Parliament of the Dominion of Canada. For years now this very day, the beginning of a new parliamentary history, had seemed the objective of all efforts. Now it had become merely the starting-point of a new and laborious series of endeavours. He was well armed for them, of course; he had seen to that. The first general election of Confederation, fought out in the previous August, had been a triumphant success for his government. The forces of the coalition had won handsomely in both provinces of Ontario and Quebec; they had better than broken even in New Brunswick. The party, in general, was full of good heart and lusty confidence. There had been, it was true, a rather unseemly row among three or four members for the Speakership. Galt, the temperamental, touchy, changeable Minister of Finance—"he is as unstable as water" Macdonald complained despairingly—had decided to mark the opening of the first federal Parliament by the emphatic device of sending in his resignation. Yet all this—even Galt's rather tiresome vagaries—was familiar enough. Macdonald could afford to dismiss it with his ironic smile. He knew that the coalition, for the present, was irresistibly powerful in Parliament. But he also knew that, beyond Parliament, an enormous, continental task still awaited it. The four provinces which had been united were only a fragment of British North America; and even in the existing union, it would be a long time, indeed, as he put it, before the gristle had hardened into bone. The process had not even begun in Nova Scotia. Nova Scotia was the violently unruly member of the union. Its opposition, he knew, made the electoral triumph look equivocal, and the future terribly uncertain. "You will have seen," he had written a few weeks earlier, "that we have carried everything before us in the two Canadas and New Brunswick. Our majority is, in fact, too large. Nova Scotia, on the other hand, has declared, so far as she can, against Confederation; but she will be powerless for harm, although that pestilent fellow, Howe, may endeavour to give us some trouble in England."[4]

"That pestilent fellow Howe"! As Macdonald settled himself in the chair to the right of the Speaker which he was to occupy for nearly twenty years and glanced with scrutinizing interest over the first House of Commons of Canada, it was to Joseph Howe that his gaze most frequently and curiously returned. On the other side was the opposition, ranged out in seven rows of beards, whiskers, moustaches, bald heads, oiled locks, and tall tile hats. On the whole, it had a rather depressingly familiar appearance. There were, of course, a number of unknown newcomers—a few unaccountable absentees. George Brown had been defeated in South Ontario; and although Macdonald probably expected that his old antagonist would quickly find another seat, Brown was never to become a member of the House of Commons of Canada. His absence was the greatest portent of change; but there were other signs of the arrival of new generations and the challenge of new problems. Prominent in the opposition—by no means a back-bencher—

was a thick-set young man with a broad, fat, rather babyish face, and a near-sighted, studious expression which gave him the air of a precocious infant. It was Edward Blake, the son of William Hume Blake, whom Macdonald had challenged to a duel nearly twenty years before. He was the most conspicuous newcomer in a phalanx of old and not very terrifying opponents. John Sandfield Macdonald, the new Premier of Ontario, who had campaigned for the unionists during the recent election, briefly and somewhat inexplicably occupied the seat of the leader of the opposition. Close to him were the familiar faces of Dorion and Holton, and the bleak, unsmiling, whiskered countenance of Alexander Mackenzie. Macdonald could afford to regard them all with the tolerant contempt of long familiarity. He had out-manœuvred them, and others better than them, a dozen times before. The real danger came from Joseph Howe. He glanced at the ageing man with the untidy fringe of hair, the tired yet still luminous eyes, and the coarse, rather bulbous, features. Here was mischief whose potentiality he could not yet calculate.

What would Howe do? He and the anti-Confederates had overwhelmed the unionists in the Nova Scotia elections, both federal and provincial. There were only two supporters of union in the new provincial assembly at Halifax; and seventeen out of the eighteen Nova Scotians who came up to Ottawa were anti-Confederates pledged to support Howe. Their mere presence in the capital was, Macdonald realized, at least somewhat reassuring, for it proved that they had no intention of boycotting the Canadian Parliament or flouting its authority. But what part would they play in it? As the House settled down into the debate on the speech from the throne, his curiosity grew. Would Howe and his sixteen followers act as an intransigent bloc? Or would they co-operate, and how far? On Friday, the second day of the debate, when Howe rose to state his position, the House and the galleries were crowded.[5] It was a respectful rather than enthusiastic audience. People were disappointed by the uneven quality of Howe's oratory, and puzzled by his odd, rather unparliamentary mannerisms. But these personal oddities and verbal infelicities scarcely mattered to Macdonald. What Howe's speech chiefly brought him was an enormous sense of relief. It was true that the old tribune kept on insisting that the Nova Scotian members had not the slightest interest in Canadian politics, that they would support neither the government nor the opposition, and that all they wanted was the repeal of the union so far as Nova Scotia was concerned. But, at the same time, Howe made it quite clear that he and his supporters had not come to Ottawa to interrupt the business of Parliament and exasperate its members. Macdonald was surprised, relieved, even a little encouraged. "We have commenced in a most amicable mode," he wrote a few days later to a correspondent in Nova Scotia. "Howe made a very good-humoured speech on the address to which he moved an amendment for the purpose of defining his position. From his tone it is very evident that he will by and by be open to reason."[6]

This was far too optimistic. Three days later, provoked by Tupper to make another explanatory statement, Howe left his listeners in no doubt that the Nova Scotian agitation for the repeal of the union would be carried on with all the force which the anti-Confederates at Ottawa and Halifax could bring to it.[7] Yet, as Macdonald had expected, Howe and his followers soon showed that they were not anti-social and unparliamentary fanatics. They kept their detached position, but they never relapsed into sullen eccentricity or deliberate obstructionism. The business of the first session of the first Parliament of Canada went promisingly forward. Macdonald himself introduced the bill which provided for the immediate construction of the Intercolonial Railway, which was to link the Maritime Provinces with central Canada. William McDougall sponsored resolutions which declared Canada's readiness —at no cost to itself—to acquire Rupert's Land and the North-West Territories. East and west, the work of nation-building had been undertaken in an impressive fashion; and the anti-unionists had not been able to interrupt or perplex it.

Yet they remained unrepentant and unconverted. Macdonald's first sense of relief was succeeded by a growing feeling of annoyance. The mere presence of a group of irreconcilable men, who were prepared to do almost anything to break the union, was a small, daily exasperation to the spirit. ". . . I must say," he wrote almost irritably to the Archbishop of Halifax, "that they tried our patience extremely. Howe talked a great deal of nonsense and some treason, but we bore with it all."[8] Yes, he had borne with it all. But now he was tired of indulgence, and anxious to be finished with suspense. "There must be an end to this kind of thing, however," he told the Archbishop grimly, "and language of the same kind will not be permitted when we assemble again." It was time for Howe to emerge from his ambiguous inactivity and make whatever last effort he had planned for the repeal of the union. Macdonald felt himself ready and anxious to meet him.

II

The riddle of Nova Scotia seemed only a symbol of the mass of uncertainties and novelties which now surrounded him. His life had become for a while a comprehensive task of settling into new conditions. Almost everything was different. He was a husband not a widower, a householder not a lodger, a citizen of Ottawa instead of a Kingstonian, and a sole, rather than an associate, Prime Minister. All these changes demanded adjustments; and the change from the widowed to the married state was perhaps the most important of all. Isabella had been dead for ten years, and for ten years before that she had been a chronic invalid. But Susan Agnes, who was nearly twenty years his junior, was a young and vigorous woman, full of vitality and naïve enthusiasms, and yet with a mind and a character which were evidently her own. He could tell easily —the signs were plentiful—that she was very much in love. She waited for him humbly in the square outside the East Block, worried over his occasional tiredness and pallor, responded quickly to his high spirits, and wondered musingly whether her heart's devotion, which was "so entirely given up to him", could be so "all-engrossing" as to be sinful.[9] She watched him proudly as he led the House. She was consciously thrilled to be "a great Premier's wife". "I do so like to identify myself with all my husband's pursuits and occupations," she wrote heartily,[10] and as a chatelaine and political hostess she had all the qualities which poor Isabella had conspicuously lacked. She thought herself a "laborious" and "awkward" housekeeper; but she presided with dignity over Macdonald's political dinner parties, and gave him the support of her grave, statuesque elegance on all public occasions.

As time went on, he began to discern at least two separate and distinct "Agneses" in her character. There was one Agnes, a girlishly excitable and pleasure-loving Agnes, who irrepressibly enjoyed a long succession of "visitors, engagements, parties, letters, and all sorts of excitement". This was the Agnes who was quick to notice the colour of the sky or the glitter of sunlight upon snow, who was sensitively aware of the atmosphere of a room or the moods of a face, who never failed to appreciate all the details, big and little, of the crowded life that she led. For this Agnes, the physical world of time and place seemed all absorbing. But there was a second Agnes, a devout, repentant, and serious Agnes, who sometimes entirely replaced the first, and for whom these temporal things could be judged only by eternal standards. This second Agnes was a woman who looked back upon her own—and other people's— "frivolities" with grave disapproval, who strove to remember the moral purpose of existence, who held up for herself the idea of a dedicated religious life. In her Anglicanism, there was a tincture of both the evangelical and the puritanical. "I am afraid," she confessed, "that my turn of mind is getting Methodistical."[11] She gave up wine—"this for example's sake"—deplored "the fashionable delineation of passion in novels *à la mode*", sighed over Mrs. John Rose's worldly sophistication, and hoped that "I may be enabled to give something of a higher tendency to the thought of the set among whom I live".[12]

Under her sober and thoughtful management, Macdonald's house began to take on a new order, decorum, and cosy comfortableness. It was the old "Quadrilateral" at the corner of Daly and Cumberland Streets, one of a terrace of houses, where he and Galt and Brydges had lived a few years before. He may very well have wished to move to larger and slightly more distinguished quarters, which would be better suited to the size of his new household and the importance of his new position; but at the moment a bigger house was something which he simply could not afford. At the beginning of his career, his professional income as a lawyer had very acceptably augmented his official salary; but during the 1860's the practice at Kingston had gradually ceased to be an asset and was rapidly becoming a serious liability. For years now he had been quite unable to give it any close personal attention; and during his long absences and the long and ultimately fatal illness of his principal partner, A. J. Macdonnell, the affairs of the firm had gone from bad to worse. It was at this most unfortunate moment that there occurred the failure of the Commercial Bank of the Midland District, the bank which his first employer, the great George Mackenzie, had helped to found thirty-five years before. Macdonald was one of the bank's shareholders and directors; he had been its solicitor since the early years of his practice. But at the moment the crucial aspect of the relationship was that his firm owed the bank considerable sums of money. A heavy obligation hovered over him. He would not know its full extent until the affairs of the Commercial Bank were finally settled. But meanwhile it was no time to be moving to more expensive quarters.

Despite this enforced simplicity and the financial worries that accompanied it, Macdonald was becoming rapidly and most agreeably domesticated. The house on Daly Street was crowded but not uncomfortably so. Old Mrs. Bernard and her son Hewitt, who had been Macdonald's secretary and who had become Deputy Minister of Justice, were permanent residents; and a room was always kept vacant for Hugh, who was away now at the University of Toronto but who came back to Ottawa regularly during the holidays. Macdonald's family, and his wife's, and the servants certainly took up most of the space; but there was enough left to permit him a separate study, and he worked there often far away from the importunate callers of the East Block, in the luxury of complete seclusion. He valued the study highly; but the room he most enjoyed was the dressing-room on the first floor, where Agnes did her sewing and her correspondence and where a cheerful fire was always burning on autumn and winter evenings. It was pleasant to drive home to these domestic comforts on November and December days after a long day in Council or the House. Winter had set in early that autumn; the wind roared in across the Ottawa River from the north-west, and there were great slanted drifts of snow on the square on Parliament Hill.

Often Agnes would be waiting for him in the antechamber of his office; the carriage or sleigh stood ready at the door of the East Block; and they would drive off together across the canal bridge and down Rideau Street through a winter dusk that was often lightened by a white blur of snowflakes. Once or twice a week, at least during the session, they would have a dinner-party; and he would notice approvingly how tactfully Agnes spoke French to the Quebec members, and with what gracious efficiency she played her rôle at the head of the table. But on most evenings there were no visitors; and he would play innumerable games of patience—Agnes reflected complacently that patience had been approved by "Albert the Good"—and lounge on the sofa reading *Phineas Finn* or Carlyle's *Frederick the Great*. On Sundays they would go to church, usually to St. Alban's, Church of England, and sometimes, by way of variation, to the "Scotch Church". In the early days at Ottawa, Macdonald had been accustomed to a number of Sunday visitors and a good deal of Sunday political talk. But Agnes discouraged these profane conversations. "I made it for months a subject of very earnest prayer," she confided to her journal, "that my husband might prevent Sunday visitors and Sunday interruptions. . . . He, my own kind dear husband, has been mercifully taught to see the right in this thing. . . ."[13]

The novelties of domestic life were matched and exceeded by the strange and unaccustomed conditions of political existence in a federal union. Even the capital itself was relatively new to Macdonald. Since the autumn of 1865, when the parliament of the old Province of Canada had moved to its new home, he had probably spent as much time in London as he had in Ottawa. And Ottawa, despite the great natural beauty of the rivers which encircled it, was a raw, overgrown, lumber town, with rows of ugly mid-Victorian terraces and semi-detached "villas" and a fringe of untidy lumber-yards, littered with stacks of boards and piles of dirty yellow sawdust. In such a setting, the Parliament Buildings stood out with incongruous magnificence; and even the Parliament Buildings, which George Brown had thought so absurdly grandiose only a few years before, were now found to be not nearly so spacious or comfortable as had been expected. The heating system, which was fed with wood instead of coal, was disconcertingly capricious; and the Commons chamber, which had been built for the one hundred and thirty assembly men of the Province of Canada, was certainly a tight fit for the one hundred and eighty-one members of the first Parliament of the Dominion.[14]

Confederation itself was not unlike a new and unfamiliar building. One was always blundering into new passages, bumping up against unexpected walls, discovering unfinished rooms; and periodically the uneasy suspicion returned that not enough provision had been made for this or that need, or that something had been completely forgotten. "The whole of our present system is an experiment," Macdonald wrote to one dissatisfied correspondent.[15] As the chief author of the experiment, he was always being called upon to explain and defend its processes, to say what could be done under the new rules and what decidedly could not. He would have to see the whole complicated process through to the end—to watch over the new system until, as he said, it had "stiffened in the mould". It was exciting and dismaying to realize that he could not yet be in the least certain how it was going to turn out.

The winter adjournment of Parliament gave a welcome temporary relief from all these perplexities. For a time, during the Christmas holiday season, many of the ministers scattered. The little town was buried in drifts of snowy peace. On his birthday, January 11, he did not go to the Departmental Buildings until late in the afternoon; and then he and Agnes drove back by sleigh over a countryside which was one even, unbroken expanse of glittering snow. They dined that night— the occasion was in his honour—at Rideau Hall. He wore the

star and the broad red riband of his order. He could catch
Agnes's surreptitious admiring glances; and it was pleasant to
see her being grandly taken in to dinner on the arm of the
Governor-General. When they left at a late hour, he and
Agnes and Hewitt Bernard were in high good spirits, and
they drove home gaily in an open sleigh, half-smothered in fur
wraps and buffalo robes, through the icy, deserted Ottawa
streets.[16]

He thrived during these days of relaxation. But they could
not last indefinitely. Council reassembled, Parliament was
due to open again early in March; and then, from one quarter
after another, really bad news began to pour in. In the previous
autumn, when it had passed its addresses to the imperial
Parliament respecting the Hudson's Bay Company, the Canadian Parliament had affected to assume that, in taking over
Rupert's Land and the North-West Territories, it need accept
only the obligation of providing government for the region. This
comfortable delusion was shattered by a dispatch which arrived
from the Colonial Office early in the New Year. The British
government stoutly insisted that the Hudson's Bay Company
held chartered rights which, until they had been successfully
challenged in the courts, could not be surrendered without
compensation. The business of western expansion was evidently
going to be extremely costly, as well as extremely difficult and
dangerous. There would be trouble and delay in the west. But
the west was not the only place where trouble and delay could
be expected. The problem of Nova Scotia suddenly emerged
from the state of ominous inactivity in which it had lain ever
since the autumn meeting of Parliament. The anti-Confederate
legislature at Halifax passed a series of resolutions which, in
scandalized and vehement tones, denounced Confederation and
demanded the release of Nova Scotia from its toils.[17] The
anti-Confederate government appointed Joseph Howe, William
Annand, H. Smith, and J. C. Troop as delegates to present this
peremptory demand for freedom at the feet of the imperial
throne. Another pilgrimage for the repeal of the union so far
as Nova Scotia was concerned would infallibly take place.

What were Macdonald and the Canadian government to do about it?

He studied the problem anxiously. Confederation was not a neat and finished job. There were loose ends lying untidily about in all directions. The long Cabinet meetings were succeeding each other rapidly now. He was "on the stretch", as Agnes called it, once more; and as he played his little games of patience in their sitting-room at night she could easily divine the worries that lay behind the drawn face and weary eyes. Early in February, Dr. Grant, who was Macdonald's physician, warned Agnes that her husband was dangerously overworking, and towards the end of the month he repeated the warning.[18] Her inward distress showed itself in a nervous and over-solicitous care; and then, just at the moment when she most wanted the house to be a refuge of comfort for him, a domestic calamity occurred. Something went wrong with the drains, and, in the middle of winter, it was difficult to have them repaired satisfactorily. The air of his study, where he did most of his business at home, was finally condemned as impure; and after protesting for days that he did not wish to disarrange the entire household, he was finally persuaded to move upstairs.[19] Yet even this shift of quarters did not stop his headaches; and for several weeks he felt out of sorts and depressed. Late in February, when the meeting of Parliament was less than a fortnight away, he had a long talk with his old friend, Alexander Campbell, in which he hinted vaguely but none the less unmistakably at retirement from public life.[20]

III

Yet, despite his troubles, he had no real doubts about Nova Scotia. He was conciliatory by instinct and long practice; but he had not the slightest intention of making compromises about the newly created Dominion of Canada. The object of Howe's mission to England was the repeal of the union so far as Nova Scotia was concerned. Macdonald refused to discuss such a subject officially. The only concessions that he ever considered making were small adjustments, chiefly financial, inside the unaltered frame of the union. He was willing to bargain about these, but about nothing more. There were those who argued that the best plan would be to persuade the Nova Scotians to give the new system "a fair trial", with the inevitable implication that if they continued to dislike the union at the end of the trial, they would be free to withdraw from it. "That, it seems to me," Macdonald wrote bluntly to Jonathan McCully, "would be giving up the whole question. The ground upon which the Unionists must stand is *that repeal is not even a matter of discussion.* I hope that the Colonial Office will be firm in this matter. If the Duke of Buckingham says at once to Howe and his confrères that they have nothing to hope or expect from the British government, I think the matter will end there; but if he should be weak enough to say—'You should give this system a fair trial for a year or two'—the consequence will be that the professional agitators will keep up the agitation for a year or two and then will return to the Colonial Office and plead their own factious course and its success as an evidence of the persistent refusal of the people to be incorporated in the union."[21]

That would be an absolutely fatal result. Surely the Colonial Office would never make such a ruinous concession. And yet, in such a matter, was it wise, he wondered, to rely upon dispatches and telegrams for the presentation of the Canadian case? Would it not be better to have a stout unionist at Westminster who could answer Howe's arguments and counteract his poisonous propaganda? He knew, of course, that such an agent could not be a member of the Canadian government, for that might be taken to imply that Canada regarded the repeal of the union, so far as Nova Scotia was concerned, as a matter for official discussion. But, beyond the limited circle of the Cabinet, there were others who were close in the confidence of the government and who might be equally suitable appointees. There was, for example, the temperamental Galt, who had resigned his portfolio at the beginning of the session, and whom it might be useful to propitiate with the offer of another job. There was also Tupper, who had disinterestedly declined a place in the first federal cabinet, but who had headed Nova Scotia's delegations to both the Quebec and London conferences. Galt, who was inclined at the time to be sulkily jealous and resentful of Macdonald, declined the post, alleging that Tupper's appointment as the second commissioner would inevitably defeat the object of the mission. Poor Tupper's unfitness, as the man whom the anti-Confederates of Nova Scotia most abominated, was the target of most of the opposition's criticism, when Macdonald got up on March 19 to explain the government's policy.[22] He defended Tupper stoutly, declaring that it was only fair for his Nova Scotian colleague to have the opportunity of vindicating his policy against its critics. When he sat down that night he must have felt fairly certain that there would be no more fuss in Parliament about the mission to England.

Physically he was feeling a good deal better than he had a month or so before. The coming of spring nearly coincided with the re-opening of Parliament; and, if the winter had been exceptionally severe, there was now ample compensation in the long, cloudless, balmy April days. He still had his unexpected lapses, his bad off-days. But he felt less depressed than before— more ready for parliamentary combat; and when, on April 6, "that sneak Parker", as he informed Tupper, brought up again the question of the mission to England, he composed himself to listen to a late debate with more equanimity and interest than he might have thought possible a month before. He pointedly took no part himself in the discussion. The debate was really beneath the attention of ministers! And the only prominent debater on the government side of the House was Thomas D'Arcy McGee. McGee was not at the top of his form—the occasion hardly required that; but, as Macdonald realized with satisfaction, he was eloquent and adroitly persuasive. He defended Tupper as a man who had risked a little temporary unpopularity in order to gain enduring fame. He promised that the Dominion would give real consideration to Nova Scotia's practical grievances. And he ended by appealing to both sides in the dispute to give time a chance to soften existing irritations.[23]

The debate drew to a close some time after one o'clock, and Macdonald drove home through the silent spring night to the "Quadrilateral" on Daly Street. It was cooler than it had been. The sunny, chill, uncertain day had ended in a sharp return of frost. A bright full moon hung high in the sky; and, as he drove along Rideau Street, the thin brittle patches of ice in the rutted road were picked out clearly in the moonlight. It was nearly half past two when he reached the house. Agnes, who had waited up, flew down to open the door for him; and he had his late brief supper in her dressing-room, while the last remains of the fire glowed in the hearth, and the gas sang serenely overhead. He was in a relaxed and cheerful mood. The Nova Scotian protest had been met and silenced for the second time, on the highest grounds, and in the most effective fashion. And, in his amused and amusing fashion, he told her something of the debate. The day had been long and full of exasperation; but it had ended at last in contentment. He lingered, savouring the peace of the silent house.[24]

He was not yet in bed before the low rapid knocking began at the front door. In a minute he flung open the dressing-room window and looked outside.

"Is there anything the matter?" he called softly.

Then he saw the messenger, his lifted frightened face pale in the moonlight.

"McGee is murdered—lying in the street—shot through the head."

Macdonald roused Hewitt Bernard. Together they drove back again, up Rideau and along Sparks Street toward McGee's lodging. Just beyond where Metcalfe Street crossed Sparks he saw the little group of still dark figures—McGee's landlady, the doctors, the police, and the printers from the Ottawa *Times*. He knelt beside the body, close to the pool of blood, to the half-smoked cigar, and the useless fallen new hat, and helped to lift his colleague and carry him into the house.[25] He listened while the witnesses told their first excited stories. He went down to the *Times* office and telegraphed to the police of the neighbouring towns. It was five o'clock and the streets were grey with dawn, when he reached the "Quadrilateral" again;

but he was back again at his office in a few hours, setting in motion all available machinery for the capture of the murderer, whom everybody expected from the start to have been a Fenian. That afternoon, when the House met, there were several tributes, moving or laboured, to the dead man; but it was Macdonald who, in his practical fashion, proposed an annuity for McGee's widow, and a small settlement for each of the daughters.[26] In the galleries his voice could scarcely be heard.[27] His face was white with fatigue, and sleeplessness and shocked regret.

The tragedy moved him deeply. McGee was dead at forty-three, "just at the beginning of his usefulness". He had been Confederation's most eloquent prophet. In the minds of many British North Americans he had almost come to stand for it; and at his death it was still ringed round with the old enemies, anti-Confederates, secessionists, annexationists, and Fenians. Macdonald and all the unionists, young and old, drew a fresh determination from the dreadful event. With almost his last breath, McGee had defended Tupper and the Nova Scotia mission; and to ensure the success of the mission had now become a duty to the dead as well as to the living. Confederation must not be destroyed "just in the beginning of its usefulness". Tupper must succeed. He must, in the first place, persuade the British government, through the Colonial Secretary, to put its foot down, flatly, firmly, and finally, upon the secessionist appeal. He must, in the second place, prevent John Bright or any other gullible member of the imperial Parliament, whom Howe and his friends could influence, from kicking up another ineffectual row in the House and thus prolonging the agitation for repeal.

Yet this, as Macdonald knew very well, was not the final objective of Tupper's journey to England. The defeat of Howe's anti-Confederate appeal to the British government and Parliament was, in reality, only a negative achievement. The ultimate goal of the Canadian government could be nothing less than the pacification of Nova Scotia—the reconciliation of the Nova Scotians to the "fixed fact" of Confederation. And the Canadian government, Macdonald also realized, could only approach anti-Confederate Nova Scotians through their own anti-Confederate leaders. Howe was the head and front of the repeal movement. Macdonald's final objective was to persuade him to abandon it and to identify himself publicly with the union through membership in the federal government. Much of the vigour of the anti-Confederate movement could be attributed to Howe's leadership, he knew; and time merely served to increase his estimate of the old tribune's importance. "The Antis have dwindled into insignificance in Howe's absence," he wrote to Tupper at the end of April, "and I see more than ever the importance of arranging matters with him."[28] The importance— and also the possibility! For Tupper, who had made occasion to see Howe several times since his arrival in England, was convinced, in his hopeful fashion, that the Nova Scotian leader would be open to reason if the anti-Confederate mission failed. Howe could then honourably lay down his arms. He could appeal for the submission of his followers. And this was exactly what Macdonald hoped to gain.

His hopes grew stronger as the summer advanced. In June, the Colonial Secretary, the Duke of Buckingham and Chandos, decisively rejected the petition for the repeal of the union, and John Bright's motion for a royal commission of inquiry on the position of Nova Scotia was ignominiously defeated in the imperial House of Commons. Tupper, who immediately announced the return of himself and the Nova Scotian delegates, wrote in a tone of confidence and jubilation. Macdonald, he insisted, must write at once to Howe. Tupper himself, immediately after his arrival, would set off through Nova Scotia to hold a series of public meetings which would finally convert the wavering inhabitants to union! Macdonald shook his head doubtfully. "Now in all this, *entre nous*," he wrote cautiously to Archibald, "I discern zeal without discretion."[29] He could not help but feel that the present was "the most inopportune time to hold such meetings, as the people have not yet recovered from the feeling of injury caused by the rejection of the motion for inquiry". As for Howe, he still believed that the Nova Scotian should make the first move. He feared to risk a snub.

Within a month he had changed his mind. For circumstances were changing rapidly also. Tupper came up to Ontario to report the results of his mission and to plead the need of action. Tilley and Archibald, who had seen Howe immediately after his arrival in Halifax, reported that the Nova Scotian leader was prepared to consider "pecuniary concessions"—or, in plain words, better financial terms for his province in Confederation.[30] This was the kind of arrangement—an arrangement which did not change the constitution vitally—which Macdonald had always himself believed possible. It was the kind of arrangement which the Colonial Secretary had discreetly hinted at, when, in the dispatch rejecting the anti-Confederate appeal, he had promised that Canada would be willing to consider all legitimate Nova Scotian grievances. Macdonald wavered. All that he now needed to meet Howe half-way was an occasion. And, as it happened, the occasion was miraculously provided for him. Down in Nova Scotia, it had been decided that the delegation to England would present its report to a convention or general caucus of all the members of the provincial Assembly as well as all the Nova Scotian Members of Parliament. The convention would then presumably plan the future of the repeal movement. It was to meet almost immediately, on August 3. Why should not Macdonald present himself in Halifax? Why should he not offer to discuss Nova Scotian grievances informally and amicably with the convention? There was just enough time. He decided to go. And Monck enthusiastically approved his decision. "I think," the Governor-General wrote, "all the evidence tends to show that you should *strike while the iron is hot*, and the iron *is* hot at the present time."[31]

IV

The trip down to Nova Scotia marked an interesting term in the history of Canadian Confederation. The Dominion was just over a year old. The federal Parliament and all the provincial legislatures had finished the first of their legislative sessions. The whole system was settling down into its own orderly routine.

He watched the process with anxious scrutiny. How far was his ideal design being realized in fact? He had planned a predominant central government. In his view the provinces were just as subordinate to Ottawa as they had once been to London. He had taken good care, in the British North America Act, to grant the federal government and the lieutenant-governors important controls on provincial legislation; and he had provided that all the great subjects of legislation should be entrusted to the federal Parliament. In fact, the legislative powers of the Dominion were very great. But they were not yet complete. There was one great gap that remained to be filled. "Property and civil rights" remained with the provinces until the laws respecting these subjects in the common-law provinces of Ontario, Nova Scotia, and New Brunswick had been assimilated in the manner authorized by section 94 of the British North America Act. Once this assimilation had taken place, "property and civil rights" could, with the consent of the provinces concerned, be transferred to the federal Parliament. He was eager to make this transfer. During the spring and early summer he had been planning for a commission which would settle "the great question of the uniformity of the laws".[32] He began to suspect, also, that despite all his careful planning, the division of power between the provinces and the Dominion was not so clear and definite as had been assumed. It occurred to him that the different governments might agree on a declaratory act which would settle the disputed points. Even this did not complete the legal structure which he was anxious to raise. The crown of the whole edifice was to be a Supreme Court. He hoped, he said, to "submit a measure for the establishment of a great Dominion court of justice, with original as well as appellate jurisdiction".[33]

This was his general programme for the completion of the new federal system. But the immediate particular object was the pacification of Nova Scotia. That must come first. On July 28, he set out from Montreal, accompanied by Agnes, Hewitt Bernard, Tupper, Cartier, and by an additional and special emissary of good will, John Sandfield Macdonald, who was both an old personal friend of Howe's and a Liberal who had opposed Confederation until it became an accomplished fact. It was nearly as large a delegation as that which sailed off down the St. Lawrence to Charlottetown nearly four years ago. But if the initial reception at the capital of Prince Edward Island in 1864 had been indifferent and unenthusiastic, the greeting now at the capital of Nova Scotia was positively hostile. There was a forbidding silence when Macdonald stepped off the train at Halifax, on Saturday, August 1; and all the members of the provincial government unanimously and conspicuously stayed away from the dinner-party which General Doyle, the Lieutenant-Governor, gave that night in honour of the visiting Canadians.[34] Yet, despite this frigid public reception, Macdonald had already gained a secret but important success. He had written to Howe, suggesting that they should meet together for a quiet talk in the General's office at Government House immediately after church on Sunday. And Howe had replied that he would be there at half past one o'clock.[35]

As he sat in the General's office, warm with August heat and tranquil with Sunday silence, Macdonald realized that, so far as Howe himself was concerned, the game was won. The man who sat before him was beaten—and knew it. The big head, with its rather coarse features and grey, untidy hair, was heavy with the dull, stupefying realization of final defeat. Despite his great talents and his greater ambitions, Howe had spent much of his life in demeaning jobs and dubious enterprises; and now, in this last and most ill-considered crusade of his career, he had been forced to recognize his complete and irremediable failure. What was he to do? His pride rejected a third appeal to the imperial Parliament—to the god that had failed. His loyalty made impossible the very thought of active or passive resistance. Why should he not discuss any remedial measures which the Canadians had to propose? Macdonald told him earnestly that the government of Canada was ready to "remove any proved grievance" concerning Nova Scotia's financial or commercial condition, and pressed him to become a member of the federal Cabinet.[36] Howe drew back. Could he carry his people with him? His unhappy doubts returned. He must, of course, wait for the convention to declare itself. He had, he told Macdonald, great hopes of the convention. Perhaps it could be persuaded to sanction friendly negotiations with the Canadians.

Macdonald withdrew to the side-lines to await developments. The General was an affable and generous host; the frivolous entertainments which Agnes liked so much and chided herself so severely for liking, continued pleasantly. And, in the meantime, the convention met and debated in a state of baffled indignation. In the end it did what all bewildered assemblies invariably do. It appointed a committee—a committee of seventeen, with Howe as chairman, to recommend a course of action for the future. If Macdonald wanted a conference, it was obviously to this body that he had to address himself; and in a short note he requested "a frank and full discussion of the position of Nova Scotia, and the best means of removing any feeling of dissatisfaction that may now exist".[37] In its reply the committee took up a stiffly formal position. It "affected to consider," Macdonald later explained to Monck, "that our visit there was an official one, and that we were charged by orders from England to make certain propositions to them".[38] Macdonald had no intention of placing himself or the government of Canada in a false position. He replied flatly that the Canadians were ready to discuss alleged grievances, but had no propositions whatever to make. This blunt announcement almost broke up the hope of a conference. But Howe still kept pressing his colleagues for a free and informal discussion; and in the end, by the casting vote of the chairman, the committee decided that it would listen to "statements" as well as accept written proposals.

By now it was Friday, August 7, nearly a week since Macdonald had arrived in Halifax. The committee's resolution, inviting the Canadians to a meeting but without specifying the time, did not reach him until nearly the middle of the afternoon; and a few more minutes elapsed before a second hurried note from Howe arrived, informing him that the appointed hour was three o'clock. By that time it was already three o'clock, and the members of the Canadian delegation were scattered on a variety of employments.[39] But Macdonald was determined to meet the committee. He spent a frantic hour in collecting the nearest available Canadian Cabinet ministers—Cartier, Kenny, and Mitchell—and in driving down to the Province Building. There, as he explained later to Monck, they were received "with sufficient courtesy". Howe could hardly be his naturally pleasant self; and at least half the members of the committee watched in sullen, disapproving silence. The atmosphere was glacial. But Macdonald spoke for some time, explaining that the Dominion could not alter the constitution, but was quite prepared to discuss financial grievances with representatives of the provincial government. Then Cartier spoke briefly, and Howe asked a few questions. The meeting was over. It had lasted about an hour.[40]

There could be no disguising the fact. He had failed to gain his objective. The convention, after having wrangled half of Friday night on the subject, did not authorize a renewal of the discussion with the Canadians. The meeting with the committee of seventeen had no sequel. Yet it was not entirely without consequences. Howe assured Macdonald that the Canadian explanations "had given considerable satisfaction, even to the violent". The convention significantly decided that the agitation for repeal could be carried on only by lawful and constitutional means; and the provincial legislature, which people had feared might refuse to work the new constitution any further, in fact continued its legislative functions in a fairly ordinary fashion. There were gains, then, even among the provincial politicians, who remained the core of the resistance movement. But with the Nova Scotian Members of Parliament Macdonald was having much more success. He had gone furthest of all with Howe. Howe and he had at least one long discussion over the week-end; and before Macdonald boarded the train for Pictou on Tuesday morning, they had reached a secret and significant agreement. "So soon as the prorogation takes place," Macdonald confidentially explained to the Governor-General, "I am to address a letter to Mr. Howe, the terms of which will be settled between us, and which, though marked 'private', he is to use among his friends, with the view of inducing them to come to his support in case he or some leading man of his party should take office."[41]

V

The government steamer, *Napoleon III*, was waiting at Pictou to carry them up the gulf. There was a day's stop at Prince Edward Island, for it was wise to take every opportunity of being courteous to the stand-offish Islanders, and a two-days' visit to Quebec, which had many pleasant memories for Agnes.[42] By August 18, they were back in Ottawa. The late summer was brilliant with cool, tranquil, cloudless days; and after the sultry weeks at Toronto, and the uncertain and exacting visit to Halifax, it was pleasant for Macdonald to slip into an easy administrative routine. A morning's work in the quiet of his study, a light luncheon at home, an afternoon's visit to the East Block for a meeting of Council or a session in his departmental office—this was his day. He was free while it was still early. As he walked down the long, cool corridors, clerks or petitioners were often waiting to beg a last-minute instruction or a brief interview; but beyond the final, importunate hanger-on was the door, and the open square of Parliament Hill, where Agnes was waiting for him. In the warm, yellow sunlight of late afternoon, they would walk together down Rideau Street and back to the "Quadrilateral".

Now his small family was complete, for Hugh, who had spent most of the summer with his Aunt Louisa in Kingston, returned to Ottawa about the middle of September.[43] Macdonald was well aware of the fact that he did not know Hugh as intimately as most fathers know their sons. The boy had lost his mother when he was seven, and for years had seen his father only infrequently and briefly; and he had grown up in Kingston under the inevitable assumption that his aunt's house was home. He was eighteen years old now—a youth who had suddenly and strangely become a man; and Macdonald began to wonder a little about his career. He had always intended to offer Hugh a place in his own law firm in Kingston. But, at the moment, there was no satisfaction whatever in making such plans for the future. The firm had been in a bad way for years. For years it had really existed on the sufferance of the Commercial Bank of the Midland District; and now that the Commercial Bank itself had failed, Macdonald's private affairs were really in jeopardy.

His family and its future welfare were often in his thoughts that autumn. He had to accustom himself to the presence of a young man who would soon be "keeping his terms" as a law student at Osgoode Hall in much the same way as he himself had kept them nearly forty years ago! An astounding novelty! Yet the prospect of Hugh's coming-of-age disturbed him far less than the thought of another event, far more imminent and perilous, to which he must look forward. It was certain now that some time in the coming winter Agnes was going to have a child. He watched her anxiously. Occasionally when she lay for long hours listless and "ailing" upon the sofa he could scarcely quiet his apprehensions for the future. But usually, as he knew well, she was supremely happy with what she called "my New Hope". "I can hardly express what a new life it has given me," she wrote. "I often think what an unsatisfactory existence women must lead who passing girlhood and having no particular vocation never realize the joys of wife and mother and spend their lives in trying to fill the void which nature has decreed they should experience."[44]

While the still September days passed by, and while he waited for Howe to give the signal they had agreed on for the letter, Macdonald took up once again the matter of the Hudson's Bay Company. He knew now, as everybody did, that Canada was not going to obtain an empire in the north-west for nothing. He had swallowed the unpalatable fact that compensation, provided by Canada, would have to be paid for the surrender of the Hudson's Bay Company's chartered rights; and whereas before he had been worried at the prospect of an overgrown colony assuming the burden of western dominion alone, he was eager now that the expansion of Canada across the continent should be completed. By the middle of September Council had reached the point of discussing the personnel of the delegation which was to go immediately to England to arrange for the transfer of Rupert's Land and the North-West Territories to Canada. There were exasperating difficulties about the matter, for, although William McDougall and Cartier—he was Sir George now and a baronet—were two certain delegates, the proposed third, Alexander Campbell, first asked for the job, and then unexpectedly declined it. Macdonald was so furious that he upbraided Campbell publicly in Council. Campbell dispatched just as much public business as it suited his convenience to do! But he, Macdonald, was blandly expected to go everywhere and to carry all burdens! He knew he could not possibly go to England in the autumn of 1868. He must stay and meet the new Governor-General, watch over the expiring efforts of Fenianism, draft his Supreme Court Bill, and get up a show of legislation for the next session. Above all he must stay to gain Howe and encourage the union cause in Nova Scotia. He stuck to his decision, though there were many influential voices which urged him to take the opposite course. "Lord Monck writes me urging very strongly that I should go to England," he confided to Rose, "but the more I think of it, the more I am satisfied that that is out of the question."[45]

It was past the middle of September before he heard from Howe. The old tribune was cautious and non-committal; but there could be no doubt that he meant business—that he hoped some positive result would issue from the correspondence. "The first step," he wrote to Macdonald, "should be for you to put in writing the substance of your oral statements to the committee. Let this be done without delay. I will then show the paper to a few friends and perhaps give you our views in writing."[46] Macdonald waited until the end of the month, for Council was to reassemble then, and he wished to base his proposals on the concurrence of all his colleagues. He warned Howe that his letter would be "merely a repetition of the statements made before the committee"; and, in fact, the lengthy communication which was finally sent off on October 6 contained nothing new.[47] He pleaded that the "purely constitutional provisions" of the British North America Act should not be lightly disturbed; he promised a generous consideration of Nova

Scotia's financial and commercial disabilities under the union. He offered to consider verbal amendments to the letter if Howe would send on his suggestions by telegraph. But Howe was amply satisfied. "Letter received, well expressed," he wired, "will write you soon."[48] This was on October 13; and for more than another fortnight Macdonald waited while Howe passed the letter about and consulted with his friends. Then suddenly the Nova Scotian broke the enigmatic silence which he had maintained all that summer and autumn in the face of the slanderous attacks of his enemies. In the Halifax *Morning Chronicle* of October 26 he began a series of public letters which advocated negotiation with the Canadians for the readjustment of the terms on which Nova Scotia had entered the union. "As you truly say," Macdonald wrote to Tupper, "Howe has not only abandoned the ship 'Repeal' but has burnt the ship. Now everything depends upon the game being played properly."[49]

Yet the game was an extremely difficult and dangerous one to play. Macdonald realized, only too clearly, that in order to win Howe and an uncertain number of his anti-Confederate friends, he ran the very real risk of alienating the faithful unionists of Nova Scotia. He had been obliged to promise that, pending the conclusion of the negotiations which he had started, he would make no federal appointments in Nova Scotia; and Tupper complained bitterly that not a single member of the union party in the province had "influence enough to get a tide-waiter appointed". Macdonald wearily agreed with much of what the resentful Nova Scotians said. He knew that he could not expect Howe to bring more than an intelligent minority of his anti-Confederates with him. He knew also that he must continue to rely on the faithful unionists for eventual success. But the brutal fact was that the unionists were already gained, and Howe was not. He must win Howe. He must be allowed the latitude necessary to win him. He pleaded for patience. "I can particularly sympathize with you and Tupper," he wrote to Archibald, "as you must hear, every day, complaints from our union friends of the manner in which they are treated by the local government and the cold shoulder given them by the government of the Dominion. This kind of thing cannot last much longer, but I do not desire, by any impatience or by yielding to the pressure of friends, to break off the understanding with Howe, which was commenced by me at Halifax and which is not yet closed. . . . The union party will have their triumph and their turn if Howe accepts the position, as he must throw himself upon the union party and cultivate their good graces in order to secure a majority in Nova Scotia. . . ."[50]

Howe would eventually need the union party. But in the meantime the union party desperately needed Howe. All that autumn Macdonald sought to gain him for the federal government by every persuasive art in his power. "From all I can learn of matters in Nova Scotia, and I hear much from both sides," he wrote, "I am satisfied that you have only to declare your will that the present constitution should have a fair trial, and your will will be law."[51] Howe had been the inspiration of Nova Scotian resistance; he was, Macdonald believed, the indispensable instrument of Nova Scotian pacification. He could bring peace alone and without assistance; and once his help had been gained the opposition of the irreconcilable provincial government became a matter of comparative unimportance. At first Macdonald had hoped that, through Howe, he could persuade Annand, Wilkins and company to sit down amicably and discuss "better terms" for Nova Scotia. But, in the end, the futility of all such hopes was borne in upon him. The existing Nova Scotian government would never negotiate. The plan must be abandoned. But, in its place, another much more brilliant and daring scheme could be substituted. The Dominion government would simply disregard Annand and his stubborn associates. The Dominion government would deal only with Howe, and the friends whom Howe might nominate, such as McLelan. All the credit for achieving "better terms" would go to Howe and his supporters, and to them alone. "This, you will say, is a bold game," Macdonald wrote to Howe, "but 'out of the nettle danger, you will pluck the flower, safety'. . . . There is a glorious and patriotic game before you; let me urge you to play it."[52]

All autumn he continued his patient exercise in persuasion. Monck finally departed for England about the middle of November. Less than a fortnight later the new Governor-General, Sir John Young, arrived by way of New York; and Macdonald, along with several other Cabinet ministers, took the morning train down to Prescott to greet him.[53] Canadian policy would not be greatly affected by these changes, Macdonald knew; but the political upset which occurred in England early in December was, he realized, decidedly more serious. Disraeli and the Conservatives, after only a little over two years of office, were defeated in the general elections; and a new government, with the formidable Gladstone as Prime Minister and two such notorious "anti-colonials" as John Bright and Robert Lowe in the Cabinet, was installed in Whitehall. Cartier, who was over in London, deep in negotiations for the cession of the Hudson's Bay Company's territories, was frankly worried that the change in government would have the most unfortunate results for Canada. Lowe, he reported darkly to Macdonald, "will not favour us very much"; and he suspected that Bright was "full of American ideas and sympathies".[54] Macdonald feared most for the Hudson's Bay Company negotiations which had just been getting nicely under way when the Conservatives went out of office. He did not really believe that the Liberals would take up the cause of Nova Scotia, and thereby disavow the policy of Confederation which originally had been their own. Yet Bright had sponsored the motion for an inquiry. His presence in the Cabinet might arouse false hopes in Nova Scotia. It was essential, in the interests of the Canadian plan, that the new British government should make its position clear at once. At Macdonald's request, Sir John Young quickly sent off a dispatch urging the new Colonial Secretary, Lord Granville, to confirm the policy of his predecessors in unequivocal terms.[55]

In the meantime, Macdonald realized, Howe was being rapidly manœuvred into the rôle which he had designed for him. At the beginning, the Nova Scotian had seemed anxious to discuss a rather frighteningly wide range of possible changes in the British North America Act. But, by degrees, these demands were forgotten, as Howe's whole energies became absorbed in the desperate struggle to convince his sullen fellow-countrymen. He dropped his concern for "constitutional questions". He began to assume—what Macdonald had always wanted him to assume—that a favourable readjustment of the financial terms of union was the one essential point in the pacification of Nova Scotia. "Better terms", Macdonald argued, could only be effectively arranged in conference; and John Rose, the Canadian Minister of Finance, stood ready to discuss the whole matter with Howe and his friend McLelan as soon as they gave the word. The meeting could not be held at Halifax, for then Rose could hardly avoid communication with the members of the provincial government. But Portland was an acceptable "neutral point"; and if agreement were secured at Portland then Howe and McLelan could "come on" to Ottawa.[56] The New Year arrived before Howe made his final decision. Rose departed by the Grand Trunk Railway for Portland. "Nova Scotia is about to take the shilling and enlist," Macdonald wrote to one correspondent, "though I am afraid it will consider itself for some time, a conscript rather than a volunteer."[57]

VI

It was a milder January than the last and lovely with clear skies, bright sun, and shimmering blue shadows on the snow. Macdonald's health was much better than it had been a year before. He was in high spirits, and almost every prospect appeared favourable. Even the approaching domestic crisis could be looked forward to with joy only slightly mixed with apprehension. Agnes was close to her time; but there was nothing in her trials which reminded him of the half-forgotten terrors of Isabella's confinements. Sometimes his wife felt "headachy" and unwell, and when he came home from Council in the late afternoon he would find that she had spent most of the day stretched out on the sofa reading a novel. But mainly she was well and confident, ready to receive callers and to preside at the dinner table; and sometimes she would venture out for a short walk with him, or he would persuade her to take a drive into the snowy countryside. His own light-hearted cheeriness was a strange contrast with his mood of a year ago. Agnes noted delightedly how often he came in "in great fun and spirits" to greet her.[58]

In fact, everything seemed to be going well. Everywhere Confederation appeared to be capturing the trophies of victory. Over in London, Cartier and McDougall grew more hopeful about the prospects of the Hudson's Bay Company negotiations; and from Newfoundland, which had almost been written off as a possible member of the union, the Lieutenant-Governor, Anthony Musgrave, wrote to Macdonald, assuring him that he thought his ministers really meant business about Confederation in the approaching session of the legislature. The timing of this new union movement, Macdonald realized, could hardly have been more fortunate. It would help to discourage and confound the repealers in Nova Scotia, just as Howe's entrance into the federal government would strengthen unionism in Newfoundland. Could he gain both the island and the peninsula in 1869? He began to plan in a mood of eager expectancy. The next session of Parliament would have to be postponed until late in the season in order to give time for Howe to join the government and win his by-election, and for delegates from Newfoundland to arrange terms of union at Ottawa. Then, about March 1, Parliament could be assembled to receive and endorse a splendid and comprehensive programme of Canadian expansion. "What a glorious programme it would be," he wrote enthusiastically to Tupper, "to go down to Parliament next session with Nova Scotia pacified, Newfoundland voluntarily joining, and the acquisition of Hudson's Bay."[59]

On Monday, January 18, Howe, McLelan and Rose reached Ottawa from Portland. The next day Howe came to lunch at the "Quadrilateral" and talked Nova Scotia affairs with Macdonald until far on in the afternoon; and on Wednesday Agnes gave a dinner party for eight in honour of the visiting Nova Scotians. It took only a few days to arrange the "better terms"; and although, as Macdonald confided to Tupper, there was "a good deal of protocolling", nothing was permitted to disturb the main basis of the plan which the Canadians had already put forward. Nova Scotia was simply to be put on a financial equality with New Brunswick. Henceforth Nova Scotia's federal subsidies were to be calculated on the basis of the rather more generous rate which had been granted to New Brunswick by the Quebec and London Conferences. These were important concessions, looked at from one point of view; looked at from another, they were simply necessary adjustments of the unfortunate irregularities of the original settlement. It was made clear that the new terms were all that the Dominion would concede, and all that the imperial government would sanction. On January 13 Granville sent off the desired dispatch to Canada rejecting the Nova Scotian demand for repeal, and confirming the new Liberal government's support of Confederation. It was the last card necessary to complete Macdonald's winning hand. "This, coming from a government of which Bright is a leading member, cuts off the last hope of the repealers, and justifies Howe's prognostications and his course."[60]

On January 30, a mild snowy day, Howe came again to the "Quadrilateral" to complete the last details of the arrangement; and after luncheon he and Macdonald went down to the East Block together. Howe was sworn in as President of the Council, and Macdonald publicly announced a government measure of "financial relief" for Nova Scotia. He had scarcely ever had a more complete, or a more carefully guarded, success to disclose. By evening everybody was talking about the wonderful news; and when he got home that night, he and Agnes spent a happy time recalling the amusing episodes in Nova Scotia's triumphant pacification. Agnes reminded him of the time, shortly after their marriage, when they had met Howe on the street in London.[61] For a few minutes the two political opponents had chaffed each other pleasantly, for they had always remained on good social terms. "Some day soon," Macdonald had insisted jocularly, "you will be one of us!" And Howe had replied, "Never! never! you shall hang me first." Well, he was "one of them" now! The victory was complete —or it would be as soon as Howe had won his by-election in Nova Scotia. He was well armed for that encounter. He carried back with him both Granville's dispatch and Macdonald's "better terms". "He will go back to Halifax," Macdonald wrote proudly to Langevin, "with the dispatch from the government of which Bright is a member, cutting off all hope of repeal, in one hand; and the substantial concessions made by us in the other."[62]

If it had not been for his worries about Agnes, he could have settled down into a state of satisfied relaxation, once Howe had left for Nova Scotia. But Agnes was very close to her ordeal. She was moving with greater difficulty now; and once, when, according to her own account, she "crept" into her husband's office, she found that he had been giving a brief sitting to a sculptor who had come to do a bust of him, and that the two were joking heartily over the bump on the sitter's large nose. Macdonald accepted few lengthy engagements that winter. He declined an invitation to the party which the Governor-General was giving in Montreal. He stayed close to the house on Daly Street, fussing over his wife protectively; and early on the morning of Sunday, February 7, when she woke him and told him that her time was coming, he first took her in his arms and held her there for a long time comfortingly. Then the doctors and nurses assumed control; and the long struggle began. It lasted while the clock ticked out a full day; and far into the grey hours of Monday morning, Agnes and the child she carried lay in peril.[63] She faced death that night and almost accepted the still peace in his eyes. But there was a final strength in her weary body which was wakened with exultance when she heard the first cry—when she knew that she and the child who was to be called Mary would live.

Chapter Two

The West in Jeopardy

I

Towards the end of February, the winter, which had been so mild and beneficent, lashed out in a sudden violent fury. The roads and railways were blocked with huge drifts of snow, and for a week, early in March, no mails whatever reached Macdonald's office in the East Block.[1] He lived in a curious state of isolation and helpless inactivity which was like a physical expression of the miserable suspense of the past few weeks. For a time it seemed that there were no foreseeable happy endings ahead. The reports of Howe's progress in his by-election contest in Nova Scotia were contradictory and a little disquieting, and Cartier's letters from London gave discouraging accounts of the negotiations with the Hudson's Bay Company. Macdonald was worried about his debts to the Commercial Bank, about his small daughter Mary, and about Agnes who seemed to recover so slowly from the dreadful crisis of Mary's birth. It was not until Sunday, April 11—nine weeks after her confinement—that she was permitted to go to church again, and they knelt side by side in thankfulness in St. Alban's.[2] Physically his wife was well once more. But how could he possibly gain real security for his small family while the tangle of his indebtedness remained unresolved? He had known now for some time that the Merchants' Bank of Canada had taken over the assets and liabilities of the old Commercial Bank. But the months went by, and no word—good or bad—came from the head office in Montreal. Finally, when he could bear the suspense no longer, Macdonald wrote directly to Hugh

Allan, the great ship-owner, who was president of the Merchants' Bank. Allan replied politely, protesting that he had left the matter in abeyance "till it suited your convenience to bring it up", but, at the same time, quite obviously expecting and welcoming a full settlement.[3] He did more. A few days later he presented the grand total of the claims against Macdonald. They amounted to $79,590.11.[4] The full consequences of Macdonald's absences from Kingston, and his debts, and Macdonnell's far heavier borrowings had now come back to him—and to him alone.

He could see no glimmer of light at the end of this long tunnel of trouble. The feeling of grinding pressure, the desperate need to scrape together some solution out of inadequate materials, was always with him now. It affected his whole outlook, although he had always tried, not unsuccessfully, to keep his public and his private life separate. He remained depressed, although in fact spring brought a return of his old luck in public affairs. On April 9, two days before he had gone thankfully to St. Alban's, Granville had cabled Sir John Young that the officials of the Hudson's Bay Company had finally accepted terms for the surrender of Rupert's Land; and less than two weeks later, on April 23, the telegraph brought the exciting news that Howe had been elected with a majority of nearly four hundred votes. Parliament reopened. The Conservatives, their numbers swollen now by the adhesion of the Nova Scotians, mustered in a mood of gay confidence. Only eight months before Macdonald had told Rose that he must stay in Canada and get up a show of legislation for the approaching session of Parliament. A show of legislation! What he had in fact was a magnificently substantial list of measures to submit to Parliament. "Better terms" for Nova Scotia, the acquisition of the north-west, provision for the prospective entrance of Prince Edward Island into union—they could all be announced in the speech from the throne.

But even this was not all. The session was scarcely a month old when it began to seem probable that still another province, Newfoundland, would soon join the federation. On May 24, the Queen's birthday, the island delegates arrived in Ottawa, and early in June it was announced that terms of union had been agreed upon. "We hope to close our session this week," Macdonald wrote triumphantly to Sir Hastings Doyle on June 16, "and a very momentous session it has been. We have quietly and almost without observation, annexed all the country between here and the Rocky Mountains, as well as Newfound-land."[5] "All the country between here and the Rocky Moun-tains"! It was an empire in itself. Yet it had its limits. Beyond the Rocky Mountains was British Columbia; and now, for the first time, British Columbia, which had been a mere speck on his mental horizon, moved up into the middle distance of his thought. With the acquisition of the north-west, the entrance of the Pacific province into Confederation became practical politics. He began to marshal his forces. They would need a new lieutenant-governor in British Columbia, "a good man at the helm", in place of the obviously unsympathetic Seymour. Who should it be but Anthony Musgrave, who was just finishing his term in Newfoundland, and who had already proved his devotion to Confederation by successfully promoting the union movement there?[6]

Yet it was not the governorship of British Columbia but the governorship of the new North-West Territories which was, at the moment, the really important office that Macdonald had to fill. By the terms of the "Act for the Temporary Government of Rupert's Land", a lieutenant-governor and a small council were to administer the new territory. Their rule must begin very shortly, for the date of the transfer of the territory was fixed for December 1, 1869. Who was to be the first governor of the newly acquired, Canadian Rupert's Land? Macdonald pondered the problem in his usual deliberate fashion, but there was never much doubt in his mind about the solution. He had, in fact, already picked his man. It was William McDougall, the former Clear Grit, the Liberal who had entered the coalition government along with George Brown, and who had held the post of Minister of Public Works in the first Cabinet after Confederation. McDougall had not been an easy colleague.[7] A tall man, heavily built, but erect of carriage, with a thick jowl, and dark, luxuriant hair and moustaches, he stood out, a somewhat

portly model of elegance, in any fashionable Canadian gathering. His public manner was composed and courteous. In the
House he spoke with restraint and consideration for others.
Yet he was, in fact, a somewhat assertive and moody individualist, who had not found political association very congenial
and who, as the record proved, had changed his loyalties fairly
frequently and with apparent ease. His importance in the
coalition Cabinet had declined, but he himself seemed unaware
of the fact. The Reformers, his political followers, were bringing
less and less support to government; but he still talked and wrote
with an air of cold command, as if he had a legion at his back.
He refused to accept Macdonald's reasonable suggestion that
the number of Ontario Liberals in the Cabinet should be reduced
from three to two. He complicated and embarrassed the task of
filling the places of the retiring Liberal ministers. He was
becoming, at one and the same time, more tiresome and less
useful.

Macdonald may have been slightly bored with McDougall's
political company. He may have been ready enough to take a
dignified method of dropping a difficult colleague. But it was
quite out of his character to make such an important appointment as that of the Lieutenant-Governor of Rupert's Land on
such purely personal grounds. He knew that the situation in
the north-west required an able first administrator; and, in
many ways, McDougall was the obvious choice. McDougall had
publicly advocated western expansion ever since the 1850's;
he, along with Cartier, had made the final arrangements with
the Hudson's Bay Company for the transfer of Rupert's Land;
and under his direction, the Department of Public Works had
already, with the consent of the authorities of Assiniboia, sent
out road-making and surveying parties to the Red River. In
the public mind, his name had long been associated with the
north-west; and he probably knew more about it than any other
man in Canadian public life. To Macdonald the appointment
must have seemed an unexceptionable one; and when, late in
the session, he finally offered the governorship of the North-
West Territories to McDougall, he can have had no inkling

of future trouble. Early in July McDougall accepted; and everybody seemed satisfied.

Yet McDougall's resignation, if it was a relief, was not an unqualified relief. It helped to make a general reconstruction of the federal Cabinet more than ever necessary. McDougall was the second Liberal minister to leave the government since the beginning of the year; and John Rose, Macdonald's old friend and crony of early days, the urbane and amusing companion of so many travels and escapades, announced, at the end of the session, that he would soon be leaving Canada to begin a career as a private banker in England. His departure was certainly the severest personal loss that Macdonald would have to bear. But it did not create the greatest political difficulty. Good ministers of finance were hard to get. But genuine Reformers were even harder. There was no doubt at all that the Liberals, in both the House and the country as a whole, had been steadily withdrawing their support from government during the past session. But, in Macdonald's view, the government had begun as a *bona fide* coalition in 1867, and as a coalition it must continue, at least until the next general election. Liberals were still necessary. But where were they to be got?

At this point, Macdonald thought of Sir Francis Hincks. Hincks was a veteran antagonist, the leader of the Reformers of Canada West in succession to Baldwin. He had retired from Canadian politics shortly after the formation of the Liberal-Conservative coalition in 1854, and had subsequently entered the British Colonial service as an imperial administrator. He had been Governor, first of Barbados and the Windward Islands and later of British Guiana. He had then been given a knighthood, but not a third appointment; and finding it difficult to live in England on the half pension to which his services entitled him, he came out to Canada for a visit.[8] Exactly fifteen years before, during the summer of 1854, he had been Macdonald's most notorious political enemy; but these old battles, if they were partly an embarrassment, were also partly a help. They at least served to remind Canadians that Sir Francis had been a very prominent Reform leader, with a record of service in party warfare which was as good as George Brown's and better than that of any of the new Liberal front-benchers. The dry, precise, ageing little man, with the mutton-chop whiskers, had once been a power in Canadian politics! Perhaps he could win back his old followers from George Brown and persuade them to give their support to the coalition government! Macdonald wondered. He hastened to show Hincks a flattering attention. He travelled down to Montreal to meet him, invited him up to Ottawa to stay at the "Quadrilateral", and organized a large public dinner in his honour at the capital.[9] Hincks, he was becoming convinced, was a real possibility for the vacant Reform post. The last of his serious worries seemed to be dissolving. It was August now, and he went off to Portland "for a fortnight's sniff of the salt water". He could hardly remember the time when he had taken a recognized formal holiday.

II

Some time during the summer—and probably soon after the session had ended—Macdonald had sent off to Hugh Allan a detailed proposal for the settlement of his debts to the Merchants' Bank.[10] The savings of a professional career which had begun nearly forty years ago in George Mackenzie's office in Kingston were, quite literally, to be wiped out. Macdonald put in all the cash which he could realize; but these liquid assets were far from being enough, and he had to fall back upon the one large piece of landed property which he had ever been able to acquire. It was a tract of land at Guelph, which he had bought long years ago, and which, as the village began to grow more populous, he had subsequently divided into town lots.[11] Upon this property, which was his biggest asset, and other lands in his possession, he offered to take out a mortgage with the Merchants' Bank for the remainder of his debt. Allan had not immediately accepted the offer. He had told Macdonald that he would submit his proposal to the board of the Bank and let him know its decision in due course. But there was no answer from Montreal when he left for his holiday at Portland

and none when he got back again at the end of the first week in
September. He was profoundly worried. He had another account
to settle—a much smaller account, fortunately—with the Bank of
Upper Canada, and some time ago the trustees of the Bank had
tentatively commenced an action against him. If they resumed
the action and secured a judgment, it would be quite impossible
for him legally to carry out the proposal he had made to Allan.
And if that arrangement fell through he knew only too well that
he was at the end of his tether.

Yet even this was not the sum of his trouble. He carried
with him always now knowledge which had begun as a
torturing suspicion and had developed into a hideous certainty.
Over six months ago—with what agonizing difficulties—his
daughter Mary had been born. Death had almost claimed her
in the moment of deliverance. And could the very desperateness
of her first struggle for existence be a portent for the future?
He had watched her as she lay, terribly tiny and fragile, upon
the pillow, with a curiosity which from the first was touched
with disquiet. For a dreadful moment, a suspicion, like a
threatening cloud, formed in his mind, only to be hurried
away by the fresh winds of his sanguine temperament. It
was absurd, at this early stage, to attach any importance whatever
to what seemed to be the little anomalies, the tiny irregularities,
in her appearance and behaviour. The child cried heartily at
times, she was fractious, she kept Agnes and himself up for
long, wakeful nights; and these small childish disorders, these
little outbursts of childish temperament, were surely only the
reassuring signs of normal, healthy growth. He almost persuaded himself; and then suddenly, as if he were a boxer with
his guard relaxed, the doubt struck him like a smashing blow
upon the face. Why did Mary lie so inertly upon her pillow?
Why did she not kick, and wriggle, and struggle to lift herself
with the strenuous eagerness of a healthy child? What was
the explanation of that frightening enlargement of the small
head, which, despite all his denials and reassurances, was always
there, in whatever light and from whatever angle he looked at
it? There was something wrong with the child—dreadfully
wrong—how wrong he did not yet know. The sickening realiza-

tion of her abnormality was a wordless secret which he and Agnes shared between them.

These were the burdens which he carried with him always now. There were days when they seemed too heavy to be borne. It was a long time since he had tried to forget his worries by drinking to excess. In the past he had drunk more often when he was happy than when he was heartsick; and for over two years now he had hardly drunk at all. When he had married and come back to Canada as the first Prime Minister of the new Dominion, he had obviously tried to effect a complete change in the conduct of his private life. This small reformation was something which he felt he owed, not only to himself, and his new country, but also to his wife, Agnes. A much more sedate and regular existence stretched before him and Agnes was certain to be the main agent of the change.

He had known from the start that she was a distinguished woman who would grace the position to which he called her. He began to realize as time went on that she was also a woman of deep religious faith and strong moral purpose. She strove earnestly for the moral improvement of others—as well as of herself. The urge towards betterment was not always a pious, private aspiration. At times it seemed to ring in the air like a command; and there were flashing hints of a steely will which flickered like a sword-blade drawn suddenly and imperiously from its scabbard. On these occasions she might have seemed almost a self-righteous and domineering woman; but she was saved from moral arrogance both by her critical intelligence and by her simple, joyous enthusiasm for life. She broke her own rules and neglected her own exacting standards with hearty human frequency. She subjected her own pious impulses to a sharp and disarming self-criticism. She realized only too well that she sometimes confused devotion to duty with love of domination, and she frankly confessed the muddle of her motives to Macdonald. "Often," she wrote contritely in her diary, "I find what I thought at first to be a principle proves itself only an evidence of a selfish love of power."[12] Macdonald, in his tolerant realistic fashion, tried to persuade her to moderate her moralizing urge, and to drop her habit of self-analysis. He

knew the weakness of her strength; but he also knew its greatness. He had come to rely heavily upon her, and upon the
supports with which she had buttressed his existence.

Then suddenly—it was just after his return from Portland,
in early September—he began drinking heavily again.[13] There
had been no letter from Allan awaiting him, and he had come
back to realize that the appointment of Hincks was not going
to be nearly such a generally acceptable solution of the ministerial difficulty as he had hoped it would be. In September
Cartier insisted on making one last attempt to persuade Galt to
re-enter the ministry; and when that failed Macdonald went
up to Toronto to talk over the matter of appointments with his
western supporters. It was annoying to encounter so much
opposition to Hincks and it was a grievous shock, when he
got back to Ottawa, to find that there was still no communication
from the Merchants' Bank. In the meantime, while the new
appointments exasperatingly hung fire, the old ministers were
certainly departing. On September 28, Macdonald came down
to the railway station to say good-bye to William McDougall,
outward bound for the Red River;[14] and the next day John
Rose came up specially from Montreal to bid them all farewell.
"It is more of a wrench to one's heartstrings writing the enclosed
than I care to express," Rose had declared when he sent in his
official resignation;[15] and to Macdonald this was a departure
which carried with it something of his own youth. He was
still in a reckless, desperate mood when he went west again to
pay court to Prince Arthur, who was visiting Canada, and who
had been travelling about Ontario attended by the Governor-
General. Despite his company, he kept on drinking, careless
of consequences; and Hewitt Bernard, who had gone west
with him, reported that he had been kept in a state of miserable
anxiety the whole time they were away.[16]

Then the bout gradually ended. It was over; but, like other
more important things that had gone before it, it left its
mark on Agnes and his relationship with her. They had
faced tragedy together that year. But it was inevitably she who
had suffered most from the appalling disappointment of her
first-born. Her "new hope" had been turned into a cruel

frustration; and although nothing could ever equal the shock of that terrible discovery, her husband's lapse into his old habits only served to confirm her sense of inadequacy and failure. Up to that time, their life together had been marked by a succession of small wifely triumphs. The improvement in his health, the praiseworthy alteration in his Sunday routine, the increasing regularity of his church-going—she had recorded them all with pride. But now she was obliged to admit defeat. That autumn she had reason for sorrow; and one dreary November Sunday, when the first thin flurries of snow were driving across the darkening landscape, she looked back with resignation on the events of the past twelve months. "What has changed with me since this day last year, when I sat writing, as I write now, in my big diary?" she asked herself. "Wonderfully little—and yet wonderfully much. . . . I ought to be wiser, for I have suffered keenly in mind since I last wrote here. Only *One*, who knows all our hearts, can tell how keenly and painfully or how for long weeks and months all was gloom and disappointment. I was over confident, vain and presumptuous in my sense of power. I fancied I could do too much and I failed signally. I am more humble now. . . ."[17] Yes, she was more humble. She was wiser than she had been. She began to have a better understanding of this complex man, her husband, who at long intervals seemed to run so quickly out of the power of self-control, and who on most occasions could draw on resources rich and varied beyond her understanding.

In the meantime Macdonald had recovered his balance. The Merchants' Bank had accepted his proposal, and he knew now that although he would face the future penniless, he could face it at least without public disgrace. The annoying question of the ministerial replacements had ended in the appointment of Hincks; and he was free to survey the political scene once more, plan for the future acquisition of British Columbia and Prince Edward Island, and estimate the prospects of the union forces in the approaching general election in Newfoundland. All these matters were certainly important to the maker of a transcontinental federation. But it was McDougall and the new empire in the north-west which were capturing the public imagination; and Macdonald found that the affairs of Rupert's Land were bulking large in his correspondence, and occupying more and more of his thoughts. Yet he did not want to make any important decisions about the north-west until his knowledge of its problems had largely increased. It was precisely for the purpose of obtaining this information that McDougall had been sent west before the actual transfer of the territory to Canada. His mission was not a rashly premature assumption of authority; it was simply a modest preliminary survey of a little-known situation. The Act under which his appointment had been made was an "Act for the Temporary Government of Rupert's Land". His government was essentially a provisional government. And nothing would be done—and in particular no western positions would be filled—until the results of his inquiries were made known. ". . . Until McDougall has time to look about him and report," he wrote to one correspondent who was enquiring about a job, "we desire to make no appointments lest they might jar with the prejudices and feelings of the people at Red River."[18] Surely this caution was sensible, and surely McDougall's mission was a wise preliminary move. Yet he remained vaguely uneasy. "McDougall goes with a large party," he wrote in one of these doubtful moments, "and I think is safe from all molestation. I anticipate that he will have a good deal of trouble, and it will require considerable management to keep those wild people quiet. . . ."[19]

He was not entirely unprepared for trouble. He did not magnify it when it came. It was about the middle of November that the American newspapers first reported that McDougall had been prevented by half-breed rioters from entering upon his prospective dominions; and a few days later a dispatch and a long personal letter from McDougall himself gave Macdonald all the first details of the ignominious repulse. The first Canadian Lieutenant-Governor of Rupert's Land had arrived at the border of his jurisdiction on October 30, only to discover that the trail to the north was barred against him. Despite protests and remonstrances, the organized *métis* continued to maintain their armed blockade; and on November 2, they completed their

effective control of the settlement by the capture of the Hudson's
Bay Company's post, Fort Garry. It was still too early to be
at all sure of the seriousness of the affair. The American
newspapers had obviously returned with zest to their favourite
habit of exaggerating every Canadian difficulty and rejoicing
in every Canadian misfortune. But, despite the confusion and
exaggeration of the reports, it was clear that Canada had
suffered a dreadful humiliation. What was to be done? Macdonald sat down to consider the appalling disaster, interviewing
people, piecing evidence together from a variety of sources.
One conclusion was unavoidable. Canada was at least partly
to blame. Dr. Schultz and the "Canadian party" at Red River,
together with Dennis, Snow, Mair and the other Canadian
surveyors and road-builders who had been sent up in advance
of the cession, had done more than he could have believed
possible to exasperate the native population. "You must bridle
those gentlemen," he told McDougall curtly, "or they will be a
continual source of disquiet to you."[20] Stoughton Dennis had
been "indiscreet", Snow and Mair "offensive", and Schultz and
his party were "disliked" and "distrusted" by the inhabitants.
Together they had made the *métis* dread the coming of Canadian sovereignty.

It was all unhappily true, he realized. But he also began to
realize that the indiscretions of a few Canadians had not been
the only incitement goading the *métis* to action, and that the
métis themselves were not the only group that was opposed or
unsympathetic to the advance of the Canadian frontier. The
affair was much more complicated and dangerous than that. It
was true, of course, that the French half-breeds formed the
active advance guard of the movement. Their strong sense
of community, their loyal belief in the validity of *la nation
métisse* gave them inspiration; and the semi-military organization
which they had developed in the buffalo hunt enabled them to
take the initiative effectively. Yet it was obvious also that they
had not acted in isolation or with complete spontaneity. On
the contrary, their resistance, Macdonald began to suspect, had
been tolerated, if not actively encouraged, by other important
groups, which were either unfriendly or positively hostile to

Canada. In his private letter of October 31 McDougall had written of "the apparent complicity" of a few of the missionary priests from old France. The officials of the Hudson's Bay Company appeared to be behaving with an equivocal inertness; and there was no doubt that the citizens of the north-western American states were watching the affair with an ominous, greedy curiosity. Canada, in fact, faced a sinister complex of antagonisms in the north-west; and, by a deplorable coincidence, nobody with any position and authority in the little colony was at hand and ready to defend Canadian interests.

William Mactavish, the Governor at Fort Garry, was seriously ill; Alexandre Antonin Taché, the Archbishop of St. Boniface, had left the settlement some time before to attend the Vatican Council at Rome. The British and French-Canadian leaders were absent or incapacitated or unwilling; but a small group of American agents, less vocal but more influential than the "Canadian party", sought, by every means in their power, to exploit the troubles at Red River for their own political purposes. Their aim was nothing less than the annexation of all or part of the British north-west to the United States; and they were well and strategically placed for the work they had in hand.[21] W. B. O'Donoghue, an Irish-American of strong Fenian sympathies who became the treasurer of the provisional government at Red River, was very close to Riel in the early stages of the revolt. General Oscar Malmros, the American Consul at Winnipeg, and Colonel Enos Stutsman, the Treasury agent at the American customs house at Pembina, were both accepted, for a time, as confidential advisers to the rebel leaders; and the editorship of the *New Nation,* the one newspaper whose publication in the colony was permitted by Riel, was given to Major Henry Robinson, an American-born annexationist. Back of these men, in the United States, was a group of journalists, politicians, and railway men, including Jay Cooke, the wealthy promoter of the Northern Pacific Railroad, who were ready to assist the movement with propaganda, political influence, and money. Back of them all was the government of the United States, which had never settled its account with Great Britain for the *Alabama* claims, and which viewed the whole north-west with an interested and acquisitive eye. From the start the American government was very curious about the troubles at Red River; and it appointed J. W. Taylor, the greatest authority in the United States on the British north-west, as a secret agent to keep the State Department informed about the development of the affair.

Macdonald suspected the existence of these American machinations. But, for the moment, he focused his attention upon the Hudson's Bay Company which, until the transfer had taken place, was the only legal authority in the region. Was Mactavish's unfortunate illness a satisfactory excuse for his curious, irresponsible detachment? Macdonald shook his head sceptically. He would never know that Malmros had reported to the State Department that many of the Hudson's Bay Company's servants desired the union of the settlement with the United States. He would never know—what Donald Smith, the chief Canadian representative of the company later confessed to its Governor, Sir Stafford Northcote—that there was some foundation for the charges levelled against the loyalty of the company's employees, and that, in particular, John McTavish, "was undoubtedly leagued with Riel".[22] He had little positive evidence as yet; but the incredible silence and passivity of the entire organization of the Hudson's Bay Company, from the head office in London down to the smallest outpost in Rupert's Land, seemed to suggest ill-will if not bad faith.

No official notification of the date of the transfer of the territory, or even of the transfer itself, he discovered, had ever been sent from the authorities in London to their subordinates at Fort Garry. "It was the business of the Hudson's Bay Company," he told George Stephen indignantly, "to instruct their officers in Rupert's Land of the arrangements as they made progress in London."[23] Yet the Company had sent no official information or instructions; and at Fort Garry, Mactavish and his officials, though they were well enough aware of what was about to happen, had maintained exactly the same misleading and provocative silence. "No explanation, it appears," Macdonald wrote to Cartier, "has been made of the arrangement by which the country is handed over to the Queen, and that it

is Her Majesty who transfers the country to Canada with the
same rights to settlers as existed before. All these poor people
know is that Canada has bought the country from the Hudson's
Bay Company, and that they are handed over like a flock of
sheep to us. . . ."[24] In such circumstances the growth of discontent was almost inevitable. Mactavish must have been conscious
of the increasing tension in the settlement. Why had he made
no use of his authority to prevent an outbreak? Macdonald's
indignation mounted. What part of all this, he asked himself
angrily, was mere neglect, and what was positive malice?

In the meantime, the Canadian government must act. In
the west, Macdonald decided, it must behave in as patient and
conciliatory a fashion as possible. In winter, a military expedition
was physically impossible, even if it were politically desirable
as a first step. Until spring came, troops could not be sent
through British-Canadian territory; and the unfriendly American government would certainly not permit them to reach their
objective through the United States.[25] All that Canada could
do at the moment was to send out emissaries of peace. The
government selected two, the Very Reverend Grand Vicar
Thibault and Colonel Charles de Salaberry. Both of them had
previously spent some time at Red River, and they were now
sent back to give their old fellow-citizens the explanations and
assurances which the Hudson's Bay Company had failed to
supply. McDougall himself must help to quiet the excitement
by cultivating the virtues of patience and kindliness. He must
remain in the vicinity, of course, and not return ingloriously
to Canada; but, at the same time, he must not even dream of
thrusting his way uninvited past the inhospitable boundary
of Rupert's Land.[26] It was a difficult and frustrating rôle, a rôle
which McDougall was not likely to find very congenial. Yet
there he was—on the spot! They would have to trust him.
They would have to pray that he would not snap in their
hands like a highly tempered instrument of steel.

It was a waiting game in the west. But, in the east, Macdonald
decided, the Canadian government must take immediate and
decisive action. Canada had very nearly blundered into a
catastrophe, and his quick lawyer's eye spotted the one sure

path away from the overhanging avalanche of responsibility that threatened to overwhelm them all. They could still escape. There was just time enough. The surrender of the territory from the Company to Great Britain, and the transfer of the territory from Great Britain to Canada would not take place finally until December 1. The fatal date was still over a week away! The authority of the Hudson's Bay Company was still the only legal authority in the north-west. The £300,000 compensation money had not yet been paid over by Canada. John Rose, in his new office in Bartholomew House—"We are between the Bank and Rothschilds," he had written a little complacently, "so we are well placed"—was waiting expectantly for orders to pay it over. But he could be stopped. Canada could refuse to accept the transfer until peace was restored, and the whole responsibility could be flung back on the imperial government and the Hudson's Bay Company. It was the one neat, quick way out. And Macdonald determined to take it. "Canada cannot accept North West," he cabled Rose on November 26, "until peaceable possession can be given. We have advised Colonial Office to delay issue of Proclamation. . . . Meanwhile money should remain on deposit but not paid over."[27]

III

On the night of December 1—the very day on which the transfer was to have been effected—Macdonald sat in the upstairs dressing-room of the "Quadrilateral", by the side of a blazing coal fire, tranquilly reading a Trollope novel.[28] The house was very still. Early in the day it had turned sharply cold after a period of thaw and rain; and now the frost gripped the deserted street outside in an icy stillness. Agnes was writing in her diary. Old Mrs. Bernard and Hewitt were playing backgammon together in their sitting-room. Little Mary, who had not cried all day, was sleeping peacefully in her cot; and downstairs, in the kitchen hall, the servants were reading the papers by the kerosene light and gossiping quietly. His mind was more at ease than it had been for weeks. Barely a fortnight ago, the first

dreadful news of the trouble at Red River had burst in upon
an unprepared Ottawa. But in the meantime he had taken the
best means to vindicate the Canadian government and pacify
the unrest. Above all, he had extricated Canada, at the very
last minute, from the frightful responsibility that was about to be
unloaded upon her. December 1 might have been a day black
with forebodings. Now it was bright with a glad sense of
release.

Everything was not settled yet, of course. The Colonial
Office had regarded Canada's refusal to complete its contract
with astonished disapproval. Granville had cabled to Sir John
Young that, in accordance with the terms of the imperial act,
the transfer to Canada and the payment of the purchase price
must legally follow the surrender of the territory to the Crown.
"Government by Company has become impossible," he wired,
"government by Canada only alternative and ought to be established promptly. . . ."[29] But how could it possibly be established
promptly, Macdonald demanded, with the half-breeds already
resisting the peaceable entrance of McDougall? A military
expedition was out of the question in the depth of winter; and,
at the moment, any assumption of authority by Canada which
was not backed up by force of arms, would simply expose
the weakness of the Dominion and invite interference from
the United States. "I cannot understand," he wrote to John
Rose, "the desire of the Colonial Office, or of the Company, to
saddle the responsibility of the government on Canada just now.
It would so completely throw the game into the hands of the
insurgents and the Yankee wire-pullers, who are to some extent
influencing and directing the movement from St. Paul that we
cannot foresee the consequences."[30] It was easily conceivable
that the American government would decide to interfere. It
was quite possible that Canada would lose its inheritance in
the north-west.

"Our case is unassailable," he declared emphatically. Granville
retreated before it. "We could not force the territory upon
Canada, if they put up their backs," he had written realistically
to Gladstone as soon as he had heard of the Canadian decision;[31] and time convinced him that it was not even desirable to

try persuasion. Responsibility for Red River, for a while at least, was deposited once more in the laps of the Hudson's Bay Company and the imperial government; and Macdonald confidently looked forward to rapid and decisive action. He may even have hoped that the imperial government would send out its own lieutenant-governor to Red River and actually convert the region into a temporary Crown colony. He certainly expected that the Hudson's Bay Company would take the most energetic steps to put an end to the anarchy in its dominions. The fact that Governor Mactavish had at last issued a "strong and well-considered" proclamation from Fort Garry gave him a good deal of satisfaction; and he was even better pleased when Donald Smith, the Company's principal representative in Canada, called on him and offered loyal co-operation in restoring order in the west. Smith was a tall Scotsman from Speyside, only five years younger than himself, with a nose almost as big as his own, a great spade of a beard, extravagantly bushy eyebrows, and calm, determined, far-seeing eyes. Why not take him at his word? A capable Hudson's Bay man at Fort Garry would at least give the feeble Mactavish "some backbone". Smith could be sent up to Red River ostensibly on instructions from his Company, and at the same time he could be commissioned, with powers larger than those of Thibault and de Salaberry, to treat for the peaceful transfer of the territory to Canada.[32] In a few days it was all decided, with the Hudson's Bay Company's hearty agreement; and early in December, only a little while after the departure of his predecessors, Smith left for the north-west.

During the first fortnight of December, Macdonald grew increasingly optimistic. "There never was much in the insurrection," he wrote rather complacently to Archibald, "but it has been tremendously exaggerated by the American newspapers which, at first, were our only source of information."[33] There were good reasons for this reviving confidence; but it was still qualified by a lingering and awful doubt. What might McDougall, in his forlorn position at Pembina, be tempted to do? From the very beginning he had tried to impress upon his incalculable western Lieutenant-Governor that, until the transfer had been completed, Rupert's Land was foreign territory, into which he could not enter without the consent of the local authorities. Even when Canada had expected shortly to assume control, this had been true. It was doubly true now, when the transfer of the territory had been indefinitely postponed, and at Canada's own peremptory request.

Power had not changed hands. There had not been even a moment's interregnum. Riel had no legal justification whatever for his provisional government; but McDougall equally had no right to proclaim Canadian rule. If, out of mere impatience, he tried to exercise an illegal authority or to use force, he would upset the *status quo* which Macdonald had effectively re-established and he might bring on the international crisis which Macdonald was desperately trying to avoid. "An assumption of the government by you," Macdonald had warned him emphatically, "of course, puts an end to that of the Hudson's Bay Company's authorities. . . . There would then be, if you were not admitted into the country, no legal government existing, and anarchy must follow. In such a case, no matter how the anarchy is produced, it is quite open by the law of nations for the inhabitants to form a government *ex necessitate* for the protection of life and property, and such a government has certain sovereign rights by the *jus gentium*, which might be very convenient for the United States, but exceedingly inconvenient to you."[34] He was exaggerating the legal position, perhaps deliberately, in order to intimidate his lieutenant. McDougall was so impulsive and high-handed! Yet, for the sake of Canadian prestige, he could not be abruptly recalled. He would have to stay on the borders of Rupert's Land. Macdonald could not quiet his apprehensions. "I very much fear," he confided to Cartier, "that he will not go the right way about settling matters."[35]

No man ever fulfilled expectations more completely than McDougall. He was reported to be high-handed. He now acted with a high hand. Before he could possibly have received any instructions in answer to his reports of half-breed resistance, he chose to assume, without any confirmation, that the north-west had been transferred to Canada on December 1. On the very day which Macdonald had ended in a peaceful fireside reading of Trollope, his western lieutenant illegally inaugurated Canadian jurisdiction on the prairies by issuing a solemn proclamation in the Queen's name. In it McDougall announced the transfer of Rupert's Land, and proclaimed his own appointment as first Canadian Lieutenant-Governor; and by another instrument, issued on the same fatal day, he empowered the ex-surveyor Colonel Stoughton Dennis to raise and equip an armed force for the chastisement of the rebels. Armed with this formidable document, Dennis began what Macdonald later called "a series of inglorious intrigues" among the Indians and Schultz's "Canadian party" which ended on December 7 in the abject surrender of McDougall's "army" to an overwhelming force of aroused *métis*.[86] Louis Riel—the man whom Macdonald had saluted at the start as a "clever fellow"—had completely triumphed. He dominated the situation as he had not done before. And he now took precisely the action which Macdonald had predicted would be the terrible result of any premature and unsuccessful attempt to assert Canadian authority. On December 8, he proclaimed the establishment of a provisional government at Red River.

Macdonald was almost in despair. It was Christmas now— of all seasons in the year! The holiday had been sadly marred by "this infernal western news", though not by that alone. In the last few weeks everything had gone wrong. Carter and his fellow pro-Confederates in Newfoundland, of whom everybody had hoped so much, had been overwhelmingly defeated, towards the end of November, in the provincial general election. There was now no prospect of the island joining Confederation; and the union with British Columbia, which a few months before he had considered such a likely possibility, must be postponed indefinitely. It was idle to dream of the Pacific Coast until Canada was in possession of Rupert's Land. And when the peaceful possession of Rupert's Land would come about, he had now not the slightest idea. The Canadian emissaries— Thibault, de Salaberry, and Donald Smith—would probably. have reached Fort Garry by this time. He still hoped that they could pacify the excitement; but it was obvious that they would encounter a most formidable opposition.

Had not the balance of probabilities tilted against Canada already? The American annexationists, realizing that the crisis of the whole affair was now at hand, would do everything in their power to prevent the Canadians from reaching a peaceful settlement. O'Donoghue and the other pro-American advisers still kept their places in the inner councils of the provisional government; the *New Nation*, which made its first appearance early in January, 1870, began a vigorous propaganda in favour of the union of the colony with the United States. Riel had the clear prospect of American aid; and already, without any external assistance whatever, he had successfully put down an armed protest against his authority in the colony. Had not the whole situation deteriorated so irretrievably that it was beyond the power of the Canadian emissaries to negotiate a peace? "As it is now," Macdonald wrote gloomily to Rose, "it is more than doubtful that they will be allowed access to the territory or intercourse with the insurgents."[37] And even if they were admitted, they would still have to confront men whose pretensions had been encouraged and whose power had been confirmed through the criminal stupidities of McDougall and Dennis. "The two together," Macdonald wrote bitterly, "have done their utmost to destroy our chance of an amicable settlement with these wild people, and now the probability is that our Commissioners will fail and that we must be left to the exhibition of force next spring."[38]

The exhibition of force! He had kept the idea in reserve from the beginning. Now it moved slowly into the forefront of his mind. Perhaps a military expedition was the only certain way of settling the whole complicated and threatening business. But it was a desperate expedient, and he dreaded its possible international consequences. He knew very well that the troubles at Red River were being watched with a steady, eager scrutiny from south of the border. The Fenians, it was reported, were in communication with the half-breed insurgents; the "Yankee wire-pullers" in the American north-west were doing everything they could, with money and propaganda, to exploit

Canadian difficulties. These guerrilla annexationists were dangerous enough in themselves; but far more ominous was the curious interest shown by the American government in the state of affairs in Assiniboia. The accounts which reached Washington of the pro-American attitude of the Hudson's Bay Company's servants aroused the interest of Hamilton Fish, the American Secretary of State. He instructed Motley, the United States' ambassador to the United Kingdom, to make inquiries; and late in January Motley subjected Sir Curtis Lampson, the Deputy-Governor of the Hudson's Bay Company, to a prolonged and surprisingly searching interrogation on the views of the Company's servants concerning the political future of the Red River colony. "I am convinced," Lampson wrote to Northcote, "that the government at Washington feel a much greater interest in this Red River affair than anyone supposes, and the settlement may possibly take a very different turn from what we supposed two months ago."[39]

Macdonald, of course, had no knowledge of this disturbing conversation. But he strongly suspected that such diplomatic manœuvres were going on. He knew that Fish was certain to be interested in the pro-American sympathies of the Hudson's Bay Company's servants and in the annexationist influences which were so strong in the inner councils of Riel's government at Fort Garry. Fish was attempting to acquire all, or a large part, of British North America, by peaceful "constitutional" means. He had inquired of Sir Edward Thornton, the British Minister at Washington, whether his government would object to what was described as a "free vote" being taken in Canada to decide the question of annexation to the United States! Any sign of disaffection, of annexationist sentiment, in any part of British North America would, of course, be valuable to him. He would, Macdonald felt sure, attempt to exploit the troubles at Red River to advance his scheme of peaceful territorial aggrandizement. This "blackguard business" of Fish's both worried and infuriated him.[40] "It is quite evident to me," he wrote to Brydges of the Grand Trunk Railway, who had informed him of another ominous conversation with an American, "not only from this conversation, but from advices from Washington, that the United States' government are resolved to do all they can, short of war, to get possession of the western territory, and we must take immediate and vigorous steps to counteract them."[41]

Yet what steps should he take? Could Canada undertake a military expedition by herself? He knew that at the moment she had neither the prestige nor power to act alone. The risks of separate action, in the circumstances, would be appalling. No, the western expeditionary force must be a mixed force, comprised both of British regulars and Canadian militia. The British government must prove to the whole world, by the convincing demonstration of military co-operation, that the United Kingdom was solidly behind Canada in the extension of its authority over the whole British American north-west. He had always been convinced that the Anglo-Canadian alliance would alone enable Canada to secure and maintain its separate political existence in North America. "British North America must belong either to the American or British system of government," he told one correspondent frankly. "It will be a century before we are strong enough to walk alone."[42] They were not nearly strong enough to walk alone yet. They needed British military assistance badly in the north-west. And yet this was the year, of all years, when anti-colonial feelings and separatist tendencies seemed to be gaining rapidly in strength.

It was the attitude of Great Britain which really worried him. He could afford to treat Galt and the other "few fools at Montreal" who were suffering from mild attacks of "independence" with tolerant contempt; but the purposes and policies of the Gladstone government were a different and a much more serious matter. From the start he had been a little suspicious of Gladstone and his colleagues. His doubts were certainly not allayed when Rose reported from London that he had been "a good deal pained to find indications of indifference" in quarters where he would not have expected to find them.[43] How serious some of these "indications" were, Macdonald probably did not realize. He almost certainly did not know that, in the previous June, Granville had actually gone so far as to enquire of the Governor-General whether there was any feeling in Canada in favour of a friendly separation.[44] He would have been appalled to learn that Sir Curtis Lampson had gone away from a recent conversation at the Colonial Office about the Red River rising with the uneasy impression that "negotiation with the United States is a possible contingency under certain circumstances".[45] Macdonald was almost certainly ignorant of all this. But at the same time he was very well aware of the equally intimidating fact that Granville and Cardwell, the Liberal Minister of War, had announced with all possible definiteness that the imperial garrisons would be immediately withdrawn from central Canada. The regulars were going in a year when their presence was as necessary as it had ever been before. All of them must not go! Some at least should remain to become part of the western expeditionary force. They must prove, to the United States, the reality of Anglo-Canadian solidarity on the North American continent. "It has got to be a fixed idea at Washington," he wrote to Rose, "that England wants to get rid of the colonies, indeed Mr. Fish has not hesitated to say so."[46] British regulars in the west would be at once a denial of American hopes and an assurance of Canadian expansion.

IV

February was a month of anniversaries. It was three years now since he had married Agnes, and a year since his daughter Mary had been born. The child had reached the first important stage in the awakening of human energy and intelligence; but her first birthday came and went, and the little struggles and accomplishments which would have delighted Macdonald's heart were so laggard and so few. "She lies," Agnes wrote in her diary, "in spite of her thirteen and a half months, still on the pillow in her little carriage, smiling when she sees me and cooing softly to herself."[47] She might walk—there was still good hope for that—but not surely with great vigour. She might do many things, but feebly, imperfectly. The terrible enlargement of her head was grievously obvious.

He came away, sick at heart, from these visits to the nursery. In his private life he had met failure after failure. That winter he carried out the arrangement that he had made with Allan and mortgaged all his assets to the Merchants' Bank of Canada. At home he lived with sorrows and worries; and at the office there seemed no end to the state of uncertainty and suspense in which he had existed ever since the troubles began in the north-west. McDougall, "very chop-fallen and at the same time very sulky", returned to Ottawa;[48] and Archbishop Taché, recalled from momentous theological debates at Rome, reached the capital, discussed the whole western imbroglio at length with Macdonald, and departed for Red River as the fourth peaceful emissary of the Canadian government. There was nothing to do now but wait for reports from these western representatives, and for the British reply to Macdonald's request for military assistance. In the meantime, Parliament opened, with Prince Arthur gracing the ceremonies, and "no end of festivities going on". A debate on the Red River fiasco was inevitable; and McDougall, who had now worked out a complete explanation of how his ruin had been accomplished by the malice and stupidity of others, took advantage of the occasion to fling the wildest accusations in all directions. Huntington and Galt, those two advocates of a very carefully qualified form of "independence", introduced resolutions supporting the treaty-making power for Canada, a customs union with the United States, and—as Macdonald explained tolerantly to Rose—"all that kind of nonsense".[49] No, there was nothing very much to be feared from the opposition of McDougall or Galt. Neither the plan for the pacification of Red River, nor the scheme for a joint Anglo-Canadian military expedition was likely to be much affected by their manœuvres. "I have got complete control of the House," he told Rose a little boastfully, "and can do with it pretty much as I please."[50]

Then the long-awaited news began to arrive from Red River. Macdonald looked at it, and looked at it again, with growing misgivings. In one sense, it was reassuring, even encouraging, yet it filled him with disquiet. Donald Smith, who had reached Fort Garry on December 27, had apparently achieved a good deal in a relatively short space of time. Within a few weeks he had somehow managed to acquire a considerable influence in the settlement; he had succeeded in appealing over Riel's head to the whole community of Red River. On January 19, a large number of citizens assembled in Fort Garry to hear him explain his mission. On January 20, a second and still more largely attended mass meeting decided that a convention, composed of twenty representatives from the French-speaking parishes and twenty representatives from the English-speaking parishes, should be called to consider the needs of the settlement and the proposals which Smith had brought. The convention, which met less than a week later on January 26, proceeded to draw up a statement—called a "list of rights"—of the claims and wishes of Assiniboia. On February 7, the list of rights was presented to Smith; and Smith then invited the convention to send delegates to Ottawa to discuss the affairs of the settlement with the Canadian government.

These were favourable results. But they had been obtained only as a result of protracted explanations and debates at Fort Garry; and these long negotiations had other and less fortunate consequences. They strengthened the political consciousness of the settlers and confirmed their improvised political institutions. Up to this point, Riel's rule had been accepted only by the French-speaking part of the community. But now the *métis* leader urged the convention to approve and reconstitute the provisional government; and the English and Scots delegates, after having obtained—incredible as it seemed—some kind of sanction from Governor Mactavish, agreed to recognize the régime and to elect Riel president. All this was disturbing enough; but it was quickly followed by a still more sinister piece of news. The irrepressible "Canadian party" in Assiniboia had chosen the peculiarly unfortunate moment of Riel's political triumph to make another suicidal attempt at resistance; and this second outbreak was as abject a failure as the first. Macdonald was deeply perturbed. "The foolish and criminal attempt of Schultz and Captain Boulton," he wrote gravely, "to renew the fight has added greatly to Riel's strength. He has put down two distinct attempts to upset his government, and American sympathizers will begin to argue that his government has acquired a legal status, and he will be readily persuaded of that fact himself."[51] It was only too true. Riel was persuaded that his government was legitimate. It was founded on popular will. It had withstood the shock of attack. It had become, in fact, what Macdonald had always feared it would become, the *de facto* government at Red River.

There was no doubt now, in Macdonald's mind, of the need of the military expedition. It would probably come to fighting yet. What did he know of Riel's purposes? Was the half-breed acting in good faith when he had agreed to send delegates to confer with the Canadian government? Or was he secretly determined, with American assistance, to continue the fight—to found an independent republic—to take the Red River colony into the United States? ". . . The unpleasant suspicion remains," Macdonald confided to Rose, "that he is only wasting time by sending this delegation, until the approach of summer enables him to get material support from the United States."[52] Canada might have a real struggle on its hands yet, he realized, and he waited impatiently for the answer of the imperial government. It came only after considerable discussion in the Liberal Cabinet, for, as usual on a Canadian matter, Gladstone was full of doubts and reservations.[53] But in the end Granville brushed these misgivings aside without much ceremony. "I see no alternative to our standing by the Canadians," he told his chief, "and if so the prompt assertion of authority is probably the safest."[54] On March 6, the official cable promising British military co-operation arrived at Ottawa.[55] The offer was, of course, accompanied by conditions—the first of a growing list of conditions. Canada must grant reasonable terms to the Roman Catholic settlers, and the transfer of the territory to the Dominion must accompany the movement of troops. Yet the matter was settled. There would be help from overseas.

It would be needed, he was more and more convinced. Before the month was out, a last and most appalling piece of news arrived from Red River. Riel had given one final proof of the fact that military power was the one solid and constant basis of his provisional government. On March 3, one of his Canadian prisoners, an obstreperous youth named Thomas Scott, was charged with having taken up arms against the provisional government (of which offence all the other prisoners were equally guilty), with insubordination, and with striking his guards. For these crimes he was tried in a summary fashion before a military tribunal, sentenced to death, and executed within twenty-four hours. Riel may have decided to strike fear into the hearts of his opponents by a savage example; or his hand may have been forced by the murderous temper of his unruly followers. But the execution of Scott, whatever its motive, utterly changed the problem of the Red River rising. It made Macdonald almost despair of a peaceful settlement.[56] He was more than ever doubtful of Riel's good faith. He feared a desperate half-breed resistance. And he was only too well aware that the execution of Thomas Scott, unlike any previous incident in the Riel rising, had aroused a passionate controversy over policy in central Canada.

English-speaking Ontario, which identified itself with Scott and the "Canadian party", clamoured for the dispatch of a military expedition to Red River, and insisted that there must be no negotiation with emissaries from the murderers of Scott. French-speaking Quebec, which instinctively sympathized with Riel and his *métis*, denied the need for force, and demanded that the government seek a peaceful settlement through negotiation with the delegates from Red River. Macdonald could have groaned in spirit. From the start the Red River affair had been full of international complications. Now it was perplexed by all the rancours of Canadian domestic politics. He foresaw a racial division in the House—an inevitable split in the Cabinet, with the Ontarios and the Maritimers demanding a military expedition, and Cartier and Langevin obstinately opposing, and himself almost torn to pieces by the struggles between the two.

It was at this inopportune moment that the rumour of a new Fenian raid burst upon Ottawa. John O'Neill, the Fenian leader at the Battle of Ridgeway two years before, was expected, according to McMicken's espionage service, to invade in force about April 15.[57] The last complication had now been added.

Yet, in the circumstances, it was an inevitable complication. Macdonald had expected it. From the very beginning of the troubles at Red River, he had feared that the Fenians would try to take advantage of Canada's western difficulties by launching an attack in the east. Now the attack was coming. And it was coming at a time when Great Britain had publicly announced the recall of the imperial garrisons from British North America, and when the western military expedition, in which she had agreed to co-operate, was being held up by annoying British conditions and stipulations. He felt like the solitary defender of a beleaguered city. "We are glad to know," he wrote to his old friend, Lord Carnarvon, on April 14, the day before O'Neill's raid was expected, "that we have in you a friend —I may almost say a friend in need—for we greatly distrust the men at the helm in England. . . . At this moment we are in daily expectation of a formidable Fenian invasion, unrepressed by the United States government, and connived at by their subordinate officials. And we are at the same time called upon to send a military force to restore order in Rupert's Land. Her Majesty's Government have been kept fully informed of the constant threats from the Fenian body for the last five years, and they have been specially forewarned of the preparations for the present expected attack. And yet this is the time they choose to withdraw every soldier from us, and we are left to be the unaided victims of Irish discontent and American hostility. . . ."[58] It was a bitter reproach, its tone perhaps heightened for Carnarvon's benefit, yet in a fashion not unjustified by the circumstances. The crisis seemed to mount about him. "We must however bear it as best we may," he ended his letter to Carnarvon, "and we intend, with God's blessing, to keep our country, if we can, for the Queen against all comers."

V

Not even the arrival of the delegates from the west could take place peacefully. On April 11, the first two of them, Father Ritchot and Alfred H. Scott, reached Ottawa; but they had not been in the capital more than two days when they were arrested, charged with aiding and abetting the murder of Thomas Scott, on warrants sworn out by ardent young Ontario patriots who deeply sympathized with the "Canadian party" at Red River.[59] In the meantime, while the first two delegates cooled their heels in custody, and Ritchot protested indignantly at this violation of their "diplomatic" immunity, the third representative, "Judge" Black, the Recorder at Red River, arrived in Ottawa. Macdonald saw him privately and unofficially at the earliest possible moment. Black was a servant of the Hudson's Bay Company, a moderate man, very different from the fanatical Ritchot and the pro-American Scott; and Macdonald hoped that, with his help, it might be possible to reduce the extreme demands which the delegation as a whole was only too likely to make. He did not want to recognize the delegates officially. He much preferred to receive them as representatives, not of Riel's provisional government, but of the convention, of the people of the north-west. The negotiations, he was convinced, must be kept at the level of informal, private discussions; and their basis could be only the list of rights which the convention had adopted after long public debate.

He began to realize that he would likely have to give way on many of these points. He was not negotiating with the representatives of a real frontier democracy. Black, Ritchot, and Scott were not simply and solely the deputies of the whole community of Red River. They were something rather less —and more. They were, to a large but indefinite extent, the agents of a remarkably astute, extremely dictatorial half-breed leader, Louis Riel, who was determined to manipulate the Red River rising in the special interests of his own people, the French-speaking *métis*. It was all over Ontario now—A. H. Scott had revealed the fact in a newspaper interview before his arrest—that the delegates had come armed with a new and revised "list of rights".[60] This second list had never been submitted for approval to the convention, or to the "legislature" of the provisional government, which was actually in session at the time the delegates left. It had simply been privately drawn up by the French-speaking members of the executive alone; and, as Macdonald speedily discovered, its terms were not only much more exacting than those of the first list, but also in some vital respects completely different. The second list included a demand that Assiniboia enter Confederation as a province, despite the fact that the convention had considered a proposal for provincial status and had expressly rejected it by a considerable majority.[61] The Red River community, democratically organized, did not want provincial status. But Riel did. And so did the French-speaking members of the executive and their clerical advisers, Archbishop Taché and Father Ritchot. Their purpose was evident. They wished to establish the character and institutions of the new western province at a moment when the French-speaking Roman Catholic half-breeds were still in a majority, and therefore at the most favourable opportunity for preparing defences against the approaching influx of Protestant, English-speaking settlers.

He realized that he would have to accept provincial status. This first western province would be an absurdly premature creation, a top-heavy, needlessly expensive establishment, which he had never expected and did not want. Yet, in the circumstances of Canadian politics, it was apparently unavoidable. It was the price that he would have to pay for the military expedition. He still doubted Riel's good faith, and feared his intentions. He still believed, despite the presence of the delegates and their apparent readiness to negotiate, in the necessity of the military expedition; and he was sustained by the welcome knowledge that Cartier emphatically agreed with him. Cartier's support was vitally necessary. But Cartier did not stand alone. Back of him, giving him political strength, were the Quebec members, his docile troop of "moutons" who usually followed him submissively enough, but who now began to show unmistakable signs of obstreperous restiveness. Like most of their fellow French Canadians, they identified themselves emotionally with the cause of Riel; they opposed the use of force against his government; and it was now rumoured on all hands that they had threatened to desert Cartier in a body if it were decided to send a military expedition to Red River.[62]

Macdonald knew very well that there was one obvious method of meeting this threat and of ensuring Assiniboia's entrance into Confederation on his own terms. With the help of the opposition, which was ready and eager to exploit the fury of Protestant, English-speaking Ontario, he could disregard Cartier's followers, authorize the military expedition, and insist that the list of rights adopted by the convention could alone be accepted as a basis for negotiation. No doubt he could do all those things. But it would mean abandoning Cartier, ruining the Liberal-Conservative party, breaking up the Anglo-French *entente* upon which Confederation itself was based. He did not even consider the possibility. At all costs—or nearly all costs —Cartier must be sustained. He must have something with which to satisfy his "moutons", and they would be satisfied only if Ritchot were satisfied. "The French," wrote one shrewd observer at Ottawa, "are earnestly bent upon the establishment of a French and Catholic power in the north-west to counteract the great preponderance of Ontario."[63] There was no way out. Provincial status—whatever its value ultimately for French-Canadian ambitions—would have to be conceded. They must negotiate on the basis of the exacting terms demanded by the executive at Red River.

On Saturday, April 23, Father Ritchot and Alfred Scott were finally discharged.[64] The negotiations with the three delegates were scheduled to begin on Monday; and on Sunday night, along with a large party, he and Agnes dined at Rideau Hall.[65] The crisis of his difficulties was at hand. It was true that the prompt muster of the militia had apparently intimidated the Fenians, for there had been as yet no real sign of John O'Neill's threatened raid. But the British government was still haggling about the terms on which it would permit imperial soldiers to be sent to the north-west; and Macdonald was now beginning to fear that the Americans, although they had used the Canadian canals freely for the transport of military stores during the American Civil War, would refuse passage on the Sault Ste. Marie Canal for the Red River expeditionary force.

He was uneasily conscious of dangers hidden or only partly disclosed, of the watchful scrutiny of a ring of pairs of eyes— eyes that were curious, or questioning, or admonitory, or hostile. The Colonial Office had sent Sir Clinton Murdoch to watch over the negotiations with the delegates; and Sir Stafford North- cote, ruddy, cheerful, and curious, the new Governor of the Hudson's Bay Company, had hastened across the ocean to protect the interests of his shareholders. He was present that night at Sir John Young's dinner party, politely pumping Macdonald for information. And there was still another interested visitor to Ottawa, who had not been invited to Rideau Hall that evening, but who had, oddly enough, been having long and intimate conversations with the delegates from Red River. It was J. W. Taylor, the special agent of the American State Department, who had found that business called him imperatively to the capital of Canada.[66]

On Monday, when he and Cartier met the reunited Red River delegation, Macdonald quickly found his worst fears realized. Ritchot was the most powerful of the three delegates, and he was both peremptory and uncompromising. He threat- ened to return to the north-west if the delegates were not given official recognition. He refused to negotiate on any other basis than that of the list of rights which the executive govern- ment had drawn up. He himself had brought a special copy of this list, different in one very significant particular from those which had been supplied to Black and Scott. The Ritchot version contained what had been included in no previous list, a demand for Separate Schools for Roman Catholics, supported by public money, on a basis of population.[67] The convention of the people at Fort Garry had made no request whatever for Separate Schools. It is not even certain that the French-speaking members of the executive ever authorized the demand; and the new clause may have been inserted by Riel alone, at the earnest solicitation of his clerical advisers. In any case, however it got into the Ritchot version, the request for Separate Schools was emphatically made at Ottawa. Macdonald knew that it would have to be conceded. He had no means of getting past these delegates to the people of Red River whose known wishes were being so freely altered. If he questioned the validity of the revised list of rights, he would merely arouse the French-Canadian members at Ottawa, imperil Cartier's position, and bring on a racial war. He gave way. "We are nearly through our troubles with the delegates," he wrote at last to Sir John Young on Wednesday, April 27, "and then we can take up the military matter."[68]

He was weak with fatigue. Yet fatigue was not the only thing that oppressed him. He was burdened with a general distress which lay heavily upon both body and spirit. For some time now he had not felt really well. Usually his trouble seemed to be nothing more than a malaise, a vague, unhappy feeling of discomfort. But sometimes, at rare intervals, there were more precise and much more disquieting symptoms. Occasionally he felt, high in his back, an odd, uncomfortable sensation of tightness, as if some organ, or organs, had been unnaturally distended; and once or twice, some terrible force—it was almost like a cruel, grasping hand—had closed briefly but agonizingly upon these stretched sensitive surfaces. He shuddered with pain and bewilderment. Yes, there must be something wrong with him. When the session was over, he would see a doctor. Yet there was another and a far more serious trouble, which, he knew now, was probably beyond the cure of any doctor. There could no longer be any real doubt that Mary's condition was irremediable. She would never be a normal girl and woman. In a sudden clairvoyant vision, which illuminated the future like a beam of harsh, pitiless light, he saw a dreary procession of treatments and manipulations, an endless repetition of hopes and doubts and deceptions, which could end only in despair. He could not even guarantee material security for this helpless, dependent being—or for Agnes, or for Hugh and himself. Everything that he had scraped together in half a lifetime of professional effort had gone to meet his obligations at the Merchants' Bank. . . . He was sick of Riel, and Red River, and these interminable negotiations. The piled papers lay on the desk in front of him. The gaze of the delegates was fixed upon him with implacable ferret-like intentness. Laboriously they worked their way through the clauses. It was Thursday night and the business was nearly finished. Tomorrow they could put the last touches to the act which would transform Assiniboia into the new Province of Manitoba.

He walked down the corridors of the Parliament Buildings and into the bar. The next morning, when Sir Stafford Northcote went down to breakfast, he was greeted by the alarming intelligence, "Bad news, Sir John A. has broken out again";[69] and, at intervals during Friday, Macdonald was seen about the House and in Russell's Hotel, obviously intoxicated, and keeping himself erect with difficulty.[70] People had half expected, Northcote went on to tell Disraeli, that the Prime Minister would "break out" once the crisis of the Red River affair was over. But Macdonald, for reasons that lay beyond the knowledge or the imagination of most, had anticipated the event. For at least a day he tried at one and the same time to continue his work and to satisfy the insatiable craving within him. But it was no use. The papers before him became a muddled chaos. The realization that this was another bout broke through the disorder of his mind, and he took the last precaution which he had taken often enough before. "His habit is," Northcote informed Disraeli, "to retire to bed, to exclude everybody, and to drink bottle after bottle of port. All the papers are sent to him, and he reads them, but he is conscious of his inability to do any important business and he does none." He did none for at least two days, while the *Globe* began charitably to denounce his drunkenness, and the government papers ascribed his temporary breakdown to pressure of overwork. Friday and Saturday and Sunday went by. The week-end was over.

Then, with a great effort, he roused himself. After all, the work of the last six months was almost finished. The military expedition, with its complement of British regulars and with Colonel Garnet Wolseley as its commander, was about to leave for Red River; and a political settlement of the north-west had finally been achieved in the Manitoba Bill. The session was nearly over. Only a little more effort was required. But it was absolutely essential that he himself should make it; and, in his absence, everything was going wrong in the House. The ministers were leaderless, intimidated, and uncertain of their following. They fumbled, hesitated, and lost direction. "The House is becoming rapidly demoralized," wrote one experienced observer, "and the government is losing its control over the members."[71] There was not a moment for delay, Macdonald realized. He must appear immediately in the House. The Bill was ready, though printed copies were not yet available to members; and on Monday afternoon, May 2, he went down to the House to make his first explanation of the Manitoba Act. He was pale, his face was drawn, and he looked and felt ill.[72] His voice, which was never very strong and sometimes indistinct at the beginning of a speech, seemed unusually feeble. But he had summoned up all his old skill in presenting an argument, all his old ingenious dexterity in avoiding pitfalls and anticipating criticisms.

"The Bill affecting Red River," he wrote to Sir John Young on May 4, "was received last night with great favour by the House, and will pass without any serious opposition."[73] The first reading was over. He was confident that the party was reunited and that the House would do his bidding. It was true that there would have to be one major amendment to the Bill for the boundaries of the new province had been somewhat curiously drawn to exclude the settlement at Portage la Prairie where the "Canadian party" was strongest, and McDougall and the opposition had leaped triumphantly upon this pointed omission. But the enlargement of the boundaries was the only important change that would have to be made; and on Friday, May 6, he waited for the debate on the second reading without much apprehension. It was early afternoon. He had come from the Council chamber only a little while before; the last caller had just left him; and he sat in his office preparing to eat the sketchy luncheon which, during the crowded days of the session of 1870, was often brought in to him. He rested for a moment, savouring the welcome peace; and then, without warning, the pain was upon him, like a wild animal, savage, implacable, immitigable. He stood up twisting, writhing, trying to bear the pain, knowing he could not bear it; and somewhere in his back, the pressure, like a great iron hand, closed inexorably on his vitals. He felt his senses whirling, spinning, dropping into a dark void of agony. He clutched the table, swayed, tried to recover his balance, and fell blindly across the carpet.

Chapter Three

Fish and Diplomacy

I

Dr. Grant, who arrived in a few minutes and found Macdonald in a state of collapse, diagnosed the disease as "biliary calculus" or gall-stones. Obviously the dreadful seizure had been caused by the passage of a stone, and there could be no doubt that the patient was in a most alarming condition.[1] His pulse barely fluttered; he was almost insensible with the pain he had endured; and, as Dr. Grant explained to the fearful Agnes, it was utterly impossible to think of moving him for a while at least. He would have to lie, almost literally, where he had fallen. The office where he had worked and eaten his hurried meals, where he had done everything but sleep, was now, by a preposterous exaggeration, to become his bedroom. In these incongruous surroundings, all the paraphernalia of the sick-room would have to be improvised and at once. It was a task that exactly suited Agnes. Her devotion to her husband, her strong sense of duty, her uneasy, recurrent suspicion that the life which she and her friends led was largely frivolous, all helped to fortify her for the work that now lay ahead. Under Dr. Grant's direction, she assumed control of the sick-room. She watched, waited, anticipated needs, and multiplied attentions with an unwearied and slavish devotion. If her nursing could accomplish it, he would live.

Yet nobody really believed that he would live. May was a month of brief recoveries and dreadful relapses during most of which his condition remained critical. Friends, assuming in secret that their old leader had not long to live, began to make discreet enquiries about the state of his affairs and discovered his almost penniless condition with horrified surprise. The general public, kept informed by a series of gloomy newspaper bulletins, was convinced that death was inevitable in a matter of days. At the end of the month he was still frighteningly weak.[2] The doctors virtually gave up all hope of his recovery. And it was perhaps the very desperateness of his condition which induced them to take advantage of a brief period of improvement to move him in a litter from the cramped quarters of his office in the East Block to the relative ease and convenience of the Speaker's chambers in the Parliament Buildings. Edward Blake, in a kindly letter of condolence and sympathy, called this migration a "march of recovery".[3] So it proved to be. Macdonald stood the little journey of June 2 well. The next day he was better again. And all during June, while Ottawa sweated and suffocated in one of the hottest summers in its history, he steadily improved. By the middle of the month, he was definitely past the crisis.[4] He would live now. The period of convalescence had begun. And for that it was best for him to get away from Ottawa, which was baked with drought and heat, and which, a few weeks later, was to be covered by a thick, grey pall of dust and smoke from a dangerously encroaching ring of forest fires.

He had to be carried on board the steamship when, on July 2, he finally left Ottawa, in company with Agnes, and Mary and Dr. Grant. The government steamer *Druid* brought them slowly down the St. Lawrence and into the cool breezes of the gulf; and it was not until the morning of July 8 that they finally tied up at Pope's Wharf in the harbour of Charlottetown, Prince Edward Island.[5] Colonel Gray, who had acted as host to the Charlottetown Conference nearly six years before, was waiting hospitably at the quayside with his carriage; and when Macdonald had been lifted ashore in an easy chair, they drove off cautiously towards Falconwood, a comfortable house on the banks of the Hillsborough, in the near vicinity of Charlottetown, which had been fitted up as a temporary residence for the patient and his family. There Macdonald rapidly improved. Within a week he was taking short walks in the grounds of

Falconwood. Now his convalescence had entered the final, not unpleasant, stages which lead towards complete recovery. And all that summer, while Europe rocked with the Franco-Prussian War, and England doubtfully considered the diplomatic future, he remained placidly fixed in the deep peace of Prince Edward Island. People respected his temporary retirement. He received few letters and sent fewer replies. He spent more time over the articles on the war in the English periodicals than he did on the ferocious controversies of the Canadian newspapers; and instead of worrying about party manœuvres in the constituencies, he followed the cavalry charges at Mars-la-Tour and Gravelotte, and watched the inexorable encirclement of Sedan.

On September 16, when they finally left Charlottetown, he walked aboard the steamship in what was almost his old jaunty style.[6] He had made a marvellous recovery; and he could have counted the summer of 1870 as one of the happiest and freest from worry that he had ever spent, if it had not been for the deepening tragedy of little Mary. The child was now a year and a half old. Her terrible physical abnormality, the enlarged head, was more conspicuous than ever; and her slow responses, at a time when a spring-like spontaneity was natural, left no doubt of the impairment of her mind and spirit. On the journey up the gulf from Prince Edward Island, she became ill; and, in the end, she had to be left at Quebec, in the care of old Mrs. Bernard, while he and Agnes came on alone together to Ottawa. The station platform at the capital was sumptuously carpeted when they stepped out of the train on the morning of September 22, and there were dozens who rushed forward eagerly to shake Macdonald's hand.[7] It was a joyful yet an awed reception. He might have been risen from the dead.

At home there was a great pile of congratulatory telegrams and letters, and oddly assorted gifts, including a basket of grapes from Moll and Professor Williamson, and a suit made of Canadian tweed and sent by an admiring Conservative woollen manufacturer. "I see," he wrote jovially in reply, "that you are resolved by sending me such an outfit to keep me politically consistent; with such a nice suit of new clothes I have no pretext for turning my coat!"[8] He smiled as he worked easily and rapidly through the huge pile of correspondence. He was flexing political muscles which had remained unused for months and which yet responded with reasonable elasticity. It was good to be back. He was not laid on the shelf yet, thank God! At the station everybody had been obviously surprised by the apparent completeness of his recovery. He had been told a dozen times enthusiastically that he had never looked better in his life. The truth, he knew very well, was a little less wonderful. He had made an extraordinarily successful recovery. There was nothing organically wrong with him now that any doctor could discover. But his strength had not entirely come back. He would have to take things easy for a while. "I shall not do much work for some months," he told his sister, "but act in the government as consulting physician."[9]

II

He picked up the old design—the union of British North America—where he had dropped it so hurriedly. On the whole, it was an encouraging moment for a reassessment. The forces which he had set in motion had travelled surely on towards their objectives during his absence. In the east, it was true, he had made no progress whatever. Both Prince Edward Island and Newfoundland had refused the better terms which had been offered them, and in the circumstances it was better to let the question of their entry into Confederation drop quietly for the moment. He would have to wait a while yet for the remaining provinces in the east; but in the west the territorial expansion of the new Dominion was about to be triumphantly completed. The Red River military expedition had reached its objective without incident, and had confirmed British-Canadian occupation of the north-west. The Province of Manitoba had been set up; and the delegates from British Columbia had come east and had agreed to the terms on which their province was to be united with Canada. These terms, of course, had yet to be ratified by the Dominion Parliament and the British Columbia legislature; and although the Red River affair had ostensibly been wound up in a satisfactory fashion, there remained a perplexing, annoying loose end—the question of an amnesty for the leaders of the rebellion, a question hideously complicated by the execution of Scott. Still, this was not an immediately pressing problem. It could be left, Macdonald thought, to "time, that great curer of evils". But the union with British Columbia was another and a much more urgent matter. Canada had, as part of the compact, agreed to begin a railway to the Pacific within two years, and to complete it within ten years, of the date of the union. "The terms can, I think," Macdonald wrote to Musgrave, the Lieutenant-Governor of British Columbia, "be fully justified on their own merits; but we may expect considerable opposition in our Parliament on the ground that they are burdensome to the Dominion and too liberal to British Columbia."[10] It would help greatly, he thought, if the legislature of British Columbia accepted the terms as they stood at once. The Dominion Parliament, when it met next winter, would hesitate to change an approved arrangement.

These were matters of tactics. He had no real doubt of a successful issue. The forces inside British North America which favoured a transcontinental union had not yet lost their potency. What worried him most, as he took stock in the early autumn of 1870, was not so much the association of the parts as the security of the whole. Confederation, as he knew very well, had been to an indefinitely large extent a response to a potential danger from the United States. That danger had not yet manifested itself in coercive diplomatic pressure, or taken the horrid shape of open war. But, on the other hand, it had never been entirely cleared away. The disputes and animosities which had grown up during the American Civil War between Great Britain and British America on one hand and the United States on the other, remained unsettled, to everybody's chronic dissatisfaction. The damages claimed by the United States for the losses wrought by the *Alabama* and the other cruisers built in British shipyards had not been honoured by Great Britain; and Canada had never got a copper of compensation for all the needless worry, expense, and loss of life which had been caused by the Fenian Raids. Canadian-American relations had been extremely bad before 1867; and the years since Confederation had certainly brought no improvement. In 1870, and particularly during Macdonald's illness, there had been, in fact, a further marked deterioration; and this, as he knew well, was the consequence of the termination of the Reciprocity Treaty which the Americans, with an angry desire for retaliation, had brought about in 1866.

So long as the Reciprocity Treaty lasted, American fishermen had been permitted to ply their trade freely within the three-mile limit of British North America. But, once the Treaty had been abrogated, these spacious freedoms came to an end. Citizens of the United States were flung back upon the privileges which had been guaranteed to them by the Convention of 1818; and by the terms of this Convention, American fishing vessels could enter the bays and harbours of Nova Scotia, New Brunswick and Prince Edward Island "for the purpose of shelter and of repairing damages therein, of purchasing wood and of obtaining water, and for no other purpose whatever".[11] The complete exclusion of Americans from the inshore fisheries of British North America was thus an unquestionable treaty right. But the provinces, realizing that American fishermen had come to take their long-accustomed fishing privileges almost for granted, decided to assert their rights of exclusion in a gradual and conciliatory manner.

During the seasons of 1866 and 1867, they permitted American fishing vessels to fish within the three-mile limit on the payment of a small fee; and for the following two years licences were again issued at somewhat higher rates.[12] But the Americans abused the licence system without scruple; when the fee was raised, only a very small fraction of them bothered to take out licences. And Macdonald decided to make an end of this régime of unappreciated indulgence. He was perfectly ready to exchange the inshore fisheries for tariff concessions in the American market, as had been done in the Reciprocity Treaty; but he saw no point in surrendering property to people who were determined to appropriate it for nothing. "We are going to put an end to all fishing licences," he had written to Rose during the previous January, "as the system has proved abortive."[13] During the summer, while he had been ill, the Canadian government had fitted out several marine cruisers to protect its inshore waters from marauders; and when he got back to Ottawa in the autumn he discovered that the American State Department had been indignantly protesting against the resulting seizure of fishing vessels, and that the fisheries had become an international issue once again.

For a while after his return, he tried to take things easily. He was determined, if it were possible, not to prejudice his complete recovery with overwork. His illness, his long convalescence, his long absence from Ottawa, all combined to invest this resumption of his old activities with something of the significance of a new departure in his career. He decided —it was in keeping with the opening of a new chapter in his life—to leave the "Quadrilateral", with its recurrently defective drainage system, for a new and more spacious house on the outskirts of the town. "I am now in the agonies of moving into Reynolds' house for the winter," he told David Macpherson early in November. "I am regularly driven out of my present one by the stench from the drains."[14] "Reynolds' house", known later as Earnscliffe, the house in which he was to spend the last years of his life, was a comfortable, rambling, many-gabled house, which stood about a mile or more north-east of town, on a great cliff fringed with low trees, overlooking the broad expanse of the Ottawa River, and the sombre masses of the Laurentian Hills beyond. The house was secluded and relatively inaccessible; and as the uninterrupted mornings and peaceful evenings succeeded each other, he began to feel progressively better. "I am, thank God, in good health and spirits," he wrote to one correspondent, "and I think have got a new lease under more easy terms than the old."[15] Yet he tried carefully not to overtax his new-found strength. "I do not do much office work," he told Archibald reassuringly, "but my attendance at Council is absolutely necessary."[16]

In Council that autumn the most important matters that came up for discussion were the problem of Canadian-American relations in general and the problem of the fisheries in particular. During the summer, while he had been convalescing, Macdonald had wondered anxiously whether Peter Mitchell, the Minister of Marine and Fisheries, was not enforcing the new policy of exclusion with more rigour than was strictly necessary; and, when autumn came, it became quite clear that Great Britain, upon whom Canada depended for diplomatic and moral support in her fisheries policy, was even more apprehensive of possible trouble with the United States. "A very unpleasant dispatch respecting fisheries has come from England," he wrote to Alexander Campbell, who had been pleading with him to go away for another holiday, "in consequence of the too energetic action of the irrepressible Minister of Marine. I must take that subject into my own hands."[17] It was easy to modify the strictness of Mitchell's policy slightly, in the hope of satisfying the British and soothing the Americans; but Macdonald had no intention of making an abject surrender of Canada's main exclusive rights in the fisheries. And what worried him now was the possibility that this ominously growing concern of the British government over the policy of exclusion really implied an anxiety to come to terms with the United States at any price.

For Great Britain, the need for a reconciliation with the United States was now more urgent than ever.[18] The Franco-Prussian War had involved England in serious embarrassments in Europe. As soon as Metz fell and the defeat of France seemed imminent, Russia took advantage of the situation by denouncing the clauses in the Treaty of Paris of 1856 which forbade her to establish naval or military bases on the Black Sea. England would have to meet this challenge without support from Europe. And why, in such dangerous circumstances, should she continue to run the risk of trouble with America? Once again, as had happened with such tragic frequency in the past, the Anglo-Canadian resistance to the United States had been weakened, at the crucial moment, by the distracting events in Europe. And once again Macdonald feared, and with reason, that the United States would attempt to exploit the British desire for appeasement by extracting ruinous concessions at Canada's expense.

He knew that important voices in the republic had urged the cession of all or part of Canada in payment of the *Alabama* claims, and that Fish, the American Secretary of State, had actually been trying, under the guise of a disinterested concern for British North American "freedom", to persuade Great Britain to abandon Canada.[19] He did not believe that even the Gladstone government could be induced to give more than a glance at this blatant manœuvre of American imperialism. No, there was no real need to fear the abandonment of British withdrawal. But, if the surrender of Canadian territory was unthinkable, could one be equally sure of the defence of other Canadian property rights? As the autumn wore on, it became obvious that Great Britain was earnestly considering the establishment of an Anglo-American Commission which would deal, not only with the problem of the fisheries, but also with all outstanding disputes between herself and the republic. Would Canadian fishing rights suffer by being included in this general agenda? Macdonald was distinctly apprehensive. He suspected that the Convention of 1818 was the weak point at which the United States would strike for the purpose of dividing Canada from Great Britain; and early in December, when President Grant gave his annual message to Congress, his fears were bluntly confirmed. "The imperial government," declared the President in a tone of mingled hostility and condescension, "is understood to have delegated the whole or a share of its control or jurisdiction of the inshore fishing grounds to the colonial authority known as the Dominion of Canada, and this semi-independent but irresponsible agent has exercised its delegated power in an unfriendly way. . . . It is hoped that the government of Great Britain will see the justice of abandoning the narrow and inconsistent claim to which her Canadian provinces have urged her adherence."[20]

III

On New Year's Day, 1871, he called another Cabinet on the everlasting fisheries question. It was deep winter now.

The Ottawa River, which had been so charming in its ruffled blue two months before, was stilled and white with ice; and the strident winds blew harshly from the north-west. "More fires," Agnes wrote in her diary, "is our war-cry, our watch-word, our hourly, nay, momently entreaty."[21] Reynolds' house, with the trees on the cliff side bent to the gale, was certainly exposed; but it was also spacious and well-appointed; and, as the night of January 1, 1871, came on, it was pleasant to think of going back to it, with its fires all crackling and its furniture all polished in readiness for the annual parade of New Year's visitors. When he got back, it was nearly dinner-time. Snow was falling now, in great, wind-blown showers, and his shoulders as he entered were thickly powdered. Inside, on the sideboard, were the remains of the sherry and the hot oyster soup with which Agnes had entertained her visitors. Over one hundred and thirty gentlemen had called to pay the Macdonalds the compliments of the season! Agnes was full of the day's doings. But she watched Macdonald's tired face with anxious interest. ". . . I think this American fishery question bothers Sir John," she wrote. "I suppose it is ticklish business as Brother Sam may show fight."[22] It was indeed a ticklish business. Council continued to prepare the Canadian case respecting the fisheries and the Fenians, as if there were a near prospect of a settlement. But nothing happened until the second day of February. Then Macdonald received a short significant note from the Governor-General, newly raised to the peerage as Lord Lisgar.

He hurried over to Rideau Hall. There on the Governor-General's desk lay a decoded cable which had arrived the day before from the Colonial Office. "If Joint Commission is appointed to consider questions pending between the United Kingdom and the United States," it read, "will Macdonald serve as Commissioner for Canada, or Rose, or both?"[23] Obviously the matter was nearly settled. The Joint Commission was a virtual certainty; and, as Macdonald had feared, its agenda would be a general one, with all questions mingled together, perhaps to the prejudice of Canadian rights and interests. He did not definitely know yet whether the British interpretation of the Convention of 1818 agreed substantially with the Canadian one, and whether he could count upon a united British-Canadian front in defence of the fisheries. This was a crucial point which must certainly be cleared up before the arrangements for the Commission were very far advanced; and there was now no time for dispatches. "Important that Canada should know," Lisgar cabled to Kimberley, "points of agreement and difference between England and herself as to fishery rights."[24]

In the meantime, while they waited for the reply from the Colonial Office, Macdonald considered Kimberley's invitation. He did not like it very much. His first impulse, as he told Lisgar frankly, was to advise the Governor-General that Canada had better not be represented on such a Commission at all. Yet, as soon as he had tentatively framed such a reply, he realized immediately that it would be impossible to submit it. ". . .We must consider," he told Lisgar, "that if Canada allowed the matter to go by default, and left its interests to be adjudicated upon and settled by a Commission composed exclusively of Americans having an adverse interest, and Englishmen having little or no interest in Canada, the government here would be very much censured if the result were a sacrifice of the rights of the Dominion."[25] No, Canada would have to be represented on the Commission, whatever dangers were involved. But what kind of a representation would be best? Should Rose and he both go? Or should one of them go alone?

Rose was one of his best friends. Rose had been active in Canadian politics for years, had resigned his portfolio as Minister of Finance barely eighteen months before, and, since his removal to England, had served Canada in a variety of ways as an interested and informed unofficial agent. Macdonald was very fond of him. Personally, he told Lord Lisgar, he "would like no better colleague to fight Canada's battle on the Commission". But no, it would not do. Rose was not a Canadian by birth. He had left the country to become a permanent resident of the United Kingdom; and he was a member of an Anglo-American banking house, which had important interests in the United States and which at the moment was vitally dependent upon the good will of the American government. Politically, it would be very dangerous for the Canadian government to sponsor him. He was unacceptable either as a sole, or as an associate, representative for Canada.[26]

There remained Macdonald himself. It was obviously his duty to go; and, although the prospect worried him, some at least of his misgivings had been allayed by the Colonial Office's cabled statement of its views about the fisheries. "It would be impossible," Kimberley replied to the Canadian cable of inquiry, "to pledge ourselves to any foregone conclusion on any particular point before entering upon negotiations, but as at present advised we think the right of Canada to exclusive fisheries within three mile limit beyond dispute and only to be ceded for adequate compensation."[27] It was true that this highly satisfactory statement was followed by a couple of qualifications. The Colonial Office was willing to compromise on the subject of fishing in bays less than ten miles wide at the mouth, and it considered that the exclusion of American fishermen from trade in Canadian ports, though perhaps justified by the letter of the Convention, was an extreme stand which might be modified. Yet despite these qualifications, the statement was a reassuring one. It would be possible, on this basis, to defend the fisheries at Washington. His colleagues would certainly expect him to represent Canada.

He did not really want to go. He had been desperately ill. He had spent a long summer in convalescence, and a long autumn relatively free of administrative routine. The strength which he had missed when he resumed his duties last September, had not yet come back. "*Entre nous,*" he wrote to David Macpherson on February 6, when his final decision had not yet been taken, "I do not feel as strong as I ought to be, and I may want to talk to my friends about the future."[28] To a person who was hinting, however obscurely, about his possible retirement from public life, the prospect of an exacting and probably ungrateful diplomatic task was definitely not attractive. "I contemplate my visit to Washington with a good deal of anxiety," he wrote to Rose. "If things go well, my share of the kudos will be but small, and if anything goes wrong I will be made the scapegoat at all events so far as Canada is concerned."[29] There was danger in his presence in Washington:

there was also danger in his absence from Ottawa. All sorts
of misfortunes were possible in the Canadian Parliament while
he was away. Yet he did not really hesitate. Probably he had
never hesitated from the start. ". . . I thought," he told Rose,
"that after all Canada had done for me, I should not shirk the
responsibility."

On Monday, February 27, he set out from Ottawa, accompanied by Agnes, Colonel Bernard, and the Deputy Minister
of the Department of Marine and Fisheries. At Washington,
no American officials and no members of the British Commission had thought it necessary to come to the station to meet
him; but Sir Edward Thornton had sent his carriage, and one
of his attachés, and the Canadians were soon comfortably
installed in the Arlington Hotel.[30] The first few days were
crowded with a succession of dinners, receptions, courtesy
calls on the American Commissioners and the officials of the
State Department, formal visits to the Senate and the House
of Representatives, and long and amiable conversations with
such notorious Anglophobes and Canadian annexationists as
Charles Sumner, Benjamin Butterworth, and Zachariah
Chandler. It was the first time that Macdonald had met Hamilton Fish, the Secretary of the American Department of State
and the head of the American section of the High Commission.
Fish was a rather sluggish-looking man, with a long, solemn
face, and a big jowl whose size was accentuated by a bristle of
beard fringing the under side of his chin. He was perhaps more
tenacious than swift in his mental processes. But there could be
little doubt that he was much superior in ability to his four
rather nondescript American associates on the Commission.

Macdonald was probably more interested in his British
colleagues than he was in the Americans. He knew most of
them, at least vaguely, by reputation, and one or two by personal
acquaintance. He may already have met the dyspeptic and
lugubrious Thornton, the British Minister to Washington, who
on rare occasions came up to Ottawa for visits; and he had seen
something of Sir Stafford Northcote, the one British Conservative on the Commission, when he had come over in the interests
of the Hudson's Bay Company, at the time of the negotiations

with the Red River delegates. The other members of the Commission, and its secretary, Lord Tenterden, were new to him. Montague Bernard, the Professor of International Law at Oxford, a slight, dapper little man who was distantly related to Agnes, seemed a friendly, kindly, rather retiring scholar. Earl de Grey and Ripon, the head of the British Commission, was physically perhaps its most distinguished member. His was a handsome and striking personality, which, outwardly at least, seemed made for leadership. His forehead was high and broad; the lines of his mouth and nose were cleanly and decisively drawn; and his dark, deep-set, piercing eyes seemed to suggest conviction, determination, and authority.

The presence of Macdonald—an indubitable colonial states-man—among these people was a slightly embarrassing novelty. It was the first time that a British North American had ever participated on terms of equality in such a general imperial negotiation; and everybody—though Macdonald probably least of all—was sensitively aware of the fact. The British ministers, Gladstone, Granville, and Kimberley, had made a consciously revolutionary decision; and the High Commissioners and many British officials regarded their daring innovation with scepticism and inquietude. Sir Edward Thornton made little secret of the fact that he would have preferred John Rose—who, after all, had been restored to respectability by his return to England— as the fifth Commissioner;[31] and Lord de Grey was disposed from the start to regard Macdonald as a member of some strange and unidentifiable species, whose habits puzzled him, and whose nature he feared would be malevolent. The mere fact that Macdonald had brought with him two officials of the Canadian civil service was looked upon doubtfully as a possible pretension towards separate status. Fish had actually been inquiring for a definition of Macdonald's position! "I shall take an opportunity for which Fish's inquiry yesterday will afford an opening," wrote de Grey in a tone of lofty condescension, "of letting Mac-donald understand that he is here as the representative not of the Canadian, but of the British government, and is in precisely the same position as any other member of the Commission. If I find any difficulty with him, I will telegraph to you, and a hint from Kimberley may be required to keep him square."[32] Certainly no nonsense could be tolerated from colonials. Macdonald must be kept very firmly in his place. De Grey hoped that Canada would not attempt to take advantage of the great concession which had already been made to it. But he instinctively feared that the Dominion would try to assert its special claims against the general imperial interests. It was exactly the counterpart of Macdonald's own apprehension. The Canadian feared that his country's rights would be sacrificed to the achievement of Anglo-American concord; the Englishman was perturbed lest the welfare of the Empire should be imperilled by the intransigence of Canadian claims. It was a curious, equivocal situation which portended trouble, and trouble came.

IV

On Sunday, March 5, just after church, de Grey came down to the Arlington Hotel specially to see Macdonald. He had a disturbing story to tell. On the previous evening, after dinner at de Grey's house, Fish had drawn his host aside and had informed him that the American Commissioners did not wish to begin a protracted discussion on the nature and extent of Canada's exclusive rights in the fisheries, but that they were prepared to buy these rights, whatever they were, and that they intended, as soon as the formal preliminaries were over, to make an offer for their purchase in perpetuity.[33] It was this astounding piece of information which had sent de Grey hurrying down to the Arlington Hotel that Sunday morning. Macdonald heard the news with surprise and disquiet. Where, he wondered, had this embarrassing notion of the sale of the fisheries come from? Who had suggested it? Although he was ignorant of the fact, it was his own chief, Lord Lisgar, the Governor-General of Canada, who had ventured to propound to Thornton the idea of granting the liberty of the fisheries for a term of years in return for an annual money payment; and Thornton, assuming, of course, that Lisgar would not have made such a suggestion, even in a private letter, without the concurrence of his ministers, had informally discussed the possibility of a sale with Fish.[34] Fish had appropriated the idea enthusiastically, and had made it his own. But to Macdonald the prospect of a sale was unexpected, unwelcome, and disquieting. He had the uneasy impression, which was to return at frequent intervals during the negotiations, of being manœuvred rapidly and expertly into a position which he did not like and had never dreamed of occupying. All he could do, on that Sunday morning in March, was to ply de Grey with arguments against a sale and in favour of commercial concessions. The Canadian Cabinet, he told his chief solemnly, "had not even taken into consideration" a "pecuniary equivalent" for the fisheries.[35] On the contrary, the Canadian Cabinet had put all its hopes in a reciprocal trade agreement which would be as close as possible to the vanished Reciprocity Treaty.

De Grey listened to his Canadian colleague with rising impatience. He had quickly conceived a slight distaste for Macdonald. From the start the Canadian's reserved, non-committal manner had inexplicably irked him. At the end of the first meeting of the British Commissioners, he had come to the rapid conclusion that Macdonald was going to be extremely difficult in his insistence on Canadian rights. He confided to Granville, in a tone of curiously childish self-satisfaction, that the British Commissioners had determined to pay Macdonald's expenses with imperial money, "as it would not do to give the Dominion government the claim to interference which would result from any charge being made on their funds".[36] He had expected opposition. Now it was coming. Macdonald was demanding a broad reciprocal trade agreement in exchange for the fisheries. But Fish, in their conversation on Saturday night, had informed him bluntly that it was quite impossible to persuade Congress to accept a broad trade agreement. What was possible, de Grey had already convinced himself, was a comprehensive arrangement in which Canada would trade her fisheries, her canals, and the navigation of the St. Lawrence for a few tariff concessions and a good-sized lump of money. It would be a good bargain, he thought. He would, of course, make an attempt to get what Macdonald wanted from the Americans. But if this effort failed—and he had little doubt of its failure—he wanted to start negotiations for a sale of the fisheries at once. Without delay, he wrote to Granville requesting permission to do so, Macdonald or no Macdonald. ". . . I expect Macdonald to be very exacting," he intimated a little irritably, "and I look forward to having a good deal of difficulty in bringing him to accept moderate terms."[37]

The next day, when the Americans informally presented their revolutionary proposal, de Grey replied on behalf of the British Commissioners that a sale of the fisheries, particularly a sale in perpetuity, would be unwelcome, and that Canada would much prefer a trade agreement in exchange for her property. Outwardly, the British front was unbroken; but when Her Majesty's Commissioners met alone, Macdonald could hardly be unaware of the chilly air of disapproval that was creeping about him. It was already strangely apparent that his colleagues were spending almost as much time arguing with him as with their American counterparts. His uneasiness grew. What did the other British Commissioners really intend? Did they mean to sell the fisheries to the United States, despite the solemn protests which he had repeatedly made in conference? He did not know, he had no means of knowing—so completely was he shut out from the familiar, confidential discussions of the "bachelor" establishment on "K" Street—that his colleagues had already determined to force his hand. But, at the last moment, some hypersensitive political sixth sense warned him of impending danger. He decided to appeal to the British government over the heads of his unsympathetic colleagues. He could not, of course, communicate directly with Granville, the Foreign Secretary—that was de Grey's prerogative. He would have to approach the British government through the regular channel of communication between the Governor-General at Ottawa and the Colonial Office. His excuse would be Kimberley's last dispatch on the fisheries, of February 16, which had been sent on to him at Washington. "Cable should be sent on dispatch to this effect," he telegraphed to Charles Tupper at Ottawa, "Canada considers inshore fisheries her property and that they cannot be sold without her consent."[88]

He was only just in time. The very next day, March 9, the Americans, as de Grey had anticipated, rejected the British proposal of a reciprocal trade agreement in exchange for the fisheries, and instead proposed purchase for a term of years. This time, however, the unpalatable dose was sweetened with a small teaspoonful of tariff concessions. Fish suggested, in deference to Macdonald's well-known wishes, that in addition to sanctioning a money payment, Congress might be persuaded to reduce or even repeal the duties on a small number of commodities—coal, salt, salt fish, and firewood.[39] It was a shrewd offer, cunningly devised, as Fish was well aware from his previous conversations with Thornton and de Grey, to win the approval of the British members of the Commission. And its success was fully up to his expectations. De Grey and his English colleagues, with that easy alacrity which characterized all their decisions about Canada, were instantly convinced that a better offer could not be expected. But neither Macdonald, nor the Canadian ministers up in Ottawa, were in the least impressed.[40] Coal, salt, salt fish, and firewood! Firewood, of all things! This niggardly little list was not even remotely comparable with the generous arrangement for which they had hoped. The Canadian Cabinet turned down the revised American offer, and Macdonald communicated the rejection to his colleagues in Washington.

He bore their not too well concealed disapproval with fortitude. For the reply to the cable to Kimberley had arrived in time. "We never had any intention," it announced conclusively, "of selling the inshore fisheries of Canada without consent."[41] Macdonald carried these fortifying words around in his pocket, prepared for any emergency. He had not long to wait. For de Grey had also received a reply—an equally satisfactory reply —to his cable of March 7 to Granville. Granville had authorized him to discuss the sale of the fisheries, and had even gone so far as to express a preference for a sale in perpetuity.[42] De Grey was elated. The supreme authority of the Empire, speaking *ex cathedrâ*, had delivered judgment. He would be able now to overwhelm the contumacious Macdonald. And, at the very next opportunity, he solemnly read the portentous words. The other British Commissioners listened approvingly and with eager interest. But, strangely enough, the heretic seemed impenitent and unabashed. Instead of capitulating, he proceeded composedly to read a second pronouncement, from the same supreme authority, which was strangely inconsistent with the first, if, indeed, it did not exactly contradict it! De Grey was mystified and annoyed.[43] He even toyed with the idea that Macdonald had falsified the words of Kimberley's cable! But this ludicrous suspicion brought no permanent comfort. The shock and bewilderment were great. It was a "floorer", as Macdonald wrote briefly and with colloquial complacency, to Tupper. He had outmanœuvred them all. It was his first great moment of triumph during the conference.

Yet had he really gained anything more than a temporary advantage? It was true that he could force his colleagues to require the Americans to produce still another offer for the fisheries. But would de Grey and the others willingly accept this virtual Canadian veto over their proceedings? In their present temper, would they not try immediately to clear up the apparent contradiction in British policy, and to their own advantage? "Lord de Grey," Macdonald wrote to Tupper, "is now, doubtless, communicating with Lord Granville as to the apparent discrepancy between his statement and that of Lord Kimberley."[44] It was only too true. De Grey was writing in reproachful astonishment to the Foreign Office. What had the British government been thinking of? And the British government, confronted with the muddle of its own making, had now to reconcile the two sincere but conflicting impulses by which it had been guided. Gladstone and his colleagues had no desire to sell Canada's property without its owner's consent; but at the same time they had a very anxious wish to reach a general settlement with the United States. In the old days the problem might have seemed insoluble. But the Gladstone government was an innovating government in colonial affairs, and it now discovered a quick way out of its perplexities. Canada's consent would be safeguarded by a special clause in the treaty providing that all articles relating to the Dominion could take effect only after ratification by the Canadian Parliament. Canada would have its say in the end; but in the meantime it could not be permitted to frustrate the negotiations at Washington. De Grey was authorized to negotiate for a settlement of the fisheries, without any restriction as to the kind of equivalent that Canada might be given for her property.

Macdonald was surprised and perturbed. He had never expected such a solution. The power of ratification was undoubtedly important for the future; but it was not the power that he wanted at the moment. So long as Canada's consent meant his own consent, given in conference to his fellow British Commissioners, he occupied a position of commanding importance. But now negotiations could be carried on, arrangements made, and even, presumably, a treaty signed and sealed, entirely without his approval! Canada was left with public and formal methods of expressing non-concurrence; and formal methods, as he knew very well, were clumsy and dangerous to use. "If a majority of my colleagues," he explained to Tupper, "should at any time conclude to accept terms which I do not approve of, I must, of course, either protest and withdraw, or remain on the Commission and trust to non-ratification of the treaty by Canada. If I take the first course it will disclose to the Americans the fact of a difference of opinion, a conflict, in fact, between Canada and England. This the Americans are anxious to establish, in order to get up a sort of quarrel between the two, and strengthen that party in England which desires to get rid of the colonies as a burden. If I continue to act on the Commission, I will be attacked for making an unworthy sacrifice of Canada's rights and may be compelled to vote in Parliament against a Treaty which I had a share in making."[45] Yet could he really vote in Parliament against a treaty which he had helped to frame? Was it conceivable that Canada could reject an agreement which had been accepted by the senior partner in the Empire? Did he even possess the option of withdrawing from the Commission or of refusing to sign the treaty? He did not know. He felt his power to influence the negotiations slipping rapidly and irretrievably away.

V

The Commission had by now got well into its stride. At first Macdonald had found in the work the relaxation of novelty. The mild March of Washington, so different from the drab late winter of Ottawa, delighted him, and for a while the politics and society of the Capitol were an amusing change. But the entertainment had been extravagantly lavish from the beginning; and it soon became a tedious superabundance. "Our life here," complained de Grey, "is rendered very intolerable by the endless feasts. We work all day and dine all night. And some wag in the newspapers says we are not a Joint High Commission, but a High Commission on Joints—the joke greatly delights the Washingtonians."[46] It also mildly amused the British Commissioners, for they accepted the sobriquet of "High Joints" and called their secretaries and assistants "cutlets". But these pleasantries did not reconcile them to the mountainous dinners. "Even in this Lenten season," Macdonald grumbled, "we are overwhelmed with hospitalities which we cannot refuse."[47] At first he found this nearly the only drawback of a pleasant situation. But not for long. The climate, which had been so charming at the outset, began to seem "relaxing", and within a month of his arrival he was anxious to be home. "I am very tired of Washington," he wrote to Colonel Gray towards the end of March, "although everybody has been very civil since I have been here; but I want to get back to my work again."[48]

There was a simple explanation for his home-sickness. He viewed the work that he had to do with growing distaste. The British Commissioners seemed to be no nearer to an agreement with the Americans; but they were perilously close to an open disagreement among themselves. The United States had, for the moment, withdrawn its offer of a "pecuniary equivalent", plus a few small tariff changes. It had apparently accepted the Canadian plan of a primarily commercial arrangement, and it now proposed, as a basis for discussion, the free entry into the American market of Canadian coal, salt, all kinds of fish and all types of lumber.[49] Macdonald was still seriously dissatisfied. The second offer was so much like the first; it was so utterly unlike the old Reciprocity Treaty, by which all Canadian natural products, without exception, had been freely admitted to the American market. Could he surrender Canada's biggest commercial asset for these trifling concessions? He did not see how he could. But his English colleagues, who were as quickly convinced on this as on the two previous occasions, decided for the third time that a better offer could not be had. Macdonald had wanted a trade agreement. Well, here was a trade agreement! Yet he still declined to accept! They could not understand it. But now there was no need for them to do so. With Granville's express authority, they could exchange the fisheries for any kind of reasonable equivalent, despite Macdonald's protests. It was time to call a halt to all this nonsense. They decided to make a definite offer to the United States, based largely on the American suggestion of free coal, salt, fish and lumber.

Macdonald had protested verbally before. He now renewed his protests in a long and somewhat formal letter to de Grey.[50] This document, without rehearsing the previous efforts of the British Commissioners to get a fair equivalent for the fisheries, concentrated on the current proposal. It condemned the proposal as insufficient and frankly predicted its rejection by the Canadian Parliament. De Grey objected heatedly, and an unpleasant row ensued, in which the leader of the British delegation openly accused his Canadian colleague of "misrepresentation".[51] Macdonald gave way. He had no intention of presenting such an obvious opportunity to a man who seemed determined to put him in the wrong if he possibly could. The obnoxious letter was withdrawn; and a short informal memorandum, briefly stating the Canadian case, was substituted for it and sent over to the British government for its information. A new struggle for the verdict of the Colonial Office was at hand. Macdonald had done all he could, but he was probably less hopeful now than he had been on the previous occasion. His position had been seriously weakened as a result of Granville's decision to give de Grey a free hand in the negotiations. And he can hardly have failed to suspect—what was, of course, the truth—that de Grey, in every private letter to England, was attacking his arguments, belittling his objections, impugning his motives, criticizing his conduct, and urging the British government to coerce him.

Yet—as he also had some reason to suspect—there was far more sympathy for his views in Whitehall than at Washington. To the shocked amazement of de Grey and his British colleagues, the Gladstone Cabinet did not at once perceive the truth in all the simple purity in which it was apparent at the "bachelor" establishment on "K" Street. Gladstone, indeed, seemed strangely unimpressed by the horrifying story of Macdonald's formal protest to de Grey. He told Granville frankly that after reading it he did not feel any more like coercing Canada. "We ought not to let our credit," he went on, "or even that of our Commission weigh a single hair in the balance. If we place a burden or an apparent burden on Canada, we shall pay for it dearly, shall never hear the last of it, nay, may perhaps tempt Canada to say, 'if gifts are to be made to the United States at our expense, surely we had better make them ourselves and have the credit of them'."[52] All these considerations suggested circumspection and delay. Gladstone was not disposed to be "hustled" into an agreement by his over-zealous Commissioners at Washington. He told Granville that the Cabinet was "of a mind to hold a little with Macdonald about the fisheries";[53] and Granville agreed that "Macdonald seems to have more to say for himself than his brother Commissioners admit. . . ."[54] The result was a cable which once again lifted de Grey's eyebrows in pained surprise. The British government would not undertake to compel Canada to accept the newest American offer of free coal, salt, fish and lumber.

Incredibly, Macdonald had won again! He had expected a final defeat. He had gained one more temporary victory. But the contest was not yet over; and de Grey and his colleagues, who believed sincerely that Macdonald's selfish obstinacy was endangering a just and necessary peace, bent themselves with grim-lipped determination to overcome his resistance. Throughout the British side of the High Commission, annoyance, suspicion, and resentment were in the air. The ambiguous relations between these five men inevitably produced misunderstandings. England and Canada had just begun the long and painful process of redefining their respective rôles in the conduct of foreign policy; and the British Commissioners at Washington were the inexperienced and easily exasperated victims of a daring experiment in imperial diplomacy. Macdonald regarded himself as the representative of a national state, with separate and important national interests which it was his business to defend and promote; and actually this was the conception of Canada's place in the Empire with which the Gladstone government had publicly identified itself. In theory, British Liberals were always protesting their readiness to welcome the growth of colonial separatism; but in practice, so long as the Empire endured, they tended instinctively to think of it as a strict diplomatic unity, with Great Britain in complete and unquestioned control.

To de Grey and his British colleagues it seemed unnatural and almost indecent that Macdonald, a mere serviceable subordinate, should actually try to employ diplomatic devices, even against themselves, in the defence of his country's special interests! The fact, communicated by Lord Lisgar, that Macdonald had inspired some of the answers to his own telegrams to Ottawa, and that the Canadian Cabinet had been willing on occasion to take lower terms than he had indicated, seemed, to the horrified de Grey, to reveal not so much a talent for diplomatic bargaining as a dreadful propensity towards "slippery" moral behaviour.[55] "Candour" was at one and the same time a duty which Macdonald owed to his colleagues and a favour which they were under no obligation to confer upon him. It never apparently occurred to de Grey that the confidences of a colonial were something which had to be requited. On at least one occasion he urged Granville to maintain greater secrecy about the private letters and cables which they habitually exchanged. ". . .I have to carry on quite as difficult a negotiation with Macdonald as with the United States Commissioners," he wrote, "and it would never do to cut me off from telegraphing to you privately without his knowledge."[56]

In the midst of this unpleasantly sultry and electric atmosphere, Macdonald and the other British Commissioners stuck to their task. In the full meetings of the Joint High Commission, de Grey was outwardly doing his best to persuade the Americans to improve their last offer for the fisheries; but privately he was bending every effort to induce the British and Canadian governments to come to terms as quickly as possible. The Gladstone Cabinet had shown a strange tenderness for Canada's interests, and an inexplicable respect for Macdonald's views. It must be rescued from these absurd delusions, if the peace were not to be lost; and Macdonald, who had been acting with irresponsible, self-seeking obstinacy, must be taught to see where his "true interests" lay. De Grey and his English colleagues set about the work in deadly earnest. Sometimes, Macdonald reported to Tupper comically, "they made speeches *at* me". Sometimes they wrote long letters, full of admonition and reprimand. More and more often, as time went on, they fell back on a judiciously compounded mixture of threats and bribes. De Grey was at pains to point out to Macdonald that if any "unpleasant consequences" were to follow the failure of the negotiations, "the people of England will not be much inclined to help the Canadians out of their scrape".[57] But these dark and sinister suggestions were suitably varied by other, very different, deliciously tantalizing hints. "I have had a talk with Macdonald," de Grey wrote Granville, "which I hope has done good; the word Privy Councillor somehow escaped my lips as a distant vision that individually I should like some day to see realized in the person of an eminent colonial minister; but I have committed no one and yet I think done what I wanted."[58] Surely the "hard, needy, greedy" colonial, in Robert Lowe's elegant phrase, would not remain insensible to this blandishment!

Yet Macdonald seemed unmoved. He kept to his course. The British government had backed him. It had agreed with him that free fish, coal, salt and lumber were not a sufficient return for the fisheries. He was determined not to make a sacrifice of Canadian property; and he was still bargaining for further tariff and other concessions from the United States, when suddenly, without warning, the whole basis of the discussion was drastically changed. On April 15, Fish informed de Grey that the current American proposal, which the British Commissioners had not yet finally accepted, would have to be withdrawn, as a result of the pressure of important vested interests in the American Congress. All that he could offer now was his original proposal of a purchase of the fisheries, not in perpetuity, but for a term of years, the amount of the payment to be settled subsequently by arbitration; and he suggested that, in addition, the United States might concede the free entry of Canadian fish. Macdonald was discomfited and deeply chagrined. His British colleagues could hardly conceal their jubilation. Macdonald, they agreed sagely, had "overstayed his market". He had "dropped the bone out of his mouth like the dog in the fable".[59] And it was almost a pleasure to confront him with the painful necessity of reaching a decision upon this last and probably final American offer. The conference was coming to an end. Most of the matters on the agenda had been settled. There remained only the wearisome problem of the Canadian fisheries. What were they to do about it?

Macdonald knew that the crisis of the whole negotiation was at hand. He had won tactical victories before. But now he was boxed in an extremely vulnerable position, and in his heart he expected nothing but defeat. Yet he maintained his stand with apparently unaltered firmness. He rejected, with the hearty agreement of the Canadian Cabinet, the new American offer of a money payment to be settled by arbitration, plus free fish. He reminded his colleagues that the Joint High Commission had originated in a proposal put forward by Canada for a diplomatic settlement of all disputed points under the Convention of 1818. ". . .What Canada desired," he told his colleagues, "was if she could not get a satisfactory equivalent for her fisheries, that she should be allowed to remain in exclusive possession of them, leaving the questions as to ports and headlands, the only matters in dispute, for adjustment by the Commission."[60] De Grey was horrified. Such a conclusion to their labours was unthinkable! The final American offer must be accepted, and Macdonald must either be persuaded or forced to yield his consent. He struggled to convince the obstinate man with argument. He even lost his temper, lecturing the Canadian, like an angry pedagogue, upon his duty as a Commissioner! But he quickly saw the futility of tirades. There was a better method available. On Sunday, April 16, after church, he came down to the Arlington as he had come exactly six weeks before, to reason with Macdonald.

Most of the interview was taken up with a long, serious recital of the reasons for Canadian acceptance of the latest American terms. Macdonald had heard these often enough before, and it was not until the conversation was nearly over that de Grey produced his astounding novelty—the last, gorgeous inducement, which the Gladstone government had authorized some time before, but which he had been keeping carefully in reserve for just such an extremity as this. As far back as February, when the Commission had first been appointed, Gladstone himself had suggested that de Grey should be provided "with the means of smoothing over any difficulties which may arise between us and Canada in the course of the negotiations by some undertaking on account of the expenses of the Fenian Raid".[61] That was when it was still hoped that the Americans could be induced to repay Canada for her losses. But it now began to look as if the United States would be able to avoid paying any compensation whatever for the raids. As a result of some singular defect in the official correspondence which had settled the terms of reference, the Americans were claiming, with a show of plausibility, that the Fenian Raids were not on the agenda of the Joint High Commission at all! It was very odd! Had the best Foreign Office in the world actually blundered? Nothing, in either explanation or apology, would ever be said to the Canadians. But the British Cabinet authorized de Grey to "hint" about the possibility of imperial compensation to Macdonald.[62] Clearly it was time to begin "hinting" now. And at the close of the long conversation at the Arlington Hotel that Sunday morning, de Grey informed his colleague of the British government's offer.

Macdonald accepted this proposal gratefully. But it did not change his attitude to the final American scheme for the settlement of the fisheries. He protested, and his protests, and those of his government, were cabled to England. The British government must finally decide. He hoped. But, at the same time, he had very little doubt as to what Great Britain's decision would be. He was only too well aware of his colleagues' eagerness to close with the American offer. He expected that they would urge the British government to accept. But even he could scarcely have imagined the desperate urgency with which de Grey and the others tried to convince the Gladstone Cabinet of the necessity of acceptance. They had tried appeals and exhortations before. What they now presented—in still another of the long list of private telegrams—was a virtual ultimatum. "If you do not back us up against Macdonald," de Grey wired to Granville, "he will be quite unmanageable, and I see no chance of coming to an arrangement."[63] This dreadful prophecy, which, de Grey assured his chief, was the collective opinion of all the Commissioners—with, of course, the exception of Macdonald—was enough to set the British government pondering deeply. Gladstone and his colleagues were eager to complete an otherwise successful negotiation. Nothing, apparently, would satisfy the Canadians; and Gladstone, reading carefully through the last protests of Macdonald and his fellow-ministers, pronounced them to be "rampantly unreasonable".[64] It was impossible to support Macdonald any longer. Yet there remained Kimberley's promise not to sell the fisheries without Canadian consent; and despite the proviso requiring ratification by the Dominion Parliament, this was still a slightly embarrassing pledge. A cabinet was held on the subject, while for days the British Commissioners in Washington waited in an agony of expectation. Then, at long last, came the eagerly awaited, the enthusiastically applauded, answer. De Grey was instructed to concede the inshore fisheries in return for a money payment, the amount to be determined by arbitration, and free fish.

VI

"Your fisheries telegram has arrived," de Grey cabled triumphantly back to Granville, "and Macdonald has yielded with a good grace which was almost laughable."[65] It was a strangely optimistic interpretation, which revealed more of de Grey's state of mind than it did of Macdonald's. Outwardly Macdonald had—at least for the moment—accepted; but inwardly his sense of exasperation, futility, and failure had now reached its culminating point. "My first impulse, I confess," he wrote to Tupper, "on the arrival of the cable message from England, authorizing the reference to arbitration of the value of the fisheries, was to hand in my resignation of my position as Commissioner, procurator, and plenipotentiary to Lord de Grey for transmission to Lord Granville. . . ."[66] It was a first impulse of disgust and anger. But it did not last the night; and by morning he had decided to remain on the Commission, even if only with a watching brief, to guard Canadian interests during the last stages of the negotiations. "It was fortunate that I did so," he explained to Tupper later, "else the articles would have been much worse than they were." Even so, they were bad enough. There was no compensation whatever for the Fenian Raids. The free navigation of the St. Lawrence—though not of the canals by which alone it was navigable throughout—was conceded for ever in return for similar rights on three remote Alaskan streams; and of all the long list of Canadian natural products, fish alone was to be admitted free to the American market. "Such are the articles," he complained bitterly to Tupper, "and a precious lot they are!" He was sick at heart. "Never in the whole course of my public life," he told Alexander Morris, "have I been in so disagreeable a position and had such an unpleasant duty to perform as the one upon which I am now engaged here."[67]

What was he to do now that the treaty was at last complete? His decision to remain on the Commission had simply postponed the difficult decision that he had to make. Should he sign the treaty or not? "Canada," he told Tupper, "is certain to reject the Treaty *in toto*." He clearly implied to Alexander Morris that he expected publicly to oppose it himself. If he signed the treaty now, how could he retain his moral right to liberty of action thereafter, how could he escape the charges of disingenuousness and inconsistency which might inflict irremediable political damage upon him? To withhold his signature was the easiest, simplest, most completely effective way of protecting himself from the inevitable accusation that he had concurred in the betrayal of his country's interests. It was the course which he first thought of taking, which many of his Canadian colleagues would have preferred him to take. But, on the other hand, there were a number of serious objections to it, all of which were pointed out to him with solemn emphasis by de Grey. He was, like all the other British Commissioners, a plenipotentiary of the imperial government, acting on behalf of the imperial government, and now instructed by the imperial government to sign the treaty. ". . .I fancy," he wrote to Francis Hincks, "it would be an unheard of thing for an envoy to refuse to carry out the instructions of his principal."[68] It might also be a highly dangerous thing politically, for the rejection of the treaty by the American Senate was a very possible result, and with it the loss of the dearly-won settlement of the *Alabama* claims. No, he could not accept such a heavy load of responsibility. He would have to put his name to the treaty.

But need he sign without explanation or qualification? He would, in fact, be acting under the orders of the British government. Was there not, he wondered unhappily, some way in which he could prove to the world in general and the Canadians in particular, that in signing he had merely done his duty as an imperial Commissioner and had in no way compromised his future liberty of action as a member of the Canadian government? Possibly, he suggested to de Grey, they might insert a paragraph in one of the protocols, stating that although the Canadian Commissioner had signed in obedience to the orders of the Queen, he considered the arrangements distinctly disadvantageous to his country. De Grey rejected this suggestion instantly and authoritatively. It would never do. Macdonald must sign *tout court*. Obviously there was only one way out. If his objections could not be indicated on the face of the treaty and the protocols, then it could only be put on record in letters between himself and the other people concerned. De Grey accepted this idea with alacrity. He promised to write a letter which Macdonald could use in Ottawa; and Macdonald set about composing formal statements of his position for Lord Granville, and the Governor-General.

This discussion—it took place early in May—was the last occasion on which Macdonald talked at length about the treaty with de Grey. Before they separated, Macdonald made a final request that the British government would not delay in honouring its principal Commissioner's pledge of compensation for the Fenian Raids. "I pressed him, therefore," Macdonald told Cartier, "to take the matter up and have it finally settled the moment he returned to England. This he promised to do. He thanked me very much for the course I was taking."[69] Gratitude may have been on de Grey's lips; but there was little in his heart. He had striven, he reasoned with himself, for a settlement in the interest of the whole Empire. Macdonald had opposed him stubbornly, from a purely Canadian viewpoint, and by methods which, he had become convinced as a result of Lord Lisgar's disclosures, were unquestionably underhand. Lord Lisgar, who had been permitted to see some of Macdonald's private communications to his Canadian colleagues, quoted from them freely in his letters to Northcote at Washington;[70] and although Macdonald's accounts of the proceedings had been in general scrupulously temperate and fair, he had made a few disrespectful remarks which affronted his English colleagues. As the proofs of Macdonald's semi-independent course increased in number, de Grey's sense of injury grew. It seemed to him monstrous that the Canadian should have dared to forward separate Canadian interests by methods which, though a commonplace for Great Britain and any other national state to pursue, were completely inadmissible in a colony. When it came to the point, colonial "nationalism" in diplomacy was nothing more or less than "treachery" to Great Britain. ". . .Macdonald," de Grey wrote to Granville in still another of those private letters from which his Canadian colleague would never have a chance to quote, "has acted with a pretty strong amount of treachery towards us."[71]

Macdonald believed that promises had been given him, and that Canada had made sacrifices which deserved reward. But de Grey felt no sense of obligation whatever. Macdonald's conduct had been simply deplorable. If he really wished to prove that he could be "of service", then let him get the treaty through the Canadian Parliament. And until that was safely accomplished, everything could be held up. How fortunate that de Grey had been so discreet in making his little hints! "I merely dandled before his eyes," he assured Granville again, "the idea of giving occasional admission to the English Privy Council to distinguished Canadian statesmen; but I was throughout the conversation, which was a short one, very careful to avoid saying anything that would bind myself or anyone else."[72] No, he was not in the least committed. Macdonald had nothing owing to him. Macdonald would get nothing. All the other Commissioners and all the secretaries —the "joints" and the "cutlets"—had been superlatively co-operative and helpful. Without exception, they all deserved well of the British government. But Macdonald was different. "Macdonald has puzzled us all," he summed up to Granville. "I do not know whether he is really an able man or not; that he is one of the duskiest horses that ever ran on any course I am sure; and that he has been playing his own game all along with unswerving steadiness is plain enough. If he gets the consent of the Colonial parliament to the stipulation of the treaty for which it is required, he will deserve reward; but if he does not, he ought to get nothing."[73]

On May 8, at ten o'clock of a brilliant spring morning, Macdonald appeared at the State Department for the final ceremony of the conference. The High Commissioners and the secretaries were all there; most of the clerks of the Department had come in to watch what was evidently an unusually solemn event.[74] The room was sweet with bright masses of spring flowers; and on the sideboard an unusual but not unappetizing morning collation—strawberries and ice cream—lay waiting to be eaten. A relaxed elated feeling of accomplishment was in the air. Macdonald alone did not share it. He was only too well aware that something that he did not want, but could not prevent, was about to be done, and done irrevocably. Even as they chatted a little nervously together, and exchanged photographs and autographs, the seals were being affixed to the two precious copies of the treaty by an awkward and extremely nervous clerk, whose operations were not assisted when Tenterden, that most invaluable of secretaries, dropped quantities of burning sealing-wax on his fingers. The poor man somewhat inauspiciously burst into tears when the work was done. But done it was, and the copies lay ready on the table. Then the final, solemn act began. Macdonald, being the junior member of the British Commission, was one of the last to sign.

"Well," he said in a half-whisper to Fish, as he took up his pen, "here go the fisheries."

"You get a good equivalent for them," Fish countered swiftly.

"No," Macdonald retorted with cheerful cynicism, "we give them away—here goes the signature!"

He signed his name with the usual small flourish under the final "d", and rose from the table.

"They are gone," he said slowly.[75]

Chapter Four

Design for the Future

I

He did not return to Ottawa as a conqueror. He did not feel like a conqueror and he did not want the pretence of a conqueror's reception. A conqueror would be expected to receive tributes and furnish reports. He had no desire to take the one or to make the other. At the back of his mind was the troubled realization that the first Parliament of the Dominion of Canada was nearing its inevitable end, and that in twelve months' time or a little more he would have to face a general election—a general election in which the unpopularity of the Washington Treaty might prove absolutely fatal to his government. A brief respite was essential to him. He did not want, for the moment, to show his hand. He had taken good care to suggest, indirectly, to the editors of the faithful Conservative newspapers, the Montreal *Gazette*, the Toronto *Leader*, the Ottawa *Times* and *Citizen*, and the rest, that they should hold back, for a few precious days at least, any expression of opinion on the Treaty. In the meantime, the Reform leaders and the Grit newspapers, assuming readily that he would support the work of the Joint High Commission, would rush forward, in their usual unthinking and intemperate fashion, to attack the Treaty. That was what he wanted. The whole Grit party must be fixed in an unchangeable position, pinned down immovably to ground which had been hastily chosen but which could not be abandoned without fear of disaster. "It is therefore," he wrote to Alexander Morris, "of very considerable consequence that Brown and the

Globe should be committed irretrievably against the Treaty."[1] In the meantime he himself would have space to manœuvre and time to consider his dispositions.

Time was valuable, whatever his final decision might be. At Washington, during the last gloomy days of conscious failure and defeat, he had talked and written as if his own public opposition to the fishery clauses in Canada were a certainty. But, despite these confident predictions, had he ever really dismissed the possibility that he might have to defend the Treaty for the sake of the Anglo-Canadian alliance by which alone Canada had survived in the North American continent? In any case, a protective silence was undoubtedly the best policy at the moment. If, in the end, he came to the conclusion that he must oppose the Treaty, then Brown and the Grits would find themselves occupying a thoroughly false position without hope of withdrawal. If, on the contrary, he finally decided that acceptance of the terms was the only possible course for Canada to take, then the delay would give him a chance to better his own position, to improve the prospects of his doubtful cause. Time would permit the violent denunciation of the Treaty in the Canadian press to burn itself out. Time was necessary also to enable the American Congress to legislate upon the subject, and the Canadian government to come to a satisfactory agreement with the British government about the promised compensation for the losses of the Fenian Raids. In six months many things would certainly be clarified, and his own chances would probably be much improved. Meanwhile he and his colleagues would maintain an unrevealing reserve.

And so, while the whole country rocked with debate over the iniquities of the Washington Treaty, he gave not the slightest indication of what the Canadian government proposed to do. It was not, of course, that he was uncommunicative about his own view of the Treaty, or about the outraged sense of betrayal which it had awakened everywhere throughout the country. In letter after gloomy letter to Lisgar and de Grey he affirmed that the violence of public disapproval exceeded even his own expectations, and that he did not yet know whether he could control the storm. "The feeling in Canada against the Treaty," he told de Grey, "has increased and is increasing and I cannot foresee the result. An utter feeling of distrust in the imperial government has arisen in the public mind and every clause in the Treaty is therefore discussed in a jealous and prejudiced spirit."[2] He was always ready to expatiate upon the endless and awful difficulties which confronted him; but, neither in private or public had he a word to say about the course which his government intended to pursue.

"The line the government takes is simply this," he told one correspondent, "that the Treaty is satisfactory to them in every respect except as regards the fisheries, and that as to the fisheries they are free to act as they please."[3] He had signed the Treaty, he reminded de Grey—and signed it expressly reserving his future freedom of action—simply because the British government had instructed its commissioners to sign. The British government had, in short, accepted responsibility for the Treaty; and if it wished the Canadian Parliament to ratify the clauses relating to British North America it must explain and justify satisfactorily the solution which it had imposed.[4] "It will be for the home government to make out a case with us," Macdonald wrote to Gowan. "After giving every consideration to the arguments of Her Majesty's government, we will have a policy on the subject which we will submit to Parliament next session."[5] In other words, if Great Britain wanted Canadian compliance in the appeasement of the United States, it would have to strengthen the Canadian government's hand. And, as Macdonald reminded de Grey, one of the first things to be done was to implement the promise of compensation for the Fenian Raids.

He had no doubt at all about the form which the compensation should take. He wanted, not a money payment, but a British guarantee for a part of the great sums of money which would have to be borrowed for the Canadian transcontinental railway to the Pacific. During the late winter, while he had been away in Washington, Parliament had ratified the terms of union with British Columbia, though only after a struggle which Alexander Morris described as the worst fight the party had had since Confederation.[6] On July 20, only a few short weeks away, British Columbia would become the sixth province of the union; and the Canadian government was committed to begin a railway to the Pacific within two years, and to finish it within ten, of this new addition to Confederation.

It was true that this formidable commitment had been explained, if not exactly qualified, by an interpretative resolution introduced by Sir George Cartier on behalf of the government, soon after the terms of union had been accepted by the House. According to this resolution, the railway was to be built by private enterprise, not by government; and the contribution of government to the project was to consist in liberal grants of land and in such subsidies of money as would not be "unduly pressing on the industry and resources of the Dominion". Was this a valid gloss upon the contract? It was highly doubtful. But even if it had not been doubtful, the Dominion was still left with an enormous and clearly defined responsibility. It must choose a company. Its own preferred plan required a commercial company, worthy to act for the nation, and to receive the nation's financial support, in what was perhaps the greatest of all national undertakings. Very soon now Macdonald and his colleagues would have to choose, and choose well, from among the various little groups of capitalists which were in the course of formation and which would soon be openly competing for the prize of the Canadian Pacific railway charter. One of them, indeed, had already appeared. Macdonald had not been back in Ottawa for six weeks, and British Columbia had not yet become a member of the union, when the first of these associations of railway promoters presented itself in his office towards the close of a sultry day in July.

It was a little group of seven people.[7] There were four Canadians—two Toronto lawyers, and two rather shadowy "capitalists", Waddington and Kersteman, who speedily turned out to have more pretensions than financial resources. These, as Macdonald probably knew very well from the beginning, were not the real men of substance in the group. The real men of substance were the three Americans, Hurlburt of New York, and Charles

Smith and G. W. McMullen of Chicago, who brought with them, not only their own financial strength, but also the support of a number of well-known American bankers and contractors. It was the first time that Macdonald had ever met McMullen, the ex-Canadian, who had grown up in Prince Edward county, and had gone off to Chicago to acquire control of the *Evening Post* and to interest himself in a variety of canal and railway undertakings. Macdonald was, of course, affable with the visitors, but he told them frankly that nothing whatever could be done at the moment. "We saw the American gentlemen who came from Chicago," he told George Jackson a few days later, "but their movement was altogether premature, and was improperly hurried by that respectable old fool Waddington."[8] The government could not act without a survey of the country and the authority of Parliament, and at the moment it had neither. Besides, Macdonald instinctively disliked a syndicate so obviously dominated by Americans. Yet the interview, he realized, was important despite its inconclusiveness. The government would have to make an agreement with a group very much like that which faced him, and in short order. It was for this reason, among others, that he wanted to clear up the matter of the British compensation for the losses of the Fenian Raids. The Treaty, the guaranteed loan, and the Pacific railway would together make a formidable instrument to develop the country and defeat the opposition. He waited comfortably for the offer from England—the offer which would reward Canada for its sacrifices and himself for his submission.

What he got instead was a hard and sudden shock. The first dispatch from the Colonial Office, which was a loftily paternal lecture on the benefits which Canada would derive from the Washington Treaty, made no mention at all of compensation for the Fenian Raids; and although Lord Kimberley alluded to the subject a few days later in a private letter to Lisgar he did so in a fashion which was surprising and annoying in the extreme. "What does Sir John A. Macdonald mean to do?" he inquired of the Governor-General. "If he is prepared to do his utmost to carry the treaty through we shall be ready to strengthen his hands with respect to the Fenian claims, but he must understand that there is no chance of obtaining concessions such as a guarantee of the Pacific Railroad. . . . The Fenian claims being omitted from the treaty are a fair subject for consideration but it is only fair to Sir John Macdonald that he should not be under the impression that further concessions can be obtained from us."[9] These hard, wary, bargaining phrases, communicated to Macdonald by Lisgar, brought both bafflement and exasperation. What did Lord Kimberley mean by "further concessions"? Why had the Colonial Office begun to quibble about the solemn engagement respecting the Fenian claims? Macdonald had believed that the promise to pay compensation was an unconditional commitment. Now it began to appear that in England it was regarded merely as a conditional liability contingent upon the ratification of the Treaty by the Canadian Parliament. The order of obligation, as he saw it, had been exactly reversed.

The fact was, though as yet he did not fully realize the truth, that the Gladstone government was viewing him with a mixture of dislike, suspicion, and cold hostility. He had opposed the settlement with the United States, opposed it persistently, and by methods unbecoming a colonial. In letter after letter de Grey and Lisgar had depreciated his services and criticized his conduct; and now their successive disclosures of his shortcomings were completed by a final and astounding revelation. Lisgar had already quoted freely from Macdonald's private communications to his colleagues in Ottawa, tearing phrases and sentences from their context in order to show his Prime Minister in a most unfavourable light; and now he transcribed a last damning extract from a confidential letter which Macdonald had written to Hincks in the last days of the conference at Washington. "Our true policy," Macdonald was alleged to have written, "is to hold out to England that we will not ratify the treaty; and I have strong hopes that in her desire to close every possible cause of dispute with the United States we can induce her to make us a liberal offer."[10]

This startling fragment handed around among a few members of the Gladstone Cabinet, provoked some very acid comment. "If I understand it rightly," Kimberley wrote, "he means to play a game for which knavery is hardly too strong a word."[11] Gladstone was equally definite in a different way. "I hope," he wrote, "the 'liberal offer' which Sir John Macdonald intends to conjure from us will be *nil*."[12] And Kimberley summed up the feeling of his colleagues accurately with the biblical quotation, "in vain is the net spread in sight of any bird".[13] The mood of suspicious niggardliness in everything that concerned Canada became a habit. The Cabinet decided that there would be no further delay in the recall of the garrisons from the Dominion, that nothing would be done to carry out the promise about the Fenian Raids until Macdonald had declared himself, and that no honour whatever should be granted him until he had got the Treaty safely through the Canadian Parliament.[14] "Payment for results," wrote Kimberley firmly, "is the safest course in his case."[15]

Macdonald was unaware of all this. But the incredible inquiry in Kimberley's letter was, in itself, sufficiently enlightening. He sat down towards the end of July to write a long private letter to Lord Lisgar which would be in effect a rejoinder to Lord Kimberley. What was he going to do about the Treaty? "The more pertinent question," he wrote, "would have been, what is the Canadian government going to do?" He promised that, when the holidays were over, the Cabinet would assemble and consider the question "in all its bearings". But he took care to remind the Governor-General that the Council had already objected to the fisheries articles and had stated its belief that the Canadian Parliament would not ratify them. "There has not been, so far as I know," he went on, "any change of opinion in the Council. . . . Meanwhile, I would venture to suggest that you should press upon Her Majesty's Government the expediency of giving satisfactory assurances as to the Fenian claims and the notice on the termination of the treaty. I hope that no attempt will be made to make the settlement of the former contingent on our acceptance of the Treaty. Such an attempt I should consider a breach of the understanding, and would at once abandon any attempt to reconcile my colleagues or the people of Canada to the adoption of the Treaty."[16]

This was plain speaking. A few days after he had finished

his letter, he went off to Rivière du Loup, for he badly needed a holiday, leaving behind him a difference of opinion which was rapidly becoming a portentous dispute. He was nettled by the condescending, temporizing communications that came from England; and Lisgar and Kimberley were annoyed by what they considered to be the deliberate non-committal evasiveness of his attitude. "It is no doubt a serious crisis in the relations of the colony with the home country," Kimberley wrote gravely to Lisgar, "but I do not despair of a satisfactory result."[17] Macdonald's letter, which had, of course, been sent on to him, was described as "very unsatisfactory", and towards the end of September he dispatched his answer to it using the somewhat formal vehicle of a secret despatch to the Governor-General for the purpose. He confessed to Lisgar that the dispatch was "controversial". It was scarcely an overstatement. The Colonial Secretary began by agreeing with Macdonald's account of the promise made by de Grey in respect of the Fenian claims. But he went on to remind his readers that compensation had been offered "if it was clearly understood to be no precedent for the future, but part of a great and final settlement between Great Britain and the United States". How then could Macdonald possibly claim that the promise made by de Grey was unconditional? "On his own showing," Kimberley continued argumentatively, "the assurance given by Lord Ripon as to the Fenian claims was contingent upon all the other questions being settled with the United States. . . . How all the questions between Great Britain and the United States can be regarded as settled, if Canada rejects an important part of the Treaty, and the fishery question is thus left unsettled, I am altogether at a loss to imagine. Her Majesty's Government will abide strictly and honourably by the promise they have given but they entirely decline to admit that a conditional promise can be construed as if it were unconditional. . . ."[18] The promise must continue to be regarded as conditional; and Kimberley implied, though he did not insist too dogmatically, that the condition could be nothing less than the acceptance of the Treaty by the Dominion Parliament.

II

Macdonald did not hurry with his answer. It was autumn now, but the American Congress had not yet met, and he had an interval which he could give to private as well as public affairs. His law firm, now Macdonald and Patton, was being prepared for its transfer from Kingston to Toronto; and late that autumn he and his family moved again, to a new house in the eastern suburbs of Ottawa, in a district which soon would be known as Sandy Hill. He had to take possession, in fact, before the house was properly finished, and in November he was laid up with a severe attack of quinsy, which he thought had probably been caused by the premature removal.[19] "I have had a run of ill luck," he wrote a little later to his old friend Alexander Campbell. "No sooner was my quinsy got rid of, than I was obliged to go to the dentist, who so bedevilled my mouth that I have had to be lanced and probed and blistered."[20] He had never enjoyed exceptionally robust health. He could look back on a long series of minor ailments, and little debilitating troubles; and he knew now, one year after his convalescence in Prince Edward Island, that the terrible illness of 1870 had left its mark on him for life. Yet he had no intention of giving up the task he had set himself. ". . .I think there is some work left in me yet," he told his friend Gowan. "I greatly desire to complete the work of Confederation before I make my final bow to the Canadian audience before whom I have been acting my part for so long."[21] At the back of his mind there was the consciousness of a definite historical rôle. There was a creator's zest for the completion of work which he knew was so largely his own, which he was determined to realize in all the finished perfection of his inner design.

That autumn he took stock of the electoral chances of the future. In Quebec province, Cartier had become alarmingly unpopular with the English-speaking population of Montreal, which before had always supported him so heartily. In Manitoba there occurred a stupid, abortive Fenian escapade, which unhappily brought Riel back again into the limelight, revived the old campaign for an amnesty for all political offenders in the Red River Rebellion, and provoked another outburst of Protestant anti-French fury in the Province of Ontario. It was, in fact, in Ontario, the most populous and politically powerful province, Macdonald's own special bailiwick, that difficulties and signs of Conservative weakness seemed to accumulate most ominously. The Ontario farmers would gain no benefit whatever from the Washington Treaty. The Ontario Orangemen had been infuriated once again by the revival of trouble in Manitoba. Worst of all, the provincial administration at Toronto, which, under Macdonald's old opponent and new ally, John Sandfield Macdonald, had been a strong support since Confederation, was now obviously weakening under the attacks of the re-invigorated provincial Liberals; and late in the autumn, after a defeat in the provincial House, Sandfield Macdonald resigned and Edward Blake formed a new Reform government. "I need scarcely say," Macdonald wrote, "that I look upon the defeat of Sandfield's administration as a most unfortunate event, of which one cannot see the results."[22] Yet the results were all too likely to be unfortunate also. Sandfield had lost power at the moment when his support was most vitally necessary. A defeat in provincial affairs was a very inauspicious prelude to a victory in a federal general election.

He badly needed new policies—policies that were positive and popular. But his new policies—the guaranteed loan and the Pacific railway—were both stuck in embarrassing uncertainty. Early in the autumn, the American railway promoters, Smith and McMullen, returned to Ottawa, bringing with them this time, as a more effective Canadian associate, the white-bearded Montreal ship-owner, Hugh Allan, the proprietor of the Allan Line of Ocean Steamships, who had just been knighted for his services to transatlantic commerce. "Allan has joined himself with a number of American capitalists," Macdonald wrote to a newspaper friend, "and they are applying to the Canadian government to be allowed to build our Pacific Railway. The government is, of course, glad to receive all such applications as they show an interest in the undertaking and indicate its value; but as yet we have come to no conclusion with respect to it. You may depend upon it we will see that Canadian interests are fully protected, and that no American ring will be allowed to get control over it."[23] It was, of course, impossible, without parliamentary authority, to make an arrangement with any syndicate; but, as he talked with the members of the Allan group, it was not merely this legal barrier that held Macdonald back. He was worried by the still obvious predominance of American capital in the syndicate and by the complete absence of any financial support from the Province of Ontario. Allan represented Montreal finance; but Toronto was Montreal's jealous and aggressive rival. And Toronto was the capital of Ontario, where, at the moment, his political weakness was most alarming.

In all these perplexing circumstances, the Treaty still remained his biggest political embarrassment. His policy was still a policy of reticence and delay. All that autumn he made no public appearances whatever, for he knew that if he accepted invitations to political dinners, he would have to speak, and speak of the Treaty, "and that it would stultify all my policy which I have carried through this whole summer if I did so".[24] Delay and silence—the silence appropriate to doubt, uncertainty, and difficulty—were best from all points of view; but, at the same time, it was absolutely essential that the Canadian and British governments should come to some agreement about the Fenian claims before the opening of the last session of the Canadian Parliament in the late winter or early spring of 1872. Late in November he finished his rejoinder to the protests of the Colonial Office. It was at least a little more conciliatory than the long letter he had written to Lisgar in July. He still harped upon the general detestation of the Treaty and the great difficulty of his own position; but he now admitted that there had been a slight abatement in the violence of popular disapproval, and he held out some hope that the Treaty might be ratified, if the British government suitably strengthened the Canadian government's hand. He denied emphatically that the promise of compensation for the losses of the Fenian Raids had been contingent upon any further action of his own or of the Canadian Parliament. The promise had been made to him during the negotiations, with the purpose of furthering the progress of the negotiations, by inducing him not to press the Fenian claims and to accept the objectionable fishery clauses. If the interminable talks had not issued successfully in a treaty, then, he admitted, it might have been claimed that the promise was void. "But," he reminded Lord Kimberley, "a Treaty has been made, and all other matters but the Fenian claims have been settled so far as the two governments could settle them, and I therefore hold that the engagement of Her Majesty's government has thereupon become absolute and unconditional."[25]

The long, solid argument of the letter perhaps made a greater impression upon the members of the Gladstone government than they were ready to admit. It was true that their unpleasant suspicions of Macdonald remained largely unaltered. They found it difficult, Kimberley confided to Lisgar, to treat him with confidence after all that had passed.[26] But at the same time it was impossible to deny the force of his argument and the pressure of his surrounding difficulties. The attitude of frigid negativism in which the Colonial Office had apparently stiffened began to be relaxed. Lord Kimberley suggested to Gladstone that the British government should be prepared to consider the substitution of a guaranteed loan for a money grant, and that it "ought not to make the assent of the Canadian Parliament to the Treaty the condition of our payment for the Fenian claims".[27] Three days later, at a Cabinet meeting which considered the problem of compensation, it was decided, so Gladstone informed the Queen, "that it would be expedient to place in the hands of the Canadian government the power of assuring the legislature that this question would be entertained and submitted to Parliament, independently of the course which that legislature might adopt with respect to the Treaty".[28] Three days later again, the dispatches and private letters embodying these proposals were sent off from the Colonial Office to Lord Lisgar.[29]

They reached Ottawa in the third week of January; and, with a swiftness that equalled or surpassed that of the Gladstone Cabinet, the Canadian government made up its mind. Macdonald had had great difficulty in holding his colleagues together, in reconciling them—and himself—to the sacrifices of the Treaty. Indeed, as time had dragged on without a decision, Lisgar had come to believe that "instead of Sir John Macdonald trying to convert his colleagues, the ablest of his colleagues are trying to convert him".[30] It had not been easy for Macdonald to accept the difficulties in which the Treaty had landed him, or to forget the slights he had received at Washington. But now the British government's air of Olympian displeasure had softened; it had shown a willingness to compromise, to meet his requests half way; and, as he wrote still another letter to Lord Lisgar on the subject, he could not prevent a slight note of triumph from creeping into his account of the past. "I therefore took the course, as you know," he reminded the Governor-General, "of urging on my colleagues not to come to any hasty conclusion, to let the Treaty be discussed on its own merits in the press, and to trust to time, liberal legislation on the tariff by Congress, and prompt action by Her Majesty's government in the Fenian matter, to afford us a justification for accepting the Treaty with all its demerits. . . . They were thus kept together and in hand, and the result has been their gradual conversion to my views. Hence the minute of Saturday."[31] The minute of Saturday was a Council decision to support the Treaty in Parliament in return for a guaranteed loan for railways and canals.

III

As soon as this decision had been taken, he started west for Toronto. It was the first of his pre-election reconnaissances in Ontario. He must try to repair, if possible, some of the damage caused by Sandfield Macdonald's defeat; he must make some specific arrangements and, in general, put new heart into his friends. For three weeks he moved rapidly about Toronto, Hamilton, and Kingston, dining urbanely with Roman Catholic bishops, trying to regain the support of the hierarchy which Sandfield Macdonald had lost, begging merchants, bankers, and industrialists for money to establish a really respectable Conservative newspaper in Toronto. Journalistic opposition to George Brown's *Globe* had been ineffective for longer years than the Conservatives cared to count; and recently, just when the need of a vigorous government press was being felt acutely again, the Conservative newspapers had seemed to become even more lamentably feeble. "The *Leader* is so completely run down as to be of no value. . . ," Macdonald complained, "the *Telegraph* is a mere blackmail paper, and the sooner it is crushed the better."[32] No, they must have something new—something distinguished, authoritative, yet lively—the *Mail!* He was busy with plans for the new paper, with Pacific railway negotiations, and with efforts to convince the Roman Catholic bishops that he could be relied upon to give the Catholic body its full share of positions in government and jobs in the civil service. "The Catholic priests are crazy to have representatives in Parliament," he observed, "and that is the best way to catch them."[33] He was certain that he had won the support of the Bishops of London and Kingston; "and I believe," he added, "the Archbishop is favourable, although from his peculiar character we cannot tell how long the impression I made on him may last."[34] Altogether the western trip had been difficult but reasonably rewarding. "I have had hard work for the last ten days here," he wrote from Toronto, "but have put heart into our friends and on the whole have made satisfactory arrangements."[35]

For a few days, while he dealt with this very familiar stuff of Canadian politics, he had almost forgotten that tangled, bungled, unlucky, vexatious affair, the Washington Treaty. He had thought comfortably that he was done with it—or almost done with it. But suddenly, without warning, the troubled international issues which it had apparently settled, were raised again in all their dangerous complexity. Early in 1872, the board of arbitration, which had been established according to the terms of the Treaty of Washington to settle the *Alabama* damages, met and began its hearings in Geneva; and to the utter consternation of everybody in England and Canada, the United States, in presenting its case, filed claims not only for all the "direct" losses which the *Alabama* had occasioned, but also for all the "indirect", "consequential", damages which, it was asserted, had led to the prolongation of the war! The

British government had never for a minute admitted these outrageous claims. The British High Commissioners at Washington had clearly understood that the United States had agreed to waive them in the coming arbitration. Yet here they were —perversely and discreditably revived! The Gladstone Cabinet prepared for resistance. It was morally certain that the arbitration would be at an end if the Americans persisted in presenting the "indirect" claims. The dearly bought settlement of the *Alabama* difficulty was in danger. The whole of the great diplomatic reconciliation between the British Empire and the United States was in jeopardy.

It was obvious to Macdonald—and to everybody else who was intimately concerned with the affair—that this put the question of Canadian ratification of the Treaty in a new and very different light. Up to this point it had been chiefly Canada which had expostulated at American diplomatic chicanery, protested against the sacrifices demanded of her, and predicted that it would prove impossible to ratify the Treaty. But now the position was reversed. Great Britain herself, by refusing to continue with the *Alabama* arbitration, might wreck the Treaty, wholly, or in large part; and if she did so, the most potent argument in favour of Canadian ratification, the plea of imperial necessity, of the desirability of a general Anglo-American understanding, would—at least for Canada—lose much of its force. Yet, for the harassed Gladstone government, it would remain a weighty argument. The Gladstone government would be anxious to save as much of the Anglo-American settlement as possible—to escape, if possible, the imputation of having repudiated the Treaty in its entirety. For Great Britain, rejection by the Canadian Parliament was now doubly to be feared. "It is more our interest than ever," Kimberley argued to Gladstone, "to come to terms if possible with the Canadian government";[36] and John Rose significantly reported that the proposal of the guaranteed loan had been received in official circles in London, "in a much more friendly spirit than I supposed it would have been".[37]

Macdonald may have enjoyed a certain ironic amusement at the change in the situation. It was now Great Britain's turn to feel embarrassment and anxiety. The Gladstone Cabinet solemnly debated the new problem in its relations with Canada. "What effect has been produced in Canada by the Alabama difficulty?" Kimberley wired privately to Lisgar.[38] Would Canada consent to ratify the fishery articles of the Treaty, even if the *Alabama* arbitration fell through? It was in her own interest to do so, Kimberley argued.[39] It was impossible, John Rose hinted, for the British ministers to come to any decision about the guaranteed loan until they had some assurance of Canada's intentions. But Macdonald was not greatly moved by these eager hints, these anxious invitations. He was not to be easily cajoled into reassuring declarations. Apart from a very general statement of solidarity with the United Kingdom, the Canadian Council remained unresponsive and uncommunicative. Lisgar, who had expected that complete assurances would be given with loyal alacrity, raged over this impudent delay. "This arises," he growled, "from Sir John A. Macdonald's jealous reticence and inveterate habit of waiting upon providence."[40] The Canadian Cabinet politely reminded the Colonial Office that it had not as yet received any reply to its proposal for a guaranteed loan.[41] Until that had been satisfactorily answered, it could obviously do nothing. The worried Kimberley promised a reply as soon as possible. In the meantime it was decided to delay the opening of the Canadian Parliament until early in April. That, it was hoped, would give time for the matter to settle itself.

Meanwhile, whether the last session opened early or late, the term of Parliament itself was inexorably approaching. Within a very few months now the general election would be upon Macdonald; and although the difficulty over the Fenian compensation made the completion of his programme impossible for the moment, he tried to set out his other policies in preparation. The *Mail*, which was soon to appear, was henceforth to be the distinguished and sonorous vehicle for the oracles of Conservative truth; and with its editor, T. C. Patteson, Macdonald carefully talked over the name, nature, and programme of the Conservative party. The very adjective "Conservative" itself seemed to him, as it had often done before, a little unfortunate, though he was sure it could not be entirely dropped. "I think, however," he wrote to Patteson, "that it should be kept in the background as much as possible, and that our party should be called the 'Union Party'; going in for union with England against all annexationists and independents, and for the union of all the Provinces of British North America, including Prince Edward Island and Newfoundland, against all anti-Confederates. . . . What think you of such a name as 'the Constitutional Union Party'?"[42] This was essentially the great national programme which he had undertaken nearly ten years before and which he was determined to complete—the union and expansion of British North America under the protection of the Anglo-Canadian alliance.

It was a political programme. But it was rapidly becoming an economic programme as well. The Canadian people were committed to the great enterprise of the settlement of Rupert's Land, to the equally great undertaking of the transcontinental Canadian Pacific railway; and the nationalistic impulse which lay back of these two great decisions, the ambition to build up a Canadian economy for the benefit of Canadians, had just been emphatically steeled by the blunt denials and disappointments of the Washington Treaty. The Washington Treaty had dropped a final curtain on all the tenaciously held hopes for a renewal of reciprocity. The United States, which seemed openly determined to starve Canada into annexation, had refused all proposals for a reciprocal trade agreement; and this conclusive rejection came at a time when Canadian manufacturing industry, which had grown rapidly during the American Civil War, was stronger, more varied, and more ambitious than it had ever been before. The manufacturers were the angry advance guard of an unorganized but potentially huge army of increasingly nationalist-minded Canadians who resented the undisguised attempt to break their hopes, who believed in the potential value of their own resources, and who were determined to develop their national economy independently of the United States, and, if necessary, by every coercive device which the United States had employed against them. The army was great; it would certainly become greater. It stood, at that moment, waiting for a political leader.

Macdonald determined to put himself at its head. "The protection of manufactures is a delicate thing to handle," he had told Adam Brown, a Hamilton mill-owner, during the previous December, "but it can be dealt with, I think, so as to weigh heavily against the Grit opposition."[48] In February, when he went up to Toronto for his first western reconnaissance, he found that the Ontario farmers, who had hoped for much and gained nothing from the negotiations at Washington, were ready and eager for retaliation against the United States. "It is really astonishing," he told George Stephen, "the feeling that has grown up in the West in favour of encouragement of home manufactures. I am sure to be able to make considerable capital out of this next summer."[44] He had, indeed, high hopes. But it would not do—it would never do—to be precipitate. Canada was still too much a country that exported raw materials and imported manufactures to accept the doctrine of tariff protection with general and unqualified enthusiasm. The very word "protection" must itself, for a while, be taboo; but the impulse towards economic nationalism was potent nevertheless; and with a sure instinct for the telling slogan, he appropriated a phrase, "National Policy", which others had used incidentally, but never so purposefully before. "The paper," he told Patteson of the *Mail*, "must go in for a National Policy in tariff matters, and while avoiding the word 'protection' must advocate a readjustment of the tariff in such a manner as incidentally to aid our manufacturing and industrial interests."[45]

Eastern manufacturing and western settlement—they were two closely related national policies. The third of the trio was the transcontinental, all-Canadian railway, which would provide the physical link between the other two. That project had advanced rapidly during the winter, but in an unsatisfactory fashion which slightly perturbed Macdonald. Early in March, Sir Hugh Allan's syndicate, the Canada Pacific Railway Company, handed in to the government its preliminary proposal to build the railway. Unfortunately, Allan had not yet got rid of his American associates, McMullen, Smith, Jay Cooke and others, most of whom were deeply interested in the obviously rival American undertaking, the Northern Pacific Railroad. Perhaps even more unfortunately, he had utterly failed to attract Toronto capitalists, or even other important Montreal capitalists, to his scheme. Brydges of Montreal, who had been general manager of the Grand Trunk Railway, and David L. Macpherson, the leader of the Toronto group of promoters, had both refused to join Allan's concern, on the ground that the Americans would exercise absolute control over it. Macpherson, not satisfied with mere abstention from the hated enterprise, proceeded promptly to form a rival syndicate, the Interoceanic Railway Company, which in its turn presented a proposal for building the Pacific railway.

What to do? How could Macdonald choose between the Montrealer and the Torontonian? Sir Hugh Allan, whom he knew much less well than he knew Macpherson, was obviously the senior of the two in age, experience, and international prestige. Macpherson was a personal friend, a very warm and devoted friend, indeed, for he had acted as chairman of the small committee which that winter had collected and donated to Macdonald a "testimonial fund" of more than sixty-seven thousand dollars, in part replacement of the heavy losses which had been discovered during his serious illness of the previous year.[46] Yes, Macpherson was a friend for whom he would like to do much. Macpherson was a good Conservative. He and his associates in the Interoceanic were far from being negligible financially and above all they were Torontonians; they represented a metropolitan, a provincial, interest which it was his business to promote and which he would neglect at his peril. He did all he could for Macpherson. He wrote to him as soon as he had received the Interoceanic Company's proposal, pointing out a few places in which it suffered fatally by comparison with Allan's scheme.[47] He did not want Macpherson to fail. But he knew, in his heart, that the Interoceanic Company could not be given the charter. He knew, with equal certainty, that Allan and his dangerous American associates could not be given the charter either. Both companies were ruled out—while they stood alone. But if they united, they could be instantly acceptable. The solution was really absurdly simple. Allan's dubious American friends would be compelled to withdraw; and their places would be taken by Macpherson's band of worthy Torontonians. A coalition between the Montreal and Toronto rings was, he told Rose, the probable answer to the problem; "and Allan will, I think, be obliged to abandon his Yankee confreres".[48]

But Allan was determined not to surrender his "Yankee confreres". Macdonald had counted on submission, but submission was refused him. For Allan had taken the one inexplicable decision in his otherwise straightforward career. A mature and successful man, who had prospered without reliance on politics, and who now, with his knighthood, his great house "Ravenscrag", and his little fleet of ocean liners, stood at the respectable summit of his career, he suddenly descended, in a moment of blind infatuation, down a dangerous course of dissimulation and intrigue. It was perfectly clear to him, when he came up to Ottawa early in the session, that the Prime Minister, the government as a whole, and the great majority of the members of both parties, were utterly opposed to the inclusion of any substantial American interest in the national transcontinental railway. It was so obvious, indeed, that he at first instructed his solicitor, J. J. C. Abbott, to prepare a bill for the incorporation of his company which would have absolutely excluded all foreigners from the directorate. Outwardly, he was prepared, in the most ostentatious fashion, to conform to public opinion; but secretly he still kept up his contacts with his American associates. He had no hesitation in attempting to evade the known wishes of the nation. He was equally ready to do everything in his power to get the better of the government plan for the amalgamation of the two syndicates.

Throughout the session, the government tried studiously to maintain a position of absolute neutrality. The rival companies were incorporated in two statutes, drawn up in almost identical terms; and by a third act the government was given authority to grant subsidies of land and money to the company which it should decide eventually to charter. On the face of it, a difficult choice seemed unavoidable; but in fact it was perfectly clear from the beginning that the Cabinet hoped to avoid this dilemma by effecting an early amalgamation of the two competing concerns. Allan professed himself perfectly ready to accept an amalgamation; but it must be an amalgamation upon his own terms. And his terms were nothing less than the presidency and a controlling interest for himself—a controlling interest which he would secretly share with his American associates. He would force the government to accept these terms; and the vulnerable point at which he intended to put the full weight of his pressure had already been cunningly chosen. It was Cartier, who was past his prime now, and none too well, who had already lost the support of the British in Montreal, and who in the circumstances of the moment could fairly readily be made unpopular with his old French-Canadian following. Cartier was still the solicitor of the Grand Trunk Railway; and the Grand Trunk, with its main lines south of the St. Lawrence, was naturally assumed to be hostile to the project of a new railway, running along the north shore of the river between Quebec and Montreal, and from thence to Ottawa. But the North Shore route was popular in Montreal. It could be made much more popular easily; and Allan, who was president of the Northern Colonization Railway, the North Shore's western extension between Montreal and Ottawa, appropriated the whole scheme and made himself its principal backer. He engaged French-Canadian newspapermen to write up the North Shore route and French-Canadian politicians to speak about it in public. He began to dispense cash with a lavish hand. "I think you will have to *go it blind,*" he wrote his friend Smith in Chicago, "in the matter of the money (cash payments)."[49] He proceeded to go it blind. The muttering volume of opposition to Cartier began to mount.

At the moment Macdonald did not properly appreciate what was happening. He was not aware of the gradual intensification of Cartier's difficulties, still less did he suspect that malice was at the back of it. He was, in fact, feeling fairly cheerfully confident, for the session was not going at all badly and he had just had an enormous stroke of luck. All during the winter the Canadian trade unions—the mere fact of their presence in numbers was a sign of the growth of the new industrialism—had been actively crusading for a reduction of working hours.

From Ottawa Macdonald had watched this so-called "Nine Hours Movement" with curious interest, his big nose sensitively keen like an animal's for any scent of profit or danger. Montreal, Toronto, and Hamilton were evidently the key centres of the working-class agitation; and at Toronto, where George Brown's *Globe* was printed and published, the strongly organized typographical union went out on strike towards the end of March. By great good luck, the *Mail* had not yet appeared, and was not involved in the resulting controversy. By even greater good luck, James Beaty, the proprietor of the *Leader*, the Conservative paper which Macdonald had described so contemptuously only a little while before, granted the strikers their demands, continued to publish his newspaper, and strongly supported the nine hours movement in its columns.

All this was highly satisfactory; but the crowning mercy was yet to come. The crowning mercy was the infatuated conduct of George Brown. Brown put himself at the head of the master printers who fought the strike, excoriated the strikers in his newspaper, and was popularly supposed to have inspired, or actually engineered, the arrest of twenty-three of their number on charges of conspiracy. As soon as their trial began, a regrettable, an almost shameful, fact was revealed. The legislatures of Canada had evidently never dealt with the subject of trade unions and their activities. The only law governing the subject in Canada was the common law; and by it the twenty-three arrested printers, merely because they belonged to a union and had gone on strike, were convicted as parties to an illegal combination in restraint of trade. George Brown had apparently won; but it was an unwanted, an unpopular, victory. He had been found guilty, in the eye of the public, of dredging up outworn and half-forgotten legal precedents in order to deal an unfair blow at opponents that were weaker than he.[50]

Macdonald seized his advantage at once. He had already concerned himself with industry; now he saw where he could espouse the cause of labour. He had a quick instinct for the kind of Tory democracy which Disraeli was to proclaim only a little later. He had been presented, as if by magic, with an opportunity of gratifying the working-men and of discomfiting the Reformers. The circumstances could hardly have been more favourable; the means lay right at his hand. Only the year before, Gladstone had rescued the trade unions of Great Britain from a somewhat similar anomalous position by passing the Trade Union Act and the Criminal Law Amendment Act. All that Macdonald had to do was to re-enact, with suitable modifications to suit Canadian conditions, the two British statutes of 1871; and the unimpeachable orthodoxy of Gladstonian legislation would remove all doubts and silence all criticisms. The situation must have amused Macdonald immensely. He could confound George Brown with William Ewart Gladstone! He could silence the disciple with the latest revelation from the master!

In the meantime, the long and involved negotiations over compensation for the Fenian losses had come to an end. On March 16, the Gladstone government finally offered to guarantee a Canadian loan of £2,500,000 for railways and canals; and at the same time it suggested, in order to remove the Canadian objection to ratifying the fishery clauses before the *Alabama* imbroglio was cleared up, that the statute of ratification should come into force only by order-in-council.[51] There were still delays, hesitations, vain attempts by the Canadian Council to get the amount increased, and other last-minute efforts at bargaining; but after the opening of the Canadian Parliament on April 11, Macdonald drew rapidly towards the end of his long exercise of patience and persuasion. He had had far greater difficulty in convincing his colleagues than Lisgar and Kimberley had been disposed to give him credit for, at least in the early stages of the deliberations. It came as a shock to Englishmen in general and the Colonial Office in particular, when Joseph Howe, one of the Cabinet ministers whom Lisgar had fondly believed to be friendly to the Washington Treaty, took advantage of an address to the Young Men's Christian Association of Ottawa, to launch out in denunciation of "England's recent diplomatic efforts to buy her own peace at the sacrifice of our interests";[52] and after that outburst, which nearly resulted in Howe's resignation, there was rather less talk about Macdonald's zealously loyal colleagues "converting" him to the necessity of the ratification of the fishery clauses. "Meanwhile," he wrote to John Rose a few days after the opening of the session, "I have screwed up my colleagues, after very many months of labour and anxiety, to the sticking point. We have finally agreed to go to Parliament this session for an Act to bring the fishery articles into force, with a clause suspending its operation until an order-in-council is issued here, Her Majesty's Government giving us the guarantee of two and half millions."[53]

In all probability he had never believed in, or hoped for, any other solution. "The great reason why I have always been able to beat Brown," he told Matthew Crooks Cameron, "is that I have been able to look a little ahead, while he could on no occasion forgo the temptation of a temporary triumph."[54] Macdonald would never be betrayed into a temporary triumph or a temporary revenge. With him the short view was lifted habitually to the long view, the gaze was steadied towards the distant objective, the eyes, wise with the remembrance of the past, sought the certainty of the future. The studied discourtesies at Washington, the long haggling with the Colonial Office, the exasperating suspicion, which he confided to Rose, that somebody was privately belittling his difficulties, were all, in the long view, merely the small inevitable frictions, the blunt familiar give-and-take of a family relationship by which Canada could alone survive as a separate and independent nation in North America. An occasional concession, a bad bargain, even something which, in the eyes of the inexperienced Canadians, could only seem an enormous diplomatic sacrifice, must all be regarded, in the long view, as a small price to pay for the indefinite continuance of the Anglo-Canadian alliance, which was the reality behind the imperial connection, and the condition and guarantee of Canada's autonomy in the new continent.

Macdonald believed he could rely on the indefinite continuance of that alliance. It was true that he had never had any very great confidence in the loyalty of Gladstone, Lowe, Cardwell, and Bright. He suspected that, in the existing British Cabinet, there were men who, in Lord Kimberley's words, made "no secret of their opinion" that England would be well rid of the colonies.[55] Yet these well-founded suspicions had never weakened his belief in the permanence of the imperial partnership. "Little Englanders" had been fairly prominent for some time now in the English governing class; and, as Macdonald had good reason to suspect, even extreme "little Englanders" were conscious of the claims of historic loyalties and obligations. Gladstone himself had admitted that the compact could never be dissolved by the action of one of the parties to it. "Let separation come if it must," wrote Kimberley, "but I will be no party to any step which tends to bring about a separation in anger."[56] The present British ministers, Macdonald realized, were simply temporary actors in a long, complex imperial drama, which had brought England greatness in the past, and which would never be permitted, even by its severest critics, to end in ignominy. Back of the Gladstone government was England and its people, and all that they had ever thought and said and done for British North America, all the effort and daring, the political wisdom and the political magnanimity—Brock leading the volunteers up the heights at Queenston, Mackenzie toiling north towards the mouth of his great river, Colonel By driving the canal through the forest towards the Ottawa River, and Carnarvon rising in his place in the Lords to move the first reading of the British North America Bill.

The third of May was a dull, cool spring day; and, when Macdonald got up to move the ratification of the Canadian clauses in the Washington Treaty, something of its uninspiring chilliness seemed to have stiffened the opening passages of his speech.[57] He often began badly, in a hesitant, feeble, not too easily audible, fashion; and on this occasion the first awkwardness was perhaps emphasized by the technical difficulty of the subject itself, and by the embarrassment of its surrounding political circumstances. It was not until after the recess for dinner that he began to warm up. By this time the long quotations were mostly finished, the legal explanations were done. The subject took hold of him, and for two and a half hours he spoke his best, defending each clause in the treaty, emphasizing the sacrifices which it called upon Great Britain to make, driving home the realization of Canada's interest in the achievement of Anglo-American peace, and ending with a personal explanation which was both a defence of his own conduct and an appeal to the mature judgment of his countrymen. "I have not said a word," he told the House, "for twelve months. I have kept silence to this day, thinking it better that the subject should be discussed on its own merits. How eagerly was I watched! If the government should come out in favour of the Treaty, then it was to be taken as being a betrayal of the people of Canada. If the government should come out against the Treaty, then the First Minister was to be charged with opposing the interests of the Empire. Whichever course we might take they were lying in wait, ready with some mode of attack. But 'silence is golden', Mr. Speaker, and I kept silence. I believe the sober second thought of this country accords with the sober second thought of the government; and we come down here and ask the people of Canada through their representatives to accept this treaty, to accept it with all its imperfections, to accept it for the sake of peace, and for the sake of the great Empire of which we form a part."[58]

Chapter Five

Blackmail

I

The brief remainder of the session was an unbroken success. The Washington Treaty passed the House by the large majority of one hundred and twenty-one to fifty-five. The Trades Union Bill, the repeal of the tea and coffee duties, the Redistribution Bill allocating the six new seats due to Ontario as a result of the recent census all slipped through with a minimum of trouble and difficulty. "We had a most triumphant session," Macdonald wrote to Rose, "not having experienced a single check of any kind. The opposition were completely demoralized and I am going to the country with good hopes of success in Ontario."[1] All the preparations were finished. The most favourable ground had been chosen, the best possible dispositions made. Even the patient propitiation of the Roman Catholic authorities was at last having gratifying results. "I cannot conceal from you the thought," wrote Archbishop Lynch genially at the conclusion of a reassuring letter, "that (now that I am warmed up about you) I will have you a good Catholic yet."[2] A most satisfactory letter! The skies seemed to smile over the home ground of Ontario. And abroad, the threatening storm on the Anglo-American horizon, instead of darkening, had cleared up with magical suddenness. The United States withdrew the "indirect" claims. The arbitration of the *Alabama* damages at Geneva continued placidly through its legal involutions. The peaceful settlement between the British Empire and the United States was saved.

Not inappropriately, the coming of peace, the achievement

of security for the new, transcontinental Canada, was marked by a change of governors-general. Lord Lisgar, the Governor who had come over as Sir John Young—a "mere Bart." in his own phrase—was now about to yield his place to "a man of high rank and the first water of fashion", the Earl of Dufferin. Lisgar's governor-generalship had coincided with the rapid political expansion of the young Dominion and the settlement of its outstanding political differences with the United States. Lord Dufferin, who was as elaborate and complimentary in his manner as Lisgar had been simple and downright, would have to preside over what was expected to be the more sober work of national organization. It was true that the projected Dominion was not yet complete. Newfoundland and Prince Edward Island had yet to come in; but the importance of their entrance into Confederation was hardly comparable to that of the acquisition of Rupert's Land or the union with British Columbia. The days of Canada's most rapid territorial expansion were past; and the task that remained, now that the United States had accepted the existence of the transcontinental northern nation, was to weld its vast domains into a working and prosperous unity. It was for this purpose—to clinch the sudden victory, to make fast the claim that had been merely staked—that Macdonald wanted another five years of power. "I am, as you may fancy," he wrote to John Rose, "exceedingly desirous of carrying the elections again; not from any personal object, because I am weary of the whole thing, but Confederation is only yet in the gristle, and it will require five years more before it hardens into bone."[3] It would require far more than five years, of course, to people the west and build up a strong eastern industry. These were long-term, comprehensive national projects, which depended, for their success, upon the inflow of men and capital, and which the Canadian government and Parliament could never realize by legislation alone. The Pacific railway was an entirely different affair. It must be built in ten years, if the Dominion kept its compact with British Columbia. It ought to be finished in less than ten years, if Canada were to give the world a convincing proof of its enterprise and resources.

Macdonald wanted to begin quickly. The Pacific railway

was his biggest task and his most important policy. But—within six weeks of the election—it had also become his principal source of anxiety. The Interoceanic Railway Company and the Canada Pacific Railway Company confronted each other in intolerable opposition. He realized that he would have to make a very earnest effort, before the elections began, to end this stupid rivalry by persuading Macpherson and Allan to unite in a joint undertaking. But what enormous difficulties confronted him! Macpherson, who still doubted Allan's good faith and who suspected that he had not, in fact, got rid of his American associates, was obviously in no mood for generous compromises. But neither apparently was Allan. Allan seemed flushed with ambition and a growing sense of power. Did he possess enough influence to force Allan to make the real concessions which were necessary to gain Macpherson's support? He was very doubtful. Within the last two months his chances of imposing a reconciliation between the two promoters and an amalgamation of their rival companies had perceptibly worsened, as he was now very well aware. His strength in Montreal, and in everything that concerned Montreal, was nothing more or less than the strength —or weakness—of George Etienne Cartier. And Cartier, the pugnacious, masterful companion of the past, was very far from being his old self, either physically or politically, in the first summer months of 1872.

Allan had, in fact, chosen his victim with extraordinary cunning. Cartier was not well. He was troubled by various disquieting symptoms, by swellings in his limbs which seemed ominously to suggest some grave disorder. But he was determined to run in the election and to run in Montreal East. Montreal and its district was his old political empire; Montreal East was his old constituency. It was all true. But it was also true that, in Montreal East, the natural public interest in the North Shore route and the Northern Colonization Railway had been so magnified and strengthened by Allan that it had now become an apparently irresistible political force directed against Cartier. Cartier, like Macdonald, had been deeply suspicious of Allan and his American connections. "Aussi longtemps que je vivrai et que je serai dans le ministère," he told one delegation which had come to ask his opinion of Allan's pet scheme of an amalgamation of the Canada Pacific and the Northern Colonization Railways, "jamais une sacrée compagnie Américaine aura le contrôle du Pacifique. . . ."[4] He had seized upon the vital defect of Allan's project as a national, Canadian scheme. But, in Montreal East, nobody would believe that the solicitor of the monopolistic Grand Trunk Railway could be a really unprejudiced witness. The thunder of Cartier's typically explosive, typically anti-American criticisms was stolen before it ever really began to roll. By the end of June it was clearly evident to most people, if not to Cartier himself, that he could not possibly win in Montreal East unless Allan and the railway interests which he represented were in some fashion appeased. "I hear on all sides," Alexander Campbell wrote to Macdonald early in July, "that the Allan North Shore interest is wanted to put Cartier in for East Montreal."[5]

By this time, Macdonald was ready to move to Toronto for the opening of the campaign. The Pacific railway, although at the moment it caused him most concern, was far from being his only worry. He expected that the general election in Ontario would give him the hardest fight of his political career. He had made all prudent preparations, he had had several strokes of real luck; but it was impossible to blink away the plain fact that every mistake that the government had made, every misfortune it had suffered—Riel, the Manitoba settlement, the bargain with British Columbia, the fatal omissions of the Washington Treaty —would be felt more severely in Ontario than in any other part of the federation. In Ontario, the new provincial administration, flushed with its triumph over John Sandfield Macdonald, and eager to complete the defeat of the Conservative party, would bring all its power and influence and patronage to bear against him. He might be defeated; he might be able to do no more than break even. And even to fight a drawn battle would, he was perfectly certain, require his constant presence in the hottest of the fighting. He would have to take to the stump, *more Americano*, as he called it, through all the central and western part of Ontario. It would mean two solid months of strenuous, exhausting campaigning. He had never done such a thing before in all the twenty-seven years of his political career; he hoped never to have to do it again. But he persuaded himself that this time it was inescapably necessary. "I only wish," he told Rose, "that I was physically a little stronger. However, I think that I will not break down in the contest. We will carry all the other provinces, I believe, with sweeping majorities."[6]

II

In the first week in July he and Agnes travelled to Toronto and settled down for what was certain to be a long summer's visit. He left his own election in Kingston to Alexander Campbell's care. There were more general and more important matters to consider, and the amalgamation of the two Pacific railways was the most important of all. A meeting of the principals involved, with himself, a benevolently diplomatic broker, hovering in the background, was surely the best means of achieving an amicable union; and he had barely established himself in the Queen's Hotel when he wrote to Montreal inviting Allan and Abbott to come up to Toronto for a personal conference with Macpherson. He had made up his mind about the broad lines of the arrangement that he wished to impose. The board of directors of the united organization would have to be a board which, from the point of view of the government, would be politically defensible; and no board would be defensible which did not reflect the political pre-eminence of Ontario. Thirteen directors, of whom Macpherson would nominate five, Allan, four, and the government the remainder, choosing one from each of the other provinces, would make a very acceptable governing body.[7] This much he would have to insist upon, for the sake of Ontario and Macpherson; but all the details of the amalgamation he left to the principals, hoping that they could reach a friendly agreement between themselves. His hopes were disappointed. Allan—it was possibly an ominous indication of the Montrealer's sense of conscious power—found it inconvenient to accept Macdonald's invitation. Abbott, his solicitor, alone put in an appearance for the conference at the Queen's Hotel; and as soon as he and Macpherson got down to a detailed discussion of the terms of the proposed amalgamation, a fundamental conflict of interest at once appeared. Macpherson utterly refused to accept Allan in advance as president of the united company;[8] Allan was plainly unwilling to grant Macpherson the nomination of the larger number of directors. There were no compromises and no agreement. Almost as soon as it began, the conference was over. And Macdonald's first attempt to secure the amalgamation had failed.

That night—it was the night of July 11—he went with Agnes to the Toronto Music Hall to keep another engagement—an engagement which was to reveal him to shining advantage in his new rôle as the "working-man's friend". A fortnight before he had received a rather shakily spelt, shakily punctuated letter from John Hewitt, corresponding secretary of the Toronto Trades Assembly, which informed him that the trades unions of Canada wished to make a presentation to Lady Macdonald "as a slight token of our appreciation of your timely efforts in the interests of the operatives of this Dominion".[9] It was a handsome, gold, jewelled casket that was presented to Agnes that night; and along with it went a laudatory address, which sketched the efforts of the Typographical Union to forward the nine hours movement, and referred poignantly to the "harsh and uncalled-for" arrest of the twenty-three printers—an arrest "instigated by the proprietor of a newspaper whose animus leads him to follow, even to the death, those who cross his path".[10]

Macdonald thanked the assembly of working-men on his wife's account and his own, promised that he would give "respectful and prompt attention" to any representations the Trades Assemblies cared to give on the subject of Canadian labour legislation, and ended up by identifying himself, in a jocular fashion, with the highly sympathetic audience before him. ". . . I ought to have a special interest in this subject," he said, while his listeners laughed their approval, "because I am a working-man myself. I know that I work more than nine hours every day myself; and then I think that I am a practical mechanic. If you look at the Confederation Act, in the framing of which I had some hand, you will admit that I am a pretty good joiner; and, as for cabinet-making, I have had as much experience as Jacques and Hay themselves."[11] It was all a tremendous success. The meeting ended in a storm of cheers and hand-clapping; outside the audience formed a torch-light procession, and a carriage carrying Sir John and Lady Macdonald, Beaty, the proprietor of the *Leader* and McCormick, the president of the Trades Assembly, was drawn in triumph through the streets. "The workingmen," Macdonald wrote proudly to Alexander Campbell next morning, "are at white heat in my favour just now."[12]

The next move in the campaign was to Hamilton, the "ambitious city", at the head of Lake Ontario. He and Hincks had decided that an important announcement of government policy was to be made there. And he was just about to leave Toronto on the following morning when a most ominous telegram arrived from Sir Hugh Allan. "It is very important," the message ran, "in the interest of Sir George and of the government that the Pacific question should be settled without delay. I send this from no personal interest but a storm is brewing."[13] It was only too obvious what had happened. Allan had been informed at once by Abbott of the denial of his demands, of the inconclusive ending of the interview with Macpherson, on the previous day. Sir Hugh had decided peremptorily to apply pressure himself. He was using threats— blatant, obviously disingenuous threats. But his power was real. Macdonald felt himself pressed, suddenly and savagely, by a force stronger and more unscrupulously wielded than he had ever felt in the past. He had only time enough, before his departure, to beg a favour of Macpherson. Would he, for the sake of peace, go and see Allan in Montreal, since Allan would not come to Toronto to see him? The only hope lay in a real meeting of the principals. Macpherson reluctantly consented; and with that Macdonald tore himself away.

Hamilton was a manufacturing town, already specializing in heavy industries in iron and steel, and in the last few years growing rapidly in population. Macdonald had decided to give it one of the six new seats allotted to Ontario by the Redistribution Bill. The town had been represented in the last Parliament by a Grit; but he was determined to regain the old seat and to win the new, and, with his new programme, he believed he had an excellent chance of succeeding. The Trades Union Bill would, he was certain, win the Hamilton mechanics. To the Hamilton manufacturers he had already been clearly hinting that the removal of the tea and coffee duties would make it necessary for the government next session to propose an increase on the tariff on articles that Canada could produce;[14] and on July 13, at a big public meeting in the city, Hincks and he made the first public announcement of the Conservative policy of incidental protection.[15] Two days later at Brantford, which was another growing manufacturing town, he repeated the announcement, dwelling proudly on the industrial growth of the country during recent years and insisting that Canada, irrespective of free-trade or any other theories, must have a commercial policy "of its own".[16] "Incidental protection" and "national policy" were the main themes of their speeches as he and Hincks travelled westward through the province. They were together at London on July 16. Then they separated and Macdonald went on to Stratford.

It was while he was still in western Ontario that the bad news began to catch up with him. There was a letter from Campbell, who had been given charge of his campaign in Kingston; there were letters and telegrams—increasingly demanding or importunate—from Macpherson, and Allan, and Cartier. Campbell wrote to inform him that Carruthers was to be the Reform candidate in Kingston, that a severe contest was expected, and that everybody hoped he would come back, establish himself at the British American Hotel, and "go into the contest as of yore".[17] He felt like a commander-in-chief of combined operations who is suddenly invited to step aside and meet one of the enemy in single combat. It was a nuisance, but, of course, he would have to go back to Kingston, at least for the nomination meeting. That was clear enough; but what was not clear, what was, in fact, shrouded in complete obscurity, was a way out of the dangerous mess of the Pacific railway affair. Macpherson had done all he had promised. He had gone to Montreal, and, on the afternoon of July 18, he had discussed the whole matter at length with Allan. He had apparently agreed to an amalgamation and had even consented to an increase in the number of directors, with himself and Allan each appointing an equal number and the government the rest. But he absolutely refused to accept Sir Hugh beforehand as president, and he insisted that the free choice of both president and vice-president should be left to the board after it had been constituted.[18]

The turning-point had been reached. Nothing had yet been settled, but an agreement was possible, if only Allan would make some concessions. And, in fact, he seemed outwardly to be prepared for compromises. Outwardly only. Secretly he was determined to get his way. He insisted that if a board as now proposed were set up, the directors appointed by the government should be given clearly to understand that they were to vote for him as president and that, in addition, over fifty per cent of the stock must be assigned to his "friends".[19] These demands were, as Macdonald knew perfectly well, dangerous and possibly fatal to grant in the circumstances. But they were demands which were no longer made by Allan alone; they were endorsed and supported by Cartier, who now, on the eve of the election, had at last realized the desperateness of his situation, and who was ready to capitulate to the man who had mastered him. On July 19, he telegraphed to Macdonald at Stratford, giving him an account of the meeting of Macpherson and Allan on the previous day, and urging that the affair must be settled "on account of elections in Ontario and Quebec".[20] Three days later, when Macdonald was at Toronto hurrying to get back to Kingston for nomination day, he received another telegram from Cartier which this time gave Allan's final ultimatum. "If the government will pledge itself," Allan had wired unequivocally, "to appoint directors favourable to me as president and to the allotment of stock as stated in my letter of yesterday I will be satisfied." And Cartier had added a desperate, importunate postscript: "Matter could be settled at once thus between him and Macpherson. Important it should be settled without delay."[21]

But Macdonald—even with Cartier's fate in the balance—was not willing to settle on Allan's conqueror's terms. He would grant nothing until he had had another conversation with Macpherson, and that was impossible at the moment, for Macpherson was still away in Montreal. Macdonald hurried on to Kingston, and the mental and physical strain to which he had been subjected for the last few weeks was only too evident on nomination day when, on a public platform at Kingston, before a large, disorderly crowd, he completely lost his temper with his opponent, Carruthers, and, as the newspapers put it discreetly, a "slight contretemps occurred".[22] He could not leave Kingston, when the struggle was fiercely and all too evenly joined; but he telegraphed Macpherson begging him to stop off on his way back from Montreal. And on July 26, their meeting finally took place. Macdonald pressed Macpherson to accept the unpalatable fact that Allan must be president on political grounds. Macpherson was stubbornly suspicious of Allan, and his American friends, and the sinister influence which they might exercise together. But he did not appear to reject the idea of Allan's presidency without qualification, and he seemed prepared to wait until after the elections for a final decision. Macdonald seized the opportunity. He telegraphed to Cartier, authorizing him to assure Allan "that the power of the government will be exercised to secure him the position of president" and postponing the settlement of the other details until after the election.[23] He had made only one promise—the presidency. And it could be argued, of course, that Allan was entitled to the presidency on grounds of age, experience, and prestige.

He closed his telegram to Cartier with the peremptory word "Answer". But for four days no answer came. And then, on July 30, a telegram from Cartier and a letter from Allan shocked him with the realization that Sir Hugh was still not satisfied, that he had made a final effort to extort the desired concessions from Cartier's weakness. The presidency—the one promise that Macdonald had thought it possible to make—was not enough for Allan. He wanted more. He insisted that he and his friends must have a clear majority of the stock and "government influence" in their favour; and he now demanded, for the first time, that if the negotiations for the amalgamation should not succeed within a brief period of two months, the charter would then be given to his own company, the Canada Pacific Railway Company.[24] In this last gambling effort, he had raised his demands to their most extravagant limit. But he had also baited them with his most seductive inducements. At the frantic Cartier's own suggestion, he had agreed that "the friends of the government will expect to be assisted with funds in the pending elections", and he had accepted a list of "immediate requirements" for Cartier, Langevin, and Macdonald, totalling sixty thousand dollars.

Macdonald stared at the telegram with amazement and apprehension. He desperately needed the money. In the mêlée of the election the rival forces surged uncertainly backward and forward, and from all over Ontario the demands for funds had become a roar in his ears. But it was utterly impossible to yield to Allan's demands. The whole agreement, into which the wretched Cartier had been betrayed by his weakness, must be instantly repudiated. In the first few moments of worried excitement, Macdonald decided that there was only one thing to do, and that was to go immediately to Montreal himself. He even began to make preparations for departure, giving Campbell hurried, last-minute directions for the conduct of the election during his absence. Then he drew back. The election! How could he leave Kingston at this moment of all others! Today was July 31. Tomorrow, August 1, the poll would begin. He had only a few hours more in which to clinch his uncertain chances of success. He could not go—not, at least, for the moment. He telegraphed instead, rejecting Allan's absurd demands, repudiating the dangerous agreement into which Cartier had been forced, throwing the whole arrangement back to the terms of his own telegram of July 26.

The next morning, in the early hours of the poll, the longed-for answer arrived from Cartier. "Have seen Sir Hugh," Cartier telegraphed. "He withdraws letter written you since you make objection to it, and relies for basis of arrangement on your telegram to me of which I gave him a copy."[25] This was definite enough, and the blessed assurance was confirmed by another telegram from Allan, in very much the same terms. A great load of anxiety rolled off his back that hot August morning; and, as the day waxed and waned, and the polling continued, his released spirits mounted mercurially. By the end of the day, the vote stood seven hundred and thirty-five for Macdonald, and six hundred and four for Carruthers.[26] He had won Kingston, and by a safe majority of one hundred and thirty-one. He was free—free of his own election contest, free of Allan's threats and his own worries for the Pacific amalgamation, free to return to Toronto and resume his command of the general election at a time when most of the contests in western Ontario were yet to come. He was free—yes. But he was also armed, as he had never hoped to be, with the sinews of war. He had rejected Allan's extreme demands. But Allan had not revoked his offer of funds for the election. The sum of twenty-five thousand dollars stood to Macdonald's credit in the Merchants' Bank of Canada. He used none of it for his own election in Kingston; but before he left Kingston for Toronto, he had already distributed a large part of it to important Conservative candidates in Ontario.

In Toronto he plunged again into the sticky fatigues of an August election. He had never worked so hard, or so continuously, or with such doubtful prospects of success. It was true that the government gained some big, popular, well advertised victories. Witton, the "labouring man", and Chisholm, his fellow Conservative candidate, captured the two new Hamilton constituencies; and Conservatives took two out of the three seats in Toronto. But, all over the province, riding after riding was falling to the opposition. Macdonald was conscious of the unpopularity of his own past mistakes and failures, of the pugnacious strength of the provincial Liberal electoral machine, of the large sums of money—he estimated over a quarter of a million dollars—which the Grits had put into the contest. Like a general desperately throwing in the last of his fresh troops, he flung his own campaign money broadcast across Ontario with reckless generosity. Already, he had approached Abbott, Allan's solicitor, for another ten thousand dollars. Hincks had been given two thousand, Carling fifteen hundred, Stephenson, Grayson Smith, and Ross a thousand each.[27] He did not know exactly where the money went. It seemed as if he could not keep himself going without constant recourse to wine and spirits; and the days slipped past him indistinguishably in a muddled confusion of effort. He knew only that the money dribbled away with incredible rapidity. It was going. It had gone. And once again—how often had it happened already? —he found himself wiring another appeal for assistance to Abbott. "I must have another ten thousand," he telegraphed on August 26. "Will be the last time of calling. Do not fail me. Answer today."[28] And Abbott answered that day—affirmatively.

The final polls were held. Six days later, on September 1, Macdonald was back in Ottawa. He had taken at least forty-five thousand dollars of Allan's money. It was a huge sum. But even so it did not represent the total of Allan's contributions to the Conservative party, as Macdonald now discovered to his dismay. Cartier had taken eighty-five thousand dollars, nearly twice as much as he himself had accepted; and Cartier and Langevin between them had been given a total amount of a hundred and seventeen thousand.[29] Macdonald felt a cold chill of uneasiness. The Conservative party had put itself in a most dangerously equivocal position. It was true that it had made only one promise—the promise of the presidency; but it had accepted sums whose size implied other and far less legitimate undertakings. At the moment when it was about to make a contract of the highest national importance, involving millions of money, the government had become deeply indebted, for purely party purposes, to one of the principal capitalists with whom it was negotiating.

III

What had the Conservative party got from this dubious, hazardous connection? It was strange, and vaguely disquieting;

but Allan seemed from the first to be followed by a grey familiar, ill-luck. Of course, he had not been the only contributor to the campaign fund and of course money alone never won elections anyway. But certainly the Conservatives had not experienced any very bountiful good fortune in the contest of 1872. They had, it was true, won the election as a whole; but only by virtue of the Maritime and western seats. Macdonald's estimate of forty-two out of the eighty-eight Ontario constituencies turned out, in the end, to be over-optimistic; and in Quebec, where Allan had spent most money and claimed to have most influence, Langevin and Cartier had been able to secure only a bare majority of the sixty-five seats. Cartier himself was defeated in Montreal East, in a constituency which, as Macdonald knew very well, was not *Rouge*, and which another Conservative might have captured with ease. It was a curious commentary upon Allan's vaunted political influence that he had been totally unable to allay the popular storm which he himself had helped so much to arouse against Cartier. Poor Cartier had given his unhappy pledges for nothing. He had yielded only to incur defeat, a defeat which must have seemed all the more bitter because it had come when his once splendid vitality had been sapped by illness, and when he faced a future which was dark with uncertainty. Macdonald had been present at the fatal interview in Montreal when the doctor had informed Cartier that he had a confirmed case of Bright's disease. He tried to spare his old colleague fatigue, and to hasten his departure for England, where Cartier was to put himself under the care of Bright's successor in the treatment of kidney diseases. But he did not believe that the greatest of all his French-Canadian team-mates would ever again take his seat at the Council board. "I cannot tell you how I sorrow at this," he wrote to Lord Lisgar. "We have acted together since 1854, and have never had a serious difference."[30]

Yet poor Cartier's defeat and illness, about which he could do nothing in any case, was not his main preoccupation at the moment. His main preoccupation was the amalgamation of the Interoceanic and the Canada Pacific Railway Companies—an amalgamation already complicated by the secret assurance given to Allan. Allan had been promised the presidency; and on no account could that engagement be disturbed. If Sir Hugh had not brought Cartier and Langevin a smashing victory in Quebec, he had at least saved them from an annihilating defeat; and they would certainly insist upon the complete and literal fulfilment of the government's pledge. It was a "political necessity", as Macdonald knew, to satisfy Quebec; but, as he also knew, it was a "political necessity" to conciliate Ontario. And since the presidency of Allan was now one of those "fixed facts" about which nothing could be done, then his first task was obviously to persuade Macpherson to accept the inevitable, in the interest of Ontario, as well as in the interest of the railway and the government. He knew that it would be a hard task; but he saw quickly that he had underestimated its difficulties. He picked the negotiations up where he had dropped them so hurriedly late in July, only to discover that in the meantime Macpherson had simply become more embittered in his opposition. Why, Macpherson inquired indignantly, did the government feel obliged to make any concessions whatever to Allan? Allan had failed it during the elections. Allan had not even been able to save poor Cartier from defeat.

Macdonald did his best. In two long letters, he tried to reason with Macpherson, pointing out that Allan had a fair claim, on grounds of seniority, to the presidency, that all the members of the Cabinet had agreed that his pretensions could not be denied, and that a scheme which, as Macpherson himself admitted, was in many other respects good, could not be rejected out of hand simply "because Sir Hugh sits at the head of the board instead of the side".[31] But Macpherson was not to be mollified. He was furious with wounded pride and mortification. He told Macdonald angrily that Allan's operations from start to finish had been nothing less than "an audacious, insolent, unpatriotic, and gigantic swindle—the greatest ever attempted in this Dominion".[32] He kept insisting that on such terms the Interoceanic Company would never accept the amalgamation; and very rapidly these confident predictions were confirmed by an official rejection. "I received this morning," Allan wired to Macdonald on October 4, "a letter from the secretary of the

Interoceanic Railway Company, Toronto, declining peremptor-ily to enter into the scheme of amalgamation."[33]

It was a crushing refusal. But Macdonald was not yet ready to give up. He thought he saw a way in which the Toronto capitalists' uncompromising position could be turned. The one legitimate objection of the Interoceanic Company was to Allan's alleged American associates; Macpherson's one valid fear was that the Pacific railway, under Allan's presidency, would inevit-ably fall under the control of Canada's most dangerous rivals. Macdonald himself had felt exactly the same fears and objec-tions. And it seemed to him that if they could only be removed, once and for all, to everybody's satisfaction, Macpherson would, in all honesty, have to give way, and the scheme could go triumphantly forward. A thorough clarification of the Canada Pacific's somewhat ambiguous position was due—if not, indeed, overdue. Government itself could help to supply the necessary reassurance. It could insist upon the inclusion in the charter of clauses which would make it impossible for foreigners to get control of the railway. But it could not possibly win Macpherson without Allan's help. Allan must make a full and complete disclosure of his affairs. The memorandum in which the Interoceanic Company had justified its rejection of the amalgamation must receive a candid, explicit, and detailed answer.

It was at this point, a few days after Macpherson's formally renewed charges had made further concealment impossible, that Macdonald received a letter from the President of the Canada Pacific Railway Company.[34] Allan was full of protestations and assurances. Yet his letter was curiously disquieting as well. He reminded Macdonald that it was Hincks who had told him originally of the visit of the Americans to Ottawa and had suggested that he get in touch with them. The implication that the alliance between Allan and his American associates had had the previous sanction of government was annoying to Mac-donald; but, bad as it was, it was not the most disturbing feature of Allan's letter. The dismaying fact which now unmistakably emerged was that Sir Hugh, despite all his previous solemn assurances, had yet to break conclusively and finally with the

Americans! He had hinted to them, he told Macdonald, of the popular Canadian suspicion of anyone connected with the Northern Pacific Railroad. He had pointed out the great and increasing difficulties in the way of American participation in the Canadian line. He had done all he could "gradually and not in too rude a manner" to prepare the way for a rapidly approaching separation. But the fact remained that he had not yet taken the final step. He was, however, just about to take it, he assured Macdonald eagerly. He would now inform his American friends that, as a result of popular Canadian opposition, their syndicate would have to be broken up.

Macdonald considered Allan's letter doubtfully. It certainly posed almost as many questions as it answered. It left Allan's good faith in doubt. It awakened fearful speculations about possible American reprisals in the future. Yet, for the moment, Macdonald could afford to put these worries aside. The main burden of Allan's letter was satisfactory. And a week later, in a formal reply to the accusing memorandum of the Interoceanic Railway Company, Allan and his principal Canadian directors solemnly protested that they had never contemplated combining with American capitalists or asking aid of them. It was possible, Macdonald believed, to build policy on the solid foundation of these assurances. If Macpherson remained obstinately sceptical of these new proofs of Sir Hugh's financial independence, then surely other and respectable Ontario capitalists would be convinced by them. And if an amalgamation of the two companies proved impossible to carry out, then the government would promote the formation of a completely new company, with a board of thirteen representative directors chosen from all six of the provinces, and free from the rivalries of the past. There remained, of course, the question of the presidency. For a moment he toyed vainly, longingly, with the idea of a new president. But, no! It would not do. The commitment to Allan could not be broken. Yet might it not be modified—just a little modified? Could Allan be made "provisional" president? "Provisional" was an agreeable word. Could Macpherson be induced to accept the provisional presidency of his rival?

Early in November, Macdonald boarded the train for Toronto.

Three weeks before, Alexander Campbell and Hewitt Bernard had been sent up as his ambassadors, and they had failed.[35] Now he was about to make a last personal effort to gain Macpherson. Safe in the Queen's Hotel, surrounded by his Toronto cronies, and far away from the dull routines of Ottawa, he began to drink a good deal. The jocular high spirits with which he approached the crucial encounter with Macpherson were fortified by a long succession of brandies and soda; and every art of persuasion which he possessed was lavished upon his obstinate fellow-Scotsman and his Ontario business associates. He told Macpherson of his plan for the "provisional" presidency. He promised that, in order to prevent the railway from falling into the financial control of Americans, the government would retain a veto on the distribution of stock for the first five years of the new company's existence. But Macpherson remained obdurate. For a little while, it was true, he wavered. But as soon as he discovered that the "provisional" presidency could mean nothing less than the presidency for a year, he drew back coldly and implacably. A whole year! It was far too much. In a year Allan could—and probably would—ruin the entire enterprise.[36] Macpherson would have nothing to do with it on such terms. The final words were spoken and written. And Macdonald realized that the long, fruitless pursuit of the president of the Interoceanic Railway was at an end.

He returned wearily unsuccessful to Ottawa. Yet he was not entirely defeated. He had, he informed Lord Dufferin, collected enough financial support in Ontario to make him virtually independent of Macpherson's refusal.[37] The formation of the new company could now be pushed forward with some prospect of success. But it would be a difficult, unsatisfactory business; and besides there were now other and more sinister perils which he could vaguely discern ahead. Allan had been hinting, not very obscurely, that it was going to be very difficult for him, at this late stage, to free himself from the clutches of the Americans; and already, Hincks reported, rumours were current in Montreal that Allan had contributed enormous sums during the elections in return for some unspecified but important promise by Cartier connected with the

Pacific railway.[38] Cartier's promise! Macdonald recalled with something of a start that he had never known exactly what the promise was. He and Cartier had agreed, by telegraph, that his wire of July 26 was to be the "basis" of the agreement. But had the rapacious Allan succeeded in extorting some dangerous additional concession? Macdonald did not know. He could not be certain that Allan would never present another of Cartier's I.O.U.'s for payment. He did not expect to see Cartier again. But he knew that the responsibility for all that Cartier had said and done during those last crucial weeks in Montreal would be his, and his alone.

"We have fixed next Tuesday for Pacific railway matters,"[39] he wrote Langevin on November 28. "There are rocks ahead of the most dangerous character, and I therefore think that you must be here without fail on that day." Early in December, Allan and a few of the directors came up to Ottawa to discuss the terms of the charter. Macdonald put on a brave front about the matter. ". . . We are making the best company we can," he wrote cheerfully to Cartier a few days before Christmas. "The thirteen directors are not all chosen yet, but they will all be settled by New Year's Day." New Year's Day![40] On New Year's Eve he was in his room at the East Block, working away at the details of the arrangement, when a card was brought in to him. As he stared at it, he realized that this was the visit he had been dreading for months past. George W. McMullen, the proprietor of the Chicago *Post*, the shareholder in the Northern Pacific Railroad, the principal American associate of Sir Hugh Allan, was waiting in the ante-room to wish him the compliments of the season! Happy New Year! Would it be—could it be—happy now?

IV

McMullen stayed in his office a solid two hours. He had a great deal to say, and he said it carefully and emphatically. He was a man who obviously knew exactly what he wanted, and, equally obviously, was determined to get it. He had about him the blunt, uncompromisingly authoritative air of conscious power. Like all successful blackmailers, he came heavily armed with documents. He produced the original contract between Allan and his American associates. He produced Allan's letters. With unsmiling satisfaction he read the more damning portions of the papers aloud while Macdonald listened in silence.

Macdonald was appalled. All his worst apprehensions, doubts, and fears about Allan and Allan's conduct were now confirmed with prodigal conclusiveness. Allan had committed errors— and something worse than errors—on a positively gigantic scale. It was as if the very grandiose magnitude of the Pacific enterprise had exaggerated every one of his defects and failings, had blown him and his vices into a size larger than life, had transformed a sober, inhibited Scottish merchant into a Roman emperor, free of restraint and drunk with power. Ambition, cunning, vanity, incredible indiscretion and incredible duplicity were all exhibited without reserve in the letters that McMullen held firmly in his grasp. Allan had boasted about his triumph over Cartier, had misreported his agreement with the government, had told, in garrulous detail, a most dangerously compromising story, compounded of truths, half-truths, and vague insinuations. During all the long months that he had been promising so profusely to break with his American colleagues, he had in fact done virtually nothing to prepare them for the end of the partnership. He had even had the sublime impertinence to demand repayment from McMullen for the $343,000 which he had paid out, chiefly to insure his own election to the presidency in a railway from which his American associates were certain to be excluded. For weeks, for months, he had carried on this unabashed double-dealing; and it was not until October 24, over a fortnight after his solemn declaration of purpose to Macdonald, that he had given McMullen the first real intimation that the syndicate would have to be broken up.

Rapidly Macdonald considered the position. He was under no obligation whatever to shield Allan, for Allan had grossly and inexcusably deceived him. A little commiseration for his fellow dupe, he felt, could be afforded. He admitted to McMullen that if all he said were true, he had been very badly used; but his tone clearly implied that redress for McMullen's grievances could be sought only from Allan. McMullen seemed unimpressed by this attitude of benevolent detachment; he obviously believed that the Canadian government was deeply implicated in the affair. He calmly pointed out the evidence which the letters supplied of the corrupt bargain between Sir Hugh and the Cabinet; and when Macdonald denied that he and his colleagues had been bribed, McMullen unpleasantly replied that, in that case, Allan must be even more of a swindler than the Americans had suspected, for he was now demanding repayment for nearly $4,000,000 which he had never expended. Macdonald made no reply. There was no use in arguing; and McMullen proceeded to state his demands. Either, he told Macdonald, the government must permit the agreement between Allan and his American associates to be carried out in its original terms, or else Allan's name must be completely omitted from the proposed new company.[41] Macdonald was staggered. He could do neither the one nor the other, he announced flatly. And then, as he expected, McMullen became very unpleasant indeed. He and his colleagues, he announced truculently, had no intention of acting as so many stepping-stones for the personal advancement of Sir Hugh Allan. If the Canadian government persisted in putting Allan in as president, if it permitted him to break faith with his American colleagues in this outrageous fashion, then the Canadian public would be promptly put in possession of all the facts.

Macdonald could only beg for time. He must, he told McMullen, consult Allan and Allan's solicitor, Abbott. McMullen acquiesced. He would withdraw now. But it was also certain that he would return—that this was the beginning, not the end, of a highly dangerous affair. Macdonald began to make discreet inquiries. From Allan, he learnt that McMullen had already been pressing him for money—a large sum, two hundred and fifty thousand dollars, was mentioned—which would include compensation for the time and thought which the Americans had given to the scheme as well as repayment for the small advances they had made to Allan's political fund.[42] Allan had jibbed indignantly at the preposterous total. The man who had been prepared to squander hundreds of thousands of dollars to ensure his appointment as president of a railway company was now unwilling to risk a smaller amount to save the railway itself from probable disaster. Allan's sudden obstinate parsimony was certainly disquieting. But even if he were prepared to meet the formidable American demands instantly and in full, could he really purchase complete safety by these means alone? Did the Americans merely want money? Or did they want something different and much more sinister? Did they want revenge—on Allan, or on the government itself? Macdonald did not know.

One thing at least was certain. There was no chance that the Americans would let the matter drop. Late in January, the pertinacious McMullen appeared again in the East Block, accompanied this time by two of his associates, Smith and Hurlburt.[43] The same ground was gone over; the same documents were produced; the same protests were made. Macdonald freely admitted the justice of the Americans' grievance. He told them that, if he were in their place, he would certainly take legal action against Sir Hugh. But, beyond this, he would concede nothing. He was not prepared to acknowledge that this was a concern of government; and he had gone so far with the new Pacific railway company that concessions were impossible, even if he had been willing to make them. All he could, and did, suggest was that the Americans see Allan and Abbott and try to reach a friendly arrangement. He bowed his visitors out, his heart full of foreboding. All during February, while he prepared for the new session of Parliament, and reopened negotiations for union with Prince Edward Island, he hoped, hoped desperately, that Allan had made a private settlement with his discarded American friends. The days went by. A reassuring silence descended over the affair. He almost began to regain confidence. And then, towards the end of February, the hard blow fell. A long threatening letter from Charles M. Smith, McMullen's principal associate in Chicago, drove home the brutal facts that no settlement had yet been made, and that the Americans were determined to get satisfaction, not only from Sir Hugh Allan, but also from the government of Canada itself. "Sir Hugh Allan *came to us* . . . ," Smith wrote bluntly. "*We* did not go to him. . . . The government alone had the address of our syndicate, and Sir Hugh's approach could not be viewed by us in courtesy or practically as resting on less than direct authority from the cabinet, and we accepted him as their representative."[44]

Macdonald knew that the end had come. Something must be done and at once. Allan must on no account be permitted to depart for England, in a vain effort to get funds, while this enormous avalanche of disaster hung suspended over their heads. McMullen was expected in a day or two at Montreal; it was probably their last chance to disarm and appease him; and Macdonald wrote hurriedly to Hincks, who was about to leave the ministry and whose home was in Montreal, begging him to bring the principals together immediately and to use all his influence to effect a settlement. Hincks replied at once reassuringly. The matter was in train at last. And three days later, a second letter brought the hoped-for relief. At a dinner in Allan's honour before his departure for England—of all ironical occasions!—Hincks had been secretly informed that an agreement had been reached. "I know no particulars," Hincks went on, "as of course conversation was impossible at the dinner, and I was quite content with the assurance that it was quite satisfactorily arranged."[45]

Macdonald nodded. In one important way, he, too, was "quite content" to know as little as possible about what had been done. As Hincks had said, it was absolutely essential for the government to keep itself clear "of all responsibility for any settlement with M.". Yet, at the same time, Macdonald secretly wished to know the truth. The whole business had been settled with such suspicious rapidity. Was McMullen really satisfied? Were they quit of the affair? He shook his head doubtfully. He feared McMullen. He profoundly distrusted Allan. "*Entre nous,*" he wrote to John Rose, "Allan seems to have lost his head altogether, and has made a series of stupendous blunders with respect to the whole matter, and the company is not yet out of the troubles caused by his imprudence. He is the worst negotiator I ever saw in my life."[46] It was a terrible indictment to have to make of a man to whom he and his country were now committed beyond repair. But the whole history of the railway had been one long, unbroken misfortune. The new board, with its elaborately graduated scale of provincial representation, and its almost complete lack of capital, was a pompous fraud. Everything depended on Allan's success in London; and Allan, as Macdonald knew only too well, was a selfish, unskilful, unreliable man. The railway and the government were far from being out of the woods. Macdonald might yet have to admit the failure of his railway policy; and in Montreal a rumour persistently circulated that the overthrow of the government at the next session was a certainty. Yet, for the moment, there was peace. There were no more frightening visits from McMullen, or threatening letters from C. M. Smith. Allan and Abbott departed for England; and down in Montreal their offices seemed sunk in unaccustomed repose.

Yet—though Macdonald, of course, was unaware of the fact— Abbott's office was not quite so undisturbed as might perhaps have been expected. Sometimes, after six o'clock, when all the clerks had departed for their dinners, the legal establishment of Sir Hugh Allan's solicitor was the scene of activities which an onlooker, if one had been present, would have found it difficult to explain.[47] Two men, one young, one not so young, entered the deserted rooms, moving very unostentatiously indeed. From the fact that the elder of the two had unlocked the outside door with a key, it might have been presumed that he was an employee, perhaps a confidential clerk, of Mr. Abbott's; and this impression would have been strengthened by the sight of the quick, systematic efficiency with which he went about his curious work. He busied himself with Mr. Abbott's files, going rapidly but carefully through the letter books, the shorthand books, the docketed packets of incoming letters and telegrams, while the younger man, who was clearly a subordinate, assisted his superior in the searches in various ways. Then, having tidied everything very carefully, they quietly departed. The younger man went ahead and got a cab. They both got in it and the cab drove away into the darkness.

V

Macdonald was in his place in the House when suddenly, without warning, the vague persistent rumours of impending trouble took the concrete form of an opposition attack. On April 2, Lucius Seth Huntington, member for Shefford in the Province of Quebec, rose in his place and moved the appointment of a select committee of seven persons to inquire into the circumstances surrounding the grant of the Canadian Pacific railway charter to Sir Hugh Allan's company.[48] Huntington was a prominent but not very commanding figure in the opposition, "a man of no great political capacity," Lord Dufferin remarked confidentially to the Colonial Secretary, "but the most agreeable speaker in Canada".[49] It was the supreme moment of Huntington's political career. Two charges, each grave in itself and graver far in combination, supplied the justification for his demand for an investigating committee. He asserted that the Canada Pacific Railway Company, ostensibly a Canadian organization, was in reality financed with American capital; and he further claimed that its president, Sir Hugh Allan, had advanced very large sums of money, including American funds, to the Canadian ministers in aid of their elections and that in return for this they had promised to award the contract for the construction of the railway to his company.

Huntington read the solemn indictment of his resolution aloud very slowly. Then, without any effort whatsoever to substantiate his charges, he sat down. What was his game? Some, including Lord Dufferin, assumed that he was hoping to provoke the ministers to angry protests—to inveigle them into an impromptu debate in which all the advantages would be on the opposition side. But Macdonald was not to be caught so easily. He did not deign to say a word himself; he imposed an absolute silence on his followers. The members were called in, and Huntington's motion, regarded as a vote of want of confidence, was rejected by a majority of thirty-one, which was one of the largest majorities which the government had obtained so far during the session. "This vote was very satisfactory," Macdonald reported to the absent Cartier, "but Council felt that we could not properly allow it to remain in that position. I accordingly, the very next day, gave notice that I would move for a committee. It was fortunate that we took that course, as we found great uneasiness among our friends. . . . It looked so like stifling an inquiry that they were afraid of the consequences to themselves in their constituencies."[50]

On April 8, less than a week after Huntington had first made his charges, Macdonald got up to move the appointment of a select committee of five.[51] Blanchet, McDonald of Pictou, and John Hillyard Cameron, Macdonald's old rival for the leadership of the party, were the three Conservatives elected to it; Blake and Dorion represented the opposition. It was a foregone conclusion that the investigating body should be divided three to two; and, in the House, interest centred more on the committee's powers than on its personnel. The session was already pretty far advanced, and the committee was almost certain to take a good deal of time in its investigation. Should Parliament not try to ensure, in some way, that the inquiry could be continued after the prorogation? And should it not empower this specially important special committee to take evidence on oath? There was no real division of opinion in the House about the desirability of either of these arrangements; but, as Macdonald saw quickly, there were technical difficulties in the way of carrying out either of them.

It was clear on the one hand that committees of the House of Commons could not survive the prorogation of the body that had created them; and, on the other hand, it was not at all certain that the Parliament of Canada was competent to empower parliamentary committees to take evidence on oath. By section eighteen of the British North America Act, the Canadian Senate and House of Commons were granted the privileges, powers and immunities enjoyed by the imperial House of Commons at the time of the union. Unfortunately, in 1867, the British House had not yet seen fit to empower any one of its special committees to take evidence on oath. This circumstance was sufficient to arouse very strong doubts in Macdonald's mind about the competence of the Canadian

Parliament. But others, including John Hillyard Cameron
and several prominent members of the opposition, were very
confident that all would be well. Macdonald yielded, and the
Oaths Bill was rushed through the House with great rapidity.[52]
He had given way here against his better judgment. He was
equally accommodating about the prolongation of the work of
the committee. He offered at the beginning to transform the
committee into a royal commission of inquiry as soon as the
prorogation took place; and when the opposition objected to
this on the ground that it would "at once place the committee
in the hands of the government", he discovered an ingenious
and unobjectionable alternative. Parliament would not be prorogued. It would simply adjourn until some time late in the
summer when the committee was certain to have finished its
investigation. It would then reassemble, in a purely formal
meeting, with the Speaker and a quorum only in attendance, for
the purpose merely of officially receiving the report.[53]

Macdonald was seriously worried. All during the debates on
the committee and its powers, he kept wondering unhappily how
the government could best defend itself. He assumed, of course,
that Huntington's charges were mainly based on the Allan-
McMullen correspondence. McMullen, he knew now, had
accepted the first instalment, twenty-five thousand dollars, of
Allan's blackmail money; but this had not prevented the Chica-
goan from closing another deal with the Liberals for the
same documents only a few weeks later. Macdonald had
doubted the blackmailer McMullen from the moment he had
laid eyes on him; and McMullen had fulfilled all his worst
expectations by double-crossing Allan and himself. The letters
would certainly discredit Sir Hugh. But they would not, he
believed, ruin the government—not, that is, unless they were
supported by other evidence. Had Huntington any further
evidence? Macdonald did not know. The member for Shefford
was in no hurry to disclose his hand to the newly established
committee. And it was only after several weeks' delay that he
suddenly handed in to John Hillyard Cameron, the committee's
chairman, a long list of the witnesses whom he intended to
call. As soon as he saw the list, Macdonald realized that the

investigation was certain to be both comprehensive and search-ing. The problem of the government's defence became more acute than ever. He himself would obviously have to make a detailed and carefully prepared statement of his own part in the whole affair; and if Huntington's witnesses began to be called, and the inquiry got seriously under way, he would have to make it very soon, in self-defence. But how could he possibly commit himself to a formal statement until he knew exactly what the unpredictable and unreliable Allan was going to say? The government's explanation would have to be based on Allan's evidence. Allan must speak first, or he might bungle or betray Macdonald's defence. But he could not speak first, for he was in England. In mere prudence, should not the whole investigation be held up until his return?[54]

Once again, as so often in the past, Macdonald's first impulse, in the face of difficulty or danger, was to seek delay. Delay was almost always useful; in this case, it seemed absolutely essential. And, moreover, it could be justified on the simplest grounds of equity. In the absence of three of the principals involved, the inquiry would necessarily be "partial" and unfair. He decided to demand a postponement on those grounds. In his capacity as one of the principal persons involved in the indictment, he appeared before the committee and made a long statement in defence of the absent Cartier and Abbott, both of whom were Members of Parliament. It was on the basis of this representation that the committee, by a majority of three to two, decided to recommend to the Commons that its proceedings should be adjourned until July 2, by which time, presumably, Cartier and Abbott would have returned. The next day, May 6, when this recommendation came before the House, Macdon-ald supported it vigorously.[55] It was a travesty of justice, he expostulated indignantly, to try men during their absence. The worst criminals in the country, charged with the most heinous crimes, could, as of right, obtain a postponement until they were prepared to meet an indictment. Why should a similar privilege be denied the ministers of the Crown in Canada? If the inquiry were continued now, Cartier and Abbott would not have a chance, until Parliament met next February, to reply to the unrefuted calumnies levied against them.

The House decided to accept the committee's recommendation. The inquiry was adjourned until July 2. But, in the meantime, an effective opening on that date had been rendered very uncertain by still another development. On May 7, Kimberley reported by cable that the law officers of the Crown had given it as their opinion that the Oaths Act was *ultra vires* of the Parliament of Canada.[56] Macdonald had dealt very fairly with his opponents here; he had, on at least two occasions, openly expressed his honest doubts as to the competence of the Canadian Parliament to pass the Oaths Act. And now the unreflecting over-confidence of the opposition had given the game into his hands once again. The imperial government would be obliged, of course, to disallow the Oaths Act. The committee would be unable to carry on the investigation in the way Parliament had clearly intended; and since it would be manifestly unfair to the accused to postpone the whole inquiry until the next session, there was every justification for appointing a royal commission to carry on the work which the committee would be compelled to drop. He had always preferred a royal commission. Now he would get it. Huntington, Dorion, and Blake had been out-generalled once again.

But there was no satisfaction at all in this small tactical success. Details did not matter. What mattered really was that the Pacific enterprise as a whole was a colossal, ruinous failure. If, in spite of all that had happened, Allan had been able to float the railway successfully in the London money market, then something of essential importance would still have been saved. But Macdonald knew now that there was very little hope of solid financial support in England. The news that came from London was gloomy, without relief. John Rose, who busied himself introducing the Canadians to his friends and acquaintances in the City, regarded Allan as "about as bad a negotiator as I have ever met";[57] and Allan himself could do nothing but report the successive refusals of all the important financial houses—Glyns, Barings, and Rothschilds—to have anything whatever to do with the project. Rose, he informed Macdonald sadly, "has uniformly told us that our mission has no chance of success".[58] Macdonald agreed with Rose. The railway in its present form was finished. Any chances that it might have had in London had been effectively killed by the publication in England of the full story of what was already beginning to be called the "Pacific Scandal". The City would have nothing to do with the enterprise. He was beaten.

He was beaten. And he stood alone. On May 20, the cable from Rose announcing Cartier's death reached Ottawa. Sir George had died in London, fighting his disease to the last with the same patient, dogged courage that he had shown in a hundred political encounters. The man whose love for Canada amounted to a blind obsession, who had grasped eagerly, while the strength slipped from him, at every bit of news from the homeland, had gone off on a longer and stranger journey than that which he had hoped and "always purposed" to take to Canada on May 29.[59] The schemes and stratagems which they shared together, the tough battles that they had fought side by side in the House, the long convivial evenings, with Cartier robustly singing his French-Canadian songs, and the endless discussions of the entwined destinies of the two Canadian peoples which had taken shape in the British North America Act and the great experiment of Confederation—they were all ended. They were ended just at the moment when the House was about to accept the terms of union with Prince Edward Island, and when all British North America—with the sole exception of Newfoundland—would be united in a single great Confederation. With almost his last breath, Cartier had given thanks for the completion of union. But now he would never see it. He had gone far too soon. Macdonald could hardly control himself sufficiently to read Rose's cable in the House.[60] He was alone now—for there would never again be anybody like Cartier—alone at a time when the burdens of solitary responsibility seemed heavier than ever. He had not been well since the session commenced. He was overworked, harassed, driven by worries.

It was too much for him. "As a consequence," Lord Dufferin wrote to Kimberley, "for the last few days he has broken through his usual abstemious habits, and been compelled to resort to more stimulants than suit his peculiar temperament. It is really tragical to see so superior a man subject to such a purely physical infirmity, against which he struggles with desperate courage, until fairly prostrated and broken down. . . ."[61] He was down indeed. Cartier's elaborately solemn funeral in Montreal, on June 13, brought the realization of his loneliness home to him with terrible force; and when, a few days later, he arrived in Quebec for the christening of the new Dufferin baby, Victoria Alexandrina Muriel May, he had obviously been drinking heavily again. "Cartier's funeral had been too much for him," Dufferin wrote, "and he was in a very bad way—not at all himself—indeed quite prostrate, but he contrived to pull himself together on the morning of the day he was to appear in church in a most marvellous manner. . . ."[62] He was weary to death of the never-ending labour and distress of office. He vainly tried, he reported to Dufferin, to resign his post on the grounds of ill health and overwork.[63] But it was plain, from the answers of his colleagues, that his retirement would bring about the instant collapse of the already shaken ministry. He squared his shoulders, pulled himself together again, as he had done on the morning of the Dufferin christening, as he had done so many, many times before. He would have to go on.

VI

He moved down to Montreal for the impatiently awaited meeting of the committee investigating the "Pacific Scandal". He wanted to be on the ground. On July 2, the day of the first session in the Montreal Court of Appeals, he wrote to the chairman, John Hillyard Cameron, reminding him that the Oaths Act had been disallowed by the imperial government, and renewing the offer, made on the floor of the House, to issue a royal commission for the continuance of the investigation.[64] He did not, of course, attend the committee's session in the Court House, nor did any member of the government; but it was a public meeting, freely reported, and very soon he knew

all about the debate which had been the chief feature of the
first day's proceedings. The committee had divided sharply on
the question of the course which it ought to take in view of
the imperial disallowance. Cameron, McDonald, and Blanchet
argued that proceedings should be suspended, since the committee was unable to take evidence on oath, as the House had
obviously intended it to do. Blake and Dorion combatted this
view vigorously, demanding that the inquiry be carried on in
the same way in which all such parliamentary inquiries had
been prosecuted in the past.[65] The wrangle lasted all afternoon,
and it was not until the second session, on July 3, that the committee finally decided, by the usual majority of three to two,
that its task must be postponed until Parliament reassembled on
August 13.[66] The chairman then read Macdonald's letter, offering to change the committee into a commission—a commission
which would be required to report to Parliament. But Blake
and Dorion would have nothing to do with this offer, and late
that evening Macdonald received their formal refusals. "I
believe," Blake wrote, "that it would be of evil consequence to
create the precedent of a government issuing a commission of
inquiry into matters of charge against itself, the commissioners
being as they are subject to the direction and control of
the accused."[67]

Macdonald had been checked. But so also had the opposition.
The inquiry was stopped dead. It looked like an interminable
stalemate. But this, as Macdonald knew very well, was not the
fact. In reality, a simple move, as easy as it would be spectacular,
was open for Huntington and his friends to make. They could
publish in the newspapers some of the evidence they had been
prevented from giving to the committee. And this, it now
appeared, was exactly what they intended to do. During the
afternoon of July 3, the rumour began to run rapidly through
Montreal that the Allan letters had been bought from McMullen
for twenty-five thousand dollars and that they would appear
the next morning in the *Herald*. There was not a moment to
lose. That night Macdonald saw Allan and tackled him firmly.
He insisted that, if any seriously damaging evidence appeared
in the press the following day, Allan must make a formal state-

ment "of all the facts as to his relations with the government, the railway, and the elections. . . ."[68] Sir Hugh, who was in no position to refuse, agreed to do so; and Macdonald felt reasonably secure. If, as the report ran, it was the Allan-McMullen correspondence which was to be published the next day, he felt that he could estimate the effect of its appearance fairly accurately, for he knew exactly what the letters contained. Publication would seriously discredit Allan; but it would not ruin the government. There would certainly be damage; but damage might in large measure be repaired by a lengthy statement from Allan with supporting documents.

The next morning, July 4, a great batch of Huntington's evidence was published in the Montreal *Herald* and the Toronto *Globe*. The public rumour and Macdonald's expectation had been quite correct. It was the Allan-McMullen correspondence which was published—nothing more, and, in fact, a little less. The documents were printed in full, but with two very significant exceptions. The two letters which Sir Hugh had written in the autumn of 1872, breaking off all connection with the Americans, were, as Macdonald explained to Dufferin, "most uncandidly omitted". He had never expected such a thumping piece of *suppressio veri* from men like Huntington, Dorion, and Blake. But he saw that manœuvres of this kind, which could easily be exposed, would quickly discredit the opposition; and he was fairly well satisfied with the long account of the whole affair which was prepared for Allan's signature during the course of July 4. "The affidavit," he told Lord Dufferin, "is very skilfully drawn by Abbott. He has made the old gentleman acknowledge on oath that his letters were untrue."[69] It was sad, but it was inevitable. Allan had brought about his own destruction and had seriously endangered others. He was expendable. It was the others whom every effort must be made to save.

On July 5, Allan's sworn statement with supporting evidence was published in the newspapers. It took well, Macdonald was immensely relieved to see. The excitement began at least slightly to subside. "The Huntington matter," he wrote three days later, "has ended in a fizzle as I knew it would do."[70] In part, of course, he was whistling to keep his courage up; but at the same time there were some good reasons for a revival of confidence. The Allan affidavit had proved that the concessions made by Cartier on July 30, 1872, had been revoked at Macdonald's instance, and that the government had compelled Sir Hugh to break with his American associates. This told in Macdonald's favour, while, on the other hand, Blake's and Dorion's refusal to accept the proffered royal commission, and the shameless "editing" of the Allan-McMullen correspondence aroused a good deal of suspicion of the validity of the opposition case. Judgment had not yet been suspended, but the scale was falling less rapidly against Macdonald than it had been.

In these circumstances, his best move was to demonstrate his eagerness to court a full inquiry. The royal commission should be established in the near future and preferably before the meeting of the adjourned session of Parliament on August 13. The meeting of August 13, which had originally been regarded as a most perfunctory occasion, had now, in the light of recent events, acquired a much greater significance. In the House, Macdonald had insisted that, in order to save the member's time and expense, Parliament would meet only *pro forma*, to receive the committee's report. But now there was no report to receive. There was, instead, a mass of highly exciting evidence which the House might like to consider, in part because its own committee had been prevented from doing so. The opposition had already begun to insist that Parliament must not be prorogued on the fatal thirteenth. Macdonald shook his head. The prorogation would take place exactly as had been agreed. But, at the same time, it would never do to give the appearance of stifling inquiry. The royal commission must be launched immediately before, or immediately after, the meeting on the thirteenth. It was over a month away. He was limp with strain and fatigue, the July sun was oppressive, and, after all that had happened, he badly needed a holiday. He stole away to Rivière du Loup, and his modest cottage by the riverside.

He was pleasantly established there when, on July 18, the opposition loosed its second and annihilating thunderbolt. On that day there appeared simultaneously in the Toronto

Globe, the Montreal *Herald*, and the Quebec *l'Evénement*, a fresh and terrible instalment of revelations.[71] There was a long statement by McMullen of his relations with Allan and the government; there was a letter from a Canadian Senator, A. B. Foster, supporting McMullen; and then, in cold black type, there appeared the telegrams which Macdonald and Cartier had sent to Abbott in the last feverish days of August, 1872. "Immediate, private," the damning words stared up at him. "I must have another ten thousand. Will be the last time of calling. Do not fail me. Answer today." How, in the name of God, had the opposition managed to obtain this appalling evidence. Had his own files been rifled? Had Abbott's office been searched during his absence in England? He shook his head in bewilderment. In his worst moments of despondency he had never even dreamed of such a dreadful disclosure. Nothing like this had ever happened to him before. "It is one of those overwhelming misfortunes," he confessed to Lord Dufferin, "that they say every man must meet once in his life. At first it fairly staggered me. . . ."[72] He was more than staggered. He had been felled to the floor. He was down and out.

Yet something must be done. The next day he roused himself and took the train from Rivière du Loup up to Quebec. Alexander Campbell had telegraphed from Montreal, suggesting a meeting of Langevin, Macdonald, and himself in Quebec city; and the three sat down together miserably to consider the disaster that had overtaken them.[73] Campbell, fresh from Montreal, was able to clear up at least one minor but baffling mystery. The theft had taken place in Abbott's office during his absence in England with Allan. George Norris, Abbott's confidential clerk, had rifled his employer's files, copied his employer's private documents, and sold the lot, as a straight commercial transaction, to the Montreal Liberals. It might be possible to persuade Norris to confess, to get him into a court for theft, to expose the despicable methods by which the opposition had acquired its information.[74] He could carry the war into the enemy's country. But what positive defence could be made of his own conduct? Everybody knew that elections were fought with money, large amounts of which could be quite legitimately spent; that throughout the English-speaking world political parties habitually received substantial contributions from their wealthy supporters; and that in Canada, where no party clubs or permanent party organizations existed, these campaign funds had been traditionally distributed by the political leaders. It was all true. There was really no indictable offence here. But, as he knew very well, this was not the crime with which he was charged. His crime was the crime of accepting campaign funds from the very man with whom he was negotiating a contract of major importance in the national interest. And for that, as he and Campbell and Langevin gloomily realized, it was difficult to devise any effective defence. They concocted a "disclaimer" which appeared a few days later in the press. They told themselves that the party must not permit itself to be panicked into a disastrous rout. The government must struggle to keep control of the explosive situation. It would press forward the establishment of the royal commission. It would resist to the last the mounting opposition clamour against prorogation on August 13.

All these measures were the merest palliatives. What confronted him in reality was an unavoidable and immediate political disaster. He could not face it, and for the next few weeks he went completely to pieces. He had been drinking a good deal in Montreal during the early days of July; and now, in a fashion which had become habitual with him in moments of acute tension, he went back to the bottle for escape from this most desperate crisis of his entire career. The days passed drunkenly with the black depression of awakening consciousness alternating with the muddled forgetfulness of stupor. ". . . Sir John A.," Dufferin confided a little later to Kimberley, "has been in a terrible state for some time past."[75] It was only toward the end of July, when the meeting of Parliament was rapidly approaching and the appeals of his friends had become increasingly importunate, that he finally roused himself, got into communication with Dufferin, who was away in the Maritime Provinces on a vice-regal perambulation, and made the necessary arrangements for the appointment of the three royal commissioners. Dufferin, as always, was courteous and sympathetically friendly; but it was plain that he took a very serious view of the situation. He volunteered the suggestion that it would be impossible to prorogue Parliament until the usual time of meeting in the winter, and that an early autumn session was absolutely unavoidable.[76] Moreover—and this was perhaps the most ominous feature of the correspondence—he announced his intention of coming back to Ottawa for the adjourned meeting of August 13. When Macdonald had parted with him in the early summer, it had been agreed that the perfunctory duty on this occasion could be performed by proxy. But no proxy could be adequate in a crisis. And Dufferin was coming back.

The brief spurt of activity was over. The drinking, which had never really stopped, was heavily resumed again. In a few days now he would have to face Parliament and the public in general. The eyes of his enemies, derisive and triumphant, would be fastened on him. He clung desperately to these last moments of respite, of seclusion. In the past, at these times, he had always tried to secrete himself, to "exclude everybody", in Sir Stafford Northcote's phrase; and now, more than ever before, he wanted to be alone, to crawl away and lick his wounds, like a dog that had been beaten and humiliated. Rivière du Loup was a small, smug, gossipy summer colony. He was conscious, everywhere, of prying eyes and sibilant whispers; and one day, when he could bear it no longer, he stole away from his modest farm cottage and took the Grand Trunk Railway train west to Lévis. Nobody knew where he was; the frantic Agnes was ignorant of his condition and his whereabouts. For a few days at least he lay, as Dufferin later informed Kimberley in horrified tones, "*perdu* with a friend in the neighbourhood of Quebec".[77] Finally, the ever-inquisitive members of the opposition got wind of the fact that he was absent from home. An interesting piece of information which might be exploited with advantage! This time mere rumour would do the trick. Early in August they industriously spread about what Dufferin called "a dastardly report" that Macdonald had committed suicide.[78]

VII

On Sunday, August 10, the suicide returned to Ottawa. He had recovered himself once more; but he seemed pale and shaky to some observers, and he waited for Lord Dufferin's arrival with the greatest anxiety. It was not until the morning of Wednesday, the day on which Parliament was to reassemble, that the hurrying Governor reached the capital. Macdonald sought an interview with him as soon as possible. Was there, at this eleventh hour, any danger of a change in the arrangements? Could Dufferin have conceivably been influenced by the rising volume of protest against the prorogation? Macdonald was aware that the opposition leaders had prepared a petition against "any attempt to postpone this inquiry or to remove it from the jurisdiction of the Commons", and that Richard Cartwright, who was in charge of the petition, was claiming the adherence of ten ordinary supporters of government as well as that of the entire Liberal opposition.

The case against any further postponement of the investigation was so strong and so popular that it found some support inside the Conservative Cabinet. But Macdonald stuck firmly to his policy of delay; and, in any case, it was now too late to change Conservative strategy. Only about a third of the Conservative Members of Parliament were in Ottawa; and the opposition had mustered its full strength. Any change in the programme would be absolutely fatal to Macdonald's government; and he presented to Dufferin the unanimous request of the ministry that Parliament should at once be prorogued in accordance with the announcement which had been made in the Commons on the Governor-General's authority.[79]

In the next moment he could have given a great gasp of relief. Dufferin saw no reason why he should not follow the advice of his responsible ministers. He agreed to prorogue. He agreed, it was true, only on condition that Parliament should be reassembled in six to eight weeks; and it was not until a second meeting had been held in the early afternoon, with all the Cabinet ministers present in solemn conclave, that he consented to lengthen the interval to ten weeks, which he might shorten by two if it seemed desirable. There was no need for fear now. The Governor-General's course was decided now, and he played his part magnificently. His extempore reply to Cartwright and the other petitioners was carefully reasoned; he carried out the prorogation with his usual dignity. There was a great protesting uproar in the Commons, and only about thirty-five Members, with Macdonald at their head, followed the Speaker to the Senate.[80] It was a nerve-wracking, exasperating episode. But it was finished. Parliament was prorogued, as he had said it would be; and next day the Royal Commission was issued to Day, Polette, and Gowan. He had about two months—two months in which the Commission could complete the inquiry, in which the popular excitement could subside, in which he could have a real chance to damage the opposition.

On September 4, the Commission opened its investigations in the Parliament Buildings at Ottawa. From then on, until the end of the month, the daily sessions continued. Macdonald was very busy. He had decided that the government, in order to protect its interests, must be represented at every examination; and although other ministers, Campbell and Langevin in particular, gave him some assistance, he carried on most of the cross-examining himself. He was determined, if possible, to drive home the facts that the government had never promised anything more than the presidency to Allan, that it had compelled him in the end to break with his American colleagues, and that the campaign funds which its members had accepted from him differed in no particular from the similar contributions given and received in all British and North American elections. He was eager, also, to expose the peculiarly dirty means by which Huntington and his friends had acquired their evidence. The opposition had trafficked with blackmailers and thieves, and had dealt in stolen goods. If he could only have the opportunity of cross-examining McMullen and Huntington! If they could only persuade or force George Norris, Abbott's confidential clerk, to reveal how the theft of the telegrams had been carried out.

But these hopes were denied. The opposition and its creatures escaped his cross-examination by the simplest of all methods. They stayed away from the inquiry. The morally righteous accusers decided that they did not quite like the idea of confronting the accused. Huntington, asserting that his first duty was to the House of Commons and refusing to recognize "any inferior or exceptional tribunal", declined the Commission's invitation to conduct the examination of the witnesses he had himself listed.[81] G. W. McMullen and Charles M. Smith, though summoned by a special messenger, remained prudently in Chicago; and Senator A. B. Foster, who, Macdonald suspected, had acted as the intermediary for the transfer of the Allan letters from McMullen to the Liberal chiefs, decided, with becoming modesty, that he would avoid the unwelcome publicity of the Commissioners' court. George Norris, as soon as he received the subpœna from the clerk of the Commission, fled with the utmost precipitancy to St. Albans, in Vermont, where he remained hidden for some days.[82] He had been well paid, expected a "government situation" as soon as the opposition got into power, and boasted that, if they did not, there were "lots of Liberals" in Montreal who would look after him handsomely. A detective trailed him all the way down to St. Albans and back again to Montreal. But he snapped his fingers contemptuously at both intimidation and persuasion. He would make no statement; he could not be got before the Commissioners; and Macdonald, on Abbott's regretful advice, decided that there was no use in trying to prosecute him.[83] In the end they had to fall back upon Alfred Cooper, a clerk in the office of J. A. Perkins, who had helped Norris do his copying. It was too late to produce Cooper before the Commissioners, even if it had been desirable to do so. But Cooper came up to Ottawa early in October and gave a long account of the affair as he knew it, which Macdonald thought might be used at the forthcoming meeting of Parliament.[84]

Parliament was to meet on October 23. And now that the Commission had finished its inquiry, Macdonald found himself looking forward to the new session with less apprehension than he would have believed possible two months ago. His doubts and terrors were, of course, by no means stilled. Far back, in some remote part of his consciousness, there remained a

BLACKWASH AND WHITEWASH.

ILLUSTRATING THE RECENT GREAT OPPOSITION SPEECHES, AND THE DOINGS OF THE JOLLY ROYAL COMMISSION.

lingering, gnawing, unappeasable suspicion that the evidence against him was not yet all in—that Cartier might have made some private promise to Allan, or that he himself, in the hectic, muddled days of the August elections of 1872, had sent still another damning telegram, of which he now had no recollection, to Abbott. Yet, after the prolonged inquiry by the Commissioners, this was scarcely a reasonable doubt. The scandal, down to its last minute details, had been exposed to the public. Surely all that could possibly be said against him had been said, and said repeatedly. It was true that the *Globe* and the other Reform newspapers kept denouncing "the eminently unsatisfactory and wretchedly perfunctory" character of the investigation, and threatening in plain terms that as soon as the session opened a new and more efficient parliamentary inquiry would be launched.[85] But neither Macdonald nor his chief, the Governor-General, was very much perturbed by these threats; the chief results of fresh investigation, Dufferin believed, would be the discovery of the "many dirty tricks" of the opposition.[86] The worst was definitely over. The "glorious reaction" which Dufferin had prophesied might even now, Macdonald considered, be setting in in his favour. The Governor-General, who appeared to be obviously sympathetic, had asked him for a personal defence which could be used in letters to England; and on October 9, Macdonald finished a long confidential memorandum on his part in the whole affair. The opening of Parliament was only a fortnight away. He was facing it almost cheerfully. "We shall have a spicy debate and a division on the address," he told Dufferin, "and there I think the matter will rest."[87] Politics, of course, were completely unpredictable; but he did not really believe that his government would be overthrown.

On Sunday, October 19, four days before the meeting of Parliament, he was suddenly and violently jarred out of his equanimity. On the previous Friday, Dufferin had returned from his holiday in Quebec, had met Day and the other Commissioners, and had spent Saturday in a very careful study of their official reports. But nothing in these outwardly formal occurrences had prepared Macdonald for the astounding communication which he received from the Governor-General on

Sunday. The letter began reassuringly. It listed the various charges of which Macdonald had been cleared. But no kindly ending followed. ". . . It is still an indisputable and patent fact," Dufferin went on, "that you and some of your colleagues have been the channels through which extravagant sums of money, derived from a person with whom you were negotiating an arrangement on the part of the Dominion, were distributed throughout the constituencies of Ontario and Quebec, and have been applied to purposes forbidden by the statutes. . . . In acting as you have, I am well convinced that you have only followed a traditional practice and that probably your political opponents have resorted with equal freedom to the same expedients, but as Minister of Justice and the official guardian and protector of the laws, your responsibilities are exceptional and your personal connection with what has passed cannot but fatally affect your position as minister."[88] Macdonald stared at the conclusion of the long sentence. ". . . *fatally affect your position as minister.*" It was true that the disturbing words were followed by warm professions of Dufferin's personal attachment and of his belief in Macdonald's great ability and patriotism. But these assurances, though perfectly genuine no doubt, did not affect the purpose of the letter. The Governor-General was plainly conveying a warning. Did he intend, as final guardian of the constitution, to intervene? And if so, should not he, Macdonald, resign instantly?

The next morning at half past twelve, he faced his chief. It was a curious interview, at once painful and ceremoniously polite, a civilized interview, in which both participants played their parts with exquisite correctness. Dufferin hated the task he had in hand. He had come to have a great respect for his Prime Minister—a more affectionate and less critical respect than perhaps his Prime Minister had for him. The Governor-General's highly complimentary style of address sometimes seemed a little "gushing" to Macdonald; but Dufferin, with his generous, romantic nature, had been almost completely won over by this exceptional colonial, who was so attentive and considerate, whose manners were so ingratiatingly charming, and who, at the same time, seemed so markedly superior to his contemporaries in ability and patriotic spirit. "Sir John is by far the ablest public man in Canada," he told Kimberley within the first year of his governorship, and time did not alter his opinion.[89] He had looked forward with "eager expectation" to Macdonald vindicating himself from the "damnable accusations" of the "Pacific Scandal". He had been only slowly and very reluctantly convinced that there was something decidedly wrong. But once this conclusion had been reached, his high standards of political conduct prompted him to act, as much for Macdonald's sake as for his own. "I had gradually brought myself to the belief," he told Kimberley, "that under certain circumstances it might eventually become my duty to intervene and to prevent the conscience of Parliament and of the country from being forced by the mere brute strength of party spirit."[90] He could not permit his present ministers to retain office by "a vitiated parliamentary majority". This was the reason for the letter and the interview. He wanted to warn Macdonald and reserve future liberty of action for himself.

Macdonald was very agitated. He might have displayed his feelings to Dufferin in some emphatic manner. But what in fact he showed was "great dignity, courtesy, and self control". He did, indeed, reproach Dufferin mildly that this important announcement had been so long delayed; and Dufferin explained that he thought it necessary to wait until he had received his Prime Minister's confidential memorandum, had seen the Commissioners personally, and had had time to study the official evidence. Macdonald accepted the explanation graciously. His first impulse after receiving the communication, he told Dufferin, was to resign. Dufferin replied that his letter had been intended not as a dismissal but as a warning, that he wished to save his Prime Minister humiliation, and that he hoped he would fall by his own hand, not another's. Carefully, as in his letter, he reviewed the situation. It had been proved beyond all question, he admitted, that the government had not had any reprehensible dealings with the Americans, and that it had not corruptly modified the Canadian Pacific railway charter in the interest of Sir Hugh Allan. But there remained Huntington's fourth charge —the charge that Macdonald and other ministers had received very large sums of money from Allan for election purposes; and this, Dufferin pointed out, had been proven and must be admitted. Macdonald could accept the minimum of blame, and beat an honourable retreat. His recovery, if he adopted such a course, even his return to power, might be remarkably swift. He himself, the Governor-General repeated emphatically, had no desire to intervene. He would intervene only if Macdonald persisted in braving out the ordeal, and in the end escape parliamentary censure only by "the skin of his teeth".

The next day, Tuesday, October 21, Macdonald and his Cabinet considered resignation. Early on Wednesday, Alexander Campbell, meeting one of the permanent heads of departments, informed him confidentially that things were "stormy", and added that Sir John was going out again that morning to Rideau Hall to see the Governor-General.[91] Macdonald could not understand the reason for this mysterious second summons. He entered Dufferin's room in some trepidation. But it was plain, from the beginning, that the Governor had a very much more agreeable duty to perform than that which he had carried out two days before. The English mail, he informed Macdonald frankly, had arrived Tuesday night. There were private letters from Kimberley in the diplomatic bag, and in one of these the Colonial Secretary had laid down the general principle that it was the business of the Canadian Parliament to decide whether it wished to withdraw its confidence from the Governor-General's responsible advisers.[92] Dufferin generously admitted that, on the basis of this opinion, he was "more straitened by the voice of Parliament" than he had imagined himself to be. Macdonald might consider the previous letter "as in some degree cancelled, although, of course," the Governor subsequently reported to Kimberley, "I did not in any sense surrender my liberty of action . . ." for the future.[93]

Still, the immediate crisis was over. The ministry must hang on, Macdonald decided, and fight out the storm. He was even confident of the outcome. Dufferin reported that the government was "very cock-a-hoop" at the opening of Parliament on Thursday, October 23; and when, after a brief adjournment to the following Monday, the debate on the address finally began, the Conservatives were described as "jubilant" and confidently predicting a majority of sixteen to eighteen. Macdonald, the Governor-General informed Kimberley, "came up to the scratch fresh and smiling". And for a little while at least, this mood of jocular equanimity lasted. Then a change, an increasingly marked change, became apparent. The strain of the debate began to tell upon Macdonald with unnerving force. He lost a supporter, then another. The majority upon which he had counted was no longer quite so certain; and, worst of all, the Liberal tactics in the debate had become a maddeningly insoluble puzzle to him. Blake, the best speaker on the Reform side, the man who had made himself master of all the intricate complications of the "scandal", had not yet spoken. What could his silence mean? Was he waiting deliberately to speak after his great opponent? What could be the motive behind such a manœuvre? Was Blake in possession of some last damning piece of evidence, some hitherto unrevealed document of a fatally compromising character, which, once Macdonald had made his defence, he would deliver like a knock-out blow to complete the rout of the Conservatives and the ruin of the government? This had been Macdonald's secret fear for months. It came back now with paralysing force. He remembered that, even after the publication of his private telegrams to Abbott, the opposition press had continued to drop hints of "fresh revelations". Had he, during his repeated insobrieties at the time of the August elections, telegraphed another terrible, though forgotten, message to Abbott?[94] Or had Cartier, in his extremity, been forced to make one last private engagement to his insatiable tormentor, Allan?

He kept silence. The debate was wearing him down, steadily demoralizing him with its unrelieved, intolerable tension. But he would not speak. His followers, with frantic and in the end almost angry entreaties, begged him to make his long-awaited statement and bring the debate to a close while there was still a chance of victory. Dufferin believed that if he had spoken in good time and forced an early division on the address, he might have won "by double figures", if not by the majority of eighteen which had been originally predicted. But Macdonald, white and shaky, sat on in silence. His strained eyes seemed fixed, with a curious dull fascination, upon a deadly blow which might yet come and which, in some way, he must try to parry or counter. All the time his majority was steadily dwindling. It sank to eight, then to six, and finally, on Friday, the last day of October, to two. On Friday afternoon, he came again to see the Governor-General. It was obvious that he had been drinking steadily and too much; but he was entirely coherent, and what he had to say was clear and only too startling. He confided to the dismayed Dufferin his fear of the final, crushing revelation which Blake might be holding in reserve.[95] He had no knowledge of the existence of another compromising document, and no notion of what its contents might be. He realized that he was lessening his chances by every hour of delay. Nevertheless he must wait until Blake had spoken. He simply would not dare to precede him.

On Monday, after a week-end for reflection, he seemed stuck in the same obstinate and dangerous inaction. His decision to wait was apparently unaltered. His physical condition was as bad as it had been. He was pale, haggard, blunderingly weak; and the muddled ineffectiveness of his direction, which was in such strange contrast with his usual superb generalship in the House, drove his followers and the Governor-General to despair. ". . . He had a preliminary skirmish with Blake," Dufferin reported to Kimberley, "on a point connected with the presentation of my dispatches to Parliament, in the course of which he said exactly the wrong things, made two or three great blunders, compromised me, and showed to everyone, as his colleague and doctor, Tupper, admitted to me, that he was quite tipsy."[96] It was a deplorable exhibition about which everybody was gossiping freely during the recess for dinner. What was going to happen? At this catastrophic rate, the long agony of the previous week would be very quickly over. The government was drifting steadily towards the rocks, and all the while the unguarded tiller swayed drunkenly from side to side.

Then, as he sat in his place after the House had reassembled that evening, a sudden and tremendous transformation came over Macdonald. He grasped the useless, ruinous folly of further delay. He began to realize, what others had suspected for days, that Blake had held back, not because he had any sensational *coup de grâce* to deliver, but simply because he hoped to unnerve his opponent with delay, and break him down through his own indulgence. Blake had almost succeeded, Macdonald reflected grimly. But he would show Blake that a moral victory was not so easily gained as that. His defence, prepared as much as he ever prepared, or believed in preparing, a speech, was ready in his mind; and he felt returning confidence, like a great masterful wave of water, roaring through his body. The packed House lay spread out round him, the packed galleries soared above his head. They were waiting, waiting for him, and for him alone. They would not be disappointed. He would speak and speak his best. He was on his feet now, his face drawn and white, his body slight and curiously frail. The applause swelled into a roar which maintained itself for long clamorous moments, and then died slowly and utterly away. He could feel the silence of acute physical tension settle like a burden upon the great room. He could see the last laggard member tip-toeing softly to his place, the reporters settling down to their note-books, Lady Dufferin bending eagerly over the railing, and Agnes watching him, her dark features strained with painful expectancy. He wetted his lips in the nervous, involuntary manner that had become habitual with him. Now.

It was nine o'clock.

VIII

"I leave it to this House with every confidence. I am equal to either fortune. I can see past the decision of this House, either for or against me; but whether it be for or against me, I know—and it is no vain boast for me to say so, for even my enemies will admit that I am no boaster—that there does not exist in this country a man who has given more of his time, more of his heart, more of his wealth, or more of his intellect and power, such as they may be, for the good of this Dominion of Canada."[97]

It was over. He had spoken for nearly five hours. The crashing roar of applause, the brief beginning of Blake's reply, the adjournment, the hand-shakings, the fervent congratulations, the pledges of unchanging support—they were all over. It was half past two o'clock, and somehow he was out of the building and driving away over the canal to the house on Chapel Street. At the street corners there were little knots of people talking excitedly. The gas lamps in many houses would burn for a long time yet while families and friends talked over every point in the speech to which they had just listened. At Rideau Hall, the Governor-General was waiting up expectantly when his wife and her guests arrived at three o'clock in the morning; and for two hours, with many dramatic gestures, Lady Dufferin retold the long argument of Macdonald's defence.

Next day, Macdonald was literally ill with fatigue. He came to the afternoon session of the House; but in a very little while he was obliged to retire, and for several hours he lay stretched out, utterly exhausted, on a sofa in one of the committee rooms.[98] He heard hardly anything of Blake's reply; he was only dimly aware of what was going on. But, through the haze of his semi-consciousness, the realization was coming home to him that, in one supremely important way, his speech had been a tremendous success. It had been—whatever its political consequences—a personal triumph, a personal victory. At six o'clock on Monday, he had been, and he knew it, a muddled, irresolute, and uninspiring leader. "Yet three hours afterwards," as Lord Dufferin privately confided to Kimberley, "he rose—pale, haggard, looking as though a feather would knock him down —and electrified the House with this tremendous oration."[99] He had done it again. He had dipped deep into those reserves for which neither he nor anybody else had ever really found the measure. He had recovered himself. He had regained and consolidated that dominion of affection and loyalty which the Canadians were so willing to concede to him. From all over the country the congratulations were pouring in; even the supposedly impartial Rideau Hall was ardently, if privately, partisan. Lady Dufferin wrote to Lady Macdonald, confiding her enthusiasms; and the Governor-General reported that "round the breakfast table at Rideau this morning there was a continuous chorus of admiration from all my English friends".[100]

It had been a personal triumph. But he knew, even as he had made the speech, that he was facing political defeat. He had regained his command. But he could not stop the rout. The defections continued. On Tuesday, he was deserted by two more followers, one of them Donald A. Smith; and on Wednesday, November 5, he and the Cabinet decided that they could no longer hope to win a majority and that they might as well anticipate defeat. That morning he waited on Lord Dufferin to submit the resignation of himself and his colleagues, and the House had barely met at half past three in the afternoon when he rose to announce the results of his interview with the Governor-General. "I have it, therefore," he said, "in charge from His Excellency to state that he has accepted the resignation of the present administration, and I have his authority to state that he has sent for Mr. Mackenzie, the leader of the opposition, to form a government."[101] It was finished. In a few minutes the House was adjourned. In forty-eight hours more or less he would have packed up his personal belongings, said good-bye to his staff, and walked out of the East Block into private life.

His government was defeated and his projected railway had been ruined. Who had won? Not Macpherson and the Interoceanic Railway Company, for their project was involved with Allan's in a common disaster. Not the Liberal party, for it had acquired power for which it was fundamentally unprepared and which it would have to exercise in most unfavourable circumstances. Not Canada as a whole, for its consolidation by means of transcontinental railways had been indefinitely postponed. The real victor was McMullen. It was the directors of the Northern Pacific Railroad, the inevitable rival of the Canadian Pacific, who had alone scored a triumph. They had discredited a Canadian Prime Minister, overthrown a Canadian government, humiliated a great Canadian party. Above all, they had postponed—for how long?—the construction of the railway which could alone defend the Canadian north-west from the economic domination of the United States. British Columbia was still an isolated outpost on the Pacific slope; the empty prairies would have to wait yet for their settlers; and the ridges of the Laurentians, primeval and unconquered, still stretched away, mile after mile, towards the north-west.

Chapter Six

The Forked Road

I

On November 6, the day after the resignation of the government, Macdonald met the Conservative Members of Parliament in caucus.[1] He hoped, if he did not really expect, that the meeting would end in the choice of a new leader. There were all sorts of reasons—cogent, solid, unanswerable reasons—for his own retirement at the moment. He had compounded great mistakes with little ones. He did not know, of course, that so close a friend as Alexander Campbell had been privately declaring that the ministry would not have been defeated "if Sir John A. had kept straight during the past fortnight".[2] But he could see the unspoken criticism of the "dull defensive" tactics of the government in the eyes of many of his followers; and he knew, too, that the miscalculations which he had made during the past two weeks were only a small part of the long and heavy count against him as the future leader of the Liberal-Conservative party. He had led it for nearly twenty years, through countless vicissitudes, and at last into a complete disaster. Around him had inevitably gathered the emotional accretions of two decades of constant struggle—the envy and hatred of his prolonged success, and the stigma and calumny of his final failure. He could never be free from the past, as a young man would be; and the past, with all its fighting, had left him tired. He would be fifty-nine years old in another two months, and he had earned a rest. He faced the long, silent rows of listening Conservatives earnestly. He begged them, for the sake of the country and the party, to choose a younger man.

The caucus refused. With an earnestness equal to his own, the assembled Conservatives insisted that they preferred to fight under his leadership. He could not help but be moved by this unanimous declaration. Even if it had been prompted merely by a generous impulse not to abandon him when he was down, it touched him, and touched him deeply. But, even in that moment of pride and gratitude, he made no permanent engagement. He told the Conservatives that he would continue to lead the party as long as they thought he could be of service; but he obviously thought—and continued to think— that his part was now a purely temporary one. A few days later, at a public dinner, given for himself and some of the other retiring ministers at Russell's Hotel in Ottawa, he returned, with as much frankness as he had shown in caucus, to the subject of his own retirement and the future leadership. "I cannot last much longer," he told his audience bluntly. "You will find young men of your party that you will be proud to follow with the same undeviating constancy that you have followed me. . . . I hope that out of the party to which I belong, there will rise a strong and successful administration. I have no doubt there will, but I hope I will never be a member of any administration again."[8]

He wanted a youthful leader. He wanted a long-term policy for the future. The Liberal-Conservatives had sustained a dreadful humiliation; and within a few months—for a general election was a certainty in the near future—they would indubitably experience a dreadful defeat. In all probability it would be years before the party could recover its self-confidence and regain the esteem and affection of the Canadian people. The last thing it could afford to do, Macdonald insisted—and the caucus agreed with him—was to risk its slowly reviving popularity by an irresponsible, factious course in opposition. "You will find," he told his audience at Russell's Hotel, describing the rôle which the Conservatives had decided to play, "that they will conduct matters differently from the late opposition. . . . You will never find us opposing any measure in the interest of the nation for the sake of opposition. I don't believe our party patience will be taxed, because I think their good measures, like angels' visits, will be few and far between; but if they are few and far between, they will be the more welcome, and we will support them accordingly. So far as I am concerned, that will be no vague promise. I have proved that before."[4]

He had indeed proved it before—during the Macdonald-Sicotte ministry. The pious resolution not to offer "factious opposition" was a highly appropriate pledge for a humiliated party to make. It was an acceptable form of public repentance; but, at the same time, it was probably the wisest decision which the Conservative party could have reached. The Conservatives would do very well to lie low for a while. They needed time to recover from defeat and to reorganize for victory. Time would give them a very necessary breathing-space. Time might also, and very rapidly, involve their opponents in most embarrassing difficulties. Already, in the light of the economic circumstances of the late autumn of 1873, it was possible to argue that if the resignation of the Conservative government was unavoidable, it could hardly have come at a more fortunate moment. The collapse of the "Prussian boom" in Europe during the spring had been followed in late September by an ominous financial crash in New York; and the record of the next two months had been a gloomy tale of financial and industrial failures, slackening trade, and falling prices. Nobody could realize as yet that this was the beginning of the "Great Depression" of the late nineteenth century. But everybody knew by now that Canada, as well as the rest of the western world, could probably expect a period of very hard times. The Conservatives were well out of it. They had troubles enough as it was. The party could not expect to take the offensive for months, and perhaps years, to come. All it could hope to do at the moment was to endure, to survive, and to wait in patience for the future.

Almost immediately, the tribulations began to descend. In December, in a by-election in Toronto, the Canadian public had a first chance to show the weight of its pent-up moral disapproval. The Liberals, with the help of a small group of patriotic, youthful publicists who denounced the corrupt partisanship of Canadian politics and described their own body as "Canada First", captured the riding easily for the Reform candidate, Thomas Moss; and this defeat in single combat foreshadowed with unhappy accuracy the virtual annihilation that was to come in the greater encounter of the following month. In the general election which took place in mid-winter, 1874, the Conservative strength in the House of Commons was reduced to about seventy seats.[5] "We have met the enemy," wrote C. H. Mackintosh of the Ottawa *Citizen* to Macdonald, "and we are theirs."[6] A little group of veterans had alone survived the fleeing disaster of the rout. A solitary square had maintained itself; but it had almost lost its weary and unwilling commanding officer. Macdonald, it was first announced, had won in Kingston over his previous opponent, Carruthers, though by only a trifling majority. The majority did not matter. The victory did. But, to the consternation of the Conservatives, the victory was immediately and sharply challenged. A formal petition, charging bribery and other electoral malpractices, was filed against Macdonald.[7] He might win the seat. But a long and exasperating legal wrangle would have to be fought out before he could prove his claim to it.

For some weeks after the election he was laid up with a bad cold, caught while he was canvassing in the rigours of mid-winter. At Kingston he had presented himself once again as an old man, who would stand faithfully behind the next Liberal-Conservative government but would not become a member of it. The idea of his approaching retirement had been very firmly planted in the minds of his fellow-countrymen; and people, including the Governor-General, were beginning to talk about his career in a retrospective, judicial fashion, as of something which must very soon be brought to a close. "It would be premature to forecast the future," Dufferin wrote cautiously about his late Prime Minister, "but I should be sorry to think that his public career was over. His health, however, is very precarious, otherwise he would be sure to come to the front, as he is certainly the best statesman in Canada. . . ."[8] A regretful, elegiac note sounded unmistakably in this generous estimate. But surely it was appropriate? In the first brief session of the new Parliament, Macdonald played a waiting, unobtrusive, non-committal rôle; and when summer came, he went off to Rivière du Loup for a long holiday, from which the importunate appeals of his followers failed to drag him. He told Tupper that the Conservatives in Toronto were pressing him to come up for a meeting or two, but that he frankly did not feel up to it. "My fighting days are over, I think," he wrote.[9]

A temporary commander, with a badly beaten army at his back, he was in no mood for adventurous forays. At Russell's Hotel he had cautioned his followers against an excess of party spirit; and he continued to keep them strictly and silently upon the defensive, even when, during the summer of 1874, an issue arose in which the national interest was clearly involved, and in which, so he was convinced, the new government was making a serious mistake. The public debate which followed must have seemed certain to tempt him to intervention. The new government—he might have argued—had blundered because it had presumptuously imagined that it could improve upon the concessions which he had wrung from the Americans in the Washington Treaty. The Liberals had always been inclined to explain the surrender of the inshore fisheries for a money payment simply as the natural result of Macdonald's diplomatic weakness and ineptitude. A satisfactory Reciprocity Treaty would have been perfectly possible—with the right negotiators! A Liberal could have obtained it—if only he had had a chance! And since, luckily enough, there was still a chance, for the amount of the money payment had yet to be settled by arbitration, George Brown, a robust and extremely optimistic diplomatist, was sent down to Washington to transmute this give-away sale into a profitable commercial arrangement. Fish, who was still Secretary of State, could hardly have been more uninterested, unco-operative, and unenthusiastic during these new negotiations; and the resulting draft treaty, which was made public during the summer, was really Brown's personal achievement. It provided that the Canadian and American duties on a wide variety of commodities, including manufactured goods as well as raw materials, were to be reduced gradually, by stages, over a period of years. From the point of view of the new industrial Canada, which Macdonald had recognized in the election of

1872, the treaty was highly contentious; and it had no sooner been made public than Canadian manufacturing associations and boards of trade began to criticize it emphatically and in detail.[10]

It seemed an obvious opportunity, particularly for a party which had appropriated the phrase "National Policy" and which had talked so much about incidental protection in the election of 1872. Tupper, sanguine and impetuous as always, was eager to accept speaking engagements and to denounce the treaty in public; but Macdonald hung back cautiously in a prudent reserve. He agreed with Tupper that the agreement was a bad one, which deserved thoroughly to be condemned; but he argued that the popular protest against its terms ought to be permitted to develop freely, irrespective of party, before the Conservatives made any too open attempt to turn it to their own uses. "The Boards of Trade and industrial meetings," he reminded Tupper, "have, without reference to politics, gone against it. Some of the leading Grit newspapers in Ontario are opposed to it. It is causing a decided split in the Grit ranks. The only thing that will heal that split is any attempt of the opposition leaders to make political capital out of it." The Conservatives would do well, he thought, to insist that they would not interpret rejection of the treaty as the defeat of the government. They would benefit themselves as well as the nation in the event. "The opposition would gain greatly by their patriotic course," he reminded Tupper, "and would prove the sincerity of what I said on behalf of the party, that our motto was country first, party afterward. This sown upon the waters would come back to us, and not, I think, after *many* days."[11]

It might have been a patriotic course. It was certainly a cautious, if not a timorous, policy. All during the autumn, the popular criticism of the draft treaty grew sharper, and an occasional Conservative, such as Thomas White of Montreal, sought to make its rejection an objective of the party.[12] But Tupper, who had been assigned the rôle of chief budget critic for the opposition, remained discreetly silent on the subject, as his chief had suggested; and Macdonald, when he discussed the proposed treaty early in the autumn with the Governor-

General, was still in a very "cautious and moderate" frame of mind. He criticized some of the treaty's definitions. He thought the "sliding scale" for the gradual reduction of duties on both sides of the border would operate unfairly on Canada. He seemed to expect that the smaller Canadian manufacturing concerns at least would almost certainly be wiped out. But, the Governor-General noted, his ex-Prime Minister was still in no mood to begin a passionate Canadian nationalistic crusade. "My impression is," Dufferin concluded shrewdly, "that Macdonald is waiting to see whether the opponents of the measure will prove sufficiently strong to make it worth his while to enter into an alliance with them. . . ."[13]

It seemed a chastened and intimidated state of mind, at once uninspired and uninspiring. "Sir John Macdonald and his party," Dufferin wrote to the new Colonial Secretary, Carnarvon, on December 8, "are entirely routed, and nobody expects them to rally during the present Parliament."[14] A year after the resignation of their ministry, the Conservatives had done almost nothing to lift themselves out of the despairing torpor of their repeated reverses; and in November, Macdonald himself met a new and sharply personal humiliation. The long dispute over the contested Kingston election case ended against him and he was unseated. In the new election, which was held the following month, in a subdued, repentant fashion, without speeches, expenditures, or any excitement, he ran again against Carruthers, and was elected.[15] But his majority—lower than it had ever been—was only seventeen! He had escaped by the skin of his teeth. And his prestige, weighed down by a year of misfortunes, had sunk lower than ever before.

He did not appear to care. For the moment he seemed sick of the ceaseless, grinding attrition of politics, and eager to be out of it. His plans for the future had been made long ago. He still kept his house in Ottawa, perhaps because property was hard to sell during the depression, and perhaps because he wanted a quiet place in which to recuperate before beginning the next phase of his existence. But there was no doubt about what the next phase was to be. He was determined to move to Toronto with his family, in the near future, and to take up the

law again where he had dropped it, so many, many years ago.
His law firm had already been transferred to Toronto, in the
wake of its principal client, the Trust and Loan Company; and
the partners—Macdonald himself, Patton, Robert M. Fleming
and Hugh John Macdonald—were now established in the Trust
Company's building, at 25 Toronto Street.[16] Hugh, who had
joined the firm immediately on the completion of his terms
at Osgoode Hall, was now twenty-three years old—a charming,
friendly, warm-hearted young man, with a good deal of his
paternal grandfather's easy-going amiability and something also
of his grandfather's enterprise and independent spirit.[17] Hugh,
Macdonald hoped and expected, would succeed him in due
course as one of the senior partners. The peaceful continuity of
the firm and the family could now be depended upon, and the
move to Toronto was simply a natural incident in a matured plan.
There was a comfortable settled air of finality about the arrangements.

II

Appearances were oddly deceptive. As the year 1875 opened,
the main trend of events appeared to be carrying Macdonald
irrevocably away from public affairs. But beneath the main
trend there was another, subterranean movement, unacknowl-
edged as yet and almost unnoticed, which was dragging him in
exactly the opposite direction. It was not so much that the
Conservatives, encouraged by the appearance of a new and
favourable set of circumstances, were recovering their confidence
and clamouring for more vigorous leadership. It was rather
that the new Liberal government had run at once into difficulties
which deepened its divisions and exposed its weakness in a
fashion that almost invited attack. Everybody knew, of course,
that the Liberals had not won office in the autumn of 1873 by
virtue of their own strength or merit. They had been swept
into power as the only available alternative to a régime which
had been rejected in a great national outburst of revulsion and
shame. The Reform party, in various important ways, was still

an Ontario rather than a Canadian party. In Nova Scotia, its leadership since the defection of Howe had been feeble; and in Quebec its members were now being pursued with undisguised hostility by ultramontane bishops and priests determined upon the extinction of "Liberalism" in all its forms. The party was still in the process of becoming a national organization; and it had taken up the burden of office at a moment when all problems of government would be hideously complicated by the coming of the depression. The completion of Confederation was the great task facing any Canadian government; and in a time of deflation and financial stringency, it was a task which had obviously become more difficult of achievement than ever.

All these facts were interesting. But there was one aspect of the Liberal party's position which interested Macdonald more than any other. A leader himself, he was incurably absorbed in problems of leadership; and for him the problem of the Grit high command had always had an irresistible fascination. He had given years of patient and rewarding study to it. It was a complex problem, of infinite ramifications, for at all times the Reform party had been, not so much a truly national or provincial political organization, as a loose association of separatist groups, of passionately independent individualists, who combined only with difficulty and usually at the tense moments of assault. The Liberals, in fact, had never solved the problem of leadership. Brown had come nearest to it. In those wonderful years from 1854 to 1858, when he had stood at the height of his enormous physical powers and at the triumphant crest of his political confidence, Brown had been a terrific, an almost unexampled, force in Canadian politics. Yet he had failed. He had remained a sectional, not a provincial, leader. He had not succeeded in welding the disparate, intractable elements of Reformism in the Province of Canada into a single efficient fighting machine. And, in Macdonald's opinion, his failure was traceable ultimately to the defects of his own impulsive and undisciplined character. He had spent himself in vain, and he had now retired into the honourable obscurity of the Senate. Alexander Mackenzie, who had succeeded him as leader, had become the First Minister in the new Reform government.

Would Mackenzie, upon whom had devolved the larger problem of creating a national Canadian Reform party, succeed where Brown had failed?

At first sight it looked as if Mackenzie would bring to the task of leadership exactly those moderating, unifying qualities which every other Reform leader, including Brown himself, had so conspicuously lacked. An obviously honest man, sensible, straightforward, caustic and pugnacious in debate, yet not too deeply committed to convictions and antipathies, Mackenzie seemed to combine authority and conciliation in exactly the desired quantities. The slight ageing man, with the wispy fringe of grey beard, the long, bleak, severe Scottish countenance, and the direct, intense blue eyes, could surely be counted upon to command respect and impose order upon his wayward and unruly followers. He was good, stout, serviceable Scotch tweed, which would wear well, stand up to hard usage, and outlast more stylish materials two to one. It ought to have been true; but, unfortunately, it was not. And the real truth, which was quite different, became rapidly apparent to a number of people, including that strategically placed but not entirely impartial observer, Lord Dufferin. "The fear has been gradually growing upon me," he wrote to Lord Carnarvon, "that my Prime Minister is not 'strong enough for the place'. He is honest, industrious, and sensible, but he has very little talent. He possesses neither 'initiative' nor 'ascendancy'."[18] It was a bluntly realistic judgment; but it was not peculiar to the Governor-General. It was held by others. It was even held by Reformers who, Macdonald noticed with delight, made little effort to conceal their opinions. He began to realize that the good old days were back again, that the Liberal party was as hopelessly divided as ever, and that the incompatibilities, jealousies, and antagonisms, to which he was so accustomed, might once again destroy a Reform government.

The new régime had begun badly. The Cabinet which poor Mackenzie had scraped together was a strangely nondescript, unimpressive group of men. Holton was not a member of it. Huntington, the "letter-stealer", at first declined a place; and Dorion, the old leader of the *Rouges*, resigned his office in a few months to become Chief Justice of the Province of Quebec. These were serious defections. But the most strangely dismaying case of all was the case of Edward Blake, the member for South Bruce. Blake, by general agreement, was the ablest of all the Reformers. High-minded, serious, widely read and extremely intelligent, he was everywhere regarded as the greatest asset that the new government possessed. Yet he had resigned his post early in the spring of 1874, after only the briefest of tenures, and just at the moment when J. D. Edgar was sent west with instructions from the Canadian government to negotiate a new agreement with British Columbia for the construction of the Canadian Pacific railway. This first hasty resignation naturally roused some doubts of Blake's fitness for the exacting and thankless tasks of party government in Canada. He suffered from bad health. He found the dull routine of administration a daily exasperation to the spirit. A reserved, sensitive, and temperamental intellectual, he was apt to feel slights keenly, and almost equally apt to hurt others by what was thought to be a distant and supercilious manner. His elaborate arguments and fine-drawn distinctions sometimes bored or puzzled his associates. His adventurously radical opinions were voiced without much apparent concern for the conventional party line. It was suspected that neither George Brown nor Alexander Mackenzie entirely approved of him, and that he repaid the disapproval of these two seniors with a not very good-natured contempt.

From the beginning, Macdonald had had high hopes of Blake. Early in 1874, several months before Blake's resignation, the inner circle of the Conservative party had become complacently aware of Edward's mutinous attitude to the Liberal leaders. "No doubt Blake is not with *us*," Patteson observed with great satisfaction to Macdonald in February, "but it does no harm for people to begin to think that he is. It all goes to undermine their stability."[19] It did indeed. People began to speculate about the warmth of Blake's party loyalty. As soon as he had resigned from the government, they passed quickly from speculations to suspicions. And in October, 1874, these suspicions became certainties. In October Blake delivered at Aurora, Ontario, a notoriously disturbing speech, and at once everybody realized that a serious revolt had broken out inside the Reform party.[20]

Macdonald was apt to regard speeches such as the Aurora speech as mere tedious irrelevancies. But he saw that on this occasion the academic exercise had its point. The address would certainly arouse the deepest antagonism in Alexander Mackenzie and George Brown. It was the speech of a worthy, serious, "progressive" undergraduate, a catch-all for most of the vaguely forward-looking ideas of the time, from Senate reform to proportional representation. It reproduced many of the notions of that other very undergraduate production, the manifesto of the Canadian National Association, the new organization of the young men of Canada First. And—what was of more interest to the *Globe* and its proprietor, George Brown—it seemed in places to reflect the influence of Goldwin Smith, the radical ex-Professor of History at Oxford, the most vehement of all the Manchester anti-colonial theorists, who had recently arrived in Toronto. In England, Smith had criticized the imperial connection from the point of view of the overburdened Mother Country: in Canada he continued the attack from the opposite approach of the colony aspiring to nationhood. He and a number of the young Canada Firsters whom he gathered about him looked hopefully to Blake as the potential leader of their movement for Canadian autonomy. Blake was a nationalist, a legal and constitutional nationalist, deeply concerned about the remaining badges of Canada's subordination to the imperial Parliament and government. But for the other form of nationalism, which emphasized the territorial expansion and integration of the country, he had little more than a parochial Ontario suspicion. He was utterly opposed to any more generous proposals for the appeasement of British Columbia. To Macdonald he must have seemed a "little Canadian"; and both aspects of his little Canadianism—his suspicion of the imperial connection and his fear of transcontinental development—were emphatically revealed in the Aurora speech. The speech would certainly annoy Brown, who twenty years before had painfully eradicated the separatist and republican notions from the great Reform party he was building. It would seriously embarrass Mackenzie, who realized that the pacification of British Columbia was a national duty of first importance.

Macdonald studied Blake and Blake's ideas with curious interest. He gave the ex-Minister, from the moment of his resignation, a separate and specially important place in all his political calculations. He had Blake's influence in mind when he suggested to Tupper that the Conservative party should not make the draft reciprocity treaty the excuse for a frontal attack on the Mackenzie administration. "The Blake section," he observed to Tupper, "would then probably be induced to vote against the treaty and thus kill Brown without killing the government."[21] Blake, Blake's abilities, Blake's prestige, and the importance of Blake's following were all, in Macdonald's opinion, worthy of the most assiduous cultivation. A little carefully tended jealousy was a wonderful solvent in politics. There would be endless opportunities for its encouragement. And one of the first occurred early in the session, when Mackenzie got up unhappily to explain the resignation of his two senior ministers, Dorion and Blake.

Macdonald was in his best jocular mood. He told the House that the government which had gone to the country a year before had been, in effect, a Mackenzie-Blake government. Blake's well-known and much respected abilities had largely ensured the success of the Liberals at the polls. Yet, once the election had been safely won, and the new government solidly established, Blake had inexplicably resigned. Was there not here more than a hint of false pretense? "Everyone knew," Macdonald went on, "what the lawyers termed the principle of 'selling by sample'. The administration goes to the country and asks—'Will you buy this article? Here is an excellent article, and one of the strongest claims of this cloth to the good housewife is that there is a strong fibre in it, coming all the way from South Bruce.' And when the people of this country, believing this to be a good kind of cloth, that would stand sun and wind or anything else, found that fibre drawn from it immediately after purchasing, it seemed, as the honourable member for South Bruce would observe, that the government had been guilty of selling under false pretences, and the people would say 'Here we have pawned off upon us the old brown stuff.'"[22]

III

The clash between the "old brown stuff" and the stout material from South Bruce was a disturbing factor in an otherwise apparently settled state of affairs. It was the one hopeful change that had taken place since the autumn of 1873. It opened up delicious possibilities. But they were possibilities only. Macdonald had no intention of altering the cautious line of conduct which he had laid down for himself and his colleagues in the bleak days following the resignation of his government. He had taken it for granted that his own leadership was merely temporary, and that the Conservative party would do well not to advertise its weakness and incur further odium by following a factious course in Parliament. Here were two good reasons for a prudent, waiting policy. The possibility of a first-rate quarrel between Mackenzie's Reformers and Blake's Liberals was obviously a third. It would never do for the Conservatives to try to exploit this internal division too swiftly. Their premature intervention would, in all probability, merely unite Blake and Mackenzie against the common enemy. No, the apple of discord must be allowed to ripen quietly and without disturbance. The Conservatives must wait.

Macdonald waited through the session of 1875 in an attitude of almost amiable expectation. He spoke less frequently and more briefly than Tupper. When he did speak, it was often upon a subordinate rather than a major aspect of the matter in hand, and what he had to say frequently amounted to little more than a jocular comment upon the conduct of the ministry in general, or a facetious flick at the sensitive relations between Mackenzie and his temperamental and imperious lieutenant, Blake.[23] There were comparatively few subjects that came up during the session which roused him to really determined opposition; and of these the most important was unquestionably the bill for the Supreme Court of Canada, which Fournier, the not very distinguished French Canadian who briefly occupied the post of Minister of Justice, introduced towards the end of the session.

Macdonald was deeply interested in a Canadian Supreme Court. The establishment of a Supreme Court and the assimilation of the laws relating to property and civil rights in the common-law provinces, and the transference of that subject to the powers of the federal Parliament had always remained in his mind as achievements which were absolutely necessary for the completion of the grand scheme of Confederation. He had himself introduced bills for the establishment of a Supreme Court in the sessions of 1869 and 1870;[24] and the speech from the throne which had opened the fatal autumn sessions of 1873 promised yet a third measure for the same purpose. All these efforts had failed. The jealous concern for provincial rights, which awoke with such mysterious suddenness after Confederation, and which was felt and voiced not only by French Canadians but also by representatives of the English-speaking provinces, had held up this whole programme. There was almost no hope that the laws relating to property and civil rights would ever be assimilated; and it began to look for a while as if the establishment of a Supreme Court was also to be indefinitely postponed. But now a reversal of fortune had come. The huge Reform majority, and the sponsorship of Fournier, a French Canadian, would almost certainly ensure the passage of the bill.

It was really Macdonald's bill. It was based upon his drafts of 1869 and 1870; and he gave it his best support in the various stages of its passage through the Commons. There was, in fact, only one feature of the Supreme Court Bill to which he objected, and this feature, strangely enough, had not been present at all in Fournier's measure as originally submitted. It had been first introduced in the debate on the third reading as an amendment, a very belated amendment, which provided that the judgment of the new Supreme Court of Canada was to be final, and that no appeal could be made from it to "any court of appeal established by the Parliament of Great Britain and Ireland, by which appeals or petitions to Her

Majesty in Council may be ordered to be heard, saving any
right which Her Majesty may be graciously pleased to exercise
by virtue of Her Royal Prerogative".[25] As soon as this amendment had been moved by a Liberal member named Irving,
Fournier got up to announce that he would be willing to adopt
it; and his endorsation converted the new clause into an integral
part of the government bill. At once Macdonald's opposition
awoke.

Why was he so disturbed? The proviso at the end of the
Irving amendment—"saving any right which Her Majesty may
be graciously pleased to exercise by virtue of Her Royal Prerogative" might seem, on the face of it, to have saved the appeal
to the sovereign in council unimpaired. This became, in the
end, the correct interpretation. But it was not the interpretation
placed at the time upon the amendment by others as well as by
Macdonald. They assumed that the new clause—the Irving
amendment became clause forty-seven of the Supreme Court
Bill—would stop appeals to British courts in all but a few
extraordinary cases; and their misapprehensions are easily explicable in the light of the great reorganization of the judicial
system which was then being carried forward in the United
Kingdom.[26] In his Judicature Act of 1873, Lord Selborne had
established a great new court of appeal, to which he intended
ultimately to transfer the jurisdiction of the Judicial Committee
of the Privy Council as well as that of the other appeal courts
and of the House of Lords. If, in accordance with these plans,
the new statutory tribunal had become the single and final court
of appeal in the United Kingdom, then clause forty-seven of
the Canadian Supreme Court Act would undoubtedly have
prevented appeals to it. This was what Macdonald feared; but
his fears, which were well founded at the time, turned out in
the end to be groundless. Lord Selborne's original design was
never completed; and the Judicial Committee of the Privy
Council was permitted to retain its historic form and its
ancient jurisdiction.

Legally, the right of appeal to the sovereign in council was
one and indivisible. There could be no real distinction, as
Macdonald and other Canadians had assumed, between ordinary

and special appeals; and, in the end, therefore, the concluding proviso of clause forty-seven ensured the continuance unchanged of the right of petition to the sovereign in council, and the practice of a reference to the Judicial Committee. The fact that the effort of the Mackenzie government to stop appeals had become inoperative as a result of the abandonment of part of the British scheme of judicial reform, was gradually realized in the next twelve months. But it was not realized in March, 1875. Macdonald attacked the Irving amendment in the light of the existing expectations and assumptions. He attacked it vehemently and repeatedly. He was obviously more moved than he had been in any previous debate in the session. He denounced the Irving amendment as "a surprise to the House, and forced upon it with indecent haste".[27] He told the Members bluntly that the amendment would probably ensure the disallowance of the Act by the imperial government, that the objectionable clause would no doubt be regarded in England as an evidence of a growing Canadian impatience with the imperial connection, and that the ultimate result of the adoption of the change might very well be the "severance of the Dominion from the Mother Country". "Those who disliked the colonial connection," he informed the House proudly, "spoke of it as a chain, but it was a golden chain, and he, for one, was proud to wear its fetters."[28]

Emphatic declarations such as this were rare. He could be counted upon to be himself, to speak his mind forcibly on basic issues. But laying down the law about the imperial connection was no real part of the game he had elected to play. His game, as he conceived it, was patiently to await the development of the discord between Mackenzie and Blake, and to promote it inconspicuously, if he could. The Supreme Court Bill was useless for this purpose, for, although Blake had taken little part in the debate on the measure, it was obviously the kind of constitutional advance in national status of which he was certain to approve. It was not here, but in the realm of territorial expansion and economic integration, that the best chance of open disagreement lay. Before the session was out Mackenzie would have to bring down his plan for the pacification of British Columbia; and its terms, Macdonald knew, were certain to be more generous than those which Edgar had been authorized to make in the spring of 1874. The Province had never given the Edgar offer any serious consideration at all. Walkem, the British Columbia Premier, had appealed over the head of the Canadian government to Lord Carnarvon at the Colonial Office; and Carnarvon, accepted reluctantly and not without qualification by Mackenzie as an impartial arbiter in the dispute, proceeded to lay down the terms of a new agreement between the Province and the Dominion.[29] The date for the completion of the Pacific railway was postponed until 1890; but, on the other hand, the federal government was required to prosecute its surveys, to spend at least two million dollars annually on the railway on the mainland of British Columbia, and, in addition, to construct immediately a line from Esquimalt to Nanaimo on Vancouver Island. Mackenzie, hedging slightly in a fashion which seemed oddly at variance with his reputation for simple honesty, accepted these terms, and on March 19 he introduced the Esquimalt-Nanaimo Railway Bill in the House of Commons. The issue was now joined. What would Blake do—Blake who had declared at Aurora that the Edgar terms went to the extreme limit of concession, who had announced that if the British Columbians were determined on secession, he was prepared to let them go?

Macdonald settled down with curious interest to await developments. For a while the domestic Liberal quarrel could hardly have been developed more promisingly. The Reform leaders were behaving like a group of eccentrically individualistic relatives, who, five minutes before giving a formal dinner party, suddenly discover that they have been plunged into a furious family row. Mackenzie and Blake went about their parliamentary affairs with the strained inattention of men who are inwardly torn between the wisdom of a compromise and the luxury of a knock-down fight. As late as the end of March it looked as if Mackenzie were still determined to resist. He had taken his stand upon the principle that the pacification of British Columbia was more important than the pacification of Blake. Would he be able to convince his own party, the

Parliament, and the nation that, in the national interest, he was right? Blake and two other prominent Liberals spoke and voted against the Esquimalt-Nanaimo Bill; but it passed the Commons with relative ease. Mackenzie was almost through his difficulties. And then, when perhaps he least expected it, he was met by a jarring, violent check. At the very last moment, when the session was almost over, the Bill was rejected in the Senate and there was no doubt that Liberal Senators had contributed to its defeat.

Macdonald had taken only the smallest part in the debate. He did not believe in interfering in the disputes of Reform leaders any more than in the quarrels of husbands and wives. He had voted for the Esquimalt-Nanaimo Bill, though most of his followers in the House and the Senate had voted against it. But he was very well aware of the important consequences that might flow from its rejection. On the one hand, the defeat of the Bill might arouse a tragic conflict between British Columbia and the Dominion; but, on the other, it might also bring the promising rift in the Liberal party to a quick conclusion. A real crisis in the life of the new transcontinental Canada could give the Conservatives their best chance of political recovery; but the first instinct of the Liberals, in the face of such a crisis, would almost certainly be to compose their differences. If the Esquimalt and Nanaimo Bill had passed the Senate, Mackenzie might have been emboldened to press forward and defy Blake. But such a course was now difficult, if not impossible. A new agreement with British Columbia was absolutely necessary. Mackenzie would need all the assistance he could get to push it through. He would need the help of the Blake wing. He would almost certainly have to come to terms with Blake; and, only a few weeks later, it was revealed that this was exactly what he had done. On May 19, Blake re-entered the Cabinet as Minister of Justice. The breach in the Liberal ranks was ended. And Macdonald was brought to the unwelcome conclusion that if the Reform government were to break up, it would break up not because of inward divisions, but because of outward attacks. How should Conservative strategy be revived in these circumstances? And how must he settle the problem of the leadership?

IV

That autumn, after another long and peaceful summer at Rivière du Loup, he moved up to Toronto. For the past eighteen months, he had been spending a good deal of time there, but as a guest and lodger, not as a householder; and in the city directory, he was listed discreetly, without specific residence, as "of Ottawa and Toronto". Now at last the definite move was made, and the transplanted Macdonald family established in a house, belonging to T. C. Patteson of the Toronto *Mail*, which stood on the east side of Sherbourne Street, a little north of Carlton Street.[30] It was a long, low, flat-fronted place, built of grey stock brick, with a single gable over the central entrance. The grounds were spacious and gently rolling; Sherbourne Street was only a peaceful sandy lane; and away to the north-east, towards Parliament Street, were open commons where Patteson had exercised his horses. It was comfortable and quiet enough on Sherbourne Street; but Macdonald had taken the house on only a short lease, and he had no intention of staying there permanently. He had his eye on a large property on St. George Street, close to University College, in a suburb which was distinguished, though perhaps not so fashionable as Jarvis Street. The St. George Street house would certainly be a large investment. But was not everything really settled? It was so obviously sensible for him to establish himself in Toronto. His firm had its head office there. He had scores of amusing friends and acquaintances in the city; and one of his old colleagues in the Conservative Cabinet, Charles Tupper, had also moved to Toronto and resumed his medical practice. They were both settling down into a species of comfortable semi-retirement. And why not?

Macdonald was getting on. They were all getting on. He was conscious of his sixty years, of time's increasingly peremp-tory reminders of its passage, of the disappearance of comfortingly familiar circumstances, of the arrival of strange and disturbing problems. "We are all getting old," he told his brother-in-law, Professor Williamson, "and have earned rest."[31] His sister Margaret, Williamson's wife, was seriously unwell that autumn; and he was worried by the prospect of the Williamsons and his sister, Louisa, continuing to live, winter and summer, in the big old farm house, Heathfield, which stood in relative isolation some distance from Kingston. It would be better, he thought, if they would all get "decent lodgings in town" during the winter.[32] He could understand the problems of the ageing, for they were, though he did not always admit it, close to his own. The needs of youth inevitably perplexed him more. Mary, the child of his mature years, made no youthful demands or assertions; but she was the tragic exception to all rules of growth and life. A wheel-chair carried her about; standing, she had to be supported; and every significant development of human childhood came to her with difficulty, imperfectly, or not at all. He fussed over her health, worried about her childish illnesses—about the painful appearance of her new teeth; and on most afternoons, in the still hour before dinner, she waited, in her heart-breaking pose of stiff composure, while he told or read her a story.

At that moment Hugh was also giving him concern. Hugh had been taught a certain independence very early by the odd circumstances of his family's existence; and as a young man he had continued to go his own way with a charming air of easy confidence. He had, it was true, dutifully accepted a place in the Macdonald-Patton firm, first as pupil and then as junior partner; but so long as Macdonald remained in Ottawa and Patton acted as the real authority in the Toronto Street office, this professional connection did not draw the father and son much closer. For years Hugh had had his own lodgings in the city and had been living a busy and agreeable existence as a sought-after bachelor and knowledgeable young man about town. Then, in the autumn of 1875, the Macdonald family arrived at Sherbourne Street. The fact that his son was now a mature man of twenty-five was forcibly borne in upon Macdonald. He became aware that Hugh was a very popular young man who had hosts of friends and knew his way about the city with practised ease. He discovered something else—something much more surprising and dismaying. He discovered that Hugh was engaged to be married.

He did not like the proposed match; and, in his characteristic brief and candid fashion, he told his son so. But it soon became clear that Hugh had not the smallest intention of altering his decision. He was obviously distressed and unhappy, for he was a warm-hearted person who had no wish to cause anybody pain; but it was also obvious that he was determined to live his own life in his own way. He would not give in, and Macdonald equally could not be won over. The atmosphere in the office in the Trust and Loan Company's building became unpleasantly, and then intolerably, strained; and Hugh, who in any case may have already reached the conclusion that it would be better for him to escape from the deep shadow of his father's immediate presence, now announced that he would leave Macdonald and Patton at the beginning of 1876 and start out on his own account. "I hope, too," he wrote at the end of the letter in which he told his father of his decision, "that you know that wherever I may pitch my tent I will always be both ready and willing to do your bidding and will always hold myself in readiness to advance your interests in any way in my power, for although I think you are acting in an unnecessarily harsh manner towards me respecting my engagement, I have no doubt that looking at the matter from your standpoint you are justified in the course you are taking, and I certainly can never forget the numbers of kindnesses done to, and favours conferred upon me, in times past."[33] Hugh was doing his best not to part in anger. But Macdonald was too wounded and annoyed to respond in kind. His note, acknowledging Hugh's letter and accepting his resignation, was curt and cool.[34] Yet, in other circumstances and different moods, he would have been the first to admit that no more frequently repeated, romantically banal situation could exist than the one in which he found himself playing the heavy father at the expense of two devoted and defiant lovers. He was getting on. All this was part of an old and endless process—of the trampling arrival of new generations, of the resigned yet protesting withdrawal of his own seniors, of his contemporaries, and even of himself.

He had said that he was going to go. He had announced, in the most public manner, and with all possible definiteness, that he hoped and expected to retire from public life. But that was two years ago; and he still led the Conservative party. It was true that many people had not yet revoked the sentence of political banishment which they had passed upon him at the time of the Pacific Scandal. It was true that even so close a friend and colleague as Alexander Galt had openly declared, in a letter made public early in September, that he thought the selection of Macdonald as leader of the opposition had been a "grave mistake".[35] Galt, of course, had found it difficult to forget the jealousy and resentment he had felt in 1867; and, within the last few months, he had been seriously displeased once again by his old leader's bland refusal to emulate his own romantic devotion to principle. Alarmed by the increasing political activities of the ultramontane priests in Quebec, Galt had sought to enlist Macdonald's help in a passionate anticlerical crusade. But Macdonald, though sympathetic, had proved extremely wary. Obviously the Conservative party benefited— though how much it would have been difficult to say—from the influence of the ultramontanes. But obviously also the political advantage of the Conservatives was only one of several very good reasons for desiring to prevent a revival of the terrible old issue of the relations of church and state.

"Mind you," Macdonald wrote shrewdly, showing more knowledge of European affairs and Roman Catholic politics than Galt would ever take the trouble to acquire, "ultramontanism depends on the life of two old men, the Pope and Bishop Bourget (in Canada). Now there can be no doubt that there is an agreement between Catholic powers that the next Pope shall not be ultramontane. In fact it is absolutely necessary for Europe that he should be a liberal Catholic, who will cure the split in the church and bring back the old Catholics to the fold."[36] For all these reasons Macdonald had advised patience. Galt, as usual, had found the advice damping to the spirit. It no doubt confirmed his belief in Macdonald's inadequacy.

PITY THE DOMINIE; OR, JOHNNY'S RETURN.

CANADA—" HERE'S OUR JOHNNY FOR YOU AGAIN, MR. MACKENZIE! YOU'LL FIND HIM APT ENOUGH, BUT FRANKLY, SIR, HE'S FULL OF MISCHIEF!"

And, at the first opportunity, he spoke out. Macdonald was wounded by his old colleague's bluntness. Yet had he the right to be hurt, when less than two years ago he had himself been publicly declaring his unfitness for the post of leader?

The truth was that in the autumn of 1875 his position in

Canadian politics in general and the Conservative party in particular had become puzzlingly ambiguous. In November, 1873, he had pleaded with his followers to choose a younger man; but by November, 1875, reference to his own imminent retirement had temporarily ceased. He had come to Toronto, was thinking seriously of buying a large property, and seemed determined to settle down gratefully in the professional and social life of the city. It was all true; but it was also true that in the autumn of 1875 he was appearing in public more frequently and speaking at greater length than anybody would have believed possible two years before. In the previous February, he had written to Dalton McCarthy, the promising young Conservative barrister in Barrie, urging him, in his own interest as well as in that of the party, to run in North Simcoe. "The reaction has certainly set in . . . ," he argued persuasively.[37] Had the events of the last session convinced him that the waiting game he had counselled would have to be drastically and immediately revised? Had he decided that a real offensive must be mounted at once? Had he really changed his purpose? Or was his new activity the result simply of the chance that had brought on several political contests together and plagued him with invitations to speak which he could not well refuse?

Certainly, the by-elections of that autumn aroused unexpected interest. They did more. They encouraged Conservative hopes. A victory in Toronto, a defeat in Montreal—at first sight there might have seemed little to awaken great enthusiasm. But the Conservatives were tremendously exhilarated by the results. It was good merely to break even with the Grits; it was better to win a seat in Toronto, where all three constituencies had gone against them in the last election; and even in Montreal there was some encouragement, for Thomas White's defeat had a curiously heartening epilogue, like a story which at the last moment is given a sudden happy twist. Macdonald went down to Montreal for the dinner given to White, as a kind of consolatory festivity, after the election was over. These dinners to defeated candidates, with their transparent excuses and vainglorious prophecies, were often extremely depressing affairs; but the White dinner was not. Macdonald, in a speech which was more obviously the speech of the evening than even the dinner committee had probably expected, fell upon the Reform party and the record of the Reform administration with the fury of a young recruit and the skill of an old campaigner.[38] No such verbal attack had been heard for years before. Yet what did it portend? Did it mean that Macdonald had now accepted the leadership on a new lease, with a permanent tenure? There were congratulations from many who looked hopefully to the future. There was grudging recognition from a few who could not forgive the inactive, waiting past. Mackenzie Bowell wrote to say that he was very pleased to learn that Macdonald had made the Grits feel that he was not "politically dead" yet. "And I am also glad to know that you have broken a silence which was being misunderstood."[39]

V

Yet how could he break silence effectively? Even if he tacitly accepted a slight extension of his "temporary" leadership, how could he escape from the cautious, defensive, waiting policy which he had followed for two years? He had never been much interested in small affairs, minor mistakes, trifling scandals. He wanted something big. And something big could be found only in the broad lines of Reform administration, in the general policies by which Mackenzie and his colleagues had tried to carry forward the task of building a separate and distinctive nation on the northern half of the North American continent. Mackenzie had certainly failed. At the end of his second year of power his failure was abundantly obvious. His growing unpopularity, his accumulating afflictions, his sheer bad luck were all plain to be seen. Yet Macdonald had to see further than this. He had to discover Mackenzie's positive mistakes. He had to offer alternatives to Mackenzie's mistaken policies. He had to persuade the Canadian people to accept his different version of the national interest. How could he yet be sure where exactly he must strike?

There was one very obvious opening. The simple-minded "little Canadianism" implicit in the amendment to Fournier's Supreme Court Bill would certainly be defended and continued by Fournier's successor, Blake; and here Macdonald decided to hit with all the strength he had. "The cardinal point in our policy is connection with Great Britain," he told the audience at the White dinner in Montreal. "I am a British subject, and British born, and a British subject I hope to die."[40] The British connection was a precious cultural inheritance. But it was also an essential political defence; and beneath the few insignificant remaining forms of the old colonial relationship, there lay the reality of a diplomatic and military alliance by which alone Canada could maintain its separateness and its autonomy on the North American continent. The potential danger to that separateness and autonomy from the United States was still very great. Before the American Civil War, he reminded his listeners at Montreal, Canada had had at least some protection in the mere fact that the southern states were strongly opposed to the annexation of more free northern territory. But now the southern confederacy had been crushed; the last inhibition had been removed from American expansionism; and the whole American people believed, as in an article of faith, in the "Manifest Destiny" of its conquest of the entire continent.

Canada could escape this peril only through the British alliance. Through the British alliance alone Canada could build up its own north-west and consolidate its transcontinental dominions. Alliance! It was the word which he had been using most frequently over the last decade to describe the probable future relationship between the United Kingdom and the country which he had wanted to call the Kingdom of Canada. England, he of course assumed, would still be the "central power" and Canada, as well as Australia, New Zealand, and South Africa, would remain "auxiliary nations". But these auxiliary nations were ceasing to be dependencies; they were becoming associated and allied powers. It would be a great mistake to imagine that their unity could be promoted by giving them representation in the imperial Parliament, or by establishing a new federal legislature for the entire Empire. These were not advances towards the future, but retreats into the past. The auxiliary British nations would be "ranged about a central power", but they would remain "separate nations" nevertheless. At Toronto he spoke of Queen Victoria as the "Queen of Canada".[41] At Montreal he told his listeners that England, Canada and the other auxiliary kingdoms would be united under the same sovereign, owe allegiance to the same crown, and be "bound together by an alliance offensive and defensive".[42]

The alliance would help to ensure the expansion and consolidation of Canada on a transcontinental scale. This was his fundamental objective; it was the end towards which the building of the Canadian Pacific railway was the most important means. And, in the failure of the Liberals to carry the design of a transcontinental railway forward very vigorously, he found the second major opening for his attack against the Mackenzie government. The Pacific Scandal had turned out to be almost too embarrassingly complete a success. It had destroyed the particular railway corporation of which Sir Hugh Allan was the head; but it also seemed, at times, to have ruined the very project of the railway itself. The scheme lay in the splintered pieces of a wreck; and when the Liberals tried to reassemble it, they found themselves embarrassed by the depression, by the quarrel with British Columbia, and by the lukewarm parochialism with which some of their ministers regarded the very idea of a transcontinental Canada. The Mackenzie government could not persuade a new group of capitalists to pick up the scheme where Sir Hugh Allan had dropped it; and, in a time of straitened finances, it could not push the railway forward too energetically as a government work. The best plan that Mackenzie could devise was to build the railway in sections, as revenue permitted, using water and road transport as far as possible meanwhile.

It was hardly a very heroic policy; and Macdonald did not fail to draw the contrast between it and the policy which he himself had been prevented from carrying out. The Conservative plan, he told his Toronto audience, would have peopled the west and kept Canadian business humming even in depression; the Liberal scheme was not really a railway at all; but simply the "pieces" of one.[43] Yet—though nobody in the Reform Cabinet appeared to be properly conscious of the fact—the transcontinental railway was still vitally necessary in the national interest. "Until that road is built to British Columbia and the Pacific," he informed his auditors at the White dinner in Montreal, "this Dominion is a mere geographical expression. . . . Until bound by the iron link, as we have bound Nova Scotia and New Brunswick by the Intercolonial Railway, we are not a Dominion in fact."[44]

Western settlement and the Pacific railway were his first two national policies. Protection to Canadian industry was again becoming the third. During the summer of 1874, when the Brown-Fish draft treaty had revived the whole question of Canadian commercial policy, he had kept silent, torn between his wish to defeat the treaty and his desire to exploit the divisions in the Reform ranks. But early in 1875, before the Canadian Parliament had even tackled the question itself, the Senate of the United States rejected the draft agreement, and it became obvious that the third effort which Canada had made since Confederation to renew the vanished Reciprocity Treaty had failed as completely as its predecessors. There was now no reason to reserve judgment; there was, on the contrary, a real opportunity for the Conservative party to declare itself, for the depression, which during 1875 began to exert its full paralysing force upon the economy, was now arousing among Canadians a passionate interest in the economic future of their country.

Macdonald felt the wind of opinion change and freshen. The public debate on commercial policy, which had begun with the publication of the Brown-Fish draft treaty, was continued in more vehement and angry accents, as Great Britain and the United States began dumping some of their surpluses on the Canadian market, and as the incidence of bankruptcies and the level of unemployment grew. Late in November the Manufacturers Association of Ontario held a special, largely attended meeting to concert efforts for the increase of the tariff;[45] and in January, the Dominion Board of Trade, a conservative body which had hitherto been more influenced by importers than by domestic manufacturers, decided to give its support to a policy of protection.[46] Long before this the Conservative party had definitely committed itself. Macdonald's pronouncements on the subject of commercial policy were more laconic and less emphatic than those made by Tupper and the Conservative candidates in the by-elections in Toronto and Montreal, J. B. Robinson and Thomas White.[47] But there was no doubt at all about his meaning. In Toronto he attacked the first Liberal budget ("It made the fortunes of the railways by the deputations that came down to protest against it") on the ground that its tariff increases imposed heavy additional charges on the consumer without affording corresponding protection to the Canadian manufacturer.[48] At Montreal he reminded his audience that the policy of incidental protection had first been introduced by the Liberal-Conservative government in the Cayley-Galt tariff of 1858-9. The party, he declared, continued to believe that the duties necessary for revenue should be imposed so as to provide incidental protection to the native producer. It was also, he insisted, a matter on which the Conservatives differed essentially from the Grits.[49]

The last point was a crucial one, which he and other Conservatives were becoming increasingly anxious to establish. There was no doubt that the Conservative party was committed to a policy of incidental protection. The only question was whether the Reform party would soon be committed to incidental protection as well. In all previous debates on the subject of commercial policy, the Reformers had certainly opposed protective duties. But now, with the loud and increasingly popular demand for a retaliatory tariff against the United States ringing through the land, they showed some signs of relieving the stiff angularity of their devotion to the principles of free trade and the practice of revenue tariffs. The Reform candidates in the Montreal and Toronto by-elections went furthest in unequivocal declarations of protectionism; but Blake was also revealing a guarded interest in the "home producer";[50] and Mackenzie, who had declared on a visit to Scotland that "the principles of Richard Cobden were the principles of civilization", returned to Canada to announce that his government would consider the wisdom of revising the tariff if the needs of the revenue seemed to require an increase.[51] The hideous possibility that the Reform party, spurred on by the "Protectionist Liberals" in the chief Canadian cities, would shamelessly appropriate the popular demand for protection in its own interest now confronted Macdonald and his outraged Conservatives; and all during that autumn a frantic attempt was made to persuade the electors that the Reform party, despite the eccentric utterances of a few of its members, was really, on its record, a free-trade party, and that nothing could be hoped from it in the present economic crisis. At the White dinner, Macdonald ridiculed the "three economic faces"—free trade at Dundee, incidental protection at Sarnia, full protection at Montreal— which Mackenzie had successively exhibited.[52] Mackenzie would apply any make-up for the sake of votes. The candid record of the Conservatives could alone be trusted.

Yet the Reform party could still falsify these confident predictions. Would it do so? The torturing uncertainty continued all autumn. It lasted into the winter. Tupper believed that the Mackenzie government had come at length to realize the peril of its situation and that it was ready to risk a *coup* to extricate itself.[53] Macdonald heard an incredible story that the administration was about to abandon the Pacific railway completely in order to claim the credit for the millions of savings which would result;[54] and in Montreal, Workman, the new Liberal member who had defeated White, announced, with the greatest possible confidence, that there would be a large increase in duties in the budget which the Finance Minister, Richard Cartwright, would bring down in February.[55] Macdonald and Tupper were convinced that the Liberals had in fact decided to raise the tariff—though Cartwright subsequently and categorically denied that such a decision had ever been taken.

In any case, there was nothing that the Conservatives could do about it. They were already irrevocably committed; and a long article supporting incidental protection appeared in the *Mail* two days before Cartwright's budget speech.[56] Macdonald and Tupper could criticize in detail, but not in principal. The Grits had been too cleverly accommodating for them. The greatest electoral opportunity of the Conservatives had been snatched away.

But had it? As February 25, the day appointed for Cartwright's budget speech, drew closer, the pressure of interested propagandists mounted steadily in Ottawa. A deputation of the "Protectionist Association" arrived from Montreal;[57] another was expected from Toronto. But these extraordinary envoys, these visitors from the outside world, were not the only advocates who worked their hardest to influence the policy of the government. While the industrial lobbyists were being received with formal politeness in government offices, Alfred Jones and the low-tariff Liberal members from Nova Scotia were threatening, in the frank intimacy of caucus, to desert the government. By the morning of February 25, the rumour was general on Parliament Hill that there was disagreement in the Liberal ranks and that the commercial policy of the government had been changed at the instance of the Nova Scotia Reformers.[58] When they walked into the Commons chamber that day, Macdonald and Tupper probably expected nothing more than a small upward increase of duties in the interest of revenue. But, as it turned out, Cartwright had rejected even such advances as these. He took his stand immovably on the existing policy. He told the House very firmly that he regarded "every increase in taxation as a positive evil in itself". "This," he announced with finality, "is no time for experiments."[59]

"This is no time for experiments." Could the Finance Minister have uttered a more inept and provocative sentence? The present was a time of profound depression, a time of unemployment and acute distress, a time when the baffled Canadians were ready to use the fiscal devices which had been so long employed against them, and when the demand for some positive attack upon the miseries of the slump had become a chorus of millions of voices. Macdonald had found his cause. He would overwhelm Mackenzie's government with the national policy of protection. With the national policy he would revenge the humiliation of the Pacific Scandal and reverse the verdict of the election of 1874.

Chapter Seven

The Picnic Grounds of Ontario

I

He took up his new position circumspectly, with an air of cautious reconnaissance. Tupper, who was the first to reply to the budget speech, moved no amendment to Cartwright's resolutions;[1] and it was left to the back-benchers, the protectionist Liberals in particular, to sponsor the first formal protests against the government's fiscal policy. Their intervention, they declared, had been prompted by the failure of the Conservatives to meet the budget with an instant challenge. They begged Macdonald to declare himself; and one of them—Devlin of Montreal Centre—promised that if the leader of the opposition would only put himself at the head of the protectionist movement, he could "catch" the entire parliamentary delegation from Montreal.[2] It was not a very tempting trap; and Macdonald avoided it with genial contempt. "I heard the threat—the dire threat—," he answered jocularly, "that the members from Montreal would go into opposition, and yet I did not see a change in my honourable friend the Premier's countenance. He did not seem to be very much frightened. . . . I thought I could see a smile—a gentle, placid smile—pass at the time over the countenance of my honourable friend who knows his power. My honourable friend from Montreal Centre is like ancient Pistol—he can speak brave words, but like the same ancient Pistol, he can eat the leek. . . . If the government are never displaced until through the aim or accident of my honourable friend from Montreal, they will remain in office much longer than either the wishes of the opposition, or the good of the country require. . . . My honourable friend from Centre Montreal gave me a warning that unless I accept his offer at once, there would be no use in my throwing my net for him. Well, Mr. Speaker, I have caught some queer fish in my time, but I am afraid that my honourable friend—as during the previous session when he sat over in that corner—is too loose a fish for me ever to catch."[3]

The insubordination of the protectionist Liberals was valuable, for it was one more indication of the growing divisions in the Reform party. The support of these rebels might be useful. But he would have them—if he had them at all—on his own terms, not on theirs; and the terms of his proposal were certain to be vaguer and more comprehensive than any they were likely to suggest. He thought their amendments incomplete and partial, for they concentrated on manufactures and neglected agriculture. He promised something more satisfactory; but it was not until March 10—a fortnight after Cartwright's speech had been given—that he formally moved the resolution which became the official opposition amendment. It was most discreetly phrased. The word "protection" was actually used, but no special prominence was given to it. There was no demand for "protective duties", but only a modest and inoffensive request for a "readjustment of the tariff". The resolution criticized the absence in Cartwright's budget of a readjustment which would "not only tend to alleviate the stagnation of business deplored in the gracious speech from the throne, but also afford fitting encouragement and protection to the struggling manufacturers and industries, as well as to the agricultural products of the country."[4]

Macdonald's intention was obvious. He hoped to occupy middle ground, with a view of two different kinds of countryside, and the best of two possible worlds. His resolution combined the not entirely compatible interests of the manufacturer and the primary producer. It sought to reconcile the logically contradictory ideas of revenue and protection. He started with the assumption, which was common to all his contemporaries, that it was impossible to impose income taxes and other forms of direct taxation in a new country like Canada and that in consequence a tariff was the only feasible method of getting revenue. Customs duties, levied at fairly high rates, could alone finance the roads, canals, and railways which were required for the opening up of the country. Public works were essential for Canadian expansion and consolidation at all times; but they had, in times of depression, the additional advantage of providing jobs for the unemployed; and to curtail or postpone such enterprises at such a moment in the interests of "retrenchment" would, Macdonald assured the House, be "a lamentable state of affairs". Money was vitally necessary; and there was only one way in which it could be got. "We must trust to our customs, therefore," he summed up, "as the principal source of our future revenue. Now, what can be more reasonable than to so adjust the tariff for revenue purposes that it will enable us to meet our engagements, and to develop our resources, the duties falling upon the articles we ourselves are capable of producing?"[5]

The "articles we ourselves are capable of producing" were not merely manufactured goods. They were also agricultural products; and one of Macdonald's first tasks was to prove to the Canadian farmer that the policy of "incidental protection" had been designed just as much in his interest as in that of the industrial enterpriser. It was true, of course—and he admitted it freely—that Canada was on an export basis so far as wheat and flour were concerned, and that the prices of these commodities were largely set in the international market at Liverpool. But he insisted that Canadian coarse grains were in another and a quite different category. They could be protected, as they were already protected in the United States; and their protection would give to the Canadian farmer his own local market, while at the same time the protection of manufactures would ensure that market's steady enlargement through the growth of Canadian industry. At the moment, the manufactures of Canada were still in their infancy. The state of the Canadian economy, in fact, corresponded exactly with that hypothetical economic condition in which—so John Stuart Mill had fortunately argued—protecting duties were justifiable. On the one hand, Canada lay open to the dumping of American goods; on the other, the United States was securely guarded against Canadian imports, despite the repeated efforts of the Dominion to negotiate a new trade treaty on mutually advantageous terms. "We are informed in the speech from the throne," Macdonald rounded off his argument by an appeal to the stern facts of the depression, "that there is a stagnation in trade. We are informed also that this has arisen, not from any fault of our own, but in consequence of the depression in trade that has taken place in the neighbouring country. That is the statement which His Excellency the Governor-General was advised by the honourable gentleman opposite to make to this House, and if it be true, I say that if there is ever a time when it is lawful, or allowable, or wise, or expedient for a government to interfere, now is that time."[6]

The issue was joined. "Never since the settlement of the great questions of the Clergy Reserves and Seigniorial Tenure," declared the editor of the Montreal *Gazette*, "have party lines been so distinctly drawn upon a clear and easily understood principle as they have been by these discussions and by the recent vote."[7] Macdonald had taken up a commodiously broad and defensible position; and the Reform government had been edged into cramped quarters, in which there was little ground for manœuvre. It was the biggest and most promising success that the Conservatives scored during the session; but at the same time it was not the only way in which their fortunes were being improved. The unhappy divisions in the Reform party, marked occasionally by the most gratifying outbursts of open quarrelling, still continued. The protectionist Liberals were openly critical of the fiscal policy of the government. Huntington, who had attacked the ultramontanism of the Roman Catholic clergy at a public meeting during the Argenteuil election, was bluntly called to account by Luther Holton, the senior English-speaking Liberal from Quebec, in the debate on the address. "Holton's escapade," Macdonald wrote to Dalton McCarthy, "has finished Mackenzie's government in Quebec, and I think the retention of Huntington in the cabinet must destroy it with the Roman Catholics all through the Dominion."[8]

Prospects were good, but not, as yet, excitingly promising.

Chance had tossed the Conservatives some unexpected favours. "Incidental protection" showed signs of becoming rewardingly popular. But it had not yet definitely proved itself; and, as for the other causes which Macdonald had tried to launch in the previous autumn, there had not, so far, been much profit in them. No new controversial measure, such as the Supreme Court Bill, had appeared to reawaken interest in the problem of the imperial connection. And the issue of the Canadian Pacific railway had become so dangerously complicated that Macdonald and Tupper, in their efforts, at one and the same time, to support the project and criticize the government, began to take refuge in the most contorted arguments. In a time of financial stress and falling revenues, British Columbia, which had captured the imagination of central Canadians a few years before, had now become a tiresome and demanding bore; and the promise to build the transcontinental railway ceased to be regarded as a statesmanlike undertaking and threatened to be damned as an utterly insane commitment. What were the Conservatives to do? They could not disown an engagement to which they had bound the country. Yet they did not want to go on supporting the increasingly costly commitments which the Mackenzie government had accepted in its reluctant and fumbling efforts to satisfy British Columbia. They were caught in a cleft stick. All that Macdonald and Tupper could do was to insist that the Conservative plan, which had been wrecked in the Pacific Scandal, of building the railway through a private commercial company would have been far more successful and far less costly than the piecemeal process of government construction into which Mackenzie had been betrayed. Macdonald believed in the railway. He believed in the pacification of British Columbia. He believed so strongly in the union and integration of the country that he may have found it difficult to criticize Mackenzie's painful but well-intentioned efforts. Perhaps significantly he had little to say on the subject. It was Tupper, more vehement and verbose than usual, who did most of the talking for the Conservatives.

Yet, despite these discouragements, Macdonald's purpose remained settled and firm. He would defeat the Reformers

and restore the Conservatives to office. And after that? Had
he really altered his decision to retire? There were signs,
during the winter and spring, that the plans he had made in
the autumn of 1873 would still be carried out. In April
occurred the death of his elder sister, Margaret, the wife of
Professor Williamson. She had been only eighteen months
older than he; and although during all the long years of his
absence from Kingston, he had been careful to keep equally
in touch with both sisters, Margaret naturally held for him a
special place. They had grown up together, and in the far-off
faded days at Hay Bay and Kingston they had shared games
and small responsibilities, from which the "baby", Louisa, had
of course been excluded. "She is my oldest and sincerest friend,"
he wrote to Williamson, "and has been so through life."[9] And
now she was dead. Should he regard her departure as one
of those reminders, those significant taps on the shoulder,
which time seemed to make so often these days? Would it not
be better for Louisa, and Williamson, and also for himself,
to admit the approach of old age, to change their lives where
it was necessary and still possible, and to give up the tasks and
properties of their prime? In Toronto, he was settling down
into an easy professional existence, as into a well upholstered
arm-chair. The new house on St. George Street, in its pleasant
rural and academic setting, with University College nearby and
the open countryside to the north and west, was at last nearly
ready for occupation. A swarm of carpenters and painters had
invaded the building and every day Agnes went up the
muddy road to mark their progress.[10] By May, he hoped, the
place would be ready for them.

Spring came, the removal was accomplished, the morning
and evening journey between St. George Street and Toronto
Street became the steady habit appropriate to the householder
and the professional man. But he could not settle down. He
did not want to settle down. The newspapers, with increasing
interest, continued to debate the merits of "incidental protection"; and, as spring waxed into summer, the first real tests of
the popularity of the new Conservative commercial policy drew
rapidly closer. By-elections were scheduled for the two con-

stituencies of North and South Ontario in the first week in July; and the Gibbs brothers were the Conservative candidates in the two ridings. The party had a new policy. But it needed a new device, a new method of presentation, which would be as fresh, as striking, as irresistibly attractive as the substance of the new policy itself. And by good luck, and at almost the last moment, the device was discovered. One hot day in June, a small deputation of the Toronto Liberal-Conservative Association presented itself in Macdonald's office. They were planning, in collaboration with the Conservatives of North Ontario, to hold a political picnic at Uxbridge, on July 1, the ninth anniversary of Confederation. Would Macdonald consent to come and address the crowd?

II

On Saturday, July 1, at half past eight in the morning, a special train of the Toronto and Nipissing Railway pulled out from the Berkeley Street Station for Uxbridge.[11] It was definitely not one of the most certain days of summer. The horizon was doubtfully smudged with clouds; but the possible unpleasantness of the weather had not apparently affected the popularity of the excursion in the slightest. There were between three and four hundred Liberal-Conservative picnickers and their ladies in the train; and the special carriage at the end, with its deep rose carpet and walnut fittings and furniture, was agreeably crowded with a little group of the more prominent guests. Macdonald and Agnes were there; so was John Beverley Robinson, the new Conservative member for Toronto West; and so were the various dignitaries of the Toronto Liberal-Conservative Association. Charles Tupper and William McDougall, who had been campaigning in Ontario South, were not of the company. But they had planned to drive north over the country roads, and it was expected that they would arrive in time for the picnic.

It was eleven o'clock when the train reached Uxbridge. During the last hour of the journey the sky had become perceptibly more threatening, and shortly after the arrival a little light rain fell. This was certainly discouraging, it promised badly for the main events of the afternoon; but it did not spoil the roaring enthusiasm of Macdonald's reception. Two brass bands—one had come up from Markham—crashed into a march tune, and before the station platform was a wide semi-circle of waiting and applauding people. The president of the Liberal-Conservative Association of Ontario North read an address of welcome; Macdonald replied gracefully for himself and the other guests; and then they all got into carriages, and the procession, with the bands at its head, moved slowly through the streets under triumphal arches, which shouted "welcome" and promised "victory". It was over half an hour before they reached the grove at the other side of the village, called Elgin Park, where the picnic was to be held. There, under the tall elms, long tables, crisp with newly-ironed cloths, had been laid out for those serious picnickers who, despite the weather, had come determined to lunch in a genteel fashion *al fresco* rather than in the steaming dining-rooms of the hotels. The tables were loaded with all the "substantials" and "delicacies" of a hearty meal—with plates of cold sliced chicken, ornamented tongues, hams in aspic, Milan soufflés, red mounds of strawberries, elaborate moulds of flummery and charlotte russe, tipsy cakes, pound cakes, piles of tea- and cheese- cakes, great misted jugs of iced lemonade and raspberry cordial, and clusters of bottles of wine.

It was high noon. Before the speeches—the main event of the occasion—were scheduled to begin, there was to be a luncheon interval of at least an hour. And, as the fickle sky gleamed and gloomed capriciously overhead, Macdonald lunched, and passed from table to table, and threaded his way from group to group, and gossiped, shook hands, acknowledged introductions, and welcomed uproarious salutes. These were the Canadians. They had come in an amiable holiday mood, to relax and chatter, to see each other, but, above all, to see him. They had dressed themselves in their best, for a memorable occasion, at once serious and entertaining; and they greeted him with a curious mixture of awe, as for a reigning monarch, and joyous familiarity, as for a beloved friend. It was a slice of the community, a cross-section of the nation, a sample of town and village and countryside.

They were all there—from the elegant young barrister, with his brocaded waistcoat and fashionably checked trousers, who had come out in the train from Toronto, to the thick-set, bearded farmer from Greenbank or Blackwater in his sagging "best" black coat and rusty top hat. Here was the wife of the harness-maker at Port Perry, in her snuff-coloured taffeta gown, with the bustle and the golden-brown satin trimming, made at home by the visiting dress-maker, on the "Little Wanzer" sewing-machine; and there was the banker's lady, expertly fitted in the "tied-back" dress that had been made for her in Toronto or London, in all the modishness of smoked pearl buttons, pleats and bows and laces, dagged edges and chenille fringe. Macdonald met them all. He shook hands with boys in wide-brimmed boater hats, and knickerbockers, and long black stockings, who were led up to him, blushing with embarrassment. He greeted little girls in two-piece taffeta costumes with miniature bows and fringes that were virtually replicas of mamma's. He bent graciously over babies in long elaborately embroidered gowns. He had a word for almost everybody. He knew so many names, remembered so many faces, recalled so many circumstances that usually, in the flashing second of a greeting, the entire form of his interlocutor's existence would miraculously take shape in his mind. He knew the Canadians better than anybody had ever known them before—and better than anybody would ever know them again.

By this time it was after half past one. He climbed the fresh pine steps of the temporary platform, crowded already with speakers, officials, and their ladies. Before him was a crowd of several thousand people—good-humoured, expectant people, who reclined on the grass, or sat on the insufficiently numerous chairs which the Conservative Association had provided, and waited for the instruction and the entertainment of the afternoon. There were several acres of hats—silk top hats, small, close-fitting feminine hats with feathers draped modishly between the curls and ringlets, old-fashioned brightly coloured sun-bonnets, curly bowlers, straw boaters, and here and there, like other enormously expanded hats, provident umbrellas and fringed pink parasols. As he watched the crowd and listened to the long succession of introductory speeches, Macdonald glanced occasionally and surreptitiously up at the grey uncertain sky. But Tupper, whose voice was hoarse with previous efforts, spoke very briefly; and McDougall, who was well aware that his speech could be only a curtain-raiser, was almost equally short. A few drops of rain had fallen, but that was all. The shower still held off relentingly when Macdonald got up to speak.

He was at his best—easy, conversational, discursive. He made some jokes. He told a few stories. He accepted occasional interruptions readily, as if they had been expected cues. His plan—if he had one—seemed infinitely flexible, his manner amiable and rambling. Yet, hidden beneath the jocular good humour of the speech was a clear and aggressive purpose. Every word was designed to put the Liberals upon the defensive. The Liberals, he told his listeners, were still harping upon the extinct issue of the Pacific Scandal, with the obvious purpose of disguising the simple fact that it was their government that was on trial. The weakness and ineptitude of the Mackenzie administration had been exposed by many tests. But its incapacity had been revealed above all by the challenge of the depression; and the mere presence of a few protectionists among the Reformers should not obscure the government's refusal to accept its economic responsibilities. "The great question now before the country," Macdonald insisted, "was as to the best means to relieve it of the existing commercial depression. And there was no use looking to Mr. Mackenzie because he was a free trader . . . and there was not the slightest use in voting for a man who said he was a protectionist unless he said he would vote to put down a government which was opposed to protection."[12]

As they drove back to Toronto in the "cars" through the long summer evening, Macdonald could feel agreeably satisfied. A smart shower of rain had come down after his own speech was finished; but the spectators, instead of bolting for cover, had stayed for the end of the proceedings. The picnic had been an unqualified social success. But—what was far more important —it had also been a huge political triumph, as the by-elections of July 5 quickly demonstrated. In South Wellington, where the Conservatives had backed a man whose protectionist principles were more certain than his party loyalty, the Reformers won; but in the Ontarios, T. N. and W. H. Gibbs were triumphantly elected. That night Macdonald went down to the United Empire Club, a club which had been founded as a Conservative counterpoise to the National Club of the Canada Firsters and Blake Liberals, and which on Wednesday was gay with lights and riotous with celebrations. "Were there ever such victories as those of N. & S. Ontario?" he wrote excitedly to Tupper two days later. "Our friends write me that W. H. owes his triumph to the Uxbridge picnic. There was a gain of eighty votes in Uxbridge alone. . . . The enthusiasm here on Wednesday night was intense. The U.E. club looked magnificent, illuminated as it was from 'turret to foundation stone'. . . . The Grits by some accident selected yesterday, the day after these elections, for a great convention for organizing. They are thoroughly alarmed by our successes, and met by G. B.'s summons. Never did a more downcast set of men meet together, jeered and laughed at as they went about the streets."[13]

It was exaggeration, of course. But it was very nearly true. Everywhere there was a sudden sharp realization that fortune, who was always unpredictable and who for a long time had been bafflingly unrevealing, had at length and decisively made up her mind. Macdonald had found his theme—the relief of the depression through a change in fiscal policy. He had discovered his method—the political picnic. All over the province, the Liberal-Conservatives were suddenly alerted, like soldiers who had been roused to action or jobless men fired by the prospect of employment. For over two years they had been sunk in apathetic discouragement. Now they were aroused and hopeful. They had a cause and a way of promoting it. Of course there had been political picnics before; but they had been local, isolated, occasional affairs, completely without general significance. The Uxbridge picnic was different. It inspired imitations throughout the province. It was the first of a long procession. On July 27, there was a picnic at Colborne, in Northumberland county; and Macdonald spoke to a huge crowd of over five thousand which had come from Belleville, Port Hope, and Cobourg.[14] On August 9, he was at Guelph and Fergus; on August 23, at St. Catharines; and a week later, on August 30, at Milton, in Halton county.[15] The picnics were becoming general, regular, frequent. They had become at once a grand circuit of entertainment and a network of musters of the Conservative clans.

The sixth picnic was at Woodstock and Ingersoll.[16] Five miles east of Woodstock, on the Governor's Road, was the village of Eastwood; and here, set in its own finely wooded park, stood Vansittart House, the comfortable red-brick country house with the tremendously thick walls and double windows which T. C. Patteson had recently acquired. Macdonald and Agnes were guests of the Pattesons for the occasion; and Patteson drove over to Woodstock in the stylish imported phaeton which he had purchased from Sir Allan MacNab's estate to bring Tupper, McDougall and the Gibbses back to Vansittart House for dinner. Macdonald drank large quantities of wine and became noisily jovial during the evening. His high spirits had been constant all during the summer. So far the picnics had drawn big crowds and awakened enormous enthusiasm. And he had no doubt that next day's affair would be fully up to the established standard of success. He was not disappointed. On Wednesday, September 6, a long procession, composed of every conceivable kind of vehicle—victorias, barouches, landaus, phaetons, buggies, surreys, democrats and spring waggons—moved slowly forward, encouraged by the blaring music of four brass bands, down the road which led from Woodstock to Ingersoll, where the speeches were to be given.

The climax of the whole series of picnics came less than a week later at Belleville.[17] The Reformers, realizing at length that jeers were hardly a satisfactory retort to these social successes of the Conservatives, began a competing series of Liberal picnics; Mackenzie, Blake, and Cartwright fired fusil-

lades of denunciations and challenges from their summer plat-
forms at Macdonald; and, as the speeches followed every few
days or every week at least, the picnic grounds of Ontario
became a kind of vast provincial debating hall in which the
accusations and rejoinders followed each other with much of
the rapidity, and with all of the appositeness and sharpness, that
would have ruled in a single debate. Each side struggled
harder and harder, as the season declined and the end of
September approached, to outdo the other in the size of its
crowds, the splendour of its arrangements, and the fighting
quality of its speeches. Undoubtedly the climax of the Conservative efforts came at Belleville. There were supposed to
have been nearly fifteen thousand people there on September
12; and, although Reform editors could very easily discount this
huge total as outrageous Conservative exaggeration, the plain
fact remained that a vast crowd—larger than any that Belleville had seen since the Prince of Wales's visit over fifteen years
before—had been at the fair grounds that September afternoon. Macdonald was elated. And one of the most welcome
sources of his satisfaction was a letter of congratulation from
Hugh. Hugh had married and had moved back to his favourite
Kingston to practise law. But he had also resumed his old
affectionate correspondence with his father as if the break of
the previous autumn had never occurred.[18]

September saw the end of the picnics. Macdonald settled gratefully down for the first autumn and winter of life in
the new house on St. George Street. He could relax and take
stock. The picnics had proved the power and popularity of
his new policy of economic nationalism; and they had awakened
and reanimated Conservatives throughout the entire province.
They had done all this. But had they not done something
else—something a good deal less eagerly acceptable—as well?
Had they not enabled the Liberal-Conservatives of Ontario to
reclaim John A. Macdonald as their political leader? In
the first of his summer speeches, he had made a few guarded,
indirect allusions to his age and the need of fresh, young blood
in the leadership of the party; but as the season went on, and
competition developed and he warmed to his work, these hints

grew less frequent. The end of the summer's campaign found him in a state of hope and well-being such as he had not known for years; and when Lord Dufferin came up to Toronto in January to deliver some speeches, he told the Governor of his exuberant good health.[19] Yet could he really lead the party again? Could he take up the burden of office again, even if only for a brief while, so as to superintend the installation of the Conservatives in power once more? In January, 1877, he became sixty-two years old. He was very nearly an old man now. He did not feel old—far from it. But the fact of his age was there. And it had been driven home to him recently with frightful force by the death of the man who was almost his exact contemporary, John Hillyard Cameron.

Cameron's death was tragic in its suddenness, as his life had been tragic in its prolonged misfortune and struggle.[20] He had spent himself in a vain effort to carry the load of obligation which he had incurred twenty years before, in the depression of 1857; and now, with some of his debts still unpaid and his family in serious trouble, he was dead.[21] Significantly, ominously, he was dead. And he was not the first of Macdonald's contemporaries to go. There was nobody but Macdonald left of all that little group of Conservatives who had gathered about "Sweet William" Draper during the troubled 1840's. William Boulton, "University Bill" as the *Globe* had once called him, had died less than three years before; but Sherwood, the arrogant, intriguing Sherwood, was over twenty years in his grave. They had both been a part of Macdonald's life; but of them all, Cameron had paralleled his own career most closely. He remembered Cameron, the prosperous and hospitable host of "The Meadows" in the brave years before the crash of his fortunes. He recalled how the kindly Rose Cameron had looked after Hugh on the days when Isabella lay utterly prostrated in the rooms in Wellington Place. He could see this, and he could see far beyond this, and back into the shadowy spaces of Owen McDougall's shop on Store Street, where John Cruickshank had opened his school for "classical and general education" nearly fifty years ago. He could see the crowded room, and the desks, and the forms, and the children, and

Cameron and himself—big boys then, and promising—sitting in lordly pre-eminence.

Cameron was gone now. But once he and Cameron had competed for Draper's approval; and Draper, after having examined their credentials, had appointed them his joint heirs. Was it not time for Macdonald to begin to consider the problem of his own successor? For some time he had been regarding young Dalton McCarthy, the Barrie lawyer, with a favourable eye, with exactly the kind of benevolently appraising eye that Draper had once turned upon himself. He had been pressing McCarthy, in a flattering fashion, to enter politics. "We in the opposition are in want of a legal man of good debating power," he had written McCarthy as far back as February, 1875, "and you would have an opportunity of securing at once a status in Parliament which you may never have again."[22] Nearly two years later, in December, 1876, the Cardwell constituency became vacant, and McCarthy agreed to contest the seat. It was regarded as a relatively safe riding; but Macdonald flung all his influence behind the candidate; and Tupper—whom he regarded as "unequalled on the stump"—went up to Cardwell to give McCarthy the benefit of his energy and experience in the campaign.[23] McCarthy was elected. McCarthy, Macdonald was convinced, had patriotism and genuine ability. And in a few years, if the Conservatives were returned to power, he might be able to lay a convincing claim to office. Yet, in the politics of the moment, these were still distant possibilities. McCarthy had yet to prove himself. And if Macdonald could persuade his followers to let him resign—and could steel himself to insist on resignation—he would need a veteran as his immediate successor. There could be no real doubt who the veteran should be. Charles Tupper would be his successor, once the Mackenzie government was overthrown and the Conservatives were back in power once more. The defeat of the Reformers, Macdonald privately decided, was something which he must accomplish himself. He must reverse the verdict of the election of 1874, as the last act of his political life. Then he could retire.

III

The Conservatives came down to Ottawa for the session of 1877 with all the superabundant confidence of a football team which has won every game in the series, or a theatrical company fresh from a successful tour in the provinces. It was a lively, argumentative, acrimonious session, crowded with accusations, revelations, scandals, and all kinds of excitement. Ever since Huntington had read his notorious resolutions in the spring of 1873, the Conservatives had burned to revenge the humiliation of the Pacific Scandal. They had almost come to believe that a victory over the Reformers would be incomplete unless it were accompanied by the discovery of a scandal among the Liberals as appalling—or nearly so—as that which had caused their own ruin. They waited with breathless eagerness for a real opportunity for moral denunciation, and in the session of 1877 they thought that they had at last discovered it. They demanded a variety of parliamentary investigations into the letting of government contracts and the uses of government patronage. They made charges against a number of prominent Liberals, including the Speaker. The Reformers ought to have been intimidated and silenced by these awful revelations. But they were not. Yelling *"tu quoque"*, they rushed forward, their faces red with righteous indignation, and laid new and similar charges against the Conservatives. They were even successful in putting Macdonald into a fresh state of embarrassment by revealing the very awkward fact that he had kept some formal control, for two years after he had left office, over a fairly large balance of secret service money.[24] He was obliged to refund a sum which had been paid out from this balance, on a claim preferred by Alexander Campbell. It was all deplorable; and the Governor-General wrinkled his nose in fastidious disgust. "It has been a very unsatisfactory session," he told Carnarvon, "the two parties bespattering each other with mud in view of the dissolution two years hence."[25]

The dishonours were even. Yet somehow Conservative prestige stood higher. Conservative purpose seemed firmer, though on both sides there was unhappy perplexity about a few great questions of national policy. The problem of the Pacific railway had divided and weakened the Liberals; but Macdonald did not dare to challenge his opponents directly and unequivocally upon the subject. He had told the audience at the picnic at Ingersoll that he did not believe British Columbia would secede; he was sure, he said, "that so strong was the feeling of the people that at the next general election they would show that the desire of the eastern provinces was to keep faith with their fellow countrymen in the west."[26] Yet he had privately informed Dufferin that, in his opinion, the famous "taxation resolution" which had been passed at the time when Parliament accepted the terms of union with British Columbia, was a gloss upon the original contract which effectively limited Canada's resulting financial obligations;[27] and in the House he made no appeal whatever for the sacrifices necessary to satisfy British Columbia. On the whole, he maintained an unrevealing silence on the subject. But his taciturnity and Tupper's garrulously involved arguments were not ineffective, from a political point of view. The Conservative criticism of government railway policy, while not aggressive enough to arouse the suspicions of central Canada, was at least sufficient to win the devotion of British Columbia. "I do not think," J. H. Gray wrote to Macdonald from Victoria, "that the people here regretted when your administration fell, because rightly or wrongly they thought they had been trifled with, but if the present one were to fall, there would be shouts of triumph and bonfires, because they believe they have been *tramped* on, *slighted*, and *deceived*."[28]

These, however, were minor triumphs. The new policy of "incidental protection" was certainly the biggest Conservative success. Macdonald had laid down propositions so broad that they could be attacked only with great difficulty. He had hoped to profit from his own flexible moderation. But he had scarcely expected to gain an additional and perhaps even more important advantage from the extreme rigidity of his opponents. Yet so it was. As Conservative policy grew more broadly accommodating, Cartwright's budgets became more narrowly doctrinaire. In 1877, he announced two new excise duties on the production of Canadian malt and beer; and the only important increase which he proposed in the tariff was a small additional specific duty on the import of tea—which, of course, the Canadians could not produce.[29] It was exactly the kind of duty in which free-traders most delighted; it could not have followed free-trade principles more undeviatingly, Macdonald claimed, even if it "had been drawn by the most rabid free-trader, the most fanatical admirer of what Carlyle called the 'dismal science'".[30] It began to look as if the Reformers had chosen the inappropriate moment of the depression to acquire the fervour and dogmatism of converts to a new religion. They had declared for *laissez-faire* at a moment when Macdonald could denounce *laissez-faire* as criminal apathy. He could stigmatize the Reformers as "flies on the wheel", who believed that economic remedies were useless and who had no remedial measures to propose. He himself had put forward a possible remedy—a remedy which was fortified by a strong infusion of nationalism. He had told his audiences at the picnics that he believed in "Canada for the Canadians". He appealed at once to their growing consciousness of national unity and their frustrated desire for economic relief.

As the session ended Macdonald was in the best of spirits. In its headlong career onward, the party had been suddenly tripped up on more than one occasion during the past session; but on each occasion also it had recovered itself quickly and pressed on. The Conservatives knew that they had got the Reformers on the run. They were aware that in the popular imagination of the Canadians the Liberal party had become the hunted and they themselves the pack in full cry. The Governor-General, watching the political chances of the future with a speculative eye, shared the common belief in the decline of the Liberals. "They have certainly lost ground at a more rapid rate than is usual," he told Lord Carnarvon.[31] He read a dull, hopeless anticipation of defeat in the obvious evidences of their fatigue and nervous strain. "Blake," he informed the Colonial Secretary, "is ill, thoroughly broken down with overwork and excitement and irritability of the brain. . . . As for

Mackenzie he looks like a washed out rag and limp enough to hang upon a clothes line."[32]

Macdonald contemplated his harried and exhausted opponents with sympathetic interest, almost with pity. His own physical and mental state was excellent. Perhaps the hard campaigning of the past year ought to have tired him. But he did not feel tired. He had never felt better. And, according to the testimony of Dr. Grant and Dr. Tupper, this sense of returning well-being had its origin in a definite physical improvement. The doctors, he told Lord Dufferin, had assured him "that his constitution has quite changed of late, and that his general health would be likely to improve from henceforth for some years to come".[33] The Governor-General himself noted slight, significant differences. During the long session, with all its dinners and entertainments, Macdonald had never once drunk wine to excess. The ex-Prime Minister had been in his best form and on his best behaviour during the session of 1877. After the prorogation, when he came to pay a polite farewell call on Dufferin, there was an air of jaunty confidence and youthful high spirits in his manner.

He was beginning to feel like a proclaimed king who was waiting only for the formality of his coronation. His journey home had much of the enthusiasm of a royal progress, and at Toronto a great reception awaited him.[34] The long platform at the Berkeley Street station, the surrounding streets, and even the roofs of the standing freight cars, were crowded with an enormous welcoming mass of people. Five hundred torchbearers marched in the procession which escorted his carriage through the heart of the city, past rows of shops and houses which were blazing with illuminations and "transparencies"; and when he came out on the balcony of the United Empire Club to address the crowd, the spring darkness was so brightly lighted with these countless fiery points of illumination that he could see the long stretch of King Street, packed and jammed with citizens. "There were ten thousand people to meet me here last Wednesday," he wrote to J. A. Macdonell. A royal welcome, which could be compared only with the welcome to royalty! "No reception like it," he continued proudly, using the now familiar comparison, "since the Prince of Wales in 1860."[35]

He was eager to get to work. "I am satisfied no time is to be lost," he confided impressively to J. A. Macdonell, "as we must have an election before another session. . . . The Grits are organizing and may make a midnight march as before. Not a moment is to be lost."[36] It was true, of course, that the Parliament elected in the winter of 1874 had still well over eighteen months of its allotted existence to run; and, although the Conservatives kept up a cheerful clamour about a dissolution, there was no certain prospect of an election before the next session. But time was running rapidly away, if it had not yet run out. The whole party must be put in a position of alert readiness for action. His second series of picnics would have to be very carefully arranged so as to cover the most ground, and do the most good, with the most economical expenditure of time. In the first week after his return from Ottawa, he sat down with Tupper to plan the summer campaign.

Tupper would be his chief aide. Tupper was his probable successor. It was time to present Tupper formally to the Ontarions, who, up until the previous summer, had never had much opportunity of appreciating his fighting qualities as a speaker. Early in June, the two friends went down to Kingston for the meeting which was to inaugurate the summer series; and Tupper, introduced as the heir-presumptive to the Conservative leadership, delivered the principal speech of the evening.[37] The town hall was packed with Macdonald's old friends and devoted followers, with people who refused to believe a syllable to his discredit, and who rejected the entire Pacific Scandal as a baseless slander. "The moral assassination policy cannot kill Sir John, Canada's ablest statesman," announced a long streamer loyally from one of the walls. It was like bringing a friend into one's parents' house, and introducing him to the family circle. As he warmed to his work, Macdonald grew more confidentially prophetic. He had long wished, he said, to retire from public life; and his friends had long resisted his retirement. "I tell you," he promised the Kingstonians, "that until my friends say that they think I have served long enough—so long as they think I can be of any use to them—it will be but a just return for what they have done for me not to desert them. I have long been anxious to retire from the position I have held, and I am sure you will say, from the acquaintance that you have formed tonight with my friend, the honourable Charles Tupper, that when I do retire, he is a man who will well fill my place."[38]

Less than a week later, on June 12, the picnics began. The tour swung west and north of Toronto, though in not too wide a range, from London, Brampton, Gorrie, Orangeville, to Markham. But this was only the prelude to more ambitious and far-flung engagements. Before the end of the month, Tupper had left for Nova Scotia, and Macdonald was ready for a new political experience—a political experience so strangely new that it might be called a political adventure. He had made speeches in Quebec city and in Montreal; but never in other parts of Quebec. Quebec was Cartier's and Langevin's territory, not his own; and even now, when, on July 4, he set out from Montreal on the afternoon train for Sherbrooke, his tour was planned to cover only the predominantly English-speaking Eastern Townships.[39] The Quebec politicians—White, Masson, Chapleau, and Langevin—accompanied and supported him on his journey; and at St. Hyacinthe, the first stop on the way to Sherbrooke, Chapleau spoke for him in French. There were other stops and speeches at Actonvale and Richmond, and darkness had fallen long before they reached Sherbrooke. But Sherbrooke was crammed with people and blazing with lights. "Sandy is no sic man as our Sir John," proclaimed one "transparency"; and another asserted that "The weevil came in with the Grits and prosperity with John A." There was a long processional carriage drive through the streets that night; and next morning Macdonald set out over the lovely countryside, with its little lakes and sudden high hills, on a packed programme of train rides, carriage drives, picnics, dinners, and endless speechifying. It was not until late on Saturday night, July 7, that he arrived back in Montreal, and at Montreal the tour climbed to its crashing crescendo of success. Five thousand torch-bearers paraded through the streets, and at Dominion

Square, where the procession ended at eleven o'clock at night, a crowd of fifty thousand people roared applause.[40]

Then, during July and early August, while Macdonald took a holiday, he and his friends tried to estimate the effects of the first phase of the campaign. "A tidal wave seems to be setting in up here in our favour," Dalton McCarthy wrote to Tupper in Nova Scotia, "and opposition stock has gone up and is going up in a manner which appears to be extraordinary. The Montreal reception seems to have capped the climax, and Mackenzie and company have returned in a very bad temper to the capital. . . ."[41] What were Mackenzie and company going to do, Macdonald asked himself curiously? Early in May, he had half expected a general election in late summer or early autumn. But August came, there was no sign of a dissolution, and Mackenzie went off on a speaking tour of Nova Scotia. Was it a reconnaissance? What kind of reception would Mackenzie get? He need hardly have wondered. "I never was at a sadder meeting—a few funerals excepted—," wrote McLelan of the Reform demonstration at Truro.[42] Confronted with these ominous signs of unpopularity, would Mackenzie dare to dissolve? Would he not postpone the general election until after another session of Parliament, in the hope of a return of better times? It was possible—even probable. Yet Macdonald had heard another and a very contrary rumour that the Reformers intended to go to the country in January. He could not be certain. The Conservative meetings, he decided, would have to continue their triumphal course through September and into October. He wrote to Tupper, begging him to return and give him his support in the autumn picnics. "My hands," he admitted wryly, "are very full of these infernal things."[43]

His hands were very full indeed. The picnics kept him so much away from Toronto during the early autumn that Mary wrote him, by dictation, begging him plaintively to return. "The house seems so dull and lonely without you," she said, "and I miss my evening stories very much. . . . Dear Father, when are you coming back?"[44] He was back for only the briefest of intervals during most of September and the early part of October. "I wish to Heavens I had your vitality," his old friend

John Rose wrote to him, "but I could no more face what you are going through than I could earn Paradise."[45] Macdonald himself, in his detached, half-amused fashion, was impressed by his own energy. "After my Eastern Townships experience," he told J. A. Macdonell, "I begin to think highly of my powers of endurance."[46] He tried to insist that the meetings at which he spoke must not follow each other on successive days, that intervals for rest and recovery were absolutely essential. But too often these precious intervening hours were taken up with conferences, private discussions, carriage drives, and long and exhausting train rides. He travelled as far north as Lindsay, Barrie, and Owen Sound. He touched the western end of the province in Essex county and its eastern extremity in Dundas and Glengarry. Early in October, as he turned from southwestern Ontario towards Toronto and home, the good weather, which had smiled so sunnily on so many of his meetings, at last began to break. His much-abused voice grew hoarse and faint. The rain poured down at Chatham on October 10, and at St. Thomas on October 12; and two days later, at Hagersville, in Haldimand county, he could make only the briefest of speeches.[47] The tour had faltered. Yet in the end it finished strong. At Hamilton, where the last great meeting was held, the sun shone once more and with the steadfast warmth and brightness of a midsummer day. Agnes came up from Toronto to meet him, and she was presented with a necklace, and made her own speech of thanks, and the crowd was greater than any he had seen outside of Montreal.[48]

IV

He carried the war aggressively into the last session of the third Parliament of Canada. It was, appropriately enough, a tense and angry period in international affairs; and the bloodless battles of Canadian politics were fought out under the lowering danger of a real conflict. Once again, twenty years after the Crimean War, Great Britain faced the real possibility of becoming involved in the quarrels of Russia and Turkey.

Late in January, 1878, Disraeli ordered the Mediterranean fleet to steam through the straits to Constantinople. In England there was immense popular support for this armed defiance of the advancing Russian armies; and for some weeks a fight on a very large scale seemed possible. Canada, which now had a coast-line on two oceans, was very much more conscious of its alarming proximity to this huge northern country, Russia, than it had been at the time of the Crimean War; and during the winter and spring occasional exciting rumours of impending attacks by Russian naval and land forces ran through the Dominion. In June, when the Congress of Berlin met to make a new settlement of the affairs of south-eastern Europe, the agitation suddenly subsided; but it had been the first serious international crisis which Canada had experienced since Confederation.

It stirred many people. It deeply affected Macdonald. He had founded the Canadian permanent force in 1871 with the establishment of the first two artillery batteries. He saw now that the existing crisis offered a favourable opportunity for strengthening and enlarging this small nucleus of a "standing army". "In a time of profound peace such a proposition would be unpopular—," he wrote to Sir Stafford Northcote, "would be objected to by the opposition of the day, and could not be carried by any ministry. And yet I am satisfied that the time has come for the formation of a regular force—closely connected with the imperial army, and worked up to the same standard of training and discipline. Without this, Canada will never add to the strength of the Empire, but must remain a source of anxiety and weakness."[49]

He was looking forward eagerly to the assumption of power. He had all sorts of things that he wanted to do with power. But power could be won only through a final, approaching struggle; and now his confidence was mixed with a tense realization that the desired trial was terribly close, that there remained only a few months in which he could make or mar his chances of victory. He was strung up to a high pitch of nervous excitement. Everybody on the Conservative side seemed in a fever from the same infection; and it was an extraordinary session,

barren of any constructive legislation, yet crowded with acrimonious arguments and violent personal attacks. "There is
the most devilish spirit with the opposition this session that was
ever seen," wrote Alexander Mackenzie severely, as if denouncing a manifestation of original sin. "I never knew anything
like it before."⁵⁰

Even Macdonald seemed to have changed. He was strangely
unlike the self-effacing, repentant, ageing man of four years
ago. There were moments when he seemed to resemble much
more closely the high-spirited, hard-drinking, hot-tempered
young politician who had fought George Brown fifteen and
twenty years before. It was true, of course, that his easy-going
urbanity never entirely departed. He intervened at moments
in the debates to soften asperities and to recall the House to its
sense of dignity. He made occasional jokes. He told stories.
He twitted Mackenzie amiably on the dizzyingly frequent
changes in his Cabinet—including the second and definitive
resignation of Blake; and when "Joe" Rymal, who was the
homespun humorist of the House, dropped his good-humoured
jibes for somewhat more acrid criticisms of the Conservative
picnics of the previous summer, Macdonald merely retorted
with one of those eighteenth-century anecdotes which he enjoyed so much. Rymal's departure from his usual, and acceptable,
type of humour reminded him, he told the House, of Boswell's
conduct on an occasion when he and Dr. Johnson had gone to
the theatre and had seen a somewhat disappointing play. The
audience made a great many noisy protests, and Boswell imitated
the lowing of a cow with such success that the spectators
encouraged his efforts by calling out *encore, encore*. Boswell
lowed two or three times; and then, in the pride of his heart,
he was emboldened to try to imitate other animals. But now
there was no applause. The attempts were ghastly failures. "My
dear Boswell," said Johnson turning impressively to his friend,
"confine yourself to the cow."⁵¹

It was all very agreeable—at intervals. But this note of genial
raillery was not dominant. Something harsher and more primitive sounded repeatedly. Macdonald tried his hardest to convict
Vail, the new Nova Scotian member of the Cabinet, of disloyal

utterances at the time of the secessionist movement. He disliked Vail. He disliked Donald Smith still more, for Donald Smith, his agent and confidant at the time of the Red River troubles, had gone over to the Reformers at the crisis of the Pacific Scandal in the autumn of 1873. Smith was now supporting a bill which the government had introduced to authorize the lease of the newly constructed Winnipeg-Pembina branch of the Canadian Pacific railway to a north-western American railway company, which would thus be enabled to provide through communication by rail from Manitoba to the east. The name of the American railway was not specified in the bill, but the government revealed the fact that it had been negotiating with a group of capitalists, headed by George Stephen of the Bank of Montreal, which was at that moment acquiring control of the St. Paul and Pacific Railroad; and Donald Smith was popularly and correctly believed to be a member of the Stephen syndicate. Macdonald attacked Smith for advocating a lease in which he had a personal interest. He attacked the government for rewarding Smith's political support in such a scandalous fashion.[52] It was a determined onslaught. Yet its bluntness and severity were hardly exceptional. Every contract, every item in the appropriations, was bitterly criticized or disputed. The debate on the tariff was endlessly prolonged. And when—as if Mackenzie had not had trouble enough at Ottawa—an important constitutional crisis erupted in Quebec, the Conservatives, with Macdonald at their head, leaped upon this new, heaven-sent issue with the evident intention of exploiting its possibilities to the full.

It was a peculiar case. Letellier de St.Just, the newly appointed Lieutenant-Governor of the Province of Quebec, had just dismissed his Conservative *Bleu* ministry, headed by de Boucherville, on the ground of its deliberate and contemptuous neglect of his office. On April 11, in a long and elaborate speech, Macdonald attacked the dismissal as a violation of the principles of responsible government.[53] Mackenzie, in his reply, took the position that the purely provincial politics of Quebec were no concern of the Parliament of Canada. He hoped to choke off the debate as soon as possible. But the Conservatives were just as anxious to prolong it. And since the government would not grant an adjournment for a third day's discussion, they continued to debate all through the night of Friday, April 12, and all through the following day until six o'clock in the evening. It was an increasingly fatigued, meaningless, and disorderly debate. Macdonald, who had directed the Conservative attack all through Friday night, had a sherry and some oysters early on Saturday morning and went to sleep on a couch in a committee room. On Monday, the *Globe* explained in scandalized tones that he had retired because he was "simply drunk, in the plain, ordinary sense of that word". Inevitably, some of the leading Conservatives got up in the House to refute these baseless slanders.[54] And inevitably the notorious debate on the Letellier affair received a fresh burst of publicity.

All this was bad enough. But there was more to come. The scandalous climax of that extraordinary session was reached on its very last day, at the moment when Black Rod was already on his way to summon the Commons to the Senate chamber for the closing ceremony of the session. On the previous evening Macdonald had reiterated his charge that the passage of the bill for the Pembina branch of the Canadian Pacific railway had been intended as a reward to Donald Smith for the "servile support" which he had given the ministry. As soon as the House met on the final afternoon, Smith rose indignantly to deny these accusations. He insisted that he had never asked or received a favour from either government, and that, at the crisis of the Pacific Scandal, he had decided to vote against the Conservative administration on grounds of conscience alone. Tupper denied his statements; Macdonald branded them as falsehoods; and in an increasingly staccato interchange which lasted through the final moments of the session, the two Conservative leaders and Smith argued furiously over the events which had preceded the fall of the Conservative government in 1873. Tupper, explosive and domineering as always, was more prominent in the mêlée than his chief. He was still shouting "coward, mean, treacherous coward!" at his opponent after the Sergeant-at-Arms had announced the messenger. But it was Macdonald who had the last word—the literally last recorded word—of the session.

"That fellow Smith," he cried hotly, after the Speaker had given orders for the admission of Black Rod, "is the biggest liar I ever met!"[55]

He might have been back in that old milling-ground—the Assembly of the Province of Canada. He might have been the still youthful Macdonald who, white with passion, had denounced George Brown on the dreadful evening of February 26, 1856! As the session ended, as the probability of an early autumn election grew more and more assured, he seemed to have recovered a young man's compelling sense of urgency, a young man's reckless determination to win at all costs. "If we fail in Ontario in the next election," he wrote to J. A. Macdonell, "then 'good-bye' to all hopes for the Conservative party. I, for one, shall give up the fight in despair."[56] This was a final effort into which he put everything of his strength and ability with hardly a moment's impatient consideration for his health. Above all, the party must be kept united; there must be no ruinous "splits" in its tightly drawn ranks. "Let us not, like the hunters in the fable," he pleaded, "quarrel about the skin before we kill the bear. It will take our united efforts to kill the bear." All that summer, while the very atmosphere seemed ominously disturbed, and periods of intense oppressive heat alternated strangely with days of frightful floods and wind-storms, he stuck to his self-appointed task. At the very beginning of the season, and again in the first fortnight of July, there were a number of huge Conservative open-air meetings and celebrations at which he spoke;[57] but this year the grand circuit of picnics was not to be so prolonged or so extended. During a great part of the summer he stayed in Toronto, dealing with his enormous correspondence, presiding over conferences, having interminable private discussions. He was the theorist of the Conservative party's strategy, the improvisor of its tactics, the arbitrator of its disputes, the prophet of its victory.

On August 17, the *Canada Gazette* announced that the third Parliament was dissolved, and that the general election would take place on September 17, exactly a month later. Immediately the tempo of the campaign quickened for the last time. Macdonald began to fit the final speaking engagements into his crowded time-table, and on August 21 he left on the night train for Kingston.[58] He was worried about his old constituency. Of his two probable opponents, one, Stewart, he had beaten before, but the other, Gunn, was an unknown and reputedly a dangerous quantity. Dalton McCarthy, who had heard a grim rumour to the effect that the Grits were boasting that Kingston would be carried against Macdonald, begged his leader to run in Cardwell, where he would hardly have to put in an appearance, and where his friends could carry on the campaign on his behalf.[59] But Macdonald considered, hesitated, and declined. He would stick to Kingston. "I shall have hard work here," he admitted, "but prospects are good."[60] On August 22, a night of thick, clinging heat, he spoke for two hours in Kingston's town hall.[61] Before the month was out, he had travelled westward as far as Toronto and eastward as far as Cornwall, was back in Kingston, and had spoken, on still another oppressively sultry night, with what the newspapers called his "vaunted vigour".[62]

What were the chances for the Conservative party? Would he really be able to revenge the defeat of 1874? Tilley, whose term as Lieutenant-Governor of New Brunswick had ended just in time, was coolly realistic about the prospects in his own province. "In viewing the position, as I see it today," he wrote to Macdonald, "we may hope to divide New Brunswick, and I say frankly that I will be satisfied with that. . . ."[63] Flour and coal duties for the benefit of Ontario millers and Nova Scotian mine-owners were not popular in the province. Tilley admitted that New Brunswick was a dangerous "weak point" for the opposition; but on the other hand he was convinced that the Maritime Provinces as a whole were sure to return a Conservative majority. Tupper agreed with him. "We have the current of public sentiment strongly in with us," he reported from Amherst, "and I will be greatly disappointed if we do not do *better* than I promised you. . . ."[64] More than sixteen out of the twenty-one Nova Scotian seats was what Tupper now predicted;

and from Langevin came a confident estimate that, in the Quebec district, the Conservatives would increase their strength from ten to fifteen or sixteen.⁶⁵ Optimism was almost everywhere. Yet what of Ontario? In Ontario he had fought the hardest battles and incurred the greatest defeat of his career. What would Ontario do now? There were some who predicted that the Reform majority would merely be reduced, others who argued that the two parties would about break even. Only a few people—such as Dalton McCarthy and Macdonald himself— really believed in their heart of hearts that the Conservatives would win a decided majority of seats in Ontario. Yet he hesitated to speak. He had an almost superstitious dread of seeming to anticipate events. Prophecies about the results in either the province or the country as a whole were foreign to his nature. And it was not until well on in the summer that Agnes, who not unnaturally wished to know whether she would be required to superintend a household removal to Ottawa in two months' time, finally persuaded him to make a sober estimate.

"If we do well," he answered briefly, "we shall have a majority of sixty; if badly, thirty."⁶⁶

He was in his committee rooms, in Kingston, on the night of September 17, when the first returns began to come in.⁶⁷ Alexander Gunn had beaten him, and by a majority of one-hundred and forty-four! For the first time in his thirty-four years of political life, Kingston had deserted her son. He could not help but feel regret; but, within a few hours, his regret was whirled away like a drop in the vast, rushing spate of his triumph. The whole province, the whole country had declared for him in an avalanche of votes. He had sworn to defeat the Grits, and he had brought about their complete downfall. He had regained power. He had revenged the defeat of 1874.

Chapter Eight

The Plan in Realization

I

"I am waiting to be summoned," he wrote to Goldwin Smith on October 1, "Lord Dufferin (*entre nous*) having told me, when here, to keep my carpet bag ready."[1] It was the end of his freedom, the end of the tranquil, almost carefree, life in the St. George Street house. "I am in good health," he reassured his sister Louisa, "but have not yet *quite* regained my strength."[2] He had certainly overtaxed himself during the election, and he spent the last few weeks of his time in Toronto in recuperative idleness, varied by busy letter-writing and by long meditations on his new government and its programme. Politically, he could hardly have asked for better fortune. The results of the general election had been favourable in every province but New Brunswick. His own check at Kingston had been retrieved by election to the two constituencies of Marquette, Manitoba, and Victoria, British Columbia; and the choice was pleasantly easy, for the appeasement of British Columbia would be one of the first tasks of his government. He would sit for Victoria; and in the Commons he would have a majority very nearly as large as that which he himself had faced in the dismal dispirited session of 1874. "I resolved to reverse the verdict of 1874," he declared proudly to Cyril Graham, "and have done so to my heart's content."[3]

On October 9, in Ottawa, at half past one o'clock, he met the Governor-General for the expected interview. It was the first official meeting in close to five years. It was also very nearly their last. Dufferin's term of office was virtually over, and he had spent a good part of the spring and summer in making a series of superlatively gracious farewell appearances. He had stayed, of necessity, to see the results of the general election; and now the installation of a new and very acceptable government was to be the last act of his governor-generalship. He greeted Macdonald warmly. He told him—with perhaps a slight enhancement of the charm of his complimentary manner—that "on personal grounds the warmest wish of his heart was gratified".[4] Macdonald, in a private letter to Tupper, dryly described the Governor-General's welcome as "gushing"; but, at the same time, he was impressed by Dufferin's good opinion, and he set a high value on Dufferin's services to Canada. He had valued them so highly, in fact, that in the previous spring he had ventured to write to Sir Stafford Northcote, suggesting that the Governor-General's term of office might be lengthened by another two years.[5] Nothing had come of this suggestion. Dufferin was going back to England in a few weeks. But he had been a good friend to Macdonald and a good friend to Canada. It was important to retain his support.

In the agreeable atmosphere of this official reunion, Macdonald was his most urbane and ingratiating self. Yet, in his usual fashion, he remained cautious. He was anxious to prepare Dufferin for the Conservative programme—to reassure him about Conservative intentions. He sketched the new government's policies in a few simple and highly tentative strokes.[6] The hope, which he had confided to Sir Stafford Northcote in the previous spring, of laying "the foundation of a standing army" had now become a more definite plan; and he suggested to Dufferin the establishment of a small permanent force of three battalions. He told the Governor-General that he was "very keen" about the Canadian Pacific railway, and eager to begin it, as a commercial enterprise, in accordance with the plan which the Conservatives had always preferred; but he also admitted that the chances of a successful company flotation were extremely small in the existing depression. He hinted that he intended to ask the British government for a guaranteed loan in aid of the railway, and he was plainly aware of the unpleasant fact that the moment when the Canadian government was contemplating an increase in the tariff was hardly the most suitable moment at which to apply for an imperial guarantee. He seemed anxious to assure the British government that Canada would not sink too deeply into the "economic depravity" of protectionism. He told Dufferin that his government planned to raise the level of the tariff to approximately twenty and twenty-five per cent, to give England a preference of about one quarter to one fifth, and to submit all its fiscal proposals to the British government before introducing them into the Canadian Parliament. He ended by insisting—not, perhaps, to Dufferin's complete satisfaction—that in all his resolutions and speeches on the subject of the tariff, he had never committed himself to pure protectionist principles.

Then they turned to the subject of the new government, and Dufferin asked Macdonald for his nominations. Macdonald told the Governor-General that his proposed Cabinet was not "cut and dry", and he went away to finish his selections. Most of the veterans were recalled to office. Tupper had confirmed his claim to the Ministry of Works by his sledge-hammer attacks on the railway policy of the Mackenzie government. Tilley's restoration to his old post as Minister of Finance would help to quiet the Maritime apprehensions about the fiscal policy of the new government. Prince Edward Island, in the person of J. C. Pope, was given a place in the Cabinet, and New Brunswick, which had done comparatively so badly in the election, had to be content with one portfolio, instead of two as before, and with the Speakership of the Senate generously thrown in as a solatium. John O'Connor stood for the Roman Catholics of central Canada; and another Pope, John Henry, who was not related to the Prince Edward Island family, represented the English-speaking minority of the Province of Quebec. Langevin, who would never enjoy so much of Macdonald's confidence as Cartier had done, was now the chief of the French-speaking ministers; and from Ontario came a respectable but rather humdrum contingent, with Alexander Campbell as its senior member.

Macdonald himself took the post of Minister of the Interior.

It was a relatively new portfolio, created as late as 1873, and invested with the management of all the important aspects of Canada's programme of expansion in the west.[7] The great main purpose for which the new office had been established was obviously the promotion of western settlement; and, in the autumn of 1878, when Macdonald assumed control, the Department had at last reached the point at which it could make an effective beginning on its real task. The painfully difficult preliminary problems, which had appeared dramatically even before the acquisition of Rupert's Land, seemed at last to have been solved. In 1876 the claims of the half-breeds and the other squatters to land grants in the new Province of Manitoba had been largely settled; and in 1877, with the signing of the last of the seven treaties with the Indians, the aboriginal title to the Canadian north-west had been extinguished, and the prairies were freed for white settlement. The task which faced Macdonald was the task of surveying this vast western empire and throwing it open for occupation. As late as April of that year, in a debate in the House, he had admitted frankly that he knew little about the provisions of the Dominion Lands Act of 1872, which was the legal framework of the settlement organization.[8] Undoubtedly he was unacquainted with the detail of the operations of the Department of the Interior. But he did not for a moment underestimate its importance. Its tremendous importance was obvious. Along with the Departments of Finance and Public Works, it was one of the three ministries specially concerned with the great business of Canadian expansion. Tupper would sponsor the Canadian Pacific railway; Tilley would introduce the new tariff; and western settlement, which was the third of the great trio of national undertakings, would have a spokesman more politically powerful than either of the other two.

On October 19, the Cabinet, now virtually complete, was announced. The new government began to settle down into harness. Macdonald had been so long away from the exasperating routines, the repeated daily annoyances, of office that he had almost forgotten their existence. But now they punctuated his days with a quickly restored irksomeness. A whole host of devoted but unemployed Conservatives hastened to present themselves as candidates for jobs in the Canadian civil service. "Five years opposition have made our friends rather hungry," Macdonald remarked to Dalton McCarthy, "and they are worrying me about office, but the departments have been all crammed by the Grits so that it will be some time before there will be any vacancies."[9] It was usually fairly easy to end the importunities of the office-seekers by a laconic and vaguely sympathetic letter, or by a short and genial interview; but, as Macdonald quickly discovered, there were some desperately immediate problems of government policy which could not be dismissed so easily. Rose, who had retained his position, all during the Mackenzie régime, as Canadian financial agent, wrote over in some haste and with all possible urgency, to remind Macdonald that in a few months' time the Canadian government would have to meet obligations amounting to over three million pounds in London.[10] Obviously there must be new financing. Obviously also a government which had sworn to use its best efforts to alleviate the slump must make a bold and impressive beginning in commercial policy; and here Macdonald gratefully picked up an idea which the Reformers had considered but never carried out. Sir A. T. Galt, who had won a title and a considerable diplomatic reputation as a result of his services in the Fisheries Commission of 1877, would be sent over to negotiate trade treaties with the principal countries of western Europe.[11] Sir Alexander's mission would, Macdonald considered, serve a double purpose. It might widen the scope of Canada's trade. It would serve notice of Canada's intention to take a more active part in the conduct of her own foreign policy.

About the middle of November, the transatlantic migration began. Dufferin said his last farewells and departed. Galt and Tilley set out for Paris, Madrid, and London. It was almost time for Macdonald to leave for Halifax, where the new Governor-General, the Marquess of Lorne, the son of the Duke of Argyll, and his wife, the Princess Louise, were expected to arrive before the end of the month. The appointment of a nobleman whose consort was a princess—the gift of a daughter, if not of a son, of the reigning Queen—was the highest compliment which Great Britain had yet paid to the young Dominion. Dufferin, as soon as he heard of it, had instantly revived his earlier suggestion that Canada should be converted into a vice-royalty;[12] and the new Colonial Secretary, Sir Michael Hicks Beach, making light of the objection that the United States might dislike the title, passed on Dufferin's suggestion with his approval to Lord Beaconsfield.[13] But Canada could no more be made a vice-royalty in 1878 than she could be made a kingdom in 1867; and in each case the fear of outraged republicanism determined the decision. The hopes of a new title were dashed; but the coming of a real princess was a certainty at any rate. At his first interview with Dufferin, Macdonald took up the problem of appropriate etiquette, and promised to have a special railway carriage built for the new exalted tenants of Rideau Hall.

Royal carriages were for royalty. His own accommodation for the journey down to Halifax was comparatively simple. "We are not going to travel to Halifax like princes but like ordinary mortals," he wrote a little tartly to an eager inquirer who was no doubt seeking a place on what he expected to be a particularly luxurious excursion.[14] There would be a Pullman, Macdonald explained, which would probably be inconveniently crowded with officials who had to be present to swear in Lord Lorne. He was tired after weeks of strenuous effort; he badly wanted a little peace on his travels; and he boarded the Intercolonial Railway train with relief—and with some bottles of brandy in his luggage. Tupper, Brydges, Hugh Allan, and an agreeable and entertaining secretary were also on board; and in this congenial company Macdonald started drinking a little too frequently and too much. The arrival at Halifax and the obvious need of putting in a presentable appearance at the Lieutenant-Governor's house, where he was to stay until Lord Lorne's ship arrived, ought to have sobered him up. But these social obligations scarcely appeared to interest him. He kept his room, in cheerful disregard of all Lieutenant-Governor Archibald's carefully arranged hospitality. He kept on drinking, to the embarrassment of the whole household, including the tremulously curious Miss Archibald. The hours—the days—went by. The ship was expected and at last announced. The reception, with all its heightened formalities, was imminent. And at last Miss Archibald, daring to do what her father no doubt considered to be beneath his own and his guest's dignity, went in the greatest agitation and implored the secretary's help. The secretary arrived, knocked boldly at the closed door and entered. Macdonald, pale, haggard, "looking more dead than alive", lay in bed; and the counterpane was strewn with a muddle of books, documents, and newspapers. The secretary stuttered out his important message. The Governor-General's ship, he quavered, was nearly in port and Macdonald must get up and prepare for the reception.

Macdonald raised himself in bed, regarded the secretary with extreme distaste, and pointed with an imperious finger to the door.

"Vamoose," he said, "from this ranch!"

II

He seemed a strange mid-Victorian statesman. Lord Dufferin, in his tactful and sympathetic fashion, had tried to explain his Prime Minister's regrettable spells of "transient weakness" on grounds of overwork, anxiety, and sorrow. Lord Kimberley, the Colonial Secretary, was inclined to be more blunt and matter-of-fact on the subject. Yet even he had confessed that it almost took his breath away to read Dufferin's account of Macdonald's extraordinary behaviour during the last days of the crisis of the Pacific Scandal. "He should have lived," Kimberley declared in amazement, "in the good old times of two bottle men, when one of the duties of the Secretary of the Treasury is said to have been to hold his hat on occasion for the convenience of the First Lord when 'clearing himself' for his speech."[15] The good old times of the "two-bottle men" had not perhaps vanished so completely as Lord Kimberley seemed to suggest. The features, soon to become almost fabulous, of eighteenth-century political life—the bibulous politicians, the drunken, corruptible electorates, the bribery, intimidation, and open violence—lingered on, in England as well as in Canada, far into the reign of the Good Queen. They lingered on; but they lingered rather as survivals which increasingly required explanation or apology. A more decorous manner of political behaviour was gaining in authority. Macdonald accepted the new austerities. But he had come of age in the florid maturity of an older and more baroque style. And in the polite, sober, provincial world of Ottawa or Toronto there were still moments when he looked oddly out of place.

Where did he belong? Lord Dufferin's comment—"Sir John is a thorough man of the world"—suggested a cosmopolitan breadth of knowledge and experience.[16] He was pleasantly at home in very different kinds of company. He knew and enjoyed different kinds of climate, mental as well as physical. He read a lot, roving freely backward in time and outward in space; and his innumerable stories—which ranged from the perfectly proper through the marginally respectable to the definitely scabrous—were not infrequently drawn from far lands and past ages. He compared Mackenzie with the Mikado, who enjoyed the prestige, and Blake to the Tycoon who had the power.[17] During one of the debates on the National Policy, he told the House cynically that the Canadian manufacturers who wanted protection reminded him of the Indian squaw who reflected sagely about whiskey that "a little too much was just enough".[18] A harsh, native, western taste sharpened some of his ancedotes; but more often their flavour was agreeably mature and subtle. He was always culling absurdities from eighteenth- and early nineteenth-century biographies, journals, and memoirs. He enjoyed repeating a blunt, teutonic comment of old George II on one of his generals, or a bantering exchange between Lord Melbourne and Sidney Smith, or a clever defence by Charles James Fox of the inconveniences and inefficiencies of the parliamentary system.[19] When he wanted to illustrate the appropriate form of retaliation against American commercial selfishness, he made use—rather free use —of Canning's famous rhyming dispatch to the Hague:[20]

In matters of commerce the fault of the Dutch
Is offering too little and asking too much.
The French are with equal advantage content,
So we clap on Dutch bottoms just 20 per cent.
  (*Chorus*) Twenty per cent, twenty per cent.

(*Chorus of English Customs House Officers and French
  Douaniers*)

(*English*) We clap on Dutch bottoms just 20 per cent.
(*French*) Vous frapperez Falck avec 20 per cent.

Lord Kimberley had placed him, with the "two-bottle men",
in the eighteenth century. There were more than a few times
when he seemed to belong most appropriately to the reigns of
George III and George IV, to the age which had closed in
1832 with the passage of the Reform Bill. He had its grace,
its urbanity, its intelligence and reasonableness, its freedom
from sanctimoniousness and cant. "Charming in conversation,
gentlemanlike, with excellent manners, quick apprehension",
he had, according to Lord Dufferin, all the surface character-
istics of the age of good talk and good breeding.[21] He had its
generous liberality of spirit as well. Poor Mackenzie, according
to the retiring Governor-General, had the "narrowness and want
of lofty generosity inherent in a semi-educated man"; but
Macdonald had always been "good-natured, placable, and magnanimous". Macdonald had never taken himself or his affairs
too seriously. In a more solemn age, he still kept something
of the jaunty eighteenth-century assumption that politics were
the affair not of ponderously instructed professionals, but of
gifted amateurs; and his successes were gained, not so much
through study and expert knowledge, as through tact, insight,
and imagination—through what Dufferin called his "great
faculty for managing other people". Here, in contrast with the
manly downrightness and simplicity which the Victorians believed they admired, his methods often seemed devious and
subtle. He could rapidly and expertly disguise his mind in the
intellectual garments of others; and it was suspected that he

adopted, almost as a matter of course, the views of his last caller, merely for the purpose of drawing out the next one. "You are sometimes, I think, oddly credulous," Alexander Campbell declared in a moment of bewildered exasperation, "or you have some arrière pensée which you do not explain —I seldom know which."[22] Yet this affectation of guileless simplicity, this shameless adoption of the mental habits of others, these clever devices of evasion and postponement were not, in the eyes of some of his contemporaries, the most puzzling features of his character. It was not merely—so they thought—a question of his occasional casual deceptions. They knew all about casual deceptions. What they could not be sure of was the fundamental seriousness of his purpose. To these mid-Victorian critics it seemed almost incredible that a man who enjoyed life so obviously, who was so frequently lacking in respectable earnestness, who seemed so ready to give up sober work and quiet repose for mere empty enjoyment, should have a really solid claim to be considered a great national statesman. He seemed to be made so incongruously for the task which he had taken up. He wore the dignity of a Prime Minister much too gaily. Surely it was a mask and he an actor.

At moments—and not only around Reform tea-tables or after family prayers in Liberal households—the dreadful charge of levity was accepted as proved. Macdonald might have been the ghost of a lean, hard-drinking eighteenth-century squire who had imprudently haunted nineteenth-century parliaments so long that he had suffered the penalty of life. Yet he did not seem bewildered or abashed by his new surroundings. If some of the mid-Victorians regarded him as the incongruous relic of an intemperate and disreputable past, he himself seemed to feel completely at home in the world in which he found himself. He got on admirably with his fellow Canadians; he evidently loved the country of his adoption. He had, in fact, a curiously sympathetic, deeply imaginative understanding of Canada and its national requirements—an understanding which seemed oddly at variance with his Regency attitude to the state and his un-Victorian want of earnestness. It was true that he looked with sceptical tolerance upon the imperfections of humanity and the limitations of government. In different circumstances he might have believed merely that the state should keep the peace and protect the frontiers; and to all projects of further governmental intervention he might have said, with Lord Melbourne, "Why can't you leave it alone?" But the circumstances which surrounded him were not those of England in the 1830's. They were the circumstances of Canada in the 1870's. And Canada was a new, huge, undeveloped, yet potentially mighty, country, where little had yet been done, and where so much might be accomplished. The only effort which was valid for his generation was an enormous positive effort on the part of the state. The only task which was relevant for his age was the continental task of nation building.

He had become a nation builder. The federal union of British North America was very largely his creation. In a national government which was as strong as he could make it, he had maintained British parliamentary institutions; and, with the help of British diplomatic and military support, he had sought to extend the territory of the new nation to its final transcontinental limits. Newfoundland alone remained aloof. He still hoped, as he had reminded Sir Stafford Northcote in the previous spring, to make his structural design complete by the addition of Newfoundland. But, apart from the second of the two island provinces, the whole of British North America had now been definitely staked out in a single claim. More, the claim had been formally acknowledged by the United States as well as by Great Britain. And the task which remained was to bind this huge, divided country together with railways, to people its empty spaces with settlers, to diversify and strengthen its simple economy with varied commercial enterprises. This was the work which he had undertaken in 1871, and dropped abruptly in 1873 because of the Pacific Scandal; and now, after five long years, he had picked it up again. It was still unfinished. If anything it had grown more difficult with the passage of time, the worsening of economic circumstances, and the mounting national feeling of frustration and failure.

As he lay in the disordered bed in Lieutenant-Governor Archibald's house on that day in late November, 1878, the annoying sounds which had issued from the secretary's lips reshaped themselves into a coherent and important message. He must get up—and at once. A new governor was about to arrive. A new government, of which he was the head, had taken office; and the whole programme of national integration and development, which, five years before, he had given up in a mood of shamed, disgusted finality, was now once more his responsibility. For many of its details he had only an uninstructed amateur's competence. He was not by inclination or training a financier, and he disowned, with cheerful frankness, any particular expertise in commercial matters. Tupper's lengthy, highly technical, immensely detailed criticisms of the Liberal government's railway policy were quite beyond him. He was not interested in the minutiae of the Canadian Pacific railway; but nobody ever saw more clearly than he the central significance of the project. "Until this great work is completed," he had told Sir Stafford Northcote, "our Dominion is little more than a 'geographical expression'. We have as much interest in British Columbia as in Australia, and no more. The railway once finished, we become one great united country with a large inter-provincial trade and a common interest."[23]

Once again, the realization of his goal and the consciousness of his purpose grew clear and certain. He got up and began to dress rapidly. Lord Lorne would be arriving at any minute. And, in a curious way, the immediacy of the Governor-General's arrival was like a peremptory reminder of the urgency of his great task. There was no time to lose. He had been given one chance and had failed. And then, by luck, and skill, and untiring effort, he had won the right to a second try. But it had taken five years to establish his claim; and now he was nearly sixty-four years old. The second chance would be the last chance. It had come late. It could not be, in the nature of things, as good, as favourable a chance as the first. But it was the last opportunity he would ever get. It lay waiting for him, and the new Governor-General, with whom, in his effort to exploit this final opportunity, he would have to be associated for the next five years, was about to make his appearance and begin their partnership. . . . He gave a few final touches to his necktie, and then, pale but erect and confident, he walked out of the room.

III

The omens seemed auspicious, as the new government and the new Governor-General settled down together in Ottawa. The immediate goals were certainly being attained. Tilley was able to dispose of his loans in London at a briefly favourable opportunity, an exceptionally favourable opportunity, Rose insisted;[24] and Galt, who was about to leave England for trade negotiations with France and Spain, seemed highly pleased with the prospects of his mission. He and Hewitt Bernard, who was to accompany him to Paris and Madrid, had found lodgings in the very London hotel in which the British North American delegates had planned Confederation in 1866. "We are all together in your old rooms at the Westminster," Galt wrote happily. "I accept this as an augury of success."[25] For a while, the augury seemed a true one. The Colonial Office was pleasantly helpful; the Foreign Office was graciously co-operative; and it was not until the eager and hopeful diplomatists reached Paris that Galt began to encounter real difficulties. Lord Lyons, the British Ambassador, who seemed to have been imperfectly instructed by the Foreign Office, met the roving Canadian Commissioner in a cool and unco-operative mood. The usual "conventional courtesies" were withheld. He "has treated me," the hypersensitive Galt raged to Macdonald, "with marked discourtesy".[26]

Macdonald smiled wryly. His old colleague's moods, he was well aware, could hardly be called lasting. And, in fact, within little more than forty-eight hours, Galt's first Parisian impressions had completely altered.[27] Lord Lyons began to be praised for his hospitality and helpfulness; and Galt discovered, to his rueful surprise, that the difficulties of making trade treaties with foreigners were not entirely attributable to the alleged dilatoriness and unconcern of the Foreign Office. The French, it appeared, had a strong bias toward protectionism. The Spaniards were worried about the position of their colonies. It was all going to be very slow and difficult, Galt began to realize; and Macdonald agreed with him. Yet Macdonald had no intention of dropping his plan for taking the initiative in the conduct of Canada's commercial relations. Galt's limited success was an argument, not for the abandonment, but for the continuation, of his mission. Perhaps the temporary appointment should be made permanent. Perhaps—over ten years after Confederation—it was now time for Canada to establish an officer, diplomatic in character and exalted in status, who would reside permanently in London, and busy himself with the promotion of Canadian interests in England and Europe.

These were matters of importance. They would have to be dealt with in the very near future. But undoubtedly the most pressing affair, the affair of the moment, was the tariff which Tilley would have to present in his budget speech. "Incidental protection" had been the main political pledge of the Conservatives, and, in all probability, the main reason for their electoral success. The promise would have to be carried out in the very first session; and late in December, when Tilley at length returned from England, the ministers settled down to the serious consideration of their plan. There were interminable sessions, beginning early in January, with the increasingly exigent representatives of the Manufacturers' Association;[28] and slowly, rate by rate, the complex schedules of the new tariff were built up. Macdonald, on the whole, took little part in these technical discussions. General policy was what interested him. Details were the concern of Tilley's department. And yet, as the details were slowly assembled and fitted together, it became gradually apparent that a certain significant change of emphasis in general policy had occurred.

What was the new tariff to be like? During the election campaign Macdonald had been usually, if not invariably, cautious and moderate in all his statements on fiscal policy. Once, at the height of the contest, he had publicly protested that he had never proposed "an increase but only a readjustment of the tariff".[29] In October, when he had accepted the task of forming a government, he had told Lord Dufferin definitely that his purpose was not protection; and on the way back from Halifax with Lord Lorne, he had insisted that the British press was quite mistaken in its assumption that the Canadian government intended anything but a tariff for revenue.[30] Literally, of course, this protest was quite justified. Revenue was bound to remain a principal object of the Canadian customs duties, for the simple reason that other forms of taxation, including income taxes, were then considered impossible of application in Canada. Money was desperately necessary. The new government had committed itself to the most costly enterprises. It had sworn to carry out the great national projects which Mackenzie and his colleagues had not been able to complete. It could not get along without a substantially larger revenue; and the only "readjustment" of the tariff which would produce the necessary funds was a "readjustment" imposing stiffer duties. The needs of the state dictated the increase; but at the same time the increase largely met the requirements of the manufacturers. The tariff became the means which would enable government and industry to co-operate in the creation of a transcontinental Canadian economy; and as the winter went on, the pressure, both inside and outside Parliament, in favour of higher duties, began to increase. The bias of government policy became clear and emphatic.

This government had, in fact, committed itself to a strongly nationalistic commercial programme.[31] It had rejected British economic theories and copied American fiscal practices in a spirit of independence and competition. The new *ad valorem* rates were fairly high; they were strengthened not infrequently with specific duties which, unlike *ad valorem* rates, would increase protection during a period of falling prices; and the twenty to twenty-five per cent British preference which Macdonald had discussed with Dufferin and Lorne was, for the moment, dropped. It was true that it had been dropped only when the preparation of the tariff was well advanced. Early in January Tilley had requested Lord Lorne to find out whether the British government would have any objection to the proposed preference.³² But the non-committal British reply and the theoretical British dislike for differential duties of any kind were not the only reasons for the Canadian government's change of plan. The Canadian government was becoming aware of the fact that in Great Britain, as well as in France and Germany, the great depression in agriculture had awakened a new interest in the protection of farming. Both France and Germany were moving towards the imposition of tariffs which would defend their farmers against the importation of cheap American cereals. What if Lord Beaconsfield, the old defender of the Corn Laws, should follow the same course? If duties were imposed on breadstuffs in the United Kingdom, then Canada and Great Britain would be in a position to exchange preferences in their respective markets; and, as Macdonald and the Conservatives had hoped in vain for years, the countries might conclude a mutually beneficial reciprocal trade agreement. It was a tempting prospect. It was all the more tempting since the grant of an unearned preference to Great Britain might provoke retaliation from the United States; and Tilley was frankly frightened of a prohibitory American duty on the import of Canadian lumber.³³ The Canadian government drew back; and early in February, when the Governor-General made a last effort to save the preference, Macdonald and Tilley refused. They were eager to discuss an exchange of tariff concessions with Great Britain. They were prepared, even with no prospect of compensation, to give England every possible advantage through favourable rates on her manufacturing specialties. But a gratuitous British preference was politically dangerous, and for the moment would have to be given up.³⁴

On February 13, Parliament opened. It was extremely cold weather, with flawless blue skies and glistening white snow—"royal weather", the newspapers called it, and fit for the Princess who now ruled the household at Rideau Hall.³⁵ The incoming trains were stuck for hours in snow-drifts; but, despite these interruptions, Ottawa was crowded with people, and for years there had not been so much stir and circumstance at the capital. On opening day, Macdonald drove his own "modest trap" up to the great entrance of the central building; and when, a few days later, he rose to speak in the debate on the address, he was at his best—laconic, easy, and humorous.[36] He could afford to be confident. The new tariff was to be the great measure of the first session; and for the new tariff he thought he could predict a tremendous reception. He had, on his side, a sympathetic governor, a large parliamentary majority, and, in Canada as a whole, an expectant and hopeful electorate. There was only one unknown element in a highly favourable situation. He did not know what England's attitude to the new tariff would be. He was concerned about England's attitude. England was such an immensely important factor in all his plans for the future that he could not afford for a moment to take her views for granted.

He expected, of course, that the British government would express a theoretical disapproval of a protective tariff. But, at the same time, he did not believe that there was the slightest likelihood of British opposition to the new duties. Yet he could not assume acquiescence. He had promised to submit his fiscal proposals to the Colonial Office for approval before introducing them into the Canadian Parliament. He would have to do so. But time was running extremely short. The deputations of manufacturers were still arriving at Ottawa. Tilley, his eyes red and inflamed with his work, was still bending over the complicated schedules. It was not until the very last moment that Lorne was able to dispatch the new tariff to London for imperial examination;[37] and the telegraphic reply was received in Ottawa only forty-eight hours before the time scheduled for Tilley's budget speech. What a characteristic reply it was! In a tone of resigned submission to invincible economic error, Sir Michael Hicks Beach informed Lord Lorne that Her Majesty's government regretted that the general effect of the new tariff appeared to be an increase of duties already high. "They deem however," he went on, "the fiscal policy of Canada to be a matter for decision by the Dominion legislature subject to treaty obligations."[38] It was the inevitable, the only possible, answer. There had been pained disapproval at Whitehall. There would probably be grumbling protests from Birmingham, Manchester, and Glasgow. But Tilley was at work on a detailed memorandum which would show how, through the determination of specific rates, the Canadian government had tried to give British manufacturers a concealed but real advantage over their American rivals.[39] And, once the memorandum was handed in, would not the matter be tactfully permitted to drop?

Macdonald had expected an easy course that session. So far as his own policies were concerned, it was all very plain sailing. But the small, local, utterly gratuitous disturbances of the Letellier affair aroused nearly as much anxiety as a first-class tempest in national politics. The Quebec Conservatives, despite the defeat of the motion of censure in the previous Parliament, continued to nurse the most rabid hatred of the Liberal Lieutenant-Governor of Quebec. Their fanatical determination to have his head, far from being diminished, seemed actually to be increased by the inconvenient constitutional fact that he had secured a premier, Joly, who, in accepting office, had assumed responsibility for the dismissal of de Boucherville and who had so far managed to retain a majority in the provincial legislature. Early in December, J. A. Chapleau wrote to Macdonald, enclosing a protestation against the action of the Lieutenant-Governor and demanding his political execution on the ground that all forty-seven of the Quebec Conservative members of Parliament were heartily in favour of it.[40] Before the month was out a deputation from Quebec arrived in Ottawa to press the same demand orally and with the greatest possible emphasis.[41] It was inevitable now that the matter would be brought up again in the new Parliament; and early in the session Macdonald's motion of censure of the previous year was introduced by Ouimet. On March 13, the night before Tilley's budget speech, it passed the Commons by the crushing majority of one hundred and thirty-six to fifty-one.[42]

What could be done? Macdonald was in a highly uncomfortable position. In his opinion, the Lieutenant-Governor of Quebec had acted in an arbitrary fashion. He told Lord Lorne that he thought Letellier had "behaved as badly as any man could".[43] Moreover, his dislike of this particular Lieutenant-

Governor was not mitigated by an extreme veneration for the office which he held. It was no part of Macdonald's creed to exalt the political consequence of lieutenant-governors. His inclination had always been to look on provinces virtually as subordinate municipal institutions; and nobody was readier than he to emphasize the fact that the lieutenant-governors were responsible "officers of the Dominion". Yet, at the same time, he knew very well that since Confederation the affairs of the provinces had been carried on in accordance with the "well understood principles of responsible government", and that, in a system of responsible government, responsibility for the actions of a lieutenant-governor was borne by his constitutional advisers. He was inclined, for this very good reason, to leave the quarrel between Letellier and his ex-ministers to the judgment of the Quebec legislature and the Quebec electorate. The other English-speaking members of the Cabinet would also have preferred to keep away from something which was not strictly their business. But the French-Canadian ministers, with what Lord Lorne deprecated as "Gallic violence", insistently demanded Letellier's dismissal. Macdonald resisted; but he could not resist indefinitely. He confided privately to the Governor-General that "it was impossible to make Frenchmen understand constitutional government".[44] But he did not propose to make the Letellier affair an occasion for imparting forcible instruction in parliamentary rules to his Quebec colleagues. Towards the end of the month the Cabinet finally decided to advise the dismissal of the Lieutenant-Governor; and on March 29 Macdonald presented their decision to Lord Lorne.[45]

He was not surprised—for he had talked the whole matter over with the Governor-General as early as their train ride up from Halifax—to learn that Lord Lorne was not prepared immediately to act on the Cabinet's advice.[46] The Governor-General was aghast at the vindictive partisanship of the French-Canadian ministers and members. The dismissal of Letellier seemed to him to be at once a repudiation of responsible government and an invasion of provincial autonomy; and he requested Macdonald to give his reasons in writing for advising such an extreme step. There was no doubt, of course —and Lorne knew it—that he would have to yield in the end or run the risk of a constitutional crisis far more serious than that which Letellier had provoked. But Macdonald was not in the least eager to apply the collective pressure of the Cabinet on his unwilling chief. He pondered the matter for a few days; and then on April 2, he returned and suggested that since the Letellier case presented a new problem, for which there were no precedents, in Dominion-provincial relations, it should be referred to the British government for settlement. The Governor-General closed readily with this offer.[47] He did not like the thought of arguing formally with his Prime Minister in documents which would have to be made public; but on the other hand he believed that somebody in authority should read the Canadian government a serious lecture on the constitutional unwisdom of the step it proposed to take. The reference to England seemed a highly convenient device to him; and for somewhat different reasons it appeared equally serviceable to Macdonald. What Macdonald wanted was delay. A delay of a few months, or even of a few weeks, might see the downfall of Joly, the return of the triumphant Conservatives to power in Quebec, and the consequent disappearance of all real reason for the political execution of Letellier. It was a definite possibility—a perhaps too obvious possibility— and the French Canadians were by now too determined, excited, and suspicious to accept postponements readily. They may have smelt a calculated delay in the wind; and they insisted that Langevin be sent over to London to urge the British government to reach a quick decision.[48] Macdonald yielded; Lorne yielded; and Langevin—with J. J. C. Abbott for company —set out.

In the meantime, the interminable debate on the tariff went on. All the conceivably relevant arguments had already been repeatedly rehearsed, on countless occasions, since the great discussions had begun in the winter of 1876. But the relentless talk continued. "Another day of profitless debate on the tariff . . .;" Macdonald reported to Lorne on March 28, a fortnight after Tilley had delivered his budget speech;[49] but nearly another month went by before the House disposed of the resolutions in committee and the bill introducing the new duties was read the first time. Macdonald took little part in these protracted proceedings; and it was not until the comparatively short debate on the third reading of the Bill that he intervened at any length. It was the kind of opportunity that always tempted him. Alexander Mackenzie, as if he too had become bored to tears by the subject, devoted most of his final speech on the tariff to a discussion of constitutional points and economic theories as advanced by such writers as John Stuart Mill and Goldwin Smith. Macdonald made the obvious retort that Goldwin Smith, who had made a stump speech in aid of the Conservatives on the eve of the election of 1878, was a repentant ex-free-trader, who had been converted from his previous doctrinaire Liberalism by the bitter experience of five years of Liberal rule. The memory of those five appalling years, Macdonald insisted, would keep the Canadian people safe in the "abiding city" of Conservatism for a good many lustrums to come. It might be, he went on, that in some distant future, and from some height of lofty impartiality, he would look down and see the position of the parties in the Canadian Parliament reversed. But that spectacle, he concluded, would not be in his time.

Mackenzie was on his feet in a moment. A thin, tight-lipped smile appeared and vanished on his face.

"I would merely remark," he said briefly, "the honorable gentleman does not mean he would look downwards. He would look upward."

The House laughed. But Macdonald would not permit this laugh to be the last.

"I always look up to my honorable friend," he answered urbanely, and the incident closed.[50] That night the Tariff Bill passed its third reading.

He had done what he had promised to do. The first session of the new Parliament ended triumphantly; and, as John Carling assured him privately, he stood at the very pinnacle of his prestige.[51] But the new tariff was only the beginning. The most difficult part of his programme still lay ahead; and, since

CLOSE OF THE PLAY AT OTTAWA.

GRAND TABLEAU.—THE TRIUMPH OF VIRTUE.

there was no time now to waste, he had planned a most strenuous summer. Parliament had authorized renewed negotiations for the construction of the Canadian Pacific railway; the Cabinet had decided to establish an important and permanent Canadian agency in London; and it was arranged that he, and Tilley, and Tupper—the most impressive Canadian delegation to cross the ocean since 1866—were to set out for England late in June to discuss these and other matters with the imperial authorities. Agnes, who was to visit England with her husband, and little Mary, who was to spend the summer at Rivière du Loup in the care of her two devoted servants, left Ottawa for Montreal on the morning of June 26.[52] Macdonald had expected, of course, to sail with his wife. But at the last moment his departure had been postponed because of the imminent dismissal of Letellier. The delay, however, would be for a few days only. He would follow in the next ship. And his mind was filled with pleasant anticipations of his near release from work, when the hard blow fell. Only a few hours after Agnes had said good-bye to him, he was struck down by a terrible attack of cholera—cholera accompanied by agonizing cramps and spasms which reminded him horribly of the pains which nearly ten years ago now had almost ended in his death.[53]

The medical men—Doctors Grant and Tupper—energetically took control. The frightened servants looked after him devotedly; and, through the hot, windless days of early July, he lay in bed in the empty house on Sandy Hill, trying impatiently to get well and worrying about the future. Only two years ago, he remembered, he had been boasting to Lord Dufferin about his good health, and the definite change for the better which had taken place in his constitution. He had relied upon the doctors, and the doctors had been proved wrong. He and they had built far too much upon the temporary well-being which he had enjoyed during the years in opposition. Had he not been well largely because he had been free from responsibility? And how far was this present attack the result of the incessant strain and overwork of the last eight months? The disappearance of the frightening cramps reassured him, and he recovered fairly quickly from the cholera. But his strength did not come back at once. He tried to shake off his weakness, as he tried to forget its ominous significance. Would he ever be able to finish the work he had set himself to do? Surely he ought never to have accepted office. He had come back, against his better judgment, because of an irresistible inner compulsion. He had realized that he alone could do the work that Canada needed at that moment. He had realized that the Canadian people believed that he alone could do it. He had come back; and in eight months he had been struck down with one of his worst attacks. How could he go forward confidently? Yet how could he give up the task? He had not much strength. And equally he had not much time.

IV

He sailed from Quebec on July 26—nearly a month later than he had planned to do;[54] and on Monday, August 4, he was comfortably established at Batt's Hotel, Dover Street, Piccadilly.[55] It was very late in the season. The House was about to prorogue, holidays and shooting beckoned delightfully ahead, and, as John Rose explained regretfully to Agnes, "all the world are flying". In fact, the days before the general exodus were so few that those who wished to show the Macdonalds some hospitality had actually to compete with their invitations. Rose, who expected to leave London in the following week for a pleasant series of visits to Scottish country houses, was quick to arrange a dinner party in his old friend's honour for Thursday, August 7. "It is entirely a scratch affair," he explained, "but the best that could be done at this season."[56] And, in order that he and his wife Charlotte, before their departure for Scotland, might both see something of the Macdonalds, he invited them down to his Surrey house, Loseley Park, for the following weekend. Saturday night could have been happily spent at Loseley. But Saturday night happened to be the night on which the much-engaged Colonial Secretary, Sir Michael Hicks Beach, had also planned to entertain the Canadian Prime Minister.[57] It was his one free evening, he confessed in some embarrassment. He had ventured to invite a few friends in to meet Macdonald; and Lord Beaconsfield would be there. As a matter of fact, Lord Beaconsfield was not there, for, as he explained to Hicks Beach, he had received "a peremptory summons to Osborne" from the Queen.[58] But it was obvious that the Colonial Secretary had done his best under difficulties and

that the Conservative political world would be largely represented at his dinner table. Macdonald made his excuses to
the Roses and dined that night at the Hicks Beach house in
Portman Square.

Already, late in the morning of the same day, he had had
his first long, confidential interview with Sir Michael at the
Colonial Office. He had faced this meeting with real trepidation.
As always in the past, so much depended upon the reception
which his plans might get in England; and this time, as he
knew very well, he had some daring proposals to make. From
what Lord Lorne had told him and from what he had himself
surmised, he knew that he had no excuse for being over-
confident. But still he hoped. For the first time since 1868 he
would have Conservatives, not Liberals, to deal with in Whitehall. His chief, Lord Lorne, had written ahead—to no less a
person than Disraeli—bespeaking a friendly welcome for his
Prime Minister and a sympathetic consideration for the Canadian projects. "Sir John Macdonald," he wrote tactfully, "is
perhaps the last Canadian statesman who entirely looks to
England, and who may be believed to be devoted to imperial
interests—notwithstanding the present tariff which is not in
accordance with recent British doctrine."[59] The present tariff,
Macdonald was quick to explain to the Colonial Secretary,
had been framed entirely to obtain revenue and to stop the
inundation of American imports. Even in its present form,
through "a somewhat complex classification of imports", the
tariff gave discreet but real advantages to British manufacturers; and these advantages could be openly and greatly
extended provided Great Britain were prepared to reciprocate.[60]
An imperial preferential system was, in effect, Macdonald's
first proposal. His second was a request for British financial
aid for the Canadian Pacific railway.[61] The railway, he tried
to impress upon Sir Michael, would for the first time provide a
safe route through British territory to the Pacific and the Far
East. It was essentially a great imperial undertaking, more
deserving of British support than either the construction of
the Intercolonial Railway, or the transfer of the Hudson's Bay
Company's territories had been.

Hicks Beach was interested, and not definitely negative in his responses. But at the same time he was hardly encouraging. Already, in two speeches given early in the spring, Lord Beaconsfield had publicly pronounced against the re-introduction of protection for British agriculture. France and Germany would try to defend their farmers with tariffs; but Great Britain, at this decisive crossroads in the history of her commercial policy, decided to take the other turning. There would be no new Corn Laws; there would therefore be no possibility of imperial preferences for cereals; and an Anglo-Canadian reciprocal trade agreement was really out of the question. An imperial guarantee in aid of a Pacific railway loan was a possible subject for discussion; but a favourable outcome of the discussion, the Colonial Secretary implied, could hardly be expected at the present moment. The Conservative government, he confided to Macdonald, had been terribly harassed recently by obstruction in the Commons; and the unpopularity of the new Canadian tariff in England would certainly be used to the full by the opposition against any government measure in aid of the Dominion. It would be quite impossible to push through a guarantee act before the close of the session, even if the British Cabinet agreed to sponsor one.[62] The whole subject had perhaps better be postponed until after the prorogation—possibly until after the now rapidly approaching general election. Macdonald resignedly accepted the suggestion of delay. He had expected, from what Lord Lorne had told him before he left Canada, that the Colonial Secretary would look unfavourably on his proposal.[63] To press it now would be to court a definite refusal.[64] He preferred to wait and pick the matter up again.

With this—and it was not very much—Macdonald had for the moment to be content. The next morning he travelled down to Guildford, and Rose's country house.[65] Loseley Park was one more proof—if, indeed, one more proof were needed —of how successfully the clever and engaging John Rose had fitted in to the second land of his adoption. It was an old, spacious stone house, built during the decade of the 1560's, at a time when the English Gothic tradition was being rapidly modified in accordance with Renaissance ideas, and when feudal irregularities were yielding place to more restrained lines and stricter symmetries. It had a special historic interest, for it had once belonged to Sir William More, kinsman of Sir Thomas More, Henry VIII's chancellor; and its great hall was beautifully decorated with the carved, inlaid, and painted panels which had been acquired from Henry VIII's fantastic palace of Nonsuch. A fairly large party, including the Galts and Hewitt Bernard, had already assembled at Loseley by the time the late guest arrived. Macdonald would have a good time —he always did on these occasions. But he had another and a more particular reason for welcoming the Roses' week-end invitation. In his long conversation with Sir Michael he had brought up the third project—the project of a Canadian "diplomatic" representative in London—which he had come to England to urge.[66] About this he was terribly in earnest. But at the same time he realized that he could hardly make any definite decision in the matter until he had talked it over thoroughly with John Rose. It was the simplest essential of courtesy and friendliness to inform Rose; and since Rose expected to leave on the following Tuesday for holidays in Scotland he would have to be told at once.

As Macdonald sat in the cool, shadowy library at Loseley, he was unhappily aware that the approaching conversation would be difficult and might be positively painful. Rose was one of his best friends. Rose had for years served the Canadian government well and faithfully as its confidential agent in London. As far back as the autumn of 1869, immediately after he had resigned his post as Canadian Minister of Finance, Rose had been "accredited to Her Majesty's government as a gentleman possessing the confidence of the Canadian government"; and six years later, during the Alexander Mackenzie régime, he had been appointed to the newly created post of Financial Commissioner for the Dominion of Canada.[67] Two governments had employed him and valued his unostentatious services. But if a Canadian "mission" were to be formally established in London, a Scotsman who had become a permanent resident of England could hardly be appointed as its first head. Indeed, Rose's name had not even been considered, and the Canadian government had selected Galt as its first choice. Galt, Macdonald knew only too well, was ambitious for himself and sensitive to the rivalry of others. He would try to extend the boundaries of his diplomatic domain to the furthest possible limits. But Rose, on the other hand, had financial connections which Galt could not hope to acquire in a hurry. Macdonald thought he saw a way of retaining Rose's services. He was extremely anxious to do so. And it was, therefore, with an extra measure of circumspection that he approached the subject of the Canadian "Resident Minister" to his old friend.

The next morning, when he took the train back to London, he felt sure that Rose's acquiescence—regretful, if not exactly reluctant—could be counted upon.[68] It had been necessary to be delicately tentative with Rose. With the Colonial Office he could press his point in a more forceful and outspoken fashion. What he had to propose was certainly extraordinary. But, then, Canada itself, in the state to which he had now brought it, was something utterly unparalleled in British colonial history. "Canada," as Galt was pointing out in the round, mouth-filling phrases of his memorandum, "has ceased to occupy the position of an ordinary possession of the Crown. She exists in the form of a powerful central government, having already no less than seven subordinate local executive and legislative systems, soon to be largely augmented by the development of the vast regions lying between Lake Superior and the Rocky Mountains."[69] Canada had grown immensely in importance. She was developing her own identity and character. And the existence of the new tariff was only one proof of the unquestionable fact that her interests—now essentially different from those of the United Kingdom—required different promotion and special advocacy. She must have a new and important representative in London—"Resident Minister" would be an appropriate title—who could speak with authority on her behalf to the imperial government, and who could promote her interests in the chancelleries of Europe.

Macdonald knew what he was about. He realized that his

proposal meant the extension of colonial responsible government into the hitherto unoccupied territory of foreign affairs. He knew, as the Governor-General knew, that this was "the beginning of a difficult question, for Canada will more and more wish to make her own treaty arrangements".[70] He did not wish to break up the diplomatic unity of the Empire. The diplomatic unity of the Empire was still essential to Canada; and he believed, as the Governor-General believed, that it might be possible "to stave off for a very long time to come any wish on the part of Canada for a separate set of representatives in foreign countries". But the existing diplomatic unity could not be maintained unless Canada were satisfied; and Canada would be satisfied only if her interests and her representatives were given the prominence and the consideration which they now desired. "The sooner the Dominion is treated as an auxiliary power rather than as a dependency," Macdonald wrote in an assertive final paragraph to Galt's memorandum, "the sooner will it assume all the responsibilities of the position including the settlement of its contribution to the defence of the Empire whenever and wherever assailed. A precedent may to some extent be found in the position of Hungary with respect to the Empire of Austria." He paused a moment, considered the last sentence thoughtfully, and slowly drew his pen through it. Yet the words remained to suggest the ultimate goal of his thoughts.

Whether that ultimate goal were ever reached or not, there could be no doubt that the nation he was creating now enjoyed a new and vastly enhanced prestige in England. He accepted the civilities and honours that were given to him as, in large measure, a tribute to Canada. But there was one distinction which he could not help regarding, in some degree at least, as a vindication of himself. It was eight long years since Earl de Grey had delicately hinted in Washington that imperial Privy Councillorships might occasionally be bestowed on particularly distinguished colonial public men. It had been eventually decided to make him a member of the imperial Privy Council, as a reward for his services on the Joint High Commission of 1871. But the honour could be conferred only by

swearing in the recipient at a meeting of the Council; and it
was obviously impossible for Macdonald to come to England
before he had fought and won the election of 1872. The award
was to be a post-electoral triumph. But fate, unfortunately,
disposed of matters rather differently. The sequel of the election
of 1872 was not the honour of admission to the imperial Privy
Council but the public disgrace of the Pacific Scandal; and as
soon as the full, dreadful enormity of the Pacific Scandal
began to be appreciated in England, Sir John Macdonald's
still ungranted honour became the subject of shocked and perplexed review. The whole question was, Lord Kimberley
admitted to Mr. Gladstone, a "very delicate one";[71] and Mr.
Gladstone agreed that it was so. Could the Queen's consent,
once granted, be withdrawn? It was hardly possible. But it
was even less possible for Her Majesty's government to be put
in the equivocal position of seeming to reward corruption. Sir
John Macdonald could hardly come over to England now and
claim admission to the Privy Council. If, unhappily, he did,
his imprudence would give rise to "very unpleasant discussions".
He would have to be asked to wait.[72]

Well, he had waited. He had waited for six long years. And
now he had come back, his disgrace obliterated in the triumph
of a new election, his place in the trust and affection of the
Canadian people emphatically re-confirmed, to obtain his reward. This time there were no doubts or reservations; there
were no hints of delay. On Thursday, August 14, ten days
after he had landed in England, he took an early morning
train down to Osborne. And at two o'clock in the afternoon,
at a meeting which was attended by the Duke of Northumberland, the Duke of Richmond, the Lord Chancellor, and Mr.
Home Secretary Cross, he was formally sworn in as a member
of Her Majesty's Privy Council.[73] He had an audience of
the Queen; and by evening the new Privy Councillor, who
could henceforth expect the words "Right Honourable" before
his name, was back in London and dining with the Scotts,
who were connections of Agnes, in Onslow Square.

He was pleased with his new honour—with the fact that
it had come, in the end, from a Conservative government. He

was gratified by the flattering reception he and Agnes had been given in London. And Agnes, of course, was enchanted by it. "It would amuse you to see how Agnes swells it . . . ," he wrote happily to his sister Louisa.[74] They went again and again to the theatre; there were frequent dinner parties; they spent a pleasant week-end at Highclere Castle, as guests of Lord Carnarvon; and both Lord Monck and Lord Dufferin sent hearty invitations, which in the end had to be regretfully declined, to visit their houses in Ireland. It was, as he told his sister, a highly agreeable succession of "civilities"; and its climax came, appropriately enough, in the first days of September, when his time in England was drawing to its close. "Lord Beaconsfield asked me to-day to give you a message . . . ," Sir Michael wrote. "He hopes you will go to dine and sleep at Hughenden on Monday next, if that day should suit you."[75] Macdonald was both surprised and delighted. When Disraeli had failed to appear at the Hicks Beach dinner, he had given up hope of meeting him. Beaconsfield was an old man. He had gone off, very soon after the session ended, to rusticate quietly at his country house, Hughenden Manor. But—and it was a new sensation in British Prime Ministers—he still felt a sense of obligation to pay some attention to the "Canadian chief". The Queen regrettably had not invited Macdonald to stay to dinner at Osborne the day he had been made a Privy Councillor; all the great houses in town were shut; the Salisburys were away at Dieppe. "This vexes me," Beaconsfield wrote in embarrassment to Lord Lorne, "as I feel your ministers ought to have been festivaled and banquetted, but what are we to do with guests who will visit London in August?"[76] There was only one thing to do, and he knew it. He invited Macdonald to come to Hughenden and Macdonald delightedly accepted.

Hughenden Manor lay in the Chiltern Hills, close to the market town of High Wycombe. Macdonald travelled down by the late afternoon train on Monday, September 1; and Lord Beaconsfield's carriage was waiting for him at the Great Western Railway station. Hughenden stood on high ground, overlooking its own park, and a small church and

churchyard. Built in the 1780's, with clean lines, sparse ornamentation, and pleasantly spaced sashed windows, it had begun
life as a typical Georgian house, unremarkable in all respects
save one. Its single peculiarity then was that it was built of red
brick with blue headers. But Disraeli was an ardent follower
of the fashionable Gothic revival; and at his orders the property
had been altered, with misplaced ingenuity, to present a spurious
Tudor appearance. Inside was a rather ornate drawing-room
with blue damask hangings and French rococo furniture, and a
small, rather ugly dining-room, where Macdonald dined alone
with Disraeli and his young secretary, Daly. After dinner they
climbed the stairs to the smoking-room, which was a kind of
auxiliary library, on the top floor of the house, and there they
talked until well after midnight.[77]

"He is gentlemanlike, agreeable, and very intelligent; a considerable man . . .," Disraeli wrote of his guest next day in
a letter to Lady Bradford.[78] It was not a bad tribute from
one veteran to another. Macdonald was certainly acquiring a
new reputation and his country a new prestige; and, as the
visit to England drew to its end, he had reason to feel not
entirely dissatisfied with its results. It was true—and he admitted it regretfully—that he had not attained the three objects
he had come to London to seek. The British government obviously considered preferential tariffs an utter impossibility;
and it had postponed consideration of both the railway guarantee
and the resident Canadian minister. Yet, on the other hand,
Tilley had had no difficulty in borrowing another three million
pounds for his immediate requirements; and from the replies
which the Canadians got to their tentative inquiries in the
city, it seemed likely that there would be capital available,
at reasonable rates, to build the Canadian Pacific railway.
London was deep in the despondency of the depression; but,
at the same time, Macdonald was conscious of a new respect
for Canada and a new interest in its future. He carried that
pleasant impression back with him, across the Atlantic, along
with the warm memory of his visit to Lord Beaconsfield; and
on September 23 he was back in his new house, Stadacona
Hall, on Sandy Hill, in Ottawa.[79]

V

Almost immediately it began—the event for which he and so many others had hoped and prayed so hard for five long and terrible years. Times began to improve. The first signs of change were admittedly timid and tentative, and he watched developments anxiously, sceptically. He had waited so long. So much depended upon a real economic recovery that he could not permit himself for a minute to indulge false hopes. And yet, as the long, warm, golden autumn of 1879 drew placidly on, he began at last to concede, even to himself, that the improvement was a miraculous certainty. Everything showed it. The harvest had been bountiful. Prices were going up. The volume of imports slowly declined, while that of exports began to rise steadily upwards. "Trade is recovering wonderfully . . . ," Lorne wrote proudly to Hicks Beach.[80] The ministers gloated. And Macdonald knew that the whole future of his government had been dramatically changed. Within a year of his accession to office, his commercial programme had been vindicated by a demonstration as convincing as it was fortuitous. The National Policy was borne away towards success on the swift wheels of an accelerating prosperity. For a time, while this good fortune lasted, he would be able to do almost anything successfully. He might even succeed—it would be the supreme piece of luck—in inducing a commercial company to take over the whole gigantic project of the Canadian Pacific railway.

If only he felt better physically . . . But somehow, despite the agreeable holiday in England, he had not recovered completely from the sharp, sudden attack of the early summer. His strength had not entirely come back; he seemed to tire easily. It was nothing serious, but it kept him depressed, and, at times, suddenly and painfully eager to be free of the cares of office. All autumn he waited, almost impatiently, for the British government's decision on the Canadian proposal for a resident minister in London. He almost persuaded himself that it would be favourable. He was fairly sure that he could count on Beaconsfield's good will. In September, soon after he had left for Canada, Beaconsfield, in a speech at Aylesbury, had spoken at some length and very favourably of Canada. Macdonald was highly delighted to know that the information which he had imparted that night at Hughenden had been used so quickly and so effectively by the British Prime Minister; and he wrote Disraeli a letter of warmly sincere thanks.[81] Surely the British Conservatives had begun a new era in colonial history. Surely they would see the needs of the "auxiliary kingdom" of Canada, and realize that "allied powers" such as Canada and Great Britain really required a "semi-diplomatic" relationship. Yet they seemed to take an incredibly long time to make up their minds. October went by. It was not until nearly the end of November that the Governor-General called in Macdonald, Tupper, and Tilley—the three ministers who had gone to England the previous summer—and laid before them a long dispatch from Sir Michael Hicks Beach.[82]

As he read it, Macdonald could not help feeling a little disappointed. The dispatch was not ungracious in form or negative in substance.[83] It merely exhibited a lack of imaginative understanding of a new and developing situation. Yet it was obvious that the British ministers believed they had gone very far—and had in fact gone quite a long way—to satisfy the Canadian demands. They graciously welcomed the appointment of the new Canadian "representative"; they predicted that his services would be valuable to both Canada and England. But he could not be, they insisted politely, an officer truly diplomatic in character. ". . . His position," Sir Michael's dispatch went on to explain, "would necessarily be more analogous to that of an officer in the Home Service than to that of a minister at a foreign court." His chief business would be to communicate with the Colonial Office on Canadian affairs; and if Canadian interests were found to be involved in any negotiation with a foreign power, it would, of course, rest with the Foreign Secretary to determine in what capacity the representative could best render his assistance. For all these obvious reasons his status could hardly be regarded even as "quasi-diplomatic" in character; and the title "Canadian Commissioner" or "Dominion Commissioner" would describe his position more accurately than the somewhat grandiose designation which the Canadian government had suggested.

To Macdonald the reasoning which lay back of this cautious, well-meaning document was obvious. The British government was frightened of condoning even the semblance of a separate foreign policy in a country for which it still felt politically responsible in the eyes of the world. There remained, as Lord Salisbury indicated emphatically to Lord Lorne, the "solid and palpable fact that if they are attacked England must defend them"; and it followed, as an inevitable corollary of this indefinite liability, "that England must decide what their foreign policy shall be".[84] No body could be more anxious than the British government, Hicks Beach insisted, to know the views of Canada and to consult her interests in every imperial negotiation affecting her. "But," he went on, "the Dominion cannot negotiate independently with foreign powers, and at the same time reap the benefit which she desires in negotiations from being part of the Empire."[85] No direct formal communication could possibly be set up between a colonial government and foreign powers. The foreign powers would certainly not accept it. Neither could the British government.

Macdonald was a little disappointed, but he did not feel that he had suffered any serious defeat. He was simply encountering the inevitable misunderstandings which await the political innovator. It was a question of words as much as of facts; and in letter after letter to his superiors in England, the Governor-General tried to ensure that his ministers' wishes were not misinterpreted. "Among sensible men here," he wrote to the Marquess of Salisbury, "there is no wish to conduct negotiations separately, but only that the interests of what Sir J. Macdonald calls 'this auxiliary kingdom of the British Empire' be pushed as the interests of an integral part of the whole."[86] The last thing that Macdonald desired was a separate foreign policy for Canada. For him the diplomatic unity of the British Empire remained at once a reality and an ideal. But, at the same time, he was convinced that it was only through a recognition of the existing political plurality of the Empire that a real and effective diplomatic unity could henceforth be achieved. The duties which had been transferred from the British government to the Canadian government, the tasks which Canada, as heir to half the continent of North America, had assumed since Confederation, were of such obvious and increasing importance that, as the Canadian Council observed in its formal reply to the Hicks Beach dispatch of November, "their discussion and settlement have become subjects for mutual assent and concert, and thereby have, it is thought, assumed a quasi-diplomatic character. . . ."[87]

The general superintending authority of Great Britain would remain formally undisturbed; but in actual fact, as the Canadian Council pointed out, the imperial government would now be "more correctly defined as representing the United Kingdom than the Empire at large". The diplomatic system of the Empire must be adjusted so as to admit these incontrovertible facts. The foreign policy of the Empire must become a collective enterprise, in which Canada and each of the other great colonial governments would have the influence which its strength and importance required. Canadian interests must from now on be accepted as a major concern of British diplomacy; Canadian representatives must henceforth play an increasingly important part in the conduct of British diplomacy; and the Canadian government, through "constant and confidential communication", must be kept at all times thoroughly informed of all that concerned it in the realm of foreign affairs. "If these essentials, proper backing and equal opportunities be given," Lord Lorne wrote to Salisbury, "we may hope to keep public men here content with the present system."[88]

The Canadian reply to the views of the British government was made at length in the formal report of the Privy Council as well as in the letters and dispatches of the Governor-General. Macdonald was determined that the Canadian case should be fully stated; but he had no intention of getting into an argument over the matter with the British government. The new Canadian representative in London would prove himself by deeds, not words; and there was no point in quarrelling about the importance of his office before it was established.

Having won the main point in the argument by getting his new officer accepted by the British government, Macdonald was quite ready to make concessions. He was even prepared to concede something in respect of the new representative's title —something, but not very much. "Resident Minister" was the title which the Canadian government had first proposed. Because of its obvious implications of diplomatic status, "Resident Minister" was plainly unacceptable to the British government. But, on the other hand, "Dominion representative" or "Canadian representative"—the pale alternatives suggested by the Colonial Office—were completely unsatisfactory to the Canadians. Instead they proposed a new designation, "High Commissioner of Canada in London". The British government considered this suggestion for some time in silence; and then, on the last day of January, 1880, the Colonial Office replied that, unless Canada considered the matter of very great importance, the title "Special Commissioner" might be preferred as more appropriate.[89]

Macdonald would have nothing to do with this last tentative proposal. Galt, he informed Lord Lorne bluntly, was not going to England for any special purpose, "but to represent Canada's interests generally". "Resident Minister" was the best designation on all counts, and since it would have to be conceded some day in any case, why should it not be conceded now? "It seems to me," he wrote tartly to Lord Lorne, "that it is a matter of no importance to the imperial government what title we may give our agent. We might call him 'nuncio' or 'legate a latere gubernatoris' if we pleased. It is, of course, for the imperial government to settle the status of our agent in England, under whatever title he may present himself. Since the title of 'Resident Minister' is objected to, I think we must adhere to that of High Commissioner."[90] They did adhere to it. They suggested, indeed, that the British government might reconsider favourably the designation "Resident Minister". Failing that—their first choice—they announced that they were prepared to accept their own alternative of "High Commissioner for Canada in London". On February 7, one week before the opening of the Canadian Parliament, the Colonial Office telegraphed that "the title of High Commissioner will be recognized under the Great Seal of Canada".[91]

It had come—and much as he wished it. One more point in his programme had been dealt with. Canada was prosperous at home and recognized abroad; and, during the winter months of December and January, while he prepared for the second parliamentary session of a successful government, his thoughts kept turning repeatedly, almost longingly, towards retirement. He did not feel quite right yet. He needed and deserved rest; and since, after a year in office, his government was even more securely established than it had been in October, 1878, he could now—and never more appropriately—step out of office. Tentatively he began to sound out his friends. What did McCarthy, and Galt, and Rose think of his intentions? It was plain, unfortunately, that McCarthy, Galt, and Rose did not take him very seriously. McCarthy, who evidently considered that Macdonald was merely tired and needed a rest, invited him up to Barrie for a few days' holiday.[92] Galt, who had himself undergone a recent and reassuring medical examination, observed philosophically that perhaps, in both their cases, the machinery was getting a little worn down. "As the old saying is, however," he concluded cheerfully, "it is better to wear out than to rust out."[93] Rose, as was his nature, offered perhaps the most consolation. Yet even Rose seemed to regard Macdonald's decision with real if unexpressed incredulity. "I am not surprised," he conceded, "that you long for a rest. Though I am six years behind you, my longings are in the same direction, but worries and responsibilities seem to thicken as one gets older. But you are a *marvel*; and how you have survived and kept up your energies and vigour, in spite of the increasing and arduous cares that have pressed upon you is hardly short of a miracle. I am not half the man that you are, and will be far less so six years hence."[94]

It was complimentary, but, at the same time, slightly exasperating. Everybody seemed to count upon his inextinguishable vitality, to rely upon his indefinite continuance in office. He pushed the matter of his retirement away—but not very far. It lay in the top drawer of his mental cupboard, as he prepared in a leisurely fashion for the new session. Parliament opened on February 12. The House of Commons proceeded onward in its usual unremarkable fashion through its usual unremarkable activities. Galt, who, in his characteristically impatient fashion, had somewhat prematurely made all arrangements to sail for England on March 26, was to be given a farewell dinner in Montreal two days before his departure. Macdonald planned to attend; and the Galt dinner was the only special event to which he was looking forward when he took his place in St. Alban's church on the morning of Sunday, March 21. He never heard the end of the service. Suddenly, with the same mysterious and frightening absence of warning, he slumped forward in weakness. He had to be helped from church.[95] His carriage brought him swiftly back to Stadacona Hall.

The faithful Dr. Grant, hastily summoned, was soothingly reassuring. The attack, in itself, was not serious. The newspapers barely mentioned it. He could return to the House almost immediately and outwardly things would go on for a while much as they had gone on before. Outwardly only. The attack had shaken him terribly. He had survived it, as he had survived others before; but it was one more unmistakable indication of the steady worsening of the general state of his health. He could not go on. He must retire now—while there was still time. Only a few weeks ago, he had been called upon to pay the government's tribute on the sudden death of Luther Holton; and Holton, the senior English-speaking member from Quebec, was almost exactly the same age as himself. As he lay on the sofa, gradually recuperating, that Sunday morning in March, he came to a tremendous decision. He would act now—at once. Within forty-eight hours the ministers were all informed of his decision. Tupper would have to represent him at the Galt dinner, and the next day, March 25, a Cabinet would consider the whole matter of the leadership.

Macpherson's letter reached him before Council met. Macpherson, Minister without Portfolio, who had been ill and was only slowly recuperating, had realized that he could not attend the Cabinet meeting; and he had spent the morning of March 24 setting down in writing his reflections on the astonishing revelation that Macdonald had made to him the night before. The words of Macpherson's letter were emphatic; its tone was one of deepest concern. "The step you said you meditated taking," he wrote, "seems to me to be fraught with such grave consequences to the Conservative party and the country that I will not allow myself to believe in its possibility. The consternation it would cause in Parliament and throughout the Dominion in the Conservative ranks would equal that which reigned at St. Petersburg on the occasion of the explosion in the Winter Palace."[96] At the moment, Macpherson insisted impressively, Macdonald's retirement was quite literally unthinkable. His work could be lightened. The Conservative majority was surely big enough to give him all the help he required. But he could not retire during the session. He ought not to think of retiring for years to come.

The next day Macdonald met the Cabinet. It was a company of Macphersons. The other ministers repeated Macpherson's words; they echoed his tone of incredulity and consternation. And, as he looked at their appalled and beseeching faces, Macdonald realized that he would have to give in. His impulsive decision to retire at once—a product of weakness and apprehension—was already losing the original force of its conviction. How could he possibly retire in the middle of the session? The bill establishing the High Commissioner of Canada in London had not yet passed the House of Commons. In England a general election was to take place within a week, and the possible return of Gladstone and the Liberals to office might complicate and embarrass Galt's assumption of his new duties. Galt—the sensitive and unpredictable Galt—would require watchful coaching for weeks. His labours had not yet been successfully started. Things were never really finished and done with. There was so much of Macdonald's programme that had not been completed. And above all there was the Pacific railway.

The railway was the one absolute essential for the Canada he hoped to build. The railway would be the means of peopling the western prairies and promoting eastern industry. It would ensure both national integration and national development.

It was the track of the future—the track of destiny. It had beaten him once. It had plunged him and his party into the worst disaster of their joint career. And the triumphant completion of the railway was something which he owed alike to each member of that indivisible trinity—Canada, the Conservative party, and himself. Now the whole country was quickening with renewed prosperity and reviving confidence. Now the chance of success was greater than it ever had been. How could he give it up?

Chapter Nine

Contract for Steel

I

It was at this point that George Stephen re-entered his affairs. He had, of course, known George Stephen before. He had known George Stephen for the sufficient reason that he knew everybody of any real importance in the business world of Canada. And George Stephen was undeniably important. Since 1850, when, a young man not yet twenty-one, he had arrived in Canada from Scotland, Stephen had certainly enjoyed an impressively solid and impressively swift success. Beginning modestly as a junior partner in a Montreal importing house, he had gradually developed a substantial interest in a variety of Canadian manufactures—textiles, steel, and railway rolling-stock; and in 1876—it was the highest distinction which the business community of Canada could award—he had been made president of the Bank of Montreal. He was a tall, thin man, with a long oval head, sunk slightly forward on his chest, a pair of deep-set, brooding eyes, and a thick beard and drooping moustaches which seemed to emphasize his melancholic and watchful air of reflection. Nobody could doubt his financial sobriety and wisdom; he would not otherwise have been made president of the Bank of Montreal. But at the same time his prestige was not founded solely on a sober record of prudence, probity, and hard work. There was about him an air of distinction which was apparent not only in externals—he was a bit of a dandy and had for some time employed a valet—but also inwardly in the imaginative daring and originality of his mind. He trusted to his first illuminating impressions; he relied upon his insights. He had courage, resolution, and unflagging enterprise. He had a sense of the present and an eye for the future.[1]

The departure of John Rose had left a gap in the circle of Macdonald's mercantile friendships; but George Stephen was not destined immediately to fill it. Macdonald got to know him well, though not with any affectionate intimacy; and their acquaintanceship, an agreeable and intellectually stimulating association, continued uneventfully until it began to be affected, in various curious ways, by still another relationship, a close, family relationship, of Stephen's. Donald A. Smith, the Hudson's Bay Company officer who had gone up to Red River in 1869 as the representative of the Canadian government, and who in 1873 had abandoned Macdonald at the final crisis of the Pacific Scandal, was a first cousin of George Stephen. The family connection, as always in Scottish households, was strong; but it was not the only tie which drew Smith and Stephen together. They became good friends, and close business associates. They prospered together—and not unequally. The knowledge and experience of the one complemented those of the other. Stephen's main interests lay in the St. Lawrence valley; Smith's beyond Lake Superior. And it was Smith who performed the crucially important office of awakening Stephen's interest both in railways and in the north-west.

The chain of events was so natural as to seem inevitable. Donald Smith, who was frequently obliged to make the long journey from Montreal to Winnipeg on Hudson's Bay Company business, acquired a deepening interest in the problem of communications between eastern Canada and the Canadian north-west. Some day, perhaps, in some dim future, a great Canadian Pacific railway would provide a transcontinental all-Canadian system of transport. But that stupendous project had been postponed—how long?—by the Pacific Scandal and the depression. Must the Canadian west wait until more favourable circumstances permitted the revival of the great scheme? Or was there another and a much simpler way of providing at least provisional communication with the settlements on the

Red and Saskatchewan Rivers? Smith was firmly convinced that there was. The materials for such a provisional system were either already in existence or soon would be. The Mackenzie government was building a branch of the future Canadian Pacific from Winnipeg south to Pembina at the international boundary. An American railway, with the ambitious title of the St. Paul and Pacific Railroad, was feeling its way slowly and with difficulty northwards towards Canada. The St. Paul and Pacific, like its great rival, the Northern Pacific, and like the Canadian Pacific itself, had passed through a series of involved financial calamities during the years of the depression. Would it not be possible, Donald Smith reasoned, to get control of it at a bargain, to persuade the Canadian government to lease running rights over the Winnipeg-Pembina branch, and thus to complete railway communication—though admittedly through American territory—between eastern and western Canada?

This was the proposal which Smith persuasively presented to Stephen; and Stephen, after a journey out to St. Paul and a trial run over the lines of the St. Paul and Pacific, eventually decided to join his cousin in the enterprise. He had begun his apprenticeship in the financing and management of western railways at a most favourable opportunity and with the most suitable associates. Donald Smith knew the west as well as any Canadian then living. James J. Hill, a Canadian by birth, and his partner, N. W. Kittson, who both became members of the new syndicate, had already had a great deal of experience in north-west transport; and Richard B. Angus, the first general manager of the organization, had acted for years in the same capacity in the Bank of Montreal. It was a tight, efficient combination of practical experience and financial power; and in the next few years it swept forward, in an easy and assured fashion, towards success. The St. Paul and Pacific Railroad was acquired, renamed, with a more precise indication of its real purpose, the St. Paul, Minneapolis, and Manitoba Railway, and pushed rapidly northward towards the Canadian border. In the meantime, the promoters, with Donald Smith acting the part of an enthusiastic and highly imprudent advocate in the

Canadian House of Commons, proceeded to negotiate with the Mackenzie government for the lease of the Winnipeg-Pembina branch.[2]

It was at this moment that Macdonald had intervened. He had the best of reasons, political and personal, for attacking the Pembina lease. The Pembina lease was a vulnerable feature of the railway policy of the Mackenzie government; and ever since the catastrophe of the Pacific Scandal, he had cordially acknowledged Donald Smith as his enemy. On the last scandalous day of the session of 1878, he and Tupper had leaped, with avenging fury, upon the Pembina lease and its defiant parliamentary defender. At the moment it was beyond their power, of course, to prevent the Mackenzie government from transferring the branch to the control of the St. Paul, Minneapolis, and Manitoba Railway. But that autumn the Mackenzie government went out of power; and Macdonald and the Conservatives were presented with an opportunity of wreaking an appropriate revenge on Donald Smith and his friends. They did exactly what might have been expected of them. They got authority from Parliament to effect a change of plan. They dispensed with the assistance of the St. Paul, Minneapolis, and Manitoba Railway and made other interim arrangements for the running of the Pembina branch.

Curiously enough, this seemed to end the whole episode. Macdonald's anger was apparently appeased. Yet, at the same time, the fortunes of Stephen, Smith, and Hill did not seem to have been adversely affected. What remained, after all the quarrelling over the Pembina branch had died away, was a growing awareness among Canadians of the opening of a new and extremely exciting chapter in the history of their own north-west. Early in December, 1878, the first train pulled out from St. Boniface, across the river from Winnipeg, for St. Paul. In retrospect, it must have seemed the train which carried the whole project of western development up the shining tracks of prosperity to success. Since then settlement had advanced on both sides of the international boundary; both divisions of the new railway system had prospered; and in the spring of 1880, after Stephen's company had been in operation under its new name for only a little less than a year, it triumphantly published a first annual report, which disclosed a considerable profit, not only from railway traffic, but also from sales of land. Stephen, who only a few years before had been as ignorant of the west as he was uninterested in railways, stood suddenly revealed, in the eyes of interested North Americans, as a tried and successful veteran of western transport. With the help of a land grant from the Minnesota legislature and a prudent reduction of the fixed charges borne by his reorganized company, he had driven a railway across the prairie and into the heart of the north-west. He had opened a whole empire for settlement. Exactly the same kind of effort—enormously, portentously magnified—must be made in the Canadian north-west, if ever the hopes of the Fathers of Confederation were to be realized. Had not Stephen shown that he was capable of it? Inevitably Stephen became the focus of the long-locked-up hopes and aspirations of those who were concerned in the project of the Canadian Pacific railway. A new future seemed to open up before him, and he began to realize his destiny. So also did Macdonald.

II

In the spring of 1880, Macdonald stood at a significant middle point in his new lease of power. It was getting on for two years since the election of 1878. It would be a good two years more, at least, before he would have to submit his record to the verdict of the Canadian people. He had not done too badly. A good part of his programme was now complete. The return of prosperity, about which even the most confirmed cavillers could hardly express a doubt any longer, had confirmed and generalized the complacent feeling of satisfaction throughout Canada; and abroad, in Great Britain and the United States, the two countries which counted most in the external affairs of Canada, conditions, though not so reassuring as at home, were certainly not serious enough to cause any real alarm.

It was true that the recent general election in England had brought Gladstone back for the second time to power, and that the approaching presidential contest in the United States had once again encouraged Republicans and Democrats to display their rival prowess in the heroic republican exercise of twisting the British lion's tail. The American government and the American Congress were in their usual state of pre-election belligerency. There had been a protest about the movement of a group of western Indians across the international boundary. A loud complaint had been made over the seizure of an American fishing vessel in Fortune Bay off Newfoundland; and it had been announced that the Bulwer-Clayton Treaty of 1850, by which Great Britain and the United States had formally agreed to a joint control of the future Panama Canal, could no longer be regarded as compatible with the oracular injunctions of the Monroe Doctrine. Macdonald refused to be alarmed by this intimidating series of demonstrations. "I have seen many presidential elections in the United States," he explained resignedly to Lord Lorne, "and at every one of them the rival parties tried to excel each other in patriotism, and that patriotism always consisted of attempts to bully England. Hence just now the angry discussion of the Fortune Bay affair, the proposed abrogation of the Bulwer-Clayton Treaty, the threatened cancellation of the fishery clauses in the Washington Treaty, and this discussion about Sitting Bull and his Sioux. All that England has to do is to play with these questions till the new election comes off and then all will be quiet until the spring of 1884 when these, or other subjects which will answer the same purpose, will be revived."[3]

England was more important. In this second, western phase of Macdonald's programme of national expansion, the attitudes of the British government and of British finance counted enormously: the view which the great mass of the British people took of Canada as a home for emigrants might make or mar the whole great scheme of western settlement. For the next few years or decades, the High Commissioner of Canada in London had a rôle of great significance to play. That was why the office had been established at that particular moment, and why Galt had hastened over to England. Macdonald took the intellectual abilities of his new High Commissioner very seriously; but Galt's personality never ceased to afford him entertainment. "Some touches of character will amuse you—if they don't bore you," he wrote jocularly to Lord Lorne, enclosing a great sheaf of Galt's letters from London.[4] Galt was always writing letters. He was the highly articulate romantic who is constantly pouring forth his soul on paper. From the moment he landed in England, he had experienced the most intoxicating succession of hopes, doubts, slights, encouragements, anxieties, and mental excitements generally. He worried about his house, his family, his expenses, his "status" in the "corps diplomatique", and the delicate problems of his introduction into the society of official London. He was appalled to discover that his present spouse, being his deceased wife's sister, could be presented at Court only with the special permission of the Queen. With remarkable precipitancy he came to the conclusion that the new Gladstone government was coldly antagonistic to the Canadian High Commissionership and that the Colonial Secretary and his whole department would do nothing whatever to enhance the importance of his office.[5]

Macdonald always placed a heavy discount on Galt's copiously temperamental effusions. Galt, he explained dryly to the Governor-General, was inclined to be a little "fidgety". "His letters show how impulsive he is," he went on. "Lord Kimberley is not celebrated for cordiality of manner and Galt jumped at once to the conclusion that the government were unfriendly. He is, I suppose, reassured by Mr. Gladstone's remark that he was glad Canada had taken the step of creating the office. That awkward business of Lady Galt's presentation has ended happily."[6] It had ended in the Queen's reaching the grave conclusion that since Galt's second marriage had been contracted in the United States, where marriages with a deceased wife's sister were unaccountably legal, Lady Galt's case might therefore be regarded as an exception from the general rule, and Lady Galt herself might be received at a royal Drawing-Room. Many—if not most—of Galt's problems were either solved or forgotten in the short interval which elapsed before their victim took up his busy pen to write again. Macdonald could afford to treat these small chronic alarms and despondencies rather cavalierly. But there were other disappointments, closely related to the principal objects of the High Commissioner's office, which aroused his serious concern. "Most unsatisfactory interview with Colonial Minister respecting emigration," Galt cabled on June 7. "He holds out no expectation of assistance. . . ."[7] Here was an important and disconcerting check. Galt's prime function in England was to arouse the interest of the British people in the Canadian north-west, and enlist the assistance of the British government in its settlement. "The most important subject which can engage the attention of the High Commissioner in England," Galt's instructions declared emphatically, "is the development of the North-West Territory."[8]

The development of the North-West Territories had become Macdonald's main concern. For a Prime Minister whose programme was national expansion on a continental scale, the settlement of Canada's prairie empire stood out obviously as the great remaining task. The preliminary work had all been done. The aboriginal title to the land had been extinguished, and the Indians—or most of them—had been settled on the reserves. The claims of the *métis* to a secondary aboriginal title, and their demand for its extinguishment by special additional grants of land or scrip had been the subject, during the winter of 1879, of prolonged inquiry and consideration.[9] All the western authorities who were consulted had pronounced firmly against the policy, which had been tried out with such very mixed results under the Manitoba Act, of making a general grant of negotiable scrip. In the old days when the west was free, the *métis* had been able to fend for themselves very well. But they were bewildered by the approach of North American civilization and vulnerable to its devices; and, according to experienced westerners, a grant of negotiable paper would merely make them easy marks for the land speculators without bringing them any permanent benefit. The negative testimony was impressively unanimous. But there was no comparable agreement among the experts as to the positive policy which the Dominion should adopt; and the small but naggingly insoluble problem of the satisfaction of the half-breeds' claims remained.

It was one of the few—the very few—complications, Macdonald could proudly boast, which troubled Canada's management and disposal of the quarter-continent which had fallen to it with the cession of the Hudson's Bay Company's territories. Whereas a good part of American expansion towards the Pacific had been piecemeal, unplanned, and haphazard, Canada was fortunately in a position to organize and prepare in advance for almost the entire process of settlement. A system of free homestead farms, comparable to that of the United States, but with somewhat easier terms and conditions, had been adopted as the staple of the federal land policy in the west; and a great, single, uniform survey for the entire region, based accurately upon the astronomical system, was being pushed forward efficiently but at headlong speed.[10] The land was ready—or nearly ready—for occupation. It needed settlers to people it and transport to get them there. The Canadian government had spent, and was prepared to go on spending, lavish amounts on immigration propaganda. Galt himself was the visible embodiment of a great new effort to capture the imagination of Great Britain and Europe for Canada and Canada's unoccupied west. Immigrants were vitally necessary. But immigrants would be helpless without transport for themselves, their effects, and their future produce. At the moment Winnipeg was the furthest outpost of the communication system. It could not be permitted to remain so. The immigrants must be carried westward to the valleys of the Saskatchewan. And for that last advance there was only one possible vehicle—the Canadian Pacific railway.

Here again Macdonald's luck held. For seven long years, despite all the lavish inducements which his and Mackenzie's governments had held out, no capitalists worthy of consideration had come forward to claim the privilege of building the Canadian Pacific railway. He had almost reached the gloomy conclusion that, even though the depression had lifted, there would never again be any offers. And then, just when the need had become really imperative, when the delay had been stretched out until it could be stretched no longer, the offers began. They were tentative, exploratory offers—in some cases mere suggestions or whispers of offers; but all during that happy June of 1880 they kept stealing in. Galt reported that the shareholders of the old Canada Company were showing a curious interest in the Pacific railway project; it was rumoured that Brassey, the fabulously successful English railway contractor, had been making inquiries; and on June 22, when the Canadian Cabinet was actually in session considering the subject, Macdonald received a telegram from a certain Lord Dunmore, announcing that he had just arrived in New York from England and was hastening up to Ottawa with an offer to build the railway.[11] After the long neglect and discouragement of the past, this sudden respectful attention was highly gratifying. Moreover, these hints and promises of British offers were not all. There was still another proposal—which had originated in Canada. It was presented by Duncan McIntyre, who now controlled the Canada Central Railway, a railway which had been planned to run from Ottawa to Lake Nipissing, and which would thus provide a vitally important link in extending the future Canadian Pacific eastward to the head of navigation at Montreal.[12] Duncan McIntyre was the principal in the conduct of the negotiations; but, as everybody knew, back of him were the directors of the St. Paul, Minneapolis, and Manitoba Railway. Back of him, and towering above all the others, was George Stephen.

It was the most important single decision of the second half of Macdonald's career. He had chosen wrongly the first time—he had chosen Hugh Allan; and total disaster had been the result. He had won the right to a second choice. It was upon him now; and this time there must be no mistake. He must not try to hurry. Every consideration must be weighed, every aspect of the problem must be thoroughly investigated; and he himself would reserve judgment until the end. He baffled his colleagues, through long days of Cabinet discussions, by his bland impartiality. He found virtues in every offer; his references to that amiable, aristocratic figure-head, Lord Dunmore, were gravely respectful. "You spoke of Lord

Dunmore," Campbell wrote, a bewildered and accusing note in his words, "as if his name added weight, great weight, to the proposal made by him and Mr. Brown, whereas it seemed to me just the sort of thing men of business and of means would not resort to, and tricksters and stock-riggers would—I mean to put forward a nobleman. And besides that he is, if I rightly understand it, a spendthrift and most probably a dupe of some knaves or other."[13]

It was all, or most of it, true, Macdonald reflected. Lord Lorne was warning him very impressively that Dunmore was a notorious speculator with "a very good heart, no head, and no money".[14] The firm which sought to impress gullible colonials with such an emissary was obviously suspect. But was Puleston, Brown, and Company, the company which Dunmore represented, to be dismissed solely on that account? Nobody in Ottawa, Macdonald discovered, could tell him anything of importance about Puleston, Brown, and Company; and this lack of significant information was another serious element of uncertainty in a foggy and treacherous situation. The hints of further British offers persisted; and now it was rumoured that Andrew Onderdonk, the contractor for the government-built section of the Canadian Pacific in British Columbia, was about to tender still another proposal.[15] Everybody was aware of Stephen's experience, immense ability, and great financial strength; and at least a few members of the Cabinet were in favour of coming to terms with his syndicate at once. But McIntyre and Stephen demanded a cash subsidy of twenty-six and a half million dollars and a land grant of thirty-five million acres. Was it possible to accept such an offer at this stage of the negotiations? Could a decision be reached while other proposals remained unexplored?

Macdonald realized that it would be highly dangerous to decide at once. The maximum terms which could be offered, the Cabinet decided, were a cash subsidy of twenty million dollars and a land grant of thirty million acres.[16] Macdonald did not believe that he could risk a subsidy of more than twenty millions. Yet McIntyre and Stephen inflexibly refused to consider anything less than the sum which they had demanded. It was a stalemate which neither side dared immediately to break; and on July 5, McIntyre wrote to Macdonald, informing him that it was the wish of his syndicate "that the subject may be considered as being closed for the present".[17] *For the present.* The words were significant. A phase of the negotiations had certainly been terminated. But it was the first phase only. Already the Cabinet had decided that the negotiations would be suspended only to be renewed in England;[18] and a committee, consisting of Macdonald, Tupper, and John Henry Pope, had been appointed to proceed to London and to examine the various offers in greater detail there. Macdonald planned to leave within a week, on July 10. He knew that Duncan McIntyre was sailing on the same day, and on the same ship; and when he left Quebec he carried with him a reassuring message from George Stephen. "Although I am off the notion of the thing now," Stephen confided to him, "should anything occur on the other side to induce you to think that taking all things into consideration our proposal is better upon the whole for the country than any offer you get in England, I might, on hearing from you, renew it and possibly in doing so reduce the land grant to some extent."[19]

Macdonald reached London and the Westminster Palace Hotel on July 19.[20] Agnes had not accompanied him; she had stayed behind at Rivière du Loup with Mary; and the journey which he had undertaken was severely, peremptorily, practical in its nature. There were few theatres and concerts; there were still fewer public dinners, and agreeable, lazy week-ends at country houses. He had come to negotiate a contract for the Pacific railway, not to renew his previous siege of the Colonial Office; and the only event of any political importance in his visit was his appearance before the Royal Commission on the Defence of British Possessions and Commerce abroad. This Commission had been established largely as a result of the Russian scare of 1878, and one of its principal objects was to investigate the division of imperial and colonial responsibilities in defence. Macdonald's evidence was cautious, and non-committal in character. With the Russian crisis safely over, and with the prospect of an enormously costly railway contract immediately before him, he knew that, at the moment, he could not run the risk of making heavy military commitments. He had not yet felt it possible to carry out the plan he had formed in 1878 of increasing the small nucleus of the Canadian permanent force; and although he had often talked in the past of an "alliance" between the "central power" and the "auxiliary kingdom" of Canada, he did not fall in with the Commissioners' evident desire to define more exactly the reciprocal obligations of the colony and the Mother Country. In his view, there already existed a moral engagement for defence between England and Canada. The pledges which had been exchanged during the conference of 1865 and the arrangements which had been made in 1871 when the imperial troops were withdrawn from Canada, constituted, as he saw it, an informal treaty for the defence of British North America. He did not believe that these commitments could be safely extended or generalized at that particular moment. It would surely be extremely unwise, in a period of peace, to raise the question of Canada's possible contribution to a hypothetical European war in which Great Britain might be engaged. That discussion, he told the Commissioners firmly, had much better be postponed until the conflict had come or was imminent.[21]

This interview was the only important interruption in his negotiations for the railway. He stuck closely, pertinaciously, to the mission which had brought him to England. He had, as he told his sister Louisa, allowed himself six weeks', or two months', absence from Canada, in which to settle the business. Time was of the essence. He hunted up John Rose, got in touch with Sir Michael Hicks Beach, the ex-Colonial Secretary, whose opinion he had come to value highly; and on the Friday of his first week in London he had a long talk with Sir Henry Tyler, president of the Grand Trunk Railway Company.[22] It was mere prudence to give the Grand Trunk one last opportunity to consider the project; but it was plain at once, if there had been any doubt about the matter, that the Grand Trunk was not, and could not be, seriously interested. So long as the old railway held to the strategy on which it had originally been planned, the natural extension of its lines was from Sarnia to Chicago and so westward south of the Upper Lakes. "I have no belief myself in any line of railway running to Fort Garry for a long time to come through British territory," Brydges, the general manager of the Grand Trunk, had written in 1872, at the time of the contest between Allan and Macpherson for the first Pacific railway charter.[23] Eight years later, as Macdonald sat in Sir Henry Tyler's office, it was plain that a railway running north of Lake Superior was just as inconceivable to Grand Trunk officialdom as it had been eight years before. In effect this settled the matter. Macdonald was prepared to compromise about many things. But he had no intention of making the slightest compromise about the route of the Canadian Pacific railway. The Canadian Pacific was to be a national railway. It must run—every inch of it— through Canadian territory.

The Grand Trunk Railway dropped out. The Onderdonk group decided that it could not compete in the short time available.[24] The other offers, of which there had been so many rumours, failed to materialize. It was—or seemed to be—a straight contest between Puleston, Brown and Company on the one hand, and McIntyre and his associates on the other. And Puleston, Brown and Company, which had seemed such a dubious organization in Ottawa, certainly took on weight and stature in London. Lord Dunmore, the agreeable and impecunious peer, faded discreetly into the background; and J. A. Puleston, who appeared to be a much more substantial and influential person, energetically took command of the negotiations for his company. On the very day of Macdonald's arrival in London, he carried the Canadian visitor off to the Speaker's gallery in the House of Commons and kept introducing him to what seemed quantities of highly important friends. He was reputed to have vast, if somewhat mysteriously undefined, backing in the City. He could apparently rely upon the support of certain influential European bankers—Baron Erlanger, M. Demère of the Société Générale, and the Reinachs of Paris and Frankfort—whose names gave to his syndicate an air of truly continental distinction. His scheme was admittedly somewhat complicated; but it had features which were extremely attractive politically. In place of the cash subsidy which he had at first requested, and which was considerably smaller than that asked by McIntyre and Stephen, Puleston finally agreed to substitute a government guarantee, for a term of years, of the interest on the very large bond issue which he proposed to float. It was attractive—it was undeniably attractive; and on one of the last days of August, Macdonald tentatively drafted a significant cable to Tilley. "Almost agreed," he wrote, "with Société Générale of Paris, equal in standing to London and Westminster Bank, at nineteen millions cash, thirty-two millions land. Instead of cash may agree to equivalent guarantee of interest for term of years not exceeding twenty. Deposit of one million sterling as forfeit. Do Council concur? Answer quick."[25]

Yet, at the last moment, he hesitated. The cable was apparently not sent. Only a few days later, on September 2, Puleston reported that the Société Générale had decided not to go ahead with the venture;[26] and this refusal, as he himself recognized, brought his scheme as a whole to an end. Had Macdonald ever really seriously considered Puleston as the principal promoter of the national transcontinental railway? There were those in the City who doubted it. "In plain English," one of Puleston's supporters wrote angrily to Macdonald, "it has been said that it was a foregone conclusion from the beginning that a certain set of people should get the business and that Puleston could not under any circumstances have got it, and much more of a stronger character."[27] It may all—or most of it—have been true. Certainly Puleston was not essential as a principal. His backers were more important than he was; and, as the event proved, they could be got without him.

But there was more than this. Puleston was an ordinary promoter. Stephen was a man of exceptional ability who had just achieved a ringing success in the very kind of enterprise which was at stake. He had, moreover, identified himself very closely with the land of his adoption; and Macdonald wanted a truly Canadian leader. The negotiations with Puleston may have been at least half serious; but early in August Macdonald and his colleagues recommenced their long discussions with McIntyre, and on August 12 the Stephen-McIntyre syndicate offered to build the railway for a cash subsidy of twenty-five million dollars and a land grant of twenty-five million acres.[28] As August drew towards its close, and Puleston was finally eliminated, Macdonald came rapidly nearer to an agreement with the Canadians; and on the morning of Friday, September 4, he sat down with McIntyre and the two Roses—John and his son Charles—to settle the provisional terms of the contract.[29] That afternoon the cable which he had come to England to send and for which all his colleagues in Ottawa had been waiting, was finally dispatched. "Best terms can be got," it read, "are twenty-five million cash, twenty-five million acres. . . . Four colleagues here concur. Hope you concur. Absolute secrecy. Answer quick. Telegraph Tilley. Sail next Thursday."[30]

III

It was done. And despite the long, grinding labour of the summer and the awful sense of his responsibility, he felt positively elated by his achievement. "I had a very pleasant trip to England and back," he reported laconically to his sister, "but was obliged to work very hard. I have been rewarded by success. And am in good health and spirits."[31] Everybody seemed to be in good spirits. There were no second thoughts, or regrets, among any of the principals involved. George Stephen wrote him, warmly welcoming him back, and assuring him that he thought there would be no difficulty whatever in coming to a final agreement on all points. "I want whatever arrangement is made," he wrote, "that it shall be *fair, creditable* to both the government and ourselves, and that not a *day* should be lost in the preparation of the contract and the act of incorporation."[32] The preliminary agreement had been signed before the delegation left England. Only a little more than a month later, on October 21, at Ottawa, Tupper, Stephen, and a few of the other principals affixed their signatures to the greatest contract in the history of Canadian transportation.

Stephen, who was to be the railway's first president, stood out from the start as the recognized leader of the syndicate.

Duncan McIntyre, who had been so prominent in the preliminary negotiations, was to be the first vice-president, and Richard B. Angus the first general manager. The other directors of the St. Paul, Minneapolis, and Manitoba Railway, Hill, Kittson and Donald A. Smith, were all important members of the new syndicate, though Smith's name, for obvious political reasons, was prudently omitted from the contract—an omission which unexpectedly infuriated the temperamental Smith and caused him to behave, so Stephen wrote disgustedly, "like a baby over the thing". The only London financial house which entered the syndicate was Sir John Rose's firm, Morton, Rose and Company. New York was represented by Morton, Bliss and Company, which was the senior of the two Morton firms, and by John S. Kennedy and Company, the organization which had been so deeply concerned in the financing of the St. Paul, Minneapolis, and Manitoba Railway. From Europe came a French-German group, headed by Kohn, Reinach and Company of Frankfort and Paris, and including the French Société Générale. Their stake in the affair was small; but Macdonald, believing that the presence of the European names would help to conciliate public opinion in French Canada, attached great importance to their inclusion.[33] But they proved suspiciously, mulishly difficult; and they finally agreed to sign on the somewhat ominous condition that if, after more mature consideration, they decided in the end to back out, Stephen would assume responsibility for their share.

Macdonald was committed now—and to the hilt. He had gambled everything on the choice of the right men. He had bought ability, energy, and experience at the expense of every other consideration. The personal rivalries and sectional interests which had counted for so much in the negotiations with Allan and Macpherson eight years before had not, on this new occasion, had any appreciable weight with him at all. He had insisted that every effort should be made to bring round Kohn, Reinach and their French associates; but this was almost his sole concession to the small tactics of Canadian political manœuvres. He had swallowed his own personal dislikes, and thrown his record for political consistency to the winds. In the past, he had attacked the St. Paul, Minneapolis, and Manitoba Railway as an alien and sinister corporation, intent upon the ruin of a truly Canadian transcontinental railway; and he had publicly denounced Donald Smith as "the biggest liar he ever saw". Yet now he had made an agreement with the very directors whom he had previously exhorted the Canadian House of Commons to repudiate. The fact that Stephen, Angus, and McIntyre were all Montrealers, that not a single Torontonian was included in the original membership of the syndicate, would make it easy for the Liberals to goad a large and important part of Ontario into opposition. It would be even easier for Blake and his supporters to reverse the rôles of the past two years, to adopt Macdonald's previous attitude to the directors of the St. Paul, Minneapolis, and Manitoba Railway, and to hold up Stephen and his friends as a gang of Americans in all but name, who were intent upon appropriating the Canadian Pacific Railway for their own alien purposes, in much the same way as McMullen and his conspirators had tried to do eight years before. In fact, of course, Stephen, Smith, and Angus were not American railwaymen attempting to invade Canada, but Canadian railwaymen who had successfully invaded the United States. It was an important difference; but it was a difference which the Liberals would try to obliterate under cartloads of abuse. There was no blinking away the plain fact. The whole scheme was vulnerable at half a dozen different and obvious points.

Yet these, as Macdonald knew very well, were not the most important defects of the scheme. Its most important defect was something far more fundamental. The project of a Pacific railway through Canadian territory was a project only less formidable than that of the Dominion of Canada itself. The Dominion and the railway would both encounter the same acute difficulties for they shared a common ultimate objective. The prime purpose of Canada was to achieve a separate political existence on the North American continent. The prime function of the Canadian Pacific Railway was to assist in this effort —to help in the building of the national economy and the national society which alone would make this ambition possible of achievement. Like Canada itself, the railway would find its most powerful rivals, its most dangerous enemies, in the continent of North America. It was, by the basic intention of its planners, in competition with all the American transcontinental railway systems in general, and with the Northern Pacific in particular. Any close or important association with American railwaymen or financiers would, as the tragic case of Sir Hugh Allan had so conclusively proved, endanger, if it did not ruin, the railway's essential character and purpose. Neither the company nor the government which sponsored it could dream of accepting too substantial an amount of capital from the United States. Neither the company nor the government could expect real friends or genuine support in any part of North America beyond the boundaries of the Dominion. The Canadian Pacific was, by design, a contender for the traffic of a continent. American railways were its natural enemies. British finance was its natural support.

Yet, at the beginning at least, British finance declined to play its necessary rôle. The Anglo-Canadian alliance, which was the basis of Canada's independence in North America, was still effective in politics. But in finance, at this stage, it exerted little force. The polite indifference to Canada which, under the Gladstone régime, ruled at Whitehall, was translated, in the City, into a cold and critical suspicion of Canadian enterprises. Morton, Rose and Company, a relatively small and inconspicuous firm, alone joined the original Canadian Pacific syndicate. No important British financial house gave the project the slightest support or encouragement at the beginning; and at least one company, the Grand Trunk Railway Company, which had its headquarters in London, maintained an unrelenting and influential opposition for years to come. The great centres of English-speaking finance, London and New York, were either indifferent or hostile to the Canadian Pacific; the press of England and of the United States varied, in its attitude, between contemptuous neglect and active malevolence. *The Times,* which had not even troubled to consider the appointment of a correspondent at Ottawa, exhibited a "sneering indifference and superciliousness" to all things Canadian, which surprised and shocked Lord Lorne.[34] The American press associations, as their record amply proved, had never missed a chance of minimizing Canada's achievements and exaggerating its troubles and difficulties.

Abroad there was little help. Help would have to come from home. And at home the nation itself was the only organization which could possibly render the required assistance. In Canada, as Macdonald had the best of reasons for knowing, the mingling of railways and politics was inevitable. The subsidy of twenty-five million dollars and the land grant of twenty-five million acres, which, in effect, made company and government the joint proprietors of the enormous patrimony of the north-west, were simply the first and most impressive pledges of a partnership which grew tighter and more inextricable with the passage of time. The government relied upon the railway for the realization of its national purposes; the railway depended upon the government for financial support and political protection. By the terms of the contract it was exempted from most forms of taxation; it was permitted to import required materials duty free; and it was given complete liberty to build what branches it desired, while at the same time it was completely protected, by one of the most controversial clauses in the contract, from all railway competition south of the international border. "For twenty years from the date hereof," the notorious clause ran, "no line of railway shall be authorized by the Dominion Parliament to be constructed south of the Canadian Pacific Railway, except such line as shall run south-west, or to the westward of south-west; nor to within fifteen miles of latitude forty-nine."[35]

To this provision, the so-called "monopoly clause", which he always regarded as the translation into railway terms of the main principle of the national policy of protection, Stephen attached, from the first, an enormous importance. "Now what do you think," he wrote bluntly to Macdonald, three days before the contract was signed, "would be the position of the C.P.R. or of the men bound to own and operate it, if it were tapped at Winnipeg or at any point west of that, by a line or lines running towards the United States boundary? What would, in such a case, be the value of the C.P.R. line from Winnipeg to Ottawa? No sane man would give a dollar for the whole line east of Winnipeg. I need not say more on this point, as it must be clear to you that *any and every line south* of the line of the C.P.R. running towards the boundary line must be owned and controlled by the C.P.R., otherwise the C.P.R. would be strangled. The fact is, that if any doubt should exist in the minds of any friends on this point I could not carry them with me, and I need not say to you, that now I am into this thing, I would not like to be forced to give it up."[36]

No, Macdonald realized, Stephen could not be forced to give it up. His company was the one potentially successful company which, in all the thirteen years since Confederation, had come forward requesting authority to build the railway. Concessions would have to be made to it, for concessions were economically vital to its success. Yet every concession, Macdonald recognized, would make his own task so much more difficult politically. The railway's privileges, powers, and exemptions were such that it could all too easily be made to appear as a gigantic and overbearing monopoly. The terms of the contract could be used to give it the dreadful aspect of a leviathan. Yet, at the moment, it was nothing but a contract. It had only a fragile paper existence. And years must pass and anything might happen, before it took concrete shape in a glittering and unbroken track of steel. Until the goal of the Pacific was reached, the partnership of government and railway, necessary but embarrassing to both, must continue. At one stroke, Macdonald had assumed a double burden. Until the success of this huge dependency was assured, he would never be free from anxiety. And he could not give up until the Canadian Pacific Railway was complete. Could he survive the ordeal? He was old and he was not too well. But in George Stephen he had acquired a helper of quite extraordinary ability. He had chosen Stephen deliberately, and he had chosen better than even he knew. Stephen was perhaps the greatest creative genius in the whole history of Canadian finance.

IV

Until the act of incorporation had been passed and the charter granted, the syndicate was really helpless; and Stephen was importunate in his demands that Parliament should be called as quickly as possible. The session opened on December 9, a good two months earlier than usual. All during the protracted and nerve-wracking negotiations of the summer and autumn, Macdonald's health had remained surprisingly good; but now at length the strain began to tell, and he fell ill again.[37] He made light of his trouble at first, assuring Louisa that it was nothing but a touch of liver, and denouncing the "confounded newspapers" which always magnified his slightest malaise.[38] But Dr. Grant counselled him not to attend the ceremonial opening of Parliament, and the Governor-General wrote a kindly note begging him to follow his doctor's advice.[39] It was Tupper, the Minister of Railways and Canals, who rose on December 14 to move the adoption of the two basic resolutions, authorizing the cash subsidy and the land grant to the Canadian Pacific Railway;[40] and although Macdonald was in his place to hear this first, formal presentation of the government's case, he did not trouble to attend when Blake and Cartwright made their prolonged and passionate attacks upon the contract. He was still not completely recovered when the House adjourned for the brief Christmas recess. Hugh and his wife and their small daughter, Daisy, came down to Ottawa for the Christmas holidays;[41] and Macdonald watched his own child, Mary, who would never properly grow up, play contentedly with the little granddaughter who was so much her junior. The brief rest helped him a little. He told his sister that he was "pretty well now". But when the House re-opened, all too quickly, on January 4, he was still, in accordance with Grant's orders, staying at home as much as possible and avoiding exposure to the cold.[42]

In the meantime the opposition to the contract had been gaining in strength and pugnacity. The company's exemption from taxation, its privilege of importing materials duty-free, its unlimited authority to construct branches, and its monopolistic control of the whole traffic of the north-west, were all vulnerable features of the agreement which perturbed even good Ontario members of the Cabinet such as Campbell and Macpherson. Blake, Cartwright, and Laurier kept hammering away at these not too easily defensible points. Yet the opposition did not by any means confine its attacks to the admittedly debatable features of the contract. Criticism was at once more positive and more basic. Once again, as in the battle over the protective tariff, the Liberals set themselves in fundamental opposition to Macdonald's whole conception of Canada's future as a nation. They had opposed the National Policy with the principle of international free trade; they now resisted the all-Canadian railway with a policy of continental transport. It would be monstrous folly, Blake and Cartwright argued, to build a railway through the unprofitable, infertile country north of Lake Superior. This criminal absurdity of nationalism ought to be abandoned at once; and instead the Canadian Pacific Railway must find its way westward through American territory south of the lake.[43]

It was this continental, anti-national position which gave the Liberal party its principal allies and its main sources of strength in the prolonged battle against the Canadian Pacific Railway. The route to which the Liberal leaders now so publicly gave their blessing was, with variations, the route which the Grand Trunk Railway had always advocated, the route which existing American railways, including the St. Paul, Minneapolis, and Manitoba, had already appropriated. At one stroke Blake and his followers found themselves reinforced by the all too powerful interests in the United States and England which were determined to spoil the chances of a national transcontinental on Canadian soil. The great American press associations began to report the speeches of Her Majesty's loyal opposition at Ottawa in the most flattering detail. The Grand Trunk Railway, which had a considerable influence in

England, as well as the power of an extensive patronage in the newspapers of Quebec and Ontario, exerted itself to ensure that Liberal criticisms of the Canadian Pacific were given the widest possible publicity. "Reports appearing English press only mention doings of opposition," Charles Rose cabled in consternation from London. "Nothing mentioned other side. Suggest seeing Associated Press."[44] Macdonald must have smiled grimly. He had been through this so often before. It was only too probable that the Associated Press was feeding England with a string of biased and disparaging cables. It could be confidently assumed that the Toronto *Globe*, *The Times* of London, and the American Associated Press would become partners in an unofficial but none the less extremely effective alliance to injure the Canadian Pacific Railway and the government which had sponsored it. But what could be done? He had tried often before to get a fair hearing for Canada in England; and he had failed.

The climax of the Liberal opposition was reached about the middle of January with the sudden submission of a rival and —on the face of it—a much better offer to build the railway. It came from a group of Canadian capitalists, resident chiefly in Ontario, who declared they were ready to accept a smaller cash subsidy and a smaller land grant than Stephen and his associates had demanded, and who professed themselves willing to forgo all the principal exemptions and privileges which had aroused so much criticism against the original contract. Macdonald regarded this proposal as a transparently fraudulent manœuvre of party politics. Up to this point he had taken only the smallest share in the debate; but, on Monday, January 17, as soon as Tupper had formally presented the new offer to the House, he arose to defend his scheme at length and to quiet the growing doubts of his followers. "We have had," he declared, recounting the history of the Liberal opposition up to the moment of the introduction of the new offer, "tragedy, comedy, and farce from the other side. Sir, it commenced with tragedy. The contract was declared oppressive, and the amount of money to be given was enormous. We were giving away the whole lands of the north-west . . . this was the tragedy . . .

The comedy was that when every one of the speeches of these honourable gentlemen were read to them, it was proved that last year, or the year before, and in previous years, they had thought one way, and that now they spoke in another way. . . . Now, Sir, the last thing that came was the farce. We had the farce laid on the table today. The tragedy and comedy were pretty successful; but the farce, I am afraid, with an impartial audience, in theatrical phrase, will be damned."[45]

He went on to damn it. The new offer was, he claimed, a flimsy imposture, concocted in Ottawa by politicians rather than capitalists, and with politics rather than transport in mind. Some of its terms were, on the face of it, an improvement on those of the government scheme. But there was a simple explanation for these bargain figures. The irresponsible authors of the new proposal had not the slightest expectation of ever being called upon to build the railway. They could promise anything. They were perfectly free to offer the most absurd conditions. Most of the new scheme could be dismissed contemptuously as mere bluff; and the features which alone gave it its semblance of authenticity were precisely those which every patriotic Canadian ought decisively to reject. The new offer, Macdonald declared, was not for a transcontinental railway at all, but simply for a prairie section, which would be connected with the American railways and from which the trade of the Canadian north-west would be run off into the United States. "Mr. Speaker," he concluded, "the whole thing is an attempt to destroy the Pacific railway. I can trust to the intelligence of this House, and the patriotism of this country, I can trust not only to the patriotism but to the common sense of this country, to carry out an arrangement which will give us all we want, which will satisfy all the loyal, legitimate aspirations, which will give us a great, an united, a rich, an improving, a developing Canada, instead of making us tributary to American laws, to American railways, to American bondage, to American tolls, to American freights, to all the little tricks and big tricks that American railways are addicted to for the purpose of destroying our road."[46]

"Your speech," J. A. Donaldson wrote him from Toronto

on January 18, "was the whole topic of conversation through the whole city today . . . the champagne corks were flying like a humming fire of artillery."[47] He had made a great effort, for the importunities of Stephen and the restlessness of his own followers had convinced him that a great effort was necessary; and once again, from some mysterious source in his being, he had drawn the necessary strength. "I was luckily strong and well when I spoke," he told Galt, "which I did in the fashion of twenty years ago."[48] The praise of his friends and the satisfaction which he himself felt in his speech helped to carry him forward. He still hoped to pull through the session. But every day his health grew more shakily unreliable; and the business of piloting the Canadian Pacific Bill through the House kept nagging at him like an obsession. "It has kept me constantly at work," he told Galt, "to the exclusion of everything else, to strengthen the weak-hearted in both Houses." The pressure from the opposition was savage and intolerably persistent. "It was six o'clock this morning before I got home from the House," he wrote to Lord Lorne on January 26.[49] The next day the Liberals occupied the whole night with a long succession of futile amendments to Tupper's main motion, and the House did not rise until eight o'clock in the morning.[50]

The pace was a killing one, but somehow he contrived to carry on. On February 1 the Bill finally passed the Commons on a division of one hundred and twenty-eight to forty-nine; and next day the congratulatory telegrams and cables began to pour in. Even Baron Reinach sent his felicitations. But the message which perhaps pleased Macdonald most was one from Alexander Morris, who, twenty years before, had preached the creation of a greater British North America and who, in June of 1864, had helped to bring Brown and Macdonald together in the coalition which had made Confederation. "I write to congratulate you," Morris declared warmly, "on the second crowning triumph of your more recent life, second only to that of Confederation. You have now created the link to bind the provinces indissolubly together, and to give us a future and a British nationality."[51]

It was done, but the doing had nearly finished him. The

illness which in some incredible fashion he had managed to keep at bay for these vitally necessary weeks, now overcame his resistance and threw him. "The long sittings at last broke me down," he wrote to Galt, "and I had to betake myself to my bed for a fortnight and am only now beginning to crawl about."[52] It was quite impossible for him to be present on the momentous occasion when the Governor-General gave the royal assent to the Bill—the Bill which, in the eyes of a good many people, would probably bring political or financial ruin to all those who had conceived it. But the thoughtful Alexander Campbell, who had kept a close superintending eye on the final adjustments to the terms, hastened to give him an account of the last episode in the story. "It will do you good," he wrote, "to know that the Pacific Railway matter is through all the stages. We had the Governor-General down yesterday. I thought it more respectful to go out to Rideau than to write, and I found him quite ready."[53] Lord Lorne had inaugurated still another of the great national policies of the transcontinental Dominion. "At last the C.P.R. is a fixed fact," Macdonald wrote from his sick-bed almost jubilantly to Galt. "Royal assent given, royal charter under the act issued, company organized, and it now remains for Stephen and Company to show what metal they are made of."[54]

The first struggle was over. But it had been a costly one. It had damaged his health badly and it had lasted an unconscionable length of time. The impatient Stephen, who had gone to England to raise funds and encourage immigration, kept insisting, in explosive and angry letters and telegrams, that the "senseless" interruptions of the "malignant" Blake and his followers had put back the whole Canadian Pacific enterprise a full year. Macdonald was not disposed to take Stephen's romantic exaggerations too seriously; but he knew that their joint programme of western development had certainly been held up by the delay. Immigration on a large scale was essential to the success of the Canadian Pacific and to the triumph of his own plans; and, in this year of rising values and exuberant economic recovery, immigration was certainly flooding into the west as it had never come before. But Macdonald was anxious, in co-operation with the British government and the Canadian Pacific, to work out a great concerted scheme of organized settlement; and before he left England in the previous September, he had handed in a long confidential memorandum on the subject to the Colonial Secretary.

He had counted upon Galt to push the plan forward. But Galt disappointed them both. The High Commissioner had spent the autumn and winter in vain attempts to interest the British Cabinet in a government-supported immigration society; and in the end he reached the characteristically gloomy conclusion that Gladstone would never consent to put a copper of public money into such a project.[55] Stephen, though he was not so easily discouraged, was no more successful; and at length he too decided that it would be better to postpone the campaign for a while and to renew it again in the autumn. "It takes time," he wrote resignedly, "to create anything in this slow moving country."[56] Another season had gone by, and one whole phase of Macdonald's policy of western expansion had scarcely even been approached. Yet he and his colleagues seemed exhausted by their efforts. Tupper was ill. John Henry Pope was ill. Galt, who was disgusted with the English climate, the cost of English living, and his own miserable want of success with the English government, begged to be permitted to resign his post.

The worst of it all was that Macdonald could not seem to make any real recovery of his own health. Parliament prorogued on March 21, and he rallied for the closing. "We had last week a parting caucus," he wrote Tupper. "It was a most enthusiastic one, and I talked to them like a Dutch uncle about working in their counties."[57] It was his last stout effort of the season, and a few days after the closing ceremonies he suffered a sudden and serious relapse. "There was no ascertainable cause for it," he wrote Tupper a little later, "but suddenly I broke down—pulse at forty-nine, and great pain and disturbance in liver and bowels."[58] Dr. Grant was obviously very much alarmed. Apparently also he was out of his depth in the complications of the case; and, perhaps as a result, was inclined to be pessimistic and discouraging. He kept fussing nervously

over Macdonald, discovering new symptoms, and reaching new
and increasingly doleful diagnoses: he told his patient frankly
that the disease might be a cancerous affection of the stomach
and that he had better put his affairs in order.[59] Macdonald
could not believe that the time had come when he must take
these gloomy warnings literally. There were days when he
felt quite well enough to escape from his bedroom, and on
one occasion at least the ministers gathered round the dining-
room table at Stadacona Hall and a Cabinet council was held.[60]
But the improvement was not continuous and steady; and
though time drifted on and May succeeded April, he still felt
appallingly tired and weak. His sister Louisa, when she came
up from Kingston for a brief visit, was shocked to see him. "I
never saw John looking what I would call old till this time,"
she wrote to Professor Williamson. "His hair is getting quite
gray."[61]

Agnes, Hugh, and Louisa were all convinced that, as soon as
he was strong enough to travel, he must sail for England in
search of better medical advice and perfect relaxation. The
Cabinet ministers emphatically agreed. "My colleagues, *en
masse*, insist on my crossing the sea," he wrote to Tupper, "and
I propose crossing in the middle of May." His condition, he
realized, was far more serious than it ever had been since the
crisis of ten years before; but, despite his weakness and the
ambiguity of the future, he had no thought now of giving up
his task. The *Globe*, with its usual tender solicitude for his
welfare, announced that his recovery could now hardly be
expected, and that he was going away for an indefinite period,
"leaving the party without a head, and still torn by dissensions
as to the succession". He authorized C. W. Bunting, who had
succeeded to the control of the Toronto *Mail*, to make a public
denial of these insinuations;[62] and, in private, he was still planning for the future of the country and the party as if he expected
to continue indefinitely in office. He begged Tupper to hurry
home, for he was worried by the uncertain Conservative prospects in the approaching by-elections in the Maritime Provinces;[63] and he assured Stephen that he intended to take advantage of his visit to England to have a long talk with Bright,

Gladstone, and W. E. Forster, the Irish Secretary, about immigration.[64]

Only a little over a year ago, he had firmly determined to
resign. But now, though his physical condition was much
worse than it had been then, the thought of retirement did
not apparently cross his mind. Strange! But it was so. The
Pacific Railway, in some mysterious fashion, had settled his
resolution. He would not admit that he was finished. He
could not desert Stephen. He would stay until the completion
of the railway was assured. "As to myself," he told Tupper,
"my remaining ambition is to see that our policy is not reversed
and that the National Policy and the C.P.R. are safe from
1883 to 1888."[65]

He sailed from Quebec on May 21, and eight days later
was in Liverpool.

V

The first benefit of his arrival was a blessed reassurance from
the consultant of his choice. Dr. Andrew Clark would not
hear of Macdonald coming to see him; he came instead to Batt's
Hotel to see Macdonald; and on June 1 he gave him a long
and searching examination. The results were better than anybody had dared to expect. Clark told both Macdonald and Galt,
who hovered anxiously in the background, that he saw no evidence of organic disease, and did not suspect any. But he also
admitted that there was great functional derangement. "My
complaint," Macdonald reported to Tupper after the examination was over, "is catarrh of the stomach, with a gouty state of
body, not amounting to gout."[66] Clark prescribed a rigidly
simple diet, but otherwise did not order any special treatment.
The great thing, after the long and unbroken ordeal through
which Macdonald had passed, was rest.

Yet rest, if he remained in a London hotel, the easy
victim of callers, was the last thing he could expect. Galt
begged him to get out of the city as soon as possible;[67] and
Agnes and Hewitt Bernard began energetically to search for a

suitable place in the outskirts of London, where he could get the desired seclusion. In the end he and Bernard rented Denmark House, a furnished cottage in Upper Norwood, for a couple of months. The place gave him suburban quiet and fresh air, it was easily accessible to London, and, as he explained to Lord Lorne, he could take a walk through the nearby Crystal Palace when it rained.[68] When they moved out there and began their temporary housekeeping, Macdonald was still extremely weak. He had, of all misfortunes, caught a bad cold soon after his arrival in England, and he could not seem to shake it off.[69] For a while Clark visited him every day and kept "stethoscoping" him regularly. The doctor was obviously concerned, but he still insisted that things would soon be all right.

July came. Macdonald had been in England nearly six weeks, and the catarrh of his chest and stomach still troubled him. "I live according to a written regimen and dietary given me by Dr. Clark," he told Alexander Campbell. "I avoid as much as possible all invitations but those that are commands."[70] Yet the commands seemed to be fairly numerous. The Duke of Argyll gave a dinner specially for the Macdonalds. They had lunch with Princess Louise, the Marchioness of Lorne, who was back in England for a visit; and there were receptions at the Gladstones' and the Salisburys'. "You will say this is a pretty good list for an invalid . . .," he admitted to Campbell. But the invalid seemed to benefit from these agreeable diversions as well as from the peaceful regularity of the life at Upper Norwood. From then on he steadily and rapidly improved; and soon the pattern which had become characteristic of his later visits to England, and which he and Agnes frankly enjoyed so much, began to re-establish itself. He dined out, he went to theatres, he met his friends and acquaintances of both political parties, he attended a royal levee and a state ball. The weather, for a good part of the summer, was dry, sunny, and even, at times, decidedly hot. There were garden parties in the sunshine, week-ends in the country, elaborate dinners with the Drapers' Company and the Lord Mayor; and on July 21, he went out to Wimbledon to a party in honour of the visiting team of Canadian marksmen who had won the Kolapore cup the day before.[71]

Yet, even in the midst of the relaxation which he had earned so dearly, he did not neglect Canadian interests. His main concern was immigration. He talked it over again with Kimberley; he tried to put in a word about it with Gladstone; he went to Lansdowne House to discuss the subject informally with the Marquess of Lansdowne and a group of large Irish landowners; and he appealed to Cardinal Manning for the support of the Irish Roman Catholic hierarchy in a plan of assisted emigration from southern Ireland.[72] The utmost the Gladstone government was prepared to do in aid of overseas settlement was to appropriate a small amount of money, in the Irish Land Act, to assist Irish peasants who wished to emigrate. The amount seemed negligible to Canadians, and the aid was just as available to emigrants who intended to settle in foreign countries as it was to those who wished to go to British colonies. Lord Carnarvon suggested that Macdonald should attend the debate on the Bill in the House of Lords, in the hope that his testimony might inspire an amendment favourable to Canada. But early in August the clause slipped through, completely unaltered, much to Carnarvon's and Macdonald's disappointment, and to Galt's angry disgust.[73]

Yet, in the main, the summer in England was an extremely happy one. Almost every mail from Canada brought reassuring news. Tupper, a burly and extremely belligerent campaigner, flung himself into the by-election contests in Nova Scotia; and on June 18—victories worthy of Waterloo day, Macpherson called them—the Conservatives captured the two constituencies of Colchester and Pictou. Tupper and Tilley went on from these successes to address a series of political meetings in New Brunswick; and Tupper, who was never inclined to underrate the good effects of his own exertions, predicted confidently that "New Brunswick would be carried tomorrow if there was an election".[74] "Governmental prospects are bright here," Alexander Campbell assured Macdonald happily, "the elections go with us, prosperity continues in business and manufacturing centres, and there is every reason, so far, to anticipate a good harvest. . . ."[75] What could Macdonald desire more? There was absolutely no reason whatever, the entire Cabinet insisted, for him to make an early return home. Tilley, Macpherson, and Campbell all urged him to prolong his stay until the middle of October. "You could not do a better thing," Campbell wrote, "for yourself or the country."[76]

But he booked a passage on September 8. He knew he must go home. George Stephen was undisguisedly pleased to hear of his early return; and George Stephen's satisfaction was significant. The Canadian Pacific was just entering upon the long period of struggle and effort which must precede its completion. The whole process might take the full ten years which were specified in the contract. He might never live to see it finished. But he was determined that he would watch over the growth of his great creation until he could watch no more. He must win the next general election. He must have another five years of power. "I have no pleasure nowadays but in work," he told Alexander Campbell, "and so it will be to the end of the chapter."[77]

Chapter Ten

Good Times

I

On the voyage home, he presided over the *Sardinian's* ship's concert—"his first appearance before the public", the programme proudly announced;[1] and when the vessel docked at Quebec on Saturday, September 17, his alert eyes and easy movements convinced the curious Canadians that he was back again on an indefinite engagement. Everybody noticed how much better he looked. His old buoyancy, the newspaper correspondents informed their readers, was back again unimpaired.[2] And, as he hurried to Ottawa and began, in his usual easy, effortless fashion, to acquaint himself with the moods of his fellow-countrymen, he realized that his own restored well-being was matched and exceeded by the exuberant high spirits of the country as a whole. Far from exhibiting any unpleasant signs of diminution, the boom was obviously at its height. Immigrants had been pouring into the west all summer. The decennial census, which had been taken during the summer of 1881, had revealed the fact that the population of the Province of Manitoba had risen in ten years from 18,995 to 65,954.[3] A veritable mania of speculation in land—something strangely new in the history of British North America—reigned at Winnipeg; and in the eastern cities, though their mood was more sedate than that of the youthful and excited west, business was obviously in a most flourishing condition. David Macpherson, who, Macdonald considered, was a sound judge in these matters, summed up the general feeling, rather regretfully, by announcing that it would have been a great year for a general election. "If circumstances should be favourable next year," he suggested, "why not have it then?"[4]

Why not, indeed? Macdonald began to make preparations for a provincial Liberal-Conservative convention which was to meet in Toronto late in November, as a first important strategic move in a rapidly approaching national campaign. In the meantime he settled down to a careful examination of the state of the Canadian Pacific Railway. The first summer's operations were over. The organization which the genius of George Stephen had called into being was grappling with the basic problems of its task; and as, one by one, the fundamental decisions were made, the grand strategy of the railway became more and more clearly apparent. Already it was evident that in the far west the directors were contemplating a line a good deal south of the route which had been projected as a result of the original surveys.[5] A main line which ran towards the future Calgary rather than towards the future Edmonton would obviously provide a better basis, both for the protection of the railway's Canadian business and for the struggle with American rivals for the traffic south of the border. This change of direction required the abandonment of the Yellowhead Pass, the relatively easy northern route, and the discovery of a new way through the Rockies and the Selkirks. It was the most daring, but not the only, innovation which the company made in its first year of operation. There was a change of nearly equal significance north of Lake Superior. There the route had been provisionally planned, in accordance with the first of Sandford Fleming's surveys, to run well inland, north of Lake Nipigon. But Stephen and his directors, in the interest of economy and speed of construction, decided to move south and build close to the shore of Lake Superior. Their first idea, which was subsequently given up, was to follow the lake-shore throughout and thus to make the branch which they intended building to Sault Ste. Marie a part of the main line. This drastic change, Stephen argued persuasively, would cut costs, and shorten time.[6] It might enable the company to complete the railway to the Pacific in only five years.

The advantages of Stephen's proposed "new departure" were
not lost on Macdonald. He had been the tenacious and unyielding sponsor of the line north of Lake Superior. He had insisted
upon it, without qualification, as an absolute essential of the
national transcontinental. The officials of the Grand Trunk
Railway had rejected the mere idea of such a line in contemptuous disbelief; even George Stephen had originally viewed
it with unhappy misgivings. But within a year of the signing
of the contract, Stephen had completely changed his mind. As
he warmed to his work, he began to realize the enormous
potentialities of the all-Canadian route. "I am sure you will
be glad to hear this from me," he wrote to Macdonald, "because
I do not think but for your *own* tenacity on that point, would
the line north of the lake *ever* have been built."[7] It would have
to be built, Macdonald had always insisted. But the prospect
of the cost and labour involved had been a formidable one. It
was a task which might drag on interminably, which might
exhaust the patience of the Canadians, ruin the railway company
and destroy his own government. The thought had haunted
him with disquieting persistence. But now, was he not half
free of its terrors? The lake-shore route might cut the labour
north of Lake Superior by as much as a half. The entire railway might be finished in 1886.

He became a convert to the "new departure".[8] It bettered his
own chances, and those of the railway. But at the same time
it helped, along with other developments since the signing of
the charter, to strengthen the opposition to the Canadian transcontinental. It was becoming increasingly clear that there was
a very real likelihood of the Canadian transcontinental becoming
a real transcontinental. It was pledged to reach the Pacific
Ocean, through territory which might have become the easy
monopoly of the Northern Pacific; and it was compelled to
seek an outlet on the Atlantic seaboard, through a long-settled
region which had been dominated by the Grand Trunk. From
the point of view of these two rivals, the nature, and the danger,
of the competition which the Canadian Pacific would offer,
were becoming clearer every day. In Ontario and Quebec, and
London, the Grand Trunk began slowly marshalling its forces

and organizing its propaganda. It could afford to take its time, for it was already solidly established on the ground in dispute. But the Northern Pacific could not permit itself such deliberate tactics. Unless the Northern Pacific could speedily effect an entrance into Canada, its hopes of gaining a substantial part of the Canadian traffic were lost. It must act, and act at once.

Macdonald watched the onward career of the Northern Pacific with growing uneasiness. He had good cause for alarm. The railway, which had been plagued for long years by recurring financial crises, emerged successfully from a final reorganization, acquired new capital, and proceeded to build westward towards the Pacific at headlong speed. The tentacles of its lines were creeping eagerly, possessively, towards the international boundary. If it could win the co-operation of some impecunious Canadian province, with a provincial railway to dispose of, or if it could get control of the interests of some Canadian railway speculator who had a charter or a half-built line that he wished to sell at a good profit, then, at a bound, it would be past the frontier and into Canadian territory. Macdonald knew that there were two or three small railways in Manitoba which could very easily be connected with the Northern Pacific, to the utter undoing of the Canadian transcontinental. He also knew that the Province of Quebec, which had relapsed from its earlier fiscal rectitude into a state of acute budgetary embarrassment, was anxious to be relieved of the burden of its provincial system, the Quebec, Montreal, Ottawa, and Occidental Railway. Chapleau, the Premier of the province, had announced flatly that he intended to sell to the highest bidder. What if he sold the Quebec lines to the Northern Pacific Railroad?

It was a frightening prospect. It meant, as Macdonald earnestly warned Stephen, grave danger ahead. The purchase of the Quebec provincial railway would place the Northern Pacific in a commanding position in the heart of central Canada. It would be put in possession of the only route by which the Canadian transcontinental could find its outlet on the Atlantic Ocean; and, by extending its Canadian lines across northern Ontario, it could connect them with the American part of its system at Sault Ste. Marie. All this was bad enough; but it was not the only mischief which could be expected to flow from this deplorable transfer of Canadian property to American hands. The Northern Pacific, by handsomely assuming the financial burdens of distressed Quebec, would ingratiate itself not only with the provincial legislature, but also with Quebec's Conservative Members of Parliament at Ottawa; and the French-Canadian bloc at Ottawa might quite possibly try to prevent the Dominion government from disallowing the legislation by which Manitoba would certainly attempt to empower its provincial railways to build to the international boundary. "The Northern Pacific," Macdonald wrote earnestly to Stephen, "are very anxious to get into Manitoba and the North West, and they think that by coming to the rescue of the Province at a moment when the syndicate people are supposed to be unwilling, they can secure a solid Quebec vote in the House of Commons against any veto of provincial legislation in Manitoba in the interest of the Northern Pacific connection."[9]

There was only one thing to do, Macdonald knew. All possible connections between the Manitoba railways and the Northern Pacific must be quickly and firmly stopped, and Stephen must be induced to prevent the Quebec, Montreal, Ottawa, and Occidental Railway from falling into the hands of his great American rival. Macdonald wrote to Stephen, informing him of the sinister rumours; he told Chapleau that the Dominion government would prefer to see the Canadian Pacific obtain the sale or lease of the Quebec lines.[10] In the meantime, the government was already proceeding, in a summary and effective fashion, to ward off inroads through the Province of Manitoba on the domain of the Canadian transcontinental. In November, Charles Tupper, as Minister of Railways and Canals, reported against the Manitoba and South Eastern Railway; and early in the new year its charter was disallowed. Macdonald had no doubts or hesitations. The Canadian Pacific must be protected, for a long time to come, against incursions from the south. The Dominion had the will to disallow. It had the power to disallow. And John Norquay, the Premier of Manitoba, had privately agreed some time before that he would do his best to prevent any interference by the province with the Dominion's railway policy.[11] "As to the monopoly cry," Macdonald wrote firmly to Martin Griffin, "it is all nonsense."

But it was dangerous nonsense, nonsense pregnant with trouble. It was no time to be getting into a row with the first prairie province. Yet, given his national policies and his commitments to the Canadian Pacific Railway, how could he possibly avoid doing so? Manitoba, which had enjoyed the comfort of steam transport for less than three years, had suddenly developed a voracious appetite for railways. There was no hope of its remaining contented with the main line of the Canadian Pacific and the main line of the St. Paul, Minneapolis, and Manitoba Railway. It would certainly want to promote settlement and to encourage competition in transport by laying down a positive network of provincial railways; and of these several might provide—and might be designed to provide—a connection with the Northern Pacific or other American systems. How often hereafter would Manitoba charter railways to the international border? How often would he be obliged to use the power of disallowance? He looked into the future with a shiver of apprehension. He began to realize how formidably complex the resistance to his grand national scheme was likely to be. He had expected the economic rivalry of the Northern Pacific; but he had not entirely foreseen how quickly it would be linked with the political opposition of discontented and ambitious Canadian provinces. Even in this year of plenty and prosperity, he was aware of the slow marshalling of the forces against him. Manitoba, he knew very well, was by no means the only malcontent province. British Columbia was not yet completely pacified. Quebec was nursing a growing dissatisfaction. But the most mutinous province of all was Ontario. Ontario had literally raised the red flag of revolt.

Macdonald was determined to fight the battle of the unified nation and the strongly centralized constitution. He made no attempt to avoid an encounter with Ontario. In fact, he appeared to welcome it. Oliver Mowat, the Premier of the province, his old pupil-at-law, was an antagonist with whom he had always found it a positive pleasure to do battle; and the provincial government at Toronto, a wealthy and powerful government, arrogantly conscious of its wide territories and its large population, assumed an independent and assertive rôle in the Dominion which it was surely in the national interest to combat. For three years now, ever since his return to power in the autumn of 1878, Macdonald had been getting more and more deeply embroiled with Oliver Mowat's government. There had been disputes over both territorial boundaries and jurisdictional limits. Macdonald believed that Mowat, in his exercise of the province's licensing power, had assumed an unwarranted legislative authority in the matter of temperance and public morals. He was convinced that Ontario, in its determined attempt to extend its boundaries to the north and north-west, was claiming territory for which it had no legal and historical right, and which would give it a dangerous preponderance in the Dominion. He opposed Mowat's Liquor Licence Law of 1877 with the federal statute, the Canada Temperance Act, of the following year. He refused to accept the boundary award, favourable to Ontario, which had been made with such suspicious swiftness in the summer of 1878 by commissioners appointed by the Liberal government, just one month before that government went out of power. He demanded instead that the whole question should be referred for a final legal settlement to the Judicial Committee of the Privy Council.[12]

In the meantime, while these disputes were simmering away in exasperation, Oliver Mowat's government had acquired a new and colossal grievance. In the session of 1881 the provincial legislature had passed an act which regulated the public use of the rivers and streams of Ontario; and this, like every other provincial statute, had been sent to Ottawa for review by the Department of Justice. The British North America Act gave the Dominion the power to disallow any piece of provincial legislation, within one year of its receipt at Ottawa; and Macdonald had always intended that this power should be used, in the national interest.[13] For him—and it was one of his most deeply held convictions—Canada was one community, with common interests, common rights, and common ideals.

"Sir," he said later in Parliament in the debate on the disallowance of the Rivers and Streams Bill, "we are not half a dozen
provinces. We are one great Dominion."[14] The Canadian
Pacific Railway was a material interest which concerned the
whole of Canada; property rights were rights which should be
equally protected throughout the nation; and unquestionably
the guardianship of these common rights and interests against
provincial encroachment was a duty which the federal government could not escape.

In Macdonald's view, the Rivers and Streams Bill peremptorily called for action by the Dominion. He regarded it as an
iniquitous piece of legislation.[15] It opened to public use the
dams, timber slides, and other "improvements" which individual
proprietors had constructed at their own expense for the floating
of their saw-logs. It had been introduced while a Conservative
lumberman was contesting in the courts the claim of a Liberal
lumberman to make use of his "improvements" and it had been
passed by a legislature with a Liberal majority, in which a
relative of the Liberal lumberman concerned had a seat. To
Macdonald it seemed an arbitrary and confiscatory enactment
which violated existing property rights in an outrageous fashion.
"The credit and fair fame of Canada," he told Meredith, the
leader of the Conservative opposition in Ontario, "are under the
charge, of necessity, of the general government and Parliament,
and a law of confiscation by its chief province is prejudicial and
might be ruinous to the credit and best interests of every man,
woman, and child in the Dominion."[16] For these reasons the
Rivers and Streams Act had been disallowed; and at once a
thunderous roar of protest split the cloudy skies of Ontario.
It was apparent that Mowat would not be intimidated into an
immediate surrender. Obviously a new fight was on.

Macdonald was concerned about Ontario. Ontario was very
much in his mind when he came up to Toronto towards the
end of November to attend the provincial Liberal-Conservative
convention. General elections were not very far away in both
the province and the Dominion; and the delegates who had
come in hundreds from all over Ontario must be sent back
to their constituencies bursting with fighting spirit. He shook

hands with them, called them by name, talked with them, watched them benevolently and hopefully as they listened to speeches and applauded the passage of resolutions; and at the end of the second day's proceedings, they crowded, nearly a thousand of them, into the pavilion of the Horticultural Gardens for the final dinner at which Macdonald was to speak. The

ANOTHER MILE-STONE PASSED; OR, FATHER TIME AS SPRY AS EVER.

walls were hung with Union Jacks and decorated with mottoes, portraits, and coats-of-arms; and over the platform, the crown and the inscription "God Save the Queen" were picked out in flaring gas jets. The diners rose, as one man, when he entered the room; and the band crashed into "See the Conquering Hero Comes".

His theme, when he got up to speak, was the theme of the nation he was creating. He had made a reality out of a dream; and the miraculous success of his policies seemed, to his auditors, to supply an incontrovertible argument against any alternative conception of Canada and its future. He dismissed, as equally false and delusive objectives, Canadian "independence" and imperial federation. Canada must remain, what it had become, an autonomous nation inside the British imperial system; and if it kept steadfastly to its first and true course, the certainty of transcontinental nationhood lay before it. He contrasted his own national policies with the international trade and railway policies of Mackenzie and Blake. He talked about his schemes for western settlement; and he revealed, for the first time, the great change of plan by which the Canadian Pacific Railway hoped to hasten the completion of the north shore route. The whole transcontinental, he told his audience —and the whole pavilion yelled applause—would now be finished in five years instead of ten. "I now have some chance," he said proudly, "if I remain as strong, please God, as I now am, of travelling over it in person before I am just quite an angel."[17]

II

As he watched over the domestic scene, and prepared for the next session of Parliament and the general election which probably lay beyond it, he looked up, every now and then, for a quick glance at the horizon of international affairs. In one direction at least, there was hardly a cloud in the sky. He had predicted that once the presidential election in the United States was safely over, the pre-election sabre-rattling against Great Britain and Canada would suddenly and mysteriously subside. He had been nearly right. Nearly, but not quite.

Most of the American crusades and grievances appeared to be forgotten; but the prospective Panama Canal, in which an interest had been revived by the activities of de Lesseps, was a clear and somewhat startling exception. Blaine, the new American Secretary of State, laid claim, in contravention of the terms of the Bulwer-Clayton Treaty, to an exclusive protectorate over the canal. The pretension irked Macdonald. For a while he contemplated the formality of a minute of council protesting against Blaine's demand. "England was an American power," he argued to Lord Lorne, "quite irrespective of the Thirteen Colonies before the United States existed; and Canada having now a larger population than the United States when the Monroe Doctrine was announced, and the certainty (humanly speaking) of a great future, has precisely the same interests to guard as the United States. That government claims the protectorate from the necessity of keeping open under all circumstances the water communication between the Atlantic and Pacific portions of their territories *via* the canal. The same necessity exists as to Canada."[18] The same necessity existed, no doubt; but Canada, independently of Great Britain, had very little power of impressing others with the importance of its requirements. The idea of a Canadian minute of council was given up;[19] and instead Lord Lorne was requested, when he went over to England in the autumn, to put the point of view of the Dominion to Lord Granville at the Foreign Office.[20]

The Anglo-Canadian alliance remained the basis of Macdonald's foreign policy. It could hardly be called a very cordial alliance during the second of Gladstone's administrations. There was a frigid air of grim historical necessity about it which seemed to chill most attempts at hearty co-operation. Macdonald drew no inspiration from Gladstone's unbenevolent detachment. He felt he could expect little good from the Liberals; he sometimes thought despairingly that all that was possible was to prevent them from doing Canada positive harm. And yet, in his heart of hearts, he knew all the time that he must not let this negative, defeatist attitude get control of his mind for a single minute. He must keep on trying, as he had tried so often before, to arouse British interest in the country he was creating. Canada wanted immigrants. She needed capital. And she saw in Great Britain the safest and most natural source of both. Great Britain must somehow be induced to believe in the Canadian north-west and to support the Canadian Pacific Railway. The brawn of British immigrants, the funds of British investors, the co-operation of the British government —they were all necessary.

It was for these purposes, in large measure, that Macdonald had established the office of High Commissioner for Canada and had sent Galt to England. But he was beginning to suspect that Galt, for all his very real talents, was not very likely to achieve the desired results. That autumn, after a highly diverting but extremely expensive tour in western Canada, the High Commissioner had gone back to his post in London. He went; but he went reluctantly, unenthusiastically, with little of his old romantic zeal for diplomacy; and in London he began once again to experience the familiar dismal succession of discomforts, illnesses, disappointments, and frustrations. Yet, curiously enough, his woes seemed to have no effect whatever on his irrepressible imprudence. He had been back in London only a month when he informed Macdonald that he intended to re-open the subject of assisted immigration with Kimberley, and that he proposed to take part—on the side of protection, of course—in the somewhat academic controversy then going on in England between "fair trade" and "free trade".[21]

Macdonald was aghast. Gladstone, for whom the verities of free trade were only slightly less impregnable than those of Holy Scripture, might take the deepest offence at Galt's bumptious hardihood. "Gladstone, if I read him aright," Macdonald wrote to Galt, deliberately exaggerating Gladstone's malignancy in order to frighten his High Commissioner, "is governed by his hates, and is as spiteful as a monkey. In a fit of rage he might denounce Canada and its future, and show the danger continually hanging over England by Canada's proximity to the United States, and the necessity of her fighting our battles. In fact there is no knowing what he might do. . . ."[22] A "fair trade" pamphlet by the High Commissioner of Canada— an intervention in British domestic politics by a colonial who claimed to be a diplomat—was an unthinkable enormity. A premature re-opening of the immigration question was, of course, a good deal less dangerous; but, even so, it would probably do some harm.[23] Macdonald had become convinced that an assisted immigration scheme, even if it were designed mainly to relieve the congestion and misery of troubled Ireland, could not be proposed, with any hope of success, unless it were preceded by a good deal of careful diplomatic preparation. Galt had already done his best; but Galt's efforts alone were plainly not sufficient. He must be assisted by others; and Macdonald had two people in mind, as unofficial and semi-official envoys. One was Archbishop Lynch of Toronto, who, he hoped, might win the good will and support of the Roman Catholic hierarchy of Ireland. The other was George Stephen.

Early in 1882, in a mood of superb assurance, Stephen departed for England. Before he left he had begun negotiations with Chapleau for the sale or lease of the Quebec provincial railways. The fact that the Canadian Pacific had now acquired a through line as far east at least as Montreal was, of course, highly distasteful to the officials of the Grand Trunk Railway. But there were other activities of Stephen's which offended them even more. The Grand Trunk Railway looked upon the territories of southern Ontario and Quebec with a jealously proprietorial eye. There were times when its spokesmen seemed almost to imply that the terminus of the Canadian Pacific ought to have remained fixed at Callander, by the east end of Lake Nipissing, exactly at the point specified in the charter. Callander had, in fact, been chosen originally as a neutral point, midway between Toronto and Montreal. Obviously the great national transcontinental could not remain suspended in the wilds of northern Ontario; and if there was any doubt on this point, it had been effectually removed by other clauses in the charter which empowered the Canadian Pacific to acquire the Canada Central, and "to obtain, hold, and operate" other railways from Ottawa as far as the Atlantic seaboard.[24] These facts were given only the most pained and loftily distant recognition by the officials of the Grand Trunk Railway. The Canadian Pacific, they seemed to say, might be permitted, if it was good, to advance respectfully from Callander as far as Montreal. But this was the absolute limit of indulgence! Yet it was a limit which Stephen seemed already to be transgressing. He and his associates were known to have acquired a considerable interest in several eastern railway properties which would give the Canadian Pacific a competitive line from Montreal into south-western Ontario, as well as a bridge across the St. Lawrence into southern Quebec. The consternation and fury of the Grand Trunk directors mounted. Their opposition to their young rival became more vehement and undisguised.

The facts had to be recognized, Macdonald knew. The Grand Trunk, despite its pious disclaimers, had become the avowed and determined enemy of the national transcontinental. "Tyler did all he could, per fas et *nefas*," Macdonald wrote angrily to Galt, "to kill our attempts to form a syndicate in 1880. . . . I have heard Tyler in a speech at the Trinity House attack our Lake Superior route, and I know he is endeavouring to keep the syndicate out of the English market. If I *live* I shall pay Sir Henry off."[25] This threat could hardly be carried out in any simple and literal fashion, for the Grand Trunk Railway had an important function to perform in the Canadian economy and Macdonald could not afford to alienate its directors, even if he had wanted to do so. But it was obvious that some kind of defence must be marshalled at once against Grand Trunk propaganda in England, for it threatened the gravest possible damage to the Canadian Pacific and the Canadian north-west. T. C. Patteson, the ex-editor of the Toronto *Mail*, had already been sent over to London to reply to the vicious attacks of what Stephen called the Grand Trunk's "paid ink-slingers". Stephen himself, who haughtily declared to Macdonald that he had gone to England to advertise his lands, not to beg for money from British investors, threw himself, with his usual furious energy, into the task of promoting the Canadian north-west as a home for British emigrants. Yet these efforts were curiously ineffectual. It was almost impossible to get any favourable publicity for Canada in the English press. " 'Jumbo', the big elephant recently bought by Barnum," declared Stephen disgustedly, "is a matter of ten times more interest to London than twenty colonies. . . . The fact is that emigration is not popular, there is an instinctive feeling that they are losing national power when they decrease in numbers, even when the emigrant goes to a British colony, and the genuine insular Britisher hates all emigration efforts, and would rather have the people remain to struggle and sometimes starve than to emigrate."[26]

If any emigration could be justified, it was emigration from over-populated and agitated Ireland. A nation of peasant farmers, Ireland had suffered far more than England from the great depression in agriculture. Widespread distress had been followed by widespread violence; and in two years the organization of the Land League and the genius of Charles Stewart Parnell had raised the problem of rural Ireland into one of the most imperatively urgent questions of the day. W. E. Forster's Coercion Bill was one answer; another was the great measure of Irish land reform which Gladstone had introduced in the session of 1881. But was there not, argued the Canadian and some British imperialists, another possible solution, a solution which would apply neither coercion nor concession, but which would solve the problem of Ireland's over-population and misery by removing its victims to a land of better opportunity? Ever since Macdonald's talk with Cardinal Manning in the previous summer, he had been hoping to persuade an influential Irish-Canadian priest to go to Ireland and enlist the support of the Irish Roman Catholic hierarchy in a scheme of assisted emigration. He invited Archbishop Lynch of Toronto to found "a new Ireland"— tempered slightly by representatives of other British nationalities—in the Canadian north-west;[27] and late in February Lynch reported that he had received permission to undertake the Irish mission.[28] He was likely to be a rather expensive representative. He hinted delicately to Macdonald that on long journeys he usually travelled with a secretary and a personal servant. "His Grace is fond of attention . . . ,"[29] Macdonald remarked significantly to Galt; and Galt dutifully busied himself in arranging courtesies in official London. Then Lynch went off to Dublin, and Macdonald waited anxiously. The appalling state of Ireland was surely, he told himself, an irrefutable argument in favour of his plan. "It seems to me," he wrote to Galt, "that Gladstone and Forster must now in desperation look to emigration as a remedy."[30]

III

At this point, there occurred a contretemps which had the most unfortunate effects on the cause of emigration in particular and Anglo-Canadian relations in general. Parliament had opened, as usual, in mid-winter. It was by now an open secret that this session was to be the last before a general election took place. "I have a sort of idea," John Rose had written early in February, "that you will take advantage of the flood tide of popularity and success and dissolve after the session."[31] It was the right decision—the only possible decision, Macdonald knew. The flood-tide of popularity and success was at its golden full. "Money is rolling in on the treasury," the Governor-General wrote complacently to the Colonial Secretary. "The number of people going to the west from Ontario alone will probably be twenty thousand this year."[32] Many old Canadian homes were affected by this exodus; Macdonald's own home was affected; and Hugh's decision to move with his wife and their small daughter to Winnipeg in the spring of 1882 was, in its way, the Macdonald family's personal endorsation of the promise of the Canadian north-west.[33] Everybody, surely, was convinced of the success of the national policy of protection. Proudly and enthusiastically the Canadians had accepted the transcontinental nation which Macdonald was bringing into being with a few triumphant passes of his enchanter's wand. He was at the height of his success. The time for him to dissolve was now.

Everybody knew it. The session was tense with the excitement of expectation; the days were full of acting, advertisement, and self-glorification. Both sides—and particularly the opposition—were striking attitudes, making declarations, and laying down general principles with the greatest possible fervour and conviction. On April 14, the Commons stayed up all night to finish its discussion of the disallowance of the Rivers and Streams Act;[34] and within the next week two slightly less prolonged debates on two equally exciting subjects had taken place. Blake proposed an amendment on the motion to go into supply, affirming Canada's right to negotiate its own commercial treaties;[35] and John Costigan, an Irish Roman Catholic member, introduced a set of resolutions on the unhappy state of Ireland which respectfully but none the less definitely requested Her Majesty to restore Irish civil liberties and to grant Ireland Home Rule.[36] Blake's motion, which revived the old theme on which Galt and Huntington had expatiated over ten years before, would, Macdonald knew, give some aid and comfort to the anti-colonials in Great Britain. But he also suspected that the consequences of the Costigan resolutions might be much worse. The Costigan resolutions, advanced at this of all inappropriate moments in Ireland's history, might drive Gladstone and his Liberal government into a state of revengeful fury.

How could he head Costigan off? Costigan was the rival of the Liberal, Timothy Anglin, for the leadership of the Irish Roman Catholics of eastern Canada. The Irish Roman Catholic vote in the approaching election was trembling in the balance; and Macdonald was well aware of the fact that if Costigan did not raise the Irish issue, Anglin or some other Liberal would unquestionably do so, and in a much more provocative fashion. Besides, why should it be contemptuously assumed that Canadian reflections on the state of Ireland were a mere impertinence? Canadians believed that their happy experience under the federal system was a strong argument in favour of a measure of Irish home rule; and, as Macdonald pointed out to Lord Lorne, a country which had suffered repeatedly from Fenian raids, felt not unnaturally that it had a legitimate interest in the solution of the Irish problem.[37]

He expected trouble. And trouble came. He thought the Costigan motion ill-timed; but he could not anticipate the full horror of its tragic inappropriateness. The resolutions passed the Canadian House of Commons on April 21. On May 6, barely a fortnight later, a new Viceroy, Lord Spencer, and a new Chief Secretary for Ireland, Lord Frederick Cavendish, arrived in Dublin to begin an era of conciliation and co-operation. Dusk was falling on that day of procession and ceremony when Lord Frederick Cavendish and his Permanent Under-Secretary, Thomas Henry Burke, were horribly murdered in Phoenix Park, within sight of the Viceregal Lodge, by a gang of murderous Irish extremists who called themselves "Invincibles". Even before the hideous tragedy in Phoenix Park occurred, there had been critical comment in England about the Costigan resolutions; but after May 6, the request of an irresponsible colonial legislature for clemency to the murderous Irish ceased to be a mere impertinence and became a positive outrage. "The people of this country," wrote Lord Kimberley coldly to Lord Lorne, "have shown wonderful calmness under immense provocation, but they are not in a temper to be trifled with by anglers for Irish votes at elections for colonial legislatures."[38] Mr. Gladstone and the Colonial Secretary made no attempt to hide their displeasure. The discussion of the Irish immigration scheme degenerated into argument and angry futility.[39] Galt was furious. He was, he declared emphatically, coming home to Canada again for the summer. He had already resigned—for the second time!

Macdonald shrugged his shoulders. He had no time for annoyance or regrets. Galt's temperament was a nuisance and assisted immigration seemed an insoluble puzzle. But the general election, on which everything depended, was now only a couple of months away. He was already deep in preparations for it; and on April 28, when the murders in Phoenix Park were still over a week away, he introduced in the House of Commons a measure which, in the eyes of his followers if not entirely in his own, was to have a decisively favourable influence upon the outcome of the election.[40] It was a Representation Bill, made necessary by the results of the decennial census of the previous year. The British North America Act provided that each province was to have as many seats in the House of Commons in proportion to Quebec's fixed number of sixty-five as its population warranted; and the census now revealed that Manitoba must be given one additional constituency and Ontario four. How, in the absence of precise instructions in the British North America Act, was this to be done? In 1872, when the first post-Confederation changes in the representative system were made, Macdonald had explained that, although population had been regarded as the basic principle of the adjustment, other factors—"interests, classes, and localities"—had also been given consideration; and, as a result of this deference to local feeling, the boundaries of the constituencies had not been permitted to cross municipal or county lines.[41] In the redistribution of 1882, on the contrary, numerical equality triumphed over local patriotism. Local divisions were cheerfully disregarded in Ontario; and townships were freely transferred, for electoral purposes, from their own to neighbouring counties. As a result of these complicated exchanges, approximate equality of population was certainly achieved. It was Macdonald's avowed object. But he had another object which, though undeclared, was no less real. The redistribution was designed to secure a party advantage. Liberal voters were to be concentrated in as few ridings as possible, thus increasing the Conservatives' chances of success. Macdonald intended, in short, to "hive the Grits".[42]

This, the opposition declared in a paroxysm of moral indignation, was a *gerrymander*. It was, the *Globe* observed, a piece of political trickery so base and shameless as to win for Macdonald "an immortality of infamy". These scarcely novel maledictions left Macdonald unmoved. He was unabashed and unrepentant. "I will unwhig that honourable gentleman," he said, quoting with relish Pitt's taunt to Fox, "if ever he goes back on Whig principles."[43] And now the preposterously incredible had happened, and the Liberals had abandoned the ancient Reform doctrine of representation by population. ". . . We, the majority of the Ontario representatives in this House," Macdonald declared with ironic unction, "are fighting the battle of representation by population against the indignant protests of the honourable gentlemen opposite." It was a diverting position to be occupying; but Macdonald evidently did not take the battle too seriously and did not mean to let it go on too long. His introduction of the bill and his rebuttal on the first evening were brief; he did not speak on the second reading at all. And he infuriated his opponents by opposing their lugubrious prophecies with comforting realism. Voters, he explained reassuringly to the opposition, could not be carted off with impunity like cabbages. The political consistency of districts was a myth which had been completely exploded by the history of the elections of the 1870's. "It shows," he concluded with smiling common sense, "that the argument to be drawn from the supposed political proclivities of any locality is worthless—there is nothing in it."[44]

He hoped and believed, of course, that there was something in it. He must win the election of 1882. Five more years of power were necessary to complete the work that he had set himself to do. "You will not forget the fact," Stephen reminded him significantly, "that the Canadian Pacific Railway is in reality in partnership with the government in the construction of the national railway. . . ."[45] It was true; but the national railway was only one of the enterprises to which his government stood committed. Macdonald's whole programme had now been presented to the Canadian people; and what he wanted, at this crucial point of mid-passage in the nation's career, was the confirmation of an overwhelming vote of approval. He could carry the huge project forward to its desired conclusion only if he had the confidence born of an emphatically favourable judgment. The judgment must confound all his enemies. It must be rendered, not only against Blake, but also against Blake's scarcely less dangerous ally, Oliver Mowat. Blake was opposing the national railway and the national policy of protection with continental transport and international free trade. Mowat was combating the ideal of a great united Dominion with provincial rights and territorial aggrandizement. Mowat threatened the division of powers which he had laid down nearly twenty years before at Quebec. The preponderance of Ontario endangered the economic and political equilibrium of the whole Dominion.

The election was now only a month away. But he felt fit and ready for it. Earlier in the spring there had been a disquieting return of his old symptoms. "I have had a warning against overwork," he had written Lord Lorne early in April, "by an attack similar to one of last spring and have been at home since Saturday last. I hope to get out tomorrow."[46] He had taken precautions then and the precautions had more than sufficed; and on May 17, when the session and the Parliament came to an end, he felt well and fairly confident. No election was ever a certainty, of course, and he knew that in Ontario he would be fought with the fury of desperation. But on the whole, he and his intimates faced the contest with comparatively light hearts. "I have no misgivings about the result of the elections," Stephen wrote robustly. "I cannot believe that the country which is now prosperous beyond all precedent wants any change in its rulers."[47] Macdonald did not really believe it either. His own position, he knew, was very strong, and Blake's recent manœuvres were a tacit admission of the fact. The acknowledged success of the national policy of protection had compelled the leader of the opposition to modify the stiff-necked rigidity of Mackenzie's and Cartwright's free-trade principles. Blake—it was a highly gratifying sight—was hedging about the tariff!

He was eager to be away—many of the ministers had already left town—but he characteristically remained until May 25, when the Royal Society of Canada, the nation's first learned association, held its first meeting in the Senate chamber. He looked his old self—genial, gracious, oddly youthful—as he and Agnes greeted the Fellows and listened to the Governor-General's opening address.[48] That night they left for Kingston; and the next afternoon, after only a brief visit to the Williamson house and a luncheon with a few personal friends, they were off again for Napanee, where Macdonald was to make the first speech of the campaign. He had decided to give up his British Columbia seat, and to return to Ontario—not, indeed, to Kingston, but to the region of the old Midland District, of which Kingston had once been the capital. He would run for Lennox, where he had lived as a boy; and he would give his first speech in Napanee, where he had gone, nearly half a century before, to establish the branch law office for his master, George Mackenzie.

The place was packed that Friday afternoon with his admirers. The main hall in town was secured, and then rejected as inadequate. The theatre, hurriedly substituted as a place of meeting, was in turn abandoned for the same reason. In the end he faced the great crowd in the open air of the market-place. It rained—a patter of drops towards the close of his speech. But the crowd did not budge. It listened in silence while he dealt faithfully with both Blake and Mowat, with national policies and Dominion-provincial relations. It was attentive. But it was far more than attentive. It was interested, warmly sympathetic, and, at the right moments, vociferously responsive. And, as the bursts of laughter and applause followed in swift and encouraging sequence, Macdonald's confidence mounted. He had been right. This time, the game was really in his hands. He had flushed Blake from the prickly covert of free-trade dogma, and the hunt was up. Blake, he told his audience, had discovered that the national policy was now enthusiastically accepted by the entire country. Blake knew that he must change his views. But he could not admit that he had changed them. "He therefore tried to hedge," Macdonald told his delighted listeners. "He tried to wear two faces under one hat—or, as the Yankee sailor said—'to steer south by north'."[49]

That night he left for Toronto. From Toronto, the capital of his rival, Oliver Mowat, he would direct the struggle for that politically dominant but politically uncertain region, the central and western part of Ontario.

IV

"We have had a hard fight in Ontario," he wrote to Lord Lorne on June 22, two days after the election, "and had to face the sectional and independence cries raised by the opposition. Still we are the victors."[50] They were indeed the victors. With one hundred and thirty-nine seats to seventy-one, they had yielded only a few inches of their commanding position. They had won in every province but Manitoba. In Ontario, where it was so important to combat Mowat's pugnacious provincialism, they had lost seats, but still retained a substantial majority; and the defeat of some of the more prominent of the Liberal leaders would certainly weaken, for a while at least, the attacks which the opposition could mount in the new Parliament. "The victory is complete," Tilley wrote jubilantly from New Brunswick.[51] Macdonald, who had made good his return to Ontario, was pleased with the results, and pleased too that he had not broken down in the struggle. But at the moment his exhaustion was extreme. "I am completely used up," he wrote to Lord Lorne. "Travelling night and day and continual 'field preaching' have been too much for a man of sixty-seven. I shall, however, soon pull myself together again."[52]

The "pulling together" process took longer than he had anticipated. In another ten days, he left for Rivière du Loup. But late in July a series of Council meetings, at which, among other things, Joseph Chapleau was made a minister and the other new appointments to the Cabinet were decided upon, called him back to Ottawa; and this brief return to the stifling summer capital ended unhappily in another prostration. "As I am not quite right yet," he wrote to Lord Lorne on July 28, immediately before his departure, "I intend to stick to the rail until I arrive at Rivière du Loup. I shall thus be able to maintain a recumbent position which is so desirable to me just now."[53] At Rivière du Loup he recuperated slowly but surely. He had promised himself a lazy, substantial, satisfying holiday —a holiday long enough to conceal for a while the inexorably rapid return of duties. And although there were often callers, and the post-bag was always full, nothing of great importance arose to trouble him. There was some discussion of the British proposal to remove the imperial garrison at Halifax for service in Egypt;[54] and, together with Lord Lorne and the Duke of Cambridge, the imperial Commander-in-Chief, he earnestly debated the unfortunate case of Major-General Luard, the officer commanding the Canadian militia, an elderly military man, who seemed imperfectly aware of the fact that he was the servant of the Canadian government, and thus subordinate to the new and energetic Minister of Militia, Adolphe Caron.[55]

Still, these were relatively minor affairs. They were small vexations in a very general contentment. It seemed that summer that nothing could go wrong with the programme of the Conservatives. Macdonald had won the general election; he was winning transcontinental dominion with the railway; and over in London he had just emerged successfully from an important round in the fight for the Canadian constitution. On June 22, two days after the general election, a crucial decision respecting the powers of the Dominion under the British North America Act was handed down by the Judicial Committee of the Privy Council.[56] The suit had been brought by an innkeeper named Russell, who had resisted the enforcement of the Canada Temperance Act on the ground that it conflicted with the provincial right to impose licences and to legislate in respect of property and civil rights. For years Macdonald had been arguing that the Canada Temperance Act was well within the authority of the Dominion and that the Ontario Licence Law was an unwarrantable exercise of provincial power. Early in the election campaign, provoked by a direct question on the subject, he had expressed his opinion openly and in the most unequivocal terms. He had boldly told his audience at Yorkville that the Ontario Licence Act was "not worth the paper it was written on". And he had gone on to promise—and the promise was not forgotten—that "if he carried the country, as he would do, he would tell Mr. Mowat, that little tyrant, who had attempted to control public opinion by getting hold of every little office from that of Division Court bailiff to a tavern-keeper, that he would get a bill passed at Ottawa returning to the municipalities the power taken away from them by the Licence Act".[57]

Now he could make good his promise. He had insisted on the constitutionality of the Canada Temperance Act. He had boasted that his judgments on constitutional questions had never been reversed. And now, apparently, he had been completely vindicated. In its decision in Russell v. the Queen, the Judicial Committee of the Privy Council had declared that the Canada Temperance Act was *intra vires* of the federal Parliament.[58] It was a judgment based upon an ample interpretation of the Dominion's residuary power to legislate for the "peace, order, and good government of Canada" in all matters

not exclusively assigned to the provinces. The Judicial Committee had, in fact, decided that the federal Parliament could
legislate under the residuary clause for genuine national objects even though such legislation might incidentally affect
"property and civil rights in the province". No judgment could
possibly have given Macdonald more satisfaction. For him the
residuary power had always been the great determining fact
in the distribution of powers at Confederation. And now it was
freed from the dangerous encroachments of "property and civil
rights". He could carry forward his programme of national legislation unimpeded. He could brush that obstructive provin-
cialist, Mowat, out of his path.

It was a lucky summer. The Conservative party was victorious and its national policies were in the ascendant.
Everything seemed made for success; and the climax of the
whole long record of accomplishment was the stupendous progress of the Canadian Pacific Railway. Nothing like such speed
of construction had been expected, or had, indeed, been conceived. To Canadians it seemed a miracle, and so, in a sense,
it was. But it was a miracle performed by a very human agent;
and in him fortune had granted the Canadian Pacific Railway
its second great gift of extraordinary ability. Macdonald had
found a financial genius in George Stephen; George Stephen
had discovered a genius for construction in William Cornelius
Van Horne. And under Van Horne, who had joined the company early in 1882, the work of exploration, survey, and
construction was pushed resolutely ahead at all points. All
that summer, as Macdonald rested in the hot sun at Rivière
du Loup, the reassuring and triumphant reports kept coming
in. On August 19, Stephen telegraphed that construction on
the north shore of Lake Superior east of Port Arthur had been
begun and was being prosecuted by a large force of men.[59]
Five days later he transmitted an even more portentous piece
of information which had come in from beyond the end of
steel just a few minutes earlier. "Just heard from Major Rogers,"
Stephen's telegram read. "He has found a good line through
the Selkirk range. No tunnel. This is good news."[60] It was
better news than they had a right to expect, for they had been

committed to the southerly route for a year, and only now had they found a practicable pass through the towering masses of the Selkirks. But Stephen and his associates assumed success; and in this golden high noon of the enterprise they seemed to be able to command it at will. Everybody marvelled at the swiftness of their progress. A long succession of important visitors—Galt, Tupper, Brydges, of the Grand Trunk Railway, and Sir John Rose—all went west that summer, inspected the miracle of construction, and reported their admiration to Macdonald. "The railroad is really most creditably built," Galt wrote from Qu'Appelle, "and being pushed with great energy. Brydges (who is not a partial witness) says he never saw such complete organization as the track laying."[61]

Yet the very speed and thoroughness of the construction hastened the arrival of a new and terrible problem—the problem of finances. From then on it was to haunt Macdonald and Stephen like an implacable and malevolent ghost. The partnership of government and company was, as Macdonald knew very well, limited sharply to a few by no means inexhaustible sources of revenue. The financial immaturity of Canada, the indifference or hostility of the important financial interests in London and New York all combined to reduce the support which the Canadian Pacific might hope to obtain. But the problem of its finances was also, and no less significantly, complicated by the methods which Stephen had deliberately adopted. Stephen was vulnerable before short-term difficulties precisely because he was a man of long-range views. His intention from the first had been to build a railway for the future. He had contemptuously rejected the practice, all too common in North American railway financing, of taking a quick and easy profit from the work of construction or the flotation of bonds. "The other plan, and the one I should have followed, had we been able to come to terms," he had explained to Macdonald in July, 1880, when his first offer to build the railway had been withdrawn, "would have been to limit the borrowing of money from the public to the smallest possible point . . . and to have looked for the return of our own capital and a legitimate profit entirely to the growth of the country and the development of the property—after the work of construction had been fully accomplished."[62]

This was the plan which had been followed in actual fact. It ensured the railway's future strength, Macdonald believed; but it also meant an initial and terrible period of weakness. The sale of common stock, the gradual acquisition of the government subsidy and the government land grant as the building of the line progressed—these were the means by which the railway obtained the sinews of construction and operation. Only twenty-five millions of common stock had been sold, at less than half of its par value; and government assistance, in lands and money, had to be earned. Inevitably a heavy initial burden rested upon the principal members of the syndicate; and, as the vastness of the whole enterprise was gradually unfolded, this burden grew even heavier than Stephen had anticipated. "The road is going to cost a great deal more money than we calculated on," he warned Macdonald, late in August, when he had just returned from a visit to the north-west;[63] and during September and October, while the work of construction was pushed forward, expenditures continued to soar in a frightening fashion. The strain upon the young organization grew heavier; the burden of responsibility which Stephen carried was never out of his mind. He became more exacting in his requirements, more impatient of government delays and technicalities, more suspicious of Cabinet ministers who did not exhibit a constant and almost uncritical devotion to the Canadian Pacific, and more furiously angry with outrageous neutrals such as Galt, who, he suspected, was secretly hostile under a mask of judicious impartiality.

Macdonald bore with it all. He knew that Stephen was a person of great creative power, infinite resource, and enormous courage. But he knew also that he was a sensitive, impatient, self-centred, and imperious man. For the task which Macdonald had entrusted to him, Stephen's good qualities vastly outweighed his defects. Yet his defects—his quick pugnacity, his arrogant self-confidence, his angry impatience with criticism—were precisely those which were most likely to increase the dislike and suspicion of the enterprise which he represented. "As I re-

marked to you on a previous occasion," Hickson of the Grand
Trunk Railway wrote to Macdonald, "your government has
created a power which believes itself to be not only stronger
than the Grand Trunk, but stronger than the government."[64]
The arrogant autocracy of Stephen was, as Macdonald knew
very well, a favourite theme of Liberal politicians. The whole
opposition press had combined to hold up the Canadian Pacific
as a frightful monster which would devour Canada's resources
and enslave its people. Obviously the government would have
to proceed with infinite caution; and the last thing which it
could contemplate at the moment was the grant of further
financial assistance to the Canadian Pacific Railway. Political
support was another matter. Macdonald could—and did—
maintain the political defences he had promised; and three
more Manitoba railway charters were disallowed that autumn.
But it was beyond his power to add, by so much as a dollar or
an acre, to the company's financial strength. Stephen—and
Stephen alone—must pull the railway through the first crisis
of its difficulties.

He counted upon Stephen, and Stephen did not fail him.
In December the president of the Canadian Pacific Railway
left for New York; from there, after a few strenuous days of
negotiations, he sailed for England. Early in 1883, it was
revealed that a strong stock syndicate had been formed in New
York, that its members had agreed to underwrite thirty millions
of Canadian Pacific stock at an average price of slightly over
fifty-two cents on the dollar, and that large blocks of the new
issue were being disposed of in London and Amsterdam. "I
must at the outset say," John Rose reported admiringly from
London, "that the result is almost wholly due to the untiring
efforts of our friend Stephen, whose zeal, energy, confidence in
himself and the enterprise seem to inspire everybody with the
like confidence."[65] Macdonald nodded happily. Stephen might
be a tempestuous and difficult colleague. He might be, as John
Rose admitted judiciously, an imperious man, intolerant of
opposition and almost incapable of compromise. He might be
all these things. He very probably was. But he was a great man
as well. Macdonald knew it; and despite the persistent and

malignant criticism of Blake, the *Globe,* and the "G.T.R. scribblers" the world would know it too in the end.

V

He caught a chill in December, and there were days when he felt far too ill to go to Council. He was sixty-eight years old on January 11, 1883; and although the chronic feebleness of his health was not likely to finish him off suddenly, it was something that he would have to make shift to live with to the end of his days. Ever since his terrible illness in the spring of 1881, he had realized that, if he wished to survive and complete his work, he must take systematic precautions to guard his health. He had always been a light eater; he was becoming an abstemious drinker. He kept a good cellar and when a correspondent in England recommended a bargain in claret, he was quick to order a couple of dozen of bottles. But the great drinking-bouts, the gargantuan insobrieties of his middle years were dwindling away now into memories. Time was galloping on. It seemed almost incredible that he had been married to Agnes for more years now than he had been married to the long-dead Isabella. "Little" Mary was a tall girl, nearly fourteen years old, and still heartbreakingly unstable and clumsy, despite all the special treatments that had been lavished upon her. Hugh, who came east for a brief visit during the winter of 1883, was now a man of nearly thirty-three. His first wife had died and he was soon to marry again.[66] How far away already that quarrel over his first engagement seemed! How incredibly distant were the days when he had been a boy in Kingston, left behind by a busy father in the care of his tall, raw-boned Aunt Louisa. And now Louisa herself was ill—so ill that that winter Macdonald nearly despaired of her life.

He knew that he must spare himself as much as possible; and he welcomed the coming of the expected mid-winter relaxation of tension. There was always a short period, between Christmas and the normal February opening of Parliament, when a brief and blessed lull occurred; and this year the session itself—the first session of a new Parliament from which some of his leading opponents had been extruded—promised to be a relatively mild affair. Throughout the country good times still continued. In Manitoba, John Norquay won a general election against an opposition, led by Thomas Greenway, which had vigorously attacked federal disallowance of Manitoba's railway charters. And in Ontario, where a provincial election had been set for February 27, the Conservative opposition was battling with such a lusty confidence that, in Macdonald's view, there was at least a chance of Mowat's defeat. A good many Ontario members of both parties were away from Ottawa, taking part in the provincial campaign; and for the first few weeks of the session, a curious holiday atmosphere pervaded the House of Commons.

Macdonald was in a most affable mood. He greeted Blake with indulgent geniality. Blake had complained, during the debate on the address, of the tedious brightness of the Conservatives' picture of the state of the nation, and had himself supplied corrective quantities of gloom. Blake, Macdonald told the House pleasantly, was darkness rather than light, shadow rather than sunshine, Rembrandt rather than Turner. "My honourable friend," he continued, "put me much in mind of an old Newcastle collier who had been boxing the compass for many years and in the exigencies of the last long voyage he had been in almost every foreign country. After a visit of seven years to the West Indies he came back to England, and when his ship was approaching the land, and when he felt the familiar sleet and storm and saw the familiar clouds, he put on his sou'wester and his peajacket and said: 'This is something like weather; none of your infernal blue skies for me'."[67]

For Macdonald, the good weather still lasted. He was determined to take advantage of it. For the session of 1883 he planned two important measures which would, in their different ways, assert the independence and authority of the Dominion. One was a Franchise Bill, designed to substitute a single, uniform federal franchise for the various provincial franchises which up to this time had been used in federal elections. The other was an Intoxicating Liquors Bill which would transfer to commissioners appointed by the federal government the whole business of the regulation of the sale of beer, wine, and spirits. A uniform, regulatory system, in the interests of national peace and order, was the avowed aim of the Bill. Its undeclared but very real enemy was Oliver Mowat and his Ontario Licence Act; and its triumphant justification was the decision in Russell *v.* the Queen. In Macdonald's opinion, Russell *v.* the Queen had confounded his opponents in Ontario. Mowat and his friends were now in disorderly retreat. Would the election of February 27 bring about their complete downfall? For a few hours, during that late night in February, it almost seemed that it might.[68] Seat after seat was falling to the Conservatives! Mowat was only a half-dozen constituencies ahead! Hopes rose dizzily—only to fall once more. The "little tyrant" was back in office again. But he was in by a greatly reduced majority. As Macdonald had predicted, he had been "run very close".[69] His complacent confidence had been rudely shaken. And Macdonald pressed his advantage and pushed his Liquors Bill forward.

Dominion-provincial relations were important. But so also were imperial relations. And ever since the passage of the Costigan resolutions and the collapse of the negotiations for assisted immigration in the previous spring, relations between Canada and England had remained in a sensitively delicate state. Improvement was urgently necessary if the Dominion was to get any effective British help in the settlement of the north-west. But how could improvement be expected from the astonishing diplomacy of Sir Alexander Galt? Galt was a highly unconventional ambassador with an irrepressible interest in new ideas and an incorrigible urge towards self-expression. A year ago Macdonald had persuaded him only with difficulty to refrain from publishing a pamphlet on "fair trade". But this time Galt evaded soothing admonitions by the simple expedient of accepting speaking engagements without notifying his home government. At Greenock, Edinburgh, and

Liverpool, he discoursed at large upon such controversial subjects as protection, Home Rule for Ireland, and Imperial Federation. The disconcerting news of his Edinburgh speech reached Ottawa late in January, barely a week before Parliament opened.

Macdonald was mildly alarmed. He told his High Commissioner that he awaited the arrival of his full report of the speech "with some little anxiety". "I hope," he went on, "you have not committed yourself too much to the project of Imperial Federation which, in my humble opinion, can never be worked out."[70] It was not that he disbelieved in the objects for which Galt had urged a federal Parliament for the Empire. He was just as firmly convinced as Galt that Canada must acquire more power and assume more responsibility in respect of those two exalted spheres of government activity, defence and foreign policy. He had established the High Commissioner's office in London. The Dominion's tiny regular force —the unostentatious, almost surreptitious "standing army" which had hitherto been composed only of artillery batteries—was now about to be augmented, as he had long intended, by the addition of small infantry and cavalry units. He entirely agreed with Galt that imperial defence and foreign policy must become a collective system; but he was sure that this could be achieved through the co-operation of autonomous governments, and not through the establishment of new federal institutions. He had no belief whatever in a Parliament for the whole British Empire. He had already said so publicly at the Liberal-Conservative Convention in Toronto over a year before. He would say so again.

Galt's direction was emphatically wrong. But so also was his pace. Galt, as usual, was in a hurry. But there was no need for hurry. There was never—or almost never—any need for hurry. Canada might spoil everything by hasty nationalistic demands or premature assertions of maturity. During the idle days of the previous summer, when, as Macdonald said, there was little else to do, a few newspapers had discussed the exciting possibility of his appointment as the next Governor-General of Canada. It would be a good time now, while Galt was talking airily about imperial reorganization in London, to spike these rumours effectively; and early in the session, in response to what was no doubt a prompted question, he dismissed the whole idea of his elevation to the vice-regal throne as a preposterous invention.[71] In his view, the office of Governor-General was the most important, but by no means the only, outward manifestation of that deep inner necessity, the Anglo-Canadian alliance. There were other public evidences of this vital connection; and he was equally reluctant to tamper with them. Old General Luard had now become so thoroughly disliked that during the winter, when the Militia Act was up for revision, the Cabinet actually considered a daring amendment which would have made imperial approval unnecessary for future appointments to the command of the Canadian militia.[72] But Lord Lorne became alarmed at this extremism, and Macdonald drew back in apprehension. He was reluctant to cut the connection between the two divisions of a unitary defence system. "The section in the Militia Bill relating to the Major-General commanding," he wrote to Lord Lorne, "will remain unaltered."[73]

Galt's pronouncements on the imperial connection had certainly been gratuitous and indiscreet; but they need not be regarded too seriously, for Imperial Federation remained a highly theoretical subject. It was very different with the burning topic of Home Rule for Ireland. Macdonald had good reason to suspect that the British press and the British government might be resentfully on the watch for unwanted Canadian advice about Ireland. "I don't know that the allusions to the Irish question and Home Rule were necessary," he told Galt, "and think that on the whole they had better, as the Yankees say, 'have been hired out'."[74] It was, on the surface, a mild, characteristically jocular rebuke; but it marked, nevertheless, a definite change in Macdonald's mind. He had at length become weary of Galt's extravagances. Galt seemed incapable of learning the first duty of a diplomatist—the duty of not meddling in the politics of the country to which he was accredited. And he had again suggested resignation—for the third time! Macdonald decided to take him at his word. "Arrangements made," he cabled, "Tupper your successor."[75] It would be very hard to let Tupper go. Everybody knew that he was not as clever as Galt; but he was loyal, and he had earnestness and force of character. "Sir C. Tupper is a man of strong temper and character," Lord Lorne warned the new Colonial Secretary, Lord Derby, "and in debate here has always been a violent and voluble speaker."[76] Macdonald would have put it differently. To him Tupper had been, quite simply, a tower of strength. He needed his support badly enough in Canada. But perhaps, in Canada's interests, it was better to have it employed in England.

The winter and the session grew old. Spring broke through the ragged drifts of snow and prorogation drew closer. He was overburdened with work, but then, at this time, he was always overburdened with work. It had not been a bad session. The Franchise Bill had run into difficulties and there would be no Factory Act. But most of his programme of domestic legislation was through; and in England the frightful consequences of Galt's indiscretions had not materialized. A mood of paternal forgiveness seemed to have extended its gentle sway over Gladstone and his colleagues. The British government appeared actually to be interested in Canada and in the settlement of its north-west. It was even possible that the British government might make a contribution in aid of emigration. A few important Cabinet ministers—including, of course, those most directly concerned with Ireland—were known to be favourable; and George Stephen, who had remained in London to promote the sale of his new issue of stock, was pressing a practical and attractive plan of assisted Irish emigration upon the attention of the Cabinet. Even so Macdonald was unprepared for the speed with which a decision was reached. On May 11 Stephen cabled giving him unofficially the gist of the British offer.[77] Gladstone's Cabinet was prepared to advance a million pounds in aid of the new company which Stephen proposed to establish as the representative of the land-holding interests of the Canadian Pacific Railway and the Hudson's Bay Company.

Macdonald hesitated. The offer was, on the face of it, exactly the kind of offer which he had been hoping for years to persuade the imperial government to make. Yet now it was his turn to exhibit something of the imperial government's calculating, self-interested detachment. "Parliament near prorogation," he cabled Stephen. "No legislation possible this season. Government favourably inclined. Await details."[78] He would await details, of course; but was he or his government likely to be very favourably inclined to such a proposal? Obviously the new interest displayed by the Gladstone administration in emigration had been largely prompted by the murderous violence which reigned in Ireland; and the very considerations which suggested the removal of Irishmen from the United Kingdom hardened the hearts of the Canadians against their reception in the Dominion. Why, Macdonald reasoned, should Canadians incur heavy additional obligations in order to transport the terrible Irish problem to Canada? Yet heavy additional obligations certainly seemed to be involved in the British proposal. The million pounds was to be advanced not directly to Stephen's new land and immigration company, but to the Canadian government; and, in Macdonald's view, Canada would therefore have to accept responsibility not only for the payment of the debt to Great Britain but also for the collection of the loans to the individual settlers. It was preposterous! Why should Canada welcome an offer of aid made partly at her own expense? It was Great Britain's responsibility and wholly within Great Britain's power to give unconditional support to Irish emigration.[79]

The argument over the assisted immigration scheme continued all during the spring and early summer. But it was an increasingly futile argument. Macdonald was not to be budged, and his mind soon turned to other things. It was July now, and he was anxious to get away for the long holiday at Rivière du Loup without which he was perfectly certain he could not carry on. He had been ill again after the prorogation. It seemed that the end of every session was punctuated by one of his break-downs; and his worried colleagues were once again taking precautions to relieve him. The burden of representing Canada abroad was being borne that summer by Tilley, Tupper, and Macpherson; and it had been arranged that when Macpherson came back, he would take over Macdonald's portfolio of the Department of the Interior. Macdonald intended to keep the superintendence of Indian affairs and the control of the Mounted Police; but the whole enormous business of land granting in the north-west, which, as he assured Lord Lorne later, was "enough for any one man—and more", would henceforth become Macpherson's direct responsibility.[80]

He had slipped from under a great load of routine. But would these—or any other conceivable arrangements—really lighten the general burden of his labour and anxiety? Tupper had told him frankly that he could not hope for real relief until he stopped work. Was the time come when he should follow Tupper's advice? At the end of the session he had faced the Commons in his usual jaunty fashion. But the effort had cost him a good deal, and more than once during the early weeks of summer he wished devoutly for complete rest. "I have nearly made up my mind to get out of office," he told Plumb. "This is a good time for it and I am breaking down. I can't conceal this from myself, perhaps not from my friends."[81]

"This is a good time for it." A year ago, even six months ago, the statement might have been true. Then he could have ended his career in a real blaze of glory. The general election had been won; the success of the National Policy and the national transcontinental had been assured; the country was gratefully rich with prosperity. But those times were irrevocably gone now, and he faced a very different future. He had delayed too long; and when the summer was over and he got back to Ottawa, it was too late.

The boom began to peter out.

Chapter Eleven

Stand Fast, Craigellachie!

I

The recession had no dramatic beginning. There was no "Black Friday" to date it, no collapse of some venerable bank or commercial house to fix its commencement in popular memory. It just began. Unheralded, unannounced, unspectacular, it could hardly have made a more unobtrusive appearance. Only gradually did people become conscious of the fact that the grey, chill, all-too-familiar presence was there. A slow but persistent decline of prices set in. The stock-market at New York began to behave in an unconvinced and highly nervous fashion; and suddenly—it was a grim foreshadowing of future deficits— J. H. Pope, who was in control at the Department of Finance during Tilley's absence, reported that the government was suddenly hard up for ready cash.[1] Macdonald, who, in the last few years, had almost come to assume that annual surpluses were a Conservative prerogative, brought the matter up, in a slightly accusing fashion, on Tilley's return; and Tilley was, of course, ready with a long and somewhat involved explanation, full of references to current and capital accounts.[2] It was not entirely reassuring; and what was happening out in the north-west was far less so. The events in the north-west were ominous, for, as Macdonald knew very well, the success of his national policies and the prestige of his government depended, to a very large extent, upon the rapid and prosperous settlement of the prairies. And out on the prairies everything seemed suddenly to have gone wrong. The hectic land boom dwindled away into

353

a sickening stagnancy. The wheat crop of 1883 was ruined by frost.

Lord Lorne and his consort were going home. Their tenure at Rideau Hall had spanned the gay morning—the forenoon and the high noon—of Macdonald's second government. They had come to stand for good times, "royal weather", blue smiling skies, favouring breezes, and beneficent showers. The country, like a hardy plant, had shot up towards maturity. Its clumsy energies had flowed vigorously into a half-dozen huge and varied undertakings. Lord Lorne had sponsored the Royal Society of Canada and the Royal Canadian Academy; he had seen the start of the "National Policy" of protection and the Canadian Pacific Railway; he had watched, with curious and sympathetic interest, the establishment of the High Commissioner's office in London, and the first beginnings of what was ultimately to become the new diplomatic system of the Empire. Everything had gone well. In those first years of the administration, success had come to seem the order of nature and failure a preposterous abnormality. Lord Lorne had brought good luck. And now he and his royal lady were departing. Macdonald watched them take their leave of Ottawa with real regret, and with something, too, of an ageing man's reluctance to accept the departure of familiar faces. "We were all unaffectedly sorry to part with you yesterday," he wrote the Governor-General, "and even the apathetic Ottawa people were stirred to the depths."[3]

The final farewells were to be said at Quebec. There the old and the new governors would exchange their powers, and the new régime would be set in motion by the usual elaborate ceremony of swearing in. Lord Lorne had gone on in advance to await the arrival of his successor; and, in a few days, Macdonald and the entire Cabinet hastened after him. It was past seven o'clock of a cool, clear evening in late October when they all put out in the government steamer *Druid* from the Queen's Wharf at Quebec to greet the new Governor-General, the Marquess of Lansdowne.[4] Far down the river, above a point of land, Macdonald could see the tremulous top lights of the Allan steamer *Circassian*. To the north, the sheer cliffs of

Quebec soared abruptly into the sky. The winking lights of the town climbed upward until they seemed to mingle with the stars; the blazing lamps on Dufferin Terrace glittered like some strange and brilliant constellation; and higher still, on both sides of the river, the sky-rockets broke in the darkness like tiny meteors. The *Circassian*, its port-holes gleaming in long, beaded rows, crept gradually, deceptively, closer to the steamship wharf on the Point Lévis side; and then, suddenly, when Macdonald hardly expected it, the huge ship was upon them, its long, sleek, darkly majestic hull towering above. There was a roar of cheers from the land; and high overhead, in the lighted quarter-deck, a tiny figure could be seen acknowledging the welcome. The *Druid* puffed importantly closer; a gang-plank was flung across the chasm between the two vessels; and Macdonald, looking tall and slim and strangely boyish in the darkness, jumped lightly into the big steamer after Lord Lorne.

Macdonald had greeted more Governors-General than he cared at the moment to remember; but, though he had no reason to expect it, he was to find in this slight dark man one of the two ablest chiefs under whom he had ever served. Now he greeted him with a formal politeness which was stiffened, at least slightly, by the very real anxiety that he felt. If he had had a voice in the selection of the Crown's representative in Canada—and he had always insisted that he preferred to have nothing to do with the matter—he would certainly never have thought of including Lord Lansdowne's name in a short list of ten. Lansdowne was an Anglo-Irish peer, with extensive estates and many tenants in Ireland, and inevitably, during the growth of the violent agrarian troubles in the island, his name had become unpleasantly well known to many Irishmen on both sides of the Atlantic. Macdonald knew that there were fierce and angry Fenians in the Canadian cities and millions more of them in the United States. "There is just a possibility," he had written to Lord Lorne soon after Lansdowne's appointment had been announced, "that, as shooting landlords is not a safe game in Ireland now, the Irish American ruffians might try it on here, trusting to our unfortunate proximity to the United States, for a chance to escape."[5]

He had carried this additional worry about with him during the summer and early autumn. He had tried, with some success, to influence the attitude of the press to the new Governor; and on the night before Lord Lansdowne's arrival, he and the other ministers had met in the Hotel St. Louis to go carefully over the arrangements for his reception. It had been decided that the swearing-in ceremony was to be hedged about with a good many careful precautions, suitably disguised with pomp and circumstance. "I think it would be well," he had written Lord Lorne, "to make a considerable demonstration on the new Governor-General's assuming the government under present circumstances."[6] When Lord Lansdowne came ashore, early in the morning of October 23, he was waiting anxiously for him. He was on pins and needles of nervousness all through the formal installation at Quebec and all during the long train journey up to Ottawa. But nothing marred the ceremonious inauguration of the new Governor's reign; and at Ottawa, which they reached just as dusk was falling, the reception on the station platform could hardly have been more satisfactory.[7] The guards and the police, he noted carefully, were out in full force; but the crowd seemed orderly by inclination and even enthusiastic in its welcome. "There was not a single sign of dissent to the cheers which rang along the platform," he reported proudly to Lord Lorne.[8]

It was a good enough augury. And yet, on the whole the auguries for Lansdowne were less hopeful than they had been for Lorne. Lorne had been accepted rapturously, on trust; Lansdowne would have to make his own way by merit. And was it not only too clear already that he would have to break a path through difficulties to win his reputation? "I fear," Macdonald had written back in July, "Lord Lansdowne will have an unpleasant reign of it."[9] Had he not spoken more truly than he knew, and with more reason than at that time he could have foreseen? Was it not growing more and more obvious all the time that the coming of the new Governor had marked a real change of circumstances, a sharp and definite shift in the winds of fortune? For weeks the signs of trouble had been accumulating on all sides; and now the final and conclusive proof of approaching misfortune had come with a crisis in the finances of the Canadian Pacific Railway. The railway, Macdonald sometimes thought, was an organization secondary only in national significance to the government itself. It was Canada, with all its aspirations, energies, and weaknesses, in little; and no barometer would ever record the vagaries of the national climate with such sensitive fidelity. Everything that happened to the railway was significant, for better or for worse. And was it not a tragic coincidence that on October 24, the day after Lord Lansdowne arrived in Ottawa, George Stephen should lodge with the Minister of Railways and Canals at Ottawa a formal petition for financial help?

Six months before there had not been the slightest sign of such weakness. Six months before, it was true, Stephen had very nearly concluded a general settlement of all conflicting interests with the Grand Trunk Railway Company in London. It was a settlement which unquestionably would have ensured a prolonged peace, for it involved the surrender of most of the Canadian Pacific's subordinate railway properties in southern Ontario and Quebec to the Grand Trunk. These were large concessions; and Stephen, at the instigation or with the approval of his associates in North America, decided in the end that he could not make them. The reconciliation was never carried through; the conflict between the two railways was renewed with greater intensity than before; and Stephen carried everything before him with a high hand. All that summer, construction was pushed forward with the furious energy which, under Van Horne, had come to be associated with the Canadian Pacific; all that summer the money which had been obtained from the sale of the thirty million dollars of stock drained ceaselessly away; and with every week that passed Stephen was driven closer and closer to the necessity of fresh financing. He still had resources left; but the time was very near when he would have to augment them largely. And, as the autumn went on, and September drifted away into October, he began to realize that the best chance had already slipped by. The New

York market was always mercurial; but that autumn it seemed to have grown more capriciously, more perversely unstable than ever. Railway stocks were in general unsettled. In September, there came a sharp break in the price of Northern Pacific, which had a damaging effect upon the quotations of other transcontinentals; and there were times also when the "bears" seemed to have picked out the Canadian Pacific as the sole victim of their rage. Yet Stephen would have to have more working capital, and quickly. Fifty-five million of the Canadian Pacific's authorized capitalization of one hundred million had already been issued. Forty-five million dollars' worth of stock was still available to him. Somehow he must convert a part, or all of it, into cash.

Late in October, immediately after Lord Lansdowne, Macdonald and the other ministers had arrived in Ottawa, Stephen reached the capital and booked a room at the Rideau Club. In the next few years the Rideau Club, Wellington Street, and the broad prospect of Parliament Hill were to become wearisomely familiar to him; but now he was only at the beginning of his prolonged ordeal of waiting upon governments and haunting Council chambers. On October 24, he talked his problems over at length with Macdonald.[10] He was seriously worried, for the first time in the history of his presidency, and he made no attempt to disguise the fact. But he was still robustly confident of ultimate success and fertile of expedient; and the plan which he presented for the solution of his difficulties was worked out in all his usual careful detail. Its essence was simple. Stephen proposed to prove, by the most convincing of all possible demonstrations, that Canadian Pacific Railway stock was a stable five per cent security. The company had, of course, decided at the beginning to pay a five per cent dividend even during the period of construction; and the dividend had so far been regularly paid. But Stephen realized that this good record could not of itself create the necessary amount of public confidence in the future of his property. He needed that confidence desperately at the moment. He could not hope to get a large supply of fresh working capital without it; and it seemed to him that the only body which could give

the public the necessary assurance was the Canadian government itself. If the Canadian government could be induced to
contribute for ten years a three per cent dividend on the
hundred million capital stock of the Canadian Pacific, then
surely he would have given the necessary proofs of permanence
and stability. The company would be left to supply only two
per cent, which, on its record, it had amply demonstrated it
could do; and Canadian Pacific shares would appear proudly
before the world as a solid, gilt-edged five per cent investment.
The government guarantee was the vital essential of the plan.
Stephen wanted it badly, and he was prepared to pay for it.
He never dreamed that he could expect any part of it as a
gift. He proposed to buy it, with cash and securities, precisely
as he might have bought an annuity for himself. As he pointed
out to Macdonald, it would take twenty-five million dollars to
pay a dividend of three per cent for ten years on the capital
stock of the Canadian Pacific Railway. He was prepared to
pay fifteen million dollars at once, and another five million
on February 1, 1884, the balance to be made up of securities
and other assets, including the government postal subsidy.

Macdonald looked favourably upon Stephen and his plan.
The Canadian Pacific, in this sudden onset of tribulations,
must be given government support. "The attempts to ruin
that enterprise and *bear* the stock are most atrocious," he told
Tupper indignantly.[11] He was angry with the unfriendly railway speculators in New York; he was even angrier with Sir
Henry Tyler and the Grand Trunk propagandist "scribblers"
in London. That the Grand Trunk should dare to attempt to
undermine the Canadian Pacific and, indirectly, the government which had created and supported it, was a piece of
effrontery so colossal that it could not be borne for a moment.
The Grand Trunk Railway was itself a stupendous monument
to government generosity and indulgence. As he reminded
Tupper, it owed Canada a debt of three and a half million
pounds sterling, together with a mere thirty years of unpaid
interest. Much of this financial support had been supplied
by Macdonald himself, in the days when he had been one of
the joint heads of the government of the old united Province

of Canada. He had never repudiated his action, never regretted it; government assistance had been necessary for the Grand Trunk Railway, just as it was now necessary for the Canadian Pacific, and for much the same reasons. But if the Grand Trunk's obligations had been waived with repeated generosity, they had never been cancelled or written off. Why, if the malicious attacks on the Canadian Pacific were kept up, should he not announce that he would enforce the collection of Canada's debt? "A threat of that kind judiciously used at the right time," he told Tupper, "would soon bring those people to their bearings."[12] He would carry the war into the enemy's camp! He urged Tupper and Rose to furnish him with proofs of the Grand Trunk's propagandist activities. There was certain to be a good opportunity of making use of such evidence during the next session.

In the meantime Stephen and his railway must be rescued. He was worried about Stephen. For the first time since that famous day in October, 1880, when the contract had been signed, Stephen looked depressed; and this, in a person of his "enormous pluck", was ominous. Action was obviously necessary at once; and the Cabinet decided without delay to accept Stephen's proposal, which, among other things, was easily defensible politically. Stephen's mercurial spirits rose with a bound; and it was with all his old gay confidence that he set out for New York on the afternoon of October 29 to get, as he told Macdonald, "Tilley's fifteen millions".[13] He never got them. At New York he was brutally awakened from his over-confident illusions. It was true that Canadian Pacific shares, like his own spirits, had jumped upward briefly.[14] For a day, on the announcement of the "new departure", they stood at nearly sixty-three dollars. But this, to a considerable extent, was because the government guarantee had been misinterpreted and magnified. The error was corrected; the price began to sag; the New York market became again what it had been for months, grudgingly unfavourable at best, and, at worst, malignantly hostile. Stephen, with despair in his heart, realized that in these circumstances it would be quite literally impossible to convert the huge total of forty-five million dollars of stock into

working capital. He had grasped too far. He must be content
with much, much less; and, within a week, he was back in
Ottawa once more with a greatly reduced programme.[15] The
government contribution of three per cent interest was now
requested, not for the whole authorized capital stock, but for
sixty-five million dollars only. It was a drastic change. It
would mean, of course, that a much smaller deposit would be
sufficient to buy Stephen's "annuity"; but it would also mean—
an extremely important point—that he would have, in effect,
only ten million dollars' worth of shares to convert into ready
money. Yet, for all his searching, he could see no better course.
Nor could the government. The bargain was concluded;
Stephen paid over his money; and, early in November, the
guarantee was announced.

For a while Macdonald hoped against hope that it would
do all that Stephen had at first expected of it. "The stock ought
to find a ready sale at seventy or more in the English market,"
he assured Tupper confidently as late as November 22.[16] But
he was whistling to keep his courage up. The stock was not
rising. It was falling, persistently. The government of Canada
had given its guarantee, and the guarantee had availed almost
nothing.[17] There was no public confidence to which the
Canadian Pacific could appeal; there was only doubt, indifference, malice, and jealousy. Stephen did not dare to issue the
new ten million dollars of stock, even though it bore the
government's guarantee for interest at three per cent. He
could do no more than pledge it in New York for a loan of
five million. His plan had failed; and he and Macdonald
knew it. The whole idea of purchasing public confidence and
support with a government dividend had proved a complete
and overwhelming failure.

Financially, the company was much worse off than it had
been before Stephen had ever conceived the notion of the
guarantee. It had paid out nearly nine million dollars—the first
instalment of the purchase price; it had given security for the
payment of the remainder; and all that it had got—or seemed
likely to get—from the whole transaction was a loan of five
million dollars. The prestige of Canada had unquestionably

suffered. The company had been dealt a savage blow; and, from the beginning of December, its position rapidly and steadily deteriorated. Stephen was appalled by the number and the venom of his enemies. He began to realize—what Macdonald had known from the beginning—that there were powerful interests in the world which had deliberately determined to effect the ruin of his railway. "You are right," he wrote to Macdonald. "We have nothing to look for from the Yankees but jealousy and bitter hostility, and as to London our friends there will do their best to feather their own nests without caring much what happens to us here."[18] He did what he could to avert disaster. He battled against his enemies with passionate energy. While the market went to pieces, he kept rushing back and forward between Montreal and New York, trying to restore confidence and stop the spreading damage. But it was hopeless and soon he knew it. "Something must be done at *once*," he wrote urgently to Macdonald, "to put the company out of discredit or we had better give up and let the government step in and carry on the business. . . ."[19]

A fortnight before this, Macdonald had made his decision. He knew what he must do. New York, London, Paris, Amsterdam—the whole investing world—had failed the Canadian Pacific. But the Canadian Pacific was a project of the Canadian nation; and, in its extremity, it had turned back to the Canadian nation for support. The support must be granted. But to push it through the Canadian Parliament would require the help of the railway's every friend and well-wisher. On December 3, he cabled to Charles Tupper in London, begging him to return to Canada. Only a few months before, Tupper had sailed for England to become the second Canadian High Commissioner. It was a job to which he had looked forward, which he was certain to enjoy. But he was not to spend the winter of 1884 in London, making the pleasant acquaintance of his new duties. He was still a member of the Canadian Cabinet and still Minister of Railways and Canals; and his place, in this new crisis, was elsewhere.

"Pacific in trouble," Macdonald wrote on the cable form. "You should be here."[20]

II

The soft, comfortable, easy-going days of the administration, the days when he had always done right, when it had been hardly possible for him to do wrong, were gone, and probably for ever. Something harder and infinitely more exacting confronted him. How would he be able to face it? Yet he assumed, and almost as a matter of course, that he would have to face it. Another year had vanished, another parliamentary session was rapidly approaching; and he was no nearer to retirement. That autumn he moved his household again and for what he must have felt obscurely was the last time. He had been a tenant, not a proprietor, during all the long years at Ottawa; but a year ago he had purchased what had once been known as "Reynolds' house" and which he renamed "Earnscliffe", the eagle's cliff. It was a roomy, rambling, gabled house which stood close to the edge of the great cliff of the Ottawa River, about a mile or so out of town.[21] He had lived there, over ten years before, during the winter between his long convalescence in Prince Edward Island and the meetings of the Washington Conference in the spring of 1871; and a year ago, in the autumn, he had moved in again for a few months while Stadacona Hall was in the throes of a thorough redecoration.[22] He liked the house, the peace of its isolation, the view up the river towards Parliament Hill, and the sombre prospect of the dark blue Laurentian Hills to the west.

The Macdonald family occupied the last weeks of 1883, with pleasant deliberation, in settling in.[23] There was nothing wrong with him that he or the medical men could detect; but he could hardly claim to feel very robust or energetic. "I am in pretty good health," he wrote to Tupper, "but feel tired every night."[24] He was not the most obvious leader for a hard parliamentary campaign; but even so, he was in as good a case as many of his colleagues. Sometimes it seemed as if the entire Cabinet had taken to haunting doctors' offices. Pope was wretchedly ill, Tilley feared diabetes, Campbell was afflicted with frightful headaches, and Macpherson had to go off every once in a while to get the "knots" taken out of him at some German spa. Even Tupper, who was so tough and resilient that he seemed at times to be made of steel and rubber, had been seriously ill in the previous spring. But Tupper had recovered. Tupper was the most vital, the most youthfully buoyant member of what Macdonald was beginning to consider a gang of old crocks. And Tupper had responded instantly to Macdonald's appeal for help in the Canadian Pacific crisis. He had left London for Liverpool at midnight on December 5; and the next day he had sailed for Montreal on the Allan liner *Parisian*.

Christmas was only a week away when Tupper reached Ottawa. At once he and Macdonald grappled with the crisis in the Canadian Pacific's affairs. By this time Stephen was nearly frantic. Railway shares in general, and transcontinental railway shares in particular, had been terribly shaken by the sudden bankruptcy of the Northern Pacific, the Canadian Pacific's chief rival. The price of Canadian Pacific stock had gone down to fifty-four; and everywhere that Stephen turned he met the bland, confident, contemptuous assumption that the company had run through its money, that it was finished, and that in a mere matter of days it would have to stop. His creditors, the owners of the floating debt that was killing the company's credit, were after him like a pack of wolves. He had run through all expedients. "Now there is no way in God's earth," he wrote, and even on paper his words were shrill with urgency, "by which these debts can be paid off but by a loan to the company by the government. . . ."[25] Even government, by itself, could not act swiftly enough for him now. He needed an immediate advance from the Bank of Montreal; but even more, if that were possible, he needed the large-scale assistance which only the Canadian Parliament could authorize.

Macdonald knew that he must intervene. The Bank of Montreal had reached its limit. It was terrified to advance a copper more. "The danger is a bear raid on the bank stock," Stephen explained to Macdonald, "on the ground of heavy advances to the C.P.R. without cover."[26] In private, Tupper assured the Bank's representatives, Smithers and Buchanan, that the government was ready to stand behind the Canadian Pacific for the repayment of the necessary advance. But Smithers and Buchanan intimated politely that Tupper's verbal assurance was not enough. They wanted more. Nothing less than a secret memorandum, initialed by Macdonald as well as by Tupper and Tilley, would satisfy the directors, so Stephen informed Tupper in some embarrassment on December 28.[27] The next day Buchanan came up to Ottawa. In the end he seemed satisfied with a letter, signed by the Minister of Railways and Canals, supporting Stephen's application; and in the end the Bank granted the advance, though only, as Stephen found out later, by the narrowest of squeaks, and over the strong opposition of several of the directors.[28] Yet the deed was done. Stephen had his money. He could meet the loans which matured in New York on January 8. But this, as Macdonald knew only too well, was only the beginning, the first slight instalment of the Canadian Pacific's bottomless necessities. There was more—vastly more—to come; and, in the middle of January, Stephen formally presented his scheme for the satisfaction of his requirements. He asked a government loan of twenty-two and a half million dollars; and for this he was prepared to mortgage the main line of the railway and all its lands not so far appropriated.

As he gazed at these stupendous totals, Macdonald was appalled. It was not that he doubted the reality of Stephen's necessities or questioned the wisdom of his plan. He and Tupper and Tilley and Pope and Schreiber had been over the mass of evidence till the figures danced before their eyes. The plan might be modified in detail; in order to improve its political defensibility, the conditions imposed upon the railway might have to be made more rigorously exacting. But that was all. In essence, the plan would have to stand, for there was no other way out. For the Canadian Pacific, the scheme was a proved financial need. But, for the Canadian government, was it not an obvious and utter political impossibility? Macdonald did not know. There was no certainty ahead. Less than two years ago, in the general election of June, 1882, he had won a majority which was amply sufficient for all ordinary purposes. But this was not an ordinary purpose of government. In the history of Canada, it was something out of all reason and all precedent. He could no longer rely upon mere parliamentary majorities for a solid basis of support. He was up against something which might cut through all parliamentary majorities, which might transform a disciplined army of Conservatives into a panicky mob of deserters. Yet how, at this stage, could he give up? He could not abandon the railway yet. He must go forward. And he knew it.

"We are going to stand by the C.P.R.," he wrote to Lord Lorne early in January, "but anticipate great opposition in Parliament, and fear some defection of own friends. But we shall face the opposition manfully."[29] In part, of course, the opposition would be real and sincere; in part it would be purely political; but, in addition, to some extent at least, it would not be opposition at all, but simply a self-interested determination to exact a suitable reward for support. In a federal and continental state such as Canada, every national undertaking seemed fated to be weighed down with a variety of embarrassing and often inappropriate additional projects, imposed on it by demanding provinces and regions. A Canadian national enterprise was like a medieval cargo which had to pay tribute to every robber baron along the toilsome trade route to its destination. This time, with an issue so tremendous and a sum so huge at stake, it was certain that every local interest, like so many steel-eyed, rubber-necked vultures, would be implacably waiting. In the previous summer, at long last, the Dominion had finally patched up a settlement with British Columbia. But, in these days, the straitened Province of Quebec seemed to have its tongue perpetually hanging out for more; and in the Maritime Provinces, which derived no obvious benefit from the new national highway, there was already a sinister suggestion that the Canadian Pacific should undertake the construction of a new line, a "short line"—shorter than the Intercolonial—to the sea.

There would, Macdonald knew, be threats, and sulks and importunities all round. Yet these, for all their exasperating complexity, were not the worst test that he faced. The worst test

was something much more serious. He would have to gamble
upon the belief which Canadians—and outsiders—held in the
future of the Dominion. The Pacific railway, which was the
condition of successful expansion across the continent, had
reached the limit of its resources and credit. It had turned,
in desperation, to the state which had given it birth. But the
state was Canada, a country of a few millions of people scattered
across half a continent; and Canada's resources and credit had
their sharply defined limits too. Was Macdonald in danger of
plunging beyond these limits to disaster? Every sign on the
commercial horizon suggested the approach of bad times, the
return of declining revenues and niggardly markets, the deepening of a depression which would be unfavourable for even
the smallest project, and might prove fatal to a giant enterprise like the Canadian Pacific. The tests, in the next few
months, would be pitilessly severe; but a real faith would
survive them. It all depended on faith in the end. Could the
Canadians—and those who could be persuaded to support the
Canadians—be kept steadfast in the conviction that the Canadian north-west was a real homeland and that a transcontinental
Canada was a viable state?

Here was the real test that he would face in the next few
months. In the next few months every propagandist device
would be employed, with all malice and without scruple, to
undermine Canada's prestige and prospects. Blake, the Grits,
the Grand Trunk "scribblers", the speculators in New York, the
correspondents of Reuters and the great American press associations—the whole great watching ring of his enemies—would
do everything in their power to misrepresent, belittle, and de-
fame the plan which he would have to sponsor. Every trumpery
criticism, every local protest, every sign of provincial or regional
discontent—anything and everything which could be used to
injure his scheme through the very destruction of Canada's
credit—would be picked up, magnified, exaggerated, twisted
out of all recognition of the truth. Provincial governments,
provincial legislatures, regional conventions and associations—
all bodies in which men gathered together as political animals—
were potential sources of danger. A serious sign of disaffection

in any part of the country would betray him. But there was one region, above all others, in which he was vulnerable. It was the north-west. Without a successful north-west his whole great plan of national expansion and integration was meaningless. If it began to seem really probable that the north-west would not become the homeland of a prosperous and contented population, then there could be no justification for the loan he was about to propose in aid of the Canadian Pacific, and no reason for the Canadian Pacific itself. It was as simple as that. Here lay the real crux of his difficulties. For, in the north-west, everything had changed in the last four months. The north-west had ceased to be his best asset, and had become his most serious liability. What he faced in the west now was failure, discouragement, and discontent.

He was not very surprised. He had always known that the elements of real trouble existed in the north-west. The Indians, the half-breeds, and the new settlers—each group represented a different but an equally explosive problem. For the first time in nearly a century, a Canadian government had been obliged to negotiate with large, organized tribes of Indians, and to attempt their settlement on reserves. The elaborate process by which this had been carried out was, of course, an old one; it had been worked out by Sir William Johnson in the eighteenth century and had been passed on, a valuable administrative inheritance, to the Canadian government in 1860, when the imperial authorities gave up the administration of Indian affairs.[30] There was nothing new about Indian reserves; but in the Canadian north-west the size of the areas involved, the numbers of Indians affected, and the solemnity and comprehensiveness of the treaty engagements accepted all helped to transform an old and rather simple undertaking into a new and awful responsibility. The costs were certainly high. During this and the previous fiscal year, the Dominion government had been spending at the rate of slightly over a million dollars a year on Indians. But it was barely six years since the last of the treaties had been signed with the Blackfoot in the autumn of 1877; and nobody as yet could feel any certainty that the new system was a success. The reserves remained an experiment—difficult, unpredictable, and highly dangerous.

Here the fears which Macdonald felt were the fears inspired by novelty. In the case of the half-breeds and the new settlers, they were the apprehensions of well remembered experience. The *métis* thought of themselves as a "nation". In the settlement process they were a nation of squatters. Macdonald knew, as any lawyer knew, that squatters were notoriously suspicious, impatient, and stubborn people, and that the settlement of their ill-defined claims was probably the most exasperating and difficult problem that could confront a land-granting department. He knew too—for the Red River Rebellion had demonstrated it with ugly conclusiveness—that the French half-breed squatters of the north-west were a sensitive, proud, impulsive lot, with a tradition of co-operation, semi-military in character, which made them extremely formidable in opposition. He knew all this; and he knew too that the dangers in the north-west must certainly have been magnified by the arrival of the great masses of settlers, who had been coming in ever since 1879.

"Settlement" was a process which he understood by experience. He had grown up in Upper Canada in the immense, unhappy disturbance of its "settlement" period. He, and his relatives and friends, had lived through privation, failure, pestilence, agitation, and actual rebellion. The troubled course of colonization could not have altered very radically in half a century; and the change, where it had occurred, was, he was inclined to believe, decidedly for the worse. Settlement had become a business, extremely commercial in character. The speculators, the land-grabbers, the predatory transients who exploited town-sites, accumulated homesteads, battened on honest and unwary settlers, were more numerous than they had ever been before. Politically they were dangerous, he was convinced, for they were skilful at organization, and ready to exploit popular discontent for their own purposes. "The truth is," he had written Lord Lorne over a year before, at the time of the disallowance of the three Manitoba railway statutes, "there is yet no real public opinion in Manitoba. The men who now lead the agitation are a ring of land sharks and homestead jumpers. In a year or two the solid mass of settlers will outvote and override the gang of speculators who now pose as 'the people of the north-west'."[31]

And now—far too early—the first great test of the north-west had come. The land boom had collapsed with demoralizing suddenness; the killing frost of September 7 had virtually ruined the crop of 1883. "Times could not be much worse than they are," Aikins, the Lieutenant-Governor of Manitoba, reported from Winnipeg on the last day of November.[32] The grumbling and dissatisfaction were very real, Aikins insisted; but he had no doubt also that they were being vigorously promoted by the new Liberal opposition, which, with Thomas Greenway as its leader, had arisen as a result of the controversy over federal disallowance. Macdonald braced himself for trouble. He had not long to wait. On December 19 and 20 a convention of westerners assembled at Winnipeg, and proceeded to organize themselves in the Manitoba and North-West Farmers' Union.[33] The "Declaration of Rights" which they adopted after a long discussion of their troubles was a comprehensive enumeration of grievances. They attacked high freight rates, the tariff on agricultural implements, the administration of the public lands, the Canadian Pacific monopoly of transport, and the Ogilvie monopoly of grain elevators. The principal author of all their misfortunes was, of course, the government of Canada.

Macdonald was worried. The agitation could hardly have come at a more unfortunate time. It coincided exactly with the crisis in the finances of the Canadian Pacific; and in both cases, unknown but obviously influential persons hastened to give the bad news as much damaging publicity as possible. Over a week before the convention held its meetings in Winnipeg, J. G. Colmer, who presided over the High Commissioner's office during Tupper's absence, telegraphed in great excitement that a dispatch had appeared that morning in all the London newspapers announcing a movement for redress of grievances among the farmers of the north-west. The agitation, the English readers were assured, was assuming "gigantic proportions"; and one inflammatory speaker was alleged to have threatened that, if grievances were not redressed, the agitators would "look to Washington". "Such reports," Colmer concluded gravely, "very harmful here."[34] They were deliberately, maliciously harmful, Macdonald knew. The propaganda against Canada was now being disseminated almost without interruption. It had become a conspiracy. John Rose reported, towards the end of December, that hardly a day passed without some dispatch injurious to the Canadian Pacific or Canadian interests in general appearing in the London newspapers. "I believe myself," he wrote, "and am assured by others, that this is part of the 'bear' movement in New York, aided by confederates here, against Canadian Pacific and all its collateral interests."[35]

Macdonald hesitated. He knew that in order to save the Canadian Pacific he must act as quickly as possible. Yet he shuddered at the possible consequences of action. He had never before performed such a crucial operation, in such unfavourable circumstances, and before the vigilant eyes of so many enemies. Adverse reports of government intentions were being carefully prepared in advance; hostile rumours of government policy were flying about from lip to lip. Stephen and John Rose begged him in desperation to maintain secrecy. He had to work out the complicated provisions of the relief bill with a wary eye for inevitable criticisms; and when Parliament met on January 17, he had to persuade his dubious and frightened followers that further aid on a vast scale could alone save the Canadian Pacific Railway. It all took time. It would take far more time—how much time he could not tell—before the measure could be pushed through Parliament. And, in the meantime, it might be too late. Stephen was at the end of his tether. When, at length, he began to realize how long it would take to grind out the relief bill, he became nearly frantic. He told Tupper bitterly that he would never have attempted to carry on if he had suspected for a moment that help might not reach him before March 1. "I am going down in the morning," he wrote Macdonald from the Rideau Club as he prepared once more to return to Montreal, "and you may be sure I will do all I can to keep things moving and in life till relief arrives, but you must not blame me if I fail. . . . I am getting so wearied

ANOTHER CASE OF "OPEN YOUR MOUTH AND SHUT YOUR EYES."

and worn out with this business that almost any change would be a relief to me."[86]

Macdonald was worn out himself. Stephen seemed to be failing him; the whole over-ambitious enterprise of Canadian nationalism was breaking apart in his hands. But his scheme was ready, and he was determined to go through with it. On the afternoon of Friday, February 1, after routine business had been finished, Charles Tupper rose in his place and introduced the eleven long resolutions for the relief of the Canadian Pacific Railway.[87]

III

The debate which followed was one of the longest and most acrimonious in the long and acrimonious history of the Canadian transcontinental railway. The opposition was determined to resist to the utmost. It was true, as Blake admitted with cynical frankness in the House, that he expected the relief bill to pass; but he and his friends and associates, in and out of Parliament, saw in the distress of the railway and the embarrassment of the government an opportunity which they could exploit with telling effect in the nation as a whole. The whole enormous indictment against the Canadian Pacific could now be presented to the Canadian people; every individual, agency, and interest which was opposed to the railway could now unite in a supreme and final effort to effect its undoing. Brydges, who had been general manager of the Grand Trunk Railway, hastened to Ottawa to "post" Sir Richard Cartwright on the iniquities of his company's terrible rival. Joseph Hickson, who had succeeded to Brydges' position, published the letters he had written to Macdonald in protest against the unjust and baneful relief bill.[38] In the Commons, Blake, Cartwright, and a long succession of Liberal speakers were attacking Tupper's resolutions with all the moral indignation of righteous men invited to condone a political abomination. To Blake the history of the Canadian Pacific was an unrelieved and unending chronicle of misdeeds. He denounced its dubious financial devices, its monopolistic methods of construction, its reckless changes of route, its lavish expenditures on railway properties outside its legitimate contract, its arrogant invasion of the territories of other railways in the east, and its own jealously guarded monopoly in the north-west.

But attacks from the outside were not the only danger which

Macdonald had to meet. He also had to cope with threatened defections from within. On February 14, while the vote on Tupper's resolutions was still some distance away, a large deputation of provincial ministers from Quebec appeared before Council to present the claims of their province for further federal assistance.[39] Four days later, John Costigan, who had sponsored the resolutions on Ireland two sessions previously, and who had, for some time, been a member of the Cabinet, sent in his resignation to Macdonald.[40] This action had nothing directly to do with the Canadian Pacific Railway; but it was timed to coincide with the crisis in the railway's finances and with the climax of Macdonald's difficulties. It was serious enough, for Macdonald had no wish to risk the alienation of the capricious Irish Roman Catholic vote. But the threatened revolt of the forty-odd Conservative members from the Province of Quebec was more serious still. The Quebec members vigorously supported the financial claims made by the government of their province, and a few obstreperous secondary leaders seemed prepared to make the satisfaction of these demands a condition of their vote in favour of the Canadian Pacific relief bill. Moreover, the news of the incipient insurrection got about, and was promptly given the widest publicity. "Further most injurious messages through Reuter," John Rose cabled from London, "stating resignation two ministers account Pacific and that forty-two French members vote against."[41]

Macdonald was not to be frightened or intimidated. He drove the Canadian Pacific loan forward with all the force which he could command. There was not a moment to lose. For the company, time was now literally of the essence. It survived from day to day, and lived from hand to mouth. "Meantime," Stephen wrote on February 16, "I do not see how we are to squeeze through and keep everything moving till relief reaches us. Our individual means of helping the company are exhausted and if we do not get help now, we must stop and the effect of that would be simply fatal to the company."[42] It would, indeed, be grotesquely tragic if the company, on the eve of its salvation, should be forced to incur the stigma of some temporary stoppage or default; and Macdonald and Stephen bent themselves to avert this disaster. Yet it was perilously close. The air was poisoned with rumours. The Cabinet, it was reported, was torn by dissension; Tilley was about to be impeached; the government would certainly fall. The campaign of misrepresentation and abuse was, John Rose insisted, terrifying the British investors all too successfully. It was even intimidating the banks. Tupper wrote to the Bank of Montreal, as he had written six weeks before, giving government backing to Stephen's request for a loan which would tide the company over the last few days until the bill was through Parliament. The bank refused the request. "McIntyre goes down to New York tonight," Stephen wrote after giving Macdonald this piece of news, "to raise by way of loan for a few days $300,000 which we think will keep us out of the sheriff's hands till Tuesday or Wednesday. I hope he will manage this, though he may not be able. In that case I do not know what we shall do. . . ."[43]

Macdonald scarcely intervened in the long debate; but he pushed the relief measure onward without pause and against all interruptions. He persuaded Costigan to withdraw his resignation. He smothered the incipient rebellion among the French-Canadian members. He wired Rose requesting him, in the name of the Canadian government, to remonstrate against the injurious dispatches which were appearing in the British press. "Message false," he cabled. "No ministers resigned. Pacific resolutions passed committee yesterday, yeas one hundred and thirty-six, nays sixty-three. Concurrence probable today."[44] It was only a day later, on February 22, that the House gave its concurrence to the resolutions; and the bill based upon them passed the Commons less than a week later, on February 28.[45] It was a Thursday, late at night; and Stephen believed that with the loan which McIntyre might obtain he could hold out until the following Wednesday. In the meantime the bill would have to pass the Senate. "I trust the Bill will get into the Senate tomorrow night," Stephen wrote urgently, "and I write this to ask you if you will kindly take such measures with your friends in the Senate as will induce them to give the Bill the utmost despatch consistent with decency, so that we may be sure of getting the money on *Wednesday.* I trust Tilley will be ready. . . ."[46] Wednesday, March 5, came; and in the afternoon the Commons trooped up to the Senate chamber to hear the Deputy-Governor, Sir William Ritchie, give the royal assent to the Pacific Railway loan.[47] It had been done, and done just in time.

At once, the tension eased. The floating debt in Montreal and New York, which had embarrassed Stephen so much, was paid off. "The Yankees are all happy now," Stephen wrote to Macdonald from New York, "having got their money from the C.P.R. . . ."[48] The repayment of the American creditors and the Bank of Montreal—the support of the Canadian Pacific credit in the international money markets—was the first object of the government loan; and it had certainly been achieved. But there was a second and still more important object, which was to ensure the successful completion of the railway, without further governmental assistance, by the spring of 1886 at latest. And as yet, as Macdonald knew very well, nobody could confidently predict that this goal would be attained. He could count upon nothing, really, but George Stephen's courage and ingenuity. The future of the railway was cloudy with doubt. But even this dark prospect was not the worst of his uncertainties. He could not yet be sure that he had not risked too much in granting the loan. At one stroke he had very nearly doubled the subsidy which had been given to Canada's first transcontinental railway. Would it be possible to convince Canada in particular and the world in general that these huge expenditures, on the part of a few millions of people, were justifiable? Would the Canadians be willing and able to prove to Western Europe and the Americas that his conception of a prosperous transcontinental Canada was a valid one? There was no sign of the depression lifting; there was every prospect of increased difficulty ahead. Could the Canadians, in time of trouble, support the burdens of nationhood? Or would this half-formed, half-empty country break apart under the strains which he had imposed upon it?

He could not begin as yet to frame an answer to the question. Political circumstances were already unfavourable.

By the time the session ended, on April 19, they had grown more unfavourable still. Organized regionalism or provincialism offered the most serious threat to the national unity upon which he had to rely for success; and organized provincialism seemed rampantly on the increase throughout the Dominion. "I had to circumvent a rather ignoble plot to cause a stampede of my French friends," he informed Lord Lansdowne in a letter recounting some of the secret history of the session, "by offering them, for their semi-insolvent province, large pecuniary aid. The plot failed, but this combination of the French to force the hand of the government of the day is a standing menace to Confederation."[49] It was not the only standing menace to Confederation at that moment, he knew very well. The country seemed full of provincial animosities and discontents. British Columbia had been pacified, New Brunswick and Prince Edward Island were quiescent; but it was nearly two years now since Nova Scotia had passed into the control of the enemy, and the government of Manitoba, though outwardly loyal, was in a restless and demanding mood. The quarrel with Ontario, and its "little tyrant", Mowat, still continued. He was so deeply committed to this struggle, and so much was now involved on both sides, that the outcome was certain to be of major significance in the political and constitutional history of the Dominion. He had hoped for a complete victory; but the time had gone by when he could indulge these hopes any longer. He could not win now. He might lose completely. The best he could do was draw even.

Over a year ago he had faced Parliament with the superb confidence born of the Dominion's constitutional triumph in the case of Russell v. the Queen. Then Mowat had been on the defensive, and Ontario's Liquor Licence Act had seemed to be in jeopardy. But now the whole position of affairs was exactly reversed. During 1883, the Judicial Committee of the Privy Council had, in its judgment in the case of Hodge v. the Queen, affirmed the complete validity of the Ontario Liquor Licence Act. It was now Blake's turn to gloat over Macdonald and cast doubts upon the constitutionality of the Dominion Licence Act of 1883. It was now Mowat's opportunity to take the offensive in support of his legislation against the pretensions of the federal act. Promptly and pugnaciously he had taken advantage of this new turn of fortune. In the course of the winter of 1884 the legislature of Ontario enacted still another provincial licence law which, among other things, imposed heavy supplementary duties upon all those who took out licences under the Dominion statute. Obviously, as Macdonald pointed out to Campbell, these differential duties were imposed, not for revenue, but as a penalty for any person who dared to obtain a federal authority. "Now the idea that any subject is to be punished in a heavy fine for obeying the law of the land," he went on angrily, "is monstrous and cannot be put up with for a moment."⁵⁰ In due course, the new Ontario licence law was disallowed; but meanwhile Langevin yielded so far as to announce that the question of the constitutionality of the federal statute would be submitted to the courts "with all convenient speed".⁵¹ A contest which revolved round taverns and tavern-keepers, and which had been undertaken at least partly for the sake of the patronage involved, was obviously nearing its end; and the Dominion's early advantage was being steadily whittled away. It had been a comically disreputable controversy; but Macdonald had always regarded it seriously. He saw—and saw correctly—its underlying significance. In the end it was to go a long way towards deciding the interpretation of the British North America Act.

The Licence Act of 1884 was the last Ontario statute which was disallowed by Macdonald's government. He still believed firmly that the Rivers and Streams Bill was an iniquitous measure; and that winter the Rivers and Streams Bill had been enacted for the fourth time by an invincibly determined Oliver Mowat. Macdonald had disallowed it thrice. But on this fourth occasion he held his hand. The whole ground of further action was being cut away beneath his feet. The dispute between the two contentious lumbermen, which had prompted Mowat's legislation in the first place, had all this time been travelling through the courts. It reached the Judicial Committee of the Privy Council, that tribunal of curiously arbitrary and contradictory judgments, early in March, 1884; and on March 7,

Dalton McCarthy, who acted as counsel for the Conservative lumberman, wrote Macdonald a long, gloomy account of the proceedings, stressing the enormous difficulty of conveying any real understanding of Canada and its economy to the minds of the members of the Committee. "In this case," he explained, "they are, I think, much influenced by an erroneous notion that they have taken up that Canada is mainly a lumbering country, and lumbering the chief employment of its inhabitants, and that the consequent use of its streams as public highways is of the first consequence to us all."⁵² Whatever their notions may have been, there was no uncertainty about their verdict. They decided in favour of the Liberal lumberman. He could float his saw-logs over his Conservative competitors' "improvements" freely and without benefit of the legislation which Ontario had tried vainly to pass on his behalf. Disallowance could not alter this decision. Disallowance could affect nothing. And it was given up.

Macdonald emerged from these encounters badly mauled. The Dominion had been beaten—almost humiliated. At a moment when it desperately needed national support, it had unquestionably lost moral authority. It had failed to vindicate the cause of unity at a time when half the provinces in the union seemed bent on pursuing a disruptive course of bluster and bullying. Quebec had got its money, Ontario had won its cases; and now Manitoba seemed quite prepared to carry its agitation to the point of endangering the Canadian Pacific and threatening the cause of western settlement. In February a delegation of the Manitoba and North-West Farmers' Union had come down to Ottawa to discuss western grievances with Macdonald; and early in March, a second convention of the union, with several hundred delegates in attendance, was held in Winnipeg to receive the mainly negative report which the delegation had brought back.⁵³ This time the proceedings were distinctly more alarming. A resolution was passed bluntly warning prospective settlers to stay away from the north-west until its wrongs were righted. There were threats of rebellion and secession. In the pages of the newspapers, it all looked extremely formidable.

Macdonald was not yet very seriously worried. "The speculators," he wrote to Lord Lorne, "who were ruined by the collapse after the boom of three years ago, and are of desperate fortunes, with some democrats, have attempted to get up a row, blustered, talked secession, and all that sort of thing; but the reaction has set in and Norquay who, with many faults and weaknesses, is loyal to the Dominion, has been sustained by an overwhelming vote, twenty to six, on certain factious amendments to the address in answer to the speech at the opening of the Manitoba session. We are doing all that we can to help them within reasonable limits, and at the opening of spring, when the people are on their farms, the agitation will be forgotten."[54] At the time it seemed a not-over-confident prediction. The Farmers' Union had discredited itself by its excesses and its flagrantly partisan tone. Tupper made a definite concession to western feeling when he announced in the House that as soon as the Canadian Pacific line north of Lake Superior had been constructed, the government would cease to prohibit by disallowance the building of railways with American connections in Manitoba.[55] Finally, interrupting the session of the Manitoba legislature for the purpose, Norquay came down to Ottawa to discuss provincial grievances in general. Late in April, after the prorogation of Parliament, Macdonald sat down with the western delegates to negotiate "better terms".

And then an unaccountable and dismaying event occurred. Norquay returned to Manitoba in May. He may have felt dissatisfied with the concessions he had secured from the federal government; he probably feared that his opponent, Greenway, would make bountiful political capital out of their alleged inadequacy. In any case, he defied Ottawa, and disavowed his own agreement; and the legislature, with the hearty concurrence of both parties and the applause of the whole province, rejected the "better terms" in their entirety. It was a hard, unexpected blow, coming at a time when the Dominion was vulnerable, and from a source which would be seriously regarded. Macdonald was dismayed and indignant. He was angry with Norquay for succumbing so tamely to the mere threat of pressure from the "demagogue", Greenway. He was frightened of the damaging publicity which would infallibly be given to this utter miscarriage of his efforts to pacify the discontented north-west. But at the moment anger triumphed over apprehension. He would show Norquay that the Dominion was not be scorned! The youngest and most insignificant of the provinces would not bully his government into submission! "As matters now stand," he wrote furiously to Aikins, "our offers for the sake of peace have been rejected, and therefore do not exist, and may never be repeated. At all events, everything is thrown over for a year."[56]

Could the Canadians, in time of trouble, support the burden of nationhood? Could the outside world be induced to believe that a transcontinental Canadian state was possible? He did not dare to attempt an answer now. Everything had gone against him in the past eight months. There was widespread discontent in Canada, hostility in the United States, and in England indifference and disbelief. He was still convinced that the surest source of support for Canada lay in the United Kingdom. But he realized that the long record of recent Canadian misfortunes seemed to deny the validity of his goal of nationhood; and he knew that virtually everything that had been said or written about Canada in England in recent years had helped to build up a solid wall of doubt and scepticism through which it seemed almost impossible to hack a way. John Rose discovered that Reuters' organization, which distributed Canadian news to many British newspapers, got its despatches exclusively from the hostile Associated Press, and had accepted this arrangement for no better reason than that the material was supplied free, or nearly so.[57] George Stephen, who, after the fiasco of the previous autumn in the United States, was anxious to secure more financial support in Great Britain, reported gloomily from London that Canada had not yet been lifted from its state of discredit, and that things Canadian were still regarded with profound distrust.[58]

But this was not all, as Macdonald soon discovered. Tilley was to meet the same distrust, in the most frighteningly serious form which it could assume. Early in June, at the moment when the legislature of Manitoba was pugnaciously rejecting its agreement with the Dominion, the Minister of Finance sailed for England, with the object of floating a new loan of five million pounds sterling, and of arranging for the conversion of an old and slightly larger loan at a reduced rate of interest. He arrived in London to find an efficiently organized propaganda campaign against Canada in vigorous operation. "A desperate effort is being made here, and successful too," he informed Macdonald indignantly, "to force down both government and Canadian Pacific Railway stocks, and the knowing ones say they will be forced still lower. All kinds of unfriendly statements are sent here from the United States and Winnipeg touching the C.P.R. and I fully expect that when the prospectus of our loan appears tomorrow we will have a heavy Grand Trunk Railway blast against it."[59] The blast was quite as heavy as Tilley expected it would be. A defamatory article in one of the financial papers described the loan as "another crutch for the C.P.R."; and a sandwich-man, advertising this diatribe, paraded for several hours in front of Barings', where the bonds were being offered to the public.[60] "Tilley has got his money," Rose explained ruefully to Macdonald, "but it required a strong whip, and we met with great opposition from certain quarters, and great lukewarmness in certain others where he and the government had the right to expect better things."[61] Macdonald had certainly expected a better rate than Tilley had been able to obtain. The whole operation, he reflected gloomily, was nothing to boast about; and it was decided to postpone the floating of the conversion loan to a more propitious time.

Before the end of June, Macdonald left Ottawa for his new summer house, "Les Rochers", at Rivière du Loup. "I was obliged to hurry away from Ottawa," he told Chapleau, "as I felt myself on the eve of breaking down. . . ."[62] He had no end of worries; and once again his physical distresses had become acute. "I am suffering much from stomachic disturbance," he wrote Tupper, "and can't throw it off, and must put up with it as best I may, but it makes life not worth living. I would leave the government tomorrow, if it were not that I really think George Stephen would throw up the sponge if I did. He was so worried and sleepless that his wife became alarmed and sent him off to the seaside."[63] Obviously Stephen was far from through his difficulties. The credit of Canada had been strained. And out in the north-west, there was an ominous fermentation, still unpacified.

He had troubles enough. But now there came an aggravation of his western difficulties which certainly he had never expected. It was ten years and more since Louis Riel had left Canada. Riel would never be forgotten, of course. He had been the creative mind and the evil genius of the Red River rebellion; he would remain an ineffaceable picture in the collective memory of the Canadians. But Riel, the man, had vanished; and the last thing that Macdonald ever anticipated was his return. He had foreseen many things. But he had never foreseen such an incredible misfortune as that. Yet now it occurred. Early in July, Louis Riel returned to the Canadian north-west.

IV

All during July and August, while he tried to rest and recover his strength, Macdonald studied the reports from the north-west with curious interest. The weather was atrocious. It teemed with rain at Rivière du Loup during most of July; it rained without ceasing when he and Lady Macdonald spent a long week-end with the Stephens at Causapscal. And, while the trees dripped and the skies gloomed overhead with sullen persistence, his own health did not noticeably improve. Campbell wrote him affectionately expressing regret at his continued illness. "If we only had a week of sunshine, we should all be better," he declared. "Why do you not relax the bow? There is no use in keeping it always bent. I would shut off everything for a month. Can you not manage this?"[64] Of course he could not manage it. His summer holidays were no longer real holidays. Fifteen years ago Rivière du Loup had been a quiet and retired village; now it had become a popular and populous summer colony. And there, as Tupper shrewdly surmised, he was "exposed" to too much work. Visitors and mails kept continually arriving. Besides, he wanted them to arrive. He would have been deeply disturbed if there had been any serious interruption in the regularity of their arrivals. His interest never ceased. He had half a dozen major problems and any number of minor difficulties to keep him constantly occupied. He could never really forget these things. He had come to live for them. And one of the most serious of his major problems during the summer of 1884 was the increasingly serious situation in the north-west.

"The news from the north-west," he admitted to Lord Lansdowne, "is a little disquieting."[65] Riel, at the request of a deputation of English and French half-breeds, had arrived in the vicinity of Prince Albert, in the District of Lorne, where the *métis* agitation had its focus; and, as Macdonald confessed, his arrival had created "rather a panic".[66] But Edgar Dewdney, the Lieutenant-Governor of the North-West Territories, wrote that he did not anticipate any real trouble; and Macdonald himself was not unduly alarmed. Yet he remained watchfully on the alert. He insisted that Riel must be kept under close observation. Riel had proved himself a successful organizer of discontent, and organizers of discontent were to be feared in the north-west, for there, as Macdonald reminded the Lieutenant-Governor of Manitoba, there were "certain uneasy elements". Inevitably, the Indians had found it terribly difficult to accommodate themselves to the revolutionary change which had taken place in their mode of existence. The *métis*, who before had been hunters of the buffalo, and carriers for the Hudson's Bay Company, had seen these old means of livelihood vanish and had betaken themselves reluctantly, and with dangerous sullenness, to the uncongenial business of farming. Even the latest arrivals, the new white settlers, had experienced a demoralizing change when they had passed, suddenly and almost without warning, from the good crops and high prices of the boom to the frosts, and failures, and deflated land-values of the depression. Every important group in the north-west had been forced to adjust itself to a new and highly unpleasant set of conditions; and the experience had been a painful one. In Macdonald's mind, this was the fundamental explanation of the unrest on the prairies. The north-west was full of disappointed and dissatisfied men. They were troubled. They were perhaps ready to make trouble for others.

Yet Macdonald did not really expect any serious disturbance. Of the three "uneasy elements" in the north-west, he put the Indians at the bottom of his list. "The last—the Indian element—," he wrote to Lieutenant-Governor Aikins, "is not to be dreaded unless there is a white or half-breed rising."[67] The Indians would do no more than follow the leadership of others; and Macdonald was inclined to believe that, if they waited for the white settlers to start a revolt, they would wait in vain. The white settlers, it was true, had blustered and talked secession; and late in June Norquay had sent Macdonald a copy of an intercepted letter from one Mack Howes to George Purvis, the President of the Farmers' Union, advocating nothing less than armed revolt. Macdonald took steps to secure the arms which Howes had proposed seizing; and he heartily approved of Norquay's decision to set detectives to watch the two agitators closely.[68] Yet he had been through these meaningless paper conspiracies often enough before. "I don't attach much importance to these plots," he wrote to Aikins, "but my experience of the Fenian business has taught me that one should never disbelieve the evidence of plots or intended raids, merely because they are foolish and certain to fail." He would keep a sharp watch out, but he did not really expect to see Howes and Purvis charging about, armed to the teeth, at the head of great masses of insurgent white settlers. Early frosts, high duties on reapers, and a railway to Hudson Bay, were the stuff of general elections, rather than revolts. There was very little afflicting the new settlers of the north-west which a bumper crop would not cure.

The half-breeds were another matter. The problem of the French-speaking half-breeds in particular stood, as he knew very well, in a category of its own. Riel was a dangerously enigmatic character; his fellow *métis* were impressionable and unpredictable people. "One cannot foresee what he may do," he warned Aikins, "or what they, under his advice, may do."[69] They had revolted once in the past; they might revolt again in the future. But Macdonald did not really fear that the Red River rising would be repeated on the banks of the Saskatchewan. He did not believe that the materials of a real revolt existed. The half-breeds had been treated with great consideration. They had been given many concessions, including the vitally important concession respecting land tenure. The holdings of the original *métis* settlers on the two branches of the Saskatchewan had been surveyed in long, narrow river lots, in exactly the fashion they desired. It was true that subsequent to the original survey, other half-breeds had squatted on lands, beyond the original *métis* settlements, which had been divided on the rectangular system of sections and townships. During 1883 and 1884 these squatters had been petitioning for a complete re-survey in accordance with their wishes. The federal government had no intention of denying these people their river lots; but the land officers believed that the existing rectangular sections could be readily divided, without the trouble and expense of a new survey, into long narrow strips, each with a river frontage.[70] They were now trying to explain their plan to the impatient and suspicious half-breeds.

There remained only one problem; but it was a problem of supreme importance. It arose out of the conviction of the *métis* that they shared with the Indians in the original title to the land of North America, and could prefer an equally valid claim for compensation. The Manitoba Act, they argued, had tacitly acknowledged this claim. The 1,400,000 acres of the half-breed grant, set aside by the Manitoba Act, had, after years of delay, uncertainty, and vexation, been finally divided; and two hundred and forty acres of land had been granted to each half-breed child, and negotiable scrip for one hundred and sixty acres to each half-breed head of a family. The troubled history of the disposition of the half-breed grant had been a most unfortunate experience which nobody, with any experience in the north-west, had any desire to see repeated. Moreover, the federal government saw no need for repetition. There was a superabundance of land for the *métis* of the north-west on whatever terms they wished to claim it. If, as Macdonald informed Lord Lansdowne, they decided to plead their Indian blood, they could obtain their share of the reserve and of the annual benefits provided by the government. If, on the other hand, they preferred to maintain the status of independent white farmers, they could acquire a homestead, and the pre-emption to another quarter-section of land on the same generous conditions as anybody else. But did the *métis* want farms? Or did they want free transferable lands and negotiable scrip, which they could sell easily for a little ready money? And was this the kind of compensation which the Dominion should think of granting to them?

Macdonald and the officials of the Department of the Interior had taken their responsibilities very seriously. They knew they were dealing with a restless and improvident people. They believed that any concessions which brought no permanent benefit to the *métis* were really valueless; and for this reason they had long ago rejected the idea of negotiable scrip. The experts were opposed to it. The whole history of the half-breed land grant in Manitoba was a warning against another such issue of paper; and those who were now demanding it in the north-west were, on the whole, an extremely doubtful lot. The émigré *métis* from Manitoba, who had squandered their previous grants and who could have no claim whatever in any future distribution, were suspiciously prominent in the agitation which was going on on the banks of the Saskatchewan; and they were aided and abetted, Macdonald was convinced, by the land sharks who had everything to gain and nothing to lose from a new distribution of negotiable scrip. "The scrip is sold for a song to the sharks and spent in whiskey," Macdonald explained to Lord Lansdowne, "and this we desire above all things to avoid."[71] It was a miscarriage of good intentions which any responsible government would try to avoid. What real benefit would these unstable and thriftless people derive from such a perfunctory solatium?

The demand, in the form in which it had been made, could not wisely be granted. Yet this did not mean that Macdonald considered the matter closed. The half-breed claims could be settled in another and a more beneficial fashion. The whole issue was a proper subject for compromise. And to Macdonald, the final proof that a satisfactory compromise was possible lay in the wise moderation of Riel's conduct since he had received the appeal to go to the north-west. The man was certainly a born leader. He had no sooner reached the settlements on the Saskatchewan than he began, with great energy and address, to knit together the various discontented elements—half-breeds, Indians, and white settlers—in one close union of protest. But he had preached only lawful courses. He gave every evidence of intending a peaceful settlement. And Macdonald was re-assured. "There is, I think," he wrote to Lord Lansdowne, "nothing to be feared from Riel. In his answer to the invitation sent to him, which was a temperate and unobjectionable paper, he spoke of some claims he had against the government. I presume these refer to his land claims which he forfeited on conviction and banishment. I think we shall deal liberally with him and make him a good subject again."[72] In such a pro-gramme, the first and most obvious need was, as Lord Lans-downe suggested, to "obtain touch" of Riel. French-speaking priests in the disaffected areas and French-speaking officials in the north-west administration were instructed to approach Riel and his discontented *métis* quietly and to sound them out. "I think the true policy," Macdonald wrote to Lansdowne after he had dismissed the idea of an issue of scrip, "is rather to encourage them to specify their grievances in memorials and to send them with or without delegations to Ottawa."

At the end of the summer, this was still the position of affairs. He lingered as long as he possibly could at Rivière du Loup; and when, after the middle of September, he at length returned to Ottawa, he carried with him the unhappy knowledge that his long holiday had not brought the hoped-for improve-ment in his health. The irritation of the "coats of the stomach", as Tupper professionally described it, kept him in a state of grumbling physical discomfort. All too frequently he felt wretched. He needed rest, he needed help; and all the time difficulties were multiplying, and the opposition was exploiting them outrageously for its political advantage. In August, Oliver Mowat, his old rival, had won what was perhaps his greatest triumph from the Judicial Committee of the Privy Council.[73] Against a battery of lawyers, led by Dalton McCarthy, who

acted for Manitoba and the Dominion, he had made good
Ontario's claim to the vastly extended boundary on the north-
west which had been awarded by the arbitrators in the summer
of 1878; and early in September he returned to Toronto in
triumph, like some fabulous eastern war-lord, laden with booty
and rich in territorial conquests. Yet even this—bad as it was—
was not all. During the summer Macdonald had come to read
the secret which was half-revealed in Stephen's disquieting
hints. He knew now that the enormous aid granted in the
last session would not be enough to secure the completion
of the Canadian Pacific Railway.

"Meanwhile," he had confided to Tupper in August, "things
are not going right. At every by-election, Dominion or local,
we are fought with the whole strength of the Grits. My
colleagues, excepting Pope, Langevin, and Caron, are not
worth a cent in counteracting this tremendous effort, and with
my failing strength and advancing years, I cannot do everything.
Next month I shall have a clear understanding with my colleagues, and they *must* work or others will."[74] Brave words!
But how could he back them up with action? Bowell, Carling,
Macpherson, and Campbell, all freely offered their resignations
in order to assist him in the work of Cabinet reconstruction.
"Take my word for it, Sir John," wrote Tupper, characteristically
stating the obvious as if it had been a discovery of his own,
"you want some fresh blood in the cabinet—young, active,
vigorous men, who, with you to advise and direct them, will
give a vigorous impulse to the party."[75] Macdonald wearily
agreed with him. He longed for young, active, vigorous men.
But where were they to be got? For years Dalton McCarthy
had seemed by all odds the most promising prospect in a small
field; and Alexander Campbell had come to assume that Macdonald's "mantle" would eventually fall upon the not unwilling
shoulders of the Barrie lawyer. But McCarthy, who had been
approached in the previous spring with an informal offer of
the portfolio of Justice, had replied, much as John Hillyard
Cameron had replied decades before, that he could not give up
his lucrative private practice while his large debts remained
unpaid. Macdonald tried him again hopefully in September;

and again he was turned down. "I am still of the same opinion," McCarthy wrote, "as to the impossibility of my giving up my business, and joining the ministry; and therefore you must re-arrange without me."[76]

There was a cold conclusiveness about this final reply which was profoundly discouraging. Macdonald realized that he had no hope whatever, for years to come, of obtaining McCarthy's assistance. He was sick and tired of the whole difficult business of Cabinet reconstruction; and, besides he still felt physically unwell. Agnes kept insisting that he must take his condition more seriously and seek more expert advice; and towards the end of September he consulted a new medical man, a Dr. Howard of Montreal. Howard prescribed a fresh treatment, seemed reasonably optimistic about his case, and then, with impressive seriousness, urged him to take a complete holiday, in the only way in which it was ever possible for him to take it, by going overseas. Macdonald pondered. Could he go? The news from the north-west had suddenly become disturbing. The growing uncertainty of the finances of the Canadian Pacific was an unutterable secret which he shared only with George Stephen. He would have to cope with these things, and cope with them soon, for there was apparently nobody else who could do so. But if the vigorous young men had failed him, if he must carry on much as he had done before, then obviously what remained of his health must be guarded jealously. Rivière du Loup had not helped him much. Perhaps London would.

He suddenly decided to follow Howard's advice. "I am obliged to go off to England," he wrote to a supporter. "My health, I am told, imperatively requires it. But I shan't give that as a reason, for it would discourage our friends."[77] There were, of course, other reasons, equally valid and much more publishable, for a visit to England. Tilley's large-scale conversion operation had still to be carried out; and Stephen, who was preparing to cross the Atlantic once again himself, argued persuasively that Macdonald could do far more good for himself, the country, and the Canadian Pacific Railway by a six or eight weeks' visit to England than he possibly could by staying unhappily at home. Macdonald yielded with a sigh of relief.

On October 8, he left Ottawa; and two days later, in the pleasant company of Stephen, he sailed for England.

V

He enjoyed a holiday in England more than any other holiday that could possibly have been offered to him. It gave him what no vacation in Canada could ensure—complete release from most of the responsibilities of office. But this great, though negative, gift of peace was not the only benefit to which he looked forward expectantly when he sailed for Liverpool. The life which opened up before him as soon as he set foot on the station platform in London was as agreeable as any he had ever experienced. He enjoyed theatres, concerts, and dinner parties. He liked good company and good talk. And every time he came to England, there were more people—old friends, new acquaintances, and unknown admirers—who were eager to welcome him back or to greet him for the first time. In the past, of course, it had been the Conservatives who had given him the most cordial formal receptions; the Liberals, except in the way of official business, had paid as little attention to him as they conveniently could. But in 1884 a strange change seemed to have come over Mr. Gladstone and his Cabinet. They had, apparently for the first time, become aware of Macdonald's existence. They began to take in the fact that here was a man who had given a lifetime of public service to a country which might, in the end, become a great North American power. Despite all their confident prophecies and candid preferences, and despite the uniformly unfavourable publicity of the Liberal press, the Dominion of Canada still seemed determined and able to enjoy an independent existence in the New World. It was odd—almost incredible! But there it was! The British Liberals came to the conclusion that the fact of Canada must be admitted, and the presence of her Prime Minister suitably acknowledged. This curious change of attitude was in part the result of the mere passage of time—time which had at least made Sir John Macdonald a familiar figure, if not exactly a colonial institution. But it may have been, to an even larger extent, the consequence of a still more fundamental change, a change in the attitude of the British people to their Empire. The foundation of the Imperial Federation League in 1884 was an evidence of this change; and it had to be admitted that there were highly respectable Liberals, such as Mr. Forster, who took a prominent part in the affairs of the Imperial Federation League. The Empire was ceasing to be something to be ashamed of, to apologize over. It was almost—if not quite—becoming a subject of pride.

Macdonald had arrived suddenly, unannounced and un-expected; and it took Mr. Gladstone, whose reflections on the subject may have been assisted by others, a little time to decide what he would do. On November 15, which was nearly a month after Macdonald had arrived at his old quarters in Batt's Hotel in Dover Street, he wrote to the Canadian, offering him, in recognition of his "long and distinguished services", the Grand Cross of the Bath.[78] A week later, on Sunday, November 23, the most memorable week that Macdonald ever spent in England began. He stayed on Sunday with the Prince of Wales at Sandringham. On Monday he was entertained at dinner in London by the Beaconsfield Club; and on Tuesday, by royal command, he went out to Windsor to receive his new honour and to dine and sleep at the castle. He was the guest of honour at a dinner given by the Empire Club, the day after his return to London from Windsor. The Marquess of Lorne—"What a good and true 'Canadian' he is!" Stephen had exclaimed—pre-sided on that occasion; and over eighty peers and commoners were present at what was undoubtedly the most elaborate and the most enthusiastic tribute which had yet been paid to a Canadian statesman. The chairman spoke handsomely in Mac-donald's praise. So did Lord Salisbury for the Conservatives, and Lord Kimberley for the Liberals. Afterwards Lord Lorne told Tupper that "no one, except a foreign potentate, had ever had such a reception".[79]

Macdonald was pleased and touched. Physically he was feel-ing enormously better. He had gone, of course, as soon as he had arrived, to consult his old physician, Dr. Andrew Clark;

but it was London, even more than medical advice and treatment, which brought back his sense of well-being. He recovered
his normal buoyant spirits far more quickly than he had in the
summer of 1881—so quickly, indeed, that Stephen was conscious
of just a shade of apprehension. He inquired solicitously, after
one large dinner which they had attended together, whether
Macdonald felt any the worse for the previous evening's turtle
soup. But Macdonald, for a man who had been suffering all
summer from a grievously "deranged stomach", accommodated
himself to the rich dishes of a succession of lavish ceremonial
dinners with extraordinary rapidity. He felt very nearly at the
top of his form. He was conquering the Liberals in 1884 as
he had conquered the Conservatives in 1879. It was true, as
had been amply evident at the Empire Club dinner, that in
Great Britain he was still, to some degree at least, the special
protégé of the Conservative party. But his new honour had
been recommended by a Liberal government. Mr. Gladstone
had unbent so far as to be positively amiable at the time of
his investiture at Windsor; and Lord Kimberley had paid him
compliments in public at the Empire Club. The amazing
fact was that for the first time Liberals and Conservatives had
combined to do him honour on an impressive scale. It was—or
it could reasonably be interpreted to be—a recognition of the
validity of his national policies, an acceptance of the idea of
the transcontinental Canada which he was trying to create.

No recognition could have come more pat. No honour could
have been bestowed at a more appropriate moment. It was
ironical, of course, that these tributes to his political wisdom,
these acknowledgments of his country's brilliant prospects
should have been made just at the moment when the materials
of the national structure seemed to be breaking apart in his
hands. In retrospect, after the possible disaster of the future,
his ovation might appear a terrible mockery. But in the
meantime it was still possible that his dream might be converted
into reality; and so long as he could struggle to achieve it, every
expression of approval was of value to him. He needed confidence as he had rarely needed it before. Ever since the autumn
began, Canada's position had seemed to be steadily worsening.

On the way over on the boat George Stephen had revealed to him in detail the desperate urgency of the Canadian Pacific's necessities. But this was not the only troubling knowledge which he carried with him across the Atlantic. Just before he left Ottawa he had received a most disquieting piece of information from the north-west.

It had come in a bulging private letter from Edgar Dewdney, the Lieutenant-Governor of the North-West Territories.[80] The plan, which Macdonald and Lord Lansdowne had advocated, had been carried out. "Touch" had been obtained with Riel. Early in September, two unofficial French-speaking emissaries, Bishop Grandin and Amédée Forget, the Clerk of the North-West Council, had sought out the *métis* leader and had persuaded him to make a statement of his demands. Dewdney had enclosed the reports of this curious interview in his letter. Macdonald studied the documents with increasing dismay. There seemed no end to Riel's incredible demands. He asked for special land grants, not only for the half-breeds then living, but also for each future generation, at intervals of eighteen years. He demanded that two million acres of land should be set aside as an endowment for the building and maintenance of half-breed schools, hospitals, and orphanages. "This is what we request for the present," ran the postscript to Bishop Grandin's memorandum of the interview, "until Canada becomes able to pay us each year the interest of the sum which our country is worth and until public opinion consents to recognize our rights to their full extent."[81] The "sum which our country is worth" was calculated in a simple and generous fashion. The value of the North-West Territories was estimated at forty cents an acre for the entire area; and the resulting capital sum was to be divided between Indians and half-breeds, at the rate of twenty-five cents an acre to the half-breeds, and fifteen to the Indians![82]

All this was disturbing enough. But there was something which disturbed Macdonald even more. The gravest revelations in the documents concerned Riel himself, his purposes and ambitions. In the presence of his fellow half-breeds, he had blustered, had insisted excitedly that his mission was purely altruistic and that he was not to be bought. Yet in private his manner significantly altered. He was much quieter. His own personal grievances were carefully enumerated. Hints were dropped about jobs for himself and his principal confederates. There was a vague suggestion of "a sum of money". What did it all mean? All during the summer Macdonald had felt certain that he could rely upon Riel's good will and his desire for a peaceful settlement. But now, in the face of these preposterous demands and this equivocal behaviour, all his confidence in the future vanished. Did this strange half-breed desire peace? Or did he intend mischief? Was he the leader of a constitutional agitation? Or was he a selfish, anarchic, black-mailing adventurer?

The problem of Riel and the north-west would confront him as soon as he got home. But so also would the problem of the Canadian Pacific Railway. All during the summer he had tried to dismiss this problem from his mind. He had sought to convince himself that somehow or other George Stephen would find a solution. He had tried to ignore George Stephen's hints and covert appeals. He could ignore them no longer. By the time he reached London, he knew the railway's real position in all its gloomy detail. Once again, after a short period of barely eight months, the company was in desperate financial straits. The government loan had saved it; but the government loan had also imposed crippling conditions which had embarrassed it ever since. Macdonald had considered it essential to prove to the hesitant and doubtful Canadians that he was not throwing quantities of good money after bad. He had guarded his investment with stiff securities. Virtually all the assets of the company were pledged in a first mortgage to the government of Canada.

The thirty-five millions of unissued common stock remained, of course. But in the circumstances of the moment they were almost useless. The government lien was too intimidating to investors. The shares were quoted at forty-five, before Macdonald left for London, and nothing that Stephen could do seemed to arrest their slow, persistent decline. New York had failed the railway. London was still coldly unresponsive to its appeals. Morton, Rose and Company was the only British firm which had so far backed the company; and Stephen was convinced that Morton, Rose and Company were giving only a timorous and ineffectual support. He and Macdonald tried, through the kind offices of a young member of the Baring clan who was a junior partner in a friendly New York firm, to secure the financial backing of the great house of Baring.[83] But these first approaches were failures. Macdonald did not know where to turn. Stephen assured him that the government subsidy and loan, paid out as the progress of the work merited, would suffice to keep construction going. But beyond this were the fixed charges of interest and dividends. And Macdonald knew now that the company could not go on meeting these payments without fresh funds. Where were fresh funds to be got?

He had talked the whole portentous problem over at great length with Stephen during the journey across the Atlantic; and once he reached London, he began another set of equally lengthy discussions on the same subject with Tupper. Tupper emphatically agreed with him that a final effort to save the railway must be made. Neither of them had the slightest doubt on that score. It was a question rather of what was the most politically acceptable form that aid could take. It was also a question—an even more fundamental question—of whether or not aid in any conceivable form could be pushed through the Dominion Parliament at its next session. Macdonald was profoundly doubtful. He shrank from the exhausting and exasperating labour involved. After only a year's respite, he must begin his work all over again, and this time under much more unfavourable circumstances. The government was not so well off as it had been in the autumn of 1883. Temporary arrangements, it was true, had been made for the loan that matured in January, 1885; but current revenues, Tilley reported from Canada, had been declining ever since the fiscal year began in July.[84] The slump had finally hit the treasury. They could confidently expect financial difficulties from now on. But grave as these financial difficulties might be, they were not likely to be so baffling as the political problems which Macdonald was certain to encounter. How was he to convince his followers —his own Cabinet—that government aid to the Canadian Pacific was necessary once again? The burly Tupper had always been a stout supporter of the railway, and Tupper could, and did, despatch a long letter to Tilley, warmly advocating the plan of relief which he and Macdonald had tentatively sketched out.[85] But this time Tupper must remain in England; and Macdonald, burdened by the momentous decision which they had taken together, must go home to face his colleagues alone. What the issue would be he literally had not the faintest idea. But he had given his word to Stephen. And perhaps at some dreadful moment in the shame and defeat of the Pacific Scandal he had made a vow with himself.

VI

Stephen sat in the pleasant library of his house in St. James's Place. He felt triumphantly elated. Even in that autumn of disasters, there was still hope; and today was a day of hope confirmed. He and his cousin, Donald Smith, by pledging their own personal credit once more, had just secured a loan of fifty thousand pounds for the railway. And now, with Macdonald committed in principle to a further instalment of government aid, Stephen could almost bring himself to believe that a way would be found through the blind jungle of difficulties which faced him. Once again the partnership of company and government, the partnership of Donald Smith, John A. Macdonald, and himself, had triumphed. They were all Scotsmen, all Highlanders, all, ultimately, sons of the same river valley. Macdonald's ancestors, on his mother's side, had come from Strathspey; and Stephen and Smith had been born in little towns close to the river in the land dominated by the Clan Grant. Stephen's fierce hatreds, his black discouragements, his radiant exaltations, were all legitimate parts of the rich inheritance he had received from Speyside; and unlike Macdonald, who had no personal memory of the country of his forbears, he was steeped in recollections of the land by which he had been shaped. He remembered the river itself, winding onward, peat-black between the high banks, and brown, like old ale, over the shallows. He remembered the great rock which had given the Clan Grant its rallying-place and its battle slogan. The rock of defiance. Craigellachie.

Stand fast, Craigellachie!

He would beat them! He and Macdonald and Donald Smith would beat them yet! Blake, the hated *Globe*, the Grand Trunk Railway scribblers, the "bear" speculators in New York—the whole malignant host of the Canadian Pacific's enemies—he would beat them all. He took a telegraph form, addressed it to Donald Smith in Montreal, and wrote a message of three words only:

"Stand fast, Craigellachie!"[86]

Chapter Twelve

Triumph and Disaster

I

The dusk of the brief January day had fallen long before the train reached Montreal. A curious balmy softness, like a false, delicious breath of spring, was in the air. The long queue of carriages moved off easily through the streets which were strangely unencumbered with snow; and the crowd waited comfortably as if it had been a night in April. There were masses of people everywhere. Macdonald could sense the enormous presence of the crowd all along the packed roads to the drill hall. The roar of welcoming applause was unbroken. There were two miles of flaming torches. High up, against the blue-black, velvety sky, the rockets burst in little showers of rose pink and daffodil yellow; and, at the Place d'Armes, a fountain, fed with hundreds of Roman candles, soared upwards and fell in cascades of golden stars. The drill shed was jammed with people. He knew he could not possibly make them hear. He told them he could have wished for a trumpet to carry his voice to all. Only a few heard his apologies and his thanks. But the rest did not seem to care. They had come, French and English, not so much to listen to him speak, as to honour him, and swell his triumph. They waited patiently and sympathetically, applauding loudly whenever there seemed a suitable opening.[1]

The day before, Sunday, January 11, he had reached the age of seventy. Two months ago, while he was still in England, he had passed the fortieth anniversary of his entrance into public life. The great celebration at Montreal was intended

399

to commemorate these two tremendous events; but it was not the first triumph that had been spread before him since his return from England. Less than a month before, on December 17 and 18, a great convention of more than four thousand Conservatives from all over Ontario had assembled at Toronto.[2] Toronto and Montreal—the two principal cities of Ontario and Quebec, the two political divisions which nearly twenty years ago had been Canada West and Canada East. Macdonald had lasted all through these political permutations and combinations. His career had spanned the history of the two sections of the old Province, and the history of the two provinces of the new Dominion. And for most of the men who crowded into the drill shed at Montreal and the Opera House at Toronto, there was no clear political memory in which his big nose, and bushy hair and tall, slight figure were not prominent. That autumn, for the first time, apparently, the English had really discovered the Canadian Prime Minister. But for the Canadians themselves there was no need of discovery or rediscovery. For forty years they had laughed at him, criticized him, forgiven him, believed in him, and followed him.

They could scarcely remember a past without him. They could hardly conceive of a future in which he would cease to be. The feebleness of his health was, of course, well-known and deeply lamented. But how could the Canadians look too seriously upon something which he himself made light of and cracked jokes about? "If John A.'s stomach gives in," he told them at Toronto, repeating a famous medical diagnosis of the political situation, "then the opposition will go in; but if John A.'s stomach holds out, then the opposition will stay out." They had not the slightest doubt that the opposition would stay out. John A. was politically indestructible. He was the monarch who had become so necessary that he would surely live for ever. And when, at Toronto, he told them that he had reached, or even passed, the culmination of his career, the great national Conservative disbelief found utterance in a single protesting cry which was heard, when it so easily might not have been heard, throughout the whole of the great auditorium.

"You'll never die, John A.!"

He had, in fact, become an old man. But, like a young man, he lived for the present and the immediate future. He rarely spoke of death; he had no interest in dwelling in the past. And it was, sometimes, with a sudden, grinding pain of recollection that he remembered what he had been through. Once, in the early days at Earnscliffe, when Agnes was still unpacking and arranging their household goods, she came upon a small mysterious box of children's toys. There was a broken rattle, a little cart, a few wooden animals. They were not Mary's—Agnes was certain of that. They seemed oddly old-fashioned to have been left behind by Daisy or some other small visitor to Earnscliffe. Whose could they be? She took them to Macdonald who was lying resting upon his bed. He looked at the box perfunctorily, incuriously, and then with a sudden pang of interest. Raising himself on his elbow, he took the small cart in his hand.

"Ah!" he said, "those were little John A.'s."[8]

And suddenly thirty years had rushed away, and he was back in the "Italian villa" Bellevue, and the soft summer breeze from Lake Ontario was blowing in from the open window, and his first-born was playing boisterously on the bed by Isabella's side . . . He did not notice Agnes's departure. The room was empty. And he was staring at the floor.

There were moments when for him, as for anyone else, what he had been through seemed too terrible to be borne. But mainly he carried the burden of his existence easily, even jauntily. There were more frequent reminders now of its dreariness; he was increasingly conscious of the almost frightening depth of experience upon which he could draw. Once, as he was on his way to his office past the rows of portraits of ex-Speakers in old Canadian Parliaments, he told his new secretary, the suave and impeccably correct Joseph Pope, that whenever he came that way he felt as if he were walking through a churchyard. Time and again there kept coming back to him the story of the old monk in the ancient monastery in Europe who had the care of the portraits of the departed members of his order, and who said one day to some visitors, pointing to the pictures of the dead, "I feel sometimes as if, after all, they were the realities, and we are the shadows."[4] Macdonald knew that there was solid reality in what he had done in the past. But it was imperfect reality—imperfect because incomplete. Deep within him there lay the inarticulate assumption that the history of Canada during its most important half-century was a plot which he, as its author, must hasten to complete. He had always known what he wanted to do. The design had been there from the beginning. All he needed now was a few years in which to finish it.

II

And yet, as he admitted to himself, the difficulties in the way of its completion were larger and more numerous than ever. The dignities which had been offered to him, the celebrations which had been given in his honour had, he knew very well, encouraged him more than he could say. But was it not a false, a fatally delusive encouragement? Had not the whole history of Canada for the past twelve months been a steady, unbroken, disheartening record of deterioration? The depression, far from lifting, had in fact steadily deepened. Manitoba had broken with the Dominion; Ontario had defied it with triumphant impunity; Nova Scotia was ominously rumbling with dissatisfaction. Some kind of trouble was brewing—was perhaps being deliberately brewed—in the north-west; and the railway which was to link all the wrangling and disconnected sections of the transcontinental Dominion together had for the second time run through all its resources, and was back once more, an embarrassed and embarrassing mendicant, upon the national doorstep. The state of the nation could hardly be worse. There could hardly be more problems than there were in domestic affairs. But, of course, domestic politics were not the only politics. There were also foreign relations.

Relations with the United States were almost never in a happy state of health. Good neighbourhood on the North

American continent was troubled by a succession of chills, fevers, and other maladies; and one of the worst of these afflictions was the everlasting problem of the fisheries, which periodically returned, like a severe case of rheumatism contracted unhappily in early childhood, to trouble the body politic with its agonies. Over twelve years ago, when he had persuaded the Canadian Parliament to accept the Washington Treaty, Macdonald had perhaps hoped that the problem of the fisheries had been successfully banished, at least for his own political lifetime. But the ancient affliction had appeared once more. It had come back in fact at the earliest possible moment at which the American government could insure its return.

In 1883, at the first legal opportunity, it had announced the abrogation of the Washington Treaty in the briskly conclusive fashion in which it had ended the Reciprocity Treaty twenty years before. The reasons for this determined haste were not, in Macdonald's opinion, hard to seek. The Washington Treaty had provided that the excess value of the Canadian over the American inshore fisheries was to be settled by arbitration; and in 1877, the arbitration at Halifax had ended in the award of five and a half million dollars to the British North American provinces. For the United States this was a preposterous sum, the payment of which was neither forgotten nor forgiven. "The truth is," Macdonald explained to Lord Lansdowne, "that the United States government have so often overreached England in diplomacy that they are dissatisfied with any treaty in which they have not gained a decided advantage."[5] Obviously the republic had not gained a "decided advantage" in these sections of the Washington Treaty. It had not got the fisheries for nothing —or next to nothing; and therefore, on July 1, at the earliest possible moment, the fisheries clauses of the treaty were to come to an end.

What to do? Macdonald had begun the consideration of this problem in the summer of 1884, when the American presidential campaign was just getting nicely under way; and he took it up again, at Lord Lansdowne's request, in December, after Grover Cleveland had been elected for his first term as President. A fair amount of time had already elapsed since the American announcement had been made; the Governor-General and Sir Lionel Sackville-West, the British Minister at Washington, were anxious to have a declaration of Canadian intentions; and Macdonald called the Cabinet together on the day before Christmas to consider the matter. Neither he nor any of the other ministers saw any reason why Canada should hurry forward anxiously with a new policy. The United States had announced the abrogation of the fishery clauses for its own purposes and without troubling itself to suggest any alternative settlement of the question. There was no need for the Dominion, like an agitated suitor desperately seeking a favourable answer, to prostrate itself in humility in Washington. Canada would always be ready to discuss a reciprocal trade treaty with the United States; it would even be willing to prolong the privileges of the Washington Treaty, for the benefit of the citizens of the republic, until January 1, 1886, in order to give another six months for negotiation. And if the negotiation failed—well, it would always be possible to fall back on the Convention of 1818, and the defence of the inshore fisheries against American depredation. Besides, there were particular as well as general reasons for waiting to discuss the matter with Cleveland rather than with Arthur. "Mr. Arthur," Macdonald confided to Lord Lansdowne, "is now engaged in the amiable work of embarrassing his successor. . . . We have a much better chance of better treatment from the new than from the moribund government."[6]

Here there was still a fairly ample margin for most contingencies. But, in the matter of the Canadian Pacific Railway, Macdonald had become a desperate prisoner of circumstances, hemmed in savagely on all sides. "I feel," Stephen confessed unashamedly, "like a man walking on the edge of a precipice, with less 'nerve' than is comfortable or even 'safe' in such a case. . . ."[7] And Stephen's feeling of inadequacy and apprehension was, at bottom, very much like his own. Two months ago, when he had been in England, talking the whole problem over with Stephen and the positive and optimistic Tupper, he had still hoped that a way out could be found. The difficulties were formidable, and he had never dreamed of underestimating them; but he had still believed that they might be overcome. He could indulge this belief no longer. It had become a stupid delusion. The financial ruin of the railway was at hand. It must have government aid. It could survive only with government aid. Yet its relief by government seemed a political impossibility.

As the January days went by and the opening of Parliament drew closer, Stephen's appeals grew more and more shrilly importunate. He kept insisting, with ever increasing vehemence of emphasis, that "the object of the present application to the government is to save the *life* of the company".[8] Late in December, the workmen at Port Arthur struck because of the delay in the delivery of their pay, and before the end of the year the stock was down to forty-three and a half at New York. There was no telling, Stephen assured Macdonald with gloomy savagery, how far it might drop. Once again the small creditors were clamouring for their money; and over in London, so John Rose telegraphed in dismay, a well organized propaganda was once more employed in battering down the credit of the company.[9] Stephen had virtually become a permanent resident of Ottawa. He drafted memoranda, arranged and rearranged figures, haunted committee rooms, and besought ministers. It was the unlimited government lien, he was convinced, which had been fatal to the success of the company; and, in his view, the only effective remedy was a measure which would pay off the government loan and convert the thirty-five millions of unissued stock into ready money. He proposed, in place of the unmarketable stock, to issue thirty millions of four-per-cent bonds; and for these, as the essential condition of their success, he begged a government guarantee of principal and interest. It was one plan for the salvation of the doomed railway. But it was only one. There were other and slightly different schemes proposed by McIntyre and Tupper. And all during January the government considered them, deliberately, critically, unenthusiastically. Stephen was nearly beside himself. "What alarms me," he wrote indignantly to Macdonald, "is the apprehension that the patient will die while the doctors are deliberating on the remedy to be applied."[10]

Yet Macdonald was convinced that haste would be far more dangerous than delay. He had expected that any proposal of further aid to the Canadian Pacific would be met by opposition; but even he had not foreseen how determined and implacable that opposition was likely to be. Before his return to Canada, a rumour of impending government assistance had begun to run in a sinister fashion through the country and, by the beginning of the New Year, a wail of alarm and protest, in which the Conservative newspapers somewhat shamefacedly joined, was ringing through the Dominion. Thomas White, the editor of the Montreal *Gazette*, wrote to say that he did not believe a measure of relief could be carried; and Macdonald's colleagues in the ministry, with their ears cocked sensitively to the protests of the back benchers and the complaints of the electorate, were convinced that such legislation could not be attempted with success. Campbell, McLelan and Bowell were all opposed to a new loan; Tilley was highly dubious. "I have heard all Stephen has to say," he wrote to Macdonald, "and I confess I cannot see how we can go to Parliament next session and ask our supporters to vote for it."[11]

At the moment, Macdonald could not see either. With a doubtful press and an unwilling Cabinet at his back, he realized that he could not risk too much too soon. "I myself fear," he wrote to Tupper on January 24, 1885, five days before the opening of Parliament, "that the *Week* is right when it says that however docile our majority, we dare not ask for another loan. The thing is hung up until next week. How it will end I don't know."[12] It was obvious by that time, at any rate, that it was not going to end in any immediate parliamentary action in favour of the Canadian Pacific. Stephen, who, with Donald Smith, had just borrowed, at the eleventh hour, the six hundred and fifty thousand dollars necessary to pay the January dividend, was begging Macdonald despairingly to assert himself. "The question is too big for some of our friends," he wrote, "and nothing but your own authority and influence will carry anything that will accomplish the object."[13] It was useless. Macdonald declined, for the moment, to impose a favourable decision. Yet, at the same time, he did not finally reject the possibility of relief. His language on the subject was curiously indecisive and non-committal. He informed Stephen, by telegraph, that there was "little chance" of any aid that year;[14] and when Blake, in the debate on the address, congratulated him ironically on the absence of all mention of the Canadian Pacific in the speech from the throne, Macdonald took the first opportunity of referring to the omission, and in phrases which were perhaps deliberately ambiguous. "There is no necessity for mentioning it," he told the Commons, "inasmuch as there is no legislation that we are going to lay before the House—that we propose to lay before the House just now."[15]

For the moment he kept his cards close to his chest. He was determined to delay. He could not be any too sure of his own strength, and he could not form an accurate estimate of the forces arrayed against him. In the game he was playing, the stakes were far too big for him to risk a false move. He would make no move at all so far as the fisheries and the railway were concerned. But there were other things in his varied and long-range programme besides fisheries and railways; and it was not the first time that he had refused an engagement at one point in order to press forward at another. He knew now where he wanted to advance. He would shake himself free, at one important point, from the hampering clutches of the provinces. For years he had disliked the fact that federal elections were held in accordance with franchises determined by the different provincial legislatures. "It is impossible, of course," he had written to Brown Chamberlin over fifteen years before, "that the elective franchise should be at the mercy of a foreign body."[16]

Fifteen years had gone by, and his conviction had simply been strengthened. The struggle between the Dominion and those "foreign bodies", the provinces, had simply grown in intensity. Mowat's victory in the boundary dispute had been followed, only a short while before the session opened, by a decision in the Supreme Court of Canada against the validity of the federal Licence Law of 1883. Mowat had successfully defied the Dominion; and Mowat's triumphant audacity seemed likely to become the fashionable model for every discontented province in the country. It was intolerable! Twice before, in two successive speeches from the throne, the government had promised a measure "for the assimilation of the electoral franchises in the several provinces". Now, for the third time, the promise was made, and this time he meant to keep it. He would prevent those insolent provincialists from meddling any longer with the laws by which the Dominion Parliament was elected!

III

The "waiting game", which he believed he so infinitely preferred, was a game played with big risks for high stakes. The stakes were nothing less than a unified, transcontinental Canada; the risks were a fatal inward division of the country, abandonment by Great Britain, and annexation by the United States. He had not thrown in his hand. With a small, but not seriously diminished, pile of chips, he was still in the game. His principal companions were players of enormously greater resources. The very fact that he continued in the game at all was a colossal gamble. He played each hand with infinite caution. His hesitations and postponements had by now become notorious. The practical man who had built a nation in a quarter century was getting to be known as a procrastinator. The realist who had always lived intensely in the immediate present had come to be called affectionately "Old Tomorrow". It was a grotesque but not unkindly misconception of which he was well aware, which did not entirely displease him; and it was never better illustrated than in the odd little episode, which prefaced, with such ironic incongruity, the most strenuous and most dangerous year in his entire political career.

It happened on the afternoon of Thursday, February 5, a week after the session opened. Blake was asking for information. Blake, like the good leader of the opposition he was, was always asking for information, on the most improbable subjects and on every possible occasion. This time his inquiries took a sharply personal turn. He wanted to know how much of the interval between the sessions of 1883 and 1884 had been spent in Canada by the ex-Minister of Railways and Canals, Sir

Charles Tupper. When, he further inquired, had Sir Charles resigned his portfolio, and when would his successor be appointed?[17] Macdonald promised that the information about the length of Tupper's residence in Canada—he had, of course, been mainly in England, beginning his new duties as High Commissioner—would be supplied "tomorrow". J. H. Pope, Macdonald went on, had been acting Minister of Railways and Canals since Tupper's resignation in June, 1884. "It is intended," Macdonald finished his reply, "to fill the office of Minister of Railways ere long." At this point, an unidentifiable voice, which the official reporter did not even notice, called out "tomorrow"![18] The House smiled. And Blake went relentlessly on with his questioning. When, he asked, had the office of Librarian of Parliament become vacant and when would a successor to Dr. Todd be appointed? "A librarian has not yet been appointed," Macdonald replied amiably, "one will be appointed ere long—I was going to say 'tomorrow' only I knew the honourable gentleman would laugh."[19]

Tomorrow was February 6; and on February 6 the news of the tragedy of Khartoum and the death of General Gordon was made public in Canada.[20] It was only the first of the military crises of 1885. But it came out of a sky which most people still thought was clear, and it shocked the conscience and stirred the indignation of the whole Empire. For a while, a great war seemed closer than it had ever done since that time, almost exactly seven years before, when the "Jingoes" had clamoured for resistance to Russia, and Disraeli had ordered the Mediterranean fleet to steam through the Dardanelles to Constantinople. What was to be done this time? Should Great Britain withdraw from the Sudan, as, indeed, Gordon had been instructed to do, or was there now any real alternative to an advance for the reconquest of Khartoum? And if a great and popular effort at retribution was to be made, what part would the Empire as a whole and Canada in particular play in it? Canada, of course, had already made a small distinctive contribution to the expedition which, in the previous October, had started up the Nile under General Wolseley for the relief of the beleaguered General Gordon. A party of Canadian "voyageurs"—lumbermen and

Indians experienced in the treacherous furies of Canadian water-ways—put their knowledge at the service of the columns which toiled up the uncharted Nile.[21] But the voyageurs, despite their usefulness and, indeed, their bravery, had been non-combatants. Was it not time for combatants, in numbers, to take over?

Macdonald remained unsympathetically aloof from the mood of belligerent patriotism which seemed for a while to be sweeping the Dominion. He held back for reasons both general and particular, theoretical and practical. As he told Tupper, the question of the mutual assistance to be given by the Mother Country and the Colonies was a question which could not be answered satisfactorily until a settlement of the much more general problem of the organization of the Empire had been carried out. Like most members of his generation, he had ideas about the organization of the Empire; but his views were not the fashionable views of 1885. He had no faith in an imperial federal parliament; what he hoped for was a league or alliance of Great Britain and the "auxiliary kingdoms" of Canada and Australia. As he saw it, a pact between England and Canada for the defence of British North America already existed. Its bases were the pledges which the two countries had exchanged in 1865, and the arrangements which they had agreed to in 1871 when the imperial troops were withdrawn from central Canada. Was it possible, now that the Dominion had so nearly come of age, to extend this agreement so as to cover other areas and other contingencies? Macdonald had always hoped that Canada would be a source of strength, not weakness, to Great Britain. At the back of his mind there had long lain the conception of a great, formal association of the self-governing kingdoms of the Empire.[22] But he knew that in this, as in so many other things, haste would be perilous. It had taken him years to establish the bare nucleus of a Canadian permanent force. It would, in all probability, take far longer to secure an acknowledgment of Canada's external obligations. He did not want to prejudice the issue by premature action. He wanted to launch his appeal when he could be certain of a favourable response.

In the meantime, in the absence of a formal agreement, each case would have to be considered on its merits and in the light of the circumstances of the time. A general war, which threatened any substantial portions of the Empire, was a war in which all its self-governing communities would obviously take part. But local defence against minor disturbances was a different matter; and Great Britain had in effect insisted upon this difference when she withdrew the garrisons from central Canada in 1871. If—which was now unhappily possible—serious trouble should break out in the Canadian north-west, Macdonald had no intention of requesting imperial military help as he had done so anxiously in 1869-70. The maintenance of peace in the north-west of North America was now Canada's business; and similarly the suppression of a small uprising in the interior of Egypt was an affair in which Great Britain and possibly Australasia might interest themselves. "England is not at war," he reminded Tupper, "but merely helping the Khedive to put down an insurrection, and now that Gordon is gone the motive of aiding in the rescue of our own countryman is gone with him. . . ."²³ This was not, nor was likely to become, a general conflict. Why should the Empire pay for the incoherence of Gladstone's foreign policy? Why should England herself indulge in further heroics in the Sudan at a time when there was already a prospect of serious trouble with Russia over the delimitation of the Russian-Indian boundary?

In the end it was an affray in the north-west frontier of India that decided the Gladstone government to cut its commitments in the Sudan. It was fear for the peace of another north-west frontier which, in all probability, caused Macdonald to blow so coldly upon the zeal of Tupper and the Canadian Militia colonels for Egyptian adventures. For over six months now, ever since Riel's return in the previous summer, Macdonald had been worried about the north-west. Since Christmas of 1884 his anxiety had been rapidly increasing. On December 30, a petition had arrived from the District of Lorne, accompanied by a covering letter from a certain W. H. Jackson, who described himself as the secretary of the "general committee".²⁴ There was no apparent connection between this petition and Riel. Jackson was known in Ottawa as the leader of the small group of white settlers who were taking part in the agitation and in his letter he referred to "the Canadian and English wing of the movement", as if it was for this wing that he spoke. The petition was in English. It briefly recapitulated the difficulties of the Indians and made the familiar demand of the *métis* for lands and scrip. It then went on to list a number of small specific criticisms relating mainly to the operation of the Dominion Lands Act; it presented a dubious historical argument, based on the Manitoba negotiations of 1870, in support of the claims of the north-west for greater political autonomy; and it ended by requesting provincial status, responsible government, and control of its own natural resources for the Saskatchewan region. Finally the petitioners asked permission to send delegates to Ottawa to lay their requests before the Dominion government in a bill of rights.

The petition was acknowledged on January 5, discussed in the Cabinet on January 9, and referred at once to the Minister of the Interior for action.[25] The period of memorials and discussions, which, as Macdonald had told Lord Lansdowne during the previous summer, gave the best promise of ending the trouble, had evidently arrived. Nothing as yet had come directly from Riel. No formal statement of the objects of his mission or the claims of his followers had yet been submitted under the authority of his own name. This was disturbing, but Macdonald had not yet given up hope. If events followed the course which they had in the Red River Rebellion, the agitators on the banks of the Saskatchewan would now probably call a large meeting or convention, draw up a bill of "rights", and appoint delegates to go to Ottawa. In the meantime, the Dominion government had decided, on its part, to make an enormous concession. Early in January the ministers came to the conclusion that they must proceed immediately to an enumeration of the north-west *métis*, with a view to granting the long-requested land and scrip. Macdonald had not changed his views about the wisdom of this dubious solatium. He regarded such grants as objectionable in principle and vicious in their probable consequences. But he decided that against his better judgment he must give in. "I do not hesitate to say that I did it with the greatest reluctance," he told the House of

Commons later. "I do not easily yield if there is a better course open; but at the last moment I yielded and I said: 'Well, for God's sake, let them have the scrip; they will either drink it or waste it or sell it; but let us have peace.' "[26]

It was at this point, when the government expected negotiations and was prepared to make real concessions, that a most disquieting piece of news arrived from the north-west. Ever since, on the eve of his departure for England, Macdonald had received the account of the interview which Forget and Bishop Grandin had had with Riel, he had been very uneasy about the *métis* leader's real intentions; and now these doubts and suspicions were horribly confirmed by still another disturbing communication from Dewdney which arrived in Ottawa late in January. Once again, "touch" had been obtained with Riel. A few days before Christmas, Father André, the local priest, and D. H. MacDowall, the member for Lorne in the North-West Council, had paid a visit to the half-breed leader in St. Laurent; and the amazing revelations of the four-hour interview which followed were now spread before Macdonald's astonished eyes. Previously, in the presence of Forget and Grandin, Riel had held forth eloquently about his altruistic purposes and merely hinted about his private claims. But now, before MacDowall and André, he was cynically, almost brutally, selfish. Quite early in the interview, he announced that he had come back to Canada to press his own personal claims as well as to advocate the interests of the half-breeds; and he left his listeners clearly to infer that he hoped, by renewing and increasing his strong influence with the *métis*, to bring effective pressure to bear on the government in his own behalf. "He then proceeded to state," MacDowall continued with his incredible narrative, "that if the government would consider his personal claims against them and pay him a certain amount in settlement of these claims, he would arrange to make his illiterate and unreasoning followers well satisfied with almost any settlement of their claims for land grants that the government might be willing to make, and also that he would leave the north-west never to return."[27]

It might have seemed enough. But there was more to come. Riel had then proceeded calmly to appraise his own political value, basing his estimates on the various efforts which, he claimed, had been made to bribe him to leave the country after the Red River Rebellion. As much as thirty-five thousand dollars had, he asserted, been offered him on one occasion by an emissary from Sir John Macdonald! "His claims," MacDowall went on, "amount to the modest sum of one hundred thousand dollars, but he will take thirty-five thousand dollars as originally offered, and I believe myself three thousand to five thousand would cart the whole Riel family across the border. Riel made it distinctly understood that 'self' was his main object, and he was willing to make the claims of his followers totally subservient to his own interests." Cynically candid about his real purposes, he was equally plain-spoken about the kind of assurances he would accept. Verbal or written promises would have no effect upon him whatever; hard cash would alone induce him to play his part. "He said, 'My name is Riel and I want material', which I suppose," MacDowall added a little sourly, "was a pun."

To Macdonald it was a shattering revelation. It made the whole agitation seem a malevolent sham. It utterly destroyed his faith in Riel's good will. "I believe," he solemnly told the House later, "he came in for the purpose of attempting to extract money from the public purse. . . ."[28] How was one to deal with such a man? How was one to cope with an agitation which seemed to be so completely the embodiment of his enigmatic personality? Could the Canadian government stoop to the dangerous devices which this self-confessed political blackmailer was openly inviting it to adopt? It could not. "Of course, that could not be entertained for a moment,"[29] Macdonald declared when he told the House of Commons of Riel's offer to accept a bribe. Riel might be ready to sell himself; but Macdonald and his colleagues could not afford to buy him. They must continue to act as if they were treating not with a self-interested American adventurer, but with a legitimate Canadian movement. They must do everything possible in reason—and even out of reason—to show their readiness to remedy popular grievances. On January 28, the Cabinet accepted the formal recommendation of the Minister of the Interior that a commission of three be appointed to make an enumeration of the *métis* of the north-west for the purpose of arriving at an equitable settlement of their claims.[80] "Government has decided to investigate claims of half-breeds," Macpherson telegraphed to Dewdney on February 4, "and with that view has directed enumeration of those who did not participate in grant under Manitoba Act."[81]

He had yielded in the west. He still hoped to dissipate the murky crisis that was developing so obscurely in the west. But in the east the collapse of the Canadian Pacific Railway was drawing closer with every day that passed. Together these disasters might mean the ruin of very nearly everything he had tried to do for the Canadian prairie country. He knew it. But characteristically he could not bring himself to accept these catastrophic conclusions. Deep in the final privacy of his being, he refused to believe that a single half-breed megalomaniac could destroy the west as a homeland for British Americans or that the track which was to bind Canada together would be permitted to fail for a few million dollars. Stephen, he was aware, still counted secretly upon his own veiled, half-whispered promises; and Stephen was prepared, up to the last moment and with his utmost effort, to do everything he could to earn the assistance which he had begged from the government. He and Donald Smith had borrowed the six hundred and fifty thousand dollars to pay the January dividend; they had endorsed a five-months note for one million dollars "to provide the company with current funds to keep it going for the next few weeks". Macdonald, implicitly if not explicitly, had required proofs that Stephen and his partner were prepared to make huge sacrifices for their own creation. And proofs had been supplied. "I venture to say," Stephen wrote reproachfully, "that there is not a business man in all Canada, knowing the facts, but would say we were a couple of fools for our pains."[82]

But was the government aid which these efforts had justified, a political possibility? Macdonald was still filled with painful uncertainty. McLelan threatened resignation; most of the other Cabinet ministers were either hesitant or opposed. John Henry

Pope and Frank Smith were strong in support of relief for the railway; and Tupper wrote from London, protesting, with more even than his usual emphasis, that the Canadian Pacific must not be permitted to go down, and that he himself was prepared to go back at once to Ottawa, either to take McLelan's place, or to give the government all the aid he could as a private member.[33] Macdonald shook his head. He missed Tupper terribly; but he realized that if the High Commissioner came back he would have to get a seat in Parliament and that the session would probably be over before the necessary by-election could be held. No, he would have to get along without Tupper. He would have to see the thing through himself. But he was weary with the toil of it; and there were times also when he was disillusioned with an enterprise which seemed such an insatiable drain upon the country and which dragged with it such a host of predatory parasites. "The Quebec M.P.s," he wrote to Tupper, "have the line to Quebec up again. The Maritimes are clamorous for the Short Line, and we have blackmailing all round. How it will end, God knows! But I wish I were well out of it."[34]

It was on March 17 that Macdonald wrote his letter to Tupper. During the next few days it began to seem increasingly probable that the Cabinet could not be persuaded to grant more aid to the Canadian Pacific. But even this was not all. At the same time, the threat of a real storm began to roar up over the horizon of the north-west. For some days, the news from the Saskatchewan had been bad. Now, with terrifying rapidity, it went from bad to worse. What was happening? Father André had kept requesting that the "indemnity" be paid to Riel; he and Crozier of the North-West Mounted Police had urged that a settlement in accordance with the "confidential communications" should be made at once.[35] Had the unbelievable really occurred? Had Riel determined to pull down the heavens because his own private demands for money were ignored? Was this the real explanation of the curious ineffectuality of the government's promise to proceed with an equitable settlement of the *métis* claims for land and scrip? Macdonald did not know, and the time for answering such questions had gone by.

He must act. On the night of March 23, Major-General Frederick Middleton, the General Officer Commanding the Canadian Militia, was sent west to Winnipeg; and next day the newspapers carried confused reports that Riel's *métis* were threatening Fort Carlton and its small garrison of North-West Mounted Police under Crozier. It had come to a fight in the west. And, at the same time, in Ottawa, the endless negotiations between the government and the Canadian Pacific Railway slowed down ominously to a stop. Stephen faced the stark fact that there would almost certainly be no government relief. "I need not repeat how sorry I am," he wrote from Abbott's office in the Parliament Buildings, "that this should be the result of all our efforts to give Canada a railway to the Pacific Ocean. But I am supported by the conviction that I have done all that could be done to obtain it."[86]

It was Thursday, March 26; and all day long alarming rumours of a clash between Riel's men and the police at Fort Carlton swept through the cities and towns and far into the Canadian countryside. At Ottawa there was no official news of an engagement, and Macdonald cabled reassuringly to London, England. But next day the telegram from Colonel Irvine, which was to end all these comforting delusions, arrived at the East Block; and that night Macdonald rose in his place in the House to announce the tiny battle at Duck Lake between the *métis* and Crozier's command.[87] The two disasters—the revolt on the prairie and the collapse of the railway—had come together in time. And together they might destroy him and his Canada. Yet the blow which they would deliver was not a single one. They were separate problems. They would have to be dealt with separately. They could even be played off against each other. And in that possibility did not there still lie a real hope? He could use the railway to defend the west. He could use the west to justify the railway.

IV

"This insurrection is a bad business," he wrote with characteristic brevity to Lieutenant-Governor Dewdney, "but we must face it as best we may."[88] For him the great danger lay not so much in the revolt of a few hundred *métis* as in the possibility of a general Indian rising. He had never believed that the Indians would start trouble; but he could not rid himself of the fear that, if once the initiative were given by others, the whole native population of the west might follow it in a bloody and destructive mob. "The first thing to be done," he wrote to General Middleton, modestly apologizing for bothering him with his "crude" strategical ideas, "is to localize the insurrection."[89] The government was already proceeding, by every means in its power, to win over the waverers and to confirm the loyalty of the well affected. Through Father Lacombe, Macdonald early secured a promise of support from the Blackfoot tribe, which occupied the territory of southern Alberta. General orders were given to distribute additional provisions to the Indians; and the investigation of the *métis* claims was now set in motion by the appointment of the necessary commissioners.

These were pacific, conciliatory measures. But the outbreak on the prairies was an armed uprising; and military force was necessary to prevent its development and to crush it at its source. For the first time in their collective history, the Canadians confidently faced a struggle on their own soil with nothing but their own resources. Macdonald had no thought of requesting the assistance of regular imperial troops; he had no need to wait, in angry futility, until the coming of spring and the opening of navigation would permit a force to fight its toilsome way through endless miles of lake and river, forest and prairie, to an uncertain encounter with a successful rebellion. He could act at once. The railway was there; citizen soldiers everywhere were clamouring for enlistment; and within only a few days of the time when the incredulous Canadians had learnt of the repulse at Duck Lake, the first national Canadian army was assembling for its journey to the north-west.

As early as March 25, the Winnipeg militia, with Hugh Macdonald among their number, had begun to move westward; and on Monday, March 30, in all the main cities of the east, the troops marched down under grey and rainy skies to the railway stations, while the bands played "Auld Lang Syne" and "The Girl I Left Behind Me".⁴⁰ "Wish you to travel night and day," Adolphe Caron, the Minister of Militia telegraphed on March 31 to the first detachments speeding westward. "I want to show what the Canadian militia can do." It was an appeal which came home as clearly, and with quite as much force, to William Cornelius Van Horne as it did to any militia commander travelling towards Winnipeg in a flat-car north of Lake Superior. Van Horne knew, and he made every one of his subordinates realize, that not only the credit but perhaps also the very existence of the Canadian Pacific Railway depended upon the speed and efficiency with which it could complete this great effort in military transport. On the night of April 4, the first companies from the east reached Winnipeg; and less than a week later, Middleton, in command of the first of the three striking columns, set out from Qu'Appelle northward for Riel's stronghold at Batoche.

Macdonald had done his work. It was up to the soldiers now. And while Caron coped energetically with the thousand details of military organization and the columns struggled over rolling prairie through the bitter cold of early spring, he took up once more the old task of maintaining Canadian confidence at home and defending Canadian prestige abroad. At home, the nation had responded magnificently. The secret fears, which had nagged at him for years, that the country was about to split apart in jagged pieces of sectional discontent and antagonism, had, in the end, been proved false. More emphatically perhaps than ever before the Canadians had revealed a sense of their identity and a belief in their future. He had not asked too much of the Dominion; he had not overtaxed the immature but growing sense of nationalism which he had nursed so patiently for so many years. The first consequence of the rebellion, in fact, was a vigorous assertion of the national will. It was much. It was perhaps even more than he had dared to expect. But it was not all. The North-West Rebellion not only gave him his supreme vindication; it also supplied his enemies and critics, both at home and abroad, with their greatest opportunity.

Abroad, the opportunity was exploited to the full. Wherever the dispatches of the American press associations went, and they seemed to go almost everywhere, Canada's western difficulties were enormously exaggerated, and her prospects painted in the most blackly discouraging colours. The news which came out of Winnipeg and was printed in most of the Canadian newspapers was, on the whole, honest and reasonably accurate. But this was not the news which the rest of the English-speaking world got, or, indeed, appeared to want. The American newspaper correspondents in St. Paul, who were familiarly known, so one Canadian editor assured his readers, as "liars on space", apparently supplied most of the information about the North-West Rebellion which appeared in the press of both England and the United States.[41] One London newspaper actually went to the extreme length of sending out a correspondent to the Canadian north-west; but *The Times* did not apparently even consider such a preposterously unnecessary expenditure. It relied instead upon dispatches which were dated, oddly enough, from Philadelphia;[42] and, as late as May 5, it was confirming its previous reports of a general Indian rising and complacently assuring its readers that Canada had a long and bloody native war on its hands. Lansdowne was astonished, as other governors-general had been astonished before him, at these evidences of indifference and misrepresentation; and Macdonald and Tupper, who knew that there was not the slightest use in attempting to correct the malevolent distortions of the American press, recommenced their old efforts to get a fair hearing for Canada in England.[43]

At home, Macdonald knew, the opposition would be even fiercer and more determined than ever. He expected the longest, hardest, most contentious session since the famous session of 1882. It was nearly three years now since the last general election; and before the despondent, twice-defeated Grits there glimmered the pale hope of a new appeal to the people. They were certain to use every ounce of strength and ingenuity to turn this session to their advantage. They would exhaust themselves in efforts. And what magnificent, unparalleled opportunities lay before them! The Washington Treaty was running out, the Canadian Pacific Railway was obviously *in extremis* and the government was about to introduce a novel and highly debatable Franchise Bill. The riches of their enemies' misfortunes were spread before the Liberals! And now, as a final gift of the bounty of good fortune, came the calamity of a rebellion. It could hardly have been worse, Macdonald realized. He knew how vulnerable he was, even at the centre of power. "The government is too old," he told Tupper. He had felt this for over a year now. He grew more and more gloomily conscious of it as the session advanced. The ministers were too old for the crisis which was upon them. They were tired and ill and timid and disillusioned.

For a while at least, he must fight a defensive battle. Controversial decisions must be postponed; the country must follow moderate courses; and in a month—in six weeks—the whole frightening aspect of affairs might be utterly changed by a stroke of good fortune in the north-west. His first, his instinctive choice was for a policy of delay; and to a large extent a policy of delay was forced upon him by the opposition. The session had opened in a deliberate, argumentative fashion. Then the news of the rebellion in the north-west seemed to transform the Grits into a pack of curs, snapping at everything and everybody, worrying each legislative bone that was thrown to them for weeks; and on April 16, when Macdonald moved the second reading of his Franchise Bill, the pack rushed in baying as if for a kill. It was only after prolonged debates, over several basic amendments, that the Bill at last got into committee; and in committee it remained for week after week while the two sides wrangled endlessly over virtually every one of its terms.

Here the prolonged obstruction ended in annoying him and stiffening his determination; but in other respects he was obviously ready to accept suggested postponements and to deal in generously conciliatory gestures. It was no time, he knew very well, to start quarrelling with the United States. The fishery articles of the Washington Treaty would, at the instance of the American government, come to an end on July 1; and, so far as the law was concerned, American privileges in the inshore fisheries of British North America would be governed once more by the terms of the Convention of 1818. In fact, in the circumstances of the moment, it would be highly injudicious for Canada to make a sudden attempt to keep American fishermen outside the three-mile limit. England was still seriously concerned over the disagreement with Russia. The Dominion had more than enough on its hands in the north-west; and, in Macdonald's opinion, the new administration at Washington, with Cleveland as President and Bayard as Secretary of State, gave far more promise of a liberal spirit in commercial policy than any of its recent predecessors.[44] He had his eye fixed, just as in 1871, upon a generous reciprocal trade agreement with the republic; and for this reason he was not inclined to reject Bayard's candidly self-interested request that the American fishing privileges under the Washington Treaty should be continued for another six months pending the possible negotiation of a new agreement. In return for this large concession, Bayard suggested that the American President, in his message to Congress, might suggest the appointment of a joint high commission for the peaceful settlement of the relations between the two countries. Beyond this no compensation whatever was offered. American fishermen might fish in Canadian waters until December 31; but on July 1, the American tariff on Canadian fish would come promptly into operation. "He appeals to us as good neighbours," Macdonald wrote dryly of Bayard to the Governor-General, "to do what he does not offer as a good neighbour to do to us."[45]

Here postponement and conciliation were obviously devices of mere prudence; but, in respect of the Canadian Pacific Railway, the policy of delay had paradoxically become a gamble of the most perilous extravagance. Within a week, the prestige of the railway had risen enormously; but at the same time it was rushing towards financial disaster with the speed of one of its own trains. In the north-west it had performed a national service with superb efficiency. The Canadian Militia had been rushed with such swiftness to their bases at Qu'Appelle, Swift Current, and Calgary that the outcome of the struggle was decided before the rebellion itself had had a real chance of getting going. In a few weeks, Macdonald was convinced, the country would begin to appreciate this; but at the moment, when the troops had not yet made contact with the rebels and when the real nature of the struggle was hardly understood, he did not believe that he could presume upon a real change in the popular attitude to the railway. Three months, two months, ago he had feared that the opposition, in the Cabinet and the party, to further aid for the Canadian Pacific was too strong for him to overcome. Now, in the face of the prodigies which the railway had performed in the national interest, that opposition was visibly declining. But had it weakened far enough to permit him to act? He did not know. He was besieged by uncertainties. And his first instinct was always to delay.

Yet, in a matter of days, delay might be fatal. The company must be saved soon or there would be nothing left to save. It was a race between the railway's creditors and the marching feet of General Middleton's militia. It was a trial of strength between the endless, acrimonious procrastinations of Canadian politics and the dauntless and devoted spirit of George Stephen. Everything he possessed had been flung into the insatiable maw of the railway's necessities. He had told Donald Smith—and Van Horne remembered it long afterwards as the finest speech he had ever heard—that if the end came they must not be found with a dollar in their pockets.⁴⁶ He had come to Ottawa because there was now no hope of assistance elsewhere; and, as he told Tupper, he had been living there almost continuously since early in December. A dozen times he had been convinced that the end had come; a dozen times he had decided that it was useless to continue the struggle further; and yet he could never quite bring himself to give in. He had sat in J. H. Pope's house, waiting for its owner, with his chin in his hand, staring into space, and muttering, "We are ruined". He had walked furiously out of the Russell Hotel, vowing that he would shake the dust of Ottawa off his feet for ever. But he had not left. He had stayed on. He had never really ceased his efforts for a moment.

Yet there were limits to human endurance; and by the middle of April he had reached the smouldering, angry conclusion that he had passed them. "It is impossible for me to continue this struggle for existence any longer," he wrote to Macdonald on April 15. "The delay in dealing with the C.P.R. matter, whatever may be the necessity for it, has finished me, and rendered me utterly unfit for further work, and if it is continued, must eventuate in the destruction of the company."⁴⁷ The destruction of the company! Was it avoidable now? "Have no means paying wages," Van Horne telegraphed to Stephen, "pay car can't be sent out, and unless we get immediate relief we must stop. Please inform Premier and Finance Minister. Do not be surprised, or blame me, if an immediate and most serious catastrophe happens."⁴⁸

On April 24, Macdonald wrote privately to C. F. Smithers of the Bank of Montreal.⁴⁹ A plan for the financial relief of the Canadian Pacific would, he explained, be brought before Parliament in the near future. But such a measure could not be passed in a hurry, and meanwhile the necessities of the railway were becoming more pressing every day. Would the Bank consent, on the strength of his private guarantee, to grant a temporary advance to the company? The Bank declined.⁵⁰ It would probably have taken a different view, Charles Drinkwater, the Canadian Pacific's secretary, wrote to Macdonald, if the legislation had actually been submitted to the House. It was the bluntest of hints; and Macdonald realized that delay had been spun out so long that a break was inevitable if he did not act at once. Yet could it be said that circumstances were yet favourable to action? On April 25 the news of the successful arrival of Colonel Otter's column at Battleford cheered the whole of Canada's anxiously waiting people. But on the same day came the disturbing reports of the stiff, indecisive engagement between Riel and General Middleton's forces at Fish Creek; and on April 30 the heavy black headlines in the newspapers shouted that Great Britain and Russia were on the eve of war. It was on the same day that Macdonald presented his plan for the relief of the railway to the Conservative caucus;⁵¹ and on May 1 he gave notice of the resolutions which he proposed shortly to submit to Parliament.[52]

It was, with minor modifications, the plan which he had discussed with Tupper and Stephen during the previous autumn. In place of the thirty-five millions of dormant common stock, which were to be cancelled by the proposed legislation, the Canadian Pacific Railway Company was empowered to issue an equivalent amount of first mortgage bonds. The essence of the plan was that the existing governmental lien upon the whole of the company's property was to be extinguished by the new bonds. They were to be delivered to government, and retained by government, as a security both for the loan of the previous year and for a new advance of five million dollars which was to be made immediately to the company. Tupper thought the plan excellent. He expected little opposition in Parliament or the country, "especially with the fact before them that but for the rapid construction of the C.P.R. the country might have been torn to pieces, and enormous waste of blood and treasure involved."[53] He was right, Macdonald knew. The rebellion was coming rapidly to an end, as he had hoped and believed it would. It was true that on May 2 Otter had suffered a hard check at Cut Knife Hill and had retired on Battleford; but, on the afternoon of May 13, Caron read in the House a triumphant telegram from Middleton announcing the capture of Batoche and the collapse of the *métis* resistance.[54] The issue of Canadian expansion had been settled, and settled for all time. The west had been won by Canadian soldiers and a Canadian railway.

But would the Canadian people be willing to pay the price of their own national survival? The party was now committed. But the measure of relief had still to be pushed through the recalcitrant and ungovernable House of Commons; and the whole management of the government's programme fell upon Macdonald. Macpherson and Chapleau were away for shorter or longer periods; Pope was ill and shaky; Campbell was repeatedly prostrated by his dreadful headaches; and Tilley departed, two months before the session ended, for the operation in England which was quickly to bring his political career to a close. For day after day of furious battle, Macdonald, the solitary fighting member of the Cabinet, faced the House virtually alone. He had every reason to break down. His record for the past few years must have led everybody, including himself, to expect a collapse. But, fed with some mysterious inner source of strength, he stood his ground. "I am holding out pretty well," he told his sister early in May, "in the hard fight we have here."[55]

He did not believe he had ever known such a savage conflict. On one occasion, shortly after the Franchise Bill got into committee, the House sat continuously for two and a half days. It was only the most preposterous of the excesses of this most incredible debate. All during May and into June every clause, sentence, phrase, and almost every word of the Franchise Bill was fought with the full strength of the opposition. Macdonald became convinced that the Liberals were exploiting the Bill, as a threat to provincial rights, with the deliberate purpose of panicking his French-Canadian followers into desertion. He grew more and more determined to fight the battle of the union and of the independent House of Commons which, in his opinion, was the union's necessary expression. The Franchise Bill became an obsession with him. "I shall not be baulked . . .," he wrote to Lord Lansdowne at the beginning of June.[56] Another week, full of petty verbal battles, went by; but by that time the end of the committee stage appeared dimly, promisingly, ahead. The government turned with relief to the suspended bills and half-forgotten measures of its programme; and finally on June 16, John Henry Pope arose to move the resolutions in aid of the Canadian Pacific Railway Company.

V

"On the twentieth," Macdonald wrote to Charles Tupper on July 27, "we closed the most harassing and disagreeable session I have witnessed in forty years. The Grits were desperate and acted like desperate men."[57] The long protesting retreat of the opposition had been fought fanatically and at every inch of the way. Blake's oratory, stripped, like a luxury liner, of all ornamentation for wartime service, had been crammed with vast formidable masses of government documents and statistical details. He had opposed the grant of further aid to the Canadian Pacific, and attacked the policy of the government in the north-west, in two enormous orations, each of which lasted well over six hours, wore everybody out with its tedious prolixity, and even plunged some of his own ardent followers into profound and noisy slumbers. Yet these heroic exploits, like the prolonged obstruction which had preceded them, had availed nothing in the end. In the end the government had staggered through. It had not, in many ways, been a very creditable session, for, as Macdonald reminded Campbell later on, the Treasury Bench had been obviously enfeebled, the whole burden had fallen on the Prime Minister, some of the work had not been well done, and the Conservatives had audibly complained.[58] Still, the government had survived. "The session is over," he wrote proudly to Tupper, "and the opposition didn't score a single point."

"I consider the passage of the Franchise Bill," he declared, "the greatest triumph of my life."[59] It was the triumph of an old man's enormous expertise in the fine points of parliamentary in-fighting. Macdonald would savour, and perhaps overestimate, this peculiarly personal success; but the victories which had been won for the railway, and in the north-west, were obviously of far greater national importance. Stephen, like one of his own prospectors in the Rockies, had at length found a good pass through what had seemed the insuperable mountain range of his difficulties; and the great house of Baring, which up to that time had regarded the Canadian Pacific with majestic indiffer-ence, now at last consented magnificently to act as agents for the issue of the new four per cent bonds. The support of the great English financial house had come late. How much easier so many things would have been if it had come earlier! But it had come at last. And with it came the apparent acceptance of Canada in England as a possible transcontinental state. The Canadians had made good their claim to the north-west with treasure, and toil, and blood. And, as Macdonald saw clearly, their own sense of their collective destiny had grown clearer and firmer during the long ordeal through which they had passed. "Canada as you will see," he wrote to Tupper, "is delirious with enthusiasm on the return of our volunteers. This has done more to weld the provinces into one nation than anything else could have done."[60]

He was—or so it seemed—nearly done with the north-west. And all that remained was to deal, in a spirit of reasonable, unsentimental clemency, with the inevitable consequences of a rebellion. The commission established by the government would have to complete its investigation of the claims of the *métis*; and the courts would have to settle the fate of the half-breed and Indian principals in the revolt. Macdonald had never believed that more than a relatively small part of the demand for scrip was legitimate; he had never believed that scrip would provide more than a brief satisfaction for those who could make good their claim to it. And, as the work of the North-West Commissioners proceeded, the accuracy of these realistic assumptions was conclusively established. Seven hundred and seventy-nine half-breeds had thought so highly of the *métis* title to the land, and their own right to participate in it, that they had signed petitions demanding its recognition. It was now revealed that of these seven hundred and seventy-nine, as many as five hundred and eighty-six could not qualify for scrip, either because they had already been granted it under the Manitoba distribution or because they were half-breeds from the United States, or squatters who were not half-breeds at all.[61] To only one hundred and ninety-three of the signatories had the North-West Commissioners granted scrip; and of these how many would derive any permanent benefit from the government's bounty? "In spite of the good intentions of government," Amyot, the French-Canadian member for Bellechasse, telegraphed from the west to Langevin, "work by Commission will be a farce, because crowds of speculators follow the Commissioners, intoxicate half-breeds, buy for a nominal sum their scrips."[62] It was for this, Macdonald reflected angrily, that the whole country had been thrown into a turmoil, that men had died, and that millions of money had been expended. It was for this that a handful of *métis* and Indians would have to pay with imprisonment or life. The last harsh episode in the affair was now at hand; and on July 20 the trial of Louis Riel, watched over by the whole nation with absorbed interest, began at Regina before Magistrate Richardson.

In the meantime, while he waited for the conclusion of the final scene in this unhappy drama, Macdonald tried to cope with the problems of the future. The reorganization of the Cabinet, postponed again and again during the past year, could not be held off any longer; there were several places—perhaps even his own place—which must be filled at once. "Now is the time for me to retire," he wrote to Tupper. "I have finished my work. Everything that I proposed to do from Confederation down to the present time has been completed."[63] It was all true; and his wish for retirement was all the stronger because it grew out of a satisfied sense of achievement and not out of the weakness and exhaustion of ill health. Yet how could he abandon the ministry now? Macpherson had already retired. Tilley was about to accept the lieutenant-governorship of his native province of New Brunswick; and for weeks past Campbell had been repeatedly requesting, in his lugubrious, put-upon manner, to be made Lieutenant-Governor of Ontario. If Macdonald left the Cabinet now, when so many others were leaving or threatening to leave, he might complete the disintegration and the ruin of the government. He would have to stay—for a while at least. He tried to persuade Campbell to defer his ambitions and postpone his resignation. And, on the advice chiefly of his Maritime friends, he got in touch with John S. D. Thompson, a Nova Scotian politician who was now on the bench, but who, before the defeat of the Conservatives in 1882, had been the main strength of the provincial government at Halifax.[64] For years—for as long, it seemed, as he could remember—he had been seeking a young, active, vigorous and able recruit for the reformation of a Cabinet of debilitated veterans. Was Thompson, of whom everyone spoke so highly, the man he sought?

On July 30, he escaped, at long last, from the stifling heat of Ottawa, and hurried down to Rivière du Loup. By now the summer was half over; and what remained of it seemed never free from the preoccupations of public affairs. The reorganization of the Cabinet, the delicate negotiations with Judge Thompson, the preliminary arrangements for a conference with the United States on the fisheries, all combined to crowd the last few golden weeks of August with their anxieties; and when, early in September, he got back to Ottawa, full of an annoyed feeling that he had earned and had been cheated out of a holiday, it was only to discover that a new and most painful difficulty was awaiting him. Campbell, who had been persuaded with considerable difficulty to remain in the Cabinet, naturally assumed that he would retain his present portfolio as Minister of Justice; but the Ministry of Justice was the one department which Judge Thompson had insisted quietly but firmly he must have if he were to enter the Cabinet. Macdonald was determined to secure Thompson's services.[65] But Campbell was a surprised and unwilling sacrifice;[66] and it was only after the most painful recriminations and reproaches that Macdonald persuaded him to accept the office of Postmaster-General. The whole episode left him feeling emotionally worn out; and he began to long once more for the only real holiday which he had ever seemed to enjoy, a holiday in England. "I have had no rest this summer at all," he wrote to Tupper, "and am half inclined to take a run across the sea. But this Riel business must be settled first, and the arrangements for the negotiations at Washington."[67]

The import of "this Riel business" had certainly increased with great rapidity during the past few weeks. On August 1, the trial of the *métis* leader at Regina had come to an end. The defence, which had been conducted by a group of the most distinguished counsel in the country, had been mainly based on the contention that the accused was of unsound mind. But Riel himself expressly and vehemently rejected the plea of insanity; the medical evidence was contradictory; and, as B. B. Osler pointed out at the time of the trial, there was a curious inconsistency between the prisoner's alleged "megalomania" and the hard, persistent shrewdness with which he had bargained for the betrayal of his "mission". "He seems," the Chief Justice of Manitoba said later, in affirming the verdict, "to have had in

· GRIP ·   Saturday, 29th August, 1885.

A RIEL UGLY POSITION.

view, while professing to champion the interests of the *métis*,
the securing of pecuniary advantage for himself."[68] In the end,
the half-breed leader had been convicted of treason; and in the
time-honoured and terrible phraseology reserved for such occa-

sions he was sentenced to death by hanging. It was this sentence, with its awful definiteness and finality, which hastened the expression of a clear and sharply divided public opinion. In Quebec a protesting demand for clemency began to be heard; in English-speaking Canada, and particularly in the Province of Ontario, it was assumed, as something about which there was no room for argument, that there would be no interference from government and that the law would be permitted to take its course.

Macdonald himself was very much of the same mind as his fellow-citizens of Ontario. Riel had been sentenced to hang on September 18; and he saw no reason why the state should make any effort to alter the infliction of this penalty. There was, on his reading of the evidence, no need for a new trial. He had confidently expected that the Appeal Court of Manitoba would confirm the decision reached at Regina; and he did not believe that the government, of its own motion, should do anything to invite further proceedings. "I don't think," he wrote to Lord Lansdowne towards the end of August from Rivière du Loup, "that we should by a respite anticipate—and as it were court—the interference of the Judicial Committee."[69] There was no appeal, as a matter of course, to the Judicial Committee of the Privy Council in criminal cases; and if the government took any special steps to "facilitate" such an appeal, English-speaking Canada, in Macdonald's opinion, would certainly take violent exception. He knew, of course, that a section of opinion in Quebec would warmly approve such a move. But he was convinced that Riel, in abandoning the faith of his fathers, had forfeited his strongest claim upon the sympathies of his French-speaking fellow-subjects. The emotional feeling in his favour did not go very deep and it could not last very long.

VI

As soon as he got back to the capital on September 10, these reasonable conclusions were shattered. At Ottawa a sense of impending crisis was in the air. Petitions for the commutation of Riel's sentence were already beginning to arrive; and—what was much worse—it was known that Langevin, with the probable support of Chapleau and Caron, would in all likelihood press for a commission of inquiry into Riel's mental state. Campbell, who was continuing as Minister of Justice pending Thompson's election in Nova Scotia, was strongly opposed to such an investigation. Riel's defence, he argued, had been based on the plea of insanity; and judge and jury, after hearing a mass of evidence on the subject, had rejected it. "How can medical men now look into Riel's mental state as it existed in February and March last?" he inquired. "We can give them no authority to hear evidence on oath which would be trying him over again and the inquiry would almost inevitably end in disagreement amongst the doctors; and leave, as regards the fate of the prisoner, 'confusion worse confounded'. . . . I do not think that such an inquiry should take place, unless the alleged insanity has intervened since the trial. . . ."[70]

With all this Macdonald agreed. But, at the back of their minds, both he and Campbell had the uneasy suspicion that for the sake of their French-speaking colleagues, the commission of inquiry would have to be granted in the end. Campbell argued that if they must yield, they had better yield at once. But Macdonald was determined, as long as possible, to avoid interference by government in the normal processes of justice. There was still a final court of appeal left, though less than a fortnight before he had counselled against inviting an application to it. On September 11, the Department of Justice telegraphed Magistrate Richardson to reprieve the prisoner; and immediately Riel's lawyers appealed to the Judicial Committee of the Privy Council in London.

In the meantime, the Governor-General left by train for the north-west. This was the journey, long planned and long and eagerly awaited, which was to be signalized by the driving in of the last spike of the completed Canadian Pacific Railway. "With that railway finished and my Franchise Bill become law," Macdonald had written, early in September, to his old friend Lord Carnarvon, "I feel that I have done my work and can sing my *nunc dimittis*."[71] There was now, he realized bitterly, not the slightest chance of his immediate retirement from the government. His work was not finished. He was caught in the toils of the Riel affair; and the Riel affair, which had arisen with such mysterious suddenness and violence, was big with menace for the future. It threatened possible ruin for much of his work. It threatened, incidentally, to spoil the ceremonial completion of the railway, for which he had struggled so long and so hard. Far out, in the mountains, construction was being held up by bad weather. The gap in the line was closing, but it was not closing fast enough; and early in October it became clear that the last spike could not be driven in before the end of the month and that if the Governor-General wished to be present for the final decision concerning Riel, he must change his plans and start east at once. Lansdowne began to hurry home; and on October 22, three days before his arrival in Ottawa, a cablegram from the Colonial Office informed Macdonald that the Judicial Committee of the Privy Council had heard counsel on behalf of Riel and had advised the Queen to dismiss his petition.[72]

Responsibility had been flung back upon Ottawa. And once more Macdonald faced the question of a special commission of inquiry into Riel's mental state. Caron was critical of the proposal; but Langevin believed that a final investigation was necessary to quiet public opinion in Quebec; and Macdonald and Campbell, who had already privately decided that they would accept Langevin's plan, if he urged it strongly, reluctantly consented.[73] A governmental interference in the administration of justice was something which Macdonald disliked on grounds both general and particular. Against his better judgment he agreed to it; but he was determined that the inquiry should be strictly limited in time, and that it should be directed towards the one question which, in the light of the legal precedents, constituted the real point of issue.

The great leading case in the whole problem of crime and insanity was the McNaghten case of 1843. In answer to a series of questions put on that occasion by the House of Lords, fourteen British judges had replied, in part, that a man must be presumed to be sane until he was proved not to be so, and "that to establish a defence on the ground of insanity it must be clearly proved that, at the time of committing the act, the accused was labouring under such a defect of reason, from disease of the mind, as not to know the nature and quality of the act he was doing; or, if he did know it, that he did not know he was doing what was wrong". The question of insanity, the judges continued, must not be put in any general or abstract fashion, but with reference to the accused's knowledge of right and wrong "in respect of the very act with which he is charged". Finally, in the fifth and last of what became known as the Mc-Naghten Rules, the judges affirmed that a medical man, even if he had been present throughout the trial and had heard all the evidence, could not in strictness be asked his opinion of the state of the prisoner's mind at the time of the commission of the crime unless the facts in the case were admitted or not disputed and the problem had thus become substantially scientific in character.[74]

On the last day of October, Macdonald rapidly completed the arrangements for the inquiry. Three medical men—Dr. A. Jukes, surgeon at the Regina prison, Dr. F. X. Valade of Ottawa, and Dr. M. Lavell, the Warden of the Kingston Penitentiary—were appointed to examine Riel. They were not invited to express an opinion on the question of the prisoner's accountability at the time of the rebellion; they were simply asked to report upon his present mental state. Lavell and Valade left Ottawa at once for the west; and to them both Macdonald gave precise and unambiguous instructions. "Remember," he pointed out to Lavell, "that the jury have decided that he was sane when his treasons were committed, and at the time of his trial. The judge approved of the verdict and the Court of Queen's Bench at Manitoba on appeal confirmed it. You cannot therefore go beyond that verdict and your inquiry will be limited to the simple question whether he at the time of your report is sufficiently a reasonable and accountable being to know right from wrong."[75] If, he continued, in explanation of the purpose of the inquiry, a criminal after conviction was found to be suffering from "raging dementia", the law was accustomed humanely to postpone the execution of his sentence; and since representations had been made that Riel's mind had lately given way, the government had decided to make an investigation into his present mental state. "I need scarcely point out to you," he reminded the two medical men, emphasizing once again the main point of the McNaghten Rules, "that the inquiry is not as to whether Riel is subject to illusions or delusions but whether he is so bereft of reason as not to know right from wrong and as not to be an accountable being."[76]

The doctors departed. There was nothing to do but wait. He was waiting now for two very different but oddly associated things—for the last act in the building of the railway, and for the final verdict in the case of Riel. It was strange how all during the troubled year of 1885 the drama of the railway and the drama of the North-West Rebellion had been so often inter-twined, and now, in the last moments of the dénouement of each, they were twisting together once more. "Doctors arrived this morning," Lieutenant-Governor Dewdney telegraphed from Regina on November 7;[77] and on the same day, far out in Eagle Pass, at the spot which Stephen had determined must be called Craigellachie, a group of intent men were watching the bearded Donald Smith drive home the last spike in the Canadian Pacific Railway. "Thanks to your far-seeing policy and unwavering support," Van Horne telegraphed from Craigel-lachie, "the Canadian Pacific Railway is completed. The last rail was laid this (Saturday) morning at 9:22."[78]

Van Horne's telegram reached Macdonald in Ottawa on Monday, November 9. If it had come a year ago, or at any time before the outbreak of rebellion in the north-west, the news from Eagle Pass would have made the day memorable with unqualified satisfaction. But now there was little spirit, and no time, for congratulations or rejoicings. Riel had been re-prieved until November 16. It was only a week away now; and the final decision on the fate of the *métis* leader was at hand. Campbell had completed his report for the Cabinet. It was, Macdonald informed Lansdowne, "a bold recommendation that Riel's sentence be carried out".[79] A telegram from Dewdney, which reached Ottawa that same Monday morning, informed Macdonald that Jukes, the doctor at the Regina gaol, had found the prisoner "perfectly accountable for his actions"; and within the next twenty-four hours the opinions of both Lavell and Valade arrived by telegraph. Lavell's examination had convinced him that Riel was a responsible being;[80] Valade drew a distinction between "political and religious subjects", on which he did not believe the prisoner to be accountable, and "other points", about which Riel seemed quite capable of distinguishing right from wrong.[81] By Tuesday, November 10, the evidence was all in; and Macdonald had made up his mind. Six weeks before he had told the Governor-General that a prerogative interference in the administration of justice was justifiable only in a case of "supreme necessity". No case of "supreme necessity" had been made out for Riel. No conclusive case of any kind had been made out. Macdonald would stick to the courts and their decisions. He would take his stand on their verdict and their sentence. And he was not to be budged.

One day later, on Wednesday, November 11, the Cabinet decided that Riel must hang. No very prolonged period of anxious debate had been necessary to reach this decision. The issue was never really in doubt. And the important question was not whether Riel's sentence would be altered or its execution postponed, but whether Macdonald would be able to carry all his French-Canadian ministers and the bulk of his French-Canadian supporters with him. Caron remained firm; Langevin was not prepared to desert his chief; and Chapleau, having spent the night after the Cabinet's final decision in composing a long memorandum in support of his dissent, decided on Thursday morning that he could not incur the responsibility of handing it in and thus helping to promote a racial war.[82] By the time Langevin left Ottawa later in the same day, Macdonald was certain that a united Cabinet would confront the mounting clamour of protest from Quebec. The French-Canadian leaders would remain faithful. But what of their followers? Langevin was met on the station platform at Montreal by five mutinous French-speaking members of Parliament. And next day nineteen Quebec members telegraphed Macdonald that they would not accept responsibility for Riel's execution.[83]

On Thursday, November 12, a special messenger, bearing the

Governor-General's warrant for the execution, left Ottawa for Regina. It was irrevocable now; and the strain and fatigue of the last few days of decision dulled Macdonald's eyes and deepened the lines on his face. His colleagues pressed him to cross the ocean for a brief rest; and he told Lord Lansdowne that he hoped to slip away so quietly that he would be aboard the ship before anyone noticed his departure. He was worn out with what he had been through; he dreaded the trouble that he knew was certain to come. But there was no panic in his heart, and no apprehension in his words. "Keep calm resolute attitude—all will come right," he wired Langevin at Quebec.[84] ". . . We are in for lively times in Quebec," he warned Lansdowne in his dry, laconic fashion, "but I feel pretty confident that the excitement will die out."[85] He could not really believe that the devotion of Quebec could be won by a man who had abjured his religion, renounced his citizenship, and shown himself perfectly prepared to abandon his followers for money. He could not really believe that the death of a single *métis* could seriously damage the work of unity through diversity which he and Cartier had carried out twenty years ago. Yet with what frightening swiftness this dreadful commotion had arisen in Quebec! Would it long survive Riel's death? Would his execution be a nine-days' horror, to be soon superseded by other excitements? Or would it remain as an indefinitely remembered injury to a people? Macdonald would soon know— or soon begin to know. "Messenger arrived seven this evening," Dewdney telegraphed on November 15.[86] Tomorrow was Monday, November 16. Tomorrow Riel was to die.

On the morning of November 16 the autumnal sun rose late but brilliant over plains which all about Regina were white with hoar frost.[87] The glare filled the land to the horizon; it formed a glittering frame for the little group of figures, dressed in sombre garments, who stood together, in still attitudes of portentous gravity, at the top of the tall structure inside the Regina gaol. And in the centre of the group Father McWilliams and Riel were saying the Lord's Prayer.

Our Father, who art in heaven, Hallowed be thy Name,
Thy kingdom come, Thy will be done, in earth as it is in

heaven. *Give us this day our daily bread; And forgive us our trespasses, As we forgive them that trespass against us; And lead us not into temptation, But deliver us from evil* . . .

And then the sprung trap gave and Riel dropped to his extinction.

Chapter Thirteen

The Revolt of the Provinces

I

WHEN the Allan liner *Polynesian* docked at Liverpool on December 1, Macdonald was greeted by two warmly cordial invitations. Both George Stephen and John Rose wanted the visitor to spend his time in London at their houses. Anne Stephen promised, her husband wrote, to "do" Macdonald quite as well as Batt's.[1] "I am all alone," John Rose assured his old friend. "You can have the whole house to yourself, breakfast and dine when you please. . . . I know it is rather far, but it may keep too many people from boring you, and there is a brougham which shall be at your sole disposal, and get you anywhere in ten minutes."[2] Even the brougham could not tempt Macdonald away from Batt's Hotel in Dover Street. Rose was one of his oldest and closest friends; and, as the postscript in Rose's letter of invitation reminded him, it was over forty-two years since they had first "foregathered". But Batt's had virtually become his London house; and part—and possibly a not unimportant part—of London's charm lay in the delicious irresponsibility which Batt's engendered. The small obligations of a private house might prove faintly irksome. He excused himself gratefully to the Stephens, and declined Rose's affectionate hospitality. He would see all three of them—and many more. But he would stop at Batt's.

London was full of excitement. The general election—they were still long-drawn-out affairs in England, lasting several weeks —had just got nicely under way; and the movement and dramatic suspense which Parnell had mysteriously succeeded in imparting to British politics, were at their height. By December 19, when the last returns were in, the English people learnt, to its consternation, that the Liberals had a majority over the Conservatives of eighty-six seats, and that Parnell's Irish Nationalists totalled exactly the same number. For the moment, the political ascendancy of the Irish leader seemed complete. Yet his "overruling position", which Macdonald bewailed in a letter to Lord Lansdowne, threatened the Conservatives much more seriously than it did the Liberals. Parnell could keep either one of the great English parties out of office; but he could not put, and keep, either one of them in. The only party to which he could give effective power was the Liberal party; and the approaching downfall of Lord Salisbury and the Conservatives seemed the one real certainty in a highly tense and ambiguous situation.

Macdonald was gravely disappointed. He had lived through the five years of the second Gladstone government without developing any overwhelming feeling of respect or gratitude; and when, in June, 1885, while the North-West Rebellion was coming to an end, Lord Salisbury had formed his first Cabinet, Macdonald had regarded the triumph of the Conservatives proudly as virtually a second Canadian victory. Now, after only six months, it was clear that the victory would likely be very short-lived. The Conservatives, almost certainly, were going out of power; and they were going out of power at a time when Canada urgently needed their support in her external relations. There was every prospect of serious negotiations, if not of actual disputes, with the United States over the inshore fisheries; there was a faint hope, which Macdonald and Stephen held in common, of an imperial mail subsidy for the Canadian Pacific steamer service between British Columbia and the Far East. In Macdonald's eyes, as well as in Stephen's, the Canadian Pacific was potentially a vast transoceanic and transcontinental system stretching all the way from Liverpool to Hong Kong. He believed that the British Conservatives would be far readier than their opponents to appreciate the importance of a great northern imperial route for traffic and defence; and he had no doubt at all, after the experience of the past, that the best hope of a vigorous defence of the fisheries lay not in Gladstone but in

Salisbury. As soon as the Colonial Secretary, Sir F. A. Stanley, got back to London after the election, he began to discuss with him the proposed joint commission with the United States.[3] He spent the New Year's week-end with W. H. Smith, the Secretary for War, at Greenlands, Henley-on-Thames; and on Monday, January 4, he went to see Lord Salisbury himself at the Foreign Office.[4]

In the meantime, in the intervals of theatres, dinner-parties and interviews, he kept reflecting on the absorbing news which was arriving from home. There was no longer the faintest doubt about the matter—Riel's execution had aroused a thunderous agitation in the Province of Quebec. On November 22, immediately after Macdonald's departure for England, an enormous mass meeting of protest had been held in the Champ de Mars, in Montreal; and a total of thirty-seven speakers competed with each other in ferocious denunciations of the "hangman's government" at Ottawa. Honoré Mercier, the provincial Liberal leader, informed the multitude that Riel was a Christian martyr sacrificed to Orange fanaticism; and Wilfrid Laurier, who for some years had been attempting to transform the anticlerical and revolutionary *Rouges* into respectable English Liberals, made the heroic but somewhat un-Gladstonian announcement that if he had lived on the banks of the Saskatchewan he would have taken up a rifle himself. The direct and immediate outcome of the meeting in the Champ de Mars was the creation of *Le Parti National*. Liberals and Conservatives co-operated in its establishment; and thus it appeared that the always dreaded, but never yet embodied, monstrosity of Canadian political life, the purely "racial", purely French-Canadian party, had at last come into existence.

Obviously, there were two important questions to be asked about *Le Parti National*, "the party of race and revenge", as the *Mail* of Toronto christened it. Would it remain a real union of Liberals and Conservatives? Would it exert any real influence in Canadian politics? As he scanned the reports in the newspapers, and read the reassuring letters from his colleagues, Macdonald began to suspect that the answer to the first question was a fairly definite no. It was surely significant that Mercier had accepted the leadership of *Les Nationalistes,* after two French-Canadian Conservatives had modestly declined it. The character of the agitation, Pope wrote to say, was becoming "more and more decidedly Rouge every day".[5] Caron was sure that the bolting Conservatives were beginning to realize that a trap had been laid for them by the opposition;[6] and Langevin believed that not more than twenty Quebec members would vote once against the party and that fewer than ten would keep up any further opposition.[7] No, it was obvious that *Le Parti National* was not going to swallow up Quebec Conservatism. *Le Parti National* was, in fact, becoming fairly rapidly a mere belligerent *ultra* wing of the Liberal party.

But were all its dangers disappearing in the process? Might not this resurgent nationalism revive the Liberal party in Quebec and fortify it for future provincial or federal victories? For this question, which was plainly the more important of the two, Macdonald had no ready answer; and it was obvious that his colleagues in Canada were equally uncertain, despite their confident predictions that the Riel agitation was a nine days' wonder which would be completely forgotten by the time Macdonald was back in Ottawa. The ministers in general, and particularly the French-Canadian ministers, wanted time. They wanted far more than nine days for the subsidence of the vast upheaval which Riel's execution had created. They suggested tentatively that "a short delay" in the opening of Parliament might strengthen their hands. Macdonald agreed with them. He told Lord Lansdowne, who was anxious to transfer the angry public debate over Riel to the legitimate theatre of Parliament, that the wishes of Langevin and the other French-Canadian ministers should be followed if possible. They had had a hard time of it, he added sympathetically. "They deserve well for the manly stand they have taken."[8]

He himself was having anything but a hard time of it in London. As usual, he had shrugged away his anxieties with enviable ease. As usual, his incredible resilience, his marvellous powers of recuperation had come effectively to his rescue; and, after a few days of complete relaxation, he emerged, as he had so often done before, looking as fresh and vigorous as if he had never seen really hard service before. He was enjoying himself immensely. He dined out night after night; he went repeatedly to the theatre; he spent two week-ends in the country; and on New Year's Eve, he was one of a large party that watched the pantomime *Aladdin* at Drury Lane. He caught a slight cold waiting on a station platform in Kent because he would insist on hurrying back to London from Lord Brabourne's country house despite the infrequent train service on Boxing Day. But this was the only misadventure which befell an elderly gentleman who had been rushing about with unsuitably youthful gusto and in apparently complete forgetfulness of the fact that he would be seventy-one on January 11 of the new year.

"What are you going to do on Christmas Day?" "little" Mary wrote to him from Canada. "I will miss you very much. I suppose you will be out in time for your birthday. . . ."[9] But by January 11 he was only two days away from Liverpool on the Cunard liner *Oregon*; and it was not until the afternoon of Tuesday, January 19, that he finally reached Ottawa. There was a welcoming reception at the City Hall; the band played "When Johnny Comes Marching Home"; and then Pat Buckley, Macdonald's favourite Irish cab-driver, drove them out along Sussex Street in his splendid four-in-hand to Earnscliffe.[10] Macdonald looked well—remarkably well. He looked, the friendly newspapers announced enthusiastically, "as ruddy as a red apple". And for once, Agnes realized gratefully, the newspapers had not exaggerated the miraculous transformation which a few short weeks had brought. "He was so tired and worried when he went away," she wrote to Louisa in Kingston, "that it quite enspirits me to see him so cheery."[11]

II

Only six months ago he had decided that the time had come for him to resign. He had told Tupper and Lord Carnarvon that he had finished his work. He had meant it; and the Canada which he had brought into being was the solid justification of his claim. The great design, sketched out gradually in the long frustrating years before 1867, had now been realized in actuality. With the exception of Newfoundland, the destined territorial limits of Canada had been reached. ". . . The Dominion cannot be considered complete without Newfoundland," he reminded Lord Lansdowne. "It has the key to our front door. . . ."[12] Some day, he was convinced, Canada must put this key in its pocket. But here his dreams of territorial expansion ended; and although he was perfectly prepared to give polite consideration to plans for the union of one or more of the British West Indies with Canada, he looked upon such proposals with inward doubt and misgiving.[13] In his view, the original provinces and territories of British North America were Canada's lawful inheritance. And in this wide, transcontinental domain he had established the institutions of a strongly centralized federal government. For nearly two decades while the law and custom of the constitution were being slowly clarified, he had watched over and defended the interests of the Dominion. He had worked out the three great economic policies—the settlement of the west, the development of eastern industry, the building of an all-Canadian transcontinental railway—by which a truly national economy, diversified and integrated, would be slowly realized. He had done his best. And his work at last was done.

Yet—and he knew it very well—he could not possibly give up at that moment. He had finished the design called Canada. But only the gaunt skeleton of the structure had been raised; and he was now called upon, almost literally, to save the half-finished fabric from abandonment or destruction. The plans, the surveys, the transport routes, the political institutions—the whole machinery of nationalism—had all been completed. But the nation itself, the populous and prosperous nation, had not yet come into existence. The meagreness of the accomplishment seemed to be a mocking refutation of the validity of the original design. In the past two years every circumstance had turned unfavourable. The depression still continued; immigration had faltered; most of the north-west was empty yet; and the country was racked with rebellion and cultural conflict. He had lost the initiative. He had been slowly and relentlessly forced back upon the defensive; and from all sides there appeared enemies who seemed determined to exploit the country's adversities and to launch the most fundamental attacks upon everything he had achieved in the past two decades.

There was danger from abroad, for the American Senate rejected the President's recommendation of a joint commission to settle the problem of the fisheries; and early in February, the inevitable occurred in England, the Salisbury government was defeated, and Gladstone formed his third Cabinet. Once again, Canada would have to defend the inshore fisheries with the uncertain co-operation of the English Liberals; and the Anglo-Canadian alliance, under the pressure to which it would certainly be subjected, might weaken or even break. The foreigners to the south, who had only grudgingly admitted Canada's separate existence and who were quite prepared to use diplomatic force to advance their annexationist ambitions, were always dangerous. In the circumstances of the moment, they were perhaps more dangerous than they had been for the past fifteen years. But, even so, were they as immediately and obviously dangerous as the enemies at home?

Macdonald did not think so—yet. Ever since he had assumed power in 1878, the enemies at home had been gradually accumulating. Everything he had done since 1878—the tariff, the transcontinental railway, the settlement of the west, the assertion of the Dominion's superintending control over the provinces —everything had provoked protests and strengthened regional discontents. Ontario had successfully defied the federal power of disallowance; Manitoba seemed determined to destroy the protection which had been granted to the Canadian Pacific Railway; and Nova Scotia was becoming more angrily impatient with her commercial and financial position in Confederation. It would never do, of course, to exaggerate the importance of these affairs. They were the ordinary sour bread and rancid butter of Canadian politics; and the one really frightening abnormality of the past year, the North-West Rebellion, had been crushed before it had had a chance to develop into a serious danger. It had been crushed. But, in dying, had it left another and possibly even greater danger behind it? The "nationalist" agitation in Quebec might provoke an equally parochial "nationalist" response in Ontario; and these two explosions of primitive feeling might destroy the cultural concord which had been one of the principal benefits of Confederation. The North-West Rebellion had begun by uniting the country in a burst of patriotism. Was it to end by dividing the nation in an outbreak of "racial" hatred? And how could a young and undeveloped country, already weakened by internal dissensions, survive a renewal, on a grand scale, of this old cultural conflict?

One thing at a time. The first issue was the issue of Riel's fate. Parliament met on February 25, and on March 1, C. J. Coursol moved for the report of the medical commission on Riel's mental state. No "medical commission" had, in fact, been appointed, as Macdonald's reply clearly revealed;[14] and there had been no formal collective "report". The government had simply requested three medical men to examine the prisoner and to give their opinion of his existing mental condition; and the replies, which were sent in separately, arrived in a very informal and piecemeal fashion, with letters following telegrams. In a twentieth-century treason case, such private and highly confidential communications would almost certainly be withheld from publication; but Macdonald's government, which dispensed information with a swiftness and a completeness rarely known in modern democracies, decided to give the substance of each expert's opinion to Parliament.[15]

It was not an unfair exercise in condensation. The omitted portion of Dr. Jukes's letter to Lieutenant-Governor Dewdney bore much more heavily against Riel than in his favour.[16] Lavell, in his telegram, had pointed out the pertinent fact that Father André was still admitting the prisoner to the sacraments, and, in his subsequent letter to Macdonald, he had described Riel as "a vain ambitious man, crafty and cunning, with powers in a marked degree to incite weak men to desperate deeds".[17] "He seeks his own aggrandisement," he concluded, "and, in my opinion, if he can attain his own ends, will care little for his followers." All these sentences, which would, of course, have given the greatest satisfaction to believers in Riel's guilt, were completely omitted from the printed version of Lavell's opinion. So also was Valade's opening statement that he did not believe

Riel to be an accountable being. But the distinction which the French-Canadian doctor had drawn between the prisoner's views on "political and religious subjects" and "other points", though blurred, had not been erased; and it was evident that he considered Riel responsible within the latter category only. The government, in short, had tried to give briefly, and in unprovocative language, the gist of each expert's opinion.

A debate was inevitable on the fate of Riel. It would, Macdonald knew, be a hazardous episode. It might bring serious trouble. But equally, with a little careful manipulation, the threat of misfortune might be turned into the gift of good luck. A debate which would satisfy the French-speaking Conservatives and embarrass the English-speaking Liberals was certainly conceivable. It would need careful planning. But planning was a congenial exercise, and early in the session Macdonald was ready with his plan. Landry, a Quebec Conservative member, gave notice of a motion deploring the fact that the government had permitted the sentence passed on Louis Riel to be carried out. There was, as Macdonald saw quickly, a good deal to be said for this particular resolution. It would give the "bolting *Bleus*" a chance to voice their dissatisfaction, and to cast what Langevin regarded as their one necessary vote against the government. It would do more than this. It would force the unhappy Liberals of Ontario to expose their serious disagreements over Riel.

On March 9, forty-eight hours before the day appointed for the debate on the Landry motion, Macdonald became ill. "I am afraid," he informed the Governor-General on March 9, "that I shall be obliged to lay up to get rid of my cold which threatens congestion."[18] The cold, which developed into bronchitis and then began to be accompanied by sciatic pains, kept him, an increasingly unhappy prisoner, in bed. But from his sick-room he could still direct the dispositions of the Landry debate; and there was a final ingenious and effective device which he now decided to use. At his request, Caron asked Langevin to move the previous question immediately after Landry had made his motion. "I shall be ready to take the floor immediately after Landry," Langevin promised.[19] And next day, as soon as Landry had sat down, he got up, defended the government's decision in a brief and somewhat formal reply, and ended by moving the previous question. At once the limits of the debate were firmly and narrowly set. The long string of fiendishly ingenious amendments by which the opposition would have continued to torture the subject and the government was abruptly cut short. The debate was focused not upon government policy in the northwest, which most Liberals could have agreed in condemning, but upon Riel's mental state and the commutation of his sentence, about which English-speaking and French-speaking Liberals were hopelessly divided.

Macdonald kept his bed. Instead of getting better, he grew steadily worse. Night after night he lay sleepless, racked with coughing or sciatic pains. The doctors prescribed sedatives and hypodermic injections; and after a brief respite of drugged sleep, he lay for long hours somnolent, his head "buzzing with opiates".[20] Yet, despite his pain and confusion, he never completely relaxed his hold on affairs. He could not help feeling worried when the Governor-General sent him a long letter questioning the wisdom of the bill which the government proposed to introduce for the better protection of the fisheries; and he was deeply suspicious of a sudden American proposal to establish a joint commission for an examination of the Canadian-Alaskan boundary. Why should such an offer be made with such zealous eagerness by a nation which seemed so strangely reluctant to accept a joint commission on trade and fisheries? Despite his pain and torpor, he was instantly alert and on the defensive; and, in a few letters to Lord Lansdowne, he quickly worked out all the main arguments on which Canada relied nearly two decades later in the final settlement of the Alaskan boundary dispute.[21]

Yet the main focus of his troubled and wavering interest was not here, but on the fate of the Landry motion. The debate—there was no doubt about it—was going well. Laurier made an eloquent speech for the opposition; and on March 17, Blake delivered a characteristically enormous oration, seven hours in length, and exactly twice as long as the speech with which a few weeks later Gladstone introduced his first Home Rule Bill. But, despite these big efforts, the opposition attack was not well sustained. The principal English-speaking Liberal leaders remained conspicuously and significantly silent; and Thompson, upon whom, as Minister of Justice, fell the main burden of the government defence, rose magnificently to his first great debating opportunity. Even Campbell was impressed; and only a few months before Campbell had observed coldly that Thompson had "the air of a man educated for the priesthood, with a nervous look and subdued manner".[22] The debate on the Landry motion changed Campbell's opinion. There was praise on all sides for Thompson's speech; and Campbell had even heard an unhappy Grit admit that the new Minister of Justice had "really smashed Blake".[23] It was true, Macdonald reflected, and true in a special sense. Thompson had "smashed" Blake in the way that Blake could be most decisively smashed—by the deeply felt but unspoken arguments of Blake's own followers. And a few days later, when the vote on the Landry motion was finally taken, it was revealed that the disaffection in the Liberal camp was even more serious than that in the Conservative. The Landry motion was defeated by one hundred and forty-six votes to fifty-two.[24] Seventeen French-speaking Conservatives voted against the government; but twenty-three English-speaking Liberals deserted the opposition.

It was, as he would have said himself, "altogether satisfactory". And, as he lay in bed and tried to cope with the gnawing pain in his leg, he could not help feeling that there were other and more general reasons for satisfaction. The session, despite his absence, was moving smoothly forward. The new and younger ministers—John Thompson, George Foster at Marine and Fisheries, and Tom White in the Department of the Interior—were all performing with tolerable efficiency; and McLelan, who had succeeded Tilley as Minister of Finance, was able to bait his budget with what everybody would certainly regard as a delectable tid-bit. The twenty million dollars' worth of bonds which the government held as security for its loan to the Canadian Pacific had now been converted into cash as a result of Barings' successful flotation of the bond issue of the previous year; and with this money, together with lands to the value of over nine million dollars, the government would be able, McLelan announced proudly, "to settle all accounts with the Canadian Pacific Railway Company".[25] The loans which every Reform politician and every Grit newspaper had denounced as a sheer gift to the railway and a total loss to the country, had been repaid within less than a year after the last spike had been driven in at Craigellachie. And Canada, fortified with twenty millions of hard cash, would be able to pay off its floating debt and escape fresh financing.

It "took well" with the public, McLelan informed Macdonald complacently. It took so well that the Liberals treated the proposal in a discreet and respectful fashion. The Liberals, in fact, were in general behaving in an unheroic and disunited way; and in comparison with the repeated and prolonged excitements of 1885, the new session was plainly a fairly tame and easy affair. "The best thing you can do for us all," Campbell wrote wisely, "is to get strong again, and in the meantime to allow us to conduct public affairs on our own judgment."[26] It was plain good sense; and despite his lust for information and his instinct for management, Macdonald let himself relax in a slow and not too easy recuperation. At the end of March he had to undergo the painful process of blistering; and a fortnight later he was admitting that a slight imprudence, such as resting incautiously on his lame leg, seemed "to awaken the sleeping demon" of his pain.[27] Yet slowly he improved. On April 20, he ventured, he told the Governor-General, to "try the atmosphere" of the House;[28] and two days later he rose in his place to propose the government bill for the representation of the North-West Territories in the Dominion Parliament.

III

The spring days lengthened, the unremarkable session drew slowly towards its close. Obviously the opposition in the House was divided and inhibited; but obviously also, as Macdonald realized very clearly, the parliamentary opposition was only a very partial expression of the dissatisfaction in the country as a whole. Resistance to the Conservative programme had not really slackened, still less had it disappeared. It had simply taken the different and possibly still more dangerous form of cultural antagonism and provincial discontent. Provincial protests were like *leit-motifs* which kept on being repeated, with incredibly persistent reiteration, by strings and brass and wood-winds, through endless varieties of orchestration, but always with the same hostile and minatory note.

The possible variations of the main themes of provincial discontent seemed literally endless. The ugly sounds kept coming back, and back, and back. Manitoba, despite the supposedly "final" settlement of its claims which had been patched up the previous year, was clamouring excitedly against the Canadian Pacific's "monopoly clause". Ontario and Quebec were quarrelling with a pugnacity which seemed to imply that "race" and religion were newly discovered subjects of dispute; and early in May, the *Mail* of Toronto which had been established fourteen years before to represent Conservatism with completeness and fidelity, began to print a series of articles on the Roman Catholic Church which sounded altogether too much like George Brown's diatribes of a quarter century ago. On May 7, the provincial legislature of Quebec began a long debate on the execution of Riel. The Quebec Liberals, with "nationalist" support and with the energetic Mercier as leader, were obviously waxing lusty and confident on the Riel issue. And everybody began to be gloomily apprehensive that the days of the Conservative government in Quebec were numbered.

Even this was not all. In the east, an angry chorus of protest grew steadily more determined and more shrill. It was over fifteen years ago that Macdonald, with Howe's help, had "pacified" Nova Scotia. But certainly no province was showing more restiveness and impatience in the spring of 1886 than Nova Scotia. Her troubles were mainly economic and financial in origin; the main objects of her dislike were the federal tariff and the insufficient federal subsidies. Certain long-run changes in the Maritime economy, such as the contraction of wooden-ship building and the relative decline of the old West Indies markets, had been unhappily accompanied and emphasized by the short-term distresses of the depression. The awful sense of permanent stagnation which resulted had bred in many people a conviction that some fundamental mistake had been made; and the old belief, which had never really died out, that Nova Scotia had been tricked into Confederation against her will and her best interests, began rapidly to gain converts once again. A new movement for Howe's old objective, the repeal of the union, was once more in being.

Macdonald had been watching the development of this agitation for some time with curious interest. The Liberal leader, W. S. Fielding, who had succeeded to the premiership of Nova Scotia two years before, had obviously been trying to make profitable political use of the movement, without identifying himself too closely with it. But his early efforts to use the bogey of secession to frighten the Dominion government into a grant of "better terms" had been unsuccessful; and in the spring of 1886 he decided upon a bolder and more aggressive thrust. On May 7, he himself moved a set of government resolutions for the repeal of the union so far as Nova Scotia was concerned. In a few days the resolutions were passed with large majorities; the provincial government announced an appeal to the people on the issue of secession; and despite Macdonald's advice to Lieutenant-Governor Richey to delay the dissolution as long as possible, the general election was fixed for June 13.[29]

"Are Nova Scotia secession resolutions serious?" Rose inquired anxiously from London. "Have they been influenced by Home Rule views here?"[30] Macdonald was always eager to counteract anti-Canadian propaganda in England, and he knew that he could return a short answer to the second of Rose's questions. "No connection between Irish Home Rule and resolutions," he cabled back. "Province applying for better terms—looks like blackmail."[31] Of course it looked like blackmail. But it was highly dangerous blackmail—how dangerous he had no means of telling as yet. He knew only that since the establishment of Confederation, and the pacification of Nova Scotia, in 1869, this was the first open attempt at the repeal of the union. He knew also that, although there might be no connection between Irish Home Rule and Nova Scotia secession, the fact remained that Fielding's agitation was reaching its climax at a time when the Liberals were in power in England and when the "Grand Old Man" of British politics was passionately espousing the cause of local liberties within the Empire.

The disaffection of Manitoba and Nova Scotia, the open quarrelling of Ontario and Quebec, all spelled trouble for the future. But this long concatenation of domestic misfortunes was not the only source of worry. There was an equal, or nearly equal, danger in the unsolved problem of the fisheries and in the unsettled relations with the United States. During the winter, Canada had decided that since all its proposals for a settlement had been uniformly rejected by the United States, it would proceed henceforth by the very different method of enforcing its treaty rights. By the Convention of 1818, American fishing vessels were permitted to enter the inshore waters of British North America for wood, water, shelter, and repairs, "and for no other purpose whatever". Why not stand on the plain meaning of these words, particularly since every invasion of the three-mile limit, for whatever purpose, made clandestine fishing ridiculously easy? The bill for tightening up the enforcement of the fishery regulations, about which Lord Lansdowne had expressed such grave doubts, was pushed forward without alteration; and in the meantime, out on the Atlantic coast, Canadian coast-guards and customs officers began to apply the existing legislation with a new vigour. Early in May, the American fishing schooner, *David J. Adams*, was seized in Digby harbour for buying ice and bait; and in the next few weeks, a few other seizures for similar infractions of the Convention of 1818 followed.

At once a great, angry roar of protest shook the United States. What did these bumptious colonials think they were doing? Bayard, with a ready reliance on the American assumption that Canada was a primitive colonial dependency, refused to concede that the Dominion had any authority whatever to give either legislative or executive effect to treaties entered into by the imperial government. Great Britain was immediately and urgently requested to prevent the offending measure from going into operation. Lord Rosebery put Canada's case forcefully to the American Minister in London; but Granville who, after an interval of fifteen years, had briefly returned to the Colonial

Office, was plainly very anxious that the seizures of American fishing vessels should cease and that the new Canadian Fisheries Bill should not become law. Macdonald was stubbornly recalcitrant under this Colonial Office pressure. Bayard's contemptuous dismissal of Canada's legislative powers had put his back up. "The present denunciation of those powers by Mr. Bayard," he told Lord Lansdowne, "is really audacious."[32] He insisted that in the circumstances Canada had no option but to protect her own property, and that the new Fisheries Bill was an entirely legitimate attempt to increase the efficiency of the protection. "After all," he reasoned with the Governor-General, "this legislation does not attempt to extend our rights but simply to improve our procedure by giving the means of enforcing those rights."[33]

The session was nearly over. Macdonald may have begun to feel that he would get the Bill through in safety. But at the last moment he had to yield. Only a few hours before the prorogation a cable arrived from Lord Granville instructing the Governor-General to reserve the Fisheries Bill.[34] "In the face of the rather impudent protest from Mr. Bayard, it will put us in a rather humiliating position," Macdonald wrote from his place in the Commons, in a final effort to avert the blow, while the last debate of the session was raging round him. "He protests against our power to legislate and we will appear tamely to acquiesce."[35] Only a few minutes later, against his own better judgment, the Governor-General did in fact publicly "acquiesce"; and although he begged Granville to explain that the Bill had been reserved solely because it was thought that it might embarrass the somewhat hypothetical "negotiations" then in progress, both he and Macdonald realized that the prestige of Canada had been dealt a heavy blow.[36] The Dominion had suffered a serious diplomatic reverse. It had been compelled to endure a grave affront to its constitutional pride.

It was bad. But it was not by any means the only misfortune of the early summer of 1886. The swift current of cultural dispute and provincial protest seemed quickening to a mill-race. The *Mail*, despite Macdonald's private protests to its editor, continued to foment religious and cultural warfare. In Quebec, Mercier's "nationalist" crusade was making such rapid progress that a Liberal victory in the approaching provincial election was now a distinct possibility; and in Nova Scotia the cause of Canadian unity was about to meet the most complete and unequivocal repudiation that it had yet encountered. Immediately after the prorogation of Parliament, McLelan and Thompson hastened down to Nova Scotia to throw the weight of their influence into the provincial electoral campaign. They utterly failed to avert the victory of the Liberals. Fielding won, won handsomely, and won on the simple and catastrophic proposal to repeal the union. "You will have seen long ere this reaches you," Macdonald wrote to Tupper on June 21, "that Fielding has defeated the Conservatives on the secession cry —horse, foot, and artillery. Never was there such a rout. McLelan has come back from this inglorious campaign and gives no intelligent account of the disaster."[37]

It was in the gloomy light of these misfortunes that Macdonald sat down, after the prorogation had brought its welcome lull, to a serious consideration of the political future. The existing Parliament was now four years old. In another twelve-month there would have to be a general election; and Lord Lansdowne was already inquiring whether he was likely to ask for a dissolution before 1886 was out. On the whole, Macdonald was inclined to favour postponement. The clean sweep which Fielding had made in Nova Scotia on the repeal issue had surprised most people, including probably Fielding himself. It was too early yet to be at all confident of how serious the secession movement might prove to be; and the fact that Gladstone, after the defeat of his first Home Rule Bill, was about to go to the country added a further and grave element of uncertainty. "A good deal will depend on the results of the elections in England," he wrote to the Governor-General. "If Gladstone succeeds, Heaven knows what he may do, if a petition is presented to the Queen asking for relief and separation."[38] Gladstone, in his infatuation with Home Rule, might give serious consideration to the Nova Scotian demands. And if so, nobody could tell what might happen to Confederation. In the meantime, however, it would be madness for the Dominion government to anticipate such a catastrophe, to challenge Nova Scotia in a general election before Fielding's purpose was made quite clear. It would be better to wait—for a while at least. And there were too many other good reasons —Riel, the racial and religious conflict, the depression and the unrest of labour—for delay. "We have rocks ahead," he wrote to Tupper, "and great skill must be exercised in steering the ship."

The work of the next six months must be a great organized effort of patient preparation. He would have to begin by giving ground. It would be highly dangerous, in the uncertain state of affairs in both Canada and England, to put too great a strain upon the Anglo-Canadian alliance; and Canada, having made its position abundantly clear in test cases such as that of the schooner *David J. Adams*, could afford to relax a little the rigour of its enforcement of the Convention of 1818. Fishing by American vessels inside the three-mile limit would, of course, not be permitted for a minute; but for the present season at least there would be no more seizures on the ground of the purchase of supplies or provisions.[39] "I have thoroughly frightened Foster," he told the Governor-General, "as to his proceedings as possibly leading to war, and he is I believe energetic in his instructions that there should not be any exhibitions of too much zeal."[40]

"This wretched fishery imbroglio", as Stephen called it, kept Macdonald preoccupied and perturbed for most of June. He could do nothing until the excitement caused by the seizures had subsided a little. He did not dare to leave Ottawa. Yet he was already planning a programme of pre-election activities which would occupy many weeks and take him very far afield. He realized that what he faced was not an election, like that of 1882, which could be carried in a rush of confident enthusiasm. The campaign which was looming up before him now would almost certainly be much more like the long and carefully organized struggle which had preceded the triumph of 1878. He invited Tupper to come back to Canada for a serious stocktaking of the wretched state of affairs in Nova Scotia. He began to feel that it might be wise to undertake a series of political meetings, something like the famous picnics of 1876 and 1877, in Ontario during the coming autumn. For the summer, his plans were made. He would go west. The Canadian Pacific was about to inaugurate its regular passenger service between Montreal and Port Moody, and what more fitting than that he, of all the ministers, should travel by the first train? The journey would give him a badly needed holiday, a knowledge of the great new country he was creating, a chance to show himself to its new inhabitants and to quiet the rising storm of their protests in Manitoba.

It was not until June 23 that Lord Lansdowne finally authorized the "western expedition". There was no hope now that Macdonald would be in time for the first "ocean to ocean" train that pulled out from the Dalhousie station in Montreal at eight o'clock on the evening of June 28. He was still working determinedly on the late afternoon of Saturday, July 10, which was the day finally set for his departure. "Awful hard work to get away," he wrote briefly to Thompson. "I have written three letters to Lord Lansdowne today."[41] It was late at night when the little party—Macdonald, Agnes, Agnes's companion, the invaluable secretary, Joseph Pope, Fred White of the Mounted Police, and the two servants—assembled in the Ottawa station. The departure had been kept a close secret until the last. There were few people in the station; and they settled themselves happily in the *Jamaica*, the special carriage, with the wonderful fine-meshed window screens to keep out the dust and mosquitoes, which Van Horne had thoughtfully provided for their comfort.[42] Then at last they were off. The lights of Ottawa dropped behind them. They were out in the open countryside, in the rich darkness of a summer night, racing north-west towards the rock and forest of the Canadian Shield. The train gathered speed. The long, lugubrious whistle of the engine died slowly and mournfully away in their wake.

IV

Macdonald watched the rapid approach of Winnipeg through the wide, curtained windows of the *Jamaica*. It was nearly nine o'clock on Tuesday morning, July 13. For two days the train had been threading its way through the dense forests of the Shield, or hugging the long, looping curves of the north shore of Lake Superior. They had done little travelling at night, for Van Horne was anxious to ensure Sir John's rest and to enable him to see the whole line by daylight. They had seen it all; and now, within the last few hours, they had watched it change suddenly and with mysterious completeness. The trees thinned out, the great scarred rocks dwindled and disappeared, the land flattened out in dead levels that stretched towards an incredibly remote horizon. The train slowed down gradually to a stop, and Macdonald got to his feet. The painful awkwardness of his leg, the unhappy, lingering after-effect of his winter's illness, still nagged at him a little. But, after only two days of holiday, he was already feeling better; and in his morning coat, grey trousers, grey top hat and favourite gay necktie, he looked very nearly his usual smart and jaunty self.[43] He moved quickly towards the end of the carriage. The first of the prairie public appearances had begun. There on the platform outside were the faithful Conservatives of Winnipeg, headed by Lieutenant-Governor Aikins and "Honest John" Norquay.

For three days they were Lieutenant-Governor Aikins's guests. They went on one long excursion, over a branch line of the Canadian Pacific, to the south-western part of the province, and, for a good part of the journey, Agnes rode adventurously in the engine. At Winnipeg there were receptions, with long queues of smiling Conservatives who wanted to shake hands, and a public meeting at the "Royal Roller Rink", which was the largest hall in town. Macdonald told his audience that when the contract for the Canadian Pacific was being negotiated in 1880 he had scarcely dared to hope that he would live long enough to travel in the flesh along the entire railway to its terminus. His friends had regretfully expected that he might have to view the completed work from the serene heights of heaven above. His enemies had naturally supposed that he would be compelled to gaze upward at it from the pit beneath. "I have now disappointed both friends and foes," he continued gaily, "and am taking a horizontal view."[44] His horizontal view, he explained, did not end at Port Moody or Victoria, but continued westward, in imagination at least, across the rim of the Pacific Ocean to the Far East. When he was last in England he had interested Lord Salisbury in a line of steamers running between British Columbia and China; and now that the elections in England were going so well for the Conservatives and the prospect of Lord Salisbury's return to power was so certain, there was a real hope that a Pacific steamship service would be soon established.

On Friday, July 16, at the very early hour which became characteristic of their morning departures, they left Winnipeg. A long, comfortable, lazy week-end was spent with the Dewdneys at Government House in Regina;[45] and it was not until Tuesday that they set out westward again. Over the gently rolling interminable prairie the train picked up speed, and they raced into Medicine Hat, in mid-afternoon, at a rate of forty miles an hour. But the darkness of the long summer day had already fallen when the train finally pulled up at Gleichen, the little station, east of Calgary, in the heart of the Blackfoot country. Chief Crowfoot, who in the dark days at the beginning of the North-West Rebellion had pledged the loyalty of his tribe to Macdonald, was waiting, a little on his dignity, for he had been led to expect the visitors nearly three hours before; and it was not until very early the following morning that the Indians, who had come to the rendezvous in full force, began to assemble for the pow-wow. The lesser chiefs—Old Sun, Eagle Rib, Medicine Shield, Running Eagle, Little Plume —sat about portentously in full war-paint and feathers. Crowfoot alone was in his oldest clothes—in memory, he informed Macdonald, of the dead Poundmaker. His face, with its well shaped features and fine lines, was shrewd and proud and intelligent. He told the listening Indians that Macdonald was the "biggest man" they had had among them for a long time. He begged Macdonald to banish the fears of the Indians for their children's nourishment and welfare. Then the Indians did a dance, and presents were distributed; and Macdonald gave Crowfoot a dark broadcloth suit with silk facings—a proper suit of mourning.[46]

Beyond Calgary the land lifted into foothills, and the foothills broke apart and thrust themselves furiously upwards in mountains. The train was stopped. Agnes and Macdonald seated themselves securely on the buffer bar—the "cowcatcher" —in front of the engine; and the wheels began to move again. The wind tore past their faces. The Kicking Horse River wound about, with sinuous agility, below them. The valley contracted menacingly into what seemed an impassable gorge and then broadened out into lush and placid meadowlands. The enormous, uninterrupted prospect began to make the view from the windows of the *Jamaica* seem narrow and unsatisfying. Agnes, with her inexhaustible vitality, preferred the hot sun and the rushing wind; and Macdonald, though he was a less frequent and less indefatigable passenger on the "cowcatcher" than his wife, kept his precarious perch for longer than he might have believed possible four months before. They travelled through Rogers Pass and past Craigellachie on the buffer bar; from it they watched the great coiling valleys of the Thompson and Fraser Rivers. On the distant sides of the canyons, the great cascades hung trembling like threads of silver. The colours of the rock-face—green, and rose, and amethyst, and deep purple—melted and mingled. Even the coming of sunset did not end the excitements of the ride; and after dinner, on the last evening of the journey out, they took their accustomed places on the buffer bar. It was black dark by now. The train was racing down the Fraser canyon towards Lytton. Above, the gloom was lit by a few stars; hundreds of feet below was the river; and the locomotive, feeling its way experimentally with the great beam of its headlight, laboriously skirted the edges of the chasm, roared through tunnels, and rattled over creaking bridges.[47]

Early on Saturday morning, July 24, they reached Port Moody; and late that night the steamer *Princess Louise* brought them to their journey's end at Victoria. "Sir John looks as gay as a lark," the correspondent of the Port Moody *Gazette* informed its readers.[48] The first, most exhilarating part of the trip was over; but its welcome relaxations were just beginning, and for over a fortnight they rested contentedly at Driard House, Victoria's most pleasant hotel.[49] Then, in a leisurely fashion, the return began. There were visits to the principal British Columbian towns. There were several stops and speeches, as they worked their way slowly back across the prairies, for the benefit of the newly enfranchised citizens of the North-West Territories. And then, at Winnipeg, came the first sharp foretaste of the hard political campaigning that lay ahead. A provincial Conservative convention had been convoked, in the hope of restoring the declining strength of Norquay's government and the waning popularity of Conservative policies at Ottawa. Macdonald defended the "monopoly clause" of the Canadian Pacific charter. It would, he hoped, be given up "speedily". But in the meantime, the national railway must be defended—and if necessary by federal disallowance—from the premature encroachments of its American rivals.[50]

On Monday, August 30, at about half past four in the morning, the Canadian Pacific engine brought the sleeping inmates of the *Jamaica* to rest at Ottawa; and the long journey, which had occupied over fifty days and covered over six thousand miles, came at last to an end.[51]

V

Back in his office in the East Block, Macdonald gazed speculatively at the hazy political horizon. "Now, I suppose," Rose wrote admiringly from England, congratulating him on his safe return, "you are like the old war horse, keen for the assault again; and may you have the fullest measure of success."[52] Macdonald was by no means sure of success. Time had crept up upon him once again; and time and the bag of troubles he carried on his back could not be shaken off now. He would have to remain in office until he had reached some kind of agreement with the United States over the fisheries; he would have to attempt to cope with the ominously spreading protest movement of the provinces. Fielding's victory in Nova Scotia had been an unqualified repudiation of the very idea of British North American unity; and Macdonald's whole conception of the national interest faced a long series of similar electoral ordeals. It had been announced that the dreaded provincial election in Quebec would take place on October 14. Beyond that there was a possible election in Manitoba and a very probable election in Ontario. And beyond all these was the definite necessity of a federal general election within the next nine months.

During September he made a few short forays of investigation into the debatable territory of southern Ontario. Ontario and Quebec were the great powers of the Dominion; and he knew that he was losing Irish Roman Catholic votes in Ontario just as he was losing French Roman Catholic votes in Quebec. At a political meeting at London, on September 16, he pointedly informed his audience that the Conservative press was completely free from party control and that he had no responsibility whatever for the editorial policies of the *Mail* of Toronto.[53] It was, he reflected gloomily, an almost wholly useless exculpation. The vast rumbling religious and racial agitation was not to be settled by such easy disclaimers. And the question was not whether he would lose support—which he was certain to do—but whether he would lose more than he gained. If Mercier and his Liberal-Nationalists triumphed on October 14, the Conservative cause in the Dominion would be seriously endangered. But if the Conservative government at Quebec were sustained, then surely Blake had no great chance of success in the approaching federal election. "A great many Protestant Liberals, especially the Presbyterian Scotchmen," Macdonald explained to the Governor-General, "are incensed at his course on the two questions of Riel and Home Rule and will only pardon him if his game succeeds in carrying Quebec. If not they will say that he sold himself without getting the money."[54] Without getting the money! If that were the result, Macdonald would be through in safety. If Quebec remained firm in its allegiance, his system of government could be maintained intact. There were times when it seemed that everything depended on the retention of Quebec.

In the meantime, while he waited apprehensively for the fateful October 14, there were other breaches in the authority and prestige of the Dominion which he must try to repair. He wanted the Fisheries Bill of last session removed from its state of suspended animation and given the force of law; he wanted a pledge of the assistance of the Atlantic Squadron of the Royal Navy in the defence of the fisheries for the season of 1887.

Lord Lansdowne, who had gone to England in the late summer, had been pressing the British government to yield on both these points;[55] and the fortunate return of Lord Salisbury and the Conservatives to power had strengthened Macdonald's hope of British support in a policy of protection. He set himself to win it. Protection, he was convinced, would now have to be continued for years. The Americans would be in no mood for diplomatic concessions for some time to come. Having just finished one presidential contest, they were virtually embroiled in a new one.

"For the next three years," he argued to Lord Lansdowne, "neither party will take any step to affect its popularity, and a supposed leaning towards England or her colonies, or the settlement of any treaty not obviously disadvantageous to England, would be unpopular. Bayard, contrary to my expectations, is endeavouring to out-jingo Blaine, both in Canada and Mexico, but neither he nor Cleveland will go in for war or interruption of diplomatic intercourse. Were Blaine in power he would do everything disagreeable short of war, and perhaps, if England had trouble elsewhere, go further. If I am right in this, the true policy would seem to be to pursue a steady course of protection to our waters, and condemnation of vessels committing undoubted breaches of the Treaty of 1818, for the next three years, before the presidential election. By that time the American fishermen will have learnt that every breach involves seizure and forfeiture and that their only course is to keep out of our waters and get their supplies elsewhere. If any weakness is shown on the part of the British government or of ours, our waters will be continually invaded and we shall have to submit to a series of diplomatic bullyings which if Blaine, or any Republican like him, is elected President, may culminate in a cessation of friendly intercourse. Nothing *can* be gained by submission. Much *may* be gained by a calm but firm assertion of our rights and their enforcement."[56]

At length, on October 14, the Province of Quebec voted. The results were certainly mixed and none too clear; but it was obvious that the Conservatives had lost and that the Liberals and Nationalists had substantially gained. There was still some hope, of course; and Langevin was inclined to believe that the Conservative government would somehow contrive to pick up a majority by the time the session began.[57] Macdonald's assessment of the future was much more blunt and gloomy. "The triumph of the *Rouges* over the corpse of Riel changes the aspect of affairs, *quoad* the Dominion government completely," he wrote to Tupper. "It will encourage the Grits and opposition generally; will dispirit our friends, and will, I fear, carry the country against us at the general election."[58] The worst—or very nearly the worst—had happened. The general election could not be delayed longer than six months; and everywhere the prospects were steadily worsening. Nova Scotia had gone. Quebec was almost certainly going. Norquay's power was obviously tottering in Manitoba; and in Ontario, Mowat stood a very good chance of improving his position at the next general election.

"What prospect your coming over?" Stephen cabled him from London.[59] "No prospect," Macdonald replied flatly. On Saturday, October 30, the Cabinet spent a long afternoon discussing the prospective dissolution, and, with only three dissentients, it was decided that the general election must take place before another session.[60] On Wednesday, November 3, Macdonald left for Toronto, to begin the rallying of the Conservative forces.[61] And less than a fortnight later, when the Conservative speaking tour in southern Ontario had just begun to get nicely under way, Mowat suddenly announced that the Ontario legislature would be dissolved and a general election held at the end of December. The tests, both federal and provincial, were coming—and coming very soon—in Ontario; and, now that Quebec was wavering uncertainly in its allegiance, the retention of Ontario began to seem the condition of Conservative survival. With White, Thompson, and Meredith, the opposition leader in Ontario, for company, Macdonald plunged into the real ordeal of a series of autumn speaking engagements. He stood the fatigues and discomforts—the long hours, the milling crowds, the suffocating rooms—with the cheerfulness of a born, and a seasoned, campaigner. "Sir John surprises me—," Thompson wrote to his wife in wonderment, "he goes through all these hardships quite gaily. . . ."[62] Even a bad cold, which unfortunately became bronchial, did not seriously interrupt the tour; and it was not until December 20 that he finally turned his face towards home.[63]

Back in the East Block, with the new year rapidly approaching, Macdonald anxiously considered the state of the nation once more. Internationally, the Dominion had gained. Late in November the imperial government agreed to give the royal assent to the Canadian Fisheries Bill; and at the same time it was decided that if an agreement with the United States had not been reached by the beginning of the next fishing season, the Royal Navy would send a cruiser to assist in the protection of the fisheries.[64] These were resounding diplomatic successes for a persevering but hard-pressed government. In the approaching general election they could be of real value. But, unfortunately, they stood virtually alone. In domestic affairs the unbroken tale of calamity had continued with the Manitoba general election on December 9 and the Ontario general election on December 28. In Manitoba, Norquay was "saved" but only, as Lieutenant-Governor Aikins admitted, after an "agony" of uncertainty; and in Ontario Mowat more than doubled his previous majority. The battered Norquay's survival could be explained, Aikins considered, by Macdonald's efforts on his behalf at the Manitoba Conservative convention of the previous August. But all during November and December, Macdonald had been expending himself, without stint, and apparently without any effect, in William Meredith's support. It was extremely discouraging. It was nearly as bad as it could be. Of the four provincial general elections of 1886, the Conservatives had lost two, drawn one, and emerged, dubious and bloody victors, from the fourth.

Yet Macdonald decided to go ahead. Postponement of the federal general election would now be regarded simply as a public admission of the gravity of his position. He might as well take the initiative with all the confidence he could muster. On Saturday, January 15, he sent the order-in-council authorizing the dissolution to Lord Lansdowne; and on Monday morning the newspapers announced that the election would be held on February 22.[65] The last fortnight of January was spent in final, frantic efforts to collect the Conservative team and put the players in good heart. Tupper, who had with

THE DOCTOR ARRIVES!

difficulty been persuaded that his presence was absolutely
essential for the recovery of Nova Scotia, did not leave England
until January 12; and Chapleau, choosing this most appropriate

moment for a violent assertion of his personality, threatened resignation if a long list of his demands were not met.[66] The team had its unwilling and refractory members. But ten days later they were all present and ready to take the field. "You may like to know," Macdonald informed the Governor-General on January 24, "that Chapleau is back into the fold."[67] And next day Tupper, looking as hearty and pugnacious as ever, arrived in Ottawa ready and willing for service.

On the last day of January, Macdonald left for Toronto by the midnight train.[68] The day had brought the news of a final and crushing misfortune. In Quebec, Mercier had finally emerged triumphant from the political muddle produced by the October election; and on January 30 a new provincial government of Liberals and Nationalists had taken office at Quebec. The governments of the two central provinces—of the "great powers" of the Dominion—were now in the hands of Macdonald's enemies. Every circumstance seemed to be in Blake's favour. Every event of the past twelve months seemed to promise his success. And yet, as the short campaign proceeded on its agitated way, Macdonald began to realize that Blake was unaccountably failing to take advantage of his enormous opportunities. The country was full of economic depression, of cultural conflict, of a sense of national frustration and discouragement. But Blake was not exploiting these possibilities. He was not making capital gains for the Liberals out of the growing volume of national discontents.

His attitude to the depression and to the vexed question of commercial policy, Macdonald noted, was characteristically uninspiring. People were now in the mood for desperate remedies—just as they had been in the years from 1873 to 1878. Macdonald had met that irrepressible human demand for action with his proposal of the national policy of protection. But Blake, in similar circumstances and with a similar opportunity, had nothing comparable to offer. In the Maritime Provinces and in certain parts of Ontario, a significant number of people, unconnected with politics, were already beginning to advocate the abandonment of protection and the substitution of a radically different policy, commercial union with the United States. Obviously no more frontal attack upon Canadian

economic nationalism could have been devised. But, if Blake
was aware of the political possibilities of the proposal, he
chose to ignore them. At Malvern, in one of his first campaign
speeches, he informed the audience that in his opinion the
size of the Canadian debt made any reduction in Canadian
taxation impossible and that therefore the tariff would continue
to give "a large and ample advantage to the home manufacturer
over his competitor abroad".[69]

It was a safe, sober, sensible announcement. But it could
hardly arouse people with the hope of drastic remedial action;
and it enabled Macdonald to hold up his opponent to ridicule
as a reluctant, half-hearted, last-minute convert to a religion
which he had previously reviled and still secretly abhorred.
Macdonald dealt largely in this kind of burlesque during the
campaign. He usually spoke last, after the other members of
the Conservative team had finished their speeches, and in a
more informal and jocular fashion. Early in the campaign the
Globe had informed its readers very impressively that the Prime
Minister was in his dotage, that Tom White had become his
virtual keeper, and that Tupper was hurrying home to take
his place. Macdonald made the most of this inspired diagnosis.
The *Globe*, he reminded his listeners genially, had reported
his suicide in 1873 and, on various occasions since, had
announced his approaching demise through cancer of the
stomach or paralysis of the brain. He had mysteriously survived
all these gloomy predictions. And, he concluded, "as he was
enjoying a few lucid moments just then before an attack of
frenzy came on," he would proceed to discuss a few of the
questions of the day.[70]

He did not usually discuss them at any length. But he stuck
to the campaign, despite its winter rigours, until the very end.
At Brockville, on Friday, February 11, the Conservative procession, reception, and speeches all took place to the accompaniment of a howling blizzard. The roads and railways were
so thickly blocked with snow that he did not reach Ottawa
until Saturday afternoon, and then he was so worn out that he
could do nothing but tumble into bed.[71] Some day he would
injure himself beyond recovery by these tremendous exertions.
Some day, perhaps; but not yet. Once again, after only a few

hours' respite, his marvellous vitality reasserted itself. That very Saturday night he addressed a crowded meeting in Ottawa. On Monday he took to the road again. And it was not until Saturday, February 19—three days before the election—that he reached Kingston, where he was once more a candidate, and finally came to rest.

VI

"After all the lies and abuse, your reward has come," the faithful Campbell wrote triumphantly on February 23. "I am fairly delighted, more I think than I felt in previous struggles. I hope Blake has a bad head-ache . . . and yourself again member for Kingston. Hurrah! Hurrah! Confound their politics, frustrate their knavish tricks!"[72] Part of their knavish tricks, Macdonald assured the Governor-General, was an unabashed reliance upon the vast organized patronage of the Grand Trunk Railway Company, and an even more deplorable acceptance, in Montreal alone, of nearly a hundred thousand dollars from the Chicago meat-packers, who had formerly controlled the Canadian market and who had evidently not taken Blake's promise about the tariff too literally.[73] Yet despite the foreigners and their gold, the "national" Canadian party had won. The old man's audacity had succeeded. "We fought with great odds against us," he wrote to G. T. Blackstock, "and would have been beaten if the elections had not been brought on when they were. With another session we were gone. I know many of our friends thought I was too bold, but boldness carried the day."[74]

It had indeed. The Conservatives, Macdonald predicted to the Governor-General, would have a majority of between thirty-five and forty when all the returns were in. This, of course, was too optimistic; but it was not a gross overestimate, and the early divisions in the first session of the new Parliament gave Macdonald majorities of thirty or slightly over. In Nova Scotia, Ontario, and Manitoba—the three "oppressed" provinces which were popularly supposed to be ripe for rebellion and secession—

the Conservatives had won; and in Quebec, despite all the efforts of Mercier and his Nationalists, they had done a little better than break even with their opponents. National unity had evidently not died on the Regina scaffold; the country was not going to split apart immediately in cultural and sectional fragments. Canadian politics—with minor changes, it was true—were apparently proceeding in their accustomed way. Things were surely as they always had been. And was not the re-election of John A. Macdonald for Kingston a significant proof of the fact?

And yet, despite this immediate and surprised sense of relief, there was something curiously unsatisfactory about the election of 1887. What, after all, had it decided? Had it done anything more than leave unsettled the question of Liberal leadership and the problem of the future programme of the Liberal party? Blake, who had now endured two defeats since he had succeeded Mackenzie, was obviously sunk deep in the gloom of disappointment and frustration; and towards the end of March he sent out a circular letter to his followers, proposing resignation from the leadership. Macdonald viewed this development with very mixed feelings. It was, of course, agreeable to have this public admission of Blake's chagrin; but, on the other hand, the prospect of Blake's retirement was definitely a disquieting one. "I hope he won't resign," he told Blackstock. "We could not have a weaker opponent than he." He had grown accustomed to Blake and Blake's little idiosyncrasies. He felt that he could go on beating Blake, every four or five years, until the end of the chapter. But a new Liberal leader was an unknown and highly unacceptable quantity. A new leader might quickly succeed in representing the vital opposition of the country far more completely and effectively than Blake had done.

In the meantime, while the Liberals were hesitating unhappily about their leader and their programme, the national dissatisfaction continued to assume different but no less dangerous forms. On March 16, in the speech from the throne which opened the new session of the Quebec legislature, Mercier announced that he intended soon to call a conference of the provinces and the Dominion to consider "their financial and other relations".

A few weeks later, on April 4, he wrote to Macdonald, drawing his attention to the announcement, and requesting "a confidential interview" on the subject.[75] This communication put Macdonald instantly on the alert. He did not like it. It seemed to him that in view of the fact that Mercier had formally made public his proposal, the time for "confidential interviews" had gone by; and, as for the proposed conference itself he viewed it from the first with the deepest suspicion. There was no provision in the constitution for such meetings and no necessity for them. Why should he negotiate with the provinces collectively rather than individually? Upon what grounds and for what reasons was this strange and unprecedented proposal being made?

He had only too much reason to question Mercier's good faith. He could not know, of course, that early in March Mercier had written to Mowat of Ontario, arguing strongly that "there should be an understanding between the provincial governments with a view to the organization of a system of common defence".[76] But he instinctively suspected that the conference would be nothing more or less than a league of malcontent provinces in organized opposition to the national policies and national leadership of the Dominion. Mercier, who owed his office to his abuse of the "hangmen" at Ottawa, was the self-confessed ringleader of this obvious conspiracy. Mowat, who had been fighting the exercise of Dominion disallowance for years, would probably be an eager partner in the alliance. Fielding, who had prudently hesitated in his campaign for secession as a result of the Conservative success in Nova Scotia in the federal general election, would no doubt gladly accept Mercier's conference as a convenient way out of his perplexities; and even Norquay, the unhappy Conservative Premier of Manitoba, who seemed to cling so desperately to office, might be driven, by the sheer weight of the anti-disallowance agitation in his province, into identifying himself with Mercier's league of discontent.

There was danger in the organization of this league. There was danger also in its basic assumption—hinted at in the Quebec speech from the throne—that Confederation was a compact which it was open to the contracting provinces to review and revise at their discretion. Macdonald replied with distant politeness to Mercier's first letter.[77] And when Mercier renewed his request, with effusive protestations of good will, Macdonald consented to an official, but not a confidential, interview.[78] This the Premier of Quebec declined; but it was plain that he intended, with or without Macdonald's co-operation, to go ahead with his project of an interprovincial conference.

No, the general election had not settled everything. It had certainly not settled everything in Macdonald's favour. He was aware of certain painful uncertainties in the political situation. He suspected that there might be lurking menaces ahead. But he had no intention of letting these possibilities intimidate him. It was spring now; and on April 13, the new Parliament met for its first session. He felt supported and comforted by its solid, manageable presence. Once again the people of Canada had sustained his government; and once again he had a comfortable majority at his back. He saw no reason at all why he should modify his conception of the rôle of the Dominion in national affairs, or alter the policies which he had devised for the nation's enlargement and integration. The Canadian voters had emphatically endorsed these policies. Why should he change them? The insurgent provinces might try to undermine the national economy, wreck the transcontinental railway, and dethrone the Dominion from its pre-eminence. But he would resist all this. They were *his* national policies. They were popular. And he would stand by them.

He could not stand by them, however, without a fight. Norquay, after a final unsuccessful visit to Ottawa, returned to Winnipeg and obviously abandoned all effort to support Dominion railway policy in the west. On April 19, he served blunt notice that Manitoba would submit no longer to federal interference with its railway legislation, and announced that a new railway, the Red River Valley Railway, from Winnipeg to the international boundary, would be built immediately by the province as a government work. The issue was now clearly and sharply joined. Inevitably it came up in Parliament, for one of the western members introduced a resolution for the deletion of the monopoly clause from the Canadian Pacific Railway charter; and inevitably Macdonald had to make a new declaration of government policy. The whole ugly business worried him. He began to discuss various possible concessions, including new Manitoba branch lines and lower freight rates, with Stephen. But he knew that at the moment he could not yield on the main point.

He defended the Canadian Pacific Railway as a great national undertaking, the axis of a transcontinental, east-west Canadian trading system, in which every province and every citizen had an interest, and which the Dominion was bound to protect and defend. "Every province," he told the Commons, "is interested in keeping that trade for ourselves, and no one knows better than the honourable gentleman opposite that the Pacific Railway charter would not have been granted, that the land would not have been given, that the money would not have been voted, and the loans would not have been made, if it had been understood by the representatives of the older provinces that the money was to be expended on an enterprise which might be bled at one hundred different points, so that by the time the traffic arrived at Montreal, it would be a miserable fragment of the magnificent stream of commerce that we had a right to expect to pass through Canada from one end to the other. . . . No; we are convinced our policy was right. We have confidence in it."[79]

He had a similar confidence in the national policy of protection. The national policy of protection, he reminded the Commons, had won an equal endorsation at the general election. There were, to be sure, increasingly disturbing signs, as spring went on, of a growing interest in complete free trade, or commercial union, with the United States. Even the Toronto *Mail* was showing a perverse interest in this new heresy. But the *Mail's* deviations from rectitude were now so numerous that they had ceased to be shocking. The paper had become a confirmed and incorrigible renegade; and Macdonald was already discussing arrangements for the establishment of a new and orthodox journal in Toronto.[80] He was not greatly impressed by the fashionable and no doubt ephemeral interest in commercial union with the United States; and the only changes which he contemplated in the protective system were changes which would round it out, strengthen it, and increase its popularity. Nova Scotia, under the tempter Fielding, had wandered away into error. Nova Scotia had been led back again into virtuous ways by Tupper at the last election. It was now the Dominion's opportunity to reward the province that had been lost, and then found, by a suitably generous treatment of her interests; and, on May 12, as the main innovation of his budget speech, Tupper proposed a scheme of substantially increased iron and steel duties.[81]

Macdonald's design was what it always had been. The country, with the Canadian Pacific Railway as its principal axis, was conceived commercially as an east-west trading system, protected mainly against competition from the south, and open at the Atlantic and Pacific coasts for the movement of men and goods and capital. The United States had always been the chief rival of this national organization; and England had been, and remained, its only great ally. Macdonald had always been deeply interested in the present and future form of the Anglo-Canadian alliance; but the imperial connection had only lately become fashionable in England; and it was not until 1887, the year of Queen Victoria's Golden Jubilee, that the British government decided to accord a new and formal recognition to the self-governing and dependent Empire. In 1887, the recently formed Imperial Federation League achieved its greatest triumph; and the Salisbury government invited representatives of the "auxiliary kingdoms" and Crown colonies of the Empire to assemble in London for a Colonial Conference. If it had been any time but the spring, Macdonald or Tupper would almost certainly have attended. But the Conference opened early in April, when the Canadian Parliament was just about to meet for the session; and it was utterly impossible for either the Prime Minister or the Minister of Finance to leave Ottawa. Alexander Campbell and Sandford Fleming, who had been the original government surveyor for the Canadian Pacific Railway, went instead. Macdonald was well aware of the fact that Fleming had had no political experience whatever and that Campbell had resigned from the ministry and was about to become Lieutenant-Governor of Ontario. He knew that they were very unlikely to act with any great initiative or energy at the Colonial Conference. He was not dissatisfied. He did not particularly want them to play a constructive part. With a country economically depressed, provinces apt for quarrelling or secession, a north-west rebellious and still half-empty, and an enormously costly railway barely completed, he was not in the mood for daring or expensive innovations. This, he considered, was definitely not a propitious moment for the working out of ambitious plans for imperial defence or imperial preferential trade; and in any case, as he had told the Royal Commission on the Defence of British Possessions and Commerce Abroad in 1880, he preferred separate arrangements between England and the individual colonies rather than a common system which bound them all. Campbell and Fleming were instructed, not to offer any new Canadian assistance to a general scheme of imperial defence, but to emphasize the contribution which Canada had already made in the assumption of new military burdens at home and in the unaided construction of the Canadian Pacific Railway. At the moment Canada still needed more help that she could possibly give. She needed it for the promotion of communications and trade on the Pacific. Above all she needed it for the defence of the North Atlantic fisheries.

As May slipped away, and Parliament adjourned for a brief spring recess, it was this final feature of Macdonald's national plan—protection against the United States—which occupied him most. A new fishing season was beginning; and, until an agreement with the United States was reached, every fishing season was full of potential trouble. But Macdonald faced the season of 1887 with much greater equanimity than he had that of 1886. His position was definitely stronger than it had been in the previous summer. During the winter months there had been some talk about a proposal of Bayard's which Lord Lansdowne found "one-sided and disingenuous" and which, he claimed, decided against Canada "all the debatable points and some which are not debatable at all".[82] Quite early in the discussions Macdonald briefly pronounced that most of Bayard's scheme was "altogether inadmissible", and there was never any real chance of its adoption.[83] No further concessions to the Americans had been made. The Fisheries Act of 1886 was law; British naval protection had been promised. In 1887 the defence of the fisheries would be stronger and more united than it had been since the Washington Treaty had been abrogated by the United States.

But defence, however concerted and successful, was not Macdonald's object. He did not want a permanent state of diplomatic friction any more than he wanted a permanent state of economic vassalage. He had always hoped for a sensible, satisfactory settlement of the fisheries dispute. He had always believed that a sensible, satisfactory settlement would be hastened if Canada only showed that she meant business about defending her property; and in the spring of 1887 the truth of this simple proposition seemed to be demonstrated. After two years, during which Bayard had "tried on" a variety of methods of settling the dispute, out of hand, in favour of the United States, the American Secretary of State finally made his first large conciliatory gesture. Through Erastus Wiman, a Canadian resident in the United States, who was soon to become notorious as an advocate of commercial union, he intimated that he would be glad to receive Macdonald or Tupper for the purpose of discussing Canadian-American relations. Macdonald accepted this indirect invitation readily enough. It was arranged that Tupper, under the guise of a holiday visit to the United States, should pay an informal call on Bayard in Washington.[84] A week after Tupper's return to Ottawa, a letter from the American Secretary of State seemed to clinch the prospect of a favourable settlement. "I am confident," Bayard wrote, "we both seek to attain a just and permanent settlement; and there is but one way to procure it—and that is by a straightforward treatment on a liberal and statesmanlike plan of the entire commercial relations of the two countries."[85]

VII

Macdonald had taken his stand. It was essentially the old ground—he saw no real reason to change it. And the question was not whether he would shift his position, but whether he could be dislodged from it. The opposition that session in Parliament was negligible; the Reformers were preoccupied with the distracting business of changing their leader. Early in June Blake finally resigned, and the Liberal and Conservative press joined in paying polite tributes to his services. The disgusted Stephen was infuriated by these respectful estimates of Blake's contribution to the national welfare. "He has done more harm to Canada ten times over than any man living," he raged, "and his record shows it."[86] Did it? Macdonald shook his head. Blake may have been politically malignant. But the record proved that he had been a singularly unsuccessful politician. Would his successor, the bookish, agreeable, and elegant Wilfrid Laurier, be any better? And would Laurier's elevation to the leadership mean any radical change in the essentially subtle and cautious policy which Blake had pursued?

On June 23, amid the festivities of Jubilee Week, Parliament was prorogued. For Macdonald there was no hope yet of an escape to the St. Lawrence. July, he knew, would have to be "sweltered out" in Ottawa. A somewhat ominous hush—the hush appropriate to anxious discussion and planning—descended upon the Liberal party. But, in the meantime, the air was loud with other ringing protests. Resistance to the Dominion and its national policies was continuing to develop outside Parliament and in virtual independence of the existing party system. In Ontario, Farmers' Institutes and Commercial Union Clubs were discussing economic partnership with the United States in a mood of growing enthusiasm; and out in Manitoba, Norquay, the renegade Conservative, was apparently preparing to carry out his provincial railway policy by main force. On July 2, in conscious defiance of the Dominion, he turned the first sod for the Red River Valley Railway. Macdonald was very angry. He determined to put a stop to these insolent proceedings at once. "Your bankrupt population at Winnipeg must be taught a lesson," he told Aikins severely, "even if some of them are brought down to trial at Toronto for sedition."[87] Peremptorily he ordered the Lieutenant-Governor to send down the offending statutes at "the first convenient opportunity"; and on July 16 the Red River Valley Railway Act was disallowed.[88]

He had, he told Aikins, no fear at all of the consequences of this uncompromising policy. But in his heart he thought differently. There was, of course, no doubt at all about the criminal lunacy of Manitoba's conduct. "When you reflect," he expostulated to John Rose, "on a legislature of thirty-five members, with a population of one hundred and ten thousand, coolly devoting a million of dollars to build a railway from Winnipeg to the frontier, between two lines owned by the C.P.R., running in the same direction, one on the east and the other on the west side of the Red River, when there is not business enough for one of the two existing lines, you can understand the recklessness of that body."[89] It was almost incredible! Nobody seemed to have the faintest sense of responsibility! Norquay was acting at least partly in self-interest; the motives of the Liberal politicians and railway speculators who were egging him on were obviously suspect; and the whole insane enterprise would very probably end in the bankruptcy of the province. Manitoba might fall. But, if she did, she would drag others down with her. Already the Canadian north-west, Canadian railways, and Canadian credit were plunging down again into ruinous disrepute. Lansdowne was gravely worried for the future. Stephen, sick at heart with the renewed and sharp decline of Canadian Pacific stock, had come to the conclusion that the monopoly clause was not worth the appalling price he had to pay for it.

When, late in July, Macdonald left for a holiday in New Brunswick, the Manitoba agitation was at its height. When he returned to Ottawa early in September, its shrill excited intensity had not diminished in the slightest. He could see no pleasant prospect anywhere. Stephen was bemoaning the fact that the drop in Canadian Pacific stock had cost the shareholders nearly twenty million dollars. The opposition newspapers—now including the *Mail*—were doing their best to whip up an interest in Mercier's approaching interprovincial conference; and there could be no doubt that the popularity of commercial union with the United States had been steadily rising all summer. The only really satisfactory intelligence that reached Macdonald during August was the news from England that Tupper's unofficial visit to the United States had resulted in an agreement to appoint a new Joint High Commission for the settlement of the outstanding Canadian-American disputes. Even the gratification produced by this announcement was qualified immediately and sharply by the darkest misgivings. Another conference at Washington! Was Canada once again to be laid as a burnt offering on the altar of Anglo-American friendship?

He was instantly on the defensive. He kept putting a long series of searching questions to the Governor-General and himself.[90] Who was to represent Canada at Washington? If he did not go himself, could the "impulsive" Tupper be trusted to act alone? Was it not probable that Joseph Chamberlain, who had been announced as the principal British Commissioner, would act in accordance with Liberal anti-colonial theories and would be ambitiously eager to get back to England as quickly as possible with a treaty in his pocket? Would the terms of reference include commercial relations as well as Atlantic and Pacific fisheries? And would the Commission be empowered to settle the controversy over Bering Sea, where the United States had been busily seizing Canadian sealing vessels as if the open ocean were a private American lake?

Obviously the powers of the Commission were the vital feature of the arrangement. Macdonald wanted them to be as wide and as explicit as possible; and when, towards the end of September, he first saw the terms of reference, he was disappointed and annoyed both by their limitations and their vagueness. "'Dolus latet in generalibus'," he wrote to the Governor-General, "and the whole thing seems to be a snare laid by the United States government to entrap England into a commission to consider the expediency of relaxing the terms of the Convention of 1818. This has long been their aim and, as it is the Magna Carta of the Maritime Provinces, must be resisted. You may think me too suspicious, but I have a lively recollection of the manner in which the United States Commissioners in 1871 at Washington, after getting the article settled respecting the *Alabama* claims, coolly refused to consider Canada's claim for Fenian invasions and outrages, on the ground that they were not authorized by their government."[91]

As October drew on, it became clear that the uncertainties of the last six months were ending. The time for expectation and apprehension was over: the time for action had come. On October 13, the Cabinet decided that Tupper would be Canada's representative at the Washington Conference and that Thompson would act as his legal assistant. "So that matter may be considered as settled," Macdonald wrote to Lord Lansdowne.[92] Once again, for the second time since Confederation, he had to face a crucially important diplomatic encounter with the United States; and at the same embarrassing moment, almost as if their movements had been deliberately timed, his domestic opponents emerged from cover to renew their attacks. On October 12, in a speech to his constituents at Ingersoll, Sir Richard Cartwright, who, since Blake's retirement from the leadership, had become the principal Liberal leader in Ontario, committed himself unequivocally to the support of commercial union with the United States;[93] and on October 20, Honoré Mercier welcomed the delegates to the interprovincial conference at Quebec.

Chapter Fourteen

The Renewal of Cultural Conflict

I

During the autumn of 1887 the newspaper attack against Macdonald's national design reached a harsh crescendo of intensity. Never before had there been such a heavy bombardment of his whole position; never before had the bombardment been sustained by so many thundering pieces of journalistic artillery. In French-speaking Canada and the Maritime Provinces, the principal newspapers had largely gone over to the opposition. In English-speaking Quebec, the Montreal *Gazette* maintained a stout defence virtually alone; and in Toronto, the capital of the "banner" province of the Dominion, the two most popular and most frequently quoted newspapers, the *Globe* and the *Mail*, had now united in opposition to everything for which Macdonald stood. In desperation, the Conservatives had decided that a new ministerial paper, the *Empire*, must be founded in Toronto; but the response to an appeal for financial support was at first so unsatisfactory that for a while Macdonald considered the still more desperate expedient of a new attempt to propitiate the *Mail*. Dalton McCarthy would have nothing to do with this proposal. "No," he wrote firmly to Macdonald, "we must start the *Empire* or prepare for defeat at the next general election —if not before that."[1]

In the meantime, the chorus of denunciation grew more shrill and sustained. The attack was now directed, not merely against this or that national policy, but against the whole conception of a separate Canadian nationality in the North American continent. Every disappointment, every misfortune, every evidence of cultural division and religious antagonism was carefully enumerated in one long, comprehensive indictment of Confederation. "Our enormous debt," the *Mail* began its portentous list, "the determination of the people of the north-west to break loose from trade and transportation restrictions in defiance of the federal authority; the exodus of population from the north-west and the far larger stream pouring out of the older provinces; the threats of secession heard in the three Maritime Provinces; the decline in our exports which are less today by five dollars per head of population than they were in 1873, although since then we have spent no less than one hundred and twenty millions of borrowed money in developing our resources; the gathering of the local premiers at Quebec to devise ways and means of allaying provincial discontent and averting provincial bankruptcy—these, to go no further, are phenomena, which, if they presented themselves in any other country, young or old, we should regard as the forerunners of dissolution."[2]

Approaching dissolution had become the main theme of the opposition press; but not of the opposition press alone. The prophecies were uniformly gloomy, the desperate significance of the existing state of affairs was emphasized by all. "It is not improbable," wrote the editor of the Montreal *Gazette*, "that the people will, sooner than many now imagine, be called on to determine whether the work accomplished in 1867 is to be undone, whether the Confederation is to be preserved or allowed to lapse into its original fragments, preparatory to absorption into the United States. The signs of the times point to the imminence of so momentous an issue."[3] The signs of the times seemed to make clear that the hour of decision was close at hand. Gloom and doubt and consciousness of failure were widespread. The air was full of a sense of impending crisis. Was it not better, argued many, to cut the national losses and to admit that the whole attempt to found a transcontinental Canadian economy had been a gigantic mistake?

It was in this despairing atmosphere that the interprovincial conference met. The circumstances of the moment gave a sinister significance to its declared purpose of amending the

British North America Act. Macdonald did not underestimate the potential danger of the conference, for he had good reason not to underrate the power of the provincial governments. In the last two decades, he had seen them become something very different from the glorified county councils which he had expected after the union. Provincial governments had grown greatly in constitutional authority, in political influence and prestige. Provincial loyalties seemed to have remained steadfast, while truly national sentiments had apparently declined in strength. Finally—and this was, perhaps, the most important point of all—some of the provinces had acquired a territorial extent and a physical power which utterly invalidated the picture which he had drawn tentatively at Confederation of the future map of British North America. He had, in all probability, looked forward to the emergence of a number of provinces, not too large and not dissimilar in size and consequence. But in the past ten years this dream of relative territorial equality had been completely shattered by the triumphant expansion of Ontario and Quebec. The final settlement of the north-western boundary of Ontario had not yet been affected by the imperial Parliament. But the enlargement was inevitable now; and, as Macdonald pointed out to Campbell, it was obvious that if Ontario were to extend as far north as Hudson Bay, so must Quebec.

"Now if you will look at the map," he continued earnestly, "and see the enormous extent of country proposed to be added to the two provinces, you will see what vast preponderance it gives them over the other provinces in the Dominion. History will repeat itself and posterity will find out that the evils that exist in other federations from the preponderance of one or more members will again happen. It is our duty as founders of a nation to look far into the future. I know it will be said that the additional territory desired by Ontario and Quebec is inhospitable in climate and ill adapted for settlement, but we used to hear the same thing of the Red River country and the north-west. I have little doubt that a great portion of the vast region asked for by the two provinces will be capable of receiving and will receive a large population."[4] The two central provinces

would become empire provinces—powerful metropolitan governments with enormous hinterlands. And Quebec, with a population of millions owing allegiance to its special customs, might
prove a barrier fatal to national unity. "I look to the future in
this matter . . .," Macdonald repeated, "farther ahead perhaps
than I should. But are we not founding a nation? Now just
consider for yourself—what a country of millions lying between
English Canada and the Atlantic will be. I have no objections
to the French as French or as Catholics, but the block caused
by the introduction of French law and the Civil Code would
be very great."[5]

He had looked into the future farther perhaps than anybody.
He had tried, with every ounce of his strength and every device
at his command, to sustain the national interest. Repeatedly he
had had to give way. The long series of engagements which
he had fought with provincial governments in the 1880's had
resulted in as many losses and draws as wins. He had had to
yield to Ontario. He was beginning to suspect that he might
have to yield to Manitoba as well. The whole difficult and
ungrateful effort to preserve the east-west transport system
from the damage which Manitoba seemed determined to inflict
upon it was breaking against Manitoba's unreasoning, almost
maniacal resistance. It was not, of course, that Norquay had
succeeded in his insane design of building a third railway from
Winnipeg to the international border. He had utterly failed
to obtain capital; and the scheme had collapsed in angry frustration for at least a season. "Norquay," Macdonald wrote wearily
to Lieutenant-Governor Aikins, "seems to have run himself
quite aground in his selfish eagerness to retain his place."[6]
But Norquay could not retain his place, Macdonald knew. He
was sinking, and sinking fast. The trouble was that he would
not sink alone.

In all probability, the Manitoba government and the Manitoba Conservative party would be dragged down with him.
He had discredited the north-west, frightened away the immigrants and capital that were necessary for its development, and
brought the Canadian Pacific Railway staggering to its knees.
"Your railway development," Macdonald declared emphatically

—·—✳GRIP✳—·—

PROVINCIAL RIGHT IS FEDERAL WRONG.

Sir John—How dare you fellows meet to conspire against ME?
Mowat—Pardon me, we met simply to take measures to preserve the rights of the provinces.
Sir John—Just so! That's what I say. It's the same thing, you little tyrant!

to a correspondent in Winnipeg, "has been paralysed and the C.P.R. prevented from getting the means to build the branches which it was their interest and their desire to build in order to bring the necessary traffic to their main line. . . . Now so great is the distrust in England as to your future that not a pound, not a cent, can be got on pledge of land grants to railways."[7] A year ago the company's common stock had been selling at the proud sum of seventy-five dollars a share; at the end of September it was quoted at a new low of forty-nine and a half. "Yesterday's advices from England about the position of the C.P.R. securities are most discouraging," Stephen wrote to Macdonald on October 4. "Barings are annoyed beyond endurance by anxious inquiries, and between one thing and another I am nearly off my head."[8] The monopoly clause, Stephen was now nearly convinced, must be given up. But he was determined not to surrender it cheaply. And Macdonald began to realize that once again, after an interval of only three years, he might have to ask the Canadian Parliament and the Canadian people to make another large concession to the Canadian Pacific Railway.

Unquestionably there were places where he would have to yield. He had given in to individual provinces before now; he would very possibly have to give in to individual provinces again. But an organized conspiracy of provincial governments was a different, and a much more scandalous, affair; and to such a conspiracy he refused to surrender. He would simply decline to recognize the interprovincial conference; he would not, by the slightest sign, admit its existence. And such a defence, though it might seem weak and ineffectual at the moment, could in the end prove completely devastating. Up to this moment, the provincial premiers had had everything their own way. They had met, to the accompaniment of a fanfare of opposition trumpets, on October 20. They had strutted about the centre of the stage in a bright spotlight of publicity, laying down general principles, formulating resolutions, and talking, with interminable volubility, about their virtues and their woes. They had abolished the federal power of disallowance, reformed the Senate in the interest of the provinces, and voted

THE OLD CHIEFTAIN [1887

themselves a large increase in the subsidies payable by the Dominion. They had done all this with a bustling, self-important, consequential air which temporarily obscured some inconvenient but highly important facts about their conference. The Dominion, of course, had not been represented: British Columbia and Prince Edward Island had neither of them put in an appearance. The interprovincial conference was not a meeting of all the governments—nor even of all the provincial governments—of Canada. Constitutionally, it was nothing.

Herein lay the masterly effectiveness of Macdonald's uncooperative silence. In the absence of support from the Dominion, what were the five malcontent provinces to do with their precious resolutions? Upon what grounds, failing the adhesion of British Columbia and Prince Edward Island, could they demand a change in the established procedure for the amendment of the British North America Act? Since Confederation the imperial Parliament had enacted amendments only at the joint request of the Senate and the House of Commons of Canada; and, obviously, so long as Macdonald and the Conservatives retained control of the two houses, no joint request for the incredible amendments proposed by the interprovincial conference would ever be sent. It was as simple as that. Macdonald waited imperturbably within the impregnable wall of his defences. It would need a revolution to destroy them. And would the Quebec Conference—this Grit caucus, this conspiracy of the discontented five—ever have the stomach to begin a real revolution? Macdonald smiled sardonically. He did not believe it.

II

In the meantime, while he waited for the provincial premiers to make the next move, he busied himself with still another section of the defence of his national system. Relations with the United States had obviously entered a most critical phase. The Joint High Commission was about to meet in Washington; and all autumn commercial union or unrestricted reciprocity with the republic had been apparently winning a great army of supporters. Unrestricted reciprocity, which was distinguishable from commercial union only by much pretentious hair-splitting, and which, like commercial union, threatened Canadian fiscal autonomy and political independence, was in fundamental opposition to Macdonald's whole conception of a separate Canadian nationality in North America. Its dangerous political implications must certainly be exposed. But at the same time it must be admitted that there lay back of it a legitimate and important aspiration, which was the natural desire of Canadians for reasonably good trade relations with the United States. Could he satisfy that aspiration? In the light of Bayard's promising letter to Tupper, was there not a real chance that it might be satisfied in the approaching negotiations at Washington?

Macdonald looked forward to the meeting of the Washington Conference with a curious mixture of eagerness and apprehension. He had worked for this conference for nearly three years. But now that it was about to assemble, he was full once more of suspicion and disquietude. He could not help but be deeply, incurably sceptical about all Anglo-American negotiations in which Canada was involved. He hardly dared to permit himself to hope for good results. And yet, on the face of it, the omens seemed undeniably favourable. The Cleveland administration appeared genuinely eager for a broad trade agreement between the two countries. Tupper, who had spent a week-end with Chamberlain talking over the Canadian case, reported that he was much pleased with the British Commissioner, and that he thought Canada had been "fortunate in his selection".[9] Thompson, who was immensely learned on the subject of the fisheries, had been placed in charge of the legal aspect of the negotiations, as principal expert adviser. Macdonald at first told the Governor-General bluntly that he hoped "no legal man will come out from England"; and when Lord Lansdowne mildly protested, Macdonald replied that Canada could have no objection to an English counsel accompanying Chamberlain, provided he kept to a properly subordinate rôle. "I want to guard against the legal conduct of matters being taken out of Thompson's hands," he wrote frankly to the Governor-General.[10] Thompson must be in control. And how strange and wonderful was the contrast between Thompson's acknowledged pre-eminence and the dubious and embarrassed status of the representatives of the Department of Marine and Fisheries whom Macdonald had had the effrontery to bring with him to Washington in 1871!

He was certainly less apprehensive than he had been in 1871. He said good-bye to Tupper almost confidently on November 15. But doubts—unpleasant, irrepressible doubts—still lingered. He had seen too many demonstrations of what he called roundly "the faithlessness of the American government". "There is no fair dealing to be expected from them," he declared emphatically to the Governor-General.[11] And within a few days—within a time so short that the event may have anticipated even his gloomiest predictions—the truth of this generalization seemed to be borne out once again. Tupper's first letters from Washington were disconcerting in the extreme. It was not, Macdonald noted gratefully, that there was any sign whatever of a break in the solidarity of the British delegation. Tupper reported that "our party is working most harmoniously and pleasantly" and that "nothing could be more satisfactory than the manner in which Mr. Chamberlain sustained our position".[12] No, thank God, the trouble was not here! The trouble was with the Americans who were conforming, in an absurdly literal way, to their reputed standard of behaviour. They had given every indication of desiring a generous trade agreement. Their Secretary of State, Bayard, had informed Tupper that, in his opinion, a satisfactory settlement of Canadian-American difficulties could be reached only through a straightforward and liberal treatment of "the entire commercial relations of the two countries". Yet now, and at the very first official meeting of the Joint High Commission, the American plenipotentiaries flatly announced that the terms of reference did not include commercial or tariff questions and that the work of the conference must be limited to the question of the proper interpretation of the Convention of 1818.

Macdonald was exasperated, extremely disappointed, but not really surprised. "All our prognostications as to the course of the United States government are more than verified," he wrote disgustedly to Lord Lansdowne, "and Mr. Bayard does not come out of it in a very creditable manner."[18] He had, of course, some sympathy for the Secretary of State's position. "I have little doubt," he remarked in a letter to Tupper, "that both he and the President were sincere at first in their desire to extend trade relations with Canada, but they feel Congress is not with them, and they wish now to avoid a second snub from the Senate."[14] The Americans, he thought, were endeavouring to extricate themselves from these political difficulties by humiliating disavowals of their past professions; and at the same time they were evidently quite prepared to use the hostility of the Senate in order to extract concessions from Canada at no expense to the United States. "The manner in which Bayard attempts to set aside his letter to you," he wrote to Tupper indignantly, "is most disingenuous. His letter should be read, not only according to its plain meaning, but also by the light thrown on it by the previous negotiations for a commission." The whole purpose of the conference, for which England and Canada had now been pressing for nearly three years, was a broad consideration of the commercial relations of the two countries. But at the last moment, and with fatal results, England had characteristically put her trust in the general declarations of a gentleman's agreement. "It is a pity," Macdonald lamented to Lord Lansdowne, "that Her Majesty's government wouldn't listen to our request to have the question of commercial intercourse specially mentioned as a subject of reference in the agreement for a conference. At present it would appear that we have fallen into a trap set for us by the United States and are now forced to enter into a discussion confined to the subject of the meaning of the Convention of 1818."[15]

This, it appeared, was exactly what the American plenipotentiaries had in view. They professed themselves to be uninterested in the privilege of fishing inside the Canadian three-mile limit. The Canadian inshore fisheries, they explained, had ceased to be of any great value to American fishermen, and what they wanted, as a support for their deep-sea fishery, were the privileges which the Canadians claimed were denied by the Convention of 1818—the privileges of buying bait, ice, and other supplies, and of transhipping fish in Canadian Atlantic ports.

Would it be possible for Canada to grant these privileges, provided the American fishing vessels took out licences for the
purpose, and provided the licences were paid for, either by fees
imposed on the vessels themselves, or by the free admission
of Canadian fish into the American market? Tupper believed
that this would be a wise arrangement to make. He drafted an
alternative proposal—a bad second-best to his original offer—
along these lines; and on December 7 he telegraphed to Macdonald for permission to submit it to the conference.

Macdonald felt extremely uncertain. For a fortnight now,
with increasing annoyance and disgust, he had been coping
with the spate of letters and telegrams from Washington. "I
am chained by the leg here just now," he wrote to his sister
Louisa, who had been pleading with him to pay a visit to
Kingston, "and cannot leave town for a moment, as the negotiations with Washington are going on and I am receiving cypher
messages hourly which require immediate answer."[16] Tupper's
request required an answer—an answer given soon, if not immediately. What was he to say to it? He hardly knew. The blunt
disconcerting diplomatic manœuvres at Washington had left
him with a profound feeling of discouragement. There was no
hope now of tariff concessions in the American market. He
would have no means of quieting the general economic unrest
which, for the moment, seemed to have been captured so completely for the commercial union movement. Tupper's proposal
aroused no enthusiasm whatever. The Governor-General was
critical of it; the ministers differed widely in their opinion of
it.[17] On December 8, after a prolonged discussion, the Cabinet
divided against it, five to four.[18]

But could he risk a complete break-up of the Conference
thus early in the proceedings? What did the British plenipotentiaries think of the proposed offer? Above all, did the Canadian
Cabinet ministers now in Washington, Tupper, Thompson,
and Foster, concur in its presentation? "Do you three agree to
proposal?"[19] he telegraphed to Tupper late on December 8.
Tupper's reply was definite and reassuring. "All three plenipotentiaries and Minister of Justice and Foster concur in the
proposal," he answered briefly. The addition of these three

names converted the narrow majority against the offer into a slightly larger majority in its favour; and on December 10, after another long discussion, the Cabinet reluctantly decided in favour of the plan.[20] The Governor-General agreed that his government could not take the responsibility of letting the negotiations fail at this stage;[21] and on December 10 Macdonald finally telegraphed to Tupper authorizing the submission of the proposal. He was at once dissatisfied and apprehensive. "The greatest care should be taken in the draft of your offer," he warned Tupper. "As you know they will make the most ungenerous use of any omission or careless expression."[22] He feared the textual chicanery of the Americans. He was worried about the reception which the Canadians would certainly give to such a niggardly settlement of the fisheries dispute. It was therefore with a real sense of relief that on the night of December 10 he received an unexpected telegram from Tupper, informing him that the Conference had adjourned for the Christmas holidays, that Chamberlain would stay a further few days in Washington for private discussions with Bayard, and would then come up to Ottawa.[23]

III

In the brief holiday interval, Macdonald had time for an anxious casting-up of the national accounts. Canada incorporated was by no means bankrupt yet; there were even a few encouraging items to be put down on the credit side of the ledger. But these were balanced by equally serious losses; and, on the whole, his position was no better than it had been in the early autumn. There was now not the faintest hope of a popular trade agreement with the United States. There was, on the other hand, every expectation of renewed trouble with the disgruntled provinces. He had no means of knowing what moves those adroit players Mowat and Mercier had in contemplation; but it was certain now, at any rate, that the game was up in the west and that the long effort to maintain a Conservative interest in Manitoba had ended in failure. Norquay, having staggered on blindly and ineffectually for so many years, finally resigned office a few days before Christmas; and although his successor, Harrison, was a Conservative, it was plain that the new government was an extremely feeble one, and that Greenway and the Liberals were certain to gain power in short order. The western attack upon Macdonald's national policy would now be directed by a new and vigorous leader, a leader uninhibited by past pledges and old political sympathies; and every effort would be made to press it home to success.

But even this was not all. The Liberal leaders were obviously continuing their absorbed, their positively fascinated contemplation of the political possibilities of commercial union or unrestricted reciprocity. Macdonald's best defence against it had now gone. He had little hope of quieting the agitation with a good trade treaty with the United States.

But, on the other hand, if the legitimate commercial aspirations back of the movement could not be satisfied, its dangerous political implications were certainly being exposed, and realized, much more fully than before. The *Empire*, the new Conservative Toronto newspaper which finally made its appearance towards the end of December, began a sustained attack on North American continentalism; and on December 30, in a speech before the Toronto Board of Trade, Joseph Chamberlain frankly assured his audience that a North American customs union would instantly compromise Canada's fiscal freedom and might pave the way for the loss of its political independence.[24] Chamberlain, Macdonald predicted gaily to Tupper, could be elected in the most Tory constituency in Canada! The whole country, he felt certain, had connected commercial union inextricably with annexation and was prepared to repudiate both. "All the federal elections," he informed Tupper complacently—too complacently, "have gone against commercial union. . . . Leading men of the opposition like Alexander Mackenzie, James Young, and John Macdonald of Toronto, and Edgar, Blake's *fidus Achates*, have denounced commercial union. The rural press of Ontario on both sides oppose it. Commercial union is a dead duck, and I think Lord Lansdowne sees now that my policy, as announced to him last spring, of allowing the cry of commercial union to blaze, crackle, and go out with a stink, without giving it undue importance, was a wise one."[25]

On the whole, his reflections, though mixed, were not more depressing than they had been. The holiday season was a pleasantly restful one. Chamberlain came up to Ottawa and there were official dinners and some long discussions of the fisheries question; but for a good part of the time he remained agreeably settled at Earnscliffe. For the first time in years, nearly all the members of his family were collected about him. Agnes, who had been west again on a visit, had brought his grand-daughter, Daisy, back with her;[26] and Hugh, who had been ill and out of sorts in the early autumn, returned to spend Christmas at Earnscliffe. It was pleasant to have the quiet, sombre house full of people and gay with children's talk; but though he loved to have the children and grandchildren about him, their presence did not make him forget his own generation. One day late in December, he and Agnes and Hugh went up to Kingston in the *Jamaica* to see Louisa. For years Louisa had been an invalid, whose hospitable instincts were excited to frenzy by the mere suggestion of a visit of her relatives. "*Now mind*," Macdonald warned her with mock severity, "if you make any attempt to provide beds for us we will turn round and return at once to Ottawa."[27] They spent the day with her, and in the evening they all went over to visit Aunt Maria Macpherson. Macdonald thought his sister looked very frail; but her courage and good spirits were as indomitable as ever.[28]

In the meantime, the second Canadian plan for the settlement of the fisheries dispute was being gradually worked out in detail. It was a comprehensive proposal which, among other things, included arrangements for a final decision of the vexed question of what bays were included in Canadian territorial waters. Its principal feature was a provision that American fishing vessels, on obtaining licences, could enter Canadian ports to buy supplies and tranship fish, and that these licences would either be issued at a substantial tonnage fee, or would be free so long as the United States repealed the duty on Canadian fish. The scheme left Macdonald coldly unenthusiastic. He considered fees for licences a troublesome, inadequate, and unpopular return for the Canadian concessions. "I would suggest," he argued to Tupper, "that if the Americans agree to a licence system at all it should be provided that licences should be issued free so soon as by treaty or tariffs we have free fish, and not before, and that the licence system should cease whenever any duties are re-imposed. . . . The Americans would pride themselves on their cleverness in getting a surrender of our claims on the bait question in such a manner that we could not terminate it, and then please the fishermen by re-imposing the duty on fish."[29] A free market for Canadian fish—the last vestige of his original idea of a trade treaty—was the only thing that really interested him. And he was reconciled to licence fees only because Chamberlain repeatedly assured him that they were a necessary part of a final settlement to which he had secured Cleveland's and Bayard's informal approval in advance.

The opening of Parliament had been set for February 23. "The fate of the conference," Macdonald wrote confidently to Lord Lansdowne, "will be determined long before this. The points for discussion are so few that they will be disposed of in a fortnight and the results, if they amount to a treaty, will at once be laid before the Senate."[30] It was, for Macdonald, a curiously naïve assumption. The State Department of the United States still had enlightening experiences in store for him, as well as for Tupper, Chamberlain, and Thompson. On January 9, the day on which the conference reconvened, the Anglo-Canadian delegates presented the proposal for which, they imagined, American approval had been secured in advance. But instead of a ready and gratified acceptance, there were unexpected requests for adjournments. The adjournments became prolonged delays; and the delays were followed by critical and inconclusive answers. The angry climax of the British delegation's bewilderment came when Bayard objected that the Canadian proposal was defective in that it did not give American fishing vessels the privilege of fishing in Canadian territorial waters. At this abrupt resurrection of a claim which the American plenipotentiaries had repeatedly and emphatically declared they had no intention of making, the burly Tupper exploded.

Chamberlain, he reported to Macdonald, was "wildly indig-nant".[31] The leader of the British delegation had come to the angry conclusion that the American plenipotentiaries were "a lot of dishonest tricksters". "I am afraid," Thompson wrote sardonically to his wife, "nothing will come of our mission but the board bills. These Yankee politicians are the lowest race of thieves in existence."[32]

Macdonald accepted this second revelation much more equably than did the furious diplomatists in Washington. He had been disillusioned by the whole wretched business. The treaty—if a treaty were ever signed—would be of almost no value to Canada and would bring no prestige to the Canadian government. He did not much care whether an agreement was reached or not; but since Canada had been manœuvred into such restricted and unfavourable ground, he was determined to dispute every remaining inch of the way. "I think the Americans are merely bargaining like costermongers,"[33] he wrote to Lord Lansdowne on February 1. He resolved to be equally tenacious. The conference, after its first salutary explosion of temper, settled down into an extremely suspicious, close-fisted examina-tion of the Canadian draft treaty, and of its much abbreviated version, the *modus vivendi*, which dealt merely with the com-mercial privileges of American fishing vessels in Canadian ports.

Virtually nothing else was discussed. Macdonald was not anxious to hasten the settlement of the Alaskan boundary.[34] Neither were the Americans. And when Tupper and Chamber-lain brought up the question of the American seizures of Canadian sealing vessels in Bering Sea, the American pleni-potentiaries, in exact imitation of their predecessors when con-fronted by the Fenian claims, replied very firmly that the Bering Sea matter was not within their terms of reference. There was nothing to do but talk of the North Atlantic fisheries —of fish, fishing vessels, fishing licences, fishing supplies, and tariffs on fish. For another ten days the mean, trivial argument continued, and then it drew sluggishly to a close. ". . . You will see that we are to have a treaty," Macdonald wrote unen-thusiastically to the Governor-General.[35] On February 15, the much-debated document was signed. On February 20, it was transmitted, with a letter of recommendation, by President Cleveland to the American Senate.

Three days later, the second session of the sixth Parliament of Canada opened at Ottawa.

IV

"I hope that you three will be able to return soon to prepare for Parliament," Macdonald wrote to Tupper on February 6. "We are quite at a standstill about legislation. I don't know what to put into the speech from the throne."[36] Two days before the opening he was still apparently undecided, for on February 21 he wrote to Lord Lansdowne, promising to settle the topics of "the speech" that afternoon and to send the draft over the next day.[37] His embarrassments and uncertainties were real, and curiously revealing. He had half a dozen subsidiary projects, most of them postponed and far from completion, by which he hoped to extend and develop the main lines of his programme. But the main lines of his programme had been laid down long before this. His most creative period as a legislator was over. All he could do—if he could do that—was to save an achievement threatened by adverse economic circumstances and fanatical human attacks. All he could do was to hang on, in the hope of better times, in the hope that his efforts would be finally justified by success. He had lost the initiative. And the initiative had been ruthlessly grasped by much more extreme and violent men. These new men were beginning to appear in federal politics. They were already very prominent in provincial affairs.

The five provincial conspirators who had met at Quebec had spent a part of the winter in glorifying the new "Quebec Resolutions" to their respective legislatures. Mowat was perhaps the most formidable member of the gang, Mercier the most sinister, and Greenway, who had replaced the luckless Norquay, would in all probability prove to be the most obstreperous. "He is so thoroughly unprincipled," Macdonald wrote of Greenway to one of his supporters in Manitoba, "that he would be sure to play a game similar to that of Norquay and be quite regardless

GRIP

SIR JOHN'S DELICATE SITUATION.

Greenway.—Drop your Disallowance Policy in Manitoba or——!!!
Stephen (C.P.R.)—Don't drop your Disallowance Policy in Manitoba or——!!!

of the evil consequences of the agitation on the Province so long as he is able to retain office."[88] It was quite certain that Greenway would quickly signalize his elevation to power by a violent effort to end the Canadian Pacific monopoly. What was the Dominion government to do? Macdonald was embarrassed by Tupper's unguarded promise, made several years ago in the House, that the monopoly would be surrendered as soon as the road was finished. He was still more embarrassed by his knowledge of the evil effects which the Manitoba agitation was having upon the Canadian Pacific, the Canadian west, and the Canadian government. But there was only one way in which the monopoly could be ended. He would have to make a financial agreement with the Canadian Pacific Railway Company—an agreement which, in the end, would probably not cost the country a copper but which, at the moment, might be very unpopular politically. Could he risk it? He decided that he would have to take the chance. And in the week before the opening of Parliament he sat down with J. H. Pope and George Stephen to work out an arrangement.

It was at this point that Thomas Greenway, accompanied by his Attorney-General, Joseph Martin, descended upon Ottawa to effect the economic liberation of his province. Greenway's arrival, which occurred early in March, could hardly have been more unfortunately timed. Macdonald and the Canadian Pacific officials had not yet by any means reached an agreement. Stephen demanded a Dominion guarantee of the principal and interest, at four per cent, of a bond issue of twenty-two and a half million dollars, based on the unsold lands of the company. Macdonald was convinced that the country could not support an issue of more than fifteen millions. The lands, he thought, must be valued at one dollar rather than a dollar and fifty cents an acre; and he and Pope and Tupper were determined that the guarantee should cover interest only, not principal, and that the rate would not be higher than three and a half per cent. Laboriously, through a series of lengthy conferences, they were working their way towards a settlement along these lines.[89] They were making progress; but unfortunately the rate of progress was not rapid enough to please the impatiently waiting Thomas Greenway.

A theatrical diplomatist, with a relish for stormy exits, Green-way suddenly and ostentatiously left Ottawa for Toronto. "I regret your hasty departure," Macdonald patiently telegraphed to him at the Queen's Hotel. "Matters making as rapid progress as possible. I hope you will return and stay for a few days. Please answer."[40] Greenway magnanimously answered. And after the receipt, by telegraph, of a further instalment of Macdonald's regrets and assurances, he still more magnanimously returned to Ottawa.[41] But he let it be known that he was in no mood to tolerate shilly-shallying; and when, on March 30, it was learnt that his departure could not be postponed much longer, Macdonald wrote a semi-official letter, informing him that there was "a good prospect of legislation by the federal Parliament during this session which will almost if not entirely remove the reasons for the exercise of disallowance" against Manitoba railway charters.[42] This was a guarded assurance; but even so, it anticipated the solution of Macdonald's difficul-ties. On the very day it was sent, Stephen telegraphed from Montreal that he must ask for more time for consideration. In the end, however, his resistance was overcome; and on April 26, Langevin rose to introduce the measure which granted the government guarantee in exchange for the surrender of clause fifteen of the Canadian Pacific Railway charter.

In the meantime, while a provincial Premier was breaking through the defences of the all-Canadian transport system, two different sets of extremists, utterly opposed in character, were beginning an attack on the national policy of protection. The agitation for commercial union had not blazed, crackled, and gone out with a stink. On the contrary, the Reform caucus, at the opening of the Parliamentary session, decided to adopt unrestricted reciprocity as the official trade policy of the party; and on March 14, Sir Richard Cartwright, the "Blue Ruin Knight" as the Conservatives loved to call him, moved in the House for "the largest possible freedom of commercial inter-course" between Canada and the United States in all the manu-factures and natural products of both countries.[43] The manage-ment of the Liberal party had passed out of the control of sober nationalists like Blake and Mackenzie and into the hands of adventurous opportunists such as Cartwright and the inexperienced Laurier. Moreover—and this, to Macdonald, was not the least important consequence of the new Liberal programme —one form of politico-economic extremism inevitably provoked another. Commercial union and unrestricted reciprocity, with their obvious threat to Canadian autonomy, naturally forced people back upon the support of England and the Anglo-Canadian alliance. North American continentalism found its logical opposite in British imperialism; and Richard Cartwright, the renegade Tory who had been so strangely transformed into a continental unionist, was now confronted by Dalton McCarthy, the Macdonald Conservative whose zeal for imperial federation seemed to be outrunning his party loyalty. Ever since the autumn, when the strength and political significance of the commercial union movement had begun to become apparent, the Imperial Federation League had been developing a new zeal and popularity in Canada. McCarthy was the president of the League; he became its parliamentary spokesman; and on April 30, he delivered in the House a considerable speech in favour of imperial preferential trade.[44]

Macdonald took no important part in the long debate on Cartwright's motion or in the short discussion which followed McCarthy's speech. He was trying to delegate more of the work of the House to his subordinates; and, in any case, his opinions were well known. He had no objection whatever to a broad commercial agreement with the United States or to an extension of preferential trade within the Empire. He had tried hard enough in the past, and would try again in the future, to secure them both. But he disliked both continental union and imperial federation, and for much the same reasons. He was convinced that each carried a threat for Canadian nationality; and in both the Cartwright and McCarthy resolutions there were, it seemed to him, serious political implications which he and his followers could not accept. Most of the Conservatives listened in discreet silence to the lame debate on McCarthy's motion. Cartwright's resolution was obviously much the more serious of the two attacks on the national policy of protection; and it was countered by an official Conservative amendment which welcomed freer trade relations with the United States provided they did not conflict with the policy "which was adopted in 1879 and which has since received in so marked a manner the sanction and approval of the people."[45] Macdonald had not the slightest intention of making any fundamental alteration in the national policy. The Canadian people had supported it in three general elections, and in both good times and bad. And now, after four stagnant years of depression, it almost looked as if good times were coming back again with a rush.

The fact was that he was beginning to feel that at least a phase of his long ordeal was over. Another parliamentary session was coming to an end. For two and a half years—ever since Riel's execution in the autumn of 1885—he had been standing with his back to the wall, warding off a ring of assailants; and now at last it began to seem that the fury of the assault was slackening. The combined onslaught of the provincial premiers had not as yet resulted in anything serious. The new Liberal leaders, like the old, had so far failed in their attacks. Best of all, there had been a sudden revival of business activity; and prices, depressed and lethargic for so long, were beginning to climb upward in a lively fashion. "The honourable gentleman," said Macdonald, referring to Wilfrid Laurier, during the debate on the speech from the throne, "has remarked the marvellous tenacity with which we proclaim the prosperity of this country. We proclaim it with considerable tenacity because we believe we are justified in doing so."[46] For the past few years the justification of this belief had been an article of Conservative faith and the substance of Conservative hopes. But had not circumstances changed at last? And was not prosperity again becoming a demonstrable fact?

Time was getting on. The great companions of the last five strenuous years of nation-building were leaving him, for their work was done. Stephen announced that he would resign the presidency of the Canadian Pacific Railway some time during the summer; and Lord Lansdowne had arranged long before to leave as soon as the current session was over. On May 22, he prorogued Parliament. He and Lady Lansdowne paid a last unexpected visit to Earnscliffe to say good-bye to Agnes and Mary;[47] and on May 23, Macdonald faced "the ablest chief"

under whom he had ever served, for the last time. "I am a bad
hand at leave-taking," Lansdowne had written only a few hours
before in a brief note of farewell, "and my difficulty does not
diminish when I feel deeply what I have to say. I do not, therefore, like to trust to this afternoon for an opportunity of saying
good-bye to you and of telling you how sorry I am to part with
you and how much I have appreciated your kindness and confidence. . . . Nor am I using an idle phrase when I say that
it has been an advantage to me not only in respect of the government of Canada to be in constant communication with one
whose experience of the public affairs of the Empire has been
as wide as yours. . . . I will not ask you not to forget us, because
I am quite sure you will remember us and not unkindly. I wish
you good-bye and as much happiness as is compatible with a
servitude from which your country will, I suspect, not allow
you to emancipate yourself."[48]

They had gone. They—and so many others—had gone or
were going. They were going with regrets or, as in Stephen's
case, with bitter resentment at Canadian ingratitude. They were
going in weariness, in illness, or in death. Thomas White, the
new Minister of the Interior, who had proved himself such an
excellent debater and administrator, died suddenly when the
session had still a month to run. John Henry Pope was ill with
what he as well as others suspected was a mortal illness. McLelan
was anxious to resign. Tupper wanted to get back to the well-
liked duties of the High Commissionership in London; and
Thompson was hopefully hinting that Macdonald might soon
find a way to fill his place and thus enable him to take advantage of an expected vacancy in the Supreme Court of Canada.
They were failing, or giving up, or backing out, or wanting to
be away. He had the disheartening and not unfamiliar sensation
that the human resources that he had painfully scraped together
were running away out of his hands.

Why should this always be so? Why was there not a small,
well-knit group of able ministers, with one recognized principal,
to whom he could surrender his leadership? His work was done.
He had created the Canadian nation. For three desperate years
he had been defending it against inward disintegration and

outward attack. Only a little over a year ago, a general election had been triumphantly won. There was still ample time for a new leader to take over, before the government would have to go to the country once more. And if he was ever to retire, if he was ever to get relief before death claimed him, this, in all probability, was his last real chance.

He talked the matter over with Stephen and with Tupper. But he could see no clear way stretching ahead. Who was to succeed him as leader? Ten years ago he had told a cheering audience at Kingston that Tupper was his appropriate and worthy successor. But that was back in 1877, and in the meantime many things had happened. Tupper had begun a new career as Canada's first diplomatist; Tilley had definitely retired from public affairs; and Langevin, the only other minister whose political career stretched back into the pre-Confederation days, had become, after Macdonald, the senior member of the Cabinet. Langevin's influence and prestige, of course, had never equalled Cartier's; but during the perilous days of the Riel crisis he had definitely grown in stature. His loyalty had preserved the solidarity of the Cabinet and prevented the open declaration of a racial war; and in gratitude Macdonald may have agreed that these services gave Langevin a good claim to the succession of leadership. But was this agreement—if it existed—still valid? And, above all, was this the moment to bring it into effect? The jealousies and antagonisms which divided the French-Canadian leaders were notorious. "The mutual distrust among them is apparently irreconcilable,"[49] Macdonald reminded Tupper ruefully. And Stephen, after a long conversation with a French-Canadian politician, reported that the Quebec members would probably prefer Tupper to any leader of their own.[50] Was this a possible solution? Before the end of the session Macdonald talked the matter over once again with the Nova Scotian leader.[51] But Tupper apparently did not believe that the understanding with Langevin should be broken, and probably preferred to go back to his London job. It was settled. Tupper resigned his office as Minister of Finance, was reappointed High Commissioner, and immediately after the session was over, left for England.

The best and most reliable of Macdonald's captains had gone. He was virtually the solitary active survivor of his generation of British North American politicians. How could he give up now? He would have to hang on, for a while at least. He would have to finish the toilsome and ungrateful job of reconstructing the Cabinet once again, and he would have to see the new Governor-General, Lord Stanley of Preston, suitably welcomed and installed. "I am afraid," he wrote to Lord Lansdowne, "that Lady Lansdowne and you have rather spoiled both my wife and myself, and that it will be some time before we become reconciled to the newcomers."[52] There were so many newcomers these days! There were so many strange faces! He was an old man with a strangely youthful elasticity of spirit. And he had stretched it to the utmost.

V

The summer was a dull and unexciting one, spent quietly at Dalhousie in New Brunswick and in a tour of Cape Breton Island. Stephen resigned the presidency of the Canadian Pacific Railway early in August and for a while Macdonald hoped vainly, longingly, that he might pay a long-desired visit to England in the ex-president's company. But this was not to be. There were far too many dangerously unpleasant situations in Canada that summer to permit his slipping away. And if the Canadian troubles had not been enough, and more than enough, by themselves, there were also the extravagances of an approaching American presidential election. American presidential elections often saw the emergence, for the benefit of millions of Anglophobe Irish Americans, of at least one or two highly acrimonious contentions between the United States and Great Britain or British North America. Macdonald took the appearance of these contentions for granted. He was convinced that they were frequently drummed up, if not virtually invented, for election purposes. But in 1888 there was no need for Democrats or Republicans to exercise their creative powers. Issues already existed. They were the still undecided fate of the Chamberlain-

Bayard Treaty and the increasingly contentious dispute over the fur-seal fisheries of Bering Sea.

The Senate had not yet accepted the Chamberlain-Bayard Treaty; and the fur-seal dispute was apparently no nearer solution than it had been in the summer of 1886, when the first Canadian sealing vessels had been arrested on the high seas. During the spring the American Department of State proposed the establishment of a close season, which would last from April to November, and during which no pelagic or open-sea fishing for seals could be carried on. This was a humane proposal ostensibly advanced with an anxious desire to protect the seals from destruction; but to Lord Lansdowne and his ministers it seemed probable that the principal beneficiaries of the plan would, oddly enough, be the American fur-seal fishermen rather than the seals themselves. The prohibition of pelagic fishing alone would totally prevent fishing on the high seas by Canadian vessels while at the same time it would generously permit the wholesale slaughter of the animals on the Pribilof Islands by the American Alaska Fur Company. The magnanimity of this offer did not greatly impress Macdonald. He somewhat grudgingly agreed that Canada was ready "to join with other governments in providing means to prevent extermination of the fur seal in the North Pacific";[53] and the negotiations dragged on inconclusively into the summer. "*Quoad* Bering's Sea," he wrote to Lord Stanley from Inch Arran House, the hotel at which he stayed in Dalhousie, "I think I can read between the lines that Mr. Bayard desires to play with the subject and postpone the settlement until after the presidential election in November. . . . Bayard or rather Cleveland dare not give the least evidence of concession now, as it would at once be used as a cry against him at the polls."[54]

He had warned the Governor-General that English-speaking countries could expect little more than calculated snubs from the United States during election time. He had learnt the truth of this by frequently repeated and bitter experience; but even he was somewhat surprised to see the completeness with which American foreign policy had apparently become the sport of American domestic politics. Cleveland and his Republican opponents were equally determined to pose as the vindicators of American rights; they were equally prepared to make use of the fisheries issue for an exhibition of republican valour. On August 21, the Senate rejected the Chamberlain-Bayard Treaty; and two days later—with the plain intention of outdoing one piece of heroics by another still more sensational—President Cleveland sent Congress a message requesting the power to proclaim a state of complete commercial non-intercourse with Canada.

It was true that the advantages of the Treaty were not completely lost, for the *modus vivendi* accompanying it was put into force; and it was almost certain that the Senate, whose anti-British thunder had been so neatly stolen, would not give its support to Cleveland's sweeping measure of economic retaliation. But it was not altogether surprising that the Canadians were somewhat alarmed by a declaration so unequivocally truculent that it might have served as a suitable preliminary to war. Macdonald characteristically tried to make light of the matter. "Cleveland, I fancy," he wrote realistically to Lord Lansdowne, "had ascertained that the Irish vote would carry New York against him, and so in desperation took an extra twist at the tail of the British lion."[55] Yet the violence of this "extra twist" settled Macdonald's plans for the late summer. "I had almost made up my mind to take a run to England," he told Stephen regretfully, "when the President's message came out. It was impossible to foresee what would be the action of the President or the Senate, and I thought it necessary to be on the spot, so that Canada might be ready to take any step that might be forced on us by such action."[56]

The American presidential election was the most important, but by no means the only, reason for his remaining on sentry duty at Ottawa. The titanic engagements of American national affairs had their minor equivalents in the alarms and excursions of Canadian provincial politics. It was a noisy and quarrelsome summer—a still more noisy and quarrelsome autumn. Collectively the provinces seemed quiescent. They were making no obvious moves to implement the reforming resolutions of the interprovincial conference. But individually the more obstreperous among their number were creating as large a commotion as ever. The legislature of Quebec had been recently passing some very controversial statutes; and the national stage continued to resound to the turbulent activities of Thomas Greenway. As soon as the monopoly clause had been repealed, he proceeded, as Stephen had always feared he would, to make an agreement with the Northern Pacific Railroad for the completion and operation of the Red River Valley Railway. And when the Canadian Pacific officials attempted, by means of an injunction, to prevent the construction of a branch of this new system, Greenway's Attorney-General, Joseph Martin, called out volunteer police to protect the work. For a brief while, there was a threat of a mimic civil war.

Macdonald kept trying, with extreme difficulty, to maintain his precarious position between these two embittered opponents, and to force each one of them to keep the peace. "The more I think over the course of Manitoba, and especially of the Winnipegers, the more astonished I am," he wrote to John Schultz, the new Lieutenant-Governor of the Province. "They seem resolved upon driving the C.P.R. into a hostile position, as they treat the company as though it were an enemy of their Province, and so blind are they to the consequences of their acts that they are urging the C.P.R. to extend their lines and build additional branches at the same time that they are passing charters and entering into negotiations with a foreign corporation to build rival lines."[57] Obviously the conduct of Manitoba was inexcusable; and if Greenway undertook to defend his extravagances with a questionable use of legislative power, Macdonald was quite prepared to resort to disallowance once again.[58] He would stand no nonsense from Greenway; but equally he was not entirely convinced by the lugubrious air of injured virtue adopted by Stephen. He reminded the ex-president that the Canadian Pacific had, on its part, been busily acquiring railway properties in the United States, and that Greenway could not be greatly blamed "for desiring to get as much railway accommodation for his Province as he can". Stephen's pessimism and Stephen's bitter disappointment at the black ingratitude of the Canadian people both betokened, he thought, a far too sensitive state of mind. "Meanwhile," he wrote with cheerful cynicism, "don't be disgusted at the ingratitude of the Manitobans. I have been long enough in public life to know how little of that commodity there exists in this world."[59]

There was another and a still harder test for his political realism that autumn. The American presidential election was rapidly approaching; and there were so many unsettled accounts between Canada and the United States that he waited for it with perceptibly more anxiety than he had four years before. "I hope Cleveland will succeed," he wrote to Lord Lansdowne, "as if Harrison is President Blaine will be, as Secretary of State, the actual government. This means continual discomfort for Canada not only for four years, but Blaine will work steadily for the presidentship for the following term, and will therefore throw himself into the arms of the Irish Americans."[60] The abandon with which both sides flung themselves into the arms of the Irish Americans and the confidence with which they both relied upon the vote-getting power of unfriendliness to England and Canada surprised and dismayed the Governor-General;[61] and even Macdonald, who thought he knew a great deal about American politics, was somewhat disconcerted by the astounding climax of the campaign. It was a relatively unknown Republican voter who succeeded in applying the methods of the *agent provocateur* to the business of bedevilling Anglo-American relations. Pretending to be a naturalized Englishman named Murchison, he wrote to the British Minister at Washington, asking his advice on how he should vote; and Sir Lionel Sackville-West—he became Lord Sackville of Knole about this time—unguardedly replied that he thought the Democratic party was still desirous of maintaining friendly relations with Great Britain and still ready to settle all questions with Canada. On October 24, the Republican managers published this letter; and two days later, annoyed with the British Minister's interference in American politics and well aware of the fact that to be credited with friendly feelings towards England and Canada was the political equivalent of a criminal charge, Cleveland kicked Lord Sackville back to England with what a supporter enthusiastically described as "your biggest boot of best leather".[62]

Macdonald had reminded Stephen that "there is no saying what the Yankees may do in stress of politics".[63] He was sorry for Lord Sackville, though he thought the net in which he had been caught was a flimsy one;[64] and he was not surprised to see Cleveland defeated and Blaine installed as Secretary of State. ". . . We must take things as they come," he had characteristically written to Lord Lansdowne, early in the campaign, when he still hoped that Cleveland would be elected; and he now tried to draw some comfort for himself and Tupper from the fact that Harrison had the two houses of Congress with him and that, if he wished for conciliation, he would not have to face the organized obstruction which had so troubled his predecessor. The ultimate fate of the Fisheries Treaty still rested in suspense. The settlement of the Bering Sea dispute had not even been begun. Altogether there were half a dozen problems in trade, transport, and communications which Macdonald still had to keep regretfully in the category of unfinished business. He was still interested in a Pacific cable and a subsidized steamship service from Vancouver to Australasia and the Far East; he was prepared to give considerable assistance to a fast line of Atlantic steamers to Montreal and Halifax. He had any number of things that he wanted to talk over with the members of the British government. Most unfortunately his visit to England, projected for that autumn, had had to be postponed. But, as he told Tupper, he had some faint hopes that the session of 1889 might be a short one. And if happily it turned out to be, he would hurry over to England in the spring.

Meanwhile, at home, there was some ground for encouragement. There were some good reasons for believing that the organized opposition which he faced was not nearly so formidable as it had been twelve months ago. The provincial premiers, having made one last vain effort to inveigle Macdonald into a discussion of the resolutions of the interprovincial conference, tacitly abandoned their attempt to reform the constitution.[65] The formal attack against the primacy of the Dominion had failed. The angry excitement over railways in Manitoba seemed to be gradually subsiding. And, best of all, the popularity of unrestricted reciprocity was apparently receding before the onrush of returning prosperity. There could surely be no doubt about it now. Times were definitely improving. "The crop in Manitoba and the north-west is very good on the whole," Macdonald wrote to George Stephen late in October, "and, as prices are good, the whole country is happy except at Prince Albert and along the North Saskatchewan where the crop can't be brought out." There were troubled spots, of course; but, on the whole, the Dominion was regaining zest and confidence. The time soon came, early in January, when he could actually inform Stephen that there was "quite a revival of a spirit of enterprise in Canada".[66]

Another year had gone by. "Today I am seventy-four years old," he wrote to Professor Williamson on January 11, "a fact which brings serious reflections. I am in fairly good health for my age, but can't expect that to last very long, as my work increases faster than my years. I must soon call a halt."[67] He must soon call a halt or death would take him before he ever had a chance to enjoy a holiday. Death had taken his sister Louisa that autumn. For long years she had been a chronic invalid; and he had fussed over her and scolded her affectionately for her imprudence, just as, in the old days at Hay Bay and the Stone Mills, he and Margaret had protectively looked after baby "Lou". Only last April the doctor had given him a fairly satisfactory report on her condition. "He speaks, however," he chided her gently, "in the strongest terms of your refusal to keep quiet. Complete rest, he says, is your best medicine, and you won't take it. . . . Now, my dear Louisa, you really must take better care of yourself, or you and I will quarrel."[68] She had resembled him physically. She had had more than a little of his gay vitality of spirit; and she had lingered on, frail, cheerful, indomitable, through years of weakness and suffering. Now she was gone; and Maria Macpherson, the dead Isabella's sister, was the last link with the past.

Everything was changing—even the physical circumstances of his daily life. Late in 1888 they moved back, from the rented quarters in which they had been living during the autumn, to an enlarged, improved, and redecorated Earnscliffe. "Reynolds' house," though comfortable enough, had been anything but spacious when he bought it six years before; but now, with a handsome new dining-room, and a small additional office built specially for himself, it had become a much more suitable residence for a Prime Minister who had many visitors, a lot of correspondence to keep up, and a great deal of entertaining to do. "It is the pride of Agnes's heart," he wrote to Professor Williamson;[69] and he himself was pleasantly satisfied with his recreated property. After three-quarters of a century he had finally secured a house which was fit for the job to which he had given his life. He had lived here for the last five years. He would probably die here. He might—who could tell?—retire to enjoy its quiet for a few years in peace.

The improvement of Earnscliffe was, in its way, the Macdonald family's farewell to the drab, defeated days of the immediate past. Macdonald could not live in the past. He had to live in the present and future; and his own and his country's perspectives were brighter and more spacious than they had been. Prosperity was coming back, and prosperity was a wonderful solvent of obstinate difficulties, a wonderful pacifier of unruly spirits. Would it not drop a golden curtain of oblivion over such extremist politicians as Honoré Mercier and Thomas Greenway? Macdonald began to indulge the hope that it would. "Mercier is killing himself in the east," he informed Stephen fairly confidently, "as Greenway is doing in the west. I hope, ere long, to get rid of both those scamps."[70]

No hope could have been more delusive.

VI

Honoré Mercier was the perfect example of the new generation of Canadian politicians, the men of provincialism and vehemence who had been flung up by the vast upheaval of the Riel agitation. In 1887, he had sought to organize a constitutional attack upon the unity of the Dominion; and now, by pushing through a settlement of the dispute over the estates of the Jesuits, he had suddenly raised an issue which seriously threatened the cultural concord of the country. The Jesuits'

Estates controversy was, in fact, exactly the kind of politico-religious dispute which had set French-speaking and English-speaking Canadians against each other in the 1850's, and against the resurgence of which the Fathers of Confederation had tried to guard in the provisions of the British North America Act. Yet here once more, its malevolent aspect apparently unaltered, was the old problem of the relation of church and state. In the past few years, all kinds of inward weaknesses and outward attacks, constitutional, political, and economic, had threatened Macdonald's national structure. And now at last had come a renewal of the old and most terrible calamity, the cultural conflict.

It was a complex matter, bristling with highly debatable points. The original Society of Jesus, which had been suppressed by papal brief in 1773 throughout the entire Roman Catholic world, had been granted large estates in New France before the British conquest of 1763. In 1800, after the last surviving Jesuit had died, the estates were confiscated to the Crown; and in 1831 they were transferred, as an endowment in support of education, to the control and management of the legislature of Lower Canada. It was not until the 1860's, when the Jesuits had re-established themselves in Canada East, that their demands for compensation for their lost estates began to be seriously pressed; and then the claims of the Society were vigorously challenged by the counter-claims of the Roman Catholic bishops, who argued that the property of religious houses suppressed by papal brief reverted to the hierarchy of the dioceses in which they were situated. Mercier determined to end the resulting controversy by a final settlement which would be backed by the authority of the Pope; and the resulting Jesuits' Estates Bill, which was passed by the Quebec legislature during the summer of 1888, settled the conflicting claims for compensation in accordance with the Pope's decision. The Act provided four hundred thousand dollars to be divided among the various rival claimants. It also put sixty thousand dollars at the disposal of the Protestant Committee of Public Instruction for Quebec.

The opposition to this measure developed slowly, but it

developed surely none the less. During the autumn and winter of 1888-9, it gradually gathered force and conviction. Why, asked Protestant newspaper editors and clerical leaders, should either the bishops or the Jesuits be given any compensation whatever? A papal brief could not confer any property rights in a British country; a new Society of Jesus could not revive the claims of a defunct corporation simply because it had appropriated its name. The whole question of the public endowment of religious bodies had been finally settled, once and for all, by the secularization of the Clergy Reserves. It was unfair and unwise to depart from this decision for the benefit of one religious communion only; and it was particularly objectionable to waive the rule in respect of property which had been transferred in trust to the province for the support of education. Finally—and this was, perhaps, the gravest part of the indictment—the authority of the papacy had been invoked to effect the settlement, and the correspondence between the Pope and Mercier had actually been printed *in extenso* in the preamble to the Bill. For all these good and more than sufficient reasons, the opponents of the Jesuits' Estates Bill began to urge the Dominion government to intervene to prevent the operation of this most iniquitous law. And in January 1889, the first important petitions requesting disallowance arrived in Ottawa.

"Am I safe in assuring the Duke of Norfolk," Tupper had inquired by telegraph a week before Christmas, "that the Jesuits' Act will not be disallowed?"[71] Macdonald replied that the matter would be settled by the middle of January. For some reason which he could not, or did not want to, explain, a few ministers evidently desired a short delay for consideration.[72] But by the middle of January, with petitions already arriving in Ottawa and a dangerous agitation under way, there was no more time for temporizing or delay, and the government hastened to announce that it had no intention of disallowing the Jesuits' Estates Act. With this decision Macdonald was in complete agreement. He did not at all approve of some of the expressions used in the preamble of the Act; he suspected that they had very possibly been placed there with the express purpose of provoking him into an unwary and unjustifiable exercise of the power of disallowance. But he was not to be caught. Disallowance was unnecessary and would be unwise. There was, as he told one Protestant clergyman, no need for the Dominion to take action in the national interest against a statute which did not in any way affect any other of the provinces.[73] The Dominion would take no action. And surely, once this decision had been firmly announced, the excitement would rapidly die away.

But it did not. Instead it grew more general and more passionate. The issue of the Jesuits' Estates Act and its disallowance would now very probably become a parliamentary matter; and—what was much more painful to bear—there was a very real probability that it would be raised, not by some Calvinistic Reformer, but by that lost leader of the Conservatives, Dalton McCarthy. McCarthy, like Mercier and Greenway, was a typical politician of the new age. Less than five years ago he had brusquely declined Macdonald's offer of the Ministry of Justice. He had evidently found a much greater interest and a more important meaning in the turbulent politics which had come into being with the depression and the North-West Rebellion than he ever would have done in the routines of administration and compromise. He had opposed Cartwright's North-American continentalism with imperial federation. Now he and his friends would confront Mercier's French-Canadian Catholic separatism with the ideal of a unified English-speaking Canada under the British Crown. "I have been asked to let you know," he informed Macdonald by letter on March 1, "that at three o'clock—or when the orders for the day are called— O'Brien proposes to say that he will take an early opportunity of moving respecting the disallowance of the Jesuits' Estates Bill."[74]

Parliament had opened on January 31. Macdonald had not looked forward to it. "I am in good health, but rather dread another session," he admitted to George Stephen; and now, when the spring and prorogation were still far away, the real trouble which justified his vague apprehensions had come. On March 15 he called a party caucus. The vast majority of the Conservative members joined him in appealing to W. E. O'Brien to drop his motion requesting the Dominion government to disallow the Jesuits' Estates Bill. But these entreaties were useless. Despite the fact that their resolution virtually expressed a want of confidence in the Conservative government, O'Brien, McCarthy and their small group of associates persisted in their decision.[75] They offered, indeed, to resign from the party; but this, of course, was the last thing that Macdonald wanted. He hoped to maintain the strength and unity of Conservatism and to prevent Canadian party politics from becoming the fanatical politics of "race" and religion. "I should be sorry," he wrote to Colonel O'Brien on March 20, "if any member should think himself bound to sever from the Conservative party because he voted for your motion."[76]

In the great debate which began on Tuesday, March 26, Macdonald took only a relatively unimportant part. The main defence of the government's position was made by Sir John Thompson; the moderate who had succeeded to the post of Minister of Justice, answered the extremist who had declined it. It was not until late on Thursday night, at the close of the third day of debate, that Macdonald rose to speak. For a few minutes he amused himself and the House by congratulating the Liberals upon the unanimity with which they were about to support the government's policy of non-interference in provincial affairs. But most of his speech was given over to an account of the politico-religious quarrels of his young manhood and to a reasoned appeal against the renewal of the desperate antagonisms of race and religion. "What would be the consequences of a disallowance?" he asked the House rhetorically. "Agitation, a quarrel—a racial and religious war would be aroused. The best interests of the country would be prejudiced, our credit would be ruined abroad, and our social relations destroyed at home."[77] That was why he hoped that the revolt of McCarthy and his independent followers would not spread. That was why, when, one hour later, the final vote was taken, he could not help feeling an enormous sense of relief. Only thirteen members— eight Conservatives, including O'Brien himself, and five Liberals —had voted in favour of the motion; and one hundred and eighty-eight had voted against it.[78] The whole difficult business was over—and well over. The "noble thirteen"—or the "devil's

dozen"—had declared themselves. The statement of their conscientious convictions was to be respected. There would be no
expulsions and no recriminations. And now, having talked the
whole matter over sensibly and decided it sensibly, the nation
would be at peace.

But peace did not come. On March 25, the day before the
debate began in the House of Commons at Ottawa, a great
mass meeting in Toronto resolved that it was the duty of
Canadian citizens to use all legitimate means to prevent the
Jesuits' Estates Bill from being carried into effect. Another
still larger meeting was planned for April 22; and the Toronto
Citizens' Committee announced that on this occasion Dalton
McCarthy would speak. It was a plain intimation that McCarthy
proposed to carry the issue of the Jesuits' Estates from the
Canadian Parliament to the Canadian people. And early in
April—as if to make the meaning of his independent course
still more explicit—he resigned from the presidency of the
Liberal-Conservative Union of Ontario. Macdonald, in a final
appeal to an old and admired friend and follower, begged him
to withdraw his resignation and to give up a senseless, primitive
agitation which threatened to divide the party and the country.[79]
But McCarthy was adamant. The fundamental question in
Canadian politics, he told Macdonald in reply, was not whether
Canada was to be annexed to the United States or not, "but
whether this country is to be English or French".[80] It was a
vague, inflammatory issue on which scores of thousands of
excited people seemed determined to take a stand. Early in
June, eight hundred representatives from Ontario met in
Toronto to form the Equal Rights Association; and on June 24,
St. Jean Baptiste's day, Mercier and a score of French-Canadian
speakers thundered a defiant rejoinder.

Macdonald's summer was settled. The Jesuits' Estates Bill
had been received in Ottawa on August 8, 1888; and for a year
from that date the Governor-General in Council could disallow
it. As the fatal, final day approached, the agitation grew shriller
and shriller. ". . . One of those insane crazes," he wrote to
Lord Lansdowne, "has taken possession of the ultra Protestants
which can only be compared with the Popish Plot or the papal
aggression agitation which ended so ingloriously in the Ecclesi-

astical Titles Act of Lord John Russell. The drum ecclesiastic
is beating in all parts of Ontario. Dislike of the French has
much to do with the excitement, which I think will soon die out,
but I shouldn't like a general election just now."[81] For a few
weeks anything might happen. He would have to stay and
keep up his protective watch over the country. Thompson
pressed him to go to England, adding reassuringly that the
ministers would "promise not to fight *much* until you could
return".[82] But Macdonald realized that the English mission
would have to be postponed once more. Would he ever see
London and the sedate, familiar front of Batt's Hotel again?
There would never be another welcoming letter from John
Rose awaiting him at Liverpool. Rose was dead. And Rose's
departure had darkened his own life and driven home the terrible
uncertainty of his hold upon it. One day, nearly a year ago
now, in a moment of depression, he had written to Lord Lansdowne that he feared they had met for the last time. What if
it should turn out to be true?

He had disappointments and worries enough. But on June
7, when he appeared before Convocation of the University of
Toronto to receive an honorary degree from its President, Sir
Daniel Wilson, he seemed as unconcerned and sprightly as
ever.[83] His physical alertness still matched his astounding
buoyancy of spirits. When Sir Daniel had finished his presentation, Macdonald jumped up, with almost "youthful alacrity"
to receive his degree; and when the ceremonies were over, he
smiled, and laughed, and shook hands with scores of people,
while the students cheered him loudly. "I wonder," he inquired
gaily of W. R. Meredith, as they were leaving the hall together,
"if this war between Queen's and Toronto will supersede the
Jesuit agitation, eh?" If only it were true! But the Jesuit agitation was something very different from a debate over matricula-
tion examinations. August 8 was approaching, and with it the
last demonstrations which the Equal Rights Association was
certain to make. He would await these final ructions imperturbably; and before the end of June he was back at "Les Rochers", at
Rivière du Loup. "The weather is delightful," he wrote to
Thompson who was still sweltering away at his desk in the

capital, "and it is all the more enjoyable when we know that there is only a sheet of brown paper between you Ottawaites and Hell."[84]

He had one strong card yet to play in the acrimonious game of the Jesuits' Estates Bill. As early as May 31, he had written to Tupper, urging him to obtain from the imperial Attorney-General and Solicitor-General an official opinion "affirming the validity and constitutionality" of the much disputed act.[85] But time went by and the answer did not come; and when finally it did arrive its wording was disappointingly defective. In the meantime the Equal Rights Association requested an interview with Lord Stanley in order to present its views in favour of disallowance; and Hugh Graham of the Montreal *Star* offered five thousand dollars in aid of a test of the constitutionality of the act before the Supreme Court of Canada. Macdonald was not entirely satisfied with the phrasing of the answer which the Governor-General proposed to give to the deputation of Equal Righters;[86] but on August 2 the interview came off quietly enough, the petitioners behaving, Lord Stanley considered, "with great moderation".[87]

"The Governor-General's answer has taken very well," Macdonald wrote to Thompson with satisfaction.[88] He was equally pleased with the Minister of Justice's "admirable paper" on Hugh Graham's petition. Finally, towards the end of August, a revised and much more acceptable version of the British law officers' opinion of the constitutionality of the Jesuits' Estates Bill arrived in Ottawa.[89] It was published on September 3, the day after Macdonald finally left Rivière du Loup for the capital. He was almost beginning to believe that the affair was at an end. The time for disallowance had gone past. The Jesuits' Estates Act was now the law of the land. Surely the ineffectual agitation against it was over, and surely the dangerous cultural conflict which it had provoked would now die away?

He was wrong. In the meantime, Dalton McCarthy had left for the west to raise the issue of the French language and Separate Schools in Manitoba and the North-West Territories.

Chapter Fifteen

The Last Election

I

He was nearly seventy-five years old. He faced the world like an old lion, less strong than he had been and conscious of his waning strength, but still powerful and proud of his continued mastery. He was tall and slight; his carriage was erect; he held himself like a young man; and his hair, waving in a fine, thin, silvery cloud, was a not too unsubstantial ghost of the curly chevelure of his young manhood. His eyes were tired and disillusioned; but his mouth was firm with strength and humour; and there was no bitterness, no mere shrewdness, no cunning in small deceptions in his face. His face was wise, and deeply experienced, and full of battle. He offered no apologies, he suffered from no vain regrets. He stood erect and determined, with an air of debonair defiance, of jaunty courage.

He had outlasted a whole political generation. The comrades and antagonists of his young manhood—MacNab and Hincks, Cameron and Foley—were dead or forgotten. George Brown, the greatest rival of his entire career, had been ten years in his grave. Tilley and Campbell and McLelan had all retired into the honourable obscurity of lieutenant-governorships; and it was half a century now since that day in the autumn of 1839 when the young Alexander Campbell had first walked into his small office in Kingston. He had seen seven governors-general come and go. He heard from some of them still, though at longer and longer intervals; and once a letter from old Lord Monck, who was so stiffened with rheumatism now that he could scarcely get about, brought back a sudden recollection of the plans and struggles of a quarter-century ago.[1] He remembered that first of July of 1867, when they had all worked away in the humid Privy Council chamber, "setting the coach in motion" in Monck's own phrase, while outside the hot sun shimmered on the terraces of Parliament Hill.

He had outlasted them all. Yet he had not exhausted his resources. He had not yet come to the end of those reserves from which there seemed always to be something else that he could draw. Campbell had spoken of his "many-sidedness". "Often," McLelan wrote admiringly, "when Council was perplexed and you had made things smooth and plain, I have thought of the expression an old farmer made about my late father when he saw him accomplish something that had puzzled all the neighbours. 'There are wheels in that man that have never been moved yet.' And so I have thought of my leader that there is a reserve force—'wheels that have not yet been moved'."[2] He had dreamed and planned and created; and his great design for Canada had been laid down, in all its essentials, long before this. But he had not exhausted his creative impulse or his creative capacity. He was still interested in general ideas rather than in administrative detail. He had a young man's zest for new constructive policies and a young man's impatience with mere competent routines. "I told Bowell just before leaving," he wrote to Thompson during the summer of 1889, "that while all my colleagues diligently attend to their several departments I cannot get them to consider, or rather to express any opinion on the general policy of the government unless I initiated it. I instanced the question of our proposed conference with the Australasian Colonies when I four times invited the attention of Council to consider it, but got nothing more than a general acquiescence in whatever I proposed. . . . Now this acquiescence is flattering enough, but it does not help me. . . ."[3]

His greatest failure, perhaps, was his failure to obtain a copious and satisfactory source of help. The Cabinet, which a few years ago had been too old, had certainly become more youthful in character as a result of the recent appointments. But had it in the process acquired a new sense of direction and purpose? Could he place any more reliance upon its unity and wisdom? He shook his head sadly. The best of the veterans were continuing to drop out of the ranks; and John Henry Pope, one of the last of them, had died after a long illness in April. Langevin, the oldest in point of service after Macdonald, was experienced, loyal, uncomplaining; but he remained an unimpressive, unimaginative man, immersed in the humdrum routines and questionable patronage of the Department of Public Works. Chapleau had fire and eloquence; but he was always restlessly attempting to extend and strengthen his political empire. "Chapleau, as ambitious and unscrupulous as ever," Macdonald wrote to Lansdowne in the spring of 1889, "is arousing his countrymen to claim for him poor Pope's succession as Minister of Railways, which I sternly refuse him, as the office would give him unlimited opportunities to job which he would eagerly avail himself of, and he will be discontented and intriguing."[4] In the end—it was a desperate remedy, for he had not administered a department for years—Macdonald had to take over the Department of Railways and Canals himself. "I was very unwilling to do this," he told Tupper later, "but could not avoid it without a *crise ministérielle*."[5] Chapleau would probably have been quite ready to precipitate a *crise ministérielle*. He was a difficult colleague—certainly more difficult than Caron. But even Caron was always getting into scrapes through sheer imprudence and obstinacy, and then, at the last moment, "recovering himself by his remarkable power of carrying a popular audience".

The others—most of them—were not much better, if they were no worse. The Irishmen, Frank Smith and John Costigan, were temperamental and very unreliable. There were encouraging times when Costigan "affected sobriety" and maintained his affectation; and there were deplorable periods when he forgot his pledges, and Macdonald threatened to call for his resignation.[6] Dewdney, who had been Lieutenant-Governor of the North-West Territories during the troubles of 1885, was one of the newer members of the Cabinet; but his appointment as Minister of the Interior had aroused a great deal of opposition among the French Canadians. Charles Hibbert Tupper, the High Commissioner's son, was another of the younger, newer ministers, whom Macdonald admired, though in a not uncritical fashion. "Charley has got the bumptiousness of his father," he wrote frankly to Thompson, "and should be kept in his place from the start."[7] All of them—even the youngest and most promising—had their crotchets, frailties, or defects. The Cabinet was a burden as well as a support; to maintain its tranquillity, he had been obliged, at the age of seventy-five, to take over the administration of a large department himself. And of the dozen and more ministers, only one man, John Thompson, had become a really strong stay and support. He admired Thompson's state papers. He relied upon him as government spokesman in the great debates in the Commons. He valued his advice.

Yet had he the right to assume that Thompson was his logical successor? Thompson was a Roman Catholic—a convert to Roman Catholicism. Did he dare—remembering the party and the nation—to step down in Thompson's favour? Did he want to relinquish the leadership yet? Politics was his profession. He had brought to it great natural gifts; he had developed them through a lifetime of experience; and there was no honourable occupation of retirement or semi-retirement which he would willingly accept in exchange for the task to which he had given his life. Tupper, who had seen more than enough of the "crass ignorance of everything Canadian" which prevailed at Washington, was eager to have him take the position from which Lord Sackville had been so unceremoniously dismissed in the autumn of 1888. "If I were Her Majesty's government," he wrote, "I would offer you a peerage and the position of minister at Washington. . . ."[8] But this suggestion, even if it had been taken up seriously, would not have interested Macdonald. He wanted neither the honour nor the job.

It was not, of course, that he had the slightest objection in principle to the grant of appropriate honours to Canadians. He had, on the contrary, always believed that "the monarchical idea should be fostered in the colonies, accompanied by some gradation of classes", and he had always hoped that the subjects of the Kingdom of Canada would be encouraged "to look forward to the Empress-Queen as the *fons honoris*".[9] But he knew

—and Agnes knew—that he could not hope to support the dignity of a title. "You may be sure," Agnes had written to Louisa on one occasion, "that he will *never* take a peerage. It would make us both ridiculous, and though we have been both very wicked often, I humbly think we have never been ridiculous! Nothing would distress me more than to see him—that most unfortunate of men—a *very poor lord.* . . . I know his mind well on the subject and am *positively certain* that he would never make so great a mistake as to be a peer."[10] He would not willingly accept the honour which Tupper—and no doubt many others—would have been willing enough to suggest in high places; and he did not particularly like the idea of the job to which Tupper hoped to promote him as a reward for his services.

The position of British minister at Washington was, he knew very well, the only suitable position of sufficient dignity which could be offered to him if he retired from active political life. But he was not like Howe, whose life had been embittered by his unhappy, unavailing search for an appropriate imperial appointment; and he was not by any means convinced that this particular appointment at Washington was one to which any Canadian ought to aspire as yet. "I greatly doubt the expediency of having a Canadian permanent minister at Washington," he had written to Tupper. "The present system of uniting the British minister ordinarily appointed with a Canadian whenever a question affecting Canada arises works more satisfactorily than the proposed change. I won't trouble you with all the arguments, but if you sit down and think it out, I am sure you will agree with me."[11] The case against Tupper's proposal seemed to him so obvious that it scarcely merited a lengthy statement. Besides, if Tupper still remained obstinately unconvinced, there was a final, and, in Macdonald's view, unanswerable argument. How could he go? "*Quoad* the Washington embassy," he wrote to Tupper a little later, "suffice it to say for the present that neither you nor I could be spared for the mission if offered and I don't know any other Canadian fit except perhaps Thompson."[12]

He could not go. He could not leave Canada. He instinctively assumed that his one rightful place was at Ottawa. It was not, of course, that he cherished a mere naïve belief in his own indispensability. Delusions about anything or anybody, including himself, were expensive pieces of mental furniture with which his mind was not encumbered. But deep within him lay the inarticulate conviction that so long as he was physically capable of doing so he must watch over the country which he had created. A long lifetime was scarcely long enough to complete the work which he had had in mind. For five years he had been kept almost continuously upon the defensive. But there were some signs now that the disrupting turmoil in the country was subsiding, and some reason to believe that the fury of the attacks against his position had declined. During the summer of 1889, he had turned again to some major items of unfinished business. The rejection, by the American Senate, of the Fisheries Treaty, had left Canadian-American relations in a highly unsatisfactory state. The Canadian east-west commercial system, transcontinental and transoceanic in extent, with terminals in Europe on the one hand and the Far East on the other, was a great undertaking which he had not yet strengthened and extended as much as he had hoped to do.

He was not an imperial federationist; and he knew that imperial federation, partly because of the unpopularity of its principal Canadian advocates, had become deeply suspect in French Canada. Ambitious schemes for an imperial defence system or an imperial customs union were out of the question; but he was just as convinced as he ever had been that the alliance with England and the association with the other developing nations of the Empire-Commonwealth were the surest guarantees both of Canada's political autonomy and its fiscal and commercial independence. "It looks like sheer insanity," he wrote, concerning the Liberal proposal of unrestricted reciprocity with the United States, "to propose practically to limit our foreign trade to the United States when there is such an immense opening for the development of our commerce with all the rest of the world. Our true policy is to cultivate closer commercial relations with England and the British colonies. Australia is already in communication with Canada for that purpose, and, if I mistake not the signs of the times, England will ere long think more of her children and less of strangers than she has hitherto been doing."[13]

He always hoped, of course, that as soon as Canada and the other colonies had demonstrated their ability to furnish the United Kingdom with the necessary supplies, Great Britain could be persuaded to establish a preferential tariff on foodstuffs. "I fear, however," he wrote to one British correspondent, "that the fetish of free trade has as yet too many worshippers in England to hope for such a result. However, the time will come, and we must wait."[14] In the meantime, while he waited, he was determined to explore the prospect of improved communications and increased trade with Australasia and the Far East. The British Postmaster-General had finally signed the contract with the Canadian Pacific for the carriage of the China mails; and during the summer Macdonald was considering the composition of a Canadian mission, headed by J. J. C. Abbott, which would visit Australasia and the Far East and discuss such matters as a Pacific cable, the Pacific steamship service, and the possibilities of improved trade relations with the different Australian governments.[15] Before the summer was over, he had realized that the Australian political time-table differed markedly from the Canadian, that the Australian legislatures would all be in session during the autumn, and that the Abbott "expedition" to the Antipodes would have to be postponed until the early spring of 1890 by which time, it was hoped, the Canadian Parliament would be prorogued.

But there was something more immediate and more important than Australia. There was the United States. And there was the urgent preliminary necessity of establishing a common policy with the United Kingdom on all the important points at issue, before the negotiations with the United States were pushed too dangerously far. ". . . I ask you for your opinion," Macdonald had written to Thompson fairly early in the summer, "as to what course to pursue *quoad* the Yankees. From Pauncefote's note to the Governor-General, it is clear that Lord Salisbury won't move, but shall wait for a move from the United States. And *they* won't move. Now shall we? And if yes, in what mode or direction? The *modus vivendi* will expire next February and our troubles will recommence. We must not like so many foolish virgins sit with our lamps untrimmed. 'I pause for a reply'."[16]

He did not have to pause very long. In a little over a week a lengthy, considered reply had arrived from the Minister of Justice. Thompson was in favour of an immediate "forward move" towards the United States. In his view, there were at least three important questions—Bering Sea, the North Atlantic fisheries, and trade relations—whose settlement was of vital importance to Canada. Macdonald agreed; but he knew that nothing serious could be done until the autumn, and he was convinced that no preliminary moves should be made until every item on Thompson's agenda had been thoroughly discussed with the officials in London. For years now he had been hoping vainly to cross the ocean to England. "I never saw anyone improve by a voyage as he does," Agnes had once told Louisa. And the sea voyage, and the London that lay at the other end of it, was a physical and spiritual satisfaction which he had been promising himself for a long time now, and which, because of one danger after another, he had been obliged repeatedly to postpone. Why should he postpone it any longer? Why should he not go that autumn, with another minister, with Thompson preferably, and have a thorough discussion of all issues outstanding between Canada and the United States?

It was a pleasant decision. But almost immediately it was qualified by unpleasant second thoughts. Was it really safe to go? "The chief difficulty would be—for instance, if you or I went—," he wrote to Thompson, "that Council might make some mistake on the Jesuit question and commit us on other matters. There would be great pressure on Council both from Quebec and the Maritimes during our absence."[17] The Cabinet, he could not help thinking, was, at the moment, a rather unhappy mixture of unreliable veterans and inexperienced apprentices. Could he depend upon it at a time when treacherous difficulties obviously still lay ahead? The Jesuits' Estates agitation, it was true, was gradually subsiding; but, as he told Lord Lansdowne, it was not subsiding "without leaving unfortunate consequences behind". "It has revived the hostile feelings," he explained, "that time had nearly extinguished between English and French, and which may lead to disastrous results."[18] Only a little while ago he had been congratulating himself that the agitation was really confined to Ontario and Quebec. But Canada as a whole had become an inflammable country through which a high wind of excitement and disputation was fiercely blowing. And before the summer was out, Manitoba, that most excitable of all provinces, had been fired by a fresh controversy.

Dalton McCarthy had gone west that summer. Early in August, he delivered two speeches, one at Portage la Prairie and one at Calgary; and at both places he expounded his now familiar message that a narrow, parochial, French-speaking "nationalism" should not be permitted, through special schools and special language privileges, to prevent the development of a true Canadian nationality. McCarthy had, of course, already expressed these views on a number of occasions and at considerable length; and the importance of the speeches at Portage la Prairie and Calgary lay not so much in the novelty of their ideas as in their immediate relevancy to the local situation in Manitoba and the North-West Territories. In respect of both time and place, McCarthy's utterances could scarcely have come more pat. His mere presence in the west seemed to precipitate the expression of convictions which westerners had reached long before, about which they had no longer any doubts, and which they were determined to put into immediate execution. Joseph Martin, the energetic Premier Greenway's Attorney-General, who had moved a vote of thanks after the Portage la Prairie speech, took advantage of the occasion to endorse McCarthy's views most emphatically. Within a matter of days, the government of Manitoba announced that, at the next session of the legislature, it would deal with separate schools and the legal status of the French language. Within another two months, the Assembly of the North-West Territories petitioned the federal government to move for the repeal of clause one hundred and ten, which defined the privileges of the French language in the North-West Territories Act.

II

It was a frustrating, disappointing autumn. Nothing seemed to be going right. Once again the long-delayed visit to England had to be given up. The mission to Australia was postponed. The great comprehensive scheme for the extension and improvement of the Canadian commercial system seemed everywhere to be running into obstacles and disappointments. The "Short Line"—the project of a swifter railway service from Montreal through the United States to the Maritime Provinces—had been one long tale of difficulties and disputes; and in October, Anderson and Company of Scotland, a firm which had virtually agreed to establish the fast steamship service between Canada, Great Britain and Europe, surrendered its option on the contract.[19] Relations with the Canadian Pacific Railway, which, on the whole, had remained so steadfastly good during all the desperate difficulties of 1884 and 1885, now seemed to be fraying rapidly under a number of rasping disagreements. There were disputes over the Short Line, over the selection of the company's lands, and finally—this was the most dismally acrimonious contention of all—over the condition of the government-constructed section of the railway in British Columbia. A long, complaining letter from Stephen, which reviewed these matters and bewailed the "unfairness and unfriendliness" with which the company had been treated, left Macdonald really "irate". "The charge of unjust treatment of the C.P.R. at my hands, and from *you*," he wrote indignantly, "seemed to me inexplicable —but an angry discussion won't help matters. . . . I wish you would read Charles Reade's novel of *Put Yourself in His Place*. I am sure if you were one of the ministry you would act as we are doing, but you, I fear, look only on matters from one point of view."[20]

There were too many of these disagreements. There were too many disappointments at a time when one might have expected fulfilment of hopes. The country was reasonably prosperous. The worst of the internal dissensions seemed to be dying away. But on all sides Macdonald's efforts to improve the external relations of the country appeared to have been brought to a standstill. The plan of reopening negotiations with the United States on a wide range of topics had been post-poned because the essential preliminary discussions with the authorities in London had not taken place, and because, until a new British minister, in place of the ignominiously dismissed Lord Sackville, had been appointed to Washington, the conduct of any serious negotiations between the two countries was virtually impossible. In the meantime, during the season of 1889, the United States had again been vigorously asserting its claim to a superintending control over the fur-seal fisheries of Bering Sea. "To please the Alaska Company and the Irish," Macdonald explained with temperate realism to Lord Lans-downe, "a revenue cutter is seizing British Columbian sealers and to mollify Lord Salisbury it allows them to escape."[21] No change in the existing unsatisfactory state of affairs occurred until late in the autumn when the new British Minister, Sir Julian Pauncefote, finally arrived in Washington. And then Blaine, the American Secretary of State, at once proposed a renewal of the fur-seal negotiations.

Macdonald, ill with one of his bad bronchial colds, was confined to Earnscliffe when the dispatch, announcing the American proposal, arrived in Ottawa. He had always feared Blaine's elevation to the seats of the mighty. "Were Blaine in power," he had prophesied to Lord Lansdowne over two years ago, "he would do everything disagreeable short of war, and perhaps if England had trouble elsewhere, go further." And now this man, whom he had always regarded as the personifica-tion of American jingoism and whom he suspected of a deep-seated hostility to Canada, was firmly installed in power. Blaine was a fact, a "fixed fact", as Macdonald would have said him-self, temporarily fixed at any rate; and it had always been his assumption that facts must be faced, with watchful cheerfulness or resignation, and the very best made of them. He told Lord Stanley that Canada would accept the American proposal, but on conditions. He stipulated that the Americans must abandon their claim to jurisdiction in Bering Sea, that Canada must be directly represented on the proposed joint commission, and that its conclusions, if any, must be subject to Canadian approval.[22]

The reply, which came quickly, was highly unsatisfactory.[23]

The United States insisted that it had never asserted the *mare clausum* doctrine and would consequently make no disclaimer. A most exasperating evasion! If the government of the United States had not asserted jurisdiction over Bering Sea, why was it instructing its officers to seize Canadian vessels in mid-ocean? In the reply which he drafted for Lord Stanley, Macdonald dealt faithfully with this important aspect of the question; but there were two other points in the American rejoinder which disturbed him only less. The first was Blaine's decided preference for an informal "diplomatic conference" rather than a commission; and the second was his blunt refusal to accept an official Canadian representative in the negotiations. Macdonald was suspicious of "diplomatic conferences", the uncertain conclusions of which could so easily be disputed or repudiated by the United States; but he looked even more darkly upon Blaine's obvious effort to depress Canada's diplomatic position. Plainly, of course, it was to the interest of the United States, in this as in all other negotiations involving British North America, to deal solely with Great Britain, the country which had little direct interest in them. But was this simple and immediate end Blaine's sole purpose? On numerous occasions and over a long period of years, the Secretary of State had shown himself consistently hostile to British North America. Might not his latest refusal be a part of the more vague and general design of embarrassing, impeding and perhaps even frustrating Canada's national development?

Even so, as Macdonald knew very well, the hope of a conference could not be given up. The only alternative was open resistance to the police authority which the Americans had been exercising in the disputed area; and the talk, which had already been going on, of sending a British man-of-war to Bering Sea to give support to the Canadian sealing vessels, filled Macdonald with deep disquietude. "I don't care to say it here lest it might be misunderstood in British Columbia," he had written to Tupper towards the end of October, "but I confess that I look with dread on the advent of a British man-of-war in the Bering Sea. A collision would not be avoided by an American officer—perhaps courted. In such a case it might not produce actual war, but Blaine would or could make it the excuse for a cessation of diplomatic or commercial intercourse."[24] Blaine's calculated snubs would have to be endured for fear of something infinitely more serious. The tactful British suggestion that a Canadian could, of course, serve as technical adviser to the Minister at Washington would have to be accepted with the best grace possible. "Canada fails to understand the United States objection to a Canadian being direct representative of Her Majesty's Government," Lord Stanley telegraphed the Colonial Office on December 13, "but to avoid delay will defer to the course decided on by Her Majesty's Government without further protest."[25]

The conference, which Charles Hibbert Tupper, the son of the old "Cumberland war-horse", would attend as Canadian adviser, would not likely be held until late in the winter. In the meantime, Parliament must be called. Macdonald had planned a fairly early opening, in the hope that Abbott would be free to depart on his Australian mission about the end of March, and in the hope also that he himself might be able to slip away before the summer was too far advanced on his long-deferred visit to England. Parliament met, according to plan, on January 16. A good deal more time would be available; but already, long before the opening, Macdonald became aware that his hope of breaking the back of the session's work in the first two months could almost certainly not be realized. It would not be an easy, uncontroversial, smoothly running session at all— far from it! The cultural conflict, like a fire in a high wind, had leaped from Ontario across the uninhabited expanses of the Precambrian Shield into Manitoba. Its fury remained virtually unabated; its character had only slightly changed. So long as the Jesuits' Estates Bill dominated the scene, the tumult had centred mainly around the power and privileges of the Roman Catholic Church; but now, with the transference of the excitement to Manitoba and the North-West Territories, the attack had come to be focused upon language and education. It was certain that as soon after the opening of Parliament as possible, Dalton McCarthy would move for the abolition of the guarantees for the French language in the North-West

Territories Act, and that a prolonged and highly dangerous debate would inevitably follow.

There was, as Macdonald knew very well, not the slightest doubt about the origins and meaning of this new disturbance in the north-west. It was the nemesis of the arrogant dictatorship of Riel. Exactly twenty years before, Riel and his spiritual advisers had sought, in the interest of the *métis* in particular and French Canadians in general, to determine in advance the structure and institutions of the first western Canadian province. They had demanded and secured a particular educational system before the citizens of Red River had even considered the subject; they had imposed provincial status upon a community which had expressly rejected it after considerable debate. This determination of the constitution of Manitoba in advance of the unmistakable assertion of its real character had not been an easy matter even in 1870. It had been accomplished only through the deliberate falsification, by Riel and his advisers, of the known wishes of the inhabitants of Red River. Even in 1870, the Red River settlement had not been simply a little French Canada in the west; and, in the twenty years since the passing of the Manitoba Act, the real character of the province had asserted itself even more emphatically. "There is no especial reason," Macdonald had pointed out realistically to Chapleau, "why a French Canadian should be preferred for office in the west. The people of Quebec will not migrate in that direction. They, wisely, I think, desire to settle the lands yet unoccupied in their Province and to add to their influence in eastern Ontario. The consequence is that Manitoba and the North-West Territories are becoming what British Columbia now is, wholly English—with English laws, English, or rather British, immigration, and, I may add, English prejudices."[26]

By 1890 the clash between law and reality had become acute. And the existing agitation was the inevitable result of the efforts of the people of the north-west to free themselves from the fetters which had been so prematurely imposed upon them. For Macdonald and the Conservative party, the agitation carried a double threat. Constitutionally, Manitoba and the North-West Territories stood in two quite different positions; and it was obvious that the danger from the North-West Territories was the more direct and immediate of the two. Within the limits imposed by the British North America Act and interpreted by the courts, Manitoba had control of its own schools and language guarantees: but in the North-West Territories, which, of course, had not yet been granted responsible government, these matters were still necessarily the concern of the federal Parliament. The Dominion was certainly more deeply involved in the affairs of the Territories than in the affairs of Manitoba; but even in respect of Manitoba and Manitoba's projected radical legislation, a position of complete detachment was going to be very difficult for the federal government to maintain. The Dominion, in addition to its general power of disallowance, possessed certain specified reserve powers in the field of education; and in the now almost inevitable controversy over Manitoba's new school legislation, these powers would be unquestionably invoked. This, however, lay still in the future. The trouble over the French language in the North-West Territories was very much in the present. On January 22, six days after the session opened, Dalton McCarthy moved to delete clause one hundred and ten from the North-West Territories Act.[27]

McCarthy justified his proposal on the simple ground that it was "expedient in the interest of unity that there should be community of language". Macdonald did not believe that community of language was the necessary condition of national unity. But he also did not believe that duality of language could be preserved in the North-West Territories by constitutional guarantees to which the mass of the inhabitants were unquestionably opposed. It was a cruel dilemma—a dilemma more cruel than that in which he and his party had been forced by the agitation over the Jesuits' Estates Bill. The Roman Catholic religion was no monopoly of the people of Quebec; but on the North American continent, the French language was their unique possession. As time passed and the second reading of McCarthy's Bill drew closer, the angry determination of the French-speaking members to defend the status of their language mounted. But so also did the resolution with which the English-speaking members prepared to ensure that the people of the north-west should have the right to determine the character of their own institutions. There was only one way out of this impossible situation; and on February 11, the day before McCarthy's Bill was to come up for second reading, the Conservative party took it. In full caucus, but with many French-Canadian supporters deeply dissatisfied, the party decided that the matter must be regarded as an open question.

On February 12, as soon as the debate began, Nicholas Flood Davin, member for West Assiniboia, arose to move in amendment that "the Legislative Assembly of the North-West Territories be authorized to deal with the subject of this Bill by ordinance or enactment, after the next general election for the said Territories".[28] Here, in the eyes of the English-speaking Conservatives, was an admirable compromise, which removed the stigma which Dalton McCarthy had placed upon the French language and safely transferred the whole contentious subject to the remote control of the North-West Legislative Assembly. The Quebec members ought to be satisfied with such a sensible solution. But plainly they were very far from being satisfied; and all hope that they could be induced to vote for the Davin amendment was quickly ended when Beausoleil, Liberal member for Berthier, moved, as an amendment to the amendment, that the language guarantees in the North-West Territories had been granted to promote good understanding and racial harmony and that nothing had since occurred to excuse or justify their abolition.[29] Immediately it became apparent that the Beausoleil amendment would become a battle slogan round which the French-Canadian resistance, irrespective of party, would inevitably rally. The next day, February 13, a second long and futile Conservative caucus failed to compose the differences between the English-speaking and French-speaking divisions of the party. The Quebec members were adamant. And in the days of debate that followed, speaker after French-Canadian speaker, of both parties, arose to identify himself with the principle of Beausoleil's amendment.

Not until the afternoon of February 17 did Macdonald enter the debate. It was Laurier's taunt that the McCarthy Bill was a typical example of harsh and oppressive Toryism which brought him to his feet. He had no difficulty in proving that it was a Conservative majority under Lord Metcalfe which had first requested the imperial Parliament to amend the clause in the Union Act of 1840 which provided that the English language alone was to be used in all the written proceedings of the provincial legislature. He had no hesitation in affirming —what he had affirmed forty years before against the determined opposition of George Brown—that the cultural duality of Canada must be accepted as the prime condition of its continued existence. "There is no paramount race in this country;" he declared firmly, "there is no conquered race in this country; we are all British subjects, and those who are not English are none the less British subjects on that account."[30] These were principles which he was ready enough to assert again and without qualification. But they were not, he realized, the only principles at stake. The susceptibilities of French-Canadians were not the only susceptibilities to be considered, and the north-west was as much involved in the agitation as Quebec. ". . . We must take great care, Mr. Speaker," he reminded the House, "that while we are calming the agitation and soothing the agitated feelings of the people of Quebec, we are not arousing the feelings of the freemen of the north-west by passing a resolution which postpones for an indefinite time, it may be for a long period, a question in which we can see, from the resolution they have adopted, that they are greatly interested."[31]

He was seeking earnestly for an acceptable compromise. But obviously also he was failing to find it. He opposed McCarthy's Bill. He rejected Beausoleil's amendment. He gave general approval to Davin's plan of permitting the citizens of the north-west to decide the matter themselves. He seemed to stand on the doctrine of self-determination. And then, towards the end of his speech, he began to qualify it with the expedient of delay. During the previous day's debate, Edward Blake had suggested that the decision concerning the French language should be postponed a while longer until the character of the north-western community was still more plainly determined. Was it not possible, Macdonald asked the House, to couple this suggestion with Davin's original proposal in a reasonable compromise?

He was desperately in earnest. But he was tired, and less effective than usual. If he had hoped to win French-Canadian approval for his vague proposal, he realized at once that he had completely failed. His followers from Quebec were bitterly disappointed at his stand; and all next day, while several unsuccessful caucuses were held, the French Canadians maintained their obstinate resistance. When, a day later, the vote on Beausoleil's motion was finally taken, every French-speaking member, with the exception of Chapleau and one or two absentees, voted in its favour; and one hundred and seventeen English-speaking members voted in a body against it.[32] What had so long been dreaded in Canadian politics had come at last to happen. Party did not seem to matter. Race stood opposed to race.

Yet, in the end, after his first fumble, Macdonald found an acceptable formula of compromise. Thompson presented it that night, for he himself was worn out by the long argument; but two days later when the House, in a much better humour, resumed the debate after the brief Ash Wednesday recess, he rose at once and accepted government responsibility for Thompson's amendment. In its opening clauses, the new resolution restated and reaffirmed the covenants in respect of the French language which were embodied in the British North America Act. It then went on to declare that it was proper, expedient and not inconsistent with those covenants that the Assembly of the North-West Territories should be empowered by Parliament to regulate, after the next general election, the conduct of its own proceedings, written and oral. The use of the French language in the courts of the North-West Territories would continue to be permitted. The territorial ordinances would be printed in both French and English as before. But henceforth the North-West Assembly would have the authority to determine the language of its own records and debates. It was a compromise; but in the light of actual conditions in the Territories, a not unreal compromise. And in a formal speech, which was the principal feature of the last two days of debate, Macdonald presented it with all the persuasive earnestness of which he was capable. "Let us forget this cry," he declared in the last sentences of his peroration, "and we shall have our reward in seeing this unfortunate fire, which has been kindled from so small a spark, extinguished for ever, and we shall go on, as we have been going on since 1867, as one people, with one object, looking to one future, and expecting to lay the foundation of one great country."[33]

Early in the morning of February 22, Lord Stanley wrote to Macdonald, congratulating him on the "brilliant division" —a division which had been so largely secured by his own great effort.[34] On the previous night, at a little after ten o'clock, the vote on Thompson's amendment had been finally taken. Fifty members—a handful of irreconcilable French-Canadian *Rouges*, a few McCarthyites, a small number of Liberals who preferred Davin's motion—voted against it; but one hundred and forty-nine people, French and English, voted in its favour.[35]

III

Four days later, Charles Hibbert Tupper, the new Minister of Marine and Fisheries, arrived in Washington for the fur-seal negotiations.

Macdonald was by no means reassured by Tupper's first reports. Blaine seemed to be pursuing a steady and determined policy of reducing Canadian participation to a cipher, conducting the negotiations on a level of calculated informality, and assuming the necessity of a close season before any effort had been made to prove it. It was plain that he did not in the least welcome a Canadian representative. He told Tupper frankly, at their first meeting, that he had not expected to see him. "I understood," he declared coldly, "that the British Government and the United States administration would agree upon a close season in the interests of this great and important industry and then submit the agreement to Canada for approval."[36] Tupper valiantly took the liberty of reminding him that unless the United States assumed Bering Sea to be a *mare clausum* of its own, it would obviously have to discuss the necessity and wisdom of a close season with all the nations interested in the fur-seal fishery. "I have never claimed the sea was a *mare clausum*," Blaine retorted. "But recollect," he added quickly, "I have never abandoned that claim which my predecessor set up."[37] In the end he agreed to submit in writing the American justification for the close season; and Tupper busied himself in preparing the Canadian reply. But it was quite evident that the Secretary of State was irritated by this deliberate and carefully recorded diplomacy. He wanted to proceed immediately to the establishment of the close season. And, in Tupper's somewhat jaundiced view, the new British Minister, Sir Julian Pauncefote, was apparently only too ready to hurry obediently after him.

Macdonald had been ill at the beginning of the year. The session had tired him out already. "I am so unwell," he wrote wearily to Bowell on March 4, "that I am completely floored, and must go to bed or I shall be ill. So you must get on as best you can."[38] He had no assurance at all that Tupper was "getting on" well at Washington. An unaccountable delay in the arrival of the letters expected from the Canadian representative aroused in him the disturbing suspicion that American agents were tampering with the mails;[39] and young Stanley, the Governor-General's son, was sent down to Washington with new and important communications. But this effort to strengthen Tupper's hand by applying a little polite pressure to the British Minister had no effect. Blaine virtually refused to give any more time to a discussion of the merits of the close season, and brusquely demanded that the Anglo-Canadian representatives present their "final proposition". On March 18, Tupper left Washington for Ottawa, bringing with him a draft convention which Pauncefote had drawn up.

The work of the session was at its demanding climax, and Macdonald was none too well. But once March 28 was past and Foster's budget speech had been safely delivered, the Cabinet settled down to the discussion and detailed amendment of Pauncefote's draft. The plan which gradually took shape was a simple one. In its main essentials, it bore a fairly close resemblance—a perhaps ominous resemblance—to the North Atlantic Fisheries Treaty, which had failed in the American Senate nearly two years before. The principal provision of the Anglo-Canadian draft was the establishment of a mixed commission of experts—with final reference to an arbitrator—which was to study the conditions of fur-seal life and, within two years, to submit a plan for the control and regulation of the fur-seal fishery. In the meantime, while the commissioners were carrying on their investigations, the capture of seals on both land and sea was to be suspended.[40]

Macdonald and the Cabinet were determined to put the unargued American case for a close season to the rigorous test of a careful and comprehensive examination. The Canadian amendments were uncompromising in the strict impartiality of their proposals; and when, early in April, Tupper returned to Washington with the revised draft, Sir Julian Pauncefote was distinctly disturbed.[41] It alarmed him to discover that the Canadians had included the American-owned Pribilof Islands in the area which the Commissioners were to investigate and to which the *modus vivendi* was to apply. He objected; and his objections perplexed and annoyed both Tupper and Macdonald. If the real purpose of all concerned was the preservation of the fur seals from extinction, then what valid distinction could be drawn between indiscriminate slaughter on the islands and indiscriminate slaughter on the high seas? Why did not Pauncefote see the force of this reasoning? Why was he yielding so readily to the persuasions of Blaine? "It may be out of place for me to say it," Tupper confided to Macdonald, "but I cannot refrain from urging that in future negotiations with the United States, no British Minister at Washington should act for us. It is apparent that there is always present on his part a desire to make his future residence in Washington as pleasant as possible, and he is to some extent therefore unable to take and keep a firm and independent position."[42]

Macdonald sighed. Clearly Sir Julian Pauncefote was not Joseph Chamberlain; and clearly the Canadian government would have to take vigorous steps itself to make its position perfectly clear in Washington. On April 11, after Tupper's report of the British Minister's objections had been received, Macdonald drafted a firm telegram to his colleague in Washington. "Council wish you to impress strongly on Sir Julian," it read, "their desire to adhere as closely as possible to the lines of our proposal."[43] A fortnight later, when Pauncefote still jibbed at the inclusion of the islands in the area to be governed by the terms of the *modus vivendi,* Macdonald telegraphed that if the British Minister insisted on the original and unamended article, the draft convention could be presented to the United States only under protest from Canada.[44] At this, Sir Julian gave in; the Foreign Office finally approved the plan; and on April 29, Pauncefote presented it to Blaine. A profound silence, lasting several weeks, followed. And then, on May 22, by the highly informal means of a press release in the American newspapers, Macdonald and Pauncefote learnt that the United States Cabinet had rejected their proposal. The news that an American revenue cutter had been ordered to seize vessels carrying on sealing in the waters of Bering Sea was included in the same dispatch.[45]

By this time Parliament had been prorogued for about a week. Though it had begun nearly a month earlier than usual, the session had ended at the accustomed time. It had been a long, exacting, dispiriting session—disagreeable to the tired and ill Macdonald and, as time went on, increasingly discreditable to the Conservative party. A month after the opening, J. C. Rykert, the Conservative member for Lincoln, had been charged with using his position and influence in Parliament for his own private gain;[46] and although these charges were not in fact substantiated by the committee of investigation, the evidence uncovered was so damaging to Rykert's character and conduct that in the end he resigned his seat. Early in May when *l'affaire* Rykert was drawing to its sorry close, a yet more unsavoury scandal, involving persons still more exalted in the Conservative party, was for the first time disclosed. Thomas McGreevy, member for Quebec West, was accused of having accepted, over a period of years, considerable sums of money in return for advancing the interests of the Quebec contracting firm, Larkin, Connolly and Company, at the Department of Public Works.[47]

What made these deplorable charges all the more dangerous was that Thomas McGreevy was Sir Hector Langevin's brother-in-law and that Sir Hector Langevin's department had always been the Department of Public Works. "If you had said," Bowell wrote to Macdonald, " 'Langevin cannot have too much *patronage—he likes it*', you would have hit the nail upon the head squarely."⁴⁸ As Macdonald knew only too well, the possibilities of jobbery inside Langevin's department were almost literally endless. Had he become really involved in something seriously discreditable?

The scandals were grave and becoming more serious; but they were not the only serious domestic problems to which he could look forward in the early summer of 1890. The government had emerged successfully—with a dignified air of wise statesmanship—from the great debate on the status of the French language in the North-West Territories. In the meantime, however, in Manitoba, one of the two opposing divisions in the cultural conflict had made another sudden and aggressive advance. During the session of 1890, the provincial legislature had abolished the legal guarantees for the French language and had established a new uniform system of non-sectarian schools to the support of which all citizens, irrespective of their religious beliefs, would be required to contribute. A disgruntled minority was opposed to both these changes. But, in respect of the language guarantees, it was obviously hopeless, after the amendment of the North-West Territories Act, to invite intervention from the federal government. The Manitoba Schools Act was a different matter. And the familiar petitions, requesting disallowance, began once more to descend upon Ottawa.

Macdonald was fresh from the long tribulations of the Jesuits' Estates Bill. He had no doubt as to the course he should take. "I am strongly of opinion," he wrote in March to a French-speaking supporter in Manitoba, "that the only mode by which the separate school question can be satisfactorily settled in your province is by an appeal to the courts. If the Bill were disallowed, the game of Greenway and Martin would be played successfully. They would probably summon the legislature again, and carry the Bill over again, and then dissolve and go to the country. The excitement would be tremendous and the question would remain unsettled, whereas a decision by the courts would finally dispose of it and the agitation consequent upon it."[49] This, of course, was the best that could be hoped for. But it would be a long time before the period in which disallowance could be exercised would be over. And it would be a still longer time before the test cases could end their protracted perambulations through the courts. Meanwhile, the opportunities for agitation would remain. The chances of embarrassment for the federal government were very real.

The danger was there. But—thank Heaven!—it was still distant. And the most pressing and immediate problems which confronted him lay in the sphere not of domestic but of external affairs. Late in June, Thompson departed for England to discuss copyrights and merchant-shipping regulations with the British officials, and also to bring up a matter which had long interested Macdonald, the appointment of a Canadian to the Judicial Committee of the Privy Council. The repeated postponement of the visit to England—which Macdonald still felt too tired to undertake—had resulted in a small accumulation of topics which would have to be discussed at the Colonial Office. They were all of some consequence; but obviously by far the most important was the unsolved question of the Bering Sea fur-seal fisheries. Since Blaine's rejection of the draft convention, and the public announcement of the American intention to police Bering Sea, relations with the United States had been nearly as bad as they could have been. Lord Salisbury and the American Secretary of State settled down to a long diplomatic argument over the freedom of the seas. A small squadron of the Royal Navy ominously took up its station at Esquimalt, British Columbia. The danger of war, the chance of a collision—such as Macdonald had always feared—which would lead to war or to a cessation of diplomatic or commercial intercourse, was greater than it had yet been.

Even this was not all. In the last little while, a most significant development had been taking place in Washington. It was becoming increasingly apparent that the United States was on the eve of a very considerable change in the history of its commercial policy. A new and comprehensive tariff measure, the McKinley Bill, was now well on its deliberate way through Congress; and the McKinley Bill provided, not only for a general and substantial increase in the American tariff, but also for the imposition of a few heavy specific duties on some of the most important cereals and other farm products which Canada exported to the United States. The McKinley Bill would be, in effect, a complete, unqualified rejection of the whole idea of a reasonable Canadian-American trade agreement. It would grievously hurt several Canadian export trades. It might ruin the barley industry of southern Ontario.

It was a bad, a politically dangerous, time. A general election was inevitably approaching. And despite Macdonald's still enormous vitality, he sometimes felt distressed by the decline of his own powers as well as by the persistence of his problems. He could never give up now. There was no way out for him. He would die in office. Tacitly he accepted his destiny; but he could not help being occasionally weighed down by the sense of his own age and weariness, and by the recurring gloomy reflection that his government's usefulness had been exhausted. "I am a good deal discouraged as to our future," he wrote to Tupper early in June. "Not that the country has gone or is going against us, but because our ministry is *too old* and *too long* in office. I am on the way to seventy-six. Langevin has aged very much and is inert and useless except in office, but he doesn't move in Quebec politics. He, Caron and Chapleau are allowing Mercier to carry the Province away from them by their want of harmony. Costigan and Colby have their frailties, as you know. Bowell is pretty hale, and yet shows age in some degree, and I fear for Thompson's health. But enough of this."⁵⁰

Enough of all this, for a while. Before June was out he was away for what he told Tupper would be a six-weeks' holiday at Rivière du Loup.

IV

During the long vacation at Les Rochers, which was less interrupted and more genuinely refreshing than any he had had in recent years, he laid tentative plans for the future. The general election would almost certainly have to be held in 1891. Further delay would be dangerous, for the provincial omens, to which he paid a good deal of attention, were foreboding trouble once again. Mercier had been triumphantly returned in the recent provincial general election in Quebec. In Ontario, where the Equal Righters, under Dalton McCarthy's inspiration, had campaigned virtually as a separate group, Meredith's Conservatives had suffered accordingly and Mowat was returned to power once more with a substantial majority. These renewed provincial Liberal successes disturbed Macdonald. It was time, at any rate, he thought, to begin making a few unostentatious preparations for the future. And early in August he paid a visit to Prince Edward Island, where he had not been since 1870, when he had spent a long carefree summer in restful convalescence at Charlottetown.[51]

Yet, as summer declined into autumn, the threat of these provincial defeats seemed to recede into the background. The real danger was something quite different. The real danger was the relentless approach of the McKinley tariff. Already Laurier, Cartwright, and Charlton were predicting economic disaster for Canada as the inevitable result of the new law. They had dragged out unrestricted reciprocity from the comparative obscurity in which it had lain for the past year with all the enthusiasm of a fresh conviction. Unrestricted reciprocity, they explained in numerous speeches, was the only panacea for the calamity that was approaching Canada; and the Liberal party was, of course, the only party which could possibly negotiate unrestricted reciprocity with the United States. Late in September, when Macdonald travelled down to the Maritime Provinces for a brief speaking-tour, talk of the McKinley Bill and its consequences had become so general and so excited that he devoted all the last part of his speech at Halifax to the question of commercial policy. The fundamental purpose of the United States, he told his audience, was to starve Canada into annexation. Reciprocity on self-respecting terms was not to be obtained from the republic. If the Canadians wished to trade freely with the United States, they must—so the Americans said in effect—either accept annexation or—what would be a virtual equivalent—separate from the United Kingdom and set up as an "independent" republic.[52]

As he rode back from Saint John, over the Short Line through a golden autumnal day, the merchants and shippers in scores of Canadian ports were frantically loading the last bulging cargoes for the United States. On Monday, October 6, the McKinley Act went into operation; and it was not until a month later, when the American congressional elections were held, that the heavy gloom which had settled down over Canada was pierced by a faint ray of hope. The Democrats had gained control of the new House of Representatives. "The rising of the people of the United States against the McKinley Bill is most wonderful," Macdonald wrote to George Stephen. "What the immediate consequences may be, can't yet be foreseen. By the rotten constitution of the United States, the present Congress, although discredited, nay repudiated, by the people, has full power until 4 March next. It will assemble on 4 December and the question is whether the Republican majority can bully it through, or whether, frightened at the hostile attitude of the electors, they may track back a bit. If the Senate is firm even after March next, the McKinley Bill cannot be repealed until 1897, but I am told that the western senators, although Republicans, will back down in the face of the angry multitude. We shall see."[53]

They would. But he did not really expect to see a repeal of the law. The persistent hostility which had been displayed, over a period of years, by both the Cleveland and Harrison administrations, had convinced him that the frustration of the Canadian national experiment had become the avowed object of both the American political parties. "Sir Charles Tupper will tell you," he informed Stephen, "that every American statesman (and he saw them all in 88) covets Canada. The greed for its acquisition is still on the increase, and God knows where it will all end. If Gladstone succeeds, he will sacrifice Canada without scruple. We must face the fight at our next election, and it is only the conviction that the battle will be better fought under my guidance than under another's that makes me undertake the task, handicapped as I am, with the infirmities of old age. . . . If left to ourselves, I have no doubt of a decision in our favour, but I have serious apprehensions, which are shared by all our friends here, that a large amount of Yankee money will be expended to corrupt our people."[54] He believed that American funds would be freely used to help the Canadian opposition. He believed that the Canadian opposition was offering advice to the Americans in the conduct of their policy of calculated denial and refusal. And he knew too that the struggle for the support of the Canadian voter would, in all likelihood, have to be carried on in the dejection and wretchedness of renewed depression. On November 7, three days after the American elections, the stock exchanges of London and Paris were reported very depressed, and the next week brought a major collapse in the security markets of all important financial capitals of the western world.[55]

In these gloomy circumstances the news that Newfoundland was successfully negotiating a trade and fisheries treaty with the United States came with a profound shock of consternation and dismay. On November 15, in response to anxious inquiries, the Colonial Secretary, Lord Knutsford, telegraphed the terms of the proposed convention, added that Blaine was apparently ready to consider a separate treaty, on a wide basis, with Canada, and suggested that one or two Canadian representatives should proceed unofficially to Washington for a conference. Two days later, after a long Cabinet meeting, Macdonald waited on the Governor-General with a draft minute of council which had been hurriedly drawn up on the subject.[56] Obviously he was deeply concerned. The effect, he declared, of these separate negotiations with Newfoundland would simply be to divide and weaken British North America by setting one colony against the other. In all probability, this was Blaine's real object. Blaine, he reminded the Governor-General, had never withdrawn or qualified his frequently expressed belief that Canada must be given no commercial privileges in American markets while she remained a British possession. Public men and newspapers in the United States made no effort to conceal their hope that the present consistently hostile attitude of the American administration to Canada would weaken and break down the Canadian desire for a separate political existence.

This, Macdonald declared earnestly, was the fundamental aim against which British North America must be always on its guard. If Great Britain permitted the signing of the separate Newfoundland treaty, the unhappy Canadian feeling of isolation and misfortune would be increased; and real and substantial assistance would be given to the United States in its commercial war with the Dominion. Separate negotiations, with different advantages and unequal concessions, would arouse jealousies and antagonisms, and weaken British North American resistance. The only effective means of ensuring Canada's survival as a separate nation—and here Macdonald expressed his deepest conviction—was the maintenance of a united front by Great Britain and the whole of British North America against the United States. As for the somewhat casual invitation to "unofficial" talks in Washington, bitter experience had made him deeply suspicious of this kind of negotiation with the United States. If the Canadian representatives presented themselves unofficially, Pauncefote, whom Macdonald believed was under Blaine's influence, would alone have any diplomatic status. "Unofficial" discussions would simply give the Canadian case away. They could, and probably would, be repudiated by Blaine at his slightest convenience.

These strong protestations had an immediate effect. It was, moreover, not simply a negative effect. And very soon it began to seem that this provoking and frightening affair might have exceptionally favourable consequences. During late November and early December, Macdonald was ill with a tenacious cold; but the news which was brought to his study in Earnscliffe appeared uniformly and—in view of all the past—almost incredibly hopeful. The Newfoundland convention was delayed until Canada could begin negotiations with the United States on its own account.[57] The United Kingdom agreed that the Canadian representatives at the proposed conference must be plenipotentiaries and not mere delegates. Pauncefote, in answer to an eager Canadian offer to start negotiations at once, reported that Blaine would not accept a formal commission until a "basis of arrangement" had first been reached, but that he had expressed "a strong desire" to conclude "a wide Reciprocity Treaty".[58] Macdonald was warily unconvinced by these characteristic evasions; but, in the critical circumstances of the moment, he knew he would have to accept Blaine's ambiguous invitation at its most favourable face value, and get the very best for Canada out of it that he could.[59] "We have held in Parliament and elsewhere," he wrote to Thompson, "that our attempts to negotiate had been so often rejected by the United States that we could not in self-respect go on our knees again, but that we were ready, whenever the United States made any sign of a desire to negotiate, to go into the matter earnestly. This suggestion of Blaine's gives us the opportunity and will prevent the opposition from stating that we have abandoned our ground and taken up theirs."[60]

On December 13, the Canadian government dispatched to London and Washington a brief statement of its comprehensive proposals for the trade discussions.[61] Three weeks later, on January 2, Lord Knutsford reported on the reception which these proposals had received at Washington. Secretary Blaine, he telegraphed, did not believe that it would be possible to obtain a formal trade commission until the prospects of its success had been assured by previous private discussions; but he was willing to enter into such private discussions with Pauncefote and one or more Canadian delegates at any time after March 4.[62] "You will observe," Macdonald explained later to Thompson, "that we had no intimation that the private and informal meeting was to be kept secret until January, when we applied for leave to publish our minute-in-council proposing a formal conference. We knew that the conference proposed by Blaine was to be unofficial and in that sense private, but had no idea that the fact of the meeting was to be kept private."[63]

The fact of the proposed meeting was, of course, not kept private. Macdonald himself made no official announcement. He did not apply to the British government for permission to publish until January 21, by which time he had nearly made up his mind to request an immediate dissolution.[64] But, in the meantime, while official statements were withheld, newspaper speculation was busy. The air was full of rumours and insinuations, for both sides felt that a general election was imminent, and each was manœuvring desperately for position. On January 14, the Toronto *Mail* announced, "on authority which leaves little reason to doubt that the rumour is true", that Great Britain had been urging Canada to compose its differences with the United States in a broad trade agreement, "and that Sir John Macdonald and his colleagues are seriously disturbed in consequence".[65] This provoked a counter-declaration from the Toronto *Empire*. The *Mail's* statement, it declared roundly, was not true. On the contrary, it was the government of the United States which had recently approached the Canadian government with a view to the improvement of trade relations.[66]

Macdonald's hand was being forced. It was of the utmost importance that he should make an official statement—and at once. He wanted permission, not merely to publish the substance of the Canadian proposal of December 13, but also to indicate that it had been inspired by the favourable attitude of the United States.[67] His necessities were the opportunities of the Liberal opposition. They were also, for somewhat different reasons, the opportunities of James G. Blaine. In these circumstances, the connection between the American State Department and the Canadian opposition, the existence of which even the Governor-General had come to suspect, was suddenly and dramatically revealed. On January 28, Edward Farrer, one of the editors of the Toronto *Globe*, had an "important though informal" interview in Washington with Secretary Blaine and Chairman Hitt of the House Committee on Foreign Affairs.[68] Blaine had found it impossible to receive official Canadian representatives until March 4; but he was evidently quite prepared to discuss trade relations with the editor of the leading Canadian opposition newspaper as early as January 28. Negotiations with official Canadian delegates must be kept strictly private; but the news of Farrer's interview was instantly given to the press and received wide publicity. The immediate consequences of the meeting—a consequence which was no doubt arranged at the meeting itself—was given wider publicity still. In a letter written on the same date, a Congressman inquired of the Secretary of State whether negotiations for a "partial" reciprocity with Canada were going on. "I authorize you to contradict the rumours you refer to," Blaine replied. "There are no negotiations whatever on foot for a reciprocity treaty with Canada. . . . We know nothing of Sir Charles Tupper's coming to Washington."[69]

All along, Macdonald had distrusted "informal" discussions. He had suspected that Blaine would repudiate them at his own convenience. Blaine had done exactly that. He had betrayed Macdonald deliberately and completely. "No, I have not seen the letter," Stanley replied, on the day of publication, in answer to Macdonald's inquiry, "but it would be quite like Blaine. . . . The more I think of the situation the more I should be disposed to advise that we should go right ahead—Blaine or no Blaine."[70] Macdonald agreed. The government was in an appalling position. It had been led up the garden path, double-crossed with cool efficiency, and then effectively prevented from uttering a word of explanation or protest. Insupportable—possibly disastrous! But there it was. Further delays or manoeuvres were pointless. The decision to dissolve, which had been taken on January 21 and withheld in the anxious, frustrating days that followed, could now be confirmed. There was every reason to take the field openly, at once, and with every ounce of resolution and confidence that he could muster. On Monday, February 2, the order for the general election was signed. When he drove home that evening with his secretary, Joseph Pope, he seemed full of energy; and far into the night he was busy outlining his election address.

The address was a reasoned defence of his design for Canada, and of its two greatest foundations, the national transcontinental railway and the national policy of protection. It was a reasoned attack upon unrestricted reciprocity which, in his view, offered the most fundamental threat to the fiscal autonomy and political independence of Canada. "The question which you will shortly be called upon to determine," he told the voters, "resolves itself into this: shall we endanger our possession of the great heritage bequeathed to us by our fathers, and submit ourselves to direct taxation for the privilege of having our tariff fixed at Washington, with a prospect of ultimately becoming a portion of the American union? . . . As for myself, my course is clear. A British subject I was born—a British subject I will die. With my utmost effort, with my latest breath, will I oppose the 'veiled treason' which attempts by sordid means and mercenary proffers to lure our people from their allegiance. During my long public service of nearly half a century, I have been true to my country and its best interests, and I appeal with equal confidence to the men who have trusted me in the past, and to the young hope of the country with whom rests its destinies for the future, to give me their united and strenuous aid in this, my last effort, for the unity of the Empire and the preservation of our commercial and political freedom."[71]

On January 21, he had sent a final appeal to Tupper in England. "Immediate dissolution almost certain," he cabled. "Your presence during election contest in Maritime Provinces essential to encourage our friends. Please come. Answer."[72] Tupper had answered yes. And on February 6, the day before the election address was finished, he was back in Ottawa once more. They would fight it out together for the last time. On Saturday, February 7, Tupper departed to fulfil an engagement at Kingston which his chief was unable to keep. And eight days later, on Sunday night, February 15, Macdonald left Ottawa for Toronto.

V

He was determined to finish what Blaine and Farrer had begun. If this was the kind of warfare that was desired, then —by good luck and good management—he could carry it effectively into the enemy's camp. He was ready to change his method; but his programme remained essentially the same. The *Times* correspondent, Colmer telegraphed from England, was now asserting that the Conservative government had virtually abandoned the plan of closer trade relations with the United States on which it had first gone to the country and had returned to the old policy of protection and imperial loyalty.

This, of course, was nonsense. The Conservative government had never officially "gone to the country" on a policy of closer trade relations with the United States. It had never had the chance. Blaine had tied the hands and stopped the mouths of the Canadians while he proceeded with complete impunity to double-cross them. Yet despite the bitter humiliation of this betrayal, Macdonald was prepared to resume the postponed negotiations as if nothing had happened. "*Times* Toronto correspondent in error," he telegraphed back to England. "Government and Conservative party have not abandoned issue on which they went to the country. They still desire to negotiate for closer trade relations with the United States, but they insist on control of their own tariffs and will not discriminate against the Mother Country."[73] These, of course, were the conditions on which Macdonald had always insisted; and the speech which he gave at Halifax on October 1, 1890—the only important speech of the previous autumn—had anticipated all the main themes of the election address of February 7, 1891.

He had not changed his programme. He did not intend directly to attack Blaine. But, by good fortune, Farrer, the intermediary between the American Secretary of State and the Canadian opposition, had been delivered into his hands. On Tuesday, February 17, at a great Conservative rally in the Academy of Music in Toronto, at which he and Tupper were the principal speakers, he attacked Farrer—and through him the Liberal party—by impugning the journalist's loyalty and calling in question the motives which lay behind his advocacy of unrestricted reciprocity. Farrer, at the request of an American friend, had written a pamphlet, in which, as he himself later explained, he had tried to view Canadian-American trade relations as an American would; and from this point of view, he had suggested several methods of economic retaliation by which the United States could bring the citizens of the Dominion to a realization of the stupidity of their trade and fisheries policy.[74] Only a few copies of this pamphlet had been printed under strict conditions of secrecy. The Conservatives, through a friendly printer, had managed to secure only a part of the proofs. But the gist of Farrer's argument, and the retaliatory methods he had suggested—tonnage duties on Canadian vessels, suspension of the bonding privileges in the United States, cutting the connections of the Canadian Pacific Railway at Sault Ste. Marie—were all clearly revealed in these few precious proof sheets.

At Halifax Macdonald had hinted that the Canadian opposition was giving aid and comfort to the Americans in the conduct of their commercial warfare against the Dominion. Now these insinuations became a definite charge. The rejection of Canadian advances, the hostility to legitimate Canadian interests at Washington, were in large measure traceable, he told his audience, to the advice which traitors like Farrer had offered to the Americans. In effect Farrer and his like had presented themselves as Canadian guides to the realization of annexation. If, they had said to the Americans, you wish to obtain the Dominion, you must concede nothing to Canada, you must put the screws on Canada, you must coerce the Canadians and bully them in every possible fashion. "In fact," Macdonald went on, summarizing the general argument of Farrer's pamphlet, "the document points out every possible way in which Canada and its trade can be injured, and its people impoverished, with the view of eventually bringing about annexation. . . . I say that there is a deliberate conspiracy, in which some of the members of the opposition are more or less compromised; I say that there is a deliberate conspiracy, by force, by fraud, or by both, to force Canada into the American union."[75]

Macdonald could play the game that Farrer and Blaine had started as well as they, or better. He had turned the tables upon his opponents. But he had done more than win by means of a sharply clever trick. He had found and stated, in a simple and arresting form, the main theme of the election. Farrer, an editor of the most important Canadian opposition newspaper, had been ready, at a time of depression and great national distress, to advise the foreigner against his country's own interests. Were not the Liberals, in advocating the closest economic relationship with the United States, really playing the foreigner's game just as effectively and by only slightly less obvious means? And was not unrestricted reciprocity nothing more nor less than a vote of want of confidence in the whole idea of a distinct and separate nation in northern North America? During the last few years, under accumulated reversals and misfortunes, the Dominion had been driven in until its back was to the wall. But the impulse to resist and to survive was strong; and that impulse had become incarnate in an old man of seventy-six, who had told the Canadians, in a final manifesto, that he purposed still to continue the work of "building up on this continent, under the flag of England, a great and powerful nation", and who would never give in until he died.

For an old man of seventy-six he was going at a killing pace. Before he left Ottawa, he had told his secretary Joseph Pope that he intended to remain in Toronto and to supervise the general operations of the campaign from there.[76] But he could not keep to his plan. He began to yield to the frantic appeals that kept pouring in from every part of the province; and quickly and inevitably he was drawn into a circuit of the battlefront, with stops at every point where the fighting was hottest. On Wednesday, February 18, the day after his arraignment of Farrer, he left Toronto for Hamilton. On Thursday, he was in Strathroy; on Friday, the guest of John Carling, in London. And on Saturday, travelling eastward again, he spoke in succession at Stratford, St. Mary's, Guelph, Acton, and Brampton.

He had done the same, or nearly the same, scores of times before; and even as recently as 1886, Thompson had marvelled at the high good spirits with which he had carried on in just such a tour as this. But Saturday, February 21, was probably as hard a day's speaking as any he had ever attempted. At Brampton people noted how hoarse he had become; and when they reached Toronto late that night, it seemed to Pope that his master looked more tired than he had usually done in the past after such exertions. Macdonald rested on Sunday, but a day's rest was not enough; and he was weary still when he started for Kingston on Sunday night. After days of mild weather in western Ontario, it had turned sharply cold again; and the thermometer stood at less than ten degrees above zero when his private car came to rest at Kingston in the early hours of

Monday morning. He was chilled through by the time he reached the British American Hotel. Most of the day he spent resting in his roomy suite in the hotel; and a reporter who came to see him in the early afternoon found him in good spirits, but still wan from the fatigues of his western tour.[77]

On Tuesday, February 24, the weather changed dramatically again. The clouds that had been piling up steadily for the past twelve hours broke in the late afternoon, the rain poured down, and by night the wind had risen to a gale.[78] He spoke that evening to a huge crowd in the Kingston Opera House; and the next day, with slush and puddles underfoot and a lowering rainy sky above, he started out for Napanee. It was nearly sixty years ago that he had gone off, a lad of seventeen, to set up George Mackenzie's branch legal establishment in the tiny frontier village of Napanee. It had been the first important move of his career; and now he was bound on what was virtually its last journey. The town, that raw, unpleasant February day, was packed with people. In an open carriage he was driven slowly down the main street, through a shouting, gesticulating crowd, to the town hall. The place was full to suffocation; even the platform was crowded. In a vague, chaotic dream he was aware of a chorus of young girls singing the national anthem, of somebody speaking, of somebody else introducing him, of himself rising slowly, desperately to his feet.[79] It was as though he stood at bay. His face was flushed, his white straggling hair was disordered; and he was conscious of nothing but the heat, and the crowds, and his own appalling weariness. Then it was over; and somehow he was stumbling towards the door, past the faces, the voices, the outstretched hands, the oppressive, indistinguishable clamour all around, and out into the street, and the open carriage, and the chill and clammy air.

When at last they reached the private railway carriage, Pope left him, with a sheaf of newly arrived telegrams in his hand, at the door of his bedroom. Only a few minutes later, when the secretary entered the room again, he found the old man lying across the bed.[80] His face was grey, grey with fatigue, grey with another kind of fatigue which was the final exhaustion of a life.

VI

The tour was stopped. The remaining speaking engagements were cancelled. In his moment of extreme weakness, his old enemy, the severe bronchial cold, had clutched at him once again. His voice was almost gone, his pulse weak and irregular; and when he breathed there was often pain over his left lung.[81] For days, while the campaign roared towards its furious conclusion, he lay and rested at Kingston; and it was not until March 4, the day before the poll, that he felt able to travel back to the capital. As soon as he reached Ottawa, he went to bed. That evening, the first election returns were brought to him as he lay there. But the short, hard cough still shook him, he tired with dismaying swiftness; and it was barely ten o'clock and the results from not more than half the constituencies were in, when he turned suddenly on his side and went to sleep.

The next day the congratulatory telegrams and letters began to pour in. The Marquess of Salisbury, Lord Lorne, George Stephen and a host of other admirers all sent their felicitations. Even the Queen, so Lord Stanley informed him, "expressed her great gratification at the result of the elections". His own feelings were much more mixed. His government had been returned to power; his own majority in Kingston was the largest in his political career. But the party had lost a few seats in both Ontario and Quebec; and although it had picked up others in the Maritime Provinces, the total majority was definitely a little smaller than it had been. Still, they were the victors; and in that year of hard distress and savage discouragement, it was perhaps wonderful that the government had even survived. "The effect of the McKinley tariff is so disastrous," he wrote to George Stephen, "that if our election had been postponed until another harvest, we should have been swept out of existence. As it was, I was surprised and grieved to find the hold unrestricted reciprocity had got of our farmers. . . . I have of course pointed out that unrestricted reciprocity meant annexation, and the movements of Cartwright, Farrer and Wiman enabled us to raise the loyalty cry, which had considerable effect.

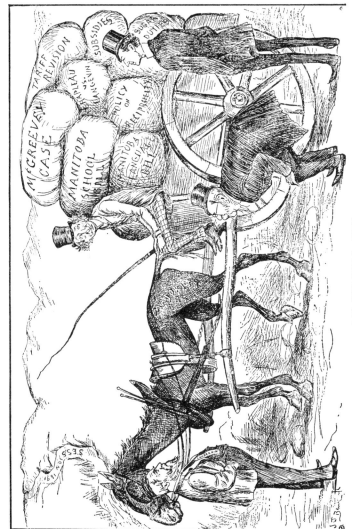

AN UP-HILL JOB.

LAURIER.—"YOUR HORSE HAS WASTED AWAY TO A SHADOW. HE'LL NEVER BE ABLE TO PULL YOU THROUGH WITH THAT LOAD!"
SIR JOHN.—"DON'T WORRY YOURSELF, MY DEAR SIR; A GOOD DEAL DEPENDS ON THE DRIVING, YOU KNOW."

Still, the farmers' defection, and the large sums sent, *beyond a doubt*, from the United States, have left us with a diminished majority and an uncertain future."[82]

His own future—a few of those closest to him began to realize—was still more uncertain. "I am slowly—very slowly—gathering myself together again," he wrote to Professor Williamson on March 10. "I have not been out of the house since I arrived here, but this is a fine day, and I shall drive to Council."[88] He had ventured downstairs for the first time the previous day and had begun work on the great unopened mass of his correspondence. His physician, Dr. R. W. Powell, cautioned him, reminding him, with the utmost earnestness, of his imperative need for rest. He listened with his usual genial courtesy; but it was plain that he intended to follow the advice only within limits. "I must attend to my work," he said seriously to Dr. Powell, "if I am at all able."[84] But he was not really able yet. Long before the business of Council was finished on March 10, he was overcome once again by his dreadful sense of weariness. He had to leave before the adjournment, to his own distress and to the deep concern of his colleagues.

The weeks went by. He spent them mainly in bed or indoors. At the end of March he told Stephen that he was "only now" recovering from his prostration. And meanwhile the time which was even partially free for convalescence was dwindling rapidly away. Early in April Sir Charles Tupper left to reopen the trade negotiations at Washington, received the rebuff of a fresh postponement from Blaine, returned once more and departed finally for England. By that time, Macdonald was deep in preparations for Parliament; and on April 29, almost before he knew it, the new session opened. He was going about more freely now; and it was with something of his old jaunty, defiant energy that he replied, on the first day of the debate on the speech from the throne, to Laurier's taunt about the Pyrrhic victory he had gained at the polls. "I tell my friends and I tell my foes: *J'y suis, j'y reste*," he answered with spirit. "We are going to stay here and it will take more than the power of the honourable gentleman, with all the phalanx behind him, to disturb us or to shove us from our pedestal."[85] Brave words!

But, as the days went by, everybody could see how feeble he was, and when he got back to Earnscliffe in the evening, or, more often, in the afternoon, Agnes knew that he was utterly done out.

During those long, dreary weeks of convalescence, he had often felt weariness and depression; but on May 12, not a fortnight after Parliament opened, he suddenly experienced fear. With two of his colleagues he went that morning to wait upon the Governor-General. The old problem, at once tiresome and dangerous, of the Bering Sea fisheries was up once more. A telegram of inquiry from the Colonial Office required an answer. He started to explain his views; and then, without warning, it became difficult for him to find or articulate his words. He was terribly conscious of his mysterious disability; but the Governor-General was conscious of it too; and making an excuse to take the telegram away with him to Rideau Hall, he promised that he would bring it back himself that afternoon to the Prime Minister's office in the Parliament Buildings. It was nearing the appointed hour when Macdonald hurriedly entered the apartments, crossed to his private room, called his secretary, and, explaining that Lord Stanley would be arriving almost immediately by appointment, asked him to go and request Sir John Thompson to attend without delay. Pope came hurrying back to say that the Minister of Justice would be there in a few minutes.

"He must come at once," Macdonald said thickly and with difficulty, "because he must speak to the Governor for me, as I cannot talk. There is something the matter with my speech."[86]

A few minutes later when Lord Stanley arrived, he found his Prime Minister and his Minister of Justice waiting for him together in curious stiff attitudes of expectancy in the inner room. Macdonald looked ill. He also seemed extremely embarrassed. In a low and not very distinct voice, he asked Thompson to speak for him; and in a very few moments the wording of the telegraphic reply was determined and the telegram itself dispatched. The sense of strain and difficulty in the room seemed to deepen. There was nothing for Lord Stanley to do but go. And then, as he turned to leave, he saw what he had not observed before, that one side of Macdonald's face was slightly drawn and twisted.[87]

The door closed upon the Governor-General. Thompson departed almost immediately after. For a few moments Macdonald was left alone, and then, as if he could bear the solitude no longer, he crossed into the outer office to speak to Pope.

"I am afraid of paralysis," he said, and there was a harsh note of apprehension in his voice. "Both my parents died of it, and I seem to feel it creeping over me."[88]

Pope called a cab. Together they walked down Parliament Hill to meet it. By that time Macdonald seemed better; and at half past six, when the doctor called at Earnscliffe, he found his patient still further improved and his speech nearly restored. Together and very gravely they talked over the ominous event of the afternoon.[89] Macdonald admitted that for some time past he had felt a slight want of power in his left arm and an occasional tingling in his left hand and fingers. Powell explained his condition, pointed out the almost inevitable consequence of continued effort, and earnestly advised complete rest. It was Macdonald's last chance; but he declined to take it. Complete rest, or an absence from Ottawa while Parliament was sitting, was, he informed Powell, utterly out of the question. He stuck to his post. He came to Council; he attended Parliament. And for a while fortune seemed to favour his magnificent audacity. He grew rapidly better. And from Monday to Friday of the penultimate week in May he was almost his old gay self again.

Friday, May 22, 1891, was a day like any other day in the Commons House of the Parliament of Canada. There was nothing to distinguish it from all the other hundreds of days he had spent there since the far-off session of 1865. Late spring had come wafted in on a breeze that was as soft and warm as that of midsummer; and Parliament Hill was heavy with the scent of lilac. "Sir John is very well and bright again," Thompson wrote that day to his wife.[90] It almost seemed that Macdonald's old parliamentary form had come back once more. He did not speak at any length; but he intervened again and again in the debate with his accustomed urbane and jocular comments. He was still in his place when the adjournment came at eleven o'clock; and he lingered for a while on the terrace outside, chatting with his Minister of Customs, Mackenzie Bowell. It was like a summer night. The laden lilac bushes rimmed the crest of Parliament Hill, and beyond that the land fell steeply away to the river below and rose on the other side to the low dark hills of the Precambrian Shield. And somewhere out there, hidden in the rock and forest, bright under the moonlight, was the railway, his railway, the track of Canada, the track of destiny, thrusting its way forward, mile after mile, towards the north-west.

"It is late, Bowell," he said. "Good-night."

Epilogue

The Sixth of June, 1891

I

IT WAS six o'clock when he reached Earnscliffe on the evening of Saturday, May 23. Parliament, of course, stood adjourned for the week-end; but he had taken advantage of the free day to call a meeting of the Cabinet, and the whole afternoon had been filled with its prolonged deliberations. Slowly he alighted from the cab; and Agnes, who had come anxiously out to the gate to meet him, saw at once, with the familiar pang, how dreadfully weary he looked. She took his brief-case—the inevitable accompaniment of his journeys home—in her hand; and when they walked up the path together arm-in-arm, it was she who was giving support to him.[1]

It was Saturday night; and by a long established rule which had become a tradition of his premiership, Saturday night during the session was the invariable occasion of a large dinner-party at Earnscliffe. The guests were all invited; in another hour or so they would be arriving. It was impossible, he told the worried Agnes, to cancel the affair at this late hour. He would preside, as he had done so many times in the past, at his own dinner table; and with the old resilience his spirits seemed to rise instinctively to meet the occasion. He was in his best form that night. It was as though he had inwardly determined that the guests at that last dinner-party would carry away with them an unspoilt memory of the geniality of their host. When Pope left him at about ten o'clock, it seemed to the secretary that the old Sir John—the Sir John not only of a few months, but even of a few years ago—had been miraculously restored.[2]

The last guest departed. He was flushed and suddenly tired. The room was warm—warm with the quickly produced heat of a spring night when the air outside is chill enough to discourage too much ventilation. Another window was flung open; and for a few moments he sat beside it, relaxed in an easy chair, while the cool air flowed refreshingly over him. It seemed nothing at the time; but next day they remembered the tiny incident, for next day he was suddenly worse again. He had contracted a cold—a slight cold only, surely; but with it those frightening symptoms, which had troubled him so much at Kingston three months ago, seemed to reappear.[3] His voice was very weak. He felt an oppressive sense of constriction across his chest; and when he coughed there came a sharp spurt of pain.

Early in the afternoon, the now seriously worried Agnes summoned the doctor. Powell gave his patient immediate relief; and for two days he succeeded in keeping him in bed, with gradually encouraging results. On the third day, Wednesday, May 27, Macdonald could bear the inaction no longer. The thought of the vast, accumulating, and accusing pile of correspondence downstairs was too much for him. He insisted that morning on going down to his study, and there, with Pope, he worked steadily through the greater part of the day. When Powell came for his evening visit, he told the doctor that he felt fairly comfortable. He was tired and weak. But then that was to be expected. He had put in a fairly full day. And it was without much apprehension, and with even a small feeling of satisfaction at a good day's work well done, that he went to bed that night. He was awakened suddenly at about half past two in the morning. He had called aloud without realizing that he had done so. The terrified Agnes was bending over him; and in a few minutes he became aware that there was little sensation in his left leg, and that the power and feeling in his left arm seemed completely gone.[4]

He lay on the bed, stretched out in stillness, and waited. Thank God, he could talk. When the doctor, hastily summoned, arrived at a little past three o'clock, he could discuss his symptoms with him with his usual laconic clarity. The left side of his face was slightly stiffened and twisted; but there was no impairment in his speech, and before the dawn of that brief night of late spring, he had already partially recovered from the effects of his seizure. By half past nine o'clock he could, with some effort, draw his left leg slowly up towards his body; and although the numbness in his left arm was more stubbornly resistant, it also seemed to be slowly passing away as the morning wore on. When Pope arrived, after the doctor had left and the breakfast hour was over, Macdonald greeted him with his usual composure. There was no fear in his eyes, and no disquietude in his voice. He discussed at some length, and with an interest which was not in the least perfunctory, two resolutions which he intended shortly to bring before Parliament. It was as if he fully expected to be back in his place in the House of Commons by the following Monday at the latest! And in one brief episode only was there a hint of his realistic awareness of his condition. He asked Pope to bring him one of his estate documents, and Pope inquired whether he wished to sign it then or later.

"Now," he replied briefly, "while there is time."[5]

Powell had requested a consultation. In some mysterious fashion a rumour of the increased seriousness of the Prime Minister's illness was already running through Ottawa;[6] and when, in mid-afternoon, Doctors George Ross and James Stewart arrived from Montreal, the grave news was amply confirmed. By four o'clock the consulting physicians were at Macdonald's bedside. His speech was unimpaired; his intellect was unclouded. He could move his left leg fairly freely now; and although the numbness in his left arm still persisted, he could lift it to his head and extend it from his body with relative ease. He was, the doctors considered, making the most remarkable recovery. But obviously a slight lesion had occurred; and, with the utmost earnestness, they explained the real state of affairs to the patient and assured him that the only way of averting a second and probably fatal seizure was complete rest in bed and entire freedom from public business for at least some weeks to come. With grave courtesy, Macdonald thanked them for their kindness and their candour. Lady Macdonald was informed.

A bulletin was drafted for publication; and at six o'clock Dr. Powell went up to the Privy Council room, met the Cabinet solemnly assembled, and informed its members of everything that had taken place.[7]

II

Macdonald spent the evening placidly reading in bed. It was, whether he was well or ill, the normal conclusion of every day; and that night he enjoyed his usual amount—about six hours—of sleep. When morning came on Friday, May 29, he was evidently feeling better still. He had a cup of tea. He moved his left arm with considerably more freedom, Dr. Powell observed, than he had even on the previous evening; and when Pope came at about ten o'clock, he reverted, with an instinctive and incorrigible impulse, to the habit of a lifetime, and demanded to see the morning's letters.[8] Pope brought up a few of them—carefully choosing those of minor importance: and a few minutes later he came hurrying in again with a piece of information of obviously much greater interest. Sir John Thompson, the Minister of Justice, had called at Earnscliffe and was waiting below. Macdonald instantly determined to seize the opportunity which this visit afforded. It was nearly a week since he had seen any one of his colleagues. He was hungry to re-establish contact, to re-impose his accustomed control; and Thompson was his favourite minister, to whom he imparted his most intimate confidences. He gave orders that the Minister of Justice was to be shown up at once.

Thompson entered the room in some trepidation. He was a worried and anxious man. His own responsibility, which was great enough before, had been magnified to an uncertain but an enormous extent within the past few days. The rumours, the bulletins, the news of the doctors' consultation had all done their disintegrating work. In forty-eight hours the character of the House had utterly changed. The government side was weighed down with anxiety; the opposition was alive with eager expectation. "The Grits," Thompson wrote to his wife that day, "are like a lot of pirates prepared to make a rush. We will have a caucus on Tuesday and rally our men." How could it be done? Without a known and accepted leader, how could the rank and file be effectively rallied? He glanced again at the man who lay on the bed before him. Macdonald's mouth was firm, his eyes were alert. He might have been recuperating from a slight illness. He was obviously better. He might even get well again. But, in his heart of hearts, Thompson did not believe it. "The probability is," he told his wife a little later, "that he will not be in the House again this session, if ever."[9]

If ever. The wordless phrase hovered in the air between them. It was the inarticulate first premise of their speculations. Who was to succeed? There was no instantly obvious first choice. There were far too few real possibilities. For months, for years, Macdonald's thoughts had trudged wearily round and round this small, closed circle of selection. He knew everything that had been said, and that could be said, for and against every conceivable candidate. A case could be made out for Langevin, for Tupper, and for Thompson. But he was aware of the disability of Thompson's religion, of the disrepute into which Langevin had fallen as a result of the recent scandals, of Tupper's unpopularity with certain important Cabinet ministers, including Thompson, and of Tupper's own preference for his work as High Commissioner in London. The idea of a stop-gap appointment, of a temporary, provisional prime minister, who would hold the government and the party together until the issue of the leadership had been settled, was an obvious idea that had occurred to him before. Late in the spring, at one of the last Cabinet meetings that he had attended, he had suggested such a plan to Thompson. "Thompson," he said slowly, "when I am gone, you will have to rally around Abbott; he is your only man."[10] Abbott had held office for only a few years, but he was a veteran member of Parliament, and an old and loyal Conservative; and the fact that he sat in the Senate, rather than the House of Commons, would have the additional advantage of giving Thompson, in the Commons, a large measure of effective control. Abbott's honour would be titular, as well as provisional. But, even so, was he worthy of it? Macdonald was not sure. His doubts and uncertainties returned. He did not feel particularly drawn to Abbott. And, even in this last extremity, he still hesitated to perform the final solemn act of naming a successor.

"Thompson," he said faintly but firmly, "some time ago I said you would have to rally round Abbott, that he was your only man. I have changed my mind now, he is too selfish."[11]

He would have spoken more. But Thompson was anxious to end the visit. The old man must not be tired. And had he not talked enough—and more than enough—already? As gently but as swiftly as he could, the Minister of Justice brought the conversation to a close and withdrew. Macdonald was left alone; but not for long. At about midday, a second visitor— Dr. Sullivan, the physician who had attended him during his break-down in Kingston in mid-winter—paid a brief call to the sick-room. Then the patient had a little milk and a few spoon-fuls of beef-tea. He was resting and reading one of the reviews, when Powell arrived at a little after half past three. For a while the doctor and his patient talked softly together. The room was very still. The whole house was hushed in silence; and outside the lawns and terraces of Earnscliffe drowsed in the hot sun of late May. Powell was putting the usual routine questions to his patient, and Macdonald was making his usual replies. And then, as if he wished merely to dispose himself a little more comfortably during this gentle interrogation, the old man leaned his head back upon the pillow. He yawned once or twice. And, in a second, he seemed to become un-conscious.

The doctor started forward. Could it be? In an instant he knew that there was no possible doubt. The man lying on the bed before him had received a second and devastating stroke. The entire right side of his body was paralysed. He was bereft of speech.[12]

It was four o'clock on the afternoon of Friday, May 29.

III

Agnes, Hugh John, and Pope were summoned at once. Hurriedly, in low tones, the doctor explained to them what had probably occurred. The stricken man was conscious of their frightened presence. He tried desperately to speak to his son; and his utter failure brought home to them all the completeness of the tragedy that had befallen him. Time was of the essence now. Death might come in a few hours—even in a few minutes. The doctor moved swiftly to give his patient quick relief, to get immediate assistance, and to send the necessary warnings. He dispatched messengers requesting two Ottawa physicians— Sir James Grant and Dr. H. P. Wright—to come at once to Earnscliffe for a consultation. He wrote to both the Governor-General and Sir Hector Langevin informing them of the sudden dreadful change in his patient's condition.

Earnscliffe waited in the strained silence of painful expectancy. It was half past six, and the rooms were rich with the golden light of early evening when Sir James Grant and Dr. Wright arrived. They and Dr. Powell were a long time together in the silent room upstairs; but if Agnes clutched at the vain hope that the length of the consultation might mean an uncertainty of diagnosis or a division of expert opinion, she was soon undeceived. The doctors were in entire agreement. The symptoms were very marked; and as Dr. Powell explained, it was obvious that "a hæmorrhage had taken place into the left hemisphere, chiefly confined to the motor area".[13] When the stroke came, the patient had been resting quietly in bed, there had apparently been no disturbance in the heart's action, and, in Powell's opinion, the damage was somewhat less serious than might have been expected. Even so, Macdonald was in a highly critical condition; and the doctors clearly feared for the worst. At eight o'clock they issued a bulletin for publication; and a little later, in a second letter to Langevin, Sir James Grant gave, without extenuation, the gloomy conclusion they had reached. "I have just seen Sir John in consultation," he wrote. "Entire loss of speech. Hæmorrhage on the brain. Condition hopeless."[14]

It was past nine o'clock when this message arrived on Parliament Hill. The House of Commons was in evening session. For most of the day the members had been discussing a Liberal resolution deploring Sir Charles Tupper's recent participation in

the Canadian general election as a breach of his duties as High
Commissioner for Canada in London. It was the same subject
that had been up a week before, on the last day that Macdonald
had attended Parliament; but the opposition had a great deal
more to say about it, and C. H. Mackintosh, the Conservative
member for Ottawa City, was endeavouring to reply to Cartwright's attack when Sir James Grant's note was brought in.
For a moment Langevin stared at the message. He passed it
swiftly to the other ministers; he crossed the floor and whispered
the news to Laurier. The House became rapidly aware that
something gravely unusual had occurred; and a minute later,
when the Minister of Public Works got up to move the adjournment, all doubts were ended. Langevin's voice was
strangely shaken. "I have the painful duty," he said, speaking
with some difficulty, "to announce to the House that the news
from Earnscliffe just received is that the First Minister has had
a relapse, and that he is in a most critical condition. We have
reports from the medical men in attendance on the right honourable gentleman, and they do not seem to believe that he
can live many hours longer."[15]

A minute later the House adjourned. It was nearly ten
o'clock. The members crowded about the Minister of Public
Works. He repeated the news; he showed Sir James Grant's
message. When there was no more to learn, Conservatives and
Liberals stood about in little groups discussing the calamity in
hushed voices; and Langevin sat in his place, the tears running
down his cheeks. He was an uninspiring man, with no great
ability except in the routines of administration and with much
too ingrained a disposition to nepotism and jobbery. But for
over thirty years, through every conceivable situation and all
possible danger, he had been loyal to Macdonald. Commonplace, mercenary, ageing, he was the embodiment of loyalty;
and in that moment it might have seemed that loyalty would
redeem him.

"For thirty-three years I have been his follower," he kept
saying over and over again. "For thirty-three years I have been
his follower."[16]

He and Thompson and Chapleau drove out that night to

Earnscliffe. Earlier in the evening, while the House was still in session, the Governor-General had called. He had informed the Queen by cable. By ten o'clock the news was speeding over the telegraph wires to every city, town, and village in Canada; and next morning, on the front pages of scores of newspapers, it was revealed to millions of shocked Canadians. In some headlines, Macdonald was referred to by his name; in others by his official title; and in still others—as if there could not be the faintest doubt as to who was meant—by pronoun only. *He is dying.* The Canadians knew the worst now. They expected him to die. They—like the physicians who had issued the first bulletin—could not see how he could long survive such an appalling shock. The Monday morning newspapers, they felt sure, would bring the news of his death. But Monday came, and the final, fatal intelligence did not appear. He still lived. The hours went by and he still lived. And gradually, as the hours mounted into another day, the Canadians began to realize that far away, in the hushed chamber at Earnscliffe, a last struggle was being waged against death itself.

IV

It was the first of June. The Ottawa valley was bathed in heat and light. For two weeks there had been scarcely any rain.[17] The sun rose blood-red at dawn and sank at night into a blood-red sky. Behind its drawn curtains, the great dim bedchamber at Earnscliffe was drowsy with summer heat; and there he lay, wasted, silent, somnolent, but still alive. His splendid vitality, which he had used and abused so often and which had never failed him yet, was fighting a final, involuntary battle for his existence. His heart's action was weak and irregular: his breathing rapid and laboured. It was painfully evident that his vital forces were close to the last point of exhaustion. Yet he lived on. Whether he willed it or no, his body continued its desperate fight for life. He could swallow the milk and beef tea and champagne which they gave him so carefully. He knew when he desired the slight relief of being moved from one side to the other of the bed.

What he felt was not mere consciousness of physical wants. Deep in its ultimate citadel, behind the thick walls of paralysis and silence, his mind was still working, imperfectly but coolly, reasonably, as it had always done. He could not speak. His whole right side was immobilized. But his left arm, which had first tingled with the threat of paralysis, was still unimpaired; and by the pressure of his left hand he could still communicate with the watchers by his bedside. It was his last contact with the world; and he used it surely, without the slightest hesitation and without a single mistake.[18] If a question were put by one of the doctors or nurses in such a way that the answering pressure might mean either yes or no, then his hand remained slack. It was only when the meaning of the slight movement had become plain and unmistakable that he gave it, if he so desired. His wishes, which came faintly but surely, and, as it were, out of endless distances, were commands which the watchers were anxious to carry out to the letter. There must be no mistake. What he wanted, must be done, and done exactly. And sometimes, to complete assurance, they put their questions in different ways, both positively and negatively. The response was always the same. He was never confused himself; he never confused them. He talked, in this strange way, with Agnes, Hugh John, Pope, Fred White, and the others who served him; and repeatedly, while his wife sat beside the bed, he answered her unuttered and unutterable question with a gentle pressure of his hand.

The room was hushed. The house was hushed. The grounds lay silent in the sunshine. The tugs which laboured up the river dragging the lumber barges behind them had ceased to blow their whistles; the bells had been taken off the horse-drawn street-cars which passed slowly up and down Sussex Street.[19] The world had drawn back, respectfully, reverently; but it had drawn back only a little way. A long procession of people came daily to make inquiries of the guardian at the gate. A short distance away, a bell tent had been pitched for the Canadian Pacific Railway telegraph operator: and every few hours the newspaper correspondents came down in a body to read the latest bulletin and to put their innumerable questions to the doctors. The whole country waited for news; and in the meantime, while it waited, it was consumed by curious and anxious speculation.

In Ottawa, Thompson wrote sardonically to his wife, the buzz of excitement was intense. What was going to happen? Who, if death came, would succeed the old chief? There was a movement in favour of Tupper, which Tupper himself quickly discouraged in an emphatic cable to his son. Langevin's declining chances were discussed. Thompson's name grew increasingly prominent; and Thompson himself, so he told his wife, was "trying to bring about an arrangement by which Abbott will be the new Premier".[20] It was all speculative, indefinite, uncertain. Nothing could be done until the struggle in the still room at Earnscliffe had ended; nothing would be done, Lord Stanley let it be known, until the inevitable and elaborate state funeral was over. Thompson, though he had determined to decline the succession himself, was annoyed at the prospect of this further and, to him, unconstitutional delay. The Governor-General, he reasoned, had no right to be without a government an hour longer than he could help.[21] Yet at what hour, in the eyes of the Canadians, would the government of the maker of their country really be over? He was ruling Canada from his death-bed. He would rule Canada until he had been buried in its earth.

For five days the eyes of the whole country were fixed upon Earnscliffe. And then, on the sixth day, Thursday, June 4, the unrevealing and monotonous gloom of the bulletins was suddenly interrupted by a ray of hope. In Ottawa, the weather, after the brief rain of the previous day, was slightly cooler; the horizon, which had been smudged with the smoke of bush fires, was clear once more.[22] And inside the dim room in the house by the cliff side, a remarkable, an unmistakable change seemed to be taking place. "Sir John Macdonald passed a fairly comfortable night . . . ," the medical men reported in their mid-morning bulletin. "His cerebral symptoms are slightly improved at the time of our consultation, owing doubtless to the fact that having lived six days since his seizure, partial absorption has had time to take place."[23] Was it possible? Was the hæmorrhage slowly disappearing? Had they the right to hope? Rapidly, as the news sped across the nation, the current of speculation changed and quickened. Inside Earnscliffe the little group of anxious people maintained their watch with breathless intentness. Still he seemed to improve. By mid-afternoon it was obvious that he was recognizing faces much more easily and naturally than he had yet done since his seizure; and one by one those closest to him came and lingered for a few moments at his bedside. Was it a last farewell? Or was it, perhaps, a first faint greeting?

For a few hours more the scales hung even; and then they tilted slowly against him. He was weaker again that night. He was weaker still at noon on Friday when Dr. George Ross, hastily summoned for the second time from Montreal, arrived to take part in the usual midday examination. "At a consultation today," the doctors declared in their two o'clock bulletin, "we find Sir John Macdonald altogether in a somewhat alarming state. His strength, which has gradually failed him during this past week, shows a marked decline since yesterday. . . . In our opinion his powers of life are steadily waning."[24] Hour after hour, as the long afternoon melted into evening, the slow decline continued. The little flame of his consciousness, which had flared up for the last time during the previous afternoon, died slowly down; and finally, after the true darkness had fallen, it flickered out.

There was another short, still summer night, with, far away, the faint roar of the Chaudière Falls. There was another red dawn, and another long, brilliant summer day, while the river, all splashed with sunshine as it had been on that first Dominion Day, flowed serenely past and away to the north-east. Then, when once more the sun had gone down behind the long blue line of the Laurentians, the last change came. Up to then his breathing had been shallow and rapid. Now it grew slower, slower still, and, as the watchers clustered around him, died away in the last, faint, lingering prolongations. He was going now. He was borne on and outward, past care and planning, past England and Canada, past life and into death.

V

Outside, in the grounds surrounding Earnscliffe, it was very still. At a little before ten o'clock, most of the newspaper men had given up their vigil. The watch had been left to two correspondents, who had strolled slowly over to the Canadian Pacific telegraph tent, and who were now strolling slowly back again. They had just reached the gate when quick footsteps were heard hastening softly towards them down the path. The lantern hanging above shed a dim light; and by it they could see Joe Pope's strained, worn face. It was exactly twenty-four minutes past ten on the night of Saturday, June 6.

"Gentlemen," Pope said brokenly, "Sir John Macdonald is dead. He died at a quarter past ten."[25]

He added, in reply to the one question which the correspondents thought of asking, that the end had come quietly and peacefully. Then he fixed Dr. Powell's last bulletin to the gate of Earnscliffe. In a few minutes the news was flashing east and west across the telegraph wires. In a few minutes more, the bells began to toll in Ottawa; and before midnight, they were tolling in most of the cities of the Dominion.

He lay, the next day, in the room in which he had died. It was not until nine o'clock on Sunday that his body was moved downstairs to the spacious, lofty room which he had added to Earnscliffe and which was hung now with heavy draperies of white and purple.[26] In his uniform of an imperial Privy Councillor and with the insignia of his orders at his side, he lay there all through Monday. The Governor-General, the ministers, a small group of his friends and associates entered one by one to stand briefly by his side. But these few people were only a small fraction of the thousands who wished to have a last glimpse of him, and who were even now hurrying towards Ottawa by train and carriage and farm waggon. A state funeral, the Cabinet had decided on Sunday night, was obviously necessary; Agnes had agreed; and as soon as Parliament opened on Monday afternoon, Langevin, the senior surviving minister, formally announced the old Prime Minister's death and formally moved that he should be "publicly interred and that this House

will concur in giving to the ceremony a fitting degree of solemnity and importance". Laurier followed in support; and it was
curious, and yet not inappropriate, that both the eulogies pronounced that afternoon should have been given by French-
speaking Canadians. Laurier, of course, was by far the more
gracefully eloquent of the two; but there was a simple, dogged
sincerity in Langevin's broken, commonplace sentences and in
his abrupt close. "Mr. Speaker," he said, "I would have wished
to continue to speak of our dear departed friend, and spoken
to you about the goodness of his heart, the witness of which I
have been so often, but I feel that I must stop; my heart is
full of tears. I cannot proceed further."²⁷

Next day, Tuesday, June 9, the body lay in state in the Senate
chamber of the Parliament of Canada. The Canadians, of all
ages and every occupation, were looking their last upon him.
They came all that day and far into the night; and early next
morning the packed queue slowed down again to a mere crawl.
It was nearly twelve o'clock and the chamber was about to be
closed to the public, when Sir Casimir Gzowski, the representative of the Queen, walked solemnly forward and laid a wreath
of roses upon the dead man's breast. "From Her Majesty Queen
Victoria," ran the inscription, "in memory of Her faithful and
devoted servant."²⁸ It was the ultimate tribute. The great room
slowly emptied. The last preparations were made. At a quarter
past one exactly the bell in the clock tower began to toll; and
slowly, with majestic deliberation, the funeral procession moved
forward.

The night, like so many of the nights of that early summer,
had been oppressively sultry. During the forenoon it grew
steadily hotter and hotter. And now the long procession moved
slowly down Rideau Street under a blue and burning sky.
Between the rows of shops and houses, draped in their folds
of black and purple, people were massed in thousands. Around
St. Alban's Church, the crowd was thickest; and as the short
service drew towards its close, the tropical atmosphere seemed
to grow ominously heavier. It was more oppressive still when
the funeral procession laboriously reformed and started back
again towards the station. A curious yellow haze hung in the

air. To the west, a great black cloud soared menacingly over Parliament Hill. There came a sudden fierce gust of wind—a violent scattering of huge raindrops. And then, in an overwhelming deluge, the storm broke upon the city.

At the railway station, the Canadian Pacific engine was draped in black and purple. Every engine and every station along the long transcontinental line of his railway was hung with mourning; and as the train swept westward towards Kingston that late afternoon, under skies cleared by the storm and golden with sunset, there were crowds on every station platform, and groups by the roadsides, and lone figures standing waiting in the fields. It was late at night by the time the train reached Kingston, but the station was packed with people. People began to assemble before the City Hall where the body lay in state, at five o'clock on the morning of June 11. People kept pouring into the town in increasing numbers as the sun climbed higher in the sky; and then, on foot and in every kind of vehicle, they followed him in thousands on his last journey over the dusty roads to the Cataraqui cemetery.[29]

"I desire that I shall be buried in the Kingston cemetery near the grave of my mother, as I promised her that I should be there buried."[30] He lay close to his parents, his first wife, his sisters, and his long-dead infant. The terraced slope rose to a slight eminence; and from there, away to the south-east, a few of Kingston's tallest towers and roofs were visible. Somewhere in that huddle of grey limestone buildings was the little shop on Quarry Street where he had begun to practise law. There, overlooking the Lake, stood the Italian villa, "Bellevue", where his firstborn had died. It was nearly seventy-one years since Hugh and Helen Macdonald and their small family of children had first set foot on the dock at Kingston. Beyond the dock lay the harbour and the islands which marked the end of the lowest of the Great Lakes; and beyond the islands the St. Lawrence River began its long journey to the sea.

A NOTE ON AUTHORITIES

The second volume of this biography, like the first, is based on materials contemporary with the events described in the text. The principal sources are collections of documents which are to be found in various archives and libraries, public and private, in Canada and Great Britain. A number of these collections have been found useful in the composition of both volumes of this biography; and for a description of such materials, the reader is referred to the note on authorities which was published in *John A. Macdonald, the Young Politician*. Here it will be sufficient to comment briefly on the nature of the evidence peculiar to *John A. Macdonald, the Old Chieftain*, and to indicate the collections which have not been listed already.

In general, the sources, both manuscript and printed, are richer and more numerous for *The Old Chieftain* than for *The Young Politician*. The evidence for the last twenty-four years of Macdonald's career is, in fact, extremely large in quantity and high in quality. Most of this material has been used very little in the past; and a substantial portion of it is here used for the first time. The Macdonald Papers, which continue to be the most important single source for the biography, are much more voluminous for the post-Confederation, than for the pre-Confederation, period. They are supplemented by valuable collections of the papers of Macdonald's principal colleagues, of which the Tupper Papers and the Thompson Papers at the Public Archives of Canada, and the Alexander Campbell Papers at the Public Records and Archives of Ontario, have been the most useful. The domestic side of Macdonald's life is illuminated by a diary of Lady Macdonald, in the possession of Mrs. D. F. Pepler, which covers the early post-Confederation years; and the political gossip of Ottawa, as it came to the attention of an informed and responsible civil servant, is revealed in the diary of Edmund A. Meredith.

The papers of the governors-general and the colonial secretaries of the period have provided some of the richest sources of material for *The Old Chieftain*. Macdonald was accustomed to write regularly and frequently to his political chiefs in much the same way as Disraeli and Gladstone reported to Queen Victoria; and the governors-general, in their turn, retailed the inner history of Canadian affairs to their political superiors, the colonial secretaries. The Argyll Papers—the correspondence of the Marquess of Lorne while Governor-General of Canada— and the Lansdowne Papers both contain a substantial number of Macdonald's letters. The Earl Granville, the Earl of Kimberley, the Earl of Carnarvon, and Sir Michael Hicks Beach, later the first Earl St. Aldwyn, occupied in turn the office of colonial secretary during a large part of the period covered by this volume; and their papers have proved extremely valuable. *The Dufferin-Carnarvon Correspondence, 1874-1878*, edited by C. W. de Kiewiet and F. H. Underhill (Toronto, the Champlain Society, 1955) has been recently published; but, in *The Old Chieftain* all references are to the original manuscripts in the Public Record Office, London. Finally, the correspondence of Sir Stafford Northcote, the first Earl of Iddesleigh, who was one of the British High Commissioners at the Washington Conference of 1871 and, for some time, the Governor of the Hudson's Bay Company, has provided some interesting information concerning the fisheries negotiations and the Red River Rebellion.

NOTES

CHAPTER ONE: *The Pacification of Nova Scotia*

(Pages 1 to 32)

[1] *Globe* (Toronto), 8 November, 1867.

[2] Diary of Lady Macdonald, 7 July, 1867.

[3] *Ibid.*

[4] Public Archives of Canada, Macdonald Papers, vol. 514, Macdonald to Bischoff, 17 October, 1867.

[5] *Leader* (Toronto), 9 November, 1867; *Globe*, 9 November, 1867.

[6] Macdonald Papers, vol. 514, Macdonald to Hill, 11 November, 1867.

[7] *Leader*, 11 November, 1867.

[8] Macdonald Papers, vol. 514, Macdonald to Archbishop Connolly, 31 December, 1867.

[9] Lady Macdonald's Diary, 11 January, 1868.

[10] *Ibid.*, 7 July, 1867.

[11] *Ibid.*, 1 December, 1867.

[12] *Ibid.*, 19 January, 24, 26 March, 1868.

[13] *Ibid.*, 17 November, 1867.

[14] Norman Ward, "The Formative Years of The House of Commons, 1867-91", *Canadian Journal of Economics and Political Science*, vol. 18 (Nov. 1952), pp. 431-451.

[15] Macdonald Papers, vol. 514, Macdonald to Cook, 3 February, 1868.

[16] Lady Macdonald's Diary, 11 January, 1868.

[17] *Debates and Proceedings of the House of Assembly of the Province of Nova Scotia, 1868* (Halifax), pp. 34-35.

[18] Lady Macdonald's Diary, 7, 27 February, 1868.

[19] Macdonald Papers, additional, vol. 2, Macdonald to Louisa Macdonald, 6 March, 1868; Lady Macdonald's Diary, 25 February, 1868.

[20] Macdonald Papers, vol. 194, Campbell to Macdonald, 28 February, 1868.

[21] *Ibid.*, vol. 514, Macdonald to McCully, 29 February, 1868.

[22] *Globe*, 20 March, 1868.

[23] *Ibid.*, 7 April, 1868; Isabel Skelton, *The Life of Thomas D'Arcy McGee* (Gardenvale, Canada, 1925), pp. 537-538.

[24] Lady Macdonald's Diary, 12 April, 1868.

[25] Josephine Phelan, *The Ardent Exile* (Toronto, 1951), pp. 296-297.

[26] *Globe*, 8 April, 1868.

[27] Journal of Edmund A. Meredith, vol. 6, 7 April, 1868.

[28] E. M. Saunders, *The Life and Letters of the Rt. Hon. Sir Charles Tupper, Bart., K.C.M.G.* (London, 1916), vol. 1, pp. 167-169, Macdonald to Tupper, 30 April, 1868.

[29] Macdonald Papers, vol. 514, Macdonald to Archibald, 4 July, 1868.

[30] *Ibid.*, vol. 115, Tilley to Macdonald, 17 July, 1868; *ibid.*, Archibald to Macdonald, 17 July, 1868.

[31] Sir Joseph Pope, *Correspondence of Sir John Macdonald* (Toronto, n.d.), pp. 67-70, Monck to Macdonald, 29 July, 1868.

[32] Macdonald Papers, vol. 514, Macdonald to J. S. Macdonald, 30 May, 1868; *ibid.*, Macdonald to Tupper, 4 July, 1868.

[33] Public Archives of Canada, Chamberlin Papers, vol. 2, Macdonald to Chamberlin, 26 October, 1868.

[34] *Globe*, 4 August, 1868.

[35] Joseph Pope, *Memoirs of the Right Honourable Sir John Alexander Macdonald, G.C.B., First Prime Minister of the Dominion of Canada* (London, 1894), vol. 2, p. 29, Howe to Macdonald, 1 August, 1868.

[36] *Ibid.*, vol. 2, pp. 29-34, Macdonald to Monck, 4 September, 1868.

[37] Macdonald Papers, vol. 115, Minutes of the Convention, August, 1868.

[38] Pope, *Memoirs*, vol. 2, pp. 29-34, Macdonald to Monck, 4 September, 1868.

[39] Macdonald Papers, vol. 115, Macdonald to Howe, 7 August, 1868.

[40] *Globe*, 8, 10 August, 1868.

[41] Pope, *Memoirs*, vol. 2, pp. 29-34, Macdonald to Monck, 4 September, 1868.

[42] Lady Macdonald's Diary, 27 August, 1868.

[43] *Ibid.*, 19 September, 1868.

[44] *Ibid.*, 21 September, 1868.

[45] Macdonald Papers, vol. 514, Macdonald to Rose, 23 September, 1868.

[46] Pope, *Memoirs*, vol. 2, appendix 18, pp. 302-303, Howe to Macdonald, 15 September, 1868.

[47] Macdonald Papers, vol. 514, Macdonald to Howe, 6 October, 1868.

[48] *Ibid.*, vol. 115, Howe to Macdonald, 13 October, 1868.

[49] Saunders, *Tupper*, vol. 1, p. 187, Macdonald to Tupper, 20 November, 1868.

[50] Macdonald Papers, vol. 515, Macdonald to Archibald, 27 October, 1868.

[51] Pope, *Memoirs*, vol. 2, appendix 18, pp. 303-304, Macdonald to Howe, 26 September, 1868.

[52] *Ibid.*, vol. 2, appendix 18, pp. 305-306, Macdonald to Howe, 4 November, 1868.

[53] *Globe*, 28 November, 1868.

[54] Macdonald Papers, vol. 202, Cartier to Macdonald, 24 December, 1868.

[55] Public Archives of Canada, Tupper Papers, Macdonald to Tupper, 2 January, 1869.

[56] Macdonald Papers, vol. 515, Macdonald to Howe, 23 December, 1868.

[57] *Ibid.*, Macdonald to Davis, 15 January, 1869.

[58] Lady Macdonald's Diary, 13 January, 1869.

[59] Tupper Papers, Macdonald to Tupper, 2 January, 1869.

[60] Macdonald Papers, vol. 515, Macdonald to White, 1 February, 1869.

[61] Lady Macdonald's Diary, 30 January, 1869.

[62] Macdonald Papers, vol. 515, Macdonald to Langevin, 25 January, 1869.

[63] Lady Macdonald's Diary, 7 February, 1 April, 1869.

CHAPTER TWO: *The West in Jeopardy*

(Pages 33 to 69)

1 *Globe*, 24, 27 February, 1869; Journal of E. A. Meredith, vol. 6, 27 February, 1869; Macdonald Papers, vol. 515, Macdonald to Howe, 8 March, 1869.

2 Lady Macdonald's Diary, 11 April, 1869.

3 Macdonald Papers, vol. 539, Allan to Macdonald, 20 April, 1869.

4 *Ibid.*, Allan to Macdonald, 24 April, 1869.

5 *Ibid.*, vol. 515, Macdonald to Doyle, 16 June, 1869.

6 *Ibid.*, Macdonald to Young, 25 May, 1869.

7 Charles Clarke, *Sixty Years in Upper Canada, with Autobiographical Recollections* (Toronto, 1908), pp. 56-59; G. W. Ross, *Getting into Parliament and After* (Toronto, 1913), pp. 23-28.

8 R. S. Longley, *Sir Francis Hincks, A Study of Canadian Politics, Railways and Finance in the Nineteenth Century* (Toronto, 1943), pp. 348-349.

9 *Globe*, 31 July, 5 August, 1869.

10 Macdonald Papers, vol. 516, Macdonald to Allan, 29 September, 1869.

11 *Ibid.*, vol. 520, Macdonald to O'Brien, 26 March, 1872.

12 Lady Macdonald's Diary, 27 February, 1868.

13 Journal of E. A. Meredith, vol. 7, 13 September, 1869.

14 *Globe*, 29 September, 1869.

15 Pope, *Correspondence*, p. 99, Rose to Macdonald, 27 September, 1869.

16 Journal of E. A. Meredith, vol. 7, 8 October, 1869.

17 Lady Macdonald's Diary, 7 November, 1869.

18 Macdonald Papers, vol. 516, Macdonald to Gray, 27 October, 1869.

19 *Ibid.*, Macdonald to Brown, 14 October, 1869.

20 *Ibid.*, Macdonald to McDougall, 8 December, 1869.

21 D. F. Warner, "Drang nach Norden—the United States and the Riel Rebellion", *Mississippi Valley Historical Review*, vol. 34 (March, 1953), pp. 693-712.

22 Northcote Papers, bundle 4, Northcote to Lampson, 20 April, 1870.

23 Macdonald Papers, vol. 516, Macdonald to Stephen, 9 December, 1869.

24 *Ibid.*, Macdonald to Cartier, 27 November, 1869.

25 *Ibid.*, Macdonald to McDougall, 27 November, 1869.

26 *Ibid.*, Macdonald to McDougall, 20 November, 1869.

27 *Ibid.*, Macdonald to Cartier, 27 November, 1869.

28 Lady Macdonald's Diary, 1 December, 1869.

29 G13, vol. 3, Granville to Young, 30 November, 1869.

30 Macdonald Papers, vol. 516, Macdonald to Rose, 5 December, 1869.

31 British Museum, Additional MSS. 44166 (Gladstone Papers), Granville to Gladstone, 29 November, 1869.

32 Macdonald Papers, vol. 516, Macdonald to McDougall, 12 December, 1869.

33 *Ibid.*, Macdonald to Archibald, 10 December, 1869.

34 *Ibid.*, Macdonald to McDougall, 27 November, 1869.

35 *Ibid.*, Macdonald to Cartier, 27 November, 1869.

36 Pope, *Memoirs*, vol. 2, pp. 59-61, Macdonald to Rose, 31 December, 1869.

37 *Ibid.*

[38] Pope, *Correspondence*, p. 119, Macdonald to Rose, 3 January, 1870.

[39] Northcote Papers, bundle 4, Lampson to Northcote, 31 January, 1870.

[40] Macdonald Papers, vol. 516, Macdonald to Rose, 26 January, 1870.

[41] Pope, *Correspondence*, p. 124, Macdonald to Brydges, 28 January, 1870.

[42] Macdonald Papers, vol. 516, Macdonald to Carroll, 29 September, 1869.

[43] *Ibid.*, vol. 258, Rose to Macdonald, 7 February, 1870.

[44] C. P. Stacey, *Canada and the British Army, 1846-1871* (London, 1936), p. 216.

[45] Northcote Papers, bundle 4, Lampson to Northcote, 31 January, 1870.

[46] Macdonald Papers, vol. 516, Macdonald to Rose, 26 January, 1870.

[47] Lady Macdonald's Diary, 1 April, 1870.

[48] Pope, *Correspondence*, p. 120, Macdonald to Rose, 21 January, 1870.

[49] *Parliamentary Debates*, 1870, pp. 449-468, 558-575.

[50] Pope, *Correspondence*, p. 132, Macdonald to Rose, 25 March, 1870.

[51] Macdonald Papers, vol. 517, Macdonald to Rose, 11 March, 1870.

[52] *Ibid.*

[53] Public Record Office, P.R.O. 30/29 (Granville Papers), Gladstone to Granville, 6 March, 1870; Royal Archives, D27, Gladstone to the Queen, 5 March, 1870.

[54] British Museum, Additional MSS. 44167 (Gladstone Papers), Granville to Gladstone, 6 March, 1870.

[55] G13, vol. 3, Granville to Young, 5 March, 1870.

[56] Pope, *Correspondence*, p. 134, Macdonald to Carnarvon, 14 April, 1870.

[57] G13, vol. 3, Young to Granville, 9 April, 1870.

[58] Pope, *Correspondence*, p. 133, Macdonald to Carnarvon, 14 April, 1870.

[59] *Globe*, 15 April, 1870.

[60] *Ibid.*, 12 April, 1870.

[61] G. F. G. Stanley, *The Birth of Western Canada, a History of the Riel Rebellions* (London, 1936), p. 95.

[62] Journal of E. A. Meredith, 19 April, 1870; Royal Archives, P 24, Curle to Ponsonby, 22 April, 1870.

[63] Northcote Papers, bundle 4, Northcote to Granville, 26 April, 1870.

[64] *Globe*, 25 April, 1870.

[65] Northcote Papers, bundle 4, Northcote to Lampson, 26 April, 1870.

[66] Stanley, *Birth of Western Canada*, pp. 118-119.

[67] *Ibid.*, p. 114.

[68] Macdonald Papers, vol. 517, Macdonald to Young, 27 April, 1870.

[69] Northcote Papers, bundle 1, Northcote to Disraeli, 28 April, 1870.

[70] *Globe*, 4 May, 1870.

[71] Journal of E. A. Meredith, vol. 7, 30 April, 1870.

[72] Andrew Lang, *Life, Letters, and Diaries of Sir Stafford Northcote, First Earl of Iddesleigh* (Edinburgh and London, 1890), vol. 1, p. 331.

[73] Macdonald Papers, vol. 517, Macdonald to Young, 4 May, 1870.

CHAPTER THREE: *Fish and Diplomacy*

(Pages 70 to 102)

[1] Pope, *Memoirs*, vol. 2, p. 76; Northcote Papers, bundle 3, McNeill to Northcote, 7 May, 1870.

[2] *Globe*, 30 May, 1870; Journal of E. A. Meredith, 30 May, 1870.

³ Pope, *Correspondence*, p. 136, Blake to Bernard, 2 June, 1870.

⁴ *Globe*, 18 June, 1870.

⁵ *Islander* (Charlottetown), 8 July, 1870.

⁶ *Ibid.*, 18 September, 1870.

⁷ *Times* (Ottawa), 23 September, 1870.

⁸ Macdonald Papers, vol. 517, Macdonald to Greer, 23 September, 1870.

⁹ *Ibid.*, Macdonald to Mrs. Williamson, 23 September, 1870.

¹⁰ *Ibid.*, Macdonald to Musgrave, 29 September, 1870.

¹¹ A. L. Burt, *The United States, Great Britain, and British North America, From the Revolution to the Establishment of Peace after the War of 1812* (New Haven and Toronto, 1940), pp. 418-419.

¹² R. S. Longley, "Peter Mitchell, Guardian of the North Atlantic Fisheries, 1867-1871", *Canadian Historical Review*, vol. 22 (December, 1941), pp. 389-402.

¹³ Pope, *Correspondence*, p. 122, Macdonald to Rose, 21 January, 1870.

¹⁴ Macdonald Papers, vol. 517, Macdonald to Macpherson, 4 November, 1870.

¹⁵ *Ibid.*, Macdonald to O'Connor, 19 November, 1870.

¹⁶ *Ibid.*, Macdonald to Archibald, 1 November, 1870.

¹⁷ *Ibid.*, Macdonald to Campbell, 1 November, 1870.

¹⁸ Kimberley Papers, Journal of Events during the Gladstone Ministry, 13 June, 1871.

¹⁹ P.R.O. 30/29 (Granville Papers), vol. 80, Thornton to Granville, 20 September, 1870, 4 October, 1870.

²⁰ G. Smith, *The Treaty of Washington, 1871, A Study in Imperial History* (Ithaca, 1941), p. 25.

²¹ Lady Macdonald's Diary, 3 January, 1871.

²² *Ibid.*, 4 January, 1871.

²³ G13, vol. 4, Kimberley to Lisgar, 1 February, 1871.

²⁴ *Ibid.*, Lisgar to Kimberley, 2 February, 1871.

²⁵ Macdonald Papers, vol. 167, Macdonald to Lisgar, 4 February, 1871.

²⁶ Public Record Office, FO.5, 1298, Rose to Granville, 9 February, 1871; G13, vol. 4, Lisgar to Kimberley, 18 February, 1871.

²⁷ G13, vol. 4, Kimberley to Lisgar, 4 February, 1871.

²⁸ Macdonald Papers, vol. 518, Macdonald to Macpherson, 6 February, 1871.

²⁹ *Ibid.*, Macdonald to Rose, 22 February, 1871.

³⁰ *Ibid.*, vol. 167, Macdonald to Tupper, 5 March, 1871.

³¹ P.R.O. 30/29, vol. 80, Thornton to Granville, 14 February, 1871.

³² *Ibid.*, vol. 63, de Grey to Granville, 28 February, 1871.

³³ *Ibid.*, de Grey to Granville, 7 March, 1871.

³⁴ *Ibid.*, vol. 80, Thornton to Granville, 22 November, 1871; Northcote Papers, bundle 4, Northcote to Lisgar, 5 April, 1871.

³⁵ Macdonald Papers, vol. 167, Macdonald to Tupper, 5 March, 1871.

³⁶ P.R.O. 30/29, vol. 63, de Grey to Granville, 3 March, 1871.

³⁷ *Ibid.*, de Grey to Granville, 7 March, 1871.

³⁸ Macdonald Papers, vol. 168, Macdonald to Tupper, 8 March, 1871.

³⁹ *Ibid.*, Macdonald to Tupper, 9 March, 1871.

⁴⁰ *Ibid.*, Macdonald to Tupper, 11 March, 1871; *ibid.*, Hincks to Macdonald, 12 March, 1871.

⁴¹ G13, vol. 4, Kimberley to Lisgar, 11 March, 1871.

[42] Macdonald Papers, vol. 167, Macdonald to Tupper, 17 March, 1871.

[43] P.R.O. 30/29, vol. 63, de Grey to Granville, 17 March, 1871.

[44] Macdonald Papers, vol. 167, Macdonald to Tupper, 17 March, 1871.

[45] *Ibid.*, vol. 518, Macdonald to Tupper, 21 March, 1871.

[46] P.R.O. 30/29, vol. 63, de Grey to Granville, 10 March, 1871.

[47] Macdonald Papers, vol. 518, Macdonald to Lisgar, 11 March, 1871.

[48] *Ibid.*, Macdonald to Gray, 31 March, 1871.

[49] *Ibid.*, vol. 168, Macdonald to Tupper, 22 March, 1871.

[50] *Ibid.*, vol. 518, Macdonald to Tupper, 29 March, 1871.

[51] P.R.O. 30/29, vol. 63, de Grey to Granville, 27 March, 1871.

[52] *Ibid.*, vol. 59, Gladstone to Granville, 12 April, 1871.

[53] *Ibid.*, vol. 63, Gladstone to Granville, 4 April, 1871.

[54] *Ibid.*, vol. 59, Granville to Gladstone, 4 April, 1871.

[55] Kimberley Papers, Lisgar to Kimberley, 6 April, 1871; P.R.O. 30/29, vol. 63, de Grey to Granville, 18 April, 1871.

[56] *Ibid.*, de Grey to Granville, 31 March, 1871.

[57] *Ibid.*, de Grey to Granville, 24 March, 1871.

[58] *Ibid.*, de Grey to Granville, 11 April, 1871.

[59] Northcote Papers, bundle 4, Northcote to Gladstone, 18 April, 1871.

[60] Macdonald Papers, vol. 518, Macdonald to Tupper, 16 April, 1871.

[61] P.R.O. 30/29, vol. 59, Gladstone to Granville, 20 February, 1871.

[62] *Ibid.*, vol. 63, de Grey to Granville, 25 March, 1871.

[63] *Ibid.*, de Grey to Granville, 15 April, 1871.

[64] *Ibid.*, vol. 59, Gladstone to Granville, 17 April, 1871.

[65] *Ibid.*, vol. 63, de Grey to Granville, 21 April, 1871.

[66] Macdonald Papers, vol. 518, Macdonald to Tupper, 27 April, 1871.

[67] *Ibid.*, vol. 518, Macdonald to Morris, 21 April, 1871.

[68] *Ibid.*, Macdonald to Hincks, 29 April, 1871.

[69] Pope, *Memoirs*, vol. 2, p. 137, Macdonald to Cartier, 6 May, 1871.

[70] P.R.O. 30/29, vol. 63, Lisgar to Northcote, 6 May, 1871.

[71] *Ibid.*, de Grey to Granville, 12 May, 1871.

[72] *Ibid.*

[73] *Ibid.*, de Grey to Granville, 5 May, 1871.

[74] Lang, *Northcote*, vol. 2, pp. 17-18.

[75] Allan Nevins, *Hamilton Fish, the Inner History of the Grant Administration* (New York, 1936), p. 490.

CHAPTER FOUR: *Design for the Future*

(Pages 103 to 128)

[1] Pope, *Correspondence*, p. 145, Macdonald to Morris, 21 April, 1871.

[2] Macdonald Papers, vol. 518, Macdonald to de Grey, 15 June, 1871.

[3] *Ibid.*, Macdonald to Gowan, 24 June, 1871.

[4] *Ibid.*, Macdonald to de Grey, 6 June, 1871.

[5] *Ibid.*, Macdonald to Gowan, 24 June, 1871.

[6] *Ibid.*, vol. 252, Morris to Macdonald, 1 April, 1871; *Parliamentary Debates, Dominion of Canada, 1871* (Ottawa, 1871), pp. 660-765, 1027-1030.

[7] *Globe*, 14 March, 18 July, 1873; Macdonald Papers, vol. 123, Names of the Parties present at the Meeting of 14 July, 1871.

8 Macdonald Papers, vol. 519, Macdonald to Jackson, 17 July, 1871.

9 *Ibid.*, vol. 77, Lisgar to Macdonald, 7 July, 1871.

10 Kimberley Papers, Lisgar Letters, Lisgar to Kimberley, 11 May, 1871.

11 *Ibid.*, Minute by Kimberley.

12 *Ibid.*, Minute by Gladstone.

13 Kimberley Papers, Lisgar Letters, Kimberley to Lisgar, 25 May, 1871.

14 Royal Archives, R51, Gladstone to the Queen, 8 June, 1871; *ibid.*, D27, Gladstone to the Queen, 5 July, 1871.

15 British Museum, Additional MSS. 44, 224 (Gladstone Papers), vol. 139, Kimberley to Gladstone, 7 June, 1871.

16 Macdonald Papers, vol. 519, Macdonald to Lisgar, 21 July, 1871.

17 Kimberley Papers, Lisgar Letters, Kimberley to Lisgar, 14 August, 1871.

18 G3, vol. 3, Kimberley to Lisgar, 23 September, 1871.

19 Macdonald Papers, vol. 519, Macdonald to O'Connor, 27 November, 1871.

20 Public Records and Archives of Ontario, Campbell Papers, Macdonald to Campbell, 19 December, 1871.

21 Macdonald Papers, vol. 519, Macdonald to Gowan, 12 October, 1871.

22 *Ibid.*, Macdonald to Carling, 23 December, 1871.

23 *Ibid.*, Macdonald to Bellingham, 10 October, 1871.

24 *Ibid.*, Macdonald to Pope, 3 November, 1871.

25 *Ibid.*, Macdonald to Lisgar, 29 November, 1871.

26 Kimberley Papers, Lisgar Letters, Kimberley to Lisgar, 20 December, 1871.

27 British Museum, Additional MSS. 44224, Kimberley to Gladstone, 15 December, 1871.

28 Royal Archives, A42, Gladstone to the Queen, 18 December, 1871.

29 G3, vol. 8, Kimberley to Lisgar, 21 December, 1871.

30 Kimberley Papers, Lisgar Letters, Lisgar to Kimberley, 11 January, 1872.

31 Macdonald Papers, vol. 520, Macdonald to Lisgar, 22 January, 1872.

32 *Ibid.*, vol. 519, Macdonald to Carling, 24 November, 1871.

33 *Ibid.*, Macdonald to Hamilton, 28 December, 1871.

34 *Ibid.*, vol. 520, Macdonald to O'Connor, 22 February, 1872.

35 *Ibid.*, Macdonald to Pope, 6 February, 1872.

36 British Museum, Additional MSS., 44,224, Kimberley to Gladstone, 16 February, 1872.

37 Macdonald Papers, vol. 167, Rose to Macdonald, 8 February, 1872.

38 Public Archives of Canada, G13, vol. 5, Kimberley to Lisgar, 10 February, 1872.

39 Kimberley Papers, Lisgar Letters, Kimberley to Lisgar, 22 February, 1872.

40 *Ibid.*, Lisgar to Kimberley, 29 February, 1872.

41 G13, vol. 5, Lisgar to Kimberley, 28 February, 1872.

42 Macdonald Papers, vol. 520, Macdonald to Patteson, 24 February, 1872.

43 *Ibid.*, vol. 519, Macdonald to Brown, 2 December, 1871.

44 *Ibid.*, vol. 520, Macdonald to Stephen, 20 February, 1872.

45 *Ibid.*, Macdonald to Patteson, 24 February, 1872.

46 *Ibid.*, vol. 539, Macpherson to Macdonald, 21 February, 1872; *ibid.*, vol. 543, Trust Deed, 27 March, 1872.

47 *Ibid.*, vol. 123, Macdonald to Macpherson, 11 March, 1872.

48 *Ibid.*, vol. 520, Macdonald to Rose, 17 April, 1872.

49 *Report of the Royal Commissioners, Appointed by Commission, Addressed to them under the Great Seal of Canada, bearing date the Fourteenth Day of August, 1873* (Ottawa, 1873), p. 195, Allan to Smith, 28 February, 1872.

50 D. G. Creighton, "George Brown, Sir John Macdonald, and the 'Workingman'", *Canadian Historical Review*, vol. 24 (December, 1943), pp. 362-376.

51 G13, vol. 5, Kimberley to Lisgar, 16 March, 1872.

52 J. A. Chisholm (ed.), *The Speeches and Public Letters of Joseph Howe* (Halifax, 1909), vol. 2, pp. 639-640.

53 Macdonald Papers, vol. 520, Macdonald to Rose, 17 April, 1872.

54 Pope, *Correspondence*, p. 161, Macdonald to Cameron, 3 January, 1872.

55 Kimberley Papers, Journal of Events during the Gladstone Ministry, 2 March, 1872.

56 *Ibid.*

57 Journal of E. A. Meredith, vol. 7, 3 May, 1872.

58 *Parliamentary Debates, Dominion of Canada* (Ottawa, 1872), pp. 344-345.

CHAPTER FIVE: *Blackmail*

(Pages 129 to 179)

1 Macdonald Papers, vol. 520, Macdonald to Rose, 18 June, 1872.

2 *Ibid.*, vol. 228, Lynch to Macdonald, 9 May, 1872.

3 Pope, *Correspondence*, p. 165, Macdonald to Rose, 5 March, 1872.

4 *Report of the Commissioners*, p. 43.

5 Macdonald Papers, vol. 194, Campbell to Macdonald, 7 July, 1872.

6 *Ibid.*, vol. 520, Macdonald to Rose, 18 June, 1872.

7 *Report of the Commissioners*, Macdonald's evidence, pp. 102-103.

8 *Ibid.*, Macpherson's evidence, pp. 28-29.

9 Macdonald Papers, vol. 344, Hewitt to Macdonald, 19 June, 1872.

10 *Mail* (Toronto), 12 July, 1872.

11 *Ibid.*

12 Campbell Papers, Macdonald to Campbell, 12 July, 1872.

13 Macdonald Papers, vol. 123, Allan to Macdonald, 12 July, 1872.

14 *Ibid.*, vol. 520, Macdonald to McInnes, 17 June, 1872.

15 *Mail*, 15 July, 1872.

16 *Ibid.*, 16 July, 1872.

17 Macdonald Papers, vol. 194, Campbell to Macdonald, 20 July, 1872.

18 *Ibid.*, vol. 123, Macpherson to Macdonald, 19 July, 1872.

19 *Ibid.*, Allan to Macdonald, 17 July, 1872; *ibid.*, Allan to Cartier, 18 July, 1872.

20 *Ibid.*, Cartier to Macdonald, 19 July, 1872.

21 *Ibid.*, Cartier to Macdonald, 22 July, 1872.

22 *Daily News* (Kingston), 26 July, 1872.

23 *Report of the Commissioners*, Macdonald's evidence, pp. 103, 199; Macdonald Papers, vol. 123, Macpherson to Macdonald, 27 July, 1872.

24 *Report of the Commissioners*, Allan's evidence, pp. 135-136; Macdonald Papers, vol. 123, 30 July, 1872.

25 *Report of the Commissioners*, p. 200.

26 T. S. Webster, John A. Macdonald and Kingston (M.A. Thesis, Queen's University, 1944), p. 121.

27 Macdonald Papers, vol. 521, Macdonald to G. Macdonald, 6 August, 1872.

28 *Report of the Commissioners*, Macdonald's evidence, p. 118.

29 *Ibid.*, Allan's evidence, p. 137.

30 Pope, *Correspondence*, p. 177, Macdonald to Lisgar, 2 September, 1872.

31 Macdonald Papers, vol. 521, Macdonald to Macpherson, 19, 26 September, 1872.

32 *Ibid.*, vol. 123, Macpherson to Macdonald, 17 September, 1872.

33 *Ibid.*, Allan to Macdonald, 4 October, 1872.

34 *Ibid.*, Allan to Macdonald, 7 October, 1872.

35 Kimberley Papers, PC/A/25a, Dufferin to Kimberley, 15 October, 1872; *Report of the Commissioners*, pp. 84-85, Campbell's evidence.

36 Macdonald Papers, vol. 123, Macpherson to Macdonald, 16 November, 1872.

37 Kimberley Papers, PC/A/25a, Dufferin to Kimberley, 27 November, 1872.

38 Campbell Papers, Hincks to Campbell, 8 November, 1872.

39 Macdonald Papers, vol. 522, Macdonald to Langevin, 28 November, 1872.

40 Macdonald Papers, vol. 202, Macdonald to Cartier, 23 December, 1872.

41 *Report of the Commissioners*, appendix, p. 89, McMullen's statement.

42 *Report of the Commissioners*, pp. 170-171, Abbott's evidence.

43 *Ibid.*, appendix, p. 89, McMullen's statement.

44 Macdonald Papers, vol. 125, Smith to Macdonald, 20 February, 1873.

45 *Ibid.*, vol. 224, Hincks to Macdonald, 25 February, 1873.

46 *Ibid.*, vol. 522, Macdonald to Rose, 13 February, 1873.

47 *Ibid.*, vol. 126, Affidavit of A. T. Cooper, 2 October, 1873.

48 Pope, *Memoirs*, vol. 2, appendix 26, p. 329.

49 Kimberley Papers, PC/A/25a, Dufferin to Kimberley, 4 April, 1873.

50 Macdonald Papers, vol. 202, Macdonald to Cartier, 10 April, 1873.

51 *Mail*, 9 April, 1873.

52 *Ibid.*, 19, 22 April, 1873.

53 *Ibid.*, 7 May, 1873.

54 Public Archives of Manitoba, Morris Papers, "C", Campbell to Morris, 29 November, 1873.

55 *Mail*, 7 May, 1873.

56 G13, vol. 5, Kimberley to Dufferin, 12 May, 1873.

57 Macdonald Papers, vol. 258, Rose to Macdonald, 1 May, 1873.

58 *Ibid.*, vol. 125, Allan to Macdonald, 9 April, 1873.

59 Pope, *Memoirs*, vol. 2, pp. 157-158, Cartier to Macdonald, 17 May, 1873; *ibid.*, pp. 158-159, Josephine Cartier to Macdonald, 22 May, 1873.

60 Journal of E. A. Meredith, vol. 8, 20 May, 1873.

61 Kimberley Papers, PC/A/25a, Dufferin to Kimberley, 29 May, 1873.

62 *Ibid.*, Dufferin to Kimberley, 21 June, 1873.

63 *Ibid.*, Dufferin to Kimberley, 13 June, 1873.

[64] Macdonald Papers, vol. 523, Macdonald to Cameron, 2 July, 1873.

[65] *Gazette* (Montreal), 3 July, 1873.

[66] *Ibid.*, 4 July, 1873.

[67] Macdonald Papers, vol. 125, Blake to Macdonald, 3 July, 1873.

[68] *Ibid.*, vol. 523, Macdonald to Dufferin, 4 July, 1873.

[69] *Ibid.*

[70] *Ibid.*, vol. 523, Macdonald to Amour, 8 July, 1873.

[71] *Globe*, 18 July, 1873.

[72] Macdonald Papers, vol. 79, Macdonald to Dufferin, 7 August, 1873.

[73] *Ibid.*, Macdonald to Dufferin, 31 July, 1873; *ibid.*, vol. 125, Campbell to Macdonald, 18 July, 1873.

[74] *Ibid.*, vol. 125, Abbott to Macdonald, 21 July, 1873.

[75] Kimberley Papers, PC/A/25b, Dufferin to Kimberley, 14 August, 1873.

[76] Macdonald Papers, vol. 79, Dufferin to Macdonald, 31 July, 1873.

[77] Kimberley Papers, PC/A/25b, Dufferin to Kimberley, 6 November, 1873.

[78] *Ibid.*, Dufferin to Kimberley, 9 August, 1873.

[79] *Correspondence Relative to the Canadian Pacific Railway Company* (London, 1874), pp. 7-29, Dufferin to Kimberley, 15 August, 1873.

[80] *Mail*, 14 August, 1873.

[81] *Report of the Commissioners*, p. 221, Huntington to Day, 26 August, 1873.

[82] Macdonald Papers, vol. 126, Ramsay to Macdonald, 22 September, 1873.

[83] *Ibid.*, Abbott to Macdonald, 10 October, 1873.

[84] *Ibid.*, Affidavit of Cooper, 2 October, 1873.

[85] *Globe*, 5 September, 1873.

[86] Kimberley Papers, PC/A/25b, Dufferin to Kimberley, 26 September, 1873.

[87] Macdonald Papers, vol. 523, Macdonald to Dufferin, 22 September, 1873.

[88] Kimberley Papers, PC/A/25b, Dufferin to Macdonald, 19 October, 1873 (enclosed in Dufferin to Kimberley, 26 October, 1873).

[89] *Ibid.*, PC/A/25a, Dufferin to Kimberley, 23 April, 1873.

[90] *Ibid.*, PC/A/25b, Dufferin to Kimberley, 26 October, 1873.

[91] Journal of E. A. Meredith, vol. 8, 22 October, 1873.

[92] Kimberley Papers, PC/A/25b, Kimberley to Dufferin, 6 October, 1873.

[93] *Ibid.*, Dufferin to Kimberley, 26 October, 1873.

[94] Morris Papers, "C", Campbell to Morris, 29 November, 1873.

[95] Kimberley Papers, PC/A/25b, Dufferin to Kimberley, 6 November, 1873.

[96] *Ibid.*

[97] *Mail*, 5 November, 1873, quoted in Pope, *Memoirs*, vol. 2, p. 194.

[98] *Mail*, 4 November, 1873.

[99] Kimberley Papers, PC/A/25b, Dufferin to Kimberley, 6 November, 1873.

[100] Macdonald Papers, vol. 79, Lady Dufferin to Lady Macdonald, 4 November, 1873; *ibid.*, Dufferin to Macdonald, 4 November, 1873.

[101] *Mail*, 6 November, 1873.

CHAPTER SIX: *The Forked Road*

(Pages 180 to 212)

[1] *Mail*, 7 November, 1873.
[2] Journal of E. A. Meredith, vol. 8, 7 November, 1873.
[3] *Mail*, 17 November, 1873.
[4] *Ibid.*
[5] E. P. Deane, "How Canada has Voted: 1867 to 1945", *Canadian Historical Review*, vol. 30 (September, 1949), pp. 227-248.
[6] Macdonald Papers, vol. 346, Mackintosh to Macdonald, 30 January, 1874.
[7] *Ibid.*, vol. 303, Petition against Macdonald's Election, 7 November, 1874.
[8] Public Record Office P.R.O. 30/6 (Carnarvon Papers), vol. 26, Dufferin to Carnarvon, 18 March, 1874.
[9] Saunders, *Tupper*, vol. 1, p. 234, Macdonald to Tupper, 24 August, 1874.
[10] *Gazette*, 13 August, 16 September, 1874.
[11] Saunders, *Tupper*, vol. 1, p. 234.
[12] *Gazette*, 19 September, 1874.
[13] P.R.O. 30/6, vol. 27, Dufferin to Carnarvon, 2 October, 1874.
[14] *Ibid.*, Dufferin to Carnarvon, 8 December, 1874.
[15] Webster, John A. Macdonald and Kingston, p. 127.
[16] *Toronto Directory for 1876, Containing an Alphabetical Directory of the Citizens and a Street Directory* . . . (Toronto, 1876), p. 281.
[17] Macdonald Papers, additional, vol. 2, H. Macdonald to Macdonald, 25 March, 1874. In this letter Hugh suggested that his father should leave the bulk of his estate to his wife and daughter, "simply giving me a trifle to show that I have not been cut off for bad behaviour".
[18] P.R.O. 30/6, vol. 26, Dufferin to Carnarvon, 16 April, 1874.
[19] Pope, *Correspondence*, p. 236, Patteson to Macdonald, 17 February, 1874.
[20] W. S. Wallace (ed.), "Edward Blake's Aurora Speech", *Canadian Historical Review*, vol. 2 (September, 1921), pp. 249-271.
[21] Saunders, *Tupper*, vol 1, p. 234.
[22] *Debates of the House of Commons of the Dominion of Canada* (Ottawa, 1875), vol. 1, p. 32.
[23] *Ibid.*, p. 649.
[24] Macdonald Papers, vol. 159. This volume contains the correspondence respecting Macdonald's Supreme Court Bills.
[25] *House of Commons Debates*, 1875, p. 976.
[26] F. H. Underhill, "Edward Blake, the Supreme Court Act, and the Appeal to the Privy Council, 1875-6", *Canadian Historical Review*, vol. 19 (September, 1938), pp. 245-263.
[27] *House of Commons Debates*, 1875, p. 980.
[28] *Ibid.*, p. 981.
[29] M. A. Ormsby, "Prime Minister Mackenzie, the Liberal Party, and the Bargain with British Columbia", *Canadian Historical Review*, vol. 26 (June, 1945), pp. 148-173.

80 *Toronto Directory for 1876*, p. 281.

81 Queen's University Library, Williamson Papers, Macdonald to Williamson, 27 April, 1876.

32 Macdonald Papers, additional, vol. 2, Macdonald to Louisa Macdonald, 14 July, 1875.

33 *Ibid.*, H. Macdonald to Macdonald, 30 November, 1875.

34 *Ibid.*, Macdonald to H. Macdonald, 2 December, 1875.

35 O. D. Skelton, *The Life and Times of Alexander Tilloch Galt* (Toronto, 1920), p. 468.

36 *Ibid.*, p. 483.

37 Macdonald Papers, additional, vol. 2, Macdonald to McCarthy, 15 February, 1875.

38 *Gazette*, 26 November, 1875.

39 Macdonald Papers, vol. 189, Bowell to Macdonald, 9 December, 1875.

40 *Gazette*, 26 November, 1875.

41 *Mail*, 8 November, 1875.

42 *Gazette*, 26 November, 1875.

43 *Mail*, 8 November, 1875.

44 *Ibid.*, 29 November, 1875.

45 *Proceedings of Special Meeting of the Manufacturers' Association of Ontario, held at St. Lawrence Hall, Toronto, 25th and 26th November, 1875* (Toronto, 1876).

46 *Gazette*, 21, 22 January, 1876.

47 For statements by White and Tupper, see *Gazette*, 27 September, 1875; *Mail*, 4 November, 1875.

48 *Gazette*, 10 November, 1875.

49 *Mail*, 29 November, 1875.

50 *Globe*, 6 November, 1875.

51 *Ibid.*, 28 July, 1875; *Gazette*, 14 October, 1875.

52 *Mail*, 29 November, 1875.

53 Macdonald Papers, vol. 282, Tupper to Macdonald, 29 January, 1876.

54 Tupper Papers, Macdonald to Tupper, 27 January, 1876.

55 *Gazette*, 29 January, 1876.

56 *Mail*, 23 February, 1876.

57 *Gazette*, 26 February, 1876.

58 *Ibid.*

59 *House of Commons Debates*, 1876, p. 261.

CHAPTER SEVEN: *The Picnic Grounds of Ontario*

(Pages 213 to 242)

1 *House of Commons Debates*, 1876, pp. 262-283.

2 *Ibid.*, p. 321.

3 *Ibid.*, p. 340.

4 *Journals of the House of Commons*, 1876, p. 490.

5 *Debates*, 1876, p. 491.

6 *Ibid.*, p. 493.

7 *Gazette*, 18 March, 1876.

8 Macdonald Papers, additional, vol. 2, Macdonald to McCarthy, 17 February, 1876.

9 Williamson Papers, Macdonald to Professor Williamson, 11 March, 1876.

10 Macdonald Papers, additional, vol. 2, Macdonald to Louisa Macdonald, 25 April, 1876.

11 *Mail*, 3 July, 1876.

12 *Ibid.*

13 Tupper Papers, Macdonald to Tupper, 7 July, 1876.

14 *Mail*, 28 July, 1876.

15 *Ibid.*, 10, 24, 31 August, 1876.

16 *Ibid.*, 7 September, 1876.

17 *Ibid.*, 13 September, 1876.

18 Macdonald Papers, additional, vol. 2, H. Macdonald to Macdonald, 22 September, 1876.

19 P.R.O. 30/6, vol. 30, Dufferin to Carnarvon, 19 January, 1877.

20 S. Thompson, *Reminiscences of a Canadian Pioneer for the Last Fifty Years* (Toronto, 1884), pp. 339-340.

21 Macdonald Papers, vol. 347, Cameron to Macdonald, 4 February, 1877.

22 *Ibid.*, additional, vol. 2, Macdonald to McCarthy, 15 February, 1875.

23 *Ibid.*, Macdonald to McCarthy, 17 November, 18 December, 1876.

24 *House of Commons Debates*, 1877, pp. 44-49.

25 P.R.O. 30/6, vol. 31, Dufferin to Carnarvon, 27 April, 1877.

26 *Mail*, 7 September, 1876.

27 P.R.O. 30/6, vol. 29, Dufferin to Carnarvon, 9 February, 1876.

28 Macdonald Papers, vol. 346, Gray to Macdonald, 14 August, 1876.

29 *House of Commons Debates*, 1877, pp. 123-147.

30 *Ibid.*, p. 402.

31 P.R.O. 30/6, vol. 31, Dufferin to Carnarvon, 5 April, 1877.

32 *Ibid.*, Dufferin to Carnarvon, 27 April, 3 May, 1877.

33 *Ibid.*, Dufferin to Carnarvon, 3 May, 1877.

34 *Mail*, 3 May, 1877.

35 Macdonald Papers, additional, vol. 1, Macdonald to Macdonell, 7 May, 1877.

36 *Ibid.*

37 *Mail*, 7 June, 1877.

38 *Ibid.*, 11 June, 1877.

39 *Ibid.*, 5 July, 1877.

40 *Ibid.*, 9 July, 1877.

41 Tupper Papers, McCarthy to Tupper, 13 July, 1877.

42 Macdonald Papers, vol. 232, McLelan to Macdonald, 20 August, 1877.

43 Tupper Papers, Macdonald to Tupper, 22 August, 1877.

44 Macdonald Papers, additional, vol. 2, Mary Macdonald to Macdonald, 12 October, 1877.

45 *Ibid.*, vol. 259, Rose to Macdonald, 24 November, 1877.

46 *Ibid.*, additional, vol. 1, Macdonald to Macdonell, 21 August, 1877.

47 *Mail*, 11, 13, 17 October, 1877.

48 *Ibid.*, 18 October, 1877; Macdonald Papers, additional, vol. 2, Macdonald to Louisa Macdonald, 22 October, 1877.

[49] Pope, *Correspondence*, pp. 329-342, Macdonald to Northcote, 1 May, 1878.

[50] Public Archives of Canada, Alexander Mackenzie Papers, Letterbook 6, Mackenzie to Cameron, 8 April, 1878.

[51] *House of Commons Debates*, 1878, vol. 2, p. 1796. Macdonald told this story accurately on the whole, but with one important mistake. Boswell's companion at the theatre on this occasion was not Dr. Johnson, but Dr. Hugh Blair. Johnson first heard the story when Boswell related it during the closing days of the tour to the Hebrides. See G. B. Hill and L. F. Powell (eds.), *Boswell's Life of Johnson* (Oxford, 1940), vol. 5, p. 396.

[52] *House of Commons Debates*, 1878, vol. 2, pp. 2556-2557.

[53] *House of Commons Debates*, 1878, vol. 2, pp. 1878-1902.

[54] *Ibid.*, pp. 2057-2067.

[55] *Ibid.*, p. 2564.

[56] Macdonald Papers, additional, vol. 1, Macdonald to Macdonell, 13 March, 1878.

[57] *Mail*, 25 May, 5, 8, 10 July, 1878.

[58] Macdonald Papers, additional, vol. 2, Macdonald to McCarthy, 21 August, 1878.

[59] *Ibid.*, vol. 228, McCarthy to Macdonald, 25 August, 1878.

[60] *Ibid.*, additional, vol. 2, Macdonald to McCarthy, 23 August, 1878.

[61] *News* (Kingston), 23 August, 1878; *Mail*, 23 August, 1878.

[62] *Mail*, 28, 30, 31 August, 1878.

[63] Macdonald Papers, vol. 276, Tilley to Macdonald, 26 July, 1878.

[64] *Ibid.*, vol. 282, Tupper to Macdonald, 6 August, 1878.

[65] *Ibid.*, vol. 226, Langevin to Macdonald, 22 August, 1878.

[66] Pope, *Memoirs*, vol. 2, p. 202.

[67] *News*, 18 September, 1878.

CHAPTER EIGHT: *The Plan in Realization*

(Pages 243 to 283)

[1] Pope, *Correspondence*, p. 245, Macdonald to Smith, 1 October, 1878.

[2] Macdonald Papers, additional, vol. 2, Macdonald to Louisa Macdonald, 2 October, 1878.

[3] *Ibid.*, vol. 524, Macdonald to Graham, 6 November, 1878.

[4] Saunders, *Tupper*, vol. 1, pp. 262-263, Macdonald to Tupper, 9 October, 1878.

[5] Pope, *Correspondence*, pp. 239-242, Macdonald to Northcote, 1 May, 1878.

[6] St. Aldwyn Papers, PCC92, Dufferin to Hicks Beach, 12 October, 1878.

[7] H. D. Kemp, The Department of the Interior in the West, 1873-1883 (M.A. Thesis, University of Manitoba, 1950).

[8] *House of Commons Debates*, 1878, vol. 2, p. 1651.

[9] Macdonald Papers, vol. 524, Macdonald to McCarthy, 24 October, 1878.

[10] *Ibid.*, vol. 259, Rose to Macdonald, 30 October, 1878.

[11] Skelton, *Galt*, pp. 515-520.

¹² St. Aldwyn Papers, PCC92, Dufferin to Hicks Beach, 8 August, 1878.

¹³ *Ibid.*, PCC13, Hicks Beach to Beaconsfield, 26 August, 1878.

¹⁴ Macdonald Papers, vol. 524, Macdonald to Coursal, 14 November, 1878.

¹⁵ Kimberley Papers, PC/A/25b, Kimberley to Dufferin, 20 November, 1873.

¹⁶ Argyll Papers, Letterbook 4, Dufferin to Lorne, 22 August, 1878.

¹⁷ *House of Commons Debates*, 1875, p. 649.

¹⁸ *Ibid.*, 1879, vol. 2, p. 1821.

¹⁹ *Ibid.*, 1878, vol. 2, 2556.

²⁰ *Ibid.*, 1876, p. 573.

²¹ Argyll Papers, Letterbook 4, Dufferin to Lorne, 22 August, 1878.

²² Macdonald Papers, vol. 195, Campbell to Macdonald, 15 July, 1880.

²³ Pope, *Correspondence*, pp. 240-241, Macdonald to Northcote, 1 May, 1878.

²⁴ Macdonald Papers, vol. 259, Rose to Macdonald, 19 December, 1878.

²⁵ *Ibid.*, vol. 216, Galt to Macdonald, 30 November, 1878.

²⁶ *Ibid.*, Galt to Macdonald, 18 December, 1878.

²⁷ *Ibid.*, Galt to Macdonald, 20 December, 1878.

²⁸ *Ibid.*, vol. 524, Macdonald to Frazer, 26 December, 1878.

²⁹ *Globe*, 26 July, 1878.

³⁰ Argyll Papers, Letterbook 1, Lorne to Hicks Beach, 3 December, 1878.

³¹ W. A. Mackintosh, *The Economic Background of Dominion-Provincial Relations*, Appendix 3 of the *Report of the Royal Commission on Dominion-Provincial Relations* (Ottawa, 1939), pp. 19-20; O. J. McDiarmid, *Commercial Policy in the Canadian Economy* (Cambridge, 1946), pp. 161-163.

³² Argyll Papers, Letterbook 1, Lorne to Hicks Beach, 1 January, 1879.

³³ *Ibid.*, Lorne to Hicks Beach, 5 February, 1879.

³⁴ *Ibid.*, Lorne to Hicks Beach, 8 February, 1879.

³⁵ *Gazette*, 15 February, 1879.

³⁶ *Ibid.*, 17 February, 1879.

³⁷ Argyll Papers, Letterbook 1, Lorne to Hicks Beach, 10 March, 1879.

³⁸ G13, vol. 10, Hicks Beach to Lorne, 12 March, 1879.

³⁹ Canada, *Sessional Papers*, 1879, No. 155, Memorandum by Tilley, 19 March, 1879.

⁴⁰ Pope, *Correspondence*, pp. 251-252, Chapleau to Macdonald, 2 December, 1878.

⁴¹ St. Aldwyn Papers, PCC61, Lorne to Hicks Beach, 26 December, 1878.

⁴² *House of Commons Debates*, 1878, vol. 1, pp. 407-408.

⁴³ Argyll Papers, Letterbook 1, Lorne to Hicks Beach, 3 December, 1878.

⁴⁴ St. Aldwyn Papers, PCC61, Lorne to Hicks Beach, 26 December, 1878.

⁴⁵ Argyll Papers, Letterbook 4, Lorne to Hicks Beach, 9 April, 1879.

⁴⁶ St. Aldwyn Papers, PCC61, Lorne to Hicks Beach, 27 March, 1879.

⁴⁷ *Ibid.*, Lorne to Hicks Beach, 3 April, 1879.

⁴⁸ *Ibid.*, Lorne to Hicks Beach, 6 April, 1879.

⁴⁹ Macdonald Papers, vol. 80, Macdonald to Lorne, 28 March, 1879.

⁵⁰ *House of Commons Debates*, 1879, vol. 2, p. 1823.

⁵¹ Macdonald Papers, vol. 199, Carling to Macdonald, 19 May, 1879.

⁵² *Ibid.*, additional, vol. 2, Macdonald to Louisa Macdonald, 26 June, 1879.

⁵³ *Ibid.*, Macdonald to Louisa Macdonald, 6 July, 1879.

⁵⁴ *Gazette*, 28 July, 1879.

[55] Macdonald Papers, vol. 162, Macdonald's Memorandum book, 4 August, 1879.

[56] *Ibid.*, Rose to Macdonald, 6 August, 1879.

[57] *Ibid.*, Hicks Beach to Macdonald, n.d.

[58] St. Aldwyn Papers, PCC75, Beaconsfield to Hicks Beach, 8 August, 1879.

[59] Royal Archives, P 25, Lorne to Beaconsfield, 1 June, 1879.

[60] Macdonald Papers, vol. 162, Confidential Memorandum on the Tariff, 25 August, 1879.

[61] *Ibid.*, vol. 216, Considerations connected with the claim for an imperial guarantee, 25 August, 1879.

[62] *Ibid.*, vol. 162, Macdonald to Walkem, 23 August, 1879.

[63] *Ibid.*, vol. 80, Lorne to Macdonald, 28 June, 1879.

[64] Argyll Papers, Letterbook 4, Hicks Beach to Lorne, 16 August, 1879.

[65] Macdonald Papers, vol. 162, Macdonald's Memorandum book, 10 August, 1879; *ibid.*, additional, vol. 2, Macdonald to Louisa Macdonald, 20 August, 1879.

[66] *Ibid.*, vol. 216, Confidential Memorandum on Canada's Representative in London, 25 August, 1879.

[67] M. H. Long, "Sir John Rose and the Informal Beginnings of the Canadian High Commissionership", *Canadian Historical Review*, vol. 12 (March, 1931), pp. 23-43.

[68] Macdonald Papers, vol. 259, Rose to Macdonald, 2 November, 1879.

[69] *Ibid.*, vol. 216, Confidential Memorandum on Canada's Representative in London, 25 August, 1879.

[70] St. Aldwyn Papers, PCC61, Lorne to Hicks Beach, 25 July, 1879.

[71] British Museum, Additional MSS. 44225 (Gladstone Papers), Kimberley to Gladstone, 2 December, 1873.

[72] Kimberley Papers, PC/A/25b, Kimberley to Dufferin, 8 December, 1873.

[73] Macdonald Papers, vol. 162, Memorandum book, 14 August, 1879.

[74] *Ibid.*, additional, vol. 2, Macdonald to Louisa Macdonald, 20 August, 1879.

[75] *Ibid.*, vol. 162, Hicks Beach to Macdonald, 28 August, 1879.

[76] Argyll Papers, Letterbook 4, Beaconsfield to Lorne, 13 August, 1879.

[77] Macdonald Papers, vol. 162; Pope, *Memoirs*, vol. 2, pp. 205-206.

[78] W. F. Monypenny and G. E. Buckle, *The Life of Benjamin Disraeli, Earl of Beaconsfield* (London, 1920), vol. 6, p. 477.

[79] Journal of E. A. Meredith, vol. 10, 23 September, 1879.

[80] Argyll Papers, Letterbook 1, Lorne to Hicks Beach, 22 October, 1879.

[81] Pope, *Memoirs*, vol. 2, pp. 207-209, Macdonald to Beaconsfield, 7 October, 1879.

[82] St. Aldwyn Papers, PCC61, Lorne to Hicks Beach, 25 November, 1879.

[83] Macdonald Papers, vol. 216, Hicks Beach to Lorne, 1 November, 1879.

[84] Argyll Papers, Letterbook 4, Salisbury to Lorne, 5 November, 1879.

[85] *Ibid.*, Hicks Beach to Lorne, 7 November, 1879.

[86] *Ibid.*, Letterbook 1, Lorne to Salisbury, 29 September, 1879.

[87] Macdonald Papers, vol. 216, Order-in-Council, 22 December, 1879.

[88] Argyll Papers, Letterbook 1, Lorne to Salisbury, 28 November, 1879.

[89] G13, vol. 10, Colonial Secretary to Governor-General, 31 January, 1880.

[90] Macdonald Papers, additional, vol. 1, Macdonald to Lorne, 5 February, 1880.

[91] G13, vol. 10, Colonial Secretary to Governor-General, 7 February, 1880.

[92] Macdonald Papers, vol. 228, McCarthy to Macdonald, 28 December, 1879.

[93] *Ibid.*, vol. 217, Galt to Macdonald, 9 January, 1880.

[94] *Ibid.*, vol. 259, Rose to Macdonald, 22 January, 1880.

[95] *Mail*, 22 March, 1880.

[96] Macdonald Papers, vol. 247, Macpherson to Macdonald, 24 March, 1880.

CHAPTER NINE: *Contract for Steel*

(Pages 284 to 316)

[1] Heather M. Donald, Life of Lord Mount Stephen (Ph.D. Thesis, University of London, 1952).

[2] *Ibid.*

[3] Argyll Papers, Letterbook 4, Macdonald to Lorne, 15 May, 1880.

[4] *Ibid.*, Macdonald Letters, Macdonald to Lorne, 17 May, 1880.

[5] Macdonald Papers, vol. 217, Galt to Macdonald, 4 May, 1880.

[6] *Ibid.*, additional, vol. 1, Macdonald to Lorne, 25 May, 1880.

[7] *Ibid.*, vol. 217, Galt to Macdonald, 7 June, 1880.

[8] *Ibid.*, Draft Instructions to Galt, n.d.

[9] *Sessional Papers*, 1885, No. 116, pp. 81-96.

[10] Chester Martin, *"Dominion Lands" Policy*, vol. 2 in *Canadian Frontiers of Settlement*, ed. by W. A. Mackintosh and W. L. G. Joerg (Toronto, 1938).

[11] Macdonald Papers, additional, vol. 1, Macdonald to Lorne, 18, 23 June, 1880.

[12] *Ibid.*, vol. 127, McIntyre to Macdonald, 21 June, 1880.

[13] *Ibid.*, vol. 195, Campbell to Macdonald, 15 July, 1880.

[14] *Ibid.*, vol. 81, Lorne to Macdonald, 24 June, 1880.

[15] *Ibid.*, additional, vol. 1, Macdonald to Lorne, 5 July, 1880.

[16] Campbell Papers, Campbell to Mills, 2 August, 1880.

[17] Macdonald Papers, vol. 127, McIntyre to Macdonald, 5 July, 1880.

[18] *Ibid.*, vol. 524, Macdonald to Dunmore, 3 July, 1880.

[19] *Ibid.*, vol. 267, Stephen to Macdonald, 9 July, 1880.

[20] *Ibid.*, vol. 163, Memorandum book, 19 July, 1880.

[21] Alice R. Stewart, "Sir John A. Macdonald and the Imperial Defence Commission of 1879", *Canadian Historical Review*, vol. 35 (June, 1954), pp. 119-139.

[22] Macdonald Papers, vol. 163, Memorandum book, 23 July, 1880.

[23] G. P. de T. Glazebrook, *A History of Transportation in Canada* (Toronto and New Haven, 1938), p. 240.

[24] Campbell Papers, Onderdonk to Campbell, 3 August, 1880.

[25] Macdonald Papers, vol. 127, Macdonald to Tilley (draft), n.d.

[26] *Ibid.*, Puleston to Macdonald, 2 September, 1880.

[27] *Ibid.*, vol. 163, Cameron to Macdonald, 8 September, 1880.

[28] *Ibid.*, vol. 127, McIntyre to Macdonald, 12 August, 1880.

[29] *Ibid.*, vol. 163, Memorandum book, 4 September, 1880.

[30] *Ibid.*, vol. 127, Macdonald to Langevin, 4 September, 1880.

[31] *Ibid.*, additional, vol. 2, Macdonald to Louisa Macdonald, 3 October, 1880.

[32] *Ibid.*, vol. 267, Stephen to Macdonald, 27 September, 1880.

[33] Macdonald Papers, vol. 127, Macdonald to Rose, 5 November, 1880.

[34] Argyll Papers, Letterbook 2, Lorne to Walker, 26 September, 1880.

[35] Glazebrook, *A History of Transportation*, p. 302.

[36] Macdonald Papers, vol. 267, Stephen to Macdonald, 18 October, 1880.

[37] Argyll Papers, Letterbook 4, Macdonald to Lorne, 16 November, 1880.

[38] Macdonald Papers, additional, vol. 2, Macdonald to Louisa Macdonald. 2 December, 1880.

[39] *Ibid.*, vol. 81, Lorne to Macdonald, 6 December, 1880.

[40] *House of Commons Debates*, 1880-1881, vol. 1, pp. 50-74.

[41] Macdonald Papers, additional, vol. 2, Macdonald to Louisa Macdonald, 23 December, 1880.

[42] Argyll Papers, Macdonald Letters, Macdonald to Lorne, 6 January, 1881.

[43] *House of Commons Debates*, 1880-1881, vol. 1, pp. 102-106, 144.

[44] Macdonald Papers, vol. 127, C. Rose to Macdonald, 8 January, 1881.

[45] *House of Commons Debates*, 1880-1881, vol. 1, p. 488.

[46] *Ibid.*, p. 494.

[47] Macdonald Papers, vol. 128, Donaldson to Macdonald, 18 January, 1881.

[48] *Ibid.*, vol. 524, Macdonald to Galt, 24 January, 1881.

[49] Argyll Papers, Letterbook 4, Macdonald to Lorne, 26 January, 1881.

[50] *House of Commons Debates*, 1880-1881, vol. 1, p. 765.

[51] Macdonald Papers, vol. 128, Morris to Macdonald, 28 January, 1881.

[52] *Ibid.*, vol. 524, Macdonald to Galt, 27 February, 1881.

[53] *Ibid.*, vol. 195, Campbell to Macdonald, n.d.

[54] *Ibid.*, vol. 524, Macdonald to Galt, 27 February, 1881.

[55] *Ibid.*, vol. 218, Galt to Macdonald, 4 January, 1881.

[56] *Ibid.*, vol. 267, Stephen to Macdonald, 7 April, 1881.

[57] Saunders, *Tupper*, vol. 1, p. 302, Macdonald to Tupper, 21 March, 1881.

[58] *Ibid.*, vol. 1, pp. 302-303, Macdonald to Tupper, 11 April, 1881.

[59] *Ibid.*, vol. 1, p. 303, Macdonald to Tupper, 21 April, 1881.

[60] Macdonald Papers, vol. 524, Macdonald to –, 18 April, 1881.

[61] Williamson Papers, Louisa Macdonald to Williamson, 3 May, 1881.

[62] *Mail*, 24 May, 1881.

[63] Saunders, *Tupper*, vol. 1, p. 304, Macdonald to Tupper, 16 May, 1881.

[64] Macdonald Papers, vol. 524, Macdonald to Stephen, 6 May, 1881.

[65] Saunders, *Tupper*, vol. 1, p. 303, Macdonald to Tupper, 21 April, 1881.

[66] Tupper Papers, Macdonald to Tupper, 2 June, 1881.

[67] Argyll Papers, Letterbook 4, Galt to Lorne, 2 June, 1881.

[68] Macdonald Papers, additional, vol. 1, Macdonald to Lorne, 20 June, 1881.

[69] Tupper Papers, Macdonald to Tupper, 21 June, 1881.

[70] Campbell Papers, Macdonald to Campbell, 12 July, 1880.

[71] *Mail*, 22 July, 1881.

[72] Macdonald Papers, additional, vol. 1, Macdonald to Lorne, 20 June, 1881.

[73] Macdonald Papers, vol. 164, Carnarvon to Macdonald, 6 August, 1881.

74 *Ibid.*, vol. 282, Tupper to Macdonald, n.d.

75 *Ibid.*, vol. 195, Campbell to Macdonald, n.d.

76 *Ibid.*, Campbell to Macdonald, 22 August, 1881.

77 Campbell Papers, Macdonald to Campbell, 12 July, 1880.

CHAPTER TEN: *Good Times*

(Pages 317 to 352)

1 Macdonald Papers, vol. 164, Programme of Ship's Concert on the *Sardinian*, 15 September, 1881.

2 *Mail*, 19 September, 1881.

3 A. S. Morton, *History of Prairie Settlement*, vol. 2, *Canadian Frontiers of Settlement*, ed. W. A. Mackintosh and W. L. G. Joerg (Toronto, 1938), p. 59.

4 Macdonald Papers, vol. 248, Macpherson to Macdonald, 4 September, 1881.

5 *Ibid.*, Macpherson to Macdonald, 9 August, 1881; *ibid.*, vol. 256, J. H. Pope to Macdonald, 19 August, 1881.

6 *Ibid.*, vol. 267, Stephen to Macdonald, 29 October, 4, 5 November, 1881.

7 *Ibid.*, Stephen to Macdonald, 27 August, 1881.

8 *Ibid.*, Stephen to Macdonald, 17 November, 1881.

9 Pope, *Correspondence*, pp. 280-281, Macdonald to Stephen, 19 October, 1881.

10 Macdonald Papers, vol. 524, Macdonald to Stephen, 6 January, 1882.

11 *Ibid.*, Macdonald to Griffin, 31 October, 1881.

12 J. C. Morrison, Oliver Mowat and the Development of Provincial Rights in Ontario: a Study in Dominion-Provincial Relations, 1867-1896 (M.A. Thesis, University of Toronto, 1947), Chapter 3.

13 W. E. Hodgins, *Correspondence, Reports of the Minister of Justice, and Orders in Council upon the Subject of Dominion and Provincial Legislation 1867-1895* (Ottawa, 1896), p. 61, Report of the Minister of Justice, 9 June, 1868.

14 *House of Commons Debates*, 1882, p. 924.

15 Hodgins, *Dominion and Provincial Legislation, 1867-1895*, p. 177, Report of Minister of Justice, 21 May, 1881.

16 Macdonald Papers, vol. 524, Macdonald to Meredith, 14 January, 1882.

17 *Mail*, 24 November, 1881.

18 Macdonald Papers, additional, vol. 1, Macdonald to Lorne, 2 November, 1881.

19 *Ibid.*, Macdonald to Lorne, 14 December, 1881.

20 Argyll Papers, Letterbook 2, Lorne to Granville, 17 December, 1881.

21 Macdonald Papers, vol. 218, Galt to Macdonald, 9, 13 December, 1881.

22 *Ibid.*, vol. 524, Macdonald to Galt, 7 January, 1882.

23 *Ibid.*, Macdonald to Galt, 27 December, 1881.

24 Glazebrook, *History of Transportation in Canada*, p. 294.

25 Macdonald Papers, vol. 524, Macdonald to Galt, 24 December, 1881.

26 *Ibid.*, vol. 267, Stephen to Macdonald, 26 February, 1882.

[27] *Ibid.*, vol. 524, Macdonald to Lynch, 9 December, 1881.

[28] *Ibid.*, vol. 228, Lynch to Macdonald, 20 February, 1882.

[29] *Ibid.*, vol. 524, Macdonald to Galt, 15 March, 1882.

[30] *Ibid.*, Macdonald to Galt, 28 February, 1882.

[31] *Ibid.*, vol. 259, Rose to Macdonald, 6 February, 1882.

[32] Argyll Papers, Letterbook 3, Lorne to Kimberley, 23 March, 1882.

[33] Macdonald Papers, vol. 524, Macdonald to Marsh, 28 January, 1882.

[34] *House of Commons Debates*, 1882, pp. 876-926.

[35] *Ibid.*, pp. 1068-1075.

[36] *Ibid.*, pp. 1033-1034.

[37] Pope, *Correspondence*, pp. 287-289, Macdonald to Lorne, 2 May, 1882.

[38] Kimberley Papers, Lorne Letters, Kimberley to Lorne, 11 May, 1882.

[39] Macdonald Papers, vol. 219, Galt to Macdonald, 27 April, 1882.

[40] *House of Commons Debates*, 1882, pp. 1202-1204.

[41] Norman Ward, *The Canadian House of Commons: Representation* (Toronto, 1950), p. 30.

[42] R. M. Dawson, "The Gerrymander of 1882", *The Canadian Journal of Economics and Political Science*, vol. 1 (May, 1935), pp. 197-221.

[43] *House of Commons Debates*, 1882, p. 1208.

[44] *Ibid.*, p. 1209.

[45] Macdonald Papers, vol. 267, Stephen to Macdonald, 8 May, 1882.

[46] *Ibid.*, additional, vol. 1, Macdonald to Lorne, 3 April, 1882.

[47] *Ibid.*, vol. 267, Stephen to Macdonald, 9 June, 1882.

[48] *Mail*, 26 May, 1882.

[49] *Ibid.*, 29 May, 1882.

[50] Argyll Papers, Macdonald Letters, Macdonald to Lorne, 22 June, 1882.

[51] Macdonald Papers, vol. 277, Tilley to Macdonald, 25 June, 1882.

[52] Argyll Papers, Macdonald Letters, Macdonald to Lorne, 22 June, 1882.

[53] Macdonald Papers, additional, vol. 1, Macdonald to Lorne, 28 July, 1882.

[54] *Ibid.*, Macdonald to Lorne, 4 August, 1882; *ibid.*, vol. 82, Lorne to Macdonald, 5 August, 1882; *ibid.*, additional, vol. 1, Macdonald to Lorne, 8 August, 1882.

[55] Argyll Papers, Letterbook 4, Cambridge to Lorne, 3 July, 1882; Macdonald Papers, vol. 82, Lorne to Macdonald, 18 July, 1882; *ibid.*, additional, vol. 1, Macdonald to Lorne, 21 July, 1882.

[56] *Mail*, 8 July, 1882.

[57] *Ibid.*, 2 June, 1882.

[58] *Report Pursuant to Resolution of the Senate to the Honourable the Speaker by the Parliamentary Counsel relating to the Enactment of the British North America Act, 1867* . . . (Ottawa, 1939), annex 3, pp. 14-18.

[59] Macdonald Papers, vol. 267, Stephen to Macdonald, 19 August, 1882.

[60] *Ibid.*, Stephen to Macdonald, 24 August, 1882.

[61] *Ibid.*, vol. 219, Galt to Macdonald, 16 August, 1882.

[62] *Ibid.*, vol. 267, Stephen to Macdonald, 9 July, 1880.

[63] *Ibid.*, Stephen to Macdonald, 27 August, 1882.

[64] *Ibid.*, vol. 223, Hickson to Macdonald, 9 October, 1882.

[65] *Ibid.*, vol. 259, Rose to Macdonald, 1 February, 1883.

[66] Williamson Papers, Macdonald to Williamson, 19 February, 1883.

[67] *House of Commons Debates*, 1883, p. 23.

68 *Mail*, 28 February, 1883.
69 Pope, *Correspondence*, p. 299, Macdonald to Galt, 21 February, 1883.
70 Skelton, *Galt*, pp. 539-540, Macdonald to Galt, 2 February, 1883.
71 *House of Commons Debates*, 1883, p. 65.
72 Argyll Papers, Letterbook 3, Lorne to Cambridge, 10 March, 1883.
73 *Ibid.*, Letterbook 4, Macdonald to Lorne, 10 March, 1883.
74 Pope, *Correspondence*, p. 298, Macdonald to Galt, 21 February, 1883.
75 Macdonald Papers, vol. 219, Macdonald to Galt, n.d.
76 Argyll Papers, Letterbook 3, Lorne to Derby, 22 April, 1883.
77 Macdonald Papers, vol. 267, Stephen to Macdonald, 11 May, 1883.
78 *Ibid.*, Macdonald to Stephen, 12 May, 1883.
79 *Ibid.*, additional, vol. 1, Macdonald to Lorne, 26 June, 1883.
80 Argyll Papers, Macdonald Letters, Macdonald to Lorne, 16 October, 1883.
81 Macdonald Papers, vol. 525, Macdonald to Plumb, 24 June, 1883.

CHAPTER ELEVEN: *Stand Fast, Craigellachie!*

(Pages 353 to 398)

1 Macdonald Papers, vol. 256, Pope to Macdonald, 23 July, 1883.
2 *Ibid.*, vol. 277, Tilley to Macdonald, 27 September, 1883.
3 Argyll Papers, Macdonald Letters, Macdonald to Lorne, 16 October, 1883.
4 *Mail*, 23 October, 1883.
5 Macdonald Papers, additional, vol. 1, Macdonald to Lorne, 9 June, 1883.
6 Argyll Papers, Macdonald Letters, Macdonald to Lorne, 26 July, 1883.
7 *Mail*, 24 October, 1883.
8 Argyll Papers, Macdonald Letters, Macdonald to Lorne, 26 October, 1883.
9 *Ibid.*, Macdonald to Lorne, 19 July, 1883.
10 Macdonald Papers, vol. 267, Stephen to Macdonald, 25 October, 1883.
11 Tupper Papers, Macdonald to Tupper, 22 November, 1883.
12 *Ibid.*
13 Macdonald Papers, vol. 267, Stephen to Macdonald, 29 October, 1883.
14 *Mail*, 30 October, 1883.
15 *Mail*, 7 November, 1883.
16 Tupper Papers, Macdonald to Tupper, 22 November, 1883.
17 *House of Commons Debates*, 1884, pp. 99-100.
18 Macdonald Papers, vol. 267, Stephen to Macdonald, 3 December, 1883.
19 *Ibid.*, Stephen to Macdonald, 15 December, 1883.
20 Pope, *Correspondence*, p. 308, Macdonald to Tupper, 1 December, 1883.
21 Macdonald Papers, vol. 525, Macdonald to Christie, 20 November, 1882.
22 *Ibid.*, Macdonald to Bate, 25 April, 1884.
23 Williamson Papers, Macdonald to Williamson, 21 November, 1883.
24 Tupper Papers, Macdonald to Tupper, 22 November, 1883.
25 Macdonald Papers, vol. 267, Stephen to Macdonald, 15 December, 1883.
26 *Ibid.*, Stephen to Macdonald, 23 December, 1883.
27 Tupper Papers, Stephen to Tupper, 28 December, 1883.

28 *Ibid.*, Stephen to Tupper, 5 January, 1884.

29 Macdonald Papers, additional, vol. 1, Macdonald to Lorne, 7 January, 1884.

30 G. F. G. Stanley, *The Birth of Western Canada, a History of the Riel Rebellions* (London, 1936), p. 207.

31 Macdonald Papers, additional, vol. 1, Macdonald to Lorne, 2 December, 1882.

32 *Ibid.*, vol. 186, Aikins to Macdonald, 30 November, 1883.

33 J. A. Jackson, The Disallowance of Manitoba Railway Legislation in the 1880's (M.A. Thesis, University of Manitoba, 1945), pp. 48-49.

34 Macdonald Papers, vol. 282, Colmer to Macdonald, 10 December, 1883.

35 *Ibid.*, vol. 259, Rose to Macdonald, 29 December, 1883.

36 *Ibid.*, vol. 269, Stephen to Macdonald, 22 January, 1884.

37 *House of Commons Debates*, 1884, pp. 84-85.

38 Grand Trunk Railway: *Correspondence between the Company and the Dominion Government respecting Advances to the Canadian Pacific Railway Company* (February, 1884).

39 R. Rumilly, *Histoire de la Province de Québec*, vol. 4, Les 'Castors' (Montreal, n.d.), pp. 132-133.

40 Macdonald Papers, vol. 206, Costigan to Macdonald, 18 February, 1884.

41 *Ibid.*, vol. 259, Rose to Macdonald, 21 February, 1884.

42 *Ibid.*, vol. 269, Stephen to Macdonald, 16 February, 1884.

43 *Ibid.*, Stephen to Macdonald, 27 February, 1884.

44 *Ibid.*, vol. 259, Macdonald to Rose, 21 February, 1884.

45 *House of Commons Debates*, 1884, p. 569.

46 Macdonald Papers, vol. 269, Stephen to Macdonald, 27 February, 1884.

47 *House of Commons Debates*, 1884, p. 664.

48 Macdonald Papers, vol. 269, Stephen to Macdonald, 21 March, 1884.

49 *Ibid.*, additional, vol. 1, Macdonald to Lorne, 26 March, 1884.

50 *Ibid.*, vol. 525, Macdonald to Campbell, 26 April, 1884.

51 *House of Commons Debates*, 1884, p. 937.

52 Macdonald Papers, vol. 228, McCarthy to Macdonald, 7 March, 1884.

53 Jackson, Disallowance of Manitoba Railway Legislation, pp. 49-53.

54 Macdonald Papers, additional, vol. 1, Macdonald to Lorne, 26 March, 1884.

55 *House of Commons Debates*, 1884, p. 109.

56 Macdonald Papers, vol. 525, Macdonald to Aikins, 6 June, 1884.

57 *Ibid.*, vol. 259, Rose to Macdonald, 23, 27 February, 1884.

58 *Ibid.*, vol. 269, Stephen to Macdonald, 26 April, 1884.

59 *Ibid.*, vol. 277, Tilley to Macdonald, 12 June, 1884.

60 *Ibid.*, Tilley to Macdonald, 19 June, 1884.

61 *Ibid.*, vol. 259, Rose to Macdonald, 18 June, 1884.

62 *Ibid.*, vol. 525, Macdonald to Chapleau, 3 July, 1884.

63 Tupper Papers, Macdonald to Tupper, 28 June, 1884.

64 Macdonald Papers, vol. 197, Campbell to Macdonald, 23 July, 1884.

65 Lansdowne Papers, Macdonald Letters, Macdonald to Lansdowne, 17 July, 1884.

66 *Ibid.*, Macdonald to Lansdowne, 10 July, 1884.

67 Pope, *Correspondence*, pp. 314-315, Macdonald to Aikins, 28 July, 1884.

68 Macdonald Papers, vol. 525, Macdonald to Norquay, 1 July, 1884.

[69] Pope, *Correspondence*, p. 313, Macdonald to Aikins, 7 July, 1884.

[70] Macdonald Papers, vol. 105, Deville to Burgess, 14 February, 1884.

[71] Pope, *Correspondence*, pp. 317-319, Macdonald to Lansdowne, 12 August, 1884.

[72] Lansdowne Papers, Macdonald Letters, Macdonald to Lansdowne, 5 August, 1884.

[73] C. R. W. Biggar, *Sir Oliver Mowat* (Toronto, 1905), vol. 1, chap. 15.

[74] Tupper Papers, Macdonald to Tupper, 13 August, 1884.

[75] Macdonald Papers, vol. 282, Tupper to Macdonald, 11 September, 1884.

[76] *Ibid.*, vol. 228, McCarthy to Macdonald, 28 September, 1884.

[77] *Ibid.*, vol. 526, Macdonald to Robertson, 4 October, 1884.

[78] Pope, *Memoirs*, vol. 2, p. 209.

[79] Macdonald Papers, vol. 282, Tupper to Macdonald, 11 December, 1884.

[80] *Ibid.*, vol. 107, Dewdney to Macdonald, 19 September, 1884.

[81] *Ibid.*, Memorandum of Conversation between Bishop Grandin and Riel, 7 September, 1884.

[82] *Ibid.*, Forget to Dewdney, 18 September, 1884.

[83] *Ibid.*, vol. 526, Macdonald to Baring Brothers, 6 September, 1884.

[84] *Ibid.*, vol. 277, Tilley to Macdonald, 3 December, 1884.

[85] *Ibid.*, vol. 129, Tupper to Tilley, 28 November, 1884.

[86] J. M. Gibbon, *Steel of Empire* (Toronto, 1935), p. 278.

CHAPTER TWELVE: *Triumph and Disaster*

(Pages 399 to 439)

[1] *Mail*, 13 January, 1885; Pope, *Correspondence*, pp. 331-332, Macdonald to Tupper, 24 January, 1885.

[2] *Mail*, 18, 19 December, 1884; Pope, *Correspondence*, p. 328, Macdonald to Tupper, 24 December, 1884.

[3] Pope, *Memoirs*, vol. 1, p. 62.

[4] *Ibid.*, vol. 2, p. 292.

[5] Lansdowne Papers, Macdonald Letters, Macdonald to Lansdowne, 7 June, 1884.

[6] *Ibid.*, Macdonald to Lansdowne, 25 December, 1884.

[7] Macdonald Papers, vol. 269, Stephen to Macdonald, 29 December, 1884.

[8] *Ibid.*, Stephen to Macdonald, 14 January, 1885.

[9] *Ibid.*, vol. 259, Rose to Macdonald, 10 January, 1885.

[10] *Ibid.*, vol. 269, Stephen to Macdonald, 14 January, 1885.

[11] *Ibid.*, vol. 277, Tilley to Macdonald, 6 January, 1885.

[12] Pope, *Correspondence*, pp. 331-332, Macdonald to Tupper, 24 January, 1885.

[13] Macdonald Papers, vol. 269, Stephen to Macdonald, 17 January, 1885.

[14] *Ibid.*, vol. 269, Macdonald to Stephen, 20 January, 1885.

[15] *House of Commons Debates*, 1885, vol. 1, p. 22.

[16] Pope, *Correspondence*, pp. 74-75, Macdonald to Chamberlin, 26 October, 1868.

[17] *House of Commons Debates*, 1885, vol. 1, p. 41.

[18] *Mail*, 6 February, 1885.

[19] *Debates*, 1885, vol. 1, p. 41.

[20] *Mail*, 6 February, 1885.

[21] G. F. G. Stanley, *Canada's Soldiers, 1604-1954* (Toronto, 1954), pp. 270-271.

[22] *House of Commons Debates*, 1886, vol. 1, p. 20.

[23] Pope, *Correspondence*, pp. 337-338, Macdonald to Tupper, 12 March, 1885.

[24] Public Archives of Canada, Department of the Interior, Dominion Lands Branch, File No. 83808, 1885.

[25] *Ibid.*

[26] *House of Commons Debates*, 1885, vol. 4, p. 3118.

[27] Macdonald Papers, vol. 107, MacDowall to Dewdney, 24 December, 1884.

[28] *House of Commons Debates*, 1885, vol. 1, p. 745.

[29] *Ibid.*

[30] *Sessional Papers*, 1885, No. 116, Order-in-Council, 28 January, 1885.

[31] Macdonald Papers, vol. 105, Macpherson to Dewdney, 4 February, 1885.

[32] *Ibid.*, vol. 269, Stephen to Macdonald, 9 February, 1885.

[33] Pope, *Correspondence*, p. 337, Tupper to Macdonald, 24 February, 1885.

[34] Tupper Papers, Macdonald to Tupper, 17 March, 1885.

[35] Macdonald Papers, vol. 107, André to Dewdney, 21 January, 1885 (enclosed in Dewdney to Macdonald, 3 February, 1885); *ibid.*, Crozier to Dewdney, 3 February, 1885.

[36] Pope, *Correspondence*, pp. 338-339, Stephen to Macdonald, 26 March, 1885.

[37] *House of Commons Debates*, 1885, vol. 2, p. 790.

[38] Pope, *Correspondence*, pp. 341-342, Macdonald to Dewdney, 29 March, 1885.

[39] *Ibid.*, pp. 340-341, Macdonald to Middleton, 29 March, 1885.

[40] *Mail*, 31 March, 1885.

[41] *Ibid.*, 25 March, 1885.

[42] Macdonald Papers, vol. 259, Rose to Macdonald, 9 May, 1885.

[43] *Ibid.*, vol. 283, Tupper to Editor of *The Times*, 20 May, 1885.

[44] Lansdowne Papers, Macdonald Letters, Macdonald to Lansdowne, 9 March, 1885.

[45] *Ibid.*, Macdonald to Lansdowne, 15 May, 1885.

[46] Gibbon, *Steel of Empire*, p. 287.

[47] Pope, *Correspondence*, p. 345, Stephen to Macdonald, 15 April, 1885.

[48] *Ibid.*, Stephen to Pope, 16 April, 1885.

[49] Macdonald Papers, vol. 129, Macdonald to Smithers, 24 April, 1885.

[50] *Ibid.*, Drinkwater to Macdonald, 27 April, 1885.

[51] *Mail*, 1 May, 1885.

[52] *Ibid.*, 2 May, 1885.

[53] Macdonald Papers, vol. 283, Tupper to Macdonald, 7 May, 1885.

[54] *House of Commons Debates*, 1885, vol. 3, pp. 1822-1823.

[55] Macdonald Papers, additional, vol. 2, Macdonald to Louisa Macdonald, 9 May, 1885.

[56] Lansdowne Papers, Macdonald Letters, Macdonald to Lansdowne, 3 June, 1885.

[57] Macdonald to Tupper, 27 July, 1885, Letter in possession of Oscar Orr, Esq., Vancouver, British Columbia.

[58] Pope, *Correspondence*, pp. 358-360, Macdonald to Campbell, 12 September, 1885.

[59] Macdonald to Tupper, 27 July, 1885.

[60] *Ibid.*

[61] *Sessional Papers*, 1886, No. 45.

[62] Macdonald Papers, vol. 106, Amyot to Langevin, 16 May, 1885.

[63] Macdonald to Tupper, 27 July, 1885.

[64] Pope, *Correspondence*, pp. 351-352, Macdonald to Thompson, 21 July, 1885.

[65] *Ibid.*, pp. 358-360, Macdonald to Campbell, 12 September, 1885; Macdonald Papers, vol. 526, Macdonald to Campbell, 14 September, 1885.

[66] Pope, *Correspondence*, p. 360, Campbell to Macdonald, 13 September, 1885; Macdonald Papers, vol. 197, Campbell to Macdonald, 14 September, 1885.

[67] Saunders, *Tupper*, vol. 2, p. 61, Macdonald to Tupper, 4 September, 1885.

[68] *Sessional Papers*, 1886, No. 43.

[69] Pope, *Correspondence*, pp. 354-356, Macdonald to Lansdowne, 28 August, 1885.

[70] Macdonald Papers, vol. 197, Campbell to Macdonald, 11 September, 1885.

[71] *Ibid.*, vol. 526, Macdonald to Carnarvon, 8 September, 1885.

[72] *Ibid.*, vol. 106, Colonial Secretary to Deputy Governor, 22 October, 1885.

[73] *Ibid.*, Campbell to Macdonald, 23 October, 1885; *ibid.*, Campbell to Macdonald, 27 (?) October, 1885.

[74] H. Barnes, "A Century of the McNaghten Rules", *Cambridge Law Journal*, vol. 88, pp. 300-321.

[75] Williamson Papers, Macdonald to Lavell, 31 October, 1885.

[76] Macdonald Papers, vol. 106, Macdonald to Lavell and Valade, 31 October, 1885.

[77] *Ibid.*, Dewdney to Macdonald, 7 November, 1885.

[78] *Ibid.*, vol. 129, Van Horne to Macdonald, 7 November, 1885.

[79] Lansdowne Papers, Macdonald Letters, Macdonald to Lansdowne, 9 November, 1885.

[80] *Ibid.*, vol. 106, Opinion of M. Lavell, 8 November, 1885.

[81] *Ibid.*, Opinion of F. X. Valade, 8 November, 1885.

[82] Pope, *Correspondence*, p. 364, Chapleau to Macdonald, 12 November, 1885.

[83] Macdonald Papers, vol. 108, Lesage *et al.* to Macdonald, 13 November, 1885; *ibid.*, Coursal *et al.* to Macdonald, 13 November, 1885.

[84] Pope, *Correspondence*, p. 365, Macdonald to Langevin, 13 November, 1885.

[85] Lansdowne Papers, Macdonald Letters, Macdonald to Lansdowne, 13 November, 1885.

[86] Macdonald Papers, vol. 107, Dewdney to Macdonald, 15 November, 1885.

[87] *Leader* (Regina), 17 November, 1885; *Mail*, 17 November, 1885.

CHAPTER THIRTEEN: *The Revolt of the Provinces*

(Pages 440 to 481)

[1] Macdonald Papers, vol. 166, Stephen to Macdonald, 29 November, 1885.

[2] *Ibid.*, Rose to Macdonald, 27 November, 1885.

[3] *Ibid.*, vol. 85, Macdonald to Lansdowne, 12 December, 1885.

[4] *Ibid.*, vol. 166, Engagement book, 2-4 January, 1886.

[5] *Ibid.*, vol. 256, Pope to Macdonald, 10 December, 1885.

[6] *Ibid.*, vol. 200, Caron to Macdonald, 26 November, 1885.

[7] *Ibid.*, vol. 227, Langevin to Macdonald, 19 December, 1885.

[8] *Ibid.*, vol. 85, Macdonald to Lansdowne, 21 December, 1885.

[9] *Ibid.*, additional, vol. 2, Mary Macdonald to Macdonald, 22 December, 1885.

[10] *Mail*, 20 January, 1886.

[11] Macdonald Papers, additional, vol. 2, Agnes Macdonald to Louisa Macdonald, 19 January, 1886.

[12] *Ibid.*, vol. 526, Macdonald to Lansdowne, 7 June, 1885.

[13] Lansdowne Papers, Macdonald Letters, Macdonald to Lansdowne, 26 May, 1884; Pope, *Correspondence*, p. 326, Macdonald to Hincks, 18 September, 1884.

[14] *House of Commons Debates*, 1886, vol. 1, p. 31.

[15] *Sessional Papers*, 1886, vol. 12, No. 43.

[16] Macdonald Papers, vol. 106, Jukes to Dewdney, 6 November, 1885.

[17] *Ibid.*, Lavell to Macdonald, 8, 9 November, 1885.

[18] Lansdowne Papers, Macdonald Letters, Macdonald to Lansdowne, 9 March, 1886.

[19] Macdonald Papers, vol. 227, Langevin to Macdonald, 10 March, 1886.

[20] Lansdowne Papers, Macdonald Letters, Macdonald to Lansdowne, 13, 17 March, 1886.

[21] *Ibid.*, Macdonald to Lansdowne, 13, 15 March, 1886.

[22] Pope, *Correspondence*, p. 360, Campbell to Macdonald, 14 September, 1885.

[23] Macdonald Papers, vol. 198, Campbell to Macdonald, 22 March, 1886.

[24] *House of Commons Debates*, 1886, vol. 1, p. 368.

[25] *Ibid.*, p. 411.

[26] Macdonald Papers, vol. 198, Campbell to Macdonald, 26 March, 1886.

[27] Lansdowne Papers, Macdonald Letters, Macdonald to Lansdowne, 14 April, 1886.

[28] *Ibid.*, Macdonald to Lansdowne, 20 April, 1886.

[29] *Chronicle* (Halifax), 10, 26 May, 1886.

[30] Macdonald Papers, vol. 259, Rose to Macdonald, 10 May, 1886.

[31] *Ibid.*, Macdonald to Rose, 12 May, 1886.

[32] *Ibid.*, vol. 86, Macdonald to Lansdowne, 4 June, 1886.

[33] Lansdowne Papers, Macdonald Letters, Macdonald to Lansdowne, 21 May, 1886.

[34] Macdonald Papers, vol. 86, Granville to Lansdowne, 2 June, 1886.

[35] Lansdowne Papers, Macdonald Letters, Macdonald to Lansdowne, 2 June, 1886.

[36] Lansdowne Papers, Letterbook 3, Lansdowne to Granville, 2 June, 1886.

[37] Pope, *Correspondence*, p. 382, Macdonald to Tupper, 21 June, 1886.

[38] Lansdowne Papers, Macdonald Letters, Macdonald to Lansdowne, 1 July, 1886.

[39] *Ibid.*, Macdonald to Lansdowne, 7 June, 1886.

[40] *Ibid.*, Macdonald to Lansdowne, 10 June, 1886.

[41] Public Archives of Canada, Thompson Papers, Macdonald to Thompson, 10 July, 1886.

[42] Macdonald Papers, vol. 288, Van Horne to Agnes Macdonald, 7 July, 1886.

[43] *Manitoban* (Winnipeg), 13 July, 1886.

[44] *Ibid.*, 15 July, 1886.

[45] *Leader* (Regina), 20 July, 1886.

[46] *Mail*, 21, 22 July, 1886.

[47] *Ibid.*, 23, 26 July, 1886.

[48] *Gazette* (Port Moody), 31 July, 1886.

[49] *Star* (Victoria), 25, 29 July, 1886.

[50] *Manitoban*, 26 August, 1886.

[51] *Mail*, 31 August, 1886.

[52] Macdonald Papers, vol. 259, Rose to Macdonald, 15 September, 1886.

[53] *Mail*, 17 September, 1886.

[54] Lansdowne Papers, Macdonald Letters, Macdonald to Lansdowne, 2 October, 1886.

[55] Macdonald Papers, vol. 85, Lansdowne to Macdonald, 20 August, 1886.

[56] Lansdowne Papers, Macdonald Letters, Macdonald to Lansdowne, 4 September, 1886.

[57] Macdonald Papers, vol. 227, Langevin to Macdonald, 15 October, 1886.

[58] Pope, *Correspondence*, p. 386, Macdonald to Tupper, 15 October, 1886.

[59] Macdonald Papers, vol. 270, Stephen to Macdonald, 4 November, 1886.

[60] Thompson Papers, Family Letters, Thompson to his wife, 31 October, 1886.

[61] *Mail*, 4 November, 1886.

[62] Thompson Papers, Family Letters, Thompson to his wife, 12 November, 1886.

[63] Pope, *Correspondence*, p. 390, Macdonald to Tupper, 20 December, 1886.

[64] Macdonald Papers, vol. 86, Colonial Secretary to Lansdowne, 26 November, 1886.

[65] Lansdowne Papers, Macdonald Letters, Macdonald to Lansdowne, 15 January, 1887; *Mail*, 17 January, 1887.

[66] Macdonald Papers, vol. 205, Chapleau to Macdonald, 20 January, 1887.

[67] Lansdowne Papers, Macdonald Letters, Macdonald to Lansdowne, 24 January, 1887.

[68] *Mail*, 1 February, 1887.

[69] *Globe*, 24 January, 1887.

[70] *Mail*, 12 February, 1887.

[71] Macdonald Papers, vol. 205, Macdonald to Chapleau, 13 February, 1887.

[72] *Ibid.*, vol. 198, Campbell to Macdonald, 23 February, 1887.

73 Lansdowne Papers, Macdonald Letters, Macdonald to Lansdowne, 24 February, 1887.

74 Macdonald Papers, vol. 527, Macdonald to Blackstock, 28 March, 1887.

75 Pope, *Correspondence*, p. 399, Mercier to Macdonald, 4 April, 1887.

76 Province of Ontario, *Sessional Papers*, 1887, No. 51, Mercier to Mowat, 8 March, 1887.

77 Pope, *Correspondence*, pp. 399-400, Macdonald to Mercier, 6 April, 1887.

78 *Ibid.*, p. 401, Macdonald to Mercier, 28 April, 1887.

79 *House of Commons Debates*, 1887, vol. 1, pp. 578-579.

80 Macdonald Papers, vol. 228, McCarthy to Macdonald, 3 April, 1887.

81 *House of Commons Debates*, 1887, vol. 1, pp. 384-407.

82 Macdonald Papers, vol. 86, Lansdowne to Macdonald, 25 December, 1886.

83 *Ibid.*, vol. 527, Macdonald to Lansdowne, 28 December, 1886.

84 Lansdowne Papers, Macdonald Letters, Macdonald to Lansdowne, 16 May, 1887.

85 Charles Tupper, *Recollections of Sixty Years in Canada* (London and Toronto, 1914), pp. 177-182.

86 Macdonald Papers, vol. 270, Stephen to Macdonald, 4 June, 1887.

87 *Ibid.*, vol. 527, Macdonald to Aikins, 25 June, 1887.

88 *Dominion and Provincial Legislation*, pp. 855-856.

89 Pope, *Correspondence*, pp. 403-404, Macdonald to Rose, 25 June, 1887.

90 Macdonald Papers, vol. 527, Macdonald to Lansdowne, 1 September, 1887; Lansdowne Papers, Macdonald Letters, Macdonald to Lansdowne, 14 September, 3 October, 1887.

91 Lansdowne Papers, Macdonald Letters, Macdonald to Lansdowne, 24 September, 1887.

92 *Ibid.*, Macdonald to Lansdowne, 13 October, 1887.

93 *Globe*, 14 October, 1887.

CHAPTER FOURTEEN: *The Renewal of Cultural Conflict*

(Pages 482 to 520)

1 Macdonald Papers, vol. 228, McCarthy to Macdonald, 3 September, 1887.

2 *Mail*, 27 October, 1887.

3 *Gazette*, 20 October, 1887.

4 Campbell Papers, Macdonald to Campbell, 3 December, 1887.

5 *Ibid.*, Macdonald to Campbell, 15 December, 1887.

6 Macdonald Papers, vol. 527, Macdonald to Aikins, 15 October, 1887.

7 *Ibid.*, Macdonald to Brown, 17 October, 1887.

8 *Ibid.*, vol. 270, Stephen to Macdonald, 4 October, 1887.

9 Pope, *Correspondence*, p. 406, Tupper to Macdonald, 15 September, 1887.

10 Lansdowne Papers, Macdonald Letters, Macdonald to Lansdowne, 18 October, 1887.

11 Macdonald Papers, vol. 527, Macdonald to Lansdowne, 3 October, 1887.

[12] *Ibid.*, vol. 176, Tupper to Macdonald, 24, 25 November, 1887.

[13] *Ibid.*, vol. 527, Macdonald to Lansdowne, 30 November, 1887.

[14] Pope, *Correspondence*, p. 406, Macdonald to Tupper, 7 December, 1887.

[15] Macdonald Papers, vol. 527, Macdonald to Lansdowne, 30 November, 1887.

[16] *Ibid.*, additional, vol. 2, Macdonald to Louisa Macdonald, 10 December, 1887.

[17] *Ibid.*, vol. 527, Macdonald to Tupper, 8 December, 1887.

[18] *Ibid.*, Macdonald to Tupper, 9 December, 1887.

[19] *Ibid.*, vol. 176, Tupper to Macdonald, 9 December, 1887.

[20] Lansdowne Papers, Macdonald Letters, Macdonald to Lansdowne, 10 December, 1887.

[21] Macdonald Papers, vol. 87, Lansdowne to Macdonald, 10 December, 1887.

[22] *Ibid.*, vol. 527, Macdonald to Tupper, 8 December, 1887.

[23] Lansdowne Papers, Macdonald Letters, Macdonald to Lansdowne, 11 December, 1887.

[24] J. L. Garvin, *The Life of Joseph Chamberlain* (London, 1933), vol. 2, pp. 333-334; W. R. Graham, "Sir Richard Cartwright, Wilfrid Laurier, and Liberal Trade Policy", *Canadian Historical Review*, vol. 33 (March, 1952), pp. 1-18.

[25] Macdonald Papers, vol. 527, Macdonald to Tupper, 15 January, 1888.

[26] *Ibid.*, additional, vol. 2, Macdonald to Louisa Macdonald, 10 September, 1887.

[27] *Ibid.*, Macdonald to Louisa Macdonald, 23 December, 1887.

[28] *Ibid.*, Macdonald to Minnie Macdonell, 12 January, 1888.

[29] *Ibid.*, vol. 527, Macdonald to Tupper, 5 January, 1888.

[30] Lansdowne Papers, Macdonald Letters, Macdonald to Lansdowne, 31 December, 1887.

[31] Macdonald Papers, vol. 176, Tupper to Macdonald, 19 January, 1888.

[32] Thompson Papers, Family Letters, Thompson to his wife, 16 January, 1888.

[33] Lansdowne Papers, Macdonald Letters, Macdonald to Lansdowne, 1 February, 1888.

[34] Pope, *Correspondence*, pp. 408-409, Macdonald to Tupper, 6 February, 1888.

[35] Lansdowne Papers, Macdonald Letters, Macdonald to Lansdowne, 11 February, 1888.

[36] Pope, *Correspondence*, p. 409, Macdonald to Tupper, 6 February, 1888.

[37] Lansdowne Papers, Macdonald Letters, Macdonald to Lansdowne, 21 February, 1888.

[38] Macdonald Papers, vol. 527, Macdonald to Daly, 31 January, 1888.

[39] *Ibid.*, vol. 271, Stephen to Macdonald, 25 February, 16, 20 March, 1888.

[40] *Ibid.*, vol. 119, Macdonald to Greenway, 20 March, 1888.

[41] *Ibid.*, Macdonald to Greenway, 21 March, 1888; *ibid.*, Greenway to Macdonald, 23 March, 1888.

[42] *Ibid.*, vol. 527, Macdonald to Greenway, 30 March, 1888.

[43] *House of Commons Debates*, 1888, vol. 1, p. 144.

[44] *Ibid.*, vol. 2, pp. 1069, 1078.

[45] *Ibid.*, vol. 1, p. 646.

⁴⁶ *Ibid.*, p. 14.

⁴⁷ Macdonald Papers, additional, vol. 2, Macdonald to Louisa Macdonald, 29 May, 1888.

⁴⁸ *Ibid.*, vol. 88, Lansdowne to Macdonald, 23 May, 1888.

⁴⁹ *Ibid.*, vol. 528, Macdonald to Tupper, 14 July, 1888.

⁵⁰ *Ibid.*, vol. 271, Stephen to Macdonald, 12 January, 1888.

⁵¹ Saunders, *Tupper*, vol. 2, pp. 117-118.

⁵² Lansdowne Papers, Macdonald Letters, Macdonald to Lansdowne, 13 July, 1888.

⁵³ *Ibid.*, Macdonald to Lansdowne, 24 April, 1888.

⁵⁴ Macdonald Papers, vol. 528, Macdonald to Stanley, 17 July, 1888.

⁵⁵ Lansdowne Papers, Macdonald Letters, Macdonald to Lansdowne, 6 September, 1888.

⁵⁶ Pope, *Correspondence*, pp. 429-431, Macdonald to Stephen, 22 October, 1888.

⁵⁷ Macdonald Papers, vol. 528, Macdonald to Schultz, 2 August, 1888.

⁵⁸ *Ibid.*, Macdonald to Schultz, 17 November, 1888.

⁵⁹ *Ibid.*, Macdonald to Stephen, 4 August, 1888.

⁶⁰ Lansdowne Papers, Macdonald Letters, Macdonald to Lansdowne, 6 September, 1888.

⁶¹ Macdonald Papers, vol. 89, Stanley to Macdonald, October, 1888.

⁶² Allan Nevins, *Grover Cleveland, A Study in Courage* (New York, 1933), pp. 428-431.

⁶³ Pope, *Correspondence*, p. 430, Macdonald to Stephen, 22 October, 1888.

⁶⁴ Macdonald Papers, vol. 528, Macdonald to Tupper, 16 November, 1888.

⁶⁵ Pope, *Correspondence*, p. 431, Mowat to Macdonald, 17 November, 1888.

⁶⁶ *Ibid.*, p. 436, Macdonald to Stephen, 12 January, 1889.

⁶⁷ Macdonald to Williamson, 11 January, 1889. Letter in the possession of W. F. Nickle, Esq., of Kingston, Ontario.

⁶⁸ Macdonald Papers, additional, vol. 2, Macdonald to Louisa Macdonald, 27 April, 1888.

⁶⁹ Macdonald to Williamson, 11 January, 1889.

⁷⁰ Pope, *Correspondence*, p. 430, Macdonald to Stephen, 22 October, 1888.

⁷¹ Macdonald Papers, vol. 284, Tupper to Macdonald, 19 December, 1888.

⁷² *Ibid.*, vol. 528, Macdonald to Tupper, 22 December, 1888.

⁷³ *Ibid.*, Macdonald to Hamilton, 26 January, 1889.

⁷⁴ *Ibid.*, vol. 228, McCarthy to Macdonald, 1 March, 1889.

⁷⁵ *Ibid.*, vol. 471, O'Brien to Macdonald, 18 March, 1889.

⁷⁶ *Ibid.*, vol. 528, Macdonald to O'Brien, 20 March, 1889.

⁷⁷ *House of Commons Debates*, 1889, vol, 2, p. 908.

⁷⁸ *Ibid.*, p. 910.

⁷⁹ Pope, *Correspondence*, pp. 442-443.

⁸⁰ *Ibid.*, pp. 443-444, McCarthy to Macdonald, 17 April, 1889.

⁸¹ Lansdowne Papers, Macdonald Letters, Macdonald to Lansdowne, 14 May, 1889.

⁸² Macdonald Papers, vol. 275, Thompson to Macdonald, 18 May, 1889.

⁸³ *Globe*, 8 June, 1889.

⁸⁴ Thompson Papers, vol. 89, Macdonald to Thompson, 4 July, 1889.

⁸⁵ Pope, *Correspondence*, pp. 445-446, Macdonald to Tupper, 31 May, 1889.

86 Thompson Papers, vol. 91, Macdonald to Thompson, 2 August, 1889.
87 Macdonald Papers, vol. 94, Stanley to Macdonald, 2 August, 1889.
88 Thompson Papers, vol. 91, Macdonald to Thompson, 14 August, 1889.
89 *Ibid.*, Macdonald to Thompson, 30 August, 1889.

CHAPTER FIFTEEN: *The Last Election*

(Pages 521 to 563)

1 Macdonald Papers, vol. 275, Monck to Macdonald, 24 September, 1890.
2 *Ibid.*, vol. 232, McLelan to Macdonald, 29 June, 1889.
3 Thompson Papers, vol. 89, Macdonald to Thompson, 4 July, 1889.
4 Lansdowne Papers, Macdonald Letters, Macdonald to Lansdowne, 14 May, 1889.
5 Pope, *Correspondence*, p. 461, Macdonald to Tupper, 7 December, 1889.
6 Macdonald Papers, vol. 528, Macdonald to Costigan, 2 May, 1889.
7 Thompson Papers, vol. 72, Macdonald to Thompson, 13 June, 1888.
8 Pope, *Correspondence*, pp. 431-432, Tupper to Macdonald, 1 December, 1888.
9 *Ibid.*, pp. 449-451, Macdonald to Knutsford, 18 July, 1889.
10 Macdonald Papers, additional, vol. 3, Agnes Macdonald to Louisa Macdonald, n.d.
11 *Ibid.*, vol. 528, Macdonald to Tupper, 16 November, 1888.
12 *Ibid.*, Macdonald to Tupper, 22 December, 1888.
13 Queen's University Library, McLaughlin Collection, Macdonald to Hallam, 6 May, 1889.
14 Pope, *Correspondence*, p. 449, Macdonald to Edgecome, 4 July, 1889.
15 Thompson Papers, vol. 90, Macdonald to Thompson, 27 July, 1889.
16 *Ibid.*, vol. 89, Macdonald to Thompson, 4 July, 1889.
17 *Ibid.*, vol. 90, Macdonald to Thompson, 25 July, 1889.
18 Lansdowne Papers, Macdonald Letters, Macdonald to Lansdowne, 28 September, 1889.
19 Macdonald Papers, vol. 288, Andersons to Macdonald, 12 October, 1889.
20 Pope, *Correspondence*, pp. 455-456, Macdonald to Stephen, 13 September, 1889.
21 Lansdowne Papers, Macdonald Letters, Macdonald to Lansdowne, 28 September, 1889.
22 Macdonald Papers, vol. 32, Stanley to Macdonald, n.d. (with enclosure).
23 *Ibid.*, Colonial Secretary to Governor-General, n.d.
24 *Ibid.*, vol. 529, Macdonald to Tupper, 22 October, 1889.
25 *Ibid.*, vol. 32, Stanley to Knutsford, 13 December, 1889.
26 Pope, *Correspondence*, p. 414, Macdonald to Chapleau, 6 June, 1888.
27 *House of Commons Debates*, 1890, p. 38.
28 *Ibid.*, p. 532.
29 *Ibid.*, p. 557.
30 *Ibid.*, p. 745.
31 *Ibid.*, p. 750.
32 *Ibid.*, pp. 875-876.
33 *Ibid.*, p. 895.
34 Macdonald Papers, vol. 90, Stanley to Macdonald, 22 February, 1890.

[85] *House of Commons Debates*, 1890, p. 1018.
[36] Macdonald Papers, vol. 30, C. H. Tupper to Macdonald, 27 February, 1890.
[37] *Ibid.*
[38] Thompson Papers, vol. 103, Macdonald to Bowell, 4 March, 1890.
[39] Macdonald Papers, vol. 529, Macdonald to C. H. Tupper, 11 March, 1890.
[40] *Ibid.*, vol. 31, Draft Convention for the North Pacific Seal Fishery.
[41] *Ibid.*, C. H. Tupper to Macdonald, 10 April, 1890.
[42] *Ibid.*, C. H. Tupper to Macdonald, 11 April, 1890.
[43] *Ibid.*, Macdonald to C. H. Tupper, 11 April, 1890.
[44] *Ibid.*, C. H. Tupper to Macdonald, 27 April, 1890.
[45] C. C. Tansill, *Canadian-American Relations, 1875-1911* (New Haven and Toronto, 1943), p. 311.
[46] *House of Commons Debates*, 1890, pp. 449-450, 638-650, 1713-1734.
[47] *Ibid.*, pp. 4500-4503, 4564.
[48] Macdonald Papers, vol. 189, Bowell to Macdonald, 23 July, 1890.
[49] Pope, *Correspondence*, p. 466, Macdonald to Chevrier, 25 March, 1890.
[50] Saunders, *Tupper*, vol. 2, p. 140, Macdonald to Tupper, 5 June, 1890.
[51] *Empire* (Toronto), 9 August, 1890.
[52] *Ibid.*, 2 October, 1890.
[53] Pope, *Correspondence*, pp. 477-479, Macdonald to Stephen, 10 November, 1890.
[54] *Ibid.*
[55] *Empire*, 11, 12 November, 1890.
[56] G 12, vol. 85, Stanley to Knutsford, 19 November, 1890.
[57] *Sessional Papers*, 1891, No. 38, Knutsford to Stanley, 25 November, 1890.
[58] *Ibid.*, Pauncefote to Stanley, 7 December, 1890.
[59] Macdonald Papers, vol. 530, Macdonald to Stanley, 8 December, 1890.
[60] Thompson Papers, vol. 118, Macdonald to Thompson, 9 December, 1890.
[61] G 12, vol. 85, Stanley to Knutsford, 13 December, 1890.
[62] *Sessional Papers*, 1891, No. 38, Knutsford to Stanley, 2 January, 1891.
[63] Thompson Papers, vol. 127, Macdonald to Thompson, 27 April, 1891.
[64] G 12, vol. 85, Stanley to Knutsford, 21 January, 1891.
[65] *Mail*, 14 January, 1891.
[66] *Empire*, 16 January, 1891.
[67] G 12, vol. 85, Stanley to Knutsford, 24 January, 1891.
[68] *Free Press* (Ottawa), 29 January, 1891.
[69] *Globe*, 30 January, 1891.
[70] Macdonald Papers, vol. 90, Stanley to Macdonald, 30 January, 1891.
[71] Pope, *Memoirs*, vol. 2, appendix 28, p. 336.
[72] Macdonald Papers, vol. 285, Macdonald to Tupper, 21 January, 1891.
[73] *Ibid.*, Macdonald to Colmer, 13 February, 1891.
[74] *Globe*, 18 February, 1891.
[75] *Empire*, 18 February, 1891.
[76] Pope, *Memoirs*, vol. 2, p. 257.
[77] *News* (Kingston), 23 February, 1891.
[78] *Ibid.*, 25 February, 1891.

79 *Ibid.*, 26 February, 1891.

80 Pope, *Memoirs*, vol. 2, pp. 257-258.

81 Public Archives of Canada, The Last Ten Days of the Life of the Right Honourable Sir John Alexander Macdonald, G.C.B., Prime Minister of Canada, by his attending physician, Robert Wynyard Powell, M.D.

82 Pope, *Correspondence*, p. 485, Macdonald to Stephen, 31 March, 1891.

83 Williamson Papers, Macdonald to Williamson, 10 March, 1891.

84 Powell, The Last Ten Days.

85 *House of Commons Debates*, 1891, vol. 1, p. 35.

86 Pope, *Memoirs*, vol. 2, pp. 258-259.

87 G 12, vol. 85, Stanley to Knutsford, 4 June, 1891.

88 Pope, *Memoirs*, vol. 2, p. 259.

89 Powell, The Last Ten Days.

90 Thompson Papers, Family Letters, 22 May, 1891.

EPILOGUE: *The Sixth of June, 1891*

(Pages 564 to 578)

1 Powell, The Last Ten Days, p. 5.

2 Pope, *Memoirs*, vol. 2, p. 259.

3 Powell, The Last Ten Days, pp. 5-6.

4 *Ibid.*, p. 6.

5 Pope, *Memoirs*, vol. 2, p. 260.

6 *Free Press* (Ottawa), 28 May, 1891.

7 Powell, The Last Ten Days, pp. 7-8.

8 Pope, *Memoirs*, vol. 2, pp. 260-261.

9 Thompson Papers, Family Letters, Thompson to his wife, 29 May, 1891.

10 Sir John Willison, *Reminiscences, Political and Personal* (Toronto, 1919), p. 193.

11 *Ibid.*

12 Powell, The Last Ten Days, p. 9.

13 *Ibid.*, p. 10.

14 *Free Press*, 30 May, 1891.

15 *House of Commons Debates*, 1891, p. 600.

16 *Empire*, 30 May, 1891.

17 *Mail*, 2 June, 1891.

18 Powell, The Last Ten Days, pp. 11-12.

19 *Mail*, 2 June, 1891.

20 Thompson Papers, Family Letters, Thompson to his wife, 31 May, 1891.

21 *Ibid.*, Thompson to his wife, 1 June, 1891.

22 *Empire*, 5 June, 1891.

23 Powell, The Last Ten Days, p. 14.

24 *Ibid.*, p. 15.

25 *Gazette* (Montreal), 8 June, 1891.

26 *Mail*, 9 June, 1891.

27 *House of Commons Debates*, 1891, p. 884.

28 *Empire*, 11 June, 1891.

29 *Mail*, 12 June, 1891.

30 Pope, *Memoirs*, vol. 2, p. 264.

INDEX